B L A C K   S E A

Ephesus

Antioch

Damascus

N   S E A

Jerusalem

Alexandria

E LOWENSTEIN

THE INTERPRETER'S BIBLE

THE INTERPRETER'S BIBLE

IN TWELVE VOLUMES

VOLUME XII

The Epistle of
JAMES

The First and Second Epistles of
PETER

The First, Second, and Third Epistles of
JOHN

The Epistle of
JUDE

The
REVELATION
of St. John the Divine

GENERAL ARTICLES

INDEXES

THE
INTERPRETER'S BIBLE

—

The Holy Scriptures

IN THE KING JAMES AND REVISED STANDARD VERSIONS

WITH GENERAL ARTICLES AND

INTRODUCTION, EXEGESIS, EXPOSITION

FOR EACH BOOK OF THE BIBLE

IN TWELVE VOLUMES

VOLUME

XII

'Εν ἀρχῇ ἦν ὁ λόγος

NEW YORK *Abingdon Press* NASHVILLE

ISBN 0-687-19218-8

Library of Congress Catalog Card Number: 51-12276

S

SET UP, PRINTED, AND BOUND BY THE
PARTHENON PRESS, AT NASHVILLE,
TENNESSEE, UNITED STATES OF AMERICA

ABBREVIATIONS AND EXPLANATIONS

ABBREVIATIONS

Canonical books and bibliographical terms are abbreviated according to common usage

Amer. Trans. — *The Bible, An American Translation,* Old Testament, ed. J. M. P. Smith
Apoc.—Apocrypha
Aq.—Aquila
ASV—American Standard Version (1901)
Barn.—Epistle of Barnabas
Clem.—Clement
C.T.—Consonantal Text
Did.—Didache
Ecclus.—Ecclesiasticus
ERV—English Revised Version (1881-85)

Exeg.—Exegesis
Expos.—Exposition
Goodspeed—*The Bible, An American Translation,* New Testament and Apocrypha, tr. Edgar J. Goodspeed
Herm. Vis., etc.—The Shepherd of Hermas: Visions, Mandates, Similitudes
Ign. Eph., etc.—Epistles of Ignatius to the Ephesians, Magnesians, Trallians, Romans, Philadelphians, Smyrnaeans, and Polycarp

KJV—King James Version (1611)
LXX—Septuagint
Macc.—Maccabees
Moffatt—*The Bible, A New Translation,* by James Moffatt
M.T.—Masoretic Text
N.T.—New Testament
O.L.—Old Latin
O.T.—Old Testament
Polyc. Phil.—Epistle of Polycarp to the Philippians
Pseudep. — Pseudepigrapha
Pss. Sol.—Psalms of Solomon

RSV—Revised Standard Version (1946-52)
Samar.—Samaritan recension
Symm.—Symmachus
Targ.—Targum
Test. Reuben, etc.—Testament of Reuben, and others of the Twelve Patriarchs
Theod.—Theodotion
Tob.—Tobit
Vulg.—Vulgate
Weymouth—*The New Testament in Modern Speech,* by Richard Francis Weymouth
Wisd. Sol.—Wisdom of Solomon

QUOTATIONS AND REFERENCES

Boldface type in Exegesis and Exposition indicates a quotation from either the King James or the Revised Standard Version of the passage under discussion. The two versions are distinguished only when attention is called to a difference between them. Readings of other versions are not in boldface type and are regularly identified.

In scripture references a letter (*a, b,* etc.) appended to a verse number indicates a clause within the verse; an additional Greek letter indicates a subdivision within the clause. When no book is named, the book under discussion is understood.

Arabic numbers connected by colons, as in scripture references, indicate chapters and verses in deuterocanonical and noncanonical works. For other ancient writings roman numbers indicate major divisions, arabic numbers subdivisions, these being connected by periods. For modern works a roman number and an arabic number connected by a comma indicate volume and page. Bibliographical data on a contemporary work cited by a writer may be found by consulting the first reference to the work by that writer (or the bibliography, if the writer has included one).

GREEK TRANSLITERATIONS

α = a	ε = e	ι = ι	ν = n	ρ = r	φ = ph
β = b	ζ = z	κ = k	ξ = x	σ(ς) = s	χ = ch
γ = g	η = ē	λ = l	o = o	τ = t	ψ = ps
δ = d	θ = th	μ = m	π = p	υ = u, y	ω = ō

HEBREW AND ARAMAIC TRANSLITERATIONS

I. HEBREW ALPHABET

א = '	ה = h	ט = ṭ	מ(ם) = m	פ(ף) = p, ph	שׂ = s, sh
ב = b, bh	ו = w	י = y	נ(ן) = n	צ(ץ) = ç	תּ = t, th
ג = g, gh	ז = z	כ(ך) = k, kh	ס = ṣ	ק = q	
ד = d, dh	ח = ḥ	ל = l	ע = '	ר = r	

II. MASORETIC POINTING

Pure-long	Tone-long	Short	Composite *sh°wa*
ִ = â	ָ = ā	_ = a	ֲ = ᵃ
ֵ = ê	ֵ = ē	ֶ = e	ֳ = ᵒ
. *or* ִ = î		. = i	ֱ = ᵉ
ֹ *or* ֹ = ô	ֹ = ō	ָ = o	
ֻ = û		ֻ = u	ֳ = ᵒ

NOTE: (*a*) The *páthaḥ* furtive is transliterated as a *haṭeph-páthaḥ*. (*b*) The simple *sh°wa,* when vocal, is transliterated °. (*c*) The tonic accent, which is indicated only when it occurs on a syllable other than the last, is transliterated by an acute accent over the vowel.

vii

TABLE OF CONTENTS

VOLUME XII

TABLE OF CONTENTS

INDEXES

MAPS

The Epistle of

JAMES

Introduction and Exegesis by BURTON SCOTT EASTON
Exposition by GORDON POTEAT

JAMES

INTRODUCTION

While the opening words of James resemble those used at the beginning of the other epistles in the New Testament, this resemblance does not extend beyond the first verse; and even this first verse has its unique features. It is unique in its vague description of the readers; in place of, say, the precise "the church of God which is at Corinth," we have the puzzling phrase "the twelve tribes in the dispersion," over which commentators have labored endlessly. Equally vague is the personality of the writer. He gives his name simply as "James," which in its original form "Jacob" was an extremely common name among Jews and early Jewish Christians, leaving his readers to decide which "James" among the many bearing this appellation is meant. He describes himself further only as "a servant of God and of the Lord Jesus Christ," thus identifying himself indeed as a Christian and further as a Christian leader (see on "servant" in Exeg. of 1:1), but this does not tell us very much. And thereafter he mentions himself only as one of those "who teach" (3:1), something already obvious from the fact that he wrote at all. (In 2:18 the "I" is of course purely rhetorical and is not to be identified with the writer.)

Equally vague again are the relationships between the writer and his readers. He speaks, doubtless, with a tone of authority which he assumes they will respect, but this authority is purely impersonal. He has not a word to say about any personal experiences he has had among them (contrast, e.g., Gal. 4:15) or any news anyone has brought him about them (contrast, e.g., I Cor. 1:11). He sends no greetings from himself or anyone else to any of his readers. The letter does not close with the customary farewell message: in fact, the epistle has no formal ending at all but simply stops abruptly and without warning.

Nor is there any hint of the occasion of the letter. Commentators have sometimes argued that 1:2-4 indicate a time of persecution; but not only is the language of these verses wholly general, but their theme is dropped immediately; contrast I Peter in this regard. Indeed, the teaching of the epistle is so free from concrete applications to any specific time or place that for the most part it is as fresh and as useful today as when it first was written; it is this very fact that gives James its enduring appeal.

I. Form and Structure

Fully as vague as the identities of the writer and readers, their relation to each other, and the occasion of the letter, is its general theme. For it has no "general theme" at all. The opening chapter is composed of a series of brief sayings, each complete in itself, whose sequence is determined not by any logical plan, but by some minor association of thought or language, often by the mere repetition of a word. The central portion, 2:1–3:12, is (apart from the isolated saying in 2:13) made up of three sections, 2:1-12; 2:14-26; and 3:1-12, treating respectively of reverence for the poor, the relation of faith and works, and sins of the tongue—themes that have no relation to one another and which might equally well have been treated in any other order. The third part of the letter, 3:13–5:6, contains what may be called "sayings-groups"; these comprise (a) compact sections, 3:13-17; 4:13-16; 5:1-6; (b) sections with less inner unity, 4:1-10 and 4:11-12; and (c) the isolated sayings, 3:18 and 4:17. The concluding part 5:7-20 resumes the style of ch. 1, being again a series of brief sayings, each complete in itself, with no general logical plan to determine their order. And, as was noted above, there is no formal conclusion to the letter; there is no rhetorical reason why it could not have

3

ended sooner or could not have continued further with additional sayings. Consequently, while the entire work undoubtedly possesses a certain unity, it lacks any formal plan—not only as a whole but in its separate parts.

James, accordingly, occupies a unique position in the epistolary literature of the New Testament. And yet very real parallels appear in portions of certain other epistles; toward the close of some Pauline letters (I Thess. 4:1-12; 5:1-22; Gal. 5:1–6:10; Col. 3:1–4:5; Rom. 12–13) and in Heb. 13 we have similar sequences of sayings-groups and isolated sayings arranged with little apparent logical order. So the form of James is not a unique creation even within the New Testament. And this form was very familiar in the contemporary Hellenistic world, where similar somewhat miscellaneous collections of general moral instructions were widely employed in teaching ethics. If these instructions were phrased throughout in the third person, such a collection was called a "gnomologium." But if the second person (singular or plural) was employed, so that the teachings were addressed—either actually or as a literary device—to an individual or to a group, then the collection was termed a "paraenesis." And in James we have a perfect example of a paraenesis; as such it was written and as such it must be interpreted.

While James is a paraenesis, as a whole and in all its parts, in many sections another highly specialized contemporary literary form is also evident—the form known as a "diatribe." For a full description of the diatribe, reference must be made to the special treatises on classic literature and rhetoric, but for present purposes it may be described adequately enough as copying the style of a speaker engaged in a lively oral debate with an opponent. The speaker is engaged in proving a point—usually in an ethical problem—but he interrupts his formal argument by quoting his opponent's arguments and refuting them, addressing his opponent directly, often in most depreciatory terms, and appealing to his listeners to agree with him. Among ancient writers on ethics who use the diatribe form Epictetus is particularly notable; among Jewish authors the thoroughly Hellenized Philo often employs it. In the New Testament, Rom. 3:1-8 illustrates the form admirably. For the use of the diatribe style in James consult the Exegesis, particularly on 2:14-26.

II. Authorship

The fact that the Epistle of James is written throughout as a paraenesis, with frequent employment of the diatribe, shows that its author must be sought among those whose literary associations were with the Greek rather than with the Hebrew world. For the antecedents of true prose paraenesis among non-Greek-speaking Jews are so scanty as to be virtually nonexistent. Partial parallels have been found in the transmission of the sayings of many of the prophets, and still more in the collections of the sayings of Jesus in the Synoptic Gospels. But in neither case were the compilers following—or forming! —a set literary form. A closer parallel exists in the wisdom literature, particularly in Proverbs and Ecclesiasticus, but the maxims in this literature are invariably in verse, not in prose. Except for Proverbs, there are no parallels at all in the Old Testament proper. In the Apocrypha, besides Ecclesiasticus, only Tob. 4:5-19 and 12:6-10 can be cited, but even in this rather remote example it is more than possible that in the original Aramaic these passages were in verse. Elsewhere in the older nonbiblical works paraenesis is represented solely in scattered passages in the Testaments of the Twelve Patriarchs and—to cite an extremely remote instance— The Story of Ahikar, a work whose essentially Jewish character and whose significant influence on subsequent Jewish literature are both quite doubtful.

And what has been said of the non-Jewish nature of prose paraenesis is even more true of the non-Jewish nature of the diatribe form; this is purely Hellenistic.

It appears, therefore, that the author of James not only could write easily and fluently in Greek but was so familiar with Hellenistic literary models that, when composing his treatise, he cast it as a matter of course into the form normally used by the Hellenistic teachers of his own time—a combination of paraenesis and diatribe. He reveals, moreover, an acquaintance with a variety of minor Greek rhetorical devices, such as alliteration, climax, etc.; the more significant of these are mentioned in the Exegesis as they occur. And he reveals in addition a knowledge of the terminology and content of the contemporary Stoic-Cynic ethics: 3:2-12 (except for vs. 9 and the last clause of vs. 6) and 4:1-2 may well have been copied verbatim from "secular" Greek works (cf. also on 1:14-15). That our Greek text of James is, as has been sometimes argued, a translation of a Hebrew or Aramaic original is therefore wholly impossible.

On the other hand, the content of James, as contrasted with its literary form, belongs unequivocally to the Hebraic-Christian, and not to the Hellenistic world. The insertion of vs. 9 and the last clause of vs. 6 in 3:2-12 convert the general teaching of 3:2-12 into something that is wholly un-Hellenistic. And the same is true of the development of the thesis of 4:1-2 in 4:3-10, producing an incongruity in 4:1-10 that has so puzzled commentators as to lead them to suspect textual corruption. James, as we have it, is unambiguously the work of a Christian author, whose rhetorical training was Hellenistic but whose religious background was firmly Hebraic.

Can the "James" whose name stands as writer at the beginning of the letter be identified with any of the other New Testament characters bearing the same name? Of these there are three (not including the James of Luke 6:16): the apostle James, who was the son of Zebedee, the second (very obscure) apostle "James the less" (i.e., "the little"), and "James the Lord's brother." Attempts to identify the author of our letter with either of the first two now belong only to the curiosities of the history of interpretation, but the theory that the third James was the author has held sway for many centuries.

He appears in Mark 6:3 (Matt. 13:55) as one of the four "brothers" of Jesus—the others being Joses, Judas, and Simon, of whom we know only the names. The exact relationship implied by "brothers" has been, and is still, the theme of often embittered controversy as among three alternatives: children of Joseph and Mary, children of Joseph by a former marriage, and cousins. The details of this controversy are for the purposes of this Commentary unimportant.

According to Mark (to a somewhat lesser degree according to Matthew and still less according to Luke), the attitude of these brothers to Jesus during his ministry lacked understanding, to say the least. In Mark 3:20-21, 31-35, alarmed at his lack of care for his health, they set out (presumably from Nazareth) to interfere ("to seize him," according to the RSV), saying, "He is beside himself." But on their arrival (in Capernaum?) Jesus refused even to see them, saying that only they who do God's will have any claim on him. (Both Matthew and Luke omit any parallel to Mark 3:20-21, presumably because its language seemed unedifying, but they give their versions of Mark 3:31-35 in Matt. 12:46-50 and Luke 8:19-21. And Luke 11:27-28 may conceivably be a softened variant of Jesus' saying in these verses.)

Then in Mark 6:1-6 (Matt. 13:53-58; the rather vague parallel in Luke 4:16-30 is quite different), at his rejection in Nazareth, Jesus declares that a prophet "is not without honor, except in his own country, and among his own kin, and in his own house" (RSV); and here, so that there can be no mistake as to who these "kin" are, they are carefully listed by Mark, with all the brothers named. (Matthew's parallel omits the word "kin" but otherwise agrees closely with Mark.)

This lack of understanding on the part of the brothers is further and acutely heightened in John 7:3-8, where the evangelist declares roundly, "For even his brothers did not believe in him," and Jesus says to them, "The world cannot hate you, but it hates me"—words of bitter reproach. And it is not to read too much into John 19:26-27 to see there a sharp criticism of the "brothers" when Jesus commits his mother to the beloved disciple as her "son."

Yet despite these unfavorable descriptions in the Gospels, the "brothers of the Lord" were by no means inconspicuous in the early church (Acts 1:14; I Cor. 9:5), while in Palestine James was accorded a position of high eminence. A special vision of the risen Christ had been vouchsafed him (I Cor. 15:7)—something hardly conceivable unless he had been prepared to receive it by genuine faith and certainly something that would be regarded by the first Christians as a proof of extraordinary divine favor. Whether or not he was formally entitled an "apostle" is uncertain, for the language of Gal. 1:19 is ambiguous, but there can be little doubt that he was often so called. And in any case, not only was he recognized as a "pillar" of the church along with Peter and John (Gal. 2:9), but he is named before the other two, as if he were the most important of the three. And this importance is corroborated in Gal. 2:12, which tells how all the Christians in Antioch, including Peter, immediately obeyed the command of James.

In Acts the picture is the same. In Acts 12:17 the local Jerusalem church is summarily described as "James and . . . the brethren." In Acts 15, while it would be perhaps too much of a modernization to say that James "presides" over the apostolic council, he is at least the final speaker and the decision he proposes is adopted exactly as he words it. And in Acts 21:18 he once more appears as head of the Jerusalem church and its council of elders; even though in what follows the pronoun is not "he" but "they"—corresponding to the fact that the decree of Acts 15:23-29 was formally adopted by the entire apostolic council—his own high authority is taken for granted.

Outside of the opening verse of our epistle, the only other mention of James in the New Testament is in Jude 1, where the fact that the "brother of James" is deemed sufficient to identify Jude and to authenticate his authority shows the prominence of the former.

Outside the New Testament, our present texts of Josephus (Antiquities XX. 9. 1) state that James was martyred by order of the high priest Annas II after the death of Festus but before the arrival of his successor Albinus, a date probably *ca.* A.D. 60-62. But there is some possibility that this section in the *Antiquities* may be a later interpolation. Otherwise the only reasonably early account of James that may have any significance is a lengthy extract from the second-century Christian writer Hegesippus, which is preserved in the *Church History* of Eusebius (II. 23). Hegesippus may be following genuine tradition when he relates how even the non-Christian Jews respected James because of his extreme and conspicuous devotion to the temple and his almost ultra-Pharisaic ceremonialism; all this, while it goes beyond what is stated in Acts 21:17-26, is not really out of accord with it. And Hegesippus may well be right in dating the martyrdom of James after the outbreak of the Jewish war against Rome (say, A.D. 66-67?), because the Christians' refusal to take part in this war (Luke 21:21; etc.) naturally inflamed beyond measure Jewish hatred of these "pacifists." But naturally there can be no positive certainty even as to the fact of the martyrdom—not to speak of its date.

It is this James, the brother of the Lord and the head of the Christian church in Jerusalem, whose name has been traditionally associated with the Epistle of James. How far can this tradition be justified?

One preliminary difficulty is immediately obvious. Whatever the exact relationship implied by "brother," James, like Jesus, lived in Nazareth (Mark 6:3) and must have been intimately acquainted with him; but there is nothing in the epistle that even hints at this intimate relationship. There is no book in the New Testament that tells us less about Christ. Nowhere in it is any saying of Jesus cited as such, and even indirect citations are very few (5:12 is really the only instance where there seems to be a definite quotation, with probable but less clear examples in 1:6-8; 2:8; cf. the Exeg.). For the teaching in the epistle, this assumed "brother of the Lord" has all but utterly disregarded the wealth of knowledge he must have had of what his greater Brother taught—and for his authorities has turned instead to the Old Testament, Jewish tradition, and Hellenistic Stoic-Cynic ethics.

A further difficulty is raised by what has been said on the form of the epistle. The brother of the Lord was a Jew of Nazareth, whose native language was necessarily Aramaic. In addition to Aramaic, he would have learned, as was the custom, some Hebrew in the local school but—this may be said with extreme certainty—no other language. On the other hand, as Nazareth lay on a thronged trade route, it may be assumed that most Nazarenes would pick up more or less Greek of some sort or

other; in the dialogue between Jesus and Pilate in Mark 15:2-4 there is no reason to suppose that an interpreter was necessary. It should also be recognized that when James became head of the bilingual church of Jerusalem (Acts 6:1), he must have attained a fair facility in speaking and perhaps even in writing Greek. But this would be the colloquial Jewish Greek of Palestine, and even this would be to him always an acquired, not a native, language; he could have felt at ease only in Aramaic and, in particular, he would use the Old Testament always either in the original Hebrew or in the Aramaic version. Can we, by the wildest stretch of the imagination, think of James in mature life as learning to write the Greek of this epistle—an epistle cast in the Hellenistic and non-Semitic form of prose paraenesis, using the equally Hellenistic and non-Semitic diatribe, characterized by familiarity with Stoic-Cynic ethical terminology, and the Greek hexameters in 1:17 and 4:5? Or that, as in 4:6, he would cite the Old Testament (Prov. 3:34) from the Greek version (LXX), which is quite unlike the Hebrew? To ask these questions is to answer them: our epistle was not written by "James the Lord's brother" nor by any other James known to us by name in the New Testament.

The name "James" at the beginning of the letter should therefore be regarded precisely like the name "Peter" at the beginning of II Peter or "Paul" at the beginning of the Pastoral epistles; the name of a great figure of the apostolic church, under whose patronage a later writer, in accord with a familiar similar and recognized custom in Judaism (Enoch, Baruch, Ezra, etc.), placed his own production. To speak of a "forgery" would be utterly unjust. The choice in this instance of James as the patron was perhaps partly due to his reputation as a stern moralist; a more immediate reason will appear in the next few pages.

III. Jewish Christianity

Even if the actual author of the epistle was not James the Lord's brother, does the content of the writing represent the special type of Christianity of which James was the recognized champion? Or in other words, does our letter teach a Jewish Christianity?

By "Jewish Christianity" here is to be understood the ideal taken for granted in the declaration of James and the Jerusalem elders in Acts 21:20-25, where a sharp distinction is drawn between Jewish and Gentile believers. There are "thousands" (literally "myriads") of the former and they are all "zealous for the law"; not merely the moral law but the "customs" (i.e., the ceremonial law) as well. So zealous are they, indeed, that they treat as an incredible slander the report that Paul has taught Jewish converts to forsake these customs; they ask him —and he agrees—to show publicly "that there is nothing in what" his enemies have been saying about him, and that he himself lives "in observance of the law."

For Gentile Christians, on the other hand, no such observance of the "customs" is required; it was sufficient for them to keep the four "necessary" points laid down in Acts 15:28-29 (and repeated in 21:25) ; if they kept these, all would be well with them. From the standpoint of non-Christian Judaism this was a miraculous, even an incredible, concession—this admission that Gentiles might be dispensed from virtually all observance of the ceremonial law and yet be regarded as inheritors of salvation. But the concession was very far from complete. It meant that in every Christian community in which there were former Jews and former Gentiles there were two sharply distinct groups of believers: those who continued to observe the Mosaic ceremonies and those who disregarded them. And—this is the important point—the former regarded themselves as representing a higher and more complete type of Christianity than the latter. In particular, the Jewish Christians simply took for granted that the seat of authority in the Christian church was in Jerusalem, the heart of Jewish Christianity. It was to "the apostles and the elders" there that the problem of Gentile converts had originally been referred for decision (Acts 15:2) , while in later days "James and . . . the elders" regard themselves as the inheritors of the apostolic council's powers (Acts 21:18, 25) .

The consequence of this Jewish Christian claim was a controversy that has left very obvious traces in the New Testament. The protagonist among those who disputed the claim was of course Paul. He refused absolutely and passionately to admit that the high ecclesiastical rank of James and the other "pillars" carried with it any corresponding spiritual authority. Their rank was given them by men, not by God, and so was to Paul a matter of utter indifference (Gal. 2:6, 9) . Therefore not only were commands from James destitute of any real binding power but—as when he forbade Jewish Christians to eat with their Gentile brethren—they actually might be commands to commit sin, so that all who obeyed him were sinners (Gal. 2:11-21) !

It is important here to realize clearly the real point at issue in Galatians. There is no hint that James—or still less Peter—taught that Gentiles could be saved only if they became circumcised and kept the ceremonies; in the entire New Testament such an opinion is attributed only to discredited Pharisaic extremists (Acts 15:1, 5). But James and the Jerusalem church, as has been said, while welcoming Gentiles as fellow Christians, regarded them as occupying an inferior position. As certainly as their Jewish brethren they would be received into the kingdom of God! But (Matt. 5:19), since they not only broke the "least" (i.e., "ceremonial") commandments of the law, but also taught others to do likewise, in that kingdom they would be the "least." Those who would be "great" in the kingdom would be those who not only kept the "great" (i.e., "moral") commandments of the law, but the "least" as well; who, indeed—for so "zealous" for the law were Jewish Christians of the second generation— went beyond the actual law to do all that the scribes and Pharisees (Matt. 23:2-3) commanded! Or as Paul puts it, Jewish Christians teach that to be complete and perfect Christians it is not enough to begin with the Spirit; men must go on and (Gal. 3:3) end with the flesh! And such a doctrine is an abomination.

It is this controversy that is responsible for the varying estimates of the brothers of the Lord that were noted above. Paul's depreciation of the authority of James finds rather more than a vigorous echo in Mark, whose narrative depreciates James himself. A portion of Mark's depreciation has been more or less mechanically copied by Matthew, but in a softened form. Still less of Mark's depreciation has been copied by Luke, and in a still more softened form; Luke may very well have been unwilling to record anything that might detract from the dignity which he would ascribe to James in Acts. But the Fourth Evangelist, to whom the freedom of Christianity from all Jewish legalism was an axiomatic dogma, goes not only beyond Mark but beyond Paul: James, far from being a "pillar," was one whom "the world cannot hate"—in poignant contrast to its hatred of Christ (John 7:7) . Here John is writing at a time when the Christians were so nearly universally Gentiles that their freedom from the "worldliness" of the Mosaic ceremonies was assumed as a matter of course. So far had this concept progressed that the (comparatively very few) Jewish believers who still clung to the ceremonies were now regarded not only as reactionaries, but as dangerous heretics against whom relentless war must be waged; compare, e.g., Ign. Mag. 9:1, where keeping the sabbath instead of "the Lord's day" is denounced as a deadly sin. And this conviction must have been immeasurably intensified by the Roman persecution of Christianity. From this persecution the Jewish Christians, because of their ceremonialism indistinguishable by the Romans from other Jews, were exempt, since at least outwardly they were members of a *religio licita;* "the world did not hate them" as it hated the church at large.

The diverse estimates of James (and the other "brothers of the Lord") in the New Testament form therefore a consistent pattern: James was praised or reproached according as his critics shared or rejected the Jewish Christian doctrine that the highest and purest form of Christianity combined faith in Christ with meticulous observance of the Mosaic ceremonies; that without such observance believers might indeed attain the final kingdom but only in a definitely inferior status.

But—and this is a matter of very great importance—while in the battle against Jewish Christianity much the most important figure was Paul, it by no means follows that rejection of Jewish Christianity involved acceptance of all that Paul taught. Nothing is more untrue to history than a reconstruction of the apostolic age, a reconstruction highly popular a century ago, that saw in it primarily a conflict between Paulinism and anti-Paulinism. The letters of Paul, the great Apostle to the Gentiles, bulk so large in the New Testament that it is easy for us to think that all Gentile Christianity was Pauline. It was not. When the author of II Peter says of Paul's letters that "there are some things in them hard to understand" (II Pet. 3:16), he speaks not only for his own and later ages but for the apostolic age as well. When Paul taught that for Christians circumcision was wholly needless, that Gentile believers were every whit the equals of their Jewish Christian brothers, this doctrine was avidly adopted. But the intricacies of the logic by which he attained this conclusion were quite another matter. When he wrote "Christ is the end of the law" (Rom. 10:4), he wrote a phrase that bewildered many. Surely, they reasoned, Paul could not mean Christ has put an end to the law "Thou shalt not kill" or "Thou shalt not commit adultery." And similarly with the phrase so basic in Paul's thinking, "We hold that a man is justified by faith apart from works of law" (Rom. 3:28). Surely, men argued, Paul could not possibly teach that if a man's belief is orthodox, his conduct does not matter.

Of course, in both instances they were perfectly right; Paul meant nothing of the sort. But Paul's real meaning could be grasped only by those who could understand his argument as an indivisible whole, a task quite beyond the capacities of almost everyone in the apostolic and post-apostolic ages. A famous saying of Harnack's (roughly paraphrased) states the facts not unfairly, "No one in the second century understood Paul but Marcion—and Marcion misunderstood him!" This saying is, to be sure, not wholly correct; B. W. Bacon observed succinctly that it should read, "No one understood Paul but John—and John did *not* misunderstand him!" But the genius of John, like the genius of Paul, soared far beyond the reach of the rank and file of contemporary Christians.

The consequence was that Paul's teaching was brought into the comprehension of ordinary believers by the explanation that by the "law" Paul meant not the moral but the ceremonial law of the Old Testament. This is the solution taken for granted, for example, by Clement of Rome. The argument of his letter is based on a myriad of citations from the Old Testament moral codes, whose eternal validity is to him an axiom. And as regards justification, Clement, whose regard for Paul was profound, is completely unconscious of any deviation from the apostle's teaching when he writes (I Clem. 10:7) that God's promise to Abraham was fulfilled because of the latter's "faith *and hospitality!*"

A still simpler solution, however, of the problem offered by Paul's "radicalism" was possible in the days when the authority of the Pauline epistles had not yet been generally accepted by the whole church, that is to say, in the apostolic age proper and in the earlier subapostolic age, perhaps until the middle of the second century. And this solution merely ignored Paul's arguments or denied their truth; cf. here perhaps II Tim. 1:15, "You are aware that all who are in Asia turned away from me"—a very curious statement when contrasted with the intense affection shown to Paul in that same "Asia" (Acts 20:37-38).

In any case, the fact is clear that we must not think of the early Christians as divided into two rival parties, Jewish Christians and Paulinists. Most believers belonged to neither of these parties but formed a broad middle-of-the-road group. They rejected circumcision and the Mosaic ceremonies on the one hand; on the other they regarded the Mosaic moral law as binding. And without attempting to phrase their conception too precisely—they certainly did not do so themselves—they assuredly regarded works as well as faith (in the sense of "belief") as essential for every Christian or would-be Christian.

To come now finally to the question at issue: Is the Epistle of James a technically "Jewish-Christian" work? Undoubtedly very much of its material is taken from Jewish sources and may even be described as "Jewish" rather than as

"Christian" (see below, pp. 9-12). But this fact does not make it "Jewish-Christian" in the polemic force of the term any more than its occasional use of traditional Stoic-Cynic ethical teaching, and its use throughout of the Stoic-Cynic literary forms of paraenesis and diatribe, make it a Stoic-Cynic treatise. Nowhere is the slightest interest displayed in the ceremonial laws of the Old Testament; indeed, these may possibly be depreciated in 1:27 (cf. Exegesis). Nowhere is there the slightest hint of two classes of Christians—the cardinal tenet of true Jewish Christianity.

The author, to be sure, takes for granted that the moral law of the Old Testament still binds Christians *as law;* in this sense Lev. 19:18 is cited in 2:8, Lev. 19:15 in 2:9, and Exod. 20:13-14 in 2:11. Paul, assuredly, would have written 2:8-11 very differently (cf. Rom. 13:8-10). But as was noted above, the theory of the binding power of the moral precepts of the Old Testament *as law* is developed by Clement far more elaborately than by James, and Clement was certainly not a Jewish Christian. And however differently he might phrase his teaching, Paul himself would heartily agree that the Old Testament precepts cited by James—"Thou shalt love thy neighbor as thyself," "Thou shalt not respect persons," "Thou shalt not kill" and "Thou shalt not commit adultery"—were, whether *as law* or not, as eternally valid for Christians as for Jews.

Wholly un-Pauline, of course, is the famous passage on justification (2:14-26). Or more precisely, this passage is wholly un-Pauline in its wording; Paul's treatment of the theme appears in Rom. 6. But, again, the presuppositions of Clement regarding the relation of faith and works do not differ at all from those set forth in James. And, again, Paul himself would heartily agree that "faith," as James defines it to mean only acceptance of monotheism (2:19), could not possibly bring justification.

We may conclude that while James is obviously not a Pauline writing, neither is it in the proper sense of the phrase a Jewish Christian writing. Its writer represents neither extreme, but is to be classed, like the author of I Clement, in the broad and nonpartisan "center" of non-imaginative but earnest and common Greek-speaking Christians.

IV. Unity and Sources

While the Epistle of James, as it stands, is unambiguously a Christian document, much of its material equally clearly is derived from Jewish rather than from Christian tradition. But was this Jewish material assembled by the writer from oral or from written sources?

This question appears to have been first raised explicitly in the last decade of the nineteenth century, when a French scholar [1] and a German scholar,[2] working wholly independently, published almost simultaneously conclusions that were identical. Both maintained that the epistle was originally a purely Jewish writing which has been converted into a Christian work by an editor who merely added "and of the Lord Jesus Christ" in 1:1 and "our Lord Jesus Christ" in 2:1. Both writers stressed in support of their theory the extraordinarily difficult grammatical problem offered by the Greek genitives in 2:1 (cf. Exegesis for details), a problem solved at once by the theory of the interpolation. And they argued further that if this interpolation is accepted, a corresponding interpolation in 1:1 may be inferred; especially since 1:1, as it now reads, contains language unique in the New Testament (cf. Exegesis). Then, since these two occurrences of "Jesus Christ" are the only explicit Christian terms in the letter, the remainder, they argued, not only represented a use of Jewish tradition, but *was* Jewish tradition and nothing else.

This theory, although treated with proper respect by subsequent writers, failed to meet with approval; it endeavored, apparently, to prove too much. But a generation later Arnold Meyer [3] revived the theory and, with a wealth of fresh evidence, restated it in a far more attractive form. Like Massebieau and Spitta, he assumed that the epistle is an only slightly Christianized version of a Jewish original, although in addition to the Christian interpolations in 1:1 and 2:1 he admitted others in 5:12 and 5:14 (cf. Exegesis).

Meyer's particular contribution, however, consisted in his attempt to explain the form and purpose of the Jewish earlier writing. Noting that in Greek, Aramaic, and Hebrew, "James" and "Jacob" are the same word (cf. the footnote to 1:1 in the ASV), he saw that if the Christian "interpolation" in 1:1 was recognized as such, the original opening words could be read "Jacob, a servant of God, to the twelve tribes in the dispersion: Greeting." This address, couched in familiar Old Testament language (for Jacob as "God's servant" cf. Gen. 32:10; Isa. 41:8; Jer. 46:27; etc.), would be ideally phrased for a letter destined to Greek-speaking Jews who, apart from the comparatively few

[1] L. Massebieau, "L'épitre de Jacques est-elle l'oeuvre d'un Chrétien?" in *Revue de l'Histoire des Religions,* XXXII (1895), 249-83.
[2] Friedrich Spitta, "Der Brief des Jacobus" in his *Zur Geschichte und Literatur des Urchristentums* (1896), II, 1-239; also published separately.
[3] *Das Rätsel des Jacobusbriefes* (Giessen: A. Töpelmann, 1930).

resident in Palestine, were quite literally "dispersed" throughout the entire Roman Empire and beyond its borders. And for a letter from Jacob to the "twelve tribes" a well-known biblical precedent was provided by Gen. 49, where Jacob addresses the "ancestor" of each tribe in turn.

The special purpose of Jacob's address in Gen. 49, moreover, is to characterize each of the twelve tribes with the peculiar vice or virtue that distinguished it. And this characterization of the tribes played a large part in later Jewish tradition. It is developed elaborately in the Testaments of the Twelve Patriarchs, where Reuben reproves fornication, Simeon reproves envy, and so on. It is developed again very fully by Philo, who equates each tribe with a special virtue or vice (for detailed reference cf. the Exegesis). Similar developments in one form or another are abundant in other Jewish material (given rather fully by Meyer). Meyer undertook to demonstrate that similar references to the twelve tribes can be detected in James, thus corroborating his thesis that James was originally a letter of Jacob to these tribes.

His major identifications are:

1:2-4: Isaac as "joy," Rebecca as "steadfastness," Jacob as "perfection through trials"; 1:9-11: Asher as "worldly rich man"; 1:12: Issachar as "doer of good deeds"; 1:18: Reuben as "first fruits"; 1:19-20: Simeon as "anger"; 1:26-27: Levi as "religion"; 3:18: Naphtali as "peace"; 4:1-2: Gad as "wars and fightings"; 5:7: Dan as "waiting for salvation," "patience"; 5:14 (in part) -18: Joseph as "prayer"; 5:20: Benjamin as "death and birth."

To these Meyer adds as conceivable, but more obscure, identifications a second characterization in 1:22-25 of Levi as "he who acts"; in 2:5-8 a very obscure allusion to Judah as "the royal one"; and in 5:12 a still more hypothetical reference to Zebulun as "oath." He finds also a number of minor references to Laban, Esau, Rachel, etc.[4]

In the short interval that elapsed between the publication of Meyer's work and the outbreak of World War II no detailed examination of his theory was undertaken by other specialists; but a summary of its contentions and a brief (rather sympathetic) analysis will be found in the commentary by Windisch (see below, p. 18), unfortunately published too soon (also in 1930) to do adequate justice to Meyer's arguments. An attempt is made below, therefore, to restate this very important theory and also to indicate the details in which it appears to try to prove too much.

[4] For a summary of Meyer's results compare the table in *Das Rätsel des Jacobusbriefes*, pp. 282-83.

That a "Letter of Jacob" really underlies our present "Epistle of James" is a very attractive hypothesis; for the first time in the long history of exegesis a really satisfying explanation has been given to the highly cryptic wording of 1:1. And that real allusions to many or most of Jacob's sons can be detected is likewise a very attractive hypothesis. Neither hypothesis, of course, is capable of rigorous proof; but in the present work it has seemed safe, at least, to accept the former hypothesis as a working theory and, as regards the latter hypothesis, to mention the more probable tribal allusions as they occur, so permitting the reader to draw his own conclusions as to their relevance.

But even if Meyer is correct in his contention that a "Letter of Jacob" forms the basis of James, it by no means follows that he is equally correct in contending that the former can be recovered by eliminating minimal Christian additions in 1:1; 2:1; 5:12; and 5:14. He seems vastly to have underestimated the contributions of the Christian editor. This appears most vividly in the long section 2:14-26 on the relative value of faith and works. While it is quite true that before the rise of rabbinism a greater emphasis was laid on monotheism as Israel's central tenet than was the case in later days, nowhere is there any evidence that the acceptance of monotheism was ever held to dispense from the observance of God's law; that "faith apart from works" was ever considered by Jews to be anything else than "barren" (2:20). Not only is the general trend of the argument in 2:14-26 one impossible in Judaism, but the details of its wording show that the argument is directed against a non-Jewish opponent—an opponent who can be identified definitely as Paul. He would be a hopelessly misunderstood Paul, no doubt, but Paul none the less—or, at least, some overenthusiastic disciple of Paul. (For a fuller discussion of the evidence consult the Exegesis.) Only one conclusion appears to be possible: 2:14-26 was written not by a Jew, but by a Christian.

Nor is 2:14-26 the only Christian passage in James. Another that may assuredly be classed as Christian is 3:1, and still others which can be so classed with a very high degree of probability are 1:6-8; 2:7-8; and 2:12 (see Exegesis). And it may be added that if the Christian origin of 2:14-26 is conceded, a still more important conclusion follows. For the general style of this long and important section is perfectly representative of the general style of the epistle as a whole; the Christian editor therefore did not content himself with a few tiny additions here and there but rewrote the whole in his own wording.

If this is correct, we have the solution of a difficulty in Meyer's theory for which he has no satisfying answer. If the "Letter of Jacob to the Twelve Tribes" was really virtually coextensive with James as a whole, we should expect to find the tribal allusions fairly evenly distributed throughout the work. But this is precisely what we do not find. Meyer detects them in 1:2-4; 1:9-12, 18-19, 26-27; 3:18; 4:1-2; 5:7, 14a-18, 19-20 (omitting the very vague references he finds in 1:22-25; 2:5-8; 5:12) —nearly all at either the beginning or the end of the letter. Or to put it differently, while James contains 108 verses, tribal allusions can be detected with any plausibility in only about 21 verses, less than one fifth of the whole. And the remaining 87 verses contain some of the most valuable and characteristic teaching of all James.

Meyer notes, to be sure, that no one writing paraenesis would tie himself down to a rigid outline; it is a characteristic of paraenetic style that it permits of all sorts of apparently unmotived digressions. It is quite true, for instance, that none of the dozen treatises that make up the Testaments of the Twelve Patriarchs confines itself rigidly to the special vice or virtue that is supposedly its theme. Yet the digressions never bulk very large; there is no adequate basis here for accepting the almost grotesque assumption necessitated by Meyer's theory, that more than four fifths of the entire work is irrelevant to its plan!

Helpful though this theory is in solving certain problems in James, it assuredly needs restatement before it can be adopted. Much more must be ascribed to the Christian editor than the theory allows; the "Letter of Jacob," instead of underlying James as a whole, underlies only portions of the epistle, chiefly at the beginning and at the end, and has been supplemented extensively by the Christian editor with further material. Furthermore, the extreme vagueness of the supposed allusions to certain tribes may very probably be accounted for by the fact that these allusions are only supposed, for the Christian editor naturally felt under no compulsion to reproduce the whole of "Jacob's" work, but would omit any part of it inappropriate for his own purpose or inapplicable to his readers. But with these modifications Meyer's hypothesis makes an exceedingly weighty contribution to the understanding of James. And perhaps without endorsing it wholeheartedly, we may recognize the arguments for it as they are given at the proper points in the Exegesis.

There remains the question of other sources used by James. Here obviously no dogmatically final conclusions can be drawn, but certain reasonably plausible statements can be made. If what seem to be the additions of the Christian editor in ch. 1 are disregarded, there is no objection to treating the remainder of the chapter as belonging to "Jacob." Its material would all be wholly appropriate in Judaism, the tribal allusions are abundant, and the sections that do not have these contain no more material than might be expected in "paraenetic digressions."

The section 2:1-13, dealing with the proper treatment of rich and poor in the synagogues, is complete in itself. Again, as in ch. 1, it contains certain touches that appear to come from the Christian editor, which should be disregarded in considering the source of the material as a whole. And this source may safely be ascribed to pre-Christian Judaism (see Exegesis); not, however, to "Jacob," for a tribal allusion to Dan detected in 2:4 (as "the symbol of distinction") is very strained, especially in contrast to the much more obvious allusion to Dan in 5:7. We have here, rather, a special little treatise on a highly specialized topic, which the Christian editor has judged useful for his readers.

We can describe 2:14-26 as wholly the work of the Christian editor.

The portion 3:1-12 is, like 2:1-13, a section complete in itself, with no connection with what precedes, although with a better connection with what follows. The opening verse, which sets the theme, is certainly from the Christian editor, and the insertion of the section may be safely ascribed to him. It is presumably, however, not his own composition and its ultimate origin is Hellenistic (see Exegesis).

This attribution of these three sections, 2:1-13; 2:14-26; and 3:1-12, to the Christian editor, whether as author or compiler, explains moreover the difference in special style between them and the remainder of the letter; each of them is a sustained analysis of a special topic, in striking contrast to the brief sayings or sayings-groups elsewhere.

In 3:13-18, on "wisdom," there is nothing specifically Christian, and the apparent tribal reference to Naphtali in vs. 18 justifies assigning it to "Jacob."

The section 4:1-10 likewise may be assigned to "Jacob." It is hard to conceive vss. 1-2 as written by a Christian to Christian readers, but they were wholly appropriate for a Jew writing to Jews; the tribal reference to Gad in vs. 1 can be verified not only from Philo but from Gen. 49:19 as well.

In 4:11-12 there is nothing Christian nor does it contain a tribal reference. Its source is therefore indeterminate, although it may well be a "paraenetic digression" in "Jacob." And no more than this can be said about either 4:13-16 or 4:17.

Similarly 5:1-6 is indeterminate. But it is unique in the epistle as having unambiguously a Palestinian setting, in which it deals with the sufferings of the "poor" in general, not specifically of the Christian "poor."

The remainder of the letter, apart from the evident Christian editing in vss. 12 and 14, may safely be ascribed to "Jacob."

Summarizing: As far as the "Letter of Jacob" can be reconstructed from James, its maximum extent appears to be 1:1 (in part), 2-4, 5 (?), 9-11, 12, 13-15 (?), 16-18, 19-21, 22-25, 26-27; 3:13-18; 4:1-10, 11-12 (?), 13-16 (?), 17 (?); 5:1-6 (?), 7-11, 12 (possibly in very small part), 14 (in small part) -18, 19-20. In this list the passages marked with (?) contain no tribal references but may very conceivably be "paraenetic digressions." At all events, these passages taken together represent the maximum extent to which "Jacob" can be disentangled from James. And as has already been observed, the absence of any really identifiable "tribal references" to (at least) Judah and Zebulun presumably indicate that James did not incorporate the whole of "Jacob" in his own work.

Of this material in "Jacob," 4:1-2 has been taken directly from some "secular" Stoic-Cynic ethical source, and there may be similar coloring in 1:13-15, but the remainder is of Jewish origin.

From the Christian editor come 1:6-8 (the teaching of Jesus); 2:1-13 (from a pre-Christian Jewish source or sources, with some Christian editing), 14-26 (the editor's own composition); 3:1-12 (vs. 1 is the editor's composition; the rest of the section is almost wholly "secular" Hellenistic); 5:12 (perhaps a few words from "Jacob," the rest from the teaching of Jesus) and 5:14 (perhaps again a few words from "Jacob," enlarged with the editor's own composition). But as has been noted, the general unity of style and vocabulary in the whole epistle indicates that the earlier material, whatever its source, has been freely rewritten by the final editor. How extensively he modified his sources it is impossible to say.

V. Purpose and Date of the Sources

The purpose of the "Letter of Jacob" is established by its opening words "to the twelve tribes in the dispersion." The phrase "the twelve tribes" shows that it was written for the benefit of full Jews, and not for the partial converts to Judaism known as "God fearers" (Acts 10:2) or "God worshipers" (Acts 16:14), a not inconsiderable class of men and women who had accepted the worship of Israel's God and had renounced idolatry, although without taking on themselves the full burden of the ceremonial laws. Moreover, "dispersion," at least in its usual sense, was the accepted and technical term to describe Jews living outside Palestine, "dispersed" throughout the Roman Empire and even beyond its limits. Of these there were very many who were Hellenized not only in their language but in their culture as well; who, while perfectly faithful to their own religion, had seen that there was much to admire in Greek philosophy and ethics.

The supreme example of this open-mindedness was Philo of Alexandria, who spent his life endeavoring to reconcile the teachings of the Greek philosophers, especially Plato, with those of Moses. And it was a similar open-mindedness, although of course on an incomparably petty scale, that appears in "Jacob's" use of Stoic-Cynic material in 1:13-15 and 4:1-2. This appears more especially in his use of Hellenistic rhetorical devices throughout, and above all in his choice of the literary form of prose paraenesis for his work. Did his readers admire the style and clarity of Greek ethical writers? Very well; he could show them that the same style and the same clarity could be utilized equally well by a faithful Jew!

But vastly more primary to the writer than his rhetorical form was his moral purpose. Good Jews, quite as truly as Greeks, were in need of concrete ethical instruction. Undoubtedly they had, as the Greeks did not have, the supreme guidance of the wholly inspired law of God; where the law spoke clearly and unambiguously, no further guidance was necessary. But—and here was the difficulty—there was an endless number of concrete moral problems on which the law spoke neither clearly nor unambiguously; and many more problems on which the law did not speak at all. Even supposing that a devout and earnest Jew should commit to memory all the various precepts contained in the Pentateuch, they would afford a very inadequate guide to the moral complexities of daily living. Supplementary help was absolutely essential.

The provision of such supplementary help was the purpose of the book of Proverbs, in the Old Testament, and, in the Apocrypha, of Ecclesiasticus and (in a more specialized form) of the Wisdom of Solomon. The peculiar aim of all three of these works, particularly of the first two, was to give concrete guidance to the perplexed soul: in the circumstances described do *this*, or don't do *that*! And the same is true of the Testaments of the Twelve Patriarchs, the work that most nearly resembles the "Letter of Jacob," and which, indeed, may have served as its model. To the same class, on the very largest scale, belong the works of Philo, for through all his allegorizing and his philosophical vagaries there runs a constant and undeviating moral purpose.

A common feature of all the works named in the preceding paragraph is their authors' willingness to utilize good moral instruction, whether from within or from without the Hebrew tradition. If a teaching can be confirmed from the Pentateuch, so much the better; but what is good is good, no matter whence it comes. Just so today learned and pious Jewish teachers are producing in all modern languages highly useful manuals of ethical guidance for the Jewish laity, supplementing the Old Testament and later Jewish traditional material with material taken from non-Jewish writers and even from the New Testament, and often—and quite rightly—pointing with pride to the unanimous teaching of Jews and non-Jews. And that there were other works of the kind written for Hellenistic Jews in the days immediately before and after the beginning of the Christian Era cannot be doubted.

Nonetheless, in the later Judaism of the second and following Christian centuries books of this kind were no longer written, and those that had already appeared fell into neglect; even the imposing works of Philo were found uncongenial. Why? The answer to this question is given by the rise and triumph of Pharisaism.

The fundamental doctrine of the Pharisees was this: The law of God, being wholly divine, must have been given not only for the time of Moses but for all future times as well. It is therefore not merely the necessary but the entirely sufficient guide for all problems that can ever by any possibility arise. The solution of many such problems was no doubt given only obscurely, but it could always be found if only the search was diligent enough. To find these solutions was the task of those technically trained for the purpose, the Pharisaic scribes; and the accumulation of their decisions formed the Pharisaic tradition, which every Pharisee was supposed to learn and follow.

While the date of the beginning of the Pharisees as a specific party is not certain, it seems fairly probable that by the time of Jesus' ministry their tradition had been accumulating its decisions for something like two centuries and had already attained formidable dimensions, not only in ceremonial matters but in purely ethical problems as well (Mark 7:6-13). But until a Pharisaic tradition had been ratified by the Great Sanhedrin in Jerusalem, something

apparently that did not happen very often, it bound only Pharisees and could be disregarded by other Jews. The change took place at the destruction of Jerusalem in A.D. 70, a destruction that included the annihilation of the Great Sanhedrin and left Judaism with no central authority. In the anarchy that threatened, the Pharisees were the sole remaining party with a definite program and with an organization prepared to carry out that program; they knew precisely what they wanted and knew precisely how to obtain it. They took immediate control of the situation, and from that time on the tradition of the Pharisees became the law of all Judaism.

All other traditions, all other attempts to solve moral problems, were therefore henceforth regarded as illegitimate; and all writings that were based on such attempts were openly or tacitly condemned and disappeared from Jewish use. The sole significant exception was the book of Proverbs, which had already been incorporated into the Old Testament and was therefore exempt from criticism.

Consequently the date of the "Letter of Jacob" cannot possibly be later than the end of the first Christian century, a conclusion corroborated by the date of James (see below, p. 15). The sole guide to the earliest limit for the date is highly conjectural. If the existence of the "tribal allusions" in "Jacob" is admitted, the frequency with which these allusions agree with those in Philo may be taken to indicate that "Jacob" knew Philo's works. (Nothing, of course, would be more probable than that a Jew cultured in Hellenism would read the works of the one Jew who was supremely cultured in Hellenism.) If this assumption is correct, Jacob cannot be earlier than the first Christian century.

No conclusion, naturally, can be drawn from the moral teaching of Jacob. As has already been observed, paraenesis is by its very nature timeless, dealing not with problems belonging to specific occasions but with wholly general truths.

One word of caution may be added: While the "Letter of Jacob," as far as it can be reconstructed, deals entirely with moral and not ceremonial rules, it would be wholly illegitimate to deduce that "Jacob" was indifferent to ceremonialism. Nowadays, to be sure, there are many "liberal Jews," who treat the ceremonial laws as no longer rigorously binding. But such a "liberal Judaism" was unthinkable in the Hellenistic period. At that time a Jew who did not observe the ceremonies would be regarded not as a "liberal," but as an apostate; open-mindedness was possible only in the intellectual realm, not in that of ritual. Philo, for instance, went to the wildest lengths of allegory to explain that even the minutest ceremony was ordained because of its moral or spiritual significance; but the theory that if this significance was adopted and practiced, its ceremonial expression might be disregarded, he would have rejected with horror. He was as faithful a ceremonialist as the most rigid Pharisee.

And this was necessarily true of the author of "Jacob" and other possible Jewish sources in James. We of course do not know that these sources ignored ceremonial matters, for we do not know what James may have omitted from these sources as unsuitable for Christian readers. But even supposing what we have no right to suppose, that we have "Jacob's" work virtually complete, he might well have thought that in what was explicitly a purely moral treatise there was no need to emphasize ceremonial rules which everyone took for granted; that every Jew would recognize what lay behind such phrases as "the perfect law," "the whole law," "unspotted from the world," etc. Precisely the same is true of the Jewish treatise most closely parallel to "Jacob" and which may more than probably have served as its model, the Testaments of the Twelve Patriarchs; it is composed almost entirely of moral and spiritual instructions and exhortations, with only the slightest incidental references to the ceremonies. Very much worth noting, in addition, is the fact that these testaments, precisely like "Jacob," were subsequently revised by a Christian editor (or editors), came to be considered a purely Christian work, and enjoyed a long popularity as such.[5]

Apart from "Jacob," the Christian editor of James used a Jewish source in 2:1-13, attacking the deference paid to rich men in the synagogues, and Stoic-Cynic material on sins of the tongue in 3:1-12. The purpose of both sections is wholly obvious. All that can be said of the date of the former is that it is prerabbinical, while the latter could have been written at any time in the Hellenistic age.

VI. Purpose and Date of James

The purpose of James, precisely like the purpose of "Jacob," was to provide concrete ethical instruction for his readers, something that they needed quite as truly as the Jewish readers of "Jacob." No doubt they had all the Jewish readers had, the supreme guidance of the wholly inspired law of God in the Old

[5] For another example of similar treatment compare II Esdras, where the addition of Christian material at the beginning and at the end, and the insertion of "Jesus" in 7:28, turned a not merely Jewish but even an explicitly anti-Christian work into a Christian writing.

Testament. And undoubtedly they had what the Jewish readers did not have: the teaching of Jesus, as wholly inspired as the Old Testament itself and as fully authoritative—indeed even more authoritative. But—and here again, as in the case of the Jews, was the difficulty—there was an endless number of concrete moral problems on which neither the Old Testament nor Jesus spoke either clearly or unambiguously; and many more problems on which the Old Testament and Jesus did not speak at all. Hence Paul and the other epistolary writers in the New Testament of necessity spent much time in supplementing the basic "inspired" teaching of the Old Testament and of Jesus with their own solutions of moral problems that arose among their readers. And the same problem is faced in the subapostolic writers as well, notably in I Clement, the Didache, and especially the Shepherd of Hermas. Precisely the same problem has been encountered at every stage of Christian history and is with us today, as witness the innumerable treatises on "Christian ethics," "moral theology," and so forth.

In early Christianity works of this kind were imperative; for as soon as the Christian mission entered the Gentile world, it entered a world of men and women whose earlier moral training had often been inadequate, when it was not wholly defective, or in its perversions worse than defective. The extensive "ethical" portions of the New Testament epistles show how elementary was the instruction that was needed everywhere. The purpose of the Christian editor of James was merely to make a further contribution to the treatment of concrete and familiar problems for his fellow believers.

There was, however—and this should be said as emphatically as possible—one purpose that the Christian editor did not have: his purpose was in no possible sense theological. In 1:1 to "God" he adds "and of the Lord Jesus Christ" and in 2:1—much more ungracefully—he converts an original "the Lord of glory" into "our Lord Jesus Christ, the Lord of glory." In 2:14-26, the only extended passage of his own composition, a perversion of Paul's justification doctrine is refuted, but in terms that do not profess to be more than sound common sense. And here and there throughout the letter, as in 1:18, language that had one meaning to Jews assuredly takes on a more profound meaning to Christians. But these are the only indications of any interest in theology.

In the older textbooks on New Testament theology there was regularly a chapter headed "The Theology of James," which was really a chapter about something that did not exist at all; the writer of James very possibly may have developed a "theology" of his own, but he has not developed it in this letter. Luther was perfectly correct when, recognizing the barrenness of "theological" content in James, he pronounced it "an epistle of straw." But Luther was also perfectly correct when he wrote: "I praise this epistle of James and consider it to be good, because it teaches no human doctrine at all and sternly declares the law of God." No one has better summarized what James attempts to do—and what it does not attempt to do.

As regards the date of James, 2:14-26 shows that it was written later than Romans, for the references to Rom. 4 are unmistakable (see Exegesis). The fact that it is written as a work of James, however, fixes a still later date for the earliest limit: a pseudonymous letter ascribed to James could have been produced only after the death of the historic James, which took place somewhere in the interval A.D. 60-66; and in addition, one must allow for the lapse of some years after A.D. 66 before James was securely recognized as a supreme figure of the Christian past. The date of the letter can hardly be earlier than A.D. 80.

On the other hand, 5:1-6, 8-9 show that when the letter was written, the apocalyptic expectations were still vivid. And 5:14 takes for granted that the Gentile Christian congregations were governed by elders; but the church polity assumed is far short of the elaboration of I Timothy and the Ignatian letters, in which visitation of the sick was primarily the task of the deacons, and spiritual ministration to all church members was the responsibility of the local bishop. Further evidence may perhaps be gleaned from the opening words of Jude, "Jude, . . . brother of James," which more than probably indicate that an epistle bearing the name of James was known to the writer. Now Jude is an anti-Gnostic work, but one written when even extreme antinomian Gnostics were still tolerated within the church (Jude 12; contrast I Tim. 1:20; I John 2:19), and so could scarcely have been written after the beginning of the second century. (But for another view on the date of Jude, see below, pp. 318-19.)

None of this evidence is very impressive. But taken together for what it may be worth, it indicates a date of the Christian edition of James somewhere between A.D. 80 and A.D. 100.

As to the place of writing there is no indication at all.

No certain external evidence for James is found until the third century; apparent citations found in second-century writers are not close enough to be convincing. But in the third century Origen quotes James as authoritative, usually without qualification or actually as "Scripture," but sometimes more guardedly as if there was doubt of its value. And even in the fourth century Eusebius, in his familiar catalogue of the books of the New Testament, classifies James not among the universally "accepted" writings but among those that were "disputed."

VII. Special Notes

A. Elders.—In early Judaism, as in many other primitive societies, the "elders" of a community were, as the name indicates, the "older men," the heads of the various families, who together exercised an unquestioned authority over their juniors. Well before New Testament times, however, the term "elder" had become simply the title of a Jewish official entrusted with authority to govern and had lost its connotation of age; an elder was not necessarily an old man and, conversely, an old man was by no means necessarily an elder (cf. the English "alderman" or "senator"). In the New Testament period every Jewish community was governed by a board of elders called a "sanhedrin" (literally, "session"), composed of seven elders in villages, twenty-three in cities, and seventy in Jerusalem. (It is this last body that is usually meant by "sanhedrin" in the New Testament, but the sanhedrins in the smaller localities appear by this name, rendered "councils" in the English version, as in Matt. 10:17.)

In theory all governmental authority was committed to these boards of elders—or rather, all executive and judicial authority. They did not have legislative authority, since the sole authoritative legislation for Israel had been given in the law of God; the task of the elders was to interpret this law in each case and to enforce it. And here no distinction was drawn between what we call "civil" and "religious" cases, for no such distinction was made in the law itself; the trial and punishment of a thief was just as truly a "religious" procedure as if the offense had been a breach of the sabbath or of the food laws. The elders were consequently regarded as acting in the name and by the authority of God; it was an office that no man could take unto himself but to which he must be duly chosen by those who were already elders and to which, after his choice, he was ordained by the laying on of their hands.

The elders, however, were in no sense religious officials in connection with public worship. They were not priests, and as elders took no part in the liturgical worship in the temple. And the same was true of the synagogues: there was no part in the synagogue liturgy that an elder might take that could not be taken equally well by any other adult male Jew. They therefore were not and never should be described as "elders of the synagogue"; their proper title was invariably that of the place (Nazareth, Capernaum, etc.) in which their authority was exercised.

In Christianity elders first appear in Jerusalem (Acts 11:30) as the local authorities of the church. In Acts 15:2, 4, 6; etc., they are named in conjunction with the apostles, and in Acts 15:23 the decree of the council is issued in the name of "the apostles and the elders" jointly. But in Acts 21:18 we have no longer "the apostles and the elders" but "James and all the elders." The development is clear if we simply remember that the identity of the name "elder" in Judaism and Jewish Christianity necessarily implies identity of office (at least in the origin); as the apostles died or sought other mission fields, their local authority was taken over by (Christian) elders.

For this stage in the development of the office of elder in early Christianity compare the commentary on the Pastoral epistles, especially on II Tim. 1:11-14; 2:1-2. It would be at this stage that the title "elders of the *church*," as in Jas. 5:14, would appear in contrast to "elders of the *place*" that designated the non-Christian Jewish officials, for the authority of the Christians was naturally limited strictly to their own community. This title in Jas. 5:14 would alone be conclusive evidence that the passage as it stands is the work of a Christian, not a pre-Christian Jewish writer.

Of still greater significance, however, is a Christian development to which Jas. 5:14 is the only New Testament passage that bears witness, but which is seen abundantly and elaborately in the post-apostolic Christian writers: in Christianity, unlike Judaism, the elders took over the conduct of worship as well as discipline. The stages in this development are obscure and probably never will be clarified completely, but before the close of the first century in I Clem. 44:4-5 it is taken for granted that conduct of the Eucharist is a monopoly of the elders; it is they who "offer the gifts." Here we have unequivocally an early stage in the evolution that was eventually to convert the elders into "priests"—something of course wholly impossible in Judaism. And this early stage is echoed in Jas. 5:14, which never could have been written by a pre-Christian Jewish author. Nor—although this is less certain—does it seem likely that Jas. 5:14 could have been written by a Palestinian Jewish-Christian author, where not only the duties but the limitations of the duties of elders would be automatically taken for granted. Only outside of Palestine and in the Gentile communities, where the title "elder"

and the duties associated with this title were completely unfamiliar, would so novel a development along wholly un-Jewish lines appear conceivable.

It should be noted, however, that in Jas. 5:14 the elders alone are named as the spiritual authorities of the community; there is no hint that there is still a higher authority above them as the single supreme pastor or "bishop." In a later stage of the evolution of the ministry all cases of sickness would be reported to him, and he would either visit the sick person himself or send elders as his representatives. Nor is there any mention of the church officers whose particular function it was to serve those in need, the "deacons" of I Tim. 3:8-13. In other words, the church organization presupposed in Jas. 5:14 is still in an embryonic stage. The elders are taking on liturgical functions—something not mentioned in the Pastoral epistles—but there is no single pastor of the local flock with his deacons, both of whom are assumed in I Timothy. And the organization of course falls very far short of that passionately defended in the Ignatian letters.

All these factors must naturally be considered in estimating the date at which Jas. 5:14 was written; but of course it cannot for a moment be taken for granted that development of the ministry went on at a uniform rate everywhere throughout Christianity. The evidence of II Timothy and Titus, for instance, shows that many churches had a "polity" far less elaborate than that described in I Timothy. Probably, however, as has been noted on other grounds, a date shortly before or shortly after the close of the first century would not be very far wrong.

B. Unction.—As will be noted in the Exegesis of Jas. 5:14, it is wholly obvious, and never should have been denied, that the anointing of the sick by the duly authorized elders, in conjunction with their prayer, is thought to have very much more than a merely physical medicinal effect; this anointing is regarded as a quasi-sacramental (or even wholly sacramental?) rite, with the twofold effects of restoration to physical health and the forgiveness of sins. On the other hand, it is likewise wholly obvious, and never should have been denied, that such anointing was very far from a universal custom in the apostolic church. The only other mention in the New Testament appears in Mark 6:13, which reads, "They . . . anointed with oil many that were sick and healed them." But neither Matthew nor Luke have anything similar in their accounts of the mission of the twelve. Luke, in fact, when in 9:6 he copies Mark 6:13 in an exact parallel, omits the mention of the anointing. Nor does even Mark attribute to Jesus any command to anoint; as far as his account is concerned, the disciples used the rite on their own initiative. If, then, the mention of unction in Mark 6:13 has not been read back into Jesus' lifetime by later tradition (cf. a similar reading back of baptism in John 3:22, 26; 4:2), in place of "they" (i.e., "[all] the disciples") we must understand "certain of the disciples." And the number of such disciples—if they existed at all—must have been comparatively few for, apart from Jas. 5:14, the New Testament is completely silent as to the practice supposed to have been initiated by them. In Acts many healings are described but in none of them does anointing play any part, not even in the healings of Christians in Acts 9:33-40; 20:9-10. In other words, while Mark 6:13 and Jas. 5:14 show that anointing the sick as a religious rite certainly existed at an early date in Christianity—very probably in the apostolic age itself—its practice was exceptional and must have been confined to a small—geographically limited?—circle (cf. perhaps the practice of baptizing for the dead in Corinth—I Cor. 15:29).

How the ceremony originated is of course unknown. But a guess may be hazarded that the widespread use of oil as an application to relieve pain, and so forth, when employed by Christians with prayer—especially when these Christians posssessed the "gift of healing" (I Cor. 12:9; etc.)—was followed so frequently by relief that the belief developed that anointing with prayer was a divinely authorized rite with a divinely wrought efficacy. In James this belief, however it originated, has developed to the point where such anointing is no longer left to individuals with a special "gift" but is confined to the regularly ordained clergy, just as in Mark 6:13 only the duly commissioned "disciples" exercise it.

The history of the ceremony in the next few centuries of Christian history is very obscure and confused, and as yet no adequate account of the facts exists. But there was certainly no orderly development of a general tradition, for such references as we find to anointing are often highly contradictory. A Roman liturgical formula of the early third century[6] has recently been identified which reads, "That sanctifying this oil . . . thou wouldest grant health to them who use it," but the context shows that the oil in question was brought by "anyone," and nothing is said in the long treatise that follows about any duty of the clergy to use this oil in visiting the sick. With a few exceptions, in fact, the evidence of the first five Christian centuries

gives the impression that anointing the sick, in so far as it existed at all, was practiced by the laity, and that the clergy at least did not discourage this practice. So Chrysostom[7] tells how in his day men and women would take oil out of the lamps in the churches, carry it home and apply it to sick persons; and he cites this custom to prove that everything in a church shares the consecration of the church itself!

On the other hand, we have the evidence of Origen,[8] who explains the "sick" in Jas. 5:14 as "spiritually sick," not physically sick, and describes the anointing ceremony as one used in absolving Christians who have sinned.

Complete acceptance of the directions in Jas. 5:14 was accordingly a very slow and hesitant process in Christian tradition, and it is probably only in the eighth century that they become definitely incorporated into the laws and liturgies of the church. In what is now known as the Greek Orthodox Church the directions in Jas. 5:14 were and still are followed literally, and unction (called εὐχέλαιον, meaning literally "prayer oil") is regarded as a "sacrament" in the fullest sense of the term. Its "matter" is pure olive oil, which has been previously blessed by the priest, and it is applied in the case of any illness, no matter how trifling. As Jas. 5:14 uses "elders" in the plural, the normal ministers of the rite are several priests acting together, properly seven in number, but in case of necessity a single priest will suffice. The "fruits" of the sacrament, as in Jas. 5:14, are twofold: physical and spiritual healing. The former often follows, since the illness may be very slight, but in any case only "if such be God's will"; if every disease were invariably healed, unction would be not only "a sacrament of healing" but "a sacrament of immortality"—something obviously not God's purpose.[9]

In Latin Christianity during the early Middle Ages the teaching and practice regarding unction was approximately the same as that just described. But in the subsequent development —the details of which are very obscure—less and less emphasis was laid on the possibility of physical healing and more and more emphasis on spiritual healing. Consequently the meaning of the rite gradually shifted until it became regarded as primarily the means for obtaining remission of sins, supplementing in a very special and unique fashion the ordinary absolution given after confession, having the

[6] Hippolytus *Apostolic Tradition* 5.

[7] *Homilies on Matthew* XXXII. 9.

[8] *Homilies on Leviticus* II. 4.

[9] For details see Frank Gavin, *Some Aspects of Contemporary Greek Orthodox Thought* (Milwaukee: Morehouse Publishing Co., 1923), 386-93.

effect of removing "the remnants of sin." The eventual result was to convert "unction" into "extreme unction" (where "extreme" is used in the sense of "final") , a rite for the dying. To be sure, the original meaning of the ceremony has not been entirely forgotten. Physical healing is in theory always regarded as a possible fruit of the sacrament, although in practice—since only those gravely ill are anointed—this is now looked on as a secondary and very unusual result. Still, persons in health but in imminent danger of death from external violence are never anointed to prepare them for their end.

Attempts to justify extreme unction from Jas. 5:14 have naturally not been lacking, usually by rendering "save" as "save from sin" and "raise up" as "raise up at the Last Day." But compare, for instance, among modern Roman Catholic commentators, Otto Bardenhewer: [10] "When the forgiveness of sins is mentioned in the second clause and the physical healing in the first, this is due to the fact that inclusive directions are given for cases of sickness; and forgiveness of sins is included only in the special instance that it may be needed."

For descriptions of other developments of the practice of unction in the various pre-Reformation Eastern churches (Nestorian, Coptic, etc.) reference must be made to the special treatises. And in certain Protestant denominations the practice has been reinstituted; exact data are lacking, but the practice is apparently always in accordance with the wording of Jas. 5:14.

VIII. Outline of Contents

[10] *Der Brief des heiligen Jakobus* (Freiburg i/B: Herder, 1928), pp. 151-52.

IX. Selected Bibliography

BARDENHEWER, OTTO. *Der Brief des heiligen Jakobus.* Freiburg i/B: Herder, 1928. The work of a vastly learned and extremely competent Roman Catholic scholar.

DIBELIUS, MARTIN. *Der Brief des Jakobus* ("Meyer's Kommentar") . Göttingen: Vandenhoeck & Ruprecht, 1921. Described as the "seventh edition" in the famous "Meyer" series, but actually a wholly new work. Extraordinarily informative, especially and uniquely as regards the literary form of the epistle.

KNOWLING, R. J. *The Epistle of St. James* ("Westminster Commentaries") . London: Methuen & Co., 1904. A volume emphasizing primarily the expository and practical elements in the interpretation.

MAYOR, JOSEPH B. *The Epistle of St. James.* 3rd ed. London: Macmillan & Co., 1910. The most elaborate commentary in English, indispensable for the thorough student. But as the general attitude toward the epistle is virtually that of the first edition (1892) , it needs supplementing from more modern works.

MOFFATT, JAMES. *The General Epistles* ("Moffatt New Testament Commentary") . New York: Harper & Bros.; London: Hodder & Stoughton, 1928. Brief, but a model of compression by a brilliant commentator.

ROPES, JAMES HARDY. *A Critical and Exegetical Commentary on the Epistle of St. James* ("International Critical Commentary") . New York: Charles Scribner's Sons, 1916. Past question the most valuable commentary in English.

WINDISCH, HANS. *Die katholischen Briefe* ("Handbuch zum Neuen Testament") . 2nd ed. Tübingen: J. C. B. Mohr, 1930. Very compressed, but a treasury of the opinions of other commentaries; the only commentary utilizing Arnold Meyer's contributions.

JAMES

TEXT, EXEGESIS, AND EXPOSITION

The Epistle of James.*—The form of James (see Intro.) is not that of a logical discourse, building up an argument to a conclusion, but is diffuse and sometimes repetitious. Therefore, sermons built upon this letter need not follow the order of chapter and verse. Passages separated in the letter may be brought together for a single sermon. The phrase "law of liberty," e.g., is found in both 1:25 and 2:12. The transitoriness of life is dealt with in 1:9-11 and also in 4:13-15. The language of James is generally so simple and direct that comment and explanation may seem to be superfluous. Indeed, an excellent way to make use of the letter in the pulpit is to read it as itself a sermon, preferably using a modern translation.

It has been demonstrated in the Exeg. that James contains a great deal of pre-Christian Jewish material; that it is most likely an adaptation by a Christian editor of the work of a Jewish author. The fact that the Christian editor considered the Jewish material appropriate to Christian purposes suggests that early Christianity and Judaism were not so far apart as in later centuries they have unfortunately tended to become. The Jewish Scriptures were the only Bible the Christians had when this letter was written. The transition from Judaism to Christianity cannot have been as difficult in all cases as it was in some. Jesus had declared that he had not come to abolish, but to fulfill, the Jewish law and the Jewish prophets. "That which is called the Christian Religion existed among the Ancients, and never did not exist, from the beginning of the Human Race until Christ came in the flesh, at which time the true religion, which already existed, began to be called Christianity." [1] This statement by Augus-

tine shows that in the early centuries of the Christian Era sharp lines of demarcation were not so commonly drawn.

George Benedict, a former rabbi, in his autobiography *Christ Finds a Rabbi*, writes:

> Some of you may be asking . . . : O Rabbi, what has Christ done for you that you are willing to turn your back on Judaism and your face to Christianity? . . . Please notice, that I have *not* turned my back on Judaism. On the contrary, I am carrying Judaism forward with me. I cannot turn my back on my mother, but I can give her my arm, to help her to walk with me while life lasts. [2]

The need for a new *rapprochement* between Jews and Christians in our time, for an overcoming of antipathies and prejudices which have too long characterized the attitudes of both groups toward each other, suggests the use of this Jewish-Christian writing as the basis of a sermon against Jewish-Christian intolerance. The fact that most of the writers of the N.T. were Jews is often overlooked. It was a famous Jew, Disraeli, who declared that "Christianity is the fulfillment of Judaism." H. G. Enelow expresses the hope "that Jesus may yet serve as a bond of union between Jew and Christian, once his teaching is better known and the bane of misunderstanding at last is removed from his words and his ideals." [3]

Sholem Asch, the Jewish novelist, besides his novels in which Jesus (*The Nazarene*) and Paul (*The Apostle*) are the central figures, has written a remarkable letter [4] addressed to Christians which, in addition to the books cited, contains invaluable material for the suggested sermon.

---

* P. 19 comprises the expositor's introduction. Text and Exegesis begin on p. 20. Editors.

[1] Augustine, *Librum de vera religione*, ch. x. Quoted by Gerald Heard, *The Eternal Gospel* (New York: Harper & Bros., 1946), opposite title page.

[2] Philadelphia: The Author, 1932, p. 263.

[3] *A Jewish View of Jesus* (New York: The Macmillan Co., 1920), p. 181.

[4] *One Destiny*, tr. Milton Hindus (New York: G. P. Putnam's Sons, 1945). See also John Cournos, *An Open Letter to Jews and Christians* (New York: Oxford University Press, 1938).

1 James, a servant of God and of the Lord Jesus Christ, to the twelve tribes which are scattered abroad, greeting.

1 James, a servant of God and of the Lord Jesus Christ,
To the twelve tribes in the dispersion: Greeting.

I. The Greeting (1:1)

1:1. Letters in the ancient world opened regularly with the name of the writer followed by the name of the recipient—or recipients—and a greeting formula, precisely as here. The name of the writer is given simply as **James,** as if no further identification was necessary. And early Christian readers would assuredly identify this James with the "brother of the Lord," the head of the church in Jerusalem in apostolic days (see Intro., pp. 5-6).

He describes himself as **a servant of God and of the Lord Jesus Christ.** In the O.T. servant of God is a very common phrase, either for any Jew as dedicated to God's service or, more particularly, for one especially consecrated to such service—the patriarchs, Moses, the prophets, etc. In the N.T., however, the title is less frequently employed; it appears for Moses (the O.T. usage) in Rev. 15:3; for any Christian, in II Tim. 2:24; I Pet. 2:16; Rev. 7:3; for a Christian leader only, in Tit. 1:1 and here. (In Acts 16:17 the speaker is a heathen.) For a Christian leader "servant of Jesus Christ" is the much more usual description (Rom. 1:1; Gal. 1:10; Phil. 1:1; Col. 4:12; II Pet. 1:1; Jude 1); the combination of both the O.T. and the N.T. titles here is unique in the N.T. But there is of course no possible thought that "no man can serve two masters," for the service of God and that of the Lord Jesus Christ are in Christian thought in every respect the same.

The recipients of the letter are described as **the twelve tribes in the dispersion.** In this Jewish phraseology **the twelve tribes** meant Israel as a whole, without regard to whether all twelve tribes still existed or not (cf. Rev. 7:4-8). But the meaning of the term in James as a Christian writing is uncertain. Some commentators have felt, not unnaturally, that the phrase should be interpreted rather literally as indicating that the epistle is addressed to Jewish Christians alone. But as there is nothing elsewhere in the letter that deals with the special problems of Jewish Christianity (see the Intro.), it is far preferable to explain **the twelve tribes** as meaning the whole spiritual Israel, i.e., all Christians. In any case, the epistle is addressed not to some particular community, but to any believer who may read it; it is a "catholic epistle" (cf. II Pet. 1:1; Jude 1).

The dispersion in Judaism was the usual inclusive term for all Jews who were "dispersed" outside Palestine, whose language ordinarily was not Aramaic but Greek (cf. John 7:35). And the word was wholly appropriate for Christians, who, in one sense, were "dispersed" throughout the Roman Empire (I Pet. 1:1) or, in another and deeper sense, were "dispersed" as pilgrims and sojourners on earth, away from their true home in heaven. The exact meaning—if any—the writer attached to the noun cannot of course be determined (cf. below).

Greeting (literally, "Rejoice") was the conventional salutation in ordinary letter writing, corresponding roughly to the modern "Dear" before "Sir." It appears in the only secular letter in the N.T. (Acts 23:26), but in Christian writings it is used only in the formal communication of the decree of the apostolic council (Acts 15:23), and here.

This opening verse of the epistle, which on a first reading appears quite uncomplicated, nonetheless offers real problems. In the first place, the designation of James as

1:1. The Twofold Service.—James called himself **a servant of God and of the Lord Jesus Christ.** In our time when we speak of service, the emphasis is upon service to our fellow men. There is no necessary contradiction between the two; indeed, to be a true servant of God is to render the highest service to men. But it

does not follow that disregard of the Godward reference is unimportant in the service of man. When one serves man as a servant of God, there is a depth of obligation and a quality of ministration not otherwise to be found. Man's service to man is usually predicated upon mutual good pleasure; you do a favor for me and I'll do a

2 My brethren, count it all joy when ye fall into divers temptations;

3 Knowing *this,* that the trying of your faith worketh patience.

2 Count it all joy, my brethren, when you meet various trials, 3 for you know that the testing of your faith produces

---

a servant of both **God** and **the Lord Jesus Christ** is, as was said above, unique in the N.T. In the second place, **Lord** as a title of Christ occurs elsewhere in James only in 2:1 and 5:14, passages that have problems of their own, while in all the other eleven instances in James—including even 5:7, 8—it is God, not Christ, who is **the Lord.** And in the third place, the bare **Greeting** is strangely cool; contrast the Christian warmth at the beginning of every other N.T. epistle. While these difficulties, if taken by themselves, would not be serious, yet they corroborate the other evidence in the epistle that our letter is a Christian revision of a Jewish work that began, "Jacob, a servant of God, to the twelve tribes in the dispersion: Greeting" (for Jacob as "God's servant" cf. Gen. 32:10; Isa. 41:8; 48:20; etc.). With this assumption everything becomes clear. The Christian editor took "Jacob" to mean "James" (the names of course are identical in Hebrew, Aramaic, and Greek) and merely added **and of the Lord Jesus Christ** to make the identification unmistakable. To the Jewish writer **the twelve tribes** was meant to recall Jacob's address to these tribes in Gen. 49. And **in the dispersion** was the correct form for use by a Jew writing in Greek to Greek-speaking Jews.

These phrases the Christian editor simply took over as he found them. In what sense he meant Christians to understand them he made no effort to explain; very probably he did not think particularly about their meaning at all. Hence the varying interpretations—none of them really satisfactory as is seen by their divergence—that have been proposed by Christian expositors.

II. TRIALS A CAUSE FOR JOY (1:2-4)

2. In the Greek the closing word of vs. 1, "rejoice," is taken up by **joy** in vs. 2; a connection that cannot be reproduced in English except by some such paraphrase as Moffatt's "Greet it as pure joy." The epistolary **brethren** was of course taken by the Christians from Jewish usage, but other religious groups employed the title similarly. The noun πειρασμός can signify either "external hardship," "trial," as here and in vs. 12, or "inner impulse to evil," "temptation," as in vss. 13-14; the writer takes for granted that his readers will distinguish between the two meanings of the word. Here the point is that **trials,** which most men regard as evils to be avoided, should be accepted joyfully by Christians; since it is by overcoming difficulties that moral progress is achieved. **All** (perhaps with the force of "complete" or "unmixed") and **various** ("of any sort"?) may be used simply for emphasis, without further special significance. Note the alliteration in πειρασμοῖς περιπέσητε ποικίλοις.

3-4. In these verses there is a skillful rhetorical climax, concluding with the rhetorical pleonasm **perfect and complete, lacking in nothing.** For the second term in the series

---

favor for you. But the servant of God must seek the good of others even if they are unresponsive and resentful. "Be merciful, even as your Father is merciful"; "For he is kind to the ungrateful and the selfish" (Luke 6:36, 35c). James, as the servant of God, was under obligation to utter truths unpleasant to the ears of those he sought to benefit. The prophet Isaiah, as God's servant, had to endure much gainsaying from the people whom he would save. It was because he was God's servant that he was undiscourageable in his service of men (cf. Isa. 50:4-9). Missionaries in their ministry of teaching and healing have

often found suspicion instead of cordial welcome among those they wanted to help. Without the love of God in their hearts, without belief that their primary obligation was to him, they would hardly persist in their service. Jesus emancipated the thought of service from all taint of meniality and put it at the heart of his religion. We too often take that great word and reduce it to the level of service stations. If a high conception of service is to be maintained, it must be rooted in God.

2-3. *The Secret of Happiness.*—The ideal of happiness which many cherish looks toward a

4 But let patience have *her* perfect work, that ye may be perfect and entire, wanting nothing.

steadfastness. 4 And let steadfastness have its full effect, that you may be perfect and complete, lacking in nothing.

---

the translation **patience** is too passive; **steadfastness** is far better. In vs. 4 **perfect** is used as a moralist's adjective, more or less equivalent to "satisfactory," to describe an ethical quality well within human attainment (cf. 3:2 and contrast Matt. 5:48).

Teaching like this is familiar in the O.T. and in later Judaism; the parallels in Rom. 5:3-5 and I Pet. 1:6-7 show that these two writers and James are each using a current maxim in his own way. But while in Romans and I Peter the terms lead to a religious climax, in James they all remain in the ethical realm; indeed, his version could have been framed by a secular moralist except for the words **of your faith**, and certain MSS omit these words, which may have been added from I Pet. 1:7. In any case, there is nothing specifically Christian in the passage.

The tribal allusions detected in vss. 2-4 are those highly appropriate for the beginning of a letter attributed to Jacob, for they are to his father, his mother, and the patriarch himself. Philo identifies Isaac with "joy" (cf. Gen. 17:17-19, where "Isaac" is explained as "laughter"), Rebecca twice with "steadfastness" (the same Greek word as in James) and Jacob with "perfection through trials" (see *Rewards and Punishments* 31-32; *The Worse Attacks the Better* 30; *Concerning Noah's Work as a Planter* 169; *On the Migration of Abraham* 200-1).

---

state of ease, comfort, and security. To be able to avoid difficulties and bask in pleasurable and undisturbed tranquillity is the *summum bonum*. They are "moved by the promptings of a nature in love with ease and superficiality." If they show any interest in religion, it is in the hope that it will be of some help in securing for them this sort of happiness. If, in spite of all, they meet difficulties or trials, these are the cause of complaint and mental misery.

James has a different ideal of happiness because he holds a different theory of the meaning and purpose of life. The purpose of life cannot be accomplished by the attainment of ease or luxurious comfort, but only in the achievement of Christlike character. Therefore, the Christian **can count it all joy** when he meets **various trials.** These test the mettle of his faith in God's overruling purpose, and when met with courage, produce **steadfastness** of character. In Rom. 5:3-5 Paul gives a similar and fuller statement of this nonhedonistic philosophy of happiness. This joy is deeper and more abiding than the superficial pleasures of the moment which pass so quickly away.

James, Paul, and Peter all join in reminding their fellow disciples what their Lord had made clear in his exposition of happiness in the Beatitudes, viz., that though life may be more difficult for one who is faithful to the Christian way, it is not less joyful, but more so than the life of selfish ease. Albert Schweitzer affirms this out of his own experience: "Existence will . . . become harder for him in every respect than it would be if he lived for himself, but at the

same time it will be richer, more beautiful, and happier. It will become, instead of mere living, a real experience of life." [5]

This is the sort of happiness which untoward circumstances have no power to diminish. Paul and Silas could sing in the Philippian prison because its bars could not prevent their serving Christ's cause. In that service they found the source of their happiness, so their trials only proved their faith and the steadfastness of their devotion. Christians are not distinguished by their immunity from the trials which are common to mankind, but in the way they meet them and what they make out of them. Theirs is no mere stoical apathy or fatalistic submission to senseless suffering, but the transmutation of adversity into spiritual victory.

4. *The Road to Christian Maturity.*—There is no suggestion here of the too-prevalent notion that when one "joins the church," "salvation" is secured, and therefore one may rest complacently in that assurance with little more to do. These words remind us of our Lord's challenge, "You, therefore, must be perfect, as your heavenly Father is perfect" (Matt. 5:48). Here and in Matthew "perfect" is the same Greek adjective. The evident impossibility of human attainment of the perfection of God, the certainty that none of us can reach the level which James suggests—**perfect and complete, lacking in nothing**—has caused most of us to dismiss this challenge as fantastically impractical. This is to miss the point completely. It is

[5] *Out of My Life and Thought* (New York: Henry Holt & Co., 1933), p. 268.

5 If any of you lack wisdom, let him ask of God, that giveth to all *men* liberally, and upbraideth not; and it shall be given him.

6 But let him ask in faith, nothing wavering: for he that wavereth is like a wave of the sea driven with the wind and tossed.

5 If any of you lacks wisdom, let him ask God who gives to all men generously and without reproaching, and it will be given him. 6 But let him ask in faith, with no doubting, for he who doubts is like a wave of the sea that is driven and tossed

III. God's Answer to Prayer (1:5-8)

5. Again, what is in the Greek the closing word of vs. 4, "lacking," is taken up by **lacks** in vs. 5. But there is a further connection; to endure trials successfully requires **wisdom**—to Jews and Christians always a God-given virtue—for which prayer must be made. And while selfish prayers are ignored by God (4:3), prayers for wisdom are certain of their answer. **Without reproaching** is well illustrated by Ecclus. 41:22, "After thou hast given, upbraid not"—such **reproaching** is an assertion of self-superiority that spoils the recipient's pleasure in the gift.

6-8. Yet even the certainty of a favorable answer to a prayer for wisdom needs qualification: the prayer must be made in true faith, not by a man whose lips and heart are at variance. The constantly changing surface of the sea is everywhere an obvious figure for instability; here **wave** would be better rendered "surge," while the participles are really synonymous in rhetorical pleonasm. The combination of vs. 7 and vs. 8 in the ASV mg. and the RSV, which take **man** as the subject of **receive**, is less emphatic than the separation of these verses in the ASV, which takes **man** as in apposition to the (unexpressed) subject of **receive**. There is no psychological theory implicit in **double-minded** (literally, "two-souled") any more than there is in Ps. 12:2, where liars are said to speak with "a double heart." **That person** (a Semitism for "such a person") is

this transcendent goal that keeps us from ever settling down in complacent self-righteousness, from the false satisfaction that we have at last arrived at holiness. To say with the man in the Gospel that we have kept all the commandments is never enough (Mark 10:20). The perfection to which we are called is not the negative absence of transgression, but the positive presence of inclusive love. Charles C. Torrey translates Matt. 5:48, "Be therefore all-including (in your good will), even as your heavenly Father includes all." [6] Since personal relations are never static, the life of love must forever expand in widening circles toward the all-including circumference which is the perfect love of God.

5-8. *Prayer and Wisdom.*—Prayer is the recourse and resource of him who sincerely desires **wisdom.** The wisdom to which James refers is not the factual knowledge which we call science, but that quality of understanding which makes one keen in discernment of moral obligation and in the apprehension of eternal verities. It is the wisdom for which Solomon prayed (II Chr. 1:8-12). It is comprised of those sound principles which, according to the book of Proverbs, originate in reverence toward God (Prov. 1:7). The phenomenal progress which

modern man has made in the accumulation of scientific knowledge has unfortunately not been accompanied by a growth in the wisdom to which James refers. As Arnold Toynbee has written, "Technical proficiency is not, in itself, a guarantee of wisdom or survival." [7]

Why is prayer necessary for the gaining of this wisdom? Because, in the Christian understanding thereof, prayer involves confession of moral insufficiency and inadequacy, and aspiration toward the perfection of God. Apart from such an attitude the attainment of **wisdom** is impossible. Christian prayer is not an attempt to change the mind of God, but the opening of the heart to the transforming influence of the Spirit of God.

Since prayer is essentially a quest, no response can be expected if the quest is not wholeheartedly and utterly sincere. Is the aspiration which is verbally expressed motivated by genuine desire? Or like Augustine, do we pray, "O God, make me pure—but not now"? Our failures in prayer are most often due to the fact that our aspirations are halfhearted; we haven't really made up our minds to "will with God one will"; we are **double-minded:** "Lead me, O God, except in the direction I do not want to go." "Save me, O God, from the consequences of

[6] *The Four Gospels* (New York: Harper & Bros., 1933).

[7] *Look,* August 17, 1948, p. 23.

23

7 For let not that man think that he shall receive any thing of the Lord.

8 A double-minded man *is* unstable in all his ways.

9 Let the brother of low degree rejoice in that he is exalted:

by the wind. 7, 8 For that person must not suppose that a double-minded man, unstable in all his ways, will receive anything from the Lord.

9 Let the lowly brother boast in his ex-

---

unstable not only in prayer but **in all his ways**, a phrase of course not to be pressed too closely. While **person** (ἄνθρωπος) might mean "man or woman," the following **man** (ἀνήρ) shows that men alone are in mind; Jewish and early Christian ethical exhortations presuppose a male audience unless women are expressly named.

While the perfectly general saying on prayer in vs. 5 has of course endless Jewish precedents, the insistence in vss. 6-8 on the necessity for perfect confidence in God's response has only late and inexact parallels in Judaism. The source of these three verses may unhesitatingly be pronounced to be the teaching of Jesus (Matt. 17:20; Mark 11:23; etc.), and in James they are due not to the Jewish source but to the Christian editor; cf. Herm. Mand. 9:5, "But if you have doubts in your heart, you will obtain none of your requests. For they who doubt God, these are the double-minded, and they will obtain none of their requests."

It is worth noting that although James is not uncommonly classed as wisdom literature, the noun "wisdom" itself occurs only in 1:5; 3:13, 15, 17, and the adjective "wise" only in 3:13.

IV. THE CURSE OF RICHES (1:9-11)

There is no direct connection with vss. 5-8, but the "trials" theme of vss. 2-4 is continued.

9-11. It is only the lowly **brother** who is praised, for of course not every poor man is blessed by the mere fact of his poverty; that a **brother** will be a *righteous* poor man is taken for granted. **Exaltation** includes present moral attainment as well as future reward. In vs. 10 interpreters differ as to whether or not the word "brother" should be

---

evil, but not from the pleasures of indulgence." How can a person with a mind so divided expect to **receive anything from the Lord?** Instead of praying "in Jesus' name," within the circle of his temper ("Not my will, but thine be done"), such a person is praying "outside of Jesus' name." It is only those who share his sincerity who pray in his name. "Prayer is the soul's *sincere* desire." Only "the pure in heart" can see God, i.e., those who are free of all duplicity.

Is it sinful to doubt? **With no doubting** is not an injunction against raising questions about facts, alleged or otherwise, nor an exhortation to blind belief. There would be no progress in knowledge and understanding in any field, including religion, if questioning were taboo. Could Ignatius Loyola have found any sanction in the teaching of Jesus for the thirteenth rule found in his eighteen rules for thinking truly and as we ought in the militant church: "To arrive at the truth in all things we ought always be ready to believe that what I see as white is black if the Church so defines it" [8] ?

Let him ask in faith, with no doubting refers to prayer, and is a warning against equivocation, against wavering in loyalty, against being a "Mr. Facing-both-ways" instead of a "Mr. Steadfast" in relation to God. It is the person who hesitates, who cannot make up his mind as to his primary allegiance, who **is like a wave of the sea . . . driven and tossed by the wind** (cf. Eph. 4:13-14; Matt. 6:24). Apart from decision of character, men are creatures of their environment, carried along in the current of the influence in which they happen to be immersed at the time. "A man without decision of character can never be said to belong to himself. . . . He belongs to whatever can make captive of him." [9] There must be unreserved commitment in the life of the Christian; he must not be a wobbler, undecided about to whom he owes allegiance (cf. Josh. 24:15).

9-11. *Sic Transit Gloria Mundi.*—That riches and the social status they afford are insecure foundations, and that distinctions based thereon are of no account in the eyes of God, is a thought which occurs repeatedly in the Bible.

---

[8] Paul Van Dyke, *Ignatius Loyola* (New York: Charles Scribner's Sons, 1926), p. 284.

[9] John Foster, *Decision of Character* (London: George Bell & Sons, 1876), p. 71.

10 But the rich, in that he is made low: because as the flower of the grass he shall pass away.

11 For the sun is no sooner risen with a burning heat, but it withereth the grass, and the flower thereof falleth, and the grace of the fashion of it perisheth: so also shall the rich man fade away in his ways.

altation, 10 and the rich in his humiliation, because like the flower of the grass he will pass away. 11 For the sun rises with its scorching heat and withers the grass; its flower falls, and its beauty perishes. So will the rich man fade away in the midst of his pursuits.

supplied after **rich**. If not, the tone of vss. 10-11 is bitter irony; present moral degradation and future punishment are the only things in which the wealthy can truthfully **boast!** If "brother" is supplied, then vss. 10-11 are meant as an affectionate but stringent warning; rich believers must constantly remember how little their riches mean. Yet this involves taking **humiliation**, which parallels **exaltation**, in the sense of "humility," which reads too much into the word. Otherwise the parallel would be imperfect, and **humiliation** would mean "loss of possessions," so that the rich brother would be either no longer rich or certain soon to be no longer rich—again reading too much into the language. Moreover, in view of 2:5-7 and 5:1-6, it does not seem that James would approve of any **rich man** at all.

The figure in vss. 10-11 is from Isa. 40:6-7 (LXX). **Grass** is herbage in general, including flowers (Matt. 6:28-30; etc.) and the **scorching heat** in Palestine is the hot southeasterly wind (sirocco), which may change the color of a landscape from green to brown in a single day.

While the teaching of these verses recalls much in the N.T., especially Luke 6:20, 24, the contrast between the righteous poor and the wicked rich is likewise so common in the O.T. and in later Judaism that a Christian origin of the passage is not particularly indicated. And the theme is also a favorite in Stoicism.

A tribal reference may be detected to Asher, whom Philo (*On Dreams* II. 35) describes, in accord with Gen. 49:20, as the type of "the worldly rich man."

To the Christian editor the language is doubtless apocalyptic, as in 5:1-6. But the wording is quite general and need not denote anything more than the reversal of status at death. Or it can be read as asserting that even in the present world the righteous poor man can rejoice in his virtue, while no rich man can have this satisfaction.

The O.T. imagery in vss. 10-11 is of course no evidence that either the original author, the editor, or the readers of this section were Palestinians.

From the Tower of Babel, the boast of Nebuchadrezzar (Dan. 4:30), to the story of the rich fool (Luke 12:16-21), it is made plain that man's glory is not God's. Recall the words of the prophet Jeremiah in this connection (Jer. 9:23-24; cf. I Cor. 1:26-29).

But why should there be this underlining of the ephemeral nature of the things men count important, this discounting of the prestige and power and wealth that they esteem most dear? What is evil in a man's satisfaction in his achievements? Is not the possibility of excelling, of outrunning others, one of the essential spurs of human endeavor? Without such stimuli, would not man sink back into indolence? Is not the biblical evaluation so "otherworldly" as to be impractical in this world? Can it be preached without a frustrating sense of unreality and hypocrisy?

The biblical emphasis upon the transitoriness of the things in which men glory is no devaluation of existence here and now, but a marking out of that in life which has enduring worth in contrast to that which fades away. Man's life has real significance only when it is concentrated upon the development and enhancement of that which is eternal. "The soul of all improvement is the improvement of the soul." Power and wealth must be used as instruments to this end; they must not be used as means by which those who have hold down those who have not. When the rich man boasts of the wealth that exalts him, in the same boasting he debases his brother who has not such wealth. "When everybody is somebody, nobody will be anybody" is his philosophy. But "to be better off is not to be better" and it is the latter which is the real business of living,

12 Blessed *is* the man that endureth temptation: for when he is tried, he shall receive the crown of life, which the Lord hath promised to them that love him.

12 Blessed is the man who endures trial, for when he has stood the test he will receive the crown of life which God has

---

V. Reward of the Righteous (1:12)

12. This verse is a saying complete in itself. It has no direct connection with vss. 10-11, but it continues the "trials" theme of vss. 2-4, restates it with greater religious warmth, and may be regarded as a final summary and conclusion of the theme. The **crown** (στέφανος) was a wreath, usually of olive or ivy leaves but sometimes of precious metals, conferred as a reward or worn simply as an ornament; not to be confused with the "diadem" (Rev. 12:3; etc.), a headband or fillet, which denoted authority. If the force of the genitive in **crown of life** is to be pressed, it is probably appositive, "the crown which is life." In the oldest Greek text **promised** has no subject, in accord with the Jewish practice of avoiding God's name when (as here) no misunderstanding is possible. Later copyists added sometimes **God**, more usually **the Lord**.

The writer appears to refer to some definite passage where the promise of a crown is recorded; possibly Zech. 6:14 (LXX; the Hebrew is quite different): "The crown shall be for those who endure" ("endure" is the same Greek verb as in James).

A tribal reference would be to Issachar, who, according to Philo (*Allegorical Interpretation* I. 80), "is the symbol of him who performs good deeds."

Nothing in this verse suggests Christian influence.

---

according to the biblical viewpoint. Men concentrate their energies upon the accumulation of things which they cannot finally retain; they run after possessions which they must inevitably give up. Tolstoy tells of a peasant to whom the devil offered all the land he could encompass from sunrise to sunset. The peasant set such a wide sweep and pushed himself to such exhaustion that, coming to the end of his course just as the sun went down, he collapsed in death. The title of the story is "How Much Land Does a Man Require?"

> Count up your conquests of sea and land,
> Heap up your gold and hoard as you may,
> "All you can hold in your cold dead hand
> Is what you have given away."[1]

12. *Should Virtue Be Rewarded?*—There are many sayings in James which recall the words of Jesus. This beatitude is similar to the beatitude in Matt. 5:10. **The crown of life** is promised to those who, because of their devotion to God, successfully stand up under the testing of their faith (see above on vss. 2-3, 4). This metaphor of the crown has given us one of the most common of Christian symbols (cf. I Cor. 9:25; II Tim. 4:8; I Pet. 5:4; Rev. 2:10). In Christian art the crown is usually pictured entwined with the Cross, which suggests that endurance of trial leads to victory, as in this verse.

[1] E. M. Poteat, "Carve Your Name High O'er Shifting Sands." Used by permission.

It is worthy of note that the Greek word for crown (στέφανος) is the name of the first Christian martyr. How appropriate his name proved to be! It was the wreath awarded to the victor in athletic games in recognition of an achievement built upon rigorous discipline. James thinks of the Christian life as one of active and strenuous moral endeavor, with the goal of that endeavor kept steadfastly in mind (cf. Phil. 3:12-14). Faith in God does not exempt one from this struggle. Rather it enables one to endure its ardors until the victory is won and an imperishable wreath received (cf. I Cor. 9:24-27).

In philosophical ethics the idea of a reward for virtue is sometimes depreciated. "Goodness for goodness' sake," "Virtue is its own reward," are maxims which are presumed to represent a level of ethical motivation which is higher than the Christian code which promises rewards (cf. Matt. 5:12). But what is **the crown of life** which is promised to those who love God? It is not compensation in a future state for deprivations suffered in the present, that "pie in the sky, when you die," which communism has averred is the promise which religion makes to the victims of injustice in order to keep them quiet here and now. It is not the sort of compensation that a calculating, materialistic individual would seek with any avidity, for it would not appeal to him. It is really "goodness for goodness' sake."

For what is goodness? Is it not that quality of

13 Let no man say when he is tempted, I am tempted of God: for God cannot be tempted *with* evil, neither tempteth he any man:

14 But every man is tempted, when he is drawn away of his own lust, and enticed.

promised to those who love him. 13 Let no one say when he is tempted, "I am tempted by God"; for God cannot be tempted with evil and he himself tempts no one; 14 but each person is tempted when he is lured

VI. Temptation, as Distinguished from Trial, Is Wholly Evil (1:13-15)

The connection with vs. 12 is by the verbal form of πειρασμός (cf. on vs. 2), which has set the "trials" theme of vss. 2-12. But the word is now used in the contrasted sense of "tempt," which sets the theme of vss. 13-18 concretely, and perhaps that of the remainder of the chapter more generally. With vs. 13, therefore, a new paragraph should have been opened in the RSV.

13. I am tempted by God is more correctly rendered "I am tempted from God," for the Greek preposition is ἀπό, not ὑπό, denoting the remote rather than the immediate source of the temptation. But the plea in any case seeks a self-excuse with which the writer has no patience. It shows total ignorance of the nature of God and of the nature of temptation as well; since evil has no attraction for God, he can tempt no one; the evil comes solely from within the individual. Here there may or may not be a polemic against a common Jewish teaching that God implants in every man two "impulses," one good and the other evil; however that may be, the author, writing as a practical moralist, is unconcerned with the ultimate origin of evil or the part it may play in God's larger plan.

14. The imagery in vs. 14 is perhaps derived from angling; the fish are **lured** from a safe hiding place and **enticed** into being caught. **Desire** (ἐπιθυμία) is properly in itself morally neutral, taking a good (Luke 22:15; etc.) or evil force only through its context.

conduct and character which in personal relations is creative of good will? The biblical terms, godliness, Christlikeness, are just this sort of goodness writ large, and the reward promised to those who seek this goodness is its achievement, nothing more or less (cf. Matt. 5:6). The reward is not something extraneous, a sort of bonus added to lure men to devote themselves to the kingdom's service; it is the culmination of devotion in the achievement of the goal which is sought. "The fruit of his suffering shall he see and be satisfied" (Isa. 53:11 Amer. Trans.). One can acquire more material goods than he can use; one can be fed-up with indulgence of bodily appetites; but can there ever be a time when friendship and fellowship with God and man will reach the satiation point?

To eliminate rewards of this sort is to accept futility as the essence of existence, and thus cut the nerve of hopeful endeavor. The Buddhist doctrine of self-negation is the logical corollary of the atheistic Buddhist conception of the vanity of life as a whole. Christian self-denial is not the negation of the self, but "self-realization through self-sacrifice." "Whoever loses his life [his self-centered concern for his personal interests] will find it [in being caught up in the larger interests of the fellowship of God's kingdom]" (Matt. 16:25).

13-15. Who's to Blame?—From Adam and Eve to the latest Homo sapiens the alibi for succumbing to temptation is invariably, "It wasn't my fault. If God made me this way, why should I be held responsible for acting according to my nature?" Today, especially, excuses for moral dereliction are found in the popular determinism which denies man's freedom of choice and thereby revokes all personal responsibility. If a man is not free to choose between alternatives, but is caught in a causal sequence which drives him to a predetermined end, then he cannot be held accountable for the results of his actions: fate or society or circumstance is responsible, not he.

The case for determinism is not without logic, and admittedly there are many factors in life which are beyond the control of the individual. No one chooses his parents, the color of his skin, the early surroundings of childhood; and all these vitally affect his destiny. But the fact remains that social relationships could not be maintained if individuals were not held, in some measure at least, to be responsible for their deeds. Moreover, the most determined determinist would probably resent being treated as if he were totally irresponsible, e.g., as an infant or an imbecile is treated.

James, in this passage, is not, however, speculating on the philosophical problem of the

15 Then when lust hath conceived, it bringeth forth sin; and sin, when it is finished, bringeth forth death.

16 Do not err, my beloved brethren.

and enticed by his own desire. 15 Then desire when it has conceived gives birth to sins; and sin when it is full-grown brings forth death.

16 Do not be deceived, my beloved breth-

But an evil connotation tended to predominate, and in Stoicism desire is one of the four cardinal vices (the others being pleasure, grief, and fear); a Stoic coloring in the word certainly exists in II Tim. 3:6; Tit. 3:3 and probably here also (cf. 4:2).

15. This vivid metaphor is of course Jewish and not Stoic; it is rightly called "purely decorative" by an able commentator and is not to be analyzed in detail; cf. the extreme elaboration in the familiar passage in Book II of Milton's *Paradise Lost*.

On the whole passage (vss. 13-15) cf. Ecclus. 15:11-12:

> Do not say, "It is through the Lord that I fell,"
> For you must not do the things he hates.
> Do not say, "It is he who caused me to sin,"
> For he has no need of a sinner.

So while the teaching of this section would undoubtedly represent common-sense Christianity, it would equally represent common-sense Judaism; there is no reason to think of it as a Christian creation. Deeper thinkers in both religions were naturally not satisfied with so superficial a dualism. That God may actually cause men to be tempted is presupposed in, e.g., Matt. 4:7; 6:13 (cf. I Cor. 10:13), and there are real parallels in Judaism (H. L. Strack and P. Billerbeck, *Kommentar zum Neuen Testament aus Talmud und Midrasch* [München: C. H. Beck, 1922-24], I, 422).

VII. All That Is Good Comes from God (1:16-18)

16-17. Vs. 16 is meant to connect vss. 17-18 with vss. 13-15; the man who says "I am tempted from God" **is deceived,** for from God come **good** gifts, i.e., *only* good gifts. But

origin of evil. He is simply uttering a warning to his fellow Christians against using specious excuses for wicked conduct. Don't blame God or the nature he has given you for the sin you may commit. In endowing man with appetites and desires, God is not tempting man to sin, for all these endowments are good and necessary to life. It is when man misdirects his desires or abuses his appetites, allowing himself to be lured into the pursuit of deceitful attractions, that evil consequences ensue. The possibility of perversion or abuse is no proof that God's endowments are evil or that he is responsible for man's misguided behavior. "All our human misery comes from mistaking where our true satisfactions lie" (cf. Ecclus. 15:11-20).

That desire is evil and the cause of all suffering is the ascetic teaching of Buddhism; it is not biblical doctrine. The God-given appetite for food and drink is not evil. It may be directed to health or dissipation. The desires associated with sex produce the best or the worst in life, the high moral achievement of the Christian home or the deep degradation of prostitution, depending on their use or abuse. What man chooses determines the good or evil outcome.

In so far as a man has an opportunity to choose, he is responsible for his choice, and he cannot lay the blame upon his Maker or upon anyone else. The margin of freedom varies with different persons. Some are more heavily handicapped than others through no fault of their own (cf. Luke 12:47-48). This should cause us to be chary of passing harsh moral judgments on others. Our real responsibility is self-criticism in the light of our relation to God (see below on 4:11-12). Spiritual death is the consequence of the refusal of this responsibility, of missing the mark in aiming our desires and affections (ἁμαρτία, the Greek word for sin, means literally "to miss the mark"). Note Paul's declaration concerning "the mark" upon which his desires were concentrated (Phil. 3:14). If the petition "Lead us not into temptation" seems to contradict James's assertion that God **tempts no one,** the translation by Tertullian may be recalled, "Do not allow us to be led into temptation" (see also Torrey, *Four Gospels, ad loc.*).

16-18. The Origin of Goodness.—David Hume posed the dilemma concerning the existence of suffering and evil in the world, "Either God is not all-good or he is not all-powerful, otherwise

17 Every good gift and every perfect gift is from above, and cometh down from the Father of lights, with whom is no variableness, neither shadow of turning.

18 Of his own will begat he us with the word of truth, that we should be a kind of firstfruits of his creatures.

ren. 17 Every good endowment and every perfect gift is from above, coming down from the Father of lights with whom there is no variation or shadow due to change.[a]

18 Of his own will he brought us forth by the word of truth that we should be a kind of first fruits of his creatures.

[a] Some ancient authorities read *variation due to a shadow of turning.*

the connection is artificial because "only," needed to make the argument clear, is not in the text, and in the Greek **good** has an unemphatic position. Moreover, what the quotation in vs. 17 really asserts is that good comes from above and not from below. Hence vss. 17-18 contain a saying that was originally independent.

The first clause of vs. 17 is in the Greek a hexameter line (compare 4:5), too nearly accurate prosodically to be accidental. It may be rendered: "Every gift that is good and every boon that is perfect"; but its source is wholly unknown. **Father of lights** describes God as the creator and so **Father** (Job 38:28) of the sun, moon, and stars, these physical **lights** figuring—perhaps none too gracefully—spiritual "light" (John 1:4-5).

The terminology in the remainder of vs. 17 is almost hopelessly obscure and the textual evidence equally so. The reading of the great Neutral uncials is that of the RSV mg., **variation due to a shadow of turning;** which is so incomprehensible that the more conventional text, followed by the KJV, which may be rendered, "variation or shadow due to turning," is presumably an attempt to elucidate it, although "shadow due to turning" still defies explanation. Possibly the text is corrupt and, to conjecture, may originally have read "variation of turning or shadow." Or the writer may have used technical astronomical terminology that he did not understand—as not uncommonly happens when preachers attempt to make a display of erudition. But the general sense is clear enough; even the sun, moon, and stars change, but God never changes.

18. God's people came into existence through no act of their own but owe their being solely to God's will, exercised through his **word of truth;** and they are thus set apart from all other men as **a kind of first fruits.** To Christians this **word of truth** could mean only "the gospel" (Col. 1:5); on Christians as **first fruits** cf. Rev. 14:4 (and II Thess. 2:13 RSV mg.).

he would have rid the world of evil." James assumes that God is all-good and that all his gifts to man are good. He makes no attempt at argument to justify the ways of God to man. Here is no discussion like that between Job and his friends. Can we agree with him that all that is good comes from God, and all that comes from God is good?

Admittedly there is a dark side to life; there are temptation and sin and pain and suffering; but these do not mean that God purposed evil for his children. The travail in the earth can be the birth pangs of the creation of the sons of God (cf. Rom. 8:19). What is evil may be transmuted into good. The endowments of God open to us unimaginable possibilities of good, of lasting joy, if we will make use of them according to his will. It is his will that all should be saved and "come to the knowledge of the truth" (I Tim. 2:4).

We can depend on God. Can he depend on us? We may change, but he is invariable in his good will toward us. Therefore, let us not deceive ourselves by the false reasoning of unbelief, or excuse ourselves from responsibility for failure to respond to his call to become what he wants us to be, the **first fruits of his creatures,** the crown of his creation.

In regard to the pain of the world, Percy Dearmer writes:

When one contemplates what human beings inflict on their bodies, what they eat and drink, what they wear and what they do to themselves and how they treat one another, one wonders whether Nature's mistake has not been that pain is not severe enough, for certainly, in spite of it and for all the warning of disease, man continues to insult his body with incredible equanimity.[2]

[2] *Man and His Maker* (London: Student Christian Movement Press, 1936), pp. 36-37.

19 Wherefore, my beloved brethren, let every man be swift to hear, slow to speak, slow to wrath:

20 For the wrath of man worketh not the righteousness of God.

19 Know this, my beloved brethren. Let every man be quick to hear, slow to speak, slow to anger, 20 for the anger of man does not work the righteousness of God.

Yet precisely similar language was possible in Judaism, where the **word of truth** would be the law (cf. vss. 21, 22-26); and for Israel as **first fruits** cf. Jer. 2:3. There may well be also a tribal allusion in **first fruits** to Reuben as Jacob's "firstborn" (Gen. 49:3).

Note the contrast between God **brought . . . forth** here and sin "brings forth" in vs. 15; perhaps an additional reason for the sequence of vss. 16-18 after vss. 13-15.

VIII. Self-Control (1:19-21)

This paragraph was perhaps intended as a special application of the principle stated in vss. 16-18. In the later Greek MSS the connection is made close by the first word of vs. 19, **wherefore**, in Greek ὥστε. But in the oldest authorities this first word is ἴστε, which can mean indifferently **know this** or "Ye know this" (ASV), and a new sentence begins with **let every man**. This sentence (vss. 19b-20) is a saying complete in itself, which the writer has provided with an introduction in vs. 19a and supplemented with vs. 21—apparently his own composition—where **word** takes up "word" in vs. 18.

19-20. The object of **hear** should not be limited to the word (vs. 21) but is perfectly general: "Be always ready to listen to anyone or anything." In vs. 20 **the righteousness of God** is "the right conduct that God demands from men," and the sense is simply "anger harms the soul"; the explanation that "anger never helps *others*" is too artificial.

19-20. *Under Control.*—For the anger of man does not work the righteousness of God. We speak of an uncontrollable temper. Is irascibility an inherited trait and therefore beyond self-restraint? If so, such an exhortation as this and similar biblical admonitions (cf. Prov. 10:19; 15:1-2; 16:32; 17:27; Matt. 5:22; Eph. 4:26, 29, 31; etc.) are a misuse of breath, blowing up a fire instead of blowing it out.

But we need to be reminded that these words of James and the other writers are directed to worshipers of God and assume that their acceptance of his sovereignty includes the submission of all habits, attitudes, and emotions to his control. The religion of a man who cannot "bridle his tongue," i.e., control his temper, is an empty pretense, declares James a few sentences farther on (vs. 26).

The person who justifies his violent temper with the excuse that he cannot help himself is quite likely indulging in a bit of rationalization. A small boy who had been passionately angry toward his mother, and who later tried to excuse himself in this manner, was asked whether he ever lost his temper toward his teacher in school. When he replied in the negative he was asked, "Why not?" "Because I don't want her to dislike me," was his answer. Quite evidently he presumed on the love of his mother, expecting her to like him no matter how he behaved; but because he had to win the affection of his teacher, he kept himself under control. That is one reason why tempers differ before and after marriage.

Anger arises out of hatred or contempt or a similar attitude toward another person, rather than out of an inherited temperament. No effort will be made to control irascibility as long as such attitudes are cherished. The cure of a bad temper depends upon a change of attitude, and this is where religion comes in. Some Chinese schoolboys were asked by their teacher why, in a fit of anger, they had smashed some of the crockery which belonged to the school cook when he served them food which they disliked. They gave the same old excuse, "We were so disgusted with the food that we couldn't restrain ourselves." The teacher then asked, "If I were to invite you to a meal in my home and served you food like that the cook gave you, would you smash my dishes?" "Oh, no!" was the spontaneous reply. "Why not?" they were asked. "Because you are our teacher." Which was to confess that they could control their tempers if they respected or loved the person involved.

If the Christian's dominant desire is to have the approval of God, then that desire will restrain him from outbursts of anger which God cannot approve. **The anger of man does not work the righteousness of God** because it is usually evoked by a clash of wills, a conflict of selfish interests, a struggle for power. God's righteousness is impartial; his justice includes

21 Wherefore lay apart all filthiness and superfluity of naughtiness, and receive with meekness the engrafted word, which is able to save your souls.

21 Therefore put away all filthiness and rank growth of wickedness and receive with meekness the implanted word, which is able to save your souls.

21. What is literally "putting off all filthiness" has been compared to the removal of soiled clothing; but this attributes too studied a figure to the writer. And still less likely is the interpretation of "excrescence of wickedness," as if wickedness was an excrescent growth on human character; there is no need to think of more than "the evil which abounds" in every man. **The implanted word,** "the word which has taken root in you," is already in the readers' hearts and yet must be continually "received," "heard attentively"; cf. vs. 25. To the Christian editor this **word** is of course the gospel, as in vs. 18.

The theme of vss. 19b-20 reappears in vs. 26, and again, much elaborated, in 3:1-12; in all small, closed religious communities talkative and irritable egotists are an endless nuisance.

While the section can be read throughout in a Christian sense, it would be even more appropriate in Judaism; indeed, **the righteousness of God** is used in a way that is conventionally Jewish (and utterly un-Pauline!). With vs. 19b cf. Ecclus. 5:11, "Be swift to hear . . . and with patience give answer."

A tribal reference here would be to Simeon, who was the type of anger (Gen. 49:5-7). Although in this Genesis passage Levi is joined with Simeon, Jewish tradition separated the two because of Levi's religious privileges (cf. on vss. 26-27).

the good of all. God is not arbitrary or arrogant or vindictive. But pride and spite are the fuel which feeds the fires of man's wrath. There is a Chinese proverb, "The man who is losing the argument strikes the first blow." This man lets his temper go, not because it is uncontrollable, but because his pride is piqued. "Love," wrote Paul, "does not insist on its own way"; therefore it is not easily provoked (I Cor. 13:5).

"The wrath of God," a phrase which Paul uses, does not imply a contradiction of God's love. This expression is a personalized symbol of moral consequence, the result of the violation of the laws of God which are utterly impartial in their working, the reaping of what is sown. The only anger which a man is justified in loosing is an anger like Christ's (cf. Mark 3:5), which is not the expression of private petulance but of public resentment against behavior or actions which cause others to suffer without blame on their part. Someone has said, "I do well to be angry at times, but I have usually chosen the wrong times."

21-24. *Worshiping in Vain.*—In the first century the Christian congregation in its Lord's Day worship followed the practices of the Jewish synagogue rather than the Jewish temple. The service consisted primarily in the reading and exposition of the O.T. scriptures, Christian writings not yet gathered together in the N.T. canon, the singing of psalms and Christian hymns, and the offering of prayers. James seems to have such a service in mind as he follows the example of Isaiah in asserting that wicked-

ness must be forsaken and righteousness must be embraced if participation in such a service is not to be in vain (cf. Isa. 1:11-17).

Primitive Christian worship was not motivated, as was the worship of pagan neighbors, by the supposed necessity of winning the favor of an impassive deity. It was not devised as a method of getting on the good side of a divine despot through flattery, or the offering of bribes on altars of sacrifice. The God the Christians knew through Jesus had no need to be cajoled into being gracious unto them (cf. I John 4:19). The difficulty was not on God's side, but on man's. It was man's response, not God's, which was hard to obtain. Man had to be brought to surrender to the persuasion of God's love, to **receive with meekness** the divine instruction, to a willingness to cleanse his heart and hands of all the **filthiness** which outraged the holiness of God. "You shall be holy, for I am holy," saith the Lord (I Pet. 1:16). "Today, when you hear his voice, do not harden your hearts" (Heb. 3:7-8).

Therefore, the practical value of church attendance, according to James, is realized only when the word heard becomes the word in action. If anyone considers himself to be a devout worshiper without carrying over into his daily living the truths he has heard, his worship is as useless as a glance in a mirror which is straightway lost to mind. Pious genuflection followed by unethical conduct is a travesty upon worship which Jesus and the prophets unreservedly condemned (cf. Hos. 6:6; Matt. 9:13).

31

22 But be ye doers of the word, and not hearers only, deceiving your own selves.

23 For if any be a hearer of the word, and not a doer, he is like unto a man beholding his natural face in a glass:

24 For he beholdeth himself, and goeth his way, and straightway forgetteth what manner of man he was.

25 But whoso looketh into the perfect law of liberty, and continueth *therein,* he being not a forgetful hearer, but a doer of the work, this man shall be blessed in his deed.

22 But be doers of the word, and not hearers only, deceiving yourselves. 23 For if any one is a hearer of the word and not a doer, he is like a man who observes his natural face in a mirror; 24 for he observes himself and goes away and at once forgets what he is like. 25 But he who looks into the perfect law, the law of liberty, and perseveres, being no hearer that forgets but a doer that acts, he shall be blessed in his doing.

IX. Hearing and Doing (1:22-25)

It is not enough to receive the word (vs. 21); one must obey the word by doing what it commands. This connection is close; but the present saying, with its figure of the mirror, is again complete in itself. God's revelation of righteousness teaches men how far they fall short, and so reveals to them their true nature. But no one must be content with a single "conviction of sin"; ceaseless self-criticism is a lifelong duty that must bring forth its fruit in good works.

22. Doers of the word is a Semitism. "Hearing" doubtless includes listening to **the word** when read liturgically, but of course it is not to be so limited (for the contrast between "hearing" and "doing" cf., e.g., Rom. 2:13).

23. The mirrors of the day were made of polished metal—silver being used for the more expensive—and were quite small, generally so made as to be held in the hand. The **natural face** is the "face as it is," with all its defects manifest; there is no thought here of any imperfection in the mirror (contrast I Cor. 13:12).

24. The Greek verbs for **observes** and **forgets** are in the aorist tense; the so-called "gnomic aorists," used in proverbs, etc., which should be rendered in English by the present tense. But **goes away** is a Greek perfect, denoting an action with enduring result, "he goes away and does not return."

25. Precisely how the Christian editor would define **the law** cannot be determined. But it would certainly include the precepts taught by Jesus (even Paul can speak of "the law of Christ" in Gal. 6:2), the Decalogue (2:8-12; perhaps excluding the Fourth Commandment) and doubtless many O.T. "moral" decrees as well; the editor's attitude

A Confucian scholar, when asked his opinion of Jesus, declared that he excelled in his power to sensitize the conscience. The word of God is sharper than a two-edged sword, and it may cause pain if it comes close to the heart. Is one of the reasons why some church members grow lax in their attendance at church that they do not want to expose themselves to **the word** which will disturb their moral and spiritual complacency?

25. Liberty in Law.—(Cf. 2:12.) Do response to the word of God and acceptance of the obligations of obedience to God result in narrowing the scope of living, in contracting opportunities for vital activity, in lessening one's enjoyment in all living things? In becoming a Christian does one have less of life, or more? It is an all too common impression that to become a Chris-

tian is to forfeit more than one gains. Francis Thompson in "The Hound of Heaven" tells of his fear "lest, having Him, I must have naught beside."

These verses suggest that obedience to the word of God is the path to freedom, for God's law is **the law of liberty,** and the road to happiness, for he who does the will of God will be **blessed in his doing.** Enrichment of life, emancipation, happiness, are the will of God for his children. His word is good news, not bad (cf. I Tim. 6:17b).

Are law and liberty at odds? Many assume them to be so. Law restricts and restrains; liberty unlocks all doors. To be able to do exactly as one pleases, "to have no master save one's mood," that is to be free. But Thomas Huxley long ago pointed out that "man's worst diffi-

| 26 If any man among you seem to be religious, and bridleth not his tongue, but deceiveth his own heart, this man's religion *is* vain. | 26 If any one thinks he is religious, and does not bridle his tongue but deceives his |

may very well be much like that of Clement of Rome, whose Christian ethic is given an almost purely O.T. foundation. The qualifying attributes in the phrase **the perfect law, the law of liberty** may be meant to contrast the Christian **law** with the Jewish law; but such a contrast would be unique in James and seems quite foreign to its tone. The remainder of vs. 25 echoes and applies the lesson implicit in vss. 23-24.

As a matter of fact, the attributes given **the law** in vs. 25 are wholly conventional in Judaism. The O.T. law is **perfect** simply because it is given by God and is therefore necessarily without flaw; the theme, e.g., of almost endless elaboration in Ps. 119. And there would be no thought of a contrast with other laws, for no comparison between God's Word and human codes was conceivable. For the O.T. law as the **law of liberty** cf., e.g., the saying of Rabbi Joshua ben Levi (*ca.* A.D. 250) in Pirke Aboth 6:2: "Thou findest no freeman excepting him who occupieth himself in the study of the law," i.e., only he who does God's will is truly free.

There is accordingly no reason to think that anything in this section is due to Christian editing.

X. Control of the Tongue (1:26)

26. The connection with vss. 22-25 may be as the application of a general rule to a specific case, but the saying here is again complete in itself. It repeats the theme of vss. 19-20, just as vs. 12 repeats the theme of vss. 2-4.

The adjective **religious** (θρησκός) is not known elsewhere in Greek literature, but the noun **religion** (θρησκεία), from which it is derived, has usually—even if not quite invariably—the special sense of "religious activity," "prayer and ceremonial," "cultus"; in Philo (*The Worse Attacks the Better* 21) this noun is used in a depreciatory sense, meaning "ritual" in contrast to "holiness." To **bridle** one's **tongue** is a common figure among Greek writers and the "bridling" meant is quite general, not to be limited, e.g., to the "anger" of vs. 19.

culties begin when he is able to do as he pleases," for then he must decide what he pleases to do. Freedom is simply an opportunity for choice; it gives no guidance as to what the choice should be.

The law of God is not the negation of freedom; it is the **law of liberty.** It is not a limitation upon vital living; it marks the direction in which life must flow if our potentialities are to be fulfilled. "I delight to do thy will, O my God" is not the exclamation of a slave, but of one who has discovered that in his service is perfect freedom, for only if we willingly conform to the God-given law of our being can we be true to our essential nature as children of God. The man who looks into **the perfect law, the law of liberty,** is the one who has discovered that his highest happiness can be attained only if he freely chooses to live in accordance with the purpose of his Creator. Restlessness, dissatisfaction, frustration, and despair are not the lot of the servant of God, but of the rebel against God. The free man knows with Augus-

tine that there is no heart's rest outside the will of God.

26-27. *Unadulterated Religion.*—If any one thinks he is religious. The notions of what makes one acceptable **before God** have been varied, confused, and contradictory. In some, great stress is laid upon ritualistic purity, e.g., in the washings described in Mark 7:3-4. The Islamic devotee must be careful to bathe according to prescribed rites before he enters a mosque. Some Christians hold that baptism is essential to salvation, that no one is truly accepted until he has undergone that rite. In other cases, the exact form of ceremonial has been held supremely important, just as in a royal court a breach of form or protocol is inexcusable. No subject dares approach his king without conforming to the prescribed court etiquette. Or it has been supposed that God Almighty does not accept the prayers of those whose theology does not conform to a certain fixed and rigid pattern. Heretics have been tortured to make them acceptable to God,

27 Pure religion and undefiled before God and the Father is this, To visit the fatherless and widows in their affliction, *and* to keep himself unspotted from the world.

2 My brethren, have not the faith of our Lord Jesus Christ, *the Lord* of glory, with respect of persons.

heart, this man's religion is vain. 27 Religion that is pure and undefiled before God and the Father is this: to visit orphans and widows in their affliction, and to keep oneself unstained from the world.

2 My brethren, show no partiality as you hold the faith of our Lord Jesus Christ,

XI. TRUE RELIGION (1:27)

27. Religion, in the Greek the opening word, is also in the Greek the last word in vs. 26 and so gives the connection. But the two verses are otherwise unrelated; vs. 27 does not state the converse of vs. 26 but introduces something new, which perhaps takes up the theme of "acts" in vs. 25.

The O.T., of course, abounds in exhortations to care for **orphans and widows,** while for the direct statement that **God** is their **Father** cf. Ps. 68:5. Yet the (liturgical) combination **God and the Father** is unusual, and many Greek MSS have simply **God** here. To a Christian **keep oneself unstained from the world** would mean "avoid the pollution of sin of any kind." The language of this verse naturally must not be pressed too far; the writer certainly does not mean to imply that **religion,** in any sense of the word, is merely philanthropy combined with (negative) sinlessness.

In neither vs. 26 nor vs. 27 does anything suggest Christian editing; in Judaism, however, **keep oneself unstained from the world** might conceivably be meant as "preserve ceremonial purity."

In either verse a tribal reference to Levi might be detected in **religion;** cf. on vss. 19-21.

XII. THE SIN OF DEFERENCE TOWARD THE RICH (2:1-13)

The first of the three longer sections of the epistle, the others being 2:14-26 and 3:1-12; contrast the brief sayings-groups or single sayings elsewhere.

This section is unified by its constant theme throughout. Yet the structure is not that of a sustained argument but is a loosely connected series of reproofs, set down apparently as they occurred to the writer's mind. The thesis is stated in vs. 1, and a

James, however, follows his predecessors, the Hebrew prophets, and his Master, Jesus, in conceiving man's relationship to God as dependent upon none of these things, but upon a simple and sincere devotion to God, demonstrated by compassionate relationship with one's fellows; cf. vs. 27 with Micah's definition of religion, "What doth the LORD require of thee, but to do justly, and to love mercy, and to walk humbly with thy God?" (Mic. 6:8.)

Such an understanding of religion is so simple that many have been unable to believe it to be adequate. But it is so difficult to practice that ceremonies with the most complicated elaboration have been found easier to offer to God in its stead (cf. Amos 4:4-5; 5:21-24).

No single definition of religion can be adequate, this definition of James no more than others; but no definition can be true to prophetic and Christian insights if the two essentials which James underlines are not prominent, viz., compassion toward one's fellows and unworldliness. To be merciful as God is merciful

is to be truly religious (Luke 6:36; cf. Hos. 6:6; Matt. 9:13; Mark 12:32-33). The ceremonies and sacrifices may do no harm if mercy is present, but without mercy **religion is vain.** "Worldliness" represents all those purposes and practices which contravene the good will of God. W. R. Inge has suggested that

what the New Testament calls "the world" is a system of co-operative guilt with limited liability. The Crucifixion was possible only by the co-operation of a cowardly governor, unscrupulous ecclesiastics, a traitor disciple, a thoughtless mob, and callous executioners.[3]

It is from such evil attitudes and behavior that the man who would be truly religious must keep himself **unstained.** Nothing less than this is unadulterated religion (cf. Rom. 12:2).

2:1-4, 9. Class and Caste in Religion.—The snobbishness, contempt, and discrimination which are attacked in this paragraph are all

[3] *A Rustic Moralist* (New York: G. P. Putnam's Sons; Toronto: McClelland & Stewart, 1937), p. 219.

2 For if there come unto your assembly a man with a gold ring, in goodly apparel, and there come in also a poor man in vile raiment;

3 And ye have respect to him that weareth the gay clothing, and say unto him, Sit thou here in a good place; and say to the poor, Stand thou there, or sit here under my footstool:

the Lord of glory. 2 For if a man with gold rings and in fine clothing comes into your assembly, and a poor man in shabby clothing also comes in, 3 and you pay attention to the one who wears the fine clothing, and say, "Have a seat here, please," while you say to the poor man, "Stand there," or, "Sit at my

---

particularly glaring example of the sin rebuked is described in vss. 2-4. The quiet tone of these opening verses then changes abruptly in vss. 5-7 to an invective like that of 1:10-11; 5:1-6; but in vss. 8-13 this invective is disregarded as if it were a parenthetical digression. Vss. 8-9 return to the original theme and lead up to a wholly general principle enunciated in vss. 10-11. And a second resumption of the theme in vs. 12 leads up again to a wholly general principle stated in vs. 13.

The adjective **royal** applied to **the law** in vs. 8 was used by Greek writers to distinguish a law properly enacted from one whose authority was defective. Very possibly, however, the Christian writer thought of Mark 12:31 as pre-eminently the law of Christ the king. And in vs. 13 Christians would inevitably recall such sayings as those in Matt. 6:12, 14-15; 18:32-33; etc. Nevertheless, the section as a whole may unhesitatingly be pronounced pre-Christian.

2:1. Christian **faith**, which has for its object **our Lord Jesus Christ**, who reigns in heavenly **glory**—for the grammar of the Greek see below—should teach us the worthlessness of the petty earthly advantages that cause **partiality**. This opening verse should be read as a command, not as a question as in the ASV mg.; the imperative belongs to the gnomic style of the epistle. **Show partiality** is literally "receive persons," a LXX phrase (Lev. 19:15; etc.) that is pure "translation Greek."

The Greek of vs. 1 closes with a series of seven words, all in the genitive case, that have been a perpetual puzzle to commentators: τοῦ κυρίου ἡμῶν Ἰησοῦ Χριστοῦ τῆς δόξης. Here the smooth English reading **of our Lord Jesus Christ, the Lord of glory** has been achieved by inserting before **of glory** the words **the Lord**, which are not in the original at all; note the italics in the KJV. Consequently, it can be argued with real force that the Christian editor has inserted into a Jewish writing at least **Jesus Christ** and probably **our** as well (since **our Lord** is far more characteristic of early Christianity than it is of Judaism); an argument that is further strengthened when the restricted use of "Lord" for Christ in James is remembered (cf. on 1:1). The original wording was then simply "the Lord of glory"; not, to be sure, an O.T. title of God, but one known to later Judaism.

2-4. Such partiality is supremely obnoxious when exhibited in a congregation assembled for worship, the time of all times when men should lay aside all worldly

---

instances of worldliness. **The faith of our Lord Jesus Christ** is not compatible with such partiality. To discriminate between persons because of their social or financial status is to pass judgments from evil motives, to **become judges with evil thoughts.** Life according to the Christian faith and life according to worldly standards are in sharp contrast here. The faith which originates in Jesus Christ disavows distinctions based upon birth, race, property, or sex (cf. Gal. 3:28).

In the world discrimination is contentiously upheld, but in the Christian fellowship there is no room for humiliation or arrogance.

For all we are Christ's creatures and of his coffers rich,
And brethren of one blood, as well beggars as earls:
For on Calvary of Christ's blood Christendom 'gan spring,
And blood brethren we become there, of one body won.[4]

Let judgment begin with the house of the Lord (cf. I Pet. 4:17). Can the followers of Christ have easy consciences so long as the churches countenance the sort of partiality which James denounces? The Greek word for partiality means literally "to receive the face,"

[4] William Langland, *The Vision of Piers Plowman.*

4 Are ye not then partial in yourselves, and are become judges of evil thoughts?

5 Hearken, my beloved brethren, Hath not God chosen the poor of this world rich in faith, and heirs of the kingdom which he hath promised to them that love him?

feet," 4 have you not made distinctions among yourselves, and become judges with evil thoughts? 5 Listen, my beloved brethren. Has not God chosen those who are poor in the world to be rich in faith and heirs of the kingdom which he has promised to

---

pride. The visitors described in vs. 2 are apparently not members of the congregation, who presumably would have their places regularly assigned (for further details see below). In the Greek the word for **assembly** is "synagogue"; not found elsewhere in the N.T. to describe a Christian congregation but always used of the building in which Jews worship. At the beginning of vs. 3 **pay attention** is literally "look upon," with the connotation "look favorably upon," as in Luke 1:48; 9:38—a Semitic usage common in the LXX. The speaker in vs. 3 does not appear to be an official appointed to attend to visitors, but is a member of the congregation sitting in a comfortable seat provided with a footstool. He rises and offers the wealthy stranger this seat but contemptuously gives the poor man only the choice between standing or sitting on the floor. The translation of καλῶς by **please** in the RSV is possible, but the more usual **in a good place** in the KJV makes excellent sense and is much more likely. The best-attested text of the words to the poor man is " 'Stand,' or 'Sit there at my feet,' " a more brusque form than that adopted in the RSV. In vs. 4 **made distinctions** may mean "had a divided mind," "were untrue to your own (better) self," "wavered in your faith," but is most easily understood as "made wrong distinctions between the rich and the poor" (see below). **With evil thoughts** is literally **of evil thoughts**, a genitive of quality.

While there are a few but very rare instances of "synagogue" to denote a Christian congregation in post–New Testament writers, the noun undoubtedly would be far more appropriate in a Jewish context. (Heb. 10:25 does not offer a real parallel.) And the discrimination rebuked in vss. 2-4 would occur far more often in Judaism than in Christianity, for there were many rich Jews. These, when traveling, would visit the local synagogues, where their expensive garments would secure them a warm welcome despite the fact that they were strangers—in poignant contrast to the reception accorded strangers of beggarly appearance. On the other hand, the Christian editor assumes that there are no rich Christians at all, and that the wealthy visitors are unbelievers.

5-7. The digression here introduces a quite different theme: not only should no special privileges be extended to the rich, but all such privileges should be reserved for the poor; it is they, not the rich, whom God has chosen as heirs of his kingdom (cf. on

---

i.e., to estimate people superficially rather than on the basis of their fundamental humanity. God's estimate is not partial to "face." He looks not upon the outward appearance, but upon the heart. An African Negro student in an American university in a speech at a student Christian conference declared, "God is he before whom white and black and red and yellow, rich and poor, can kneel and say, 'Our Father.' " But Gandhi, when he was in South Africa early in his career, went to a Christian church where his English friend C. F. Andrews was to preach, only to be turned away at the door by an usher because his skin was not white. The opponent of caste in the Hindu religion found caste at the door of a Christian church. An Anglican minister in the same part of the world was put in jail in 1947 because he broke the color bar. Is South Africa the only place in Christendom where such things occur? An Italian missionary in a mission in an American city supported by a wealthy congregation averred, "They want us to be saved, but they don't want to associate with us." The words of James are unequivocal: **If you show partiality, you commit sin.**

5-7. *Is Religion the Opiate of the People?*— In the time of James the brothers in the Christian fellowship were mostly of humble origin, though there are names of well-to-do Christians in the N.T., e.g., Barnabas (Acts 4:36-37), Lydia (Acts 16:14), and Philemon. The oppression to which James refers most likely was at the hands of rich and powerful persons who were not members of the church.

6 But ye have despised the poor. Do not rich men oppress you, and draw you before the judgment seats?

7 Do not they blaspheme that worthy name by the which ye are called?

those who love him? 6 But you have dishonored the poor man. Is it not the rich who oppress you, is it not they who drag you into court? 7 Is it not they who blaspheme that honorable name by which you are called?

1:10-11). In both the present passage and in 1:10-11 is voiced the experience of the early church that it was almost exclusively among the poor that its message was welcomed. **Listen** is in the diatribe style of an oral debate and does not indicate that the epistle itself was written to be preached like a sermon. **Kingdom** occurs only here in James.

Since it is among the poor that nearly all converts are made, discrimination against them calls forth the sharp rebuke in vs. 6a. And in vss. 6b-7 specific faults of the rich are detailed. They **oppress,** "lord it over," the poor (cf. 5:1-6), and they so control the courts that poor men cannot obtain justice—complaints familiar at all times and in all places. There is no hint here of technical religious persecution; while the **you** of course are Christians, and are doubtless thought of as especially singled out for bad treatment, other poor men who were not believers would not fare much better. In vs. 7 **that honorable name by which you are called** (literally, "called upon you"), to the writer and his readers, must be "Jesus," "Christ," or perhaps specifically "Christian." And as the rich men **blaspheme** this name, they must be thought of as unbelievers.

In vss. 2-4, therefore, the Christian assemblies are described as open to the public—at least for certain services, if not all—and as freely visited by even hostile outsiders. So in this context the overgracious welcome extended to rich men would apparently be in the hope of winning them as converts or at least of convincing them that Christians are harmless and should be treated kindly—a hope that to the writer would in either case be wholly vain.

These verses, which break the connection between vss. 2-4 and 8-13, may safely be ascribed to the Christian editor. They are, however, composed almost entirely of Jewish material. As was noted on 1:10-11, the antithesis between the godless "rich" and the righteous "poor" has abundant precedents in both the O.T. (especially in the Psalms) and later Jewish literature; early Christianity simply made more acute what was already a Jewish commonplace. And **rich in faith** is a good rabbinical phrase. But the doctrine that the poor *as such* are the sole heirs of the kingdom is not known in Judaism and may well be due to the Christian editor; to him also may be attributed the sole appearance of **kingdom** in the epistle.

Vs. 6, however, contains nothing that limits its application to Christians, as was noted above. And much in vs. 7 has abundant O.T. parallels; for "called by [God's] name" cf. Deut. 28:10; Isa. 63:19; Jer. 14:9; 15:16; for "blasphemy of [God's] name" by

But the days came when Christians were rich and powerful and corrupted by worldly ambition, cupidity, the pride of life, the love of power. There has been some historical justification for Lenin's sarcastic definition of religion as "one aspect of the spiritual oppression which falls everywhere upon the masses who are condemned to eternal labor for others by their need and loneliness" [5] and for the dictum of Karl Marx, "Religion is the opium of the people."

Nicholas Berdyaev, the Russian Christian philosopher, exiled from Soviet Russia, wrote:

[5] Nicholas Berdyaev, *The Origin of Russian Communism* (London: Geoffrey Bles; New York: Charles Scribner's Sons, 1937), p. 195.

Christians, who condemn the communists for their godlessness and anti-religious persecutions, cannot lay the whole blame solely upon these godless communists; they must assign part of the blame to themselves, and that a considerable part. . . . Have Christians done very much for the realization of Christian justice in social life? Have they striven to realize the brotherhood of man without that hatred and violence of which they accuse the communists? . . . Betrayal of the covenant of Christ, the use of the Christian Church for the support of the ruling classes, human weakness being what it is, cannot but bring about the lapse from Christianity of those who are compelled to suffer from that betrayal and from such a distortion of Christianity.[6]

[6] *Ibid.,* pp. 207-8. Used by permission.

8 If ye fulfil the royal law according to the Scripture, Thou shalt love thy neighbor as thyself, ye do well:

9 But if ye have respect to persons, ye commit sin, and are convinced of the law as transgressors.

10 For whosoever shall keep the whole law, and yet offend in one *point,* he is guilty of all.

8 If you really fulfill the royal law, according to the scripture, "You shall love your neighbor as yourself," you do well. 9 But if you show partiality, you commit sin, and are convicted by the law as transgressors. 10 For whoever keeps the whole law but fails in one point has become

---

unbelievers cf. Isa. 52:5; Ezek. 36:20. Nonetheless, the identification of the rich *as such* with blasphemers, like the identification of the poor *as such* with the heirs of the kingdom, has no known parallel in Jewish teaching. The Christian editor, consequently, has introduced vss. 5-7 in order to adapt the Jewish original of vss. 1-4, 8-13 to Christian conditions, where any "rich" man was necessarily an unbeliever.

8-9. Disregarding vss. 5-7, vss. 8-9 return to the theme of vss. 2-4 and continue it directly. In vs. 8 an objector, in diatribe style, offers an excuse: "In the kindly attention we pay to rich men, despite their faults, we demonstrate that we love them like ourselves; and so we fulfill the supreme commandment of Lev. 19:18." To this excuse the writer, continuing the diatribe style, replies in vs. 9: "Such behavior would be admirable if true! But do you pay the same kindly attention to the poor men likewise? If not, your obedience to Lev. 19:18 is vitiated by your violation of Lev. 19:15!" And the wholly general principle in vss. 10-11 sums up and reinforces the argument of vss. 8-9. Obedience to one precept in the law is no excuse for disobedience to another precept; the breach of any commandment of the law is rebellion against God, who gave the law; and so is rebellion against the law in its entirety. Here **in one point** is a correct expansion of the Greek, which has only "in one"; in Jewish phrasing "the law" is an inclusive term and a single precept in it is not called "a law." For the inverted order of "adultery" and "murder" cf. Luke 18:20 (not Matt. 19:18, and probably not Mark 10:19); Rom. 13:9. It is so found in certain (not all) MSS of the LXX.

10-13. What is stated as a principle in vss. 10-11 is then repeated as an adjuration in vs. 12: "As you will be judged by your obedience to every precept in the law, beware lest you violate *any* of them!"—where, of course, in the context Lev. 19:15 is concretely in mind. And this context gives the general truth in vs. 13 the specific meaning, "If you show the poor no mercy [vss. 2-4], God will show you no mercy"; while on the other hand **mercy triumphs over judgment,** "merciful acts turn God's condemnation from those who perform them." And this verse brings the section to an appropriate conclusion.

If Christians are to maintain untarnished the **honorable name** which they bear, they must stand with the oppressed, not with the oppressors; they must follow in the footsteps of the prophets and of their Lord, as James follows in his insistence that justice and mercy must characterize those who profess to serve the Lord of glory (cf. Isa. 3:13-15; 10:1-2; Jer. 5:26; Luke 20:46-47).

8-17. *Pious Excuses for Unchristian Behavior.*—"The worst is the corruption of the best." A rotten lily smells worse than a decayed weed. The Christian religion which contains within it the promise of the highest moral achievements has been used to cover up some of the world's worst evils. Here are two examples of its perversion: (*a*) Discrimination in favor of the rich is excused as practicing the law of love.

(*b*) Heartlessness toward the needy is excused as unimportant so long as one has faith.

James punctures the pious rationalization that partiality toward the rich is really an illustration of obedience to the command to love one's neighbor. Should not one be kind to such people? Certainly the law of love is not prejudiced against the rich. But this law is inclusive of all, and we cannot practice it toward the rich man if at the same time we are discriminating against the poor man. The interests of the one are not to be served at the expense of the other. A Christian's conduct must be consistent, for it is presumably under the control of a single dominant motive; therefore, love for one cannot involve disparagement of another. **The royal law has one intention,** the good of man, and it does not matter

11 For he that said, Do not commit adultery, said also, Do not kill. Now if thou commit no adultery, yet if thou kill, thou art become a transgressor of the law.

12 So speak ye, and so do, as they that shall be judged by the law of liberty.

13 For he shall have judgment without mercy, that hath showed no mercy; and mercy rejoiceth against judgment.

guilty of all of it. 11 For he who said, "Do not commit adultery," said also, "Do not kill." If you do not commit adultery but do kill, you have become a transgressor of the law. 12 So speak and so act as those who are to be judged under the law of liberty. 13 For judgment is without mercy to one who has shown no mercy; yet mercy triumphs over judgment.

For the Christian conception of **the law,** every precept in which binds believers, cf. on 1:25, where the phrase **the law of liberty** is also discussed. There is no reason to think that in vs. 12 any contrast is implied between the stricter Jewish law and the milder Christian law; the point is simply that since true liberty is to do God's will, violation of God's will is doubly inexcusable, an offense against self as well as against God.

As was noted above (p. 35), the attribute "royal" given to Lev. 19:18 suggests Christian wording, since Judaism gave no such supreme prominence to this precept; yet in vss. 8-11 this commandment is not treated as all-inclusive but simply as one among others, of which all are of equal and independent obligation. And vs. 10 is of course thoroughly Jewish, although the parallels in later Jewish writers have generally the converse form, "He who has kept one commandment has kept them all." For the possibility of Christian influence in **the law of liberty** (vs. 12) cf. on 1:25. Vs. 13 has ample parallels in the O.T. (Prov. 14:21; etc.), the Apoc. (Tob. 4:10, "Alms delivereth from death"; Ecclus. 3:30, "Almsgiving will make atonement for sins"; etc.), and later Jewish sources.

To summarize what has been said about this work of the Christian editor in this section: In vs. 1 "Jesus Christ" is certainly due to the Christian editor and probably "our" likewise. Vss. 5-7 have been interpolated by him; although the material is Jewish, he has intensified the religious contrast between "rich" and "poor" and he has introduced "kingdom." And "royal" in vs. 8 may well be his addition.

We may ask, however, how far the section with his modifications was really suited to Christian conditions. In its Jewish form it dealt with a constantly recurring evil in the discrimination made between rich and poor *Jewish* visitors in the synagogues. And in later Christian ages—including the present day!—the section in its original extent (without vss. 5-7) was and still is equally applicable to precisely the same discrimination between visitors in our churches. But when the editor wrote, there were no wealthy Christians; so he was obliged to treat the visitors in question as unbelievers. Can we think that rich non-Christians, whether Jews or pagans, visited the Christians' services so often as to make so drastic and uncompromising a warning needful? Or did the content of the section so appeal to the editor that he used it without much reflection? (Cf. on 4:1-2.)

---

which particular commandment is violated; for if one violates the law's intention, one is guilty of violating the principle which underlies all the commandments of God. There is no necessity for casuistical calculation as to obedience or disobedience to a specific enactment if one is loyal to this principle.

Paul's famous simplification of the complicated system of the six hundred odd laws of Pharisaism, "Love is the fulfilling of the law" (Rom. 13:10), is similar in import to James's exhortation to **so speak and so act as those who are to be judged under the law of liberty.**

It is immaterial what the particular offense against the person of another may be—adultery, murder, theft, slander—if the basic principle of love is violated. Nor is there any need for the multiplication of specific laws for the one who has genuinely accepted the law of love as the rule of his relationships.

How strange the perversion of Christian teaching which presumed that the law of love was a relaxation of the moral requirements of the law of Moses, that the gospel relieved men from an obedience which had proved itself too rigorous for human frailties, instead of what it

14 What *doth it* profit, my brethren, though a man say he hath faith, and have not works? can faith save him?

14 What does it profit, my brethren, if a man says he has faith but has not works?

XIII. Faith and Works (2:14-26)

The theme may conceivably be regarded as a generalization of that in vss. 1-13, where the proper treatment of rich and poor is a special "work" that should follow from true "faith" (vs. 1). But the present section naturally forms a complete and independent whole in itself.

It is made up of three separate and parallel arguments, vss. 14-17, 18-19, and 20-26, the first and third ending with virtually identical phrases. And the tone throughout shows the writer's impatience with a theory which he regards as so futile that its falsity ought to be obvious to everyone.

The argument in this section as a whole reveals the writer as an earnest, common-sense moralist, unconcerned with the deeper spiritual problems of the relations between God and man, but wholly concerned with everyday conduct. Doctrine such as his would not produce great saints—let alone great mystics—nor was it designed to do so. Most Christians are neither saints nor mystics, but men and women desiring to fulfill properly the tasks of daily life, who become confused by what seem to them to be theological subtleties and who can understand only teaching that deals with their immediate needs. Such teaching James gives them, that and no more.

In support of the view that the origin of vss. 14-26 is pre-Christian can be adduced the absence of anything specifically Christian in the passage and, furthermore, the fact that the relative value of faith and works was a real subject of debate in non-Christian Judaism. For the former point compare below. As regards the latter point, the Jewish data are assembled in Strack-Billerbeck (on Rom. 4:2-3 in *Kommentar zum Neuen Testament,* III, 186-201). They show that the centrality of faith was by no means without recognition, although this appears much more clearly in the pseudepigraphs than in the rabbinical writings. And this "faith" was, of course, primarily acceptance of monotheism (as in 2:19), with which was coupled acceptance of God's reward of the righteous and punishment of the wicked (cf. Heb. 11:6). But such faith was never held to be a barren intellectual tenet; it must result in a life in which this belief was the driving power, a self-surrender to God's revelation. And there are many passages in the pseudepigraphs and in Philo that hold up Abraham as the supreme exemplar of such faith.

The sole passage that appears to imply that men can be saved by faith is II Esdras 9:7, "Every one that shall be saved . . . by his works, or by faith, whereby he has believed." But even here it does not appear that the author means more than he does in II Esdras 13:23: "Such as have works, and faith"; i.e., that both works and faith contribute to salvation, so that a deficiency in one is compensated for by the presence of the other—something very different from the assertion of the opponent in James that faith *alone* dispenses from all need for works. When in II Esdras 8:32 we read, "Thou shalt be called merciful, to us who have no works of righteousness," the language is merely that of self-abasing penitence; there is no antithesis, expressed or implied, of "but because we have faith." The real attitude of the writer is seen in the language of the angel in

really is, an enhancement of the depth and scope of moral obligation (cf. Matt. 5:20, 43-48). How strange also that the Christian doctrine of forgiveness should have been used as a concession to evil, on the presumption that God indulges the faults of those who are dutiful in their prayers. **Judgment is without mercy to one who has shown no mercy** are the stern words of this letter, but they are not more stern

than the words of Jesus when he commented upon this same matter (Matt. 18:23-35).

The second perversion of Christian teaching which James attacks is the notion that a confession of faith guarantees salvation regardless of the conduct of the believer; in other words, that the recital of a creed makes a man acceptable to God despite his behavior toward his fellows. Antinomianism is an aberration that has

II Esdras 7:77, "Thou hast a treasure of good works laid up with the Most High, but it shall not be showed thee until the last times." In other words, even though "Esdras" bewails his lack of good works, he nevertheless has them in abundance; and it is these that will bring his reward.

Indeed, we may well ask how a "faith-not-works" doctrine could possibly be taught in Judaism, whose very essence was belief in the unique gift to Israel of God's law; obedience to which (in "works"!) was utterly obligatory on every Israelite. If so utterly un-Jewish a theory was taught by any who professed and called themselves Jews—a supposition for which there is no evidence at all—they must have been eccentrics whom no one could take seriously. But the length of the argument in James and its passionate tone show that the writer is refuting an argument that at the moment was of burning importance, something impossible in Judaism.

Nor can a place for the "faith-not-works" antithesis be found in pre-Pauline Jewish Christianity, as is sometimes argued. The early Jewish Christians undoubtedly put a wholly new emphasis on the central importance of faith; but in Paul's controversy with the "Judaizers" he never gives the slightest hint that justification by faith *alone* was a doctrine already held by many. In Gal. 2:16, no doubt, he argues that this is what Peter logically *ought* to believe. But obviously this is not what Peter actually *did* believe; if Peter had accepted Paul's teaching, Paul would have said so. And the argument in Galatians would have read very differently.

That the opponents against whom James inveighs regarded themselves as Paulinists ought never to have been disputed; it is with Paul, and only with Paul, that the antithesis "faith not works" enters Christianity. The declaration that "a man is justified by faith apart from works of law" (Rom. 3:28) is a Pauline coinage, inseparable from Paulinism as a whole; and it is echoed in 2:18, where "faith apart from . . . works" uses the same Greek preposition. And when 2:23 insists that Gen. 15:6 must be interpreted by Gen. 22:1-14, we surely have an attempt to meet the argument in Rom. 4:7, which treats the assertion of Gen. 15:6 as complete and final in itself.

James, of course, misunderstands Paul, as multitudes of later Christians have likewise misunderstood him. Faith, in its Pauline sense, is no mere intellectual acceptance of monotheism that demons can share with men; it is a self-surrender of the whole individual to God; which cannot possibly be "dead" or, in its moral results, "barren." And Paul's use of justification is likewise misunderstood. To Paul this is the initial act in the spiritual life, by which God accepts the believing soul, pardons it, and starts it on its way. To James justification belongs not to the beginning, but to the progress or even to the end of the spiritual life; what he says is, in effect, that no one can attain to heaven unless he has good works as well as faith.

In other words, the polemic in James is not directed against true Paulinism but against a distortion of what Paul taught; a distortion that Paul himself rejects as blasphemous (Rom. 3:8; 6:1-2). But the fact that Paul rejects this distortion of his message shows that it was current; and it was in this distorted form that it was known to James. It is more than likely that the latter had no firsthand acquaintance with the apostle's letters—it is, of course, not to be supposed that these were in circulation throughout the entire apostolic (or even the subapostolic) church. James would have known of Paul's teaching only through reports of Paul's enemies or—what would be still more harmful to the apostle's reputation—perversions of his doctrine by professed adherents (II Pet. 3:15-16).

It is sometimes argued that 2:14-26 contains nothing specifically Christian. Precisely the same is true of Paul's own major argument in Rom. 4:1-22. It is not until the closing verses (vss. 23-25) of this chapter have been reached that Paul applies to Christians what, he holds, has been true from the beginning of creation. To be sure, Abraham was justified not by faith in Christ but by faith in God, but this is immaterial; the fact remains that Abraham was justified *by faith*. And so Paul's doctrine that Christians now are justified by faith is not a violation of fundamental O.T. teaching but is a return to

15 If a brother or sister be naked, and destitute of daily food,

16 And one of you say unto them, Depart in peace, be *ye* warmed and filled; notwithstanding ye give them not those things which are needful to the body; what *doth it* profit?

17 Even so faith, if it hath not works, is dead, being alone.

18 Yea, a man may say, Thou hast faith, and I have works: show me thy faith without thy works, and I will show thee my faith by my works.

Can his faith save him? 15 If a brother or sister is ill-clad and in lack of daily food, 16 and one of you says to them, "Go in peace, be warmed and filled," without giving them the things needed for the body, what does it profit? 17 So faith by itself, if it has no works, is dead.

18 But some one will say, "You have faith and I have works." Show me your faith apart from your works, and I by my

---

what had long been forgotten. And, to James as a former Jew, it is the O.T. basis of Paul's argument that is all-important; it is with this alone that he need concern himself.

There may be added finally the summary of one of the ablest commentators on James of the understanding of Gen. 15:6 ("Abraham believed God and . . .") in Judaism, James, and Paul (M. Dibelius, *Der Brief des Jakobus* [Göttingen: Vandenhoeck & Ruprecht, 1921; "Meyer's Kommentar"], p. 168) : in Judaism Abraham's faith was reckoned to him *as a work* for righteousness; in James his faith *and* his works were reckoned to him for righteousness; in Paul this faith was reckoned to him *instead of works* for righteousness.

14-17. The direct address to the readers in the question **What does it profit?** is in diatribe style, which is maintained through the whole section. Vss. 15-16 have been aptly described as a "little parable," which finds its application in vs. 17. In vs. 16 **be warmed** implies "by proper clothing." The Greek of vs. 17 emphasizes **dead** by adding "in itself" (cf. **being alone;** for some reason the RSV omits the qualifying phrase) : "not only does such 'faith' have no outward effect, but it actually does not exist at all." It should be noted that the writer does not charge his opponents with antinomianism but with lack of moral effort; they praise virtue (vs. 16) but do not practice it.

18-19. The arguments in vss. 18-26 disregard vss. 15-17 altogether; the initial **but** in vs. 18 looks back to vs. 14—or, perhaps more precisely, is in contrast to the "faith-not-

---

plagued the churches from James's time to this. But the N.T. as a whole certainly gives no leeway for such an interpretation. There is only one answer to James's question, **Can his faith save him?**—if his faith does not issue in deeds consonant therewith.

What significance has membership in a church if one does not honestly seek to live in accordance with the principles upon which it is founded? What is the profit in pious words like **go in peace** if they are dissociated from merciful conduct? That this seemingly obvious truth is overlooked by some members of the Christian fellowship is illustrated by an experience which D. C. Macintosh reported:

It may be ironical, but it is nevertheless true that the Cross of Christ has been very commonly used by his supposed disciples to encourage them in not bearing the cross themselves. . . . As an extreme illustration of this I recall a man of business whose methods were recognized by the whole community, including himself, as deviating widely from honesty and justice, and who said, in conversation

about the Christian life: "I know that I am not living a good life; but then I'm not trusting in my own merits for salvation. I'm trusting in the merits of Christ, and in his death as my substitute on the Cross. And when I told this to the minister who was here before you, he said I was all right." [7]

One can imagine what James would say about such a confession of faith.

18-26. *The Demons Are Monotheists.*—The demons **believe that God is one,** but such faith does not change their demonic character. They are no friends of God, as Abraham was (vs. 23) ; so when they think of God they shudder. Faith in God which is poisoned by fear and superstition, which has no transforming effect upon one's outlook, attitudes, character, and activity, is **barren.** Someone has said that in many instances "the living faith of the dead has become the dead faith of the living." A nationwide census in the United States would undoubtedly find a small number registering as

[7] *Social Religion* (New York: Charles Scribner's Sons, 1939), p. 98. Used by permission.

19 Thou believest that there is one God; thou doest well: the devils also believe, and tremble.	works will show you my faith. **19** You believe that God is one; you do well. Even

works" theory that the author is refuting. The opening phrase of vs. 18, **but some one will say,** undoubtedly suggests the common device (especially in diatribe style) of introducing an opponent's objection, to which the writer is about to reply. And the RSV apparently accepts this theory by enclosing only the next sentence in quotation marks. But what follows is not a reply to this statement but a continuation of its argument; the pronoun **you** throughout vss. 18-26 represents the advocate of the "faith-not-works" doctrine, and the **some one** (or **I**) is the supporter of the writer's thesis. (The **I**, however, is not quite the writer himself, who assuredly does not mean to proclaim the excellence of his own works.) Consequently, if quotation marks are to be supplied after **say,** the quotation should continue to the end of vs. 26. Or perhaps it is more accurate to say that as the writer elaborates his argument he forgets to close his quotation (cf. Gal. 2:14-21).

Vs. 18, therefore, must be taken as a unit. The opponent's contention is assumed without being stated explicitly. And to it **some one** replies with a demand that the opponent cannot satisfy, since the merely mental attitude implied in faith "separated from" or **apart from** (not **without**) works obviously cannot be "shown." On the other hand, works *can* be shown; and their existence proves that faith must underlie them. Here, naturally, the writer takes for granted that both he and his opponent are Christians; he is not thinking of the possible value of good works performed by unbelievers. Note the rhetorical skill in the chiastic order in this verse: in its first clause the sequence is **faith . . . works,** in the second, **works . . . faith.**

What the writer assumes that his opponent means by **faith** appears in vs. 19; he identifies it simply with pure intellectual orthodoxy in the basic dogma of both Judaism and Christianity, belief that **God is one.** Such orthodoxy he approves with the ironical "Good—as far as it goes!" But it does not go very far! Such "faith" has no moral value, for it is shared by the demons—and it makes them **shudder!**

While vs. 19 can be read as a question, beginning, "Do you believe?" to take it as a statement, **you believe,** is simpler.

atheists if the question, "Do you believe in God, or are you an atheist?" was on a questionnaire. But it is also certain that many of those who would register as believers in God are not much affected morally or spiritually for the better by the belief which they profess. Stanley Jones reports a man remarking to him, "I believe in God, but not sufficiently to influence my conduct except perhaps now and then." One wonders whether God does not respect honest atheists more than such theists. Voltaire is reported to have said, "In the arguments for belief in God there are difficulties; in the arguments against belief in God there are absurdities," but how much place did God have in the life of Voltaire? When he was observed removing his hat on passing a church, he replied to those who asked him why he did so, "We salute, but we don't speak."

It has been claimed by some commentators that James was attacking the teaching of Paul, who advocated a "faith-without-works" doctrine. Some who have presumably taken Paul's side in this supposed controversy have further claimed that his teaching on "justification by faith alone" (*sole fidei*) represents authentic Christianity, while James represents only a slightly modified Judaism. That there were those who perverted Paul's teaching into antinomianism is evidenced in Paul's own letter to the Romans (6:15). That Paul repudiated this misrepresentation of his teaching is no less certain. That James may have come across advocates of this antinomian "faith" is possible, but in attacking them he is not attacking Paul, but consciously or unconsciously sharing Paul's reprobation of such a caricature of Christian faith.

This misunderstanding of the relationship between Paul and James has arisen in reference to the use of the word **works,** in Paul's letter, as in Romans 3:28, and in James, as here in vs. 18. The word is the same, but the usage differs. The point of attention is not the same. In James, attention is directed to the question as to whether a profession of faith is valid if there

20 But wilt thou know, O vain man, that faith without works is dead?

21 Was not Abraham our father justified by works, when he had offered Isaac his son upon the altar?

22 Seest thou how faith wrought with his works, and by works was faith made perfect?

23 And the Scripture was fulfilled which saith, Abraham believed God, and it was imputed unto him for righteousness: and he was called the Friend of God.

the demons believe — and shudder. **20** Do you want to be shown, you foolish fellow, that faith apart from works is barren? **21** Was not Abraham our father justified by works, when he offered his son Isaac upon the altar? **22** You see that faith was active along with his works, and faith was completed by works, **23** and the scripture was fulfilled which says, "Abraham believed God, and it was reckoned to him as righteousness"; and he was called the friend of

20-26. The third argument takes a new turn, combining the Greek diatribe style with a rabbinical appeal to proof texts. For the form of the question in vs. 20 cf. Rom. 13:3. The sarcastic address to the opponent, **you foolish fellow,** is in diatribe style; here **foolish** is literally "empty" (cf. "Raca" in the RSV mg. of Matt. 5:22). There is a wordplay in the Greek ἔργων ἀργή, which might be reproduced in English by translating, "faith apart from works does no work."

In vs. 21 for **Abraham our father,** when Christians are meant, cf. Rom. 4:16; Gal. 3:7; I Clem. 31:2. In this verse and in vs. 23 Abraham's faith and God's blessing in Gen. 15:5-6 are treated as merely preliminary to and prophetic of the events of Gen. 22:1-14, where the far more explicit blessing is given only after the patriarch's faith has manifested itself in a supreme "work." (Apparently the point also in I Macc. 2:52, "Was not Abraham found faithful in temptation, and it was reckoned unto him for righteousness?") It is with this "work" that the writer associates the title **friend of God,** although this title does not occur in Genesis, but comes from II Chr. 20:7; Isa. 41:8—an association due perhaps to a slip of the writer's memory, perhaps to some Jewish tradition that God gave the title to Abraham because of his willingness to sacrifice Isaac. There-

are no deeds to substantiate it (**works** is equivalent to deeds). In Romans, Paul is concerned with the question: How does one come into right relationship with God? Does one, as he, when a Pharisee, had formerly supposed, have to earn God's good will, or buy his favor, by offering up a spotless record with all the six-hundred-odd laws of the Jewish code marked plus? (**Works** here represents earned credits.) No, he replies, he is "justified by faith." That is to say, all he has to do is to respond wholeheartedly to the love which God has freely offered to him. God does not treat him as a bookkeeper would, but as a Father would. If in gratitude he responds to God's grace, i.e., if he has faith, then he comes at once into the circle of God's family, he is adopted as a son, i.e., he is justified. In Paul's usage "faith" is not mere belief in God (see above), nor is it the profession of a set of doctrinal beliefs about God. It is not synonymous with the recital of any creed. Faith is a personal response in genuine gratitude to the grace of God which Jesus proclaimed and manifested in his life, death, and resurrection. It is a relationship of trust, loyalty, gratitude, and affection.

That Paul's understanding of the gospel implied a toleration of a less responsible ethic than that of Judaism, he specifically denied. "Do we then overthrow the law by this faith? By no means! On the contrary, we uphold the law" (Rom. 3:31). That Paul was at one with James in insisting that the only acceptable evidence of the presence of faith was manifestation in life of the deeds of love is as clear as I Cor. 13 or Rom. 12 can make it. It is the realization of, and openhearted response to, the love of God which is the motivating power which makes it possible for one to live on a level of ethical relationships higher than ever before.

For as the body apart from the spirit is dead, so faith apart from works is dead, writes James. "If I have all faith, so as to remove mountains, but have not love, I am nothing," writes Paul (I Cor. 13:2). The expressions differ, but their purport is the same.

Both writers quote the same verse concerning Abraham (Gen. 15:6) and seem to draw dissimilar conclusions from it. But here again it must be remembered that they are demonstrating different propositions. Paul's controversy

24 Ye see then how that by works a man is justified, and not by faith only.

25 Likewise also was not Rahab the harlot justified by works, when she had received the messengers, and had sent *them* out another way?

26 For as the body without the spirit is dead, so faith without works is dead also.

God. 24 You see that a man is justified by works and not by faith alone. 25 And in the same way was not also Rahab the harlot justified by works when she received the messengers and sent them out another way? 26 For as the body apart from the spirit is dead, so faith apart from works is dead.

---

fore (vs. 22), Abraham's **faith** was no mere mental attitude but was always **active** (imperfect in the Greek) **along with his works,** working with them (contrast **barren** in vs. 20); and by these works it was **completed** (aorist in the Greek), "attained perfection." This (vs. 23) is how Gen. 15:6 must be understood! And so (vs. 24), not **faith alone** justifies but **works**—although, of course, these must always be accompanied by faith; the writer naturally does not think of justification by works alone (cf. on vs. 18).

Note that in vs. 22 the "you" is singular, addressed in diatribe style to the opponent, but in the summing up of vs. 24 "you" is plural, addressed to the readers—a distinction not noted in the RSV.

A second proof text (vs. 25) is Josh. 2:1-21, which tells of Rahab's **works,** that these were the outcome of faith (cf. Heb. 11:31) being taken for granted; in Jewish tradition **Rahab** was used as an example of repentance, was said to be a proselyte and sometimes was even made the wife of Joshua (contrast Matt. 1:5). And vs. 26, recalling the language of vs. 17, states the final conclusion. The figure, however, should not be overstressed as if the writer meant to say that **faith** is the **body** enlivened by **works** as the **spirit** (or vice versa); he means simply that death is as complete in one case as in the other.

---

was with those who claimed that the Gentiles could not come into the favor of God unless they earned that favor by the observance of the hundreds of laws in the Jewish code, especially the rite of circumcision. He quoted the verse in order to show that it was Abraham's attitude of trust in God that brought him into right relationship with God at a time when the rite of circumcision had not even been instituted. James's controversy was with those who claimed that faith in the existence of God was all that was needed to make one a Christian. He quoted the verse to show that anyone who has faith in God, who is in right relationship with God, will demonstrate the reality of that faith and relationship by conduct which is consonant with that faith. Both propositions are of the essence of the gospel.

25. *The Reclaiming Mercy.*—The mention of **Rahab the harlot** in this connection would be startling if we were reading this verse with eyes unaccustomed to the Bible or if the word prostitute were used in the text as in Goodspeed's translation. Does this reference, as well as the similar reference in Heb. 11:31, reflect the influence of the attitude which Jesus took toward those who were condemned to the lowest position in the social and moral scale? "Can any good come out of Nazareth?" asked Nathanael. "Can any good be found in such a depraved

person?" would be a more common query. But Jesus found a spark of potential goodness in Mary Magdalene, and James and the author of Hebrews see in Rahab a heroine of the faith. Obviously, in the view of Jesus and of James, respectability and faith are not equivalents. Society directs its sternest condemnation against the hot sins of passion, but often condones the coldly calculated selfishness of those who keep "within the law." More than one person has considered himself a good Christian because he was self-disciplined in his personal habits, while at the same time he was ruthless in his personal ambition. Jesus encircled the outcasts in the sweep of his grace, but a great many people have been estranged from his church by the snobbery of pious churchgoers.

T. E. Jessop in his unconventional study of the Christian ethic remarks:

Christianity has been called, with a fine one-sidedness, "The religion of all poor devils." Whatever His Church may have done, Christ never confused the elect with the *élite*. His way of living for the most part removed Him from good circles. . . . He shocked the respectable. . . . He was blowing sky-high those notions about morality which were as current in His day as they are in ours. . . . Christianity is less an exposure of obvious badness than an indictment of obvious goodness.[8]

[8] *Law and Love* (New York: Student Christian Movement Press, 1940), pp. 11-12, 16.

3 My brethren, be not many masters, knowing that we shall receive the greater condemnation.

3 Let not many of you become teachers, my brethren, for you know that we who teach shall be judged with greater strict-

XIV. Sins of the Tongue (3:1-12)

A section complete in itself, with no connection with what precedes. The theme is stated in vs. 2b: **If any one makes no mistakes in what he says he is a perfect man.** To this theme is prefixed in vss. 1-2a a special application of the principle to contemporary Christians, an application that is ignored in the remainder of the section. What follows is an elaboration of the theme in a series of figures: control of something large by something small (vss. 2c-5), fire (vs. 6), taming animals (vss. 7-8), incongruous behavior (vss. 9-12). See further on section as a whole under vss. 9-12 below.

3:1-5. The opening warning in vss. 1-2a rebukes a highly specialized form of the tongue's sins, those committed by believers who pose as teachers but who are not qualified for the responsibility of the office. Such men may do infinite harm. This warning reflects the democracy of the early church, where anyone might feel himself moved to teach (I Cor. 14:16-23; etc.). Consequently there was a constant danger not only of formulated "false doctrine," but of all manner of reckless utterances, for whose effects the self-constituted "teacher" would be responsible. It is therefore far safer to avoid so grave a responsibility; every man commits too many sins in his daily life (vs. 2a) without adding to them the special sins to which teachers constantly expose themselves.

The first clause of vs. 2 continues vs. 1, and the word **mistakes** should be followed by a period and not by the **and** of the RSV, introduced without authority in the Greek;

The thought of Helen Wodehouse is also pertinent at this point:

We think we must climb to a certain height of goodness before we can reach God. But He says not "At the end of the way you may find me"; He says "I am the Way; I am the road under your feet, the road that begins just as low down as you happen to be." If we are in a hole the Way begins in the hole. The moment we set our face in the same direction as His, we are walking with God.[9]

3:1. The Responsibility of the Teacher.—The KJV translates διδάσκαλοι as **masters,** but teachers were masters in those days. The RSV adds the phrase **who teach,** which is not in the original, but undoubtedly this represents and emphasizes the meaning of the author.

In a day when there is a scarcity of candidates for the ministry and the teaching profession it would hardly seem appropriate to make use of this text for a sermon. Yet it has in it a greatly needed emphasis which makes it appropriate even as a text for a sermon to the students in a teachers' college or a theological seminary.

James was not trying to keep others out of a profession which he wanted to monopolize. He made this statement because of his keen awareness of the heavy moral responsibility which as a teacher he had to carry. His warning was against aiming at the prestige of the teacher's

[9] Dorothy Berkeley Phillips, ed., *The Choice Is Always Ours* (New York: Richard R. Smith, 1948), p. 44.

vocation without being aware of this necessary burden. Let no one enter this profession without having his eyes open to the obligation involved therein.

Why should anyone desire to be a teacher or a minister? It used to be popular to be a teacher, and the profession carried perquisites and a prestige in the community which made it attractive to many. Such was also the case with the ministry. A modicum of prestige still obtains. But those who enter these professions primarily because of the perquisites or prestige supposedly connected with them are forgetting that the teacher and the preacher deal with the most precious thing in the world, human personality, and that any mishandling or misdirecting of the persons entrusted to their care will bring upon them the heaviest condemnation.

A vocation once signified a call from God to serve one's fellows. Now the word is used to mean the way one earns his living. A profession was once considered primarily as a form of public service. Now many think of it as connoting social prestige or high financial rewards. It is not uncommon to hear teachers declare that their jobs involve the presentation of facts to their pupils, but not the moral responsibility for the conduct or character of those whom they teach. Is this a healthy situation? Does not the sense of divine vocation and moral obligation which James manifested in this verse need to be reintroduced as motivation into the profession of teaching, and indeed into all the vocations?

2 For in many things we offend all. If any man offend not in word, the same *is* a perfect man, *and* able also to bridle the whole body.

3 Behold, we put bits in the horses' mouths, that they may obey us; and we turn about their whole body.

4 Behold also the ships, which though *they be* so great, and *are* driven of fierce winds, yet are they turned about with a very small helm, whithersoever the governor listeth.

5 Even so the tongue is a little member, and boasteth great things. Behold, how great a matter a little fire kindleth!

6 And the tongue *is* a fire, a world of iniquity: so is the tongue among our members, that it defileth the whole body, and setteth on fire the course of nature; and it is set on fire of hell.

ness. 2 For we all make many mistakes, and if any one makes no mistakes in what he says he is a perfect man, able to bridle the whole body also. 3 If we put bits into the mouths of horses that they may obey us, we guide their whole bodies. 4 Look at the ships also; though they are so great and are driven by strong winds, they are guided by a very small rudder wherever the will of the pilot directs. 5 So the tongue is a little member and boasts of great things. How great a forest is set ablaze by a small fire!

6 And the tongue is a fire. The tongue is an unrighteous world among our members, staining the whole body, setting on fire the cycle of nature,*b* and set on fire by hell.*c*

b Or *wheel of birth.*
c Greek *Gehenna.*

the theme saying (vs. 2*b*) beginning with **if** should be printed as a separate sentence. The definition of a **perfect man** as one who **makes no mistakes in what he says** is, despite Matt. 12:37, somewhat superficial; an accomplished hypocrite's words may be irreproachable, although belied by his acts and still more by his thoughts (cf. the use of "perfect" in 1:4; also cf. below). The concluding clause of vs. 2 leads directly into the obvious figure in vs. 3, which suggests in turn the equally obvious figure in vs. 4, while vs. 5*a* applies the imagery of these figures to the theme. In this application we should expect, "The tongue, although a little member, accomplishes great things"; but the writer, who throughout the section is thinking only of the harm the tongue can do, substitutes for "accomplishes" the depreciatory **boasts** to connote selfish haughtiness. In vs. 3 the first word is probably **if** (RSV) rather than **behold** (KJV), but the text is not quite certain. In the Greek of vs. 5 note the alliteration μικρὸν μέλος . . . μεγάλα.

6. In vs. 5*b* the contrast of small and great is taken up again with the figure of **fire,** which is developed in vs. 6; to begin a new paragraph with vs. 6 (so the RSV) breaks the continuity. The wanton destruction caused by a forest fire is familiar wherever there are forests. The punctuation of vs. 6 is disputed, and the Greek is so obscure that the text may be corrupt. But the simplest rendition is, "And the tongue is a fire; that world of unrighteousness, the tongue, is set among our members." Here "world of unrighteousness" is preferable to **unrighteous world;** the tongue is a universe in which every sort of unrighteousness exists; every man must remember the infinite possibilities of evil of which his tongue is capable! The next phrase, **the cycle of nature,** was perhaps originally a highly technical term of some sort but, despite minute research by specialists (cf. the several commentaries), no parallel has been discovered that throws any real light on the usage here. Certainly no reference to any recondite teaching is implied by

If one is unwilling to accept this personal responsibility, should he not hesitate to enter these professions?

2-12. *The Power of Words.*—"Talk is cheap." "Words, words, nothing but words." "He's just a talker." These sayings illustrate a common depreciation of the importance of speech. But are there any things in the world more potent for good or ill than words?

Speech is the faculty which differentiates man from the animals. It is the sign of personality. Self-consciousness is manifest only in speech. Thought is impossible without words which are the counters of ideas. Action is preceded by thought. As Heine put it, "Thought precedes action as lightning does thunder." But thought is prompted by verbal suggestion. All co-operation between human beings depends for **its**

7 For every kind of beasts, and of birds, and of serpents, and of things in the sea, is tamed, and hath been tamed of mankind:

8 But the tongue can no man tame; *it is* an unruly evil, full of deadly poison.

9 Therewith bless we God, even the Father; and therewith curse we men, which are made after the similitude of God.

7 For every kind of beast and bird, of reptile and sea creature, can be tamed and has been tamed by humankind, 8 but no human being can tame the tongue — a restless evil, full of deadly poison. 9 With it we bless the Lord and Father, and with it we curse men, who are made in the likeness of

---

the writer, who takes for granted that his readers will know what he means. Therefore, no matter what the origin of the phrase, we should treat it as used popularly and translate it accordingly; the KJV's **the course of nature** gives a clear and simple sense and must be about right: the orderly course of human affairs is set on fire—made destructive to mankind—by evil tongues. And a tone of intense religious seriousness is added by the final phrase, **set on fire by hell.**

7-8. In these verses the third figure is developed: the tongue is more vicious than any of the lower animals. For no matter how wild they may be, they can be tamed—in fact, they all have been tamed—by men; but no man can tame the tongue! Even poisonous serpents can be controlled but not the poisonous tongue; it never rests and its poison is deadly.

9-12. The fourth figure differs from the others in admitting that good may come from the tongue as well as evil. But this very fact brings a new reproach; such incongruity of behavior is a revolt against nature, where everything pursues an orderly course of good or bad (vss. 11-12). Undoubtedly the analogy is imperfect; fire, e.g., can warm as well as destroy. But in an argument of this kind such criticism would be pedantic.

As a whole the wording of this section is neither Jewish nor Christian, but is Hellenistic. As was noted above, the theme of the section (vs. 2), which defines perfection as freedom from faults in speech, represents a superficial moral standpoint. It is, however, precisely the type of adage that would be inculcated by a Hellenistic rhetorician whose sole interest would be in correct language. And the series of illustrations that follow, all drawn from nature, more than suggest figures that might be found in a handbook for the use of speakers; as a matter of fact, the imagery of the horse and that of the ship are actually found combined in Greek writers, while that of the destructiveness of forest fires is quite common. And in so obvious an illustration as that of vs. 12, there is no reason to think that Matt. 7:16 was in mind, still less to suppose that vs. 11 was suggested by Exod. 15:23-25. Only the last clause of vs. 6 and all of vs. 9 are Jewish or Christian additions, the latter (vs. 9) presumably suggested by the opening words of vs. 10.

---

success on verbal communication. No undertaking which involves others is ever begun without an exchange of words. No plans can be made or completed if no words are spoken. One of the greatest obstacles to world-wide co-operation is the diversity of languages which makes mutual understanding so difficult. If anyone is deaf and dumb, he must find some method of communication. The cultural solidarity of a group is based upon a common language. Character is revealed by one's speech. "Out of the abundance of the heart his mouth speaks" (Luke 6:45).

Thus James is not far wrong when he places such great emphasis upon the tongue. **The tongue is a fire** which can inflame a mob to a dastardly lynching. **The tongue is a little mem-** ber, but it can inspire a nation to heroic action. Hot words start quarrels, destroy friendships, break up homes, instigate wars. On the other hand, words of comfort can rescue a soul from despair; bold words can strike powerful blows for justice; inspired words can start feet marching toward the goal of human brotherhood. Someone has said, "A word spoken at a solemn moment may be a mightier force for good or ill than any bodily act whatever." And Pindar wrote, "Longer than deeds liveth the word." [10] Think of the reverberations of the closing sentence of Lincoln's Gettysburg Address. Think of what might have happened in Britain if there had been no one like Churchill talking about "blood, sweat, and tears." The effect

[10] *Nemean Odes* IV.

10 Out of the same mouth proceedeth blessing and cursing. My brethren, these things ought not so to be.

11 Doth a fountain send forth at the same place sweet *water* and bitter?

12 Can the fig tree, my brethren, bear olive berries? either a vine, figs? so *can* no fountain both yield salt water and fresh.

13 Who *is* a wise man and endued with knowledge among you? let him show out of a good conversation his works with meekness of wisdom.

God. **10** From the same mouth come blessing and cursing. My brethren, this ought not to be so. **11** Does a spring pour forth from the same opening fresh water and brackish? **12** Can a fig tree, my brethren, yield olives, or a grapevine figs? No more can salt water yield fresh.

13 Who is wise and understanding among you? By his good life let him show

---

But the opening warning in vss. 1-2*a* certainly comes from the Christian editor. It is so specialized an application of the general teaching of the section and so poorly integrated with what follows that it cannot be thought to be part of the Hellenistic material. And in Judaism, at this period, to become a teacher ("rabbi") involved such long and rigorous study and training that there was no need to warn "many" against undertaking it. A stage in Christian organization is therefore presupposed, despite 5:14 (cf. the Intro.), prior to the full development of the official teaching ministry, such as is suggested by Matt. 23:8, 10.

As a matter of fact, not only the opening warning but the insertion of the entire section may be ascribed to the Christian editor. As in 2:14-26, there are no tribal references in the passage; it is unique in the epistle in its almost purely Hellenistic wording throughout. Its opening warning is to the writer the primary reason for its insertion. And it admirably prepares for and reinforces the following section in vss. 13-18.

Of course it is impossible to tell whether the Christian editor took the material in the section directly from some Hellenistic source or whether he found it already utilized by some Jewish predecessor; the point is simply that it was not part of the original "Letter of Jacob."

XV. True Wisdom (3:13-18)

Intellectual ability, when used rightly by a humble and devout soul, is a heaven-sent blessing; when used wrongly by a selfish egotist, it does indescribable damage.

---

which Jesus has had upon history has been mediated by words; the effect which Hitler had upon his people was likewise mediated. "Both glory and disgrace come from speaking," said Sirach (Ecclus. 5:13). Is it any wonder that Jesus said, "By your words you will be justified, and by your words you will be condemned"? (Matt. 12:37.)

"Sticks and stones may break my bones, but names can never hurt me." Is this proverb really true? The wounds in the body made by stones may heal, but the hurt in the heart made by an insult may endure for a lifetime. "Many have fallen by the edge of the sword; but not so many as have fallen by the tongue" is Sirach's truer dictum (Ecclus. 28:18).

If a man's religion gives him no control over his tongue, so that his words will edify and not corrupt (cf. Eph. 4:29), then his religion is useless, for it has failed at a most crucial point (cf. on 1:26). **From the same mouth come**

blessing and cursing. My brethren, this ought not to be so.

A little poem by Beth Day, written *ca.* 1855, and entitled "Three Gates of Gold," is worth quotation here:

> . . . Make it pass,
> Before you speak, three gates of gold:
> These narrow gates. First, "Is it true?"
> Then, "Is it needful?" In your mind
> Give truthful answer. And the next
> Is last and narrowest, "Is it kind?"
> And if to reach your lips at last
> It passes through these gateways three,
> Then you may tell the tale, nor fear
> What the result of speech may be.

13-18. *To Be Clever, or to Be Wise?*—As indicated above (1:5-8), James shares the general biblical conception that wisdom is not simply knowledge (science) or cleverness or astuteness, but rather a profound understanding of what

14 But if ye have bitter envying and strife in your hearts, glory not, and lie not against the truth.

15 This wisdom descendeth not from above, but is earthly, sensual, devilish.

16 For where envying and strife is, there is confusion and every evil work.

his works in the meekness of wisdom. 14 But if you have bitter jealousy and selfish ambition in your hearts, do not boast and be false to the truth. 15 This wisdom is not such as comes down from above, but is earthly, unspiritual, devilish. 16 For where jealousy and selfish ambition exist, there will be disorder and every vile practice.

While connected only rather vaguely with the preceding section as a whole, this one resumes directly the opening warning in vss. 1-2a: the grave responsibility incurred by all who pose as teachers. Consequently, although vss. 13-18 contain nothing specifically Christian, the passage presupposes for the original Christian readers a small closed community that may be distracted by rival teachers who contradict one another; cf. Paul's analysis of "wisdom" in I Cor. 1-4.

13-15. The opening question in vs. 13 and the answer that follows (diatribe style) set the theme: the man who is genuinely wise remembers his moral responsibilities toward others. **Wise and understanding** is rhetorical pleonasm; the two adjectives are as indistinguishable in Greek as they are in English (for **wise** cf. on 1:5). True **wisdom** displays itself in a **good life**, particularly in "gentleness" to the opinions and even the faults of one's neighbors (**meekness** gives a wrong sense in modern English; in Elizabethan English "meek" and "gentle" were commonly used as synonyms). If (vs. 14) anyone forgets this and is so absorbed in a sense of the sole correctness of his own opinions and a resulting feeling of his own superiority as to feel **bitter jealousy** of his rivals and **selfish ambition** to be recognized as an exclusive leader, then when such a man claims **wisdom,** he is a liar. Such (vs. 15) is not the wisdom that God gives; it is **earthly,** with no heavenly element; it is **unspiritual,** "psychic" (cf. I Cor. 2:14, etc.; Jude 19), "merely animal." And still worse, it is **devilish,** the kind of "wisdom" displayed by demons. ("Demonic" would have been a better translation than **devilish,** since in the more recent English versions "devil," as distinct from "demon," has been rightly reserved for Satan.) Note the climax in the triad "earthly, animal, demonlike," as in 1:15.

16-17. The result is **disorder** in the community, a disorder that may well produce any **vile practice.** In sharpest contrast are the results of **the wisdom from above,** which the writer describes in a list of eight terms, a device taken from the practice of the Hellenistic teachers of rhetoric and ethics. These made their pupils memorize lists of virtues or vices, to be used in moral instruction for guidance in learning good conduct

---

the good life is or ought to be. Such wisdom produces concord and harmony between persons and groups. It contrasts sharply with that calculating egoism which is the cause of social **disorder and every vile practice.**

The established laws of human growth through mutuality are **the truth,** i.e., the divine wisdom, in which the genuinely wise man shares, but the counterfeit of wisdom which is **earthly, unspiritual, devilish** contravenes these laws and makes **selfish ambition** the mainspring of conduct. The **wisdom from above** is genuine, considerate of the feelings of others, willing to yield for the sake of peace, reasonable, full of compassion and kindliness, unambiguous, and without duplicity.

The shrewd, the cunning, the smart operator is convinced that the highest sagacity is what the sophisticate calls "enlightened selfishness,"

the "know-how" of manipulation of men and circumstances for the satisfaction of greed. To gain his ends this smart man will not scruple to lie, dissemble, cheat, or bribe if he thinks he can avoid detection. A good part of the cleverness on which he prides himself is his ability to "cover up," to "get by." If his ambition can be achieved only by disloyalty to his friends or by cruelty to his victims, that may be regretted, but it is the price "the realist" pays to win the only success worth having in this world.

To make a fortune or to gain power, how can one afford to be too scrupulous? It may be unethical for a physician to raise his fees in an epidemic, but it is only good business to raise prices when food is scarce. In a review of a book a British critic suggested that "even so popular a slogan as 'the end justifies the means' is no longer in tune with the anti-ethics of the

17 But the wisdom that is from above is first pure, then peaceable, gentle, *and* easy to be entreated, full of mercy and good fruits, without partiality, and without hypocrisy.

18 And the fruit of righteousness is sown in peace of them that make peace.

17 But the wisdom from above is first pure, then peaceable, gentle, open to reason, full of mercy and good fruits, without uncertainty or insincerity. 18 And the harvest of righteousness is sown in peace by those who make peace.

---

and avoiding evil conduct. But in rhetorical instruction these lists served a much wider purpose, being memorized to use as general lists in praise or blame. Such lists are not found in the O.T. and appear to be foreign to Palestinian Judaism in the N.T. era, but were freely adapted to Jewish use in Hellenistic Judaism (e.g., Wisd. Sol. 7:22; 14:23-26) and are quite common in the N.T. (e.g., Rom. 1:29-31; I Tim. 3:2-4; etc.; cf. the section on "Ethical Lists" in the "Word Studies" in Burton S. Easton, *The Pastoral Epistles* [New York: Charles Scribner's Sons, 1947], pp. 197-202). The present list is arranged partly by alliteration; five of the terms begin with epsilon and three with alpha. Unlike many of such lists, however (e.g., that in I Tim. 3:2-4), it is not a commonplace, or general list, more or less imperfectly adapted to the context, but is made up of terms all strictly relevant to the theme: the true **wisdom** is **pure**, "unmixed with evil," the basic quality underlying all those that follow; **peaceable**, not causing the **disorder** of vs. 16; **gentle**, respectful of the feelings of others (the Greek adjective here differs from that in vs. 16 but in this context is indistinguishable from it); **open to reason**, not obstinate in clinging to its own opinions; **full of mercy** to those who are in the wrong and so aiming to win them back to the truth, thus producing **good fruits; without uncertainty**, or perhaps better, "single-minded," aiming only at the truth; **without insincerity** (RSV), or perhaps more clearly, **without hypocrisy** (KJV), a similar quality but with the accent on the moral rather than on the intellectual element.

No attempt is made in this list to lead up to a climax, which is supplied in vs. 18: the purpose of life is to attain righteousness, not only in one's self but in one's relationship to others, so helping them to attain righteousness also. And they who **make peace**, as the fruit of their sowing, will reap this **righteousness** as their **harvest**.

---

times. Today we are learning to say, 'the means justify themselves provided they are dirty enough.' "

But this is **devilish and false to the truth**, says James. And is he not on the demonstrable ground of experience when he declares that this devilish cleverness leads only to **disorder**, to social chaos, and to every sort of villainy? Dishonesty, no matter how astute, undermines the structure of good faith and mutual confidence upon which all human transactions must ultimately depend. When that structure falls, all must suffer in the final debacle. Ruthless ambition provokes the opposition of others, and the struggle for power becomes more and more disastrous when in our time men have invented infernal machines to support their scheming. If men will not learn the wisdom that is peaceable, reasonable, merciful, and sincere, they will end by destroying themselves with the bombs their cleverness has devised.

In our modern education we seem to be preoccupied with the accumulation of knowledge, to the neglect of the wisdom which alone can save us from the misuse of that knowledge. Rabbinical literature has a phrase descriptive of those who know much, but who still remain fools: they are "asses laden with books." "Knowledge is power," but how that power shall be used so as to be beneficent and not maleficent is the question. We have more knowledge than ever before; do we have more wisdom? Going faster and farther, we may yet be going astray. Grapes are not picked from bramble bushes, nor can the good society be harvested from the sowing of dragon's teeth. "The harvest uprightness yields must be sown in peace, by peacemakers" (3:18 Goodspeed).

18. "Blessed Are the Peacemakers."—"Pacifist" is a term that has not been in wide repute in this century of wars. But the word is from Latin roots that are the equivalent of the Greek terms in this sentence, makers of peace. As to the means to be used to achieve peace, there is room for difference of opinion, but can there be any dispute that the vocation of every Christian, whatever his status in society, is to make peace, to strive to secure those conditions and

4 From whence *come* wars and fightings among you? *come they* not hence, *even* of your lusts that war in your members?

4 What causes wars, and what causes fightings among you? Is it not your passions that are at war in your members?

Here, it should be noted, **righteousness** is not thought of in Pauline terms as "the righteousness of God" (Rom. 3:21), the gift bestowed by God on those who have not merited it by their works, but in O.T. terms as the quality men attain by their works and which God rewards.

While the Christian editor may very well have seen in vs. 18 a reference to Matt. 5:9, this reference is very vague and there is nothing else in the section that suggests a Christian origin. A tribal reference to Naphtali may be detected; cf. Philo (*On Dreams* II. 36): "Naphthali is the type of peace, for his name, being interpreted, means 'wideness' or 'what is opened'; and all things are widened and opened by peace as, on the contrary, they are closed by war."

XVI. Wrongful Desires (4:1-10)

"Peace," the key word of 3:18, suggests **wars** as its opposite; but where in the last section only the special harm done by false wisdom was in point, the far greater harm wrought by wrongful desires in general is now the theme.

The section is strangely lacking in unity. The writer begins in vss. 1-2*b* with an aphorism found so frequently in substance among Stoic moralists that it may well have been taken from some Stoic teacher. The development that follows, however, is purely religious and in terms impossible to Stoicism but wholly appropriate in Judaism.

4:1-2*b.* A further problem is raised by the inappropriateness of the opening aphorism to Christian readers. In vs. 1, no doubt, the **wars** and **fightings** (terms frequently coupled

---

relationships that will make possible good will, concord, and co-operation instead of hatred, strife, and conflict?

Isaiah cries, "How beautiful upon the mountains are the feet of him that bringeth good tidings, that publisheth peace" (Isa. 52:7); and Jesus gives his blessing to the peacemakers; they, as sons, are close to the heart of God. Paul writes of "the ministry of reconciliation" (II Cor. 5:18). Can the church's responsibility be made more plain?

T. Z. Koo has illustrated the meaning of peace by the use of three Chinese characters, all similarly translated "peace." The first, *ping,* suggests equality. Peace obtains where no one seeks to domineer over another. The second, *an,* is an ideograph representing a woman under a roof. Peace obtains when homes are unmolested and tranquil. The third, *ho,* is a character combining two elements, mouth and grain. Peace obtains when all have sufficient to eat.

Righteousness implies right relationships between human beings. These relationships can never be secured without arduous labor any more than a harvest can be reaped without sowing and cultivation. If a farmer gave no more thought, time, and effort to secure his harvest than many members of the church of Christ give to the establishment of social justice, would he ever reap a harvest?

Fortunately a keener conscience seems to be developing among church people concerning the relevance and practicability of Christian principles in business, industry, politics, in every field of human relationships. This is illustrated in the symposium *Laymen Speaking,* edited by Wallace C. Speers, who declares it to be his own conviction that "there is a pattern of workability for the world contained in the laws of God for human conduct." Melvin J. Evans, an industrial engineer, tells of an intensive study of human problems in business which led to the discovery that "industrial difficulty [could be] traced directly back to lack of balanced character on the part of the people involved. . . . If these people are men of wisdom, a great company inevitably results; if they are petty chiselers, the opposite effect must be expected." As an industrial consultant and "trouble shooter," Evans declares: "If one pursues a program of this sort to its ultimate conclusion, we finally come face to face with the realization that Christ laid down the laws for man in the most perfect form, and that it is only through him that the higher stages of spiritual development can be reached." [11]

4:1-3. *What Causes Wars?*—The logical consequence of the pursuit of selfish ambition is

[11] New York: Association Press, 1947, pp. 23, 146-47, 151. See also Hugh Martin, *Christian Social Reformers* (London: Student Christian Movement Press, 1927).

2 Ye lust, and have not: ye kill, and desire to have, and cannot obtain: ye fight
and war, yet ye have not, because ye ask
not.

2 You desire and do not have; so you kill.
And you covet[d] and cannot obtain; so you
fight and wage war. You do not have, be-

[d] Or *you kill and you covet.*

---

by Greek writers and hardly to be distinguished), if they stood alone, might be understood to mean only the quarrels and factional disputes in the communities, as in 3:16.
But in vs. 2 it is clear that the words were meant quite literally: of "wars" actually
"waged," of "fights" that actually result in "killing." Surely no reproach could be more
grotesquely unsuited to members of the early Christian churches! So strongly has this
appealed to commentators that all kinds of devices have been devised to soften the
language; even a drastic and wholly arbitrary emendation of the text to read "envy"
in place of **kill** (i.e., in the Greek substituting φθονεῖτε for φονεύετε, a suggestion first
made more than four centuries ago by Erasmus).

The solution of the difficulty, however, lies not in such evasions of the problem but
in recognizing that the opening aphorism was not framed originally by a Christian or
even a Jewish moralist but by a Stoic, who was using the conventional language of his
system; something seen further by the occurrence in vs. 1 of one Stoic cardinal vice
"pleasure" (somewhat pointlessly rendered **passions** in the RSV; here the KJV's **lusts** is
better) and in vs. 2 of another Stoic cardinal vice **desire** (cf. on 1:15); that these two vices
cause "wars," "fightings" and "killings" was, as was noted above, a Stoic commonplace,
widespread because of its obvious truth. And this wholly general Stoic teaching could
be taken over unchanged by a Jewish moralist; for murders were certainly not unknown
in Judaism, while—even apart from the great rebellion of A.D. 66-70—there were various
Jewish insurrections in the first century A.D. that were quite literally "wars" and "fightings"
(e.g., Acts 5:36-37).

---

a clash between the egoists whose interests and
appetites collide. Two men desire the same
object which they are unwilling to share. One
or the other cannot have it, so they fight to
decide possession. As between two individuals
or two nations, wherever prestige, power, and
possessions are sought as the highest good in
life, conflicts will inevitably occur. In such conflicts it is the possessors of material power that
will prevail; wherefore, with all your getting,
get material power! In nationalism this power
is glorified, and it is the nation which deems it
has superior power and covets more which
provokes wars. It is so also in private quarrels.

Can war be eliminated without a change in
the goals which are sought by men and nations?
You ask wrongly, to spend it on your passions,
says James. There must be a radical redirection
of the energies and ambitions of men. They
must seek "the kingdom of God and his righteousness" instead of all these things that the
nations seek.

Is it practical to expect such a change? Well,
where will the road we have been traveling
take us? Eugene O'Neill, the playwright, is reported to have remarked in an interview:

If the human race is so stupid that in two thousand years it hasn't had brains enough to appreciate that the secret of happiness is contained in
one simple sentence which you'd think any school

kid could understand and apply, then it's time we
dumped it down the nearest drain and let the ants
have a chance. That simple sentence is: For what
shall it profit a man if he gain the whole world
and lose his own soul?[1]

A British publisher, turned author, in a documented indictment of our modern civilization
asserts that a way of life based upon love,
mercy, and respect for personality is the only
vision that can save man from total destruction.[2] The strange paradox of life appears to
be that when men desire satisfactions which
contradict their spiritual nature, they find
satiety rather than bliss; that when nations
make power and possessions their goal, they
destroy themselves in seeking to conquer others.
The stories of the widow's cruse and barrel of
meal, and the feeding of the five thousand in
Galilee, whatever one may think about their
miraculous aura, surely convey the truth which
has been demonstrated time and time again,
viz., that life shared is life multiplied, that
good will can create conditions where there is
more, not less for all. Will mankind ever learn
this lesson?

**1b. *Your Cravings Which Are at War Within
Your Bodies*** (Goodspeed).—These words ac-

[1] United Press dispatch, New York, September 2, 1946.
[2] Victor Gollancz, *Our Threatened Values* (London:
Victor Gollancz, 1946).

3 Ye ask, and receive not, because ye ask amiss, that ye may consume *it* upon your lusts.

3 You ask and do not receive, because you ask wrongly, to spend

---

The Christian editor has therefore simply taken over the work of his Jewish predecessor unaltered because of the value of what follows. If he thought about the matter at all, he may have considered the aphorism to be addressed to his readers, not as Christians, but as ordinary human beings (it is perhaps worth noting that he does not speak to them here as "my brothers"), who as human beings were capable of the worst crimes if they gave rein to their lower nature.

In vs. 1 **your members** are "your bodies" as in 3:6; the desire for pleasure in men's minds causes their bodies to commit acts of violence on all who interfere with gratifying that desire; "wars without come from wars within." (A Stoic might also speak of various irreconcilable kinds of pleasure causing conflicts and confusion within the mind of an individual, but this is not the point here.) In vs. 2 the punctuation of the first two sentences is debated by commentators but that in the RSV gives much the best balance: it gives perfect parallelism to these sentences, which first state the cause of the disorder and then relate the disastrous effect.

2c. But in the concluding sentence the philosophical phrasing is dropped abruptly. A Stoic would have continued by exhorting men to learn self-contentment and self-control by suppressing all pleasure and desire; then they will be free from the vices that these cardinal evils create. The writer, however, contradicts the Stoic principle point-blank: desire for what we do not have is not necessarily wrong at all! Our fault is rather that we try to gain by evil means what God would give us if we asked him for it in prayer! This startling incongruity between the first two and the third sentences of vs. 2 is simply the incongruity between Stoicism and Judaism (or Christianity); while Stoic and Jewish moralists could agree in many details, the two systems themselves are radically incompatible.

3-4. After the rather awkward beginning of his own analysis in vs. 2c, the writer applies something of the Stoic terminology in Jewish setting. While it is wholly true that God answers prayer, it is not at all true that he literally grants every petition; certainly not the petition of sinners for means to continue and multiply their sins. And such sinners are those who seek only self-indulgence in their "pleasures." They are indeed

---

cord with modern psychology's description of inner conflicts unresolved by any integrating principle, purpose, or loyalty. F. W. Foerster, a Christian philosopher exiled from nazi Germany, in a lecture described this situation in these words: "If the wild, indeterminate, infinite appetites of man are separated from their spiritual law, anarchic chaos will ensue. Physical vitality let loose without spiritual control leads to destruction."

There is a sort of chain reaction within man's soul, just as James describes it here: lust, incapable of satisfaction, leads to sadistic impulses, which, heated by a vision of pleasures beyond reach, turn to violence, cruelty, and murder.

3. Desires that Are Self-Defeating.—You ask and do not receive, because you ask wrongly, to spend it on your passions. Ask for what? For pleasure, for happiness, for abiding satisfaction? But abiding happiness cannot be secured through selfish indulgence. John Macmurray

has well said that "the best cure for hedonism is the attempt to practise it." [3] (The Greek word translated "passions" above gives us the English word "hedonism.") George Jean Nathan, a modern hedonist, has expressed his philosophy of life as follows: "The best that man can hope and strive and pray for is momentary happiness during life, repeated as frequently as the cards allow. . . . To me, pleasure and my own personal happiness—only infrequently collaborating with others—are all I deem worth a hoot." [4]

Does not this confession reveal a decidedly pessimistic undertone in this man's pursuit of happiness? What pleasures there are, are only transient, and death puts an end to all of them; so try to forget death or it may poison what

[3] *Interpreting the Universe* (London: Faber & Faber, 1933), p. 158.
[4] Albert Einstein, John Dewey, and others, *Living Philosophies* (New York: Simon & Shuster, 1931), pp. 224, 222.

4 Ye adulterers and adulteresses, know ye not that the friendship of the world is enmity with God? whosoever therefore will be a friend of the world is the enemy of God.

5 Do ye think that the Scripture saith in vain, The spirit that dwelleth in us lusteth to envy?

it on your passions. **4** Unfaithful creatures! Do you not know that friendship with the world is enmity with God? Therefore whoever wishes to be a friend of the world makes himself an enemy of God. **5** Or do you suppose it is in vain that the scripture says, "He yearns jealously over the spirit

---

(vs. 4) **unfaithful creatures!** This last phrase is an admirable rendition of a Greek noun that means literally "adulteresses," using the familiar O.T. imagery of Israel, the bride of God, who is unfaithful to her marriage vows. But the term puzzled later Christians who did not remember this imagery. To them the noun meant women, not men and women indifferently, and they therefore altered the Greek text to read as it is translated in the KJV, **adulterers and adulteresses**—which of course introduces a wholly irrelevant concept into the passage.

Friendship with the world is enmity with God. This succinct saying, introduced as if familiar to the readers with **do you not know that,** may very well be a current maxim from some source or other. Its use of **the world** (as in 1:27) as the totality of evil is common in the N.T., but is common likewise in Judaism to describe everything lying outside the community of God's people (I John 5:19; etc.). In the present context with vs. 3, it refers particularly to the illegitimate "pleasures" that tempt the readers; anyone who seeks such pleasures—even if he prays God to give them to him—is making himself an **enemy of God.** The writer, however, does not say—and this should be carefully noted—that all pleasure in itself is wrong or an improper object of prayer; in neither Judaism nor Christianity is such an ultra-puritanical asceticism set forth as the true and only ideal. And the same is true even in Stoicism, although the Stoics did not use the word "pleasure" for approved pleasurable emotions, but the noun χαρά, which is rendered "joy" in the N.T. But to the writer of James possibly legitimate pleasures are not in mind here; only the wholly evil pleasures of "the world." And God and "the world" are antinomies between which no compromise is possible; the choice between them is the terrible responsibility of every individual.

5-6. The sequence of the writer's thought in these verses is extremely difficult for modern readers to follow and has been the cause of endless perplexity to commentators.

---

little pleasure you have. Have contact with others only in so far as they can be used to extract a modicum of pleasure, otherwise disregard them.

How meager a prospect for real happiness is here held out. Man is a social being. His life depends upon others, as others depend upon him. His deepest satisfactions come in the interdependence of friendship and fellowship. Loneliness is hell. But these satisfactions cannot be enjoyed by one who is willing to collaborate with others only so long as he can use them for his own personal ends. As soon as they discover they are being used, they will turn against him. No thoroughly selfish person ever had a friend. He may ask for friendship, but he can never obtain it; for he asks wrongly to use it for his selfish pleasures.

4-6. The False Friendship of the World.— Whoever wishes to be a friend of the world makes himself an enemy of God. Friendship

with the world is equivalent to the adoption of this hedonistic philosophy as one's own. It is to live an egocentric, self-indulging, parasitic life, indifferent to the consequence of such a life on oneself or on others. It is to espouse the accumulation of wealth, of prestige, and of power to domineer over others as the standard of success (cf. Luke 12:16-17; 22:24-25). John Cowper Powys declares himself a proponent of this philosophy:

It is necessary to undermine with skepticism (*a*) the duty of serving humanity (*b*) the pursuit of truth. . . . A person who has found the secret of a thrilling life of happiness, why should he bother with a lot of people? He has no wish to convert them, no wish to change them, no wish to gain their admiration. His only wish concerning them is that they should take themselves off and leave him alone.[5]

[5] *In Defense of Sensuality* (New York: Simon & Schuster, 1932), p. 91.

6 But he giveth more grace. Wherefore he saith, God resisteth the proud, but giveth grace unto the humble.

which he has made to dwell in us"? 6 But he gives more grace; therefore it says, "God opposes the proud, but gives grace to the

---

Apparently the writer assumes that his readers will gather his meaning sufficiently from the citation in vs. 5, which he quotes as if it were familiar to everyone; it may well be, in fact, that if we knew the exact meaning and the context of the passage cited, the problem would be solved. But although described as **scripture**, there is no such text in the O.T., the Apoc., or in any Jewish writing that has survived; nor does rabbinical literature contain any parallel. This fact, of course, is of no great importance in itself, for to early Christians "scripture" often embraced much more than the later church accepted; cf. John 7:38; II Tim. 3:8; Jude 14-15; etc.

In any event, the words cited form, like 1:17a, a Greek hexameter: πρὸς φθόνον ἐπιποθεῖ τὸ πνεῦμ' ὃ κατῴκισ' ἐν ἡμῖν. The correct translation, however, is uncertain, as in the Greek πνεῦμα ("spirit") can be either the subject or the object of the verb. In the former case (cf. KJV) the meter may be reproduced by rendering: "Zealously yearns for God the spirit he planted within us." In the latter case we have (cf. RSV) : "God zealously yearns for the spirit he planted within us." In either case there can be little doubt that "the spirit he planted within us" is a reference to Gen. 2:7, where "the breath of life" has been interpreted as **the spirit,** the divine spark in each human being.

As to choice between the alternatives, the second is undoubtedly rhetorically preferable, for it assumes the same subject for both verbs and also the same subject for the verb in vs. 6. And it gives a comprehensible, even though not a very smooth connection with vs. 4; the responsibility of each individual for his choice between God and "the world" is immeasurably heightened by the fact that a wrong decision involves rejection of God's yearning love for his soul. This alternative may therefore be adopted.

There is a bare possibility, incidentally, that the citation is from a lost Jewish work called *Eldad and Modat* (cf. Num. 11:24-29) , mentioned in Herm. Vis. II. 3. 4.

In vs. 6 the connection is so very obscure that textual corruption may be suspected. But the underlying thought seems to be that God, since he yearns for every human soul, gives **more grace** (cf. Rom. 5:20?) , "special help" to those fitted to receive it by their

---

But this is to defy God. To conduct one's life in accordance with this point of view is to be **an enemy of God.** Does it follow that to "submit . . . to God" (vs. 7) involves the surrender of any prospect of happiness? Is the friend of God condemned to a dull existence which is a drab alternative to the bright, though fleeting, pleasures of the hedonist?

On the contrary, Augustine, an erstwhile hedonist, testified in his *Confessions* that he was attracted to the Christian way because he found within it a joy untainted by the dregs of dissipation. In the epilogue to *Romola,* George Eliot makes Romola say:

There are so many things wrong and difficult in the world, that no man can be great—he can hardly keep himself from wickedness—unless he gives up thinking much about pleasure or rewards, and gets strength to endure what is hard and painful. My father had the greatness that belongs to integrity; he chose poverty and obscurity rather than falsehood. And there was Fra Girolamo [Savonarola] . . .

he had the greatness which belongs to a life spent in struggling against powerful wrong, and trying to raise men to the highest deeds they are capable of. And so, my Lillo, if you mean to act nobly and seek to know the best things God has put within reach of men, you must learn to fix your mind on that end, and not on what will happen to you because of it. And remember, if you were to choose something lower, and make it the rule of your life to seek your own pleasure and escape from what is disagreeable, calamity might come just the same; and it would be calamity falling on a base mind, which is the one form of sorrow that has no balm in it.

In a symposium conducted by *Life* [6] on "The Pursuit of Happiness," the concluding remarks made by Betty Barton, who has been a paralytic because of an automobile accident, were as follows: "We are so suffocated with things and with distractions that the real pursuit of happiness is impossible. . . . Happiness is primarily an inner state, an inner achievement. In other

[6] July 12, 1948.

7 Submit yourselves therefore to God. Resist the devil, and he will flee from you.

8 Draw nigh to God, and he will draw nigh to you. Cleanse *your* hands, ye sinners; and purify *your* hearts, ye doubleminded.

9 Be afflicted, and mourn, and weep: let your laughter be turned to mourning, and *your* joy to heaviness.

humble." **7** Submit yourselves therefore to God. Resist the devil and he will flee from you. **8** Draw near to God and he will draw near to you. Cleanse your hands, you sinners, and purify your hearts, you men of double mind. **9** Be wretched and mourn and weep. Let your laughter be turned to mourning and your joy to dejection.

---

humility. And to prove this the writer quotes Prov. 3:34 (cf. I Pet. 5:5) exactly according to the LXX (the wording of the Hebrew is somewhat different; see the English texts of Proverbs). But while God so helps **the humble, the proud,** those who love themselves and therefore "the world," will receive no such help, but rather are treated by God as his enemies.

Therefore, while there remain real obscurities in vss. 5-6 that may never be entirely clarified, the general purpose of these verses in the writer's argument against unlawful "pleasures" and "desires" is to insist on the deadly evil of such temptations and to help his readers to overcome them.

7. No doubt these evil desires are very strong; but God is stronger and he gives his strength to all who **submit** themselves to him. **The devil** (cf. on 3:15) knows this; and so he will **flee** in panic from all who **resist** his advances. In the Testaments of the Twelve Patriarchs cf. Naphtali 8:4; "If you work that which is good, my children, . . . the devil shall flee from you"; Simeon 3:5: "If a man flee to the Lord, the evil spirit fleeth from him"; Benjamin 5:2: "If you do good, even the unclean spirits will flee from you."

8-10. God's help (vs. 8) is immediately at hand if men draw near to him by repentance—by rejecting the false "pleasures" and "desires" in which they have indulged themselves, their sins and their **double mind,** which tries to serve God and the "world" simultaneously (cf. 1:8). **Cleanse your hands,** originally an actual washing for cere-

---

words, I would like to close by saying that the Kingdom of Heaven is within us." One recalls the words of Paul, "The kingdom of God does not mean food and drink but righteousness and peace and joy in the Holy Spirit" (Rom. 14:17).

7-10. *Draw Near to God and He Will Draw Near to You.*—In the gospel the final word is not condemnation, but an appeal for change of mind and heart. No matter how defiant or rebellious a man has been, if he will turn to God, if he will submit himself to the Lord, he will be welcomed and lifted up. When the cheap joys of self-indulgence turn into the sadness of disgust, when laughter turns to tears as the things falsely prized turn to ashes, draw near to "God who gives to all men generously and without reproaching" (1:5). "Thou hast made us for thyself and our hearts can never find repose until they rest in thee."

Cleanse your hands, you sinners. Warfield M. Firor, a surgeon associated with Johns Hopkins Hospital, in commenting on the general confession, which contains the words "We have left undone those things which we ought to

have done; And we have done those things which we ought not to have done; And there is no health in us," suggests that this absence of health means that "there is no source of spontaneous control for our spiritual lives. . . . We are disoriented; we have lost our bearing; our spiritual awareness is atrophied." If we are to be restored, we must be penitent, but according to Firor, penitence is not remorse. "Remorse is the scrutiny of one's errors without hope." One has gone too far, so one thinks, to turn around. "Repentance is the scrutiny of those same mistakes with hope." "The genius of Christianity lies in the fact that it demonstrates renewal. We have the capacity of being restored, renewed. There is no other teaching in the world which is so full of the concept of renewal." [7]

9-10. *Be Wretched and Mourn and Weep.*—Scott Fitzgerald was the novelist of the dissipated youth of his generation and a sharer in their feverish pursuit of sensations. Not long before his death at a comparatively early age

[7] Wallace C. Speers, ed., *Laymen Speaking*, pp. 36, 37, 38.

| 10 Humble yourselves in the sight of the Lord, and he shall lift you up.

11 Speak not evil one of another, brethren. He that speaketh evil of *his* brother, and judgeth his brother, speaketh evil of the law, and judgeth the law: but if thou judge the law, thou art not a doer of the law, but a judge. | 10 Humble yourselves before the Lord and he will exalt you.

11 Do not speak evil against one another, brethren. He that speaks evil against a brother or judges his brother, speaks evil against the law and judges the law. But if you judge the law, you are not a doer of |

monial purity, is of course used figuratively, as in Isa. 1:16; etc. (cf. I Tim. 2:8), of proper outward behavior, just as **purify your hearts** refers to proper inward attitude. The **laughter** (vs. 9) and the **joy** brought by the "pleasures" must be utterly renounced and turned into penitential sorrow; the language, however, should not be interpreted as directing penitential practices such as fasting, sackcloth, etc. Only in this way will (vs. 10) the true happiness be found that comes from God's approval.

After what has been said above regarding the entire inappropriateness of the aphorism in vss. 1-2 for early Christianity, it should be clear enough that this section has been taken by the Christian editor from the earlier Jewish work; there is, indeed, nothing specifically Christian in any of its wording. The tribal reference is to Gad, the type of "wars and fightings," or as Philo (*On Dreams* II. 35) states it, of "attack and counterattack" (cf. Gen. 49:19).

XVII. SPEAK NO EVIL (4:11-12)

11-12. A little section that is complete in itself. But there is a certain connection with vss. 1-10, since evilspeaking is one result of evil desires and of pride. And there is a more direct relation to 3:1-12, which rebukes sins of the tongue; all of 3:1–4:12 has, in fact, a certain unity of theme.

Evilspeaking of others is forbidden by **the law.** Here, if any specific precept is in mind, Lev. 19:16-18 is the most likely passage, but the writer may well be thinking of the general tenor of God's law as a whole. He who violates that law affirms that it is not

---

he wrote a confession in which he called himself a "cracked plate." He wrote of finding himself consistently in valleys of depression and of trying to climb uphill to recover from moral and spiritual bankruptcy. He must have found that the old proverb, "It costs far more to indulge one bad habit than to exercise many good ones," is pretty close to the truth. The coarse laughter was turned to mourning and the cheap joys to dejection. Emile Durkheim describes this condition as common to our times:

> From top to bottom of the social scale, violent but indefinite and unfocused desires are aroused. Nothing could possibly appease them. . . . [Men] thirst for novelty, for unknown delights, for nameless sensations which nevertheless lose all their zest as soon as they are experienced. Then, let the slightest reverse occur and men are powerless to bear it. . . . [They] discover how futile the whole uproar was and realize that any number of these novel experiences piled up indefinitely has not succeeded in accumulating a solid capital of happiness on which they might live in times of trial.[8]

[8] Quoted in *The University Observer*, Winter 1947 (Chicago: University of Chicago Press), pp. 58-59.

It may be paradoxical, but it nevertheless is true that the only real exaltation and emancipation of the human spirit come through humbling oneself to God.

11-12. *Contra Bigotry.*—The words of Jesus recorded in Matt. 5:22 and 7:1-5 are brought to mind by these words of James. Paul is concerned with the same problem in Rom. 14. The three passages might well be dealt with together. Why these strictures against judging others? Is it possible to go through life without passing judgment upon other people? If we are to have dealings with other people, do we not have to estimate critically their characters and abilities? Why should such necessary discrimination be condemned? Moreover, is not the author of this letter constantly passing judgments which now he forbids to his readers? Only a few sentences above he uses such expressions as "unfaithful creatures," "you sinners," "you men of double mind."

"Physician, heal thyself." Should he not take some of his own medicine? But James, as Jesus and Paul, was not prohibiting the moral appraisal which is necessary in human relation-

12 There is one lawgiver, who is able to save and to destroy: who art thou that judgest another?

13 Go to now, ye that say, To-day or tomorrow we will go into such a city, and continue there a year, and buy and sell, and get gain:

the law but a judge. **12** There is one lawgiver and judge, he who is able to save and to destroy. But who are you that you judge your neighbor?

13 Come now, you who say, "Today or tomorrow we will go into such and such a town and spend a year there and trade

---

a binding law and so not God's law at all; when he slanders his neighbor, he, consciously or unconsciously, **speaks evil against the law** as well as against that neighbor **and judges the law** as worthless. And so he sets himself up against God, not only in condemning the law that God gave but in arrogating to himself the authority to pronounce judgment on men, something that God alone can do infallibly. He (vs. 12) is the sole judge **who is able to save and to destroy** (Ps. 75:7); in comparison, what value has the opinion of any human being? Here the **one lawgiver and judge** (in the late Greek text that underlies the KJV the words **and judge** were omitted) was obviously—even to the Christian editor—God and not Christ.

Nothing in this section suggests a Christian rather than a Jewish origin; the correspondence with similar Christian teaching (Matt. 7:1-5; Rom. 14:4; etc.) is no greater than would be due to the common theme and the common O.T. background. And for a close rabbinical parallel Strack-Billerbeck (I, 227) cites Rabbi Jochanan (d. 279): "The slanderer is like one who denies God" (citing Ps. 12:5).

XVIII. Sinful Self-Confidence (4:13-16)

13-16. Again a little section complete in itself. Conceivably one further example of sins of the tongue may have been in the writer's mind; but any real connection with what precedes is so tenuous that this section is practically independent.

The opening word **come** begins an imperative demand for the readers' attention, which is heightened by the following **now,** the two words together insisting on the great

---

ships. He was concerned with that hypercritical, condemnatory attitude which is taken toward other people on the basis of an assumed superiority to them; that malicious and ungenerous criticism which is not really directed toward their welfare or improvement, but is rather a means of self-justification and self-aggrandizement. This sort of defamatory attack on others is possible only to those who have forgotten that they too are under the judgment of God. This is a source of intolerance which is itself a manifestation of self-righteousness and moral conceit.

A most subtle and deceptive temptation is the temptation to be contemptuous toward those who are adjudged morally or religiously inferior, because it is a temptation that corrupts those who are striving to fulfill their own moral and religious duties. It is the temptation to which the Pharisee in Jesus' parable succumbed (Luke 18:9-14). In the pursuit of goodness beware lest you assume the role of a self-righteous judge. Such an assumption of moral and spiritual superiority corrupts goodness at its heart, for genuine goodness is self-effacing, full of sympathy and kindliness, tenderhearted and

forgiving (cf. Eph. 4:31-32). Before God, who is good? Even Jesus raised that question in regard to himself (Mark 10:18). Before God, who dares claim the right to condemn his brother?

Intolerant persons often claim that they are representing God in the strictures they pass upon their fellows, but actually they are usurping his throne. Bigots cover their lust for power over the souls of others with a cloak of piety and orthodoxy. Dogmatists, with the assurance of infallibility, read those whom they deem unorthodox out of the fold. But they forget that **there is one lawgiver and judge;** they forget that they are not God (cf. 5:9). The cruelty of the self-righteous is most terrible because it is dressed in the garb of doing good. Intolerance not infrequently reaches its most acrimonious stage in the persons of those who profess to be followers of Christ.

13-16. *Sub Specie Aeternitatis.*—The church folk of an earlier generation used to add the initials "D. V." (for *Deo volente*) when writing a letter which involved future appointments. They followed literally this injunction in James, not to make any plans without the reservation,

14 Whereas ye know not what *shall be* on the morrow. For what *is* your life? It is even a vapor, that appeareth for a little time, and then vanisheth away.

14 whereas you do not know about tomorrow. What is your life? For you are a mist that appears for a little time and

importance of what follows. (In the Greek the opening verb is in the singular although many persons are addressed, a conventional and perfectly correct Greek usage.) It should be noted carefully that in what follows the writer does not denounce commerce as evil in itself nor does he deny that tradesmen and merchants may be pious and God-fearing men; he does not even assert that there is anything sinful in the desire to **get gain.** What he reproves is so complete an absorption in the affairs of this world that God is forgotten.

With the first clause of vs. 14 cf. Prov. 27:1. Whether the Greek ἀτμίς should be rendered **vapor** (KJV), **mist** (RSV) or "smoke" is indeterminate and wholly unimportant; the figure is perfectly clear.

The theme of the section is reached in vs. 15. Contrary to what might be expected, Jewish parallels to this teaching are very scanty; it was not the Jewish custom to qualify statements about plans for the future with a reverent formula like this. And the same is largely true of the N.T. as well; the only exact parallel appears to be I Cor. 4:19b (but cf. also Rom. 1:10; 15:32). On the other hand, the formula "if the gods will" was so common in the Hellenistic world as to be conventional; we have here a case where it was felt that Jews and Christians could learn something from Gentiles even in matters of religion. **The Lord** here is God, not Christ.

If the Lord wills, we shall live and we shall do this or that. This pious practice is no longer common. The question remains, however; has the thought behind the practice lost its validity?

There are, generally speaking, three ways of estimating man's life and activities. First, since life is fleeting, the time for experiencing its sensations is so brief that one must be alert to taste them all. "Gather ye rosebuds while ye may!" *Carpe diem.* "Let us eat, drink, and be merry, for tomorrow we die." Yang Chu, an ancient Chinese philosopher, estimated life in this fashion:

One hundred years is the limit of a long life. Not one in a thousand ever attains to it. Yet if they do, still unconscious infancy and old age take up about half this time. The time he passes unconsciously while asleep at night, and that which is wasted though awake during the day, also amounts to another half of the rest. Again, pain and sickness . . . fill up about a half, so that he really gets only ten years or so for his enjoyment. . . . We ought, therefore, to hasten to enjoy life and pay no attention to death. . . . Allow the ear to hear what it likes, the eye to see what it likes, the nose to smell what it likes, the mouth to say what it likes, the body to enjoy the comforts it likes to have, and the mind to do what it likes.[9]

This is the Epicurean or materialist evaluation of life.

Second, since life is fleeting, self-indulgence or involvement in the various activities of man-

[9] Yu-lan Fung, *A Comparative Study of Life Ideals* (Shanghai: The Commercial Press, 1925), pp. 82-84.

kind can give only truncated satisfactions. The desire for life is fatefully destined to disappointment as man moves on through sickness and old age to death. Therefore, to avoid disillusionment, ennui, and despair, do not love life. Turn your back on it. Don't throw yourself into something that is meaningless and a cheat. Then at least you won't be life's dupe. This is the Stoic or Buddhist evaluation of life.

Third, granted that life is fleeting, that it is a **mist that appears for a little time and then vanishes,** still it is more than that. There is God, and man's life may be linked to the Eternal. There is the seen, but also the unseen; there is the temporary, but also the eternal. If one lives in the light of the eternal, then he need never suffer disillusionment or defeat. The temporary finds its significance in relation to the eternal, and all the experiences of life here and now have value because of this relationship. This is the Christian evaluation of life (cf. II Cor. 4:16-18).

In this Christian conception of life the material and physical side is not disvalued or denied, but it is subordinated to the spiritual. When Jesus declared that life was more than meat or raiment, he did not dismiss meat and raiment as of no account. "Your heavenly Father knoweth that ye have need of all these things" (Matt. 6:32). James does not enjoin his readers against engaging in trade. Rather, he avers, man's business should be conducted in acknowledged dependence upon God. The economic activities in which men engage are the necessary

15 For that ye *ought* to say, If the Lord will, we shall live, and do this, or that.	then vanishes. 15 Instead you ought to say, "If the Lord wills, we shall live and we shall do this or that." 16 As it is, you boast in your arrogance. All such boasting is evil. 17 Whoever knows what is right to do and fails to do it, for him it is sin.
16 But now ye rejoice in your boastings: all such rejoicing is evil.	
17 Therefore to him that knoweth to do good, and doeth *it* not, to him it is sin.	

In vs. 16 ἀλαζονεῖαι (plural) is "braggings" or **boastings** (KJV), rather than the paraphrase **arrogance** (RSV), and the self-confident assertions of vs. 13 are meant; in themselves they are bad enough, but to *boast* about such worldly assurance is a further aggravation.

There is no trace of Christian influence in this section; in Matt. 6:34, which is sometimes compared with it, the theme is trust in God despite what seems to be a gloomy future, not disregard of God when the future is bright. A closer parallel could be found in Luke 12:16-21, but even there the emphasis is quite different; the selfish covetousness of the rich man in the parable is rebuked, not his lack of trust in God for the enjoyment of his riches. And it scarcely needs to be said that plans like those of vs. 13 would be far more common among Jews than among early Christians.

XIX. SINS OF OMISSION (4:17)

17. An isolated aphorism (cf. 1:12) with no real relation to what precedes or to what follows. It is apparently because of the independence of this saying that the RSV has omitted the connecting particle **therefore**, although there is no authority in the Greek MSS for this omission. But the translation is better without the particle, for commentators have puzzled endlessly about its force; perhaps the best explanation is that it is a familiar quotation from some well-known source in which the particle connected the saying with something omitted in James. All that can be said about the saying's position here is that the writer felt (quite correctly) that it was well worth citation; and he inserted it more or less at random at this point.

supports of life on this planet, but they are not the end or purpose of living.

Dostoevski, through his Grand Inquisitor, comments on the first temptation in the wilderness and the reply of Jesus, "Man shall not live by bread alone":

For the secret of man's being is not only to live but to have something to live for. Without a stable conception of the object of life, man would not consent to go on living, and would rather destroy himself than remain on earth, though he had bread in abundance.[10]

For the Great Illusion of human history has been precisely this, the belief that man can be satisfied with bread. He can be bought with it, no doubt; suborned by it, corrupted by it, but never satisfied by it. He eats thereof and is not satisfied. Were he beast of the field, he might be, but then he is not—he is man.

Whether the use of D. V. in letters is ever revived or not, can mankind succeed in conducting its affairs without reference to the will of God, without discrimination between the purpose of life and the means of life, between

the temporal and the eternal? In an interview not long before his death Charles P. Steinmetz, the scientific genius, said:

Someday people will learn that material things do not bring happiness and are of little use in making men and women creative and powerful. Then the scientists of the world will turn their laboratories over to the study of God and prayer and spiritual forces.

17. *Sins of Omission.*—Whoever knows what is right to do and fails to do it, for him it is sin recalls the saying of Jesus, "That servant who knew his master's will, but did not make ready or act according to his will" will receive a more severe punishment than the servant who did not know (Luke 12:47).

When one becomes a Christian, one voluntarily takes upon himself responsibilities and obligations which ordinary persons do not acknowledge. The ordinary person recognizes responsibilities within the circle of certain limited relationships, but what lies beyond that circle is not his concern. No one can be forced to become a Christian. The duties which inhere in the Christian vocation can only be assumed willingly. No one need be in the dark as to

[10] *The Brothers Karamazov* (New York: Modern Library, Inc., 1929), p. 312.

5 Go to now, *ye* rich men, weep and howl for your miseries that shall come upon *you*.

5 Come now, you rich, weep and howl for the miseries that are coming upon you.

The verse should not be overstressed, as if James meant that righteousness is composed solely of knowing and doing, or as if only he who knows can sin. In substance such a saying could come from any serious ethical teacher of any antecedents, although of course **sin** belongs to the Jewish or Christian vocabulary, not to the Hellenistic. But if the particle **therefore** discussed above really does indicate that the verse is cited from some familiar source, it is easier to think of this source as belonging to the rather abundant Jewish literature than to the comparatively scanty Christian literature; to predicate the existence of a Christian writing, well known for a while but now completely lost, is always hazardous.

XX. JUDGMENT ON THE RICH (5:1-6)

With no attempt at connection with what precedes, the theme of 1:9-11 and 2:1-7 is resumed abruptly. The highly oratorical language is much in the style of O.T. prophecy and still more in the style of Jewish apocalyptic, with a further parallel in Wisd. Sol. 2.

5:1. The lamentations are not, as in 4:9, expressions of humble repentance but of unavailing remorse and terror; while the **rich** in 1:9-11 can just conceivably be thought of as "brethren," in the present passage (and most probably in 1:9-11 as well: cf. on

---

what is involved. Certainly Christ wants no blind followers. But when anyone of his own free will makes the choice of adherence to Christ, he cannot refuse to carry out the obligations of that relationship without sinning against his Lord.

Not infrequently the Christian vocation is equated with respectability, and all that is required of a member of a church is to live a decent and inoffensive life and not break the accepted taboos. No wonder many people declare it unnecessary to have relationship with a church in order to be good. If goodness is simply respectability, then these critics of the church are correct in their appraisal. It is not necessary to become a church member in order to keep out of the hands of the law.

But if the Christian life is what Jesus asserted it to be in his challenge to his disciples, then it is a different matter, for the conditions of discipleship which he laid down are not so easy. "If any man will come after me, let him deny himself, and take up his cross, and follow me" (Matt. 16:24). To refer to only one of the conditions, "to take up his cross," is precisely to assume responsibilities toward God and man which ordinary persons do not acknowledge or accept. Jesus did not have to leave Nazareth and go to Jerusalem in order to maintain a reputation for respectability. No one can be required by law to "go the second mile." No one can be forced to accept responsibilities beyond his family or nation, but anyone who follows Christ cannot close his ears to the call to "go . . . into all the world, and preach the gospel

to every creature" (Mark 16:15). This missionary obligation which is upon the church as a whole cannot be refused by the individual Christian without disloyalty to Christ, without committing sin.

Perhaps one of the reasons for irresponsibility on the part of many church members lies in the failure to make plain to candidates for church membership the seriousness of the obligations which are involved in that membership. Thus their subsequent indifference to any but a minimum of Christian responsibilities does not appear sinful in their eyes. Jesus held off would-be disciples lest they commit themselves to a relationship whose obligations they did not really comprehend (cf. Luke 9:57-62). We seem to be glad to gain church membership on almost any terms. P. T. Forsyth quotes Kierkegaard as saying,

For long the tactics have been to induce as many as possible, everybody if possible, to enter Christianity. Do not be too curious whether what they enter is Christianity. My tactics will be, with the help of God, to make clear what the Christian demand really is if no one entered it.[1]

5:1-6. On the Side of the Oppressed.—Shall we speak on a terrific passage like this? Even to read it in a church service would be to rasp the eardrums of many worshipers. Upton Sinclair once read this bit of James to a group of ministers after attributing it to Emma Goldman, an anarchist agitator. The ministers re-

[1] *Positive Preaching and Modern Mind* (New York: G. H. Doran, 1907), Introduction.

2 Your riches are corrupted, and your garments are moth-eaten.

3 Your gold and silver is cankered; and the rust of them shall be a witness against you, and shall eat your flesh as it were fire. Ye have heaped treasure together for the last days.

2 Your riches have rotted and your garments are moth-eaten. 3 Your gold and silver have rusted, and their rust will be evidence against you and will eat your flesh like fire. You have laid up treasure[e]

[e] Or *will eat your flesh, since you have stored up fire.*

2:1-7) they are denounced as a class without exception, all rich men being regarded as necessarily sinners.

2-3. In the Greek the verbs here are in the perfect; **the last days** have already begun and with them all earthly values have lost their meaning. Orientals spend large sums on expensive garments, for men quite as much as for women, and moths are therefore a constant danger; one moth can destroy a fabric so as to render it wholly useless. The writer uses this familiar fact to illustrate the transitoriness of riches as this world passes away. Just so in vs. 3 he uses the figure of **rust** all the more pointedly because in this world rust scarcely affects **gold** and harms **silver** only very gradually. And in the Judgment this (supernatural!) rust will be revealed as **evidence** of the worthlessness of all that has been treasured; and by a bold further figure this rust is represented as extending its corrosive power from the gold and silver to the men themselves, so that the riches actually become the means of tormenting their owners, who had thought of them as bringing happiness!

The punctuation of vs. 3 is uncertain, since its concluding phrase (**you have laid . . . days**) may be read either as a subordinate clause or as an independent sentence. In the former case (RSV mg.), **fire** is the object of the following verb, whose transitive force is indicated in the RSV mg. by rendering it **stored up,** and the figure of the torturing **rust** is continued directly. In the latter case (RSV text) the verb is used as an intransitive, indicated by the RSV's rendition **laid up treasure.** The meaning is so nearly the same

acted with indignation against the effrontery of her diatribe and declared that she ought to be deported![2]

It is sometimes said that ministers should stick to "the simple gospel" in their preaching, leaving social and economic questions strictly alone. William Gordon, a Tory of colonial times, complained against his minister's preaching on independence for the colonies, "I most heartily wish that he and many others of his profession would confine themselves to gospel truths." But a good deal of the Bible would have to be discarded if social and political issues were to be tabooed. The Bible as a whole is on the side of the oppressed, and in God's name protests against injustice in every form. Do these words of James differ fundamentally from the mordant words of Amos?

They hate him who reproves in the gate,
And loathe him who speaks the truth.
Therefore because you trample upon the weak,
And take from him exactions of grain,
Though you have built houses of hewn stone,
You shall not dwell in them (Amos 5:10-11 Amer. Trans.)

[2] See *The Profits of Religion* (Pasadena, Calif.: The Author, 1918), pp. 287-90.

Consider also the words of the other prophets, e.g., Mic. 6:10-11, or Isa. 3:13-15, or Jer. 5:26. And what about the words of Jesus as recorded in Luke 20:46-47, or his parable of the rich man and Lazarus? (Luke 16:19-31.)

Those who would cultivate piety at the expense of just dealing get small comfort if they read the Scriptures. Nowhere in them can it be found that a man can be in right relationship with God if he is acting unjustly toward his fellows. The cries of those who have been defrauded arise to **the ears of the Lord of hosts.**

Your riches have rotted apparently refers to the accumulation of things which must finally be discarded as useless. If these things had been shared with the needy, they might have usefully worn out, rather than rotted in useless decay.

Wine and meat are decaying in the palaces
    While on the street are the corpses of those who
    have frozen to death

are lines translated from a poem by Tu Fu, an eighth-century Chinese poet.

Are the churches in our land filled with members whose sense of justice is so keen, whose acceptance of social responsibility is so conscientious, that the words of James and the

4 Behold, the hire of the laborers who have reaped down your fields, which is of you kept back by fraud, crieth: and the cries of them which have reaped are entered into the ears of the Lord of Sabaoth.

5 Ye have lived in pleasure on the earth, and been wanton; ye have nourished your hearts, as in a day of slaughter.

for the last days. 4 Behold, the wages of the laborers who mowed your fields, which you kept back by fraud, cry out; and the cries of the harvesters have reached the ears of the Lord of hosts. 5 You have lived on the earth in luxury and in pleasure; you have fattened your hearts in a day of slaughter.

---

in either case that the difference is insignificant; but the marginal rendition is perhaps preferable because the active voice (used here) of the Greek verb is normally transitive, even though there are exceptions (Luke 12:21; II Cor. 12:14).

The apparent relation of vss. 2-3 to Matt. 6:19 is purely superficial, much greater in the traditional English versions than in the Greek. Quite different Greek words are used for "rust"; indeed, the noun employed in Matt. 6:19 (βρῶσις) may not mean "rust" at all but rather "worm" as in the RSV mg. And in Matt. 6:19 the point is the possible destruction of "riches" in the present life, so that if "rust" is the correct translation, not gold and silver so much as utensils of iron or bronze are meant; if "worm" is right, the reference is more general, but certainly not to gold and silver. In either case, the saying in Matt. 6:19 is not addressed to "rich" men but to persons of very moderate means. In James, however, truly "rich" men are meant, who preserve their wealth as long as they live. And the warning expresses apocalyptic certainty; at the Judgment, riches, which to the writer could have been gained only by fraud and crime, are not only useless but bring eternal condemnation to their owners.

4. A specific sin of the wealthy is defrauding workmen of their pay, a grave crime in Judaism, where "the wages of him that is hired shall not abide with thee all night until the morning" (Lev. 19:13; cf. Deut. 24:14-15). The two sentences in this verse are in parallelism, with little distinction between "mowing" and "harvesting" (cf. the KJV's **reaped down** and **reaped**) but with a telling distinction between the "outcry of the wages" (a vivid figure) and the "outcry of the men." **The Lord of hosts** is simply "the Almighty [Judge]," a familiar O.T. title (Isa. 5:9; etc.), added for solemnity, with no thought as to whether the **hosts** are angels, stars, or other possible alternatives.

5-6. The thought of the rich preparing their doom by their own acts is continued; through their **luxury** and their **pleasure** (not the Stoic technical term for this vice) they have **fattened** their **hearts** like the fattening of cattle before their **slaughter**. And the climax is reached in vs. 6; the selfishness of the rich has culminated in murder. Here

---

prophets are no longer relevant? How shall the challenge of a godless communism be met if godly churchmen consider that their religion has little to do with how they make or spend their money, but only with the amount they put in the collection plate? In the trial of the president of a stock exchange a prominent financier, who was also an active churchman, was called into court as a witness. He was asked whether he was aware of the illegal activities of the stock exchange official. When he answered in the affirmative, he was asked why he did not try to stop him. "It's a man's own business what he does with his money," was his reply. But is there any matter that is set forth more clearly in the Bible than the responsibility for administering what goods God may have entrusted to us in such a way as to serve, not private greed or luxurious ostentation, but the common welfare?

The early Christian preachers of the gospel had no uncertainty at this point. Here are the words of Clement of Alexandria (150-215):

I know that God has given us the use of goods, but only as far as is necessary. . . . It is absurd and disgraceful for one to live magnificently and luxuriously when so many are hungry.

And Ambrose (340-397):

How far, O rich, do you extend your senseless avarice? Do you intend to be the sole inhabitants of the earth? Why do you drive out the fellow sharers of nature, and claim it all for yourselves? The earth was made for all, the rich and poor, in common. Why do you rich men claim it as your exclusive right? . . . Property hath no rights. The earth is the Lord's, and we are his offspring.[3]

[3] Quoted in Upton Sinclair, *The Cry for Justice* (Philadelphia: John C. Winston, 1915), p. 397.

6 Ye have condemned *and* killed the just; *and* he doth not resist you.

7 Be patient therefore, brethren, unto the coming of the Lord. Behold, the husbandman waiteth for the precious fruit of the earth, and hath long patience for it, until he receive the early and latter rain.

6 You have condemned, you have killed the righteous man; he does not resist you.

7 Be patient, therefore, brethren, until the coming of the Lord. Behold, the farmer waits for the precious fruit of the earth, being patient over it until it receives the

---

τὸν δίκαιον, "the righteous," is not **the righteous man** in the sense of a particular individual, but a generic term (cf. "the poor" in 2:6), *any* righteous person who has so suffered. Such men have been **condemned** and **killed** by being deprived of their livelihood; while barely possible, it is not at all necessary to think of extreme instances such as corrupt use of the law courts to have righteous poor men condemned to death. The final clause of this verse, pointing the utter helplessness of the poor to resist, heightens the guilt of the oppressors. Some commentators prefer to take this clause as a question, "Does he not resist you?" in the sense of "Does he not bear testimony against you in God's presence?" But would any reader so understand it?

While the Christian editor throughout is naturally thinking primarily of the hardships suffered by Christians, there is nothing at all specifically Christian in the wording; ample Jewish parallels exist. In particular, to identify **the righteous man** (vs. 6) with Stephen is wholly arbitrary and artificial; his martyrdom was scarcely a crime of the "rich" against the "poor." Even more out of the question is the identification of this "man" with Christ; how could a reader detect so obscure an allusion? This is, of course, not to say that the Christian editor or Christian readers might not think of Christ and the Christian martyrs as *included* in the wholly general language. It should be noted, moreover, that this section in James is unique in presupposing a Palestinian background. For it was only in Palestine that harvesting the crops (vs. 4) was done by hired workmen; elsewhere in the Roman Empire fields were worked by slaves. And the Christian editor was not a Palestinian.

XXI. PATIENCE OF THE RIGHTEOUS (5:7-11)

While the **therefore** connects this section with vss. 1-6, the following exhortation is quite general; patience under any form of hardship or distress is enjoined, not merely under oppression by the rich. As the end of the world is at hand and the righteous will soon receive their reward, they can disregard their present troubles and wait patiently with sure confidence.

7. Brethren who are believers (contrast "the rich" in vs. 1) should follow the example set by all farmers, who do not become impatient during the long interval between seedtime and harvest but wait unhurriedly for the crop, here described as

---

How did it happen that the religion of the Bible, which is so predominantly concerned with the establishment of just and compassionate human relationships, became in the course of its European development primarily interested in what happens on the other side of the grave? Bernard in the twelfth century cried: "The church is resplendent in her walls, beggarly in her poor. She clothes her stones in gold and leaves her sons naked." [4] Who can say that there was no basis for Lenin's indictment which he wrote in 1905:

[4] Apology to William of St. Thierry. See J. A. C. Morison, *Life and Times of St. Bernard* (London: Chapman & Hall, 1863), p. 148.

Religion teaches those who toil in poverty all their lives to be resigned and patient in this world, and consoles them with the hope of reward in heaven. As for those who live upon the labors of others, religion teaches them to be "charitable"— thus providing a justification for exploitation and, as it were, also a cheap ticket to heaven likewise. [5]

The question comes again: Shall we dwell on a terrific passage like this in James? If not, why not?

7-11. Holding Out to the End.—**Behold, we call those happy who were steadfast.** The Chinese have a striking expression descriptive of the man who turns back after he has put his

[5] *Religion* (London: Martin Lawrence, n.d.), p. 11.

8 Be ye also patient; stablish your hearts: for the coming of the Lord draweth nigh.

9 Grudge not one against another, brethren, lest ye be condemned: behold, the judge standeth before the door.

10 Take, my brethren, the prophets, who have spoken in the name of the Lord, for an example of suffering affliction, and of patience.

early and the late rain. **8** You also be patient. Establish your hearts, for the coming of the Lord is at hand. **9** Do not grumble, brethren, against one another, that you may not be judged; behold, the Judge is standing at the doors. **10** As an example of suffering and patience, brethren, take the prophets who spoke in the name of the

---

precious because figure and fact are combined; the infinite reward of the righteous is really in mind. Palestine has two rainy seasons; in October-November **(the early)** and April-May **(the late) rain.** But the language by itself in no way proves a Palestinian origin of the passage, since "former and latter rain" is a fixed phrase in O.T. language (Deut. 11:14; etc.) and might be used by any Jew (or Christian) anywhere (cf. 1:10-11).

8-9. In times of hardship tempers are apt to wear thin and "grumbling," not merely against oppressors but **against one another,** is only too likely to occur. But this temptation must be resisted resolutely (cf. 4:11-12) at all times, above all now when judgment is so near at hand. Even to the Christian editor **the Lord** in vss. 7-8 and **the Judge** in vs. 9 must have meant God, not Christ, for it would be very awkward to understand "the Lord" in vs. 4, these verses, and vss. 10-11 as having different senses (cf. Mal. 3:1).

10-11. The writer thinks presumably not only of the actual O.T. account of the **suffering and patience** of the **prophets,** but even more of the many Jewish traditions regarding their afflictions (cf. Heb. 11:36-38). In vs. 11 **the steadfastness of Job** (RSV; cf. on 1:3) is much better than **the patience of Job** (KJV), which has become a traditional phrase in English; for while Job was constantly steadfast in his moral integrity, his protests against his sufferings can scarcely be described as "patient." Very possibly, however, the writer was not thinking of the whole book of Job but only of Job 1:21; 2:10; he certainly did not mean to encourage his readers to imitate Job's passionate

---

hand to the plow. It may be translated, "Before half the road is traveled he runs away." The temptation to give up before the goal is reached comes inevitably to all the followers of Christ. James is here seeking to "strengthen . . . the weak hands, and confirm the feeble knees" (Isa. 35:3).

In a world like ours the harvest of righteousness does not come overnight. The forces of evil seem ever more potent than the powers of good; they have the most money, the political and social power and prestige; they do not scruple to use means to gain and maintain their power which are denied to those who serve the cause of Christ. So sometimes this cause seems utterly hopeless and, as at the time of the Crucifixion, Christ's dismayed disciples forsake him and flee.

Be patient, therefore, brethren, until the coming of the Lord. . . . Establish your hearts, for the coming of the Lord is at hand. James is not asking his readers to submit supinely to injustice or oppression without protest. That is not the point of this paragraph. In the face of all their difficulties and disappointments, he is beseeching them to be steadfast in their loyalty

to their Lord. Whatever happens, let them not surrender to evil, for the vindication and ultimate triumph of their Lord is at hand. **Establish** (vs. 8) is the same word which appears in Luke 9:51, "He steadfastly set his face to go to Jerusalem," and in Luke 22:32, "When once thou hast turned again, establish thy brethren" (ASV).

For the Christians of that time history was foreshortened, and they expected its climax before long in the coming of Christ. Even so, they were tempted to disheartenment as the parousia was delayed, and they were in need of encouragement. The writer of II Peter is attempting to meet this same situation (II Pet. 3:3-10). The followers of Jesus constituted a small and insignificant minority in the mighty Roman Empire, and the forces arrayed against them seemed overwhelming. But if they would only hold on a little longer, when the Lord appears his truth would be vindicated. **God's power would be supreme and they would be saved.**

Two millenniums have gone by since these words were written, and **the coming of the Lord** which was promised has not eventuated.

11 Behold, we count them happy which endure. Ye have heard of the patience of Job, and have seen the end of the Lord; that the Lord is very pitiful, and of tender mercy.

11 Behold, we call those happy who were steadfast. You have heard of the steadfastness of Job, and you have seen the purpose of the Lord, how the Lord is compassionate and merciful.

outbursts. The difference between **the purpose of the Lord** (RSV) and **the end of the Lord** (KJV) is the difference between two possible meanings of the Greek noun τέλος, which, precisely like "end" in English, can mean either "the end in view" and so "purpose," or "end" in the simple sense of "termination." Obviously no final choice between the two alternatives is possible; but "the happy ending that the Lord gave to Job's sufferings" (Job 42:10-17), something familiar to every reader, suggests the meaning adopted in the KJV. This meaning also seems much more in accord with vss. 7-8. The other meaning, "the purpose for which the Lord caused Job to suffer," is by no means obvious in the O.T. text and would have to be explained in James by the remote passage 1:12.

It seems almost incredible that this section should ever have been treated as an original Christian exhortation; how could a Christian writer seeking examples of steadfastness content himself with O.T. prophets and Job, ignoring completely the supreme model of the sufferings and steadfastness of Christ? (To interpret **the end of the Lord** in vs. 11 as "the death of Christ" is out of the question.) While the writer of Hebrews in his ch. 11 likewise draws elaborately on the O.T. in his long list of the heroes of faith, it all leads up to the Christian climax in "Jesus the pioneer and perfecter"

What appeal, therefore, can such words have for us today? Can we find courage in this expectation which was not fulfilled? Among Christians today there are those who expect a denouement like that described in II Pet. 3:10. But there are others, aware of geologic time and the modern understanding of history, to whom such hopes are but a fantasy.

Christians are no longer an insignificant minority. They have place and power in the councils of state, in the marts of business, in the general affairs of the world. But, as yesterday, they are under the grave temptation to grow halfhearted in their devotion to their Master, to surrender their hope of the kingdom of God, to lay down their weapons without having won the victory for righteousness.

Do we not need a constant reminder that to make such a surrender is to deny our Christian faith? Basic in that faith is confidence in the victory of God and in the vindication of Christ and the way which he revealed. Such a confidence was the essential element in the early Christian belief in **the coming of the Lord**. How or when he might come was uncertain, but that he would come in victory was sure. Is it not hypocrisy to call ourselves Christians if we believe the gospel of our Lord to be only a pretty dream? Unless we believe that our salvation, individual and social, depends upon our obedience to the laws of God as these are engraved in the structure of life; unless we believe that these laws cannot be broken, though we may break ourselves upon them if we defy them, why should we bother to call ourselves Christians at all?

The prophets, Christ, the apostles, faced far more discouraging situations than we face when they called upon their generation to turn to God. Practical people ridiculed them as visionaries and hardened their necks against them.

"Come and let us smite him for his speech
And let us pay no more heed to any of his words!"

they said to Jeremiah (18:18 Amer. Trans.). "Away with this man, and release to us Barabbas" (Luke 23:18), was the cry against Jesus. But will we vote for the high priests and Pilate against Jesus? Do we believe that their way is really practical rather than his? We must believe in the victory of Christ, **the coming of the Lord,** or else give up the whole human race to despair and self-destruction. No other way but God's way will really work! [6]

The reference to Job (vs. 11) recalls the cynical appraisal of Satan that Job's devotion to God was not genuine, but rather the result of the material favors which he enjoyed. "Does Job serve God for naught?" The cynic is sure that there is no such thing as a genuinely religious person; no such thing as a man of high integrity and loyalty to God. All who practice religion do it from calculated selfishness. Put the pressure on, take away all the tangible bene-

[6] See John Macmurray, *The Clue to History* (New York: Harper & Bros., 1939).

12 But above all things, my brethren, swear not, neither by heaven, neither by the earth, neither by any other oath: but let your yea be yea; and *your* nay, nay; lest ye fall into condemnation.

12 But above all, my brethren, do not swear, either by heaven or by earth or with any other oath, but let your yes be yes and your no be no, that you may not fall under condemnation.

(Heb. 12:2). One may note also the contrast between vss. 10-11 and I Pet. 2:18-24. The only possible conclusion is that the present section in James was originally written not by a Christian but by a Jew; the Christian editor has simply taken over the work of his Jewish predecessor unaltered.

A tribal reference—the first since that to Gad in 4:1-2—can be detected in vs. 7 to Dan; cf. Gen. 49:18, "I have waited for thy salvation, O LORD" (KJV). A reference to Issachar, who in the Greek (not the Hebrew) of Gen. 49:15 is described as a "farmer" (the same Greek word as in vs. 7 here), is too obscure, while a reference to Issachar already appears in 1:12.

XXII. SWEARING FORBIDDEN (5:12)

12. There is no connection between this verse and vss. 7-11; to argue, e.g., that suffering causes profanity misses the point entirely. For the writer is not concerned with what we call "profanity," the reckless use of holy names to add emphasis, but with oaths taken to assure truthfulness, the opposite of which would not be "profanity" but "perjury." The danger of the use of such oaths is that men come to feel that if these are omitted, there is no binding necessity to speak the truth.

The **above all** that introduces vs. 12 emphasizes the importance of the saying to the writer's mind. But surely there is exaggeration here; can it be held that the use of

fits of such devotion, and they will turn and curse God to his face. The book of Job is a protest against this cynical appraisal of mankind. Granted that the cynic may be right in many cases, even in the majority of cases, yet one man who remains steadfast is sufficient to refute his generalization.

The Bible's answer to the cynic is not given in the form of a theoretical argument, but in a demonstration in the lives of persons who actually possess the quality which the cynic denies. The prophets Jeremiah and Amos under extreme pressure refused to sell out. They and others like them are an incontrovertible rebuttal of the cynic's taunt, "All that a man hath will he give for his life." We do not have to confine ourselves to the Bible for the demonstration that there are persons who cannot be bought at any price. In the persecution which the Huguenots of France suffered, the reply which some of them made to the demand to recant was, "We are willing to sacrifice our lives and estates to the king, but our consciences being of God we cannot so dispose of them." **Behold, we call those happy who were steadfast.** "You may burn my body and scatter the ashes to the winds of heaven; you may drop my soul into the regions of darkness, but you will not get me to support what I believe to be wrong." These words of Abraham Lincoln call on all of us to prove the cynic wrong, to belong

to the company of men like Job and the prophets, who refuse to give in, regardless of the pressure.

You have seen the purpose of the Lord. Goodspeed translates, "You have seen what the Lord brought out of it [i.e., Job's steadfastness], for the Lord is very kind and merciful." This most probably refers to the final restoration to Job of what he had lost in the beginning. Does James imply that endurance always is climaxed by such a restoration and that God's mercy guarantees such a happy ending on earth? The Jewish author of the basic work would hardly make such a guarantee as a reward to faithfulness. His spirit would be that of Shadrach, Meshach, and Abednego: "If our God, whom we serve, is able to deliver us, he will deliver us out of the furnace of flaming fire. . . . But even if not, be it known to you, O king, we will not serve your gods, nor prostrate ourselves before the image of gold which you have set up" (Dan. 3:17-18 Amer. Trans.).

12. *Honesty Is the Essential Policy.*—Let your yes be yes and your no be no, that you may not fall under condemnation. Again the words of James recall the teaching of Jesus (Matt. 5:33-37). Why is the swearing of oaths forbidden? The reference is not to what we call profanity, but to the practice of supporting a statement by an appeal to God. By swearing an oath of this sort a man's word is supposedly

oaths is the superlative sin, greater than all the others rebuked in the epistle? The extreme emphasis shows that this verse comes from the Christian editor, who (even though the saying has real parallels in Judaism) feels that here, where the relation to Matt. 5:34-37 is unmistakable, he is speaking with the direct authority of Jesus and therefore that what he is writing has unique importance. Conceivably, perhaps, the Jewish original had here, "But swear not at all, my brethren, lest you come into judgment" (a thoroughly rabbinical teaching), and the Christian editor has enlarged and emphasized what his predecessor wrote.

The verse may be paraphrased, "Abstain from all oaths, for they weaken a man's sense of obligation to speak the truth on all occasions; learn to make a simple 'Yes' or 'No' completely binding." Commentators note that the force is perhaps not quite the same as in Matt. 5:37, which means, "Never say more than 'Yes, yes' or 'No, no,'" where the doubling of the reply is conceivably to add emphasis; but this is fine spun and the distinction is of no consequence.

authenticated. If God is called to witness the assertion, the speaker will not dare to violate his word and, therefore, in that particular case at least, his word is to be trusted. If his word is not thus attested, one had better receive it with caution. *Caveat emptor.* In other words, where oaths are used, basic honesty founded on principle is not assumed. Whether the truth will be told or not will depend upon the circumstances. If the occasion is important enough, let the awesome fear of God be invoked and the words of the speaker be guaranteed by some such oath as "Heaven strike me dead if I am not telling the truth."

In the Sermon on the Mount and here the essential point is that no extraneous support afforded by oaths is needed by one who is really honest. The honest man's unsupported "Yes" or "No" can be fully trusted. Even with an oath, who can trust a man whose life is not built on the rock of sincerity?

The biblical emphasis upon honesty and sincerity needs to be recovered. "Thou desirest truth in the inward parts," says the psalmist (Ps. 51:6). Jesus apparently considered hypocrisy the chief menace to religion and morality. Consider his "woes" against duplicity as recorded in Matt. 23. One of the prime marks of the new life of the Christian, according to Paul, is honesty. "Therefore, putting away falsehood, let every one speak the truth with his neighbor, for we are members one of another" (Eph. 4:25). John, the seer, condemns all liars to the lake of fire which is the second death (Rev. 21:8).

Without honesty, the bottom drops out of all other virtues. Love is acclaimed the supreme quality of the Christian life, but Paul, who says that of faith, hope, and love, the greatest is love, also declares that love must be without hypocrisy (cf. "Your love must be genuine" [Rom. 12:9 Goodspeed]). Love that is not genuine is worse than no love at all. Honesty is the essence of moral courage, as was demonstrated in the life of Jesus. A white lie could have saved him from the Cross, but he would not utter it even though his life was at stake. The early Christians made their impression upon their contemporaries not simply because of the love they exemplified ("Behold how these Christians love one another"), but quite as much, if not more, by the integrity of their lives. Martyrs could have saved their lives by equivocation, but they would not. The transformation of the Greek word *martys*, meaning witness, into the present word martyr, meaning one who gives up his life for a cause, is evidence of this impression.

The opposite of honesty is deception and fraud. An American criminologist has stated that fraud is the most widespread criminal practice in our land, prevalent in respectable business circles as well as in the underworld. Is there not a widespread cynicism among us as to the reliability of the press, the advertisers, the lawyers, the politicians, or even the preachers? "Who knows what or whom to believe?" is a common question. Are we growing less honest? Certain it is that the structure of society is upheld by mutual trust; and apart from common agreements supported by good faith, all social and business relationships become suspect and undependable. See what happened in Germany when its rulers adopted the big lie as their propaganda weapon and the spy system undermined confidence of neighbor in neighbor. Truth is the first casualty of war, and war is the ultimate negation of all ethics.

Christ called his disciples "the salt of the earth." Christians today need to give an effective demonstration of simple and courageous honesty in order to help save our society from rotting at its core. Are Christians today distinguished for their integrity? Do people accept their "Yes" or "No" without other guarantee because they know that they are honest on

13 Is any among you afflicted? let him pray. Is any merry? let him sing psalms.
14 Is any sick among you? let him call for the elders of the church; and let them pray over him, anointing him with oil in the name of the Lord:

13 Is any one among you suffering? Let him pray. Is any cheerful? Let him sing praise. 14 Is any among you sick? Let him call for the elders of the church, and let them pray over him, anointing him with

XXIII. Total Consecration (5:13)

13. Again there is no logical connection between this verse and the preceding. The teaching that every emotion, joyful or sorrowful, is to be consecrated to God is of course fully as familiar to Judaism as Christianity. **Suffering** is a wholly general term, including both sorrow and sickness. At the end **let him sing psalms** (KJV) is an undue restriction of the verb rightly rendered **let him sing praise** (RSV). The translation in the KJV may have been influenced by the puritan insistence that the (divinely inspired) psalms alone were legitimate in Christian worship, but such a teaching was unknown to early Christianity; cf. "psalms and hymns and spiritual songs" (Col. 3:16).

XXIV. Sickness (5:14-18)

The theme was evidently suggested by "suffering" in vs. 13. When sickness occurs, two methods of relief are to be employed. The primary method is prayer: a theme continued beyond its application to sickness and generalized in vss. 16-18.

14. We have here something unique in James: a concrete reference to the official organization of the Christian community under the rule of **elders,** who had been formally ordained to their office (for details see the note on "Elders" in the Intro., pp. 15-16). Here it is evidently presupposed that by virtue of their ordination their prayer would have a particular efficacy. (**Pray over him** means, of course, "pray standing over the sickbed.") And then a second and distinct method of relief is directed: **anointing him with oil in the name of the Lord.** While it is perfectly true that the use of oil as a medicine was widespread in the ancient world (cf., e.g., Luke 10:34), it is not true at all that oil was regarded as a cure for every disease, no matter what its nature. Consequently, since here its use is commanded in all cases of sickness, something more than a merely medicinal effect is assumed; that the oil, when applied by the duly authorized elders of the church, in conjunction with their prayer, is believed to have a quasi-sacra-

principle, not simply on occasion? Ought it not to be so?

A sermon on this text will be enriched if Richard C. Cabot's book *Honesty* [7] is consulted. It ought to be in every minister's library.

13-14. *The Ministry of Healing.*—Is any among you sick? The Christian church, since the days of the Great Physician, has always been compassionate toward the suffering and the sick. Disease was not accepted fatalistically as the will of God, nor was suffering taken as an irremediable constituent of life. The hope of relief from noisome diseases and for the insane was generated when Jesus touched the lepers and cured those possessed of demons. It has been under the influence of Christian ideals that medicine has made its greatest progress. Christian medical missionaries in the Orient and Africa pioneered the creation of a new

[7] New York: The Macmillan Co., 1938.

attitude toward the sick and new methods and institutions for their cure. When David Livingstone went to Africa he said that his Master was a Teacher and a Physician and an imitation of him, even though a poor one, was what he hoped to be.

That faith in God can be an important factor in health has been rediscovered in recent years, and the new science of psychotherapy confirms some of the ancient Christian insights as to the relationship of mind and body. Prayer with and by the sick does not seem as irrational as the materialists of an earlier generation assumed. A man's total attitude to life, his faith or lack of it, affects his bodily condition. An integrating loyalty to God produces mental balance. A bad conscience can make one ill. Confession of sins may bring mental and bodily relief, and a sense of forgiveness can create new vigor for living.

15 And the prayer of faith shall save the sick, and the Lord shall raise him up; and if he have committed sins, they shall be forgiven him.

16 Confess *your* faults one to another, and pray one for another, that ye may be healed. The effectual fervent prayer of a righteous man availeth much.

oil in the name of the Lord; 15 and the prayer of faith will save the sick man, and the Lord will raise him up; and if he has committed sins, he will be forgiven. 16 Therefore confess your sins to one another, and pray for one another, that you may be healed. The prayer of a righteous

---

mental (or even wholly sacramental?) healing effect is unmistakable and never should have been denied (for further details see the note on "Unction" in the Intro., pp. 16-18). Here, however, it should be noted that the wording of vs. 14, after the opening question is past, is purely Christian and therefore **the Lord,** who gives healing, is Christ (Acts 3:6, 16; 9:32-34; etc.).

15. The emphasis shifts from anointing to prayer as the medium of healing; so completely so that the suggestion may be hazarded that the Jewish original of vs. 14 read, "Is any among you sick? Pray over him." The continuation of this teaching by vs. 15 makes not only good sense but certainly smoother sense than the present text; it is really plausible to argue that here the purely Christian directions about the elders and the anointing have been inserted into a passage that originally appealed to the universal Jewish (and Christian!) belief in the universal efficacy of prayer.

Save has the very common meaning "deliver from sickness," "heal" (Matt. 9:21; etc.), and **raise him up** likewise means "raise from the sickbed," "cure" (Matt. 9:5; etc.), while forgiveness of the sick man's sins is associated with healing because of the general belief that sickness is due to sin (Mark 2:5; John 9:2). The writer leaves this promise without qualification, although both he and his readers know perfectly well that not all cases of sickness will be healed; here as always when the efficacy of prayer is taught, the condition "if it be God's will" is to be tacitly understood. Nonetheless, everyone knows that where intense and vivid faith exists—and that such was the case when James was written may be taken for granted—extraordinary cures occur.

16. This verse continues the teaching of vs. 15, and **healed** has (at least ultimately, as one result of the forgiveness that follows confession) the same physical connotation as "save" and "raise up" in vs. 15; in every case of sickness there must be confession of sins (by the sick man) and prayer (by those visiting him but of course not excluding his own supplications). But "the elders of the church" are now not mentioned; not only is prayer **for one another** but confession is likewise **to one another.** This teaching is supported solely by texts drawn from the O.T. (vss. 17-18) and is therefore apparently of Jewish (rather than Christian) origin—an additional argument for holding that the

---

In the book *Body, Mind and Spirit*, by Elwood Worcester and Samuel McComb, it is stated:

It is now an ascertained fact that, other things being equal, the sick person who prays for himself and has others pray for him has a better chance of recovery than he who refuses the hope and stimulus that prayer can bestow. Through prayer we are united to God, and this union means increase of comfort and peace, which in turn help on the process of Nature's healing virtue.[8]

The whole discussion in this book is of high value in this connection.

[8] Boston: Marshall Jones Co., 1931, p. 308.

16b-18. Shall We Pray for Rain?—The reference to Elijah, who, because he was a righteous man, was able by praying to effect a drought that lasted three years and six months, is hardly as effective an encouragement to prayer as it was in days gone by. Our knowledge of modern science, the existence of weather bureaus and meteorologists, make us skeptical of such a tale. Have our changed notions as to the workings of nature affected our ideas of prayer? Undoubtedly, and sometimes disastrously. Many have lost all confidence that prayers, even of a righteous man, have any real effect.

This passage may well be taken as a point of departure in dealing with this change in mental

17 Elias was a man subject to like passions as we are, and he prayed earnestly that it might not rain: and it rained not on the earth by the space of three years and six months.

18 And he prayed again, and the heaven gave rain, and the earth brought forth her fruit.

19 Brethren, if any of you do err from the truth, and one convert him;

man has great power in its effects. 17 Elijah was a man of like nature with ourselves and he prayed fervently that it might not rain, and for three years and six months it did not rain on the earth. 18 Then he prayed again and the heaven gave rain, and the earth brought forth its fruit.

19 My brethren, if any one among you wanders from the truth and some one

mention of elders and anointing in vs. 14 is a Christian insertion into a Jewish original. It may be worth noting, however, that in the Jewish parallels collected in Strack-Billerbeck (IV, 576) confession of sins is enjoined only on those at point of death, and is associated with physical healing only in the sixteenth century.

17-18. The reference is to I Kings 17:1; 18:1, 42-45, as modified in later Jewish tradition. The O.T. text itself speaks only of a prophecy of Elijah, not of a prayer; but cf., e.g., Ecclus. 48:3, "By the word of the Lord he shut up the heaven." And **three years and six months** does not agree with "in the third year" of I Kings 18:1, but the phrase in James appears also in Luke 4:25. Possibly it is only a conventionally used round number; more probably the text is influenced by the "year, two years, and half a year" of Dan. 7:25; 12:7, a period appropriated in apocalyptic symbolism to denote the duration of evil (Rev. 12:6, 14; 13:5).

What Elijah accomplished, James emphasizes, was not the magical performance of a superhuman being but the act of a man in all regards exactly like ourselves, who simply used such prayer as we can likewise use. **Prayed fervently** (vs. 17) is in the Greek "prayed with prayer," a combination hardly idiomatic in good Greek and due doubtless to the writer's familiarity with the Greek version of the O.T., where similar combinations, representing an overliteral rendition of the Hebrew, are common. The combination really means only "prayed"; while of course any such effectual prayer would be "fervent," the addition of **fervently** or **earnestly** is a gloss not actually warranted by the text.

The tribal allusion in vss. 17-18—or possibly in the Jewish original of vss. 13-18 as a whole—would be to Joseph, who in the Testament of Joseph and other Jewish tradition is treated as eminently a man of prayer.

XXV. RECALL OF THE ERRING (5:19-20)

19-20. The concluding saying in these verses was possibly suggested by the mention of sin and confession in vss. 15-16, but this saying is complete in itself.

The wording is wholly Jewish; cf. Prov. 24:24-25, which may be rendered, "He who says to the wicked man, 'You are righteous,' peoples shall curse him, nations shall abhor

climate in order to show that a purified and more reasonable understanding of prayer is possible. William R. Inge writes:

If we think that we should like to control events by our prayers, let us consider how we should like the idea of our neighbour being able to control them by his. I once had a letter from a good lady who said, "I am praying for your death. I have been very successful in two other cases." . . . Providence does not begin where nature leaves off. Things are not specially "providential" because they suit our convenience. . . . If the order of nature is not broken by so-called supernatural interventions, the

probable reason is that the Author of nature is satisfied with the regular operations of His own laws.[9]

Inge defines prayer as "the elevation of the mind (or soul) to God," and quotes George Meredith, "He who rises from his knees a better man, his prayer has been granted."

19-20. The Ministry of Reconciliation.—The writer of this letter has leaped from subject to subject without obvious connection between his

[9] *A Rustic Moralist* (New York: G. P. Putnam's Sons; Toronto: McClelland & Stewart, 1937), pp. 78-80. Used by permission.

20 Let him know, that he which con-
verteth the sinner from the error of his
way shall save a soul from death, and shall
hide a multitude of sins.

brings him back, **20** let him know that whoever brings back a sinner from the error
of his way will save his soul from death
and will cover a multitude of sins.

---

him: but to those who rebuke the wicked man there shall be delight, and a good blessing
shall come upon them"; Lev. 19:17, "Thou shalt surely rebuke thy neighbor, and not
bear sin because of him" (ASV); Pirke Aboth 5:26, "He who leads many to virtue,
through him shall no sin befall." And for **cover . . . sins** cf. Ps. 32:1; Prov. 10:12; and
especially the familiar passage I Pet. 4:8, "Love covers a multitude of sins." While the
resemblance between Jas. 5:20 and I Pet. 4:8 is not close enough to indicate a dependence
of either writer on the other, it at least more than suggests that the language was familiar
in late Judaism and so in early Christianity.

The only debated problem in the interpretation is whether the "sins" that are
"covered" in vs. 20 are those of the one turned from error or those of the one who
turns him from error. The answer given only too often depends on the theological
presuppositions of the interpreter; the question being phrased thus, "Can a man who
performs the good work of converting an erring soul by this act cover a multitude of
his *own* sins?" According to strict "evangelical" teaching, good works, though ever so
numerous, can never atone for sins, though ever so few; consequently traditional
Protestant exegesis has usually insisted that the whole of vs. 20 must be applied to the
converted man, so that **save his soul from death** and **cover a multitude of sins** both mean
the same thing. But we have no right to assume that the writer of James thought in
these terms—as Luther long ago pointed out with perfect accuracy—and it seems far
more natural to read the two final clauses of vs. 20 as referring to two persons, not one;
to turn a sinner from error confers a double benefit, and helps not only the "converted"
soul but the "converting" soul as well. The parallel with Prov. 24:24-25 points in the
same direction. If, as there is no reason to doubt, this section was originally written by a
Jewish author, such would certainly have been its original meaning; and the Christian
editor would scarcely have thought of giving the saying a wholly new force.

---

themes, and now at the end his conclusion appears abrupt and in no sense climactic. Yet in
a way the final paragraph serves as an excellent
ending to the discourse, for it concludes on a
note of hope for those who go astray, rather
than on a note of fatal condemnation. The
hard words about renegades and the double-
minded are not retracted, but the possibility of
turning such persons from error to the truth
is held out.

Responsibility for this ministry of reconciliation is laid upon the ordinary Christian, not
just upon the minister or priest. **My brethren,
if any one among you wanders from the truth
and some one brings him back.** . . . There was
no sharp division between clergy and laity in
those days, and the rapid spread of Christianity
in the Roman world can be largely attributed
to the fact that the humblest of Christians accepted the responsibility of witnessing to the
gospel among pagan neighbors. Anyone who
found the pearl of great price enthusiastically
told others about it without waiting for an
official of the church to do it for him.

T. R. Glover [10] has pointed out that Jesus was
able to give to his disciples a compassionate concern for people whom society condemned as
hopeless, a concern which they handed on to
their successors and which the church has not
ever wholly lost. Jesus' parables of the lost
sheep, the lost coin, the lost son, his association
with publicans and sinners, the missionary passion of the early church, these all represent the
peculiar genius of Christianity and have made
it what it is. The state deals with the criminal
in terms of condemnation and punishment; the
church sees him as a wandering brother who
must be redeemed.

A Christian church is not a social club with
an exclusive membership; it is open to all on
the sole terms of repentance. Neither is it simply
an ethical culture society for the self-improvement of its members. It is the reconciling agent
of the kingdom which knows no boundaries; it
is the servant of the abundant love of God which
is for all peoples. He "reconciled us to himself

[10] *The Conflict of Religions in the Early Roman
Empire* (12th ed.; London: Methuen & Co., 1932), p. 130.

It is perhaps possible to detect a tribal allusion to Benjamin in vss. 19-20, for Philo (*On the Change of Names* 96) in his discussion of Benjamin's birth (Gen. 35:16-18) similarly uses "death" and "soul" in combination. While the resemblance is not very striking, we may at least note the appropriateness of concluding the tribal allusions with Jacob's youngest son; cf. the fact that these allusions began with Jacob's father, his mother, and Jacob himself (1:2-4).

The epistle closes, as is not unusual in paraenesis, with no indication that the end has been reached; there is no attempt to conclude with a climax and there is no farewell to the readers.

and gave us the ministry of reconciliation" (II Cor. 5:18). If a church in its rank and file does not function in this manner, then it is recreant to its high mission. Too many church members either have no faith to share or else lack enthusiasm to share it. They are willing to delegate that responsibility to the paid employees of the church. Perhaps they no longer believe that it is a matter of life or death, as James believed; no longer believe that to wander from the truth is disastrous. But can anyone look about him today and not tremble at the desperate state of the world which has traveled so recklessly the broad way to destruction? Is not the choice before us Christ or chaos?

The First Epistle of

PETER

Introduction and Exegesis by ARCHIBALD M. HUNTER
Exposition by ELMER G. HOMRIGHAUSEN

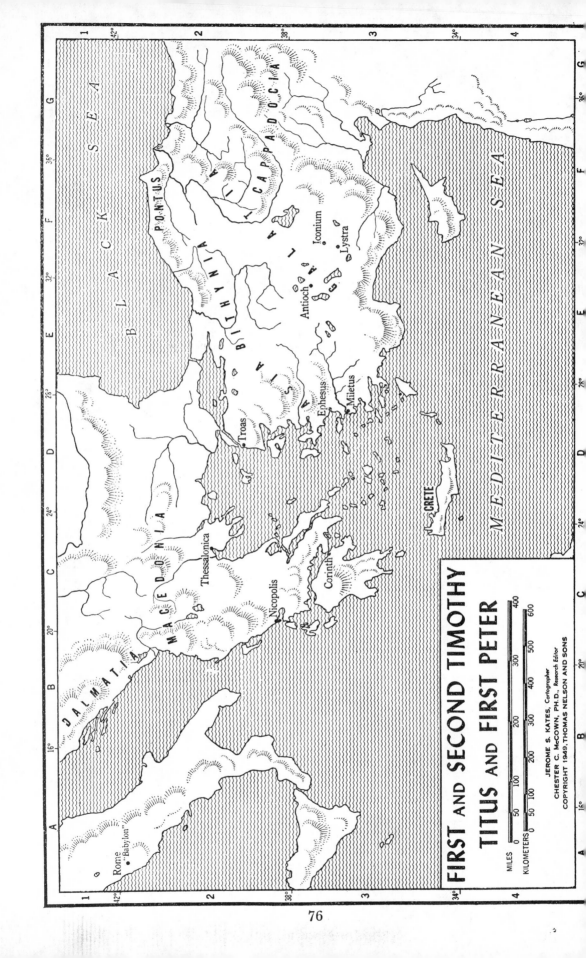

FIRST AND SECOND TIMOTHY
TITUS AND FIRST PETER

MILES
0   50   100   200   300   400

KILOMETERS
0   50   100   200   300   400   500   600

JEROME S. KATES, Cartographer
CHESTER C. McCOWN, PH.D., Research Editor
COPYRIGHT 1949, THOMAS NELSON AND SONS

I PETER

INTRODUCTION

This little letter has been variously described as "the Epistle of Courage," "the Epistle of Pilgrimage," and "the Epistle of Hope." All three titles can be justified. No one can fail to hear the note of courage that rings through it: courage in the teeth of trial and suffering, "not a grey, close-lipped stoicism" but the "true valor" of Bunyan's Christian that "come wind, come weather" will meet all life's ills and accidents in the strength of a superb faith in God and an unwavering trust in Christ. Nor can anyone miss the pilgrim note. "One idea haunts the whole epistle," it has been truly said; "to the author, as to the patriarch Jacob, life is a pilgrimage." Yet the dominant theme, it may be noted, is neither courage nor pilgrimage. It is hope: not the wistful, nebulous optimism that in the end things will turn out all right, which so often passes for hope; but religious hope, hope that rests not on man but on God, the living God who is known by his mighty acts, the God who raised Jesus Christ from the dead and gave him glory that our faith and hope might be in him, and who holds out to the faithful pilgrim at his journey's ending the promise of an inheritance incorruptible and undefiled and that fadeth not away.

Among the shorter writings of the New Testament there are few more attractive than this. "The First Epistle of Peter," says B. H. Streeter, "is one of the finest things in the New Testament." [1] "This gallant and high-hearted exhortation," writes J. W. C. Wand, ". . . breathes a spirit of undaunted courage and exhibits as noble a type of piety as can be found in any writing of the New Testament outside the gospels." [2] "An Epistle truly worthy of the chief of the Apostles," said Calvin, "full of apostolic authority and majesty."

But can we believe that this epistle comes to us charged with the authority of the chief of the apostles? Tradition, as we shall see, answers "Yes"; but we live in an age of criticism which will accept nothing on mere authority, and it is not surprising that many scholars have rejected the verdict of tradition. Moreover, the whole question of the date of the epistle is bound up with that of authorship. We must therefore, first of all, see whether external and internal evidence supports the Petrine authorship.

I. Authorship

"Peter, an apostle of Jesus Christ," the epistle begins. Very near its ending (5:12) we read, "By Silvanus, a faithful brother as I regard him, I have written briefly to you." The letter purports to have been written by the apostle Peter with the help of Silvanus, who is probably Paul's old comrade, called, in Acts, Silas for short.

External evidence supports this claim. Indeed, there is no book in the New Testament which has earlier or better attestation, and attempts to shake the strength of that evidence (e.g., Streeter, *The Primitive Church*) have not succeeded. All the relevant testimony cannot be given here, but these are the four chief pieces:

(a) Clement of Rome, writing *ca.* A.D. 95, echoes the language of I Peter. (Lightfoot counts twelve parallelisms and Harnack

[1] *The Primitive Church* (New York: The Macmillan Co., 1929), p. 124.

[2] *The General Epistles of St. Peter and St. Jude* (London: Methuen & Co., 1934), p. 1.

twenty.) Barnabas and Hermas also seem to have known I Peter.

(b) Polycarp, who died ca. A.D. 155, is steeped in the language of I Peter.

(c) Irenaeus, who wrote ca. A.D. 185, testifies, "Peter says in his epistle, 'Whom though you see him not, etc.' " [3]

(d) Eusebius, the father of church history, who classified the sacred writings as "accepted," "disputed," and "spurious," placed I Peter in the first category.

The absence of any reference to I Peter in the Muratorian Canon (a list of books deemed canonical in Rome toward the end of the second century) is probably due to the fragmentariness of the document. Clearly the epistle was reckoned canonical from the time when the word "canonical" began to have any meaning. In the words of "The Thirty-nine Articles," it is one of the books "of whose authority there was never any doubt in the Church." And the church's unanimity about its authority is very hard to explain unless its claim to Petrine authorship be really true.

Does a study of the internal evidence confirm or refute this claim?

Many modern scholars reject the testimony of tradition. They challenge the Petrine authorship on four main grounds:

(a) The letter shows a command of the Greek language incredible in a person like Peter.

(b) It is clearly indebted to Paulinism.

(c) It does not bear the marks of one who had known Jesus and heard his teaching.

(d) It implies a time when the mere profession of Christianity was a crime—that is, the first decade of the second century.

If these objections can be sustained, there is obviously an end to the Petrine authorship. We must examine them one by one.

(a) Peter (the first objection runs) could not have written the Greek of this epistle.

It is possible to exaggerate the excellence of the Greek; yet it must be admitted that the writer of I Peter could write Greek freely and with some literary skill. Could Peter have done this? Although we do not know much about his literary attainments, the New Testament does not lead us to believe that Peter was a skilled writer in Greek. A Galilean like Peter must have had some understanding of the koine, or common Greek, which was the lingua franca of the age; but there is no basis for supposing that he could write the language with a sense for correctness and idiom.

If then we were shut up to the view that Peter must have written this epistle without

[3] *Against Heresies* IV. 9. 2.

help from another, the case for the Petrine authorship would have to be abandoned at once. But the letter expressly tells us that in the writing of it Peter had the help of Silvanus. "By Silvanus . . . I have written briefly to you" (5:12). Thus, it seems clear, Silvanus had a share in the composition of the epistle. We may well believe that in this case Silvanus acted as a trusted secretary who was given considerable scope in interpreting his master's mind. Furthermore, we have evidence that Silvanus was just such a person as could have written the good Greek of the letter.

To begin with, there is no reason for disputing the identity of this man with the Silvanus who is named as the joint author, with Paul and Timothy, of the Thessalonian epistles, nor again his identity with the Silas of Acts. Now this man was clearly a person of considerable gifts and ability. We know that he was a member of the mother church in Jerusalem and was sent by them as an accredited delegate to the church at Antioch (Acts 15:22, 32). Further, we know not only that he was a Roman citizen (Acts 16:37), but that he was a coadjutor of Paul during the momentous second missionary journey which took the gospel to Greece and Europe. A man who was chosen to draft and convey the apostolic decree to the Gentile churches, who could preach the gospel in Greek to Gentiles, who had journeyed far and wide on Gentile soil with Paul, was clearly one well able to write the Greek of I Peter. We need therefore worry no more about "the good Greek" of the epistle. We may reasonably hold, with most English-speaking scholars, that in I Peter the voice may well be Peter's voice, though the literary hand is the hand of Silvanus.

(b) But (the objector will proceed) the epistle is too full of Paulinism to be the work of Peter.

The objection seems fair enough till you ask, "What precisely is Paulinism?" Then it becomes much less cogent. For the time is past when scholars could picture Paul as a spiritual pioneer voyaging alone through strange seas of thought, and practically every idea in his epistles could be set down as the invention of his own seminal mind. We are now able to see that a great deal of what we once labeled "Paulinism" is really common, apostolic Christianity.[4] But, to come down to particulars, what evidence is there in I Peter that the writer has borrowed freely from Paul? The usual answer is that the letter shows clear knowledge of both Ephesians and Romans. But I think we may at once affirm that the case for the dependence of

[4] See Archibald M. Hunter, *Paul and His Predecessors* (London: Student Christian Movement Press, 1940).

I Peter on Ephesians is, to say the least, highly dubious. When one examines the alleged parallels, one finds that they amount to no more than a few phrases like "blessed be God" (which any pious Jew might have used), and some instructions to husbands and wives, masters and slaves, which, as Weidinger and Dibelius have shown, were derived from a common ethical tradition used by all the apostolic writers. The case for a dependence of I Peter on Romans looks at first sight to be stronger. Examined in detail, it loses impressiveness. For of the eight passages listed by Sanday and Headlam as showing Peter's dependence on Romans, two are Old Testament prophecies, two give lists of common Christian duties, a fifth is semiliturgical, a sixth depends on thought rather than words, and the last two are quite doubtful.[5] None of them is enough to prove Peter's dependence on Paul. On the other hand, there are such decided differences between I Peter and the Pauline epistles as to make any case for dependence extremely precarious. It is not only that the great Pauline doctrines like justification by faith are conspicuous by their absence, but that even in small details like the nuances of words (compare, for example, Peter's use of the words "grace" and "soul" with Paul's), Peter gives no hint that he had sat (spiritually) at the feet of Paul.

On the other hand, to say all this is not to say that here and there we may not find a phrase in I Peter which may have sprung originally from the brain of Paul. After all, Silvanus, who helped Peter in the writing of this letter, had been too long in the company of Paul not to have caught something of his "great accents." Could any man live long with Paul and not find himself using some of his phrases? Besides, it is probable that the Epistle to the Romans, written about A.D. 56, was already a treasured possession in the church at Rome, where, as we shall see, I Peter was almost certainly written.

In fine, the second objection is no more decisive than the first.

(c) The third objection may be handled more briefly. To say that the epistle shows little knowledge of the life and teaching of our Lord is simply not true. Let us recall, first, that the epistle runs to no more than 105 verses and, second, that its main purpose was not to reveal the writer's knowledge of Jesus, but to fortify a suffering church; and then, I think, we may well marvel at the number of references there are to Jesus' life and of quotations of his teaching.

The writer implies that he had seen Jesus (1:8) in a way that his readers had not. In 5:1

[5] See Wand, *General Epistles of St. Peter and St. Jude*, p. 19.

he probably claims to have been a witness of the Transfiguration (see Exeg.), as he expressly claims to have been a witness of Jesus' sufferings. Moreover, his language shows a knowledge of the foot washing (5:5; see Exeg.) and of the trial of Jesus (2:21-24), while his command, "Tend the flock of God" (5:2), is most easily interpreted as a reminiscence of the command which the risen Jesus had given to Peter (John 21:17). As for the moral teaching of Jesus, we shall see, when we come to consider the theology of the epistle, that there are at least ten echoes of Jesus' sayings in the Gospels. So far then from marveling at the meagerness of the references to Jesus in the days of his flesh, we are surprised to find so many, and would rather argue that these references point the other way, and are confirmatory evidence that Peter stands behind this letter.

(d) The last objection, which incidentally involves also the question of date, is that the letter implies a time when the mere profession of Christianity was a crime, that is, a time about the beginning of the second century, which Peter could not possibly have lived to see.

The references to suffering and persecution in the letter are as follows: 1:6; 2:12, 15; 4:12 ff.; 5:9. All these are of a quite general character except 4:12 ff.: "Beloved, do not be surprised at the fiery ordeal which comes upon you to prove you . . . . But rejoice in so far as you share Christ's sufferings, that you may also rejoice and be glad when his glory is revealed. If you are reproached for the name of Christ, you are blessed, because the spirit of glory and of God rests upon you. But let none of you suffer as a murderer, or a thief, or a wrongdoer, or a mischief-maker; yet if one suffers as a Christian, let him not be ashamed, but under that name let him glorify God."

This passage (note especially "if one suffers as a Christian") must have been written, so it is argued, in the time of Pliny, *ca.* A.D. 112, because Pliny's famous rescript to Trajan is the first evidence we have of Christians being punished for the mere profession of Christianity.

But this is surely a very rash conclusion. For, in the first place, the word "suffer" is quite general and need not involve more than public malevolence and abuse such as was the lot of Christians from the earliest days of the faith. But suppose we grant that the context demands that we take "suffer" in the sense of "be punished by the state," we have no right to declare dogmatically that such punishment was first inflicted in the time of the Emperor Trajan. On the contrary, as J. V. Bartlet has pointed out, if Paul was condemned to death by Nero in A.D. 62, the mere profession of Christianity must have become a crime very generally. In short, there is nothing in the language of I Peter which compels us to believe that it could not have been written before the beginning of the second century.

To sum up: We have surveyed both the external and the internal evidence. External attestation, as we have seen, is very strong. The general tone and temper of the epistle suggests that it comes down to us from the early days of the faith, nor can any of the objections raised against Petrine authorship be sustained. We may therefore safely accept the tradition which links this epistle with the apostle Peter. The only qualification we need make is that probably Silvanus had a large share in the actual composition of the letter. Peter wrote, as we have seen, with the help of Silvanus; and in a case like this, remembering of course that the apostle probably had no great facility in Greek, we may suppose that the usage was exactly the same as that which still prevails in Eastern life—the great man dictates to his secretary the terms of his proposed communication, perhaps revises it rapidly, and maybe adds a few words of his own.[6]

II. Date and Place of Writing

Where then did Peter write his letter with Silvanus' help? The clue is to be found in 5:13, which may be rendered, "She that is in Babylon elect together with you saluteth you." "She" *might* be Peter's wife or even some noble patroness of the church—a primitive Countess of Huntingdon, as it were! But scholars are practically unanimous that "she" designates the local church from which Peter wrote. "Your sister-church in Babylon," Moffatt boldly and rightly translates. The real crux is the meaning of "Babylon." Can this be the once-renowned city on the Euphrates? This is just possible; but since there is not a scrap of evidence that Peter ever was there, scholars are fairly well agreed that Babylon here must be, as it is in Revelation (see Rev. 14:8; etc.), a cryptic name for Rome.

From our discussion of the authorship it will be obvious that the letter must have been written some time in the sixties of the first century, that is, within the lifetime of Peter, who, according to a tradition there is no reason to doubt, was martyred in the reign of the Emperor Nero. The Neronian persecution broke out in A.D. 64, and many scholars, who think that we must allow time for the persecution to have spread from Rome to the provinces, date the letter about A.D. 67. Two facts incline us

[6] For fuller statements of the case for and against the theory of Petrine authorship see the commentaries of Selwyn and Beare, cited below, p. 85.

to put the letter just before the outbreak of the actual persecution. One is the fact that it is still possible for Peter to counsel loyalty to the emperor (2:13-17). The other is that the language of the epistle suggests an impending rather than an actual persecution. Peter is preparing his readers for a blow that is about to fall rather than one that has already fallen. It seems likely, then, that Peter wrote just after the martyrdom of Paul in 62, but just before the great outrage of 64, in expectation that the local authorities in Asia Minor would enforce the law against the Christians; for this reason he used "Babylon" for Rome as a precautionary disguise.

III. Occasion and Readers

We need not dwell on the occasion of the letter. Its purpose was to fortify the Christians in Asia Minor to stand fast in their Christian loyalties against the worst that persecution could do. This Peter does by recalling the noble example of their Lord in the face of unmerited suffering and death, and by pointing his readers to the heavenly inheritance laid up for all those prepared to follow in the steps of Christ.

And now, last of all, a word on the readers. These are described in the first verse of the epistle as "the exiles of the dispersion in Pontus, Galatia, Cappadocia, Asia, and Bithynia." These five countries—or rather provinces—roughly correspond to what is known as Asia Minor. The word "dispersion" might at first sight suggest that the readers were Jews dispersed throughout Asia Minor. Closer study of the epistle will show that the greater number of the readers must have been originally pagans (see, e.g., 2:10; 4:3). On the other hand, it is also morally certain that in this case, as in the case of the Pauline churches, there must have been an original nucleus of Jewish Christians. But this is a secondary matter, as F. J. A. Hort observes, compared with a right understanding of the way in which Peter applies to the whole collection of Asiatic churches, Gentiles and Jews alike, the language which the Old Testament uses to describe the privileges of the people of God:

The truth is that St Peter, as doubtless every other apostle, regarded the Christian Church as first and foremost the true Israel of God, the one legitimate heir of the promises made to Israel, the one community which by receiving Israel's Messiah had remained true to Israel's covenant, while the unbelieving Jews in refusing their Messiah had in effect apostatised from Israel. This point of view was not in the least weakened by the admission of Gentile Christians in any number or proportion.

In St Paul's words they were but branches grafted in upon the one ancient olive tree of God.[7]

One final point to remember: I Peter is probably a circular letter like Ephesians. Look again at the Asiatic provinces named in the opening verse, and pick them out carefully on a map. Why this particular order? It can hardly be fortuitous. It is an old suggestion, but one which has never been bettered or disproved, that the order in which these provinces are named represents the circular route which the bearer of this letter was meant to take. He would begin in Pontus and go around the Christian churches in Galatia, Cappadocia, and Asia, ending his journey in Bithynia.

IV. Summary of Contents

A short paraphrase of the letter will best summarize its contents.

After greeting the churches in Asia Minor as the true Israel of God, Peter breaks into a recital of their *blessings* as God's redeemed children:

"Thanks be to God who by Christ's resurrection has kindled in our hearts a living hope of a heavenly inheritance. Let your present trials serve only to purify your faith; the reward of faithful endurance is final salvation. This is the salvation which prophets of old longed to see and into which even angels desire to look. So, remembering you have been redeemed by the sacrifice of the sinless Lamb of God, live holy lives and love one another heartily. You are newborn children of God; so be done with evil and grow up into that spiritual temple of which Christ is the cornerstone. To some the stone is a stumbling block; but you who believe in him are God's own people, summoned to declare the wonderful deeds of him who called you out of darkness into light." (1:3–2:10.)

Next, Peter describes their *duties* as Christians in the world:

"Let your good conduct silence your heathen critics. Be subject to the civil authorities as divinely ordained. Let servants obey their masters even if it means innocent suffering: by so doing, they will follow in the steps of Jesus whose suffering has redeemed them from sin. Let wives be submissive to their husbands, and show that modesty in dress and gentleness of spirit which God approves. (Such a woman was Sarah of old.) Husbands, for their part, should be considerate and chivalrous to their wives. And all should be sympathetic, loving, forgiving, as the psalmist counsels. Suffering for righteousness' sake is blessed. So make Christ Lord

in your hearts; be ready to answer all who ask why you are Christians; and follow Christ who died for sins and went and preached to the spirits in prison. The saving of Noah's household by water in the days of the Flood has now its counterpart in Christian baptism. Live henceforth not for the flesh but for the doing of God's will. If your former pagan neighbors, surprised at your behavior, abuse you, leave them to the Judge of both living and dead. Since the end is near, be sober and prayerful; above all, show love and hospitality, and use your gifts for men's service and God's glory." (2:11–4:11.)

Finally, Peter deals with their *trials* in the world:

"Do not be surprised at your coming ordeal. Remember Christ also had to suffer. In suffering of this kind there is blessedness and, at last, glory. Judgment is beginning, and if it starts with the church, what will happen to unbelievers? As your fellow elder and a witness of Christ's sufferings, I bid you elders tend the flock of God willingly, eagerly, and selflessly. On the great day the chief Shepherd will reward you. Cast all your worry on God who cares for you. Be vigilant—the devil walks abroad—and be ready to suffer with your Christian brothers elsewhere in the world. When your suffering is past, God will restore and strengthen you." (4:12–5:11.)

So with a commendation of Silvanus, his trusty secretary, and a greeting from the Christians in "Babylon," Peter rounds his letter off with some greetings and a blessing.

V. Theology of I Peter

A. *Relationship to the Earliest Christian Tradition.*—In the First Epistle of Peter we seem to be in touch with primitive Christianity. The letter does not read like a document emanating from the end of the first century or the beginning of the second. Alike in its doctrine and in its church organization, it shows no sign of the later ecclesiastical developments; rather, it reminds us of the faith and practice of the earliest church as portrayed in the opening chapters of the Acts of the Apostles.

This is the first impression the letter makes on us, and the impression grows stronger and stronger as we study the letter more closely.

What was the Christian tradition in the earliest form we can discover by the methods of modern scholarship? To answer that question one must summarize the findings of some recent research. If there is one thing that New Testament scholars are making clearer than any other, it is that the essence of the earliest gospel was a story, or rather, a proclamation—the

---

[7] *The First Epistle of St Peter* (London: Macmillan & Co., 1898), p. 7.

proclamation of Jesus Christ, crucified and risen. We err gravely if we suppose that the heart of the earliest gospel was the Sermon on the Mount or any similar ethical manifesto. For the first Christians the primary thing was the Cross on the hill and the empty tomb rather than the Sermon on the Mount. It was only to people who had already accepted the message of the crucified and risen Lord that the apostolic preachers transmitted the sayings of the Sermon on the Mount and other ethical teaching. What was preached in the first instance was what God had done for men in the life, death, and resurrection of Jesus the Messiah.

In the beginning, then, was the proclamation. Afterward, as a sort of corollary, came the ethics or moral teaching. In other words, the earliest Christian tradition had two strands, a primary and a secondary. The primary strand was the proclamation, or to give it its Greek name, the *kerygma* (which means, by the way, not the act of preaching, but the thing preached). The secondary strand was the teaching (that is, of Jesus), or to give it its Greek name, the *didachē*. These two strands—the proclamation and the teaching, or more simply, the gospel and the commandment—we can trace in the Gospels; for Mark, properly understood, is simply an expansion of the *kerygma,* and the excerpts from the sayings-source called Q, which we can discover in Matthew and Luke, represent the *didachē*.[8]

We have now to show that both these strands are fully represented in I Peter. But to begin with, let us summarize the *kerygma* as it has been laid bare by modern scholarship:

God's promises made to his people in the Old Testament are now fulfilled.

The long-expected Messiah has come.

He is Jesus of Nazareth, who

went about doing good and wrought mighty works by God's power;

was crucified according to the purpose of God;

was raised by God from the dead and exalted to his right hand.

He will come again for judgment.

This message, with an appeal to all who heard it to repent, be baptized, and receive the forgiveness of their sins, was in essence the message of the earliest apostles, Peter among them.

Now it is obvious that this message finds expression in I Peter. To be sure, Peter's primary

[8] For the proof of all this the reader should study C. H. Dodd, *The Apostolic Preaching and Its Developments* (London: Hodder & Stoughton, 1936). See also the article, "The Gospel in the New Testament," Vol. VII, pp. 3-31.

aim is not to expound that message; he is writing to men and women who had already heard and accepted it. His real aim is to exhort them to stand fast in the face of suffering and persecution. Nevertheless, the authentic notes of the *kerygma* ring out in the course of his exhortation.

"The old prophecies are fulfilled in the gospel" is the meaning of those rather difficult verses, 1:10-12: "The prophets who prophesied of the grace that was to be yours searched and inquired about this salvation; they inquired what person or time was indicated by the Spirit of Christ within them when predicting the sufferings of Christ and the subsequent glory. It was revealed to them that they were serving not themselves but you, in the things which have now been announced to you by those who preached the good news to you through the Holy Spirit sent from heaven, things into which angels long to look."

This good news or gospel, as Peter goes on to say in his letter, centers in Jesus the Messiah. It is not that Peter sets out to prove Jesus is the Messiah—a procedure that might not have carried very much conviction with Gentiles who had not the requisite messianic background, and to whom χριστός (the Greek for the Hebrew Messiah) would mean simply "smeared." Rather, it is the cumulative way in which Peter sets out Jesus as the fulfillment of the Old Testament yearnings for a Savior which gives meaning to the clause, "The long-expected Messiah has come."

If Peter—as also Paul in his epistles—does not dwell on the preaching and healing ministry of Jesus, he is very insistent that the death of Jesus was "according to the will of God," as revealed in the Scriptures. In the pre-Pauline creed which Paul quotes in I Cor. 15:3, the first article was that "Christ died for our sins according to the scriptures." The scriptures are not specified, but beyond all reasonable doubt Isa. 53 is meant. Peter is therefore simply expanding that first article when, in 2:21-24, he describes the passion of Jesus in language which takes us back to the great prophecy of the suffering servant of the Lord (see Exeg.).

"Jesus was raised by God from the dead and exalted to his right hand." There is hardly need to adduce proof that this clause of the *kerygma* occurs in I Peter. The letter begins (1:3) with a *Te Deum* for the living hope that God has given us by raising Christ from the dead; later, Christians are described as those who, through Jesus Christ, are believers "in God, who raised him from the dead and gave him glory" (1:21); and ch. 3 ends with a reference to "the resurrection of Jesus Christ, who has gone into heaven and is at the right hand of God, with angels, authorities, and powers subject to him" (3:21-22).

The testimony of the apostolic preaching to Christ generally ended with a clause affirming the expectation of his second coming as judge. This element is well attested in I Peter. Peter speaks of the time when Jesus Christ shall be revealed in his glory (1:7, 13; 4:13; 5:1), bids his readers look forward to the day when "the chief Shepherd is manifested" (5:4), and refers to "him who is ready to judge the living and the dead" (4:5).

It is clear, then, that the first and primary strand of the earliest Christian tradition, the *kerygma,* controls the thought of I Peter.

We turn now to consider the second strand, which we have called the *didachē,* that is, the tradition of Jesus' moral teaching which was treasured as a guide and pattern for Christian living. The following parallel columns will tell their own story:

I Peter	Ethical Teaching of Jesus
1:13. Therefore gird up your minds.	Luke 12:35. Let your loins be girded.
1:17. If you invoke as Father, etc.	Luke 11:2. When you pray, say: Father, etc.
2:12. That . . . they may see your good deeds and glorify God on the day of visitation.	Matt. 5:16. That they may see your good works and give glory to your Father who is in heaven.
3:9. Do not return evil for evil or reviling for reviling; but on the contrary bless.	Luke 6:28. Bless those who curse you, pray for those who abuse you.
3:14. If you do suffer for righteousness' sake, you will be blessed.	Matt. 5:10. Blessed are those who are persecuted for righteousness' sake.
4:5. They will give account to him who is ready to judge the living and the dead.	Matt. 12:36. I tell you, on the day of judgment men will render account for every careless word they utter.
4:14. If you are reproached for the name of Christ, you are blessed.	Matt. 5:11. Blessed are you when men revile you . . . on my account.
5:6. Humble yourselves therefore under the mighty hand of God, that in due time he may exalt you.	Luke 14:11. He who humbles himself will be exalted.
5:7. Cast all your anxieties on him, for he cares about you.	Matt. 6:25 ff. Do not be anxious about your life. . . . Your heavenly Father knows that you need them all.

Nor is this all. When Peter says that "the prophets . . . searched and inquired about this salvation" (1:10), he is echoing Christ's great beatitude of Luke 10:23-24, "Blessed are the eyes which see the things that ye see; for I tell you that many prophets and kings have desired to see those things which ye see, and have not seen them." When he applies to Christ Ps. 118:22, "The very stone which the builders rejected has become the head of the corner" (2:7), he is simply doing what he had heard his Master doing in Jerusalem (Mark 12:10). When he bids his fellow elders "tend the flock of God" (5:2), we recall the command of Christ to Peter, "Feed my sheep" (John 21:17). And when he says, "Put on the apron of humility to serve one another" (5:5 Moffatt), surely it is Christ's deed and word recorded in John 13:4 ff. which is in his mind.

Once again, then, it is clear that though he did not set himself to expound the *didachē* of his Master, Peter's thought is colored and controlled by the words of him who spake as never man spake. The epistle is penetrated and pervaded by both elements, or strands, the *kerygma* and the *didachē,* which made up the original and unchanging content of the church's common faith in the earliest days. Ever since, despite all changes of theological climate, faithfulness to that gospel and commandment is the test of "a standing or falling church."

B. The Doctrine of God.—The doctrine of God in I Peter is just such as we might have expected from the apostle. It is the Jewish conception of the living God, creator of all things (4:9), transcendent and holy (1:15), long-suffering and gracious (3:20; 5:10), who had chosen Israel to be his own people. Thus far Peter is the Jew; but Peter was one who had learned in the school of Jesus to call God "Father," and who had experienced the mightiest of God's mighty acts in the resurrection of Jesus Christ from the dead; and these two facts transform his whole idea of God. For now God has become for Peter, as for all the early Christians, "the God and Father of our Lord Jesus Christ" (1:3), and when they kneel in prayer, it is this Father-God whom they invoke (1:17). Yet, if God is Father, he is *holy* Father, for Peter time and again insists that we must approach him with reverence and awe (1:17; 3:2, 15), and he has hardly called him Father when he insists that he is also Judge (1:17). But— and this is perhaps the characteristic note of the epistle—God is the God of the Resurrection, the God whose abundant mercy was supremely shown when he raised Christ from the dead and gave him glory, that our faith and hope might be in him (1:3, 21).

C. The Doctrine of Christ and His Work.—
In I Peter many titles are applied to Christ.
For example, he is the Living Stone, the Chief
Shepherd, the Just One. But for Peter, Jesus
Christ—he never uses the simple name Jesus—
is pre-eminently the Lord (2:3; 3:15) and the
Risen One (1:3, 21; 3:21), who has trodden the
path of the Suffering Servant (2:21-24) and is
now in the highest place that heaven affords
(3:22). If we go on to examine details, we find
that for Peter, Jesus Christ is the Pre-existent
One (see 1:20: Only that can be manifested
which was in being before it was manifested),
the Sinless One (1:19), and the head of the new
people of God which is the church (5:4). More
significant perhaps, he is one to whom the name
of Lord given to Yahweh in the Old Testament
can be applied (2:3; 3:15); he is one who, so
far as men's salvation is concerned, stands side
by side with the Father and the Spirit (1:2).
But most significant of all, possibly, is the brief
phrase in 1:21, "who by him do believe in
God." Peter does not mean that his readers did
not believe in God before they believed in
Christ. He means that the only adequate form
of belief in God is belief in God through Christ.
The God in whom the Christian believes is the
God who is the Father of our Lord Jesus Christ,
the God who gave him up for us, who raised
him from the dead and exalted him to his right
hand.

The references to the atoning death of Christ
are to be found in 1:1, 18-19; 2:21-24; 3:18. All
of them are intensely practical: in other words,
Peter holds up Christ in his death to his readers
as an example of how suffering should be borne.
But his own view of the Atonement is far from
being a merely "exemplarist" one. Observe too
how varied are the ways in which Christ's
death is conceived. In one place Christ is the
Christians' Paschal Lamb (1:18-19), in another
he is the Suffering Servant of God (2:22), and
it is just possible that in 2:24 he is thought of
as the Scapegoat (see Lev. 16:20 ff.).

When we try to sort out Peter's thoughts
about the death of Christ, we find him saying
three things: (a) Christ "bore" the sins of
men, that is, took upon himself their consequences (2:24); (b) Christ "ransomed" men
from their sins (1:18-19); and (c) Christ by his
blood covered men's sins so that they might
enter into covenant with God (1:2).

Christ's death, then, is central to Peter's conception of Christianity. Its purpose was twofold:
to bring us to God (3:18) and to enable us to
live righteously (2:24). But if there is no clear-
cut doctrine of atonement, two words—"sacrifice" and "substitution"—describe the author's
approach to Christ's work. In all the main

references the thought of Christ's death as an
expiatory sacrifice is implicit. Furthermore, the
thought of substitution lies at the heart of both
2:24 and 3:18. As James Denney puts it, "Whoever says 'He bore our sins' says substitution."[9]
Nor are the two ideas mutually exclusive.[10]

D. The Doctrine of the Spirit.—The doctrine
of the Holy Spirit is not so prominent in I Peter
as it is, say, in Paul's epistles; but there is
enough evidence to show that in this, as in other
doctrines, Peter represented what has been
called "central Christianity."

In 1:12 the words "the Holy Spirit sent from
heaven" no doubt refer to the day of Pentecost
(Acts 2). Christians are "elect," Peter says, in
virtue of their consecration by the Spirit (1:2)
—a reference doubtless to the reception of the
Spirit at baptism. They form "a spiritual house"
(2:5) in which Christ is the chief cornerstone,
and their function is to offer "spiritual sacrifices"
to God. On them as Christians the Spirit of God
rests (4:14). And that there is no hard and
fast line of demarcation between the Spirit of
the new dispensation and that which wrought
in the seers of the old covenant is shown by
the reference in 1:11 to "the Spirit of Christ"
which inspired the prophets "who prophesied
of the grace that should come unto you."

E. The Doctrine of the Church.—If the actual
word "church" (ἐκκλησία) does not occur in
the epistle, the thing itself is everywhere present.

Peter speaks of the church in three ways. To
begin with, like the other New Testament
writers, he thinks of it as the true *people of
God*. The old people of God had comprised
only Jews; the new one embraces both Jews and
Gentiles. "Once you were no people," he tells
them, "but now you are God's people" (2:10),
and he applies to the Christian church the
various titles of honor which had once belonged
to the old Israel (2:9-10).

Second, he speaks of the church as a *spiritual
temple* (2:5). (Some such conception had been
in his Master's mind; see Mark 14:58; John
2:19.) In this spiritual temple Christ is the
chief cornerstone, and believers, who are also
"living stones," are aligned to him in a spiritual
unity. And with this description is combined
another: Christians are not only the stones of
which the temple is built; they are also the
body of priests in the temple who offer the
spiritual sacrifices which are its primary purpose
(2:5).

Finally, the church is *the flock of God*. Centuries before, Ezekiel had pictured the Messiah

[9] *The Death of Christ* (London: Hodder & Stoughton,
1903), p. 100.
[10] See O. C. Quick, *Doctrines of the Creed* (New
York: Charles Scribner's Sons, 1938), p. 235.

and his church under the similitude of a shepherd and his sheep (Ezek. 34). Jesus himself had regarded his disciples—the church in nucleus—as the "little flock" (Luke 12:32) of which he was Shepherd, and had looked for a time when "other sheep" would be included in it (John 10:16). Now in I Peter we see the thing come to pass; for Peter speaks of the church as "the flock of God" (5:2) and of Christ as "the chief Shepherd" (5:4).

People, temple, flock—so Peter conceives of the church, whose rite of initiation is baptism (3:21), defined, one might translate, as "not the removal of dirt from the body but the pledge of a good conscience toward God," and whose sacred function it is to "declare the wonderful deeds of him who called you out of darkness into his marvelous light" (2:9).

F. The Christian Hope.—No account of the theology of I Peter could be complete without a reference to that "hope" which glows through it and which has led many to call it "the Epistle of Hope." This hope is (in Paul's phrase) "the hope which is laid up for you in heaven," and it rests on the resurrection of Jesus Christ from the dead (1:3).

For Peter the end of all things is at hand and the supernal kingdom of God is near—nay, has already begun with Christ's death and resurrection. Peter's favorite name for this "salvation ready to be revealed in the last time" is "the revelation of Jesus Christ" (1:7, 13; 4:13): the unveiling of Christ in all his celestial glory. Indeed, "glory" (one of the epistle's commonest words) is a synonym for that final salvation which comes with Christ's second coming (4:13; 5:1), and a "crown of glory" is the reward that is promised to Christ's faithful ones (5:4). That there will be a last judgment, when the faithful will be rewarded and the wicked will receive just retribution for their sins, Peter does not doubt (4:5, 17-18).

Of the nature of that heavenly world Peter has little to say, but that little is suggestive. He calls it the Christians' "inheritance"—a new and better Canaan—a country beyond the reach of ravaging armies, beyond the taint of pollution, and beyond the change and decay that mark this mortal sphere—in his own words, "incorruptible, and undefiled, and that fadeth not away" (1:4), the home of God's elect.

> If thou canst get but thither,
>   There grows the flower of peace,
> The Rose that cannot wither,
>   Thy fortress, and thy ease.

> Leave then thy foolish ranges;
>   For none can thee secure
> But One who never changes—
>   Thy God, thy life, thy cure! [11]

VI. Outline of the Letter

I. Salutation (1:1-2)
II. The blessings of God's redeemed children (1:3–2:10)
  A. Doxology for the risen Christ (1:3-9)
  B. The prophets and the gospel (1:10-12)
  C. Exhortation to holy living (1:13–2:3)
  D. The cornerstone and the new temple of God (2:4-10)
III. The duties of Christians in the world (2:11–4:11)
  A. Believers and unbelievers (2:11-12)
  B. Christians and the state (2:13-17)
  C. The duty of slaves (2:18-20)
  D. The *Imitatio Christi* (2:21-25)
  E. Husbands and wives (3:1-7)
  F. Recapitulation (3:8-12)
  G. The Christian answer to persecution (3:13-17)
  H. Our example, Christ (3:18-22)
  J. Exhortation to pure living (4:1-6)
  K. Ethics for the crisis (4:7-11)
IV. The trials of Christians in the world (4:12–5:11)
  A. A call to Christian constancy (4:12-19)
  B. Exhortation to elders (5:1-5)
  C. Concluding exhortation (5:6-11)
V. Conclusion and blessing (5:12-14)

VII. Selected Bibliography

BEARE, F. W. *The First Epistle of Peter.* Oxford: Blackwell & Mott, 1947.

BENNETT, W. H. *The General Epistles* ("The New Century Bible"). Edinburgh: T. C. & E. C. Jack, 1901.

BIGG, CHARLES. *A Critical and Exegetical Commentary on the Epistles of St. Peter and St. Jude* ("The International Critical Commentary"). New York: Charles Scribner's Sons, 1901.

CRANFIELD, C. E. B. *The First Epistle of Peter.* London: Student Christian Movement Press, 1950.

HORT, F. J. A. *The First Epistle of St Peter I.1–II.17.* London: Macmillan & Co., 1898.

MOFFATT, JAMES. *The General Epistles* ("Moffatt New Testament Commentary"). New York: Harper & Bros.; London: Hodder & Stoughton, 1928.

SELWYN, E. G. *The First Epistle of St. Peter.* London: Macmillan & Co., 1946.

WAND, J. W. C. *The General Epistles of St. Peter and St. Jude* ("The Westminster Commentaries"). London: Methuen & Co., 1934.

WINDISCH, HANS. *Die Katholischen Briefe* ("Handbuch zum Neuen Testament"). 2nd ed. Tübingen: J. C. B. Mohr, 1930.

[11] Henry Vaughan, "Peace."

I PETER

TEXT, EXEGESIS, AND EXPOSITION

1 Peter, an apostle of Jesus Christ, to the strangers scattered throughout Pontus, Galatia, Cappadocia, Asia, and Bithynia,	1 Peter, an apostle of Jesus Christ, To the exiles of the dispersion in Pontus, Galatia, Cap-pa-do'ci-a, Asia, and Bi-

I. SALUTATION (1:1-2)

Peter salutes the Christians scattered throughout Asia Minor, reminds them of their election, consecration, and forgiveness, and prays for them increase of grace and peace.

The Catholic Epistles.—The letters, or the *ad hoc* tractlike messages of Peter, James, John, and Jude, written to fellow Christians of their time, are called "general" or "catholic" epistles. Whereas Paul's letters were addressed to individual churches or persons, these seven epistles were termed by Origen and other church fathers "catholic" or "universal" because they were addressed to the faithful of the Dispersion, or to Christians in general.

Three views have been held regarding the terms "general" or "catholic." These seven letters are so designated (*a*) because of their common apostolic and authoritative authorship; (*b*) because of their universal acceptance by the churches of their time as canonical; and (*c*) because of their generally acceptable doctrinal content. Perhaps all three reasons are involved in their designation: authorship, acceptability by the churches, and content of Christian truth. In any case, these letters are directed to all Christians, and their inclusion in the Bible is evidence of the catholic, ecumenical, and universal nature of the Christian revelation. These letters stress works (James), love (John), hope (Peter), and pure faith (Jude), four of the great elements in the holy, catholic faith of the Christian church. They also give us a clear glimpse into the varied characteristics and problems of the churches, the basic ingredients of a truly Christian faith, and the foundational principles of Christian ethical action in a non-Christian world.

Christian Letters.—Letter writing is one of the high arts of man. But the kind of letter writing found in these epistles is unique. Christians in this generation have experience of the encyclical letter written by one church to another, or by a Christian leader to a group of Christians, because such letters have been writ-

ten in our time. Such a letter was written by the theologian Karl Barth to French Protestants during the Nazi occupation of France. While not canonical or catholic in the scriptural sense, letters like these have become common in our day. During World War II messages of comfort, assurance, exhortation, and sympathy passed between individual Christians and churches across battle lines. They were catholic or general in spirit and attested to the reality and the unity of Christians in faith, hope, love, and good works, whether they lived in the state of dispersion (displaced persons), or in some modern "Pontus," "Galatia," or other unfriendly land. Pastoral letters too, by church leaders, have been dispatched to Christians widely scattered, sorely confused by the enigmatic nature of the historical situation, and tested and persecuted by "corsairs" and their "new orders."

The Roman Catholic Church has long used the papal encyclical to provide its members with an authoritative pronouncement of the church on matters of great concern. Its encyclicals on marriage, labor, and education are but a few which have appeared in relatively recent times. That church has also issued more personal letters or epistles to its clergy and its people who were confronted with persecution and even martyrdom.

Such letters are not uncommon in ecumenical circles today. The World Council of Churches has from time to time spoken to Christians a counseling word regarding many matters. While these messages do not claim the authority of a Roman encyclical, they do express the Christian mind on relevant matters with a view to guiding Christians as they confront bewildering conditions and baffling decisions.

**1:1-2. *The Greeting.*—The apostle packs into his greeting to the exiles of the Dispersion an

1:1. Peter, an apostle of Jesus Christ: Peter is the Greek form of the Aramaic surname *Cephas* (or "Rock") given him by Jesus (Mark 3:16; Matt. 16:18; John 1:42). He designates himself simply an apostle, i.e., the commissioned envoy or messenger of Jesus Christ. He has no need to amplify or to defend his apostolic credentials, as Paul sometimes had. He is an apostle beyond any possible contradiction.

To the exiles of the dispersion in Pontus, Galatia, ... (RSV; KJV is less accurate). The phrase describes the Christian church in the parts of Asia Minor mentioned. They are (*a*) exiles, i.e., exiles from their true fatherland which is in heaven, and have here no abiding city. (Yet it may be added, if Christians must say with Samuel Rutherford, "Fie, fie, this is not like my country" they are not absolved from the duty of trying to make their home-from-home, which is this world, a fairer and a better place.) (*b*) They are **of the dispersion.** The Greek word *diaspora* denoted originally "the Jews dispersed in the world outside Palestine." Here it is applied figuratively to the Christians who, through the Jews' rejection of the Messiah, have become the true Israel, and form a dispersion from the heavenly Jerusalem.

Pontus, Galatia, Cappadocia, Asia, and Bithynia: A rough name for the area we know as Asia Minor. These five districts formed four Roman provinces, for Pontus and Bithynia counted as one.

---

amazing wealth of Christian truth. It practically encompasses the major elements of the biblical revelation: God the Father and Ordainer, Jesus Christ the Savior and Lord, and the Holy Spirit, the Consecrator, Perfecter, and Sanctifier. It issues from a genuine apostle of Jesus Christ and is directed to members of the churches. It wishes them a multiplication of **grace** (divine favor), and **peace** (divine benediction and blessedness). And it is offered in the clear and fervent spirit of one who writes with a passionate concern and love for the recipients of his letter.

The greeting from beginning to end is set within the context of a God-initiated revelation which was made known through Jesus Christ and effectuated by the Holy Spirit. Peter, the author, is what he is not by any special merit of his own but by the authority of Jesus Christ, whose apostle he is. The members of the churches to whom he writes are Christian not by right of their religious endowments but because of their divine election. The greeting sets the entire contents of the letter in the atmosphere of the eternal. It starts with the divine initiative.

Greetings like this still have a place in the intercourse of church with church, and in the official judicatories of the churches. But not often do we see the decisive nature of the Christian faith set forth in such short compass at the beginning of official documents or pastoral declarations as it is set forth in I Peter. The greeting (1:1-2) is a little *Summa* of the Christian faith which forms the foundation of everything Peter discusses in his letter. It also proclaims in inspiring fashion the high faith which binds apostle and people together. And it preaches the basic kerygma, the gospel, which

is aimed to cheer the Christian exiles who are on the verge of despair.

1a. Peter, an Apostle.—Peter, a letter writer! Granting all that some critics [1] have said about the "good Greek style" of this letter and its "extensive literary vocabulary," which makes its Petrine authorship questionable, no reader can escape its Petrine personality, faith, and spirit. Silvanus was on hand no doubt (5:12) to give Peter's message the literary refinements it needed. But that Peter would venture at all to write is an amazing fact. We are grateful that his name appears among the literary immortals. He who was once described as "unlearned and ignorant" (Acts 4:13) by ecclesiastical leaders has a niche in the hall of canonical writers. The journey from fisherman to apostolic writer was a long and difficult one in his case. Would that he had written more, for he had so much to say! He was one of the intimates of our Lord. He had walked with him "from the beginning." He had given up his occupation to join the peripatetic company of Jesus. He had ventured farther with Jesus than any one of the twelve. He tried to walk on the water, he shared the Transfiguration, he made the great confession, he protested his unfailing fidelity, he severed the ear of a soldier in the arresting party. Worst of all, he had failed most tragically, as he reverted to his old self and denied his Lord thrice with an oath. Yet he had wept bitterly at the look of Jesus, had run breathlessly to view the open tomb, made a humiliating yet bold comeback as he vowed thrice to love the risen Christ without superficial boast, preached him fearlessly in the face of imprisonment and martyrdom, opened the

[1] Among them F. W. Beare, *The First Epistle of Peter* (London: B. Blackwell, 1947).

Pontus lay on the south coast of the Black Sea. When Christianity came to it, is not clear; but in Pliny's time, the first decade of the second century, there were numerous Christians there. From this part of Asia Minor hailed Aquila (Acts 18:2), and here in Sinope, one of its seaports, was born in the second century Marcion, the famous heretic.

Galatia is the central part of Asia Minor. Originally the name described the wild mountainous country around Ancyra (modern Ankara) inhabited by Gallic immigrants; but in 25 B.C. the Romans had enlarged the land into a province by adding territory in the south and east, notably Pisidia and Lycaonia. This was the country evangelized by Paul during his first missionary journey (Acts 13–14). Peter, no doubt, is thinking of the Roman province.

Cappadocia lay inland, east of Galatia and south of Pontus. It had been made a Roman province in A.D. 17. Jews from Cappadocia were present in Jerusalem on the day of Pentecost (Acts 2:9).

Asia, the land extending along the east coast of the Levant and comprising the famous cities of Ephesus, Smyrna, Miletus, etc., became a Roman province in 133 B.C.

---

church to Gentiles when he saw the undeniable work of the Spirit in Cornelius, and—according to tradition—sealed his apostleship with a martyr's death by crucifixion with his head downward.

What memories this name "Peter" brings to mind! He, an immortal writer of eternal truth; **an apostle of Jesus Christ;** a living evidence of the power of Jesus Christ; a teacher of the Christian community; a man with an authoritative message for the saints; an unlettered and impulsive fisherman transformed by the invading power of Jesus Christ. This massive and elemental man of conflicting impulses had become the rocklike man Jesus recognized him to be once he had been steadied and shaped by grace and a disciple's passion. He could swear and weep and orate and rebuke and lose his temper. All of this potent personal power was now directed by a new power: Jesus Christ. Peter was an apostle—one sent—by Christ; he was an authorized agent, commissioned to undertake a definite mission. He would not boast about his office; he was "an" apostle, not "the" apostle. His authority was derived, not self-existent. The final authority resided in Jesus Christ. His commission was received from his Lord. Though the apostle's position was to be respected in the church, apostleship for him was more a function than an office, more a means than an end. The great reality was Jesus Christ, who had invaded and pervaded his life in a growing and penetrating encounter until he was no longer the man Simon Peter, but **Peter, an apostle** not merely of Jesus the Galilean, nor of Christ the Word, but of that unique historical event and Person: Jesus Christ, the Word made flesh, whom he had preached at Pentecost.

1b. To the Elect Exiles.—Technically the exiles were Jews living outside the homeland, but Peter is addressing his letter to the new

Israel, which included Gentiles now members of the household of God who were dispersed into strange lands. **Strangers** and **exiles** they were in the earth. They were like Abraham, their father, who was "a stranger and a sojourner" (Gen. 23:4); like Jesus who had "nowhere to lay his head" (Matt. 8:20); like the psalmist who lamented, "I am a stranger with thee, and a sojourner, as all my fathers were" (Ps. 39:12). The children of God are often victimized by forces which drive them hither and yon; they are aliens in a hostile world, for their citizenship is in heaven (Phil. 3:20). They are ever aware of the fact that this world is not home, that this world can guarantee them no peace, that the order of this world is in conflict with God's eternal order, and that the secular life lacks the essential dimension without which life is bounded by birth and death.

Christians know they are pilgrims who live in a vale of soul-making, in an earthly school of life's perfecting, in a place where even the Son of man is "made perfect through suffering." They know the truth of the words of the writer of the Epistle to the Hebrews, who reminded his friends that God lovingly chastises his children to make them "partakers of his holiness" (Heb. 12:10), to bring them, if they are exercised or taught thereby, to maturity.

Human existence is set within the context of eternity; its origin and meaning and destiny are in things unseen and hoped for. Otherworldliness is justly unpopular, because no one wishes to be branded unrealistic, utopian, idealistic, or unsocial. "Pie in the sky by-and-by" elicits scornful laughter because it is indicative of a kind of escapism from the responsibilities of this life. Yet the truth of the matter is that men—all men—are pilgrims, born to a restless and troubled life. Man's life is short and precarious; he dimly surmises that **Pontus**, whether

2 Elect according to the foreknowledge of God the Father, through sanctification of the Spirit, unto obedience and sprinkling of the blood of Jesus Christ: Grace unto you, and peace, be multiplied.

thyn'i-a, 2 chosen and destined by God the Father and sanctified by the Spirit for obedience to Jesus Christ and for sprinkling with his blood:

May grace and peace be multiplied to you.

The seven churches of the Revelation all lay in this district, and Ephesus and its neighborhood was the scene of Paul's extended missionary work during his third journey.

Bithynia lay cheek by jowl west of Pontus along the Black Sea. It had been united in 64 B.C. with Pontus to form a single province of which Pliny the Younger was governor in A.D. 110-12, when he wrote his famous rescript to Trajan about the Christians. During Paul's second journey he "assayed to go into Bithynia: but the Spirit [of Jesus] suffered them not" (Acts 16:7). In this district lay towns like Nicaea and Chalcedon, destined to win fame in later church history.

One final point: Why are the names of these provinces given in this order? I Peter is a circular letter, and this is the circular route its bearer would follow. He would begin in Pontus (possibly at Sinope) and travel around the Christian communities in Galatia, Cappadocia, and Asia, ending his journey in Bithynia.

2. Elect (KJV); **chosen and destined** (RSV): On this word **elect** depend the three following phrases. The readers' choice, consecration, and forgiveness were all part of God's great plan. **Father . . . Spirit . . . Jesus Christ.** Note the trinitarian sound and symmetry of Peter's words and cf. II Thess. 2:13-14, "God chose you . . . unto salvation

---

the United States or Russia or Fiji, is not his eternal abode, that the earth, however bountiful and beautiful, cannot ultimately satisfy the deepest needs of men, that human existence is a broken and frail thing.

The Christian knows all this and more. Exile though he is, he does not give way to despair. Because his life is centered in an abiding home, he accepts his dispersion life and brings the reality of his heavenly citizenship to bear upon this fleeting condition and thus blesses the world. Further, he is not surprised at dispersion, since he knows that the eternal order of his heavenly life and the human order of this world are in conflict. The ancient apologist expresses it well, when he says: "Christians inhabit their own land but as sojourners. They share in all things outwardly as citizens, and endure all things as strangers. Every foreign land is theirs, and every land is foreign." [2] Yet they bring something of home into their short and temporary abodes. The eternal conditions the temporal, the abiding makes its impact upon the transient, the reality of heaven makes the earth meaningful.

2. Elect and Destined by God the Father.— The divine initiative had sought them out while they were sinners and alienated from the household of God. God in Christ was prior to their response of faith. What they now are they had been made by a power beyond their own human energy or initiative. On the surface they may

appear a rather pathetic group of aliens without dignity or promise. Their peculiarity did not reside in what they were as human beings. The eye could see they were like other common people. They possessed no superior qualities in themselves. Yet these are special people who are different from others. It was God's marvelous counsel and favor which was at the basis of their status and vocation; as his love had chosen Israel (Deut. 4:37) of all peoples to perform a unique ministry as prophet, priest, and king to all mankind, so had his love continued to elect the new Israel. In the life of the Christian, as in the life of the church, there is something strongly mysterious at work. The whole Christian movement is not at the mercy of men, nor is it something which men support and protect. The sovereign and holy love of God in Christ Jesus is the unshakable foundation of all things. "If God be for us, who can be against us?" (Rom. 8:31.)

Election has been a doctrine of contention when it is meant to be a comforting reality. It lifts the heart of despairing man by fixing his faith in the faithful and loving purpose of God, and vouchsafes to those who are called "the only comfort in life and in death." [3] What finer security is granted to man than a sense of his call to sonship with God which is based upon a God whose infinite wisdom understands our thoughts afar off and whose tender mercy seeks our salvation **through sanctification of the**

---

[2] Epistle to Diognetus 5:5.

[3] *Heidelberg Catechism*, Question and Answer 1.

in sanctification of the Spirit . . . to the obtaining of the glory of our Lord Jesus Christ" (ASV). This is as yet "the trinity of experience," out of which sprang the later dogma. The early Christians found by experience that they could not express all that they meant by the word "God" till they had said, "Father, Son, and Spirit." Christians were then, as they still are, people who are seeking, finding, and doing the Father's will with the companionship of his Son by the strength and guidance of the Spirit.

Through sanctification of the Spirit means "in virtue of hallowing by the Spirit" (a subjective genitive). Probably a reference to reception of the Spirit at baptism.

Unto obedience and sprinkling of the blood of Jesus Christ (KJV); cf. the RSV, **for obedience to Jesus Christ and for sprinkling with his blood.** The purpose of their election was that they might be obedient to Christ and might be forgiven by his sacrifice. The reference to **obedience** and **sprinkling** takes us back to the inauguration of the covenant at Sinai, especially to Exod. 24:7, 8: "And he [Moses] took the book of the covenant, and read in the audience of the people: and they said, All that the LORD hath said will we do, and be obedient. And Moses took the blood, and sprinkled it on the people, and said, Behold the blood of the covenant, which the LORD hath made with you

---

Spirit and **sprinkling of the blood** on Calvary on our behalf! The common tendency among men, even Christians, is to judge the church by the standards of the market place. But the secret of the elect community is not to be found in its external or organizational aspects. Seen from the "inside," it cannot be judged by what it seems on the surface. As Manson says to the bishop in Charles Rann Kennedy's play, *The Servant in the House,* "I am afraid you may not consider it an altogether substantial concern. It has to be seen in a certain way, under certain conditions. Some people never *see* it at all. You must understand, this is no dead pile of stones and unmeaning timber. *It is a living thing."* [4]

The church therefore is one, holy, apostolic, and catholic. It is made so by its Head, who was sent from God. It has been brought into being not by human ingenuity but in the foreknowledge and by the will of God. It may consist of people with no reputation, many of them dispersed among the nations, many of them pretty poor Christians, most of them apparently rather impotent; but they are

> Elect from every nation,
> Yet one o'er all the earth. [5]

God's great design and his unfailing promise encompass them behind and before. He accepts them as his co-workers in the accomplishment of his glorious goal.

Not only are the exiles elected, they are **chosen** for a definite purpose: **unto obedience and sprinkling of the blood of Jesus Christ.** The high estate of sonship with God is not only an undeserved gift, it is also a responsibility. "We are saved to serve." "To whom

[4] New York: Harper & Bros., 1908, Act 2, pp. 67-68.
[5] Samuel J. Stone, "The Church's one foundation," st. ii.

much is given, of him will much be required" (Luke 12:48). The elect are hallowed people; they are set apart and ordained for God's purposes. They are motivated by the Spirit of God who generates faith within them, creates the virtues of the "new man in Christ," nurtures the people of God toward their full stature in Christ, possesses them and infills them with all the fullness of God. And their election is to result in a life of obedience to Jesus Christ, because they have been bound to him in a blood covenant. The old covenant was sealed by sprinkling half the blood of the sacrifice upon the altar and half upon the people (Exod. 24:6-8) as they pledged obedience to Yahweh; so in the new covenant the new relationship between God and man was sealed by the sacrificial death of Jesus Christ. Christians are people who are conscious of having been purchased at great cost; hence their lives are no longer their own. They belong to Jesus Christ. Their vocations are to be channels of obedient service. They are a "holy priesthood" (2:5, 9), a people with a divine mission to perform. They are characteristically: (*a*) forgiven of God through Christ's sacrifice, (*b*) conescrated to obedient service to him, (*c*) conscious of utter dependence upon the cleansing and maturing power of the Holy Spirit.

The election of the elect is not a once-for-all procedure; in Peter's mind election and **sanctification** go together. The election has started, and yet it is being continued by the power of the Spirit, who not only calls but continues to make the election more effective. Election is an act, but it also involves a process. The distinguishing quality of the Christian and of the church is that there is at work in them a spirit different from that which operated in the world (4:17-18). The lack of the power of the Spirit in the modern church has been called the

3 Blessed *be* the God and Father of our Lord Jesus Christ, which according to his abundant mercy hath begotten us again unto a lively hope by the resurrection of Jesus Christ from the dead,

3 Blessed be the God and Father of our Lord Jesus Christ! By his great mercy we have been born anew to a living hope through the resurrection of Jesus Christ

concerning all these words." Here the sacrificial metaphor of sprinkling is to be interpreted spiritually. It means: with a view to sharing in the blessings of Christ's sacrifice which inaugurated the new covenant between God and his people. For *the blood is the life,* and Christ's blood means his sinless life consecrated to God in death for us men and for our salvation.

Grace: The normal greeting in a Greek letter was "joy" (χαίρειν). Here χαίρειν becomes χάρις, **grace,** i.e., God's unmerited love to men. "Grace," says James Denney, "is the first and last word of the Gospel; and peace—perfect spiritual soundness—is the finished work of grace" (*The Second Epistle to the Corinthians* [London: Hodder & Stoughton, 1894], p. 11).

II. The Blessings of God's Redeemed Children (1:3–2:10)

A. Doxology for the Risen Christ (1:3-9)

This section might be summarized: "Thanks be to God who has given us a living hope of a heavenly inheritance in the risen Christ! Present trials should only test and purify your faith. Though you have not seen Christ, you love him and joyfully believe in him, and your joy is a foretaste of your final salvation."

3. Peter's salutation passes into doxology, just as Paul's does in II Corinthians and Ephesians. The fact of the Resurrection had made all new in Peter's own life—had turned

blind spot in modern Christianity. We are possessed of buildings and organizations and programs and money, but we often lack the effective power of the Spirit.

In a real sense Christianity is the creation of the Holy Spirit ever since Pentecost. We no longer live in "the days of his flesh," we live in the era of the Spirit. Jesus considered it necessary that he go away, that he send his substitute, so that his followers might come to know him in fuller measure, in all his glory, in his God-manhood. Unless the Spirit takes of the things of Jesus in the gospels and reveals, interprets, and applies them, we may know a great deal about him, but we may not know him as he is. Christians are to work out their salvation "with fear and trembling" (Phil. 2:12), because God is at work in them; they are to make their calling and election sure (II Pet. 1:10).

2b. Grace and Peace Be Multiplied.—We can never have enough of grace and peace. If James Denney is right when he says that "grace is the first and last word of the Gospel; and peace—perfect spiritual soundness—is the finished work of grace," [6] then these gifts are life's greatest boons. Peter is wishing for his friends that the astonishingly new and wonderfully powerful love of God-in-action, which broke into the

[6] *The Second Epistle to the Corinthians* (London: Hodder & Stoughton, 1894), p. 11.

world through Jesus, would increase in their spirits. As it had burst in upon those who walked with the Lord, it had literally offered them release from old enslavements by its forgiveness, and lifted new horizons for them through its shining light of risen truth. Peter is praying that their lives may remain open to the influx of that divine power so that it may complete what it had started. And he hopes that the deep blessedness and conviction of being undergirded by the good will of God may continue to save them from insecurity and a sense of futility. Let the **grace** of Jesus Christ, which reconciles God and man, and the **peace** of mind that results from it, be multiplied!

3. Hope Is Rooted in Praise.—The main theme of hope is introduced by a prayer: **Blessed be the God and Father of our Lord Jesus Christ!** Prayer is man's final submission to the God whose character has been made known in Jesus Christ. Through it we say "Yea" and "Amen" to God as we confide in his will, which is our peace, our joy, and our very life. Prayer has been called the highest affirmation of faith which we make on our knees. In this magnificent prayer the writer of the epistle embarks upon his exhortation to his friends. All true knowledge of God begins with prayer. Reverence toward God is the beginning of wisdom about life and history. The sum of all that the Chris-

tragedy into triumph—so that it is altogether fitting that his epistle should begin with this paean of it.

The God and Father of our Lord Jesus Christ: Cf. II Cor. 1:3; Eph. 1:3. For Peter, as for Paul, God had revealed his glory and grace supremely in Jesus Christ so that henceforth they could not speak of him but in terms of Christ. It was a case of "like Son, like Father." Maltby has said of the early Christians, "When they said their prayers to God at night, there was another Face on the screen of their minds, and they fell asleep thinking of Jesus" (quoted by Frederic Greeves, *The Christian Way* [London: Student Christian Movement Press, 1945], p. 39).

According to his abundant mercy: Cf. the Scottish paraphrase:

> 'Tis from the mercy of our God
> That all our hopes begin.

It is in the inconceivable compassion of God that our redemption takes its origin.

Hath begotten us again, i.e., regenerated and renewed us. The verb (ἀναγεννήσας) is found in the N.T. only here and in 1:23. For the idea see Mark 10:14-15; John 3:7, and for the apostolic testimony to the reality of the new life see, e.g., Rom. 6:4-5 ("newness of life"), I John 3:14 ("we have passed from death unto life").

---

tian affirms about life is rooted and grounded in the primacy and the glory of the God and Father of our Lord Jesus Christ. Here is no anxious speculation about the existence of a Supreme Being, no hazy human groping after divine reality; on the contrary, Peter is definite in his conviction that God and Christ are inseparably united, and that the Christian rests his all upon God who was in Christ.

Peter also makes it clear that of all the things for which he is thankful, there is one thing that is paramount: the gift of Jesus Christ. His shout of praise magnifies the redemptive event that took place in and through Christ. This event is the all-qualifying center; and all other gifts are of subordinate importance. It is significant to note that he does not dwell upon the state of affairs in the culture of his day. Here and there we get indirect hints as to the religious attitude and moral practices of the times, but these are never magnified. Contrary to modern students, who are often long on analysis and short on prognosis, Peter starts with God, not with man. His letter is written to strengthen "the feeble knees" (Heb. 12:12). He seems to take for granted a world of tribulation to which the gospel has come with its wonderful hope. No mention is made of possible persecutions about to fall upon Christians. Rather, he starts with trumpets sounding the advent of the gospel of God. **Blessed be the God and Father of our Lord Jesus Christ,** who has done great things. This is the starting point of the Christian faith in a day of anxiety and imminent danger.

3b. The Living Hope.—"Faith, hope, love abide, these three," wrote the great apostle (I Cor. 13:13). But even though love is "the greatest of these," and even though faith is primary in the Christian's life, without hope, faith and love "must mount on broken wing." Faith in the God and Father of Jesus Christ, and communion in that love, "all loves excelling," may provide life with its highest joy and peace. But what if there is no prospect for faith and love? This trinity is like the three legs of a tripod; each supports the other and each must be kept in proper relation to the other.

Man is created with a capacity for memory; he is endowed with the power of present insight; and he is constituted with the power to anticipate and plan for the future. Hope is an essential element in human life; without it even the finest and best which earth can yield is shrouded with a deadly miasma of futility. Lacking a realizable future, our most meaningful experiences of—and our most profound confidences in—reality are but tantalizing projections of our fancy. Of what value is the education of man, the cultivation of his implanted capacities, the arousal of his noblest potentialities, if he at last is enveloped in the dark night of death and the unfeeling grave of extinction? Had the gospel brought only the revelation of God's saving truth and his redeeming grace for the present, it would have aroused man's spirit only to plunge him into a deeper despair in the consciousness of a hopeless future.

(*a*) How astonishingly marvelous and new was the gift of hope to those first Christians! **According to his abundant mercy,** not according to man's merit, has this living hope come to the world. The Resurrection and all that it meant to human life and history had been no myth, no fable, no dreamy possibility generated

A living hope: As "living waters" are those that flow from a perennial spring, so a living hope is one which no trials and tribulations can ever quench.

By the resurrection of Jesus Christ from the dead: This clause is to be taken with hath begotten us again. It is by Christ's resurrection that God has kindled this inextinguishable hope in us; nay, we may go further and say that without the Resurrection, there would have been no Christian church. Christianity is an Easter religion. Its theism is resurrection theism.

---

by the wisdom of men. It was a free act of the merciful God who did something for men which they could not do for themselves, however hard they tried or however fervently they yearned. The gospel which generated hope in those early Christians was a sheer gift; it was not deserved; and it was something which no amount of human energy or substance could pay for.

The gift of this living hope can be appreciated only by those who know the bondage of fear which held the pagan masses of that day captive. Those who were economically and politically well situated were surfeited with the fed-up life of luxury, or unsatisfied with the aimless and bankrupt pursuit of meaningless philosophical speculation. They knew nothing of real hope or joy or peace. While Greco-Roman civilization abounded with beauty, with courage, and with intellectual vigor, it was indeed a world without hope. Old age was faced with fear; life was continually threatened with misfortune and tragedy; and early death was to be desired above a life that at last had to end.

To such an age, and to every such age permeated by the frustrating sense of despair and futility, the merciful action of God in opening up the true destiny of life by the resurrection of Jesus Christ is his greatest gift. This act is indeed history's greatest miracle.

(b) This hope is a living and active reality; it produces the "life of hope" in which the eternal power of God is at work. This living hope is anchored in One who is alive even now; it is not the product of man's wishes, nor is it set upon the passing and perishing hopes of this timebound world.

(c) This living hope, this life of radical hopefulness, is a new creation, and can be compared only to the birth of a new life. All men are to be born twice: once physically, and again spiritually. Once they come into life in this world; again they must be born again to the world order of the kingdom of God. Peter uses a strong word here: begotten. This birth into the new life in Christ, which involves being raised with him into "heavenly places," is crucial, decisive, and miraculous. It is God's creative work. No one brings about his own physical birth; he is born by the action of powers not his own; and no one brings about

his own spiritual birth; he is born anew, or begotten, by the action of powers beyond his own. Theologians have argued over the parts which God and man play in this spiritual rebirth. For those who speak from experience, as did Peter, and who know the stirrings of the living hope within them, there is no doubt about the fact that God took the initiative and hath begotten us again unto a living hope.

(d) This living hope is based upon the Resurrection. Easter is a unique personal event; it is not like the inevitable recurring springtime. Nor is it in a category with hatching eggs, prolific bunnies, or the bright new togs of the Easter parade. The Resurrection means that Jesus was raised from the dead, and all that he said and did and was came alive by a creative act of God. This is what we celebrate every Lord's Day. Easter means: Jesus Christ lives. The light and the life and love of God that shone in and through him are real and true and abiding. The Resurrection "is the crowning triumph of life in the created universe." [7]

In the beginning God created order out of chaos; then he brought light into darkness, after which he fashioned human life in his own image; and finally by the Resurrection he brought the "consummation of reconcilement." Jesus Christ is not only a historical figure; he lives now and is with his own always. He is the assurance and pledge that the future is meaningful, that "all things work together for good to them that love God" (Rom. 8:28), that the last word is with the life that he generates, that those who are incorporated into his life may face the future with the spirit of triumph and confront their trials without dread.

Early Christians were characterized by the spirit of triumph. Their worship and their work were done in the spirit of joy and anticipation. They were already "raised with Christ" (Col. 3:1) and enjoying the life of hope. Their "new look" made pagans inquire as to the secret of their new life. Their acceptance of suffering in the belief that they shared it with Christ was unheard of in the Greco-Roman world. Nothing could daunt them; the dimension of eternity

[7] *The Speaker's Bible*, ed. James Hastings, *et al.* (Aberdeen: Speaker's Bible Offices, 1924), I and II Peter, p. 14.

4 To an inheritance incorruptible, and undefiled, and that fadeth not away, reserved in heaven for you,

from the dead, 4 and to an inheritance which is imperishable, undefiled, and un-

---

4. To an inheritance: The Greek word (κληρονομίαν), to a reader of the Greek O.T., would inevitably recall Canaan, the God-given inheritance of the Jews. Here, of course, not the "old Canaan" (to use Watts's phrase), but the celestial Canaan is in Peter's mind: a Canaan that is "incorruptible, undefiled, and unfading"—three splendidly sonorous epithets suggesting that supernal country which, in contrast with the old Canaan, is beyond the ravages of war, the taint of pollution, and the change and decay that mar this terrestrial sphere (cf. Matt. 6:19-20).

Reserved in heaven for you: Cf. Col. 1:5, "The hope which is laid up for you in heaven." **Reserved** means "preserved" or **kept** (RSV), and the perfect tense of the verb in the Greek (τετηρημένην) indicates that the "reservation" still holds good; for it is **in heaven,** beyond the reach of earthly accidents. On the verse as a whole perhaps the best, as it is the most beautiful, comment is Henry Vaughan's hymn, "My soul, there is a country."

---

and the far goal of human life were dominant in their thinking. Unlike many whose anxieties over things make them miserable, these pioneers of the Christian way kept things in their proper place. The center of gravity in their lives was a triumphant, living Person.

4. An Assured Inheritance.—Readers of this letter knew the meaning of **inheritance.** God had given Israel the inheritance of Canaan (Deut. 15:4), the Promised Land. This was home, the Holy Land, the sacred abode of God's people. But Canaan was often ravaged by alien armies, and its fields were often wasted by insects and drought. A "fatal flaw" afflicts all life. It silently affects our highest joys, and fills us with a melancholy sadness. No inheritance is immune to its ruthless and permeating influence. Nothing lasts, nor does it escape corruption, except the **imperishable,** enduring, and **incorruptible** inheritance of that new Canaan which cannot be ravaged by enemy forces, eaten by omnivorous insects, blighted by the blasts of desert wind, or corrupted by the corrosives of decay. "The Lord is the portion of mine inheritance" (Ps. 16:5).

This inheritance is **undefiled,** free from the pervasive taint of impurity. The inheritances of men, whether of popularity, fame, fortune, or power, are shot through with the vice of injustice and the poison of pride. Men sell conscience for coins, women sell honor for gain, and Judases sell Christ for a price. The Greek word *amiantos,* which means **undefiled,** refers to a mineral found among the rocks and made into a fire-resisting fabric. Though soiled, it turned pure white when placed in the fire. Romans paid generously for it; in it they wrapped the remains of their dead, so that in cremation the precious ashes would be preserved

in a fabric unaffected by the consuming fire. The Christian's inheritance is free from the taint of defilement; it is unaffected by the fiery judgment. It **fadeth not away;** its brilliance and splendor are not affected by the years. Like the ancient maranth, the flower which seemed dead though it was alive and enduring, so the inheritance of the Christian knows nothing of the law of transiency. It maintains its original brightness and beauty.

Reserved! Fully assured! No disappointment! "In my Father's house are many mansions: if it were not so, I would have told you" (John 14:2). So said Jesus concerning the future. It is the word of an authority. "I would have told you, if it were not so." It is not at the mercy of arbitrary powers; it is kept for us, and it will be certainly bestowed. The Christian is an heir. The N.T. abounds with the idea: "Heirs together of the grace of life" (3:7). "Heirs of salvation" (Heb. 1:14). "Heirs of the kingdom" (Jas. 2:5). "Heirs according to the hope of eternal life" (Tit. 3:7). The Christian may now know that he is a child of God and a member of his Father's house, yet "eye hath not seen, nor ear heard, neither have entered into the heart of man, the things which God hath prepared for them that love him" (I Cor. 2:9). What the Christian will come into is more significant than what he has already experienced. The "best is yet to be." And while already in this life he tastes of that inheritance, he will come into such a possession of it as he has never dreamed of here, where "we see through a glass darkly" and where we know only "in part" (I Cor. 13:12). The anticipations of earth are hardly comparable with the full inheritance to be acquired.

5 Who are kept by the power of God through faith unto salvation ready to be revealed in the last time.

6 Wherein ye greatly rejoice, though now for a season, if need be, ye are in heaviness through manifold temptations:

fading, kept in heaven for you, 5 who by God's power are guarded through faith for a salvation ready to be revealed in the last time. 6 In this you rejoice,[a] though now for a little while you may have to suffer

[a] Or *Rejoice in this.*

---

5. Who are kept by the power of God through faith: lit., "Who in God's power are garrisoned through faith"—as though God's power was the stronghold or fortress (cf. Luther, "A mighty fortress is our God") and our faith the garrisoning force.

Unto salvation ready to be revealed in the last time, i.e., the final deliverance from sin and death to come at "the revelation of Christ" and the consummation of all things.

6. Wherein (i.e., this being the situation, wherefore) **ye greatly rejoice:** The Greek verb might be taken also as an imperative, "Wherefore rejoice" (cf. RSV mg.).

For a season (KJV) is less accurate than **for a little while** (RSV); and **manifold temptations** (KJV) than **various trials** (RSV). Trials or tests of character and faith, not allurements to evil, are meant. Peter does not say that these trials are certain to come: **if need be** means "if it comes to that." The persecution which had broken out in Rome, or was threatening, may spread, he thinks, to more distant parts of the Roman Empire. This summons to joy in the midst of suffering takes its origin from our Lord himself (Matt. 5:11-12), is exemplified in apostolic history (e.g., Acts 5:41, where the apostles rejoice that they are counted worthy to suffer for the name), and finds abundant illustration in later Christian history. "Radiance amid the storm and stress of life," said Baron von Hügel to Rufus Jones, "is the one indispensable mark of those canonised as saints" (quoted in J. F. Rowntree, *et al., Inner Light* [London: Allen & Unwin, 1931], p. 294).

5-9. *A Glorious Salvation Now, and Yet to Come.*—Our incorruptible, undefiled, and unfading inheritance is kept secure for us from all eternity by the perpetual vigilance of God. Nothing that happens to us in this life can touch this boon of surpassing value.

This may be true of the treasure, but what of us? We are **guarded,** "garrisoned," by the power of God. We are not saved from the wounds of battle, nor are we spared the pains of our mortal existence, but we are personally surrounded and undergirded by a providence that is directed toward each of us personally. God's faithfulness will see us through, and guide us until the complete and perfect **salvation** is inherited.

Salvation, the fullness of all that God wills us to have and be, is not only carefully secured for us, but it is real, and it is **ready to be bestowed** upon us in full in the "great day" when this incomplete state of salvation will be made perfect. Let there be no confusion of the glory, the brilliance, and the perfection of salvation beyond time and history with the shadowy and childish experience of salvation in time and history. Let there be no promise of a complete "peace of mind," of any solution of all human problems, or of a perfect integration of personality this side of the *eschaton,* the last hour. Heaven may and does send its warm currents of eternal life to touch upon the cold and barren wastes of our chill mortal shores; but heaven is heaven and earth is earth. How can the finite know the fullness of infinity, or the sinful the dimension of holiness, or the temporal the blessedness of him who neither slumbers nor sleeps and in whose presence a thousand years are as a day? Would that we might recapture the wonder of a **salvation . . . to be revealed in the last time,** a salvation carefully kept for us, and imminently ready to burst with its reality upon us who have only envisioned it as a dream.

But is salvation then purely eternal? Is there no relation between the **last time** and this time? And what of these sufferings through which we are passing—are they meaningless? Because of this glorious salvation to come we may rejoice greatly. Our joy has a future reference; it is fed by the unfailing spring of divine faithfulness; it is a deep blessedness which nothing that happens today and tomorrow can affect. Rejoice—now! And the trials? They last but a little while, are insignificant in the light of the glory that is **to be revealed.** "Our light affliction . . . is but for a moment," as the apostle Paul put it (II Cor. 4:17). Even the stake, cruel as it was, lasted only for "a time." Concentration camps were episodes in the lives of modern saints. The tyrant's triumph is limited, and his power is in the control of him whose "is the kingdom, and the power, and the

7 That the trial of your faith, being much more precious than of gold that perisheth, though it be tried with fire, might be found unto praise and honor and glory at the appearing of Jesus Christ:

8 Whom having not seen, ye love; in whom, though now ye see *him* not, yet believing, ye rejoice with joy unspeakable and full of glory:

various trials, 7 so that the genuineness of your faith, more precious than gold which though perishable is tested by fire, may redound to praise and glory and honor at the revelation of Jesus Christ. 8 Without having seen[b] him you[c] love him; though you do not now see him you[c] believe in him and rejoice with unutterable and exalted

[b] Some ancient authorities read *known*.
[c] Or omit *you*.

7. **The trial of your faith:** The Greek word (δοκίμιον) translated **trial** means "the tried [or proved] part," i.e., what is genuine in your faith (cf. RSV; also Jas. 1:3). There follows an analogy between the testing of character and the refining of gold, of which the point is that if temporal gold is worth the trouble of refining, how much more the faith which has eternal value. **Unto praise:** God's, not man's. Was Peter thinking of his Master's "Well done, thou good and faithful servant, . . . enter thou into the joy of thy Lord"? (Matt. 25:21.) "We should endeavor so to live," said the agnostic John Stuart Mill, "that Jesus Christ would approve our life." **At the revelation of Jesus Christ,** i.e., at the Second Advent which would end their trials; but Peter, instead of using the usual word "parousia," speaks of the unveiling of Christ.

8. **Whom having not seen, ye love:** A hint that the writer had himself seen Jesus. We may compare Peter's claim in Acts 10:39, "We are witnesses of all things which he did both in the land of the Jews, and in Jerusalem." Peter's readers, however, share in the beatitude pronounced by the risen Christ, "Blessed are they that have not seen, and yet have believed" (John 20:29). In the N.T. there are three ways of apprehending Christ: (a) the physical sight of the eyewitness, such as Peter himself had enjoyed; (b) the apprehension granted to the eye of faith, as here; and (c) the beatific vision (cf. I Cor. 13:12; I John 3:2). On "the magnetism of the unseen Christ" we have the well-known testimony of Napoleon: "An extraordinary power of influencing and commanding men has been given to Alexander, Charlemagne and myself. But with us the presence has been necessary. . . . Whereas Jesus Christ has influenced and commanded His subjects without His visible bodily presence for eighteen hundred years" (see E. G. Selwyn, *The First Epistle of St. Peter* [London: Macmillan & Co., 1946], p. 131).

glory, for ever" (Matt. 6:13). But what is even more important is that these trials are indications of the precious nature of salvation. Those who suffer "for righteousness' sake" may rest assured and rejoice in the very fact, because only the righteous feel the opposition of unrighteous powers. The fact that Jesus Christ suffered was proof that he was loyal to his Father's will. His treasure was in heaven; in loyalty to it he eschewed all the treasures of earth; for it he surrendered his own will in Gethsemane. The followers of Christ may well rejoice in suffering, for therein they share in the life he lived and in the redemptive action which he inaugurated and still continues.

But more, such trials are also meant to discipline and prove us. They yield "the peaceable fruit of righteousness unto them which are exercised thereby" (Heb. 12:11). Faith is refined by trials, as gold is refined by fire; a faith refined by trials is more precious than gold

refined by fire. For gold, however valuable to the contemporaries of Peter, was of little worth when compared with salvation. The whole world is not to be compared with the value of the soul. Discipline is painful, but its major purpose under God's providence is to mature and temper us, and above all to make us fit for his praise at the last. "Well done, good and faithful servant" (Matt. 25:23). When the course has been run, the fight fought, and faith kept to the end, then at the revelation of Jesus Christ the faithful suffering servant will be fully rewarded. Such a conception of suffering, seen in the light of a final salvation, is sufficient to see the Christian through his trials and sorrows.

These reasons are not strong enough to keep the Christian faithful. There is one more valid than any Peter can command: Jesus Christ. While the readers of this letter had not seen Jesus (**without having seen him**) they loved him,

9 Receiving the end of your faith, *even* the salvation of *your* souls.

10 Of which salvation the prophets have inquired and searched diligently, who prophesied of the grace *that should come* unto you:

joy. **9** As the outcome of your faith you obtain the salvation of your souls.

10 The prophets who prophesied of the grace that was to be yours searched and

---

With joy unspeakable and full of glory: The joy of the Christian believer has two marks: (*a*) it far outpasses the power of human telling; and (*b*) it is "glorified," i.e., irradiated with (divine) glory—the glory which shall be revealed at the consummation of all things (5:1). Here the believer experiences an earnest of the glory to come at Christ's second advent. Paul has this thought too. In Rom. 8:30 he writes, "Them he also glorified"—the boldest anticipation of faith in the N.T.—and in II Cor. 3:18, "We all, with unveiled face, beholding the glory of the Lord, are being changed into his likeness from one degree of glory to another." We need add only that feelings of joy and glory often attend conversion (see William James, *Varieties of Religious Experience* [London: Longmans, Green & Co., 1915], pp. 248-56).

9. As the outcome of your faith you obtain: This clause gives the reason for their joy. With an anticipation hardly less daring than Paul's in Rom. 8:30, Peter speaks of his readers as already in possession of salvation. But of course this emphasis on the "here-and-nowness" of salvation fits in well with the doctrine of "realized eschatology" (see Vol. VII, pp. 148-49, 656-57) in the Synoptic Gospels, Paul's conception of justification by faith, and John's doctrine of eternal life as a present possession of the believer in Christ. **End** (τέλος) may be either (*a*) temporal: "result" or "outcome"; or (*b*) logical: "issue" or "consummation."

B. The Prophets and the Gospel (1:10-12)

The theme of the following three verses may be put in a sentence, "The yearnings and searchings of the old prophets find their fulfillment in Christ and his redemption."

---

and believing on him they rejoiced greatly with joy unspeakable. Christ is the final motive and goal of salvation. Some saw him in the flesh, and we all shall see him one day at his revealing. We rely upon the testimony of those who did see him in the flesh, and we also know him through the realizing power of faith. Through personal faith we have a "personal affection and devotion" to him in the heart. Faith's "fair vision" will one day "change into sight," we sing. But faith is more than a "fair vision"; it is a unique personal relationship to a Person who lived and taught and suffered and wept and died. In the Incarnation the invisible Word became flesh, and some were given the privilege of seeing and touching the Word made flesh; in the Resurrection, and particularly in the Ascension, the man Jesus of Nazareth was taken up into the invisible world so that the "heavenly place" is no longer a vague realm of bodyless spirits. Jesus Christ is in that world; he was raised to sit at the right hand of God the Father. We may no longer see him in the flesh, but we set our faith upon a living Lord, who is like unto us even now, and in that unseen world is our advocate before the Father.

Not only was the Word made flesh, but the flesh has been raised into the heavenly places of the spiritual world in Jesus Christ. Our faith is not set on a vague series of propositions, but upon a person. The reason for the Christian's joy, which defies words to express (**unspeakable**), is his warm relationship to the Christ who though unseen is real, and his utter confidence in the Christ who lives and reigns at the heart of things. As the eleventh-century hymn puts it:

> But what to those who find? Ah, this
> Nor tongue, nor pen can show:
> The love of Jesus, what it is
> None but his loved ones know.[8]

The glorious outcome of such a faith is **the salvation of your souls.** Faith in Christ is no vain thing; it is the way to man's highest joy, now and in all eternity.

10-12. Salvation Sent from Heaven.—How can we rightly value **this salvation?** Peter maintains that the **prophets . . . searched and inquired** about it. Indeed, the angels long to

[8] "Jesus, the very thought of thee," tr. Edward Caswall.

| 11 Searching what, or what manner of time the Spirit of Christ which was in them did signify, when it testified beforehand the sufferings of Christ, and the glory that should follow. | inquired about this salvation; 11 they inquired what person or time was indicated by the Spirit of Christ within them when predicting the sufferings of Christ and the |

But the verses are difficult, and a paraphrase may clarify them: "It was nothing but this hope of salvation which mightily exercised the prophets of old. They strove to learn when and how would be fulfilled those mysterious things to which the Spirit of the Messiah, speaking in them, pointed. That Spirit spoke of the Messiah's sufferings and the glories to follow them. They knew, these olden prophets, that these things would be fulfilled not in their own generation, but in some blessed future one. And that fulfillment you now enjoy in the gospel."

10. The prophets are the O.T. prophets, and not (as Selwyn argues) those of the apostolic church. **Inquired and searched:** in the Greek two synonyms denoting a prolonged search. Dan. 9:24-27 is perhaps an example of such "search." **The grace that was to be yours:** Peter means God's grace shown in all the blessings of the gospel. In his speeches recorded in the early chapters of Acts, Peter is at great pains to show that Jesus the Messiah is the fulfillment of all the hopes of the O.T. prophets. Indeed, as C. H. Dodd has shown in his *Apostolic Preaching* (London: Hodder & Stoughton, 1936), the first plank in the apostles' platform was that the life, death, and resurrection of Jesus and the outpouring of the Spirit were the fulfillment of the prophecy. We cannot today state the argument from prophecy in the precise form used by the earliest preachers; what we need is a restatement of the argument from prophecy which will show that Jesus and the church are the fulfillment of the spiritual principles of the O.T., that in fact the O.T. is one great question, to which the N.T. supplies the answer. For praiseworthy attempts to do this very thing see A. G. Hebert, *The Throne of David* (New York: Morehouse-Gorham, 1941); W. J. Phythian-Adams, *The Fulness of Israel* (London: Oxford University Press, 1938); and R. V. G. Tasker, *The Old Testament in the New Testament* (Philadelphia: The Westminster Press, 1947).

11. The Spirit of Christ which was in them: With this phrase cf. Paul's "the Spirit of Christ" (Rom. 8:9); "The Rock was Christ" (I Cor. 10:4). The N.T. writers identify the Spirit of Christ, who controlled their lives, with the Spirit of Yahweh, who inspired the prophets.

The sufferings of Christ, and the glory that should follow: If we ask what particular scripture in the O.T. predicted Christ's sufferings and triumphs, Isa. 53 leaps immediately to mind. There not only the humiliation and death of the servant are described, but in the last three verses his vindication and victory. But, in fact, there is no evidence that the Jews held the doctrine of a suffering Messiah, or interpreted Isa. 53 in a messianic

---

get a peep into it. History and heaven are concerned about this matter of salvation. Christians are the fortunate recipients of something which has been the object of earnest speculation and anxious inquiry for centuries by all living spirits. Of all peoples, those of the O.T. community were inspired by the Spirit of God to inquire about God's salvation which would include all men. In that messianic community it was the prophets especially who were given to see in a measure and to speak about the suffering and the glory of the world's Redeemer. The prophets but anticipated this salvation; they saw it from afar as Moses saw Canaan from Pisgah; Christians know it from experience.

Jesus once spoke of the "prophets and kings" who desired to see, and could not, the things which his disciples saw, and to hear the things which they heard (Matt. 13:16-17; Luke 10:23; 24:44). While Abraham and Isaiah, according to John's Gospel, had intimations of the coming Messiah's glory, it is true that those who know only the prophetic hope are, in spite of their Spirit-inspired insight, not as fortunate as are the simplest Christians who live in the messianic era and know Christ's grace and presence.

The Gentiles are no afterthought in the redemptive work of Christ; God thought of them from the beginning. The gospel is no

12 Unto whom it was revealed, that not unto themselves, but unto us they did minister the things, which are now reported unto you by them that have preached the gospel unto you with the Holy Ghost sent down from heaven; which things the angels desire to look into.

13 Wherefore gird up the loins of your mind, be sober, and hope to the end for the grace that is to be brought unto you at the revelation of Jesus Christ;

subsequent glory. 12 It was revealed to them that they were serving not themselves but you, in the things which have now been announced to you by those who preached the good news to you through the Holy Spirit sent from heaven, things into which angels long to look.

13 Therefore gird up your minds, be sober, set your hope fully upon the grace that is coming to you at the revelation of

---

sense. It was our Lord who first fused in his own conception of his messiahship the sublime figures of the Son of man and the servant of Yahweh. In this passage by **the glory that should follow** Peter means, no doubt, the Resurrection, the outpouring of the Spirit, and the expansion of the church as the fulfillment of the closing verses in Isa. 53.

12. They did minister the things: Peter here sees the O.T. prophets as serving God not for their own sakes or times, but for ours; they were doing work, the full import of which was hid from themselves and is disclosed only now in the gospel. **Through the Holy Spirit sent from heaven:** The primary reference is to the descent of the Spirit on the day of Pentecost described in Acts 2.

Things into which angels long to look: The Greek word for **look** (παρακύψαι) means to "peep" or "peer into" (cf. Luke 24:12; John 20:5, 11). In I Cor. 4:9 Paul speaks of the apostles as "a spectacle" for the angels (cf. also Eph. 3:10). The blessings of the gospel are here said to excite the envious interest of the angels.

C. Exhortation to Holy Living (1:13–2:3)

Truth for the apostolic writers is always "truth in order to goodness." So, having dwelt on the gospel, Peter now considers the sort of life his readers ought to live. The sum of this exhortation is: Live holy and pure lives, (*a*) because God your Father is holy (vss. 13-17); (*b*) because you have been redeemed at infinite cost by Christ (vss. 18-21); and (*c*) because you have been born anew (vss. 22-25).

13. Wherefore gird up the loins of your mind: In the East to **gird up the loins** is to tuck up one's skirts into the belt in readiness for action. The metaphor had been used

---

makeshift plan which just came into being haphazardly; on the contrary, God planned everything as it has come out, and as it will be consummated. He laid hold of the prophets and gave them of the spirit of Messiah, to be the pointers to his glorious redemption. Yet they did not enter into it. It was all for **you**, says Peter. God is no arbitrary force; he serves all men by providing a gospel of salvation through a companion sufferer on life's pilgrimage, who was exalted to high heaven on our behalf. And through the same Spirit this gospel was preached to you; indeed, it was **sent from heaven.**

Such a salvation even **the angels long to** glimpse. Perfect angels who know nothing of the agony and anguish of guilt and despair know little of the wondrous gospel of forgiveness and eternal life. What can an elder brother know of the joy of a prodigal redeemed from a pig sty by his father's love? What can perfect

spirits understand of the marvelous grace of God and its wondrous power to redeem sinners? There is, says Charles Wesley,

> A song which even angels
> Can never, never sing.[9]

1:13–2:3. *Good News and Good Conduct.*— Peter does not permit his readers to remain on a mountaintop ecstatically viewing the blessed hope of the future, or contemplating the precious inheritance that is reserved for them. With a suddenness that is breathtaking he plunges them into the practical implications of the salvation in which they rejoice now and will enter hereafter.

Dorothy L. Sayers, the English lay theologian, dramatist, and detective story writer, once defined the seven most conspicuous "virtues" of ordinary church members as respectability,

[9] "There's a Friend for little children."

14 As obedient children, not fashioning yourselves according to the former lusts in your ignorance:

Jesus Christ. 14 As obedient children, do not be conformed to the passions of your

---

by our Lord, "Let your loins be girded and your lamps burning" (Luke 12:35; cf. Browning's lines from "The Statue and the Bust") :

> And the sin I impute to each frustrate ghost
> Is—the unlit lamp and the ungirt loin.

Our equivalent would be, "Roll up your sleeves" or better, "Brace yourselves."

Be sober: Not "Don't indulge immoderately," but "Keep calm": sound counsel in time of crisis. So Paul, when some readers in Thessalonica became morbidly excited about Christ's second coming, bade them "study to be quiet" (I Thess. 4:11) .

Hope to the end for the grace (KJV) or **set your hope fully upon the grace** (RSV) : Prefer the latter. Τελείως means "completely" or "fully." **The grace that is to be brought:** lit., "that is being brought," as though the coming grace cast its shadow before it. **The grace** is the final expression of "God's love in action" which the Christians will experience when Christ is "unveiled" in all his majesty as judge and redeemer.

14. As obedient children: Despite its emphasis on Christian freedom, obedience is one of the cardinal virtues of the N.T. **Not fashioning yourselves according to the former lusts in your ignorance** (cf. RSV) . This means, "Don't relapse into your former bad habits when you were pagans." The Jews with the law could hardly plead **ignorance;** therefore it is likely that Peter has Gentiles here primarily in his eye.

---

childishness, mental timidity, dullness, sentimentality, censoriousness, and depression of spirits.[1] No one of these so-called "virtues" is listed by Peter. The Christian ethic was to him something new and nonconformist, and it was based upon the Christian's sense of new life which was rooted in a living Christ and in the order of which he was the center.

Wherefore is a call to arms. Like Paul's "therefore" in Rom. 12:1, it links Christian faith and action and relates the grace of the gospel to the conduct of the believer on the dusty road of life. In the light of the Christian's dignity and destiny he has a high vocation to fulfill. "To whom much is given, of him will much be required" (Luke 12:48) . There is no favor without a corresponding debt of gratitude to be discharged. This man Peter had a muscular faith: it was learned in companionship with the Jesus who went about doing good, who washed the disciples' feet, and performed countless works of mercy; it was made dynamic by the will to serve a Christ who had loved Peter utterly, in spite of his terrible failure.

Gird up your minds. Pull yourself together mentally; go in for some hard thought. People in Peter's day who wished to engage in some strenuous activity pulled up their long robes and tucked them into their belts. Today we roll

[1] *Creed or Chaos?* (New York: Harcourt Brace & Co., 1949), p. 23.

up our sleeves and take off excessive clothing. Being a Christian who is saved by grace does not excuse one from hard theological thinking. We must be able to give a reason for the hope that is within us (3:15) ; we must wrestle with the meaning of salvation in a confused age. The cry for less theology is not in harmony with the demands of the gospel. Individual Christians and congregations ought to be intelligent about the meaning of the gospel in the light of the times. The church is the community in which Christ's mind is being formed and his truth is taken seriously; the church is a high community of rigorous thinking on the part of those who have girded up the loins of their minds.

Men are to love God with their minds, and the gospel is the good news that truth has come to rescue them from the slavery of error and the darkness of falsehood. The light of revealed truth is the source of liberty. A real church is a teaching church. It refuses the superficial demand of sentimental people for sermons that entertain but do not instruct and for an easy Christianity which makes no demands upon the mind. If the church is to be saved from becoming a "blind leader of the blind," it must gird up its mental loins and become a militant teacher of the truth that sets men free from crippling superstition, blinding ignorance, and damning error.

Be sober; keep cool; keep steady. Impetuous

15 But as he which hath called you is holy, so be ye holy in all manner of conversation;

16 Because it is written, Be ye holy; for I am holy.

17 And if ye call on the Father, who without respect of persons judgeth according to every man's work, pass the time of your sojourning *here* in fear:

former ignorance, 15 but as he who called you is holy, be holy yourselves in all your conduct; 16 since it is written, "You shall be holy, for I am holy." 17 And if you invoke as Father him who judges each one impartially according to his deeds, conduct yourselves with fear throughout the time

---

15. But as he who called you is holy: Better, "Like the Holy One who has called you." A reminiscence of Isaiah's distinctive name for God, e.g., "Thus saith the Lord GoD, the Holy One of Israel" (Isa. 30:15). **Called:** A reference to the readers' conversion, when God summoned them to a new life of holiness, of separation from sin and progress toward moral perfection. (Cf. Matt. 5:48, "Be ye therefore perfect, even as your Father which is in heaven is perfect.")

16. It is written: The quotation is from Lev. 11:44-45. Christianity, no less than Judaism, summons to holiness; but the holiness it demands is not ritual and outward, but inner—the holiness of "the pure in heart" who shall "see God" because they are like him.

17. And if you invoke as Father: As in Rom. 8:15 and Gal. 4:6, the reference here is probably to the corporate recitation of the Lord's Prayer, which in its Lukan form (probably original) begins simply, "Father" (Luke 11:2). **Who without respect of**

Peter counsels his friends twice (4:7; 5:8) to avoid the excesses of their pagan world, a world which literally glittered with seductive allurements to sensuality. Live the plain life, admonishes the old veteran, and keep your eyes on **the grace that is coming to you at the revelation of Jesus Christ.** This sobriety does not refer only to alcoholic excesses; rather it instructs the Christian to hold himself back from an intoxication with anything which would rob him of his poise, his sanity, his reasoned judgment. There is an intoxication of the body, of the mind, and even of the spirit which may lead one to an unbalanced and "drunken" life. Kipling pleaded with his beloved Britain not to be "drunk with sight of power,"[2] lest it lose its ability to make responsible judgments.

Be hopeful! Set your hope on the grace that is coming to you when Jesus Christ is revealed; and set your hope absolutely and unreservedly on the gracious action of God in Christ. There are temptations on every hand to build up hopes for the future out of the events in history, or out of the aspirations of men; but they are illusory and unreliable.

Hope perfectly! Let your hope be rightly informed and correct. Do not allow it to become perverted one way or another. Keep it set on the maximum and on the ultimate; all intermediate and temporal hopes will deceive. And do not allow the discouragements of the

[2] "Recessional."

times and the delays in its fulfillment to cause your hope to be dimmed. There is only one hope for the world: Jesus Christ the Lord, who is still to be fully revealed in all his glory. The crucified, risen, reigning, and coming Christ is the one bright prospect for the world's redemption. To him the Christian clings for good and for all.

Be obedient! **As obedient children** who owe their all to God they will do what befits such people. They live by no human ideal, nor do they strain to obey cold commandments. Obedience is to a gracious Person, and in doing his good pleasure men will find their highest joy and peace. They fashion themselves inwardly and outwardly, not according to the prevailing customs and mores of society. They do not engage in the loose and lusty living of their Gentile pre-Christian days, when they were ignorant of the higher life. Nor do they use God to give them "peace of mind" or a "happy feeling inside," thus putting man and his wishes at the center instead of God and his gracious purpose. Churches and Christians who make God a master butler, and who refuse to practice the spiritual disciplines, soon cease to possess the primary quality of God's children and lose their cutting sense of life direction. The Christian must put on the whole armor of God and engage in battle. "All things are yours," Paul wrote to the Corinthian Christians (I Cor. 3:21-22); the Christian is a child of God and heir to all that is his Father's. "This is my

18 Forasmuch as ye know that ye were not redeemed with corruptible things, *as* silver and gold, from your vain conversation *received* by tradition from your fathers;

of your exile. 18 You know that you were ransomed from the futile ways inherited from your fathers, not with perishable

---

persons judgeth: Cf. Peter's words in Acts 10:34, "God is no respecter of persons." A judge might allow his judgment to be swayed by other things than the strict merits of the case, e.g., the social standing of his client or a fat bribe. **Father who . . . judgeth:** There is no antithesis between God's fatherhood and his sovereignty. Peter is simply reminding his readers that if God is their Father, he is also one who cannot palter with sin but must judge it. On the other hand, it is a comforting thought that our judge is "the God and Father of our Lord Jesus Christ." **Sojourning** (παροικίας): Better, **exile** (RSV), i.e., from their true home which is in heaven. **With fear** means "reverently."

18. Forasmuch as ye know that . . . : The Christian's holy living should spring from a realization of the costliness of his redemption. **Redeemed:** The basic idea of the Greek word (ἐλυτρώθητε) is of ransoming (cf. RSV) from slavery into freedom—a rite that was sometimes accompanied by a sacrifice. Peter, no doubt, derives the metaphor from his Lord, who had spoken of his atoning sacrifice as "a ransom for many" (Mark 10:45). Here Peter does not adumbrate a doctrine of atonement, but is content to state the cost of it. The price of redemption was not perishable **silver and gold,** but the lifeblood of the sinless lamb of God.

From the futile ways inherited from your fathers: Peter describes the degradation of the old life in two striking epithets: first, it is ματαία, **futile,** a fumbling, groping life which makes no effective contact with reality and whose mournful verdict at the end must ever be *vanitas vanitatum,* all is vanity; and second, it is πατροπαράδοτος, utterly traditional and conventional, destitute of moral initiative or originality. How different, he would say, is the life that Christ has touched, how new and fruitful and effective!

Father's world . . ."; and because it is, all things good, true, and beautiful are the Christian's by inheritance. But with the "worldliness" of the world, and with a secular, covetous lust for the satisfactions which this world can give man's sensuous "flesh," there can be no compromise; only ceaseless warfare is in order here, to keep the body under (I Cor. 9:27). Obedience is the one antidote to the world's corrosive processes. The child of God is no longer fashioned **according to** [his] **former lusts** which were given free play in his pre-Christian days. Only a stronger obedience to Christ can master the pull of an appeal to the lower life.

Be holy! Because the God **who called you is holy,** you are called—and privileged—to be holy. Would that we could put ancient words through a cleansing process by which they would lose their odor of bad associations! The stereotyped "Holy Joe" has no attraction for anyone; he is an artificial "saint" who is denatured of real humanity. Or he wears a halo of sanctity which makes his religiousness forbidding, if not repulsive. Holiness too has been associated with a sanctimoniousness which frowns upon simple pleasures and feeds on the dry crumbs of ascetic negativism. It may even smack of hypocrisy;

for many a "holy" person wears a mask of sinlessness behind which he hides a pit of writhing sins like pride, envy, etc. All too often it is associated with monks living and praying in monasteries, with retreatants attending quiet places to cultivate the "spiritual life," with aspirants after a perfection which puts them beyond the possibility of sin.

What a travesty on this key word of the Scriptures! To **be holy** means to be separated or set apart for a special and unique purpose. God is holy in his person because he is in a class by himself, and he stands over against man as "absolute authority." [3] He is not merely the majestic central power behind and in and through all things. The prophets make it plain that he is altogether right in his being, attributes, and actions. God is God, not something or someone else.

Because God is holy, therefore Israel too is a holy, a separated, a peculiar people, who have been called to perform a unique role in history, to be the "chosen" agency through which God reveals himself to men and works out the ad-

[3] See Walther Eichrodt, *Theologie des Alten Testaments* (3rd ed.; Berlin: Evangelische Verlagsanstalt, 1948), I, 139-46.

19 But with the precious blood of Christ, as of a lamb without blemish and without spot:

20 Who verily was foreordained before the foundation of the world, but was manifest in these last times for you,

21 Who by him do believe in God, that raised him up from the dead, and gave him glory; that your faith and hope might be in God.

things such as silver or gold, 19 but with the precious blood of Christ, like that of a lamb without blemish or spot. 20 He was destined before the foundation of the world but was made manifest at the end of the times for your sake. 21 Through him you have confidence in God, who raised him from the dead and gave him glory, so that your faith and hope are in God.[d]

[d] Or so that your faith is hope in God.

19. But with the precious blood of Christ: The phrase, as Selwyn says (*First Epistle of Peter*, p. 145), describes "the nature of the ransom-price (blood, not money), its costliness (precious, not perishable), and its religious significance (sacrificial and Messianic)." Christ is conceived as the Christian's paschal lamb, and the figure sets forth Christ as the flawless sacrifice (cf. Exod. 12:5; John 1:29-34; Rev. 13:8).

20. Destined before the foundation of the world, i.e., before Creation, God had intended Christ as Redeemer; cf. Acts 4:28, where Peter explains Christ's death in terms of the predetermined plan of God, and Eph. 1:4 ("He chose us in him [Christ] before the foundation of the world"). **Manifest,** i.e., in his incarnation, resurrection, and exaltation. **At the end of the times:** Peter regards the Christian Era as the last period in the religious history of man.

21. Through him you have confidence in God: Observe that here the brethren believe in God, not because the Son has revealed the Father (Matt. 11:27), but because the Father has revealed the Son—revealed him by raising him from the dead. The Resurrection is God's mightiest act, the act which more than any other reveals him as the living God. A verse like this seems to bear the Petrine mark upon it, for it was the Resurrection which wonderfully restored Peter's shattered faith. **Gave him glory,** i.e., honored by exalting him (cf. Acts 3:13, "The God of our fathers glorified his servant Jesus").

vance section of his redemptive purpose for all mankind. Israel was not holy by reason of its own ethical efforts; it was holy because God chose it. The character of Israel's God was reflected in its life and work. Israel's sin and shame and Israel's glory are in proportion to its faithfulness in letting the kingdom and the power and the glory of God shine through it.

Peter makes clear that members of the Christian church are the new Israel; they are "saints," called to be holy . . . in all . . . conduct. The character and purpose of the God and Father of the Lord Jesus Christ is so impressed upon them that they are "set apart" and "called out" for a special vocation and destiny. They too are in a class by themselves among men. Says W. E. Sangster: "The church's *one* privation . . . is *holiness*."[4] What the church needs is the quality of saintliness, of goodness in the "inward parts." Had the church this quality, it would experience revival, know spiritual power, conquer atheism and agnosticism, produce great leaders, move toward church union, and have "ebullient joy."

[4] "The Church's One Privation," *Religion in Life*, XVIII (1949), 493-502.

How long could the world really ignore a holy church? The church fails of impressiveness in the world largely because there is not enough difference between the people inside and those outside to strike a contrast. Sangster asks for no holiness found in retreat, or in spiritual ecstatics, or in hypocritical perfectionism, or in the cult of holiness; rather he calls for a holiness at home by the washtub as well as in a chapel.

Be fearful! But let your fear be inspired by and directed toward God. He has allowed men to address him as Father, but that does not give men the right to slap him on the back or treat him as an indulgent old gentleman who has lost all power of making impartial moral judgments. Grace abounds, especially where sin is most heinous; but Christians have no right on that account to continue to live without obedience to the moral law. Love is not sentimentality which permits anything to go; the holy love of God alone shows up the damning and diabolical character of man's unloveliness, as the light reveals the filth of dark alleys and the masterpiece puts the fraud to shame. "Reverence" or "proper respect" for God is the beginning of

22 Seeing ye have purified your souls in obeying the truth through the Spirit unto unfeigned love of the brethren, *see that ye love one another with a pure heart fervently:*

23 Being born again, not of corruptible seed, but of incorruptible, by the word of God, which liveth and abideth for ever.

22 Having purified your souls by your obedience to the truth for a sincere love of the brethren, love one another earnestly from the heart. 23 You have been born anew, not of perishable seed but of imperishable, through the living and abiding

---

22. The RSV is much clearer and more accurate than the KJV here. Peter's meaning is: "Your obedient acceptance of the [gospel] truth has cleansed your souls and made them ready for true love of the brethren; so let your love for one another be spontaneous and fervent." **The truth** is "the gospel"; cf. II Thess. 2:10, 12, 13. **Love of the brethren:** Not vague "brotherly love" but "brother-love"—the family spirit in a Christian community, "that noblest jewel in the diadem of early Christianity" (Gunkel).

23. Being born again: The general sense is that Peter's readers have been born anew through the gospel. **Seed,** the Greek σπορά, may mean either "seed" or "sowing." If we prefer the first, we may find the explanation in the parable of the sower, "The seed is the word of God." **By the word of God, which liveth and abideth:** This is explained in vs. 25*b* as **the good news which was preached to you,** i.e., the gospel.

---

wise thinking and living; it gives us a deterring fear, lest we treat God's judgments lightly, and saves us from that godless living which collapses in the day of testing.

But "reverence" toward God will also give us that authentic sense of "wonder, love, and praise" for his infinite love which took the initiative for our redemption and which paid the utmost price for our salvation. Anyone who has stood at the foot of the "wondrous cross" and has been overwhelmed by meeting such "love and sorrow" will sink into silent worship as he repeats the grand verse:

> Were the whole realm of nature mine,
>   That were a present far too small;
> Love so amazing, so divine,
>   Demands my soul, my life, my all.[5]

Peter expresses his own experience when he says that Christianity is a redemption, a deliverance, a freedom, which is personal and centers in a person. It centers not in a ritual, a table of laws, a system of philosophy, but in a God who "so loved the world, that he gave his only begotten Son" (John 3:16) ; and also in a Son who so loved erring men and so obeyed his holy Father that he did what needed to be done to bring them together. By his suffering and through his broken body and poured-out life he satisfied all parties and conditions, so that in his lifetime the "transcendent origin" became an event in history. The great work of redemption which was ordained by God **before the foundation of the world** was manifested once and for all. It cannot happen again. Calvary

[5] Isaac Watts, "When I survey the wondrous cross."

has something mysteriously final and finished about it; it marked "the end of the times" of preparation, indeed the end of preredemptive history. From then on men have lived in a new era: A.R., After Redemption. We live in the time between redemption and consummation. What God had in mind from all eternity came to birth in Bethlehem, to fulfillment on Calvary, to victory at the Resurrection, to exaltation on the mount of Ascension, and is even now coming to consummation. This grand sweep of God's glorious gospel staggers the mind, humbles the heart, and subdues the whole being in silent adoration. And yet, writes Peter, this whole drama of redemption which begins in all eternity is brought to bear upon individuals. It was all **made manifest . . . for your sake,** as though the Eternal One serves the lone individual with all that is at his disposal. This is the way—even Jesus Christ. By him we have come to believe in God as Father and to trust him. Even so, let no one who has experienced so great a redemption, centering in the Christ who was raised and glorified by God, forget that his faith and his hope are in God—not in himself. Had not God raised and glorified Christ Jesus, how could we have any confidence and hope?

Love one another from the heart. Sincere and genuine love of Christian for Christian is one of the hallmarks of the Christian's conduct. Brotherly love is of the very essence of the Christian community. Peter knew what love meant from bitter experience. He had seen it in Jesus; he had experienced it in his own restoration. There is an orthodoxy of charity which few churches apply to their members, yet it is every bit as im-

24 For all flesh *is* as grass, and all the glory of man as the flower of grass. The grass withereth, and the flower thereof falleth away:

25 But the word of the Lord endureth for ever. And this is the word which by the gospel is preached unto you.

2 Wherefore laying aside all malice, and all guile, and hypocrisies, and envies, and all evil speakings,

word of God; 24 for
"All flesh is like grass
and all its glory like the flower of grass.
The grass withers, and the flower falls,
25 but the word of the Lord abides forever."
That word is the good news which was preached to you.

2 So put away all malice and all guile and insincerity and envy and all slander.

---

24. This is taken from Isa. 40:6-8 (LXX). Peter's meaning is: "You have read in Isaiah of a word of God which abides when all else fails and falls. Well, that word is the gospel." And the gospel is sempiternal because its center is "Jesus Christ the same yesterday, and to-day, and for ever" (Heb. 13:8).

2:1. **Wherefore:** i.e., since you are born again. The sins enumerated are, it is implied, survivals of the old bad life. **Malice,** the inclination to harm one's neighbor. **Guile,** the inclination to get the better of him unfairly. **Hypocrisies, . . . envies, . . . evil speakings:** The three plurals probably mean, "All sorts of hypocrisy, etc."

---

portant as the orthodoxy of doctrine. Truth and grace belong together indeed, and when separated the Christian life may degenerate into a rigid doctrinaire theology, or into sentimental and amorphous altruism. Many a sad church controversy could have been avoided if Christians had kept "faith" and "love" together. Love for the brethren is a requirement of the Christian's confession of faith. John makes that clear in his first epistle (I John 4:20); faith and works are twins; the relation to God and the relation to the neighbor are bound up in one great law. This love is active and intense; it is without guile or hypocrisy; it partakes of the kind of love that was in Jesus Christ. Fervent love for the brethren issues from the "purifying" effort of the Christian as he "obeys" the **truth** and is moved by the power of **the Spirit.** Those who vow to become followers of Christ yield themselves in obedience to that body of truth which must end in the life of love. "Truth is in order to goodness," declares a great confession of faith; for the truth that is in Christ Jesus is no mere abstract set of doctrines. Rather it is that personal and dynamic reality about God and man which is aimed at the conversion of persons. "Faith, hope, love abide, these three; but the greatest of these is love" (I Cor. 13:13). Love is the greatest thing in the world; it is the objective of truth. **You have been born anew . . . through the living and abiding word of God.** This love is the acid test of the Christian life. Peter's dramatic charge to mental effort, to sobriety, to hopefulness, to antiworldly struggle, to holiness, to reverence,

means little if anything unless brotherly love is genuine. The presence of this love attests to the fact that one has new life within him, generated by the living, abiding, and imperishable **word of the Lord**—which is the **good news.**

One of the chief characteristics of the early church was the love that Christians bore one toward another. Faced with cruel persecution and pagan derision, Christians needed each other. And their cohesive loyalty was generated by Jesus Christ, who "loved his own . . . to the end" (John 13:1). This love is the full fruit of the word of God. And **that word is the good news which was preached to you.** The new life in Christ is initiated and matured not by any human agency but by the glorious power of the living and imperishable word. We are dealing here with no mundane matter, nor are we dealing with the liturgies of mystery religions or the philosophies and speculations of men; we are dealing with a revelation.

Put away all malice and all guile and insincerity and envy and all slander. Be done with all of it. The Christian is "born" to a new order and community of life; he is "crucified" and "dead" to the old age. It is not enough to strive for the positive virtues of Christian discipleship; there are unchristian habits and attitudes and customs to be discarded. Greco-Roman culture was saturated with a pagan spirit against which the Christian had to contend night and day. He was in a veritable spiritual warfare against degrading and disintegrating practices and ideas which threatened his personal integrity and his social relations.

2 As newborn babes, desire the sincere milk of the word, that ye may grow thereby:

2 Like newborn babes, long for the pure spiritual milk, that by it you may grow up

---

2. Like newborn babes, long for the pure spiritual milk: The sense is, "Long for the milk of the gospel as a babe for his mother's breast." The adjective **newborn** might imply that the readers' conversion was very recent; but the point of the simile is surely the ardor of the suckled child. Ἐπιποθήσατε, the Greek word rendered **desire** (KJV) or **long for** (RSV), is the same word as in the Greek version of Ps. 42:1, "As the hart panteth after the waterbrooks, etc." The crux here is the adjective λογικόν. It may mean (a) rational; (b) metaphorical; (c) belonging to the word (KJV); (d) spiritual (RSV); cf. Rom. 12:1, the only other place where the word occurs in the N.T. Our choice seems to lie between (c) and (d), nor is there much difference between them. On the twin grounds that λόγος in the N.T. always means "word," and that Peter is probably catching up 1:23, the KJV is preferable, the **milk of the word**—**the word** being the gospel. **Sincere** (ἄδολον): The word in the papyri regularly means "unadulterated"; cf. RSV **pure.**

That by it you may grow up to salvation: The words **to salvation**, not in the KJV, are probably part of the true text, and the meaning is, "That [feeding] on it [the milk of the word] you may grow up to salvation," salvation being a mature state, not something achieved *per saltum* at conversion.

Because the Christian was faced with such a world and animated by the mind of Christ, Peter admonished him to dissociate himself from all the evil and wickedness of the pagan world, from the devious deceitfulness of the unstraightforward, from the pretending duplicity of those who conceal their evil motives behind a friendly face or gesture, from the slanderous back-chat of those who are always disparaging others. "A man that is characteristically deceitful, cunning, and crafty, cannot be a Christian." [6] It is the work of the gospel to ferret out and reveal hostility toward others, deceitfulness, false appearances, hatred of those who surpass us, unkind and vicious talk. The gospel aims to probe the hidden motives of the heart, bring them out into the clear, and have them judged and condemned in the light of Jesus Christ.

Grow up to salvation. Peter would remember the time when he and his friends were quarreling about position and prestige. Jesus dramatically set a child in their midst and addressed them with the humiliating and edifying truth: "Except ye be converted, and become as little children, ye shall not enter into the kingdom of heaven" (Matt. 18:3). He was also reminded of the injunction given him at the Galilean seaside: "Feed my lambs" (John 21:15). **Newborn babes** famishingly crave and ardently seek the mother's breast for nourishment. They are uninhibited in their eagerness to find the source of their existence and growth into physical maturity. It is so by their very

nature. They cry out for milk that not only satisfies the hunger, but really nourishes the growing body. Those who have really **tasted** the goodness and **kindness of the Lord** have developed a hunger and thirst for the nourishment of the spirit that cannot be satisfied with anything that is adulterated, or with anything that is a substitute. The Christian faith is such that everyone who wishes the satisfactions that it promises to give must come to receive it with a hungry faith and a famishing thirst. We are "saved by faith," by reception, by trust.

And it might be well to provide nourishment in the right form. No one gives a baby solid foods. And certainly no one gives him acid for milk; neither does he give the craving soul a philosophy for the gospel. The formula must fit the stage of growth, although at every stage the eager spirit of a hungry infant crying for pure milk provides a vivid and proper symbol of desire.

The word **salvation** has a divine meaning, but here Peter reminds his friends that while salvation is a free gift of God's grace, it is also a development toward a perfection which requires long and hard discipline. As children are not meant to remain infants but to grow in stature, so the Christian is under compulsion to develop from birth into maturity. When the Christian or the church ceases to yearn for growth in "grace and knowledge," both are on the way to senility. The impotence of the Christian movement in any age may be traced to its lack of the hunger and thirst for the things that truly satisfy life. A self-satisfied church is no longer Christian. A Christian who no longer aspires to perfection is a fraud. The apostle

[6] Albert Barnes, *Notes, Explanatory and Practical, on the General Epistles of James, Peter, John and Jude* (New York: Harper & Bros., 1865), p. 153.

3 If so be ye have tasted that the Lord is gracious. 4 To whom coming, *as unto* a living stone, disallowed indeed of men, but chosen of God, *and* precious,	to salvation; 3 for you have tasted the kindness of the Lord. 4 Come to him, to that living stone, rejected by men but in God's sight chosen

3. If so be ye have tasted . . . : The RSV is much better. If means "seeing that," and the words that follow echo Ps. 34:8, "Taste and see that the Lord is good [kind]." So the meaning is, "Seeing you have accepted the psalmist's invitation and found that the Lord (i.e., Christ) is good." The thought of Christ as "the bread of life" lies close to hand.

D. The Cornerstone and the New Temple of God (2:4-10)

From exhortation Peter turns to speak of Christ and the church under the figures of the cornerstone and the new temple of God. Both conceptions go back to the Lord himself; for Christ had applied to himself the psalmist's words about "the stone which the builders rejected" and, in a saying which has come down to us only in the garbled version of his enemies, had prophesied that he would "build" a new shrine or temple, "made without hands," for the worship of the new people of God (cf. Mark 14:58; John 2:19).

Summary: Christ our Savior is a living stone, nay, the cornerstone in the new temple of God, and you, his worshipers, are to be living stones in that temple, built around him. He has made you priests unto God. To you who believe belongs the honor that is his, but to those who disbelieve he is like a stone in the path to trip over. You Christian believers have inherited the spiritual vocation of the old Israel: you are the new people of God, called to manifest his glories in the surrounding darkness and to be worthy of the great mercy which God has shown you.

4. To whom coming (προσερχόμενοι): The participle is present, denoting repeated action. The Christian is always coming to Christ afresh, for "the perseverance of the saints consists of ever-new beginnings." The RSV translates the word in connection with οἰκοδομεῖσθε as another imperative. **A living stone:** the origin of what we may call "the

Paul was an eager man who had not yet apprehended the riches of grace that are in Christ, but pressed on "toward the mark for the prize of the high calling of God in Christ Jesus" (Phil. 3:14). His life was animated by a restless passion to "attain unto the resurrection of the dead" (Phil. 3:11). Peter is convinced that this eagerness to grow up rests ultimately upon whether one has **tasted** [of] **the kindness of the Lord.** Those who have no taste for music, or education, or world peace seldom work at it. And those who have no taste for the things of God will seldom stir themselves toward growth into the stature of Christ.

4-10. *Becoming God's Own People.*—A. N. Whitehead once declared that "religion is what the individual does with his own solitariness." [7] True as this statement is about the uniqueness and loneliness of personal religious experience, it hardly does justice to the sociology of religion generally, or to the social nature of the Christian faith particularly. Not only are men born into a religious community, or a community with religious institutions and symbols and meanings; the community itself is the bearer and channel of historic religion. No individual creates his religion out of nothing; he inherits a religion and either conforms to it, transforms it, or leaves it for another. Christianity comes to us through the Christian community, and without a relation to the Christian community our individual Christianity becomes either impossible or tenuous and incomplete. Jesus Christ has a body, which is the church. There is no disembodied Christianity. Those who are related to Christ as Lord and Savior relate themselves to the church. Christianity is a social faith, for it embodies itself in a unique and organic community of fellow believers.

Peter had caught the mind of Christ in this matter. He was a Jew who believed passionately in the Lord's covenant relation with his people. In fact, so strong was Peter's attachment to the Jewish church that it took a special revelation to convince him that Gentiles could become members of the new covenant. Even then, in spite of that experience, he found it hard to break through his Jewishness and to have fellow-

[7] *Religion in the Making* (New York: The Macmillan Co., 1926), p. 16.

5 Ye also, as lively stones, are built up a spiritual house, a holy priesthood, to offer up spiritual sacrifices, acceptable to God by Jesus Christ.

and precious; 5 and like living stones be yourselves built into a spiritual house, to be a holy priesthood, to offer spiritual sacrifices acceptable to God through Jesus

---

stoneship of Christ" is to be found in his application to himself of Ps. 118:22 (Mark 12:10-11), "Have you not read this scripture: 'The very stone which the builders rejected has become the head of the corner'" (cf. Acts 4:11, where Peter repeats the application). If we ask, "Why *living?*" the answer is, "Because Christ is the living and life-giving One." The words **rejected** and **precious** prepare us for the actual quotation from Ps. 118 in vs. 7.

5. Like living stones be yourselves built into a spiritual house: The KJV takes the Greek verb (οἰκοδομεῖσθε) as an indicative; the RSV as an imperative. As Christ, the cornerstone in the temple, is called a **living stone,** so also can believers by virtue of their connection with him. Possibly there is an implied contrast between them and the lifeless stones in pagan temples. **A spiritual house: House** here bears its ecclesiastical sense of temple. (So Jesus had said, "Your house [i.e., the temple] is left desolate.") It is **spiritual** because it is indwelt by God's Spirit. **A holy priesthood:** Read εἰς before this phrase and translate (with RSV) **to be a holy priesthood.** Note how the metaphor changes: stones become priests. The phrase defines the *vocation* of the church; it implies the priesthood of all believers. **Spiritual sacrifices, acceptable to God by Jesus Christ:** Peter contrasts the sacrifices which the Christian offers with the material sacrifices offered on Jewish and heathen altars. Prayers and praises, righteousness and mercy, love and beneficence and obedience are in mind (cf. Rom. 12:1). Such sacrifices are **acceptable** because offered to God together with the supreme self-sacrifice of Christ (cf. Heb. 13:15, "Through him then let us . . . offer up a sacrifice of praise to God").

---

ship with Gentile Christians at Caesarea (Acts 10:44–11:18). Yet he had heard Jesus speak of himself as the life-giving Vine of the branches, as the Shepherd who gives his life for the sheep, as the Bread and Wine of the new covenant. He had taken part in the Holy Communion, the fullest expression of the Christian faith, marking Christianity as communal. He had heard Jesus declare that he would build his church upon the rocklike confession of faith in him as the Son of the living God. Little wonder, then, that at last the veteran apostle should speak of the **living stone** which was intended by God to be the solid **cornerstone** of a **spiritual house** or community, composed of **lively stones** destined to perform redemptive functions among men and to be a unique incarnation in the social world.

Peter here affirms faith in the living church. He had come a long way in understanding the meaning of the church according to the mind of Christ and the power of the Spirit. Resting solidly in the O.T. covenant community, Jesus Christ had infilled that community with a profound and universal significance. It now included all races and classes of men. Peter used all the words he could recall in his attempt to describe that church: "obedient children," "temple," **spiritual house, priesthood, race, nation.** To climax it all he spoke of Christians as **God's own people.**

In this strong but short message to scattered and harassed individual Asian Christians, the apostle sets forth a gospel which is indeed founded upon a Rock and which incorporates the Christian into stimulating and supporting fellowship. The unsettled and vacillating Peter could speak about both with the authority of experience. Time and again he had boasted of his self-sufficiency, only to fail and be re-established by the steadfastness of Christ. Those three years with Jesus had introduced him into a fellowship which was an inevitable and necessary part of the faith that centered in Jesus Christ. He knew now that no Christian can live in isolation from his brethren, and that there can be no free-lance Christianity which acts as though the body of Christ is unimportant or does not exist.

However living the stones in the house of Christ may be, they must "come" to the Cornerstone if they would find a place in the pattern of God's design; by themselves they lack the larger context. No individual Christian makes a church. Paul thinks of Christians as members of the body of Christ; members mean absolutely nothing when severed from the body. So Peter declares that Christians must **come** to the building, not once in a first "careless rapture" of conversion joy, but again and again and with increasing surrender, so that Cornerstone and stones may be cemented and fused together

6 Wherefore also it is contained in the Scripture, Behold, I lay in Sion a chief corner stone, elect, precious: and he that believeth on him shall not be confounded.

7 Unto you therefore which believe *he is* precious: but unto them which be disobedient, the stone which the builders disallowed, the same is made the head of the corner,

Christ. 6 For it stands in scripture:

"Behold, I am laying in Zion a stone, a
    cornerstone chosen and precious,
and he who believes in him will not
    be put to shame."

7 To you therefore who believe, he is precious, but for those who do not believe,

"The very stone which the builders rejected
has become the head of the corner,"

---

6. The **scripture** is Isa. 28:16. But notice two things: (*a*) **shall not be confounded** is the LXX version of the Hebrew, which means "shall not make haste"; (*b*) Peter adds the words **on him.** Now the interesting fact is that in Rom. 9:33 we read, "Behold, I am laying in Zion a stone that will make men stumble, a rock that will make them fall; and he who believes in him will not be put to shame." This is a mixture of Isa. 28:16, just quoted by Peter, and Isa. 8:14, which occurs in this same section of I Peter (2:8). Did one apostle copy from the other? No; Rendel Harris has shown that the collocation of the two quotations and their peculiarities of reading are to be explained by the fact that both writers are drawing from a collection of *testimonia,* i.e., an anthology of messianic proof texts from the O.T. which was current in the early church (see also on Rom. 9:33). The **cornerstone,** of course, is the Messiah. We should perhaps note that a cornerstone is not the top stone, as at the head of a gable, but the stone at the extremity of the angle which controls the design of the edifice and is visible (cf. Eph. 2:20). In the N.T. Christ is both foundation stone (I Cor. 3:11) and cornerstone. The former implies the *dependence* of Christians on his person and work; the latter stresses the *cohesion* of believers in the body of Christ.

7-8. Unto you therefore which believe he is precious: But the ASV mg. is better: "For you therefore that believe is the honor." "Honor" echoes ἔντιμον, "honorable" or

---

into a glorious edifice which reveals the glory of God in Christ.

Much is said here (vss. 4-10) about the foundation of the church, the nature of the church, and the function of the church. The foundation of the Christian community is a solid and living reality: Jesus Christ. Without him the church is an impossibility. This Christ is no cold stonelike doctrine or institution, although he is central, unshakable, and massive. He is no abstract myth, no ephemeral ideal. He is alive to all that stirs the human heart, and is sensitive to all that moves the heart of God. Christians worship no dead Christ. From him the entire edifice gets its stability, its trueness, its design; upon him the entire house ultimately rests. All stones are built and cemented into this Cornerstone so as to become an integral part of the whole structure. Nor is this Christ a human religious genius aspiring to build a pantheon to his own memory; on the contrary, God long beforehand took the initiative and began laying a stone throughout Israel's history. At last a Son appeared in whom the Father was "well pleased." He is **precious** in God's sight, because in him as in no other was God's will

so perfectly done and his love so fully revealed. And he is **precious** to believers who have come to know the unique value of his revelation of the Father, and his power to lift human burdens and infuse life with strength and hope. So precious was he to Paul that he could shout, "For to me to live is Christ" (Phil. 1:21).

Precious as this stone is to God and to believers, it is a threat of doom to those who reject it as the cornerstone of thought and life. It dare not be treated lightly or defiantly by individuals or groups who prefer to build their lives on other foundations, and integrate them into other edifices of fellowship. Towers of Babel come at last to nought, for they are based upon assumptions and principles which are not in line with those truths and standards which abide the corrosion of time and the tempests of history. To live against Jesus Christ is to court disaster. Nations that kiss the Son (Ps 2:12) and assent to Christ are blessed. That which bows not to him in adoration and obedience faces a dark and desperate future. For Christ is judge of men and nations.

Theologians have long debated about the nature of the church, only to become more and

8 And a stone of stumbling, and a rock of offense, *even to them* which stumble at the word, being disobedient: whereunto also they were appointed.

9 But ye *are* a chosen generation, a royal priesthood, a holy nation, a peculiar people; that ye should shew forth the praises of him who hath called you out of darkness into his marvelous light:

8 and

"A stone that will make men stumble,
    a rock that will make them fall";
for they stumble because they disobey the word, as they were destined to do.

9 But you are a chosen race, a roya priesthood, a holy nation, God's own peo ple,[e] that you may declare the wonderfu deeds of him who called you out of dark

[e] Greek *a people for his possession.*

---

precious in vs. 6. The meaning is that Christian believers share in the honor of Chris whom God has exalted to be the cornerstone in his temple. On the other hand, the **disobedient** (i.e., unbelievers) are not only chagrined to find the rejected stone, Christ in the chief place of honor, but even find it, as Isaiah predicted, **a stone of stumbling—**a loose stone left about by the builders over which a careless man will trip.

On this description of Christ two comments may be made: First, the reference here and elsewhere in the N.T. to Christ as a stumbling stone is a moving witness to the "scandal" of the Cross in the earliest days of the faith. Second, Christ cannot be taken or left: as Selwyn says, "To those who refuse belief, He is a constant anomaly, meeting them in unexpected places and challenging their indifference" (*First Epistle of Peter*, p. 164) **For they stumble** [at the stone] **because they disobey the word. The word** is the gospel.

Whereunto also they were appointed (KJV) means simply, **as they were destined to do** (RSV). The thought is that God ordained that they should stumble because of their disobedience; the reference is to the rejection of Christ by the Jews. Here is divine predestination, as in Rom. 11:11. But Peter does not say that they stumbled irretrievably and we may believe that, like Paul, he cherishes the hope of their ultimate conversion.

9. But ye. Emphatic: You, my readers. Peter proceeds to apply title after title conferred on the old Israel to the church as the new Israel of God. **A chosen race:** So Israel

---

more bewildered at its mystery and its complexity. Pragmatic people are inclined to think of the church as a building or an institution. Both are right, for the church is both "visible" and "invisible." It exists in visible form and it also exists in invisible reality. It is not something to which people come, as though the church were something apart from life; nor is it something which consists only of people, as though the church were only a human creation. Peter is aware of the mystery of the church and its divine nature, but he is also conscious of the fact that it is composed of real persons who are **living stones.**

For an individual to be reckoned a member of the church is a solemn and solid reality. His solitariness is surrounded by the glory of fellowship with Christ and with his community of divine destiny. He is given a place in the drama of divine redemption. He is a member of the living household of God's family, an initiate into God's redemptive **priesthood,** an elect of God's **race,** a citizen of God's **holy nation.** Those who are voluntary members, who **come** to the **living stone,** which is Christ, are enhanced with a new dignity and invested with a high vocation.

Indeed, they who once were nothing—**no people** —are made into children of the most high God From "pig sty to royal palace," from "rags to riches," might be the theme of their autobiographies. The various religions of the world have all erected their temples. The Christian faith reared the Gothic cathedral, perhaps the "most magnificent creation which the mind of man has thrown out of itself." [8] But what religion can fashion such a temple of living persons as that which Jesus Christ has built in all the world? This "house not built with hands" is ecumenical and embraces the consecrated lives of peoples in nearly every part of the inhabited globe. The temple in Jerusalem may lie in dust, but the "spiritual house" of a living Christ continually attracts to itself persons who gladly allow themselves to be builded into the living walls of Christ's increasing and growing city.

This church is primarily a spiritual reality with a spiritual purpose. It is a holy and **royal priesthood, a chosen generation** or **race, a holy nation,** and a **people of God** in a special sense. The terms refer to all members of the church,

[8] Quoted in Hastings, ed., *Speaker's Bible*, I and II Peter, p. 112.

10 Which in time past *were* not a people, but *are* now the people of God: which had not obtained mercy, but now have obtained mercy.

ness into his marvelous light. 10 Once you were no people but now you are God's people; once you had not received mercy but now you have received mercy.

---

is called in Isa. 43:20. **A royal priesthood, a holy nation:** So, again, Moses styles Israel in Exod. 19:6. They are **royal** as belonging to the king; priests, because they offer up spiritual sacrifices. **God's own people:** The phrase means literally "a people for [God's] possession." The KJV's **peculiar** (from the Latin *peculium:* a slave is private property) is an attempt to render this (cf. Isa. 43:21, "This people have I formed for myself; they shall show forth my praise"). **That ye should shew forth the praises:** Privilege implies responsibility: the new people of God must take up the task left unfulfilled by the old, viz., to declare the excellences (or **wonderful deeds**) of the God who had called them out of heathen darkness into the marvelous light of salvation (cf. the words of Jesus, "Ye are the light of the world. . . . Let your light so shine before men" [Matt. 5:14-16]).

10. **Which in time past were not a people:** Hitherto they had been **no people** but mere "units in the medley of nations that could all be classed as 'heathen.'" Now they are **the people of God.** Formerly they had been proudly and falsely self-sufficient, but now they have become the humble recipients of God's mercy. So, says Peter in effect, are Hosea's words fulfilled, "I will have mercy on her that had not obtained mercy; and I will say to them which were not my people, Thou art my people; and they shall say, Thou art my God" (Hos. 2:23).

Nothing could show more clearly than these two verses the claim of the early Christian church to be the true people of God, heir to all the promises made to the old Israel. Still, to this day, that is, or ought to be, the root idea of the church, viz., the people of God, living under God's fatherly rule, whose function it is to declare his mighty acts in Jesus Christ to all men, and whose duty it is to live by his law.

---

for we find here no distinction between laity and clergy. They are associated by reason of their calling and their common new life; they are destined to reveal and fulfill the purpose of God for the whole human race. They are commissioned to be a kingly community of persons who mediate between God and man, who worshipfully make God central in life and use their gifts for the service of mankind. They are a great company of many kinds of people bound together by cohesive ties and set apart to become a "world-unifying, world-comprehending and world-glorifying society in which humanity will realize its true ideals and know the plentitude of its life." [1]

Christians in the church are also a people of God's own possession, or as Weymouth translates, "a people belonging to God." In a special sense they are God's peculiar treasure, his favorite object of affection. God not only wills the church to be, but through Jesus Christ he reveals his jealous love for it. "Christ loved the church, and gave himself for it." (Eph. 5:25). His relationship to the church is as intimate as that of husband and wife. And he wishes the church to be as a glorious bride who might be presented before him in splendor,

"not having spot, or wrinkle, or any such thing; but . . . it should be holy and without blemish" (Eph. 5:27).

The function of the church derives from its nature. To be sure, its primary business is to be the church, i.e., a genuine community of living disciples of Christ. Not that they will possess any of the qualities of the Christian life in perfection, but that they shall witness to that differential in spirit which faith in Christ makes. Further, they are to be a priestly community in which the worship of the God and Father of Jesus Christ will be not only a stated form of liturgy but a constant attitude, until all of life shall be brought into a sacramental relation with the Creator, Judge, and Redeemer. Moreover, they are to be a priestly community constantly engaged in prayer and intercession for themselves and all men, sacrificial mediators between God and man, and between man and man, with the hope of bringing about the life of reconciliation and love. And they are to be a joyous community, constantly and gratefully declaring the "wondrous works" of a God who has called them out of the darkness of an existence without knowledge of the true God into the life of love and truth and hope. The whole church is to be a witnessing community,

[1] Hastings, ed., *Speaker's Bible,* I and II Peter, p. 125.

| 11 Dearly beloved, I beseech *you* as strangers and pilgrims, abstain from fleshly lusts, which war against the soul; | 11 Beloved, I beseech you as aliens and exiles to abstain from the passions of the flesh that wage war against your soul. |

III. The Duties of Christians in the World (2:11–4:11)
A. Believers and Unbelievers (2:11-12)

11. Beloved, i.e., by God. **As aliens and exiles.** The first of the two words in Greek, πάροικος, denotes a person living in a foreign country where he has not the rights of a citizen—a noncitizen or alien. The second word, παρεπίδημος, means a person staying for a time in a place which is not his permanent home—a pilgrim or exile. Here both words are used figuratively of the Christian who resides on earth but whose real home is in heaven. This is a note that modern Christianity has largely lost. Modern Christians are so much concerned with setting in order "this house of our pilgrimage" that sometimes they tend to forget that their true destiny lies elsewhere. Here, as elsewhere, *in medio veritas;* our task is to try to hold a true balance between a this-worldly and an otherworldly view. **Fleshly lusts:** The carnal side of man's nature is here contrasted with **the soul,** or spiritual side. (Paul's name for the latter is not soul, but spirit.) **War against:** The same metaphor as in Rom. 7:23.

through its corporate testimony and the testimony of every member. Thus the church takes the gospel into the home and work and society. In this way the gospel about the mighty works of God is proclaimed to and in the world. Worship, witness, and loving service are the great hallmarks of the Christian church, and the three of them issue from the mighty act of God in bringing deliverance to "captives" and to those who "sit in great darkness." The Christian's "spiritual sacrifices" (Rom. 12:1) of life and work, when seen in this context, take on dignity and nobility, for they are joined with that of the great High Priest who served God and man so perfectly and so completely on Calvary.

11-12. *The Warfare and Witness of the Christian.*—Peter addresses his fellow Christians with the characteristic Christian term, **beloved.** Though seldom used in the so-called "free" churches today—because apart from the historic liturgies it seems to have become either meaningless or sentimental—it nevertheless is uniquely Christian. Christians are to address each other in love; and the teacher or preacher of Christian truth and morality must speak "in love." Christian truth, supremely incarnate in Jesus, must be spoken with responsibility toward and with concern for the person addressed. Preachers of a former day would address their congregations with the salutation "Beloved," and proceed to speak as kindly and concerned pastors to the people to whom they were bound with the bonds of Christian concern, and for whom they exercised a shepherding responsibility. There is compassion and there is strength in Peter's solicitous exhortation **Beloved, I beseech you.** Into these words he poured all the feeling which Jesus Christ had generated in him. For Peter knew the "look" of Jesus that made him weep. Peter knew the tenderness of his Lord, who had not lost confidence in him in spite of his dastardly denial.

Is the Christian faith a bid for otherworldliness? Or does it make men socially responsible? "Opium" is what Karl Marx called religion, insisting that it soothed men with the expectation of a glorious heaven but made them oblivious to the hard realities of a social order which frustrated the coming of an era of justice. Perhaps Peter has a word to say on this burning issue. Christians, says he, are both **pilgrims** and **strangers.** As Abraham (Gen. 23:4) was both stranger and sojourner, so are the children of God. They have here "no lasting city" (Heb. 13:14). Their "citizenship" is in "heaven" (Phil. 3:20). They never receive the promise fully in this life, for they live and die in faith. Christians are temporary residents on earth. They are in the world but not of it (John 17:15).

The first Christians used the Greek word for **strangers** (*paroikous*) to describe the congregations or parishes of which they were members. They were like a nation within a nation, at once rooted and grounded in eternity and also resident **aliens** in the world community. Because of this dual character the church has often been tempted to become otherworldly, ascetic, mystical, escapist on the one hand, or secular, this-worldly, unspiritual, expediently humanistic on the other. A church which forgets that its people are residents, even though **aliens,** who in the words of the old spiritual, "ain't got long to stay here," will fall into heresy, be bereft of its power, forfeit its Christian character, and cease to be a church. It dare not become so invisible

12 Having your conversation honest among the Gentiles: that, whereas they speak against you as evildoers, they may by *your* good works, which they shall behold, glorify God in the day of visitation.

13 Submit yourselves to every ordinance of man for the Lord's sake: whether it be to the king, as supreme;

12 Maintain good conduct among the Gentiles, so that in case they speak against you as wrongdoers, they may see your good deeds and glorify God on the day of visitation.

13 Be subject for the Lord's sake to every human institution,*f* whether it be to the

f Or *every institution ordained for men.*

---

12. Maintain good conduct among the Gentiles: Peter passes from the inner purity to its visible fruits (Hort). The Greek word καλήν rendered **honest** (KJV) and **good** (RSV) means morally beautiful. The reference to the Gentiles seems to imply that there were not a few Jews among his readers.

That . . . evildoers: The early Christians were accused of all sorts of enormities— sedition, immorality, ritual murder. "Hated for their crimes," says Tacitus; "This new and noxious superstition," comments Suetonius.

They may see your good deeds and glorify God: We cannot miss the clear echo of Matt. 5:16, "That they may see your good works, and glorify your Father which is in heaven." Peter believes that the best witness for Christianity is a good Christian life: one saintly life is worth a dozen stout volumes on Christian apologetics. **In the day of visitation,** cf. Luke 19:44: Any time of crisis when God visits men in judgment or in blessing; not necessarily the Judgment Day.

B. Christians and the State (2:13-17)

13. Here begins the moral code which bulks so large in this epistle. The first section on the duty of the Christian toward the civil powers resembles Rom. 13:1-7; but there

---

as to lose its visible reality. And it dare not become so conformed to the world that it loses its nature as a colony of heaven.

Christians are engaged in a warfare from which there is no discharge. There are forces that war against the real personality of a man. **Fleshly lusts** are powerful enemies that infect our natural bodies and pervert them. What God created good is enslaved by diabolical and satanic powers until that which is fashioned in God's image is alienated from God. Peter is not saying that the body and all that it represents is evil; rather he is warning against the **fleshly lusts** that use the body in order to make man's ego self-sufficient and autonomous. Here is the major conflict of history. Into this holy encounter between God and the evil one for the possession of man's soul, Jesus entered. The decisive victory has already been won on Calvary. Jesus Christ is Lord. The warfare continues, however, as the full consequences of that victory are being brought on to a conclusion. The mighty battle for man's liberation and restoration is still in progress. The Christian is called upon to enlist in the army of Christ and to engage in that warfare.

Christians, meanwhile, may be severely criticized, may even be called **evildoers.** In Peter's day they were accused of incest and cannibalism,

because they loved one another and partook of the body and blood of their Lord in Holy Communion. In other days they were accused of disloyalty to government and disinterestedness in the *status quo.* In modern times some Christians have been sent to prison for obeying God rather than men. And some have been martyred for refusing to give reverence to some Caesar who would be God. Heb. 11 could be rewritten by supplying the names of twentieth-century heroes and heroines. The worldly man whose only standards are secular may indeed hate the Christian as the crowd hated Jesus and shouted for his crucifixion. What then? A **conversation honest among the Gentiles**—conduct upright and consistent: there is no other way by which such antagonism can be met. When the judgment of God falls upon men, or they are visited by some arresting experience, they may be led to **glorify God** by reason of the very **good works, which they shall behold.** Who knows what the power of influence may effect? Certainly in a day when the words of the Christian community have outrun its exemplary living, the church itself is in peril of that judgment which begins "at the house of God" (4:17). **Dearly beloved, I beseech you.**

13-17. The Dimensions of Christian Citizenship.—Christians are "colonists of heaven"

14 Or unto governors, as unto them that are sent by him for the punishment of evildoers, and for the praise of them that do well.

emperor as supreme, 14 or to governors as sent by him to punish those who do wrong

---

are also clear differences. It is likely that both Peter and Paul were drawing from a common source.

The gist of Peter's advice is: "Be loyal subjects. The civil powers have their place in God's providential scheme, and law-abiding conduct will silence slanderers."

Every ordinance of man: Better, with RSV, **every human institution.** The Lord here is Christ. **The king** is the Roman emperor, although the Romans themselves refused to call him *rex*. If we are right in our dating of the epistle, the reigning emperor at this time was Nero!

14. Governors, e.g., procurators like Pontius Pilate. **Punishment . . . praise:** The purpose of government is (negatively) to suppress evil, and (positively) to encourage good. Note that in the view of both Peter and Paul the state is concerned not with economics alone but with the good life. Brunner may call the state "organized selfishness"; but the alternative to it is anarchy, and the state's functions are necessary to promote the

---

(Moffatt), eschatologists, finalists, eternalists, but they are obligated to take seriously their relationships with people, groups, and institutions in this world. These relationships are never to be treated casually. Peter makes it clear that Christians are to **be subject** to all men and to every man **for the Lord's sake.** The Lord is concerned about secular life; for his sake Christians are to fulfill their divine calling and vocation by relating the eternal to the temporal, the sacred to the secular. There is no place in the Christian vocation for the ascetic attitude which disdains the secular or condescends on occasion to deal tenuously with it. And there is no place here for an "autonomous and individualistic spiritual life" which cultivates its piety with no concern for everyday matters. Nor is there any room for a dual loyalty in the Christian calling: to God in certain matters and to Caesar in others. Christians are of choice to subject themselves to the whole human order of persons and institutions, with freedom and with identity. They are to serve one another; to seek the welfare of others; to submit themselves to one another in the fear of Christ (Eph. 5:21). They are to be keepers of their brethren and to regard others more highly than themselves. Being **for the Lord's sake,** such concern for the whole human order saves the Christian from serving others merely to win personal power and influence. It also saves him from an abject servility which denatures life of personal integrity. Gratitude to God is the source of humility, of service to the neighbor, and of a sense of divine vocation to the world in the spirit of identification with humanity.

Following his declaration of the Christian principle of free and responsible identity with the human order **for the Lord's sake,** Peter sets forth the major relationships about which the Christian must be concerned: **The king,** supreme earthly authority; **governors,** as lesser authorities; **all men; the brotherhood; God.**

The Christian, wherever he lives, is not a "man without a country." He must acknowledge and bear his responsibility to governmental authority and its lesser authorities in the political realm. Whether that authority is a king, a congress representing the will of the people, or a tyrant such as Nero (who was emperor of Rome at the time Peter wrote these words), the Christian is to **honor** this power as **sent** by God properly to order human society, to keep social life from chaos, to be a deterrent to evildoers, and to be a rewarder of those who do right. The state is not a church, nor is its purpose to redeem men for time and eternity. Yet it is more than an expedient provision by God for the restraining of man's sinful propensities and actions; it is also meant to provide opportunities for the free proclamation of the gospel and the expression of the Christian life. It may not be itself a redemptive agency, but it is meant to serve the purposes of that redemptive agency which is the church. **For the Lord's sake** the Christian is bidden to honor the state and its authority. His rightful relation to it is a part of his discipleship. In no wise does this require that he must serve incumbents of a political authority who decree what is unjust and contrary to God's command. **For the Lord's sake** we are to **honor** the state for what God intended it to be; Christians may continue loyal to a state authority, even while in higher loyalty they resist those in office who assume divine prerogatives or deliberately seek to use the state for ends that are contrary to the God who provides for the state. The Christian

15 For so is the will of God, that with well doing ye may put to silence the ignorance of foolish men:

16 As free, and not using *your* liberty for a cloak of maliciousness, but as the servants of God.

and to praise those who do right. 15 For it is God's will that by doing right you should put to silence the ignorance of foolish men. 16 Live as free men, yet without using your freedom as a pretext for evil; but live as

---

good life. Arnold J. Toynbee has said that so long as original sin remains an element in human nature, Caesar will always have plenty to do.

15. With the thought of this verse cf. Seneca (here surely *saepe noster*—almost a Christian!) : "Persistent good will conquers evil." The **foolish men** are the slanderers of vs. 12. Being foolish and ignorant, they were all too ready to believe and say the worst about the Christians. God's way to "muzzle" (the word used in the Gospels when our Lord silences an evil spirit) such people is active well-doing.

16. As free . . . : "The Christian is to obey authorities, not in any servile spirit, but as a free man, whose freedom consists in loyal service to God, and therefore includes obedience to those who are doing God's work" (W. H. Bennett, *The General Epistles*

---

is first a Christian, and in the light of that absolute loyalty a responsible patriot who seeks to conform the state to its divine purpose.

Some of us no longer live under authoritarian states as did Peter; we live in some form of democratic government. To us, application of Peter's injunction is even more pertinent since Christian citizens in a democracy are all charged with the duty of responsible co-operation. No longer are we subjects of a king; rather are we citizens who must exercise social responsibility along many lines. Individual relationships with the state are more ramified and complex in a democracy. There, in a sense, every man is a king, although it is the sum total of citizen opinion and action which is finally decisive. It is highly important, therefore, where the will of the people, enlightened by truth, is authoritative, that Peter's injunction should strike home with peculiar force. Subjects may be tempted to let the king and his governors do it; citizens in a democratic state may be inclined to say that as individuals they count for little, or they may be tempted to manipulate state authority for their own ends without any reference to **the Lord's sake.**

The problem of obedience to Christ and to Caesar has always been with Christians. Here the principle is announced that the disciple of Jesus Christ should submit himself to the laws of the state, even when the **king** is Nero. And yet Peter failed to follow through this principle of action, for he is St. Peter precisely because he defied Nero to death. One's submission to the state must always be **for the Lord's sake,** not because the state has an absolute value in itself. For when Caesar demands what is Christ's, even the pinch of incense offered to his image— harmless as it may seem—borders on an act of worship in which the Christian cannot partici-

pate. "The Incarnation has made deification forever impossible." [2] But what if Caesar professes Christian faith? Even then the Christian must not think that the tension between Christ and Caesar is past. Had the church in the early centuries of her history remembered that, the whole course of history might have been changed. A Christian Caesar may put the force of the empire behind the Christian movement, but the inevitable secularization of the church and the gradual absorption of prevailing standards may in the end prove harmful to the unique and independent nature of Christianity. A church which has become a phase of secular culture gradually loses its religious substance.

To honor **all men** means to recognize the worth of every person. It means to be done with cynical contempt, with that sneering disdain which cumulatively is worse than murder. To honor a man is to see in him one for whom Christ lived and died, to recognize in him a person, and to perceive in him a worth that goes beyond class, wealth, race, cultural status, or nationality. To **love the brotherhood** is to practice a genuine affection for all who are in Christ, regardless of their differences in background and experience, their denominational affiliations, or their peculiar ways of expressing their piety. Love for the Christian fellowship is implied in the nature of the gospel; it is the mark of that higher citizenship which is nothing less or other than Sonship with God, who in Jesus Christ loved the church and gave himself for it. Above all, Christians are to **fear God,** not in abject dread, but in holy reverence. Peter uses words found in Prov. 24:21, but as a Christian he deliberately uses a different verb

[2] Hugh Ross Williamson, *The Seven Christian Virtues* (London: Student Christian Movement Press, 1949), p. 44.

17 Honor all *men.* Love the brotherhood. Fear God. Honor the king.

18 Servants, *be* subject to *your* masters with all fear; not only to the good and gentle, but also to the froward.

servants of God. 17 Honor all men. Love the brotherhood. Fear God. Honor the emperor.

18 Servants, be submissive to your masters with all respect, not only to the kind and gentle but also to the overbearing.

[Edinburgh: T. C. & E. C. Jack, 1901; "The New Century Bible"], p. 217). **Not using your liberty for a cloak of maliciousness:** A warning against antinomianism, i.e., the belief that Christians are emancipated by the gospel from the obligation to keep the moral law, a danger of evangelical Christianity in all ages.

17. Four short commands, probably to be taken in two pairs: (*a*) **Honor all men** (i.e., show the courtesy due to personality as such); but **love the brotherhood** (i.e., your fellow Christians). (*b*) **Fear God. Honor the emperor.** With the last two clauses cf. Prov. 24:21, "My son, fear thou the LORD and the king." The whole verse is a motto for him who would be at once a good citizen and a good churchman.

C. The Duty of Slaves (2:18-20)

Summary: "Slaves must serve their masters faithfully, even bad ones. Patient endurance of wrongs wins God's approval." The writer will go on to say (vss. 21-25): "It is also a following in the steps of Christ who, as the servant of the Lord, endured obloquy and death for our salvation."

18. Servants: The Greek word (οἰκέται) means household servants, who were normally slaves. **With all fear:** The RSV's **with all respect** is better. **The froward:** An

---

to make clear that kings may be honored, but only God is to be feared. Man's relation to God is unique, because God is in a class by himself.[3] "The fear of the Lord is the beginning of wisdom" (Prov. 9:10). It may be added that the love—grateful reverence—of God is wisdom fulfilled. Mere dread of God makes men cringe before him as slaves; mere sentimental love toward God makes men careless and irresponsible. Calvin observed that some men "feel only the forced and servile fear which divine judgment extorts; . . . the wicked, . . . knowing that he [God] is armed with power for vengeance, . . . tremble in dismay on hearing his anger."[4] Servile fear is based upon a wrong conception of God and is disastrous. Only an enlightened faith in the God and Father of our Lord Jesus Christ gives man a proper perspective on himself, a true attitude toward God, and a dynamic incentive to lead a holy life. Clement of Alexandria regarded the fear of God as like the attitude of a child to its father, or of a citizen to the good magistrate.[5]

Such conduct as Peter describes may not be deliberately designed to "win friends and influence people," but in **the will of God** it puts to silence those who are critical and even hostile to the Christian faith. Jesus prayed for the for-

giveness of those who crucified him, saying that they did not know what they were doing. In a real sense those who go against Christ and his church are foolish people; they are ignorant of the fact that they are rejecting him who is their friend and benefactor. Christian love issues from gratitude to God, and bears a wordless witness more potent than words.

But even more—Christians are free men in Christ. Not bound ultimately by any earthly authority, they may be tempted to use their freedom for license. In Christian history there have been some who believed they were beyond the law. Peter cautions all such to remember that for the Christian there is no use of **liberty for a cloak of maliciousness.** There may be times when for conscience' sake the Christian must revolt against an unjust government. Positive rebellion there must be in such a case; but the free man in Christ must not use his freedom to engage in downright **evil.** The Christian is to demonstrate to a world that often makes its freedom licentious and wicked that there is a freedom which is responsible. The problem of the use of power in our modern world ultimately goes back to the individual's use of personal power. The highest freedom is that which God gives a person; the highest use of freedom is that which issues in righteousness and justice, not in wickedness.

18-25. *Christian Servants and Their Vocations.*—Peter raised no questions about the in-

[3] See Emil Brunner, *One Faith* (New York: Charles Scribner's Sons, 1936), p. 2.

[4] *Institutes of the Christian Religion,* Book III, ch. 2, section 27, 1:63; 2:127.

[5] *The Instructor* I. 9.

19 For this *is* thankworthy, if a man for conscience toward God endure grief, suffering wrongfully.

20 For what glory *is it,* if, when ye be buffeted for your faults, ye shall take it patiently? but if, when ye do well, and suffer *for it,* ye take it patiently, this *is* acceptable with God.

19 For one is approved if, mindful of God, he endures pain while suffering unjustly. **20** For what credit is it, if when you do wrong and are beaten for it you take it patiently? But if when you do right and suffer for it you take it patiently, you have

archaic English word to translate the Greek σκολιοῖς, which means literally, "crooked," and so, "perverse," "unreasonable," "cross-grained," **overbearing** (RSV).

19. A difficult verse. Literally, it means: "For this is grace, if on account of conscience of God a man endures griefs, suffering wrongfully." What does "grace" (χάρις) mean here? The clue to the meaning is in Luke 6:32-34, of which this passage may well be an echo. There χάρις occurs three times in the sense of "favor" before God. (In the LXX it is the regular word for the approbation and good will of a superior, especially the approval and favor of God.) Here, then, Peter says that those who are willing to suffer innocently find "favor" with God. The second crux is the meaning of "conscience [συνείδησιν] of God." Either the word bears its technical sense of conscience—in that case the meaning is "through a conscientious sense of duty toward God"—or it is used in the sense of "consciousness," i.e., awareness of God. This seems better, and **mindful of God** is a good paraphrase of it.

Grief: The abuse, beating, and torture which masters often inflicted on slaves.

20. For what glory is it . . . : Better, **what credit is it . . .** (RSV). **Buffeted:** The Greek word (κολαφιζόμενοι) is used of the treatment meted out to our Lord after the ecclesiastical trial, "And some began . . . to buffet him" (Mark 14:65). As Peter exhorts to patient suffering in face of wrong, there comes back to him the memory of how the supreme Sufferer had carried himself in such a situation.

stitution of slavery, probably because he saw little hope of correcting it by a head-on revolution. That method had been tried only to make the lot of the slave even more intolerable. Entrenched as the system was, what could a handful of Christians do to abolish the accursed relationship of master and slave?

Perhaps Peter also was more concerned about the imminent end of the human order than he was about social reform. He therefore was anxious to counsel his friends on the attitude and conduct of the Christian in an existing situation. He has little to say to masters, since there were few in the churches to which he was writing; and no doubt he regarded the relationship of the slave or domestic servant to a master as more difficult than the reverse.

The practical-minded apostle therefore (*a*) goes straight to the task of giving his friends instruction on how to live out their Christian vocations in the servant-master relationship in which they monotonously lived from day to day and from which there was no escape; (*b*) he offers them counsel regarding the attitude and conduct of Christians and their relation to the example of Jesus, who died the death of a slave (capital punishment for criminal Greco-Roman slaves was crucifixion) and lived the

life of a servant; and (*c*) he holds high the rewards and reasons for such conduct.

Christians in every age live in a social situation that is saturated with maladjusted and imperfect relationships. We may in the twentieth century have little of the older slavery left, but there is much in our age which smacks of a new slavery.

(*a*) About slavery in N.T. times there is much to relate. It was an accepted institution; even the noble Aristotle had argued that some men were born to be slaves. The system was foundational to Greco-Roman civilization. Slaves had no rights; they were owned by their masters. Their marriages were not legal, nor were their children considered their own. The lot of masses of such slaves, whether attached to the land or to some industry, was appalling.

To be sure, there were domestic servants whose position was much better. Among them were teachers, doctors, secretaries, and musicians. It is evidently to such as these that Peter directs his counsel. They were often regarded with esteem and honor. Some of them were free men. Even so, their status kept them in their places, and their economic dependence kept them constantly anxious about their future. Resentment, hostility, and even hatred burned

21 For even hereunto were ye called: be- | God's approval. 21 For to this you have
cause Christ also suffered for us, leaving us | been called, because Christ also suffered
an example, that ye should follow his steps: | for you, leaving you an example, that you

---

D. The Imitatio Christi (2:21-25)

In what is one of the noblest parts of the epistle Peter bids the slaves take as their example in patient suffering the Lord himself who, to redeem them, chose the destiny of the suffering Servant. In verse after verse we catch clear echoes of Isa. 53, the chapter in which Jesus had seen his own passion (and triumph) prefigured; in which, too, the early church had sought the clue to the secret of his death (see the references to Jesus as "the servant of God" in the early speeches in Acts). In the last verse, however, the metaphor changes to that of the shepherd—a figure that also had been in Jesus' mind.

The following parallels show the dependence of this section of I Peter on Isa. 53:

I Peter 2:21-25	*Isaiah 53 (LXX)*
Vs. 21. Christ also suffered for us.	Vs. 4. He bears our sins and is pained for us.
Vs. 22. Who did no sin, neither was guile found in his mouth.	Vs. 9. He did no sin nor was guile in his mouth.
Vs. 23. Who, when he was reviled, reviled not again; when he suffered, threatened not, but committed himself to him that judgeth righteously.	Vs. 7. And he, because of his affliction, opens not his mouth. (Here probably Peter blends Isa. 53 with his memory of how Jesus actually comported himself in the face of his foes.)
Vs. 24. Who his own self bare our sins, etc.	Vs. 12. He himself bare the sins of many (cf. also vs. 11: And he shall bear their sins).
Vs. 24b. By whose stripes ye were healed.	Vs. 5. By his stripes were we healed.
Vs. 25. For ye were as sheep going astray.	Vs. 6. All we like sheep have gone astray.

21. Hereunto: To patient suffering. **For us** (KJV): The variant reading **for you** (RSV) is preferable. The Greek word for **example** means a child's "writing copy."

---

within the breast of many a domestic servant. He did his work grudgingly and with little enthusiasm. Like many a modern member of industrial mass society, he worked at something for which he had little relish, and he looked upon the master class with suspicion because it had the power to determine his economic fortune and destiny.

The institution and the situation being what they are, the Christian, says Peter, is conscientiously to accept the servant-master relationship in the "fear of God," and to do his work in the spirit of a Christian workman, whether his master is good and gentle or crooked and perverse. He is to perform his daily tasks with a personal integrity that is finally accountable to God, not to any human authority. The quality of his work is after all not dependent upon the conditions under which he does it. Nor is he to do it merely for the sake of pleasing another.

Modern industry is discovering that attitudes toward work and toward the conditions under which it is done make a great difference in the quality of the output and in the spirit of the laborer himself. If the Christian refuses to put his hand to anything until he finds an ideal master or the most favorable conditions, he is demanding the impossible. Besides, work in-

fused with that redemptive quality which Jesus put into his may always have to suffer from a world that carries on its vocations in the spirit of competition or under duress. Jesus did what he had to do under human conditions that at last broke his body. The servant-master relationship in some form may be with us until the end, with its inevitable chain of authority and responsibility. Civilization may legislate conscience into law and abolish some of the humiliations and indignities involved, but there will always be need for this higher sense of divine vocation to lend the proper attitude and dignity to the person who works under another's direction. Only a realization of the presence of God, only his sanctification of what we do in unjust situations, can lend any meaningfulness to the tasks we are asked to do which smack of servility. Only such an offering of our tasks and of ourselves in them is **acceptable with God.**

(b) Christian attitudes and Christian conduct are the result of being called to the kind of life that produces them—**for . . . hereunto were ye called.** Above all, they are related to the life and work of Jesus Christ. The Christian owes everything to his Lord who **suffered** for him, who made a new life possible by taking upon himself the form of a servant and subjecting

22 Who did no sin, neither was guile found in his mouth:

23 Who, when he was reviled, reviled not again; when he suffered, he threatened not; but committed *himself* to him that judgeth righteously:

24 Who his own self bare our sins in his own body on the tree, that we, being dead to sins, should live unto righteousness: by whose stripes ye were healed.

should follow in his steps. **22** He committed no sin; no guile was found on his lips. **23** When he was reviled, he did not revile in return; when he suffered, he did not threaten; but he trusted to him who judges justly. **24** He himself bore our sins in his body on the tree,^g that we might die to sin and live to righteousness. By his wounds

^g Or *carried up . . . to the tree.*

---

22. Who did no sin: Cf. 1:19, "A lamb without blemish and without spot." Both passages affirm the sinlessness of Jesus Christ.

23. Who, when he was reviled, reviled not again: Here, as has already been suggested, we have a blending of Isa. 53:7 with the memory of Christ's own majestic endurance of the taunts and insults of his foes. **Committed himself:** We think instinctively of Luke 23:46, "Father, into thy hands I commend my spirit," the last word from the Cross.

24. Who his own self bare our sins: If we ask in what sense Christ bore our sins, the answer is, he took the blame of them and suffered the curse of them, which is separation from God. This interpretation is confirmed by the words **on the tree,** which take us back to Deut. 21:22-23 (cf. Gal. 3:13, "Cursed is every one that hangeth on a tree"; cf. also Acts 5:30; 10:39). This is far more than a mere exemplarist view of the Atonement. It is also possible that the words **in his own body** recall the Levitical scapegoat who, on the day of Atonement, had Israel's sins symbolically transferred to him and was then driven away into the desert (Lev. 16:20-22).

That we, being dead to sins, should live unto righteousness: This clause describes the aim of Christ's atoning work—"He died to make us good." **Being dead** (ἀπογενόμενοι) means "having departed from," "having ceased from."

---

himself to unjust suffering for the sins of men. He **did no sin, neither was guile found in his mouth: who, when he was reviled, reviled not again; when he suffered,** he did not threaten retaliation. He submitted himself to God who judged rightly, and he bore in his body **our sins . . . on the tree.** By his stripes we are healed.

Peter uses quotations from Isa. 53:5-6 to describe what he had seen with his own eyes: the buffeting, the mocking, the crucifixion, the silent bearing of the sins of men in body and soul; and all of it was done so that by this mighty and vicarious death we might enter into the new world of eternal life for which Jesus lived and died, putting an end to the world of sin which he allowed to put an end to him.

Here is no cold systematic credo concerning the Atonement which stands by itself, isolated from life. Peter is a Christian who scrupulously relates reality to action, truth to life, the work of atonement to the daily work and attitude of the Christian. The life of the Christian is not only inaugurated by this great Redeemer; it is also guided by him. The way in which he saved men is exemplary, and we are to **follow in his steps** by living and working redemptively in our vocations and in whatever situation we find ourselves.

> Must Jesus bear the cross alone,
> And all the world go free?
> No, there's a cross for every one,
> And there's a cross for me.⁶

(*c*) The reward of such attitudes and conduct is that they are **acceptable with God.** Ultimately this is the highest commendation men can receive. Peter would emphasize that truth, for it grew out of his experience in those early days of the church. To obey God rather than men became the supreme principle of his life. Jesus had counseled his disciples against a human righteousness that did no more than was expected of men (Luke 6:32-35). "What do ye more than others?" (Matt. 5:47.) The Christian, Peter knew, "goes the second mile," he "turns the other cheek," he "loves the enemy." And he has his reward in simply being Christian— the result of which is his willingness to go beyond the standard of "eye for eye."

Another reward which the Christian enjoys is the knowledge that he has been brought back from his aimless and foolish life of rebellion and isolation to the true **Shepherd** and the fold. Again the experiences of Peter, the sheep-like man who was so often betrayed by his sheepish appetites, is brought into play. He

⁶ Hymn by Thomas Shepherd, *et al.*

25 For ye were as sheep going astray; but are now returned unto the Shepherd and Bishop of your souls.

3 Likewise, ye wives, *be* in subjection to your own husbands; that, if any obey not the word, they also may without the word be won by the conversation of the wives;

you have been healed. 25 For you were straying like sheep, but have now returned to the Shepherd and Guardian of your souls.

3 Likewise you wives, be submissive to your husbands, so that some, though they do not obey the word, may be won without a word by the behavior of their

---

By whose stripes ye were healed: Less literally, the RSV: **By his wounds you have been healed.** The Greek word for "stripes" is μώλωψ, which means "a weal," the mark left by a lash—a word that recalls the scourging of Christ and would have a grim ring for a slave. On the whole verse Theodoret comments: "A new and strange method of healing. The doctor suffered the cost, and the sick received the healing" (see Selwyn, *First Epistle of Peter,* p. 181).

25. For ye were as sheep going astray: This is Isa. 53:6; but with the words **ye . . . are now returned,** lit., "ye were turned back" (cf. Ps. 23:3, "He turned back my soul" [LXX]). Peter turns from the thought of Christ as the suffering Servant to that of the Shepherd of the sheep. This title, too, Jesus had applied to himself and his "little flock" (see Mark 6:34; 14:27; Luke 12:32; John 10:11 ff.; cf. Heb. 13:20; Rev. 7:17).

Shepherd and Bishop of your souls: Bishop is ἐπίσκοπος, i.e., **Guardian** (as the RSV translates) or "Overseer." The word is not yet used in the ecclesiastical sense it was to acquire.

E. Husbands and Wives (3:1-7)

Summary: "A Christian wife will obey her husband, even if he is a pagan, hoping to win him for Christ by her conduct. Before God, character means more than outward

---

knew what it meant to be healed by the stripes inflicted by his obstinacy and carelessness upon his Lord. The marvel of his restoration could never be forgotten. Once "far off," he had **returned.** He knew himself to be the recipient of a favor which bound him to Jesus with an unbreakable bond of gratitude.

But is there no further consequence of Christian conduct? Peter may not have been able to envision its effects upon the evil order of the times. The relations which existed between masters and servants were to be transformed by the power of the gospel. Slaves who became Christians knew a liberty and a personal integrity which revolutionized society from within. Through the fellowship of the Christian community, differences between slaves and masters were tempered and transcended. Philemons and Onesimuses, though masters and slaves, were brothers in Christ; they were fellow recipients of the grace of Christ; they worshiped in the same service; they partook of the same Communion; they sat at the same love feast. And though they maintained their social differences, their relations one to another took on a new character. In time the internal experience expressed itself in a changed external status.

While the life and faith of the Christian may not bring about immediate results in terms of

social reform in a day like that in which Peter lived and wrote, over the years they must inevitably have a profound effect in society if persisted in with tenacity and fidelity. But times differ, and there are periods when the Christian will express his conviction in other ways. This injunction of the first century must never be interpreted to mean that he must always employ the indirect method of social change, and practice only a suffering patience in the face of adverse conditions. While the inner revolution alone is radical and essential and lasting, there are occasions when the Christian will practice a holy impatience and choose to suffer as he attacks injustice in the name of a Christ who cleansed the temple and boldly challenged the corrupt powers that lent their support to the evil. "Thy will be done" is not a dumb submission to the *status quo;* it is a high resolve to do the will of God come what may. Under certain conditions we may even have to suffer deliberately, although all suffering must be redemptive in motive and aim, and must be undertaken and endured only in full obedience to Jesus Christ.

3:1-7. *Christian Wives and Christian Husbands.*—Peter's lengthy and detailed counsel to Christian wives may imply that women outnumbered men in the churches to which he

2 While they behold your chaste conversation *coupled* with fear.

3 Whose adorning, let it not be that outward *adorning* of plaiting the hair, and of wearing of gold, or of putting on of apparel;

wives, 2 when they see your reverent and chaste behavior. 3 Let not yours be the outward adorning with braiding of hair, decoration of gold, and wearing of robes,

---

adornment in a woman. (Remember the holy women of old.) On the other hand, the Christian husband will treat his wife considerately, not only because she belongs to the weaker sex, but because she is a coheir with him of eternal life."

Peter does not talk like a modern sex equalitarian; but there breathes through his advice the very spirit of Christian chivalry.

3:1. Likewise refers to 2:18. **To your own husbands:** Peter means that in a home the husband should be head of the house, and that the wife should recognize the fact. **If any obey not the word:** Here **the word** is the gospel, and the clause means, "If any are not Christians." In the next clause, however, **without the word** (KJV) is literally, **without a word** (RSV) and admits of two interpretations: either (*a*) without the word of the gospel, i.e., the wife is not to preach to him; or (*b*) without a word being spoken, i.e., she need not argue—the mere sight of her conduct will suffice. The latter explanation is perhaps better. **Won:** Converted, won for Christ. History offers many examples of husbands being converted through the influence of their wives, e.g., Clovis, king of France, through his wife Clotilda, and Ethelbert of Kent, through his wife Bertha.

2. When they see your reverent and chaste behavior: Cf. Shakespeare (*The Winter's Tale,* Act 2, scene 2) :

> The silence often of pure innocence
> Persuades when speaking fails.

3. Whose adorning, let it not be . . . : Christian women, Peter says, should be distinguished not so much by outward ornamentation as by inner beauty of character. Of

---

addressed this letter. This sounds rather modern. No doubt more women than men were attracted to the person and gospel of Jesus Christ. Our Lord was especially gracious in dealing with women, with his mother, with Mary, with the woman at the well of Samaria, with the Syrophoenician, and with many others. The lot of women was difficult in those days; they were definitely regarded as inferior to, indeed the property of, men. They had few rights, they could be easily divorced, they were for the most part circumscribed in their privileges and possibilities. And yet, as so often has been the case in Christian history, even in pre-Christian times women have been almost unbelievably influential by reason of their home relationships, even in those societies where they had little or no status beyond the home. Many of these wives to whom Peter was writing no doubt were married to pagan husbands. Their position seemed to be even more difficult than for those who were not Christians at all. Pagan husbands of Christian women could make life most miserable for their wives. Peter's counsel to the wives therefore is far from a reiteration of the worldly mores of the time; he is acknowledging the

dignity and influential vocation of the Christian wife. He had little reason to write Christian husbands who had non-Christian wives; they would be most likely to lead their wives into the faith.

Likewise, or in the same way in which the Christian servant and citizen accepts his situation, so the Christian wife accepts the relationship of husband to wife. There is nothing said here about inferiority and superiority; what is maintained is rather the fact that the relationship which exists between husband and wife is to be respected and submitted to, so long as it does not run counter to Christian convictions. But the outward conformity is to be infilled with a new meaningfulness. Instead of a passive submission to the marriage vow, there is to be an active acceptance of the marriage relationship in a new spirit. Peter provides no source materials for those who would argue, as between men and women, an "equality" which is blind to the fact that there are real differences. What he does say is that while there is no male or female in Christ (Gal. 3:28), there is a difference in function between the sexes which Christian faith does not eradicate. And

4 But *let it be* the hidden man of the heart, in that which is not corruptible, *even the ornament* of a meek and quiet spirit, which is in the sight of God of great price.

4 but let it be the hidden person of the heart with the imperishable jewel of a gentle and quiet spirit, which in God's sight

---

course, he is not urging carelessness in dress. He is warning against ostentation in coiffure, jewelry, and clothes. Cf. Isaiah's trenchant denunciation of the daughters of Zion who "are haughty, and walk with stretched forth necks and wanton eyes, walking and mincing as they go, and making a tinkling with their feet, . . ." (Isa. 3:16-24). Cf. also I Tim. 2:9-12, which closely resembles this passage. Neither Peter nor Paul would have approved the modern woman's virtuosity in cosmetics.

4. The hidden man of the heart (KJV). Since women are in question RSV's **the hidden person of the heart** is better. The phrase is equivalent to Paul's "inner man" (Eph. 3:16) : the real self, hidden in the heart and soul. We may also recall Paul's description of the true Jew (Rom. 2:28-29) : "He is a Jew who is one inwardly, and circumcision is that of the heart." Robert Burns in "The Epistle to Davie" writes:

> The heart aye's the part aye
> That makes us right or wrong.

With the imperishable jewel of a gentle and quiet spirit: The Christian woman's charm should be that of character, not of make-up. That is what God approves. **Spirit** (πνεῦμα) is here used in the same sense as it bears in Luke 9:55, "Ye know not what manner of spirit [disposition] ye are of." **A gentle and quiet spirit** has been defined as one which "neither worries other people, nor allows itself to be worried." More than any other Christian group, the Quakers know the secret of Peter's words.

---

he also recognizes the reality of mixed marriages in which one party may not be a Christian.

As Christian wives, they are not to flout the laws of the land, nor make their Christian faith an occasion to break up their marriages. They can within even a "mixed" situation act the Christian role and see their relationship to their husbands in a new way. They may redeem this most intimate relationship between man and woman from its pagan perversion by an inward attitude. They can remove some of the prejudice of non-Christians by their conduct, and by their gracious, **meek and quiet spirit** use their Christian liberty in Christ to help break down the wall of misunderstanding and ignorance which separates the non-Christian from the gospel. They would not only give no offense thereby; they would positively preach the gospel through their winsome characters.

All too long have we harbored the half-truth that preaching of the Word is done only by clergymen who proclaim the gospel from church pulpits. True, they preach representatively for the church, for it would be bedlam if every member of the congregation were to preach publicly at one and the same time. But every Christian is a witness to the gospel both in life and in speech. Peter is declaring sound truth when he writes that a Christian wife may preach the Word effectively to a non-Christian husband

who is not obedient to the Word of God. The wordless example of a wife may penetrate a husband's heart where repeated verbal argument and appeal only make his mind the more impenetrable. **A meek and quiet spirit,** a behavior that is simple and dignified, yet tempered with a proper respect, not craven fear, for her husband may preach more eloquently and effectively than the golden-mouthed preacher who addresses his multitudes.

Such behavior is in the great tradition of noble womanhood. **Sarah** was the matriarchal pattern. And she was no submissive lamb to the father of the faithful—Abraham! She assumed her place at his side with dignity and with grace. She granted that Abraham was "head of the house," but in her was not one shred of the groveling dumbness of a browbeaten wife. She **hoped in God,** and she adorned herself with the eternal garment of a true womanly spirit born of her wifely vocation under God. If the line of Christian heroes is long and venerable, the line of Christian heroines is equally as long—if not longer.

But let Christian women—and all women—remember that if they would be attractive and admired and influential, an extravagant adornment of the body is hardly the way to accomplish that end. The vanity of women, as well as of men, is an age-old characteristic. Braided

5 For after this manner in the old time the holy women also, who trusted in God, adorned themselves, being in subjection unto their own husbands:

6 Even as Sarah obeyed Abraham, calling him lord: whose daughters ye are, as long as ye do well, and are not afraid with any amazement.

is very precious. 5 So once the holy women who hoped in God used to adorn themselves and were submissive to their husbands, 6 as Sarah obeyed Abraham, calling him lord. And you are now her children if you do right and let nothing terrify you.

---

5. An appeal to the example of the **holy women** of old, especially Sarah, wife of "the father of the faithful." **Who trusted in God:** The Greek is not "believed" but **hoped** (RSV). It may be that the verb is significant; for as one commentator puts it, every Jewish mother hoped that she might be the mother of the Messiah.

6. **As Sarah obeyed Abraham, calling him lord:** Sarah is cited as the mother par excellence of the Hebrew race as the chosen people, and the reference is to Gen. 18:12, where she calls Abraham "my lord." It must be admitted, however, that such phraseology does not come easily to a modern Christian wife!

Whose daughters ye are, lit., "whose children ye have become, if. . . ." Just as Paul regards all Christians who accept the grace of God in Christ as "sons of Abraham," because they have a faith like his, so Peter regards all Christian wives who are "subject to their husbands" as "daughters of Sarah."

If you do right and let nothing terrify you: The second half of the clause echoes Prov. 3:25 (one of Peter's favorite chapters, for it is quoted again in 5:5). Peter is apparently thinking of some attempt (by a pagan husband?) to scare a woman out of her Christian faith. Justin Martyr (*Second Apology*) tells of a pagan husband who

---

hair, jewels, and clothing have ever been the stock in trade of women; so have their charms been enhanced and their appeal made more fetching. Christianity does not frown on any of these when used in moderation; on the contrary, it decries slovenliness and filthiness. Surely God approves of beauty of every kind, and especially in its human form. However, there is a danger in making the outward all-important, and especially in substituting it for the real beauty of the inward spirit. "The Lord looketh on the heart" (I Sam. 16:7). Women may *obtain* a beauty of sorts at the corner drugstore in the form of cosmetics; they may *attain* real beauty of character and spirit only by patiently putting on the apparel of God's grace as it is known in Christ. The true glory of man is the reflection of the glory of God in the face of Jesus Christ.

Christian husbands, however, are not to be without Peter's counsel. They are to live with their wives **according to knowledge, to give honor unto the wife, as unto the weaker vessel,** to honor their wives **as being heirs together of the grace of life,** to the end that their **prayers be not hindered.** While a husband may be the "head of the house," the number one in point of responsibility in marriage, he has no right to act the dictator or tyrant. Far better were he number two; then his obligation would be the lighter. Whereas the Christian wife is obedient,

but not humiliatingly submissive, so the husband is the head of the house but not arbitrarily authoritarian. He is to live with his wife in the knowledge of the gospel; and the gospel has much to say about love for the neighbor. Surely his wife is his best and nearest neighbor. Will not one who knows God and God's concern and purpose for each individual respect accordingly that best and nearest of all his neighbors? He will not use her as a means, nor will he rule over her as though he were God. If he is to regard her as **the weaker vessel,** because of the limitations of her physical strength, he has no right to regard her as spiritually, morally, or intellectually any weaker than himself. She—with him—is a joint heir of grace, and is therefore his equal in the fundamental relationships of life. This joint heirship is the declaration of woman's emancipation. If husband and wife are equals here, then the day of their inequality for the Christian is finished, in the home, in the church, and in any society that is seeking to be Christian. What Peter envisioned in that first century is even now more clearly seen. Yet the declaration of women's rights which he here proclaims has still to be fully realized.

Husbands are also counseled that the treatment of their wives is related to their spiritual condition and growth. The spiritual or prayer life may be definitely hindered by self-centeredness in marriage. A Christian home can be built

7 Likewise, ye husbands, dwell with *them* according to knowledge, giving honor unto the wife, as unto the weaker vessel, and as being heirs together of the grace of life; that your prayers be not hindered.

8 Finally, *be ye* all of one mind, having compassion one of another; love as brethren, *be* pitiful, *be* courteous:

7 Likewise you husbands, live considerately with your wives, bestowing honor on the woman as the weaker sex, since you are joint heirs of the grace of life, in order that your prayers may not be hindered.

8 Finally, all of you, have unity of spirit, sympathy, love of the brethren, a tender

---

denounced his wife to the authorities as a Christian, because she left him on account of his drunkenness and immorality.

7. Having described the good Christian wife, Peter now considers in one verse the good Christian husband.

Dwell with them according to knowledge: Bennett describes the knowledge as "the true spiritual enlightenment, which would be aware of the needs and claims of the wife, and would regard them as sacred obligations" (*General Epistles*, p. 226; cf. also RSV).

Bestowing honor on the woman as the weaker sex: Christian chivalry in a sentence. **Vessel** (KJV) is in Greek σκεῦος, which was also used in the sense of "body," i.e., "person" (cf. the Scots' "puir body"; also I Thess. 4:4). The ancient world agreed that woman was "the weaker sex." "Lighter tasks," said Plato in *Republic* (V. 457 A), "are to be given to women than to men because of the weakness of their sex." And though modern woman may often object to the phrase, nevertheless, in its most obvious sense, the physical, it remains true.

As being heirs together of the grace of life: An exquisite phrase, **life** here being life in its Johannine sense, "eternal life," life of a new quality, life with eternity in it; in short, a synonym for salvation. **The grace of life** therefore means the free gift of eternal life. (Cf. Rom. 6:23, "The free gift [χάρισμα] of God is eternal life in Christ Jesus our Lord. Paul and Peter are at one in this definition of salvation.)

That your prayers be not hindered: Probably the husband's prayers are chiefly in Peter's mind; but the general thought of the passage is that, in Burns's words, "a correspondence fixed wi' heaven" cannot subsist save on the basis of "the sacred lowe o' weel-placed love" between husband and wife. So married love and the love of God are joined in a beautiful unity.

F. Recapitulation (3:8-12)

Peter now addresses his readers, not in distinct classes, but as a whole community. He exhorts them to "unity of spirit, sympathy, love of the brethren, a tender heart, and a humble mind," and he ends with a beautiful quotation from Ps. 34.

8. Be ye all of one mind: The Greek word (ὁμόφρονες) denotes likeness of sentiment and disposition rather than of opinion.

---

only on the foundations of spiritual equality between husband and wife. And while marriage is a gift of God for the happiness and welfare of mankind, it is more than an end in itself: it may really be a means of grace through which husband and wife enter more fully into companionship with God. God wills that mankind shall be a family living together in peace, in truth, and in grace. Little wonder, then, that the whole context of biblical revelation is set so deeply within the context of the family. Marriage and family life are God's laboratory—his basic church—through which the spiritual education of the race is achieved.

Peter has little to say about rights, but much about duties, always of course linking up duties with corresponding blessings and rewards. The modern age has grown so self-conscious and self-centered that it is fast losing its willingness to lose itself for the sake of anything but immediate and personal reward. "It is small wonder when a marriage, in which both partners are obsessed with their rights, does not prove much of a success." [7]

8-12. *Finally, Inherit a Blessing.*—Let us remember that this letter was written to Christians

[7] C. E. B. Cranfield, *The First Epistle of Peter* (London: Student Christian Movement Press, 1950), p. 74.

9 Not rendering evil for evil, or railing for railing: but contrariwise blessing; knowing that ye are thereunto called, that ye should inherit a blessing.	heart and a humble mind. **9** Do not return evil for evil or reviling for reviling; but on the contrary bless, for to this you have been called, that you may obtain a bless-

Having compassion one of another: In the Greek this is one word, συμπαθεῖς, "sympathetic" (cf. RSV), and it signifies community of all feelings, whether of pleasure or pain (Bigg). Instead of φιλόφρονες (**courteous** [KJV]), the best MSS (followed by RSV) read ταπεινόφρονες, "humble-minded."

9. Not rendering evil for evil, . . . but contrariwise blessing: Cf. Rom. 12:17, "Recompense to no man evil for evil," and I Thess. 5:15, "See that none render evil for evil unto any man." Both Peter and Paul are echoing our Lord's words in Luke 6:27-28, "Love your enemies, do good to them which hate you, bless them that curse you, and pray for them which despitefully use you."

Knowing that ye are thereunto called: The best text omits "knowing" (εἰδότες). Moffatt well renders the Greek, "For this is your vocation, to bless and to inherit blessing." The principle of the passage is that "the Christian hope is also the Christian rule." As Jesus had often said, "Forgive, and ye shall be forgiven," so Peter here says, "Bless, and ye shall be blessed." To bless is to wish well, and to turn the wish into a prayer.

in Asia Minor who by their conversion had separated themselves from the "old" life. To be a Christian in those days and amid their circumstances demanded at that point a clear-cut break. If Peter writes with a passionate tone that sounds dogmatic, one can appreciate his reason for doing so. He brings this section to a ringing conclusion by demanding of his readers those qualities which are integral to the Christian way of life.

He does not make them an option for the Christian; they are a part of the Christian's vocation, "to bless and to inherit blessing" (Moffatt). While we may have to endure trials, we are also called to a life blessed and blessing. To illustrate his point Peter quotes from Ps. 34:12-16, which is a veritable hymn of life for those who—though they may suffer—stand clearly in God's favor, their movement out upon the world integral with God's movement, partaking of the very nature of God.

Be like-minded. So our Lord prayed in the upper room—"that they all may be one" (John 17:21). Not that Christians should slavishly conform to doctrinal or other rigid standards, but that they should be profoundly united in "sentiment and disposition" (see Exeg.). This unity is no "spiritual luxury, but . . . something essential to the true being of the Church."[8] The common loyalty of Christians to their Lord does not eliminate real and tense differences among them, whether of race or nationality or economic status; but it holds them together in a higher bond. It must ever be stronger than all our divisions. When those divisions become more evident than that unity, we commit sin; our

interests become more important than the lordship of Christ. Tensions within the church ought to drive Christians not to bitter conflict but to greater humility and penitence, lest Christ be dishonored and the Christian witness weakened.

Be compassionate. Feel with and for each other. Shed for each other "the sympathetic tear." [9] And "rejoice with those who rejoice" (Rom. 12:15). As members of the same body who share the disease or health of the whole, so let Christians identify themselves with each other in an organic, familial, and personal way (cf. I Cor. 12:26).

Be loving brothers. Jesus made the love of his disciples for one another the sign of discipleship (John 13:35). And John regarded brotherly love as a true indication that the Christian had passed from death to life (I John 3:14).

Be tenderhearted. Our time has seen an eruption of violence and brutality on a universal scale. War, revolution, and tyranny have ravaged whole populations. Young lives have been brutally mutilated, homes have been ruthlessly destroyed, populous cities have been made a shambles. Refugees, orphans, displaced persons number into the millions. So accustomed we may be to these matters that we are in danger of becoming hardened into insensitivity. If Friedrich von Hügel was right in saying that Christianity is the religion that has taught people to care, then Peter's appeal comes home to us with inescapable force. The Christian who has learned pity from Jesus, who taught that God marked the sparrow's fall, will be tender-

[8] *Ibid.*, p. 75.

[9] Thomas Gray, "The Alliance of Education and Government," l. 37.

10 For he that will love life, and see good days, let him refrain his tongue from evil, and his lips that they speak no guile:

11 Let him eschew evil, and do good; let him seek peace, and ensue it.

ing. 10 For

"He that would love life
and see good days,
let him keep his tongue from evil
and his lips from speaking guile;

11 let him turn away from evil and do right;
let him seek peace and pursue it.

10-12. Peter quotes Ps. 34:12-16 in the Greek version of the O.T. But the first verse of the quotation in the LXX runs, "Who is the man that wishes life, loving to see good days?" By **life** the psalmist meant "a happy life on earth." Peter *may* here mean "eternal life."

Let him seek peace and pursue it: We recall the Lord's "Blessed are the peacemakers" (Matt. 5:9). In both passages peacemaking is a positive thing. The peacemakers are not

---

hearted not only to the unfortunates among men, but to all dumb and helpless creatures. To inflict needless pain upon anybody or anything is the very negation of Christian pity. The sensitive heart is the wellspring of creative concern.

Be humble-minded! Of all the qualities of the Christian life, this one must have been most difficult for Peter's readers to express. The Greeks had little respect for the diffident Milquetoast; they worshiped virility in all its physical perfection. To be humble-minded was not the fashion. The slavish person cowered in the presence of others; he was inferior; he lacked the force of an aggressive self-assertion. But Christians must be done with that egoistic pride which looks with condescension and even disdain upon others, with that autonomous self-centeredness which breaks communion with others. The Christian is "poor" and "meek" in spirit because he is a creature, a sinner, and a disciple of One who did not avariciously grasp after equality with God but emptied himself and took upon himself the form of a servant (Phil. 2:7). Jesus "came not to be ministered unto, but to minister, and to give his life a ransom for many" (Matt. 20:28). He was "lowly in heart." He died for others. Of that knowledge is born the Christian's knowledge that he has no reason to be proud of himself. If he boasts, he boasts "in the Lord." It is only the humble-minded who shall be exalted; only they are assured a part in the Lord's glory (Matt. 23:12).

Do not render evil for evil, or reviling for reviling! On the contrary, bless. Jesus taught his disciples to "bless those who curse you" (Luke 6:28). Paul reiterated the same truth in his own words: "Being reviled, we bless" (I Cor. 4:12). The natural inclination of men to want revenge on those who mistreat them is reversed. A new redemptive relationship must be set up to counteract evil. To give way to revenge is to

feed one's pride, to take God's right into our control, to perpetuate and even increase the wrong, and to disobey Christ. The "new man in Christ" injects a new spirit into old human relations.

The Christian life has a twofold aspect: It is moved by a sense of mission, and it is possessed of a sense of satisfaction. It is at once a blessed gift that fills life with joy and peace, and a high responsibility that drives life with divine purpose and a will to serve. One of the most difficult problems of the Christian is this: How can the disciple of Jesus Christ live up to such high demands? Being a Christian is hard, since it counters the basic desires of the "natural man." Motivation comes from two truths: Man's high calling to a life of eternal meaningfulness and dignity, and the marvel of God's gift to a prodigal race. The ultimate motivation is in that "unspeakable gift." The Christian ethic rests upon it.

He that would love life. . . . Peter follows rather freely the LXX of Ps. 34, which in the original of vs. 12 reads, "He who loves life and desires to see good days," i.e., life in this world. Even austere Calvin writes: "It is indeed a desirable thing, since God has placed us in this world, to pass our time in peace."[1] But Peter seems to go beyond the psalmist by putting into the words **love** and **life** a full Christian meaning. To **love life** may voice a pagan philosophy which finds satisfactions only in secular pleasures, whether gross or refined; to **love life** in the Christian sense is to rejoice in the eternal kind of life which Christ gives here in this world and which is fulfilled in the age to come. In a day when many were so cynical about life that they found it a curse rather than a blessing, the Christian's love of life was good news in-

[1] John Calvin, *Commentaries on the Catholic Epistles* (tr. John Owen; Grand Rapids: W. B. Eerdmans Publishing Co., 1948), p. 104.

12 For the eyes of the Lord *are* over the righteous, and his ears *are open* unto their prayers: but the face of the Lord *is* against them that do evil.

12 For the eyes of the Lord are upon the righteous,

and his ears are open to their prayer.

But the face of the Lord is against those that do evil."

---

those who merely practice the negative virtue of nonresistance to evil; they overcome evil with good, and create peace where there is discord and strife, make up quarrels and reconcile enemies.

12. The face of the Lord: The divine Presence manifested, whether in judgment (as here) or in mercy.

---

deed. And in a day when "good days" faced the constant threat of the end, the Christian hope of eternal life was one of the greatest boons.

But he who desires such a good life must be watchful on the one hand and persistent in purpose on the other. To **refrain** [the] **tongue from evil** means more than avoiding profane, obscene, slanderous, and false talk. While it is the mark of Christian courtesy to refrain from saying unkind and unclean things, it is even more the mark of Christian character to watch the heart out of which the lips speak. Let heart and lips be in harmony; therefore no double talk or guile (cf. Jas. 1:26; 3:2). Jas. 3:5-6 calls the tongue the "world of iniquity . . . among our members, [which] defileth the whole body." Moreover, the good life avoids the evil deed; it does not use pious words and then engage in evil actions. Religion and ethics belong together (Rom. 12:1). Every semblance of evil is to be resisted as a plague, for what it does to the life, and for what it may do to our witness. But the very resistance comes of being possessed of an eager spirit: a spirit that pursues the **peace** which so easily escapes us. That **peace** is a prize to be purchased at cost. It does not come to those who simply sit and wait. It is not a passive attitude of unconcern, nor is it a state of existence where one is unmolested by strife. It is a calm at the heart of a storm. It is security in the midst of peril. It is the prize of man's striving and the gift of God's grace.

The providential care of God indeed surrounds all men; his rain and sunshine bless good and evil alike. But for those who are in right relationship with him—"in Christ," as Paul would say—there comes a deeper consolation and assurance. For them God's "eyes," "ears," and "face" take on a new significance. God keeps watch over them; he hears their prayers; he looks upon them with approval. No better assurance can be offered to any person than the assurance that there is such a gracious God, the Father of our Lord Jesus Christ. Without this intimate and personal relation of God toward us, life, however good from

a secular point of view, would be ultimately empty and futile. The affirmation that nothing can separate us from the love of God gives life a meaning that is infused with joy and peace. There is real comfort in the fact that there is One who does not forsake his own on the hard and often irrational pilgrimage of life. Not only will he comfort us with his presence and his love; he will be our avenger. He is no passive God; he takes an active part in history. His face is "for" or "against" men. The evil shall not prevail, nor shall it have its ultimate triumph over the righteous.

The Christian's life with God is indestructible. The powers of evil would assail Peter's readers. The very thought struck fear into their hearts. To allay that fear he insisted that they simply could not be harmed. Essentially nothing could hurt them. The body might be bruised and even destroyed. Indeed, they might be called upon to suffer terribly. But if they were as zealous as the Zealots—fanatical Jewish religious nationalists—they would come upon an inward power that could make them forget the pain. Athletes, though badly hurt, many a time choose to continue in the spirit of the game rather than to admit that they are injured. Soldiers in the heat of battle are seldom aware of their wounds. If Peter were writing to Christians today, he would perhaps suggest that if Christians had the fanatical zeal of Nazis or Communists, they would be more invulnerable and irresistible and far less concerned about their little discomforts. Jesus drank his cup to the dregs because it was his "meat" to do the Father's will. He told weepers along the Via Dolorosa not to weep for him (Luke 23:28). Though bruised with cruel beatings, he carried his cross to Calvary with a high sense of purpose, while those who wept were moved only by the sight of his physical suffering. There is an indestructibility about a purposeful and holy life which "evil" cannot harm. As the "gates of hell" cannot prevail against the true church, so the gates of evil cannot prevail against the true life.

13 And who *is* he that will harm you, if ye be followers of that which is good?	13 Now who is there to harm you if you are zealous for what is right? 14 But even
14 But and if ye suffer for righteousness' sake, happy *are ye:* and be not afraid of their terror, neither be troubled;	if you do suffer for righteousness' sake, you will be blessed. Have no fear of them, nor

G. THE CHRISTIAN ANSWER TO PERSECUTION (3:13-17)

Summary: "As a general rule, the best defense is an upright life. But if persecution should arise, it is blessed to suffer for righteousness' sake. Be unafraid; let Christ be Lord of your heart; be ready to give a courteous and intelligent answer to those who ask why you are Christians; and let your good conscience and life shame your libelers."

13. This recalls Isa. 50:9 (LXX), "Behold, the Lord will help me. Who will harm me?" **Followers,** lit., "zealots" (ζηλωταί) and so, "enthusiasts." It is enthusiasts for goodness, not Laodicean lovers of it, who are promised immunity from harm. "No heart," said Sir John Seeley in a famous sentence in *Ecce Homo,* "is pure that is not passionate, no virtue safe that is not enthusiastic." But does not Peter's dictum conflict with the flagrant facts of experience? Is it not often true that obloquy, suffering, and even death are the portion of "the enthusiast for good," the **zealous for what is right?** The answer may be that Peter is thinking of such a saying of Christ's as "Be not afraid of them that kill the body, and after that have no more that they can do" (Luke 12:4). In other words, he is thinking of real, as distinct from physical, harm. It is told that "Woodbine Willie" (G. A. Studdert-Kennedy) was once asked whether prayer would render a man invulnerable to shot and shell. His reply was that fellowship with God through prayer would make a man sure that though his body was shattered, his soul would be untouched.

14. But and if ye suffer for righteousness' sake . . . : The Greek verb is in the optative mood, and a more accurate rendering would be, "if ye should suffer" or **even if you do suffer.** The suffering is a possibility, not a certainty. The sentence is a clear echo of Matt. 5:10, "Blessed are they which are persecuted for righteousness' sake."

3:13–4:6. *But If You Suffer for What Is Right.* —Christians must be alert to the hardships involved in their high calling. Bitter experiences should be no surprise to them. But there is a way to meet such battle wounds with an understanding that will not only make us more than conquerors, but will also make our suffering witness effectively for Christ. And it will make us maturely perfect as children of God. The strength for bearing such hardships comes of the suffering Servant, Jesus Christ; the result of bearing them triumphantly will be life in the spirit (4:6).

Suffering of one kind or another comes to all men, whether they are Christians or not. But the lot of those who pursue the cause of right may lead to suffering in the "flesh," to bodily pain and discomfort, at the hands of those who love "darkness rather than light" (John 3:19). "To suffer *for righteousness,*" writes Calvin, "means not only to submit to some loss or disadvantage in defending a good cause, but also to suffer unjustly, when anyone is innocently in fear among men on account of the fear of God."[2] The suffering meant here is suffering which comes to one because he is a Christian.

[2] *Ibid.,* p. 106.

No Christian should court bodily pain, as abnormal persons sometimes do, getting a kind of satisfaction out of it. Nor should he welcome suffering in order to pride himself on his martyrlike religious zeal. The early church had to discourage this will-to-martyrdom by which fanatical Christians hoped to gain a martyr's accolade, total forgiveness, or immediate entrance into heaven. Impatient Peter wisely implies that the Christian may well run into suffering simply and solely **for righteousness' sake,** because the way of the Christian and the way of the world are not compatible.

Then he indicates how it should be met. For one thing, says he, you may consider yourselves **blessed** or **happy.** Such pain was the kind which Christ endured as he did his Father's will. The dregs of the cup he drank were bitter. Be assured that your faith is authentic if it partakes of that cup **for righteousness' sake.** You are sharing in the very sufferings of Christ; your pain is not destructive but constructive. Even the Son of God was made "perfect through suffering" (Heb. 2:10). What you suffer may bring you closer to God and bring your neighbors closer to life in the spirit. Indeed, such redemptive suffering is a part of Christ's con-

15 But sanctify the Lord God in your hearts: and *be* ready always to *give* an answer to every man that asketh you a reason of the hope that is in you, with meekness and fear:

be troubled, 15 but in your hearts reverence Christ as Lord. Always be prepared to make a defense to any one who calls you to account for the hope that is in you, yet do it

---

Have no fear of them, nor be troubled: These words and the first part of the following verse are derived from Isa. 8:12-13, "Fear not their fear, neither be troubled. Sanctify him Lord, and he will be thy fear" (LXX).

15. For **the Lord God** (KJV) read, with the best MSS, **Christ as Lord** (κύριον δὲ τὸν Χριστόν). The phrasing is from Isa. 8:13, but for "him" (i.e., Yahweh), Peter has **Christ**. In other words, for Peter, as for the early Christians generally, Christ had the value of God. Monotheists though they were, they found it possible to apply to Jesus titles and honors applied in the O.T. to God himself. **Sanctify** (KJV), **reverence** (RSV): Acknowledge as holy. **In your hearts** is not in Isaiah. Christ is to inhabit the secret shrine of their hearts.

Answer: The Greek ἀπολογία means any **defense** (RSV) or self-justification, formal or informal. We find the word in Acts 22:1; 25:16; II Tim. 4:16, of Paul's speeches in defense of himself, and it had been applied by Plato to Socrates' famous defense of himself. **Who calls you to account for:** The Greek phrase (αἰτεῖν λόγον) suggests a rational and intelligent explanation. **The hope that is in you:** We might have expected "the faith that is in you"; but, as Bigg observes, in Peter's mind the two words are nearly identical. **With meekness and fear:** Better, with RSV, **with gentleness and reverence.** What sort of answer did Peter expect his readers to make to inquirers? It must have been simple and brief: The main facts about Christ, perhaps the few great truths which prove themselves to all religious men, and certainly the personal testimony of the answerer. Today, when paganism is rampant in our world and the Christian church often finds its teaching openly challenged, the same "readiness" is demanded of him who would be a Christian in strong earnest.

---

tinuing ministry to the world. It is a kind of badge of honor by which we are joined in Christ's redemptive work. And surely **it is better, if the will of God be so, that ye suffer for well doing, than for evildoing** (3:17). The way to meet such suffering is to understand it in the light of the sufferings of Christ, and in the light of the relation of suffering to the life of righteousness.

Moreover, instead of being afraid of those things which so promptly fill the heart of the non-Christian with fear, instead of trembling before the threats of evil-bent persecutors, the Christian is to fear God alone. Peter hardly means to make such a blanket statement as that Christians should not fear what other people fear, but that they should not be terrorized by what men may do to them. The fear of God drives out all other fears. "The fear of the Lord is clean" (Ps. 19:9). The only real danger to life is not what men can do to us in the flesh, but what God, the ultimate judge and redeemer, can do to us in the end. We are overcome with fear, we think ourselves lost, when men seem to have more power to injure us than God has to save us. God alone is our ultimate security.

"Let not your heart be troubled: ye believe in God, believe also in me" (John 14:1). The troubled mind is born of a fear of man which has become a substitute for a simple trust in the God and Father of our Lord Jesus Christ.

Therefore **sanctify,** hallow, **reverence Christ in your hearts** as Lord of this world. Peter quotes from the LXX of Isa. 8:12-13, where the prophet told the people during the Syrian invasion not to cherish a greater sense of reverent awe toward the aggressors than toward God. "Your sacred loyalty," writes Peter, "is to your Lord Jesus Christ, as the sacred loyalty of those Jews was to God. In your hearts enthrone the One who alone is holy, who is not a man or a thing, who is in a class by himself, possessed of the ultimate quality before which all creation bows in silent fear." As J. B. Phillips summarizes Peter's advice: "Concentrate on being completely devoted to Christ in your hearts."[3] Only a holy flame of passionate love for him can consume the unholy flame of the hate that blazes up against you. Only the power of a concentrated purpose and devotion can hold life

[3] *Letters to Young Churches* (2nd ed.; New York: The Macmillan Co., 1953), p. 205.

16 Having a good conscience; that, whereas they speak evil of you, as of evildoers, they may be ashamed that falsely accuse your good conversation in Christ.

17 For *it is* better, if the will of God be so, that ye suffer for well doing, than for evildoing.

with gentleness and reverence; 16 and keep your conscience clear, so that, when you are abused, those who revile your good behavior in Christ may be put to shame.

17 For it is better to suffer for doing right, if that should be God's will, than for doing—

---

16. **That, whereas they speak evil of you:** The KJV here translates an inferior text. The best text ἐν ᾧ καταλαλεῖσθε means, literally. "wherein you are spoken against," i.e., as the RSV renders, **when you are abused.** The translation **revile** is better than **falsely accuse;** and **behavior** is better than **conversation.** The phrase **in Christ,** which occurs some 164 times in Paul, probably takes its origin in such teaching of Christ as is recorded in John 15:4, "Abide in me, and I in you." In some instances a mystical meaning may be uppermost: Christ is the spiritual atmosphere of the believer's soul, so that he dwells in Christ, and Christ in him. But the clue to most passages is in the Hebrew conception of "corporate personality," according to which the head of a society stands for the society itself. Thus in I Cor. 12:12 Paul (as Calvin observed) "calls Christ the church." To be **in Christ** is therefore to be a member of the redeemed society (i.e., the church) of which he is the head, and the phrase is a synonym for "being a Christian" (for "the Bible knows nothing of solitary religion"). For a good discussion see *Christianity According to St. Paul* by Charles A. Anderson Scott (Cambridge: The University Press, 1927), pp. 151-58; also see Vol. VII of this work, pp. 26-27, and Vol. IX, pp. 472-73.

17. **If the will of God be so:** Lit., "If the will of God were so to will," the optative mood of the verb in Greek suggesting a contingency, not a certainty. If God should ordain suffering for you, says Peter, better be found doing right than wrong.

---

together when the world tries to tear it apart. The eye that is "single" brings light to the whole body (Matt. 6:22).

But it is not enough to cherish Christ in the heart; the believer is also to **be ready always** with **an answer** or **a defense** concerning **the hope** that he cherishes, or the faith that he embraces. Silent devotion is not enough; the Christian must express his faith in terms of witness, and **be ready** to do it without hesitation whenever opportunity offers. He must speak out, whether before civil magistrates or before non-Christians who are curiously interested in the Christian faith. If there is any stalwart **hope . . . in him,** he will be able to give an intelligent and meaningful account of it. Christianity is no sanction for unintelligent ranting; on the contrary, it demands both passionate zeal and reasonable faith (1:13; Mark 13:11).

And let the reply be given in **meekness and fear,** not in arrogance and pride. He who speaks about God ought to be reverent, and he who speaks as a Christian to men ought to be tactful, wise, and gracious. A contemptuous and truculent attitude toward inquirers and critics gets nowhere; it weakens the case and sets up a barrier between witness and hearer. The Christian living in a day of rampant and even hostile paganism may be inclined to cherish his

devotion to Christ in private; and he may look with loathing contempt and aloof antagonism upon non-Christians: but if he has the gospel in his heart, he will be filled both with a sense of reverence toward this that God has committed to him and with a sense of loving concern for his neighbors.

A Christian must also have a **good conscience** as he meets suffering in his pursuit of right. When "spoken against," his **good behavior in Christ** ought to put his critics **to shame.** Nothing negates a good verbal witness to the gospel like bad personal conduct. A good confession and a good conscience go together. A good conscience gives integrity to a good confession. And even if such good conduct does not make converts to Christ, it may shame the opposition out of its misrepresentations. Innocent suffering for right is an argument hard to refute; indeed, it may convert. But even so, there is something intrinsically right about suffering **if the will of God be so. For it is better to suffer for doing right . . . than for doing wrong.**

The real inspiration for the innocent sufferer, however, is in the redemptive suffering of Jesus Christ by which he has brought us to God, and in the shining example of his obedience to the will of God, even though such obedience meant bodily pain. The Son of God endured his human sufferings with patience and trust, so that

18 For Christ also hath once suffered for sins, the just for the unjust, that he might bring us to God, being put to death in the flesh, but quickened by the Spirit:

ing wrong. 18 For Christ also died[h] for sins once for all, the righteous for the unrighteous, that he might bring us to God, being put to death in the flesh but made alive in

[h] Some ancient authorities read *suffered.*

H. OUR EXAMPLE, CHRIST (3:18-22)

In this difficult passage Peter begins with an appeal to the example of Christ on the Cross, goes on to speak of his preaching to the "spirits in prison," is led to speak of Christian baptism, and ends with attention fixed on the risen and exalted Savior.

Summary: "Consider our supreme example Christ, whose innocent suffering has brought us back to God. Consider too how in Hades he offered salvation to those who had disobeyed in Noah's day. As water was the means of saving Noah, so now the water of baptism—combined, of course, with an appeal to God for a clean conscience—saves you, in virtue of the resurrection of Christ who is now at God's right hand."

Vss. 18-22, as Bennett observes, set forth a threefold activity of Christ: In vs. 18 he redeems men by his passion on earth; in vs. 19 he preaches to the spirits in prison; and in vs. 22 he receives the submission of angels in heaven.

18. For Christ also hath once suffered for sins: For **suffered** (ἔπαθεν) it is better with RSV to read **died** (ἀπέθανεν); but there is no real difference of meaning. Both refer to the Passion. Three things are said of Christ's death: (*a*) it is atoning—"in respect of sins"; (*b*) it is vicarious—**the just for** [ὑπέρ] **the unjust;** and (*c*) its aim is to restore the broken fellowship between God and man—**that he might bring** [conduct] **us to God.** Peter undoubtedly holds up Christ in his passion as an example, but his view of the Atonement is far more than merely "exemplarist." **Once,** as in Heb. 9:28, distinguishes Christ's single sacrifice from the repeated deaths of the victims under the Levitical system.

That he might bring us to God: The basic idea is that of access to God, which is in the final analysis, "the be-all and end-all of religion." Peter means that in virtue of Christ's death we are enabled to get "through" to God, to pass from dis-grace into grace.

Being put to death in the flesh, but quickened by the Spirit: "The flesh is the sphere or element in which death took place; similarly, the spirit is the sphere of resurrection, the element of life that made it possible. In virtue of one aspect of His being, Christ died;

all who have similar bitter experiences may have the comfort of his companionship and the stimulus of his example. Thus our little lives, so often beset by terrible afflictions, are subsumed and incorporated into the context of eternity. Suffering may be accepted and made a means of grace.

Peter of course thinks of Christ's suffering as more than an example: The once-for-all suffering and death of Christ, by reason of the sins that unrighteous men laid upon him, is the way by which God seeks us for himself (cf. Rom. 6:9; Heb. 7:27; 9:12, 26, 28; 10:10). He was righteous, yet he voluntarily assumed the consequences of and involvement in unrighteousness, and so suffered death; but he was **quickened by the Spirit** to triumph over the death that comes to all mortals who live in the flesh. It is through such a vicarious and unique event of suffering that we are reconciled to God. Such an act, initiated by God, lays a claim upon our lives, requires of us to live and die for and with Christ. The weakness and pain of the flesh

are not the last word about life; the last word rather is the resurrection power of the Spirit. This does not mean that the fleshly body has no share in the life of the Spirit; it means that the unholy and frail aspects of that body are crucified with Christ, and that thereafter the Spirit raises it a "spiritual body." The "old man" dies and the "new man" comes to life in the Spirit. We bear in our bodies the dying of our Lord, that his raised life may become manifest in us (II Cor. 4:10). The "flesh" in this case is the outward man, and the Spirit is the agency of the new life (I Cor. 15:42 ff.). Christ's innocent suffering **for righteousness'** sake at the hands of unrighteousness not only "leadeth . . . to repentance" (Rom. 2:4), but his physical undoing even to death is met by the resurrecting power of the Spirit. Let that strengthen you in your suffering; and even though your bodies be done to death, as you seek to be obedient to God, know that the Spirit will raise you to a new life. In this we have at least some shadowing forth of the way in which

19 By which also he went and preached | the spirit; 19 in which he went and preached
unto the spirits in prison; |

---

in virtue of the other and higher, He was raised again. . . . Spirit means here the Divine vital principle, in a higher potency than it attains in man, and thus characterized by an essential and indestructible energy" (H. R. Mackintosh, *The Doctrine of the Person of Jesus Christ* [Edinburgh: T. & T. Clark, 1912; "International Theological Library"], p. 46).

19. In which he went and preached to the spirits in prison: In which, i.e., in the spirit, as distinguished from the flesh, his human life. But what is meant by preaching **to the spirits in prison?** The passage is one of the darkest in the N.T., and exegetes have differed about the interpretation of every word. Two attempts to avoid the most natural meaning of the words must first be put aside.

(*a*) We must reject Rendel Harris' brilliant cutting of the Gordian knot. He suggests that by a textual error (haplography), the word "Enoch" has fallen out after "in which also," i.e., what Peter wrote was ΕΝΩΚΑΙΕΝΩΧ, "in which [spirit] Enoch also went and preached to the spirits in prison." The reference would then be to the apocryphal story that Enoch made a proclamation of doom to imprisoned angels (Enoch 6:4 ff.). There is no MS evidence for the theory; the introduction of Enoch interrupts the course of the argument; and it is hard to harmonize Harris' theory with 4:6. But both Moffatt and Goodspeed accept Harris' conjecture.

(*b*) Nor can we accept Selwyn's view that Christ, in the course of his passion and resurrection, "made proclamation" to the powers of evil. "What St. Peter and St. Paul assert of these powers of evil, as their divine Master had asserted it before them, is that in Christ's death their end was sealed" (*First Epistle of Peter*, p. 360). This "mythological" view as expounded by Selwyn can be carried through only if we wrest the meaning of the Greek words in a most unnatural way.

The simplest meaning is that our Lord descended between his passion and resurrection, to preach to certain spirits imprisoned in Hades. (Hades, or Sheol, was no longer regarded as the abode of pithless shades, but partly as a place of punishment and partly as an intermediate state.) But who were the imprisoned spirits? Just possibly the fallen angels of Gen. 6:1-4. Much more probably Peter meant the spirits of the rebellious generation who perished in the Flood (Gen. 6:12 ff.).

Christ effects redemption for men. Through self-giving identification (even to death) with man the unrighteous, Christ the righteous enabled the unrighteous to become righteous. The purity of heaven took on in him the impurity of earth, so that the impure might become pure. Many a devout soul has expressed it in words similar to those of the great apostle, "He died for me, that I might live in him."

> I know not how that Calvary's cross
>   A world from sin could free;
> I only know its matchless love
>   Has brought God's love to me.[4]

It was in the power of the Spirit that Christ **went and preached unto the spirits in prison** (vs. 19). Biblical scholars have propounded a long series of interpretations regarding the identity of these **spirits** (see Exeg.). Be it said

[4] Harry Webb Farrington, "I know not how that Bethlehem's Babe." Copyright 1924 by H. W. Farrington. Used by permission of The Hymn Society of America.

only that Peter refers by way of *illustration* (vs. 20) to the disobedient people who perished in the Flood. To these Christ preached in the Spirit, whether between his crucifixion and his resurrection or in his preincarnate life. The age of **Noah** was critical indeed, for out of that end and beginning time in history, only **eight souls were saved,** saved by the very water which destroyed so many and purged the world of its filthy sin.

These wicked spirits of an evil age were imprisoned and confined by their own choices. God waited and wrestled patiently with men for 120 years (Gen. 6:3). Yet Noah's contemporaries could not or would not discern the signs of the times, repent, and believe. They rejected the man of faith. They ridiculed his ark and refused the means of escape it provided. For Peter this dramatic historic event was of utmost significance. It spoke of the patience of God. It proclaimed the shame of man's procrastination and the folly of his failure to heed the

20 Which sometime were disobedient, when once the long-suffering of God waited in the days of Noah, while the ark was a preparing, wherein few, that is, eight souls were saved by water.

to the spirits in prison, **20** who formerly did not obey, when God's patience waited in the days of Noah, during the building of the ark, in which a few, that is, eight persons,

How did this tradition of a ministry of Jesus in Hades originate? In Acts 2:27 Peter applies to Jesus the words of Ps. 16:10, "Because thou wilt not leave my soul in hell, neither wilt thou suffer thine Holy One to see corruption." This seems to indicate that the early church was thinking of what happened to Jesus between his death and resurrection. Moreover, Jesus had applied to his own ministry the great words of Isa. 61:1, where the Lord's servant is sent "to proclaim liberty to the captives" (Luke 4:17-18).

Bearing these two passages in mind, we may do a bit of guessing. Two questions must often have exercised the mind of the earliest Christians: (a) Where was Christ's spirit in the interval between his death and resurrection? (b) What was to be the fate of those who had died before the gospel was preached? An answer is supplied in 3:19 and 4:6 ("This is why the gospel was preached even to the dead"). Christ went down "in the spirit," says Peter, into Hades, between his death and resurrection, in order to offer salvation to sinners who had died without hearing the gospel and getting a chance to repent.

The tradition of Christ's descent into Hades and of the harrowing of hell soon became a part of the church's theology (cf. the Apostles' Creed, "He descended into hell"). Thus also in the apocryphal Gospel According to St. Peter (ca. A.D. 130), among the wonders attending the Crucifixion we read the question, "Hast thou preached to those who have fallen asleep?" To which the answer was heard from the Cross, "Yes." And in the Middle Ages the harrowing of hell was a common theme in popular poetry and theology; cf. the lines of Spenser's hymn:

> Most glorious Lord of life, that on this day
> Didst make thy triumph over death and sin,
> And having harrowed Hell, didst bring away
> Captivity thence captive, us to win.

If we ask what value this tradition has for us today, the answer is that wherever men are, Christ has power to save.

20. Were disobedient: Noah's contemporaries refused to listen to his call to repentance. **Waited** (ἀπεζεδέχετο): The tense of the Greek verb suggests "waited, waited,

warning of God's prophet. But even more, it revealed the scope and sweep of the eternal Christ's dominion over the living and the dead of all ages, and the inescapable kingship of him who was dead but is alive forevermore (Rev. 1:18).

In short, at the darkest point in human resistance to God, Christ the victorious Lord was preached, indicating that his victory was not his alone, but one that penetrated even to the realm of the most disobedient dead. (See also John 5:25-29; 8:56; Matt. 27:52 ff.) These verses are therefore not the foundation for faith in Christ's descent into hell; that article of faith may be deduced from other passages (Eph. 4:8-10; Acts 2:27, 31; Rom. 10:6-8). It is rather the vast range of Christ's descent and ascent that are here accentuated. Peter has no inten-

tion of dealing with the subjects of purgatory, or a second opportunity beyond death, or a universal salvation. The whole passage is an illustration of a practical truth. He is indicating how Christ in his suffering death is not taken captive but is victor through the Spirit; has indeed taken "captivity captive" and manifested his triumph not only in our world, but in that world which is beyond our world.

So, he goes on, as **Noah** was **saved** out of—yes, by and **through**—water, Christians are saved in a like figure (*antitypon*). For them baptism is not merely a **putting away of the filth of the flesh**, but a serious and efficacious act which cleanses the spirit. The water which saved **Noah** was also the water which destroyed the ungodly. The very instrument and power which **saves** men may at the same time be a furious **enemy**

21 The like figure whereunto *even* baptism doth also now save us, (not the putting away of the filth of the flesh, but the answer of a good conscience toward God,) by the resurrection of Jesus Christ:

22 Who is gone into heaven, and is on the right hand of God; angels and authorities and powers being made subject unto him.

were saved through water. 21 Baptism, which corresponds to this, now saves you, not as a removal of dirt from the body but as an appeal to God for a clear conscience, through the resurrection of Jesus Christ, 22 who has gone into heaven and is at the right hand of God, with angels, authorities, and powers subject to him.

---

waited." One interpretation of Gen. 6:3 made God grant the antediluvians a respite of 120 years. **Eight souls:** Noah and his wife, his three sons and their wives (Gen. 7:13). **Were saved by water:** Lit., with RSV, **through water;** they escaped through the Flood.

21. This saving through water at once suggests to Peter Christian baptism which he calls an ἀντίτυπον or "counterpart" (so Moffatt) of the water of the Flood. Peter insists that the primary significance of baptism is not physical, but moral and spiritual; but the exact translation of the Greek words συνειδήσεως ἀγαθῆς ἐπερώτημα εἰς θεόν is difficult. Ἐπερώτημα has been translated **answer** (KJV), "interrogation" (ERV), **appeal** (RSV), "inquiry" (Alford), "craving" (Weymouth and Goodspeed), and "prayer" (Moffatt). No certainty is possible; but the choice seems to lie between (*a*) a prayer to God for a good (clean) conscience; and (*b*) a pledge to God proceeding from a clear conscience. The first (*a*) may be interpreted to mean the prayer, appeal, or request which the baptized person makes to God for a good conscience. But (*b*) is to be preferred, and the explanation is to be found in the practice of baptismal vows. There is papyri evidence that ἐπερώτημα was used for the formal question and assent of two contracting parties. It could thus apply to the Christian's formal "confession" of his faith (cf. Rom. 10:10). We have to think of some solemn interrogatory before baptism, "Do you believe . . . and will you promise to renounce . . . ?" The whole proceeding of question and answer could thus be summarily called "a pledge to God proceeding from a clear conscience."

Through the resurrection of Jesus Christ: Again the characteristically Petrine emphasis on the central importance for salvation of the risen Christ.

22. Who . . . is at the right hand of God (cf. Rom. 8:34): The position of supreme honor, the highest place that heaven affords. It is not a dead Christ in whom we believe,

---

to those who spurn it. The consuming fire of rejected love is devastating. And as Christ was raised to the heavens and sits **on the right hand of God** clothed with power, authority, and honor, **angels and . . . powers** being **subject unto him,** so the Christian who suffers **for righteousness' sake** may bear up under his trial because he is borne up by the resurrecting power of the Spirit. No man then can place limitations upon Christ's redemptive activity. Those who suffer death with him through the symbolism of baptism are brought to new life. The saving power is not in the water, but in the power of Christ's atonement and **resurrection,** to which the Christian makes **answer.** The word so translated in the KJV—used of the question asked of the candidate for baptism, "Dost thou renounce . . . ?"—is a most difficult word. It may mean the promise or pledge of the baptized to maintain **a good conscience** and to renounce the "world"; or it may mean his

appeal for some pledge or assurance on God's part of full forgiveness and **a good conscience** (see Exeg.). As baptism involves both the offer of God's forgiveness and man's repentance and faith, it results in justification before God and in a conscience that is infused with a desire to be clean.[5]

Peter now turns (4:1-6) to consider the positive implications involved in being raised by the power of the Spirit. Christians are to live a new life by being changed in mind, in associations, and in conduct. They are not only to be conformed to Christ's death; they are to be

[5] For other interesting interpretations of this difficult and obscure passage see Calvin, *Commentaries on the Catholic Epistles;* James Moffatt, *The General Epistles* (New York: Harper & Bros.; London: Hodder & Stoughton, 1928; "Moffatt New Testament Commentary"); and others, such as Harris, Selwyn, Bigg, Lumby, and those mentioned in the Exeg. See especially the interesting sermon on "Spirits in Prison," by James S. Stewart, in *The Strong Name* (New York: Charles Scribner's Sons, 1941), pp. 24-34.

4 Forasmuch then as Christ hath suffered for us in the flesh, arm yourselves likewise with the same mind: for he that hath suffered in the flesh hath ceased from sin;

2 That he no longer should live the rest of *his* time in the flesh to the lusts of men, but to the will of God.

4 Since therefore Christ suffered in the flesh,[i] arm yourselves with the same thought, for whoever has suffered in the flesh has ceased from sin, 2 so as to live for the rest of the time in the flesh no longer by human passions but by the will of God.

[i] Some ancient authorities add *for us*; some *for you*.

but a living; and not only a living Christ, but a Christ enthroned. **Gone:** The Ascension; cf. Acts 1:10-11.

Angels and authorities and powers, i.e., various classes of angels—all made subject to Christ, who is "personally participant in the sovereignty of God."

J. Exhortation to Pure Living (4:1-6)

Summary: "Christ is your example in suffering which, humbly borne, purifies from sin. Live henceforth to do God's will. Once you lived like profligates, and now your pagan neighbors expect you to continue so and revile you when you refuse. They will have to give account to him who judges both living and dead. It is because judgment embraces the dead that the gospel had to be preached to them, so that though they were once judged in the experiences of their earthly life, they may yet attain unto spiritual life."

4:1. Forasmuch then looks back to 3:18. The words **for us** (KJV) should be omitted. **Arm yourselves likewise with the same mind:** For an expansion of this military metaphor see Eph. 6:10-17. **Mind** (KJV) is **thought** (RSV) or principle. The Christians are to arm themselves by taking the same view of their suffering as Christ took of his.

For he that hath suffered in the flesh hath ceased from sin (cf. Rom. 6:7; "He who has died is freed from sin"). Peter's meaning here seems to be that patient endurance of suffering has moral value. As Robert Leighton beautifully puts it, "Affliction, sweetly and humbly carried, doth purify and disengage the heart from sin, wean it from the world and the common ways of it (*A Practical Commentary upon the First Epistle of St. Peter* [London: Society for Promoting Christian Knowledge, 1853], II, 271).

2. That he no longer should live ...: The Greek might equally well be rendered "that we no longer should live...." **The rest of his time in the flesh:** The remainder of his earthly life (cf. RSV).

Human passions: These are, in John's phrase, "the lust of the flesh, and the lust of the eyes, and the pride of life" (I John 2:16). **The will of God:** We live according to the

transformed by "arming" themselves with his mind (see Phil. 2:5). They are to equip themselves not only with his spirit of humility and patience in suffering, but with his purpose, which sought always to do the will of his Father (John 4:34). There was about it a militant spirit which is an "invincible weapon" (Calvin) to subdue the "flesh."

Yet this persistent set of mind will not free one completely from sin; but it will enable the Christian to participate more fully in the Spirit (4:14). It will cleanse him who suffers for righteousness' sake. The cost of his loyalty will sharpen his sense of right and tone up his conscience. The higher drives out the baser. Baptized—and therefore buried with Christ—he is justified before God and has thus far died to sin; he is finished with it as the central motive of his life. He may not be free from the assaults of sin, but he will have done with the

lusts of men in his obedience **to the will of God.** In God's sight the sinner is justified—made right; but in actuality the forgiven sinner must strive to become what he is in reality before God. **No longer** will he run with the old crowd; no longer will he waste his time pursuing **the lusts of men**; no longer will he conform to **the will of the Gentiles** (pagans); no longer will he walk or live in the gross sins of the flesh, or in the **idolatries** of the mind and heart. There is a past in the Christian's life. Somewhere along the line there is a break with the life of "sin." There is also a future in the Christian's life, and a way into it.

Peter sets forth six human passions found in the society which he knew: plain sensuality; sexual lust; carousing, usually associated with drunkenness; dissipation associated with drinking; revelry; idolatry, or worship of forces and objects usually associated with natural or vital-

3 For the time past of *our* life may suffice us to have wrought the will of the Gentiles, when we walked in lasciviousness, lusts, excess of wine, revelings, banquetings, and abominable idolatries:

4 Wherein they think it strange that ye run not with *them* to the same excess of riot, speaking evil of *you:*

5 Who shall give account to him that is ready to judge the quick and the dead.

3 Let the time that is past suffice for doing what the Gentiles like to do, living in licentiousness, passions, drunkenness, revels, carousing, and lawless idolatry. 4 They are surprised that you do not now join them in the same wild profligacy, and they abuse you; 5 but they will give account to him who is ready to judge the living and the

will of God when, in the words of Lancelot Andrewes, "His will is our law, His word our rule, His Son's life our example, His Spirit rather than our own soul the guide of our actions" (*Sermons*, II, 203, as quoted by Selwyn, *First Epistle of Peter*, p. 210).

3. Ironical. "You have had plenty of opportunity in time past for doing the things which the Gentiles delight in—pursuing, as you did, a course of indecency, debauchery, hard drinking, revelry, carousing, and abominable idolatry."

The will of the Gentiles suggests that the majority of Peter's readers were Gentiles. Lax Jews, however, sometimes fell into the evil ways of their pagan neighbors.

4. **Wherein they think it strange** (ξενίζονται): The Greek verb means "entertain" or "surprise." Here, as in Acts 17:20, **they are surprised** (RSV) is the meaning.

The same excess of riot: Ἀνάχυσις means "flood" and ἀσωτία is from the same root as the word used of the prodigal son's "riotous living." Moffatt translates, "It astonishes pagans that you will not plunge with them still into the same flood of profligacy."

5. **Who shall give account . . .** : It is not stated whether the judge is God or Christ. Peter may here be echoing a word of his Master's, "But I say unto you, That every idle word that men shall speak, they shall give account thereof in the day of judgment" (Matt. 12:36).

The quick and the dead, i.e., all generations of men. The phrase is found on Peter's lips in Acts 10:42: "It is he which was ordained of God to be the Judge of quick and dead"; cf. II Tim. 4:1, "I charge thee . . . before God, and the Lord Jesus Christ, who shall judge the quick and the dead." The phrase **the quick and the dead** was perhaps already semicreedal. Since in these last two passages Christ is the Judge, the reference in this verse may be to Christ also. We are reminded of the parable of the last judgment in

istic powers; and profligacy, or sheer wasting of time and money and energy on aimless living.[6] He makes no attempt to catalogue all the **lusts** and **idolatries** of his time, but exempts nobody from complicity in any of them. His concept of the radical perversion of the human heart is realistic and unsentimental. The Jews had corrupted their own high religion by mingling it with Gentile practices. The danger to the Christian community was in some sense even greater. We have little conception of the impurity and pride of life in the Greco-Roman empire of the first century: and to stem it, not the stern figure of the prophets, but the loving figure of Christ. Little wonder men thought it **strange** that Christians were marked for "their charity and their chastity."[7] **The time**

past of their lives, the remembrance of their sins, their meaningless existence, their sinful squandering of hours and days—of months and years—in unreal and unwholesome living, might well have nerved them on to redeem the little time that was still left. The memory of a life that was a sin not only against life but against God may itself have served to stimulate them to greater effort. At any rate, their life and conduct were now so authentic that the people with whom they once associated wondered at them, and in jealousy, envy, or ridicule "spoke evil of them" (4:4). But let all who will, talk and gossip and oppose. And give an account of it to God. That some there are who ignore him is no proof that he is not, or that he is not sovereignly righteous. There is a Judge whose jurisdiction is total. No areas are exempt from his just and judicial reign, whether past or present, whether in life or in death. Dying may remove a man from the earthly scene, but it

[6] See M. R. Vincent, *Word Studies in the New Testament* (Grand Rapids: W. B. Eerdmans Publishing Co., 1946), I, 659, for interesting studies in these words.

[7] Moffatt, *op. cit.*, p. 148.

6 For, for this cause was the gospel preached also to them that are dead, that they might be judged according to men in the flesh, but live according to God in the spirit.

7 But the end of all things is at hand: be ye therefore sober, and watch unto prayer.

dead. **6** For this is why the gospel was preached even to the dead, that though judged in the flesh like men, they might live in the spirit like God.

7 The end of all things is at hand; there-

Matt. 25:31-46. For an excellent discussion of our Lord's teaching about judgment see T. W. Manson, *The Teaching of Jesus* (Cambridge: Cambridge University Press, 1931), ch. viii. His conclusion is that in Jesus' view the judgment is (*a*) universal in its scope, embracing all people and all generations; and (*b*) the criterion is strictly ethical and religious in character. Each individual is judged on his own merits; and his merits are determined by the disposition of his will toward the kingdom of God as it is manifested in his day and generation.

6. Cf. 3:19, with which this passage must be taken. In 3:19 the idea of our Lord preaching to the dead was applied to a particular class, viz., the wicked contemporaries of Noah. Here it is generalized. **The dead** are those who died before Christ came, but who heard the gospel in the abode of the dead. **That though judged in the flesh like men, they might live in the spirit like God:** We find the same contrast between flesh and spirit as in 3:18. The dead have already suffered some judgment in their life on earth. Now they have the gospel preached to them in Hades in order that they may have the chance of full and final salvation, i.e., life with God and as God lives. We can only guess at what Peter means by their judgment **in the flesh:** perhaps "trials, persecutions, and death" are in his mind. Selwyn quotes Wisd. Sol. 3:4, "Though they be punished in the sight of men, yet is their hope full of immortality." Note also that in I Cor. 11:30-32, Paul speaks of bodily illness and death as "judgments."

K. ETHICS FOR THE CRISIS (4:7-11)

Convinced that the end of the world is near, Peter now counsels his readers how to live in view of the approaching crisis. "Keep cool; be loving; practice hospitality; whatever your gift, use it as servants of God and for his glory."

7. The end of all things is at hand: Like most of the earliest Christians, Peter believed that the world's end could not long be delayed. That knowledge, he says, should

---

will never remove him from God's dominion. The dead are not gone and forgotten; nor is God the Lord only of those now living. So is the Christian assured concerning his own beloved dead, who die before the end (4:7). He is assured too that his own death will not separate him from the God whose eternal reign will deal with evil in every corner of the universe. And above everything else, he is assured that all souls are in the hands of that righteous God. No doubt Peter shared with Christians of his time the view that Christ preached to the O.T. saints who had seen the promise "afar off." Some have suggested (see Exeg.) that he referred to Enoch's mission of doom to **the spirits in prison** (3:19), while Christ's mission (4:6) was one of hope. Enoch preached to fallen angels; Christ, to human spirits in the world of disembodied spirit. Whatever the interpretation, this Christ is Lord of all men, and Judge

of all men, **the quick and the dead,** the saint and the sinner. Before his face, and by his power, the blessed shall **live according to God in the spirit.**

4:7-11. *Because the End Is at Hand.*—No wonder Peter raises a warning finger at Christians who settle down to a life of static complacency. Because the final issue is postponed, there are those who tend to become involved in a routine of church affairs and pious religious observances. Religion becomes a "business as usual" affair, a set of holy habits. Lacking the sense of **the end,** they have about them no alertness to the unexpected; they look for no "coming" of the Lord. They are spiritually domesticated and regular persons, while the Christian is one who lives on the edge of the ever-new and the ever-becoming. He has about him a sense of crisis. He lives between the old and the new. He takes life seriously, and with

8 And above all things have fervent charity among yourselves: for charity shall cover the multitude of sins.

fore keep sane and sober for your prayers. 8 Above all hold unfailing your love for one

---

make them **sane and sober** (RSV) unto prayer. In similar circumstances Paul urged the Christians in Thessalonica to "study to be quiet" and to "be sober" (I Thess. 4:11; 5:8).

8. Above all . . . have fervent charity among yourselves: Above all—because **love** (ἀγάπη) is the cardinal Christian virtue. **Charity** (KJV) is a word that has come down in the world of words. Nor is **love** (RSV) itself a perfect rendering; for all sorts of nuances cling to it. Ἔρως, the other Greek word for love, is the love which craves, and, at its worst, lusts. Ἀγάπη is the love which seeks not to possess but to give. "Caring" conveys something of its meaning. ("Christianity is caring, most of all, it is caring.") For the rest, if definition is difficult, we have its character matchlessly portrayed for us in I Cor. 13. (Vss. 1-3 treat of its necessity; vss. 4-7 of its nature; and vss. 8-13 of its never-failing character.)

Love covers a multitude of sins: A simple saying that has puzzled the exegetes. We have an echo of it in Jas. 5:20. Two passages of Scripture help us to its meaning: Prov. 10:12, "Hatred stirreth up strifes: but love covereth all sins"; Luke 7:47, "Her sins, which are many, are forgiven; for she loved much." What then does it mean? (a) We may at once dismiss the popular interpretation, "Love is blind to all faults." (b) Others explain: "Love atones for other people's sins." This is a true idea supremely exemplified in the love of Christ for sinners. (c) Others again explain: "Love atones for the manifold faults of the lover." This last is probably to be preferred. It is in line

---

an eye to that which is always ready to break into his ordinary existence with fresh revelations from beyond.

To be sure, there are some who at the other extreme make the far-off end the center of the Christian faith. By constantly thinking about it and waiting for it as the solution of life's predicaments and the consummation of all their hopes, they do little about relating it to the business of daily living. The result is spiritual complacency, a pious anticipation which fails to take life seriously because it fails to take seriously the end in time. For the end can mean nothing apart from the point at which men live. The pure eschatologist all too often neglects to make clear the relation between the future hope and the present life. If it is dangerous to forget the end, it is equally dangerous to separate it from the threshold situation between this moment and the next.

To all the complacent, therefore, whatever the cause, Peter's trumpetlike words sound a reveille which for him must have been reminiscent of the staccato proclamation of Jesus, "Repent, for the kingdom of heaven is at hand" (Matt. 4:17).

There is an end! This world does not carry within it its own finality. It is a created world; it is bounded by a beginning and an end. One day "heaven and earth will pass away." The drama of man's life—individual and corporate —will come to a climax. It will be both an end and a beginning, a "termination and a consum-

mation." [8] It will be the final termination of the old order and the ultimate consummation of the new order inaugurated in and through Jesus Christ. It will be the Day of Judgment and the day of mercy. And it is already at work in the present; the powers of "the age to come" (C. H. Dodd) extend themselves backward into the lives of those who are members of the kingdom. The new age is even now judging and saving the old. The end is the glorious goal that throws its promising light before it. **The end . . . is.**

But is the end near? Was Peter wrong in holding that he lived in the "last days," seeing that the centuries since have disproved such an immediate hope? Like his first-century Christian friends, he may well have misunderstood the exact calendar time of the final end, but he did not misinterpret the imminence of the real and inevitable end. The immediate presence of that end is integral to the entire N.T. Paul writes to the Romans, "The night is far spent, the day is at hand" (Rom. 13:12). I John 2:18 says: "Children, it is the last hour." And the last book of the Bible concludes with the overture and the response: "Surely I am coming soon. Amen. Come, Lord Jesus!" (Rev. 22:20.) All of them are talking about something which is considerably more than a future date. They know that the end of the old world began when the beginning of the new world moved into it with saving grace and judging truth in Jesus Christ.

[8] Cranfield, *First Epistle of Peter, ad loc.*

9 Use hospitality one to another without grudging.

10 As every man hath received the gift, *even so* minister the same one to another, as good stewards of the manifold grace of God.

another, since love covers a multitude of sins. **9** Practice hospitality ungrudgingly to one another. **10** As each has received a gift, employ it for one another, as good stewards

---

with the Jewish idea that almsgiving atones for sin; it is true to the technical meaning of **cover** (atone) ; and it is consonant with Luke 7:47. In the last analysis, however, we ought not perhaps to divide between (*b*) and (*c*) ; for love has this atoning effect whether for our own sin or that of others.

9. Use hospitality . . . : Not social entertainment, but board and lodging for traveling Christians is meant. This new conception has been called "one of the greatest contributions of the Christian church to the society of the time." **Without grudging:** Hosts and hostesses were not to let travelers feel that their entertainment was "a great bother."

10. Gift (χάρισμα) : lit., "grace-gift," i.e., a gift originating in God's grace. This is a favorite word of Paul. Probably the particular gift meant here is "the wherewithal to entertain." The man who has it is to use it for the good of his fellows. **As good stewards of God's varied grace:** Paul thinks of Christian ministers as "stewards"; cf. I Cor. 4:1,

---

In the "fulness of the time" this unprecedented event of the Incarnation, Atonement, and Resurrection had occurred. Something new had come into history. The end and goal of life had been revealed. And that end was always at hand. All human history since the day of Jesus Christ on earth is but an epilogue in which there can be nothing in the "after a while" which is not already in the "now." We live in the time of the end, in the time of fulfillment; one day it will come around to its beginning again and be fully consummated when Christ who was incarnate in humility will be manifested in glory. So has the end of the world already been pronounced. All the world's crises and tragic events only indicate its continuous ending and the inevitable conclusion toward which it moves. And while these events reveal the transiency of this world, they also point toward the sure victory of Christ, which though now hidden, and seen only by the "eyes of faith," will at the conclusion be made cosmically manifest.

We human beings are constantly made aware of this end in individual life, whether by calamities, serious illnesses, frustrations, or the imminence of death. Man's finitude, which he has fashioned into sinfulness, and which is so arrestingly symbolized in death, daily appraises him of that end which only the beginning of the day of Christ can change from the day of death into the day of life.

What difference does this imminent end make in life? Because the end is at hand always, it makes a world of difference: In mind, in spirit, in attitude toward others, in vocational service, and in preaching and teaching. In a word, this sense of living "between the times,"

on what is at once the edge of the old and the edge of the new, gives life a unique tone and temper, and makes the chief end of man the glory (or manifestation) of God. For God's is the final **glory and dominion for ever and ever.**

The Christian in whom there is a sense of crisis between the old and the new has a sound mind. He does not give way to loose or sentimental thinking; he does not succumb to propaganda born of panic; he does not go into mental hysterics. His eyes are not always on the future end; they are fixed upon the end in every situation. He does not fold his hands in pious inactivity as he waits for the coming of the Lord. Nor does he work in the present with no sense of purpose. He does not misuse his mind by fanatically predicting the time of Christ's advent; nor does he use it to draw a blueprint of "the shape of things to come." Knowledge of the ever-present end of all things keeps him **sane and sober.**

Such sanity makes for sobriety of spirit, for realism in judging the issues and the conditions of life. It makes possible true and effective **prayer.** Jesus once warned those who prayed amiss that they knew not what they asked (Matt. 20:22) . They lacked the sobriety to which Peter would admonish all Christians. The Pharisee who prayed within himself was far from being **sober** (Luke 18:11) . Living in the time of the end ought to make for sound knowledge about the God who hears and answers prayer. As Moffatt puts it: "Your prayers must not be wild screams or reasonless cries." [9] One might add: "Your prayers must be made in sincerity and in truth." Says Cranfield: "To be sober unto

[9] *Op. cit.,* p. 152.

11 If any man speak, *let him speak* as the oracles of God; if any man minister, *let him do it* as of the ability which God | of God's varied grace: 11 whoever speaks, a[ ] one who utters oracles of God; whoever renders service, as one who renders it by

---

"stewards of the mysteries of God." Stewardship, he says, implies not only a trust, but trustworthiness. So Peter insists that his readers must be **good** (or honorable) **stewards** **The manifold grace of God**: There is "an infinite variety" in God's bounty; Rom. 12 and I Cor. 12 show what is meant.

11. Peter now singles out two aspects of this sharing of gifts: (*a*) teaching and (*b*) practical service.

As the oracles of God (ὡς λόγια θεοῦ): Λόγια meant oracular utterances, and could be applied to the Ten Commandments or O.T. scripture generally. The speaker is to speak with gravity and authority, as one who transmits divine truth and not as one who purveys his own private notions.

---

prayer means avoiding all that would fuddle the mind, impair alertness, warp the vision and obstruct communion with God, whether intemperance of the body or preoccupation with the cares of the world and the deceitfulness of riches or smug self-righteousness or whatever else it may be." [1]

Above all hold unfailing your love for one another. The Greek word here suggests no wishy-washy philanthropy offered impulsively and spasmodically by a superior to an inferior; it means a tough, strenuous, **fervent**, persistent love. It is a love that endures like the strength of a long-distance runner. It is a love that strains like a horse in full gallop. It is no luxury; it is a necessity which is bound up with the Christian hope. "Faith, hope, love abide . . . but the greatest of these is love" (I Cor. 13:13). Yet the three dare not be separated. The blessed **end of all things** generates a love among the brethren which is directed by a mind guided by truth.

Such love covers a multitude of sins. Love always tends to cover and to minimize the sins of those for whom it is concerned. The love of Christians in Paul's N.T. churches must have "covered" his sins against those same churches in his unregenerate days. "Love bears and endures all things" (I Cor. 13:7). It thinks the best, not the worst. And the source of such constraining love is found in Christ; he loved the unlovely and covered their sins. In Ps. 32:1 God is regarded as the great coverer. Where love is genuine, there forgiveness takes place, past sins are forgotten, sinful tendencies are countered by encouraging helpfulness, and the accumulated mass of sinful actions meets the antidote of the forgiving, cleansing, and healing power of God. A loving Christian and a loving church may do much to neutralize and remove the sins of the individual and the community.

This love will show itself in concrete acts of

[1] *Op. cit.,* p. 94.

hospitality, done **without grudging**. In Peter's time hotels were few and far between. Inns were expensive and immoral. Traveling Christians found lodging in the homes of their fellow believers. No doubt the entertaining of itinerant preachers and journeying Christians became a burden which fell heavily upon the faithful. What is more, since church buildings were few, homes were used for fellowship and services of worship. In fact, the missionary cause both past and present owes an incalculable debt to those whose homes have been thrown wide in a persistent and enduring love, practiced without murmuring. Many a parsonage, manse, and missionary compound holds within it an interesting and noble story of guests entertained for the kingdom's sake. Our Lord put new meaning into such hospitality by relating it to himself: "I was a stranger, and ye took me in. . . . Inasmuch as ye have done it unto one of the least of these my brethren, ye have done it unto me." (Matt. 25:35, 40.)

It is the same solemn sense of **the end of all things** that involves every Christian also in a life of responsibility. There is no exception to the rule, for God takes every life seriously, and he expects everyone to take his gifts seriously. And everyone has **received** some **gift**, some special capacity or benefit through which he may serve God and the community. These "talents" are not to be hidden away in the earth out of fear; nor are they to be employed only in private pursuits. We do not administer God's **manifold grace**, but we are permitted the unbelievable privilege of serving as **good stewards**, guardians, and dispensers of the gifts of that grace.

These gifts, of course, differ greatly, but each is a precious benefaction. They are as varied as the ability to preach and the capacity to deal with children, as the art of making friends and the grace of entertaining guests in a home (see Rom. 12:3-8; I Cor 1:7; 7:7; 12:1–14:40; I Tim.

giveth; that God in all things may be glorified through Jesus Christ: to whom be praise and dominion for ever and ever. Amen.

the strength which God supplies; in order that in everything God may be glorified through Jesus Christ. To him belong glory and dominion for ever and ever. Amen.

Whoever renders service: Peter means one who gives practical Christian service—almsgiving, attention to bodily wants, etc. **As . . . by the strength which God supplies:** He is to act "in humble dependence on God." Χορηγέω, the Greek verb rendered **giveth**, had three meanings: (a) lead a chorus; (b) supply a chorus (i.e., produce a play at one's own risk); and (c) generally, "supply" with the idea of liberality.

That God . . . : A doxology rounding off this section. **Through Jesus Christ:** In three of the apostolic benedictions glory is given to God through Christ: Rom. 16:27; Jude 25; and here. **To whom** refers to Christ, as in Rev. 1:6. **Amen** means "This is really so" rather than "So be it." Borrowed from synagogue worship, it is an affirmation rather than a petition.

4:14; II Tim. 1:6 for a description of these gifts). Since they all issue from the same source and are designed for the same purpose, the persons who possess them are not to use them selfishly, for personal aggrandizement. They are gifts of the Spirit, given to the church for the purpose of building up the community for the ministry of the Word, and for the development of the Christian-in-community into a genuine fellowship in Christ (Eph. 4:12).

Good stewards, said Jesus, are "faithful and wise" (Luke 12:42). They are not to spend recklessly what belongs to another, nor are they to devote their trust to unnecessary and immoral ends. Whether they are stewards of the "mysteries of God" (I Cor. 4:1-2), or of the **manifold grace** [God's varied grace] **of God,** their position and the charge committed to them should make them responsible, especially in the light of the crisis of the times. And how **manifold** indeed that **grace!** Grace "is the activity of the heart of God." Inevitably it expresses itself in a multitude of forms. Whatever its manifestations, it is the personal power of God in redemptive action, working in ways that are past finding out.

Grant us such grace that we may work Thy Will
And speak Thy words and walk before Thy Face,
Profound and calm, like waters deep and still:
    Grant us such grace.

Not hastening and not loitering in our pace
For gloomiest valley or for sultriest hill,
    Content and fearless on our downward race,

As rivers seek a sea they cannot fill
    But are themselves filled in its embrace,
Absorbed, at rest, each river and each rill:
    Grant us such grace.[2]

[2] Christina G. Rossetti, "Grant Us Such Grace that We May Work Thy Will," from *Gifts and Graces.*

The implications of this responsibility for the preacher and for the man engaged in practical Christian service are singled out by Peter for especial consideration. What does it mean to preach the gospel, if one has the gift for such proclamation or presentation, and if one preaches in the full consciousness that **the end . . . is at hand?** Real preaching is not a facile talking about God, not even with the golden tongue of an angel. It is not a discussion of what we may know about God, of the religious consciousness, of the development of our capacity for religion. On the contrary, real preaching is done only by one who is burdened by a message given him of God. It is a preaching of the Word. It is humble utterance by one who knows that he is under commission and constraint. It is a form of speech which conveys the living Word of God to its hearers not by any trick of psychology or genius of oratory, but by its sheer nature as a witness to something beyond itself. A preacher speaks boldly, as though he were an oracle of God, and yet he speaks humbly because he knows that he is dependent upon the Spirit of God to make his preaching effective.

As for the person who has the gift of practical service, he is to engage in such service with the consciousness that his strength is supplied by God. Whether he dispenses charity to the poor, exercises the office of a deacon in a congregation, provides for a homeless family, or gives of his abundance through a church treasury, he is to regard himself as a **steward.** Even the energy with which he performs these services, together with the means which he shares, are gifts of God. His ministry is not from above down; rather is it the disposition of bounties by a steward of things every one of which belongs to the God "from whom all blessings flow." Only as both giver and receiver are related to

12 Beloved, think it not strange concerning the fiery trial which is to try you, as though some strange thing happened unto you:	12 Beloved, do not be surprised at the fiery ordeal which comes upon you to prove you, as though something strange were

IV. The Trials of Christians in the World (4:12–5:11)
A. A Call to Christian Constancy (4:12-19)

Summary: "Your impending ordeal should not surprise you who know that Christ had to suffer. As you share his suffering, rejoice, assured of future glory. No Christian must get into trouble for such crimes as murder and theft; but if anyone suffers because he is a Christian, let him glorify God for it. The judgment which is beginning will touch God's family first. What the fate of unbelievers will be, who knows? Our duty is plain: to do right and to trust in our Creator."

12. **Beloved,** as in 2:11, introduces a new section. **Think it not strange** (KJV); better, **Do not be surprised** (RSV): Jews were used to persecution; Gentiles were not, and might find their persecutions hard to reconcile with their status as Christians. Let them remember that the purpose of such persecutions was to test their faith. **Fiery trial** (πυρώσει): The allusion is to the fire by which gold is tested, and the word is probably

---

God can the pride be taken from the one and the indignity from the other.

Peter then adds a concluding word which sums up all that he has tried to say. The end, as well as the dynamic of it all, is **that in everything God may be glorified through Jesus Christ.** Thus the full nature and purpose and power of God will be manifested, openly shown and declared. God himself will make his way into life through all these channels, and the thin line between the seen and the unseen will become transparent. Mind and affection and spirit and service will become sacramental with the presence of the living God, who comes to us uniquely through him who is the central source of our saving knowledge. "He that hath seen me hath seen the Father" (John 14:9). "The only begotten Son, which is in the bosom of the Father, he hath declared him" (John 1:18). Jesus Christ is the key to our knowledge of God. **To whom be praise and dominion** [reign, sovereign sway, regal domain] **for ever and ever. Amen.** So be it! Verily it is so! In the glorification of God is the glory of his children.

12-19. Meeting the Fiery Ordeal.—Peter addresses his readers affectionately about the **ordeal** that is already upon them. Earlier he dealt with possible sufferings to come; now, after a pause in his writing, he comes to grips with the actual trials which they are enduring. He speaks first about the ordeal itself (vss. 12-16), and then about the sure deliverance that is theirs (vss. 17-19).

To establish an identity of feeling with his readers he uses the salutation **Beloved.** He takes them into his confidence. He feels what they feel; he addresses them with kindness; he vicariously bears their pain. And he has a right

to speak on the subject; for he knows from personal experience what it means to be hounded by secret police, to suffer imprisonment for his faith, to live the precarious life of the persecuted. "Dearly beloved" is still a solicitous salutation used by ministers who speak the truth in love to God's people.

This **ordeal** is a reality in our time. In several areas of the world the church is "under the Cross." Many Christians in Nazi Germany suffered intimidation, imprisonment, concentration camp, and exile from their native land. Some were martyred. The full story of Christian heroism under European and Asian dictators in the twentieth century may never be fully known.

The early church endured ten persecutions through the first three centuries of its history. Everyone has heard of the catacombs, the lions in the arena, and the burning of Christians on tar-daubed crosses. Those ages of the martyrs must not blind us to the fact that the faithful in the O.T. community too, as well as in the long history of the Christian Era, had to pass through the **fiery ordeal.**

Think it not strange. "The disciple is not above his master" (Luke 6:40). The followers of a Christ who suffered at the hands of a world of men that hated and crucified him can hardly hope to escape the same kind of ordeal. There were three crosses on Calvary. On two of them society was pronouncing judgment upon men whose consciences were too hardened to allow them further freedom and life. On the middle cross society put out of the way One whose life was too sensitive for men to tolerate. The world's judgment on Christ still reveals its sinful character. The spirit of the world is not friendly to the spirit of Christ, and those

13 But rejoice, inasmuch as ye are partakers of Christ's sufferings; that, when his glory shall be revealed, ye may be glad also with exceeding joy.

14 If ye be reproached for the name of Christ, happy *are ye;* for the Spirit of glory and of God resteth upon you: on their part he is evil spoken of, but on your part he is glorified.

happening to you. 13 But rejoice in so far as you share Christ's sufferings, that you may also rejoice and be glad when his glory is revealed. 14 If you are reproached for the name of Christ, you are blessed, because the spirit of glory*j* and of God rests upon

j Some ancient authorities insert *and of power.*

---

derived from Prov. 27:21. "Fire is the trial for silver and gold." The point is not so much the fierceness of the heat as the refining power of fire, and "trial by fire" would be a better translation than **fiery trial.**

13. For inasmuch as (KJV): Better, **in so far as** (RSV); cf. Phil. 3:10, "That I may know him . . . and the fellowship of his sufferings"; also Rom. 8:17; II Cor. 1:7; Col. 1:24. Christians share in **Christ's sufferings** through their experience of like persecution and obloquy; but the burden of the mystery of suffering is lightened, first, by the remembrance that it was shared by the only Son of God and, second, by the hope of the joy that shall be ours when Christ's glory is revealed.

14a. If ye be reproached for the name of Christ, happy are ye: This is Peter's version of Matt. 5:11, "Blessed are ye when men shall revile you . . . for my sake." **For the name of Christ:** Because they were Christians and so bore the name of Christ. In the Acts we hear several times of the apostles suffering for the name, e.g., Acts 5:41; 9:16; 21:13.

For the Spirit of glory and of God resteth upon you: The Greek is τὸ τῆς δόξης καὶ τὸ τοῦ θεοῦ πνεῦμα—a very difficult phrase. It seems to be inspired by Isa. 11:2, "The Spirit of the Lord shall rest upon him." Two translations are possible: (*a*) "the Spirit of glory, yes, the Spirit of God." Charles Bigg explains: "He is the Spirit who enables us to glorify God through suffering. He rests upon the Christian as the Shechinah rested on the tabernacle, and brings a foretaste . . . of that glory which is fully given at the Revelation" (*A Critical and Exegetical Commentary on the Epistles of St. Peter and St. Jude* [New York: Charles Scribner's Sons, 1901; "International Critical Commentary"], p. 177). (*b*) The other rendering is Bengel's, "The Spirit of the Glory and of God." "The Glory" is a title of Christ conceived as the Shekinah or "visible presence" of God among men; cf. Jas. 2:1 (with J. B. Mayor's note on it). This is preferable. "The Glory" is to be taken as a title of Christ, much like Emmanuel or the Word.

14b. On their part he is evil spoken of . . . (KJV): Omit, as no part of the true text.

---

who are "in Christ" cannot escape the tension. At times that tension breaks out into overt acts of violent antagonism. To be reconciled to God involves one in a life unreconciled with the world. One is called out to be a Christian; he no longer drifts "along on the stream of this world's ideas of living" (Eph. 2:1).[3] The new life of the Christian is not only at odds with the old life; it is a rebuke to the life that is not centered in God. Strange when Christians are not persecuted! For Christians to be so safely conformed to the world and its course of living that they run into no trouble at all may well be an indication that they have denatured their way of life of its radical, world-judging, and world-changing spirit. They are no longer able to see the difference between what

[3] Phillips, *Letters to Young Churches,* p. 106.

is Christian and what is not. Or perhaps the N.T. conception of the Christ has been conveniently toned down, maybe even lost through a dangerous ignorance of the nature of Christianity. Christ is no serviceable addendum to human life; he is the radical center to which life must be reconciled and conformed.

Nor is **the fiery ordeal** to be regarded as a tragedy. There is no such thing as tragedy in the economy of God. In God's world nothing comes by chance, and nothing that happens is a dead loss. "All things work together for good to them that love God, to them who are the called according to his purpose" (Rom. 8:28).

The ordeal is a test. The refiner's fire (Prov. 27:21) does not consume the gold; it consumes the dross (1:7). Those who **are reproached for the name of Christ**—the character, the reality,

15 But let none of you suffer as a murderer, or *as* a thief, or *as* an evildoer, or as a
busybody in other men's matters.

16 Yet if *any man suffer* as a Christian,
let him not be ashamed; but let him glorify
God on this behalf.

you. 15 But let none of you suffer as a murderer, or a thief, or a wrongdoer, or a
mischief-maker; 16 yet if one suffers as a
Christian, let him not be ashamed, but

---

15. Let none of you suffer: The verb does not define the nature of the suffering or
the manner in which it is inflicted. The crux in this verse is the meaning of ἀλλοτριεπίσ-
κοπος. Here are some suggested renderings: **busybody** (KJV); "a meddler in other men's
matters" (ASV); **a mischief-maker** (RSV); "a revolutionary" (Moffatt); "informer"
(Jülicher); Calvin and Beza took the word to mean "a coveter of other people's money."
The word means literally, "an overseer of what belongs to other people." Probably the
KJV's **busybody** is as good a rendering as any. No doubt many Christians, misapprehend-
ing what was involved in their duty to be "the light of the world," tended to meddle in
matters which were no proper concern of theirs and thus irritated those around them.
(This tendency of course was not confined to the first Christian age.) When the situation
was very delicate for the Christians, such conduct might well start "an incident," and
Peter therefore solemnly warns against it.

16. Yet if any man suffer as a Christian: This verse is often made an argument for
a late date for the epistle. It points, so the argument runs, to a time when the mere
profession of Christianity was a crime in the eyes of the state and therefore implies a
state of affairs that did not exist till the time of Pliny's rescript to Trajan, *ca.* A.D. 110.

---

the very essence of Christ's person and work
and cause—ought to think of the ordeal as a
testing or examination of their faith. It is
like the wind and the rain that beat upon the
house of life (Matt. 7:25). It is like the winnow-
ing fan that separates the wheat from the chaff
(Luke 3:17). It is like the discipline that corrects, matures, and causes the children of God
to become "partakers" of the "holiness" of God
(Heb. 12:10). Such tests reveal weaknesses; they
strengthen and confirm character; they develop
hidden powers. "Great souls nearly always wear
crowns that have been fashioned in the fires of
great sorrows." [4]

Such an ordeal may indeed **rejoice** the heart
because it brings the sufferer into a close relationship with **Christ's sufferings.** A mutual sharing of pain creates an understanding fellowship.
And when the pain is borne for the same cause
and is suffered from the same enemy, its bearers
are united in person, in mission, and in destiny.
The sufferings of Christ were unique, and in
a real sense complete; his followers are only
partakers of their Lord's pain. But to understand pain in the light of the Cross is to gain
strength to bear it. To see it as a sharing of the
cause which brought him pain is to make pain
meaningful with the purpose of Christ. To
regard suffering as companionship in what
Christ endured is to set one's burden within the
context of eternity. And can anyone deny that

Christ enters into our ordeal far more profoundly than we can enter into his? Peter is
writing from experience; for he had heard Jesus
speak of these things (Matt. 5:10-11), and he
himself had endured **the fiery ordeal** (Acts
5:41). He knew at first hand that there is no
greater joy open to the human heart than the
privilege of having some part in Christ's purpose
and of participating in his love. So every ordeal
of the Christian may be made not only bearable
but joyous in the thought that it is shared with
Christ, until the day when all this suffering
shall be brought to its harvest in **glory.**

By the same token, reproach **for the name of
Christ** may be borne as a blessing. Outright
persecution is one thing; sneers and cutting
remarks may be harder even to endure than
bodily injury.

> Universal reproach, far worse to bear
> Than violence. [5]

They penetrate to the core of one's life and
create loneliness, isolation, and despair. Yet
even so, and even then, **the spirit of glory and
of God rests upon you**—as real and as present
as was the Shekinah in the O.T. God does not
forsake his own. **The spirit of glory and of God**
is God-in-action, assuring them of his presence
in their suffering, glorifying them through their
meaningful pain, and giving them in their
hearts "the earnest of the Spirit" (II Cor. 1:22),

[4] J. H. Snowden, *Is the World Growing Better?* (New
York: The Macmillan Co., 1919), p. 28.

[5] Milton, *Paradise Lost*, Bk. VI, 1. 34.

17 For the time *is come* that judgment must begin at the house of God: and if *it* first *begin* at us, what shall the end *be* of them that obey not the gospel of God?

18 And if the righteous scarcely be saved, where shall the ungodly and the sinner appear?

under that name let him glorify God. 17 For the time has come for judgment to begin with the household of God; and if it begins with us, what will be the end of those who do not obey the gospel of God? 18 And

"If the righteous man is scarcely saved, where will the impious and sinner appear?"

But there is absolutely nothing in the language to compel such a conclusion. **Christian** was, in origin, a nickname meaning "a partisan of Christ," and was current in Antioch about the middle of the first century (Acts 11:26). Why it could not have been current in Asia Minor, say, fifteen years later, is a question which those who insist on a late date for I Peter must have difficulty answering. Nor does the word **suffer** necessarily mean "punished by a magistrate." The word is quite general. In the previous verse, Peter had warned his readers against suffering as criminals or bad characters; now he deals with suffering for the mere fact of being a Christian, for being "a partisan of Christ." Such suffering was no new thing: in the earliest days of the faith we read that the apostles rejoiced "that they were counted worthy to suffer dishonor for the name" (Acts 5:41). Here Peter bids his readers do precisely what he and his friends did then—"glorify God in this name" (ASV).

17. The meaning seems to be that the sufferings of the Christians are the beginning of the final **judgment**. Peter says in effect: "If even you, the children in God's family, have because of sin to be subjected to such sore trial, how awful must be the doom of God's enemies—that doom from which his mercy saves you!" **Household of God**, i.e., the church.

18. This is Prov. 11:31 (LXX). **Scarcely** (μόλις), i.e., with difficulty.

---

his pledge of a glory which is yet to be **revealed**, his offer of a power that can inspire and mature and glorify through any and every ordeal. "Let theirs be the blasphemy who reproach and persecute you," some pious soul has added as his footnote; "yours the doxology!"

But let no one think that any ordeal is meritorious for its own sake. Surely the **murderer**, the **thief**, or the **evildoer** dare not claim the comfort of that blessed suffering which is experienced for the sake of the Christ who died in a murderer's stead, and between two thieves. Note that Peter also mentions the **busybody in other men's matters**. The meddler, the gossip, the news peddler, the obnoxious Christian, all are included in this category; perhaps too the radical revolutionary. The Greek word used here occurs nowhere else in the N.T. Moffatt makes much of this last meaning of the term, and suggests that Christians at that time laid themselves open to accusation as seditionaries and members of a secret society which sought to overthrow the government. Christians who believed in the imminent end of all things might well have been accused of making light of social obligations, particularly as between slaves and masters. They might even have engaged in disobedience toward the authorities who were persecuting them. But the term is given here a practical turn: it indicates any person who interferes with the business of others, who pronounces glibly and authoritatively about things in which he is not expert, who tactlessly criticizes existing customs and institutions and thereby arouses tempers. A good many people with unimpeachable intentions but mistaken zeal bring upon themselves social disfavor because of their "busybodiness." Usually they regard themselves as martyrs when badly treated. There are militant Christians who are always straining at gnats in matters of doctrine as they argue with others; zealous evangelistic Christians who do not exercise love in dealing with non-Christians; moralistic Christians who make faith a matter of rules and regulations and seek to impose them upon others; dogmatic Christians who will not listen to the convictions of other Christians just as sincere. These are busybodies, and if they suffer criticism and unpopularity from their fellow Christians, they have no right to regard their sufferings as blessed. They may have faith so as to remove mountains, but if they lack love, they are nothing (I Cor. 13:2). It is easy to be a martyr; it is less easy to know when martyrdom partakes of the sufferings of Christ.

| 19 Wherefore, let them that suffer according to the will of God commit the keeping of their souls *to him* in well doing, as unto a faithful Creator. | 19 Therefore let those who suffer according to God's will do right and entrust their souls to a faithful creator. |

---

19. This is a summary. Suffering, a part of God's discipline, is to be borne with stanch faith in God the creator, and to be accompanied by active beneficence. **Them that suffer according to the will of God:** "Those who suffer because God wills it."

Commit the keeping of their souls (παρατιθέσθωσαν): The Greek verb is that used of a man "depositing" his money in the safekeeping of a friend while he goes from home. But the phrase reminds us of Jesus' word on the Cross, "Father, into thy hands I commit my spirit" (a quotation from Ps. 31:5, with the word "Father" added). **In well doing:** Active beneficence, which is the proof that faith in God is sincere. **As unto a faithful Creator:** Omit **as** with RSV. The divine title **Creator** is found also in Rom. 1:25, but nowhere else in the N.T. **Faithful:** The epithet implies one who can be trusted "to keep

---

Wherefore, adds Peter, to be called a "Christian" is nothing to be **ashamed** of. Though the term was first used to deride and ridicule the followers of Christ, the apostle counsels his readers **under that name** to glorify God. Christians at that time were a definite kind of people who were distinguishable from others. Their commitment to Christ made a difference in their living. And even though some may not have suffered bodily pain, all were marked as bearers of the name, and were the object of all sorts of wild and vicious rumors. They were talked about because they were different.

What then does it mean to be a "Christian"? To bear the name of Christ? Does it single one out from the crowd and subject him to hardships and hostilities from those not so committed? Does the bearing of the name, and the consequent discomfort that it brings, fill the modern "Christian" with any sense of pride? Does it fill him with a deep delight in the fact that by his way of steadfast faith and courageous witness he may really manifest God to the world? The bearing of the name of Christ is the highest honor that can come to any man. The popular and loosely used term "Christian" has little distinctive meaning now. Perhaps suffering at the hands of critical outsiders might rescue it from its meaninglessness. The fiery ordeal through which Christians of our time are passing may be the furnace that will consume the dross and restore its luster.

The time is come. The **judgment** of God has begun because the final era has been inaugurated. Since God's new order has moved into history, the old is being judged. The ordeal of suffering is a part of the sifting and dividing process which will continue until the last assize, when the judgment will be complete (see Mark 13:8, 13). Christians are the first fruits of that judgment; judged and chastened of the Lord (I Cor. 11:32), they are to regard their painful

experiences as part of God's process of bringing his purpose to pass. The judgment is sure, constant, and cumulative. It has begun, it is continuing, and it will become more severe. "If they do these things in a green tree, what shall be done in the dry?" (Luke 23:31.) The new age will not be thwarted. The living Lord of this world cannot be denied his right. None can escape him. There are no islands of immunity. The moral will of God is not a trifling matter. The wickedness of men does not have the last word. Neither does the superhuman evil of "principalities and powers." There is comfort in the sovereign righteousness of God. We live in no arbitrary world, but in one where the will of that God is ultimate. And the **judgment** begins at his **household.** It always has—and it always must. The church must be the first to repent of its sins, and the first to be cleansed of its unrighteousness. As the church, so the world. This is where Isaiah (10:12), Jeremiah (25:29), and Ezekiel (9:6) said it must begin. "Begin at my sanctuary" was the word that came to Ezekiel regarding the restoration of Israel. This is where the Lord of the temple began as he drove out those who had defiled it. The cleansing and redeeming process must begin with those who are sensitive to the sovereign demands of God upon men. **The household of God** is the community of penitence and faith. It is the society of those who have been humbled by the law of God and raised by his grace. It is the fountain and source of God's new race of men. Having passed under the judgment, it "has passed from death to life" (John 5:24).

The **judgment** therefore should hold no terror for the Christian. It should assure him of God's activity in history and in personal life. He sees in the ordeal it brings the sure indication that Christ is winning through; that the way of the transgressor is hard, and increasingly

5 The elders which are among you I exhort, who am also an elder, and a witness of the sufferings of Christ, and also a partaker of the glory that shall be revealed:

5 So I exhort the elders among you, as a fellow elder and a witness of the sufferings of Christ as well as a partaker in the

---

that which I have committed unto him against that day" (II Tim. 1:12). On the whole verse Bengel comments finely: *Haec una patientium cura: bene et agere et pati. Cetera curabit Ille:* "Let those who suffer have one care—to do and to suffer well. The rest will be His care" (*Gnomon Novi Testamenti* [Stuttgart: J. F. Steinkopf, 1860], *ad loc.*).

B. EXHORTATION TO ELDERS (5:1-5)

Summary: "I, Peter, your fellow elder and witness of the sufferings of Christ, charge the elders to shepherd God's flock faithfully and selflessly. Let the younger submit to them; and let all show mutual deference."

5:1. The elders which are among you I exhort: Since these men "exercise the oversight" (vs. 2; some ancient MSS omit the words), they are church officials; but vs. 5 implies also that they were actually *older* men (which is the literal meaning of the word). In N.T. times the government of a local church was in the hands of a body of men called almost indifferently **elders** or "overseers." **Who am also an elder** (KJV): Better, **a fellow elder** (RSV). Mark the modesty and humility of the title. Peter might have styled himself "an apostle"; instead, he calls himself their **fellow elder**—one who knew and felt the responsibilities and difficulties of an elder.

---

hard; that God's unsparing redemption is at work. He is to regard himself fortunate in his present suffering, for the procrastinating unbeliever will have a difficult time of it in the future. Better the acceptance of suffering now; it will be worse in the days ahead. If **the righteous . . . is scarcely saved,** what about the lot and doom of the **ungodly?** The alternatives are stark, and they are inescapable. Since the issue is of salvation, it is of supreme importance that the trial regarding it be severe. The gate is strait and the way is narrow (Matt. 7:14). Peter knew from experience how Satan seeks to "sift" the disciples of Christ as wheat (Luke 22:31), how sore it is even for the righteous to hold on through life. But "what is impossible with men is possible with God" (Luke 18:27).

Endure the ordeal of suffering then **according to the will of God,** by committing **the keeping of [your] souls,** as Jesus did (Luke 23:46), **to a faithful creator.** Holding true by persistent faith and dogged hope is rather grim business unless one can be assured of a love that will not let him go and of a victory that is sure. Peter may have watched the ordeal of his Lord on Calvary from afar. He saw how he endured his cross (Heb. 12:2), and how at the last without bitterness he committed himself into the hands of his faithful Father. So we are to commit ourselves **in well doing,** not in idleness or mere patient endurance, with no passive spirit, but with the eager readiness of an active and aggressive discipleship, to him who cares for us (5:7). The test of discipleship is in that obedience. In such surrender of our lives to

him God will not only "keep" us, but will work within us exceeding abundantly above all that we can ask or think. As **faithful,** he will not go back on any of his promises. He will not reverse his will to redeem his people. He is the Father Almighty, who combines within himself both omnipotence and fatherliness. He has created us, and sustains all things by his providential power and he is at once the God and Father of our Lord Jesus Christ. "Trust," says the apostle, "in that almighty love. He is not only willing but is able to comfort and support you, and at the last to crown you with glory and honor."

What makes this word so authoritative is that it comes from the once-faithless Peter, who in the crucial moment sinned against God's Christ, and went out and "wept bitterly." A man of well-nigh constant faithlessness, he had at last come to rely upon and commit himself in martyrlike discipleship to One who was truly faithful. "Lord, thou knowest all things; thou knowest that I love thee" (John 21:17). He knew the ground of life's ultimate confidence.

5:1-4. *About the Shepherds and the Flock.*— "So," writes Peter, "because the fiery ordeal is upon us Christians, because the judgment has begun at the household of God, because we are to commit our souls in well doing to our faithful Creator—there is urgent need that we bear one another's burdens. If the righteous scarcely be saved, if even they have difficulty in persevering, then surely they ought to support one another with pastoral concern. Let the elders or pastors therefore take seriously their duty to be examples, their positions of leadership, and

2 Feed the flock of God which is among you, taking the oversight *thereof,* not by constraint, but willingly; not for filthy lucre, but of a ready mind;

glory that is to be revealed. **2** Tend the flock of God that is your charge,[k] not by constraint but willingly,[l] not for shameful

[k] Some ancient authorities add *exercising the oversight.*
[l] Some ancient authorities add *as God would have you.*

A witness of the sufferings of Christ: A delicate hint of his higher rank and claim on their respect; he had been an eyewitness of the Savior in his passion. This interpretation of the word **witness** is more natural than the view that Peter was a witness of Christ's sufferings in virtue of the sufferings he had himself endured for his name, or the view that **witness** here means no more than "fellow preacher."

And also a partaker of the glory that shall be revealed: This might mean that Peter was an heir of the promise of glory made by Jesus in such a saying as Matt. 19:28. But Selwyn is probably right in finding here a reference to the Transfiguration, when Peter, James, and John had been granted a foretaste of the glory that shall belong to Jesus and the redeemed at his final triumph. Peter "had experienced, and was known to have experienced, a special revelation of the glory which had been restored to Jesus at the ascension . . . and would be manifested to all when He came again at the End" (*First Epistle of Peter,* p. 229).

2. Feed the flock of God which is among you: For **feed** read **tend** (RSV) or "shepherd." The words recall Christ's charge to Peter in John 21:16, "Feed my sheep" (cf. Paul's charge to the Ephesian elders in Acts 20:28). In the O.T., God, or his Messiah, is

---

their attitudes toward the members of the congregation, as they exercise their pastoral oversight of the flock of God."

There is something rather personal and autobiographical about vs. 1. Peter speaks of himself as **a fellow elder, a witness of the sufferings of Christ,** and **a partaker in the glory that is to be revealed.**

As a fellow elder he assumes no favored position among his colleagues. He makes no claim to being the first among the apostles. He makes no mention of his peculiar relationship to Jesus. He assumes no superior position. On the contrary, he places himself on an equality with his fellow elders and modestly assumes his part in the pastoral oversight of God's people. How the impetuous and boastful Peter has been changed! Certainly this is all far removed from those who claim as his successors to be the only vicars of Christ.

He is also a witness to **the sufferings of Christ.** Not only had he observed the Master's passion and death; he had become a witness to his pentecostal presence and power. The sufferings of Jesus must have made a deep impression upon Peter. By his denial he had contributed to that burden (see Mark 14:29, 32-42, 50, 54, 66-72; Luke 22:31, 61). Yet the suffering Servant endured it all, and even prayed for those who crucified him. In the garden he accepted the cup, and consecrated himself "for their sakes" as a Shepherd who gives his life for the sheep. The constraining power of the love of Christ no doubt gave Peter his pastoral concern. His love

for Christ was the one quality that made the risen Christ entrust his lambs and his sheep to Peter's care (John 21:15-17).

And he is **a partaker in the glory that is to be revealed.** Peter had already had a preview of the glory of Christ on the mount of Transfiguration (Mark 9:2-8). But even more, he was already sharing in a glory (4:14) which all Christians shared, and which would be fully revealed in the end (John 13:36). The apostle never fails to indicate that behind and beyond the sufferings of Christians in this world there is an ultimate glory. He is a man of invincible hope.

Critical times lay heavy strains upon personal life. Anxiety increases when the stability of society gives way to disintegration or revolution. An ordered environment makes for smooth living, but a disordered world tends to rob even the Christian of his peace of mind. Such times and conditions call for a pastoral ministry to persons. The tension in personal life is increased when the individual seeks to live conscientiously. He finds himself in a strange and hostile world. The Christian who is bent on doing the will of God needs strong inner resources and steadying outer relationships. The rapid developments in pastoral psychology and in professional psychiatry bear witness that both the science of medicine and the church of Christ are continuing with greater intensity than ever before the long history of their concern. Nothing presses more urgently upon a troubled generation than the need of a ministry brought

3 Neither as being lords over *God's* heritage, but being ensamples to the flock.

gain but eagerly, **3** not as domineering over those in your charge but being examples to

---

commonly called the shepherd, and the community of the faithful his flock (see, e.g., Ezek. 34:12-23). In the N.T. Jesus the Messiah calls himself the shepherd (John 10:14 ff.; Luke 15:3-6; 19:10) and his band of disciples the "little flock" (Luke 12:32; Matt. 10:16). If we ask what Peter means in this context by "tending," the answer (in Henry Alford's phrase) is, "leading, feeding, and heeding."

Taking the oversight thereof (KJV): The words are omitted by two of the best MSS (cf. RSV).

Not by constraint . . . : Not out of a stern sense of "needs must" but with hearty alacrity. **Not for filthy lucre:** The elders were probably paid, on the dominical principle that "the laborer is worthy of his hire" (Luke 10:7), and the Pauline one that "they which preach the gospel should live of the gospel" (I Cor. 9:14). What Peter forbids is not reasonable remuneration but a sordid lust for money (cf. I Tim. 3:8; Tit. 1:7).

3. Not as domineering over those in your charge: "Domineer" (κατακυριεύοντες) is the same Greek word which Christ applies to the rule of the "great ones" among the Gentiles (Mark 10:42). The word κλῆρος, originally "a lot," came to mean "a share won in a lot"; then (in classical Greek) an allotment of land assigned to a citizen by the authorities. Here it denotes "an allotted sphere of pastoral care," a **charge**.

---

back to the "cure of souls." Men and women without any Christian convictions at all are yet aware of the judgment that has fallen. The "fiery ordeal" calls for very few asterisks or footnotes. Even the righteous will scarcely be saved without the constant encouragement of pastoral counsel and the healing influence of the fellowship.

The term **the flock of God** has been used uniquely in the Hebrew-Christian tradition to describe the people of God. References to the flock, the shepherds, and the sheep are numerous in the O.T. God is Israel's shepherd (Isa. 40:11; Pss. 23; 80; 95). Sheep? His people, like sheep, often wander far from Shepherd and fold (Isa. 53:6; Ps. 119:176). They pathetically lose themselves (Num. 27:17; I Kings 22:17). They were meant to live with one another. And to that end God gave to kings and religious leaders the responsibility of being undershepherds (II Sam. 5:2; 7:7; Jer. 12:10; Ezek. 34:1 ff.). But they often exploited the flock and turned traitor to their trust (Jer. 23:1; Ezek. 34:1-10; Isa. 56:11; Zech. 11:16 ff.). In such a case God himself will be the Shepherd of his flock (Jer. 31:10; Ezek. 34:15) and provide dependable shepherds for it (Jer. 23:4; Ezek. 34:23), until one day a princely counselor will tend the flock of God (Mic. 5:2 ff.).

Our Lord enriched and fulfilled ("filled to the full") the image. He regarded himself as the good Shepherd, who was to give his life for the sheep (John 10:11). He was no hireling whose major concern was financial pay and the avoidance of physical danger while protecting the sheep from their enemies (John 10:11-18).

He came to seek and to save the lost (Luke 19:10). And other sheep he had which were not of that flock. To them all he would be the door of the fold through which they might go in freedom to find pasture and through which they might return in safety after the long day to find succor and rest. What better metaphor can be used even in an industrial age to describe the nature of the church, the characteristics of its people, the ministry of Christ to and among those who have heard his voice and accepted him as their Shepherd? We may not like being compared with sheep who reveal themselves as stupid and docile creatures, prone at times to panic in the face of enemies. Quite often we act like defiant prodigals who demand our rights and our properties. Even so, the prodigal was nothing other than a stubborn black buck who insisted on being his own shepherd as well, and who thought he could find life in riotous living with "other sheep" in another fold. More frequently, however, men like sheep go astray through sheer stupidity. Juicy tufts of grass—or sensate pleasures—lure them on and, following the lead of appetite, they find themselves at the close of the day lost, alone, and far from shepherd, flock, and fold.

Let undershepherds beware of minimizing or underestimating the sheep of God. Politicians may say, "The public be damned!" because they discredit the worth and the ability of the average man. Not many ministers have had the effrontery to say anything similar about the people of the church—though some impatient parsons have treated their people with scant courtesy, and have undertaken to run the church

4 And when the chief Shepherd shall appear, ye shall receive a crown of glory that fadeth not away.

the flock. 4 And when the chief Shepherd is manifested you will obtain the unfading

---

4. And when the chief Shepherd shall appear, i.e., at the Second Advent. With this beautiful title for Christ (only here in the N.T.) compare "the good shepherd" (John 10:11, 14) and "the great shepherd of the sheep" (Heb. 13:20).

Ye shall receive a crown of glory that fadeth not away: The metaphor is that of the garland worn by victors at the games, but it is doubtful whether **that fadeth not away** is a quite accurate rendering of the Greek word. In 1:4 the word is ἀμάραντος, which means "unfading," "never withering"; here it is ἀμαράντινος, which means, literally,

---

without them, usurping the central place which belongs to the good Shepherd, and exploiting for their own prestige and power what is not theirs but God's. None other than Peter warns and admonishes that the flock of God is God's, not man's; that Christ is its true Shepherd; that it is an organic life, not an organization of things; that undershepherds occupy a responsible and privileged position in co-operation with and under the authority of Another; that the protection, nourishment, and healing of the flock is the undershepherd's major responsibility; that shepherds care for only a small but integral portion of the great flock; and that in spite of the frequent irresponsibility of human shepherds, the good Shepherd will not forsake his sheep.

The duties of **elders,** older persons (see Exeg.), or persons charged with the oversight, pastoral care, instruction, and leadership in Christian communities, are in part clearly set forth. They have not changed; in fact, they are becoming more urgent as time moves on. Broadly speaking, those who are elders are charged with the responsibility of leading the immature into the full meaning of the Christian way of life. While they may not be fully mature themselves—who can claim maturity in Christ if men like Paul could not fully achieve it?—because of their age and experience they cannot avoid assuming roles of leadership in the growing Christian community. But whether aged or not, every member of the body of Christ is meant to minister to every other member. The "priesthood of believers" is the brotherhood of mutuality. Some may hold special positions in the church as pastors and teachers, counselors and preachers; but it is the duty of every Christian to exercise his ministry of helpfulness to every fellow Christian and to every neighbor, whoever he is and wherever he lives. Moreover as the body of reconciliation, the church not only cares for its own members, but also for all men in the name of the Savior and Redeemer of the world.

Let elders, then, **tend** the particular **flock** of God that is in their immediate care. The local church is not to be despised; it is part of the great church. Let them exercise their ministry **willingly,** freely, democratically, and exemplarily. The solemn **charge** is to **feed** the sheep, a word which still resounded in the soul of Peter from the day of his restoration at the Galilean lakeside. To **tend** means to nourish by a proper diet, to protect with vigilant watchfulness, to heal from the bramble hurt, and to strengthen for the possible assault. Tending refers to the whole vast range of service which God requires for the spiritual maturing of his people. Those who engage in this work ought to be equipped to undertake its heavy responsibility and its exacting service; and they ought to remember too that they are working at holy things, and that they are working with God. In the task allotted to them they have been entrusted with an "inheritance." Theirs is a part of God's **heritage,** assigned them as a plot to cultivate with utmost care.

This ministry is not to be undertaken with a sense of legal **constraint.** One cannot be forced into a ministry of compassion. Since it is a ministry of love, it cannot be coerced. It is the love of Christ that constrains the true minister and priest. It is an inward necessity that is laid upon him (I Cor. 9:16). The shepherd's heart is learned from the heart of Christ, who had compassion upon the multitudes that were "as sheep having no shepherd" (Matt. 9:36). The gift of pulpit speech, the capacity for theological intelligence, the grace of personal charm, the clerical ancestry of one's forebears, do not make the real pastor. Nor can the ecclesiastical laws and pronouncements of church courts and clergymen make of an official minister or nominal churchman a real pastor or a burden-bearing member of Christ's family. The inner constraint is necessary. No doubt it is difficult to engage in pastoral work; it taxes one's vitality. Some shrink from personal counseling because of the cost in time and energy. Social pressures may push one into the ministry; pastoral customs may force the minister to do

"made of amaranth," i.e., a genus of plants sometimes called immortelles because they long retain their freshness; cf. Milton's "Lycidas":

> Bid amaranthus all his beauty shed,
> And daffodillies fill their cups with tears,
> To strew the laureate hearse where Lycid lies.

If this interpretation is correct, we may here have a passing reference to the garden of the heavenly paradise. "To the mind of every Christian reader," says an older commentator, "the thought of the στέφανος ἀμαράντινος which the grace of our Lord gives to us, suggests at once the remembrance of the στέφανος ἀκάνθινος which our sin gave

---

pastoral work; baptisms, weddings, and funerals may imperiously demand attention. But unless these "tendings" of the flock are done with a willing spirit, they lack the authentic touch of the work of him who "went about doing good," who consecrated himself for our sakes, and who was deeply satisfied with "meat" after a noontime conversation with a woman at the well of Jacob (John 4:5-34).

There is another reason for Peter's injunction to serve **willingly**. Leaders of congregations in those days were often singled out by the authorities for persecution. As a result, there were some who avoided the pastoral office because of the danger involved. To volunteer was an invitation to trouble. Nevertheless, urges Peter, enlist in the army of Christ. The call to Christian leadership is never an invitation to untroubled comfort.

Pastoral work also must be done **eagerly** and not for the sake of **filthy lucre**, or for **gain**. The worker, to be sure, is worthy of his hire. The ministry is to live by its service. Peter is not speaking about a "paid ministry" as over against one that is supported by the work of its own hands or by voluntary offerings. He warns against the use of the office of the ministry for mere material gain, for personal prestige, or for popular acclaim. There are congregations that have been centered in popular preachers. And there are ministers who use their spiritual offices for personal advantage. The religious man is easily self-deceived. He may be doing effective work in a church and fail to realize that his real ambition is to make a "success" of the church rather than a Christian congregation of the flock of God. There is no escaping this perennial temptation to make the church of God into an institution of man. The danger of professionalism is ever present in the life of every servant of Christ. The only antidote to the poison of ambition is to cultivate the **ready**, the "zealous" **mind**, which seeks only to serve Christ.

Nor is the elder to "lord it over" the charge committed to him. Power corrupts even the religious man. And there is no corruption so odious as the abuse of that which purports in public to be benevolent and disinterested. There is nothing so disreputable as a corrupt religion. Jesus warned that this spirit was to be found among the Gentiles, who loved to rule over men. Said he, "It shall not be so among you" (Mark 10:43). The power motive knows no limits, and its spirit is an ever-present threat to every church. Authority there must be, but even in churches that are ruled by bishops, the dominating spirit of undemocratic autocracy and tyranny must not obtain. The church of Christ is no civil government. The authority of God's household is one of truth and love that leads to persuasion. It must be commensurate with the nature of the good Shepherd and his dealings with his sheep. And should it come to pass that strong action is needed to deal with elements that would disrupt and pervert **the flock of God**, let the authority then exercised for the peace of the church be done in the truth and the love of the great Shepherd himself. Every elder must combine within himself the qualities of loving care and genuine authority. The history of the church abounds with examples of men, "dress'd in a little brief authority," [6] who usurped the place which should be occupied by the Shepherd. There are differences of gifts in the church, but they issue from the same Spirit. There is no place for "bosses" who run it as a government or a business. While Christ is no friend of disorder and chaos, he might well decry the efficiently successful church that has lost its democratic nature.

And be **examples**. As is the clergy, so is the church. The pastor is the person: the chief Christian person in the flock. He is everyman's Christian. As the good Shepherd did not drive his sheep, but went on before them in the way (John 10:4), so must the pastor of a congregation. It is no longer possible to say, "Do as I say, but not as I do." The spiritual level of a congregation will hardly rise any higher than the level of the spiritual integrity of the minister. Word and life must correspond; the word without the life is sterile; the life without the

[6] Shakespeare, *Measure for Measure*, Act II, scene 2.

5 Likewise, ye younger, submit yourselves unto the elder. Yea, all *of you* be subject

crown of glory. 5 Likewise you that are younger be subject to the elders. Clothe

---

to Him" (Robert Johnstone, *The First Epistle of St Peter* [London: T. & T. Clark, 1888], p. 388) .

5. Ye younger: The reference here is to age, not official rank. Younger men are to defer to their elders.

Be clothed with humility (ἐγκομβώσασθε) : The Greek verb, found only here in the N.T., is very interesting. The noun ἐγκόμβωμα (derived from κόμβος, "a band" or "a knot") signified an apron worn by slaves and regarded as a mark of their status. Here, therefore, the verb means "put on the apron of"; so indeed Moffatt renders, "Put on the apron of humility to serve one another." The word conjures up vividly the supreme example of humility when the Son of God, about to do the work of a servant, "took a towel, and girded himself" (John 13:4) .

For God resisteth the proud . . . : From Prov. 3:34; also quoted in Jas. 4:6.

---

word is meaningless. "Be ye followers of me, even as I also am of Christ" (I Cor. 11:1; see also II Thess. 3:9; I Tim. 4:12; Tit. 2:7; Phil. 3:7) .

He was shepherd and no mercenary,
And tho' he holy was and virtuous,
He was to sinful men full piteous.
His words were strong but not with anger fraught,
And love benignant he discreetly taught,
To draw mankind to heaven by gentleness,
And good example was his business.
But if that anyone were obstinate,
Whether he were of high or low estate,
He would be sharply checked with altered mien.
A better parson there was nowhere seen.
He paid no court to pomps and reverence,
Nor spiced his conscience at his soul's expense,
But Jesus' love which owns no pride or pelf
He taught—but first he followed it himself.

Thus Chaucer described the parson in his *Canterbury Tales.*[7] Where **elders** have served others sacrificially they have again and again wielded a power beyond that of rulers who dominated men by force.

When the chief Shepherd is manifested these faithful ministers will receive the **unfading crown of glory.** Theirs will be the highest prize which God can offer to any mortal. That Christ is the **chief Shepherd** is a concept unique and central to the Christian faith. The shepherd-God is beautifully and satisfyingly celebrated in the classic sentences of Ps. 23. He is perfectly incarnate in the ministry of our Lord. Jesus claimed the title for himself and won his right to it by loving his own to the end, by giving himself for the defense and the freedom and the life of his sheep, by offering them the food and the pasture that nourish unto life eternal, by providing them with his "substitute" (Holy Spirit) continually to tend, feed, shepherd, lead, and unite them through his person, his love,

[7] Prologue, "The Parson."

his care. None may assume his place. All under-shepherds must serve under his wise and faithful leadership. The **chief Shepherd** alone can glorify the undershepherd's task. He alone can proffer **the unfading crown of glory.**

5a. Youth and Age in the Church.—Just why Peter should call attention to the relationship of youth and age in the church is an interesting question. We know from I Clement that there was trouble in the Corinthian church on this matter toward the end of the first century. Perhaps there were tensions between conservative age and revolutionary youth even in Peter's day. Earlier in this letter he mentions the relationship of masters and servants, wives and husbands (2:18–3:7), exhorting servants and wives in particular to be Christian in their stations in life. The apostle Paul counsels his friends regarding the duties of parents to their children (Eph. 6:4) . Yet he also writes Timothy not to be ashamed of his youthfulness as a minister (I Tim. 4:12). He should not allow members of his congregation to discredit him because of his age.

The emphasis upon youth is a rather late phenomenon in the church and in the world. It arose toward the end of the nineteenth century with the development of adolescent psychology and the discovery of the importance of youth in education, economics, and politics. In some respects the "youth movement" belongs to the twentieth century. The church has taken cognizance of this emergence and has provided for youth fellowships, student movements, camps and conferences, caravans and work projects, and even "youth churches." The tension between youth and age has intensified. It has not always been easy for the generations to understand each other. The one has stood for a religion of tradition and order, while the other has stood for a religion of action and unconventionality. The increase in the number of

one to another, and be clothed with humility: for God resisteth the proud, and giveth grace to the humble.

6 Humble yourselves therefore under the mighty hand of God, that he may exalt you in due time:

yourselves, all of you, with humility toward one another, for "God opposes the proud, but gives grace to the humble."

6 Humble yourselves therefore under the mighty hand of God, that in due time

---

C. CONCLUDING EXHORTATION (5:6-11)

Summary: "Be humble—so God will exalt you. Be watchful—the devil is abroad looking for victims. And be ready to pay the same tax of suffering as your brethren in the world. When your suffering is past, God will strengthen you."

6. Humble . . . exalt: Cf. our Lord's word in Luke 14:11, "For every one who exalts himself will be humbled, and he who humbles himself will be exalted." **The mighty hand of God:** A common O.T. phrase for the divine activity, whether in deliverance or, as here, in judgment. **In due time:** "Not thy fancied time, but His own wisely-appointed time" (Leighton, *First Epistle of Peter*, II, 461).

---

older people has not eased the situation. The general education of youth through school, press, and radio has made them more alert and informed than ever, and they have become even more restless with a static religion which seems to do nothing. Youth is more and more aware of its role as well as of its possible fate in the precarious social situation.

The impetuosity of youth is felt in the ranks of the ministry. Ecclesiastical authority is concentrated largely in the hands of the "elders." Youth is subdued in the presence of entrenched power and superior experience. This tends to a self-assertiveness, a critical attitude, and even a hostility that is not becoming to the fellowship of Christ. Peter is not pleading for the squelching of the much-needed enthusiasm and freshness of youthful religion in the church; but he is counseling younger churchmen to **submit** themselves to their brethren, and particularly to those who are wise and experienced.

The gospel appeals to youth; it has its revolutionary aspect (cf. Acts 17:6, where Christians were spoken of as those who "have turned the world upside down"). But zeal without knowledge may become fanaticism, even as knowledge without zeal may become dead. There is a wisdom of the Christian past, and there is a stability in the Christian heritage which dare not be thrown to the winds in radical recklessness. The old and the new need to balance each other in the church. There is a pertinent word here for Christian sects that would ignore the church's long history and start a new Christianity on their own. There is a valid admonition here for impatient younger Christians to be careful lest they cut themselves off from the holy catholic church and become less than fully Christian. And indirectly there is counsel for older churchmen to listen to youth, to think in larger than traditional church terms, and to

make themselves worthy of their esteemed position in the church by befriending youth. God still has much truth to break forth from his Word. And the church is composed of all ages.

5b-11. Some Closing Remarks.—Before concluding his letter with some personal references, the veteran apostle counsels his friends to be **humble**, be trustful, be **watchful**, and be hopeful. And all because God's is the **dominion**—the reign, the rule—**for ever and ever. Amen.**

Be **humble.** Humility is the foremost grace of the Christian life. The apostle insists that the admonition to be humble be placed first in his list. The world around these early disciples exalted the pagan virtues of physical perfection, manly courage, and proud self-control. Humility was inconsistent with the prevailing ideal of the perfect man. Self-criticism and the spirit of dependence upon God were regarded as anything but conducive to the fullest expression of human life.

But true **humility** is not servility. It is not a sense of worthlessness which degrades human nature. The humble person does not think more lowly of himself than he ought to think. Humility is not self-depreciation, nor is it a mere sentiment. It must never be a false modesty meant to win from our impressed friends praise for our humility.

Real humility, or lowliness of mind, is "the highest virtue, mother of them all." [8] It is a sense of lowliness which results from a vision of life's greatness. There can be no humility where there is no awareness of failure to achieve the highest. Humility results when a man realizes that all he is and has is derived, whether from God or from his neighbors. Above all, humility of spirit results when he is aware of the fact that he is saved by the unconditioned and free grace of God in Christ. Humility

[8] Tennyson, *Idylls of the King*, "The Holy Grail."

7 Casting all your care upon him; for he careth for you.

8 Be sober, be vigilant; because your adversary the devil, as a roaring lion, walketh about, seeking whom he may devour:

he may exalt you. 7 Cast all your anxieties on him, for he cares about you. 8 Be sober, be watchful. Your adversary the devil prowls around like a roaring lion, seeking

---

7. Casting all your care upon him; for he careth for you: The two words for **care** are different in the Greek. We should render the first **anxieties** (RSV) or "worry." The verse recalls Ps. 55:22, "Cast thy burden upon the Lord, and he shall sustain thee." Possibly Peter had also in his mind the Lord's great words about worry and its cure (Matt. 6:25-34). In the words **he careth for you** "is the central truth that Christ was manifested to reveal" (Masterman, as quoted in A. S. Peake, *A Commentary on the Bible* [London: Thomas Nelson & Sons, 1919], p. 911). The message of the gospel at bottom is that in Christ we have the supreme proof that God cares for us; and it is because he has cared, and cares, for us that we are to care for others.

8. Be sober, be vigilant: Though the Christian casts all his anxiety on God, he is not thereby absolved from the duty of watchfulness. **Be vigilant** ("watch"): The very command that Christ had given Peter and his two friends in the Garden of Gethsemane (Mark 14:38). **Your adversary the devil** (ὁ ἀντίδικος ὑμῶν διάβολος): Ἀντίδικος in its

---

acknowledges its sins and with childlike simplicity accepts the free forgiveness of God with joy and hope. A like humility is to be found in the minds of great scholars, artists, and teachers. Faced with the almost limitless areas of knowledge, beauty, and truth, they have forgotten their own excellences and "waited" with meekness upon the glory of the ideal and the as yet unknown. Such humility makes for strength, not weakness.

For Peter the supreme example of humility is Jesus, who knew that he came from God, that he went to God, had all things put into his hands by God, yet took a towel, and girding himself with it stooped down to wash his disciples' feet (John 13:1-17). Jesus was humble in that he was not ashamed to do a slave's task. He was humble even though and precisely because he was peculiarly conscious of his relationship to God and of his power in God. Real humility toward one another rests ultimately upon real humility before God. Yet while he was humble before God, Jesus was not a coward before men. So should Christians be humble as they suffer **under the mighty hand of God.** Humility must always be seen as **under the mighty hand** of him who is an enemy of pride, self-centeredness, and man-centeredness (see Prov. 3:4 LXX); but the hand that brings down **the proud** will in due time **exalt** those who live and walk under its strong direction, correction, and protection.

The term "God's hand" is used in many parts of the Bible to indicate the ways in which God "handles" his people. Sometimes his hand warns, at other times it succors; again it resists the proud, and then it raises up the fallen. His hand opens and satisfies "the desire of every

living thing" (Ps. 145:16); his hand portions out bitter sufferings (4:12-19). Perhaps there is no finer statement concerning the Christian's confidence in the hand of God than that set forth in Answer 26 of the *Heidelberg Catechism:*

That the eternal Father of our Lord Jesus Christ, who of nothing made heaven and earth, with all that is in them, who likewise upholds and governs the same by his eternal counsel and providence, is for the sake of Christ his Son my God and my Father; in whom I so trust, as to have no doubt that He will provide me with all things necessary for body and soul; and further, that whatever evil He sends upon me in this vale of tears He will turn to my good; for He is able to do it, being Almighty God, and willing also, being a faithful Father.

We are to be humble-minded and sweet-spirited, even when the everlasting arms that support us and the fatherly hands that deal with us seem like the arms and hands of an enemy. In a sense we share the humiliation and the sufferings which even God's Son endured. **In due time** these arms and hands will raise you up. "Blessed are the poor in spirit: for theirs is the kingdom of heaven" (Matt. 5:3).

Be trustful. Face life with a positive faith in the reliable and life-bearing goodness of God. Cast all your anxieties onto his shoulders. The true and living God cares. And he cares for each of us. How many anxious people have been consoled and comforted by these simple words! And no wonder. They contain the heart of the gospel. They reveal the nature of the ultimate reality, the finality beyond which none can go. Their burden was the essence of the ministry of Jesus Christ. "Ye believe in God,

9 Whom resist steadfast in the faith, knowing that the same afflictions are accomplished in your brethren that are in the world.

someone to devour. **9** Resist him, firm in your faith, knowing that the same experience of suffering is required of your

---

primary sense means "an adversary at law," as in Matt. 5:25. It came to mean "an enemy" generally. Here the word answers to the Hebrew שׂטן and means "the Enemy." **As a roaring lion:** The simile is derived from Ps. 22:13, the **roaring** being of course the rage of hunger. **Walketh about:** Better, **prowls around** (RSV). Job 1:7 has Satan "walking up and down" in the earth.

Seeking whom he may devour (KJV) translates ζητῶν τίνα καταπιεῖν. The RSV reads **seeking someone to devour.** Either translation is possible; the difference in the Greek is only that of accentuation on one word. In another and earlier time of trial, "the Enemy" had tried to make Peter his prey: "Simon, Simon, behold, Satan hath desired to have you, that he may sift you as wheat" (Luke 22:31). But Christ had prayed for him and prevailed. Now, "converted," Peter obeys his Lord's command, "Strengthen your brethren."

9. The cure for temptation is a solid faith in God. **Knowing that the same afflictions are accomplished in your brethren that are in the world:** That is a possible translation

---

believe also in me" (John 14:1). All men believe in a God of some kind; but until they see and know and trust the living God in gracious action in Jesus, they will lack the final comfort of life. The great God in whom "we live, and move, and have our being" cares. The final ground of existence is benevolent. It is none other than the God and Father of our Lord Jesus Christ. If a man can believe that with all his heart, mind, soul, and strength, he shall be relieved of the great terror, the dread of that abysmal depth of nothingness which at the last swallows up our hopes and our aspirations. A new convert gave a reason why she refused to learn more than the first two words of the Lord's Prayer—"Our Father." She said: "If a Father is in control of all things, and he cares for me his child, then all life takes on a different meaning." The God of creation is the God and Father of our Lord Jesus; but the glory of it all is that he is my God. He is near; he "worries" about me; he involves himself in my anxieties. "Such knowledge is too wonderful for me" (Ps. 139:6). As Moffatt says, "**His** and **you** are emphatic." [1]

And who does not have anxieties? Some there must be, for they go with that freedom in which we have been created and with the contingencies that are a part of our human existence. But when anxieties become terrors they consume their bearers with fear and uncertainty. Human beings have their cares, whether of family or health or vocation or economic security or social prospect. The older we grow the larger are our relationships and the heavier are our responsibilities. And the more are the cares that accumulate. It is not cares as such that crush

and kill; rather is it the lack of resources to bear them, and the failure of the bearer to share them, that break men down.

Cast your burdens upon God, Peter commands, and do so with a strong determination and without hesitation. Be done with them as with a deadly plague. Make no compromises with any of them. Be done with the whole lot of them. The shoulders of God are inviting and broad, and his heart is generous and big. He is willing to take all burdens, even those trifling ones men think too insignificant to mention. The secret burdens we hesitate to confess; those sins that do so easily entangle us (Heb. 12:1); those pet cares we dangerously fondle—are to be dealt with drastically and without reservation. Nothing is too small and nothing is too bad to take to God. Unshared anxiety denies the loving care of God; it makes man his own savior; it rejects the proffered help of the Father; and it robs life itself of that intimate relationship between God and the human soul which is the very heart of meaningful living.

Be sober, be watchful. To trust God and cast one's **anxieties** upon him is no indication that there is nothing more to do. Being a Christian may give you inner peace, but it offers you no permanent place in a rest camp. There is a fight on. The Christian is to put on the whole armor of God—not to fight the major battle, which has been won, but to engage the enemies of his Lord who constantly environ him day and night, and who prowl around the flock seeking to kill and to destroy, **roaring** for their prey, ready to pounce upon the unwitting sheep, and to **devour** the unwatchful lamb.

No doubt Peter recalls his own experience.

[1] *The General Epistles*, p. 167.

10 But the God of all grace, who hath called us unto his eternal glory by Christ Jesus, after that ye have suffered a while, make you perfect, stablish, strengthen, settle *you*.

brotherhood throughout the world. 10 And after you have suffered a little while, the God of all grace, who has called you to his eternal glory in Christ, will himself restore,

of the Greek, but there is a better one. The key word is ἐπιτελεῖσθαι. This verb does mean "accomplish," but it can also mean "pay tribute." Thus Xenophon speaks of "paying the tax of old age" (τὰ τοῦ γήρως ἐπιτελεῖσθαι), in loss of sight, memory, etc. If we adopt this meaning here, as Moffatt does, we may translate, "Knowing that you pay the same tax of suffering as your brethren in the world." The RSV is close to this. Peter's readers are not alone in their affliction; and the knowledge that their Christian brethren elsewhere in the world are being made to pay a similar terrible tribute ought to nerve them to constancy.

10-11. There are verbal similarities between these two verses and II Thess. 2 (**grace, called, eternal, perfect**), which perhaps point to the pen of Silvanus.

The God of all grace: The God whose characteristic it is to supply grace to fit every need. **Called:** At baptism. The words **in Christ** may be connected either with **called** or with **glory. A while:** Better, with RSV, **a little while.**

Thrice in the garden of Gethsemane he had dozed off as Jesus prayed with great earnestness. When later that evening the maidservant questioned him about his connections with this Galilean, he had again been taken off his guard. And Jesus had cautioned his disciples about their possible failure when the last things should occur (Mark 13). Peter himself had heard the whisper of that sinister voice which lulls the follower of Christ into a dangerous forgetfulness of every warning.

That the Christian life is no "bed of roses" he well knew by this time. It was a strenuous way. Jesus had spoken of the "tribulations" of this world. He had spoken of the disciples as sheep sent into a world of "wolves." From experience Peter had come to see that he who would follow Jesus must "take up his cross daily" (Luke 9:23). The table was prepared by the Shepherd for his own even in the presence of enemies (Ps. 23:5). Because the issues were so crucial and the values at stake so precious, the life of the Christian had to be achieved by a costly decision and a perennial vigilance. A pearl of this kind comes high; it takes the precious collection of a lifetime to acquire (Matt. 13:45-46).

And there is an enemy. A modern biblical scholar publicized the fact that the damning reality of evil had found its way back into theological thought, and did it by giving his article the title, "Satan Returns from Holiday." His Satanic Majesty has returned not only into our thinking but into our situation. Whatever our interpretation of this diabolic reality that makes beasts of men and seeks to liquidate everything for which Jesus Christ stands, it is no mere impersonal force. It appeals to

persons and becomes incarnate in them individually and corporately. And it is real. Is there no Antichrist? No restless, prowling, slinking, devouring power that wants to sift the unstable Peters as wheat? To finish off the Christian cause? To create panic in the minds and hearts of faithful, loving, and hopeful people? Peter is no professional theologian; he offers us no answer to the age-old enigma of evil. He does not tell us how evil got into God's world, whether **the devil** is a personal reality whose power is co-equal with God's, or whether evil is permitted of God as a necessary concomitant of creation itself. As a practical-minded Christian, all he knows is that there is a sinister power at work in the world; that it is like **a roaring lion** on the prowl to prey upon the sheep of the fold; and that the Christian has to be on the alert lest he lose his precious new life in Christ. As Eivind Berggrav put it in a moving address at the Amsterdam Assembly of the World Council of Churches: There is a God; there is a law; there is an enemy; and there is a victory.

All this means that there is a way to meet this threatening power of evil. One must keep cool. To get all fussed up is to lose a calm sense of judgment. Superficial enthusiasm is also of little help in the precarious situation. The Christian must keep a clear head and a sane mind. Eternal vigilance is the price of freedom for the children of God. "Awake thou that sleepest" (Eph. 5:14). "Watch and pray, that ye enter not into temptation" (Matt. 26:41). "The children of this world are in their generation wiser than the children of light" (Luke 16:8). Why should being religious make one blind? Why should good people be good for

11 To him *be* glory and dominion for ever and ever. Amen.

12 By Silvanus, a faithful brother unto you, as I suppose, I have written briefly, exhorting, and testifying that this is the true grace of God wherein ye stand.

establish, and strengthen[m] you. 11 To him be the dominion for ever and ever. Amen.

12 By Sil-va'nus, a faithful brother as I regard him, I have written briefly to you, exhorting and declaring that this is the

[m] Many ancient authorities read *restore, establish, strengthen and settle.*

Make you perfect, stablish, strengthen, settle you: The last verb should possibly be omitted. Moffatt renders, "repair, recruit, and strengthen." **Perfect** (καταρτίσει) is the word used of "mending" holes in nets (Mark 1:19) or of setting a broken bone. The meaning is "amend" or **restore;** cf. Bengel's comment: "Perfect—so that no defect remains in you; stablish—so that nothing will make you stumble; strengthen—so that you may overcome every hostile power" (*Gnomon Novi Testamenti, ad loc.*).

V. CONCLUSION AND BLESSING (5:12-14)

These last three verses are possibly from the hand of Peter himself, just as Paul ends II Thessalonians and Galatians with an autograph message.

12. By Silvanus, a faithful brother as I regard him, I have written briefly to you: **Silvanus** is beyond reasonable doubt the man who bears that name in Paul's epistles,

---

nothing? If Christians are to be as "tangy" as salt and as penetrating and exposing as light, then they ought to be prophetic pioneers who are constantly fighting the decaying and the darkening effects of evil.

This devil must be resisted with courage fortified by **steadfast . . . faith.** He must be countered in the heart, in the mind, in the body. And he must be resisted at the very beginning of his assault. To give an inch is to begin a contest that may end in surrender. John Bunyan in *The Holy War* knew that the senses are the gateways to Mansoul. The eyegate and the eargate must be guarded. But mere resistance is not enough. It lacks dynamic unless it is offensive and issues from a positive faith. Soldiers in battle must have a rationale for the campaign. Without the knowledge that life's battles are part of the holy warfare, morale and the determination to resist the enemy would soon collapse.

But be hopeful. For in their resistance Christians are not alone. Others share the same wounds and engage in the same struggle (vs. 9). The battle line runs around the world. The wounds are not in vain, nor is the contest futile. The church today enlists its millions in the ranks of Christ. The fact of common sufferings for the sake of the faith will inspire rather than deflate the spirit of the saints. And while we do not glorify military matters in the church, yet in this spiritual warfare we may sing

> Onward, Christian soldiers!
> Marching as to war,
> With the cross of Jesus

> Going on before.
> Christ, the royal Master,
> Leads against the foe;
> Forward into battle,
> See his banners go!
>
> . . . . .
>
> Onward, then, ye people,
> Join our happy throng,
> Blend with ours your voices
> In the triumph-song;
> Glory, laud, and honor
> Unto Christ the King;
> This through countless ages
> Men and angels sing.[2]

The pain has an end. The battle will not go on forever. And when the consummation is come, those who were wounded in the strife will be restored, established, and strengthened. The gracious God of life will mend you like old broken nets (Mark 1:19), or put you up like a veteran ship of many a voyage into drydock for overhauling. He will give you secure foundations, and internally renew your strength.

After such a prospect, in the light of such hardships, who does not want to sing the Doxology? It is God who brings it all to pass. God's is the battle; God's is the cause; God's be the glory **for ever and ever.** So may it be! Yea verily! **Amen.** Were it not for God, life's battle would not be worth the candle. But since it is his campaign, anything can be endured. Through Christ we are enabled for all things (Phil. 4:13).

12-14. *Final Words.*—Did Peter take pen in hand and, like Paul (Gal. 6:11; I Cor. 16:21;

[2] Sabine Baring-Gould.

13 The *church that is* at Babylon, elected together with *you,* saluteth you; and *so doth* Marcus my son.

true grace of God; stand fast in it. **13** She who is at Babylon, who is likewise chosen, sends you greetings; and so does my son

---

and who is called Silas in Acts, a man who had been in the Christian church almost from the first, who had accompanied Paul on the second missionary journey, and who was probably a man of considerable culture. But what does **by** (διά) mean? On its narrowest interpretation it would mean simply that Silvanus was the bearer of the letter—Peter's postman, as it were. But the preposition can also mean that Silvanus was a good deal more than the postman, that he was the draftsman of the whole letter; and that is the more probable view.

As I suppose (KJV): This translation suggests some hesitation—a hesitation which is not in the Greek verb (λογίζομαι). Translate, "as I reckon" or **as I regard him** (RSV). **I have written** (ἔγραψα) is the Greek epistolary aorist which looks at the matter from the viewpoint of the *receiver* of the letter. In English we use a present or, as here, a perfect tense. **Briefly:** 105 verses; Peter felt that he could have said a good deal more on this important subject.

This is the true grace of God wherein ye stand: It is better (with the RSV) to split it into two independent clauses: **This is the true grace of God; stand fast in it.** The grace Peter's readers had received at their conversion, and in the blessings of their subsequent Christian life, was no delusion (as in the face of persecution they might be tempted to imagine), but the genuine grace of God.

13. The church that is at Babylon is, literally, **she who is at Babylon** (RSV). **She** might just conceivably be Peter's wife, but is almost certainly the particular church which Peter represented at the time (cf. II John 13). And **Babylon** almost certainly does not here designate the famous city on the Euphrates (we have no evidence that Peter was ever there), but is, as in Revelation, a cryptic name for Rome.

Marcus my son: In a spiritual sense, of course. There is no reason to doubt that John Mark, the earliest evangelist, is meant. Col. 4:10 and Philem. 24 testify to his presence

---

et al.), add these final sentences? Since **Silvanus** had acted as Peter's secretary and was about to deliver the letter in person, he would hardly agree to writing his own commendation. He was a transparent amanuensis to his colleague, and the two worked together as a team. Writing for the "big fisherman" must have been difficult; but putting down Peter's declarations and exhortations must have been even more trying. How much the Christian faith owes to its secretaries, its writers, and its translators of the thoughts and experiences of others! Had it not been for Silvanus, how meager would be our direct testimony of Peter! And what the Christian faith owes to its couriers! Silvanus belongs to a vast company of faithful, genuine Christian brothers who have remained in the background and sought only to perform their responsibilities devotedly, sometimes under those less talented than themselves.

Exhorting and declaring belong together. Peter had declared the gospel of God's true grace, and he had exhorted his hearers to **stand fast in it** and live it out. The *kerygma* (message) and the *didachē* (ethical teaching) dare never be separated. The gospel is **the true grace**

of God; it is not the creation of man, nor is it at the mercy of "change and decay." Man's understanding of it may be fragmentary, and his trust in it may be meager. Therefore he needs to "grow in grace, and in the knowledge of our Lord and Saviour Jesus Christ" (II Pet. 3:18).

The church **at Babylon** sends greetings. The church exists even in Babylonian Rome. That church too is of the elect company of God's people. In that center of proud pagan culture and of far-flung political power Jesus Christ has his followers. His lordship is coming into its own even in that lordly metropolis. His city is in the making in that great city of man. And across the vast stretches of land and sea it greets others of God as fellow members of a common family. They are **elected together with** each other, not through anything human, but through the initiating mercy of God. Christian unity takes place between people of varied languages and customs and places. And that unity is realized only as Christians recognize their common "election" as children of God.

And so does my son Mark. How this young

14 Greet ye one another with a kiss of charity. Peace *be* with you all that are in Christ Jesus. Amen.

Mark. **14** Greet one another with the kiss of love.

Peace to all of you that are in Christ.

---

in Rome with Paul, and we know from Acts 12:12 ff., as from the testimony of Papias, that Peter and Mark were close friends and coadjutors.

14. Greet ye one another with a kiss of charity: Peter expects his readers, after they have heard his letter, to renew their fellowship with this loving token. Paul's phrase for it is "a holy kiss." The kiss of peace (*osculum pacis*) was a customary greeting among early church members. Later, owing to abuse, it was discontinued; but in the Western church it was customary at the Communion service until the thirteenth century, and in some of the Eastern and Western churches to this day it is retained in a modified form.

Peace be with you all that are in Christ Jesus: As Peter had begun his letter with a "peace be unto you," so now he ends it with another; only he adds the words **that are in Christ Jesus,** as if saying, "Peace be to you; but remember that true peace can be only to those who are firmly linked to Christ by faith, and linked to one another in that loving fellowship which is in the church."

---

man had traveled in terms of physical and spiritual distance! From a raw youth in whose mother's house the early Christians met, on through some rather strenuous missionary experiences with Paul and Silas, to "sonship" with Peter. And at last he writes the Gospel that bears his name but contains the memoirs of Peter. The gospel literally made individuals creative, and it effected an ecumenical fellow-ship. Witness here the **kiss** that was customary as a symbol of **love** and communion. In Did. 14:2 it would have been the sign of reconciliation between estranged Christians. That Judas used it indicates that it was customary among the disciples (Mark 14:44; Luke 7:45). By that token, to those **that are in Christ Jesus,** let there be peace! For he indeed is peace, between God and man, and between man and man.

The Second Epistle of

PETER

Introduction and Exegesis by ALBERT E. BARNETT
Exposition by ELMER G. HOMRIGHAUSEN

II PETER

INTRODUCTION

The author of II Peter was an ardent advocate of orthodoxy. Christian truth had been given authoritative conceptual formulation in the teaching of the founders of the church. This teaching supplied the only sound guidance for building Christian practice. False teachers were using membership in the church as a façade for the promotion of destructive heresies. The consequence of their error had been widespread licentiousness. Because of these pietistic but theologically unsound errorists, the way of truth had been defamed (2:2).

The author was no doctrinaire. He nevertheless believed that wholesome religious experience deserves and requires a sound theological and historical foundation. "Cleverly devised myths" may attract the uninstructed but will make no appeal to those who are "established in the truth." Possessing this stability, believers escape "the error of lawless men" (3:17) and become the beneficiaries of the promise that Christ will himself grant them "all things that pertain to life and godliness" (1:3-4).

I. Authorship

When Irenaeus (ca. A.D. 185) quoted words "said by Peter," he invariably had in mind passages from I Peter.[1] His introductory formula, "Peter says in his epistle," implies that he recognized only one epistle as by Peter. He may have known only one epistle under Peter's name. Conceivably, however, he knew II Peter but rejected its authenticity. Contemporary leaders in the West, such as the author of the Muratorian canon, Tertullian, and Cyprian were similarly silent regarding II Peter.

Clement of Alexandria was an Eastern contemporary of these Western leaders. Eusebius says that in his *Outlines* Clement gave "concise explanations of all the canonical scriptures," including "disputed" writings such as "Jude

and the remaining Catholic epistles, and the Epistle of Barnabas, and the Apocalypse known as Peter's.[2] His statement clearly implies an acquaintance with II Peter. Clement's extant writings, however, contain no quotations from II Peter and reflect no acquaintance with it.

The earliest explicit reference to II Peter is made by Origen (A.D. 217-51). He says that Peter "left only one epistle of acknowledged genuineness." Without trying to account for or refute current skepticism about the authenticity of a second epistle under Peter's name, he says simply, "This is doubtful."[3] Eusebius (ca. A.D. 325) included II Peter in his New Testament with the other Catholic epistles. He recognized, however, that its canonization was the outcome of its being "read in public in most churches" rather than the result of any certainty of its authorship by Peter. Only I Peter, he says, is recognized "as genuine and acknowledged by the elders of olden time." II Peter is used "along with the other scriptures," despite the tradition that "it was not canonical."[4] The judgment prevailing in the church caused Eusebius to describe II Peter, along with James, Jude, and the two shorter Johannine epistles, as "disputed, nevertheless familiar to the majority."[5]

Athanasius[6] and Augustine[7] both recognized II Peter as canonical. Neither says anything about its authenticity. Essentially the same position is taken by the third council of Carthage (A.D. 397). Jerome at about this time expressed the judgment that Peter "wrote two epistles which are called Catholic." Because of differences in style, however, he says that II Peter "is considered by many not to have been by him."[8]

The epistle names Peter as its author. Its mes-

---

[1] Cf. *Against Heresies* IV. 9. 2 (I Pet. 1:8); IV. 16. 5 (I Pet. 2:16); V. 7. 2 (I Pet. 1:8).

[2] *Church History* VI. 14. 1.
[3] *Commentary on John* V. 3.
[4] *Op. cit.* II. 23. 25; III. 3. 1, 4.
[5] *Op. cit.* III. 25. 3.
[6] *Festal Epistles* XXXIX. 5.
[7] *On Christian Doctrine* II. 8. 13.
[8] *On Famous Men* I.

sage is said to be from "Simon Peter, a servant and apostle of Jesus Christ" (1:1). This ascription is further emphasized by the author's allusion to Jesus' prediction of Peter's martyrdom (1:14; cf. John 21:18-19), his claim to have been with Jesus "on the holy mountain" on the occasion of the Transfiguration (1:17-18; cf. Matt. 17:5; Mark 9:7; Luke 9:35), and his implicit reference to I Peter as also written by him (3:1).

This zeal of the epistle for its own authenticity creates more doubt than confidence and other data fail to support its claim. Differences in style from I Peter create insuperable difficulties for the view that the two epistles have a common author. Although both are probably pseudonymous, a stronger case can be made for the authenticity of I Peter. The possibility of Petrine authorship is definitely eliminated by data which locate the second epistle in the second century: (a) the incorporation of Jude as its second chapter; (b) the author's implicit classification of himself with a generation to whom "the fathers" were known by tradition (3:2, 4); (c) the recognition of Paul's letters as scripture (3:16); (d) the allusion to heretical misuse of Paul's letters (3:16).

Because he felt he wrote in Peter's spirit, this unknown Christian leader of the second century felt justified in attributing what he wrote to Peter. That this was legitimate by current literary standards is shown by the titles of other second-century writings such as the Gospel of Peter, the Acts of Peter, the Teaching of Peter, and the Preaching of Peter. Peter symbolized original and authoritative Christianity. By his authority, therefore, our author condemned heresy.

II. Reading Public

The epistle is addressed "to those who have obtained a faith of equal standing" with the apostles "in the righteousness of our God and Savior Jesus Christ" (1:1). The first readers are further described as having received I Peter (3:1), and as belonging to the religious community in which Paul's letters were accorded the status of "the other scriptures" (3:16).

No local church was in the author's mind, nor was a particular group of churches. The heretical trends condemned are church wide, not local. Accordingly, the epistle is a message to Christendom. Its readers were any and all Christians to whose attention the little homily might come. The late and restricted use of the epistle reflected in early Christian literature and the difficulty with which it achieved a place in the canon of the New Testament suggest that its popularity and circulation prior to canonization were limited.

III. Date

That II Peter belongs to the middle of the second century is indicated by the historical situation reflected in its allusions and by the relatively extensive body of Christian literature with which it shows acquaintance. The author knew and accepted the tradition that Mark's Gospel was essentially Peter's.[9] He took for granted his readers' familiarity with the Synoptic account of the Transfiguration (1:17; cf. Matt. 17:5; Mark 9:7; Luke 9:35). His reference to Jesus' prophecy of Peter's martyrdom suggests an acquaintance with John 21, and therefore with the four Gospels as a published collection (1:14; cf. John 21:18-19), since John 21 was probably written at the time our four Gospels were published under the title of The Gospel (ca. A.D. 125). Paul's letters had also been collected and published, and our author and his readers revered them along with "the other scriptures" (3:16). The heretics who twisted Paul's letters "to their own destruction" could easily have been followers of Marcion (ca. A.D. 144). The author's severe attitude toward backsliders may well reflect familiarity with the impressively similar attitude of the author of Hebrews (2:20-21; cf. Heb. 6:4-8; 10:26-31). His acquaintance with Jude and I Peter is also clearly evident (2:1–3:1).

IV. Place of Composition

Such data as relate to the matter suggest Rome as the place of composition: the author's abhorrence of heresy, his irenic picture of the relations of Peter and Paul,[10] his reference to Peter's martyrdom (1:14), the suggestion that Peter collaborated with Paul in instructing the churches by means of letters.[11] The reference to Mark's Gospel as embodying Peter's message and as written to enable the church to recall after his death what he taught also tends to locate the epistle at Rome.[12] I Peter and Jude were Roman documents. Their strong influence on II Peter creates the probability of its origin at Rome. The data are not decisive, however, and the place of the origin of this epistle must remain uncertain.

V. Purpose

The author of II Peter was an ardently orthodox Christian of the middle of the second century. Peter epitomized for him the faith of the

---

[9] 1:15; cf. I Pet. 5:13; Eusebius op. cit. III. 39. 15.

[10] Cf. I Clem. 5:3-7; 6:1; Ign. Rom. 4:3; the Muratorian canon; Irenaeus Against Heresies III. 1. 1; Tertullian Scorpiace XV.

[11] 3:1, 15; cf. Heb. 5:12; I Clem. Salutation and 47:1-7.

[12] 1:15; cf. Irenaeus op. cit. III. 1. 1; Eusebius op. cit. II. 15. 2; III. 39. 15.

apostles. He had been aroused by the propaganda of false teachers, whose appearance Peter had foreseen and against whom he had forewarned the church (2:1). Because prophecy and apostolic teaching were the foundations of Christian stability, the author wrote for the purpose of arousing Christians generally to "remember the predictions of the holy prophets and the commandment of the Lord and Savior through your apostles" (3:2).

He finds in the author of Jude a kindred spirit and largely incorporates that epistle as the heart of his own manifesto. Like the earlier writer, he regards serious variation from traditional Christian beliefs as involving moral deterioration. The Old Testament, viewed as consummated in Christian revelation, and the traditional Christian message, understood as being the commandment of the Lord through the apostles, supplied the norms for orthodoxy (1:12-21; 2:21; 3:16). Abandonment of traditional teaching and morality proved the imminence of the day of the Lord.

The forms of heresy specifically protested against are rejection of the expectation of the Second Coming (3:3-7) and a perversion of Paul's teaching on freedom (3:16). Skepticism regarding the fundamentals of Christian tradition is the basic problem. Insistence on the Second Coming meant essentially the affirmation of belief in the validity of the traditional Christian message as against the cleverly devised myths of heretical leaders (1:16; 2:10). Adventism typified orthodoxy. II Peter stresses adventism because it stood for the original faith to which he felt fidelity was so imperative. The epistle is a plea for loyalty to the tenets of primitive Christianity. Heretical teachers have ridiculed certain of these emphases and distorted the meaning of others. The outcome has been the introduction into the church of "destructive heresies" ("destructive sects," Goodspeed). Those who "follow their licentiousness" face the threat of "swift destruction."

The traditional faith of the church, by contrast, provides guidance for the achievement of salvation. It embodies "all things that pertain to life and godliness." It plots a clear course for those who desire to "become partakers of the divine nature." Heretical speculations originate in "the impulse of man," not in the guidance of the Holy Spirit. Traditional Christianity, however, rests upon "the prophetic word" and "the commandment of the Lord and Savior" faithfully transmitted by the apostles.

The heresy explicitly attributed to the false teachers is disbelief in the Second Coming. Their skepticism, however, shows the nearness of the end. This gives compelling urgency to the plea that believers should "be zealous to be found by him without spot or blemish, and at peace."

VI. Outline of Contents

I. Salutation (1:1-2)
II. The traditional faith as the guide to salvation (1:3-21)
    A. Knowledge of Christ enables believers to appropriate his own glory and excellence (1:3-11)
        1. Christ entrusted the revelation to the apostles (1:3-4)
        2. Men must appropriate these truths (1:5-7)
        3. Guarantees of admission to Christ's kingdom (1:8-11)
    B. Peter's testimony to the truths of the apostolic message (1:12-21)
        1. Peter bequeaths a record of Christ's revelation (1:12-15)
        2. The apostolic record rests on eyewitness testimony (1:16-19a)
        3. The apostolic tradition embodies divine revelation (1:19b-21)
III. Instead of salvation, unorthodox teachers bring destruction (2:1-22)
    A. Heretics successors to the false prophets of the Old Testament (2:1-10a)
        1. Doctrinally unsound, morally corrupt (2:1-3)
        2. History foreshadows the doom of errorists (2:4-10a)
    B. The lawlessness of heretical teachers (2:10b-22)
        1. Lust and irreverence determine their behavior (2:10b-16)
        2. Their promised freedom is slavery to sin (2:17-22)
IV. Prophecy and tradition determine the duty of Christians (3:1-18)
    A. Orthodox Christianity supported by prophets and apostles (3:1-10)
        1. Criteria for the condemnation of heresy (3:1-2)
        2. The flood a type of the coming judgment (3:3-7)
        3. Psalm 90:4 supports belief in the Second Coming (3:8-10)
    B. The times require that Christians live worthily (3:11-18a)
        1. Certainty of the Parousia makes godliness a necessity (3:11-13)
        2. Paul's letters support the expectation of the Second Coming (3:14-18a)
V. Benediction (3:18b)

VII. Selected Bibliography

Bigg, Charles. *A Critical and Exegetical Commentary on the Epistles of St. Peter and St. Jude* ("International Critical Commentary"). New York: Charles Scribner's Sons, 1901.

Case, Shirley Jackson. "Second Peter," *The Abingdon Bible Commentary*, ed. F. C. Eiselen, Edwin Lewis, and D. G. Downey. New York and Nashville: Abingdon-Cokesbury Press, 1929.

LUMBY, J. RAWSON. *The Epistles of St. Peter* ("Expositor's Bible"). New York: A. C. Armstrong & Son, 1893.

MAYOR, J. B. *The Epistle of St. Jude and the Second Epistle of St. Peter.* London: Macmillan & Co., 1907.

MOFFATT, JAMES. *The General Epistles* ("Moffatt New Testament Commentary"). New York: Harper & Bros.; London: Hodder & Stoughton, 1928.

WAND, J. W. C. *The General Epistles of St. Peter* New Testament Commetnary"). New York: Harper & Bros.; London: Hodder & Stoughton, 1928.

II PETER

TEXT, EXEGESIS, AND EXPOSITION

Authorship and Christian Truth.—The arguments for and against the Petrine authorship of this letter are carefully set forth in the Exeg., above. There are some weighty names on both sides of the controversy. They have conscientiously examined the tone, style, vocabulary, and Christian truth contained in the epistle. And they have compared the situation out of which it emerged in the light of that which is presupposed in I Peter. About all these important matters the preacher and teacher ought to know. Honest scholarship and honest exposition go together. There is a close association between the truth about authorship and the authority of the truth in Christianity. The chief question we must ask ourselves about II Peter is: Does definite Petrine authorship alone establish the truth which II Peter seeks to convey? If the answer is affirmative then this piece of literature, of all that is contained in the Bible, will have to be used with great caution.

However, II Peter is in the Bible! It is in the canon, or list of approved writings regarded by the church as the word of God. And it is so in spite of the fact that no other N.T. writing won so limited and hesitating a recognition.[1] It did communicate something which to the mind of the church was in harmony with the whole word of God. It revealed aspects of the nature of Jesus Christ, of the holiness of truth, of the character of the true church, and of the dangers involved in the perversion or distortion of gospel truth which, if deleted from the Bible, would leave something to be desired.

John Dow puts it this way:

But the pseudonymous letter is not a discredited document. Its truth remains just as the wisdom put in the mouth of Shakespeare's characters remains. It is an endeavor to capture and preserve the Petrine faith and tradition and to keep alive sound doctrine and wholesome Christian living in an age when agnostic heresies and other corrupting philosophies were abroad. It breathes Christ and awaits his consummation.[2]

And John Calvin writes: "The doubts respecting this Epistle mentioned by Eusebius, ought not to keep us from reading it." He continues by saying that "it has nothing unworthy of Peter, as it shews everywhere the power and the grace of an apostolic spirit . . . ; not that he himself wrote it, but that some one of his disciples set forth in writing by his command, those things which the necessity of the times required." Calvin believed that in his old age Peter may have "allowed this testimony of his mind to be recorded" for those Christians who wished it, so that when he was dead the good might be supported and the wicked suppressed in his apostolic name. So Calvin wrote his *Commentary* by allowing himself "the liberty of using the word Peter or Apostle indiscriminately."[3]

No fraud or fiction is involved in such a conception of the authorship of II Peter. Pseudonymity was a device whereby the spirit and perhaps the funded wisdom of some widely recognized and highly esteemed person were used to proclaim truth with authority. What we have in this letter may not be from the actual hand or the immediate dictation of Peter the apostle, but what we have is Petrine in character and spirit. The situation to which the letter is directed is different from that which obtained when I Peter was written, but the new situation would inevitably involve somewhat different emphases regarding the Christian message.

[1] James Moffatt, *The General Epistles* (New York: Harper & Bros.; London: Hodder & Stoughton, 1928; "Moffatt New Testament Commentary"), p. 175.

[2] In *The Speaker's Bible*, ed. James Hastings, *et al.* (Aberdeen: Speaker's Bible Offices, 1924), I and II Peter, p. 307.

[3] *Commentary on the Second Epistle of Peter*, tr. John Owen (Edinburgh: Calvin Translation Society, 1855), pp. 363-64.

1 Simon Peter, a servant and an apostle of Jesus Christ, to them that have obtained like precious faith with us through the righteousness of God and our Saviour Jesus Christ:

1 Simon Peter, a servant and apostle of Jesus Christ,
To those who have obtained a faith of equal standing with ours in the righteousness of our God and Savior Jesus Christ:[a]

[a] Or *of our God and the Savior Jesus Christ.*

I. SALUTATION (1:1-2)

II Peter, like Jude, is addressed to Christians as such, without reference to their place of residence. In the salutation the author accredits himself, designates his audience, and prays for the multiplication to them of the blessings of **grace and peace.**

1:1. The author presents himself as **Simon Peter, a servant and apostle of Jesus Christ.** "Symeon" rather than "Simon" is a possible rendering. (Sinaiticus and Alexandrinus read "Symeon," but Vaticanus reads "Simon.") Elsewhere in the N.T. Symeon is used of Peter only in the reply of James of Jerusalem when Barnabas and Paul gave the church an account of their missionary labors (Acts 15:14). Symeon is regularly used in the LXX and appears five times in the N.T. with no reference to Peter. Simon is a Hellenized rendering of Symeon and is first found in relatively late Jewish books (Ecclus. 50:1 [180-175 B.C.]; I Macc. 15:24 [125-100 B.C.]). On the basis of strong textual support for Symeon, and because of the historical improbability that Simon would be altered to Symeon, interpreters like J. B. Mayor and Charles Bigg accept Symeon as original and regard it as a convincing credential of authenticity. The more Jewish form of the name represents for them Peter's resumption in old age of the name familiar to his youth. Acceptance of the textual accuracy of Symeon does not, however, require this interpretation. It would more probably represent an aspect of the pseudonymity of the letter. The author clearly wishes to be identified with the author of I Peter (cf. 3:1-2). The use of

So, regardless of the authorship of the document, we are confronted with an actual epistle which is a part of the canon. Though its authorship has been debated by competent scholars and unquestioned Christians it has stood the test of use by generations. It speaks about matters which were once dangerous to the Christian faith, and are dangerous still. It calls attention to the subtle ways by which the Christian heritage may be sabotaged by the infiltration of those who denature the faith of its normative historical content. It warns about the devastating effects of divorcing the gospel from ethics. And it exalts the lordship of Jesus Christ in all his majesty and power.

1:1a. The Christian Leader's Credentials.— The writer mentions three basic aspects of his life and status to impress upon the readers his right to address them humanly, sympathetically, and authoritatively on matters of Christian faith and conduct. First, he identifies himself as a real man by the name of **Simon.** And to identify himself more concretely, he uses the familiar Jewish name by which he was known ("Symeon," Moffatt) to his kin and friends. He wishes to be known as that Simon the son of Jonas, the hard-working fisherman, the unvarnished, human, faithful Jew, born a member of the Old Covenant. To be a Christian is first of all to be a man, one who has a name that identifies him with a time, a place, a people, and a religion.

Second, he wishes to be known as a "slave" of Christ. Like those whom he was addressing, he was not his own since the love of Christ had claimed him in body, mind, and soul. Christ was his master and lord. The Christian's enslavement to Christ Jesus, however, is not a surrender to annihilation but a release into true humanity. It is death that leads to life. To belong to Christ is not extinction but resurrection, not degradation but exaltation.

Make me a captive, Lord,
  And then I shall be free;
Force me to render up my sword,
  And I shall conqueror be.

. . . . . .

My heart is weak and poor
  Until it master find;
It has no spring of action sure—
  It varies with the wind.

It cannot freely move
  Till Thou hast wrought its chain;
Enslave it with Thy matchless love,
  And deathless it shall reign.[4]

[4] George Matheson. Used by permission of McClure Naismith, Brodie & Co.

167

Symeon rather than Simon contributes to that identification. The precedent of Acts 15:14 also gives verisimilitude to the author's pose as protagonist of apostolic orthodoxy.

Jude introduces himself as "a servant of Jesus Christ" (vs. 1). The author of I Peter writes as "an apostle of Jesus Christ" (1:1). Both letters are consciously in the mind of the author of II Peter, and he understandably combines their phrases in designating himself as **a servant and apostle of Jesus Christ** (for **servant** see Exeg. on Jude 1). **Apostle** is used in the strict sense and suggests that the author was one of the twelve. The correlation of servant and apostle calls attention to a primary emphasis of the author. **Servant** describes the relationship which faith establishes between all Christians and Christ as Lord (2:1; cf. I Cor. 7:22; Eph. 6:6; Col. 4:12; II Tim. 2:24; I Pet. 2:16; Rev. 1:1; 2:20; 7:3; 10:7; 19:2, 5; 22:3, 6). Each of the twelve as a Christian was a servant of Jesus Christ. By describing himself as **servant and apostle,** the author identifies himself religiously with his readers and at the same time claims authority for what he writes. This collocation of terms prepares for the assertion that readers of the epistle have **obtained a faith of equal standing** with that of the apostles. Faith is thus more important than official status and is made the credential for such authority as the official exercises. The humblest believer enjoys a relationship to Christ equal in saving effectiveness to that sustained by Jesus' first associates.

The addressees of the epistle are **those who have obtained a faith of equal standing with ours.** The faith of Christians generally is described as obtained, as being of equal standing with that of the apostles, as owing the impartiality of its benefits to **the righteousness of our God and Savior Jesus Christ.** Each of these affirmations about the faith of every Christian requires exposition.

In II Peter faith means primarily the truths that compose the message of salvation proclaimed by the apostles. These truths must be believed and relied on, however; and faith accordingly has the secondary meaning of the receptivity of spirit that causes men to accept and to be governed by the gospel. **Obtained** applies to both aspects of faith. The truths constituting the apostolic message were originally obtained from Christ and were passed on to subsequent generations by the apostles. The inward grace to believe and rely on these truths is individually obtained by persons from Christ, whose "divine power" grants a man "all things that pertain to life and godliness" (vs. 3). It is in effect their "call and election" (vs. 10; cf. Eph. 2:8-10).

Ours refers to the apostles, not to Jewish Christians. The author is concerned with the relationship of ordinary Christians to the apostles. Their faith is **of equal standing.** Men of faith neither wish nor enjoy precedence over one another. But faith of equal standing must be of standard quality. A faith at variance with apostolic standards would

---

Tiro was the slave of Cicero. That fact gave him a reputation and a name. He understood his master, was fond of him, and served him with enthusiasm. He really became great through his relationship with the great Cicero. Enslavement to the highest and best is a creative and regenerative [5] experience.

Third, the writer calls himself an **apostle.** He is a member of that inner circle who were associated with Jesus. He has a unique authority. Simon (Symeon) Peter is a combination of names that illustrates the history of the Christian life: The first indicates his pre-Christian state, the second indicates the new character which has been given him by his Lord and Savior. In a real sense, Symeon Peter is every Christian's name: He is both "old" pre-Christian

[5] See T. R. Glover, *The Disciple* (Cambridge: Cambridge University Press, 1942).

historical man and "new" Christ-man who is like every Christian, whatsoever the accident of his racial and national past.

1b. Our Common, Given, and Precious Faith. —Peter, one of Jesus' inner circle, courteously puts himself on the plane of his readers. He does not say "you" and "mine," but **those** and **ours.** Venerable as his name would be to those who received his letter, he breaks down the barrier between clergy and laity, between Gentile and Jewish Christians, between apostle and simple believer. Peter, in spite of being an apostle, and in spite of having a more developed faith, was the recipient of the same kind of faith which was given to those whom he addressed. There is no place for classes in the Christian household, nor is there any reason for making a distinction between the Christian faith of clergy and laity, of Christians at home

not be of equal standing. In the preservation and faithful transmission of the Christian message the apostles rendered later generations a service of great importance. The value of that message is undiminished by the passage of time. Only "false teachers" will regard it as outmoded and antiquated. Orthodoxy as represented in this message constitutes the only sure guide for distinctively Christian religious experience. Because of their service in this respect, the apostles deserve the reverence in which the church holds them. Those who "despise" their "authority," therefore, are properly kept "under punishment until the day of judgment" (2:9). The present epistle is itself written to cause men always to "remember . . . the commandment of the Lord and Savior through your apostles" (3:2). They invite "swift destruction" who follow the "destructive heresies" of "false teachers" (2:1).

The **equal standing** of the faith of Christians is due to **the righteousness of . . . Jesus Christ,** who for believers is both **God and Savior. The righteousness of . . . Jesus Christ** describes him as being completely impartial in dealing with men. Call and election (vs. 10) are from him, but favoritism never affects his relationships with men. Salvation is planned for all men. God, as Christ reveals him, desires that all men believe and rely on the gospel. The common faith of Christians is of equal value for all who share it. Those who meet the conditions embodied in the apostolic message obtain **a faith of equal standing** because of the impartiality of Christ in his bestowal of blessing and in his judgment of worth.

Our God and Savior Jesus Christ (RSV) is significantly different from the more familiar reading, **God and our Saviour Jesus Christ** (KJV; ASV, Goodspeed, Moffatt, and R. A. Knox, along with ERV, support the reading of RSV). In the one instance one person is mentioned, in the other, two. The problem of correct rendering is both textual and historical. The reading of the KJV is based on MSS that show the definite article before both "God" and "Saviour." The critical texts of Nestle and of Westcott and Hort

---

and Christians abroad, or between Christians of Jewish extraction and of Gentile background whatever the color of their skin or the language they speak. Peter, like many a Christian after him, had learned his lesson through the manifestation of the Spirit of God at work in people he once thought unclean. At some Joppa (cf. Acts 10) every Christian has been initiated into a common faith. This is the secret of Christian fellowship.

But this faith is something given. It is obtained as a divine gift, and not attained as an acquired skill. The first can come only *to* us, the latter can be developed *out* of us. This faith and the life that it effects is "obtained by lot," or "allotted" to us (Moffatt). It is an offer **in the righteousness of our God,** or in the equity or impartiality of God, in his great generosity which shows no favoritism. The apostle Paul refused to boast about his Christian experience; he wrote, "Let him who boasts, boast of the Lord" (I Cor. 1:31). Paul regarded Christ as "the source of your life in Christ Jesus" (I Cor. 1:30).

This faith is in a Person. And that Person is both God and Savior; he is both man (Jesus) and God (Christ). The strong phrase **in the righteousness of our God** is found only here in the N.T., although it is implied throughout the Christology of the N.T. (see the observation

of Thomas, John 20:28). When II Peter was written the church's faith was becoming more clearly defined. The important fact is that both the faith and the fruits of "life and godliness" (vs. 3) which it brings are rested deep in a person-to-person relationship of love and trust between Jesus Christ and the believer. Alexander Maclaren writes that had Christianity taken this truth seriously, it

would have been delivered from mountains of misconception, and many a poor soul would have felt that a blaze of light had come in upon it. . . . The object of trust is the living Person, Jesus Christ, and . . . the trust which grapples us to Him is essentially a personal relation entered into by our wills and hearts far more than by our heads.[6]

As we are vitally related to Christ, his righteousness may indeed become ours, not through a mechanical "imputation" but through a living trust. The righteousness of God is given to us in Christ Jesus through faith.

Such faith is **precious.** The word occurs often in the letters of Peter. Precious to the writer of the First Epistle is the "trial of faith," the "blood of Christ"; precious to the writer of the Second Epistle is the **faith,** the "exceeding great

[6] Alexander Maclaren, *Expositions of Holy Scripture* (New York: George H. Doran, 1915), I and II Peter and I John, p. 172.

2 Grace and peace be multiplied unto you through the knowledge of God, and of Jesus our Lord,

2 May grace and peace be multiplied to you in the knowledge of God and of Jesus our Lord.

show the definite article only once, before "God." In four other instances II Peter uses the definite article once with two nouns clearly referring to Jesus (vs. 11; 2:20; 3:2, 18). If the text accepted as correct in the present instance shows the article only once, the author's customary usage would require that it refer to Jesus as our God and Savior. In addition to strictly textual evidence, two arguments favor the RSV reading: (a) if two persons are meant, the reader is left uncertain whose righteousness accounts for the equal standing of the faith of all Christians; (b) the tendency to call Jesus Christ "God" became increasingly widespread from the end of the first century onward—e.g., convinced of the reality of the Resurrection, Thomas addresses Jesus, "My Lord and my God" (John 20:28); Ignatius of Antioch (in the salutation to his letter to the Ephesians) uses the phrase "Jesus Christ our God," and in the same letter refers to Mary as having conceived "our God, Jesus Christ" (18:2); the author of the Pastoral epistles thinks of Christians as awaiting their "blessed hope, the appearing of the glory of our great God and Savior Jesus Christ" (Tit. 2:11-13; cf. I Clem. 1:1). The fact that "God" and "Jesus our Lord" are clearly distinguished in vs. 2 does not reduce the probability that the reading in vs. 1 which describes Jesus Christ as our God and Savior is original. Ignatius salutes "the church . . . at Ephesus in Asia" as "united and chosen through true suffering by the will of the Father and Jesus Christ our God."

2. In the knowledge of God and of Jesus our Lord is the distinctive addition of II Peter to the formulas of I Peter and Jude. The point seems to be that grace and peace are multiplied within the sphere designated as the knowledge of God and of Jesus our Lord. Knowledge (ἐπίγνωσις) is one of the primary emphases in this epistle. The word occurs here and in 1:3, 8; 2:20. Elsewhere in the N.T. it is found nine times in Paul's letters, twice in Ephesians, once in Hebrews, and four times in the Pastorals. Interpreters of equal competence differ as to whether ἐπίγνωσις and γνῶσις, both translated "knowledge," express significant shades of meaning. J. B. Lightfoot argues that ἐπίγνωσις denotes "a larger and more thorough knowledge" than γνῶσις. He is convinced that Paul employs the terms to contrast complete with partial knowledge (Rom. 1:21, 28; I Cor. 13:12). By ἐπίγνωσις he thinks Paul designates "the goal and crown of the believer's

and precious promises" (vs. 4). Here faith is precious because it is the channel through which all the wonderful riches of God are made available to the believer. As a city regards its aqueducts precious because through them its life-giving water is supplied, so is faith precious to the Christian. The isolated city of Berlin depended utterly upon the airlift at the time of the blockade in 1948. How precious to its people was the hum of airplane motors going and coming day and night. So precious is the life line of faith to the believer. Faith is the one essential means of receiving the gift of life. Paul calls it a "shield," and Peter in his Jerusalem address regarded it as the means by which God purified men's hearts. Indeed, Peter continues (vss. 5-6) by saying that out of faith all the virtues and graces of life flow.

Faith in Jesus Christ is precious only to those who know what it brings to life and what it makes of life. It brings another world into this. It brings the unseen into the seen.

2. Grace and Peace Be Multiplied.—No one is born into a mature Christian life in an instant. This vast world of possibility which Christ has opened up for us is something into which we grow; its glories are multiplied in us through that peculiar knowledge of God, and of Jesus our Lord. And the chief realities of that dimension of life are grace and peace. Grace is the greatest word in the N.T. and in the human vocabulary. It is distinctively Christian, for while the Greeks knew the aesthetic meaning of grace and graces and graciousness, they never applied it to the God in whom men live and move and have their being. The real meaning of grace came through Jesus, in whom grace was seen in act, heard in speech, and observed in personality. To grow in the grace of God in Christ is to come into an increasing experience of the fact that God is good and that he wills the highest well-being of all people. This grace creates peace—a deep sense of blessedness in the soul. It provides that essential assurance

3 According as his divine power hath given unto us all things that *pertain* unto life and godliness, through the knowledge of him that hath called us to glory and virtue:

3 His divine power has granted to us all things that pertain to life and godliness, through the knowledge of him who called us to[b] his own glory and excellence,

[b] Or *by*.

---

course," which consists in "the complete appropriation of all truth and the unreserved identification with God's will." It signifies in his judgment the "perfection of knowledge," especially the knowledge of God. (*Saint Paul's Epistles to the Colossians and to Philemon* [rev. ed.; London: Macmillan & Co.], p. 137; *Saint Paul's Epistle to the Philippians* [rev. ed.; London: Macmillan & Co., 1894], p. 86.) In the comment on Rom. 10:2, Sanday and Headlam express the judgment that Lightfoot's definition of ἐπίγνωσις leaves "nothing to add." The term means, they say, "a higher and more perfect knowledge, and hence is used especially and almost technically for knowledge of God, as being the highest and most perfect form." (*The Epistle to the Romans* [New York: Charles Scribner's Sons, 1920], pp. 46, 81, 283; cf. Archibald Robertson and Alfred Plummer, *The First Epistle of St Paul to the Corinthians* [New York: Charles Scribner's Sons, 1911], p. 299.) J. Armitage Robinson, on the other hand, defines ἐπίγνωσις as "knowledge directed towards a particular object, perceiving, discerning, recognizing," in distinction from γνῶσις, which is knowledge "in the abstract." (*St Paul's Epistle to the Ephesians* [London: Macmillan & Co., 1903], pp. 248-54. "The evidence of the papyri" is said by J. H. Moulton and George Milligan to bear out Robinson's definition; see *The Vocabulary of the Greek Testament* [London: Hodder & Stoughton, 1914-19], Part III, p. 236.) Both shades of meaning were conceivably in the author's mind. With God or Christ as the object, all of the powers of personality are engaged in the attainment of knowledge, with the result that knowledge profounder than human intelligence achieves is possessed. Revelation also contributes to the completeness of such knowledge.

II. The Traditional Faith as the Guide to Salvation (1:3-21)

A. Knowledge of Christ Enables Believers to Appropriate His Own Glory and Excellence (1:3-11)

Vss. 3-7 show how the knowledge of Christ actually works. On the one hand, Christ's divine power committed to the apostles the truths that have to do with salvation (vss. 3-4). On the other, what was thus bestowed must be appropriated and developed by human effort (vss. 5-7). The two aspects of the functioning of **knowledge** form the basis of the present comment and that which follows it.

1. Christ Entrusted the Revelation to the Apostles (1:3-4)

3-4. Us, like "ours" (vs. 1), refers to the apostles. Simon Peter, speaking in his dual role as servant and apostle of Jesus Christ, describes the apostles as the recipients of a

---

about the ultimacy of God's love and purpose which removes the enervating anxiety that eventually consumes and frustrates life.

The writer prays a great prayer for his readers. Perhaps this is the highest form of intercessory prayer. For if one has an assured inner knowledge of God's grace which makes for peace, he has God's greatest boon and life's best possession.

3-4. All Things We Need.—(*a*) Has God provided man everything necessary to live the good life? The N.T. answers, "Yes!" It strikes the positive note. It may tell us that we "see through a glass, darkly" (I Cor. 13:12) and that

we know only "in part" (I Cor. 13:9), but it never despairs of life's possibilities or disparages the resources that are available for the living of the godly, the reverent, the truly human life. The Bible may stress the dark nature of God's judgment; even more it stresses the promising nature of God's will to give men fullness of life. These **things** have been granted to everyone in superabundance; God has done more than we can "ask or think" (Eph. 3:20). We are dealing here with a love that passes knowledge and with a generous power to share that beggars description. Our God is no stingy deity begrudging anything he may give his children; he is lavish be-

revelation from Christ. This revelation became the content of the apostolic message, "the commandment of the Lord and Savior through your apostles" (3:2). "A faith of equal standing" (vs. 1) with that of the fathers, who long ago "fell asleep" (3:4), is the heritage of subsequent generations. The service of the apostles lay in their faithful transmission of the truth, the "splendid trust" (Goodspeed), of which Christ made them custodians (II Tim. 1:14). Christ, who called the apostles, calls his followers in later times, and **his divine power** impartially grants them **all things that pertain to life and godliness, through the knowledge** of himself.

Two considerations show that Christ, not God, is spoken of in vs. 3. **Knowledge** is of Christ (vss. 2, 8), and persons **called** will be "provided . . . an entrance into the eternal kingdom of . . . Jesus Christ" (vs. 11). **Divine power** is exercised by Christ because he is our God as well as Savior (vs. 1).

The knowledge of himself is the means by which Christ grants believers **all things that pertain to life and godliness** (cf. Col. 1:9-12). This knowledge is both historical and mystical. It has to do with the Jesus of history and the Christ of faith. The life Jesus lived on earth was a divine self-manifestation. Through it God's character and his will for men were revealed. The message of the apostles reported this revelation. Under the guidance of that message, believers achieve an inward, mystical knowledge of Christ. By moral and spiritual fellowship with Christ men **become partakers of the divine nature.** The importance and authority of apostolic tradition grow out of the guidance it affords for the experience of this inward fellowship with Christ and the profound knowledge of him in which it issues. The destructive heresies of false teachers (2:1) bring swift destruction, not saving knowledge.

Life and godliness are elements in the religious development of believers that find parallels in the **glory and excellence** of Christ. The glory and excellence of Christ are shared by men as life and godliness. By means of a saving knowledge of Christ, **his divine**

---

yond understanding. All that a person really wants for life and of life God has granted to men by his divine, self-generated power. Best of all, he has freely given *himself* so that all men may be filled with the fullness of God. What more could God give us for the living of life to the full? What more can he give than himself in Christ?

(b) How does God call us into the good life? He **called us to** [by] **his own glory and excellence.** God is not a passive Being silently contemplating himself; he is an aggressive God of energy who by his very nature is continually seeking and calling men. "He did not leave himself without witness" (Acts 14:17). He has made man restless until he rests in God. He has endowed nature with signs of his power and his providential presence. In Christ Jesus he came to seek and to save those who were lost from their relationship with him, and thus were lost to life. In Christ, the Light shone into the darkness. The life that was in him was the light of men. That light is an energetic power; and the darkness did not put it out.

How does God call men? Through nature, conscience, and historical event. They witness, and so compel men to recognize the glory and energy of God that infills all things. But the glory and virtue of God as seen in Jesus Christ are the most potent preachers; they arrest men

and challenge them by a new quality of life. The glory and the virtue they see in him shame them out of their pseudo life and call them into the life they know to be the life. **Glory** and **virtue** are still God's angels summoning men to himself. Who can describe glory? It was the supernatural light that was upon the cherubim and lay upon the ark and the mercy seat. The glory of God is "the irradiation and the perpetual pouring out and out and out from Himself, as the rays of the sun stream out from its great orb, pouring out from Himself the light and the perfectness and the beauty of His own self revelation." [7] The glory of God is the splendor of God shedding itself abroad in the delicacy of love. God rayed out his pure self in such fullness in Christ that John wrote, "We beheld his glory, . . . full of grace and truth" (John 1:14).

The **virtue** of God is the energy of God. Plants are said to possess "virtues," powers of healing or of death. Jesus Christ not only revealed the glory of God, he also possessed power over himself, over nature, and over others. On one occasion someone touched his garment and he said that virtue (energy) had gone out of him. He was possessed of power; by it he performed signs and wonders; by it he spoke with authority; by it he forgave sins; by it he healed

[7] Maclaren, *op. cit.*, pp. 180-81.

4 Whereby are given unto us exceeding great and precious promises; that by these ye might be partakers of the divine nature, having escaped the corruption that is in the world through lust.

4 by which he has granted to us his precious and very great promises, that through these you may escape from the corruption that is in the world because of passion, and be-

---

power endows them with moral and spiritual effectiveness. Qualities of newness and eternity characterize the lives of all who enjoy inward fellowship with **him who called us to his own glory and excellence** (cf. John 17:3).

The glory and excellence of Christ compose the goal toward which believers strive with the aid of his divine power. **Glory** includes all attributes that definitely show Jesus' divine sonship. The apostles who were with Christ on the holy mountain were eyewitnesses of his majesty, or glory (vss. 16-18). **Glory** is an equivalent for **the divine nature,** fully revealed by Jesus; but men may also share in it. Believers, other than the apostles, may behold the glory of the Lord and thereby be progressively changed into his likeness, a metamorphosis brought to pass not by their own unassisted effort, but "from the Lord who is the Spirit" (II Cor. 3:18; cf. Rom. 8:29; I Cor. 11:7; 15:49; Eph. 4:24; Col. 3:10). **Excellence** or **virtue** is the moral goodness implicit in glory. The emphasis on the moral content of glory distinguished orthodox Christianity from heretical teaching. The moral energy involved in glory finds expression in the ways enumerated in vss. 5-7. In their effort to approximate the glory and excellence of Christ, believers are saved from a sense of futility by their experience of the availability of Christ's assistance (cf. II Cor. 3:18).

---

the sick; by it he restored men to their rightful selves; by it his whole ministry was marked; and by it he was raised from the dead.

From what we know of the nature of light, we can say that it has both a glory and a power. It issues from one great source, the sun. There is no mightier physical power on earth than that of the sun; yet it works quietly and silently and surely as it summons men to life and labor each new day, even as it summons the dormant life of nature into new being at springtime. God in a greater sense calls and beckons men to himself by raying out his glories and energizing beauty, truth, and goodness. And so adequate and perfect are his glory and virtue in Jesus Christ that to the sincere they utterly satisfy the deep needs of hearts, minds, and spirits. No doubt Peter was fascinated and at last captured by the grace and virtue of him who one day passed and said, "Follow me." He could not help responding. When others left off following Jesus at the close of his ministry, it was Peter who said, "To whom shall we go? thou hast the words of eternal life" (John 6:68). He might have added, "Where, in whom, can we find such glory and such virtue?"

Indeed the highest form of divine glory is radiated from Jesus Christ. He is very light of very light, the express image of God's self. And Christ Jesus is the virtue, the healing power of God in its most available and highest form. To as many as "receive" him, he still gives the "power" to become the sons of God. It is the church's high vocation so to present the glory

and the virtue of Jesus Christ that men may behold and welcome his redeeming work in their lives.

(c) And what does God give to those who respond to his call? Through his **great and precious promises** which have been fulfilled and confirmed in Christ Jesus, the Christian now has an escape from the corruption of worldly passion which disintegrates and ruins life, and a power to partake of the very nature of God. The three great words in this statement are: **Promises, escaped, partakers.** In a true sense they are essential aspects of the Christian faith: (i) God's revelation of himself through hopeful and redeeming promises and their fulfillment; (ii) man's escape from the power of perverted desires and their damning effects; and (iii) participation in the very life and purpose of God.

A promise is an assurance given by someone to another. He who promises has the power to fulfill, and he who is to receive waits with anticipation. In a real sense, men live by promises! Life is perennially unfulfilled. If this is so on the lower levels, how much more true is it on the highest? God has created deep yearnings in the human spirit. He has given men promises about satisfying these yearnings. Little wonder then that Peter refers to the promises of God as **exceeding great and precious.** They are of inestimable value in buoying up and "enhoping" the spirit of man. The promises to which he refers are assurance of forgiveness and of eternal life: all those things that **pertain** to man's com-

They alone participate in God's nature who, through Christ's promises, **escape from the corruption that is in the world because of passion. Corruption** denotes a condition in human life just the reverse of participation in the divine nature. Decomposition such as the physical body undergoes after burial is the literal meaning of the term. Here it connotes moral deterioration and the consequent forfeiture of immortality. This corruption consists in and results from **passion** (ἐπιθυμία). **Passion, or lust,** signifies desire for the forbidden (cf. Rom. 7:7-8; Gal. 5:16; Col. 3:5; Jas. 1:14-15) and is constantly under condemnation (2:10, 18; 3:3). The government of life by sexual appetite causes corruption and the forfeiture of life. All who believe in and rely on "destructive heresies" (2:1) instead of "the commandment of the Lord . . . through [the] apostles" (3:2) experience corruption.

The **precious and very great promises** invite men to become **partakers of the divine nature** (cf. I John 3:2). By the appropriation of the gifts immediately bestowed by Christ the granting of surpassingly **precious** gifts is guaranteed. Moral victory and immortality are assured. Stoicism taught that all men were automatically partakers of the divine nature. The various mystery cults proposed by liturgical acts and emotional

---

plete salvation. The promises of God have been confirmed in history by the ministry of Jesus Christ and implemented by the power of God's life-giving and indwelling Spirit.

Karl Marx called religion an opiate. He regarded it not only as a drug which anesthetizes the agonized human spirit and desensitizes it to social injustice and personal anxiety; he, like some psychologists, also regarded it as an escape, a mechanism by which man isolates himself from this evil world, whether through mystical piety, rational orthodoxy, aesthetic liturgism, sentimental idealism, or unworldly monasticism. There is a measure of truth in the accusation. Some kinds of escape are immoral; they are the practices of an abnormal religion. However, there is an escape involved in being a Christian; it is an escape from the corrupting and degrading and ruining powers of unholy lust and diabolical desires. Human nature without God in it is subject to decay. This realistic view of the absolute corrupting power of godless living is taken only by those who know the contrasting, powerful, godly living which actually saves life from death. There is no salvation in trying to escape the world. We never escape from the "world in lust" by some miraculous once for all act; we must escape it through continual struggle. Only by a growing, fuller participation in the divine nature can the Christian succeed in escaping the lust that is in the world which the Christian inhabits.

That we can be partakers of the divine nature is a rather bold affirmation. Yet the N.T. makes clear that believers do experience a life of communion with God through the Spirit. Of all the religions of the world, Christianity is unique in this: It exalts the eternity, infinity, and unchangeableness of God; but it also elevates lowly, finite, space-bound, sinful humanity to the level of union with God himself. It is God who has made it possible for persons to partake of his nature. To partake of God's **nature** does not mean to become absorbed into deity, as some mystical religions hold. This would dissolve personal identity and make communion between the I and Thou impossible. Rather it means an intimate relation with God's Spirit: his moral character, his holy purpose, his saving love, his healing light, his yearning concern for justice, his suffering compassion, his pure righteousness, his victorious and universal rule. In this sense, the Christian life is not an imitation of Christ, as though he were a sort of copybook pattern. In one of our hymns we sing, "Thy nature, gracious Lord, impart. . . ." [8] We partake of Christ's **nature.** We do not take Christ as an external model; we receive him as an internal power. Paul put it thus: "I live; yet not I, but Christ liveth in me" (Gal. 2:20). He had experienced a participation in or vital communion with Christ. Three phrases in I and II Peter bring out the same idea: **Partakers of the divine nature** (vs. 4); "partakers of Christ's sufferings" (I Pet. 4:13); and "partaker of the glory that shall be revealed" (I Pet. 5:1). A Christian has a nature in common with Christ: he suffers in common with Christ; and he will partake of a glory in common with Christ.

Yet, in all this, he is "becoming"; he **has** not yet arrived. As the energy and light of the sun are ever given and never possessed apart from the central source, so the Christian is ever growing and becoming as he receives the gifts of God's love. The Christian does not possess the divine nature; he continually partakes of it.

(*d*) The divine call to life and the divine gifts for life are received **through the knowledge of him.** To be sure, this knowledge has to do with historical facts; but it has more to do with

[8] Charles Wesley, "O for a heart to praise my God," st. v.

5 And besides this, giving all diligence, add to your faith virtue; and to virtue, knowledge;

come partakers of the divine nature. 5 For this very reason make every effort to supplement your faith with virtue, and virtue

---

experiences to enable men to become such partakers. With these pagan conceptions in mind our author insists that by the knowledge of Christ and the consequent sharing of his own glory and excellence believers become partakers of the divine nature. He has in mind essentially what Paul called "participation in the Spirit" (Phil. 2:1; cf. II Cor. 13:14).

2. MEN MUST APPROPRIATE THESE TRUTHS (1:5-7)

Appropriation of Christ's promises requires **effort** on the part of men. The character of this effort is specified in vss. 5-7.

5. Human **effort** must expand what Christ's divine power grants. **For this very reason** refers to the desirability of taking the steps required for fulfillment in the experience of individuals of the promises of Christ. **Faith** is fundamental. The seven qualities enumerated in vss. 5-7 **supplement** it. Here, as in vs. 1, faith involves right belief. It has ripened into conviction, however, and supplies motivation and guidance for action (cf. Heb. 11:1, 3). Because apostolic tradition embodies the commandment of the Lord (3:1), believers must know and accept that tradition. Only so can they follow the way of truth (2:2). This is negatively illustrated by the fact that they who adopt destructive heresies usually become licentious (2:1-2). Faith as defined in apostolic teaching is thus required of all who desire to share Christ's blessings.

But **faith** produces fruits, **virtue, knowledge, self-control,** etc. To alter the figure, these are a superstructure reared on faith as the foundation, or the implements which faith must possess and use. The Greek word translated **supplement** (ἐπιχορηγέω) suggests the idea of exceptionally generous provision. (E.g., the word occurs in a papyrus account of a complaint lodged by a Greek husband against his wife. Said he, "I for my part provided for my wife in a manner that exceeded my resources" [cited by Moulton and Milligan, *Vocabulary of Greek Testament, s.v.*].) The verb as here employed suggests that faith, the original and basic gift of God in and through the apostolic tradition, requires the superaddition of qualities which come, partly at least, by human **effort.**

---

that saving knowledge by which the whole life is transformed. It is one thing to know the Bible as a book; it is something more to know it as the Holy Bible, as a personal revelation, because we have heard God speak to us through it. There is an impersonal knowledge of things and events; there is an intimate knowledge of persons. I may know science, but I may also know my son. The knowledge of which Peter writes has to do with the personal more than with the propositional. Christianity has to do with things and events and creeds and institutions; but to know only these and not the living Christ is to be deficient in the knowledge that saves.

5-11. *Add to Your Faith!*—Peter was a practical man of action. He might be termed an "activist." **Diligence** was a part of his being. No doubt his fervent sense of duty was inspired by his eagerness to please his Lord. Whether fishing or mending nets, whether vigorously professing his loyalty to Jesus even to death or taking the sword to defend him in the Garden,

this man of action was up and doing. There is little of the contemplative in him. In this spirit he tells his fellow Christians to work at their Christan faith. And give **all diligence,** he writes, because there is a zeal of the Lord that has done wonders for us. Match God's zeal with your zeal! For this very reason (vs. 8) the diligence must not be spasmodic but constant, and it must involve our whole being—our all! Moffatt mentions a cynic's estimate of nominal Christian experience as "an initial spasm followed by chronic inertia." [1] Paul was also mindful of the fact that Christians had to work out the human implications of their salvation with fear and trembling, because God was at work. Such gifts demand duties; such privileges demand obligations. There is a time to wait, and there is a time to make haste. Jesus well knew this sense of urgency: "I must work the works of him that sent me, while it is day: the night cometh, when no man can work" (John 9:4). There must be no dallying. Opportunities must not be neg-

[1] *The General Epistles,* p. 181.

| 6 And to knowledge, temperance; and to temperance, patience; and to patience, godliness; | with knowledge, 6 and knowledge with self-control, and self-control with steadfast- |

God's grace, however sufficient, must be given maximum effect by the earnest endeavors of believers.

Virtue is a translation of the same Greek noun (ἀρετή) which in vs. 3 is translated "excellence." It is the opposite of "corruption" (vs. 4). Instead of helping men escape from this corruption, heretical teachers encourage licentiousness and the swift destruction that must ensue (2:1-2). Orthodoxy reverses this process. Faith looks toward virtue. Believers are called to Christ's own glory and excellence (or virtue). Virtue is equivalent to the moral energy generated in believers by faith.

The **knowledge** to be superadded to **virtue** is intelligence, sagacity, practical wisdom (γνῶσις in distinction from ἐπίγνωσις in vs. 3). The thought has two aspects: (a) The moral energy generated by **faith** contributes to the development of an understanding of God's will. Where moral and religious values are concerned, the good man thinks more clearly and discriminatingly than the licentious man. The will to do God's will enables a man to know whether the teaching is from God (John 7:17; cf. John 15:15). (b) Of equal importance, virtue must function under the guidance of intelligence. Zeal for God which is not enlightened spells tragic waste (Rom. 10:2). Under both aspects the demand is for the close correlation of conscience and practical wisdom. Faith requires both moral initiative and the intelligence to grasp and effectively execute its insights.

6. Self-control (ἐγκράτεια) in the broadest sense describes mastery of the appetites. More narrowly, it signifies the restraint of sensual impulses, especially sexual desires. It is apparently used in this latter sense here. Self-control is contrasted with the licentiousness and greed of false teachers (2:1-3). It is the outgrowth of virtue and **knowledge**. Where virtue, guided by knowledge, disciplines desire and makes it the servant instead of the master of life, self-control may be said to supplement faith. Heretical teachers, "who indulge in the lust of defiling passion" (2:10; 3:3), illustrate "intemperance" (ἀκρασία), the opposite of self-control (cf. I Cor. 7:5). In their case, appetite overwhelms reason, violates virtue, and dominates life in its entirety.

Steadfastness (ὑπομονή) describes a quality of spirit which is adamant to the aggressiveness of evil from without. The word is employed in later Jewish writings to

lected. Without effort the Christian calling will not be confirmed, nor will that which was begun be perfected and matured. "Nobody goes to heaven in his sleep." No one "oozes" into the kingdom of God. It is hard to become a Christian, and equally hard to remain one. **Diligence** may lack glamour, but it is the only way to honor God's high calling.

To be sure, by faith and faith alone we are justified. But faith must be "up and doing" or it atrophies. Workless faith is faith in a vacuum; it is in danger of becoming only an inner relationship with God divorced from the total life of man and from the social environment. Faith and works are not opposites at enmity against one another; they are correlatives. Indeed, faith must be added to if we are to be kept from that blindness and shortsightedness which forgets the grace of God (vs. 9) that initially forgave us our old sins. Works have a way of confirming and establishing our **call and election**. We learn by doing. Doing what Christians ought to do

helps to give us greater assurance of our new life in Christ. Life is a unity, and faith is related to the whole of it. The Christian life is a pilgrimage into perfection; therefore faith is not a static single act of acceptance, a once for all and finished acceptance, but a living and growing relation that infuses the whole of life and persists through the full extent of it.

Faith must be added to, although this does not create faith. It must be supplemented. Each grace is interrelated with all others, and each seems to flow out of another. Faith may be regarded as the central theme of a symphony, with all the graces to support and amplify it. So faith should be expressed through **virtue**, manliness, chivalry, resolve, the heroism of one who is armored for the struggle and fortified by the Spirit to "endure hardness, as a good soldier of Jesus Christ" (II Tim. 2:3). **Virtue** must not be blind recklessness; it must be guided by sound **knowledge**. Knowledge means insight and understanding; it means wide ac-

7 And to godliness, brotherly kindness; and to brotherly kindness, charity.

ness, and steadfastness with godliness, 7 and godliness with brotherly affection, and

---

describe the martyr spirit (IV Macc. 1:11; Pss. Sol. 2:40). It also denotes the quality in Joseph's character that fortified him against the wiles of the Egyptian temptress (Test. Joseph 10:1). As such, it constituted inner conviction sufficiently resolute to determine conduct. It regularly has to do with the repulse of attack from the outside (cf. Rom. 5:3; II Cor. 1:6; 6:4; II Thess. 1:4; Jas. 1:3; Rev. 2:2). Lightfoot distinguishes between two similar Greek terms as follows: ὑπομονή (here translated steadfastness) is "the temper which does not easily succumb under suffering," whereas μακροθυμία (translated "forbearance" in II Cor. 6:6) is "the self-restraint which does not hastily retaliate a wrong. The one is opposed to *cowardice* or *despondency,* the other to *wrath* or *revenge.*" (*Epistles to Colossians and Philemon,* p. 138.) The sequence, self-control and steadfastness, is effective and thoroughly natural.

Godliness (εὐσέβεια) indicates that the incentive to steadfastness is definitely religious. In turn, steadfastness contributes to a piety in which moral values are exalted. That Moses "endured" is explained by the fact that he saw "him who is invisible" (Heb. 11:27). The "ungodly" (cf. 2:5-6; 3:7) lack the quality of reverence for God. As in vs. 3, godliness comprehends the feeling of reverence for God and the practical phases of Christian living involved in church membership. It is "operative, cultive piety" (Moulton and Milligan, *Vocabulary of Greek Testament, s.v.*).

7. Brotherly affection (φιλαδελφία) means literally the love brothers by common descent have for one another. Early Christians thought of themselves as having become sons of one Father through their spiritual union in Christ. Brotherly affection for them signified the love Christians should have for each other as members of the church (cf. Rom. 12:10; I Thess. 4:9; Heb. 13:1; I Pet. 1:22; I John 5:1). The emphasis is definitely on a consciousness of responsibility within and for the Christian group. A proper sense of this responsibility requires avoidance of attitudes and practices that might destroy unity or bring the brotherhood into disrepute.

Love (ἀγάπη) is more inclusive and universalistic than brotherly affection ("spirit of brotherhood," Goodspeed). It transcends the confines of the Christian community. It describes the right Christian attitude and behavior toward all men as persons. This is the moral term regularly employed in the N.T. to describe the character of God. It

---

quaintance with the truth; it means a well-instructed mind. But knowledge of a certain kind may puff a man up; so it must be tempered with self-control. In 2:10 ff. and 3:3 reference is made to certain people who had knowledge which resulted in pagan conduct. Positive self-control and not ascetic self-negation is meant here. The word also implies the power to endure difficulties. Self-control, or temperance, should lead to steadfastness, the power to hold out in hope when life is difficult, the assurance that all things can be wrought into a pattern for good when God is in control. This is not a social attitude of dumb submission to things as they are, a grim determination to endure what comes to all men. It is a positive attitude of hopeful and creative steadiness. Steadfastness must be related to godliness; and godliness is piety in the best sense of the word. Piety is not a sentimental and emotional religiosity; it is strong awareness of the God-relatedness of all life. It is that attitude which sees all things

in their relation to God and receives all things from God. But godliness cannot be dissociated from brotherly affection. Much religion has become unacceptable because religious people cultivate a personal piety unrelated to love for the neighbor. There is always the danger of cultivating inward religion, even in luxurious sanctuaries, and forgetting the desperate needs of the community. Finally, brotherly affection must flow into love. "The greatest of these is love" (I Cor. 13:13). Love here is the real and final thing; it is that catholic largeheartedness which is characteristic of the Christian faith. It is love for all men, and it is love such as was in the heart of Jesus Christ.

This series of seven graces is a unity. They are beads upon a chain; each is distinct and separate, yet each is bound to others by a golden thread of unity. In these the Christian is to excel. He seeks to appropriate them with all diligence. The discipline involved in such appropriation and growth will make his life rich

8 For if these things be in you, and abound, they make *you that ye shall* neither *be* barren nor unfruitful in the knowledge of our Lord Jesus Christ.

9 But he that lacketh these things is blind, and cannot see afar off, and hath forgotten that he was purged from his old sins.

brotherly affection with love. 8 For if these things are yours and abound, they keep you from being ineffective or unfruitful in the knowledge of our Lord Jesus Christ. 9 For whoever lacks these things is blind and shortsighted and has forgotten that

---

describes God's treatment of men as exclusively determined by consideration for their true welfare. In the exercise of love men become "imitators of God, as beloved children" (Eph. 5:1), truly "sons of your Father who is in heaven" (Matt. 5:45). Here, as elsewhere in the writings of early Christianity, love is the ultimate fruitage of faith (cf. I Cor. 13:13; II Cor. 6:6; Gal. 5:22; I Thess. 1:3; II Thess. 1:3-4; I Tim. 6:11; I Pet. 3:8; I Clem. 1:2-3; 62:2; Barn. 2:2-3; Herm. Vis. III. 8. 1-11). The issue of mature faith is invariably the kind of love for men as persons that gave the Cross its significance (cf. Rom. 5:6-11).

3. Guarantees of Admission to Christ's Kingdom (1:8-11)

8. The necessity of possessing **these things** enumerated in vss. 5-7 and to be achieved, at least in part, by human "effort" is now stressed. **These things** must be **yours and abound.** The Greek phrase (ὑπάρχοντα καὶ πλεονάζοντα) describes two emphases: (*a*) actual possession as one's own of the Christian graces enumerated, and (*b*) continuing growth in those graces.

Personal possession of these things and the multiplication of them by use safeguard believers against **being ineffective or unfruitful in the knowledge of our Lord Jesus Christ.** The foundation of the life of godliness is knowledge of Christ (vs. 3). By means of this **knowledge** (ἐπίγνωσις) Christ grants believers "all things that pertain to life" (vs. 3). This knowledge is developed, however, by human effort (cf. vss. 5-7). Knowledge, then, is the root, not the goal, of the Christian life. The goal is Christ's "own glory and excellence" (vs. 3).

Ineffective describes persons who avoid labor for which they should assume responsibility. In the present instance they fail or refuse to "make every effort to supplement . . . faith with virtue" (vss. 5-7). **Unfruitful** describes persons barren of moral and spiritual activities. Active employment of the knowledge Christ grants can alone prevent such failure and futility.

9. Lack of **these things** indicates that one is potentially **blind and shortsighted and has forgotten that he was cleansed from his old sins.** This is the negative statement of the thought of vs. 8. The Greek word translated **blind** (τυφλός) is frequently employed to describe a psychological rather than a physical condition. It is mental blindness (cf. Matt. 15:14; 23:17, 19, 24, 26; John 9:39-41; Rom. 2:19; Rev. 3:17). The corresponding verb means to darken the mind in the sense of blunting discernment (cf. John 12:40; II Cor. 4:4; I John 2:11).

---

and effective not only in terms of influence upon others but in his knowledge of Jesus Christ. The blindness, lack of insight, shortsightedness of many Christians can be largely traced to the fact that they never add to their faith any of the disciplines of Christian living. They lack that large confirmation.

8-21. *Remembering These Things!*—Some **things** are very important for Christians. To be sure, they are things already known (vs. 12); indeed, the disciples of Christ are **established in the present truth** of them to some extent. With-

out a knowledge of them it is impossible to become a Christian, to remain a Christian, or to grow into maturity as a child of God.

Since these things are so crucial, and since Christians are inclined to forget them, it is right that they are to be heard over and over again. Preachers and churches may seem to be saying the same old things repeatedly, *ad nauseam,* but there is no other way to keep the Christian faith alive. This is so because the memory is capricious. We remember a hurt but we forget a favor. Even Christians are prone to forget

10 Wherefore the rather, brethren, give diligence to make your calling and election sure: for if ye do these things, ye shall never fall:

he was cleansed from his old sins. **10** Therefore, brethren, be the more zealous to confirm your call and election, for if you do

The word translated **shortsighted** is really the participle of the verb meaning to blink the eyes, or turn them away from the light, or reduce vision by screwing up the eyes. It explains the origin of blindness. Blindness results when the eyes look elsewhere than at the graces on which they should focus. Instead of proceeding from the knowledge with which the life of the Christian is originally endowed, here is an instance of refusal to make the effort prescribed in vss. 5-7. Such a person becomes **blind** because he closes his eyes to duty or deliberately turns them away. Persons really called (vs. 3) may refuse to confirm their **call and election** (vs. 10), and that refusal brings blindness. Instead of their minds being blinded by "the god of this world," as Paul said of "those who are perishing" (II Cor. 4:3), these believers are made blind by their own inertia.

The lack of **these things** also shows that the believer **has forgotten that he was cleansed from his old sins.** The language and symbolism refer to the significance of Christian baptism (cf. Luke 3:3; Acts 2:38-39; Rom. 6:3-11; I Cor. 6:11; Eph. 5:25-27; Tit. 3:5; I Pet. 3:21; Barn. 11:11; Herm. Mand. IV. 4; IX. 4-7). **Old sins** ("former sins," Goodspeed) refer to definite wrong acts committed prior to baptism, not to the inherited depravity of human nature. These are pictured as **cleansed** or washed away. This cleansing was regarded as both necessary and effective. Christ's death made it possible. The benefits of his atoning death were personally appropriated by repentance and faith and were actually conveyed to the individual at baptism. Growth in the "glory and excellence" of Christ followed this cleansing, and participation in "the divine nature" would reward believers who lived daily under the spell of the "precious and very great promises of Christ" (vs. 4). Blindness and forgetfulness endanger this whole process. The reader is being warned of the seriousness of sins committed after baptism (cf. 2:20-22; Heb. 6:4-8; 10:26-31).

10-11. These verses are an exhortation in view of the blessings and dangers just pointed out (vss. 8-9). **Be the more zealous** has essentially the same force as "make every effort" (vs. 5). Employment of the aorist imperative of the Greek verb σπουδάζω ("to exert one's self," or **be the more zealous**) emphasizes the urgency of the issues. **Calling**

the pit from whence they were digged, the bottom rungs of the ladder by which they have climbed, the solid events of history to which their faith is anchored. Christians must be aroused to remember. It is only by constantly relating our contemporary faith to the norm of revelation events that Christian experience can be saved from going stale or becoming something less or other than genuinely Christian. Persistent remembrance of these sources of faith is essential to prevent heresy and degeneration.

The word of God is a living thing; it is essentially a story to be told by word of mouth from generation to generation. Yet it was preserved in written form to pin it down to a definite set of events in history. Men like Peter have always been concerned about keeping Christianity a historical faith, lest it soar off into the rootless realms of gnosticism. They have felt so keenly the need to save Christianity from becoming an intellectual or mystical system

that they have done their utmost while still **in this body** and before their **departure** to keep alive the memory of these things that have happened in history.

The generations of Christian leaders, like Peter, rise and pass away. There is no automatic transmission of their faith to the oncoming generation. They know that life is a pilgrimage and that they will pass on and leave the precious faith to those coming after. Everything depends upon the bridging of that gap between the generations with the **things** that must be remembered. Older people are rightly concerned about the next generation and its confrontation with the things of the Christian faith.

The author has a realistic conception of his own pilgrimage; he knows he must die. But he regards his decease as a Christian who looks forward to putting off his old body and to putting on a glorious new body. He links his *exodus* and his *entrance*, and regards his transition from earth to heaven as something akin to

11 For so an entrance shall be ministered unto you abundantly into the everlasting kingdom of our Lord and Saviour Jesus Christ.

this you will never fall; **11** so there will be richly provided for you an entrance into the eternal kingdom of our Lord and Savior Jesus Christ.

---

and election, though real and effective, require stabilization by man's self-exertion. Christ calls and elects but man must **confirm.**

The Greek word for **election** (ἐκλογή) occurs six other times in the N.T., five of them in Paul's letters (Acts 9:15; Rom. 9:11; 11:5, 7, 28; I Thess. 1:4). It describes God as selecting persons to be the beneficiaries of the gifts of his grace. The happy outcome of the tortuous course of Paul's thought in Rom. 9–11 appears in 11:32, where the divine intention is seen unwaveringly to be to have mercy upon all. That is the point of view in II Peter. Christ is described (vs. 3) as having called us. The "things that pertain to life and godliness" are granted by him. Imperative though it is that men **confirm** them, **calling and election** describe salvation as ultimately requiring God's initiative and power (cf. Phil. 2:12-13). Strictly, election precedes calling. They are called who have been "selected." (Cf. Rom. 8:30, "Those whom he predestined he also called." Paul thinks of foreknowledge and predestination as activities of God in causing men to be "conformed to the image of his Son," the divine aspiration for all men [Rom. 8:29; cf. 11:32].) This order is ignored here and calling and election are viewed as halves of God's fixed purpose for men. Christ calls men to "his own glory and excellence" (vs. 3). By "precious and very great promises" he encourages them to confirm this call by effort on their part (vs. 4). Divine power, in other words, supports men in their effort to achieve their true destiny, to "become partakers of the divine nature" (vs. 4).

Effort to confirm your call and election has a twofold outcome: (a) **you will never fall;** and (b) **there will be richly provided for you an entrance. . . . You will never fall** ("stumble," ASV and Goodspeed; "make a slip," Moffatt) refers to the danger that threatens the blind and forgetful believer (cf. vs. 9). The premium is on spiritual surefootedness. The Greek verb πταίω refers to the surefootedness of a horse. It is used figuratively in Rom. 11:11; Jas. 2:10; 3:2; cf. ἀπταίστους, Jude 24. The **zealous** are assured of being kept from types of error that jeopardize salvation as they possess and grow in the virtues enumerated in vss. 5-8. The believer is conceived to be traveling toward **the eternal kingdom of our Lord.** "The gate is narrow and the way is hard, that leads to life" (Matt. 7:14). Ineffectiveness, blindness, shortsightedness, and forgetfulness imperil safe arrival (vs. 9). To be steady on his feet and reach his divine destination, the traveler must possess "these things" enumerated in vss. 5-8. The **effort** to possess them will **confirm his call and election** and guarantee that he **will never fall.**

The promise of vs. 8 and the exhortation of vs. 10 look toward the divine assurance (in vs. 11) that the believer will be **provided . . . an entrance into the eternal kingdom of . . . Jesus Christ.** If the believer will supplement his faith as directed (vss. 5-8), **there will be richly provided** (the verb in both instances is ἐπιχορηγέω) for him an entrance

---

what he saw on the mount of transfiguration. No sooner does he complete his statement about **his departure** than he mentions the **power,** the **glory,** and the **majesty** of Jesus Christ of which he was an eyewitness (vss. 16-17).

Jesus was concerned about the problem of keeping his memory alive. The Lord's Supper was instituted, in part at least, that his followers through the ages might remember his broken body and his shed blood—his incarnation and atonement—as they ate of the broken bread and partook of the crushed fruit of the vine. In short, this Christianity is no bodiless, ethe-

real, unhistorical philosophy; it is the gospel of the Son of God who personally loved us and gave himself for us and who for us men was made man.

The Christian revelation is unique in this respect: it centers in an incarnation. The Son of God became man; he assumed our human life; he took upon himself the form of a natural man. While God is spirit and truth, the God we know is the God and Father of our Lord Jesus Christ. And he that has seen Jesus has seen the Father (John 14:9). This Christianity is a most personal matter. It is solidly rooted

12 Wherefore I will not be negligent to put you always in remembrance of these things, though ye know *them,* and be established in the present truth.

12 Therefore I intend always to remind you of these things, though you know them and are established in the truth that you

into the eternal kingdom. God's rich provision complements the believer's effort. Three things are said about the kingdom: (*a*) it is eternal; (*b*) it is the kingdom of our Lord and Savior Jesus Christ; (*c*) entrance to it is future, is morally conditioned, and is divinely provided. Orthodox Christianity took these assumptions for granted (cf. Matt. 6:10; 25:31-46; etc.). They are emphasized here because scoffers ridiculed them (see 3:3-4). Delay, admittedly regrettable, must not, however, weaken the confidence of those who share the faith of the apostles.

B. Peter's Testimony to the Truths of the Apostolic Message (1:12-21)
1. Peter Bequeaths a Record of Christ's Revelation (1:12-15)

12. Therefore introduces a conclusion based on the crucial importance of the counsel contained in vss. 10-11. Because believers may so confirm their call and election as to have "richly provided . . . an entrance into the eternal kingdom," the author promises **always to remind you of these things.** He has in mind the precious and very great promises through which they may escape worldly corruption and become partakers of the divine nature (vs. 4). He also has in mind the graces by which faith must be supplemented (vss. 5-7).

These things are constituent elements of **the truth** in which believers are **established** (cf. vss. 1, 8). Because they are established, the author's task is to **remind,** not inform (cf. Jude 5). Christian tradition had preserved Christ's specific commission to Peter: "When you have turned again, strengthen your brethren" (Luke 22:32). The Greek verb (στηρίζω), translated "strengthen" in Luke 22:32, is here translated **established.** The truth in which believers are established came to them through the agency of the apostles, of whom Peter is the spokesman. It is equivalent to "the faith which was once for all delivered" (Jude 3), "the holy commandment delivered to them" (2:21), the faith common to the apostles and subsequent generations of believers (1:1). The historical, doctrinal, and ethical content of orthodox Christian teaching is viewed as a unity, the truth in contrast to the cleverly devised myths (vs. 16) and the destructive heresies of false teachers (2:1; cf. I Pet. 1:22-25).

and grounded in history. God meets us in the person of Jesus Christ. Since Peter and his associates had walked and talked with this Jesus, they could not stand by and see what they had seen and heard and touched be denatured of its marvelous personal quality. When Christianity gets away from personal and historical reality it soon ceases to be uniquely Christian.

But why this emphasis upon the **things** of the Christian faith? Why this concern lest Christ Jesus be denatured of his historical character, lest the **Christian** faith be divorced from its factual roots? The author makes it clear when he says that he and his associates in preaching the gospel offered no **cunningly devised fables.** They made known the **power** and **coming of our Lord Jesus Christ** as eyewitnesses. This gospel they preached was true. It is not a humanly invented piece of fiction created in the minds of hypersensitive men. This **power** and **coming,** or dynamic and advent, were—and are—real,

and they brought—and bring—something which, while beyond history, is nevertheless effective and observable in history.

The experience at the mount of transfiguration was evidence that heaven and earth had met, that God had spoken in approval of his Son, that Jesus Christ had received honor and glory from God the Father. This genuine experience based upon personal observation and the hearing of the **voice** convinced the disciples that Jesus was the Messiah, that he was unique, that it all pointed both to what prophecy had foretold and to the glorification of Jesus Christ that was yet to come. The contention of the author is that Jesus Christ, as historic man and also as majestic Son, must never be divided. Any such attempt endangers the gospel. Nor dare the Christian church ever doubt that its faith rests upon the testimony of the prophets and the apostles who were eyewitnesses to these things.

13 Yea, I think it meet, as long as I am in this tabernacle, to stir you up by putting *you* in remembrance;

14 Knowing that shortly I must put off *this* my tabernacle, even as our Lord Jesus Christ hath showed me.

15 Moreover I will endeavor that ye may be able after my decease to have these things always in remembrance.

have. 13 I think it right, as long as I am in this body,*c* to arouse you by way of reminder, 14 since I know that the putting off of my body*c* will be soon, as our Lord Jesus Christ showed me. 15 And I will see to it that after my departure you may be able at any time to recall these things.

c Greek *tent.*

13-15. As long as he is **in this body,** the author of II Peter promises to **arouse** his readers **by way of reminder** because it is **right** that he do so (cf. 3:1). Paul had corresponded with his churches in similar spirit (cf. Phil. 3:1). The welfare of believers and the responsibilities of apostleship require a comparable service of Peter. The urgency of his decision to write grows out of the further fact that **our Lord Jesus Christ showed** him that **the putting off** of his body would **soon** take place. The author writes as though he were fulfilling the prophecy of John 21:18-19. He apparently knew the Fourth Gospel with ch. 21 appended. The alternative is to suppose that the present reference is to a vision experience of the sort familiar in the narrative of Acts (cf. 1:2, 11; 4:8; 9:5-9; 10:9-16; 12:7-11; 16:9; 18:9; 22:11; 23:11; 27:23).

But death could not still the apostle's voice. He proposes to **see to it** that after his **departure** those who have counted on him to remind them of these things will **be able at any time to recall** them. He assures them by his letter that the historical life and message of Jesus and the revelation he committed to the apostles will continue to supply faith with unshakable foundations and that he will bequeath to posterity a documentary record of that revelation. II Peter itself hardly satisfies that promise. The Gospel of Mark satisfies it admirably. The author of II Peter probably knew and accepted the tradition reported by Papias and confirmed by Irenaeus that Peter's reminiscences were Mark's principal source and that Mark's Gospel was actually Peter's (Eusebius *Church History* III. 39. 15; V. 8. 3; VI. 14. 5-7; Irenaeus *Against Heresies* III. 1. 1; see also Vol. VII, pp. 630-31). Irenaeus explains the origin of Mark's Gospel: "After their [Peter and Paul's] departure, Mark, the disciple and interpreter of Peter, did also hand down to us in writing what had been preached by Peter." Irenaeus and II Peter use the same Greek word for the decease (ἔξοδος) of Peter, and Irenaeus probably understood II Pet. 1:15 to refer to that Gospel as Peter's.

What is more, Jesus Christ and prophecy belong together. That prophetic word pointed to the coming of the Messiah. Prophecy is not the product of human speculation; it is a gift of the Spirit. In spite of the fact that there were many prophets, prophecy itself is a unity. In general, the prophets were in agreement with each other. Now this prophetic promise is fulfilled. The Messiah has come. This is historic fact. It is verifiable. It is simply impossible, says the author, to have the Christmas spirit without the birth of Jesus, the resurrection hope without the resurrected Jesus, the experience of the Holy Spirit without these historical **things.**

The Christian's mind is a perennial battleground in which memories and ideas and a Presence contend for attention. To forget these **things** concerning the Lord Jesus Christ—the terms are always used together in II Peter—is to be on the dangerous path that leads to heresy

and loss of the faith; to remember continually the things concerning Jesus Christ in ever fresher understanding through the power of the Spirit is to make one's election and calling more certain.

Creative remembrance of these **things** makes for the effective and fruitful knowledge of Jesus Christ (vs. 8). They must be made one's very own through personal appropriation; no second-hand knowledge will suffice. And they must **abound** through an ever-increasing and continuing meditation and reflection. To lack these **things** is to lose the power of spiritual insight, to become circumscribed in vision, and to forget the fact that one has been **cleansed from his old sins** through **our Lord and Savior Jesus Christ.**

Remembering these **things** and translating them into obedience with **diligence** and zeal helps to confirm one in his call to discipleship and in his sense of being chosen. Such memory,

16 For we have not followed cunningly devised fables, when we made known unto you the power and coming of our Lord Jesus Christ, but were eyewitnesses of his majesty.

16 For we did not follow cleverly devised myths when we made known to you the power and coming of our Lord Jesus Christ, but we were eyewitnesses of his majesty.

2. The Apostolic Record Rests on Eyewitness Testimony (1:16-19a)

Continuing his insistence on the historicity of the apostolic tradition, Peter now says that these things to be remembered have as their foundation the testimony of those who were with him on the holy mountain.

16. We refers to the apostles (cf. "ours," vs. 1). Their testimony, incorporated in the four Gospels, was no mosaic of **cleverly devised myths. Eyewitnesses of his majesty** vouched for that testimony. In Luke 1:2 the term translated "eyewitness" is αὐτόπτης. He is one who sees with his own eyes. In II Peter the word is ἐπόπτης, a term employed in the Eleusinian mysteries to describe the initiate who had reached the highest level of insight. Both shades of meaning were probably in our author's mind. The apostles knew the objective facts and they also knew their inner significance. False teachers (2:1) and scoffers (3:3) had probably ridiculed the expectation of "an entrance into the eternal kingdom" (vs. 11) and also "the promise of his coming" (3:4) as based on spurious prophecies (**cleverly devised myths**). **Myths** is the term used in the Pastorals to describe the basis of the "endless genealogies" of the Gnostics (cf. I Tim. 1:4; 4:7; II Tim. 4:4; Tit. 1:14). The intention of II Peter is to suggest that **cleverly devised myths** more accurately describes the message of the scoffers than that of the apostles. Our author retorts that the "precious and very great promises" of Christ implicit in Christian experience were supported also by objective, historical evidence. Those who were with Christ reported what they saw, and written Gospels embodied that report.

The **majesty** of which the apostles were **witnesses** was the "visible splendor of the divine majesty as it appeared in the transfiguration of Christ" (J. H. Thayer, *A Greek-English Lexicon of the New Testament* [New York: Harper & Bros., 1887], *s.v.;* cf. Luke 9:43, "the majesty of God"; Acts 19:27, "her magnificence," meaning that of "the great goddess Artemis"). II Peter interprets the Transfiguration as a guarantee to the apostles of the Second Coming, which scoffers ridiculed (3:3). It was a sort of foretaste of the Parousia. It is conceivably viewed as a fulfillment of the promise that the apostles would not "taste death before they see the kingdom of God come with power" (Mark 9:1). The expectation of the Second Coming is for our author a symbol of traditional Christianity. It stands for old-fashioned faith. The credibility of this expectation is guaranteed and underwritten by the testimony of **eyewitnesses of his majesty. The power and coming** of Christ, made known by the apostles, refer to the eschatological appearance of "the Son of man coming on the clouds of heaven with power and great glory" (Matt. 24:30). **Power** (δύναμις; cf. vs. 3) and **coming** (παρουσία) are used in identical connections in vs. 16 and Matt. 24:30. The power is that of the risen Christ (cf. Rom. 1:4), and this

---

diligence, and zeal do not *create* the **call** and the **election**, but they **confirm** them and make the reality of God's initiative in Jesus Christ more certain. To live out the Christian imperative establishes the Christian faith. "If any man will do his will, he shall know" (John 7:17). The venture of faith confirms the authority and the reality of the Christ who calls. To center one's eyes upon Christ in holy obedience will keep one from falling. Such concentration will provide the faithful with **an entrance into the eternal kingdom of our Lord and Savior Jesus Christ** (vs. 11).

To **pay attention to this** is to discern the **lamp** of life as it shines in the **dark place of** this world, pointing to the inevitable dawning of God's day of fulfillment. To concentrate on that **lamp** and that **dawn** will cause the **morning star,** that harbinger of the rising sun and the growing light, to rise in the heart. Prophetic promise, historical fact, personal experience, and future hope are combined in this beautiful sentence (vs. 19b).

16-21. *No Devised Myths.*—Christianity according to Peter is a real and genuine religion. Lofty as may be its claims it does not rest

17 For he received from God the Father honor and glory, when there came such a voice to him from the excellent glory, This is my beloved Son, in whom I am well pleased.

18 And this voice which came from heaven we heard, when we were with him in the holy mount.

19 We have also a more sure word of prophecy; whereunto ye do well that ye take heed, as unto a light that shineth in a

17 For when he received honor and glory from God the Father and the voice was borne to him by the Majestic Glory, "This is my beloved Son,^{d} with whom I am well pleased," 18 we heard this voice borne from heaven, for we were with him on the holy mountain. 19 And we have the prophetic word made more sure. You will do well to

^{d} Or my Son, my (or the) Beloved.

---

power is to be demonstrated with finality at the Second Coming (cf. Mark 8:38; 9:1). *Parousia* is explicitly used of the Second Coming in 3:4, 12; Matt. 24:3, 27, 37, 39; I Cor. 15:23; I Thess. 2:19; 3:13; 4:15; 5:23; II Thess. 2:1, 8, 9; Jas. 5:7, 8; I John 2:28.

17-18. The writer assumes the readers' familiarity with the Synoptic accounts of the Transfiguration (cf. Matt. 17:1-13; Mark 9:2-13; Luke 9:28-36). He emphasizes the premonitory relation of Transfiguration to Second Coming, an emphasis peculiar to him. This was probably his inference from the fact that accounts of the Transfiguration succeed references to the Second Coming (cf. Matt. 16:28; Mark 9:1; Luke 9:27).

19a. The prophetic word refers to O.T. prophecy. The prophets supposedly spoke with unanimity about the coming and saving mission of Christ (I Pet. 1:10). The thought is essentially the same as that of Acts 3:21, where the risen Christ is regarded as residing in heaven "until the time for establishing all that God spoke by the mouth of his holy prophets from of old." Proof by prophecy served to make the O.T. in effect a Christian book (cf. Jude 14).

The prophetic word is here viewed as making more sure by the voice borne from heaven. The passage may be interpreted in either of two ways. The translation, We have the prophetic word made more sure (RSV; cf. Moffatt and Goodspeed) suggests that O.T. prophecy is authenticated by the voice borne from heaven . . . on the holy mountain. On the other hand, the translation We have also a more sure word of prophecy (KJV) suggests that the prophetic word needs no confirmation, but itself witnesses to the truth of the gospel. The latter translation seems more likely. Apostolic tradition draws support from the Scriptures. The voice heard on "the holy mountain" had the same origin as that heard in antiquity by the prophets. The inspiration of the prophets was generally assumed. Their word did not need to be confirmed. Scoffers, however, ridiculed the primitive Christian expectation of the Parousia (3:3-4), and Peter sustains the traditional faith by claiming that the prophetic word authenticates the voice borne from heaven on the holy mountain.

---

upon the creations of men's imaginations but upon something solid and substantial. It is not the product of such arbitrary and wishful speculation as characterized so much of the religious mythology of Peter's day as of ours. Nor is it a fanciful embellishment of a simple historical fact into a mountain of fabulous theories about the future.

The power of Jesus Christ and his sure advent, his regal arrival, were seen by the eyes of real people who were present. In the days of his flesh they saw that majesty which will someday be manifested in all its fullness. This Jesus received honor and glory from God the Father on the mount of transfiguration. They heard

the approving voice speak to and of him. The majesty was indeed hidden; but it was seen and heard. It was not created by an individual; it was witnessed by a group.

What is more, it was promised by the O.T. prophets. They did not speak by and in their own human powers; they were moved and inspired by the Holy Spirit. No prophecy was uttered as a private opinion. Prophets were not gifted individualists; they did not talk as private citizens. They were carried away by something divine. They received what they gave. Their prophecy was of God. The prophets were all related to a certain line of truth; what all of them said formed a harmonious pattern. What

dark place, until the day dawn, and the day-star arise in your hearts:

20 Knowing this first, that no prophecy of the Scripture is of any private interpretation.

pay attention to this as to a lamp shining in a dark place, until the day dawns and the morning star rises in your hearts. **20** First of all you must understand this, that no prophecy of scripture is a matter of one's

---

3. THE APOSTOLIC TRADITION EMBODIES DIVINE REVELATION (1:19b-21)

19b. Prophecy of scripture meant more, not less, to those who had been with Christ and had heard the voice borne from heaven. That should show less privileged believers their duty to **pay attention** to the prophetic word as to **a lamp shining in a dark place.** Comparison of the prophets to a lamp shining in a dark place brings to mind the description of John the Baptist as "a burning and shining lamp" (John 5:35). Early Christians, like the prophets, pictured the messianic age in terms of light (Rom. 13:11-14; cf. Isa. 60:1-3). **The day** refers to the Second Coming and the inauguration of that age (cf. vs. 16; 3:4). The verb translated **dawns** (διαυγάζω) describes the sunlight breaking through the darkness of vanishing night. The Second Coming will so affect the world (cf. Mal. 4:2; Rev. 22:16).

Literally, **the morning star** precedes the sunrise. Reversal of that order is due to the author's shift of attention from the Parousia, which is objective and future, to the present illumination of the inner life of the believer by the Spirit. The figure of the morning star portrays religious experience (cf. II Cor. 4:4-6; I John 2:8). The emphasis is on immediacy and inwardness (cf. Rom. 2:15-16; 5:5; 8:27; II Cor. 1:21-22; Eph. 1:18; 3:16; Col. 3:15). This experience of the light-bringing Spirit by believers is comparable to the luminous vision of the apostles, who were "eyewitnesses of his majesty . . . on the holy mountain" (vss. 16, 18). The literal order of the imagery employed is (a) the prophetic word, likened to **a lamp shining in a dark place,** (b) the Second Advent (the day dawns), (c) **the morning star rises in your hearts,** the inner light due to the Spirit's indwelling. The order of experience would be prophecy, inner transformation, the Parousia. The prophecy of scripture is a lamp shining in a dark place in the twofold sense that it forecasts Christ's messianic return and prepares man's spirit to respond to the Holy Spirit. In turn, the indwelling Spirit is like the morning star in that he illuminates the meaning of prophecy for the believer. The climax of history and of religious experience will be the Parousia, when the day dawns. The author's complete thought is that the **sure word of prophecy,** inwardly clarified and authenticated by the Spirit, will guide believers like a lamp shining in a dark place, until the day dawns (cf. John 16:13; Rom. 8:26-27; II Cor. 4:4-6; Eph. 1:18).

20-21. Because the prophets were **moved by the Holy Spirit,** their words were a message from God. The prophetic word is timelessly authoritative for the reason that its authors were God's spokesmen. Since prophecy never came **by the impulse of man,** it cannot be **a matter of one's own interpretation. One's own** describes individuality, or

---

they said about God is not to be wrested from its context and added to by false teachers who read into or out of prophecy something that simply is not true. It must be allowed to be itself.

The O.T. prophets are to be interpreted by the fulfillment of their prophecies in the N.T., and particularly by their fulfillment in Jesus Christ. No **interpretation** of prophecy is valid unless it is given in the power of the Spirit. Prophecy is a unique work among men. Peter provides us with no indication as to how the Spirit inspires or interprets prophecy, but he does insist that the prophets were **moved** by the

Spirit; and because that is so, those who interpret what they prophesied cannot understand prophecy without the Spirit's aid. "God is his own best interpreter." It is false prophets, unwilling to abide by the principle of Christ-centered continuity or God-inspired initiative in prophecy, who secretly produce destructive heresies and change the very nature of the Christian religion.

It is well for Christians to pay attention to the message and proper interpretation of the prophetic word, for it is **as . . . a lamp shining in a dark place, until the day dawns and the morning star rises in** [men's] **hearts.** As the

21 For the prophecy came not in old time by the will of man: but holy men of God spake *as they were* moved by the Holy Ghost.

2 But there were false prophets also among the people, even as there shall be false teachers among you, who privily shall bring in damnable heresies, even denying the Lord that bought them, and bring upon themselves swift destruction.

own interpretation, 21 because no prophecy ever came by the impulse of man, but men moved by the Holy Spirit spoke from God.*e*

2 But false prophets also arose among the people, just as there will be false teachers among you, who will secretly bring in destructive heresies, even denying the Master who bought them, bringing upon

e Many authorities read *moved by the Holy Spirit holy men of God spoke.*

---

difference from another. Here it is contrasted with the **sure word of prophecy.** Scripture is viewed as objective and fixed in meaning. Discovery of that meaning, not the imposition upon it of the point of view of the interpreter, is the duty of believers. Whimsical interpretation is the mark of heretical teachers (cf. 2:1). The Spirit of Christ taught the apostles the true meaning of scripture and continues to give the apostolic message the validity of revelation (cf. Luke 24:25-27, 44-48; Rev. 1:1-2; 5:1-14). The proper understanding of scripture will always therefore require divine guidance. To make it a matter of one's own interpretation invites disaster. With only their own ingenuity for guidance, "the ignorant and unstable twist [the Scriptures] to their own destruction" (3:16).

III. Instead of Salvation, Unorthodox Teachers Bring Destruction (2:1-22)

A. Heretics Successors to the False Prophets of the Old Testament (2:1-10*a*)

The existence of **false prophets** in former times makes understandable the appearance of **false teachers** in the church. True identification of the latter compares in importance with the sound interpretation of the Scriptures (cf. 1:19*b*-21). Accordingly, the whole of ch. 2 is an exposure of their characteristics.

1. Doctrinally Unsound, Morally Corrupt (2:1-3)

2:1. The reference to **false prophets . . . among the people** has to do with ancient Hebrew history (cf., e.g., Deut. 13:1-5; 18:20; Jer. 5:31; Ezek. 13:3; Luke 6:26). Their existence prepares the church for the detection of its own **false teachers** (cf. Justin *Dialogue* LXXXII). Compounds with ψευδο- (pseudo-) mean "sham," "counterfeit": "false Christs" (Matt. 24:24); "false apostles" (II Cor. 11:13); "false brethren" (Gal. 2:4). The message of such men, like their character, is untrustworthy.

As the natural outcome of treating prophecy as a matter of "one's own interpretation" (1:20), the errorists **bring in destructive heresies,** which appear when men assume that "prophecy . . . came by the impulse of man" (1:21). Whimsical interpretation, secrecy, and divisiveness characterize such teachers and are the marks of falsity (cf. Jude 4). Interpretation of the Scriptures in the light of apostolic tradition protects the church against heresies and establishes criteria for the detection of false teachers.

The Greek word for "heresy" (αἵρεσις) literally means any selected course of activity or thought (cf. Acts 5:17; 15:5; 26:5). The corresponding verb means "to capture."

---

morning star appears before the dawn, so the pre-Christian prophetic word throws light upon man's pilgrimage and causes the dawn of hope to rise in the soul until the day itself in Jesus Christ shall be manifest in all its glory.

2:1-22. *False Prophets.*—There have been and there will be **false** teachers of the Christian faith. The world is full of teachings of one kind or

another, and these teachings or systems of religion and philosophy have their place. The writer is not referring to them. Rather is he warning against those who pose as teachers of the truth but who twist and even pervert it into something other than it is. They **secretly bring in destructive heresies.** This is fifth-column subversion; against it the church must be on

Intellectually, it described the mind as convinced or "captured" by given opinions. It came to mean the tenets of a party or sect which varied from those traditionally held by the church. The heresies denounced in II Peter are destructive in the sense that they foster **licentiousness**, contempt for **the way of truth, greed, false words,** and lead to **destruction** in the impending judgment (vss. 2-3). Ignatius of Antioch warned against heresy in very similar terms: "I beseech you therefore (yet not I but the love of Jesus Christ) live only on Christian fare, and refrain from strange food, which is heresy. For these men mingle Jesus Christ with themselves in specious honesty, mixing as it were a deadly poison with honeyed wine, which the ignorant takes gladly in his baneful pleasure, and it is his death" (Ign. Trall. 6:1-2; cf. Ign. Eph. 6:2). As in Phil. 1:28, destruction is the opposite of salvation. The church is regarded as the custodian of sound teaching. Views peculiarly one's own, in the sense of being at variance with apostolic doctrine, endanger sound morality and threaten salvation itself.

Denial of **the Master who bought them** constitutes the nature of the heresy **secretly introduced** by the **false teachers** (cf. Jude 4). The denial could be a rejection of orthodox Christology in its entirety. More probably it represented repudiation of specific tenets. With Ignatius and the authors of II John and Jude, the actuality of Jesus' humanity was the point at issue. In II Peter it could have been the atoning significance of Jesus' death: they denied **the Master who bought them.** The thought looks back to an earlier reminder that believers "were ransomed . . . with the precious blood of Christ" (I Pet. 1:18-19). II Peter uses the verb ἀγοράζω, whereas λυτρόω is used in I Peter. There are conceivable differences between "purchase" and "redeem," but illustrations from the papyri suggest that the terms had become synonymous (cf. Moulton and Milligan, *Vocabulary of Greek Testament, s.v.*). Conceivably the author of II Peter preferred the word Paul used (cf. I Cor. 6:20; 7:23) because the false teachers he has in mind "twist" Paul's letters, along with the other scriptures, to their own destruction (3:16). The frequency of ἀγοράζω in Revelation (cf. Rev. 5:9; 14:3-4) might also have figured in its use here since the false teachers also scoff at the idea of the Second Coming (3:3-4).

The verb **bought** (ἀγοράσαντα) describes Christ as having made men the "private property" of God by shedding his blood for them. The author shares the serious view of sin held by the author of Hebrews, who speaks of the apostate as one who has "spurned the Son of God, and profaned the blood of the covenant by which he was consecrated" (Heb. 10:29).

Swift destruction is identical in meaning with **their condemnation** and **their destruction** (vs. 3). As in Jude 4, 15, 17, O.T. prophecy and apostolic teaching make the doom of heretics certain and terrible. The Second Advent will be the occasion of the

---

guard with an eternal vigilance, must therefore engage in theological thinking. Theology is not only a system of thought formulated on the basis of the Scriptures as implemented in experience; theology is also a persistent and necessary function of the church. Every creative idea proposed as Christian must be put to the test of the mind of the church.

False prophets are referred to time and again in the Bible (I Kings 22:12; Jer. 14:14; Matt. 24:24; I John 4:1). Their teachings were taken seriously and soundly denounced. What a person believes is of utmost importance, for it determines his attitude and his conduct. Right thoughts precede right actions; they determine the release of the emotions. They express themselves in social relations, in daily work, and in the life of the home. A world-renowned professor of theology was once asked about the impor-

tance of religious education. He replied, in effect, that the communication of a false theology about God and man is more destructive than the intemperate use of alcohol. The latter affects the body, the former affects the spirit. Heresy may have a blighting, a damning effect upon young life. There can be no easy tolerance of such poisonous influences in the church. The gentle Jesus spoke sternly about the false teachers of his day. Peter's warning was learned from his Lord.

Such heresies also divide the church, as they did in Corinth. They confuse Christians who do not have the theological discernment to detect their falsehood. Often the perpetrators of such heresies bring serious criticism upon the truth because they teach one thing and live another. The glorious gospel is brought into disrepute by its "disciples'" conduct. They will exploit

2 And many shall follow their pernicious ways; by reason of whom the way of truth shall be evil spoken of.

3 And through covetousness shall they with feigned words make merchandise of you: whose judgment now of a long time lingereth not, and their damnation slumbereth not.

themselves swift destruction. 2 And many will follow their licentiousness, and because of them the way of truth will be reviled. 3 And in their greed they will exploit you with false words; from of old their condemnation has not been idle, and their destruction has not been asleep.

---

destruction. It is described as swift (ταχινός, used only here in the N.T.) in the twofold sense that the Parousia is imminent and will come suddenly (cf. 3:7). There is a touch of grim humor in the warning that whoever brings destructive heresies into the church brings swift destruction upon himself in "the day of judgment and destruction of ungodly men" (3:7). The play on ἀπώλεια (**destruction**) is intentional and effective.

2. Those who follow heretical teachers in denying the Master will naturally **follow their licentiousness.** Jude had treated sexual laxity as the correlative of heresy (cf. vss. 4, 6, 8, 13, 16, 18, 23). II Peter is equally emphatic that one implies the other (vss. 7, 10, 12, 14-15, 18-19, 22; 3:3, 17). The authors of both epistles insist on the moral necessity of accepting apostolic teaching about Christ. Denial of it has practical consequences of the most serious character. Use of the plural of the Greek word for licentiousness may imply that the errorists practice sexual indulgence in a variety of ways or else that "their lascivious doings" (ERV) are constantly repeated and habitual.

In Acts 9:2 the disciples are described as persons "belonging to the Way" (cf. Acts 22:4; 24:14). Says R. J. Knowling: "The term may have originated amongst the Jews who saw in the Christians those who adopted a special way or mode of life, or a special form of their own national belief, but if so, the Christians would see in it *nomen et omen*—in Christ *they* had found the Way, the Truth, the Life, John xiv. 6" ("The Acts of the Apostles," *The Expositor's Greek Testament* [London: Hodder & Stoughton, 1910], II, 230). **The way of truth** is a similar designation of Christianity. **Truth** describes apostolic tradition in contrast with destructive heresies. Paul had quoted Isa. 52:5 to say that because of unworthy Jewish conduct "the name of God is blasphemed among the Gentiles" (Rom. 2:24). The same Greek word is here translated **reviled.** II Peter may consciously apply Paul's condemnation to the later situation. His thought is that orthodox Christianity **will be reviled** because of those who follow the licentiousness encouraged by false teachers.

3. Jude had described the heretical teachers of his day as abandoning themselves "for the sake of gain to Balaam's error," and as "flattering people to gain advantage" (vss. 11, 16). II Peter similarly relates the **false words** of false teachers to the use of religion to exploit people because of **greed.** "Licentiousness" and "lust" for money (Moffatt so renders πλεονεξία) are both expressions of sensuality. They illustrate equally the false character of those who **secretly bring in destructive heresies** (cf. vs. 15; I Tim. 6:5; Tit. 1:11; Irenaeus *Against Heresies* I. 13. 3; Eusebius *Church History* V. 18. 2). The Greek word translated **exploit** (ἐμπορεύομαι) means to trade or traffic in something. The term suggests the contrast Paul drew between "men of sincerity . . . commissioned by God" and "peddlers

---

people by using them to build up their own egos, fortunes, reputations, and followings. Like Pied Pipers their smooth words will lure the seekers after new teachings and lead the innocent to the slow but sure disintegration of their minds, affections, and wills. Forsaking **the right way,** like Balaam, they go **astray** (vs. 15). Promised **freedom** from the law of God, they become enslaved to the law of lust (vs. 19). And the worst tragedy is that those who once **escaped the defilements of the world through the knowl**

edge of our Lord and Savior Jesus Christ . . . are again entangled in them and overpowered, the last state has become worse for them than the first (vs. 20). It would have been better for them never to have known the gospel and its way than to have known it and turned back from it. Those who rise high fall hardest! False teachers like their disciples are like dogs that turn back to eat their own vomit, and like washed pigs who turn back to the dirty wallow.

The list of terms used of such heretics is a

4 For if God spared not the angels that sinned, but cast *them* down to hell, and delivered *them* into chains of darkness, to be reserved unto judgment;	4 For if God did not spare the angels when they sinned, but cast them into hell*f* and committed them to pits of nether *f* Greek *Tartarus*.

of God's word" (II Cor. 2:17; cf. Jas. 4:13). The false teachers were extortionate, not reasonable, in their demands for money. They were essentially "peddlers," not prophets. They traffic in sex as though it were godliness, and the many who follow their licentiousness with religious fervor pay them in accordance with their extortionate demands.

The condemnation of false prophets never became a dead letter. Because it expressed the unchanging character of God, it is relevant whenever heresy appears. Jude had supported his denunciation of heretics by citations of prophetic predictions (cf. vss. 4, 14-15). II Peter is content to assert that **from of old their condemnation has not been idle.** This idea of the certain and cumulative character of divine punishment had been forcefully stated by Paul, who conceived of the impenitent as "storing up wrath" for themselves "on the day of wrath when God's righteous judgment will be revealed" (Rom. 2:5). The false teachers of the time of II Peter scoffed at the orthodox belief in the Second Coming. They, however, not **their destruction,** have been **asleep!** Delay has created in them a false sense of security and has encouraged them to assume that the Second Coming is fictitious. Orthodox Christian belief, however, teaches that the existing world is "stored up for fire, being kept until the day of judgment and destruction of ungodly men" (3:4-7).

2. History Foreshadows the Doom of Errorists (2:4-10a)

The three instances of God's punishment of sinners which are cited are a rearrangement and embellishment of Jude 5-7. In addition to the certainty of punishment, II Peter stresses God's determination to **rescue the godly from trial.** Jude's historical illustrations are the Exodus, the offending angels, and the punishment of Sodom and Gomorrah (Jude 5-7). II Peter follows the more chronological sequence: **the angels when they sinned;** the **flood** sent **upon the world of the ungodly,** paralleled by the preservation of Noah; God's **turning the cities of Sodom and Gomorrah to ashes,** paralleled by the rescue of **righteous Lot.** The three illustrations compose the content of a single conditional sentence. Their effectiveness is reduced somewhat by the heaviness of the grammatical structure. To the protasis, **If God did not spare the angels when they sinned,** a logical apodosis would have been, "he will not spare contemporary false teachers and their followers." The actual apodosis, shaped by the case of Lot, appears in vs. 9: **The Lord knows how to rescue the godly from trial, and to keep the unrighteous under punishment until the day of judgment.**

4. In Jude 6 the sinning angels are divinely "kept . . . in eternal chains in the nether gloom until the judgment of the great day." In II Peter, **God . . . committed them to pits of nether gloom to be kept until the judgment.** Some MSS of II Peter read **chains** instead of **pits,** in agreement with Jude. This probably resulted from an adaptation of the text of II Peter because the Greek word for pits (σιροῖς) so closely resembled the word for chains (σειραῖς), although δέσμος is the word for chain actually used by Jude. **Pits** (RSV) and **chains** (KJV) both belong to the imagery of the book of Enoch. The author of II Peter may have had in mind such passages as Enoch 10:4-6; 19:1; 54:5, while Jude

long and arresting one: Licentious, greedy, exploiters, libertine (despising authority), passionate (since they live by base desires), **bold, wilful,** revilers, **irrational animals, creatures of instinct,** revelers (even in the daytime), carousers, dissipaters, **unsteady,** lustful, **waterless springs,** boastful, liars (promising what they cannot give), dogs, pigs. Such strong language sounds strange to our humane ears, perhaps

because we no longer sense the diabolical danger of false teachings.

One serious charge stands out against these purveyors of heresy: They deny **the Master who bought them** (vs. 1). It may be that Peter is recalling his own "heresy" when he denied his Lord. In a real sense, most Christian heresies have to do with Jesus Christ. In him God has given men his decisive and adequate revelation.

5 And spared not the old world, but saved Noah the eighth *person,* a preacher of righteousness, bringing in the flood upon the world of the ungodly;

6 And turning the cities of Sodom and Gomorrah into ashes condemned *them* with an overthrow, making *them* an ensample unto those that after should live ungodly;

gloom to be kept until the judgment; 5 if he did not spare the ancient world, but preserved Noah, a herald of righteousness, with seven other persons, when he brought a flood upon the world of the ungodly; 6 if by turning the cities of Sodom and Gomor'rah to ashes he condemned them to extinction and made them an example to

---

was recalling 54:3-4 (cf. II Baruch 56:13). Whatever the reading, the point is that if angels who sinned were confined in nether gloom until the judgment, assuredly heretical teachers and their immoral followers should know that "their destruction has not been asleep."

5. Jude used the story of the Exodus but not the story of the Flood. II Peter's employment of the flood story here and in 3:6 may, however, have been indirectly due to Jude, since in Genesis (6:5–9:17) it immediately follows the account of the sin of the angels (Gen. 6:1-4). It appeals to the author of II Peter because it offers the opportunity for his own emphasis on God's unfailing mercy. True, God **did not spare the ancient world.** Instead, he **brought a flood** upon it. Nevertheless, he **preserved Noah,** thus showing unforgettably that he **knows how to rescue the godly from trial,** but without creating doubt of his determination finally to bring the unrighteous to judgment (vs. 9). This exhibition of mercy as parallel to divine judgment marks an advance of II Peter over Jude. Denunciation is inadequate as an expression of the Christian point of view; there must be comfort too. The author may have had in mind the collocation of judgment and mercy in Wisd. Sol. 10:6, "While the ungodly were perishing, wisdom delivered a righteous man" (ERV).

Because Noah was **a herald of righteousness,** he was preserved when God destroyed **the world of the ungodly.** In Jewish and early Christian tradition Noah was known as a herald of righteousness (see such descriptions of him in Josephus *Antiquities* I. 3. 1; I Clem. 7:6). This illustration requires the readers of II Peter to choose between contemporary heresy and apostolic orthodoxy. The consequences of their choice will follow as certainly as those illustrated in the fate of Noah and **the ancient world.**

6. The sequence of punishment by water and then by fire involved in the citation of the reduction of **the cities of Sodom and Gomorrah to ashes** resembles that of III Macc. 2:4-5: "Thou didst destroy those who aforetime did iniquity, . . . bringing upon them a boundless flood of water. Thou didst burn up with fire and brimstone the men of Sodom." The sequence also prepares for 3:6-7, where destruction of "the world that then existed" by water serves to warn that "the heavens and earth that now exist have been stored up for fire."

Sodom and Gomorrah are described as turned **to ashes** and **condemned . . . to extinction** as **an example to those who were to be ungodly.** The thought is that God will invariably treat sinners as he treated the cities of Sodom and Gomorrah in antiquity. From of old, therefore, the condemnation of sinners has not been idle (vs. 3).

Any Christianity not taking the revelation seriously is less than Christian. Any religion refusing the best is surely inadequate. Christianity maintains that eternal life consists in knowing the only true God and him whom God has sent.

But even more, there is a heresy which is the contradiction of the divine event in Christ Jesus: it is the denial of or the refusal to admit that "God was in Christ, reconciling the world unto himself" (II Cor. 5:19). It is the unwillingness to admit that he gave "his life a ransom for many" (Mark 10:45). In short, it is human autonomy, or man-centeredness, which does not start its life and thought with the God who in Christ Jesus provided the way to a *new* order and to a *new* life. In a sense, there are only two religions in the world: one is a human system by which man seeks to make himself acceptable to God; the other is that divine action by which God has provided man with justification and reconciliation. One is of man, the other of God.

7 And delivered just Lot, vexed with the filthy conversation of the wicked:

8 (For that righteous man dwelling among them, in seeing and hearing, vexed *his* righteous soul from day to day with *their* unlawful deeds:)

9 The Lord knoweth how to deliver the godly out of temptation, and to reserve the unjust unto the day of judgment to be punished:

10 But chiefly them that walk after the flesh in the lust of uncleanness, and despise government. Presumptuous *are they,* self-willed, they are not afraid to speak evil of dignities.

11 Whereas angels, which are greater in power and might, bring not railing accusation against them before the Lord.

those who were to be ungodly; 7 and if he rescued righteous Lot, greatly distressed by the licentiousness of the wicked 8 (for by what that righteous man saw and heard as he lived among them, he was vexed in his righteous soul day after day with their lawless deeds), 9 then the Lord knows how to rescue the godly from trial, and to keep the unrighteous under punishment until the day of judgment, 10 and especially those who indulge in the lust of defiling passion and despise authority.

Bold and wilful, they are not afraid to revile the glorious ones, 11 whereas angels, though greater in might and power, do not pronounce a reviling judgment upon them

---

7-8. God's rescue of Lot is cited for the encouragement of orthodox Christians who reject destructive heresies (cf. Wisd. Sol. 10:6; I Clem. 11:1). Because Lot was **greatly distressed by the licentiousness of the wicked** God rescued him. Vexation at the evil around him marked Lot as **righteous.** Because he reacted as a righteous man should, God stood by him and delivered him from the revolting situation by which he was **distressed** and **vexed.** Righteous men will always be fortified in the midst of trial by the certainty of divine rescue. God never abandons the faithful man.

9-10a. The references to Noah and Lot in vss. 5, 7 are supplementary protases to the principal protasis of vs. 4. They determine the form of the apodosis of vs. 9 in the interest of II Peter's primary emphasis on redemption. Noah and Lot stood alone but undismayed, and God preserved the one and rescued the other. God, who so acted in crises of antiquity, will deliver the righteous in all conceivable crises. He **knows how to rescue the godly from trial.** But **the unrighteous** he will **keep . . . under punishment until the day of judgment.** They will, in effect, get a foretaste of the punishment which will become their permanent destiny after the Second Coming (cf. 3:3-7; Matt. 10:15; 11:22, 24; Luke 16:23-29; I Pet. 3:19; Jude 6-7).

B. The Lawlessness of Heretical Teachers (2:10b-22)

1. Lust and Irreverence Determine Their Behavior (2:10b-16)

10b-11. In Jude 8 the antinomian errorists "reject authority, and revile the glorious ones." II Peter elaborates that picture and describes them as indulging in **the lust of defiling passion,** despising **authority,** and as being so **bold and wilful** as to be unafraid **to revile the glorious ones.** The two descriptions agree in making irreverence their essential sin. They condone licentiousness as religious. They revile the glorious ones in the sense of attributing to them their own licentious passions (cf. Gen. 6:1-4). Whereas reverence for the divine presence keeps angels humbly silent, the heretics, with brazen effrontery, express **reviling** judgments, overlooking that judgment is a divine prerogative.

The awful consequences of false teaching are set forth in three historical illustrations: The angels, the Flood, and Sodom and Gomorrah. Whatever men may think about these punishments that befell men and angels in times past, Peter is setting forth an eternal truth: false life produced by false teachings ends in suffering and disaster. To emphasize the illustration, he cites the favored angels who because of their station might have been spared. But their *pride* proved their undoing in **Tartarus,** the place of imprisonment. If this happened to angels, then what may happen to men? *Disobedience* was the sin of those who ridiculed Noah, his warning and his invitation to life. *Sensuality* was the false spirit in the residents of

12 But these, as natural brute beasts made to be taken and destroyed, speak evil of the things that they understand not; and shall utterly perish in their own corruption;

13 And shall receive the reward of unrighteousness, *as* they that count it pleasure to riot in the daytime. Spots *they are* and blemishes, sporting themselves with their own deceivings while they feast with you;

before the Lord. 12 But these, like irrational animals, creatures of instinct, born to be caught and killed, reviling in matters of which they are ignorant, will be destroyed in the same destruction with them, 13 suffering wrong for their wrongdoing. They count it pleasure to revel in the daytime. They are blots and blemishes, reviling in their dissipation,*g* carousing with you.

g Some ancient authorities read *love feasts.*

---

12. The thought of Jude 10 is poorly related and somewhat confused in its meaning. II Peter leaves the reader in doubt as to how and by whom the false teachers will be **caught and killed.** Instead of contrasting two levels of knowledge, as Jude had done, he emphasizes the brutishness of the errorists, saying in effect that men who live at the brute level will share the destruction normal for brutes. Jude's thought is more nearly that of Rom. 8:5-6 and I Cor. 2:14; II Peter's seems to be that the heretical teachers completely lack what the Spirit might impart. They represent themselves as spiritual but confuse the thrill of animal instinct for the presence of the Holy Spirit. They are **irrational** in the sense of lacking the divine life implanted by the Spirit. Lacking this, they remain exclusively **creatures of instinct.** Destruction is involved in being creatures of instinct; appetite makes possible the ensnarement of animals. Men who lapse into animalism bring upon themselves **the same destruction** that overtakes animals.

13. These . . . will be destroyed (vs. 12) becomes the keynote of vss. 13-16. **Suffering wrong for their wrongdoing** supports that basic assertion. "The hire of wrong-doing" (ERV) is suffering wrong. The thought is that the rewards or wages of sin are deceptive. Balak hired Balaam but never paid him (Num. 24:11; cf. II Pet. 2:15). Similarly, destruction (i.e., death) defrauds false teachers of the material rewards for which they sacrificed all other values (cf. Luke 12:19-21). Licentiousness and greed cannot make men rich toward God. The licentious and greedy unhesitatingly "revile the glorious ones" by regarding lust as angelic. They nevertheless feel aggrieved when God inflicts **suffering . . . for their wrongdoing.**

Again, these false teachers and their followers **count it pleasure to revel in the daytime.** "Revelry" and "pleasure" refer to luxurious sensuality. **The daytime,** lit., "the day," may contrast day with night, as in the RSV; but it may describe the brevity and transiency of sensual satisfactions. On this latter view the better translation would be, "They find pleasure in the indulgence of the moment" (Goodspeed). This would draw the contrast not between day and night so much as between "the voluptuousness of a day" and "the bliss of eternity" (Christopher Wordsworth, "The Second Epistle of St. Peter" in *The New Testament in the Original Greek* [London: Rivingtons, 1867], II, 92). Bernhard Weiss expresses the same view: "Clearly reference is made to this [i.e., destruction of sensual life by sensual indulgence], when it is said that they merely consider the voluptuousness of each day as pleasure, with which their souls are fed, although life passes away like a short day, and what will come after this will show them sufficiently that they have been cheated out of the reward of their immorality" (*A Commentary on the New Testament,* tr. G. H. Schodde and Epiphanius Wilson [New York: Funk & Wagnalls Co., 1906], IV, 310). The prevalent view, however, favors **the daytime** as the translation (cf. KJV, ERV, ASV, and Moffatt). On this view "day" and "night" as metaphors for spirituality and sensuality would probably be in the author's mind. His exhortation is that believers abstain from sensual indulgence because the new age of light had been inaugurated (cf. Rom. 13:12; I Thess. 5:5, 8; etc.).

Jude 12 had described the errorists as "blemishes on . . . love feasts." The best MSS of II Peter make no reference to love feasts in this context. These occasions are, however, probably in the author's mind. They would offer opportunity for the Christians of

14 Having eyes full of adultery, and that cannot cease from sin; beguiling unstable souls: a heart they have exercised with covetous practices; cursed children:

14 They have eyes full of adultery, insatiable for sin. They entice unsteady souls. They have hearts trained in greed. Accursed chil-

antinomian tendency to "carouse" with their fellow church members (cf. I Cor. 11:27-34). They had not withdrawn from the church and so could exploit its celebrations. If love feasts were the occasions Peter had in mind, the phrase **reveling in their dissipation** would represent an effective play on words. The Greek words for dissipation and love feast are respectively ἀπάτη and ἀγάπη. Two letters make the difference between worship and carousal! Instead of participating in the agape in accordance with its spirit, they make it an occasion for dissipation. For this reason **they are blots and blemishes.** Clement of Alexandria described this misuse of the agape: "There is no limit to epicurism among men. For it has driven them to sweet-meats and honey-cakes, and sugar-plums. . . . But we who seek the heavenly bread must rule the belly. . . . For 'meats are for the belly,' for on them depends this truly carnal and destructive life; whence some, speaking with unbridled tongue, dare to apply the name *agapè* to pitiful suppers, redolent of savour and sauce. . . . But such entertainments the Lord has not called love feasts." (*The Instructor* II. 1.)

14. The Greek word translated **insatiable** literally means "unable to stop." II Peter applies this description to the eyes of false teachers. Indulgence does not satisfy them. Adulterous looking perpetually engages them. Every woman is a potential adulteress to them. Whenever they see women, they have licentious thoughts. Their eyes are in this sense **full of adultery** (cf. Job 24:15; Matt. 5:28-29). **Entice** has the sense of catching with bait. In vss. 14, 18, the "bait" is **licentious passions of the flesh.** The false teachers encourage men to believe they are religious when in fact they are "lured and enticed by . . . desire" (Jas. 1:14). They probably assumed that true spirituality makes bodily indulgence of no moral significance. The deeply spiritual might even express religion in sexual indulgence. Only **unsteady souls** are enticed by such bait. People "established in the truth" (1:12) cannot be so deceived. In their effort to fortify unsteady souls in their licentiousness, the false teachers go so far as to "twist" Paul's letters to substantiate their error (3:16).

The motive of the false teachers is covetousness, not service. Their false words are intended to exploit, not enlighten (vs. 3). The word translated **trained** (γυμνάζω) means to exercise body or mind. The English word "gymnasium" is derived from it. The author of Hebrews described the spiritually mature as persons having "their faculties trained by practice to distinguish good from evil" (Heb. 5:14). Instead of being so trained, the **hearts** of the errorists are said to be **trained in greed.** Greed, like licentiousness, typifies the unregenerate life.

Accursed children looks back to the earlier description of the errorists as inevitably **suffering wrong for their wrongdoing** (vs. 13). Because they are divinely accursed, they are doomed (cf. Gal. 3:13). They deserve execution at the hands of God (cf. II Thess. 2:3; Eph. 2:3). The reward for their apostasy is ultimately rejection by God (cf. Deut. 11:26; Ps. 109:18). This exclamation both summarizes the assertions of vss. 13-14 and introduces the further description of vss. 15-16.

Sodom and Gomorrah. Living in a luscious valley which supplied them with all good things, they defected through sheer appetitism. Ezekiel says of them: "This was the iniquity of thy sister Sodom, pride, fulness of bread, and abundance of idleness" (Ezek. 16:49). The end was the same in each case. What men—and angels— sow they also reap.

Yet the picture is not all dark. A slight shaft

of hope shines through the gloom. Peter mentions the character of Lot, who, though not especially **righteous,** was **rescued. The Lord knows how to rescue the godly from trial, and to keep the unrighteous under punishment until the day of judgment** (vs. 9). Thank God for Noahs whose **righteous** souls are **vexed . . . day after day** by what they see and hear in the world about them. Nonconforming dissenters,

15 Which have forsaken the right way, and are gone astray, following the way of Balaam *the son* of Bosor, who loved the wages of unrighteousness;

16 But was rebuked for his iniquity: the dumb ass speaking with man's voice forbade the madness of the prophet.

17 These are wells without water, clouds that are carried with a tempest; to whom the mist of darkness is reserved for ever.

18 For when they speak great swelling *words* of vanity, they allure through the lusts of the flesh, *through much* wantonness, those that were clean escaped from them who live in error.

dren! 15 Forsaking the right way they have gone astray; they have followed the way of Ba'laam, the son of Be'or, who loved gain from wrongdoing, 16 but was rebuked for his own transgression; a dumb ass spoke with human voice and restrained the prophet's madness.

17 These are waterless springs and mists driven by a storm; for them the nether gloom of darkness has been reserved. 18 For, uttering loud boasts of folly, they entice with licentious passions of the flesh men who have barely escaped from those who

---

15-16. The right way is synonymous with "the way of truth" (vs. 2). Salvation is in both instances the destination. Only by following the apostolic rule of life may believers expect to reach that goal. The false teachers and their followers have forsaken this right way and **have gone astray** in the variety of ways specified. Greed is the particular variation from the right way which marks them as having **followed the way of Balaam** (for **the way of Balaam** see Exeg. on Jude 11). II Peter deliberately contrasts the right way and the way of Balaam. These ways lead in different directions and must not be confused with each other. The writer emphasizes the necessity of seeing clearly in this respect by showing that **a dumb ass** possessed sounder prophetic vision than a religious official whose moral sense had been perverted by **gain from wrongdoing** (cf. Num. 22:21 ff.). With fine irony the errorists, despite their claims of prophetic revelations and superior spirituality, are shown to be subasinine.

2. Their Promised Freedom Is Slavery to Sin (2:17-22)

17. II Peter substitutes **waterless springs and mists** for Jude's "waterless clouds" (Jude 12). **For them** he reserves **the nether gloom of darkness**, which in Jude 13 "has been reserved for ever" for "wandering stars." Darkness is a more appropriate penalty for wandering stars than for waterless springs. The writer is concerned, however, with the point rather than the details of the imagery. He means to say that an eternally dark future is in prospect for leaders whose guidance is unsound. **These** for whose description Peter borrows and embellishes Jude's analogies are the false teachers of vss. 10*b*-16. The effect of their teaching on "unsteady souls" is examined in vss. 17-22.

18. The loudness of their **boasts of folly** suggests the substitution of fervid enthusiasm for moral sanity. "Unsteady souls," susceptible to the enticement of **licentious passions of the flesh** to begin with, mistake the **loud boasts of folly** for religious certainty. The participle in this phrase **(uttering)** is a form of the verb usually employed of significant prophetic utterances. Madness and folly, not revelation, characterize what the false teachers say. Florid rhetoric obscures their abandonment of the right way. R. A. Knox illuminates the meaning by his translation, "Using fine phrases that have no meaning, they bait their hook with the wanton appetites of sense." Boasts of folly share the transiency (cf. Rom. 8:20; Eph. 4:17) of licentious passions of the flesh. No reliance can be placed in them.

The pertinence of the figure of **waterless springs** appears in the charge, **They entice with licentious passions of the flesh.** They arouse expectations which they cannot satisfy. Springs without water lure, but disappoint, the thirsty traveler. Passions of the flesh include all phases of human nature which are put to wrong uses (cf. Rom. 13:14; Gal. 5:16, 19, 24; I John 2:16) —the prostitution of the powers of human life. Persons **barely escaped from those who live in error** are the recent converts from paganism. Such people

19 While they promise them liberty, they themselves are the servants of corruption: for of whom a man is overcome, of the same is he brought in bondage.

20 For if after they have escaped the pollutions of the world through the knowledge of the Lord and Saviour Jesus Christ, they are again entangled therein, and overcome, the latter end is worse with them than the beginning.

live in error. **19** They promise them freedom, but they themselves are slaves of corruption; for whatever overcomes a man, to that he is enslaved. **20** For if, after they have escaped the defilements of the world through the knowledge of our Lord and Savior Jesus Christ, they are again entangled in them and overpowered, the last state has become worse for them than the

have not been taught to associate goodness with religiousness. They therefore are easily deluded. R. A. Knox understands **those who live in error** to refer to false teachers rather than to Gentile pagans. Those **who have barely escaped** are conceived to be persons reclaimed from heresy to orthodoxy, upon whom heretical teachers continue to urge their teaching. He accordingly translates, "Those who have had a short respite from false teaching." But however **barely escaped** is understood, the reference is to persons who have made limited progress in Christian living. They need constantly to be reminded of the precious and very great promises of Christ (cf. 1:3-15). If ὄντως, instead of ὀλίγως, is read, however (with many MSS), the reference is to mature believers, not catechumens, and the translation would be, **Those that were clean escaped from them who live in error** (KJV).

19-22. Freedom (ἐλευθερία) had been one of the great emphases of Paul. (The noun occurs six times in Paul's letters. Elsewhere in the N.T. it is found in Jas. 1:25; 2:12; I Pet. 2:16; and here. The adjective occurs fifteen times in Paul's letters, and elsewhere in the N.T. in Matt. 17:26; John 8:33, 36; Eph. 6:8; Rev. 6:15; 13:16; 19:18. The verb occurs five times in Paul's letters, elsewhere in the N.T. only in John 8:32, 36.) By it Paul meant fundamentally the privilege of being governed by the promptings of the Holy Spirit, by whom he conceived God's will to be directly communicated to his own spirit. He invariably established limitations within which freedom must be exercised. The freedom he commended as superior to legalism meant the opposite of antinomianism in that it was freedom for which "Christ has set us free" (Gal. 5:1). That being the case, it could never become an opportunity for the flesh, but rather for service under the Spirit's guidance (Gal. 5:13-17). But the false teachers "twist" certain elements in Paul's letters that are admittedly hard to understand (3:16). Among those elements so twisted, Paul's emphasis on freedom was almost certainly equated with licentiousness. That makes preposterous their promise of freedom, who **themselves are slaves of corruption** (cf. 1:4; Rom. 8:21; Gal. 6:8). The promise of freedom is under the circumstances the equivalent of "entrapment" with the bait of licentious passions of the flesh. They actually offer servitude, as their own slavery to **corruption** demonstrates. By contrast, the precious and very great promises of Christ demonstrably bring about the believer's escape from corruption and his participation in the divine nature (1:4).

The heretical teachers are **slaves of corruption** on the principle that **whatever overcomes a man, to that he is enslaved.** He is enslaved by having been overpowered by **the defilements of the world** (vs. 20). Corruption is his master.

Slaves of corruption may escape **the defilements of the world through the knowledge of our Lord and Savior Jesus Christ.** Although unsteady (vs. 14; cf. vs. 18), persons

they are like the light which resists and fights the darkness, like the salt which wages war against decay and putrefaction. Living against the pagan tide of their times, they are the saving salt and healing light of every situation. They help to turn the course of events toward righteousness and truth. They do not stand

well with the world, but they are not bereft of the power and consolation of God's rescuing power. Evil does not have the last word; it is held in control. It cannot get beyond certain bounds. It is kept under by the regulative power of God until the day of judgment. There is no escape for the unrighteous—

21 For it had been better for them not to have known the way of righteousness, than, after they have known *it,* to turn from the holy commandment delivered unto them.

22 But it is happened unto them according to the true proverb, The dog *is* turned to his own vomit again; and the sow that was washed to her wallowing in the mire.

3 This second epistle, beloved, I now write unto you; in *both* which I stir up your pure minds by way of remembrance:

first. 21 For it would have been better for them never to have known the way of righteousness than after knowing it to turn back from the holy commandment delivered to them. 22 It has happened to them according to the true proverb, The dog turns back to his own vomit, and the sow is washed only to wallow in the mire.

3 This is now the second letter that I have written to you, beloved, and in both of them I have aroused your sincere mind by

---

barely escaped from those who live in error are not helpless. Only when their own wills consent are they overpowered. When they escape the defilements of the world in the first instance, it is owing to Christ's divine power (1:3, 9). The divine power which enabled them to escape can also keep them from being **again entangled . . . and overpowered.** The condition of those who permit themselves again to become entangled and overpowered is **worse for them** than their earlier condition as pagans for the reason stressed in Christian tradition: that persons who become partakers of the Holy Spirit and then commit apostasy crucify the Son of God on their own account; they cannot again be restored by repentance (Heb. 6:4-8; 10:23, 26-31; cf. Matt. 12:43-45). One group of persons is under discussion in vss. 18, 20-22: **men who have barely escaped from those who live in error** are the same as those who **have escaped the defilement of the world.**

The holy commandment (cf. Rom. 7:12, where the reference is to the Tenth Commandment) is II Peter's equivalent for Jude's "the faith which was once for all delivered to the saints" (Jude 3). Adherence to apostolic orthodoxy is for both writers the condition of remaining in **the way of righteousness.** Apostasy leads to becoming **again entangled . . . and overpowered.**

The proverbs in vs. 22, one from Prov. 26:11, the other from a nonbiblical source, suggest the spiritual states of repentance and apostasy. Repentance brings "escape from the corruption that is in the world because of passion" (1:4). Furthermore, it opens up the glorious possibility of participation in the divine nature. Repentance, however, does not preclude apostasy. Believers can accept the destructive heresies of false teachers and follow their licentiousness (vss. 1-2, 14). **To turn back from the holy commandment delivered to them** is the supreme tragedy. The author of II Peter writes to warn all who have **known the way of righteousness** of the dangers of such a lapse.

IV. Prophecy and Tradition Determine the Duty of Christians (3:1-18)

Attention is now shifted from the libertines to the orthodox. After the lengthy denunciation of unsound teachers (ch. 2), the author returns to the theme of 1:5-21. Reference to "the holy commandment delivered to them" (2:21) prepares the readers for the shift from a negative and denunciatory to an affirmative and constructive mood.

A. Orthodox Christianity Supported by Prophets and Apostles (3:1-10)

1. Criteria for the Condemnation of Heresy (3:1-2)

3:1. The earlier letter to which II Peter is represented as the sequel is clearly I Peter: **This is now the second letter that I have written to you.** Differences in vocabulary, style,

---

there is a day of reckoning. This good word is to make the righteous patient in adversity and hopeful in seeming tragedy.

3:1-18. *Christ's Sure Coming and Its Implications.*—The key message of ch. 3 is the coming

of Christ, which is associated with the fiery dissolution of **the earth and the works that are upon it** (vs. 10). Every admonition issues from this inevitable end which the prophets predicted and the apostles commanded (vs. 2).

and content are too unmistakable for both letters to have been written by the same hand. Certain common emphases do, however, enable the later writer, with some degree of realism, to regard what he writes as complementary to I Peter.

The author of II Peter says that in both letters he has refuted destructive heresies by norms supplied in the commandment of the Lord . . . through your apostles. I Peter is less explicitly a refutation of heresy than Jude and II Peter. Like II Peter, however, I Peter appeals to the authority of prophets and apostles (I Pet. 1:10-12; cf. II Pet. 1:4, 16-21; 3:2), makes much of Noah's salvation (I Pet. 3:19-21; cf. II Pet. 2:5; 3:5-7, 9-15), makes the Passion and Ascension historically fundamental (I Pet. 1:21-25; 3:18-22; 4:1, 13; 5:1; cf. II Pet. 2:1), and repeatedly stresses the Second Coming as of central significance in apostolic tradition (I Pet. 1:4-7; 4:5-7, 13, 18; 5:4, 10; cf. II Pet. 1:11, 19; 2:9; 3:4, 7-8, 10-13).

The reference to arousing the readers by way of reminder looks back to 1:13. The object of the reminder is here your sincere mind. Mind is the faculty of feeling and desiring as well as of understanding (cf. Matt. 22:37; Mark 12:30; Eph. 4:18; Heb. 8:10; 10:16; I Pet. 1:13). It is an equivalent for the inclusive conception of "spirit" (Col. 1:21). The adjective sincere occurs in the N.T. here and in Phil. 1:10. The noun εἰλικρίνεια is used by Paul to describe what God brings about in man by his indwelling Spirit (II Cor. 1:12; cf. I Cor. 5:8; II Cor. 2:17; Phil. 1:10). That the author of II Peter is speaking to orthodox church members is indicated by the address beloved (cf. Jude 17). He thinks of their state of mind as undistorted by destructive heresies and undefiled by licentiousness. He credits them with having a sincere mind on the ground that they are "established in the truth" (1:12).

The author is urgent about the whole matter, because he takes this end and its terrible consequences and accompaniments seriously. Little wonder, then, that he repeats in this letter what is found (see Intro.) in the first (vs. 1), and that he seeks to arouse their minds to remember and to understand (vss. 1-3). He bids them not to ignore (vs. 8) the matter. Since all this will happen, he urges them to live holy and godly lives, to live in a waiting attitude of hope, as well as in a hastening attitude of diligent obedience. And they are to beware lest they be carried away with the error of lawless men and lose [their] own stability (vs. 17). Effort at growth in grace and knowledge of Jesus Christ is the only antidote to the persuasive errors which pull one away from true knowledge. A vigorously growing and maturing faith which is centered on the one great reality —Jesus Christ—is the best immunity to that corrosive power of heresy which ends in an existence burned up in the consuming fires of divine judgment.

Surely the writer speaks in this chapter to a condition which is still with us. He had his ear to the ground, as we would put it, and listened to what people were saying. He was not like the preacher who seeks to answer questions in his preaching which the people in the pew are not asking!

(a) He knew the persistent queries which were being made about Christian doctrines. One of the most persistent had to do with the Christian hope. "What about Christ's coming?" History has been moving along for quite some time and there is no sign of it. Birth and death are still the monotonous boundaries of life. Where is the promise of his coming?

The worldly-minded, secular scoffers seemed to be right. They did not take the spiritual world seriously, and therefore had no stake in the larger fulfillment of life and history. And these earth-bound people have their contemporaries. They are not interested in a second coming of Christ. Even Christians whose hope has been long delayed are inclined to lose their interest in it. Many are no longer held by the literalism of the early church's faith. Scientific method has flattened out reality until it takes on the prosaic nature of continuity. Any idea of an interference from beyond in the world of inflexible process is ridiculed as an absurdity. The Second Coming is a theological curiosity, a kind of religious threat which is wielded by fire-and-thunder evangelists, a sheer fiction of fearful and fevered minds. After all, year succeeds year, and generation succeeds generation, and century succeeds century. There has been nothing new under the sun, and there will not be anything new in the future. The horizontal mind of the secularist, the closed mind of the naturalist, the unwilling mind of the pagan, cannot see anything in the fulfillment of that which was started in Palestine years ago.

(b) What is the answer to his type of mind— whether Christian or secular? Peter posits three

2 That ye may be mindful of the words which were spoken before by the holy prophets, and of the commandment of us the apostles of the Lord and Saviour:

way of reminder; 2 that you should remember the predictions of the holy prophets and the commandment of the Lord and

---

2. Jude had supported the expectation of a Second Coming by "the predictions of the apostles" (Jude 17). For the same purpose, II Peter combines the testimony of prophets and apostles (cf. 1:12-21). On the authority of prophets and apostles, Peter "made known . . . the power and coming of our Lord" (1:16).

Down to this point attention has been focused on heretical denial of the power of the "Master who bought them" (2:1). Interest is now shifted to the coming of the Lord. This shift is explicitly indicated in vss. 3-7 and is implicit in vss. 1-2. In view of the Second Coming, Peter has twice written to arouse believers to **remember the predictions of the holy prophets and the commandment of the Lord . . . through your apostles.** The commandment of the Lord (cf. 2:21) reflects the conception of Christ as Master. (The verb "command" [ἐντέλλομαι] is used of Jesus in Matt. 17:9; 28:20; John 15:14, 17; Acts 1:2; 13:47. The corresponding noun [ἐντολή] is used of his teaching in John 13:34; 14:15, 21; 15:10, 12 [cf. I John 2:3-4, 7-8; 3:22-24; 4:21; 5:2-3; II John 4-6].) All that Christ commanded rather than a particular commandment is given significance for II Peter by the imminence of "the last days" (vs. 3; cf. Matt. 28:20). In view of the impending last days Christ's commandment through the apostles becomes an authoritative rule for the guidance of the thought and action of believers. The apostles are viewed as belonging timelessly to the church at large. Instead of having transmitted "cleverly devised myths" (1:16), the apostles, as successors to the O.T. prophets, dependably passed on the gospel to the church.

---

strong arguments which still have some weight. First, there is the argument from history. Have all things continued as they were? Has history gone on as usual? A great many things have taken place which do not conform to the iron-clad law of uniformity. What about the Flood? People thought things would go on and on, with business as usual. *But*—historical process is not continuous; there are breaks now and then. "Acts of God" we still call them, because there is no explaining their occurrence. So **the day of the Lord** may come as a trumpet blast at midnight. Crises do occur. There is such a thing as contingency in creation. Today the scientist himself no longer believes in an absolute law of cause and effect. Though nature is faithful and predictable, he will not absolutely guarantee that effect will definitely issue from cause.

Second, Peter replies with the law of contrast. In effect he says that we must never confuse time with eternity, the time of man with the time of God. God sees time quite differently from man. Man's outlook is limited. With God there is no "long" or "short" time. With him **a thousand years are as one day.** The real things are not measured by time; God's holy purposes do not follow a time schedule. Relativity is now a commonly accepted concept. A sufferer finds time long on his hands; a lover finds time short. Delay on God's part in the

fulfilling of his purpose must not be regarded as unconcern for its fulfillment (vs. 9).

Third, Peter answers the critics with the argument of opportunity. He looks upon this delay, this slowness of God as an evidence of his long-suffering. God does not wish that any should perish. There was a rabbinical saying that if the Jews were penitent for one day only, the Messiah would come. What might happen to our world if all men for one day only were really penitent! Meanwhile the Almighty is stretching the calendar, so to speak, so **that all should reach repentance.** Like Gabriel in *Green Pastures*, the righteous are much too anxious to blow the horn of final judgment, whereas the Lord is patient in the hope that men everywhere may come to a knowledge of the truth and be saved. He does not force repentance. Many like Luther have marveled at the patience of God in the face of man's evil and sin. His judgments strike slowly in history, but they do strike; only then, after evil has made itself abhorrent, is the cleansing spirit of repentance generated. Charles Beard, the historian, said that one of the truths he had learned from his study of history was that

> Though the mills of God grind slowly,
> Yet they grind exceeding small.[2]

[2] Longfellow, "Poetic Aphorisms: Retribution." From the *Sinngedichte* of Friedrich von Logau.

3 Knowing this first, that there shall come in the last days scoffers, walking after their own lusts,

4 And saying, Where is the promise of his coming? for since the fathers fell asleep, all things continue as *they were* from the beginning of the creation.

Savior through your apostles. 3 First of all you must understand this, that scoffers will come in the last days with scoffing, following their own passions 4 and saying, "Where is the promise of his coming? For ever since the fathers fell asleep, all things have continued as they were from the beginning of

2. THE FLOOD A TYPE OF THE COMING JUDGMENT (3:3-7)

Here the author embellishes Jude 17-18 to stress the portion of the apostolic message dealing with the Parousia.

3. The identical clause used in 1:20 to introduce the exhortation to a proper appreciation of prophecy is now employed to assert the relevance of that phase of the commandment of the Lord having to do with the promise of his coming. **The last days** refers to the troubled period preceding the end (cf., e.g., John 6:39-40, 44, 54; 11:24; 12:48; Acts 2:17; II Tim. 3:1; Heb. 1:2; Jas. 5:3; I Pet. 1:5, 20; I John 2:18; Jude 18; Clem. Rom. 14:2; Barn. 16:5). Christian tradition associated the appearance of the Antichrist and pretenders in general with the last days (cf. Matt. 24:5; I John 2:18). II Peter on that basis argues that **scoffers** by their very **scoffing** testify to the validity of **the promise of his coming**.

4. The first Christians did not expect to die. When a few Thessalonian converts had "fallen asleep," Paul assured the church that these would be at no disadvantage by

This is only another way of saying that men may become impatient with the evil state of affairs and wish a radical change, but the patience of God offers them every opportunity before his corrective power makes itself felt. In personal experience, every Christian knows that God has not dealt with him after his sins, but has been long-suffering and patient. The Flood came only after "the wickedness of man was great on the earth" (Gen. 6:5). The French Revolution was brewing for three generations before it boiled over into madness. The present revolution and violence in the earth are the result of long-standing causes which have been active for generations. No one can say that God has not been patient with us, waiting for that godly repentance to appear which is the beginning of human transformation. And so will it be before the Day comes! Let no one mistake God's slowness for forgetfulness!

(c) What kind of persons then are we to be? Peter closes his remarks about Christ's coming and the fiery dissolution of **all these things** with a reference to **persons**. The contrast is strong between the **things** that shall be dissolved and the kind of **persons** we ought to be in the light of the end. Things are not permanent, but persons are. After all, things are to serve persons and take on significance, take on even a sacramental nature, as they are used for persons and by persons for high ends. "Seek ye first the kingdom of God, and his righteousness; and all these things shall be added unto you" (Matt. 6:33).

Few passages of the Bible have greater relevance to our generation than these words from II Peter. Sophisticated theologians used to raise an eyebrow as they read, **the heavens shall pass away with a great noise, and the elements shall melt with fervent heat.** It sounded rather preposterous. But now a **great noise** of which Peter had no inkling has actually been heard, and **fervent heat** has melted the bodies and the cities of men! The very words themselves are no longer a laughing matter.

Little wonder that our author held such a serious view of life and history. For him, life was not to be taken frivolously. Because of the grave possibilities which confront us, he writes, **what sort of persons ought you to be in lives of holiness and godliness, waiting for and hastening the coming of the day of God** (vss. 11-12). He is not seeking to frighten people into being good; he is merely trying to indicate how a Christian should live in an age which expects such a glorious—and awful—conclusion. Surely he must live a spiritually prepared life. He ought also to live in an expectant mood as he waits and works for **new heavens and a new earth in which righteousness dwells.** He ought to be a person of integrity, a man of peace who acquiesces in the will of God, ever on his guard lest he be taken in **by the error of lawless men and lose [his] stability in the truth.**

And let him **grow in the grace and knowledge of our Lord and Savior Jesus Christ** (vs. 18). For, as indicated above, a growing life which is entering more and more into the won-

5 For this they willingly are ignorant of, that by the word of God the heavens were of old, and the earth standing out of the water and in the water:

creation." 5 They deliberately ignore this fact, that by the word of God heavens existed long ago, and an earth formed out of

---

comparison with the majority who would live "until the coming of the Lord" (I Thess. 4:13-18) . But Paul was sure that neither he nor most of his contemporaries would "sleep." Rather, they would be "changed, in a moment, in the twinkling of an eye, at the last trumpet" (I Cor. 15:51-52) . As time passed and the expectation of **the fathers** (i.e., the founders of the church) that they would themselves witness the Parousia failed, Christians found this phase of their tradition increasingly problematical. On the basis of the death of the fathers and the failure of their expectation that not all would sleep, the scoffers of II Peter's time denied the validity of **the promise of his coming.** Further, they generalized that **all things have continued as they were from the beginning of creation,** and concluded that the orthodox expectation of a kingdom of God on earth was fantastic.

5-6. The author attacks skepticism as to Christ's return with utmost vigor. He shows indisputably that the Parousia was an essential item in the Christianity of the apostles (vss. 10, 12; 1:16; cf. Matt. 10:23; 16:28; 24:3, 27-31, 34, 42; Acts 1:11; I Thess. 4:16-17; II Thess. 1:7-9; Jas. 5:8-9; Rev. 2:5, 25; 3:11; etc.) . Then he justifies the expectation of radical

---

derful generosity of God in Jesus Christ, and is appropriating more and more of the truth that is in him, is becoming inwardly immune to the thrusts of error. Health is the best enemy of disease. If these are the words of Peter, they reveal the adventurous nature and quality of the Christian's life, even in old age. There is something of the spirit of Paul in the writer, of him who had not yet fully "apprehended" what was in store, but who continually pressed on toward the undiscovered country of personal enrichment (Phil. 3:13-14) . Christ opens up the real possibilities of life; he generates a hopeful anticipation regarding the future. As growth is of the very essence of natural life, so growth is of the very essence of life with God-in-Christ. To grow up, to become mature as a Christian, is to come into a deeper consciousness of Christ's love and favor. The growing Christian should realize the assurance of that love. The growth itself is a daily progress, not in some occult mystical experience but in a practical awareness and inner assurance which gradually transform life by their power.

We are to **grow** in the **knowledge** of Christ. We are to pass from a "bowing acquaintance" to a closer friendship, "where all restraints are laid aside," as Maclaren puts it, and we come into a relationship of "perfect confidence." [3] Paul could shout, "Oh, to *know* Christ," and by it reveal that insatiable thirst for the truths about God and himself and history and the future which were concentrated in Jesus Christ. Such an impatient scholarship is the secret of youthfulness. It is the undying flame that lights

[3] *Expositions of Holy Scripture,* I and II Peter and I John, p. 237.

the human spirit. Anyone who has come to sit at the feet of Jesus and learn "the one thing . . . needful" (Luke 10:42) will be enrolled in a school that is never out.

Peter also implies that growth is a duty. There is no alternative. The Christian is engaged in a strenuous race, in perpetual warfare. There is no place for arrested development in his life or in the life of the church. Infantile Christian experience is the plague of many a Christian! Little wonder that he lacks the stature of God's child, or that he is pushed and pulled by counter propaganda. Is it enough to insist that people make a public confession of faith once only? Is there no place for insisting upon the discipline of growth in a Christian's life? Does the Christian life stop at the time of confirmation, or public profession of faith?

Peter does not mention the means by which this growth takes place. Surely he would insist upon prayer, sharing in the Holy Communion, entering into corporate worship, remembering the ancient events of God's people, practicing the Christian life in the daily round, and calling to mind the life and words and works of Jesus Christ. Even Christian service can be a "means of grace" by which one may **grow in grace** and **knowledge.** And he would regard quiet meditation as essential. The means of spiritual growth are many indeed; they include books and tracts and fellowship with other Christians and a long list of ways through which the undeserved kindness and the immeasureable truth of God-in-Christ enter into life and change it "from glory into glory."

5-15. *Three Worlds.*—William Moorehead finds in these verses a description of three

6 Whereby the world that then was, being overflowed with water, perished:

7 But the heavens and the earth, which are now, by the same word are kept in store, reserved unto fire against the day of judgment and perdition of ungodly men.

8 But, beloved, be not ignorant of this one thing, that one day is with the Lord as a thousand years, and a thousand years as one day.

9 The Lord is not slack concerning his promise, as some men count slackness; but is long-suffering to us-ward, not willing that any should perish, but that all should come to repentance.

water and by means of water, 6 through which the world that then existed was deluged with water and perished. 7 But by the same word the heavens and earth that now exist have been stored up for fire, being kept until the day of judgment and destruction of ungodly men.

8 But do not ignore this one fact, beloved, that with the Lord one day is as a thousand years, and a thousand years as one day. 9 The Lord is not slow about his promise as some count slowness, but is forbearing toward you,[h] not wishing that any should perish, but that all should reach

[h] Some ancient authorities read on your account.

alteration of the framework of earthly life by recalling how the antediluvian world was deluged with water and perished. He charges that the scoffers deliberately ignore this fact of the Flood. They are only pretending when they represent all things as having continued as they were from the beginning of creation.

7. Actually, prophecy and apostolic testimony combine to show that the God who formed an earth . . . out of water and by means of water, and once destroyed it, will destroy by fire the heavens and earth that now exist (cf. Enoch 83:3-5; Isa. 29:6; 30:30; 34:4; 51:6; 66:15-16; Dan. 7:9-10; Joel 2:30-31; 3:15-16; Nah. 1:5-6; Mal. 4:1). In their stead he will establish his kingdom. Apostolic tradition leaves no basis for doubt in these matters so far as faithful church members are concerned.

3. Psalm 90:4 Supports Belief in the Second Coming (3:8-10)

The argument is now directed to orthodox believers who may be inclined to become impatient at delay. They must not permit impatience to lead them to overlook the truth implicit in Ps. 90:4.

8. The vivid contrast implicit in the opening clause is obscured by the translation, But do not ignore this one fact, beloved. Literally, the author urges, "This one fact must not escape you." You in vs. 9 is emphatic and is contrasted with "they" in vs. 5. "They [i.e., the scoffers] deliberately ignore" the fact that God made and can destroy the earth. This one fact which must not escape believers is God's eternity. With man a thousand years is an eternity. With the Lord, however, one day is as a thousand years, and a thousand years as one day. Faith orients man to eternity, whereas scoffers remain children of time. Believers are for this reason undisturbed by the delay of the Parousia. Applied to the problem of "the promise of his coming" (vs. 4), Ps. 90:4 means that to God all events are present, including "the end of all things" (I Pet. 4:7). The ascription of this outlook to Peter suggests familiarity on the part of the author with John 21:18-19.

9. His promise refers to "the promise of his coming" (vs. 4). Some count slowness with regard to his promise as indicative of indifference, carelessness, impotence. Believers,

worlds.[4] For the apostle, all history is divided into three great and clearly defined sections.

There is first of all the old world, the antediluvian world which the Flood inundated. Skeptics at the time of this writing were saying, "Where is the promise of his coming?" (vs. 4). Things had gone on as usual. The generations

[4] The International Standard Bible Encyclopedia, ed. James Orr, et al. (Chicago: Howard-Severance Co., 1915), IV, 2357-58.

had come and gone and everything remained the same. The forces of history had been continuous, and they seemed destined to continue without interruption or break. All this sounds rather modern, for the skeptical mind fortified by the scientific method believes only in the continuity of natural processes and the inviolability of nature's laws. Catastrophe is unlikely. Yet Peter reminded his critics that the Flood had overwhelmed a generation.

10 But the day of the Lord will come as a thief in the night; in the which the heavens shall pass away with a great noise, and the elements shall melt with fervent heat, the earth also and the works that are therein shall be burned up.

11 *Seeing* then *that* all these things shall be dissolved, what manner *of persons* ought ye to be in *all* holy conversation and godliness,

12 Looking for and hasting unto the coming of the day of God, wherein the heavens being on fire shall be dissolved, and the elements shall melt with fervent heat?

repentance. 10 But the day of the Lord will come like a thief, and then the heavens will pass away with a loud noise, and the elements will be dissolved with fire, and the earth and the works that are upon it will be burned up.

11 Since all these things are thus to be dissolved, what sort of persons ought you to be in lives of holiness and godliness, 12 waiting for and hastening[i] the coming of the day of God, because of which the heavens will be kindled and dissolved, and the

[i] Or *earnestly desiring.*

---

however, know that forbearance, not slowness, explains the seeming delay (cf. Rom. 3:25; 11:32). Christ's desire that **not . . . any should perish, but that all should reach repentance** accounts for the apparent slowness about his promise. Accordingly, believers will "count the forbearance of our Lord as salvation" (vs. 15), and so as belonging to the genius of his promise. Delay of the Parousia ought on this basis to fire believers with evangelistic fervor, not make them easy prey for the skeptics. Christ delays the end to give **all** the opportunity of salvation. Believers must make his promise of advantage to as many as possible.

10. The certainty of "the promise of his coming" remains. **The day of the Lord will come,** and, as apostolic tradition pictured, **as a thief in the night** (cf. Matt. 24:43-44; Luke 12:39-40; I Thess. 5:2, 4; Rev. 3:3; 16:15). II Peter embellishes the primitive emphasis on certainty and unexpectedness with vivid details (cf. I Thess. 5:1-11; II Thess. 2:1-17): **the heavens will pass away with a loud noise, . . . the elements will be dissolved with fire, . . . the earth and the works that are upon it will be burned up.**

B. The Times Require that Christians Live Worthily (3:11-18a)
1. Certainty of the Parousia Makes Godliness a Necessity (3:11-13)

11-13. The dissolution of **all these things** being certain, the urgent consideration becomes, **What sort of persons ought you to be in lives of holiness and godliness?** The answer to the question is implied in the terms in which it is asked. The certain dissolution of all these things requires men to live lives of holiness and godliness. Because scoffers assume the permanence of things as they are, they do not **wait for new heavens and a new earth.** The temporal and transient occupy their attention. But holiness and godliness belong to the eternal order. Like "faith, hope, love" (I Cor. 13:13), they abide when **the elements . . . melt with fire. Lives of holiness** refer to ways in which holy living manifests itself. The reference is fundamentally to "life and godliness" (1:3) for which Christ endows men. The qualities by which the lives of believers should be characterized, therefore, are fully exemplified in Christ's "own glory and excellence" (1:3). As specified for men, these qualities are listed in 1:5-7.

But there was another world: **the heavens and earth that now exist** (vs. 7). This is the present order of things. But—this world **is stored up for fire,** it contains within it the power by which it can be consumed. The world is in the custody of a fiery power, reserved as it were for fire. (See the references to God and the consuming fire associated with his coming: Ps. 50:3; Isa. 66:15-16; Dan. 7:10-11.) Paul seems to take up the same theme in II Thessalonians (1:7).

From what we now know of the chemical composition of the elements it is not at all unlikely that the world could be consumed by some kind of fire. However, it seems that Peter here has no reference to an utterly annihilating fire which would end time and reduce all things to ashes. He is using the word to denote a kind of transformation, through judgment and mercy, of creation into something glorious (but see Exeg.). As the Flood did not merely bring an end to the

13 Nevertheless we, according to his promise, look for new heavens and a new earth, wherein dwelleth righteousness.

14 Wherefore, beloved, seeing that ye look for such things, be diligent that ye may be found of him in peace, without spot, and blameless.

elements will melt with fire! 13 But according to his promise we wait for new heavens and a new earth in which righteousness dwells.

14 Therefore, beloved, since you wait for these, be zealous to be found by him with-

---

The godly life involves **waiting for and hastening the coming of the day of God.** The verb translated "waiting for" (προσδοκάω) describes the direction of the person's mind. Expectancy, whether hope or fear or intellectual anticipation, is the mood with reference to the day of God. Steadfastness (1:6), not scoffing (vs. 3), is the mark of the godly man's waiting (vss. 2, 8-10). The verb translated "hastening" (σπεύδω) means either "to hasten" or "to desire with earnestness." **Hastening** probably expresses the writer's thought. In apostolic tradition prayer was thought to bring about the earlier coming of the kingdom (Matt. 6:10; cf. I Cor. 16:22). The universal proclamation of the gospel of the kingdom must precede the end, and will presumably hasten it (Matt. 24:14; cf. Acts 3:19). Conversely, the sins of men delay the coming (vs. 9; cf. C. G. Montefiore, "Rabbinic Conceptions of Repentance," *Jewish Quarterly Review,* XVI [1904], 209-57). **Lives of holiness and godliness** are the most universally effective way for bringing about the day of God ahead of schedule. Living as though the kingdom had come, even though it is yet to come, will shorten the period of waiting. This is in effect to say that the universe is moral, not mechanistic, and that a God of righteousness, not blind fate, determines the course of history.

The coming (*parousia*) ordinarily refers to a person. Here, however, it refers to **the day of God.** The sense is the same. The day of God is the occasion of Jesus' second coming. **The day of God** (cf. Jer. 46:10; Rev. 16:14) is synonymous with the more usual "day of the Lord" (vs. 10). The advent of this day will cause **the heavens** to be **kindled and dissolved.**

The **promise** which inspires believers to **wait for new heavens and a new earth** is identical with the "precious and very great promises" mentioned in 1:4. It is corroborated by the apostolic and prophetic word (1:19-21; cf. Rev. 21:1; Enoch 91:16; Isa. 65:17; 66:22). Not only so, but Christ's divine power which now grants believers "all things that pertain to life and godliness" (1:3) authenticates the promise. Believers will therefore wait instead of despairing. While waiting, they will live **lives of holiness and godliness,** because **righteousness dwells** in the new heavens and new earth for which they wait.

2. PAUL'S LETTERS SUPPORT THE EXPECTATION OF THE SECOND COMING (3:14-18a)

In conclusion, Peter urges maintenance of the primitive Christian expectation of the Second Coming. He regards this hope as the sure safeguard against moral lapse. However confusing his doctrine of freedom, "our beloved brother Paul" wrote clearly and frequently regarding it.

14. Therefore introduces Peter's final emphasis (cf. 1:10, 12). Paul had popularized this way of enforcing his reasoning, using the term twenty-one times in his genuine letters.

---

old, but was the occasion for a new beginning, so fire may be the end of the old dross and the creative event which will purify and refine the gold.

A third world is the new world (vs. 13). It is the **new heavens and . . . new earth, wherein dwelleth righteousness.** Peter, like those of his day, looked for Paradise restored. This vision is similar to that in Revelation, where the "first

heaven and the first earth had passed away, and the sea was no more" (Rev. 21:1). Such language is highly figurative, and is not to be taken literally. How life could be sustained on earth without the sea would be rather difficult to imagine. What it means is that the final stage of life will involve a fundamental change in the heavens and the earth, that is, in the world as we know it. The end will be both an end to

15 And account *that* the long-suffering of our Lord *is* salvation; even as our beloved brother Paul also according to the wisdom given unto him hath written unto you;

16 As also in all *his* epistles, speaking in them of these things; in which are some things hard to be understood, which they that are unlearned and unstable wrest, as *they do* also the other Scriptures, unto their own destruction.

out spot or blemish, and at peace. 15 And count the forbearance of our Lord as salvation. So also our beloved brother Paul wrote to you according to the wisdom given him, 16 speaking of this as he does in all his letters. There are some things in them hard to understand, which the ignorant and unstable twist to their own destruction,

---

Beloved denotes that the author's appeal is to orthodox church members (cf. vss. 1, 8; Jude 3, 17, 20). Since Christians **wait for these**—i.e., "new heavens and a new earth" (vs. 13)—they will **be zealous to be found by him without spot or blemish, and at peace.**

Since you wait for these refers back to vs. 12, where believers are described as "waiting for and hastening the coming of the day of God." Waiting describes the characteristic and unflagging attitude of expectant confidence regarding the promise of his coming (vs. 3). Waiting Christians, however, live neither idly nor negatively. They are **zealous**—i.e., they exert themselves—to hasten the coming of the day of God (vs. 12) by immediately embodying the righteousness of the **new heavens and . . . new earth** of Christian expectation. **Without spot or blemish** contrasts believers with licentious errorists, who in 2:13 have been described as "blots and blemishes." The dissipation and carousing encouraged by those who scoff at the promise of his coming can have no place in the lives of faithful church members.

At peace describes the inner serenity and optimistic outlook on the future with which believers **wait**. Peace originates and is multiplied in believers, "in the knowledge of God and of Jesus our Lord" (1:2). It is both the foundation and the outcome of a life of spiritual purity and moral consistency. It is diametrically in contrast to the outcome of life for scoffers (cf. 2:1-3, 17).

15. The forbearance of our Lord has earlier been interpreted as evidencing the desire that "all should reach repentance" (vs. 9). **Salvation** must refer to the opportunity of salvation—i.e., the forbearance moves us to repentance (vs. 9). **Our beloved brother Paul** had so interpreted forbearance (cf. Rom. 2:4; 3:25; 9:22; 11:22). This reference to Paul reflects the author's fraternal and at the same time reverential attitude toward the apostles (cf. vs. 2; 1:1). **To you** is an equivalent for "those who have obtained a faith of equal standing with ours" (1:1). Paul's letters are viewed as intended for Christians in general, instead of merely for members of churches in the localities where he had labored.

16. Moreover, Paul's letters are classified with **the other scriptures.** The point of view is substantially that of the Muratorian canon (*ca.* A.D. 190), where Paul's letters are described as "hallowed by being held in honor by the Catholic Church" (Henry Bettenson, *Documents of the Christian Church* [London: Oxford University Press, 1944], p. 41). So conservative a scholar as J. B. Mayor admits that the assumption of the existence of "a collection of later writings known to the writer as Scripture, of which St. Paul's epistles formed a part . . . can hardly be conceived as possible before the middle of the second century" (*The Epistle of St. Jude and the Second Epistle of St. Peter* [London: Macmillan & Co., 1907], p. 168; see also A. E. Barnett, *Paul Becomes a Literary Influence* [Chicago: University of Chicago Press, 1941], pp. 222-28).

Paul's letters, although accorded scriptural status, admittedly contain **some things . . . hard to understand** ["knotty points," Moffatt], **which the ignorant and unstable twist to their own destruction.** The ignorant and unstable are evidently the same as the "unsteady souls" (2:14; cf. 1:12) enticed by errorists (2:10-22). Paul had found it difficult to make the difference clear between the freedom of the faith-approved life and the licentiousness of antinomians (cf. Rom. 6:1–7:6; I Cor. 6:13-20; 9:1-23; Gal. 2:17-21;

17 Ye therefore, beloved, seeing ye know *these things* before, beware lest ye also, being led away with the error of the wicked, fall from your own steadfastness.

18 But grow in grace, and *in the* knowledge of our Lord and Saviour Jesus Christ.

as they do the other scriptures. 17 You therefore, beloved, knowing this beforehand, beware lest you be carried away with the error of lawless men and lose your own stability. 18 But grow in the grace and knowledge of our Lord and Savior Jesus

---

5:1-24; 6:7-10). Antinomians of the time of II Peter apparently undertook to justify their moral laxity on the basis of Paul's rejection of legalism in the interest of guidance by the Holy Spirit (2:1-3); cf. Jude 8, 19-20). By their misreading of Paul's letters (cf. 1:20), they bring about their own destruction.

17. The exhortation of vs. 14 is resumed. **Knowing this beforehand** looks back to the assumptions of 1:20 ("First of all you must understand this") and 3:1 ("I have aroused your sincere mind by way of reminder"). Believers are enabled **to be found . . . without spot or blemish** while waiting for new heavens and a new earth because of the foreknowledge divinely provided them in inspired prophecy and the apostolic tradition. Peter's first epistle (3:1) and Paul's letters combine to make the prophetic word (1:19-21) more sure. Prophecy and apostolic tradition complement each other as bulwarks against **error** (cf. Jude 14, 17-20). Foreknowledge, however, provides no automatic protection against error. Believers must **beware** ("be on your guard," Goodspeed) to avoid being **carried away** (cf. Jude 1, 21, 24). II Peter, like Jude, insists that believers must exert themselves if divine provisions for their safety are to become effective.

Lawless describes the character of the **error** by which "righteous Lot" was "greatly distressed" (2:7) and by which believers are in danger of being **carried away**. It designates men who to gratify lust violate all restraints, human and divine. Licentiousness threatens **stability**. Nonmoral Christians, like pagans, have fallen into this error (cf. 2:18). Their purely emotional piety makes their licentiousness doubly dangerous to the stability of other church members (cf. Jude 4, 8, 19).

Peter's warning against loss of **stability** corresponds to Jude's admonition against falling (Jude 24). The Greek noun στηριγμός is used in the N.T. only here. The corresponding verb, however, occurs six times in Paul's letters and four times in Luke-Acts. The meaning usually given is "firmness." Charles Bigg thinks it designates "a strong foundation" (*A Critical and Exegetical Commentary on the Epistles of St. Peter and St. Jude* [New York: Charles Scribner's Sons, 1901; "International Critical Commentary"], *ad loc.*). Souter uses the word "support." If it is so understood, grace and knowledge (vs. 18) compose the strong foundation which is endangered by **the error of lawless men.** The emphasis on **stability**—contrast "unsteady" (2:14) and **unstable** (3:16)—refers back to the earlier description of believers as "established in the truth" (1:12). Loss of stability begins in skepticism regarding "the truth that you have" and eventuates in licentiousness.

18a. Kinship between Peter's thought and that of Gal. 5:4 appears in the alternative to loss of stability here described: **But grow in the grace and knowledge of our Lord and Savior Jesus Christ.** Two translations are defensible: (*a*) **Grow in grace, and in the knowledge of our Lord** (KJV); cf. R. A. Knox, "Grow up in grace, and in the knowledge of our Lord." On this basis knowledge denotes personal communion with Christ (cf. 1:2, 8) and constitutes the condition of growth in grace. (*b*) **Grow in the grace and knowledge of our Lord** (RSV; supported by ERV, ASV, Goodspeed, and Moffatt). This translation makes grace and knowledge the gifts of our Lord, in agreement with the

---

the old and a fulfillment of the old. Heavens and earth there will be, but they will be changed, renewed, remade. The end will not be some fanciful place absolutely different from what we knew; it will be new yet it will be like

the old. We have here the same idea in the affirmation, "I believe in the resurrection of the body and the life everlasting." The two seem contradictory, yet in revelation they are always one.

To him *be* glory both now and for ever. Amen.

Christ. To him be the glory both now and to the day of eternity. Amen.

---

statement of 1:3. Knowledge, on this basis, corresponds to the sense of 1:5-6 rather than of 1:2, 8, and denotes acquaintance with the truth contained in apostolic tradition. It is the outcome of Christian instruction rather than of mystical experience. It stands in contrast with destructive heresies (cf. 2:1). Perhaps the two constructions are both present in Peter's thought in the sense that he regards orthodox instruction as the prerequisite of valid religious experience.

This prayer looks back to the initial prayer of 1:2 and to the reminder of 1:3 that Christ bestows salvation on believers by means of "the knowledge of him who called [them] to his own glory and excellence." The process of growth is resolved into stages in 1:5-11. Deepening communion with Christ, kept sound by the believer's acceptance of apostolic teaching, sustains **stability**. **Grace** and **knowledge** are the roots of Christian stability. From these roots the believer advances toward maturity. **Your own** points to the true foundation as distinguished from that on which the libertines base their lives. The latter have no stability.

V. Benediction (3:18b)

18b. In Jude the doxology is addressed to "the only God, our Savior through Jesus Christ our Lord" (cf. I Pet. 5:11). Here the address is directly to **our Lord and Savior Jesus Christ** (cf. 1:1, where Jesus Christ is referred to as "our God and Savior"). Peter's doxology may contain snatches from an early Christian hymn in which Christ is equated with God. Pliny wrote Trajan that Christians in Bithynia "were in the habit of meeting on a certain fixed day before it was light, when they sang in alternate verses a hymn to Christ, as to a god" (*Letters* X. 96).

The day of eternity occurs only in this instance in the N.T. It is probably a reminiscence of Ecclus. 18:10, where the "few years" of a man's life are, by comparison with "the day of eternity," like "a drop of water from the sea, and as a pebble from the sand." Thus, **day of eternity** means simply "eternity," and is an equivalent for Jude's "forever" (Jude 25). Moffatt regards **day of eternity** as a variant for "the day of God" (vs. 12), and "the day of the Lord" (vs. 10). He makes it synonymous with "the day of judgment" (vs. 7); see his *The General Epistles* (New York: Harper & Bros.; London: Hodder & Stoughton, 1928; "Moffatt New Testament Commentary"), p. 213.

18b. To Him the Glory Now and to the Day. —Calvin calls this a "remarkable passage."[5] It proves the divinity of Christ. It is an ejaculatory ascription which reveals the mainspring of Peter's life. The very thought of Christ made him shout. It brought out his whole being in a mighty affirmation of triumphant faith.

There is high Christology here. Putting Christ

[5] *Commentary on II Peter*, p. 426.

on an equality with God, the aged apostle says that: (a) Christ is central and crucial; (b) Christ shares **the glory** of eternal God; (c) Christ is to be glorified **now**; and (d) Christ is the glory of that eternal day which encompasses and fulfills all our days.

Amen seals what he writes with a mighty "Yea." What he has set down he believes to be true. So by an oath he authenticates his faith.

The First, Second,
and Third Epistles of

JOHN

Introduction and Exegesis by Amos N. Wilder
Exposition by Paul W. Hoon

I, II, AND III JOHN

INTRODUCTION

The epistles of John have had their special appeal to the church from early days in connection with the picture of the aged John, the last survivor of the twelve, giving his repeated and unvarying paternal counsel to a new generation of believers, "Little children, love one another."[1] This picture received a memorable formulation for modern readers in Browning's "A Death in the Desert." Here John, dying in concealment and attended by a few adoring followers, themselves on the verge of condemnation to the arena, dwells on his survival as one who can testify as an eyewitness to the great events of the gospel story and to the historical Jesus, now already belonging to a distant past. When my ashes scatter, says John,

> there is left on earth
> No one alive who knew (consider this!)
> —Saw with his eyes and handled with his hands
> That which was from the first, the Word of Life.
> How will it be when none more saith, "I saw"?

However it stands today as regards the question of the authorship of these epistles, their appeal will continue to rest on the simplicity of their testimony that God is love and that love is the test of religion.

These writings have several special relationships which further suggest their significance. They are numbered among the Catholic or General epistles. They must also be studied in relation to the other writings traditionally assigned to the Johannine canon, including the Fourth Gospel and Revelation. Their subject matter, again, brings them into close relationship with a considerable number of antiheretical writings both within and outside the New Testament. They are also illuminated when

studied in relation to various writings that originate in or have to do with Ephesus and the Roman province of Asia. Finally, their formal character suggests comparison with other compositions of the period.

I. Contents and Occasion

The view proposed in the present Introduction and Exegesis is that the three epistles have a common author and illuminate each other. In III John the writer who speaks of himself as "the elder"—which may or may not refer to his age—addresses a certain "beloved Gaius," whom he praises for hospitality to itinerant missionaries. Evidently the elder is supervising evangelical activity in the region. Couples or teams of missioners go through the area visiting the household churches and witnessing to the pagan populace, not, however, accepting sustenance from the latter. Gaius is encouraged to continue his entertainment of such travelers. At the same time it is brought to his attention that in a neighboring Christian group known to both Gaius and the writer a certain Diotrephes has boycotted the elder and his emissaries and even acts to exclude from the fellowship those who would welcome them. He is insubordinate and slanderous, and his motive is construed as ambition. He is not charged with any particular error, nor can we say what office he may have held or claimed. Quite possibly Gaius is encouraged to entertain a team excluded by Diotrephes. The Demetrius who is commended in vs. 12 may be the bearer of this letter. We may conclude that the extreme measures practiced by Diotrephes and the tenor of the letter reflect a breach that goes deeper than would be caused by an individual case of arrogance, deeper even than any conflict between general and local authority. In the light of I and II John it is likely that the troublemaker belonged to the party of the errorists

[1] Jerome, *Commentary on Galatians* III. 6. 10; cf. I John 3:11; 4:7; II John 5. When asked why he did not vary his testimony, John is said to have answered, "Because it is a commandment of the Lord, and if it be done, it suffices."

209

identified in those letters. The advances of the elder are met with disaffection, and his supporters may even be in the minority in some of the Christian groups in the area. Diotrephes may well be a conscientious leader of a strong party in numerous household churches which looks on the elder and his teaching as inferior or divisive.

Here II John may help us. This is a letter to a congregation, addressed under a graceful figure, carrying the greeting of the elder and a sister church. The recipients are warned in the most drastic terms against the advanced views of those who recognize Jesus Christ, but not his coming in the flesh. Any visitors who hold such views are not even to be greeted, much less afforded hospitality. The emphasis on love and the commandments suggests that the erroneous views are associated with unchristian practices. In this letter the boycotting is on the side of the elder and his sympathizers, and heretical views are explicitly mentioned. The two letters reflect a common situation. The similarity in their conclusions, which alike anticipate a visit of the elder, encourages the view that they were carried by the same messenger. III John 9 may refer to II John and may anticipate that Diotrephes will prevent its reaching the church. The preservation of the two letters together argues for their being companion pieces. Even so, III John 9 more probably refers to some earlier communication which had met a rebuff, and which contained a more detailed plea. II John itself is rather a brief charge carried by missioners to one of the congregations in the disaffected area to encourage support of the elder's cause, a congregation where there is reasonable hope that the letter will be received. The intransigence and exclusiveness of the procedure urged on the congregation suggest that the party of the elder may have been thrown on the defensive. The error in view is not necessarily something new—despite vs. 7—but the schism in the region has declared itself and the problem of authority has taken on a critical form.

The situation in I John is illuminated by the briefer letters. Here the elder, though he does not name himself or use the epistolary form for so general a communication, writes a pastoral letter with particular groups in mind. He deals with the same error characterized in II John and with the same situation of division reflected in III John. Missionary bands would presumably take this pastoral with them to numerous groups and on repeated tours in the given area. On one such tour they also took II and III John in view of local emergencies. The direct address to the readers in I John 2:12-17 does

not mean that only one church is envisaged, though like other passages, it indicates the author's sense of relationship to his readers. The withdrawal of the party attacked (2:19), and the victory of the point of view favored (4:4), require caution in interpretation. The other two epistles and the words, "the world listens to them" (4:5), suggest a cleavage rather than an exodus. In some household churches the errorists will have been in the minority and will have withdrawn. In others the group favoring the elder will have been excluded. Both sides practice a boycott where they are able to command the situation. The elder is attempting to meet the various local situations by resourceful moves and appeals. Our knowledge of similar dangers and attempts to deal with them in this period illuminate the present case.[2]

Modern analogies of the situation are found where, as in the frontier days in the West or on the mission field, a variety of aggressive sects are found tending to make inroads on each other or where in such circumstances there may be a struggle for power between the local leadership and the home base or missionary board. Edward Shillito in commenting on the reports of James H. Rushbrooke after his visits to the Baptist churches in the Baltic states wrote:

Among other things, he gave us an understanding of the free churches in eastern Europe, whose champion he was. I had never read the Epistles of St. John with so much understanding as I had after hearing Dr. Rushbrooke tell of his travels among the little Apostolic churches, always suspected and sometimes persecuted by other Christians.[3]

II. Analyses and Outlines

The first epistle does not lend itself easily to a tabular outline, as appears in the disagreement of those who have sought to analyze the movement of thought. An earlier commentator compared its course to that of the river Meander, which flowed through the province of Asia, while the adjective "cyclical" has been applied to it by modern students. Apart from the prologue and epilogue, it is helpful to distinguish the two chief polemic sections, 2:18-27 and 4:1-6. An illuminating lead is found in the observation that the theme of love dominates the central part of the epistle (particularly 3:11–4:21), while the earlier section is more concerned with righteousness and obedience, and the closing part with faith and confidence. Yet these notes overlap. The reader will observe that two particular themes recur: (a) real fel-

[2] Walter Bauer, *Rechtglaübigkeit und Ketzerei im ältesten Christentum* (Tübingen: J. C. B. Mohr, 1934), ch. iv.

[3] *The Christian Century*, LXIV (1947), p. 509.

lowship with God requires righteousness, and this goes back to the beginnings of the gospel; (b) the faithful are given repeated reassurance of their victory over the world and of the grounds for confidence in the face of divine judgment.

The three epistles can be outlined as follows:

I JOHN

I. Prologue (1:1-4)
II. The ethical test of fellowship with God; the light and the darkness (1:5–2:17)
    A. Fellowship with God and its test (1:5-10)
    B. Knowledge of God and obedience (2:1-6)
    C. Love and the true light (2:7-11)
    D. Charge to young and old: love for the Father and the world (2:12-17)
III. The deniers of the faith; truth and falsehood (2:18-27)
    A. The Antichrist and the last hour (2:18-23)
    B. Summons to faithfulness (2:24-27)
IV. The children of God and of the evil one; life and death (2:28–3:24)
    A. The children of God and the second coming of Christ (2:28–3:3)
    B. The children of God and of the devil (3:4-10)
    C. Hate and death in the world; life and love in the faith (3:11-18)
    D. Confidence before God in the truth (3:19-24)
V. The false spirits and the Spirit of God (4:1-6)
    A. The denial of Christ come in the flesh (4:1-3)
    B. The victory of the children of God (4:4-6)
VI. God's love and our confidence: the witness of the Spirit (4:7–5:12)
    A. God's love and our love for one another (4:7-12)
    B. The grounds of our confidence (4:13-18)
    C. The children of God and his commandments (4:19–5:5)
    D. The witness of the Spirit (5:6-12)
VII. Epilogue: closing affirmations and charge; the true God and eternal life (5:13-21)

II JOHN

I. Address and greeting to the church (vss. 1-3)
II. Summons to love (vss. 4-6)
III. Warning against error (vss. 7-11)
IV. Conclusion (vss. 12-13)

III JOHN

I. Address and greeting to Gaius (vss. 1-2)
II. Gaius and the itinerant missionaries (vss. 3-8)
III. Recalcitrance of Diotrephes (vss. 9-11)
IV. Commendation of Demetrius (vs. 12)
V. Conclusion (vss. 13-15)

III. Epistolary Form and Style

Both II and III John are letters in the strict sense, as is indicated alike by their form and content. I John has no epistolary introduction and herein resembles the Epistle to the He-

brews. But unlike Hebrews, it also lacks the concluding features of a letter. James ends similarly but has an initial salutation. The full outward marks of a letter or epistle were not originally given this writing, nor were they added later, as was sometimes the case, especially when authorship by an apostle was to be assigned. Yet the composition has some of the marks of a letter. Though there are no concrete indications of the identity of the author or the recipients, yet the writer visualizes those whom he addresses and their situation, and writes them with warmth and authority. Such recurrent phrases as "My little children, I am writing this to you" (2:1), and the interchange of "we" and "you," mark the personal character of the communication. Circumstances (2:19, 26; 4:4) and issues (3:17, 20; 5:16-17) are referred to which suggest the author's concern with the situation in the churches of a particular area. His thought, however, deals somewhat generally with the Christian life as a whole and the larger concerns of his day. What we have, then, is most probably a "pastoral" (Westcott), a "religious tractate" (Windisch), "an informal tract or homily" (Dodd) addressed to numerous groups of Christians in the region with which the writer has special relationships.

The style of the epistle is marked by simplicity of syntax after the impressive opening. As with the Fourth Gospel, clause is added to clause and statement to statement with a minimum of connectives or dependent relationships. Similarly, the movement of thought and succession of themes is cumulative and linked together rather by the fundamental insights than by conscious composition. We find here a special form of the hortatory or "paraenetic" style familiar to us in the religious discourse of the age, marked by personal appeal, contrasts of right and wrong, true and false, and an occasional rhetorical question. The use of parallelism is so marked in parts as to convey a ceremonial character, and the writer has his own locutions which give a peculiar stamp to the work.

A noteworthy instance of these locutions recurring throughout the epistle is illustrated by the following: "*This* is the message . . . *that*" (1:5); "By *this* we know . . . *by*" (3:24); and "In *this* is love . . . *that*" (4:10). See also 2:5, 25; 3:8, 10, 11; 4:9; etc. In such cases a demonstrative is given first place in a sentence, looking forward to its definition or explanation usually after some particle or conjunction (ἵνα, ὅτι, ἐάν, etc.). This is one of the features which by its frequency distinguishes the style of the epistle from that of the Gospel of John. This writer is also fond of anticipating a positive statement by a negative, e.g., "I write to you, *not* because you do not know the truth, *but* because you know it" (2:21; see also 2:7; 3:18; 4:10; 5:6; and II John 1:5). He also "uses the conditional sentence in a variety of rhetorical figures which are unknown to the gospel."[4] Dodd cites the following passages among others: 2:1, 29; 3:20; 5:9. Characteristic also of the style is the reminder of matters of common knowledge expressed by such terms as "we know," "you know," "if you know," "as you have heard," "what you heard from the beginning."

A more important aspect of the style of the epistle, however, and one which affects profoundly our view of its composition and interpretation, is the formal and rhetorical character of certain passages. The writer appears to quote recurrently and then to enlarge upon units or fragments of poetic material whose style is distinct from his own. This material is characterized first of all by its couplet form or parallelism, differing in character, however, from the parallelism familiar to us in the poetic books of the Old Testament or the Synoptic Gospels. The cogency of the argument rests partly on our knowledge of similar phenomena in the Fourth Gospel, especially the prologue, partly on similar ceremonial forms in Hellenistic literature of the time, and partly on the illumination of the movement of thought in the epistle when these elements are noted. In any case, the special character of these passages is to be recognized as a distinctive aspect of the composition. The matter can best be illustrated by presenting two sections written in this special style or drawn from the supposed source as identified by two scholars. The first[5] is as follows:

Every one who does right is born of him (2:29b)
Every one who commits sin is guilty of lawlessness
   (3:4)
  No one who abides in him sins (3:6a)
  No one who sins has . . . seen him (3:6b)
He who does right is righteous (3:7b)
He who commits sin is of the devil (3:8a)
  No one born of God commits sin (3:9a)
  No one who does not do right is of God (3:10b)

As von Dobschütz points out, each of these four couplets exhibits antithetical parallelism. There is, moreover, a close relationship between the first and third couplet, as between the sec-

ond and fourth. Study of this passage will disclose a surprising balance of thought in which simplicity of statement is combined with a highly artistic formulation. These lines are interrupted in the text of I John by other matter which, however, can be recognized as comment and paraphrase, and which bears the watermarks of the writer's particular style. If the text of I John 2:28–3:12 is written out with the above lines set apart as quotations and presented in special type,[6] the sense of the passage and the movement of thought become easier to grasp.

Rudolf Bultmann independently reached practically identical results with this section of the epistle. Quoted below is a different passage from his more complete analysis of the writing.[7]

He who says "I know him" but disobeys his commandments
  is a liar, and the truth is not in him (2:4);
but whoever keeps his word,
  in him truly love for God is perfected (2:5a).
He who says he is in the light and hates his brother
  is in the darkness still (2:9).
He who loves his brother abides in the light,
  and in it there is no cause for stumbling (2:10).
But he who hates his brother is in the darkness
  and walks in the darkness (2:11a).

Here again, as the Greek shows even more clearly, the balancing of similar and antithetical terms, phrases, and conceptions, and the aphoristic and lapidary form indicate that we have poetic material which can be distinguished from the reworking it receives from the writer of the epistle. Bultmann's study of this source begins with a full discussion of the section 1:5-10 which stands in the epistle almost unaltered, beginning with the words, "God is light and in him is no darkness at all." Typical in this section is the initial phrase, "If we say" (ἐὰν εἴπωμεν). Typical in the section 2:4 ff. cited above is the present participle used substantively, "he who says" (ὁ λέγων), which varies elsewhere, i.e., in the section adduced by von Dobschütz, with "every one who" (πᾶς ὁ ποιῶν). It is at least clear that there are considerable and sometimes continuous elements in the epistle whose style distinguishes them from that of the author both with respect to poetic structure and syntactic usage. A further element appears in the writer's use of formulas drawn from the common tradition of the Gospel.[8]

[4] C. H. Dodd, "The First Epistle of John and the Fourth Gospel," *Bulletin of the John Rylands Library,* XXI (1937), 134, 135; cf. Rudolf Bultmann, "Analyse des ersten Johannesbriefes," *Festgabe für Adolf Jülicher* (Tübingen: J. C. B. Mohr, 1927), p. 143.
[5] Ernst von Dobschütz, "Johanneische Studien, I," *Zeitschrift für die neutestamentlichen Wissenschaft,* VIII (1907), 4.
[6] *Ibid.,* p. 6.
[7] "Analyse des ersten Johannesbriefes," *Festgabe für Adolf Jülicher,* p. 157.
[8] Otto A. Piper, "I John and the Didache of the Primitive Church," *Journal of Biblical Literature,* LXVI (1947), 437-51.

IV. Background

To understand the message of I John it is important to appreciate the background it shares with the Gospel of John (see Vol. VIII, pp. 440-42). Here, however, several matters must be emphasized. In contrast with the Gospel the epistle has almost no allusion to the Old Testament and lacks evidence of Semitic style. It reflects more directly than John a Hellenistic milieu; see, e.g., the term "anointing" (χρῖσμα, 2:27; etc.), and the sacramental idea that God's "seed" (σπέρμα, 3:9) makes the believer sinless, as well as the dualism which it shares with the Gospel. This Hellenistic background is not Greek, properly speaking, but Oriental-Gnostic. We have sufficient evidence of a religious outlook in the East neither Jewish nor Greek, though influencing both, to which the new faith early accommodated its message in ways quite distinct from Jewish Christianity or Paulinism. This outlook had its own prophets, its own conception of salvation, and its own oracular poetic forms. These religious conceptions had deep roots in a long past for multitudes of men. They answered to certain perennial needs of the soul more satisfyingly at various points than the Jewish terms in which the gospel was first formulated. This world view, with its contrasts of light and darkness, life and death, truth and error, was more philosophically appealing, and its story of the redeemer or light-bringer was familiar often in grandiose and moving formulation, associated with rites of baptism and with oracular discourse and hymns. Christianity in this atmosphere took on a kindred expression, and within the church teachers arose who espoused ambiguous forms of the gospel, often of a dangerous character.[9]

For men of this background the Jewish idea of creation was inadequate to account for the world. Things arose through generation or emanation from God in a long series, and the world was separated from him by a radical alienation. The soul, though of divine origin, was a prisoner here in a domain of darkness, and could be saved only by a revealer who would descend from the world of light and usher it into eternal life. When such conceptions found their way into Christianity there was danger especially at two points. God's final sovereignty over the world as a whole was de-

preciated and his final purpose in history was lost sight of. Moreover, the salvation of the soul made too little of the ethical factor in either God or man. Thus several supreme achievements of the Old Testament were forfeited. Particularly uncongenial to men of this background were the Jewish conceptions of the resurrection.

The exaggerated dualism of this outlook also had as its consequence the conviction that the divine redeemer in descending to earth could not be thought of as subjecting himself to a real embodiment in the flesh or to the humiliation of suffering in the body. Thus there were Christian teachers who denied that Christ was really born as a man and died on the Cross; he only seemed to do so. Hence they are spoken of as the Docetists ("seemists"). Jesus was not to be identified with Christ. A common view was that Christ's divine nature came upon him at his baptism and left him just before his passion. The epistles of Ignatius and the apologists testify to the concern the church had with this error. It represented often a well-meant attempt to safeguard the Incarnation on the Godward side but it emptied the mission of Christ of its essential element. Thus we can appreciate the vehement repudiation of the Docetists in our epistle, as later in Irenaeus, who speaks of "these blasphemous systems which divide the Lord, as far as lies in their power, saying that he was formed of two different substances." [10]

But Docetism was only one aspect of the extravagance and variety of Christian teaching that prevailed in the time and region with which our epistles are concerned. All the writings which bear upon the churches of Asia in this period show that diverse impulses and patterns existed. The authors of the deutero-Pauline writings, Revelation and I Peter, as well as Ignatius, evidence the disorder. The Gnostic tendencies were accompanied by arrogance toward less sophisticated brethren and at times by libertinism.

The task of the author of our epistles in these circumstances is well suggested by E. C. Hoskyns and Noel Davey:

The author of the Johannine writings, like St. Paul, is faced by a riot of disordered religious romanticism. . . . When [he] writes, spiritual romanticism has entered the Church, and is there confidently declared to be the essence of the Christian religion. He is therefore less concerned with spiritual romanticism in the world than he is with

[9] See B. W. Bacon, *The Gospel of the Hellenists* (ed. Carl H. Kraeling; New York: Henry Holt & Co., 1933), chs. ix, x, xi; Ernest Percy, *Untersuchungen über den Ursprung der Johanneischen Theologie* (Lund: Hakan Ohlsson, 1939); Hugo Odeberg, *The Fourth Gospel* (Uppsala: Almquist & Wiksell, 1929); Rudolf Bultmann, *Das Johannesevangelium* (10th ed., No. 4; Göttingen: Vandenhoeck & Ruprecht, 1937-40; "Meyer's Kommentar").

[10] *Against Heresies* III. 16. 5; cf. III. 16. 8: "Their doctrine is homicidal, conjuring up, as it does, a number of gods, and simulating many Fathers, but lowering and dividing the Son of God in many ways."

its appearance in the Church; and he is compelled to put forth his whole pastoral and literary energy in order to recover the control of the Church by the Life and Death of Jesus.[11]

Part of the background of our letters is, of course, also the evangelical tradition going back to Jesus and the primitive church. To this our writer makes constant appeal in connection with both belief and conduct.

V. Message and Doctrine

The message of I John, alluded to in II and III John, resumes the common faith of the apostolic age, but it is conditioned by the special situation to which it is addressed and by a special perspective shared with the Fourth Gospel. The situation in question leads the writer to dwell chiefly upon the character of the Christian life, its ethical tests and endowments, and upon the radical conflict between the church and the world in the last days.

The great theme dealt with and prominent both at the beginning and end of I John is that of the "true God" (versus "idols") and of fellowship with him. "God is light and in him is no darkness at all" (1:5). God is love and only so can he be known. The ground for our knowledge of God and fellowship with him, and the ground of the message itself, is the revelation of God's eternal life (so, "the word of life," 1:1) in his Son. "In this the love of God was made manifest among us, that God sent his only Son into the world, so that we might live through him" (4:9). The reason for the insistence on the confession of Jesus as Christ come in the flesh is that only here is the true knowledge of God and sharing of his life possible. For it is in "Jesus Christ the righteous" (2:1) and in the love of God exhibited in his love that we meet the Father as he is and works. Only here are eternal life and victory over the world secure. In the light of the Fourth Gospel we can see that our epistle connects victory over the prince of this world with the death of Christ without special emphasis on or mention here of his resurrection (3:8; 4:4; cf. John 12:31-32). Thus the errors of the Gnostic Christians arising from their dualistic world view are corrected, while much of their outlook and language is shared.

The fateful character of the crisis in the church is interpreted in eschatological terms. This is the last hour, the time in which the Antichrist manifests himself. Denial of the Incarnation is associated with lovelessness and hatred, the children of the devil are contrasted

with the children of God, and the inspiration of error with the Spirit of God. The "world," meaning first of all the world of men, is "in the power of the evil one" (5:19), and is related to darkness, error, and death. The children of God are to abide in him, keeping the new yet old commandment of love. They have an understanding, an anointing, an inner testimony, the Spirit, and the forgiveness of sins. Particularly in baptism and the Lord's Supper is the testimony confirmed to them; for the children of God have fellowship not only with Christ the medium of the Spirit but with the Christ who really endured the passion (5:6-8). The evangelical tradition is clear in the view of Christ as expiator and advocate, and in the expectation of his second advent. The common apostolic message and familiar formulas of faith and conduct, together with echoes of the teaching of Jesus, can be recognized in the writing.[12]

VI. Relation of I John to the Gospel of John

Early Christian tradition and the great majority of modern scholars have agreed on the common authorship of these writings, even where the author has not been identified with the apostle John.[13] The situation has changed in more recent study. Following on earlier investigations, especially by H. J. Holtzmann, a number of contemporary scholars of the first rank, including Dodd, have been led to the conclusion that the author of the epistle could not well be the same man who wrote the Gospel.[14]

The similarities of these two writings over against the rest of the New Testament impress all readers. We meet certain words, phrases, and conceptions here that are absent or rare elsewhere. Thus we note the repeated use of abstract terms like light, life, truth, and love; the fondness for radical antinomies; repeated phrases such as "abiding in," "walking in," "knowing (or doing) the truth," "of the truth," "of God," "of the world"; basic conceptions of the interrelations of God, the Son, knowledge, love, and rebirth. The reader also soon comes to recognize the style of these writings, as it has been characterized in the case of the epistle above. All in all, there is a combination of simplicity and elevation which differs from the flexible discourse of Paul and from the more

[11] The Riddle of the New Testament (New York: Harcourt, Brace & Co., 1931), pp. 231-32.

[12] C. H. Dodd, The Johannine Epistles (New York: Harper & Bros.; London: Hodder & Stoughton, 1946; "Moffatt New Testament Commentary"), pp. xxvii-xliii; Piper, "I John and the Didache of the Primitive Church."
[13] So Westcott, Jülicher, Wrede, Brooke, Law, Bacon, Bernard, Percy, Howard.
[14] So Bauer, von Dobschütz, E. F. Scott, Moffatt, Riddle, Dibelius. Windisch also inclines to this view. See discussion of this question, Vol. VIII, pp. 461-62.

concrete vocabulary and formal features of the Synoptic Gospels. The two writings have at least a very close relationship to each other if they are not by the same author.

But very real differences appear in the writings under close inspection.[15] The matter has been most recently canvassed by Dodd, who relates his study to that of A. E. Brooke in the latter's *Critical and Exegetical Commentary on the Johannine Epistles*.[16] Dodd calls attention in I John to grammatical and syntactical peculiarities, distinctive idioms and rhetorical features (including the absence of Aramaisms), and significant features of the vocabulary. In summing up he says:

The style of the Epistle has a strong general similarity to that of the Gospel, but is on the whole more monotonous and narrower in range, while it nevertheless uses certain idioms and figures which are absent from the Gospel; and it lacks a whole range of idioms which are characteristic of the Gospel, and are plausibly held to indicate a Semitic character from which the Epistle is free. Its vocabulary overlaps with that of the Gospel, but lacks a large number of highly significant terms characteristic of the latter. While these facts cannot be said to disprove identity of authorship, they leave it in grave doubt.[17]

It is, however, the alleged disparity of religious ideas between the two writings that has occasioned the most discussion. The epistle is practically devoid of all reference to the Old Testament. The ideas of the Second Coming and the Last Judgment show no signs of being spiritualized as in the Gospel. The epistle has an interpretation of the Antichrist which is *sui generis*. Furthermore, it construes Christ's death specifically in terms of expiation, and repeatedly connects the forgiveness of sins with it. The Gospel ordinarily thinks of Christ's death in connection with his being "lifted up" and the consequent making available of the Spirit and eternal life to his followers. Again, the epistle identifies Jesus himself with the Paraclete, as one who in heaven will intercede for his own, while in the Gospel the Paraclete returns to them on earth in the form of the Spirit.

[15] H. J. Holtzmann—Walter Bauer, *Evangelium, Briefe und Offenbarung Johannes* (3rd ed.; Leipzig: J. C. B. Mohr, 1908; "Hand-Commentar zum Neuen Testament"), pp. 319-22; C. H. Dodd, "The First Epistle of John and the Fourth Gospel," *Bulletin of the John Rylands Library*, XXI (1937), 129-56, and *The Johannine Epistles*, pp. xlvii-lvi; and Hans Windisch, *Die Katholischen Briefe* (2nd ed.; Tübingen: J. C. B. Mohr, 1930; "Handbuch zum Neuen Testament"), pp. 109-11.

[16] (New York: Charles Scribner's Sons, 1912; "International Critical Commentary") pp. i-xxvii.

[17] "The First Epistle of John and the Fourth Gospel," *op. cit.*, p. 141. Used by permission.

These differences are quite marked. It is true that the special circumstances that occasioned the epistle and its different literary form would account for some of them. It is quite possible that the author of the epistle had something to do with the editing of the Fourth Gospel or that he used strata of tradition also present in John. But we shall probably do the most justice to the epistle in all its aspects if we recognize its independent character. This carries with it also rejection of the idea that the epistle was a covering letter or addendum to the Gospel.

VII. Origin and Literary History

The unknown elder writes at some time during the first decade of the second century to churches in the Roman province of Asia in circumstances described above, assuming acquaintance on the part of his readers with the Fourth Gospel or its type of Christianity. It is understandable that I John, as a pastoral tractate carried by itinerant missionaries throughout the region, lacks a true epistolary form and explicit designation of the writer. The three writings indicate that the problem of the time was as much one of social control in the churches as of heterodoxy. They reflect a period of luxuriant and uncontrolled diversity of faith and leadership and the means pursued by the more responsible leaders to establish norms for faith, conduct, and fellowship based on the revelation which was from the beginning.

The three writings having been so closely associated in their origin were no doubt preserved together. In the middle of the second century, when the Fourth Gospel began to receive wider recognition as apostolic, I John (with its apparent corroboration of the apostolic authorship of John and this epistle in 1:1-3) and therewith the other two letters became closely associated with that Gospel, and their survival was thereby assured. Their literary history is closely related to that of the Gospel and our conclusions as to their authorship hinge closely upon our evaluation of the Johannine tradition in the early church in connection with the Fourth Gospel and Revelation. It is only toward the end of the century that we begin to have clear references to one or more of these epistles by name and as written by John. Later (Origen, Eusebius) the tradition betrays some uncertainty as to the apostolic standing of the two shorter letters and distinguishes their authorship from that of I John. Some modern scholars have agreed with this, identifying the elder of II and III John with the author of Revelation, and relating I John to the Fourth Gospel. The tradition was motivated in this conclusion by the fact that II and III John, being written by an "elder," could not easily be assigned to the apostle John, who was taken to be the author of the Gospel and I John. But the three epistles of John are in all likelihood by the same writer, the elder, and the survival of the two briefer epistles can best be accounted for on the view that the three formed a corpus from the beginning. The references in the church fathers to only one letter (Irenaeus: "the epistle of John"; he, however, quotes from two), or to two (the Muratorian fragment and Clement of Alexandria) do not prove otherwise since they might be referring to the whole corpus.[18] That the elder is not the apostle John would appear from his self-designation and from the tenor of the shorter letters and the situation reflected there. The eyewitness of I John 1:1-3 is best understood as a reference to the continuous testimony in the church going back to the initial revelation. That the elder is not the "elder John" of

[18] Edgar J. Goodspeed, *An Introduction to the New Testament* (Chicago: University of Chicago Press, 1937), p. 324.

second-century tradition is likewise probable.[19] In any case, the authorship of the epistles is to be distinguished from that of Revelation.

VIII. Selected Bibliography

BROOKE, A. E. *A Critical and Exegetical Commentary on the Johannine Epistles* ("The International Critical Commentary"). New York: Charles Scribner's Sons, 1912.

DODD, C. H. *The Johannine Epistles* ("Moffatt New Testament Commentary"). New York: Harper & Bros.; London: Hodder & Stoughton, 1946.

FINDLAY, G. G. *Fellowship in the Life Eternal.* London: Hodder & Stoughton, 1909.

HOLTZMANN, H. J., and WALTER BAUER. "Johanneische Briefe," *Evangelium, Briefe und Offenbarung des Johannes* ("Hand-Commentar zum Neuen Testament"). 3rd ed. Leipzig: J. C. B. Mohr, 1908.

LAW, ROBERT. *The Tests of Life: A Study of the First Epistle of St. John.* 3rd ed. Edinburgh: T. & T. Clark, 1914.

WESTCOTT, BROOKE FOSS. *The Epistles of St. John.* 3rd ed. London: Macmillan & Co., 1892.

WINDISCH, HANS. *Die Katholischen Briefe* ("Handbuch zum Neuen Testament"). 2nd ed. Tübingen: J. C. B. Mohr, 1930.

[19] B. W. Bacon, *Gospel of the Hellenists*, pp. 3-51.

I JOHN

TEXT, EXEGESIS, AND EXPOSITION

1 That which was from the beginning, which we have heard, which we have seen with our eyes, which we have looked

1 That which was from the beginning, which we have heard, which we have

---

I. PROLOGUE (1:1-4)

Though this pastoral message begins with no epistolary salutation nor with the usual expression of devout good wishes, the announcement of the great blessings of eternal life, fellowship, and joy shared with the readers serves a similar purpose. The

---

1:1-4. *The Prologue—A Christian Manifesto.* —The meaning of the prologue is best grasped by taking vs. 3 as the main theme, which vss. 1-2, 4 elucidate. The author declares in vs. 3 that his purpose in writing the epistle is to **proclaim** the message of the reality of God revealed in Christ. Because this epistle was occasioned by the need of dealing with heresy and misconduct, argument and denunciation frequently appear. But the author does not first engage in apologetics; he knows that error is best met by confronting it with the truth it

denies. (The words "proclaim," "testify," "testimony," appear nineteen times in the epistles.) Debate may interest and controversy illumine, but only the proclamation of positive convictions can enlist commitment and establish men in faith. The gospel has no place for the false tolerance which alleges that one idea is as good as another, nor for the fashionable attitude which supposes that a man is mistaken in the degree that he is positive. The gospel is a "manifesto." It proclaims that which was **manifested** (vs. 2) in Christ.

upon, and our hands have handled, of the | seen with our eyes, which we have looked
Word of life; | upon and touched with our hands, concern-

---

supreme realities of eternal life and fellowship with God, known in immediate, tangible experience, and aspects of a revelation going back to the beginning, are invoked here in the prologue, both as a ground and sanction for the practical exhortation that makes up so much of the epistle, and as a makeweight against current errors which can claim no such authority or antiquity. The appeal to ultimate beginnings echoes or suggests not only the prologue of the Fourth Gospel with its "Word" which was "in the beginning . . . with God" (John 1:2), but also the first phrase of Genesis and the divine utterance that brought the world into existence. The epistle has thus an august exordium, and one which takes the reader immediately into the secrets of the divine counsels and the sharing of the divine life. This attitude of thought determines the mood and level of concern of the epistle throughout and even the high sobriety and oracular character of its rhetoric.

The construction of the long first statement running through the third verse occasions some difficulty. Not only is it interrupted by a parenthesis, vs. 2, but the syntax and bearing of the important phrase, **concerning the word of life,** are unclear. The clue to the passage is found when we begin with the words of the third verse and relate the preceding clauses to it: **That which we have seen and heard [concerning the word of life] we proclaim.** The theme of the proclamation is further described in vss. 1-2. It includes **the life** (vs. 2), and it concerns the whole **word of life** or revelation of life (vs. 1), but it is not to be identified only or precisely with these. For the pronoun used in vss. 1 and 3 for the object of the proclamation is neuter and cannot therefore refer specifically to either **life** or **word.** What is proclaimed as tangibly experienced is the primal divine reality manifested both as life and truth.

1:1. The Greek tense of the last two verbs, **looked upon and touched,** reinforces their emphasis on actual personal observation, while the different (perfect) tense of the preceding verbs—repeated in inverse order in vs. 3—brings out the continuing significance

---

The content of the proclamation is on the loftiest possible plane here and throughout the epistle. Even when the author descends to specific points of controversy or exhortation, he sets them within the over-all context of the fundamental ideas of Christianity. Indeed, I John may be called an epistle of ideas, and the cast of the author's mind has been aptly described as "metaphysical," "absorbed." [1] Significantly, among all the N.T. writings I John alone does not contain a single proper name or a single definite allusion—historical, personal, or geographical. Consider the massive ideas of the epistle, and the dignity, even majesty, with which they are presented: life, love, truth, righteousness, light, forgiveness, obedience, belief, knowledge of God, prayer, assurance, regeneration, sin, darkness, fear, the world, hatred, the Antichrist, the Second Coming. The grandeur of these themes rebukes those interpreters of the gospel who reduce Christian preaching and teaching to trivialities and who give men stones for bread. Great religion, as great art, always deals with ultimate truths. The Finnish com-

[1] G. G. Findlay, *Fellowship in the Life Eternal* (London: Hodder & Stoughton, 1909), p. 377.

poser, Sibelius, in an interview concerning his methods of composition, said he strove that through all his music there might run "the golden cord of truth."

But a message, however lofty, must be personally believed and experienced if it is to avail. Thus language grammatically cast in the first person—such as that of the prologue, **we have heard, . . . we have seen, . . . we have looked upon and touched with our hands**—always marks authentic religion. Personal experience must seal the truth the mind holds (cf. Expos. on 5:10a). The Christian message, further, is verified in objective history as well as in subjective experience (cf. Expos. on 4:2). It is also corroborated and tested by reference to the abiding, collective witness of the Christian fellowship through the centuries (cf. Expos. on 4:13-18). The singular pronoun "I" has its rightful place in proclamation; but the language of Christian conviction rises to its height in the plurals of the prologue, or of the *Te Deum:* "The Apostles, . . . the Prophets, . . . the Martyrs, . . . the holy Church throughout all the world doth acknowledge thee." All who believe may possess the testimony of those who have gone before,

of the witnessed facts. Those who have **heard** and **seen** are still ruled by that experience and are thus constituted as witnesses (cf. Acts 4:20). We may compare the words of Ananias to Paul after his conversion, "For you will be a witness for [Christ] to all men of what you have seen and heard" (Acts 22:15), and Paul's own words: "Am I not an apostle? Have I not seen [ἑόρακα] Jesus our Lord?" (I Cor. 9:1.)

A question of the greatest importance arises here and it is related to the matter of the authorship of the epistle. To whom does the **we** refer? (*a*) Is it an "editorial" we, and is the writer in effect saying "I"? (*b*) Or does the **we** refer to a restricted group of original eyewitnesses of the events of the life of Jesus, among whom he is one? The latter view is widely held and appears to be confirmed by the apparent contrast with **you** in vss. 2 and 3. (*c*) Or does the **we** really stand for all believers, whether original eyewitnesses or not? In this case the writer is referring to the "abiding witness" experienced in the church and borne by the church in unbroken solidarity through the generations. This is the view which is preferred here, in the light of the use of "we" in the epistle as a whole and in the Gospel of John. In 4:14 the elder writes, "And we have seen and testify that the Father has sent his Son as the Savior of the world." Here "we" is used as in 1:1-4. But the preceding verse, 4:13, shows that it refers to all true believers, including those addressed, "By this we know that we abide in him and he in us, because he has given us of his own Spirit." The readers share the truth with the writer, "I write to you, not because you do not know the truth, but because you know . . ." (2:21). The author of the Fourth Gospel speaks of the common experience of all, "And the Word became flesh and dwelt among us; . . . we have beheld his glory. . . . And from his fullness have we all received" (John 1:14, 16). Where a group has a strong sense of solidarity it is natural to speak of absent members sharing in events that were actually witnessed by part of the group. So

---

and find themselves made one with the "myriads of souls, redeemed by Him from themselves and from the world . . . who with linked hands stretch back to touch Him through the Christian generations." [2]

The reality of God has been uniquely revealed to men in **the word of life.** While the gospel in one sense is a message, a word, in a deeper sense it is the communication of life through the Word. "Life" is thus the fundamental theme of the epistle, and with this theme it opens (1:1) and closes (5:13, 20). Man ever seeks life—in primitive or civilized ways, on physical, cultural, or religious levels. What distinguishes man as man is his capacity for and urge after fuller, richer life; and history is but the story of his seeking. Christianity alone satisfies this elemental urge and answers to man's deepest need with the only true life. Legend relates that early Christian martyrs during an era of imperial persecution were taken to North Africa and put to work in the salt mines for the remainder of their years. But with their implements of labor they cut on the walls of the mines the words, *vita, vita, vita,* "life, life, life." In their heroic way they proclaimed the heart of the gospel, the eternal life they had found in Christ.

1-2. *God in Christ Is Ultimate Reality.*—The concepts of eternity and history, of reality and

revelation, of God's primal life and human life in Christ, are combined in these words: **That which was from the beginning, . . . the life was made manifest.** The Christian message of life is no innovation or invention. It is not at the mercy of shifting fashions of thought. It is the revelation of Reality as Reality always has been and will be. All atheisms or skepticisms ultimately break themselves against the eternal Reality of the universe. But in Christ the eternal has invaded time, and ultimate Reality has disclosed itself for human eyes to see and mortal ears to hear. Accordingly, because God chose to reveal himself in history, Jesus is not an accident or an incident in discontinuity with human life, but the deliberate self-revelation of the divine in the context of human life (cf. 5:10-12). Further, because ultimate Reality has decisively declared its character in Christ, the Incarnation forever qualifies the nature of the universe as unalterably and eternally Christlike. The Christian claim is that every religious meaning found in Jesus Christ can be ascribed to God, and that God was as fully present in Jesus as it is possible for God to be present in human life. Christian faith thus challenges every doubt of the reality of God by summoning men to behold the Jesus of history: "Our certainty of God may be kindled by many other experiences, but has ultimately its firmest basis in the fact that within the realm of history to which we ourselves belong, we encounter the man Jesus as an un-

[2] James Stalker, *The Life of Jesus Christ* (New York: Fleming H. Revell Co., 1891), p. 151.

2 (For the life was manifested, and we have seen *it,* and bear witness, and show unto you that eternal life, which was with the Father, and was manifested unto us;)

ing the word of life — 2 the life was made manifest, and we saw it, and testify to it, and proclaim to you the eternal life which was with the Father and was made manifest

---

Polycarp in his Epistle to the Philippians (9:1) reminds his readers, long after the time of Paul and the apostles, of the virtues which "you also saw before your eyes, not only in the blessed Ignatius . . . but also . . . in Paul himself, and in the other Apostles." As Benjamin W. Bacon says with regard to our passage, "So strong . . . is this feeling of solidarity with the past that in it the lines of demarcation between one era and the next are obscured" (*The Gospel of the Hellenists,* ed. Carl H. Kraeling [New York: Henry Holt & Co., 1933], p. 57.

The common and abiding witness has to do first of all with the life of Jesus and his resurrection (here see especially for **touched with our hands,** Luke 24:39, the same Greek verb, and John 20:27). But **the word of life** refers more widely to the whole revelation of God from **the beginning,** of which "the word of the cross" (I Cor. 1:18) or "the word of this salvation" (Acts 13:26) is the culminating aspect. Thus the **word of life** here is not the personal "Word" of John 1:1-3, 14 or Rev. 19:13. As B. F. Westcott says, "The personal interpretation of *'the word of life'* is not supported by any parallel" (*The Epistles of St. John* [3rd ed.; London: Macmillan & Co., 1892], p. 7). Westcott has in mind such passages as Phil. 2:16; Acts 5:20. The author is speaking of the eternal purpose and revelation of God which conveys life to men. So in Isa. 55:11 we read of "my word . . . that goeth forth out of my mouth: it shall not return unto me void" (ASV). Those, therefore, that have **seen and heard** have had possession, in Christ's life and death and resurrection, of God's primal and eternal life and truth.

2. In the prologue of the Fourth Gospel it is in its aspect of "life" that the personal Word is related to men, "In him was life, and the life was the light of men" (John 1:4). In I John too, though the "word" has the somewhat different sense of "revelation," it is through it that **life** is opened to men, **the eternal life which was with the Father.** The

---

doubted reality." [3] Jesus Christ is the center of history. Once and for all the ultimate Reality of the universe emerged in history and was apprehended in such a way that it is declared to be the climax and the criterion by which all else is to be judged. History is not inevitable progress toward a future climax of good in this world; the climax has already occurred. Jesus' words on the Cross, "It is finished" (John 19:30), mark the end of one age and the beginning of a new one (cf. 2:8).

2. *Eternal Life Now.*—The invitation of the gospel is to live in the eternal life of the new age now. (The phrase **eternal life** is the Johannine equivalent of such phrases in the Synoptic Gospels as "entering the kingdom of heaven," "being saved," "inheriting eternal life," and of being "in Christ" in Paul's writings; cf. Exeg. on 2:24.) While it is true that our author shares the eschatological expectations of early Christianity, which included life after death (cf. Expos. on 2:17; 5:10*b,* 12*b*), a distinctive aspect of the Johannine conception of eternal life is that it is a present possession and ex-

perience. In this connection the adjective "eternal" must not be permitted to mislead us. "Eternal" means not what is future in terms of time but what is unending and what is of the character of the life Christ lived. (A. E. Brooke suggests that in popular language the adjective "spiritual" gives the meaning of the Greek αἰώνιος better than "eternal." [4])

This conception corrects a common perversion of the gospel. Expositors often interpret eternal life as future immortality and withhold the richest gift Christianity offers to men—life with God now. It defines the true measure of life as qualitative rather than quantitative. Length of years is not life, and to speak of "long" or "short" lives is false; one ought rather to speak of large and small lives, poor and rich lives, empty and full lives. Man's need is to add life to his years rather than years to his life. This conception thus confronts men with judgment upon the kind of life they are now living. Millions of people, it has been said, long for immortality who do not know what to

[3] Wilhelm Herrmann, *The Communion of the Christian with God,* Bk. II, ch. i, sec. 3.

[4] *A Critical and Exegetical Commentary on the Johannine Epistles* (New York: Charles Scribner's Sons, 1928; "International Critical Commentary"), p. 6.

3 That which we have seen and heard declare we unto you, that ye also may have fellowship with us: and truly our fellowship *is* with the Father, and with his Son Jesus Christ.

4 And these things write we unto you, that your joy may be full.

to us — 3 that which we have seen and heard we proclaim also to you, so that you may have fellowship with us; and our fellowship is with the Father and with his Son Jesus Christ. 4 And we are writing this that our[a] joy may be complete.

[a] Other ancient authorities read *your*.

---

word **eternal** (αἰώνιον) means first of all unending, not timeless, but takes on qualitative overtones from its Christian use in connection with the new age or age to come. It is in the events narrated in the gospel that this **life** is **manifested** and proclaimed, and the idea of love is therefore implicit in the term.

3. This is confirmed by the emphasis now on **fellowship** as the goal of the message. This term with its sense of active and intimate partnership—both the mutual relationship of the believers and their common relationship **with the Father and with his Son Jesus Christ**—anticipates here at the beginning of the epistle the crowning theme of love, and helps us to recognize that the **word of life** refers specifically to the revelation of the love of God, of which the church had had such concrete experience.

4. Eternal life, fellowship, and now **joy** are all interrelated in the tidings. **Our joy** is the joy of all (many of the MSS, indeed, read here "your joy"), and its connection with "fellowship" reminds us of John 15:10-11. So Ignatius writes to the Magnesians (7:1): "Let there be in common one prayer, one supplication, one mind, one hope in love, in the joy which is without fault."

---

do with themselves on a rainy afternoon! In the hearts of how many Protestant Christians today would the author's purpose in writing this epistle find response, "That you may know that you have eternal life" (5:13)? "Immortality" is a present experience. Christian faith declares not merely a resurrection after death, it insists above all on a resurrection with Christ now. A man may know whether he possesses eternal life, and if he does not possess it before he physically dies it is questionable whether he will possess it after he dies. When the Christian lives in eternal life through faith (5:13) and love (3:14), he becomes a source of life to others (cf. John 7:38). His vitality is infectious; he radiates life to all whom he touches. Of F. D. Maurice it has been said:

He lived as few men have ever lived in the Divine. He was . . . "a spiritual splendor." The Divine embraced him. . . . It was this more than anything that made him the spiritual power that he was. In the presence of Maurice it was hardly possible to doubt of a Divine sphere,—of a spiritual life.[5]

3. *Eternal Life Means Divine and Human Fellowship.*—Because the life of eternity is to abide in love (cf. 3:11-18; 4:7–5:2) it can be lived only in community. Thus fellowship is both the goal and the source of the proclaiming of the Christian message. Human nature is made

[5] John Tullock, *Movements of Religious Thought in Britain During the Nineteenth Century* (New York: Charles Scribner's Sons, 1893), p. 293.

for fellowship. Man seeks fellowship on various levels—of self-interest, hobbies, cultural tastes and intellectual interests, political affiliation, patriotic loyalty, causes of social good will. But fellowship of men with God and with one another through Christ is the richest fellowship, and alone fulfills the purpose of life as fellowship: "so that you may be sons of your Father who is in heaven" (Matt. 5:45). Individual religion is a contradiction in terms. Our spiritual life is inevitably mutual. Mysticism has its place in the Christian life; but the most mystical of Christians—the author of this epistle—does not err when he habitually uses the plural "we" (which together with "us" and "our" appears twelve times in these four verses alone). Divine-human fellowship of believers with one another in Christ constitutes the true fellowship of the church and exposes by contrast cheap forms of so-called "fellowship" in which churches "specialize." Too often churches are little more than religious clubs whose fellowship consists of entertainments, friendly smiles, and diffused geniality. The true nature of the church's fellowship is portrayed in Jesus' metaphor of the vine and the branches (John 15:1-6), and in Paul's figure of the body (Rom. 12:4-5; I Cor. 12). The true mark of the church's fellowship is self-sacrificing love manifest in mutual service, prayer, labor, helpfulness (cf. 3:16-18; 5:15-16).

4. *Eternal Life Means Joy.*—Joy motivates, informs, and issues from fellowship (vs. 4), but it is a holy joy. Walter Pater relates that a

5 This then is the message which we have heard of him, and declare unto you, that God is light, and in him is no darkness at all.	**5** This is the message we have heard from him and proclaim to you, that God is light and in him is no darkness at all.

II. The Ethical Tests of Fellowship with God; the Light and the Darkness (1:5–2:17)

This first section of the body of the epistle is characterized by its contrast of light and darkness, as the following polemic section, 2:18-27, to which it leads up, is marked by the contrast of truth and falsehood, and the subsequent section, 2:28–3:24, by the contrast of life and death. Walking in the light and obedience to the commandments of God are brought into close relationship to each other and serve as ethical tests of those who make false claims to that fellowship announced in the prologue. The section closes with a charge to Christians faced with the great crisis of the end time, whose particular manifestation in the Antichrist is presented in the following section.

A. Fellowship with God and Its Test (1:5-10)

The more general "word" or revelation invoked in the prologue is spoken of now in its more immediate aspect as the **message,** and the theme of the divine "life" gives way to that of the **light** as one that lends itself better to the ethical considerations now to be pursued. The same transition is found in the prologue to the Gospel of John when it speaks of the personal Word, "In him was life, and the life was the light of men" (John 1:4), the ethical significance of this "light" being clearly brought out in John 3:19-21. Light symbolism is universal in religion, and is particularly marked in the Johannine writings. The background for its use here is found both in Jewish and in pagan Hellenistic writings. Light realized as a priceless good suggested not only illumination and revelation, but also security and joy. These various aspects may be illustrated from the O.T.: "The Lord is my light and my salvation" (Ps. 27:1); "In thy light shall we see light" (Ps. 36:9); "But unto you that fear my name shall the Sun of righteousness arise with healing in his wings" (Mal. 4:2). But the term inevitably took on a moral connotation in Israel and elsewhere. "The children of the light" (Luke 16:8; John 12:36; Eph. 5:8*b*), who bear "the armor of light" (Rom. 13:12), and in whom is found the "fruit of light" (Eph. 5:9) are those who "walk in the light" in the sense of showing a life and conduct that accord with the gospel.

The parallelism in the present section is to be noted. Vss. 6, 8, 10 match each other even in the formal detail of the phrasing. Vss. 7 and 9 answer to vss. 6 and 8, and there may have been a similar balancing member to vs. 10 in the source that appears to be used here.

young Roman officer named Marius called on some Christian friends one evening, and in the garden of their villa heard them singing in what was to him a new way. "It was the expression not altogether of mirth, yet of some wonderful sort of happiness—the blithe self-expansion of a joyful soul in people upon whom some all-subduing experience had wrought heroically, and who still remembered . . . the hour of a great deliverance."[6] Those who truly behold the word of life are ruled by so great an experience that they can but sing their joy.

5-10. Tests of Religious Experience.—The author's concern in this passage, to prescribe

moral tests for judging whether a believer lives in eternal life, marks his distinctive genius in combining so profoundly the mystical and ethical aspects of religion and provides a permanently valid criticism of religious experience in general and—as here—of the claim to enjoy fellowship with God in particular. For religion always needs tests. Without them it is often distorted into mere emotionalism or liturgical formalism, into barren creedalism or self-centered piety. We need tests for religious faith and moral character no less than we need tests to measure intelligence, aptitudes, physical health, personality.

5, 7. Walking in the Light.—The moral test for religious experience is laid down in the

[6] *Marius the Epicurean* (New York: E. P. Dutton, 1934; "Everyman's Library"), p. 196.

5. At the head of this series of contrasts appears the antithetical couplet, **God is light, and in him is no darkness at all.** The way in which it is introduced relates it to the proclamation in the prologue and suggests that a well-known formula is being cited to which all readers would agree. The actual identification of God or his Son or Messenger with **light** goes back into the syncretism of the East. In the Fourth Gospel and in these epistles the mythological associations of the term have been lost. The life of God appears in the world as the "true light" (2:8; John 1:9) in the Incarnation. In the expression, "the light of the world," we have something different: a comparison rather than a metaphysical statement (John 8:12; 9:5; cf. 12:46). But in the present case God himself is defined as light absolutely (the only similar definitions: "God is love," I John 4:8, 16, and "God is spirit," John 4:24). That **God is light** is not meant to exhaust his nature, but in view of its thought context it is more than a figure of speech. Thus Philo can say: "God is light, and not light only, but the archetype of every other light, or rather more ancient and higher than any archetype" (*On Dreams* I. 75). All the rich significances of light for man are connoted, overlapping at many points with those of life and truth. The term is not to be unduly moralized. Yet in these epistles and in the Fourth Gospel

---

correlative statements that **God is light** and that the Christian must **walk in the light.** The definition that **God is light** may be taken to signify that as light by nature cannot be self-contained but must communicate itself, so the divine nature is by necessity self-revealing. That God is light signifies that, against all forms of despair and nihilism, God is a God of meaning and his meaning can be apprehended by his creation. This universe is a universe of warmth and light, not of chill indifference, darkness, or hostility. God needs responsiveness from his creation as light needs the eye to be seen. Light in its manifold beauty and meaning in the physical creation is an intimation of the perfect beauty of holiness in the moral order. As physical light makes objects visible in their true character, so God's nature is such that he reveals everything in the moral and spiritual order in its true character. For things to be seen as they really are, they must be beheld *sub specie aeternitatis.* How life is changed in hours of such vision! Mists of anger, prejudice, and fear that becloud our sight are dispelled. Purposes can be judged, goals clarified. People can be viewed in their true relation as fellow children of God. Most of all, we ourselves are delivered from self-deception. "All things assume a different aspect in the Light of God; but nothing looks so different as we ourselves do."[7] Light supremely symbolizes the sheer goodness of God (the word "god" is a shortened form of the word "good") in which **is no darkness** of moral imperfection. The author is primarily interested not in the metaphysical, mystical, or aesthetic implications of the concept that God is light, but in its moral implications. His conception of God is intensely ethical.

[7] Robert Law, *The Tests of Life: A Study of the First Epistle of St. John* (Edinburgh: T. & T. Clark, 1909), p. 65.

To **walk in the light,** accordingly, means to live in the moral presence of God in such a sincere way as to know one's character as it truly is in the moral judgment of God. As light is "reality" (cf. Exeg. on 1:6), to walk in the light means to live in the reality of moral truth about oneself. Only thus do we **live according to the truth,** with the "truth . . . in us" (vs. 8). This conception corrects such erroneous and sentimentalized interpretations of walking in the light as holding a vague belief in God's providence or as emotionally enjoying God's benign favor. Thus to walk in the light requires rigorous honesty with God and the acknowledgment and confession of sin. The identity of darkness with refusal to acknowledge sin in vss. 8a, 10a signifies complacency and pride. The identity of light with confession of sin in vss. 7a, 9a signifies repentance and humility. To shun darkness and walk in light in this sense is ever man's need. The central problem of man's salvation is always that

somehow the darkness of his mind must be broken through so that he can . . . begin to see things as they really are—God as He really is, himself as he really is. . . . The saving revelation must be such that at one and the same time it shows man the truth and makes it possible for him to be sincere with it.[8]

This problem is partly solved by bringing men to acknowledge the reality of sin in life, to pierce through the sophistries with which we so easily explain away or excuse sin, and to face and confess sin in ourselves (cf. Expos. on 3:4-10). The Gnostic heresy of denying sin has its counterpart in every age, and in our age particularly man is characterized by nothing so much as by an easy conscience. The reality of

[8] H. H. Farmer, *The World and God* (New York: Harper & Bros., 1935), p. 196.

6 If we say that we have fellowship with him, and walk in darkness, we lie, and do not the truth:

6 If we say we have fellowship with him while we walk in darkness, we lie and do

---

the terms **light** and **darkness** are governed by the conception of the divine revelation of love in Christ. The emphatic repudiation of any **darkness** in God in the second half of the verse may be aimed at heretical teaching. Irenaeus in his criticism of the Gnostics continually points out the inconsistency in their teaching that evil arose in the divine order, and reproaches them for conceiving of the ultimate God as one "who allows a stain to have place in his own bosom. . . . For if they hold that the light of their Father is such that it fills all things which are inside of Him, and illuminates them all, how can any vacuum or shadow possibly exist within that territory which is contained by the Pleroma and by the light of the Father?" (*Against Heresies* II. 4. 2, 3.)

6. False claims of some among those addressed are apparently quoted, in an ascending order of seriousness: **we have fellowship with him** (vs. 6); **we have no sin** (vs. 8), i.e., we do not sin or cannot sin; **we have not sinned** (vs. 10), i.e., we are not guilty. These false claims are met by a corresponding series of double accusations, likewise in ascending order: **we lie and do not live according to the truth** (vs. 6); **we deceive ourselves, and the truth is not in us** (vs. 8); **we make him a liar, and his word is not in us** (vs. 10). The Christian experience of salvation is sometimes so intense that it can result in overconfidence. Moreover, it was a central teaching of the gospel that the new age had come in some real sense—that new age in which God would wash away men's sins and give them

---

sin may be vivified by citing the results of psychiatric and psychological research, which reveal undreamed depths of evil and uncivilized drives in human nature (cf. Expos. on 3:11-18; 4:1, 3). The reality of sin may also be vivified by citing the testimony of disaster in society, as in personality, that befalls man when he resists the moral will of God (cf. Expos. on 2:3-6; 4:1, 3, 17, 18). The testimony of great literature—Aeschylus, Dante, Goethe, Shakespeare, Milton, Hawthorne—also underscores the reality of sin. Acknowledging sin in general, however, is a different matter from confessing one's own sin; and confessing one's specific sins is a still different matter from confessing one's sinfulness (cf. vss. 8*a*, 9*a*, 10*a*). "Sin" is too blanket a term, and we often use it precisely because its generality makes confession less painful. Actually sin is first known in concrete *sins,* and men truly walk in the light only when they are willing to confess that they are liars, cheats, scandalmongers, or that they are sensual, covetous, jealous. Such confession is infinitely more than mere psychological catharsis; it is an act by which men enter into reality. But while confession of this kind is painful, it is not degrading, and when it is sincere, man receives forgiveness and cleansing (vss. 7, 9). A distinguished philosopher has written: "To fall on our knees and supplicate for . . . pardon and help seems to me not an abdication of our manhood, but . . . an act of wisdom and of an enlightened will." [9]

6, 8, 10. *Walking in Darkness.*—The problem of salvation, i.e., of bringing men to walk in the light, is further solved by confronting them with the results of walking **in darkness.** Darkness brings uncertainty, frustration, futility, purposelessness (cf. Expos. on 2:9-11). **We lie,** i.e., we substitute falsehood in speech and thought for truth. Observe how often "saying" or "he who says" is the author's target in this epistle (1:6, 8; 2:4, 6, 9; 4:20). In vs. 6 to **lie** is to **not live according to the truth.** Morally, words are acts and they determine character. **We deceive ourselves.** Man's need is always to know himself as he really is. Salvador de Madariaga asks:

Who can tell where sincerity merges into humility, and where it folds itself over and becomes hypocrisy, and where it touches self-righteousness? When does generosity become ostentatiousness, kindness weakness, or weakness heroism, or heroism love of display? And how often do modesty's eyelids fall over the glowing eyes of pride? [1]

Distinctions in moral self-knowledge are essential to character, but they are impossible to him who does not live in the light of God. Note the frequent use of "we." The author displays no self-righteousness in his castigation of self-righteousness. Darkness is a state possible even for those who warn against it. **We make him [God] a liar, and his word is not in us.** We register the superficiality of our conception of God and of our belief in God. We childishly

[9] Paul Elmer More, *Pages from an Oxford Diary* (Princeton: Princeton University Press, 1937), ch. xxv.

[1] *Englishmen, Frenchmen, Spaniards* (London: Oxford University Press, 1928), p. xii.

7 But if we walk in the light, as he is in the light, we have fellowship one with another, and the blood of Jesus Christ his Son cleanseth us from all sin.

not live according to the truth; **7** but if we walk in the light, as he is in the light, we have fellowship with one another, and the blood of Jesus his Son cleanses us from all

---

a new heart. The Christian "born anew, not of perishable seed but of imperishable, through the living and abiding word of God" (I Pet. 1:23), or belonging to the "new creation" (Gal. 6:15; II Cor. 5:17; cf. Rom. 6:7), would all too easily be inclined to think that the possibility of sin was transcended. Influences of the Gentile world also enhanced this temptation. Irenaeus' characterization of certain Gnostic Christians later is pertinent here: "And they declare that they themselves are perfect, by the fact that they maintain that they have found their Bythus [i.e., the Maker of All] . . . and they desire themselves to be regarded as 'the perfect,' because they have sought and found the perfect One, while they are still on earth" (*Against Heresies* II. 18. 3, 6).

Religious experience on the emotional or the mystical side can all too easily lead men to overlook its ethical tests. We cannot **have fellowship with** God, who is "light," if we **walk in darkness.** To **walk in the light** (vs. 7) or the **darkness** carries a more significant sense than merely doing right or wrong. Walking in the light means letting our lives be ordered by reality, by things as they are. It means sincerity; and Jesus' parable of the "lamp of the body" (Luke 11:34-36) is very appropriate. If we make the claim of fellowship with God and disingenuously ignore the real state of things, i.e., **walk in darkness,** then we consciously **lie,** and **do not the truth.** This last phrase seems a curious one. To "do the truth" means to guide one's conduct in the light of things as they are and as the gospel shows them. John 3:21 is apposite, "But he who does what is true [the same Greek construction here] comes to the light, that it may be clearly seen that his deeds have been wrought in God." It is of great interest that neither passage speaks of "good deeds" as such, but rather of deeds "wrought in God" or of doing **the truth.**

7. Thus it is our sincerity rather than our works that brings us toward the light and into fellowship with God, and **with one another.** This candid view of things as they

---

defy the moral universe. We blaspheme. At the same time we reject the meaning of God's revelation in Christ. "The sinner who justifies himself does not know God as judge and does not need God as Saviour." [2] This is to say, we do not have fellowship with God.

6-7, 9. Fellowship with God.—The way to bring men into fellowship with God is to proclaim—as John proclaims ("This is the message")—the blessedness of walking in the light. Such blessedness includes **fellowship with one another.** Men enjoy the deepest levels of friendship only when they live without deception and are willing to be known to one another as they really are, in their faults and sins as in their virtues and goodness. This is true with nations and races as with individuals. Only in God's light revealed in Christ can men be delivered from the curse of racial pride and national self-righteousness. Christian fellowship above all is possible only among those who believe in a God of pure goodness and who accept the obligation —despite their failures—to be good like him. The richest fellowship in life is fellowship in

goodness. **If we confess our sins,** God becomes known as **faithful and just, and will forgive our sins.** The great truth of the gospel is that while men are enjoined to acknowledge their sins they are not condemned to bear them, and that peace of mind and soul is possible only when men confess their sins and by doing so enable God to free them from sin. Against the attitude that flippantly denies the reality of sin or tries to ignore or repress it, the gospel declares simply, **confess.** That God is **faithful** means that God's character is unchangingly self-consistent. The unalterable structure of the universe is of justice and forgiveness. God never acts in contradiction of himself, and in all experiences we may depend on him to be unalterably just and forgiving toward us. Because God is faithful he can thus be an object of our faith. That God is **just to forgive** means that God's mercy is the function of his righteousness rather than vice versa. The author's thought here is crucial. It is that God forgives because his moral goodness cannot tolerate sin, rather than that God is morally good because he forgives sin. The distinction is not academic. The latter concept would interpret God's goodness as the result of

[2] Reinhold Niebuhr, *The Nature and Destiny of Man* (New York: Charles Scribner's Sons, 1941-43), I, 200.

8 If we say that we have no sin, we deceive ourselves, and the truth is not in us.

9 If we confess our sins, he is faithful and just to forgive us *our* sins, and to cleanse us from all unrighteousness.

10 If we say that we have not sinned, we make him a liar, and his word is not in us.

sin. **8** If we say we have no sin, we deceive ourselves, and the truth is not in us. **9** If we confess our sins, he is faithful and just, and will forgive our sins and cleanse us from all unrighteousness. **10** If we say we have not sinned, we make him a liar, and his word is not in us.

---

are leads us to recognize our insufficiency, and to welcome the assurance of cleansing. That these traditional formulas bearing on Christ's expiation of sin (cf. below 2:2; 4:9-10; 5:6, 11) were more than formulas is evident when we see how the ideas of washing and purging evoke gratitude and emotion in the Gospel of John, particularly 13:10 and 15:2-3. This same feeling of value appears in 3:1 of this epistle. "See what love the Father has given us." In 1:7 the work of Christ is brought into relation with the continuing sin of Christians (cf. 5:16a), and the word **all** is to be understood in this context. Bultmann is probably correct in holding that the original form of this verse in the source read, "But if we walk in the light, as he is in the light, we have fellowship with him" (i.e., with God), the clause ending here. Similarly, in vs. 9 the author has added the words **and cleanse us from all unrighteousness.** The source envisaged a once-for-all forgiveness at conversion; our author sees a continuous forgiveness and cleansing.

8-9. To say expressly now that **we have no sin** is to **deceive ourselves,** and to show that the right understanding of the gospel of grace has not come home to us. The confession of our sins interestingly parallels walking **in the light** in vs. 7, i.e., they both indicate a recognition of things as they are. The assurance of our forgiveness is assigned to the fact that God is **faithful and just** (δίκαιος) ; i.e., God's righteousness is the very ground of his grace. This takes us back to the foundation stone of the Epistle to the Romans, which describes the gospel as the revelation of "the righteousness of God" (Rom. 1:17; 3:21) .

10. To go the length of denying past sin and present guilt is not only to becloud ourselves with sophistry but to give the lie to God himself. The warning of the author is here raised to an awesome level. So in Matthew's version of the parable of the eye as the "lamp of the body" Jesus suggests the extreme peril of falsehood, "If then the light in you is darkness, how great is the darkness!" (Matt. 6:23b.) The elder here exposes pitilessly the real purport of spiritual complacency or cynicism, as Paul does in Rom. 2:1–3:20. The fact is that the Christians in question, as many since, were in the position not merely of being tempted to spiritual pride by their abundance of visions or esoteric

---

his conveniently blotting out sin, instead of locating his goodness precisely in his recognition of and redemptive dealing with sin. The former concept interprets forgiveness as the expression of God's essential moral nature which, because he is faithful, cannot contradict itself. This distinction governs the Christian conception of God. It defines the nature of Christ's expiation and intercession (cf. Expos. on 2:2) . It corrects the teaching and preaching of the church which so often interprets forgiveness as a breach in God's self-consistency, or which sets God's justice and mercy in opposition to one another. The author of this epistle is often called the "apostle of love." He is no less the "apostle of righteousness." "So long as the Church lays up this Epistle in its heart, it can never lack a spiritual tonic of

wholesome severity." [3] **He . . . will . . . cleanse us from all unrighteousness.** Man's sin ever needs a double cure, moral renewal as well as forgiveness, purity of life as well as release from guilt (cf. Expos. on 2:28–3:3, 4-10). The unqualified affirmation that God cleanses man of all unrighteousness is typical of the author's perfectionism (cf. 2:5, 14b; 3:6a, 9; 4:12b, 18; 5:18) . However, the significance of perfectionism as conceived in this epistle lies not so much in the dubious claim that human nature can be made sinless, i.e., fully sanctified (a claim the author is unwilling to make—cf. 1:8, 10; 2:2; 5:16-17) , as in what the author is trying to say about the moral grace of God, viz., that God's grace is utterly transforming and perfecting and

[3] Law, *Tests of Life,* p. 69.

2 My little children, these things write I unto you, that ye sin not. And if any man sin, we have an advocate with the Father, Jesus Christ the righteous:

2 My little children, I am writing this to you so that you may not sin; but if any one does sin, we have an advocate with the

---

knowledge, but also of holding a superficial view of the real character of life even for the Christian. As Paul teaches, there is still death, anguish, and sin in the world even for those who are a "new creature." Satan has still to be crushed under our feet (Rom. 16:20), and the "desires of the flesh . . . and the desires of the Spirit . . . are opposed to each other, to prevent [us] from doing what [we] would" (Gal. 5:17). Failure to recognize these things means that God's **word is not in us**; we have not seen ourselves and the world in the light of his revelation (cf. 5:10*b, c*).

B. Knowledge of God and Obedience (2:1-6)

The writer turns now to a more direct and intimate form of address to his "little children" (τεκνία μου, as in vss. 12, 28; etc., and John 13:33) and uses "I" instead of "we." It is in keeping with this, no doubt, that he passes from the theme of disingenuousness and self-deception prominent in his source to the plain test of deeds and obedience: keeping Christ's commandments (vs. 3), walking **in the same way in which he** [i.e., Jesus] **walked** (vs. 6). This is the ultimate test of our pretensions and the best check on our spiritual condition. It is all too easy to fall into illusions about ourselves if we make too much of our religious feelings, even those of an elevated kind. A selfish heart has

---

is able to bring man to realize the purpose of life in becoming a child of God. In the latter sense, as distinguished from the former, this epistle may be called perfectionist and its meaning for our age be understood. Cults and philosophies of "self-expression," "self-development," "self-improvement," "self-fulfillment," abound in the fields of education and culture, psychology of personality, etc. These are essentially superficial except in so far as they comprehend man's need of self-realization in moral terms and in terms of fellowship with God.

2:1a. The Apostle's Loving Concern.—The affectionate tenderness of the words, **my little children**, is implicit throughout the epistle, most significantly in passages warning against sin, as here. Such tenderness keeps righteousness from becoming exacerbating harshness and makes love truly redemptive. Moreover, sinners are often like children—immature, ignorant, impulsive—and as a wise father unites gentleness with firmness, so the Christian teacher and pastor deals tenderly with those he corrects and rebukes. **I am writing this to you so that you may not sin.** A great deal of religion must be plain "preventive religion." It is one thing to cure moral sickness; it is another to prevent it. How many pursuits of life do men carry on that people may not sin? And how many do they carry on that people may sin! Is not the worst sin causing others to sin, and the next worst failing to do all one can to prevent people from sinning? These words pronounce judgment on purveyors of vulgarity, warmongers, agents of organized vice,

corrupt leaders of government, advertisers who debauch minds and bodies for profit, cynical-minded educators. But they also pronounce judgment on Christian people who put forth so little energy to prevent sinning. Much "preventive religion" is admittedly prudish and blue-nosed; but the battle against sin must be unceasing.

1bc. Sinlessness in Relation to Forgiveness.—**That you may not sin; but if any one does sin:** The inconsistency of these phrases is characteristic of the author's mind and presents the problem of perfectionism (see Expos. on 1:6-7, 9) in a different form. Throughout the epistle the requirement and possibility of sinlessness are affirmed, most pointedly in 3:9 (cf. also 1:9; 3:6a; 5:18); at the same time the author clearly refuses to permit any man to say that he is without sin. This problem is hardly solved, as some commentators have suggested, by distinctions between tenses of Greek verbs, between mortal and venial sins. Indeed, theologically it is probably insoluble in that it presents the central paradox of the gospel—that man is summoned to sinlessness of life at the same time that he is assured of the forgiveness of God in Christ for the sins he is required to confess; a paradox which in turn roots in the paradoxical mystery in God of the relation of divine righteousness as it condemns sin to divine mercy as it forgives sin. Practically, however, the problem is solved in that to affirm the tension between the requirement of sinlessness and the assurance of forgiveness—and to confront men with this

many disguises, and an uneasy conscience goes to great lengths to justify itself both with emotional patterns and systems of rationalization. Thus the elder challenges all such sophistries, writing in very downright terms farther on: "Little children, let no one deceive you. He who does right is righteous, as he is righteous" (3:7). This searching criterion appears throughout the N.T.: at the conclusion of the Sermon on the Mount (Matt. 7:17-21); in Rom. 2:6, 13; and in James's emphasis on deeds (1:22-27; 2:14-26). It remains true that any such simple appeal to deeds is not sufficient by itself. It is also necessary to show just what kinds of deeds are righteous or sinful and why. Earnest consciences can be deeply baffled about problems of conduct even with all the light that the gospel sheds. This is one reason why ethics in the N.T. is never finally a matter of a "works-righteousness" or code. The Spirit interprets our duty to us in various situations. But even more necessary where right deeds are enjoined is a motivation for their performance. In his own way this writer, like Paul, and indeed like James, rests his appeal to works upon the endowments of faith. For his present purposes he points out that our obedience is the test of our pretended faith, but his basic theme is that true faith is the source of our right conduct.

The elder is faced with a perennial problem. The gospel gives assurance of forgiveness and cleansing (1:7, 9). Here the danger of another sophistry appears, which in Paul's circles took the blatant form: let us "continue in sin that grace may abound" (Rom. 6:1,15). The elder in our present passage recognizes that **if any one does sin, we have an advocate with the Father, Jesus Christ the righteous;** but we may not presume upon this. For as he goes on to say, the only way in which **we may be sure that we are in him** (vs. 5), and so know that we can benefit by his intercession, is by our manner of life, which must be like his. In connection with this argument he takes up again the source used in 1:6-10, quoting from it in 2:4-5. We recognize it by its form: a false claim is repudiated, again in a double clause (vs. 4), and a positive statement (vs. 5) balances the negative one.

2:1. But **if any one does sin** (i.e., commits an act of sin [aorist tense]; contrast habitual sin in the present tense, 3:6, 9 and 5:18) **we have an advocate.** The Greek term translated **advocate** (παράκλητος) was used of a party who took one's side in a lawsuit or trial. This term has so different a reference in the well-known passages John 14:16, 26; 15:26; 16:7 that its use here is taken as marking one of the theological differences which argue in favor of assigning the two writings to different authors. Here, in the epistle, Christ as the Paraclete intercedes in heaven with the Father for his followers (as in

---

tension—does avail in experience to save men from moral discouragement and despair without at the same time relaxing the moral demands that make for character and validate faith by works. That is the heart of this passage, and the author's success in solving the problem practically, if not logically, is instructive for us. The assurance of forgiveness and intercession is the theme of vss. 1-2; the moral demands of the gospel the theme of vss. 3-6.

If any one does sin. Forgiveness is offered to all men. The invitation of the gospel is universal. The same great note is struck as in John 3:16, "whosoever believeth." **We have an advocate.** The plural **we** (contrasted with the singular "I write") marks the moral lapse of one as affecting all (cf. Expos. on 5:14-16). As Jesus vicariously suffered for others, so the Christian man does not want to be exempt from responsibility for the sin and suffering of his fellow men. John Woolman so took on himself the sin and

suffering of others that near the end of his life he dreamed of being so mingled with the gray mass of suffering humanity that his individual identity was lost and he could no longer reply when his name was called.

1c. Jesus Christ—Our Advocate.—Advocate means "pleader." The term is primarily legal, but it means more, as Brooke suggests, "the help of anyone who 'lends his presence' to his friend." [4] The helpfulness of our advocate lies in his being **Jesus,** a man who knows our humanity; **Christ,** who as God's anointed is uniquely acceptable to God; **righteous,** one who will represent no case "which justice does not approve [although] compassion prompts it." [5] **With the Father.** God is "faithful and just" (1:9), but he exerts his justice as a father and not merely as a judge (cf. Expos. on vss. 20-23). May not the present advocacy of Jesus be under-

[4] *Johannine Epistles*, p. 26.
[5] Findlay, *Fellowship in Life Eternal*, p. 118.

2 And he is the propitiation for our sins: and not for ours only, but also for *the sins* of the whole world.

Father, Jesus Christ the righteous; 2 and he is the expiation for our sins, and not for ours only but also for the sins of the whole

---

Heb. 7:25; 9:24; Rom. 8:34). In the Gospel it is the Spirit sent to the followers on earth, as "Comforter" (KJV) or "Counselor" (RSV) or Paraclete. The two conceptions are brought close together in Rom. 8:26, where it is "the Spirit himself" who "intercedes for us."

2. The present advocacy of Christ rests upon his **expiation** (cf. 4:10). The writer invokes here a familiar formula of the tradition testifying in various forms to the universality of the redemption wrought by Christ (cf. II Cor. 5:19; I Tim. 2:5, 6). The Gospel of John does not employ the precise term used here, ἱλασμός, but the world-wide effect of Christ's work appears in John 1:29; 3:16; and 11:51-52. Moreover, when the Fourth Gospel presents Christ as sanctifying himself in order to sanctify his disciples "through the truth" (John 17:19), the same idea of the removal of defilement is conveyed as in the term **expiation**. What is distinctive in the present passage is that the **expiation** continues for postbaptismal sins; for those followers, i.e., who, though they are not sinless, yet do not "walk in darkness" (1:6, 8, 10), and who seeing things as they truly are know that they stand in need of it. Conversely, it is only because those in the world "walk in darkness" (1:6; 2:11) and have "loved darkness rather than light" (John 3:19) that they fail to lay hold of **the expiation** which is **for the sins of the whole**

---

stood in light of his intercessory prayer for his disciples while on earth (cf. Expos. on 5:14-16)? And are not our prayers for forgiveness effective only in so far as he gathers them up in his? Is not his present intercession also of a character with his unfailing love for his disciples of which John writes in 13:1: "Jesus . . . having loved his own who were in the world, . . . loved them to the end"? Does he not still love men "to the end"?

And didst Thou love the race that loved not Thee?
   And didst Thou take to heaven a human brow?
Dost plead with man's voice by the marvellous sea?
   Art Thou his Kinsman now? [6]

2. *Jesus Christ as Expiation.*—Jesus is our advocate, however, because he is also **the expiation for our sins** (cf. 1:7; Expos. on 3:16a; 4:7-12). The whole work of Christ—his incarnation, his earthly ministry, his resurrection and ascension—are signified by expiation, though especially his death; and all was undertaken by God (4:10) to forgive and cleanse us from all unrighteousness (1:9). We limit the richness and grandeur of Christ's expiation when we confine it to his death. His whole life was an act of atonement and provides a means of cleansing (cf. vs. 6; Expos. on 3:2-3). **Not for ours only but also for the sins of the whole world** (cf. Expos. on 4:14-15). These words hold a mysterious, metaphysical meaning. Theology has attempted to interpret the cosmic significance of Jesus' sacrificial life and death in various ways; but that in an ineffable way his

[6] Jean Ingelow, "Kinsman."

life and death have decisively availed with the moral order of reality is the burden of unbroken witness from the cry of John the Baptist, "Behold, the Lamb of God, who takes away the sin of the world!" (John 1:29), to the song of John on Patmos, "Worthy is the Lamb who was slain" (Rev. 5:12). The author of this epistle knows this meaning. He sees Jesus' death as a decisive death grapple with the devil in which once and for all the power of sin has been shattered (cf. Expos. on 3:7-10). The relevance of this insight to a world that seems increasingly to be possessed by the power of evil drives the Christian to ask: where else but in Christ can men find the salvation they so desperately seek from the disaster their sins have brought and threaten—still more tragically—to bring?

The atonement of Jesus is universally effective because the sins it exposes and redeems are universal and timeless in character. Men in every generation and in every place sin the same sins that brought Jesus to his death in Jerusalem. Pride is pride in the first century or the twentieth; expediency is expediency in a Roman Pilate or a totalitarian dictator; prejudice is prejudice in a Jewish Pharisee or a white American Protestant. And cruelty, cowardice, violence, hatred of truth, conventional piety, the indifference of the masses, treachery, greed—these corrupt men in every age and land. But as sin was unleashed on Jesus in its full reality and in a form intelligible to every man, so it was met by love suffering in a way that all men everywhere in every age can comprehend. "Suffering is a language that everybody under-

3 And hereby we do know that we know him, if we keep his commandments.

world. 3 And by this we may be sure that we know him, if we keep his command-

---

world. "The Gospel 'speaks to our condition,' " says C. H. Dodd, "when it assures us, not only that God loves the world and is ready to forgive our sin, but that His love has been expressed concretely and objectively in history to provide a means of sterilizing human wickedness and effecting a forgiveness which is not merely an amnesty or indulgence but a radical removal of the taint" (*The Johannine Epistles* [New York: Harper & Bros.; London: Hodder & Stoughton, 1946; "Moffatt New Testament Commentary"], pp. 28-29).

3-5a. A new false claim, **I know him,** is now repudiated (cf. Tit. 1:16, "They profess to know God"). Knowledge or gnosis was the chief goal and hallmark of Hellenistic religious philosophy in this period. The Christian apologists were at pains to insist on the limits of knowledge even in the faith, quoting Paul, "Now I know in part"

---

stands," a German Jew has said, and Jesus' suffering is the universal language of love. There is that in the heart of every man which can respond to Jesus. The Oriental and the Occidental, the peasant and the scholar, the Negro and the white man, the child and the grandparent, the woman and the man, the successful and the broken, the rich and the poor, the Catholic and the Protestant—all behold in Jesus that which speaks to them. Said an Indian woman on hearing her first sermon about Jesus by a Christian missionary: "I have known about him all my life, and now you have told me his name."

History verifies the Christian claim that Jesus is the world's Savior. If the claim had not been valid, it would long ago have been exposed as false. The sheer goodness and sanctity of Jesus have sufficed to save and cleanse men in every generation if they confess and believe. In comparing Jesus and Marcus Aurelius, Ernest Renan writes: "Marcus Aurelius and his noble masters left no lasting impress on the world. . . . Jesus remains for humanity an exhaustless source of moral new birth. Philosophy does not suffice for the multitude: They must have sanctity." [7] Jesus' saviorhood continuously avails for those who, though they are not sinless, yet do not "walk in darkness." This is typically the Christian's plight, and the gospel meets it by assuring us that while we are sinners we are nevertheless under a dispensation of grace that perpetually deals with our sins. This assurance has particular relevance for modern Christians living in a world whose political and social life inevitably requires choices between lesser and greater evil rather than between clear-cut good and evil. It enables us to act, knowing that despite the sin in which our actions frequently involve us we are yet mercifully accepted by God because God knows our plight. At the same

time we are delivered from the self-deceiving assumption that our course of action is morally perfect, and from the self-righteous judgment that another's course is not as good.

Thus while the author is concerned to lay down moral obedience as the test of knowledge of God in the following verses, he does not err where he prefaces his injunction to keep the commandments with a majestic announcement of the expiation and intercession of Christ for man's sin. For the truth is, the most powerful incentive to ethical living is the assurance that despite our wrong we are forgiven, and that despite our unlovableness we are beloved. Experience of parenthood teaches us that forgiveness brings children to goodness as punishment and condemnation never can; and as with a human father, so with the heavenly Father. Theologically, John Baillie puts this truth clearly:

Salvation begins by tackling the guilt of my sin rather than its power over my will, and offers me forgiveness before it offers me holiness. . . . I am accepted "just as I am" and without being fit; and it is my acceptance while still unfit that alone has power . . . to make me fit. I am not saved because I have become sinless; I am saved, while still a sinner, because Christ is sinless and . . . bare my sins in His own body on the Tree. But this being saved while still a sinner is the beginning of my ceasing to be a sinner.[8]

Poetically, Longfellow expresses this evangelical truth in his poem, "Divina Commedia," in which he imagines himself accompanying Dante into the world of the dead. But as he hears from the confessionals "rehearsals of forgotten tragedies" and "lamentations from the crypts below," a voice celestial begins to hymn the great words, "Although your sins are as scarlet, they shall be white as snow."

3-6. *Moral Nature of Eternal Life.*—While obedience and knowledge of God are the im-

---

[7] *Life of Jesus* (Boston: Little, Brown & Co., 1929), p. 415.

[8] *Invitation to Pilgrimage* (New York: Charles Scribner's Sons, 1942), p. 67.

4 He that saith, I know him, and keepeth not his commandments, is a liar, and the truth is not in him.

ments. 4 He who says "I know him" but disobeys his commandments is a liar, and

---

(I Cor. 13:12) , and rejecting all presumptuous explorations of "the deep things of God," and the claim of some teachers that they had acquired, not a partial, but a universal knowledge of all that exists (cf. Irenaeus *Against Heresies* II. 28. 9) . Here, then, the elder counters with the test of **his commandments, his word.** The pronouns that follow, **him, his,** refer most naturally to Christ in view of the antecedent in vss. 1-2 and the invocation of Christ's example in vs. 6. But the original reference in the parallelistic source cited in vss. 4-5a was to God, and this gives the pronouns a double sense. The basic issue here is evidently that between a knowledge that turns to pride, and love as it exhibits itself in keeping **his word,** i.e., in living out the gospel and the **commandments** that go with it. That knowledge can be set over against love appears in I Cor. 8:1-3: " 'Knowledge' puffs up, but love builds up. If any one imagines that he knows something,

---

mediate theme of these verses, the parallelism of the phrases **know him, love for God, abides in him,** indicates the larger theme of the epistle. These phrases, indeed, are alternate ways of describing the relation of man to God that John more mystically calls "eternal life." And that nothing less than "eternal life" is made to depend on keeping God's commandments is the measure of the epistle's intensely ethical character, and a mark of the author's genius in being able to balance so perfectly the elements of forgiveness and moral demand in the gospel.

His commandments . . . his word. The Greek word for commandments appears eighteen times in the epistles (six times in vss. 3-8) . It means the moral expression of God's nature of which eternal life is the experience. The commandments are "his," i.e., God's, not man's, decree. They are not historical, but "from the beginning." Though plural, they are one in nature, having a moral unity signified by **his word.** The commandments are communicated to man by the dynamic expression and claim of God's will revealed in Christ. More concretely, the commandments are the moral law of Israel expounded and comprehended in the two great commandments of Jesus (cf. Rom. 13:8-10) .

To **keep his commandments** means acknowledgment of the givenness, the objectivity of the moral will of God. Man did not invent the commandments; he received them. He cannot repeal them, he can only obey or disobey them. Woodrow Wilson is said to have remarked that the moral laws of the universe do not threaten, but they operate! The forms taken by the sanctions of what we perhaps too impersonally call "moral order" vary in different ages and cultures, but the fact of the "moral order" itself never alters. To wage war rather than to renounce it may have been considered "right" in the past, whereas today war is generally acknowledged to be "wrong"; but the consciousness of

something being "right" and something being "wrong" is common to all ages and cultures.

Recognition of and conformity to the moral will of God is implacably binding on all life. In so far as progress can be detected in history, it consists in man's increasing appreciation of the claim of morality upon his total life. In statecraft as in private life, in law as in education, in marriage as in economic life, the morality of the universe relentlessly operates. Albert J. Beveridge always advised law students to study the Ten Commandments before studying modern authorities, and to continue studying them throughout the years of their legal practice. The advice to study the commandments holds for every area of life.

To "keep his commandments" suggests the necessity of discipline in personal living (cf. Expos. on 1b-5) . Emotionalized religion without discipline becomes sentimental, and intellectualized religion becomes sterile. The discipline of the party member in politics, of the scientist in research, of the athlete in his games, exposes and shames the lack of discipline in many Christians today. Protestantism is often weak where Roman Catholicism is strong because it does not generally have orders of discipline in its church life. Moral discipline is the path to Christian character. A successful coach said of his athletes: "They do not go into training; they stay in training." The Christian is always in training, and each man must build "his own world as a gymnasium for his moral will." [9]

4-5. *Knowledge Through Moral Obedience.*— True knowledge of God is never primarily intellectual or mystical, as the Gnostics claimed; it is acquired through all the faculties of personality, and distinctively—in the thought of this epistle—through the will put forth in obedience

[9] John Oman, *Grace and Personality* (3rd ed. rev.; Cambridge: Cambridge University Press, 1925), p. 64.

5 But whoso keepeth his word, in him verily is the love of God perfected: hereby know we that we are in him.

6 He that saith he abideth in him ought himself also so to walk, even as he walked.

the truth is not in him; 5 but whoever keeps his word, in him truly love for God is perfected. By this we may be sure that we are in him: 6 he who says he abides in him ought to walk in the same way in which he walked.

---

he does not yet know as he ought to know. But if one loves God, one is known by him." Indeed, it is at this point that the word **love** makes its first appearance in the epistle. **Love for God** ("love to God," Moffatt) has its fulfillment in fellowship, as the expressions, to be "in him" (vs. 5b) and to abide "in him" (vs. 6), indicate. To have the truth in one (vs. 4b), as the parallelism shows, means the same thing. For "truth" in the Johannine vocabulary has the sense of shared reality rather than correct knowledge (cf. 1:6, 8).

5b-6. By this we may be sure: As frequently with this phrase, it is not clear whether **this** refers backward or forward. The different punctuation in the two versions above illustrates the ambiguity. In this case the reference is probably forward, but the preceding thought is also in mind. **He who . . . abides in him** merely characterizes in different terms the one in whom **truly love for God is perfected** (vs. 5a). And to walk **in the same way in which** [Jesus] **walked** is to obey his commandments (vs. 4) and to keep his word (vs. 5a).

---

and love (see Expos. on 3:4-10; 4:7-12; 4:19–5:5). Similar claims of a Gnostic sort have been made in every generation. The emphasis on education in our time has led many people to suppose that the best Christian is the most educated Christian. Similarly, numerous cults and theosophical systems prey on credulous minds with false promises of esoteric knowledge and unlocked mysteries. Moral obedience as a pathway to God, however, is always superior to possession of knowledge through reason or through pseudo sciences of the supernatural.

C. F. Andrews writes that the vision of God became radiant to him just in proportion as the test of seeking to do God's will in daily life was sincerely applied.[1] Theologically this is true because God's most essential nature is moral love, and only moral love—rather than reason or mystical contemplation—can best know moral love. Psychologically and practically, human experience teaches that we learn by doing better than by thinking. Action, more than thought or emotion, vitally apprehends and consolidates meaning as personal possession. Thus Jesus characteristically cast his injunction to love God in terms of action: "Not every one who says to me, 'Lord, Lord,' shall enter the kingdom of heaven, but he who does . . ." (Matt. 7:21); "Every one then who hears these words of mine and does them . . . and does not do them . . ." (Matt. 7:24, 26); "If any man's will is to do his will, he shall know . . ." (John 7: 17; cf. also John 14:21-24). In terms of history

[1] *What I Owe to Christ* (New York: Abingdon Press, 1932), p. 14.

and culture these verses pronounce condemnation on our unchristian society. Western civilization is nominally Christian—we say "we know him"; but in virtually every area of life we disobey his commandments. In war we kill. We dishonor marriage and parenthood. In our greed we covet and steal. In our manners and morals we falsely swear and blaspheme. We worship the scientific and materialistic gods of our own hands. We secularize the sabbath. We pay lip service to the love of God and man but renounce it in our common life. We resent commandments and we reject the moral order. May it not be that pagan and atheistic movements in our world are actually the judgment that God is pronouncing through history upon a culture that pretends to **know him** but that in reality **is a liar** in whom **the truth is not?**

In a wider sense our pathetic faith in knowledge as the maximum good is a contemporary form of the Gnostic fallacy. The new empires, it has been said, are to be empires of the mind; knowledge is power; a nation's strength lies in knowing more, knowing it first, and knowing it fastest. Thus faith in education and science is our main reliance; all the evils in the world could be cured if men would only think, a prominent educator has said. The answer to this fallacy is the insight of Christianity—that love is sovereign over knowledge, and knowledge must be morally controlled. Unless life is conformed to the moral order the intrinsic "lie" on which our culture is built will destroy us.

6. *The Imitation of Christ.*—We ought to **walk in the same way in which he** [Jesus]

7 Brethren, I write no new commandment unto you, but an old commandment which ye had from the beginning. The old commandment is the word which ye have heard from the beginning.

7 Beloved, I am writing you no new commandment, but an old commandment which you had from the beginning; the old commandment is the word which you have

C. Love and the True Light (2:7-11)

The plain test of obedience to the "commandments" has been stated. The present section reflects on the fact that the commandment (now in the singular) or word, while it is as old as the gospel itself, takes on a new character in the present situation of the church when the power of the gospel over the world is becoming manifest. Resuming his antithesis of light and darkness and his parallelistic form, the writer now repudiates another false claim. In this case it is the claim to be in the light on the part of him who hates his brother.

7. Commandment (ἐντολήν) would appear at first to refer to the same term in the plural, used in 2:3-4, just as word (λόγος) refers to this same term used with an ethical bearing in 2:5. But I am writing you picks up the phrase of 2:1, and the exhortation in terms of light and darkness recalls 1:5-10. The commandment in question refers, therefore, generally to the whole ethical instruction of the opening of the epistle, though the term here in the singular points to its summary in the law of love. This demand is

walked. The highest form of devotion to the commandments of God is to live as Jesus lived. Commandments are best understood and most readily obeyed when beheld incarnate in a human life rather than when heard or read. In Jesus the commandments are actualized in such a way that no man can misunderstand or evade them. Men need the inspiration of a person more than the sanctions of a law. Discipline without inspiration can become a hard Spartanism. Men are won for the Christian life not by urging them to obey laws but by drawing them to live in imitation of Jesus' example and in fellowship with his presence. And the more faithfully men walk as he walked, the more surely they find his spirit cleansing them from sin and bringing them into a true knowledge and love of God.

7. Beloved.—The recurring note of gentleness suggests the Christian way to handle controversy and contention, as in this passage. Remember that while the author is called "the apostle of love," he yet had enemies; but he deals with them, as another great Christian urged, by "speaking the truth in love" (Eph. 4:15).

7-8. Moral Commandments, Old and New.—The moral instruction of Christianity is old to us in the sense in which it was old to the author's hearers; we, as they, have heard it from the lips of parents, pastors, teachers, friends, from our earliest days. But because it is old to us, familiarity can dull its edge and power. People can become inoculated with small doses of religion in such a way as to become immune to the real thing. Thus often the preacher's task is first to proclaim and elucidate the old rather

than to open up the new. The claims of Christian morality confront men with sacredness and majesty because they inhere in that which is from the beginning. The commandment is grounded in God's changeless being, as old as creation and as eternal as God himself. When men disobey the commandment they defy eternity and dash themselves against the structure of Reality. Right and wrong are the grain of the universe. The British statesman, Lord Morley, traveled from England to give an address to the students of a Canadian university. As he came to the rostrum to speak, his first words were: "Gentlemen, I have traveled four thousand miles to tell you that there is a difference between right and wrong." God sent Jesus to proclaim as part of his message to us that the difference between right and wrong is from the beginning.

The commandment is new in the sense that God is a living God and his moral law is a living law. Forms of the law become outworn and set aside, as the later prophets laid aside ceremonial laws of primitive Judaism as irrelevant to inward character. But the reality of the moral law itself ever confronts men with "newness." The commandment is new in the sense that it partakes of the new order of reality, of the new age revealed and ushered into history in Christ. A divine action has taken place in him, a new realm of light (vs. 8) has been brought into being that has profoundly changed the character of human existence in this world. Is there not a touch of autobiography in John's thought here? John has lived through a day of new creation. He has seen "the kingdom of God come

8 Again, a new commandment I write unto you, which thing is true in him and in you: because the darkness is past, and the true light now shineth.

8 Yet I am writing you a new commandment, which is true in him and in you, because[b] the darkness is passing away

[b] Or that.

not **new** or questionable for it has always been an essential aspect of the **word** or revelation as his readers had known it **from the beginning** of their Christian lives. But it is even older than that since for the Christian all revelation is one, and God's disclosure of himself in Christ is only the climax of what has gone before. The phrase **in the beginning,** while it must be interpreted variously according to its context in the epistle, yet always carries some sense of that eternal precreative life of God, which like the **true light** envelops and conditions all that occurs in the world.

8. Yet it is also a new commandment. The **again** of the KJV is somewhat misleading in that it suggests an additional or contrasting **commandment.** The writer probably has in mind Jesus' words in the Fourth Gospel, "A new commandment I give to you, that you love one another" (John 13:34). In any case, as the following verses show, the essence of the **commandment,** old and new, is love of one another (3:11), here particularly directed to love of the brother. The expression **which is true** introduces an explanation of why the charge can also be called **new:** because, viz., **the darkness is passing away and the true light is already shining.** The passing away of the darkness, or of the old world (vs. 17), the bringing to nothing of the "things that are" and of "the rulers of this age, who are doomed to pass away" (I Cor. 1:28; 2:6), is an expression of the vivid eschatological consciousness of the church. "The night is far gone, the day is at hand. Let us then cast off the works of darkness and put on the armor of light" (Rom. 13:12). **The true light** is used in John 1:9 more specifically of the personal Word of God, whose coming as a peacemaker is beautifully anticipated in Test. Levi 18:3, 4:

> Lighting up the light of knowledge as the sun the day. . . .
> He shall shine forth as the sun on the earth, . . .
> And there shall be peace in all the earth.

The contrast between old and new is partly that between the old and new covenants (II Cor. 3:7-8). But the elder is also saying that the **old commandment** of the gospel takes on a new aspect in the new circumstances of the church. It is new **in him,** i.e., in Christ, for the meaning of the way of love in him is newly perceived and corroborated. And it is new **in you** as the faithful grasp its present applications in the throes and victory of the final crisis.

with power" (Mark 9:1). Probably within his lifetime Jesus has died and risen, the apostolic church has been established, the leaven of Christian love has begun to work in the world. The contrast of human life before and after the spirit of Christ has been brought to it is so marvelous that only the conception of a new age is adequate to describe it. In his teaching Jesus placed the morality of the O.T. in an entirely new light. "You have heard that it was said. . . . But I say to you . . ." (Matt. 5:38-39). Jesus gathered up the entire moral law of the gospel in his own new commandment of love: "A new commandment I give to you, that . . . even as I have loved you, . . . you also love one another. By this all men will know that you are my disciples." (John 13:34-35.) Jesus' conception of "love" as the fulfillment of morality was so

new that a new word had to be found to express it—the Greek ἀγάπη. Jesus' death sealed his new commandment with new meaning—a vicarious and redeeming meaning—and gave it new authority and power. The newness of the love revealed on the cross is continuous. The love of Calvary is an "ever-flowing fountain."

The commandment is also new **in you** (vs. 8), i.e., in Christian believers. Thus Paul writes that "if any man be in Christ, he is a new creature: . . . all things are . . . become new" (II Cor. 5:17). Jesus' commandment of love daily speaks new claims, impels to new duties, reveals fresh light to man's conscience; it is inexhaustible in its challenge and meaning. The commandment is new in the sense that so few people have really lived it; but when they have, life and light have broken with startling freshness

9 He that saith he is in the light, and hateth his brother, is in darkness even until now.

10 He that loveth his brother abideth in the light, and there is none occasion of stumbling in him.

11 But he that hateth his brother is in darkness, and walketh in darkness, and knoweth not whither he goeth, because that darkness hath blinded his eyes.

and the true light is already shining. 9 He who says he is in the light and hates his brother is in the darkness still. 10 He who loves his brother abides in the light, and in it[c] there is no cause for stumbling. 11 But he who hates his brother is in the darkness and walks in the darkness, and does not know where he is going, because the darkness has blinded his eyes.

[c] Or him.

9. The rhetorical parallelisms of these verses—in the same vein and no doubt from the same source as 1:5-10—speak only of love and hate; but coldness, contentiousness, and a spirit of superiority are implied in the heightened contrasts. It is clear that many of the fellowship are tempted by the schismatics or false Gnostics to a loveless arrogance of the kind referred to by Irenaeus: "They tell us that . . . they have sublime knowledge on account of which they are superior to others (*Against Heresies* II. 10. 3). Such men "call the light darkness"; though "the Sun of righteousness" has arisen "with healing in his wings" (Mal. 4:2), they are **still** in the night. Vs. 11 drives this home and, like Jesus in John 12:35-36, fearfully pictures the blinded progress and shrouded destiny of the lost. They deceive themselves (1:8) and, like a man on a dark night, they meet pitfalls and go astray. As we read in the Epistle to the Ephesians with regard to the Gentiles, "For they live blindfold in a world of illusion, and are cut off from the life of God through ignorance and insensitiveness" (Eph. 4:17-18; tr. J. B. Phillips, *Letters to Young Churches: A Translation of the New Testament Epistles* [New York: The Macmillan Co., 1948], p. 106).

10. **In the light,** on the other hand, there are no pitfalls, and **he who loves his brother** not only has the light but abides in it. The KJV (cf. RSV mg.) follows a reading **in him** in which the occasion of stumbling refers not to the light, but to the individual in question. Here the meaning is that such a one is not the occasion of any offense to others as are the troublemakers who spread confusion in the church.

upon the world. History ever waits for Christian people who will live the commandment of love in the face of war, greed, prejudice, expediency.

9-11. *Hatred Versus Love.*—These verses resume with a new construction the antithesis between light and darkness originally introduced in 1:5, 7. Love of the brethren replaces consciousness of the moral reality of God as the equivalent of light, and hatred replaces refusal to acknowledge sin as the equivalent of darkness. The absolutist character of the author's thought is plain here. He recognizes no intermediate states between love and hatred. This moral version of the original religious antithesis again marks the epistle's ethical character. We are never permitted to forget that the religious experience of ultimate reality has to do with perfectly concrete situations in human life where the alternatives of love and hatred are being forever presented to men in their social relations with one another.

He who hates . . . is in the darkness and walks in the darkness, and does not know where he is going, is blinded in his eyes. These four statements describe the condition, the course, and the issue of the life of the man who hates. His inward darkness of alienation from God determines his outward conduct; as he is, so he walks. The true nature of his actions is concealed from himself. The loveless person **does not know** that he is unloving; he imputes to others the faults in himself. He also does not know the inevitable disaster to which his walk leads. In one sense he walks in darkness because the darkness has blinded him; in another sense he is blind because he has walked in darkness. He who refuses to see, at last cannot. Consistent hatred progressively destroys the capacity for good. Lastly (by implication from vs. 10), he causes others to stumble. Hatred unnerves others and causes them to lash out; vindictiveness often injures the innocent; revenge poisons motives in others; the hypocrisy of the Christian who says he is in the light and hates his brother shames the church, repels the earnest seeker, and edifies the cynic.

12 I write unto you, little children, because your sins are forgiven you for his
name's sake.

12 I am writing to you, little children,
because your sins are forgiven for his sake.

D. Charge to Young and Old; Love for the Father and the World
(2:12-17)

The continuity with the foregoing is evident in the expression **I am writing to you**
(cf. vss. 7-8), and in the renewed address, **little children** (cf. vs. 1); but it is also evident
in the theme. Forgiveness, knowledge of God, the indwelling word: these are again
confirmed to the readers. The elder is most earnest in bringing home to them reminders
of what they already know and assurance of the great things that are already theirs.
Those addressed would seem to be to some extent uncertain of their true attainments
and thus easily tempted to secure more specious tokens of their advance in the religious
life. They are being solicited to a popular if not faddish version of knowledge and
illumination, as the next section makes clear. Over against this the writer now states
his assurance, subsequently to be emphasized, that they already have the decisive
knowledge (vss. 20, 21) and anointing (vs. 27). But his concluding charge (vss. 15-17)
shows that their temptation, as all temptation, involves finally the issue of ultimate
devotion, whether to the Father or the world.

12-14. There is much diversity of opinion among interpreters with regard to details
of this passage. There are six assurances to various groups. Do we have a double series
with three members in each, corresponding to the age groups: **children, fathers, young
men?** This is an attractive view and suggestive, if not of "the seven ages of man," at least
of three of them as they exhibit the graces of the gospel in the Christian family. Irenaeus
distinguishes several phases of life, all of which, he argues, Christ passed through and
sanctified "that he might be a perfect Master for all." "For he came to save all through
means of Himself—all, I say, who through Him are born again to God—infants, and
children, and boys, and youths, and old men." This may well reflect the present passage
in I John, particularly since "boys" are included (besides "children"), although "old

---

This analysis is philosophically and ethically
valid. Within the context of Christian revelation, hatred disqualifies a man for knowledge
of God and communion with him. How can the
unloving man know God, who is love? Physi-
ologically, psychologically, emotionally, it is also
valid. Hatred can injure physical tissue and
induce disease. A physician has said that half a
dozen bitter words, and the very pepsin of the
stomach loses its power. Hatred unbalances and
inflames the mind. It subverts thought to passion and undermines intelligent judgment. One
commentator paraphrases "he . . . walks in the
darkness" as "he cannot think straight"![2] Socially, hatred sunders fellowship and isolates
personality. Tennyson writes:

And he that shuts Love out, in turn shall be
Shut out from Love, and on her threshold lie
Howling in outer darkness.[3]

Hatred violates life's law of mutuality and contradicts God's will of brotherliness. Politically

and socially, he who hates is in darkness and
does not know where he is going. A nation is
whipped up to hatred in war, or an ideology
inculcates hatred between classes or races. For a
time hatred can be effective in achieving short-
term goals, but the final end is destruction.

But **he who loves his brother abides in the
light, and . . . there is no cause for stumbling.**
(The epistle's teaching of love for the brethren
reaches its height in 3:11-18; 4:7-12, 16-21; cf.
Expos.) Love brings its own illumination to
difficult decisions and vexing relations. Love
makes clear its own mandates, unfolds its own
wisdom, brings its own guidance. He who loves
radiates light that enables others to walk in the
light and not stumble. Nathan Söderblom described a saint as a man who makes it easier for
one to believe in God. Such radiance, while
unwitting, partakes of divine light, and augments the world of light into which God un-
ceasingly strives to bring his creation.

12-14. The Richness of Christian Experience.
—The warning in the Exeg. against permitting
the precise literary structure of these verses to
govern the interpretation of their religious
meaning clarifies the elder's purpose here—to

[2] C. H. Dodd, The Johannine Epistles (New York:
Harper & Bros.; London: Hodder & Stoughton, 1946;
"Moffatt New Testament Commentary"), p. 36.
[3] "To ———, I send you here a sort of allegory."

13 I write unto you, fathers, because ye have known him *that is* from the beginning. I write unto you, young men, because ye have overcome the wicked one. I write unto you, little children, because ye have known the Father.

13 I am writing to you, fathers, because you know him who is from the beginning. I am writing to you, young men, because you have overcome the evil one. I write to you, children, because you know the Father.

---

men" replaces **fathers** (*Against Heresies* II. 22. 4; cf. II. 24. 4). Against the view that three age groups are present to the writer's mind may be urged: (*a*) **Little children** (τεκνία) refers elsewhere in the letter to all Christians addressed (vss. 1, 28; 3:7 [doubtful], 18; 4:4; 5:21). (*b*) The corresponding term which introduces the second series, vs. 13, **children,** is a different one, viz., παιδία. If it is meant to identify an age group, why is not the same term repeated as in the case with **fathers** and **young men?** In vs. 18 "children" (παιδία) refers to all Christians addressed, as it does in John 21:5 and in some MSS in 3:7. (*c*) It is a question whether the forgiveness of sins is specially appropriate to **little children** (vs. 12), particularly if infants are thought of as included. With these considerations in mind, many conclude that only two special age groups are distinguished within the whole body of believers, viz., **fathers** and **young men.**

Yet the elaborate parallelism of the passage—in this case the work of the elder himself and not of his source—should put us on our guard against too precise an interpretation. The elder appears actually to be addressing all Christians and his shifting categories carry a *double-entendre,* as the very ambiguity of τεκνία and παιδία suggests. Whatever the ages of the readers, the elder can properly say to all of them: **Your sins are forgiven; you know him who is from the beginning; you have overcome the evil one.** Thus Augustine here sees all Christians addressed as though they all could be viewed under each particular age group: as children, since they are reborn in baptism; as fathers, since they acknowledge Christ as the Father and Ancient of Days; and as young men, since

---

appeal to the richness and variety of religious experience as a means of confirming his hearers in the faith. The shifting categories of the verses suggest two viewpoints from which to interpret religious experience: from the viewpoint of growth—**little children, young men, fathers** (but cf. Exeg.) ; and from the viewpoint of qualities of spiritual life common to all stages of growth—**sins . . . forgiven,** knowledge of **the Father . . . who is from the beginning,** being **strong** to **overcome the evil one** through the abiding presence of the word of God.

Religious living is growth. The obvious comment on the worn-out controversy as to whether salvation comes through sudden conversion or gradual growth is that it comes through both, and more normally through the latter. It has been said that if people are regularly given religion as food they will not need it suddenly as medicine. E. Stanley Jones writes that in his experience as an evangelist he has found that six people are converted through gradual growth for every four who are converted suddenly.[4] Because religious growth is vitalistic it is also mysterious, and we must beware of dogmatic, hard-and-fast classifications of stages and types of religious experience. The warning in

[4] *Victorious Living* (New York: Abingdon Press, 1936), p. 56.

the Exeg. is permanently valid. Overschematized elaborations of religious experience are unreal whether in ministers' sermons, in books on the theology and psychology of religious experience, or in charts of religious educators. Religious growth is not a matter of physical age or of intellectual development. People advanced in years are often religiously still in kindergarten. Many with a high I.Q. are spiritually illiterate. Learned professors and brilliant scientists often do not know the ABC's of Christian doctrine or ethics. The most important question to be asked about a Christian congregation and about a Christian man is whether they are growing in apprehension of the meaning of Jesus, in experience of eternal life, and in moral devotion to the Christian commandments. All other measures of progress are secondary.

Mysticism often speaks of the quality of "simultaneity" in religious experience, by which is meant the apprehension and possession of differing meanings at one and the same time. The mystical cast of John's mind, together with his conception of eternal life as a present possession, may permit this thought to be taken as the key to interpreting the categories of vss. 12-15. In varying degree all believers experience forgiveness of sins, knowledge of God, and victory over evil at each stage of religious growth.

14 I have written unto you, fathers, because ye have known him *that is* from the beginning. I have written unto you, young men, because ye are strong, and the word of God abideth in you, and ye have overcome the wicked one.

14 I write to you, fathers, because you know him who is from the beginning. I write to you, young men, because you are strong, and the word of God abides in you, and you have overcome the evil one.

---

they are strong and robust. Dodd (pp. 38-39), who says that "the threefold arrangement is probably not much more than a rhetorical figure," calls attention to the passage in the *Corpus Hermeticum* XI. 20 which teaches (in Dodd's words) that "the true mystic . . . has experience of all grades and stages of existence at once."

The formulas in which the **young men** are addressed are of particular interest. The background of such passages, says E. G. Selwyn, "is the social life of the Hellenistic towns, where the . . . νέοι or νεώτεροι were trained as a recognized group in the Gymnasia. . . . The address to νεανίσκοι in I Jn. ii. 13, 14 was no doubt in line with the ethical aims emphasized in the better Gymnasia, where σωφροσύνη [sobriety] was an accepted ideal" (*The First Epistle of Peter* [London: Macmillan & Co., 1946], p. 436).

A subsidiary problem in these verses is the changing tense: γράφω, **I write** (KJV) or **I am writing** (RSV) in the first three members, versus ἔγραψα, **I have written** (KJV) or **I write** (RSV) in the last three. The translation of the latter form in the KJV suggests that the elder refers either to an earlier writing, or looks back upon what he has written up to the point now reached in this epistle. The latter is the probable force of the tense here employed. The RSV regards the aorist as "epistolary," equivalent to a present.

The assurances of these verses are in most cases already familiar to us. The forgiveness of sins **for his name's sake** (KJV) echoes the connection of "name" and "forgiveness"

It can belong to age to conquer as to youth to know, and to youth to be innocent as to childhood to be strong. Innocence and purity characterize children, but paradoxically the more mature a Christian becomes the more childlike his heart and life (cf. Matt. 18:3). Consciousness of sins forgiven humbles one into consciousness of the further need of sins to be forgiven (1:5-10) and inspires purity. Frederic W. Farrar writes of a Roman Catholic chancellor of Paris, Jean de Gerson (1369-1429), as the author of Thomas à Kempis' *Imitation of Christ*. In a stormy period of medieval history his labor and virtue greatly molded men and events. But at the end of his life, unable to reform a corrupt priesthood and sordid episcopate, rejected, forced to wander in disguise and poverty, the great chancellor who had been

the support of mighty Councils, and the terror of contumacious Popes, takes obscure refuge in a Tyrolese Monastery of Celestine monks, and there passes his last days in humility and submission, seeking only the society of little children, and leading them to . . . uplift for him their little white hands with the prayer, "O my God, have pity on Thy poor servant, Jean Gerson." [5]

Knowledge of God is also common to all, but particularly to children and fathers in the faith

[5] *The Imitation of Christ* (6th ed.; London: Methuen & Co., 1926), pp. xx-xxi.

(vss. 13ac, 14). In religion as in life there are two kinds of knowledge: the naïve knowledge of the least advanced (vs. 13c), and the profounder knowledge of the aged (vss. 13a, 14) who have passed beyond doubt and inquiry into final serenity and peace. The mind of childhood —its desire to learn, its capacity to know simply and intuitively, its credulous awareness of the spirit world—has its counterpart in religious experience. Similarly, knowledge which the mature man has harvested from the experience of the years and wrested from the labors and battles of daily life is paralleled in religion by knowledge of God as the one abiding reality. When men know God they know all that is worth knowing; if they know all else, but do not know God as Father, they are still ignorant.

Strength to overcome evil through the abiding power of the word of God, peculiarly appropriate to youth, is available to all Christians (cf. Expos. on 5:4b-5). The victory of Christ appropriated through faith defends the young Christian from falling, nerves the arm of the mature Christian to "fight the good fight," and enables the advanced Christian to persevere to the end. To bring men to live in the strength of the victory that "overcomes the world" (5:4), and to claim the strength of Christian manhood, youth, and childhood for the war against evil, is the unending task of the church.

| 15 Love not the world, neither the things *that are* in the world. If any man love the world, the love of the Father is not in him. | 15 Do not love the world or the things in the world. If any one loves the world, |

---

in Peter's call to baptism in his sermon at Pentecost (Acts 2:38). The overcoming of **the evil one** (cf. 5:18; John 17:15) suggests Christ's prior victory over "the ruler of this world" (John 12:31) which has introduced the new age in which the Father can be truly known and sins forgiven (Jer. 31:31-34).

15. Commentators generally insist that the term **world** (κόσμος) in the following verses and usually in the Gospel of John refers not to the order of creation (including man), but to men's life as alienated from God. **Do not love the world** appears, indeed, to suggest a markedly different aspect of the world (κόσμος) from those sayings which speak of God's love of the world (John 3:16) or of Christ as the Savior of the world (4:14). There are passages—and some in this epistle—where the meaning of the term is evidently narrowed so as to refer to the world in its human aspects; thus 3:1*b*, "The world does not know us," and 4:5: "The world listens to them" (yet contrast 3:17; 4:17). Certainly the meaning of the term varies in different passages.

But in our present passage **world** means more than "mankind fallen away from God." The greatness of this writer's perspective can easily be missed. For him there is a great contrast between God and the creation. Eternal life and the true light and the Spirit belong to the original order ("in the beginning") from which "the Son of God has come and has given us understanding" (5:20). The world is created and loved by God, and Christ has come to save it. But it is ephemeral, subject to decay and death; moreover, it has fallen under the control of the evil one, and therefore into darkness. The world of men and the world of nature were closely interrelated in the thought of ancient men. Thus in our present passage not only the lusts of a fallen humanity but a love of the creature and the creation is disparaged over against the primal and everlasting ground of existence, the Father and his purpose. The true majesty of the charge appears when it is not unduly moralized and when it is related to such passages as Isaiah's contrast of

---

15-17. God Versus the World.—The key to these verses lies in the profound cleavage between the world and the Father, and in the consequent choice every man must make between them. Men cannot live without consciously or unconsciously having to choose some reality to which they give ultimate devotion. They must and will love something. To refuse to choose is itself a choice. They may offer their ultimate devotion to God, the devil, the world, mammon, the state, a political party, truth, beauty, their own lower desires. But life requires decision and the Christian life demands decision. However, decisions once made must be constantly reaffirmed. The situation the elder faced we face: people are brought up as Christians but their enthusiasm fades, religion grows nominal, moral obligation becomes oppressive, sharp distinctions between Christian and pagan practices are no longer tolerated. In such a situation the fundamental dualism of the gospel must be asserted: **Do not love the world; . . . love . . . the Father.**

John employs the term κόσμος **(world)** more than twenty times in this epistle, and his meaning in each usage must be carefully distin-

guished. In the present passage the **world** is set in opposition to God in a semimetaphysical sense and means: the creation as contrasted with the Creator—**all that is in the world . . . is not of the Father;** the creation as ephemeral and mortal, contrasted with the eternal quality of life experienced by him who does the will of God—**the world passes away, . . . he who does the will of God abides forever;** the creation as fallen within "the power of the evil one" (5:19) and alienated from God who alone is good—**lust . . . pride** are **not of the Father.**

15-16. On Loving God Alone.—The injunction to love the Creator and not the creature is the burden of all religion and the core of the Hebrew-Christian heritage. Man perversely seeks to secure his existence in the finite rather than in the infinite; but God who alone is reality makes man to dwell in safety (Ps. 4:8), and God alone is worthy to be completely loved. Life is but the experience of learning where the soul's safety finally lies, and it teaches us that neither nature nor beauty, nor the work of our hands or minds, nor material possessions, nor even love of husband or wife or child can offer final harbor to the human soul. Augustine's

16 For all that *is* in the world, the lust of the flesh, and the lust of the eyes, and the pride of life, is not of the Father, but is of the world.

love for the Father is not in him. 16 For all that is in the world, the lust of the flesh and the lust of the eyes and the pride of life, is

---

the withering grass and fading flower with "the word of our God [which] shall stand for ever" (Isa. 40:6-8).

Such an emphasis is indeed exposed to the modern reproach of a false otherworldliness, and this passage has often been used to fortify such a piety. But the gospel in its ultimate apprehensions can both qualify the importance of man's creaturely life and its setting and sanctify these. The power of this epistle, as of the N.T. as a whole, arises out of the sense of disparity and consequent tension in which the august life of God is contrasted with the created order. The word or revelation of life with which it is concerned is good news just because it speaks authentically of the ground and source of all that exists, and exists so precariously and transiently. The great hold of this epistle and the Gospel of John has lain in the effectiveness with which everlasting life and the days of our years are both contrasted and brought together. Therefore, to restrict the sense of **world** here to human life as alienated from God is to dwarf the paradox and the grandeur of the writer's outlook.

16-17. The lust of the flesh, i.e., the flesh's lust, refers to all the cravings of unregenerate man, as in I Pet. 2:11 and Eph. 2:3 (**flesh** in Paul's sense, not confined to sen-

---

words are not unworthy to be set beside John's verses: "God is the only reality, and we are only real in so far as we are in His order and He in us." [6]

Further, only when we first love the Creator can we love creatures as they should be loved, and only when we first live in God do we know how to live in the world. This paradox is the Christian answer to the charge of otherworldliness so often leveled at religion. Admittedly, Christians have corrupted the paradox: in the name of loving God they have been guilty of morbid asceticism, callousness to social injustice, Philistinism in art, unhealthy attitudes toward sex. But love of God alone sanctifies all other loves—love of beauty, of work, of fatherland, of nature, of family. Augustine has written: "If bodies please thee, praise God on occasion of them, and turn back thy love upon their Maker; lest in these things which please thee, thou displease. If souls please thee, be they loved in God: for they too are mutable, but in Him are they firmly established." [7] Christianity is not "escape from reality"; it is laying hold on Reality and living in Reality.

16-17. The Evil Lusts.—The world as evil is a complementary concept to John's profounder apprehension of the world as created and mortal. It includes acknowledgment of the reality and power of the devil at work in life (cf. Expos. on 3:4-10; 4:1, 3; 5:19b) and recognition of the lusts which the spirit of evil kindles in

man (see below). Observe that John does not speculate about the origin of evil as we do; like Jesus, he simply affirms its reality and reign. Further, in contrast to our modern, naïve faith that evil is being cleaned up like "a bad patch on civilization," [8] John gives us to think that the world will continue to lie within the power of evil (cf. 5:19) until God brings evil finally to pass away. Evil is not something men will conquer in the future when they "build" or "bring in" the kingdom of God. Evil is conquered only in the sense that it already has been overcome in the life and death of Christ (3:8b), in the sense that the kingdom has come, and in the sense that only he who believes in Christ and loves his brother has emerged from mortality and in the power of Christ's victory is able to overcome the world.

In the three forms of the power of the world as evil to tempt and capture the human soul, specified in vs. 16, some interpreters find a parallel to the threefold temptation of our Lord in the wilderness (Luke 4:1-13), and to the temptation of Eve (Gen. 3:6). In John's thought the world as evil is characterized by (a) **the lust of the flesh.** This phrase does not mean bodily appetites of themselves: "The evil significance of the phrase lies in 'lust,' not in 'the flesh.'" [9] John's insistence that Jesus Christ came "in the flesh" (4:2) implies a sacramental conception of physical flesh and requires us to believe that the bodily appetites are in them-

---

[6] Quoted by Evelyn Underhill, *Collected Papers* (New York: Longmans, Green & Co., 1946), p. 128.

[7] *Confessions* IV. 11, 12.

[8] John S. Whale, *Christian Doctrine* (New York: The Macmillan Co., 1941), p. 36.

[9] Law, *Tests of Life,* p. 149.

suality, though this is prominent). **For the lust of the eyes** a passage in the Testament of Reuben (ch. 2) is illuminating. It speaks of the "seven spirits of deceit" which are "appointed against man" of which one is the "sense of sight from which ariseth desire" (cf. also Ezek. 20:7-8). Jesus strictly warns against the eye as the occasion of temptation in the Sermon on the Mount (Matt. 5:27-29). The third phrase, **the pride of life,** is also general enough to encourage various applications. The Greek word for **pride** here connotes vainglory, insolence, and display, while that for **life** refers particularly to possessions

selves wholesome. Their degradation comes from the soul. Lusts of the flesh consist in the lower vitalities and passions of human personality unredeemed by God with which primal evil finds affinity (cf. Expos. on 3:4-10; 4:1, 3). In philosophical thought lust of the flesh can take the form of naturalism, and evil consists not so much in the fact that men hold a naturalistic conception of life as in the fact that some men want to hold such a conception. Naturalism denies any divine origin or meaning to life and attempts to interpret everything in terms of physical nature. It interprets history in terms of materialism. It interprets man as a creature exclusively within the order of nature. Thus naturalistic anthropology conceives man as merely an animal evolved from other animals; naturalistic biology reduces man to chemistry and endocrinology; naturalistic psychology conceives man as a creature of highly developed reflexes whose behavior is exclusively reaction to environment. **Lust of the flesh** takes cultural expression in the modern belief that true reality is mainly or exclusively sensory; and the culture mothered by this belief is spoken of as "sensate —empirical, utilitarian, hedonistic." [1] In our age the physical senses—with the assistance of reason—have been made the arbiter of the true and the false, the valuable and the valueless, the real and the unreal. "Scientism" as distinguished from science, is one element in sensate culture, the prevalent faith that science and technology afford the only knowledge and resources men require for individual and social salvation. Materialism, another cultural expression of lust of the flesh, infects virtually every area of modern civilization and has shaped a society based on the primacy of material values. Greed also has become "the besetting sin of a bourgeois culture," in which we are tempted to "regard comfort and security as life's good." [2] Gluttony, alcoholism, hedonism—living for sensual pleasure—are other expressions of lust of the flesh. Writes a modern sensualist: "I appeal to youth. . . . With concentrated purpose follow the deepest inclinations of your being, and snatch, snatch at happiness with passionate eagerness. . . . The secret of life is to live by the

senses with an ardor passionate and religious." [3] The publication of the Kinsey reports [4] reflects the devastation wrought by an animalistic conception of sex in American morals and mores. It would appear that American standards of sex morality approach those which prevailed in Roman civilization in the period of its decay. In personal living **lust of the flesh** consists in man's primitive drives, animal impulses, and ancestral instincts unexpelled or unsanctified by the love of God. Against these every man must battle: "Wherever he stands, at the beginning or the end of things, a man has to sacrifice his gods to his passions or his passions to his gods." [5]

(*b*) **Lust of the eyes** "includes every variety of gratification of which sight is the instrument." [6] Captivation by the outward show of things without regard to their real value; covetousness; surrender to the glittering, the glamorous, the dazzling; vulgar display and pretentiousness; sensationalism in advertising; love of gadgets—"this gadget civilization" ours has been called—these are modern counterparts. In less crude forms **lust of the eyes** is the temptation of taste, and takes the form of love of novelty for novelty's sake, grotesqueness, "colossalism" in art and architecture. "Pliny's 'Not being able to make our values beautiful, we make them huge,' is as applicable to our culture as to the sensate culture of Rome." [7] In a more sophisticated form, "art for art's sake" becomes **lust of the eyes.** The relation of aesthetic culture to the spiritual life is always a problem. But surely the sense of beauty, like all else, is of God; and in so far as art is unsanctified by the love of God and unchastened by the beauty of holiness, it becomes idolatry.

(*c*) **Pride of life** is the egotistical passion to live in conscious superiority to one's fellow men according to the standards and values of the world. Such egotism appears in people of every age and station in society, from politicians to movie stars, from giants of in-

[1] Pitirim Sorokin, *The Crisis of Our Age* (New York: E. P. Dutton & Co., 1941), p. 274.

[2] Niebuhr, *Nature and Destiny of Man,* I, 191.

[3] Llewelyn Powys, *Impassioned Clay* (London: Longmans, Green & Co., 1931), pp. 95, 119.

[4] *Sexual Behavior in the Human Male* (Philadelphia: W. B. Saunders Co., 1948); *Sexual Behavior in the Human Female* (Philadelphia: W. B. Saunders Co., 1953).

[5] Joseph Conrad, *Notes on Life and Letters* (Garden City: Doubleday, Page & Co., 1921), p. 16.

[6] Law, *Tests of Life,* p. 150.

[7] Sorokin, *op. cit.,* p. 255.

17 And the world passeth away, and the lust thereof: but he that doeth the will of God abideth for ever.	not of the Father but is of the world. 17 And the world passes away, and the lust of it; but he who does the will of God abides for ever.

or "style of living." Thus everything from "conspicuous expenditure" to a presumptuous trust in outward securities is suggested. All of these things—which in view of the immediate sequel are indirectly charged to the schismatics—are under doom, **but he who does the will of God abides for ever.**

dustry to ecclesiastical dignitaries. It takes such forms as the craze for publicity in our publicity-conscious age, vulgar ostentation in dress and possessions, unholy professional ambition, lust for fame. It is

the vainglory of life—the self-conceit, the desire for praise and deference, the delight of being thought an important . . . person, of wielding power over others, of being in the lime-light; all the empty vanities of fashion and custom and title and office and uniform and status, the little snobbish impostures into which men tumble . . . . It matters not that . . . before God it will all avail us nothing. The mean little ego will still have us out on our stage, prancing and strutting and posturing.[8]

17a. God Alone Abides.—We may not be able to believe that **the world passes away** in the eschatological terms of John's expectation of the literal second coming of Christ (cf. Expos. on 2:18; 2:28–3:3; 4:17, 18), but we can understand that the world passes away in terms of the movements of history. The inherent transiency of all human things is the message of literature and the testimony of history. In our age specifically, reasonable men must contemplate the possible destruction of human life and the extinction of civilization on this planet. If the **world** is conceived in moral terms, then in so far as human life is characterized by lust of the flesh and of the eyes and by pride (cf. Expos. on vss. 16-17) the world passes away by self-destruction. It cannot be otherwise; good cannot finally tolerate evil. In personal experience man is involved in the decay and transiency of life. He is time-bound. He seeks escape from the temporal and mortal:

Change and decay in all around I see;
O Thou, who changest not, abide with me.

Man seeks escape through knowledge. A character in a modern story says: "I want to study astronomy . . . because I can no longer stand the thought of time. It feels like a prison to me, and if I could only get away from it altogether

I think I should be happy."[9] He seeks the eternal through beauty, and the poet can write:

The rose whose beauty glads thine eye to see,
Blossomed in God 'ere time began to be.[1]

But the experience of eternal life in God who is **from the beginning** alone offers fruition of communion with the eternal; it alone enables man to live in the eternal and the temporal world at the same time; it alone enables him to see persons, things, choices from the viewpoint of eternity; it alone enables him to "cram today with eternity."

17b. Obedience to God, and Eternal Life.—Opposed to the world is God, and opposed to the doom which falls on him who loves the world (cf. Expos. on vss. 16-17) is the immortality of eternal life: **he who does the will of God abides for ever.** The will of God is the constituent principle of life and the universe, and permanent value resides only in what is within God's purpose. Only in so far as man attaches himself to God's will does he belong to the order of immortality. Everything not within God's will simply "passes away," i.e., dies. But in Johannine thought the doing of God's will is only part of living in the eternal life of God appropriated through faith and manifest in love. And must one not reckon with the possibility that the converse of vs. 17 is also true, that he who rejects the gift of this life, who does not do the will of God, but lives by the lusts of the world, is destroyed? It may be that belief in the infinite mercy of God enables one to believe in the universal restoration of all souls after death, and certainly judgment belongs to God alone; at the same time, all that is of the world "passes away," and "wide is the gate, and broad is the way, that leadeth to destruction" (Matt. 7:13). Ought we not be more sparing in the assurance that men will "live forever"? Future immortality is accordingly bound up with the kind of life one lives in this world. Mere hope of immortality, ability to logically prove the case for immortality, even religious faith in immortality

[8] H. H. Farmer, *The Healing Cross* (New York: Charles Scribner's Sons, 1939), pp. 183-84.

[9] Isak Dinesen, *Seven Gothic Tales* (New York: Smith & Haas, 1934), p. 182.
[1] Angelus Silesius, "The Imitation of Christ."

18 Little children, it is the last time: and as ye have heard that antichrist shall come, even now are there many antichrists; whereby we know that it is the last time.

18 Children, it is the last hour; and as you have heard that antichrist is coming, so now many antichrists have come; there-

III. The Deniers of the Faith; Truth and Falsehood (2:18-27)

This passage is the first of two polemical sections directly concerned with those who are deceiving the church. The other section is a shorter one, 4:1-6. The writer has already, indeed, spoken of dangers *within* the fellowship. He now speaks of men who "went out from us," specifies the crux of their heresy, identifies it with the Antichrist of the end time, and fortifies the readers in their own better knowledge which they have all along had "from the beginning." With a warning and a promise which link this topical section to what has preceded and which introduce the topic of the Second Coming (2:28–3:3), he returns to his earlier theme of the tests of fellowship with God, treated in new terms in which love and divine sonship dominate (2:28–3:24). In the present section, since he is clarifying a concrete church situation, he has no occasion to use his rhetorical style or source except in vs. 23, but rather makes generous drafts upon the confessional formulas of the church: the coming of Antichrist, the acknowledgment of Jesus as Christ, and the promise of eternal life.

A. The Antichrist and the Last Hour (2:18-23)

18. It is the last hour follows naturally from the statement that "the world passes away" (vs. 17 and cf. vs. 8), though the present eschatological line of thought differs

do not *per se* bring one to abide forever. Rather, immortality is intimated to us in the experience of doing God's will in daily life. In this sense immortality is not reserved until we physically die; it is an aspect of eternal life we may enjoy now.

18a. The Last Hour.—The doctrine of the last hour reflects an eschatological conception of history derived from apostolic thought going back to Jesus himself (cf. John 6:39-40, 44, 54; 11:24; 12:48; I Pet. 1:5). The author believes he is living in the last hour of the old age, and that the new age—soon to culminate in the literal second coming of Christ—is already existent. The author's skill in avoiding the cruder aspects of the doctrine of the last hour and in laying hold on its permanent significance well bears out Findlay's comment concerning John's mind, "He had both *sight* and *insight*."[2] At the same time, it discredits all in our day who would use biblical language and thought forms to support their own particular apocalyptic time charts of history and who pervert religion to excite curiosity. The warning still applies, "It is not for you to know the times or the seasons, which the Father hath put in his own power" (Acts 1:7).

In terms of history last hours come. Epochs and cycles of history contain within themselves mortality and finality. The historian Arnold Toynbee writes at length of what he significantly calls "the rhythm of disintegration" and reports

[2] *Fellowship in Life Eternal*, p. 53.

that of twenty-six civilizations he has identified, sixteen are dead and nine of the remaining ten have broken down.[3] Eschatology is a historical as well as a theological concept. In a specific, tragic sense the decades of war of the twentieth century may be a last hour. "While after the first World War the mood of a new beginning prevailed, after the second World War a mood of the end prevails."[4] People have often spoken of an "ultimate stage of history" in which choices were presumably to be made that would decisively determine human destiny. But in our century, it would seem, man for the first time in history is in an hour when, if his decisions are not morally and intelligently made, there may be no more hours.

Philosophically, life can be conceived as always in its last hour. The philosophy of existentialism, whose spread has been spurred by the catastrophes of the past decades, sees the human situation as always perilous, ambiguous, and disposed to tragedy; in every choice presented to man's will his existence is at stake and his destiny is being forged. Religiously human life is always in its last hour. The eschatological meaning of history—from the Christian point of view—is the meaning of every human life. The gospel ever brings men individually as well

[3] *A Study of History*, Abridgement of Vols. I-VI by D. C. Somervell (New York: Oxford University Press, 1947), pp. 548-54.
[4] Paul Tillich, *The Protestant Era*, tr. J. L. Adams (Chicago: University of Chicago Press, 1948), p. 60.

somewhat from the dualism which, as we have seen, governs the writer's view of "the world." Here the distinction is between the old age and the new rather than between the world and eternal life. The traditional apocalyptic eschatology of the church is employed, and appeal is made to what the readers **have heard.** The familiar signs of the **last hour** or "last time" (Jude 18) were to include hatred (vss. 9, 11), falsehood (vs. 4), apostasy, and the appearance of the Antichrist. "And then many will fall away, and betray one another, and hate one another. And many false prophets will arise and lead many astray. And because wickedness is multiplied, most men's love will grow cold" (Matt. 24:10-12). The Teaching of the Twelve Apostles has a similar version which includes mention of the Antichrist: "For in the last days the false prophets and the corrupters shall be multiplied, and the sheep shall be turned into wolves, and love shall change to hate; for as lawlessness increaseth they shall hate one another and persecute and betray, and then shall appear the deceiver of the world as a Son of God" (Did. 16:3-4). The point to notice in I John is that the Antichrist does not *follow* the deceiving prophets and "spirits" (4:1), but is identified with them or their lie. The actual term **antichrist** appears only in I and II John in the N.T. but the same figure is in view in the "man of lawlessness" of II Thess. 2:3-4, in the great agent of sacrilege in Mark 13:14 and its parallels, and elsewhere. In our epistle he is identified with the "spirit" of heresy (4:3) or error (4:6) rather than with an apostate Jewish pretender or a blasphemous world ruler. Thus the author speaks of **many antichrists** and of the "spirits" of "many false prophets" (4:1) as **already come.** He has in mind disturbers of the life of the churches generally and pretenders to messiahship or divinity in various parts of the empire. Words assigned to Jesus in the Gospels bearing on these events were thought of by the evangelists as fulfilled in their day. Thus in Matthew, among the features of the great tribulation which will immediately herald the advent of the Son of man, Jesus says: "Then if any one says to you, 'Lo, here is the Christ!' or 'There he is!' do not believe it. For false Christs and false

as collectively "face to face with God in his kingdom, power and glory," and the preaching of the church accordingly must be "directed towards reconstituting in the experience of individuals the hour of decision which Jesus brought . . . . 'The time is fulfilled and the Kingdom of God has come. Repent, and believe the Gospel.' " [5] The gospel couples what has been called "the good news of damnation" with "the good news of salvation"; it permits no heresy of delayed-action discipleship; it thus imposes a great constraint and urgency upon the church.

18b-19, 22. The Symbol of the Antichrist.— The spiritualization of the traditional symbol of the Antichrist is another instance of the author's ability to infuse timeless meanings into a historical thought form. This suggests the task set for every interpreter of the gospel: not to confuse the husk of form with the kernel of content, but with imagination and insight to reinterpret Christian truth in terms of its abiding meanings. In essence, the Antichrist is an idea or person in history that denies God revealed in Christ (vs. 22), i.e., denies the whole Christian revelation, the gospel (cf. Expos. on 4:1, 3, 4-6). Antichrist thus is not the spirit of honest doubt but of willful error in face of

palpable truth. "I am the spirit that denies," says Mephistopheles in *Faust.*[6] A certain desperation and fatefulness characterize the appearance and recognition of Antichrist, for man stands helpless before evil and would yield to despair except for the faith that in the last hour of extremity the Lord will come. The complacency and apathy so often displayed by the church in face of world conditions are judged by this insight. Many Christians have never entered into any feeling for the terrific moral struggle going on in life and in the universe. A critic once called the novelist Galsworthy "a toy Socialist." So there are many "toy Christians" who play with religion instead of fighting for it.

While embodied in persons, Antichrist is essentially a false idea, an untrue belief, the "spirit of heresy or error." Thus it becomes evident that the true battlefield between God and evil is the human mind, and so the cliché, "It does not matter what a man believes so long as he leads a decent life," is seen to be ridiculous. Only belief in decency makes a man decent. Every man in the long run lives by his faith, and his faith determines what he is. Moreover, he lives down to his beliefs as well as up to them. Remember that the false teachers whom John calls **antichrists** were also morally reprobate; their

[5] C. H. Dodd, *The Parables of the Kingdom* (New York: Charles Scribner's Sons, 1936), pp. 205, 204.

[6] Part I, scene 3.

19 They went out from us, but they were not of us; for if they had been of us, they would *no doubt* have continued with us: but *they went out,* that they might be made manifest that they were not all of us.	fore we know that it is the last hour. **19** They went out from us, but they were not of us; for if they had been of us, they would have continued with us; but they went out, that it might be plain that they all are not of us.

prophets will arise and show great signs and wonders, so as to lead astray, if possible, even the elect" (Matt. 24:23-24; cf. Mark 13:21-22; Luke 21:8). The church fathers, rightly or wrongly, supply the names of Dositheus, Simon Magus, Judas Galilaeus, and later, Montanus, as having made messianic claims. Origen knows of only a few. It is evident that the elder adopts the powerful dramatic symbol of the Antichrist here, and spiritualizes it to suggest what is at stake in the present trial of the church, feeling free as others before and after him to reinterpret it. Convinced that the great final conflict is under way, he looks about for manifestation of "the spirit of antichrist, of which you heard that it was coming" (4:3b), and identifies it with the sway of falsehood and hatred and with the denial that **Jesus is the Christ** (vs. 22).

19. The cleavage and disaffection which had declared themselves within the churches concerned are interpreted as an exodus of the false pretenders and teachers. The two shorter epistles do not indicate that these groups thought of themselves as outside the church, but the elder is concerned to show that "they are of the world" (4:5), which explains the hearing they get in the world, and to maintain that their repudiation of

---

denial of truth issued in hatred of the brethren. Belief molds character. The power of ideas multiplied by modern means of communication is the great fact of our century. Charles Demant writes: "The important lesson of totalitarian movements is that human power is generated not by advice, but by dogma. Men are moved not by exhortation, but by affirmations." [7] Printing presses, motion pictures, radio propaganda, win battles that guns never can. Consider what the ideas of *Mein Kampf* and *Das Kapital* have done to the world. The Nazi assault and the Communist challenge to Western civilization were directly the result of ideas. The church's task lies here. The true weapons of the church are never those of the world but weapons of religious faith, moral example, and intellectual appeal. The victory of Gandhi in India, unparalleled in military and diplomatic history, was a victory of ideas, of truth.

The **antichrists** [who] **were not of us . . . went out, that it might be plain that they all are not of us.** The antichrists once were Christ's; but **they went out.** The greatest danger to Christianity often lies not in its declared enemies but in its false friends. Why do Christians "go out"? Because of petty jealousies in church life; because of bitter doctrinal differences; because of weariness or boredom in living the Christian life. More often Christians "go out" because they have never really grasped the truth and power of the life Christ can bring men to

live. To say, as some people have said, that communism and its leaders are the idea and the embodiment of Antichrist is a distorted religious judgment and an oversimplified historical judgment. Nevertheless, it is significant that Stalin studied for the priesthood before he turned revolutionist, and that communism in its original ideological form was called a Christian heresy, "a leaf taken from the book of Christianity—a leaf torn out and misread." [8]

Antichrists employ the name and use the means of religion to propagate the antithesis of religion. Antichrist signifies "one who opposes Christ by assuming the guise of Christ." [9] The faith is ever imperiled by those who undermine Christian truth with corruptions of Christian truth. One thinks of Christians who hinder social and economic reform by enjoining a false peaceableness; of Christians who permit the sacred sanctions of the gospel to be used to prosecute war; of those who justify obscurantism in thought and theology with a false, literalistic conservatism; of so-called Christian movements such as the Ku Klux Klan which thrive on unchristian prejudice and hatred; of religious groups which attempt to tyrannize men's souls into salvation; of modern paganisms which employ the cultus of religion to foment mystical zeal and fanatical loyalty.

The fact that the schismatic antichrists went out is proof that nominal membership in the church is insufficient to preserve men in the

---

[7] Quoted by H. G. G. Herklots and Henry Smith, *Pilgrimage to Amsterdam* (New York: Morehouse-Gorham Co., 1947), p. 38.

[8] Arnold J. Toynbee, *Civilization on Trial* (New York: Oxford University Press, 1948), p. 236.

[9] Law, *Tests of Life*, p. 321.

20 But ye have an unction from the Holy One, and ye know all things.

21 I have not written unto you because ye know not the truth, but because ye know it, and that no lie is of the truth.

20 But you have been anointed by the Holy One, and you all know.[d] 21 I write to you, not because you do not know the truth, but because you know it, and know that no lie

[d] Other ancient authorities read *you know everything.*

---

fellowship and instruction (cf. III John 9-10) shows plainly that **they all are not of us,** indeed, that they were **not** [ever] **of us.** Ignatius says of dissidents in the same region: "For these are not the planting of the Father. For if they were they would appear as branches of the Cross (and their fruit would be incorruptible) by which through his Passion he calls you who are his members" (Ign. Trall. 11:1-2). The closing purpose clause of this verse is elliptical in the Greek, as is indicated in the italicized words in the KJV, and implies providential necessity. It is all to the good, the writer means, that the issue should be clarified (cf. I Cor. 11:19).

20-21. As he leads up to his final criterion in vs. 22, the elder makes appeal to the revealed understanding of the matter on the part of his readers. By a kind of play on words he reminds them that they too have **an unction** (KJV) or "chrism"—Greek: χρῖσμα (cf. ἀντιχριστός). What he has in mind is basically the gift of the Holy Spirit (cf. 3:24; 4:2; etc.). Some commentators believe that the word is chosen in view of a special rite of anointing which may have been used by the offenders in line with Hellenistic practice and was thought of as conferring superior truth. The use of oil (χρῖσμα) in baptism by the church at a later time may well have been encouraged by the present passage. The word is not used in the N.T. outside the present chapter. As Dodd has shown, the use of this

---

truth. The epitaph **they went out** describes many modern Christians whose faith has lapsed because their original commitment was exacted too cheaply and whose original loyalties were established too weakly. Contrast the costly demand Jesus imposed on those who would follow him with the easygoing, conventional way many churches receive people into membership. The mortality rate of Protestant church membership is a scandal. Attention and energy might be better directed toward establishing and confirming believers in the faith than spent in movements of mass evangelism. Earnestness of commitment is more important than numerical church membership.

But schism is not always evil. Secession can be part of the divine purpose of "making plain" (vs. 19) who genuinely constitute the church. So-called religious tolerance ceases to be a virtue when it sacrifices solidarity in the truth for nominal fellowship. There is a legitimate conservatism that must hold to the truth which is "from the beginning," that has no alternative but to expose the error of those who in the name of a false emancipation or false progress deny the truth. Observe that the antichrists were not irreligious atheists; they were theists, but not Christians (cf. Expos. on II John 9).

20-23. *Believing or Denying Christ.*—But while there are many antichrists and liars (vs. 18), *the* Antichrist, *the* liar is he **who denies that Jesus is the Christ, . . . he who denies the Father and the Son. No one who denies the Son has**

the Father. He who confesses the Son has the Father also. These words express the great christological thesis of the epistles—that everything depends on whether men believe in Jesus Christ. On some issues there can be honest difference of opinion; but on the fundamental issue, the full meaning of Jesus as the Christ and as the Son of God (also as the Savior of the world [vs. 2; 4:10, 14] and our Advocate [vs. 1]), there can be no compromise. The choice is between nothing less than truth or falsehood, and it determines man's entire "interpretation of life and of the world" (cf. Exeg. on vss. 22-23).

Christology is the heart of theology, and Christian thought is faithful to the gospel only when it first addresses itself to the ancient question: "but who do you say that I am?" (Matt. 16:15). "The Christological debates of nineteen centuries are a monument to the uniqueness of him whom Christians know as the Incarnate Son of God." [1] Significantly, the dominant doctrine in the greatest of all Christian confessions, the Nicene Creed of A.D. 325, is the Incarnation. Of one hundred and one Greek words, eighty-four are concerned with the Son.

The confessional formula, "Jesus is the Christ," is a verbal epitome of the doctrine of the Incarnation and, in answer to the Docetists, signifies the unity of the divine Christ with the human Jesus (cf. Expos. on 4:2, 14-15; 5:6-12). This unity was probably most in question by

[1] Whale, *Christian Doctrine,* pp. 108-9.

245

22 Who is a liar but he that denieth that Jesus is the Christ? He is antichrist, that denieth the Father and the Son.

is of the truth. 22 Who is the liar but he who denies that Jesus is the Christ? This is the antichrist, he who denies the Father and

---

pagan term is bold, and W. A. Karl may be right in thinking that it points to an emphasis on ecstatic experience in the Christian life of these believers (cf. Gal. 4:6). The "chrism" is properly one which "abides in" the Christian and "teaches" him "about everything." This suggests that the gift of revelation in question, received at a given time, presumably at baptism (ἐλάβετε), is closely related to the true word of God, which likewise "abides in you" (cf. vss. 27 and 14b, also 24). **The Holy One** may refer either to God (John 17:11) or to Christ (John 6:69; cf. Rev. 3:7; etc.). The MSS differ in the last phrase of vs. 20 (cf. KJV and RSV), but modern textual critics prefer the reading favored by the RSV, **you all know.** The writer desires earnestly to awaken his readers to their deepest convictions and counts on the widespread insight of the laymen of the church as a bulwark in a perilous situation. He also is insisting that the knowledge is not reserved to a few (cf. I Thess. 4:9).

22. The liar may mean only the liar in question, but the interconnection in the epistle of falsehood, darkness, the Antichrist, and the evil one shows that the term is to be taken more absolutely here as the liar par excellence. The denial that **Jesus is the Christ** is not the Jewish refusal to recognize Jesus as the Messiah; this denial would hardly be made by members of the church. The sense of the denial is illuminated by 4:2: it is the denial that "Jesus Christ has come in the flesh." The form "Jesus is the Son of God" (4:15) conveys the same point. The Docetists made a separation between the

---

the errorists; Jesus as a historical person would hardly be disputed. So it still is in our age. Only uninformed or opinionated minds will dispute the historicity of Jesus. The evidence for the historical Jesus is as reliable as the evidence for any other similarly notable figure in history, such as Julius Caesar or Napoleon. Further, many modern men will concede the perfection of Jesus' humanity, that Jesus was a great teacher, or brilliant thinker, or moral hero, the perfect Man. Some will go further and concede that in a semiphilosophical sense he perfectly incarnated "ultimate values," that he is the "norm of humanity," etc. But to believe that in Jesus of Nazareth God was fully present is a different matter. Our modern Docetism may concede the significance of Jesus' humanity; it rejects the union of divinity with his humanity.

However, beyond the issue of Jesus' divinity lies the profounder issue Findlay defines in these words: the errorists "recoiled not from a crucified Messiah, but from *a humanized God.*"[2] They could perhaps accept Jesus of Nazareth as the Christ; they could not accept Jesus of Nazareth as "God" (4:15). They might believe in the Godlikeness of Christ; they could not believe in the Christlikeness of God. This is still the ultimate issue. So much in our modern world strikes at the thought of a Christlike God: the brutality and savagery of human life in history; the incalculable dimensions of the physical universe science has revealed that stag-

ger the mind and chill the heart; the fashionable belief in God as eternal beauty or reason, as cosmic energy, as absolute being or divine oversoul—modern equivalents of first-century Gnostic abstractions; the affront to reason offered by the Cross, that God could suffer such shame; the affront to reason and taste offered by the Incarnation, that God could be born in a stable; the shock to reason, that in one event in history God has disclosed himself as he has nowhere else (cf. Expos. on 4:2). But the scandal to our modern age is the message of the gospel: the Incarnation "represents an eternal fact in the heart of God."[3] "He who has seen me has seen the Father" (John 14:9).

It is the glory of Christian devotion that, at the summit of attainment, we frail mortal creatures seek and find a human Face in the Deity to welcome us.

<blockquote>
A Man like to me
Thou shalt love and be loved by for ever: a hand like this hand
Shall throw open the gates of new life to thee! See the Christ stand![4]
</blockquote>

The unique meaning of Jesus' revelation consists in the disclosure of God as Father. Men may know other aspects of God's nature through other revelations, but no one who de-

[2] *Fellowship in Life Eternal,* p. 319.

[3] Whale, *op. cit.,* p. 116.
[4] R. Newton Flew, *The Idea of Perfection in Christian Theology* (Oxford: The Clarendon Press, 1934), p. 215. Used by permission.

23 Whosoever denieth the Son, the same hath not the Father: [*but*] *he that acknowledgeth the Son hath the Father also.*

the Son. **23** No one who denies the Son has the Father. He who confesses the Son has

---

earthly Jesus and the heavenly Christ. There were various theories about the Christ or the Son of God in his relationship to Jesus, and the elder no doubt repudiates more than one kind as he appeals to the early Christian confessions of faith. These verses sound very harsh and dogmatic to us (and cf. 5:10, 12). As a matter of fact, the impulse of the writer was not that of an inflexible orthodoxy: it was an appeal to the abiding dynamic witness of the Spirit, which quickens and leads into all truth. This Spirit was indeed related inseparably to the old oral confessions of the church (cf. Acts 8:37, RSV mg.), but these evidently were already taking various forms, and the meaning of the term **Christ,** for example, had changed markedly. What is crucial is the interpretation of life and the world in terms of the gospel: Jesus of Nazareth and his whole story. To misconceive Jesus and to dissolve the bond between him and the Christ—i.e., the Son of God or Word of God—is, of necessity, to misconceive God himself.

23. No one who denies the Son has the Father: He is unable either to recognize the Father as he really is or to "abide in" him (cf. vs. 24b). The writer is not speaking of doubt, but of denial. Denial carries with it responsible refusal of recognized reality and obligation. This animus against the gospel is interpreted by the elder in keeping with his dualistic as well as with his eschatological outlook. It is a refusal of the "true light," which antedates the world and thus can arise only from those who "walk in darkness" (1:6), and it represents the Antichrist or "spirit of antichrist" (4:3), which is the climactic challenge of evil in the end time. The writer believes that just as it is by the

---

nies the Son has the Father. "No one comes to the Father, but by me" (John 14:6). This claim once and for all distinguishes Christianity from mere theism. What is at stake is not the existence of God but the nature of God. This claim stipulates that the truest knowledge of God comes not through reason or mystical initiation but through faith (and love, cf. Expos. on 4:7-12). The fatherhood of God cannot be demonstrated by logical argument. It cannot be inferred from the aesthetic experience of beauty, or deduced from the fact of law in nature or moral purpose in history. It hinges solely on the Son's revelation of the Father. The area of experience which best illumines the fatherhood of God is human parenthood and childhood; and we are encouraged to trust the analogy of human parenthood as an intimation of divine fatherhood as far as our minds can take us, if—but only if—we have first been brought to interpret it with the mind of Christ. There are depths in God which we cannot comprehend, as there are colors in the spectrum the human eye cannot see. But God revealed as Father in Jesus offers all that our minds can comprehend or our hearts will ever need for communion with him. To know God as Father is not a matter of abstract thought but of experienced possession: **He who confesses the Son has the Father also** (vs. 23). What is finally involved is not theological controversy but religious experience.

23. *Importance of Faith and Creed.*—The author's insistence on belief and doctrine in these verses complements his equally intense ethical concern evident throughout the epistle. These two fundamental emphases are most clearly expressed in 3:23, which has been called the key verse to the epistle: "This is his commandment, that we should believe . . . and love." Belief is hardly less central than love in all authentic interpretations of Christianity, and the elder's frequent use of confessional formulas (1:7; 2:1-2; 3:5, 8b; 4:2, 14; 5:1, 5, 13, 20; II John 7) underscores the importance of creeds in the life of the church (cf. also Acts 8:37; I Cor. 12:3). The statement of the Exeg. is correct, that the elder argues for no "infallible orthodoxy" (vss. 22-23). At the same time, there is a minimum of belief which a man cannot reject and still call himself Christian. Only spurious and shallow religion deprecates creeds. When held, declared, and interpreted under illumination of the Holy Spirit (vs. 20), creedal confessions serve to divide falsehood from truth, confront men with the challenge of truth, and lead them to embrace those truths in the gospel which cannot be understood until they are first believed. Creedal confessions tax men to love God with their mind as with every other faculty, and provide the framework of thought that guarantees permanence to religion: "The religion which makes its appeal to the sense of the beautiful, and speaks to the fancy in legends,

24 Let that therefore abide in you, which ye have heard from the beginning. If that which ye have heard from the beginning shall remain in you, ye also shall continue in the Son, and in the Father.

the Father also. **24** Let what you heard from the beginning abide in you. If what you heard from the beginning abides in you, then you will abide in the Son and in the

Spirit of God that men perceive the significance of Christ and know the Father, so it is by corresponding evil forces in the soul that men resent and deny them (cf. I Cor. 12:3). Thus the denier is identified with **the antichrist**, just as in 4:1-3 the disavowal or cursing of Christ (see below) is connected with "spirits" in the sense of the "controls" of false prophets. That the Son is the medium to the knowledge of the Father is a variant on a very important early Christian formula, of which we have an example in Matt. 11:27= Luke 10:22, and which is the basis of much instruction in the Fourth Gospel. The confession of Christ as the basis of our relation to God, moreover, takes us back to the crucial antinomy of Jesus himself in Matt. 10:32-33 and its parallels. **No one who denies the Son has the Father** is merely a new and somewhat mystical version, in the light of a changing theology, of Jesus' warning, "For whoever is ashamed of me and of my words in this adulterous and sinful generation, of him will the Son of man also be ashamed, when he comes in the glory of his Father with the holy angels" (Mark 8:38). The italics in 23*b* in the KJV reflect the fact that this half of the verse had dropped out of some of the MSS on which that version was based.

B. Summons to Faithfulness (2:24-27)

24. As in vs. 20, the **you** is strongly emphasized in the Greek by its position, and here also by its irregular construction. Contrast with the heretics is intended. The indwelling

or to the imagination in symbols, may do well for a season . . . ; but only the religion which addresses and exercises the reason will continue to live."[5] Creeds correct error and define truth. "It is just as much idolatry to worship God according to a false mental image as by means of a false metal image."[6] Creeds provide the grammar of religion, and are to religion what grammar is to speech. They kindle faith, offer the joy of conviction, and inspire loyalty. Studdert-Kennedy once remarked that the Apostles' Creed ought to be repeated to the roll of drums and the flourish of trumpets; and Calvin and other Reformers declared that the Nicene Creed should preferably be sung!

While vss. 18-23 are a polemical section, observe that the author's denunciation and appeal are informed with wisdom, poise, good taste, and high-mindedness. He appeals to the best in those whom he addresses; he credits them with the best motives; he has confidence in their character and attainments (vs. 20). He does not override their judgment or conscience, but trusts the truth of what he writes to carry its own self-evidencing appeal. He spurs his hearers to further achievement by appreciation of what they have already attained; and he is more con-

cerned to bring them to live by what they already know than to impress or intrigue them with new knowledge they do not yet have. Finally, the elder appeals not to the loyalty of a few favorite friends or to the authority of the resident pastor in charge, but to the collective conviction and common sense of the general body of laymen who have held true. The intelligence, good will, and devotion of the laity are often a safer court of appeal in a controversial church situation than the professional clergy. Demetrius in III John 12 is a good case in point!

24-27. *Summons to Faithfulness.*—The title of this section suggests by implication a perennial temptation in the Christian life, the temptation to faithlessness. Sometimes people are sources of temptation, as the deceivers (vs. 26) were to John's hearers. The cynic, the casuist, the sophisticate, the hypocrite, the worldling often wear the guise of Christianity. Slogans also tempt Christians to be faithless: "You've got to be realistic," "legitimate self-interest," "business is business," "see a bit of life," "if you don't look out for yourself, no one else will," "one religion is as good as another," "you don't need to go to church to be a Christian," etc. Experiences of adversity, of disillusionment, of frustration, also tempt the believer to waver. People become atheists more often through emotional devastation than through intellectual conviction. John Wesley once said that an earth-

[5] A. M. Fairbairn, *The Philosophy of the Christian Religion* (New York: The Macmillan Co., 1902), pp. 4-5.
[6] William Temple, *Christian Faith and Life* (New York: The Macmillan Co., 1931), p. 24.

25 And this is the promise that he hath promised us, *even* eternal life.

26 These things have I written unto you concerning them that seduce you.

Father. 25 And this is what he has promised us,*e* eternal life.

26 I write this to you about those who

e Other ancient authorities read *you.*

---

of the word or revelation or "chrism" (vs. 27) is to be safeguarded as it guarantees our indwelling **in the Son and in the Father.** We find ourselves here amid familiar Johannine conceptions, all suggestive of participation in the divine life, which is also "eternal life" (vs. 25), and fellowship with or possession of (vs. 23) the Son and the Father. The Fourth Gospel and the epistles vary these expressions in numerous ways, all of them, however, conveying that sense of the new covenant relationship with God now realized, for which Paul has his own favored formulas: in Christ, in the Spirit, Christ in us, the Spirit in us. The double mutual abiding appears in John 15:5, "he who abides in me, and I in him," where it is closely related to the indwelling word, "if you abide in me, and my words abide in you" (John 15:7). II John 9 affirms that "he who abides in the doctrine of Christ has both the Father and the Son." Later in the present epistle such mutual indwelling is connected with the Spirit (4:13) and with love (4:16). The dominating mystical sense of the Christian experience here described, together with its connection with the Lord's Supper, appears in John 6:56, where also the promise of "eternal life" is found in the context, as here in vs. 25.

25. This refers both backward and forward; Christ has promised us **eternal life,** which is viewed as only another way of describing our abiding "in the Son and in the Father." Ignatius combines Pauline and Johannine language when he speaks of the believers as "found in Christ Jesus unto true life" (Ign. Eph. 11:1).

26-27. As in vs. 21, the RSV **I write** conveys the sense of the "epistolary" Greek aorist tense here, translated by the English perfect in the KJV. The author refers to his discussion of the false teachers now being concluded. The RSV also brings out a special shade of the participial construction that follows with its reference to **those who would deceive you** (KJV: **them that seduce you**). In vs. 27 the elder praises his readers in a courtesy expression that reminds us of similar expressions in Paul (e.g., I Thess. 4:9), but as in vs. 21, his purpose is also to renew their confidence in their own earlier experience and to

---

quake in Spain uncovered more atheists than all the inquisitions of the Pope. Social catastrophes such as economic depression, war, revolution, weaken the will and courage to believe. Said a Christian woman who had devoted her mature years to the cause of peace, only to see her labors crash at the outbreak of World War II, "There is nothing left for me to do but to curl up like a viper and sting myself to death."

24-26. *The Christian's Experience of God.*—The secret of resisting evil and error lies in continuing communion with God and in the abiding experience of his life in the human soul: **Abide in the Son and in the Father. And this is what he has promised us, eternal life.** The mystical nature of this experience of eternal life defies analysis. However, it is characterized by continuity and permanence. Significantly, the Greek word for **abide,** μένω, occurs more often in the Gospel and Epistles of John than in all the rest of the N.T. Communion with God is not a matter of fitful, occasional prayer; it is a habitual state of mind, the permanent disposition of the soul. It is marked on man's

part more by the consciousness of being possessed by God than by the consciousness of possessing God. Indeed, on the deepest level of religious experience men speak more as if God were holding them than as if they were holding on to God. A coat of arms portrays a human hand clinging to the cross; beneath are the words, "I hold, and I am held."

The experience of abiding in God means recollecting and reappropriating what was once received: **Let what you heard from the beginning abide in you.** Such recollection enables one to draw from past experience truth and inspiration that have always been latent but unappropriated. How different is the meaning of the parable of the prodigal son or of the good Samaritan at the ages of five and fifty! Recollection serves also to preserve the simple essentials of Christian faith. It holds the believer to what is fundamental, and saves him from capitulation to the merely novel. More than one man has been saved from faithlessness by recalling what he heard "from the beginning," perhaps at his mother's knee, or from a wise teacher or good

27 But the anointing which ye have received of him abideth in you, and ye need not that any man teach you: but as the same anointing teacheth you of all things, and is truth, and is no lie, and even as it hath taught you, ye shall abide in him.	would deceive you; **27** but the anointing which you received from him abides in you, and you have no need that any one should teach you; as his anointing teaches you about everything, and is true, and is no lie, just as it has taught you, abide in him.

mobilize their own resistance to the heretics; perhaps he also wishes to indicate why he need not analyze the issues more fully himself. The last half of vs. 27 raises difficulties because the text varies and the syntax can be read in more than one way. The RSV takes the main verb as an imperative, **abide in him,** though many commentators construe the form here as indicative, as does the KJV. But the future tense (KJV) is to be rejected. The whole verse characterizes further the "chrism" first mentioned in vs. 20. It is received from him (i.e., Christ; cf. John 16:7); it **teaches you about everything** (cf. John 14:26); it **is true** (cf. John 14:17); **and is no lie** (cf. vs. 21); and its present and past instruction agree (cf. vs. 7).

pastor. For the Christian, communion with God centers in Christ, in the Son (cf. vs. 23; 1:3). A Christian mystic has said that he would rather be saved in Christ than lost in God. Jesus' metaphor of the vine and the branches (John 15:1-11), clearly suggested here, once and for all distinguishes Christian experience from pantheism, nature mysticism, Oriental mysticism, reabsorption into the absolute, etc. It also decisively rebukes all false humanistic self-reliance: "Apart from me you can do nothing" (John 15:5). Communion with God is an individual, personal experience, not secondhand: **If what you heard . . . abides in you, then you will abide in the Son and in the Father. . . . I write this to you.**" Even the collective experience of the church, strengthening as it is, cannot be a substitute for one's own experience, nor the parent's for the child's, nor the minister's for the layman's.

27. The Holy Spirit as Teacher.—The **anointing** refers to "the Holy one" of vs. 20, identifying the chrism as the Holy Spirit (cf. Expos. on 3:22; 4:1, 13; 5:7-8, 10*a*). The distinctive office of the Spirit in this passage is expressed in the words **His anointing teaches you about everything, and is true, and is no lie.** The verb teaches, διδάσκω (in the present tense here), denotes continuousness. The experience of eternal life means growth in truth as well as possession of truth; the injunction, "Let what you heard from the beginning abide in you," is no justification for religious infantilism or intellectual obscurantism. "Abiding" means "something more than 'standing still.' It is the 'abiding' of the son who grows up in the house." [7] "In understanding be men" (I Cor. 14:20). While the basic certainties of Christianity defend the believer from error and evil, "A real

belief in Christ, besides answering questions, starts them." [8]

At the same time, while faith in Christ starts questions, the Spirit as truth—in still another sense—answers them. Life in God is both intellectual adventure and fruition. This twofold aspect of eternal life is an experience of the Spirit as he teaches; it is also a foretaste of the richer experience of God's life and truth in the world to come. This conception of the Spirit as the teacher of truth corrects the note of diffidence and query—if not apology—so often present in Christian preaching and teaching. B. H. Streeter confesses that for years he had approached the study of Christianity by asking the wrong question, "Is Christianity true?" [9] That approach implied that Christianity is a question, whereas it is intended to be an answer, and had placed him in the false position of being anxious to save religion instead of letting religion save him. The authentic note of the gospel is Paul's word: "The Son of God, Jesus Christ, . . . was not Yes and No; but in him it is always Yes" (II Cor. 1:19). The anointing teaches **about everything** (RSV) or **of all things** (KJV) in the sense that it reveals all truth in the gospel, kindles all faith, inspires all virtue necessary for the salvation of the human soul. The Spirit teaches of all things in the sense that the Spirit alone enables a man reliably to appraise the truth of every situation in life, and in the sense that the Spirit alone relates the relevance of the gospel through the mind to all life. A modern scholar writes:

There is no situation before which the Christian religion breaks down and confesses itself unable to

[7] Brooke, *Johannine Epistles,* p. 61.

[8] H. S. Talbot, quoted by T. R. Glover, *Jesus in the Experience of Men* (New York: Association Press, 1921), p. 168.

[9] *Reality* (New York: The Macmillan Co., 1926), pp. ix-x.

| 28 And now, little children, abide in him; that, when he shall appear, we may have confidence, and not be ashamed before him at his coming. | 28 And now, little children, abide in him, so that when he appears we may have confidence and not shrink from him in |

IV. THE CHILDREN OF GOD AND OF THE EVIL ONE; LIFE AND DEATH
(2:28–3:24)

The transition from the polemic section falls here. The break after vs. 29 in the chapter division and in the spacing in the RSV and the ASV is unfortunate. Not only are vss. 28-29 linked with 3:1-3 by the theme of the Second Coming and the idea of the Christian as one born of God (3:29; cf. **children of God,** vss. 1-2), but the latter conception here enters the epistle and dominates the whole present section, 2:28–3:24. Moreover, the theme of "confidence" of 2:28 continues through 3:3 and recurs in the closing paragraph, 3:19-24, of this part of the writing. Those who recognize a source in I John agree that the author now resumes its use in 2:29*b*. It is now recognizable in the formula, πᾶς ὁ ποιῶν (**every one who does**) with variations, 2:29*b*; 3:4*a*, 7*b*, 8*a*, 10*b* (and cf. 3:6*a*, *b*; 9*a*). What is of special interest in this new development in the epistle is the deeper characterization of the believers as **born of God** or **children of God** (cf. 5:1). The author is concerned with ultimates, and with the origins of visible things in the invisible, and of passing things in the everlasting. Hitherto he has spoken of those who "know God," who "have" God, who "abide in God," in whom God's word abides. But now he speaks of those who are **God's children** and who are **born of him** and who have God's **seed** in them, and sets these over against those who are the **children of the devil.** His peculiar outlook and greatest thought appear here, just as they appear in his initial emphasis on "eternal life" and on "that which was from the beginning." Our Christian life and its powers and potentialities rise not merely out of God's purpose and revelation, but out of his eternal being. Here the elder finds his necessary final sanction for his case against the error that threatens to subvert the believers. That error also is an ultimate error; the false teachers are antichrists whose impulse is spiritual, i.e., diabolical, just as their lie is an eternal lie, and those who believe it are the **children of the devil.** This ultimate view of the situation had also been introduced in the great antithesis of light and darkness in the opening of the epistle, for in the categories of the times this antithesis, like that of life and death now to be introduced, as that of truth and the lie, referred to antagonisms deep in the order of existence. This same world view is represented in the Epistle to the Ephesians: "For we are not contending against flesh and blood, but against the principalities, against the powers, against the world rulers of this present

do or say anything. . . . What other philosophy of life has a relevant word to speak on big things and little things, pleasant things and unpleasant things, wealth and poverty, suffering and health, life and death? . . . The view of God and his relation to the world which Christ opened up to us takes in wars and the welfare of babies, earthquakes and ants, flaming nebulae in the heavens and the microbes that infest a wound, the soaring mind of a saint and the foul practices of a concentration camp.[1]

Because the teaching of the Spirit **is true, and is no lie** (RSV), and deals with **all things** (KJV), the Spirit accordingly is the supreme teacher whose illumination underlies all other

[1] Leslie D. Weatherhead, *This Is the Victory* (New York and Nashville: Abingdon-Cokesbury Press, 1941), p. 118.

teaching. The Spirit is simply God present in the mind bringing men to view the world and life within his eternal truth. Thus education without religion is a contradiction in terms; religion must inform all intellectual disciplines as it alone sanctifies art.

2:28–3:3. *The Marks of God's Children.*—The conception of eternal life as being born of God, and of Christian believers as children of God (cf. Expos. on 3:7-10; 4:7-12; 5:1*a*), governs the interpretation of this section and is part of the distinctive Johannine world view. This concept, perhaps in part borrowed from Hellenism, and introduced into the stream of Christian thought, represents the endeavor of early Christianity to find a concept intellectually adequate to express the difference between those who have and have not believed in Jesus, and the

darkness, against the spiritual hosts of wickedness in the heavenly places" (Eph. 6:12). Of course the writers of the N.T. do not think of evil or the evil one as ultimate in the sense that God is ultimate. But the operation of evil, of darkness, of death, roots in a power which antedates human life (3:8a), and can be overcome only, as it is now being overcome, by the victory of God's primal life. This has been effective on earth through his Son, and by means of an eschatological transaction now drawing to its close in a struggle in which they are all participants since they are "born of God" and are thus victorious by their "seed," their "unction," and their "faith."

A. The Children of God and the Second Coming of Christ (2:28–3:3)

From his warning against deceivers the elder now passes to a plea for righteousness and consecration, especially in view of the Second Coming. The transition is natural since the "last hour" of the preceding section suggests the imminent advent of Christ. The hortatory note here is combined with a threefold assurance to those who "must all appear

---

difference between the church's life and the life of the world.

When the Christian compared himself with his former self, how were the new vision of truth, the new aims and affections that arose out . . . of a new nature to be accounted for? Or, when he compared himself with the "World lying in the Wicked One," how came it that he saw where others were blind, worshipped where others scoffed; that he stood on this side, others on that, of a great gulf going down to the foundations of the moral universe? [2]

The explanation could only be that the very primal life of God himself had been communicated to man. Something of this consciousness of contrast always characterizes authentic Christian experience. Those whom the elder addresses—and with whom he includes himself—recognized the contrast between their present and former state to be nothing less than the contrast between life and death (cf. 3:14; 5:11-13, 20). The contrast may consciously be that vivid or less vivid, as there are gradations in consciousness of eternal life (cf. 3:2). There are also fluctuations in awareness, times when our hearts "condemn us" (cf. Expos. on 3:19-24). But always in different accents the Christian fellowship exclaims, **We are God's children now.**

The children of God possess God's very nature, and in them a new kind of humanity has emerged which the world does not comprehend or receive: **The world does not know us.** The church should be the embodiment of divine life, and the more faithfully it lives this life and shows it forth the less it can expect to be recognized by the world. This is no justification for a false otherworldliness or for want of effort to convert the world. But the church only cheapens itself when it seeks recognition by the world on the world's terms. Sensationalism and bad taste in "church advertising," e.g., cheap popularity, compromise on issues of pub-

lic morals—any form of surrender to the flattery or lusts of the world perverts the church's mission and corrupts its life. The concept, **children of God,** does not mean all men. In a general, genitive sense all men are children of God by virtue of their creation. But too loose a use of the phrase "the children of God" obscures the distinction the gospel is obligated to make between those who do and those who do not believe in Jesus Christ. The distinction, however, is one of fulfillment as well as of contrast. Christians covet for every man who is a child of God by creation the richer experience of being a child of God by redemption, because God in his deepest nature as Father and man in his fullest stature as son are realities apprehended only through faith in Christ.

The children of God are those who do right (2:29; cf. Expos. on 3:7-10). Religion has its mystical aspect, but it must come to terms with the hard fact that one important mark of a true Christian is simply that he **does right.** Of this we **may be sure!** Such straightforward words are appealing. They cut through all the sophistries with which men love to beguile their conscience. They hew a plain path for thought and decision. A helpful, practical rule for the Christian life is simply to do right. But "right" as revealed and defined in Jesus: as **he is righteous.** Man too cleverly deceives himself as to what is right, or moral choices are often too complicated; the desire to do right may be present, but "right" in a particular situation is difficult to ascertain. Jesus is the absolute. He helps us know "right" through concrete rules and commands, e.g., "Do not lay up for yourselves treasures on earth" (Matt. 6:19); through his example, "You also should do as I have done to you" (John 13:15); most helpfully through his mind informing our minds and his spirit companioning with us, "I am with you always" (Matt. 28:20).

2:28–3:3. The Second Coming.—The experience of being a child of God is equivalent to

---

[2] Law, *Tests of Life,* p. 202.

29 If ye know that he is righteous, ye know that every one that doeth righteousness is born of him. | shame at his coming. 29 If you know that he is righteous, you may be sure that every one who does right is born of him.

before the judgment seat of Christ" (II Cor. 5:10): the confidence of the righteous (2:29); the divine adoption and begetting (3:1); the promise of the new creation (3:2).

28. The advent of Christ is spoken of as his appearing and his **coming** (παρουσία). The latter term in such a context had become a technical one in the church for the Second Coming, as Paul's characteristic usage shows, and such a passage as Matt. 24:3, where the disciples ask Jesus, "What will be the sign of your coming [Parousia] and of the close of the age?" The absence of the term and the minimizing of the idea in the Gospel of John are significant for the relation of the two writings. Paul also uses the term "revealing" (ἀποκαλύπτειν) of Christ's advent, and this term, like "appearing" or "becoming manifest," offers us a more available conception of the same great reality. If we cannot easily anticipate today the Second Coming on the clouds, we can appreciate and accept the manifestation of that which is hidden, whether in judgment or grace, as one of the laws of life, personal and social. Jesus' parables of the hidden leaven and the word spoken in secret and the stone that is rejected suggest the great reversal by which truth and he that is true assert their final authority and judgment over all existence. The connection of shame with rejection at the Judgment is illustrated by Jesus' words in Mark 8:38. The elder, however, speaks rather of **confidence** in this emergency (cf. 4:17), using a Greek term that has very rich connotation throughout the N.T., and which suggests not only assurance but freedom from inhibition and liberty of spirit. It appears below in 3:21 and 5:14.

29. **If you know** evidently has the sense of "since you know." Participation in God's nature (the pronouns in this verse refer to him rather than to Christ) places us on his side in his visitation, however appalling it may be (cf. Matt. 7:23). The idea of our

abiding **in him** and enables the believer to have confidence **when he [Christ] appears . . . and not shrink from him in shame at his coming** (cf. Expos. on 3:19-24; 4:17, 18). Reinterpretation of the doctrine of the second coming of Christ for the modern mind requires us to understand that the Second Coming implies a first coming. Pascal wrote that humanity can be divided into two classes—those for whom Christ is yet to come, and those for whom he has come. Many people use speculation about future revelation to avoid the hard challenge of revelation that has already taken place; or they vaguely expect someday to confront Christ in his meaning, forgetting that he has already confronted them. Man cannot face with confidence the final coming of Christ if he does not know that for him Christ has come. But more, Christ has not merely already come: in the profoundest sense he still abides; he has not departed to come again. By his resurrection and the gift of his spirit he came to his people never to leave them again (cf. John 14:15-18, 23; 16:16-22).

In a deeper sense the final appearing of Christ is the consummation of a revelation continuously being made. The crisis of his coming is a present experience as well as a past event and future certainty. As eternal life is offered now as well as promised hereafter, so the "manifestation" (the epistle's characteristic expression for "Parousia," "appearing") of Christ even now continuously confronts man with judgment. The Parousia as judgment is ever being anticipated in the experience of the believer. But inasmuch as judgment is essentially the declaration of a man's true status, "the manifestation of that which is hidden" (cf. Exeg. on 2:28), so judgment is self-judgment in the light of Christ's meaning. Men reveal what they are by their response to Christ, and write themselves down by what they think of him. Samuel Butler came down to breakfast one Christmas morning with the remark, "Well, today is the birthday of the hook-nosed Nazarene." Charles Lamb, in discussing with friends what character in history they would most like to have met, said of Jesus: "There is only one person I can ever think of. . . . If Shakespeare was to come into this room, we should all rise up to meet him; but if that person was to come into it we should all fall and kiss the hem of His garment." [3] Judgment of Christ is also self-judgment in terms of moral

[3] William Hazlitt, *Sketches*, quoted by James Marchant, ed., *Anthology of Jesus* (New York: Harper & Bros., 1926), p. 339.

3 Behold, what manner of love the Father hath bestowed upon us, that we should be called the sons of God: therefore the world knoweth us not, because it knew him not.

3 See what love the Father has given us, that we should be called children of God; and so we are. The reason why the world does not know us is that it did not

---

abiding in God, carried over from vs. 27 and the earlier parts of the letter, is now deepened by the idea of being begotten of him (cf. I Pet. 1:23; John 1:12-13), and this conception dominates the later parts of the epistle. Our fellowship with him is grounded in eternity.

3:1. John's term for **sons** (τέκνα) brings out this idea of divine offspring as it does in Rom. 8:15-17, "When we cry, 'Abba! Father!' it is the Spirit himself bearing witness with our spirit that we are children of God, and if children, then heirs." Paul uses another term for sons (υἱοί) in the similar passage, Gal. 4:5-7, where the idea of adoption is stressed, as also the contrast between slaves and sons. In both cases the assurance for the future connected with sonship is stressed as it is in the present context. That **we should be called children of God** (cf. Matt. 5:9) calls to those unable to help themselves (cf. Eph. 1:3-8) for wondering scrutiny of the **love of the Father. And so we are** stresses the fact that a real act of begetting and new creation has taken place, falsely claimed for themselves, no doubt, by the rival groups. Believers are viewed in the N.T. as children or sons of God in a special sense not covered by the pagan idea that all men are "his offspring" (Acts 17:28), or even by the Hellenistic conception that those who are reborn by the mysteries or by gnosis become the sons of God. The distinction goes back to the idea of

---

reality. "Judgment is not the assigning of a character to men from without; it is the revelation of character from within; . . . it is self-revelation, self-classification, self-separation." [4] In Jesus' parable of the sheep and the goats (Matt. 25:31-46), judgment consists in the king's revelation of self-knowledge to both the righteous and the wicked of what they had done and failed to do. As a present experience, judgment similarly exposes self-deception and brings a man to behold himself as he really is in the sight of God. As such it is not something the Christian needs to fear but something he desires and needs. Thus he may have confidence even now and need **not shrink . . . in shame** from Christ as he comes.

The second coming of Christ will be a future historical event. That the world did not end at the time John and other apocalyptic thinkers expected does not mean that it will not end. Because the span of God's purpose is beyond man's mind all attempts to interpret signs of the times at particular periods of history as foreshadowing the imminent end are futile and artificial; they only betray the poverty and pride of man's knowledge. But "the eternal purpose to comprehend the universe in Christ as its head" [5] will be brought to pass in history as it already prevails in eternity.

Reinterpretation of the Second Coming permits us to ascribe to man's life after death the qualities John ascribes to it at the Parousia. **We shall be like him** means transfiguration; **we shall see him as he is** means beatific vision. The reserve of vs. 2 warns that these are clothed in mystery. However, in one sense transfiguration is qualification for vision, and to become **like him** cannot be postponed to the future life. We may believe that our vision of Christ after death will correspond to the degree of Christlikeness of character God has enabled us to achieve in this life. The extent to which we are enabled to abide in him now is an intimation of our communion with him hereafter. In another sense, in so far as we **see him** now we shall **be like him** hereafter. We assimilate that which we behold. The goodness and beauty of Christ on which we gaze are transferred to us and become part of us. Thus, to behold Jesus and to hope to be like him purify character as nothing else can (3:3). If the hope of seeing again those whom we "have loved long since, and lost awhile" on this earth—a child or wife or parent—holds men steady and keeps them pure, how much more the hope of communion with Christ!

3:1. God's Fatherly Love.—The consciousness of being born of God is bound up with the consciousness of the fatherhood of God, and specifically of the Father's love: See [**Behold** KJV] **what love the Father has given us, that we should be called children of God** (cf.

[4] Law, *Tests of Life*, pp. 329-30.
[5] Emil Brunner, *The Divine-Human Encounter*, tr. A. W. Loos (Philadelphia: Westminster Press, 1943), p. 141.

2 Beloved, now are we the sons of God, and it doth not yet appear what we shall be: but we know that, when he shall appear, we shall be like him; for we shall see him as he is.

3 And every man that hath this hope in him purifieth himself, even as he is pure.

know him. 2 Beloved, we are God's children now; it does not yet appear what we shall be, but we know that when he appears we shall be like him, for we shall see him as he is. 3 And every one who thus hopes in him purifies himself as he is pure.

the divine purpose and choice settled upon Israel as God's son. The second part of our verse echoes a familiar Johannine theme. "They have not known the Father, nor me," says Jesus (John 16:3; cf. 17:25; the **him** here can refer to either), and this is related to the lot of the disciples (John 15:18-19).

2-3. These verses well reflect both the certainty and the sobriety of the Christian expectation with regard to the conditions of the life to come, as well as its moral conditions. **We know** shows that the author is alluding here again to a common formula of the church's eschatological tradition. **We shall see him as he is,** while it refers to Christ, reminds us of the many passages in the Bible which always postpone the face to face seeing of God to the new age. "No man hath seen God at any time" (John 1:18). Though the disciples in the days even of Christ's flesh had "beheld his glory" (John 1:14), yet Jesus' prayer for them had included the petition, "Father, I desire that they also, whom thou hast given me, may be with me where I am, to behold my glory" (John 17:24). "For now we see in a mirror dimly, but then face to face" (I Cor. 13:12).

Selwyn (*First Epistle of Peter*, p. 131) interestingly indicates four stages of seeing: (*a*) hope, in the O.T.; (*b*) physical sight of the original followers (contrasted with the later Christians, I Pet. 1:8); (*c*) faith (II Cor. 5:7); (*d*) the beatific vision (as here and Matt. 5:8).

We shall be like him recalls the various teachings as to the transfiguration of the faithful in the consummation: the "change" of "our lowly body" (Phil. 3:21; cf. Rom. 8:19, 23); our appearance "with him in glory" (Col. 3:4). This change "into his likeness" that accompanies our "beholding the glory of the Lord" begins already in this life (II Cor. 3:18). Like beholds like. There are two senses possible here in connection with the last clause of vs. 2. Either our seeing Christ **as he is** will transform us (as the last passage quoted teaches; also parallels from the Gnostic writings), or it will evidence our likeness to him. In any case, the great hope is an incentive to our present imitation of his holiness, as the thought of his appearing is an incentive to "abide in him" (2:28).

Expos. on 4:7-12 for comment on the epistle's teaching of God as love). The wondrous nature of the Father's love consists in its givenness. The language of Christian devotion is never that of pride in anything we have earned or merited, but of gratitude for something we have received. Those who receive this love are no longer aliens, orphans, or servants, but are pronounced and made children in nature. All the rich meanings of filial relationship are signified—intimacy, dependence, trust. But God did not give his love in order that men might be called sons. "The greatness of His love . . . was manifested in this, that He allowed Himself to be called their Father." [6] The sublime wonder of the Christian revelation is that the universe has declared itself to bear toward men the character of fatherly love revealed to our minds and lived out before our eyes in Christ. Jesus "brought a new revelation and because it was new, he needed a new name for God. But he did not look for it in the courts of kings or search for a word to express majesty and power. He preferred for us the risks of intimacy rather than the chill of distance, and gave us the name 'father.' " [7] The mission of the church is to bring all men to be seized by the divine love which the church itself has come to know: **Behold** means "beholden," "to be held by." The task of religion is so to thrust before men's eyes the glory of God's love in Jesus' life and death that they cannot resist it. When once they have really seen it, they are beholden by it, and are moved to respond in adoration and joy, "My

[6] Brooke, *Johannine Epistles*, p. 80.

[7] W. R. Maltby, *The Significance of Jesus* (New York: Harper & Bros., 1929), p. 57.

| 4 Whosoever committeth sin transgresseth also the law: for sin is the transgression of the law. | 4 Every one who commits sin is guilty of |

B. The Children of God and of the Devil (3:4-10)

The call to purification in vs. 3 leads on now to a clarification of what sin really is. Since it has the character of anarchy, the sinner is not **of God** but **of the devil,** and, it is implied, cannot face the Second Coming or share the hope connected with it in the same way as the **children of God** (referring to 2:28–3:3). Our passage contrasts two kinds of men: **the children of God** and **the children of the devil.** Behind this contrast we may recognize two sources: (a) the current Hellenistic distinction between the enlightened and unenlightened; (b) the biblical distinction between men belonging to the new age and the old. Corresponding to these contrasts were pagan and biblical ideas of sonship to God. The Hellenistic religious philosophy could view the "spiritual man" or Gnostic as born or reborn of divine "seed" (σπέρμα) through an initiation rite or by ecstatic knowledge. The Jewish and Jewish-Christian background had its analogies, e.g., "Thou art my Son; this day have I begotten thee" (Ps. 2:7), in which the Messiah or his people were viewed as adopted or given a gracious status in the context of God's purpose. In the N.T. we see how the idea of sonship is interpreted more and more in terms of a divine begetting, in which especially God's "word" has the chief role, "You have been born anew, not of perishable seed but of imperishable, through the living and abiding word of God" (I Pet. 1:23; cf. Jas. 1:18). In John 1:12-13 the pagan realistic conception is much more prominent, as it is in our passage.

Our author uses the conceptions of his day not only to give vivid expression to our kinship and fellowship with God, but also to show the incompatibility of sin. His thought here, though in alien terms, is very close to that of Jesus: "Every sound tree bears good fruit, but the bad tree bears evil fruit. A sound tree cannot bear evil fruit" (Matt. 7:17-18). So he says here: **No one who abides in him sins** (vs. 6); **No one born of God commits sin; for God's nature [seed (KJV)] abides in him, and he cannot sin because he is born of God** (vs. 9). The sharp distinction between two kinds of men in this passage

---

heart thou hast bound in love of Thy Name, and now I cannot but sing it." [8]

4-10. Moral Dualism in the Epistle.—The dualism of John's thought—apparent throughout the epistle—is sharply focused here in the antithesis between **the children of God** and **of the devil.** Even the literary style of these verses, with their strong blacks and whites, their "bold dialectical hyperbole" (cf. Exeg. on vss. 14-15), serves the author's purpose to present his world view in terms of the moral cleavage between good and evil. Previously his dualism has taken the forms of antitheses between light and darkness, truth and the lie, the world and the Father. Here his dualism assumes a profoundly moral character expressed in three ways: in a metaphysical form (a "supramundane category," cf. Exeg. on vss. 12-13) that conceives moral anarchy in the universe contending against God; in a doctrinal form elucidating the relation of the Incarnation to the existence and activity of evil; in the practical form of ethical contrast between people who commit

[8] Richard Rolle, quoted by Underhill, *Collected Papers,* p. 217.

sin and people who do right. In other passages the author appears to be aware that life does not in fact correspond to a moral chessboard with its blacks and whites divided by rigid lines (cf. vs. 19; 1:5–2:2; 5:16-17). But here the essential polarity of ethical religion must be boldly set forth.

The clauses **sin is lawlessness; sin is of the devil; the devil has sinned from the beginning; the works of the devil,** contrasted with their counterparts, **he who does right is righteous, is born of God; God's nature abides in him; and he cannot sin,** mark the metaphysical form of the elder's dualism and suggest its aspects. Evil exists and is part of reality as righteousness exists and is part of reality. Righteousness is antecedent to evil, because evil defined as lawlessness implies a prior order of law against which evil rebels. While in one sense **the devil has sinned from the beginning,** in another sense it is impossible to accord to evil the same eternity which the Christian revelation ascribes to God as he is "from the beginning" (cf. 1:1). Both evil and good are constitutive principles; both possess a generative power and are able to

5 And ye know that he was manifested to take away our sins; and in him is no sin.

6 Whosoever abideth in him sinneth not: whosoever sinneth hath not seen him, neither known him.

lawlessness; sin is lawlessness. 5 You know that he appeared to take away sins, and in him there is no sin. 6 No one who abides in him sins; no one who sins has either seen

---

has naturally contributed to the discussion of predestination in Christian theology, especially when related, as it must be, to the similar theme in John 8:31-47. No one can read these two writings, however, without noting that the freedom of men to respond to the gospel is also largely assumed. The Bible often uses the conception of reprobation as a spur to repentance or as a retrospective explanation of impenitence and obduracy. We note that the present section has intermittent quotations from the author's source. Recognition of this is illuminating, for where the *source* refers to God, the *comment* introduced by the elder may refer to Christ, and the ambiguity of the pronouns (him, his, etc.) is explained (thus vss. 6-7 and cf., above, the sudden shift between 2:29a and b).

4. To purify ourselves (vs. 3) means to refrain from disobedience of the divine law. The gravity of sin or sinful acts is emphasized by the identifying of them with **lawlessness,** a term which seems to have connoted sin in all its enormity and blasphemy if we judge by the characterization of the Antichrist in II Thess. 2:7-8 as "the lawless one," and his activity as "the mystery of lawlessness." Matt. 24:12 also cites the increase of lawlessness as one of the signs of the messianic tribulation. The enlightened and elated schismatics may well have made much of the fact that they were now above all law, without appreciating that they were not "without law toward God but under the law of Christ" (I Cor. 9:21). Irenaeus speaks of heretics who suppose "that, from the nobility of their nature, they can in no degree at all contract pollution, whatever they eat or perform" (*Against Heresies* II. 14. 5); and elsewhere of those for whom good and evil are only matters of human opinion (*op. cit.,* II. 32. 1).

5-6. Again a formula of the early preaching: **He appeared to take away sins**— though the plural is used here to suit the theme of postbaptismal sins (contrast John 1:29), and the concern with deeds rather than disposition, which appears again in the phrase **the works of the devil** (vs. 8). The Johannine view that salvation is connected with the manifestation of the Son of God apart from a special emphasis on his death alone, and that we are assimilated to his nature by vision is reflected here: **No one who**

---

impart themselves to human nature; and every man must draw his life and power from one source or another (cf. Expos. on 4:1, 3). Dynamic evil is in contest with dynamic good. The devil works and has sinned; the Son of God appears and destroys. Lawlessness resists the commandments of God. The doctrine of predestination is a witness to the way in which the generative and dynamic aspects of good and evil in human life have impressed thought.

The words, Jesus **appeared to take away sins, and in him there is no sin.** . . . The reason the **Son of God appeared was to destroy the works of the devil** who **has sinned from the beginning,** represent the doctrinal form of the elder's dualism. The contest of good and evil implicit in all life has been made explicit in the Incarnation and Atonement, and the superhuman potency —though not the reality—of evil has been decisively broken: "Now shall the ruler of this world be cast out" (John 12:31; cf. Expos. on 4:1, 3; 5:1b-5). Only a being incarnating good

as the devil incarnates evil could achieve this victory; thus **in him . . . is no sin.** The positive result of this decisive contest is the act of "begetting" that occurs in those who have seen and known Christ in his appearing (vs. 6) and in whom **God's nature abides** (vs. 9).

From this derives the palpable fact that **the children of God . . . do right,** and **the children of the devil** commit sin, and in appealing to this fact—**by this it may be seen**—the elder's thought takes the third, practical form. The human situation validates both Christology and metaphysics and visibly illustrates the truth of the elder's insight into the moral nature of reality.

4-10. *The Scope and Power of Sin.*—The injunction **let no one deceive you** underscores the importance of grasping this profound world view, and in its widest sense is addressed to all men who seriously inquire into life. Failure to grasp the cleavage between good and evil and its consequences for thought and life is—to put

7 Little children, let no man deceive you: he that doeth righteousness is righteous, even as he is righteous.

8 He that committeth sin is of the devil; for the devil sinneth from the beginning. For this purpose the Son of God was manifested, that he might destroy the works of the devil.

him or known him. 7 Little children, let no one deceive you. He who does right is righteous, as he is righteous. 8 He who commits sin is of the devil; for the devil has sinned from the beginning. The reason the Son of God appeared was to destroy the

---

sins has . . . seen him. In him there is no sin refers to Christ; the doctrine of his sinlessness as distinguished from that of his righteousness appears in Matthew and Paul's letters but takes on a dogmatic character in the Johannine literature (cf. John 8:46). It follows that **no one who abides in him sins.** (The present tense of **sins** is indicative of habitual state or repeated action.) This is explained in vs. 9.

7. Another false claim of the deceivers is implied, a claim to be **righteous;** and the simplest test, that of deeds, is proposed as in 2:3-4, 6, though the example of Christ (**as he is righteous**) sanctions and defines that righteousness. It is of interest to find a similar ethical test and a similar validation of the divine commandments in an outstanding Moslem mystic. "Al-Hujwiri," writes Joachim Wach, "repudiates all antinomianism: 'I reply that when you know Him, the heart is filled with longing and His command is held in greater veneration than before.'" For faith involves both "verification in the heart" and "observance of the divine command." Further, "the law is never abrogated"— this is addressed to those heretics who assert that obedience is transcended when a certain stage of love has been attained ("Spiritual Teachings in Islam: A Study," *Journal of Religion,* XXVIII [1948], 269).

8. We meet here the conception of two kinds of men of which we have spoken above, well illustrated for us in the commentary on Jesus' parable of the tares, "The good seed

---

it mildly—to be "deceived." Evil in the human situation cannot be known for what it is nor appraised in its malignity and power unless it is viewed within the context of a moral universe. One great deception of our era is the fancy that evil has no metaphysical roots. "Deceivers" tell us evil is merely an evolutionary overhang or cultural lag; that it is the result of faulty economic systems (so communism) or of insufficient education (Gnosticism in modern dress); that it is psychological immaturity or biological disequilibrium; that it results from failure to apply the scientific method; or that it is simply the invention of priestcraft. Recent history has partly exposed the superficiality of all such positivistic thinking. In any case, the answer is the blunt words of the epistle: **Sin is . . . from the beginning.**

Sin in personal terms similarly cannot be appraised for what it is unless viewed within the context of a moral universe. Because the universe is governed by moral law, **sin is lawlessness.** Sometimes sin may be described in general terms of disposition and motive, but other occasions require sin to be defined in plain, homely, concrete terms of lawlessness. However, sin is never an isolated act but the outward expression of inward evil. Man is not a sinner because he commits sin; he commits sin because he is a

sinner (vs. 8); and every sin contains the essence of all sin, a fact which men continually overlook by calling sins "peccadilloes," "foibles," "failings," as if something not quite right were not quite wrong. It must be remembered, too, that sin is omission as well as commission. In man's not doing right (vs. 10*b*), as in his doing wrong, his affinity with evil is revealed. Moreover, sin involves guilt: **Every one who commits sin is guilty.** Men too readily dismiss the sense of guilt as an unhealthy complex; guilt is a sign of the conscience at work. At the same time, the gospel's message of forgiveness is addressed to men's guilt; for "the ravages wrought by . . . guilt are no less in the modern soul than they were in the ancient, and . . . the denizens of our brave new world are no less disturbed by it than were King Oedipus or Mary Magdalene or Lady Macbeth."[9] Schemes for dealing with evil are inadequate unless based on the redemption wrought in Christ. How do men mistakenly handle evil? By pretending that it does not exist, e.g., Christian Science; by repression; by distraction; by Stoic acceptance; by trying to educate it away; by meeting evil with evil; by despairingly yielding to it.

7-10. *Victory over Sin.*—Positively, **the children of God** are those who believe that Christ

⁹ Baillie, *Invitation to Pilgrimage,* p. 61.

9 Whosoever is born of God doth not commit sin; for his seed remaineth in him: and he cannot sin, because he is born of God.

works of the devil. 9 No one born of God commits sin; for God's*f* nature abides in him, and he cannot sin because he is*g* born

f Greek his.
g Or for the offspring of God abide in him, and they cannot sin because they are.

---

means the sons of the kingdom; the weeds are the sons of the evil one, and the enemy who sowed them is the devil (Matt. 13:38-39). The idea of the false brethren as offspring of Satan has an analogous expression in Ignatius' plea to the Ephesians "that no plant of the devil be found in you" (Ign. Eph. 10:3). We find a fuller statement of the ideas of the present verse in John 8:44 and its context, where Jesus says to his adversaries: "You are of your father the devil, and your will is to do your father's desires. He was a murderer from the beginning, and has nothing to do with the truth, because there is no truth in him." The elder and his source here are concerned with the mysterious depth and malignancy of sin; and the eschatological situation intensifies the tragic conflict. The harshness of language and the very terms have their background in rabbinical polemic and exegesis (W. F. Howard, *Christianity According to St. John* [Philadelphia: The Westminster Press, 1946], pp. 87-93). A recent translator of the epistles of the N.T. (Phillips, *Letters to Young Churches,* p. xiii) has this to say with regard to their authors:

We can hardly be surprised to find in these writers a condemnation of "false teachers." This condemnation may strike us at first as odd and even un-Christian. We commonly suppose that all roads of the human spirit, however divergent, eventually lead home to the Celestial Benevolence. But if we were seriously to think that they do not, that false roads in fact diverge more and more until they finally lead right away from God, then we can at any rate sympathise with what may seem to us a narrow attitude.

The necessity and rightness of a negative judgment on men and even passionate arraignment are not in question, but only who it is that can properly assume the role of judge and when. What may be unchristian for a modern sectarian may be Christian for the author of I John, just as what may be disinterested indictment by a Milton or a Lincoln may be tinged with personal bitterness in another man.

The second sentence in vs. 8 is only one of the notable passages in the N.T. which interpret "the work of Christ" in terms of the overthrow of Satan and his servants; cf. the temptation narrative in the Gospels; Luke 10:18; John 12:31; Acts 10:38; Col. 2:15. The Gospel of John and this epistle sometimes use the Greek term here translated **works** and its corresponding verb to refer to supernatural works, whether of God (John 5:17; 9:4; 14:10) or of Satan, as here, or even of Cain as in vs. 12. The sense of divine or diabolic agency as an aspect of human action corrects any oversimple moralism and recognizes a dimension in ethics confirmed by modern pathology. On the use of ἔργον in John see Hugo Odeberg (*The Fourth Gospel* [Uppsala: Almquist & Wicksell, 1929], p. 148). This deeper sense of **the works of the devil** corroborates the understanding of λύειν, **destroy**, held by many of the early fathers, as "to deprive of supernatural power" or "to break the spell of." **The Son of God appeared** not merely to cancel the evil results of the devil in the world but to break his spell (see Otto A. Piper, "I John and the Didache of the Primitive Church," *Journal of Biblical Literature,* LXVI [1947], 444).

9. As "a sound tree cannot bear evil fruit" (Matt. 7:18), so **no one born of God commits sin.** The reason is that God's **seed [nature (RSV)] remaineth in him.** As we

---

has destroyed **the works of the devil** (vs. 8*b*), and who through faith appropriate his victory (cf. Expos. on 4:4-6; 5:4*b*-5). One must behold evil in its full power and malignity—**sin is;** yet evil is broken in the event in which **the Son of God appeared.** An accurate construction of the

reality of evil delivers men from shallow thought and false optimism; faith in the meaning of the Incarnation correspondingly delivers them from despair and cynicism. The child of God is **he who does right** and enters the lists against evil as did Jesus, who was righteous (vs. 7*b*). Wil-

10 In this the children of God are manifest, and the children of the devil: whosoever doeth not righteousness is not of God, neither he that loveth not his brother.

11 For this is the message that ye heard from the beginning, that we should love one another.

of God. 10 By this it may be seen who are the children of God, and who are the children of the devil: whoever does not do right is not of God, nor he who does not love his brother.

11 For this is the message which you have heard from the beginning, that we should

---

have seen, the metaphor of begetting is employed, as Hellenistic parallels and John 1:12-13 indicate. The metaphor, however, is only a graphic way of emphasizing the divine origin of that new creaturehood which every Christian properly possesses. Paul has his own way of saying that those who have been crucified with Christ are no longer "enslaved to sin. For he who has died is freed from sin" (Rom. 6:6-7). What the figure of the **seed** stands for, apart from an imparting of the divine life itself, is best suggested by the life-giving word or message of which it is also said that it abides in us (2:14; cf. 2:24).

10. This verse in its second part states again the test of vs. 7, i.e., righteous action, and then equates this with the love of the brother, which becomes the theme of the next passage. **By this** points both backward and forward. Ignatius, writing to the Christians of Smyrna of "those who have strange opinions"—in particular, who do not believe on the blood of Christ—says that "for love they have no care, none for the widow, none for the orphan, none for the distressed, none for the afflicted, none for the prisoner, or for him released from prison, none for the hungry or thirsty" (Ign. Smyr. 6:2).

C. Hate and Death in the World; Life and Love in the Faith (3:11-18)

The division of men into two classes according as they have their origin in God or the devil continues to dominate the thought here, but love and hate replace righteousness and sin as the respective traits. At the same time the connection of love with life is illustrated by Christ, who in love gave his life, while the connection of hate with death is illustrated by Cain, who in hate committed the first murder. This act is viewed as typical of the attitude of the world to the believers. These considerations are set forth by the writer as he both continues his exhortation to the imitation of Christ and confirms the confidence of his readers.

11. In 1:5 the original **message**, ἀγγελία (peculiar to this epistle), is represented as a declaration, here as an imperative. The **message** is "the word of truth, the gospel of your salvation" (Eph. 1:13). But the very nature of the good news is such as to have

---

liam James has written: "If this life be not a real fight, in which something is eternally gained for the universe by success, it is no better than a game of private theatricals . . . . But it feels like a real fight, as if there were something really wild in the universe which we . . . are needed to redeem." [1] The children of God are those who find salvation from sin by being conformed to Christ's nature through vision and knowledge of him (vs. 6). Appropriation of Christ's victory and enlistment in the battle for righteousness issue from the forgiveness and renewed power to do right which the grace of God in Christ has wrought through faith in the soul of the believer. The struggle for righteousness in human life can be won only by those

[1] Quoted by Garfield Morgan, "Christ—The Lord of His Event," in G. Bromley Oxnam, ed., *Creative Preaching* (New York: Abingdon Press, 1930), pp. 224-25.

who through grace have been brought to live in the righteousness of Christ, who are **righteous, even as he is righteous.**

11-18. Hate and Death Versus Love and Life. —The author's "ultimate view" of "antagonisms deep in the order of existence" (cf. Exeg. on 2:28–3:24) is carried forward in these verses, and his conception of the dualistic nature of reality now takes the ethical form of antithesis between love and hatred (illustrated by Christ and Cain), and the religio-metaphysical form of antithesis between life and death.

11, 14. The Metaphysical and Ethical Nature of Love.—The command we should love one another is grounded in the message which is from the beginning. Accordingly, love is a requirement which the universe itself imposes upon man. Ethical love is not an option, nor an invention of priests or moralists, nor an evolu-

12 Not as Cain, *who* was of that wicked one, and slew his brother. And wherefore slew he him? Because his own works were evil, and his brother's righteous.

13 Marvel not, my brethren, if the world hate you.

love one another, **12** and not be like Cain who was of the evil one and murdered his brother. And why did he murder him? Because his own deeds were evil and his brother's righteous. **13** Do not wonder, brethren,

---

its outcome in a fellowship of mutual love. Vs. 16 below summarizes both the message and its corollary. It is the special concern with the crisis in the fellowship which leads the writer to speak now of mutual love in particular rather than of righteousness in general or "walking in the light" as heretofore. For the same reason, no doubt, the immediate scope of obligation is narrowed to the church; **love one another,** as in Jesus' parting commandment to the intimate circle of his disciples (John 13:34); or love the "brother" (3:10, 14, 16-17; cf. 2:9-11). Perhaps the "old commandment" (2:7) or **message** which the readers had **heard from the beginning** was: "You shall love your neighbor as yourself" (Mark 12:31), but Jesus' citation of this passage from the law has been adapted to special circumstances in our Johannine versions of it. The increasing self-awareness of the Christian movement, partly occasioned by persecution, and the present dangers of broken fellowship explain this limitation of the scope of love. That love to the wider world was not absent is suggested by the missionary activity that provides the setting for all these epistles, as well as by references in I John and the Gospel of John to the world as the object of God's love and Christ's redemption.

12-13. In the first clause of vs. 12 the form of the KJV indicates the awkward ellipsis in the Greek. Jewish and early Christian writings show how the first murder in the Bible prompted such theological reflection as is assumed in the present passage. We note that Cain, though he lived so early, is already **of the evil one,** for the devil "was a murderer from the beginning" (John 8:44). And as the text shows, it is the fact that Cain is **of the evil one** and **his own deeds were evil** which explains the act of murder. Here we have again the Johannine sense of **deeds** (ἔργα) as supernatural, as "wrought" either "in God" or in the evil one. This conception reminds us of the Pauline view that it is Christ or the Spirit that acts in us if we live by faith. The apparent works-righteousness of I John (2:6; 3:7; etc.) should not therefore mislead us. But Cain's act was directed against Abel because the latter's deeds were **righteous.** More than jealousy is intended

---

tionary sport. Love confronts men as a Christian categorical imperative from the heart of Reality. However, Christian love is not merely a philosophic concept. It has its meaning in the life of man with man, it is love . . . for the brethren (the words "brother" or "brethren" appear seven times in these verses alone, eighteen times in the epistles). "Brother" here means fellow believer, and the author's conception of the church as a fellowship of love rebukes and corrects lesser conceptions of the church commonly held. It also sets the task of the church in the world—to be a nucleus or "first fruits" (Rom. 11:16) of a redeemed humanity, a school of charity whose members winningly exhibit the love whose validity is universal for all men. No worldly power, wealth, efficient organization, can atone for the absence of love in the church. Conversely, no limit can be set to the possibilities for brotherhood in history if the love of which the church is custodian is believed in and lived. Christian love, while embodied in the

church, is applicable to all human relations and can meet the demands of every individual and social situation without losing its dignity, power, and eternity.

12-13, 15. Cain, a Study in Evil.—The author develops his theme pictorially rather than dialectically, and hatred as the antithesis of love is symbolized by the contrast of **Cain who was of the evil one and murdered his brother** with Jesus who "laid down his life for us." Cain was **of the evil one.** Hatred and murder root in diabolic reality, and he who hates partakes of and augments the reign of evil. Evil character mothers evil acts. Cain **murdered** because he **was of the evil one.** But morally, if not literally, **any one who hates his brother is a murderer.** Hatred issuing in actual murder differs from incipient hatred, felt but restrained, only as a mild attack differs from a virulent attack of the same malady. But evil acts also mother evil character: **Why did he murder him? Because his own deeds were evil.** Outward action shapes inward

14 We know that we have passed from death unto life, because we love the brethren. He that loveth not *his* brother abideth in death.

15 Whosoever hateth his brother is a murderer: and ye know that no murderer hath eternal life abiding in him.

that the world hates you. 14 We know that we have passed out of death into life, because we love the brethren. He who does not love remains in death. 15 Any one who hates his brother is a murderer, and you know that no murderer has eternal life

here. Cain hated Abel precisely because the latter's **deeds** were **righteous** and, in this context, righteous toward Cain. The parallel with Christ and the Christian is in the writer's mind. So Kierkegaard says of Christ, "He was and is regarded as an enemy by sinners—because he is the 'friend of sinners'" (*The Gospel of Suffering and the Lilies of the Field*, tr. David F. Swenson and Lillian Marvin Swenson [Minneapolis: Augsburg Publishing House, 1948], p. 22). The Fourth Gospel teaches that the darkness shrinks from the light and hates it; and Jesus observes that because he has given God's word to his disciples, therefore "the world has hated them because they are not of the world, even as I am not of the world" (John 17:14). The elder draws the same conclusion here.

14-15. The better text followed by the RSV omits **his brother** (KJV) in 14*b*. The antithetical parallelism in vs. 14, following the chiasmic pattern (*a, b, b, a*), evidences the use of the source. The following verse is partly from the source, and its first and last members have a close relationship to the members of vs. 14. It would appear that the bold dialectic and hyperbole of the source used here and there in the epistle (cf. 3:6, 8*a*, 9*a* above) determine the depth of the meditation and the supramundane categories which give the composition such a breath of eternity, and which are yet so different from the corresponding terms of other parts of the N.T.

The movement of thought here is illuminated by a passage from the Testaments of the Twelve Patriarchs, which may be translated, "As love desires the quickening of the dead . . . , so hate desires to put the living to death" (Test. Gad 4:6). Hatred partakes of the character of murder, as anger and contempt do in Jesus' saying, Matt. 5:21-22. Moreover, while he **who hates his brother** is devoid of **eternal life,** we, since **we love the brethren,** have now already in this age **passed out of death into** [this same eternal] **life** (cf. John 5:24). In 2:9-10 much the same thing is said in terms of light and darkness rather than life and death: "He who says he is in the light and hates his brother is in

disposition, and successive evil deeds cumulatively mold character (cf. Expos. on 2:9-11). Hatred is always potentially present when love is absent: not loving in vs. 14 becomes hate in vs. 15. Human nature morally tolerates a vacuum no more than physical nature. Motivation to evil inheres in the fundamental repugnance evil bears to good. **Cain . . . murdered his brother . . . because . . . his brother's** [deeds were] **righteous.** The cosmic struggle between good and evil going on in the universe is reenacted in the moral battles each man fights. The metaphysical repugnance of evil to good has its moral and psychological counterpart in daily life. It is possible for men to be so possessed by evil that the contemplation of goodness goads them to madness and impels them to destroy that which could save them. Men resist goodness because it judges them, and rather than accept judgment they will destroy the judge. The lineage of Abel and Cain extends to Jesus and the Pharisees, to Savonarola

and the church of his day, to Joan of Arc and her judges. Every man belongs to the brotherhood either of Cain or of Christ. **Do not wonder, brethren, that the world hates you.** Those who love must expect to be hated. If the hostility of the world is not aroused the Christian probably is not really living in love. At the same time, deliberately to seek hostility in the name of love is only a subtle form of pride. The Christian must learn to distinguish between a legitimate consciousness of inward integrity in face of persecution (cf. Matt. 5:11-12) and moral inflammation of the ego.

14-15. *Eternal Life Is Ethical Love.*—The antithesis between hatred and love is virtually interchangeable with, and culminates in, the antithesis between life and death: **We know that we have passed out of death into life, because we love the brethren,** i.e., "No one who hates or murders has eternal life." The author's personal testimony joined with the corporate experience of the apostolic fellowship (**we**

16 Hereby perceive we the love *of God*, because he laid down his life for us: and we ought to lay down *our* lives for the brethren.

abiding in him. 16 By this we know love, that he laid down his life for us; and we ought to lay down our lives for the breth-

---

the darkness still. He who loves his brother abides in the light, and in it there is no cause for stumbling." We see how closely in the mind of the author light is related to life, and darkness to death. He who "walks in the darkness" (2:11) is the same as he who **remains in death.** The test of it in both cases is hate of the brother; moreover, both *act* their hate (for in 2:10*b* the true reading and sense may well be that he who hates his brother injures him: "There is . . . occasion of stumbling in him") , and the destination of both is destruction (2:11*b*; 3:15*b*) .

16. By this we know love. Love here is used absolutely; the expansion in the KJV, **of God,** is not called for. The tense used shows that our knowing goes back to a past revelation, clarified by the words, **he laid down his life for us.** Contrast with Cain the

---

know) impressively marks the "new age"—long anticipated in Hebrew history—as having been brought to pass through living in the love which Jesus has incarnated, communicated, and commanded: **We have passed . . . into life.** For implicit in vs. 14 is the recollection of a time when the author and his fellow Christians were in death, and the life they experience through ethical love is so different and so possessively real that only hyperbolic language can describe the contrast. This experience of eternal life through Christian faith and love for the brethren has been called "realized eschatology," which means that the final decisive revelation of Reality has already occurred in Christ, and that men may live in Reality now as well as in the future (cf. Expos. on 1:2) . The significant point here, however, is that the realization and appropriation of the eternal life of the new age take place through love.

The problem set for every man born into the world is to pass out of death into life. Answers to this problem have included knowledge, that to know is to possess life; aesthetics, that to behold and create beauty is to find life; mysticism, that through contemplation or initiation into divine mysteries men enter into life; materialism, that to live by the senses is life. Over and against these stands the message of the gospel, that love for one's fellow men is life. Even on sub-Christian levels this truth is valid. Love of husband and wife, of parent and child, of friend for friend, of humanitarian for his fellow men, always brings richer, more abundant life. Psychology validates this insight. Hatred or want of love brings disease and destruction to human personality; love means health and growth. Adolph Meyer significantly describes the "shut-in personality" as the "beginning of dementia praecox." Every man who finds his center in himself rather than in others is on the way to madness. In dealing with our enemies

love is the only way to life. Hatred can end only in death. "There is nothing to do with men but to love them. . . . Task all the ingenuity of your mind to devise some other thing, but you never can find it. To hate your adversary will not help you; . . . nothing within the compass of the universe can help you, but to love him." [2] History verifies this insight. Collectively, those who will not love remain in death. Arnold J. Toynbee conceptualizes man's passion to immortalize himself and his cultures —to pass from death into life—in the symbols of "saviours" who have attempted in history to deliver disintegrating societies from death: "The Saviour with the Sword," "The Saviour with the Time Machine," "The Philosopher masked by a King." But these have all failed, and only Christ, "The God incarnate in a Man," conquers death. [3]

16a. Jesus' Love Is the Absolute.—By this we know love. The redeeming truth is this: The character of the love that brings men into life has been once and for all definitely revealed in Christ. Before Christ men had known love such as Jacob's, David's and Jonathan's, the patriot's, the martyr's, and the prophet's; but until **he laid down his life for us** the fullness of love was wanting. Do men today understand that Jesus' love is absolute? The modern mind, it has been said, comprehends the love of Plato or Freud better than the love of Christ. The love of Jesus is absolute because it is indistinguishably one with the eternal love of God and is of the nature of eternal Reality (cf. John 10:11-18; 13:1-5; 15:13-14) . At the same time it is manifest and visible in concrete action on the plane of history (John 19:12-16) . The essence of absolute love is self-denial to the point of death

[2] Orville Dewey, quoted by Mary W. Tileston, *Daily Strength for Daily Needs* (Boston: Little, Brown & Co., 1900), p. 178.
[3] *Study of History,* pp. 588-89.

murderer is intended; where Cain deals death, Christ in effect gives life. We are reminded of Peter's discourse in Solomon's porch: You "asked for a murderer to be granted to you [i.e., Barabbas], and killed the Author of life" (Acts 3:14-15). Christ, like Abel, is the victim of the "deeds" that spring from "the evil one," but the analogy stops there. The closest parallels to this theme of our endowment with love by God are found in 3:1 and 4:9. The same expression for Christ's vicarious work is found in John 10:11 and 15:13. The obligation on Christ's followers is similarly concluded by Paul, "And he died for all, that those who live might live no longer for themselves but for him who for their

---

for others (vs. 16a). The Cross was the inevitable issue of the kind of life Jesus lived. (Observe how the author relates the Atonement to the Incarnation here.) Jesus denied himself, however, not for a principle or a cause, but **for us,** i.e., for people. The pagan in John's world could live in heroic self-denial—the athlete (I Cor. 9:25-27), the orator, the warrior. So in our day the scientist, the artist, the soldier, can be capable of great self-denial. But mere self-denial is not love. Only when man surrenders that which has value for his own life in order to enrich the life of another does he love. Jesus' love is defined in terms of action (**he laid down his life),** not in terms of reason or emotion. Emotion is the least reliable element in personality, and if we love only when we feel like it or when we are loved (cf. Matt. 5:46) our love will be fitful and incomplete. Love is essentially a resolute disposition of the will regardless of feeling. Jesus' love is universally intelligible; it speaks to men of every nation, class, and race; and we must have faith in the capacity of men to respond to it. As an ignorant African woman said after hearing her first Christian sermon by a missionary, "There! I always told you that there ought to be a God like that."[4]

16b. Moral Constraint of Jesus' Love.—Such love means inescapable obligation: **we ought.** All the grammatical indicatives of the gospel, it has been said, are actually imperatives, and Jesus' laying down of his life is an imperative inescapably binding on all Christians. Christian song joyfully exalts the love of Christ, but mingled with joy and gratitude is always obligation:

> Love so amazing, so divine,
> *Demands* my soul, my life, my all.

We do not simply contemplate or receive the love of Christ; we are above all conscripted by it. Such love also means imitation: **He laid down his life; . . . we ought to lay down our lives.** Every life ought to be an "imitation of Christ." Only by living in such love as Jesus' love can we know from the inside the new life he brings. On certain tragic occasions self-

[4] Harry Emerson Fosdick, *The Meaning of Prayer* (New York: Association Press, 1915), p. 3.

denying love for people may mean literal martyrdom, death. But life is not always tragic, and what counts is the principle of steadily being willing and ready to deny oneself. The author of these words did not—so far as we know—lay down his life in an act of heroic martyrdom; yet one feels that he was always prepared to do so.

Such love is binding on all Christians in the total fellowship of the church, in all relations, with all people. The author's use of five plurals (four of them nominative) in vs. 16 alone, and the phrase **if any one** in vs. 17, may be taken to signify the comprehensiveness of the obligation to love for all believers. A common sin in the church is the tacit assumption that sacrificial love, for example, has a reality for a foreign missionary that it cannot have for the stay-at-home layman, or that to lay down one's life has a meaning for the spiritual hero that it does not have for the ordinary churchman. But this is false. Love is expressed on different levels of intensity and in different vocations. But the principle and the nature of love hold equal meaning for all Christians. All relations must be conducted and governed by the love that characterizes the church. No relation is exempt, whether with one's family, with employer or employee, with one's fellow citizens, or with people of other nations and races. Love as defined in this passage is a totalitarian claim upon the church as a whole as well as upon believers as individuals. The corporate conscience of the church is bound to no less high a standard than the individual conscience. The tragedy of the church so often has been its unwillingness to exemplify as an institution the obligation of love it enjoins upon its members— to lay down its life for others. One thinks of the church's greed. Karl Marx is reputed to have said that the Church of England of his day would more readily pardon an attack upon one of its thirty-nine Articles of Religion than upon one thirty-ninth of its income, and the point of the remark applies to all denominations. One thinks of social complacency. The Protestant churches in the United States in many instances have become so identified with the racial prejudices of the white bourgeois that to insist on racial brotherhood within its membership would

17 But whoso hath this world's good, and seeth his brother have need, and shutteth up his bowels *of compassion* from him, how dwelleth the love of God in him?

18 My little children, let us not love in word, neither in tongue; but in deed and in truth.

ren. 17 But if any one has the world's goods and sees his brother in need, yet closes his heart against him, how does God's love abide in him? 18 Little children, let us not love in word or speech but in deed and in truth.

---

sake died and was raised" (II Cor. 5:15). **To lay down our lives** in the literal sense is only the extreme demand that may be made upon our devotion. Windisch well instances the language of Rom. 16:4.

17-18. The application of the rule surprises us by its down-to-earth practicality, and the first reaction may be to see it as an anticlimax. But our "living" (βίον), **goods,** is an essential part of our "lives" (vs. 16), and is to be shared along with life itself. The same Greek word appears in 2:17, "the pride of life," i.e., vainglory in material possessions. It is evident that "private property" for the Christian, as God-given along with everything else, is a vital element in that sharing of life which fellowship (κοινωνία) involves. Indeed, Paul uses the latter term in this sense almost as often as in the larger sense. The elder is using here a widespread injunction of moral teachers of his age, and has in mind the coldheartedness of the Gnostic Christians; but this naïve test of the Christian calling is taken as obvious throughout the N.T. (Matt. 25:35-45; Luke 3:11; 10:30-35; II Cor. 9:6-11; Jas. 2:15-16). Part of the meaning of vs. 18 is expressed in Shakespeare's line, "They do not love, that do not show their love" (*Two Gentlemen of Verona,* Act I, scene 2). But **truth** is added to **deed** to make clear that even where acts are performed they must be genuine (cf. Matt. 6:2-4). This imperative, stressed by the appeal, **little children,** does more than apply vs. 17. It refers to the whole foregoing section and serves as a transition to what follows, vss. 19-24.

---

in some respects require a laying down of life. One thinks of the church's changing, compromising witness against war. Howard Spring writes:

Whether "Christendom" cares to face the fact or not, Jesus was a pacifist and would have had no part or lot in this bloody shambles which besets us. . . . It becomes increasingly difficult for an effective "opposition" to be staged to any State activity in the modern world. For the Churches to stage one against the Moloch of our supreme and suicidal devotion would be to court almost certain extinction. But what a death! . . . What could not spring from the ashes of such a phoenix! [5]

17-18. *The Proof of Love.*—Vs. 17 poses a question answered by vs. 18. The author knows well the perennial temptation to substitute talk about love for deeds of love. He also knows the subtler temptation—often of pride or ostentation—to substitute deeds that appear to be loving, for **love . . . in truth.** Paul's words in I Cor. 13 parallel John's thought here: "Though I speak, . . . though I give, . . . but have not love. . . ." Sometimes a closed heart is revealed in the closed hand, but an open hand does not necessarily always mean an open heart. Religion needs to be guarded from overspiritualization

by down-to-earth practical tests. The religious experience of eternal life and the claims of Christian ethics must on occasion be abstractly dealt with in thought, but they all come to this: to practical helpfulness to a person in need. Every day for a number of years William Ellery Channing fed with his own hands two poor old women who fancied that people wished to poison them and would accept their food from him alone. But the principle of sharing one's goods with people in need means more than charity to individuals. In its widest sense it is a Christian ethic applicable to the economic ordering of human society. This ethic asserts the inherent sacramentalism of the gospel which conceives the material as "good," not as bad. (Note the significance in vs. 17 of the word **goods.**) Thus Christianity has been described as the most materialistic religion in the world. This ethic also establishes the meeting of **need** (vs. 17)—rather than the making of profits—as the main motivation of a truly Christian economic order. It further establishes concern for human welfare in **God's love** (vs. 17*b*), and thus distinguishes the Christian approach to economic problems from mere secular social concern. Accordingly, this ethic rebukes those who suppose that an economic system motivated by a desire to serve human need can succeed with-

[5] *And Another Thing . . .* (New York: Harper & Bros., 1946), pp. 33, 94-95.

| 19 And hereby we know that we are of the truth, and shall assure our hearts before him. | 19 By this we shall know that we are of the truth, and reassure our hearts before |

D. CONFIDENCE BEFORE GOD IN THE TRUTH (3:19-24)

The theme of confidence before God with the conditions of that confidence appears at the end of this main section as at the beginning (2:28), though there it had special reference to the Judgment. The basic condition is that of safeguarding our divine sonship, which means to "abide in him" (vs. 24; 2:28) and to be "of the truth" (vs. 19). The test of this is presented in a twofold way as "keeping his commandment": (a) holding the faith of the gospel of love in its full sense, recognizing, i.e., that Jesus is the Messiah, the Son of God; and (b) loving one another. The passage concludes with the first reference in the writing to the Holy Spirit, offered as a final evidence of our sonship in the subjective aspect.

19-20. Of the truth here (cf. John 18:37) signifies *origin* and is chosen rather than "of God" (vs. 10) or "of light" (John 12:36) in view of vs. 18. Real love to God and man in us derives from the reality of love in God. "Behind this wondrous new creation of human kindness and tenderness, of unbounded self-surrender and unwearied service to humanity, which the Apostolic Churches exhibited, there is a *vera causa*" (G. G. Findlay, *Fellowship in the Life Eternal* [London: Hodder & Stoughton, 1909], p. 293). This makes for confidence even if our **hearts condemn us,** for God as the "true God" (5:20) **is greater than our** ["poor"] **hearts, and he knows everything.** Here we have one way of understanding this passage.

The difficulty of these verses is such that scholars commonly present several interpretations as almost equally likely. The differences between the KJV and the RSV indicate some of the ambiguities. For one thing, the better MSS differ in significant ways. Furthermore, the connective words between vss. 19 and 20 (ὅτι ἐάν) lend themselves to two different translations: **for if** (KJV) or **whenever** (RSV). The Greek future verb

---

out any religious or metaphysical foundation. At the same time it also rebukes those who would condemn an economic philosophy that would meet human need, merely because it is not nominally religious.

19-24. The Christian's Confidence.—This passage is best understood by remembering that while the author was a mystical thinker who bequeaths to us many profound insights into the nature of God and of human life, he was first a pastor of people and churches. His fundamental aim in this epistle is to establish people in the Christian life rather than to engage in theological controversy. Moreover, he conceives the experience of eternal life normally to be such that one can be certain of possessing it (cf. Expos. on 4:13-18). Thus while the author has taken pains in the preceding verses to prescribe practical ethical tests of the experience of eternal life, he is equally concerned in vss. 19-24 to encourage those who have been born of God and to deepen the assurance of those who are **of the truth.** The theme of this passage is accordingly expressed in the words **By this we shall know, . . . and reassure our hearts, and have confidence before God . . . and abide in him.**

Man's need of confidence before God is well known to all pastors and counselors of people, as it was to the elder. Despondency is sometimes as dangerous as sin, and life brings many experiences when **our hearts condemn us.** Indeed, the more advanced a believer is in the Christian life the more sensitive he can be to doubt and misgiving. (The elder's choice of the word **heart** probably signifies the whole consciousness of man, not merely his moral sense.)

Sometimes we suppose that our hearts condemn us when actually the mystery of God's presence is the explanation. Jesus said that God's Spirit—as the wind—"blows where it wills . . . but you do not know" (John 3:8). Our ignorance of the working of God's Spirit must not be allowed to lead us to self-condemnation. Truly, "in God's education of the human spirit into a rich personal sonship to Himself there is a place for darkness and mystery." [6] Our shifting, unstable emotional life can also destroy our confidence. Moods affect the religious consciousness as all else, and Christian literature abundantly testifies to feelings of depression and desolation in even the lives of saints.

[6] Farmer, *The World and God,* p. 90.

20 For if our heart condemn us, God is greater than our heart, and knoweth all things.

him 20 whenever our hearts condemn us; for God is greater than our hearts, and he

---

(πείσομεν) translated **assure (reassure** RSV) should perhaps have the sense (with the following particle ὅτι) : "convince . . . that . . . ," requiring a statement as sequel. In this case we would then translate as follows: "By this we shall know the truth, and convince our hearts before him that even if our hearts condemn us, God is greater than our hearts, and he knows everything." The sense here is that if we love our brethren in truth (vss. 16-18), we then have the means of convincing our timorous hearts that God knows our basic sincerity. But commentators rightly see something of a *non sequitur* in this version. That **God is greater** than our hearts we know already. Moreover, a second ὅτι before μείζων **(greater)** has to be ignored as a repetition of the first at the beginning of vs. 20.

The translation in the RSV avoids these difficulties. Here too the reference of **by this** is backward. **By this we shall . . . reassure our hearts before him whenever** (ὅτι ἐάν) **our hearts condemn us.** Here there is a stop; and then follows an explanation of why the timorous scruples of conscientious Christians are to be overruled: **For God is greater than our hearts, and he knows everything.** Other readings are possible. Findlay restates a persuasive and quite different view with a long history going back to the early fathers (*ibid.*, ch. xviii). In this view vss. 20 and 21 are in antithetical parallelism: "if our hearts condemn us" is contrasted with "if our hearts condemn us not." In vs. 20 he who has a bad conscience is *warned,* not comforted, by the thought that God's judgment is far more searching than his own. This interpretation has much in its favor. But is this negative note to be expected at this point? Throughout the epistle the elder addresses himself to believers who need to be encouraged to lay firmer hold on what they already know and have experienced. Excessive scruple or self-condemnation is a temptation to them to follow heretical ways and is the very opposite of that confident spirit of joy and trust in fellowship to which he summons them (1:4) and for which they are ready. He is dealing with a perennial problem. Against any timidity or self-reproach he appeals

---

Martin Luther once began a prayer, "O God, art thou dead?" Religious growth, wrestling with new truth, progress into moral and intellectual maturity, also bring such hours. Many a firm believer has passed through atheism and doubt. The experience of new wine bursting old wineskins is not always pleasant. Again, the sheer pathos of human life—the suffering, the folly, the evil of men—can trouble a religiously sensitive person. Shadows of pain and doubt can darken the light. A character in a novel by Thomas Wolfe is described as she beholds for the first time without pretense the pathos of life:

She was sorry for all who had lived, were living, or would live, fanning with their prayers the useless altar flames, suppliant with their hopes, . . . casting the tiny rockets of their belief against remote eternity, and hoping for grace, guidance, and delivery upon the spinning and forgotten cinder of this earth. O lost.[7]

The spectacle of other people who become confused and despairing can make the Christian confused. Again, the spirit of the age can undermine certainty. The atmosphere in which the apostolic church found itself toward the close of the first century was one of intellectual confusion. Today the atmosphere tends more toward anxiety, nervousness, and despair. Writes a modern critic: "The temperamental cards of our time are all stacked in favor of despair. . . . The genius that has molded the mind of the present is almost wholly destructive. . . . This mood of . . . despair has penetrated millions of minds."[8] More specifically, seemingly unanswered prayer (does the elder obliquely refer to unanswered prayer in vss. 21-22?), perplexity about a course of action, the clouding of faith by old guilt patterns and fears, the deposit of memory of evil in the subconscious mind—these can cause our hearts to condemn us.

To the need of assurance the elder answers, **God is greater than our hearts, and he knows everything.** Certainty of acceptance by God can exist even amid feelings of condemnation. Moreover, this certainty can actually change our

---

[7] *Look Homeward, Angel* (New York: Charles Scribner's Sons, 1929), pp. 59-60.

[8] Van Wyck Brooks, quoted by Paul Wolfe, Helen A. and Clarence Dickinson, *The Choir Loft and the Pulpit* (New York: H. W. Gray Co., 1943), pp. 15-16.

21 Beloved, if our heart condemn us not, *then* have we confidence toward God.

knows everything. 21 Beloved, if our hearts do not condemn us, we have confidence be-

to the greatness of God's knowledge, as Peter appeals to Christ: "Lord, thou knowest all things; thou knowest that I love thee" (John 21:17). In the last analysis God is our judge and we refer ourselves to him (I Cor. 4:4-5); our human hearts and consciences are often clouded by old guilt patterns and fears which can be almost as crippling as disobedience. The elder is really stating in his own way Paul's theme of justification by faith. It has its dangers, but he has safeguarded it by the tests he provides.

21-22. The thought here runs parallel with that of Paul as he surveys the prospect that opens out before those who "have peace with God through our Lord Jesus Christ" after justification has been once and for all established (Rom. 5:1-5). Paul's thought turns to hope; the elder's to **confidence,** and especially to confidence in prayer. The same thought reappears in 5:14-15 (see below). The answer to prayer comes **because we keep his commandments and do what pleases him.** It would be a mistake to place all the

hearts so that whereas our hearts once condemned us, they **do not condemn us** and **we have confidence before God.** Observe the nature of this assurance. It centers in God, not in ourselves; it is objective, not subjective: **God is.** The first step in overcoming spiritual discouragement is to contemplate God, not our own emotional troubles. Fénelon writes:

The whole basis of your trouble is that you cannot get out of yourself. Do you hope to get out of it by always communing with yourself, and feeding your sensibility . . . ? You only make yourself pity yourself by all this introversion. But the slightest glance toward God would calm your heart far better . . . . David . . . said, "I saw always God before me," and again, "My eyes are always raised to the Lord, that he may keep my feet from snares." The danger is to his feet, yet his eyes are on high. It does less good to think of our danger than to think of the help of God.[9]

The sheer greatness of God's being and life offers the final refuge to man's troubled soul: **God is greater than our hearts.** At times we feel overcome by the ineffable greatness of God; but actually God's greatness comforts and steadies us:

As the marsh-hen secretly builds on the watery sod,
Behold I will build me a nest on the greatness of God:
I will fly in the greatness of God as the marsh-hen flies
In the freedom that fills all the space 'twixt the marsh and the skies:
By so many roots as the marsh-grass sends in the sod
I will heartily lay me a-hold on the greatness of God.[1]

God . . . knows everything. The Christian is assured that the divine Mind fathoms the depths

[9] *Christian Perfection,* tr. Mildred W. Stillman (New York: Harper & Bros., 1947), pp. 97-99.
[1] Sidney Lanier, "The Marshes of Glynn."

of human consciousness, and comprehends the native endowments of personality and the conditioning factors of environment that make a man what he is. The Christian is assured that God can disentangle good from evil in character, can understand the intentions of our hearts as well as our outward deeds. Moreover, God knows everything with the knowledge of love, and we must say of God's mind what we say of God's will, that he never comprehends or judges man—as he never acts toward man—in any way save love. This assurance, however, is not merely an abstract, theological conviction; it is a child's personal experience of the Father's love. The important thing in religion, it has been said, is not the theological belief that God is omniscient but the personal experience that God knows me.

God's power thus to save men from self-condemnation issues in what may be called legitimate self-confidence. The elder elsewhere warns against self-deception (1:8); here he warns against unjustified self-accusation. In authentic Christian experience there are times and states when **our hearts do not condemn us** and **we have confidence before God,** when believers may know that they **abide in him, and he in them.** The Christian must remember that there is a status of gracious acceptance by God to which he is entitled and can attain; at the same time he must remember that he always needs and can receive the continual forgiveness of God. This self-confidence and acquittal, however, are grounded in keeping the two fundamental **commandments** of the gospel: **believe, love.** Obedience to these commandments distinguishes confidence before God from mere feeling. Man's emotional nature is proverbially unstable, and yet many people appeal to feeling, rather than to moral action (love) or to commitment to God in faith (believe), as the basis of their confidence. Again, keeping of

22 And whatsoever we ask, we receive of him, because we keep his commandments, and do those things that are pleasing in his sight.

fore God; 22 and we receive from him whatever we ask, because we keep his command-

---

emphasis on such moral conditions. Right actions are only an index of our being at one with God in our desires, of our asking "according to his will" (5:14). For **all who keep his commandments abide in him, and he in them** (vs. 24). This is confirmed for the Johannine outlook by John 15:7: "If you abide in me, and my words abide in you, ask whatever you will, and it shall be done for you." It is only at a very deep level of consecration that the promise is not misleading, as with Jesus' similar sayings with regard to the role of faith in prayer. The clue appears in Paul's explanation that at least in what concerns our own Christian fulfillment it is not we but the Spirit of God that does the praying (Rom. 8:26-27).

---

these commandments saves self-confidence from becoming pride. Our hearts do not condemn us when on the one hand we do not make light of any hold on truth or faithful obedience we may have won, when we do not engage in artificial self-depreciation or manufactured penitence; and when on the other hand we do not presume to be better than we are, when we do not say "we have no sin" (1:8) or "we have not sinned" (1:10).

22. Petitionary Prayer.—Confidence in the validity of petitionary prayer is one aspect of confidence before God, and likewise issues from obeying the commandment to believe and love: **We receive from him whatever we ask, because we keep his commandments and do what pleases him.** (Petitionary prayer is also referred to in 5:14-15, confessional prayer in 1:9, intercessory prayer in 5:16; cf. Expos.) The elder's conception of prayer throughout the epistle is instructive in that he never argues for the efficacy of prayer or urges men to pray. He simply assumes that confident prayer is an essential, normal part of the Christian life, and that God's answer to such prayer is always to be expected: "He hears us" (5:14); "We have obtained the requests made of him" (5:15); "If any one . . . ask, . . . God will give" (5:16). As noted in the Exeg., such language can be misleading if one does not understand that prayer in Johannine thought is grounded in man's union with God's nature through faith and love, and that the believer accordingly receives from God whatever he asks precisely because he asks only what God desires to give (cf. John 15:7, 13-15). Indeed, it is God himself who puts into the believer's heart the very petitions he offers. It is in this sense that the assurance of having already received from God whatever we ask can be asserted, and it is doubtful whether John could write so mystically and profoundly of prayer if this assurance had not been verified in his own experience.

Only as profound a conception of prayer as this can do justice to the Christian interpretation of the responsive grace of God and shame us from our doubts of God's loving concern for human life. In the light of this conception our doubts are exposed as reflections of our own spiritual poverty rather than as valid reasons for not praying. It also teaches us the conditional nature of prayer, i.e., that prayer is real and effective when it rises from a life that in its total action and attitude is in harmonious fellowship with God: **we receive from him whatever we ask, because we keep . . . and do.** Such fellowship rests on more than moral conditions, but at the minimum it must include certain moral conditions. We are the same people in prayer we have been all along, and if our everyday living is not morally governed by obedience to God, it is doubtful whether our aspirations in prayer can avail with God. At the same time prayer is natural and inevitable in the truly Christian life. When a believer lives in the kind of fellowship with God that John pictures, so far from needing to be urged to pray, he cannot help praying.

The dynamic power of genuine Christian prayer must never be underestimated. When the Christian's life corresponds to his prayers, and vice versa, nothing is impossible. Friedrich Heiler quotes from Kierkegaard the sentence: "The archimedean point outside the world is the little chamber where a true suppliant prays in all sincerity—where he lifts the world off its hinges." [2] In the Johannine sense prayer is indeed "the archimedean point outside the world," in that the quality of life underlying true Christian prayer transcends the world and time and participates in eternal life. This conception of prayer answers to a deep, psychological need in human personality—the need of affirmation rather than question or argu-

[2] *Prayer*, tr. Samuel McComb (New York: Oxford University Press, 1932), p. 279.

23 And this is his commandment, That we should believe on the name of his Son Jesus Christ, and love one another, as he gave us commandment.

ments and do what pleases him. 23 And this is his commandment, that we should believe in the name of his Son Jesus Christ and love one another, just as he has com-

---

23. The "commandments" of vs. 22 are not then only or chiefly moral, as has been said. Underlying them is the confession which testifies to our sonship, our being "in God" and "of the truth." The construction here, **believe in the name** (πιστεύσωμεν τῷ ὀνόματι), calls for several comments. The aorist tense is to be preferred (the present is found in some MSS) and suggests that reference is being made to the act of confessing Christ through baptism, at which belief in the name of Jesus was the current formula. The dative construction, rather than the frequent form (εἰς with accusative) found in 5:13, lays stress on belief in the message suggested by the name. "Belief" in the Johannine writings carries an overtone of commitment or faith in the deeper sense, whether the object of belief is Christ himself (or his name, as 5:13 again) or the gospel message

---

ment; the need of realization rather than petition; the need of being able to believe that God is giving what we ask for. (Note the present— not future—tense: "we have confidence," **we receive . . . whatever we ask.**) It has been pointed out that the language of Ps. 23 is not that of asking for gifts in the future but of realizing the possession of gifts already received: "He leadeth me beside the still waters. He restoreth my soul: . . . for thou art with me; . . . thou preparest, . . . thou anointest." This is psychologically far sounder than to say, "I beseech thee to lead me, to restore me," etc. We can learn from John's conception of prayer the wisdom of receiving and possessing from God what we ask for as well as the wisdom of asking only for what he desires to give.

The source of our confidence before God, however, is not finally ourselves; rather, "we know . . . by the Spirit which he has given us" (vs. 24b). The Spirit is God present in the human soul kindling and informing our faculties of awareness (cf. Expos. on 4:1, 13; 5:7-8).

23. *Belief and Love.*—The (plural) "commandments" (vs. 22) are summarized in the (singular) **commandment** (vs. 23), **that we should believe in the name of his Son Jesus Christ and love one another.** This verse has been called the theme of the entire epistle, and puts in concise form the content of the message of eternal life which ever and again the author would proclaim. The command to **believe** is aimed at the Gnostic Docetists who deny that Jesus is God's Son and the Christ come in the flesh, and the command to **love** is aimed at the Gnostic Antinomians who felt themselves to be above the moral claim of love. But as so often in the epistle, the author speaks to every age as well as to his own. For this commandment once and for all indissolubly connects religion and morality, theology and ethics, faith and works, mysticism and morals; and all who in any way sever

one from the other stand convicted of violating his [God's] **commandment.** The injunction to believe and love is indeed *the commandment.* Sanctions attach to believing and not believing, and to loving and not loving, that do not attach to any other commandment. This of course does not mean that Christianity would force people to believe and love against their will. But it does mean that the necessity of believing and loving is written into the constitution of the universe and of human life, and whether or not men believe and love determines their destiny. In this sense Jesus himself commanded men to believe and love. He set before them fateful questions and pressed for decision. He required men to decide for God or mammon, love or selfishness, the truth or the lie, humility or self-righteousness, faith or unbelief, an eternal or an earthly life. "The sphere which these questions occupy is all-embracing," and man is called to decide "whether he will be on God's side and the Eternal's, or on the side of the world and of time." [3]

To **believe in the name of his Son Jesus Christ** thus means to accept and affirm as binding upon all life—including one's own—the total truth of the Christian revelation. It is to declare that the meaning of Jesus' life and death and resurrection is absolute and sovereign. Fairbairn writes: "Christ's person . . . does not simply denote a figure which once appeared under the conditions of space and time, . . . it also stands for a whole order of thought, a way of regarding the universe, of conceiving God and man in themselves and in their mutual relations." [4] Significantly, the commandment places love after belief, for love issues from belief. Belief in God in the Johannine sense is belief in a God whose most essential nature is

[3] Adolf Harnack, *What Is Christianity?* tr. T. B. Saunders (New York: G. P. Putnam Sons, 1901), p. 154.
[4] *Philosophy of Christian Religion*, p. 16.

24 And he that keepeth his commandments dwelleth in him, and he in him. And hereby we know that he abideth in us, by the Spirit which he hath given us.

4 Beloved, believe not every spirit, but try the spirits whether they are of God: because many false prophets are gone out into the world.

manded us. 24 All who keep his commandments abide in him, and he in them. And by this we know that he abides in us, by the Spirit which he has given us.

4 Beloved, do not believe every spirit, but test the spirits to see whether they are of God; for many false prophets have gone

---

associated with his name and titles as here. This is why belief can be presented as a command. In John 6:29 belief in Christ is presented as a "work of God," commanded, but the term for work (ἔργον) brings out more clearly the supernatural assistance necessary if one is fully to commit oneself to Christ.

24. This verse picks up the thought of vs. 22, as has been indicated above. But the fact that the obedient **abide in him** has as its correlative that God abides in them, evidence of which is given in the activity of the Holy Spirit. Rom. 5:1-5, to which allusion has been made, points to the same ground of assurance.

V. The False Spirits and the Spirit of God (4:1-6)

We have here a second polemic passage. The groups attacked and their false doctrine are probably not different from those envisaged in 2:18-27. This is suggested by their association again with **antichrist,** and by the statement that the disturbers have gone out into the world (cf. 2:19; II John 7a) with stress on the fact that they are **of the world** and therefore "not of us" (2:19). The erroneous doctrine is not stated in the same terms. In the earlier section the "liar" is "he who denies that Jesus is the Christ" (2:22), amplified in the same verse as "he who denies the Father and the Son." Some have supposed that an Ebionite denial of Jesus' messiahship is all that is intended here (so Maurice Goguel). But the second part of the verse makes it likely that Docetic-Gnostic issues are involved. Thus the normative confession of vs. 2 is our guide in both cases: **Jesus Christ is come in the flesh** (cf. II John 7). What distinguishes the present passage is the designation of the sources of the error as **spirits** and their mouthpiece as **false prophets.** In appealing to the evidence of the Spirit in 3:24, the writer is led to repudiate false claims to it and to assign a confessional test (so 4:13-15; 5:6-9). But the importance of a sound Christology as the basis either for confidence or for brotherly love has been evident even in the nonpolemic parts of the epistle, and in the passage that immediately precedes the present section, i.e., 3:23a.

A. The Denial of Christ Come in the Flesh (4:1-3)

4:1. God has given us the Spirit (3:24) which is "his own Spirit" (4:13), and we can believe its "witness" (5:7), but we are not to **believe every spirit,** i.e., not to accept

---

love; and (as is made clear in vss. 11-18; 4:7-21; 5:1-3) love of one's brother is engendered by love of a God who is love. To love ethically, in brief, is to partake of metaphysical reality, and brings confidence to one's soul because one is united with God. On this point Findlay writes of the difficulties of Christian belief—*solvitur amando,* they are solved by loving.[5] A Christian may not be able to define his belief logically in terms of thought, or be able to argue cogently against doubt, but if his belief issues in works of love, it is real; and in his heart he knows it. When he loves he knows he is **of the truth** and

his heart is reassured even if his intellect is troubled.

4:1-3. *The Menace of False Prophets.*—The challenge of Gnosticism to the early church must be especially borne in mind in understanding this second of two polemic sections. The elder cites the popularity of Gnostic **prophets** who **have gone out into the world** as evidence of diabolic spirits whose activity expresses evil in its supernatural reality and power. These spirits mysteriously find affinity with primal impulses of evil in human personality, and are able to possess and use men as their mouthpieces. The same supernatural,

[5] *Fellowship in Life Eternal,* p. 291.

the message of such as true. In the view of the age there were many evil spirits which led men into sin and error; the reality of their supernatural impact is everywhere recognized in the Jewish and Christian literature, and especially assigned to the "last hour." Just as the "evil one" stands over against God, so the Antichrist stands over against Christ, "the spirit of error" over against "the spirit of truth" (vs. 6), and the **false prophets** over against the true. In the N.T., as in the O.T., the prophet is the bearer of revelation, the mouthpiece of "spirits," and to him the believers looked for dynamic and novel oracles rather than to the evangelist or teacher. Examples of the role of prophecy in the N.T. are offered in Acts 11:27-28; 13:1-3; 21:9-12; Rev. 10:11; but above all in I Cor. 12 and 14, where the contributions to the meetings of the church of those who have the gift of prophecy are considered. The church of the second century evidences a widespread hunger for new revelations and visions, but what was offered to meet this need too often took the form of irrational deliverances and esoteric schemes.

The supernatural is not always the divine. The rebuke of false prophets who give deceptive assurances of safety in Jer. 14:14 illustrates the O.T. background: "The prophets prophesy lies in my name; I sent them not. . . . They prophesy unto you a

---

diabolic reality that fathers "children of the devil" (3:10), who sin by hating and murdering (cf. Expos. on 3:12-13, 15), also begets false prophets who sin by misleading men into error and denial of truth. Evil attacks belief as well as morals.

1, 3. Supernatural Evil.—The strangeness of John's thought forms—employed by many thinkers of his time—must not be allowed to obscure the permanent meaning of these verses: that the supernatural is diabolic as well as divine, and Christian people must be on guard against the spirit of evil as it uses and speaks through **false prophets.** This meaning is valid for our age as for every age because evil still possesses a dynamic, invasive power, and it is healthy to be reminded that antichristian spirits are still real and at work: **the spirit of antichrist . . . now . . . is in the world.** In our time the acknowledgment of the supernatural reality of evil has taken the form of a reassertion of "the demonic," by which is meant a "structure of evil beyond the moral power of good will, producing social and individual tragedy."[6] Modern conceptions of the demonic derive from Greek thought with its concepts of fate and tragedy as well as from Christian thought with its concepts of evil and original sin. But common to both is the realization of a supernatural, diabolic power that attacks man on the deeper, nonrational levels of his being, and that can control his existence and determine his fate unless broken by an equally superhuman agency of good. The response of modern thinkers and writers to the Christian concept of "the demonic" reflects a growing awareness in our time of the structural character of evil and underscores the timeless validity of John's insight.

But as the spirits of evil speak and work through false prophets, so in our time "the

[6] Tillich, *Protestant Era*, p. xx.

demonic" is manifest in particular individuals and particular movements. Political saviors who incarnate demonism that palpably partakes of evil are an example. A newspaper correspondent reported having visited the studio of a German artist in World War II and having been shown a portrait of Goebbels, the German minister of propaganda. The portrait was of Satan, with the face of Goebbels, drawn against the livid background of the inferno. When asked what Goebbels thought of it, the artist replied, "He loves it. The more sinister I made it, the better he liked it. He knows that this picture is a personification of evil, but he is in love with evil." Often such political saviors are false prophets in that they believe that man is unto his fellow man as a wolf, that struggle is the law of life, that war—not peace—is man's natural state, that naked power—not ideas or ethics—determines human destiny. A minister of war in a totalitarian state once said: "To the meaningless idealisms—Liberty, Fraternity, Equality—we oppose the realities—Infantry, Cavalry, Artillery." There are also the false prophets of racism who exalt biological and racial inheritance, and who ground values in the absolute of blood; false prophets of materialism who deny any spiritual dimensions to life and affirm that only the material is real; false prophets of secularism, mouthpieces of a new worldliness who locate man's happiness and destiny in the world of space, time, matter, and history; false prophets of humanism who declare that man is the master of things; false prophets of scientific rationalism who believe that man's salvation lies within the power of his own intellect. Again, and one recognizes this with reluctance, there are those who pretentiously declare the sanctions of institutionalized religion to be ultimate—specifically those who assert the claim of Roman Catholicism to decide what is error and

2 Hereby know ye the Spirit of God: Every spirit that confesseth that Jesus Christ is come in the flesh is of God:

out into the world. 2 By this you know the Spirit of God: every spirit which confesses that Jesus Christ has come in the flesh is of

---

lying vision and divination, and a thing of nought, and the deceit of their own heart." The church found it necessary to set up criteria and controls, a difficult thing to do since it involved the danger of smothering vitality. In one of his earliest letters Paul writes, "Do not quench the Spirit, do not despise prophesying, but test everything" (I Thess. 5:19-20). The passages I Cor. 12:1-11; 14:1-5, 24-33 well document the discrimination of spirits viewed there as a peculiar gift, and set up the test: "No one speaking by the Spirit of God ever says 'Jesus be cursed!' and no one can say 'Jesus is Lord' except by the Holy Spirit" (I Cor. 12:3). Here, as in our present passage, the false prophet is known by his reaction to Jesus; in Matt. 7:15-20 and in The Teaching of the Twelve Apostles 11:8-12, by his unrighteous conduct and greed; in the O.T. by flattery and popularity.

2-3. "Jesus is Lord" was the appropriate formula in Paul's situation, but in the new circumstances in Asia it did not fully meet the danger. The test for the errorists of the present crisis was to affirm (a) that "Jesus is the Christ" (2:22), meaning not only

---

what is truth (vs. 6), and who would substitute the infallibility of a hierarchy for the free activity of the human mind confessing that "Jesus Christ has come in the flesh" (vs. 2). Surely the spectacle of men and movements in our century whose power is clearly derived from evil inspiration verifies the elder's analysis of the human situation. The variety and popularity of contemporary false prophets should not surprise us; it is still true that "the world listens to them" (vs. 5). In every age the lie contends against the truth, evil against good, false prophets against true prophets, the spirit of Antichrist against Christ.

1. Test the Spirits!—Against this background the elder writes: Do not believe every spirit, but test the spirits. Side by side with positive Christian faith is a healthy skepticism that inquires into the claims of men and movements to be inspired. (Significantly, no less than nine times does the author of this epistle offer his readers tests by which they may assure themselves that they are of the truth, introduced with such a phrase as in vs. 6, "By this we know. . . .") The command, do not believe, . . . test, is as relevant under certain circumstances as the commandment, "Believe, . . . love" (3:23). The mind of the Christian is not a soft mind, and faith is the farthest thing from gullibility. But observe: the Christian is to test the spirits not in order to see whether they agree with his own opinions but to see whether they are of God. The false inspiration the Christian rejects is sometimes matched by false inspiration manifested in bigotry or prejudice in himself. One's own thought is too subjective and unreliable; it is always the objective reality of God revealed in Jesus to which the Christian mind turns for light and truth.

2. Confession of Christ the Christian's Absolute.—The creedal nature of this test is obvious, and is another instance of John's appeal to dogma in the life of the individual believer and of the apostolic fellowship (cf. Expos. on 2:23). Further, Christology again is the heart of the matter. The only valid viewpoint from which to judge the meaning of swirling currents of thought is the truth of Christ. The Incarnation is the essence of the test John lays down: "the self-revelation of God in the historical Jesus and in his deed" (Exeg. on vss. 2-3). One is not justified in defining in too precise terms what John means in each confessional formula he employs. But observe the conjunction of the two words, Jesus Christ. "Jesus" signifies the human, historical character of our Lord; "Christ" signifies his divine character. The union of these two words, signifying the divine-human nature of our Lord, is thus a verbal epitome of the doctrine of the Incarnation, and constitutes an answer to "false prophets" in every age who would separate them. Thus every time we use the phrase "Jesus Christ" we not only commit ourselves to the total Christian revelation; we also recapitulate in our own thought the momentous doctrinal struggles through which the church has successfully passed under such inspired thinkers as John; and we are reminded of the thinker's toil, the apostle's witness, the martyr's blood offered up to preserve the gospel to us.

The words, Jesus Christ has come in the flesh, suggest the dynamic activity of God who has broken into physical, historical existence from another, different sphere of being. The soul of the universe, it has been said, has looked at us through the eyes of Jesus. The tense of the words has come (the Greek perfect) conveys

3 And every spirit that confesseth not that Jesus Christ is come in the flesh is not of God: and this is that *spirit* of antichrist,

God, 3 and every spirit which does not confess Jesus is not of God. This is the spirit

---

that the historical Jesus was the Messiah, but that he was Messiah in the sense of the Son of God (as this came to be understood in the later first century and in the Gospel of John particularly); and (*b*) that **Jesus Christ** in this sense **has come in the flesh.** A standard formula of confession, at least in the second generation of the church, appears in Acts 8:37, all the more significant since it is a gloss: the Ethiopian eunuch responds to Philip's invitation with the words, "I believe that Jesus Christ is the Son of God" (RSV mg.). **Come in the flesh** in our present passage only specifies what is taken for granted in that typical formula, thus countering the Docetic error which distinguished the two natures of Christ, to use a later phrase, in a way that falsified the gospel (see Intro., pp. 213-14). Our recognition of the evolving character of the confessions of Christ in the N.T. should safeguard us from too dogmatic a use of polemic passages like the one under discussion. What would seem to be the heart of the matter here, and in continuity with the simpler confessions of Acts and Paul, is insight into the self-revelation of God in the historical Jesus and his deed. As Paul says, it is only by the Holy Spirit that such an insight finds utterance. So the elder writes that **every spirit** which makes the confession is **of God.**

The opposing **spirit** refuses the confession, and being **not of God** is of antichrist. Like Paul in the passage quoted (I Cor. 12:3), the writer is not concerned with intermediate positions, with attitudes to Christ marked by varying degrees of honest doubt, uncertainty, or indifference. He is speaking here, be it noted, of "spirits" not men—i.e., of

---

the idea of a decisive, constitutive advent, once and for all accomplished, through which has been introduced into history a new order that stands as salvation and judgment over against the human order (cf. Expos. on 1:1-4). In this connection the grammar of this phrase is typical of N.T. language which habitually prefers not the substantive noun but the active verb predominantly in the aorist or perfect tense. God's relation to man is not static but dynamic; God always acts toward man, but in Christ he has supremely and decisively acted. He **has come.**

The words **in the flesh** further declare that in a particular person in history who lived and died at a certain time, Reality has revealed itself. This insight decisively distinguishes Christianity from all mythology, and establishes its truth in historical realities. To many this has been the stumbling block of the gospel. Lessing once said: "Particular facts of history cannot establish eternal truths. There is the ugly wide ditch over which I cannot get, oft and earnestly though I spring."[7] One can sympathize with such intellectual difficulty. Nevertheless Christ must be believed in as **come in the flesh,** or he cannot be comprehended in his full meaning. "It is an act rather than a thought which sets the Christ above history, and being an act, it is more indubitably in history than a mere thought."[8]

[7] Quoted by John S. Whale, *Christian Doctrine*, p. 57.
[8] Niebuhr, *Nature and Destiny of Man*, II, 92.

That Christ came **in the flesh** once and for all sanctifies the material. The dichotomy between the spiritual and the material is false and untenable from the Christian point of view. Consider the implications of this insight for Christian attitudes toward sex. Consider also the answer this insight enables us to make to the challenge of materialism—philosophical, economic, practical—in our age. The Christian answer to the challenge of materialism is not to surrender to the Gnostic fallacy of declaring that matter is evil. Instead, it is to spiritualize and ethicize the material. The Incarnation is in one sense an event; in another sense it is also a process eternally going on whose consummation needs our thought and labor. The object of faith and the basis of Christian certainty is not ultimately a dogma but a person. The confession that stamps a man as "of God" or "not of God," is not of the fact of the Incarnation but of the Incarnate Christ: **Jesus Christ . . . in the flesh.**

2-3. Those Who Believe and Deny.—The distinction in vss. 4-6 between two kinds of men who find affinity with the two kinds of spirits is partly anticipated in vss. 2-3; the response of men to Jesus Christ determines whether they are "of God" or "not of God" (vs. 6) and disposes them as being of true or false spirits. This insight is valid first in a retroactive sense, in that faith in the Incarnation alone enables men to comprehend the true meaning of history. From the Christian point of view the Incarna-

whereof ye have heard that it should come; and even now already is it in the world.	of antichrist, of which you heard that it was coming, and now it is in the world already.

the primal impulses that control men. Where he baldly contrasts men as "children of God" and "children of the devil" in 3:10, it is by a practical test of love and righteousness. In any case it is the emergency that justifies the dualism, as in the case of Jesus' words, "He that is not with me is against me" (Luke 11:23). The redemptive cause of God was at stake, as it is in particular crises throughout history. Attitudes pro and con are finally determined by ultimate creative or destructive factors in the soul. In the language of the time the "great refusal" could best be expressed as the work of the **spirit of antichrist**, whose virulent manifestation was expected in the end time which had now **already** overtaken men.

An important textual variant to vs. 3a, witnessed by many of the church fathers, reads, πᾶν πνεῦμα ὃ λύει τὸν Ἰησοῦν. This has usually been translated, "every spirit which divides Jesus," i.e., makes a distinction between "Jesus" and "Christ," as the Docetists did. The Latin fathers so understood this reading, as is evident in their translation *solvit* for λύει (so Vulg.). The reading has been rejected by modern scholars not only because of the contrary witness of the Greek codex MSS, but because it does not make clear sense to say "divide Jesus" (as it might if it read, "divide Jesus Christ"). But Piper ("I John and the Didache of the Primitive Church," *Journal of Biblical Literature*, LXVI [1947], pp. 443-44) well argues that λύει here had the sense not of divide, but of exorcize or anathametize (cf. 3:8; Matt. 16:19; I Cor. 12:3; Ign. Eph. 13:1; 19:3). Misunder-

---

tion and Atonement represent the fulfillment of history, only in the light of which can the subsequent movements of history be understood. Thus a modern historian writes that the Crucifixion and its consequences are the greatest new event in history, and that they determine the future course of history.[9] The contrast of this viewpoint with differing interpretations of history—e.g., Marxian materialism—illustrates the cleavage between those who are of God and not of God. The "redemptive cause of God" (cf. Exeg. on vss. 2-3) can be comprehended in its purposefulness and be brought to pass in actuality only by those who take their stand within the Christian revelation.

The destiny of each human soul individually, however, as well as the destiny of men collectively, is also at stake. To confess or not to confess that Jesus has come in the flesh defines the perpetual crisis in which each man finds himself, and presents the fateful choice ever set before him. Jesus forever offers himself as the rock of salvation on which man may secure his existence (Matt. 7:24), or as the stone of judgment that will grind him to powder (Matt. 21:44). The emergency that in John's circumstances compelled his use of the harsh dualism—of Christ or of Antichrist, of God or not of God, of the spirit of truth or of the spirit of error—is in the largest gospel sense the perpetual emergency of the human soul. The impulses that lead men to choose evil will always remain

[9] Toynbee, *Civilization on Trial*, p. 237.

mysterious. Jesus himself acknowledged this mystery in saying that the gospel was "hidden . . . from the wise . . . and revealed . . . to babes" (Matt. 11:25). "Destructive factors in the soul," "primal impulses" of evil (cf. Exeg. on vss. 2-3), appear to some thinkers to be so strong as to justify the doctrine of predestination. Some modern thinkers locate these factors in the subconscious depths of the mind; thus C. G. Jung writes that

man has never yet been able single-handed to hold his own against the powers of darkness—that is, of the unconscious. Man has always stood in need of the spiritual help which . . . religion held out to him. . . . Man is . . . helped . . . only by revelations of a wisdom greater than his own. It is this which lifts him out of his distress.[1]

The fact is that people often believe or fail to believe as by a natural affinity. Writes Edwin Arlington Robinson:

> There is a faith that is a part of fate
> For some of us—a thing that may be taught
> No more than may the color of our eyes.
> It was a part of me when I was born.[2]

Nevertheless, the power of choice still lies within the freedom of the human soul. Every man can **test**, believe not, or **confess**.

[1] *Modern Man in Search of a Soul* (New York: Harcourt, Brace & Co., 1933), pp. 277-78.
[2] *Cavender's House* (New York: The Macmillan Co., 1929), p. 25. Used by permission.

| 4 Ye are of God, little children, and have overcome them: because greater is he that is in you, than he that is in the world. | 4 Little children, you are of God, and have overcome them; for he who is in you is |

standing of the Greek term led to the many textual variants that exist, including our common reading. On this view the heretics are accused of presuming to "break the spell" or annul the authority of Jesus by demonic power.

B. The Victory of the Children of God (4:4-6)

The distinction between the two kinds of spirits is carried over now into one between two kinds of men, those **of God** and those **of the world**. The use of parallelism is so clear (vss. 5, 6*a, b*) that we can agree with the view that the elder is here depending on his rhetorical source, no doubt as a way of corroborating his general antithesis and the lessons he draws from it. The citation is introduced by his own observation, **Little children, you are of God, and have overcome them.** The phrases from the source may be arranged so as to bring out its balance of thought and form:

Vs. 5 (*a*) They are of the world,	Vs. 6 (*a*) We are of God.
(*b*) therefore what they say is of the world,	(*b*) [missing]
(*c*) and the world listens to them.	(*c*) Whoever knows God listens to us.

The writer enforces the last clause (vs. 6*b*) by repeating it in its negative form, and then concludes the whole passage (vss. 1-6) in his own summary: **By this we know the spirit of truth and the spirit of error.** The background of the contrast of those of God and those of the world is found in various passages in the Fourth Gospel. Listening and not listening to Christ's word is the theme of John 8:43, "You cannot bear to hear [ἀκούειν, the same verb] my word" (cf. John 8:47). The world's refusal to **listen to us** has its background also in the teaching of John 15:19, "If you were of the world, the world would love its own; but because you are not of the world, . . . therefore the world hates you" (cf. 3:13). Passages like these make it clear that the term "world" means more (as has been said apropos of 2:15-17) than just the life of men apart from God. It has quasi-metaphysical connotations, as is indicated by its close association with the devil and the Antichrist.

4. The overcoming (of the "false prophets" and the "spirit of antichrist") refers first of all to the rejection of the temptation occasioned by the deceivers, but more

4-6. Victory over Error and Evil.—The dualism of John's thought evident throughout the epistle—the world versus God, Christ versus Antichrist, truth versus error, love versus hatred, belief versus denial—underlies this passage; but now it takes the practical form of antithesis between the two classes of men who in a concrete historical situation exhibit their affinity with **the spirit of truth** or **the spirit of error.** John designates the two classes thus: **Little children, you are of God** and **They are of the world;** and he describes the victory of the former in the words **you . . . have overcome them.**

Any victory assumes a previous struggle, and a good test of the life of a Christian congregation is whether it has ever met head on the challenge of anti-Christian prophets. Of how many Christian congregations could it be said that they have ever overcome anything? Too often churches seem unaware of the need to pitch in and help win the ceaseless struggle going on between the spirits of good and evil in human life, and instead tend to measure their vitality by the test the elder specifically disavows—whether they are successful in persuading the world to listen to them (vs. 5). The temptation the elder commends his hearers for rejecting—too ready accommodation to pagan ways and teaching—is the temptation to which churches so often yield. The bald dualism of John's thought is a wholesome reminder that sometimes sharp lines must be drawn, struggles must be waged, men must stand up and be

5 They are of the world: therefore speak they of the world, and the world heareth them.

6 We are of God: he that knoweth God heareth us; he that is not of God heareth not us. Hereby know we the spirit of truth, and the spirit of error.

greater than he who is in the world. **5** They are of the world, therefore what they say is of the world, and the world listens to them. **6** We are of God. Whoever knows God listens to us, and he who is not of God does not listen to us. By this we know the spirit of truth and the spirit of error.

---

concretely to the withdrawal of the latter from the fellowship (2:19). So the elder interprets the schism reflected also in II and III John. Despite the widespread struggle in the conventicles and churches of the area, "I rejoiced greatly to find some of your children following the truth" (II John 4). This was the victory. It is due to him **who is in you,** i.e., God, who is stronger than the evil one. This has been demonstrated by Christ, who, as he is about to be "lifted up," announces, "Now shall the ruler of this world be cast out" (John 12:31). For this reason the writer can also say: "This is the victory that overcomes the world, our faith" (5:4).

5-6. The assurances of vs. 4 are spoken to counteract any misunderstanding or dismay at the popularity of the heretical teaching. **The world listens to them** because the world loves "its own" (John 15:19). But **whoever knows God listens to us.** In another connection Paul writes that human wisdom is understood by the human spirit but God's wisdom by the Spirit of God. "Now we have received not the spirit of the world, but the Spirit which is from God, that we might understand the gifts bestowed on us by God" (I Cor. 2:11-12). But this "is not a wisdom of this age or of the rulers of this age" (I Cor. 2:6). **By this** (ἐκ τούτου, not the usual formula, ἐν τούτῳ) points back to the whole passage, not to the immediately preceding or following thought.

---

counted and confess what they believe (cf. Expos. on 2:15-17). But while the church struggles it must also be confident of victory. Or more accurately, it must live in the power of the victory Christ has already won (cf. Expos. on 2:12-14; 3:7-10; 5:1b-5).

Apparently the victory of the children of God in this instance issued in the withdrawal of the deceivers from the fellowship of the church (cf. Exeg. on vs. 4), and sometimes outright schism is truly victory. But sometimes schism is tragedy rather than victory. The appeal to tradition to unmask falsely inspired prophets can be misused to expel the truly inspired prophets and can rob the church of that freedom of the Spirit that is its very life. The problem of the tension between authority and freedom, between tradition and inspiration, is most safely solved not by excluding but by reconciling in love and truth those who claim to be inspired. "The Church fares best when apostle and prophet stand together as the firm foundation of its life." [3] The negative response of the world to the message proclaimed by the children of God—**he who is not of God does not listen to us**—points the differences between hearing (KJV) and listening (RSV). Those who are of the world may hear, but they do not listen. How much agony have true prophets

suffered, and how greatly has the redemptive cause of God been hindered, precisely because men refused to listen. However, to expect that the world will refuse to listen is no excuse for making the message of the gospel dull, or for rationalizing one's inability to secure the attention of men. It is true that affinity with truth or error in men's souls will incline them to listen or not listen; but the more inclined men are not to listen the more resourcefully and energetically the church must proclaim its truth.

The power of God is the source of the church's life and the cause of its victories: **he who is in you is greater than he who is in the world.** Believers can confidently say, **We are of God,** and meet all evil in God's invincible strength. At the same time such confidence is saved from becoming pride by understanding that all inheres in God's greatness. The marks of those who are of **the spirit of error** are plain: **They are of the world, . . . what they say is of the world, and the world listens to them. . . . He who is not of God does not listen to us.** All fits together: evil character, false thinking, false speaking, rejection of truth, worldly-mindedness. The worldly man's lips utter what he is. Like seeks like. The world speaks to its own and listens to its own; it has its own language, lives by its own values, bestows its own rewards. Tragically, there is comradeship in evil as in good, in error as in truth.

[3] Dodd, *Johannine Epistles,* p. 106.

7 Beloved, let us love one another: for love is of God; and every one that loveth is born of God, and knoweth God.

7 Beloved, let us love one another; for love is of God, and he who loves is born of

VI. God's Love and Our Confidence: the Witness of the Spirit (4:7–5:12)

This concluding section of the epistle proper does not lend itself easily to outline. The writer here tends to weave together his previous themes, though in a positive form and with special emphasis on the certainties of faith known in the Spirit. In 4:7–5:5 the commandment of love and its larger implications are considered for themselves apart from the polemic aspects which condition the earlier discussion in 3:11-18. Likewise in what follows, the renewed insistence on the true confession and the witness which confirms it (5:6-12), the note is positive, and the elder's thought returns finally to the theme of eternal life with which he began.

A. God's Love and Our Love for One Another (4:7-12)

As 4:1-6 relates to the first rule of the double commandment in 3:23, "We should believe in the name of his Son Jesus Christ," so our present passage develops the second, viz., that we should **love one another.** This rule has already been presented in 3:11-18, where love and hate are contrasted in a larger context dealing with the conditions of confidence before God (2:28–3:24; cf. also 2:9-11; 4:17). In the present passage the motive for mutual love is the knowledge of God and the sharing of his life which that knowledge makes possible. Yet our love is rather the sign of our fellowship with God than its condition. By it is certified our divine sonship. The elevation of the epistle and its freedom from a commonplace moralism are seen in two facts: (*a*) rewards and punishments, as in the teaching of Jesus, are subordinated to higher sanctions; (*b*) the appeal to the will is subordinated to the appeal to spiritual vision or faith. The final ground of all that the writer has had to say about love is now wonderfully brought out in the statement, not only that love is of God, but that God is love. The evidence for these claims is then adduced, together with an appeal for mutual love based on imitation and gratitude.

7. Love is of God: The Gnostics might say that wisdom or power is **of God** but hardly **love,** whose involvements would not fit with the divine detachment. The deity

---

7-12. *Divine and Human Love.*—The word **love** is used as a noun or verb twenty-five times in vss. 6-21, and the concept it expresses—like a symphonic theme with variations—receives here the most beautiful and profound treatment of any passage in the epistle. But observe, the concern that leads the mind of the elder to compose our present passage, and the thought with which he begins and concludes it, is **love one another.** The implications of this injunction culminate in the author's outstanding contribution to Christian theology—the doctrine that **God is love.** At the same time the author's purpose is predominantly hortatory and ethical rather than theological. He is first commending love, not speculating about God. John's mystical apprehension of the nature of God rises to its height in this passage, but still it is informed with intense ethical concern.

(*a*) The statements **love is of God** and **God is love** are basic to a logical understanding of John's thought here and constitute his definition of the essential nature of ultimate Reality.

This definition, however, rests on the Christian revelation of Reality: **The love of God was made manifest among us, that God sent his only Son into the world; . . . he loved us and sent his Son to be the expiation for our sins.** From these issue derivative assurances, injunctions, promises: **He who loves is born of God and knows God; we . . . live through him; . . . we . . . ought to love one another; . . . if we love one another, God abides in us and his love is perfected in us.**

The grandeur of John's insight that God is love and the majesty with which he develops this theme in these verses correct the sentimentality and shallowness with which we often speak of God's love. When one confesses that God is love one is subscribing to nothing less than the Christian view of the universe and of the meaning and destiny of human life. The boldness and loftiness of John's declaration that God is love, further, can be appreciated only when compared with other answers men have made to the question "What is God?" Certain

8 He that loveth not, knoweth not God; for God is love. | God and knows God. 8 He who does not love does not know God; for God is love.

was thought of in paganism as the object of mystical desire (ἔρως) rather than its subject. Vs. 10 constitutes a direct denial of the general Hellenistic view that love is first of all an impulse that goes out from the material to the spiritual order. No, **in this is love . . . that . . . he loved us** (vs. 10). We would not otherwise have known what love is (cf. vs. 19). Therefore **he who loves** shows thereby that he is **born of God and knows God.** He is the true Gnostic! In his love he has an empirical knowledge of God which disposes him to a deepening understanding of God's action and revelation, far superior to any merely rational wisdom or esoteric mysticism.

8. He who does not love has not even *begun* to know God (so the Greek tense implies, as also in I Cor. 8:2: "does not yet know [i.e., begin to know] as he ought to know") **For God is love.** This supreme affirmation is a hard saying even to "men of good will" today, and is one of those things that "the natural man does not receive" and "is

Oriental religions reply that God is a changeless unmoved Being engaged in self-contemplation without concern for human life. Pagan religions have deified fecundity or sexual life force as God. Ancient and modern Hellenism have conceived God as pure Mind, Wisdom, or Beauty. Moralistic religion has conceived God as Righteousness. Ancient and modern science has conceived God as Energy. The insight of Johannine thought (implicit throughout this epistle but explicit in 4:7–5:3) surpasses these in defining God's essential nature as love and represents the highest conception of the divine nature man can hold. This conception, accordingly, requires one to believe that the divine love is eternal and unchangeable; it is "that which was from the beginning" (1:1). It requires one to believe that love governs all other attributes in the Godhead: "To say 'God is love,' implies that *all* His activity is loving activity. If He creates, He creates in love; if He rules, He rules in love; if He judges, He judges in love." [4] One must believe further that God's love is dynamic; it acts and has decisively acted. God's love is not passionless benignity; it has been **made manifest among us; . . . God sent his only Son.** God's love is moral. Our knowledge that God is love depends on the moral mutuality of our lives with our fellow men. (Observe the first person plurals of vss. 7-12.) God's love has its ultimate issue in bringing men to live in his eternal life: **that we might live through him.**

(*b*) John's conception of God as love was the result of his mind's reflecting on the meaning of God's self-revelation in Jesus Christ and on the meaning of that revelation as the apostolic church experienced, verified, and announced it. Thus the declaration in vs. 8 that **God is love** is followed immediately by his setting forth of the Christian basis for that declaration: **In this the love of God was made manifest among us,**

[4] *Ibid.*, p. 110.

that God sent his only Son into the world. . . . **In this is love, not that we loved God but that he loved us and sent his Son to be the expiation for our sins.** John's declaration of the nature of Reality, in other words, rests exclusively on Jesus' historical revelation of Reality. Only within that revelation can one say that God is love, and only within that revelation can one understand how God is love. The Incarnation and Atonement constitute this revelation (cf. Expos. on 1:1-2, 7; 2:2, 20-23; 3:4-10, 16*a*, 23; 4:2). An additional aspect of the Incarnation and Atonement dealt with here lies in John's description of Jesus as God's **only begotten Son.** By the modifier **only begotten** John is conveying the magnitude of God's gift as the measure of his love. The full being of God's nature is conceived as present in Jesus. Other values in life can intimate God's love; only Jesus actually and fully communicates God's love.

John's insight that only within the Christian revelation can men confidently believe that God is love assigns the proper limits to what other areas of human experience can tell us of God and corrects our thinking as we survey them. Nature is often sentimentally interpreted as offering evidence of God's love. But at the most, nature can only establish the existence of God and reveal a divine intelligence, purpose, and energy. So far from witnessing to love in the universe, nature more readily witnesses to cold unconcern or brutal struggle. History cannot be reliably appealed to as evidence of cosmic love. Tragedy, frustration, and destruction loom too prominently. One may be able to infer a supernatural purpose from history; whether or not that purpose is benign is another matter. Man's individual experience in everyday life is indistinct and uneven in its revelation of God's love. The right kind of family life comes closest to assurance of divine love. Jesus appealed thus to family life (Luke 11:11-12). But multitudes of

9 In this was manifested the love of God toward us, because that God sent his only begotten Son into the world, that we might live through him.

10 Herein is love, not that we loved God, but that he loved us, and sent his Son *to be* the propitiation for our sins.

9 In this the love of God was made manifest among us, that God sent his only Son into the world, so that we might live through him. **10** In this is love, not that we loved God but that he loved us and sent his Son

---

not able to understand" (I Cor. 2:14) : (*a*) Love here is not merely an attribute of God but defines his nature, though in a practical rather than philosophic sense. God's nature is not exhausted by the quality of love, but love governs all its aspects and expressions. (*b*) The term used here for **love**—ἀγάπη—is in effect a Christian creation. Greek-speaking Judaism took over the commonplace pagan term to translate Hebrew words expressive of the love of God and the love of neighbor, and the church then filled it with the meanings implicit in the Christian experience. (*c*) The present verse requires a personal view of God, going beyond the dynamic conception of God suggested by the term λόγος, light or spirit, as used in pagan religious teaching at this time. Thus the significance of God, not only for nature and history, but for personal religion and ethics, was revolutionized.

9-10. The love of God was made manifest among us (not **toward us,** KJV; cf. John 1:14). The initiative of God in terms of his **only begotten Son** recalls John 3:16; cf. Rom. 5:8-9. One aspect of vs. 10 is beautifully illustrated in the Odes of Solomon 3:3-4, "I should not have known how to love the Lord, if He had not loved me. For who is

---

people do not enjoy such experience, and human life in its totality includes much evidence that seems to deny divine love. Middleton Murry writes of his reflections when he walked about London during a night air raid in World War I.

> The great city seemed to be washed clean of humanity. . . . The idea that people should love one another, the fact that sometimes they did love one another, and dearly, seemed like a strange dream, out of which I had suddenly awakened. Nothing really mattered. You went on loving . . . just as you went on sleeping, or eating . . . ; but it had not the faintest relevance to the destiny of the universe. A tribe of people had been born with this odd faculty of love; they might just as well have been born with an extra and useless finger . . . : that was the order to which this torturing idiosyncrasy belonged.[5]

Philosophy can speculate that God is love. It can attempt to infer a divine love from the meaning of human love, or magnify human love into an absolute, or posit a benignant, divine being whose nature responds to man's mystical desire, somewhat as pagan and Gnostic thought conceived human love (*erōs*) to be projected toward God (cf. Exeg. on vs. 7). In contrast to the claims offered by these areas of human experience that God is love, Christian faith says with John, **In this the love of God was made manifest, . . . not that we loved God but that**

[5] *Reminiscences of D. H. Lawrence* (New York: Henry Holt & Co., 1933), p. 83.

he loved us. Ultimately the only safe ground on which to believe and assert that God is love is God's self-revelation in Christ. Love as God's nature is thus unconditioned and objectively real, prior in its initiative to man's aspiration, and alone able to satisfy man's craving for God precisely because it antedates and kindles that craving.

(*c*) A theological interpretation of what John means by the declaration that God is love, however, is no more important than understanding the consequences and imperatives that flow from it. **He who loves is born of God.** One might expect John to write, "He who is born of God, loves." Here, however, he reverses his usual train of thought and interprets love as the condition as well as the sign of sonship to God (cf. Exeg. on vs. 7; Expos. on vs. 16). **He who loves . . . knows God. He who does not love does not know God.** (Cf. Expos. on 2:4-5.) These words, originally addressed to Gnostics who pretended to a mystical knowledge of God independent of moral content, mark John's break with pure mysticism and constitute a profound contribution to religion in that they define man's highest destiny in terms of ethical love for his fellow men rather than in terms of mystical contemplation of the deity. "The secret of the LORD is with them that fear him," the O.T. proclaims (Ps. 25:14). John would add, "The secret of the Lord also is with those who love him, and who love their brother." The highest knowledge of God is not gained through in-

11 Beloved, if God so loved us, we ought also to love one another.

12 No man hath seen God at any time. If we love one another, God dwelleth in us, and his love is perfected in us.

to be the expiation for our sins. 11 Beloved, if God so loved us, we also ought to love one another. 12 No man has ever seen God; if we love one another, God abides in us and his love is perfected in us.

---

able to distinguish love, except the one that is loved?" (Cited in A. E. Brooke, *The Johannine Epistles* [New York: Charles Scribner's Sons, 1912; "International Critical Commentary"], p. 119.) Or as Rudolf Bultmann has written, "Only he who is already loved can love, only he who has been trusted can trust, only he who has been an object of devotion can give himself" (*Offenbarung und Heilsgeschehen* [München: Evangelischer Verlag, 1941], p. 58).

11. **Beloved:** The last of the six occasions when this form of address is used, frequently in a context dealing with mutual love, as in this instance. The motive to love here is not only gratitude, but imitation and action proper to those who are the sons of God (Matt. 5:45).

12. Knowing God by the Gnostic path could reach its goal in the claim to behold him in mystic vision. The temerity of this claim is no doubt to be condoned, in view of the fact that some of great nobility of spirit from Plato on have made it. But the Bible, more aware of the disparity between Creator and creature, assigns this goal to the *eschaton* (so Matt. 5:8 of the "pure in heart" and I Cor. 13:12), save in the modified sense of 1:2 and John 14:19. But **if we love one another,** the life of God in its essential character is ours: God abides in us (cf. 3:24). Indeed, **his love is perfected in us** in the

---

tellectual endeavor, devotional exercises, or aesthetic contemplation. These may afford some knowledge. An artist, though morally dissolute, can learn something of God as beauty; a scientist, morally unconcerned for the uses of his discoveries, can learn of the laws and powers of the physical universe and know God as intelligence or energy. But God as love, God as he most essentially is, can be known only by the man whose life is so loving that it morally qualifies him to know. And further, only by such a man can God be *known,* not respected or admired or acknowledged. **Know** means intimacy, fellowship, adoration. In the second century a band of Christians was arraigned before a Roman magistrate who demanded of their bishop, "Who is the God of the Christians?" The bishop's reply laid down the qualification for knowing the God of Christian faith, "If thou art worthy, thou shalt know."

Let us love one another. . . . God is love, . . . he loved us, . . . we also ought to love one another. These words locate the inspiration and motivation for ethical love in the divine *agapē*. Other motives by contrast are seen to be inadequate. Self-interest—enlightened or otherwise—as an ethical rule of life is exposed as inadequate because it contradicts the love of God. "God is reality, and reality is against all who would interpret life by self-love and self-will."[6] The attractiveness or responsiveness of those to be loved is an

inadequate motive. The essence of Christian love is that it is to be directed precisely toward the unlovable, the unlovely, even toward the hostile (cf. Matt. 5:44-48), for such is the character of the love God has revealed to us. The claim of need ranks high in the scale of motives that impel men to love one another. Jesus appealed to this motive in the parable of the good Samaritan (Luke 10:30-37), and John appeals to it in I John 3:17. But the claim of need is known in pagan religion as well as in Christianity, and in humanism and positivism as well as in religion. Moreover, men can be repelled by need as well as be attracted by it; the ratio in the parable of the good Samaritan is significant—only one out of three men on an average can be expected to respond to need. A motive greater than the unreliable emotions of human personality is necessary. An American journalist in China watched a Catholic sister cleansing the gangrenous sores of wounded soldiers in a hospital. "I wouldn't do that for a million dollars," the visitor said. Without pausing in her work the sister quietly replied, "Neither would I." Only the love of God revealed in Christ can inspire man to bring his noblest love to the gravest need. Hope that love will be successful in social terms on the larger scale of history is also an inadequate motive. Naïve, utopian faith in the effective strategy of love is belied by the facts of history. "The final justification for the way of *agapē* in the New Testament is never found in history. The motive

[6] Oman, *Grace and Personality*, p. 225.

| 13 Hereby know we that we dwell in him, and he in us, because he hath given us of his Spirit. | 13 By this we know that we abide in him and he in us, because he has given us |

sense that it is realized or brought into actuality. This is a much greater outcome than the alleged vision of God, which in any case is impossible here (John 1:18) and is only one aspect of the final consummation.

B. The Grounds of Our Confidence (4:13-18)

The writer now establishes the certainty of our abiding in God by bringing together various earlier considerations and combining them all with the present deeper treatment of the theme of love. This certainty is then considered with reference to the great test of the Judgment. These verses are taken as a unit, though the connections backward and forward are very close. In what follows (4:19–5:5) it is not fear, but the alleged difficulty of the commandments, over which our faith and fellowship with God are victorious.

13. By this: The phrase looks forward. Not only does our mutual love prove that God abides in us, but the experience of **his own Spirit** adds a concrete corroboration. So the

to which Christ appeals is always the emulation of God or gratitude for the *agapē* of God.[7]

In contrast to lesser motives and principles is the author's profound insight into the heart of the gospel: **Let us love one another; for love is of God. . . . God is love. . . . He loved us and sent his Son. . . . We also ought to love one another.** This insight expresses the distinctive Christian interpretation of the relation of religion and ethics. For thought, it simultaneously establishes morality in religion and defines religion as inescapably moral. The ultimate sanctions of ethics inhere in divine Reality at the same time that Reality can be known only morally. For the practical decisions and actions of everyday life it defines man's duty and destiny as the conforming of his life to nothing less than the eternal character of the universe: In Jesus' words, "Love . . . that you may be sons of your Father who is in heaven. . . . Be perfect, as your heavenly Father" (Matt. 5:44-45, 48). The purpose of love in the universe is to be fulfilled in every action: **his love is perfected in us,** i.e., brought into actuality, consummated in action. It is in our relations with our fellow men that **God abides in us.** While the vision of God has ever been the goal of man's search, **no man has ever seen God;** vision is not the most important thing; it is subordinate to the real presence of God in the soul. We can have communion with God without vision of God. And this communion is nothing else than the experience of eternal life in everyday life: **that we might live through him.**

13-18. *Great Assurances.*—John's frequent use of the Greek word παρρησία meaning **confidence**

(thirteen usages in the epistles out of thirty-one in the N.T.) signifies a deep conviction, implicit throughout his letters, that comes into clear expression in vss. 13-18, the conviction that people of Christian faith can be certain of living in the eternal life of God if their experience meets specified tests (cf. Expos. on 3:19-24). Thus the language of vs. 13, **By this we know that we abide in him and he in us, because . . .** is characteristic of John's mind and answers to a perennial need in human life—the need to be sure of God and of living in God. In every age man needs to lay hold of Reality on which he can stake his existence and of whose possession he can be indubitably sure, and we can take heart in realizing that Christian people in apostolic times needed to be encouraged as we need to be encouraged, that they as we "out of weakness were made strong" (Heb. 11:34). John proclaims this reality to be the indwelling, eternal life of God, and vss. 13-18 define the tests of its possession.

13. *The Presence of the Spirit.*—The first test is prescribed in vs. 13b: **he has given us of his own Spirit** (for further comment on John's conception of the nature and work of the Spirit cf. Expos. on 2:27; 3:22; 5:7-8, 10a). John's appeal to the presence of God's Spirit in the human soul accents the objective nature of this test and rebukes man's preoccupation with his own subjective moods and feelings. The tense of the verb **has given** also suggests definiteness and certainty; people ought to be able to recognize the Spirit of God as having acted in their lives. The fundamentally religious nature of this test also places in their proper light the conventional, peripheral tests of religious experience commonly appealed to, e.g., nominal church

[7] Niebuhr, *Nature and Destiny of Man,* II, 88.

14 And we have seen and do testify that the Father sent the Son *to be* the Saviour of the world.

15 Whosoever shall confess that Jesus is the Son of God, God dwelleth in him, and he in God.

of his own Spirit. 14 And we have seen and testify that the Father has sent his Son as the Savior of the world. 15 Whoever confesses that Jesus is the Son of God, God

writer recurs to the point touched on at 3:24. As Paul says, "When we cry, 'Abba! Father!' it is the Spirit himself bearing witness with our spirit that we are children of God" (Rom. 8:15-16).

14-15. A third proof to the Christian that **God abides in him, and he in God** is the true confession he makes. The required insight can come only from God. To recognize the Father and his working certifies true sonship. But this proof is closely related to the witness of the Spirit (vs. 13). For it is by God's **own Spirit** that we **testify that the Father has sent his Son** and that any man **confesses that Jesus is the Son of God.** "No one can say 'Jesus is Lord' except by the Holy Spirit" (I Cor. 12:3). It is to such witness of the Spirit that the present writer refers in 5:9, "This is the testimony of God that he has borne witness to his Son."

We have seen and testify expresses the common and abiding witness of the church, as in 1:1-5, and not that of a special group of eyewitnesses. For corroboration note the use of "we" in vss. 13, 14, 16 and in John 1:14, 16. Here the "testimony of men" is added to the "testimony of God" (in the Spirit); cf. 5:9. The form of the confession varies from those employed above ("Jesus Christ has come in the flesh," vs. 2; "Jesus is the Christ," 2:22); Jesus is now seen as **Savior of the world** (cf. John 4:42) and confessed as the **Son of God.** The elder invokes various current formulas of confession understood as typical of the church from the beginning and as embodying insights without which true fellowship with the Father and with one another was impossible.

membership, the acknowledgment of polite society that one is a Christian, etc.

14-15. *Personal and Corporate Testimony.*— **And we have seen and testify. . . . Whoever confesses.** These words point to further grounds of man's confidence of abiding in God, and underscore the importance of testimony in the Christian life. The believer's inward witness of the Spirit is complemented by the external witness of the historical apostolic fellowship. But while one's own Christian assurance can be corroborated by the tradition and heritage of the church, the danger is that the content of tradition will remain secondhand. Every believer must ultimately appropriate, define, and confess his own faith: **whoever confesses.** For in making his testimony, his own confidence is made strong. "Preach faith until you have it," Peter Bohler advised the youthful John Wesley. Confession and testimony also kindle and strengthen the confidence of others. And the issue of true confession is nothing less than communion with God: **Whoever confesses, . . . abides . . . in God.** (Cf. Expos. on 1:1-2.)

14-15. *Jesus, Son of God, and Savior.*—The content of confession again is Christocentric: **The Father has sent his Son as the Savior of**

the world. . . . Jesus is the Son of God. (All that has been previously written of the centrality of the Incarnation in John's thought applies to the confessional formulas here; cf. Expos. on 1:1-2; 2:20-23; 3:16a, 23; 4:2; 5:1a, 10b, 12b.) The redemptive aspect of the Incarnation is distinctively stressed here (as in 2:1-2), together with the universality of the claim that Christ's saviorhood exerts on all men: **Savior of the world.** The church has no more sacred task than to announce this claim, and finds here the dynamic of its missionary endeavor (cf. Expos. on III John 6b-8). Missionary concern, observe, is not something tacked on to the gospel, nor something to be artificially aroused; on the contrary, it inheres in the very purpose and act of God himself—**the Father . . . sent his Son as the Savior of the world**—and in what we have found and declare Christ's saviorhood to be in our own experience—**we have seen and testify.** We proclaim Jesus as Savior to all men because we have known God to save us in him. Nothing less than this can really inspire and sustain the missionary endeavor of the church. Motives of self-interest, political or economic strategy, mere good will or social sympathy, will not suffice. The true motivation of missions lies in the mind

16 And we have known and believed the love that God hath to us. God is love; and he that dwelleth in love dwelleth in God, and God in him.

abides in him, and he in God. **16** So we know and believe the love God has for us. God is love, and he who abides in love

---

16. We know and believe the love God has for us: Note that in this sentence the love of God takes the place of the twofold abiding in vs. 13a above. The writer is interweaving these conceptions. The same two verbs, "know" and "believe," in the same perfect tense occur in John 6:69 and are there translated more meaningfully. Peter replies to Jesus' challenge, "We have believed, and have come to know, that you are the Holy One of God." The passage is relevant since the learning process here too is connected with discernment of the Mediator, **we have seen . . . that the Father has sent his Son** (vs. 14). The second sentence in the verse parallels vs. 12b very closely. The phrase there, "his love is perfected in us" or "comes into actuality in us," brings out vividly the full meaning of the mutual abiding here mentioned. The greatest themes of the epistle are focused in

---

and heart of the eternal God as we have experienced his saving action in our own lives.

16. Living in God's Love.—The note of confidence implicit throughout the epistle rises to its height in the eloquence and boldness of speech of this verse: **So we know and believe the love God has for us. God is love.** The conjunction of **know** and **believe** is significant, and the double emphasis is characteristic of the note of assurance that sounds through the N.T. from beginning to end. The men of the N.T., it has been said,

were simply and magnificently sure. They tell of being "grounded" in the faith; of being built upon a foundation; of having "a hope both sure and steadfast"; of how "the foundation of God standeth sure." These men . . . are sure of something. Their whole message and outlook are grounded on certainty.[8]

The conjunction of **know** and **believe** also reminds us that people can believe in God's love without fully knowing it, and can know God's love without fully believing in all that is bound up with it. Familiarity with the Christian affirmation that God is love has dulled its grandeur and boldness for some people; others hold the assurance of God's love merely as a theological concept, or as hearsay. Conversely, people can know the love of God in their own experience without comprehending fully the belief bound up with it. The metaphysical and ethical implications of God's love for man's thought and life often escape them. The Christian experience of the love of God can be corrected and kept vital and growing only when men both know and believe.

The love God has for us. God is love: The nature of God is again defined substantively

(not adjectivally) as love. The word **love** here is a noun denoting essence (cf. Expos. on vss. 7-12). However, the declaration that God is love is set within the context of thought of union with God, rather than (as in vss. 7-8) of knowledge of God or (as in vs. 12a) of man's ethical love of his fellow men: **he who abides in love abides in God, and God abides in him.** John's feeling for the ethical nature of love is still present. But now, in loftiest strain, the elder's thought rises above even the conception of God's love as something known by the human mind or as apprehended in action by the will. Now love is mystically conceived as the very life of God in the life of man and abiding in love as the union of man's nature with God's nature. This is an unconditioned experience John is writing of, something *sui generis*. The mystical experience of divine love in its fullest dimensions is above knowledge or morality, though it includes both. Only the greatest category of all—the eternal life of God himself—is adequate to comprehend and express it. Such a profound, mystical conception defies analysis and is suggestive rather than logical. Three modes of love are suggested: the love God imparts to us, our love of God, our love to our fellow men. But in whatever relation love becomes real, it is one and the same love and shares the character of the divine *agapē*. The insight that love is of God has led some interpreters to believe that whenever men live in love—whether or not in the distinctively Christian sense of *agapē*—they experience the life of God. "All deep human love strikes down somewhere into the Divine, though it may strike darkly and with a dim feeling after Him who is not far from any one."[9] If love is of a whole and is always of God, whoever loves experiences at least in part the life of God.

---

[8] Raymond Calkins, *The Eloquence of Christian Experience* (New York: The Macmillan Co., 1927), p. 15.

[9] Findlay, *Fellowship in Life Eternal*, p. 370.

17 Herein is our love made perfect, that we may have boldness in the day of judgment: because as he is, so are we in this world.

abides in God, and God abides in him. **17** In this is love perfected with us, that we may have confidence for the day of judgment, because as he is so are we in this world.

---

this verse. It is clear that God is defined as love only in the light of the coming of Christ, and that our love is identified with divine fellowship only as love is understood in this context, i.e., that of the Christian *agapē*.

17. Two corollaries from our abiding in the love of God are now drawn, one with regard to anxiety in face of the Judgment, the other with regard to fear in general. **In this** may refer backward. In that case the meaning is: The perfection of the divine love is achieved among us in the twofold abiding; so great is this love, e.g., that even **in the day of judgment** we shall be boldly confident. **In this,** however, probably looks forward: Our glad boldness **in the day of judgment** (which is even now upon us) is a supreme instance of the full realization of the divine love in our midst. The anguish of the great final confrontation with the Judge cowed the hearts of these Christians (2:28-29; 3:19-20). Since the Antichrist was at work, the coming of the Lord was imminent. Confidence at his appearing is assured in 2:28 to those who "abide in him." For those who are like the Judge have nothing to fear from him (2:29). So here: **We may have confidence for the day of judgment, because as he is so are we.** We are like him (though we are **in this world** while he is so no longer), since we too abide in God and love one another. The thought of our peace of heart in the Judgment has its direct relevance to those occasions in which the modern Christian finds his conscience shaken by the judgments of

---

Nevertheless, in John's thought Christian confession and human experience must be kept together. The significance of the parallelism of vss. 15, 16 must be borne in mind: **Whoever confesses . . . Jesus, . . . abides . . . in God; . . . he who abides in love abides in God.** The Christian revelation of the meaning of love is not intolerant, but it is unique. Its relation to other forms of love is one of correction and fulfillment. All other kinds of love must be measured against the decisive revelation of the perfect love men behold in Jesus, which surpasses and crowns all that men have meant by love in word or act before or since.

17. *Confidence Before Divine Judgment.*— Abiding in love brings **confidence for the day of judgment.** John's expectation of a literal, imminent judgment was not historically fulfilled; but his conception of human life as essentially transient, as being ever exposed to divine judgment, and as ultimately to be confronted with final judgment, is timelessly valid (cf. Expos. on 2:15-17; 2:28–3:3). John's concept of the Day of Judgment may be paralleled in our thinking by the prospect of death. And death can be confidently faced—as John declared the early Christians could confidently face the Second Coming—only if men live in the eternal life of God by abiding in love. (Two qualities of such love are specified here: **perfected,** i.e., being brought into full reality; and Christlike, **as he is so are we in this world.**) It is healthy and necessary to face the fact that we

shall die, but it is not healthy or necessary to fear dying. Fear of death is best overcome when set within the context of Christian faith and Christian ethics—the faith that God is love and the experience of eternal life through living in ethical love. When men thus believe and live, one can say of them what was said of the early Christians—that one could talk to them about dying without modulating into the minor key. But in one sense man is even now being judged with the same judgment he will encounter at death, in that the reality of his moral situation is known by God, and in that man's duty is to know that situation as far as he can, i.e., "walk in the light" (1:7). Thus when a man consciously lives in the spirit of Christian love—and John would have us believe that we can know whether or not we are living in love—he is living as God intends him morally to live, and he is saved from fear of judgment.

Anxiety caused by crises in our personal experience also parallels the anxiety man feels in facing judgment (cf. Expos. on vs. 17). Adversity, temptation, persecution, suffering, are forms of judgment in that they lay bare the precariousness of human life and test and reveal character. Confidence in meeting such experiences again rises from love. The solution of all problems and the resolution of all difficult situations usually will be found to lie ultimately in meeting life with the spirit of love. Trust in God's love, love of God through all experiences of suffering and adversity, love manifest in a

18 There is no fear in love; but perfect love casteth out fear: because fear hath torment. He that feareth is not made perfect in love.

18 There is no fear in love, but perfect love casts out fear. For fear has to do with punishment, and he who fears is not perfected

---

God in our own time, and in his own private circumstances. "Can thine heart endure . . . in the days that I shall deal with thee?" (Ezek. 22:14.)

18. The elder presents one after another all but impossible levels of Christian attainment: the fixed conviction that God is love and only love; unshaken confidence in the *hora novissima* when "men shall go into the caves of the rocks, and into the holes of the earth, from before the terror of Jehovah, and from the glory of his majesty (Isa. 2:19 ASV) ; and now **perfect love** which **casts out fear.** And yet these ideals do not here seem unreal or fanatical, so persuasively grounded are they in the victorious life of the church. The epistle describes a moral stature and human greatness such that the perennial foes of mankind, in particular here **fear,** are dwarfed or banished. Since fear shrinks away while love unites, there can be **no fear in love;** at least **perfect love casts** it out. Since it is the love and fear of God which are chiefly in view, **fear has to do with** his **punishment,** and is an aspect of his discipline (literally, **fear hath torment**). But as the preceding verse has made clear, the one **who fears** is he who **is not perfected in love** and therefore shrinks away from God.

---

will resolved to seek the good of others at cost to oneself, love of others driving out all self-pity —love in these and other ways makes for confidence. "There is nothing that so lifts a man, . . . so arms him for the battle of life, as a pure and noble passion of the heart." [1]

John's conception of judgment is also paralleled in human experience by events in certain epochs of history when the evil resident in life is revealed in its power and consequences, and disaster for man and his works results. The wars, revolutions, and crises, the despair, confusion, and disintegration of man's moral and cultural life in our century, must be interpreted as the reaction of a moral universe to human sin and as judgment at work in and through the events of history. The difficulty of meeting these events with confidence is underscored by the anxiety and despair evident in much modern drama, poetry, art, philosophy, and in the alarming increase in mental disease and suicide. Significantly, our age has been called a neurotic age. The only final source of confidence for living with dignity and serenity in an age of anxiety is the eternal life of God—appropriated through faith and love—that transcends time and history. Without self-righteousness and yet with confidence, the Christian man can meet history's days of judgment knowing that his mortal life is hid in the safety of the eternal life of God.

18. Love Overcomes Fear.—Punishment by God at the Day of Judgment is one construction of this verse. Love casts out such fear in that through abiding in love man experiences God's

[1] *Ibid.*

love to be so essential and comprehensive in his divine character that nothing is possible to him except the forgiveness, discipline, and correction of a loving Father. As by loving people we become experimentally assured of the goodness behind their actions toward us, so by living in love we become assured of the goodness of God's actions toward us. The more two people love each other the less they will be likely to be afraid of what the other may do, and the more we are perfected in love the less we become afraid of God.

In a wider, semipsychological sense **love casts out fear.** Fear, the most self-centered of all emotions, can be analyzed as a heightened awareness of self occasioned by what are deemed to be threats to the self. Thus our classification of various kinds of fear is actually a classification of various kinds of threats to the self, e.g., claustrophobia, monophobia, myctophobia, pathophobia. The cure for fear lies partly in eliminating external threats to the security of the self; but it lies more in eliminating excessive consciousness of the self. Love supremely does this. The essence of love is self-denial and self-surrender, outgoingness from self into life and people and God. Love thus casts out fear because it casts out unhealthy self-consciousness. It organizes personality on a higher, wider plane than self-centeredness; it unites the self with man and God. Indeed, the principle may be laid down that the presence of fear in human personality denotes ethical and religious maladjustment somewhere—in John's words, **he who fears is not perfected in love.**

In man's social life, in relations between

19 We love him, because he first loved us.

in love. 19 We love, because he first loved

C. The Children of God and His Commandments (4:19–5:5)

If our abiding in the love of God lifts us above every kind of fear, it also reassures us as we recognize the difficulty of God's commandments. His judgment will be based on his requirement of love, but neither requirement nor judgment need intimidate us. For in responding to his love we have been **born of God,** born from above, and have taken on his nature. But **whatever is born of God overcomes the world,** whether its fear or its selfishness or its disobedience. But this rebirth and overcoming all hang upon our being able to recognize God's love in Christ. Hence the emphasis upon the true confession that Jesus is **the Christ** (5:1) and **the son of God** (5:5). This leads in the following section to the elder's final clarification of the confession.

19. To prepare for this second reassurance the elder returns to his insistence on the priority of God's love for us (vss. 10-11), **We love, because he first loved us.** (The KJV's **we love him** follows an inferior reading.)

---

groups and classes and nations—as between individuals—love casts out fear. Want of love, evident in suspicion, duplicity, hatred, and aggression, begets fear. Most of the tensions between classes and races in society are basically rooted in fear, and only love expressed in imaginative sympathy, fair-mindedness, and good will can cast out fear. Fear itself is a form of punishment. It is the painful consciousness of a wrong relation to God and to man. But while John writes penetratingly of fear and love, observe that he never appeals to fear in order to persuade men to love. On the contrary, he appeals to love in order to dispel fear. This insight rebukes those who would threaten men into being saved or terrorize them into being virtuous. In religion as everywhere else the appeal to fear is unhealthy and self-defeating. In the profoundest sense only **love casts out fear.**

4:19–5:5. *Necessity of Faith and Love.*—Belief and love comprise the heart of the gospel for John, and as they underlie the Christian life in general so they provide the basis of Christian confidence in particular (cf. 3:19-23; 4:14-18). The highest form of confidence—developed in this passage—the ability to keep God's commandments and to overcome the world (cf. 2:15-17), likewise depends on belief and love: **Every one who believes, . . . and every one who loves . . . is born of God [and] overcomes the world.**

19. *We Love, Because He First Loved Us.*— This verse cites the act of divine revelation in which the Christian believes, and through which has been expressed and defined the character of the love he practices. The priority of God's love to man's (**he first loved us**) means that the primal love of the universe is the ground of human love. The word **first** has in part the meaning of "from the beginning" (1:1), and

suggests the eternal unconditioned character of God's love. While God loved us in a decisive act in the incarnation and atonement of Christ, he has always been loving. His existence and nature have never been anything other than love. But his love is not a general benevolence shed forth on all creation; it is the personal love of a personal God for persons: **We love, because he first loved us.** "Love is a personal thing, called out by persons, and exercised by persons. . . . Nothing but a personal Incarnation, and the self-sacrifice of the Incarnate, could either adequately reveal the love of God for man, or call forth the love of man to God." [2]

But God's love is prior to man's love in terms of action as well as of existence. Elsewhere John has used nouns to describe God's love (4:7-8); here he uses the active verb, and in the aorist tense, **he first loved us.** Christianity is distinguished from all other religions—even from those which ascribe love in varying degree to the Godhead—by the act of God in entering into the world, into history and time, and despite man's unlovableness and hostility, actively undertaking his salvation. God's action thus sets before man the decisive event of history, and on man's response of faith depends his own destiny and likewise the destiny of human society. Man's love is accordingly but response to God's love; and without God's act man would stand there unsaved and despairing. Only the action of God could inspire man to believe or love: **We love because he first loved us.** "Because" implies causation. But as God's love was most manifest in an act, so man's love is truly love only when it is action. Love as emotional pity or a philosophical concept does not share

[2] W. R. Inge, "Confessio Fidei," *Outspoken Essays,* 2nd Ser. (New York: Longmans, Green & Co., 1922), p. 46.

20 If a man say, I love God, and hateth his brother, he is a liar: for he that loveth not his brother whom he hath seen, how can he love God whom he hath not seen?

21 And this commandment have we from him, That he who loveth God love his brother also.

us. 20 If any one says, "I love God," and hates his brother, he is a liar; for he who does not love his brother whom he has seen, cannot[h] love God whom he has not seen. 21 And this commandment we have from him, that he who loves God should love his brother also.

[h] Other ancient authorities read how can he.

20-21. The passage 4:20–5:3 constitutes a digression challenging the false pretension of the loveless schismatics, **I love God,** after the manner of 1:6 and 2:4, where similar claims are repudiated: "We have fellowship with him"; "I know him." What distinguishes the present argument is that, in keeping with this climactic theme of the espistle, it is formulated in terms of the love of God, whereas the earlier discussion was in terms of light and darkness, truth and falsehood (yet see 2:5a).

He who does not love his brother whom he has seen, cannot love God whom he has not seen. This follows from the fact that "God is love" and that all love is "of God." (The reading in the KJV, **How can he love God?** is probably to be rejected.) The theme, which reminds us of Matt. 25:40, sets a question mark over against all religion dissociated from ethical expression. "Feelings may be delusive. The proof that love is real, in the full Christian sense, lies in the overt action to which it leads (cf. iii. 17 . . .). There is no real love to God which does not show itself in obedience to His commands" (Dodd, *Johannine Epistles,* p. 123). In support of the test the double great commandment (Matt. 22:37-39) is invoked in vs. 21.

---

the character of God's love. But when man loves as God loves, his love has the power and vitality and authority of the universe behind it. Let it be remembered, in the active struggles and labors and decisions of everyday life, that the Divine is not only loving, love is also divine; that Omnipotence is not only loving, love is also omnipotent. Does not history verify this truth? Love has reached the height of power and sanctity when it has been motivated by God's love in Christ. Other noble acts and expressions of love, e.g., the life and death of Socrates, do not attain the grandeur nor avail with the power of Christ's.

Our personal experience corroborates John's insight that **we love, because he first loved us.** As John could not have written this sentence unless he had found it true in his own heart, so we cannot comprehend its meaning until it has been brought to pass in our own experience. Here also the "we" of apostolic witness must become the "I" of personal experience: "I love, because he first loved me."

4:20-21. *The Test of Love for God.*—These verses offer a permanently valid test of religious experience. The logic is simple, clear, and inescapable: the proof of love of God is love of one's brother, and nothing less than the fundamental commandment of Christianity (Matt. 22:37-39) is invoked (4:21). Types of relations that falsify the claim of loving God are outright

hatred (4:20a), want of love of one's brother in general, want of love of a specific individual, want of love of a specific individual who stands in the relationship of a brother in Christ (5:1-2). The condemnation pronounced on him who loves falsely is twofold: First, **he is a liar,** i.e., a hypocrite, a man who lives in self-deception, one who consciously or unconsciously is living in illusion and unreality. Secondly, he **cannot love God;** hatred or want of ethical love disqualifies a man for life with God; he is rendered unable—he **cannot love God.** Christian *agapē* possesses a unity; it is of such a nature that failure to love in one relationship cancels love in other relationships and brings a man ultimately into death (3:14). The blunt realism of John's thought in these verses exposes all forms of false religion (cf. also 1:6; 2:4, 9, 22; 3:14b, 15, 17; 4:3, 8; 5:10b). While his interpretation of Christianity is generally speculative, mystical, theological, he yet makes all to depend on what one does ethically about people, and even more practically on how one lives with the people with whom one associates in everyday life. Religion as intellectual knowledge or creedal affirmation, as psychological hygiene or aesthetic appreciation of beauty, as emotional feeling or devotional practice, must come to terms with **the commandment we have from him, that he who loves God should love his brother also.**

5 Whosoever believeth that Jesus is the Christ is born of God: and every one that loveth him that begat loveth him also that is begotten of him.

5 Every one who believes that Jesus is the Christ is a child of God, and every one who loves the parent loves the child.

5:1. The chapter division here is misleading. The elder knows how to appeal to common observation. In vs. 20 above he refers to the very human preference we have for those who are near us over those who are out of our sight. Here he cites a popular adage, "Love the parent, love the child." In the present connection it means that the love of God and the love of the Christian brother (individually and in the singular here) go together. For the latter is **born of God** and his true confession evidences it (cf. John 1:12-13). No one, on the other hand, who denies that **Jesus is the Christ** "has the Father" (2:22-23), i.e., can claim that he loves the Father. Only "he who confesses the Son has the Father also" (2:23). To believe, here, means to give assent to a doctrine; but the parallel uses of the verb show that moral insight and commitment are included.

5:1a. The Necessity of Faith.— (Cf. Expos. on 2:20-23; 3:23; 4:2, 14-15; 5:4b-5, 10b, 12b.) Whereas doing righteousness in 3:7-10 and love of one's fellow men in 4:7 are declared to be evidence of sonship to God, here belief in Jesus as the Christ is declared to render a man a child of God. Man can enter into certain kinds of relation with God in other ways than by belief in Christ. The philosopher can be convinced by thought that ours is a theistic universe; the artist can know God as beauty; the moralist can know God to be moral. But only God's self-revelation in Christ laid hold on by faith can bring man in his total being—with his mind and emotions and will—into the intimate experience of God's life and love that Christianity describes with the figure of Father and child. Further, only faith that Jesus is the Christ, and the truth revealed to such faith, can convince men that this world is really a home, that people are meant to live in it together as a family, and that the noblest pattern of family life is the pattern of God's purpose for human society.

1b-5. Ways of Loving God.—When man believes that Jesus is the Christ he enters into the distinctive solidarity of Christian fellowship, and love of the brethren prevails: **every one who loves the parent loves the child.** As in a human family, he who loves the parent who begat him naturally loves the other children whom his father has begotten, so every Christian who is a child of God through faith loves his fellow Christians because he loves his heavenly Father. The elder's use of this analogy upholds a beautiful ideal for the church and by contrast shames the church for all want of tenderness in the relations of its members. As children's quarrels, jealousy, vanity, disfigure family life and wound parents' hearts, so they injure the unity of the church and wound God's heart. Within groups in a congregation, between congregations, between denominations, as lovelessness is a denial of the faith and an offense to God, so love is proof of faith and a cause of joy to God. But surely this ideal should not be confined to the Christian church alone. Is it not also the ideal for all humanity?

But as love of God becomes real when it is expressed in love for man, so the converse also can be said to be true: that love of man becomes most real and fruitful when it is rooted in love of God: **By this we know that we love the children of God, when we love God. . . . For this is the love of God, that we keep his commandments.** The inseparability of the two forms of love here—ethical and religious—justifies the observation that except for passing references in 2:5, 15, only in this verse in the entire epistle does John write specifically of man's love to God as determinative of his love to his fellow man. This fact rather conclusively indicates that the gravest problem John faced was immoral antinomianism among the heretical schismatics he has in mind. But at the same time it proves that his deep ethical concern—evident throughout the epistle—is not so much a reaction provoked by a particular historical situation as an essential part of his total conception of the gospel. Men have loved God in many ways. Philosophy speaks of *amor intellectualis Dei,* the love of the intellect for God. Mysticism speaks of the affectional love of God: "He may be fully loved who cannot be defined . . . . By the affection He may be secured and kept, but by the thought never." [3] Medieval symbolism liked to stress the place of mystical, affectional love of God by characteristically placing near God in painting and sculpture the cherubim—the spirits of divine knowledge—but nearer still, the seraphim—the spirits of adoring love. Surely the devotion of the mystic and the mind of the

[3] *The Cloud of Unknowing* (New York: Harper & Bros., 1948), p. 36.

2 By this we know that we love the children of God, when we love God, and keep his commandments.

3 For this is the love of God, that we keep his commandments: and his commandments are not grievous.

2 By this we know that we love the children of God, when we love God and obey his commandments. 3 For this is the love of God, that we keep his commandments. And his commandments are not burdensome.

2-3a. If "every one who loves the parent loves the child" (vs. 1), then **we know** [that] **when we love God we** [also] **love the children of God. By this** refers backward. Our knowledge here is based on the analogy of the family. The usual interpretation deduces our love of one another from our love of God, but this does not agree with the elder's usual view (cf. 3:14, 17-19; 4:20). For him our love to man is the test of our love of God, though he certainly thinks of the two as inseparable. The analogy of family love in vss. 1b-2 is safeguarded by the closing clause of vs. 2. The love of the divine Father requires also that we **obey his commandments** (Greek: ποιῶμεν; not τηρῶμεν, **keep,** as in the KJV). **For this is the love of God** (i.e., love to God), **that we keep** (τηρῶμεν, with the sense of cherish) **his commandments.** Love and obedience go together (cf. 2:5; II John 6; John 14:15, 21).

3b-4. Here the thought of the difficulty of God's commandments arises and the elder again offers reassurance as he has already done in connection with the Judgment. The Gospels speak paradoxically of the ethic they enjoin: "Unless your righteousness exceeds that of the scribes and Pharisees, you will never enter the kingdom of heaven" (Matt. 5:20); and yet, "They bind heavy burdens, hard to bear, and lay them on men's shoulders"

---

scholar belong within the order of saints. Nevertheless, the noblest way of loving God lies in action of the will. But ethical action of the will becomes Christian love only when it is impelled by the prior love of God. E.g., philanthropy without religion is good; but philanthropy inspired by religion is better. Children in a Chinese village declined to accept needed medicines offered them by a government station, and instead walked an extra distance to get them from a missionary. On being asked why, they replied, "The medicines are the same, but the hands are different." Service motivated and governed by the love of God is different. But love manifest in acts of the will still is not enough. One must distinguish between action and resolution of the will. This distinction may be taken as one interpretation of the two different verbs John uses in 5:2-3, **obey his commandments, keep his commandments** (cf. Expos. on 2:3-6; 3:23). **Obey** means occasional acts; **keep** means permanently to resolve upon, to cherish. Men of prayer often speak of "willing" God's will as well as of "doing" God's will. To do God's will is not always the same as desiring God's will; and desiring God's will is not the same as willing his will. To keep and obey God's commandments alone is to love God with the commitment of our total being.

And his commandments are not burdensome (cf. Expos. on 2:7-8). The Christian man has been born of God, and **whatever is born of God overcomes the world.** Because the believer shares

God's nature he is endowed with God's power to obey God's commands. Christian experience corroborates this truth. The true saint is one who by nature finds it harder to disobey than to obey God; he so lives in the nature of God that to fulfill God's commandments is as natural as it was previously to deny them. Christianity affirms that the deepest truth about human nature is that man is made for obedience to God's commandments, and that his peace and happiness lie in surrendering his being to God alone. Jesus' metaphors—the wearing of the yoke, the bearing of the cross, the driving of the plow—tell us that man does not become his best until a demand is placed upon him which he accepts. The analogy of family life also illumines this truth about human nature. An eminent psychiatrist has said that children need rules and discipline for emotional health as much as they need bread and butter for physical health. So the children of God need the discipline of commandments for spiritual and moral health. The word "discipleship," practically as well as grammatically, implies discipline. The paradox that God's commandments are not burdensome also illumines the nature of man's freedom. While the possibility of freedom lies in the fact of man's free will, freedom itself is an achievement that results when a person out of freedom of choice submits himself to God. Any lesser object to which submission is made—the state, mammon, pleasure—does not really free man. God's commandments are not burdensome in

4 For whatsoever is born of God overcometh the world: and this is the victory that overcometh the world, *even* our faith.

4 For whatever is born of God overcomes the world; and this is the victory that over-

---

(Matt. 23:4). Jesus speaks of the narrow gate and the extreme sacrifice. Yet he is quoted as saying, "My yoke is easy, and my burden is light" (Matt. 11:30; cf. Deut. 30:11-14). The Christian yoke can be spoken of as easy partly because so far as it is a law it is a "law of liberty" (Jas. 1:25) or a law in the performance of which one feels oneself free. In Paul's terms the "law of Christ" means freedom from law. But the deeper explanation lies in the endowment of the disciple with the powers of the age to come, or with the Spirit, or in Johannine language with the new birth: **For whatever is born of God overcomes the world.** This is stated here with the utmost generality: the subject is in the neuter; the verb is in the present tense. The elder is citing his source. The basic insight is that whatever represents the expression of the divine life and light necessarily vanquishes death and darkness. The true reality necessarily vanquishes the lie. God and whatever was in the beginning with God necessarily vanquishes the world. This general principle is articulated in the epistle with reference to particular forms of the "world" and its resistance: (a) It is appealed to with reference to the overcoming of sin (as here) in 3:9, "No one born of God commits sin; for God's nature ["seed" KJV] abides in him, and he cannot sin because he is born of God" (cf. 5:18). (b) It is cited with reference to the work of the Antichrist in the church in 4:4. (c) In John 16:33 Jesus' words, "I have overcome the world," refer first of all to its "tribulation" but also to everything connoted by the "world." Something of this larger meaning is implied in vss. 4b and 5 here.

The second part of vs. 4 relates the universal principle to the experience of the readers and the household of faith generally. **Victory:** metonymy for "means of victory."

---

that they alone among all other claims comprehend man's deepest need and serve his largest good. Can we not say that God's need of man's obedience is as great as man's need of God's commands? The love of God is manifest in this, it has been said, that he chose to limit his divine freedom and imperil his divine purpose by according to man freedom to obey or disobey his divine will. His love as his will thus needs the obedience of our wills. As our hearts are restless until they find rest in God, so God's heart is restless until we permit him to possess us; and as in his service is our perfect freedom, so in our service is his freedom made perfect.

This is the victory that overcomes the world, our faith. Who is it that overcomes the world but he who believes that Jesus is the Son of God? The declaration that faith in Jesus as the Son of God enables the believer to overcome the world is comprehended in its full meaning only when all that John means by **the world** is recalled from the general content of the epistle (but specifically from 2:15-17; 4:1-6), and when his vivid figure of "the whole world" as lying "in the power of the evil one" (5:19) is anticipated. For **the victory that overcomes** matches at every point the assaults and temptations of **the world.** It is victory of joy over unhappiness (1:4); of fellowship over loneliness (2:19; 3:13; 4:5); of honesty over moral pride and self-deception (1:6-10); of righteousness and holiness over sin (2:1-2, 12-13; 3:8-10; 5:18); of purity over worldly lusts (2:15-17); of truth over error (2:20-27; 4:1-6; 5:20); of confidence over fear, doubt, and discouragement (2:28; 3:2, 19-22; 4:17-18; 5:10, 14); of love over hatred (2:10; 3:14-18; 4:7-21); of eternal life over time and death (1:2; 2:17, 25; 3:14; 4:9, 16-17; 5:11-13, 20). The attack the world delivers upon man comes in many ways from within and without: from evil inclinations and primal passions from within which, if unconquered by divine power, align man with demonic evil and bring about his destruction; and from without, in such forms as hostility (3:13), temptation (2:15; 5:21), persecution, and martyrdom (3:16). But the battlefield on which the believer overcomes the world is ultimately not that of thought or theology but the sphere of his daily living. John's metaphysical conception of the world must not be permitted to obscure the fact that it is on the battlefield of ordinary circumstances that Christian faith wins or loses, and the crown of Christian character is gained or lost.

4b-5. Faith Is the Victory.—Victory is won by faith, and **he who believes that Jesus is the Son of God . . . overcomes.** This profound concep-

5 Who is he that overcometh the world, but he that believeth that Jesus is the Son of God?

6 This is he that came by water and blood, *even* Jesus Christ; not by water only, but by water and blood. And it is the Spirit that beareth witness, because the Spirit is truth.

comes the world, our faith. 5 Who is it that overcomes the world but he who believes that Jesus is the Son of God?

6 This is he who came by water and blood, Jesus Christ, not with the water only but with the water and the blood.

Thus, **our faith,** in the sense of both belief and discernment with the accompanying endowment of "life," is the means by which we *have overcome,* or by which we *definitely overcome,* **the world.** (The verb **overcomes** is in the aorist tense.) The victory gained over the schismatics (4:4) is part of what is meant.

5. Who is it that overcomes? Now the great principle is related to the individual, and in the form of a direct question; and **our faith** (vs. 4) is formulated as in 4:15, supplementing the confession of 5:1. This leads to the next section in which the truth and the meaning of the confession are established.

D. THE WITNESS OF THE SPIRIT (5:6-12)

In this section the meaning of the true confession is brought out against erroneous views: it is insisted that Jesus was not only a Spirit-filled Revealer but a Redeemer who particularly through his death made the eternal life of God available to men. The validity of the true confession is then referred to the witness of God himself, offered both in the gospel story and in the life of the church. We shall follow the verse enumeration of the KJV rather than the RSV.

6a. Jesus Christ **came by water and blood** (omitting with KJV and RSV the addition "and Spirit," found in the Sinaitic and Alexandrine codices and elsewhere); the emphasis in 6*b* shows that there were those who denied that he came *by* **blood** and *with* **the blood.** The two Greek prepositions whose difference is indicated here in the RSV are significant: (*a*) Christ came into his power and authority *by* his baptism with water on which occasion the Holy Spirit descended upon him, *and by* the baptism of his passion (Luke 12:50), which was the hour in which he was glorified (John 17:1-5; cf. Rom. 1:4). (*b*) Christ came **with the water and the blood,** i.e., he brought these, and what they stood for, viz., the benefits of baptism and the Lord's Supper. The **water,** therefore, stands for Christ's own endowment with the Spirit *and* his gift of the Spirit to the church (John 3:5). **The**

---

tion exposes the shallowness of other ways in which men try to deal with their perennial foes. Flight from the world, misreading life to persuade oneself that evil is nonexistent, anesthetizing oneself with literature or art, distracting oneself with pleasure or cynical bargains struck with the world—these turn out to be futile. Or stoical courage, mere optimism that the good in life will arithmetically outbalance evil, trust in luck, faith in progress, confidence in oneself and one's powers—these also do not avail. To those who attempt in these ways to deal with the world, Christianity offers the invitation of faith in Jesus as **the Son of God.** But such faith is faith in the total Christian revelation and all that religiously and ethically is bound up with it. Above all, it means appropriating and living in the very life of God himself, which alone delivers man from evil, time, and mortality.

6-12. *Evidence for the Incarnation.*—The key to understanding this rather difficult passage lies in the author's concern to cite the evidence for the truth of the Incarnation. Faith in the Incarnation has just been declared to be the means and pledge of victory over the world (vss. 4-5), and its truth cannot be too strongly attested. The truth John invites men to confess is declared in the opening and closing words of this passage: **He . . . came, . . . Jesus Christ. . . . And . . . God gave us eternal life . . . in his Son.** The remainder of the passage amplifies and certifies this declaration; it explains the ways in which believers find it to be real; and it describes the consequences that issue from accepting or rejecting it.

6. *Significance of the Crucifixion.*—Before he marshals his evidence, however, John pauses to stress the relation of Jesus' death to the Incarnation: Jesus Christ came **not with the water only**

7 For there are three that bear record in heaven, the Father, the Word, and the Holy Ghost: and these three are one.

7 And the Spirit is the witness, because the

---

blood stands for Christ's entrance into his supreme power and glory *and* for the benefits of his death (cf. 1:7) available to the church, especially in the Supper. Emphasis is placed upon Christ's coming **by** and **with the blood** (cf. John 19:34-35), since his death on the Cross or its significance was denied by the Docetists and the followers of the Baptist, as well as by other groups.

6b (7 in RSV). Here the Spirit as it operates both in the heart of the believer and in the life of the church is defined as **the witness,** testifying to the true manner of Christ's coming and to the benefits so conferred (cf. 3:24; 4:13). It is because the **Spirit is truth**— and not "of error" (4:6)—that he bears witness to Jesus Christ "come in the flesh" (4:2). We are reminded of Christ's parting discourse with his disciples in the Gospel of John: "But when the Counselor comes, whom I shall send to you from the Father, even the Spirit of truth, who proceeds from the Father, he will bear witness to me" (John 15:26).

7. This verse in the KJV is to be rejected (with RSV). It appears in no ancient Greek MS nor is it cited by any Greek father; of all the versions only the Latin contained it, and even this in none of its most ancient sources. The earliest MSS of the Vulg. do not have it. As Dodd (*Johannine Epistles,* p. 127n) reminds us, "It is first quoted as a part of I John by Priscillian, the Spanish heretic, who died in 385, and it gradually made its way

---

but with the water and the blood (cf. 2:22-23). This emphatic parenthesis is aimed at the heretics who maintained that it was impossible and incredible that God should suffer and that Jesus' passion was not an essential part of salvation. John's blunt repudiation of this heresy is part of the great doctrinal struggle the church has often fought to preserve the central truth of the gospel—that Calvary reveals the suffering love of God as well as the loving suffering of a man.

Father, if He, the Christ, were Thy Revealer,
  Truly the First Begotten of the Lord,
Then must Thou be a Suff'rer and a Healer,
  Pierced to the heart by the sorrow of the sword.

Then must it mean, not only that Thy sorrow
  Smote Thee that once upon the lonely tree,
But that to-day, to-night, and on the morrow,
  Still it will come, O Gallant God, to Thee.[4]

But the elder's emphasis on Jesus' passion is also a corrective to certain tendencies among the early Christians to believe that metaphysical or mystical knowledge of God is salvation. In their endeavor to absorb what was of value in Hellenistic thought, and to use and shape Gnostic categories to their own purposes, the early church was tempted to emphasize the revelatory —as distinguished from the redemptive—meaning of the Incarnation. But John profoundly saw that Jesus came not merely as Enlightener

[4] G. A. Studdert-Kennedy, "The Suffering God," from *The Unutterable Beauty.* Used by permission of Hodder & Stoughton, Ltd., and Harper & Bros., publishers.

(with the water) but above all as Redeemer (with . . . the blood), that men need to be saved not from ignorance as much as from sin, that man's need lies not so much in deficiency of knowledge as in corruption of character and enslavement of will, and that the most basic category with which to interpret and understand the meaning of Christ must include his death as well as his birth and life. So today man's trouble is not that the darkness of his mind needs to be taken away; it is that his guilt must be removed, his passions cleansed, and his will possessed and redirected by God. "There was that in the . . . Love of God which water could not, which only blood could express. There was that in the need of man which water could not, which only blood could adequately meet."[5]

7-8. *The Threefold Witness.*—Having thus made explicit the redemptive meaning of the Incarnation, the author cites the evidence that attests to its validity: **There are three witnesses, the Spirit, the water, and the blood.** These witnesses may first be understood as referring to historical events and manifestations through which the eternal life of God was communicated and made known to men in Jesus. The Spirit decisively entered into history in our Lord's birth, baptism, ministry, death, and resurrection. **The spirit is the truth,** and truth has once and for all been revealed in its full nature in Christ. Men experienced the Spirit of God before Jesus, but never so fully and really as after Jesus. The water signifies the event of Jesus' baptism, and

[5] Law, *Tests of Life,* p. 122.

8 And there are three that bear witness in earth, the spirit, and the water, and the blood: and these three agree in one.

Spirit is the truth. 8 There are three witnesses, the Spirit, the water, and the blood;

---

into MSS of the Latin Vulgate until it was accepted as part of the authorized Latin text." (For a fuller statement see Brooke, *Johannine Epistles,* pp. 154-65) . The mention in the true text (vs. 8) of the **three witnesses** which **agree** naturally led to an interpretation along trinitarian lines, and this occasioned the present gloss which appears in various forms in MSS and quotations from the fifth century on.

8. Thus **three witnesses** are now identified, **the Spirit, the water, and the blood.** In the life of the church this meant the objective evidences of the true understanding of the faith: in holy inspiration, in the rite of baptism, and in the rite of the Lord's Supper. No doubt the terms had a more mystical connotation, however, suggested not only by the Johannine teaching concerning the water of life and the cleansing blood (1:7), but by the quasi-Gnostic ideas which lay back of them. The elder finally rests his case on the surpassing force and self-evidencing authenticity of the Christian experience. It is for this reason that he has declared that "the Spirit is truth," i.e., reality, whether known in the rites of the church or in the depths of the soul. It is here that the passage still speaks to our modern condition. The threefold character of the witness is stressed in line with the recognition in the Jewish law that the agreement of three witnesses was to be held conclusive (Deut. 19:15; cf. Matt. 18:16) .

---

the blood signifies Jesus' death on the cross, indisputable facts of the gospel record and historically known to have happened. Over against the desire of the heretics to accept as historical only what they choose, or to pervert the events of the Incarnation and Crucifixion into mere allegory or myth, John stoutly defends the full historicity of the total gospel (cf. Expos. on 4:2) . But equally valid is the evidence of the continuing influence of these witnesses in the life of the church, through which the original meaning of the Incarnation is re-presented to and recaptured by men, and through which God's eternal life in the presence of Jesus is received into the life of the believer. The activity of the Spirit as teacher (2:20, 27) and as the revealer of truth (4:6) has previously been described. But as other forms of "holy inspiration" (cf. Exeg. on vs. 6) in the church marked the action of the Spirit, so throughout the centuries even until today all actions of the Spirit attest to the Incarnation. The child kneeling at his confirmation, the scholar investigating the nature of "the historical Jesus," the artist exalting Jesus in color and song, the parent building a Christian home life—these reveal the Spirit at work, and constitute evidence. A prayer of "Thanksgiving for the Work of God's Spirit" includes these words:

. . . for the work of thy Spirit within and beyond the bounds of thy visible Church, we thank Thee, O Lord. For the work of thy Spirit in the history of the world, through peaceful advance, and through pain and tumult. . . . For the work of thy Spirit . . . through . . . heroes and leaders, in statecraft,

law and industry. . . . For the work of thy Spirit in the slow triumph of truth over error . . . . For the work of thy Spirit in the spread of education, and in the development of a fuller life. . . . For the work of thy Spirit in the deepening sense of human worth in all nations and classes, and in the growing reverence for womanhood and childhood. . . . For the work of thy Spirit in the Church, which will not cease until it joins all nations and kindreds and tongues and peoples into one great family, to thy praise and glory, we thank Thee, O Lord. Amen.[6]

The water and the blood also signify the sacraments of Baptism and the Lord's Supper, rites in which the meaning of Jesus' baptism and death is perpetually retained and continually offered to men. The sacraments recall to the memory of believers the historical events to which they refer, and thus they perpetuate the historical evidence of the Incarnation. But the sacraments are more than memorials. They further testify to the abiding effect of Jesus' life and death, and above all re-present to believers the eternal life of God that Jesus ever offers to men. In the act of experiencing and responding to this re-presentation, the witness of the water and the blood is established in the believer's own consciousness. "Each Communion is not a stage in a process by which His coming gradually draws nearer. . . . It is a re-living of the decisive moment at which He came." [7] This conception of the sacraments marks the high

[6] From *A Book of Prayers for Students* by permission of the publishers, The Student Christian Movement Press, Ltd.

[7] Dodd, *Parables of the Kingdom,* p. 204.

9 If we receive the witness of men, the witness of God is greater: for this is the witness of God which he hath testified of his Son.

and these three agree. **9** If we receive the testimony of men, the testimony of God is greater; for this is the testimony of God

9. **If we receive the testimony of men,** i.e., generally where three witnesses agree, or such testimony to Christ as that of the Baptist in John 5:32-36, yet **the testimony of God is greater** (again, John 5:34, 36). It is **greater** or more valid because a father can speak more authoritatively with regard to his son than can anyone else—again the elder appeals to common observation. Indeed, "no one knows the Son except the Father" (Matt. 11:27). But vs. 9b and its connection are not altogether clear; **which** translates an inferior reading. In any case the emphasis falls on the varied, objective, and continuous

place that symbolism holds in religion and thought, and the strangeness or obscurity of John's figures of the blood and the water must not lead us to dismiss them as unintelligent or irrelevant. Religion, as life, is impoverished without symbolism; the truly religious man brings something of the mystic and the poet to his devotion. Consider how Jesus deliberately chose the symbols of water, bread, wine, light, vine, shepherd, to convey his meaning to men. Actually symbols can convey undertones and overtones of meaning that logic cannot express. At the same time, symbolism must not be used as an escape from thinking. This lofty conception of the sacraments also rebukes the church for the want of dignity and beauty with which the rites of Baptism and Holy Communion are often administered, for its failure to instruct believers in the sacred meaning of these symbols, and for its unhealthy subjectivism which conceives the appeal of the church to be made primarily through the personality of the preacher or through elaborate church programs rather than through the offer of eternal life in Jesus objectively mediated to men through the historical sacraments. Preaching has a central place in the ministry of the church. But the sacraments are visible words—*verba visibilia*—as preaching is the spoken word. And both utter the divine Word of Life.

9-10a. Three Kinds of Testimony.—Another viewpoint from which to approach "the varied, objective, and continuous attestation" (Exeg. on vs. 9) to the Incarnation that John desires to cite is that of testimony. The testimony is threefold, **the testimony of men, the testimony of God,** and the testimony that **he who believes in the Son of God has . . . in himself.**

The testimony of men may be taken to mean the continuing witness and tradition of the apostolic church expressed through its preaching, dogma, rites, and through the unique influence of its life in a pagan world. We, too, are heirs of this original testimony (cf. Expos. on 1:1-4). But we are heirs also of Christian testi-

mony in all generations, including our own. Indeed, does not every Christian owe the genesis of his faith and religious experience in one way or another to the testimony of men?

To Thee, Eternal Soul, be praise!
Who, from of old to our own days,
Through souls of saints and prophets, Lord,
Hast sent Thy light, Thy love, Thy word.[8]

But we, too, are part of this same testimony, and have our part to play in making it known. By our words we testify, and the spirit of the apostolic gospel must find expression through us: "We cannot but speak of what we have seen and heard" (Acts 4:20). We testify to other things in life that hold meaning for us, e.g., music, travel, love for our country. Why should we hesitate to speak our word of witness to him who holds supreme meaning—Jesus Christ and his gospel? If it is said, "I will let my life speak," the Christian replies, "Yes, action is the decisive witness. But it is hardly less important to seal the meaning of what we do with words that explain why we do what we do." Further, our own faith is deepened, defined, and strengthened by witnessing to it. It is reported that every Christian convert in a missionary diocese in North India is taught to put his hand on his head every morning to remind himself of his baptism, and to repeat the words, "Woe is me if I preach not the gospel." By deed, likewise, the life of the individual Christian is part of the testimony of men. The Christian is called to show forth the spirit which has been described as characterizing the true saint: "The saint is not a professor who puts to society a convincing set of arguments. He puts before men a life and an embarrassing invitation which they must decide to accept or reject."[9]

The testimony of God is the witness he has borne to the Son through the preparation of Jewish prophecy for the advent of Christ,

[8] Richard Watson Gilder.
[9] Douglas V. Steere, *On Beginning from Within* (New York: Harper & Bros., 1943), p. 17.

10 He that believeth on the Son of God hath the witness in himself: he that believeth not God hath made him a liar; because he believeth not the record that God gave of his Son.

10 He who believes in the Son of God has the testimony in himself. He who does not believe God, has made him a liar, because he has not believed in the testimony that God

---

attestation to his Son that God has offered to all beholders, beginning with the mighty works and other signs performed by Jesus in his ministry (John 5:36).

10. But apart from such outward testimonies there is an inward one (cf. John 5:38). It is his who places his faith (here πιστεύειν εἰς), not in a doctrine, but in a person, **the Son of God**—the Son, i.e., of him who testifies. Then (vs. 10b) we have the converse; and we recognize the familiar source (see, e.g., John 3:18-21) used by the elder both by its antithetical parallelism and its resonant generality. This clause concerns him **who does not believe God** (πιστεύειν with the dative), i.e., who does not trust God's word. So demonstrative is the evidence of the truth of God's witness that any such man can be thought of only as having made up his mind **that God is a liar** in this particular attestation and false in all his ways.

---

through the supernatural signs and powers accompanying Jesus' birth, life, death, and resurrection, and through the fact of Jesus' continuing presence and power in history. This testimony **is greater** because it bears the authority and sanctions of the entire Christian revelation (but see Exeg.): "This is the testimony, that God gave us eternal life, and this life is in his Son" (vs. 11). This testimony is external and objective, as compared with the subjectivity of human testimony. It is also prior, and elicits the testimony of men rather than vice versa. Men do not impute to Christ their own confession of him as truth, or read back into Jesus' life their own opinions, and then find that God verifies them; rather, their confession of Christ as the truth only acknowledges and answers to the truth God has previously revealed and to which he has testified.

10a. The Witness of Inward Experience.— But while the Christian may in part be persuaded of the truth of the Incarnation by the testimony of God and men, ultimately he is made most sure by **the testimony in himself** when he **believes in the Son of God**. External evidence cannot be a substitute for inward experience, and objective evidence needs to be complemented with subjective conviction (cf. Expos. on 1:1-2). Religion does not err when it appeals to personal experience, despite all the risks in doing so. The author of this epistle knows these risks well. In fact the entire epistle in one sense is a critique of false kinds of religious experience (cf. especially Expos. on 1:5, 7; 4:1-3). Nevertheless, John does not hesitate to rest the case for Jesus' divine meaning and for the validity of the gospel on the testimony of inward experience wrought by the Spirit: **He who believes . . . has . . . testimony in himself.**

So still the experience of the heart brings its own testimony. Tennyson describes it thus:

I found Him not in world or sun,
  Or eagle's wing, or insect's eye;
  Nor thro' the questions men may try,
The petty cobwebs we have spun:

If e'er when faith had fallen asleep,
  I heard a voice, "Believe no more,"
  And heard an ever-breaking shore
That tumbled in the Godless deep,

A warmth within the breast would melt
  The freezing reason's colder part,
  And like a man in wrath the heart
Stood up and answer'd, "I have felt." [1]

The inward assurance is wrought by faith. Logic and reason do not suffice to bring to men the final truth of the Incarnation. It has been said that there are some truths in religion you cannot understand until you believe them—*Credo ut intelligam*. It is also true that there are some truths you cannot experience until you believe them: only **He who believes . . . has . . . testimony in himself.** But such belief is "not in a doctrine but in a person" (Exeg. on vs. 10). The Christian believes **in the Son of God**, not in the Incarnation as a theological concept. Such belief is wrought by the Spirit, baptizing the believer with Jesus' own presence and bringing him to experience inwardly the truth he acknowledges with his mind and confesses with his lips, i.e., the testimony of God and the claim of Christ to be the Son of God are to the believer self-evidencing and self-authenticating.

10b, 12b. Penalties of Disbelief.—The consequences of rejecting the truth of the Incarnation

[1] *In Memoriam*, Part CXXIV.

11 And this is the record, that God hath given to us eternal life, and this life is in his Son.

12 He that hath the Son hath life; *and* he that hath not the Son of God hath not life.

13 These things have I written unto you that believe on the name of the Son of God; that ye may know that ye have eternal life, and that ye may believe on the name of the Son of God.

has borne to his Son. 11 And this is the testimony, that God gave us eternal life, and this life is in his Son. 12 He who has the Son has life; he who has not the Son has not life.

13 I write this to you who believe in the name of the Son of God, that you may know

---

11-12. This is the testimony—referring to that inner kind which the believer has "in himself" (vs. 10*a*) —**that God gave us eternal life.** Here the benefits and content of the testimony are defined in terms of that favorite conception of **eternal life** which dominates the Gospel (cf. John 3:15-16; 17:2) and this epistle (1:2; 2:25). The tense of **gave** shows that the elder has the historical life of Christ in mind. **This life is in his Son;** cf. John 20:31. It follows that **he who has the Son has life** and only he (cf. John 3:36). Note the movement of thought in this last part of the epistle proper. The difficulties of the demands of God upon us are envisaged. Reassurance is found, however, in the evidence that we abide in God—evidence found in our own love, in our true confession, and in the activity of the Spirit within us. Our abiding in God is then modulated to the conception of our being born of God, and this finally to that of eternal life, with which the epistle began. But all these formulations of status and salvation are insistently related to a non-Docetic grasp of the significance of Christ.

VII. Epilogue: Closing Affirmations and Charge; the True God and Eternal Life (5:13-21)

13. This verse can be taken with what precedes as a more emphatic restatement of vs. 12 and as the real conclusion of the epistle proper. It rings like the closing verse of the Gospel of John (20:31, not counting the appendix, ch. 21). But it is also transitional to what follows in its emphasis on sure knowledge; **that you may know** (ἵνα εἰδῆτε; cf. vss. 18-20).

I write this to you (aorist tense, as in 2:26; etc.) **who believe in the name,** i.e., who place your confidence in him who has the name and authority of Son of God. The same construction is used and the same kind of "believing" is indicated as in vs. 10*a* above, but the phrase added here, **in the name of,** draws attention to the particular formula of confession with all that is implied in it as brought out in vss. 6-12. It is in the light of this true faith that the great affirmations that follow can be made.

---

are described in vss. 10*b*, 12*b*. **He who does not believe God, has made him a liar** (cf. Exeg. on 2:21-22). Those words should frighten the man who ignores or rejects the gospel, for they convict him of blasphemy and insult. The pretensions of his refusal of the meaning of the Incarnation are seen to be ridiculous, as if little man were shaking his fist at the universe and crying, "Liar, liar!" Further, **He who does not believe . . . has not the Son** and **has not life.** Everything hinges on believing or not believing, and the man who does not believe is shut out from what the Son uniquely offers—eternal life. There have been—and perhaps can still be—other, lesser forms of communication of God's life to

the human soul. But life as revealed and offered in Christ is utterly unique, and Christianity only injures that which constitutes its most distinctive nature when it offers itself in any less bold language than John employs here. Only "as many as received him" (John 1:12) have found and still find that "in him was life" (John 1:4).

13-21. *The Closing and Opening Theme of the Epistle.*—This final section significantly opens and closes with the central theme of the epistle (continuing the thought of vss. 11-12): **I write this . . . that you may know that you have eternal life. . . . This is the true God and eternal life** (cf. Expos. on 1:2). Despite the many and varied ideas the author has dealt with,

14 And this is the confidence that we have in him, that, if we ask any thing according to his will, he heareth us:

15 And if we know that he hear us, whatsoever we ask, we know that we have the petitions that we desired of him.

that you have eternal life. 14 And this is the confidence which we have in him, that if we ask anything according to his will he hears us. 15 And if we know that he hears us in whatever we ask, we know that we have obtained the requests made of him.

14-15. The Christian life means a joyful confidence and uninhibited utterance, whether in witness (Acts 4:13; etc.; II Cor. 3:12), in the approach to God (Heb. 10:19), or, as this epistle stresses, in the Judgment (2:28; 4:17), and in bringing petitions before God (3:21-22 and here). In the Gospel of John this latter theme is prominent, "If you abide in me, and my words abide in you, ask whatever you will, and it shall be done for you" (John 15:7; cf. John 14:13-14; 11:22, 41). Note the conditions set here for God's answer to prayer: **If we ask anything according to his will. He hears us:** in the sense of consent (cf. John 9:31; 11:41). **And if we know that** this is true, viz., that **he hears us** in this sense, then **we know that we have obtained the requests.** We already possess them (cf. Mark 11:24). At a given level of selflessness and in the light of Jesus' prayers this hard saying becomes meaningful (see on 3:21-22 above and Dodd, *Johannine Epistles, ad loc.*).

and the occasional excursions into which he has been led, his main purpose in conceiving and writing this letter has been steadily kept in mind—to communicate eternal life. And the effect of reading and studying his words is strangely that of experiencing deepened life in the soul. To Christian people all through the centuries this epistle has brought life. It has nourished souls, kindled faith, inspired love. And one would covet for all readers of this epistle the fulfillment of Law's statement that is at once a definition of the eternal life the gospel offers and a promise of its reality:

Every hour of His [Jesus'] history belonged to the eternal order. Every word He spoke, every deed . . . He did, was an outgoing of Eternal Life. The Divine nature was in it. And in whomsoever it exists . . . the possession of that nature which produces thoughts, motives and desires, words and deeds, like His, is Eternal Life.[2]

14-16. *Concerning Prayer.*—John wishes to make clear that when one shares this eternal life, one may have confident certainty of its possession: "you may know that you have eternal life." (Observe that the declarations "we know," "you know," occur seven times in vss. 13-21.) This certainly is described in various forms in the epistle (cf. Expos. on 2:28–3:3; 4:17). Here it takes the distinctive form of confidence in God's response to petitionary and intercessory prayer (vss. 14-16). The attitudes of naturalness in asking God for his help, and of simple earnestness in lifting our petitions to him, are suggested by the plain words **If we ask anything, . . . whatever we ask, . . . requests made**

of him. All true prayer springs from a sense of need: "Your heavenly Father knoweth that ye have need" (Matt. 6:32), and no need is beyond prayer. It has been said that anything worth worrying about is worth praying about. The only condition laid down is **according to his will.** (Similar conditions are laid down in 3:22; John 14:14; John 15:7.) Christian prayer is active identification with the divine will, the lifting up of our will to God's desires, not the persuasion of God's will to fulfill our desires. Thus prayer is but a devotional expression of the same principle by which the Christian man habitually lives, and his prayer is effective because it represents the kind of life he lives. A noble Jewish saying quoted by Brooke is apropos: "Do His Will as if it were thine, that He may do thy will as if it were His."[3] Such prayer, far from restricting God's will, releases and perfects it. God is essentially disposed not to ignore but to hear, not to deny but to grant requests: **he hears, . . . God will give.**

Christian prayer, while including petition, is in essence the fellowship of person with person: **he hears us, . . . God will give him.** It is a heavenly Father to whom we pray, not a life force or cosmic mind; and men stand in relation to God not as things but as personalities. All the rich meanings of fellowship, friendship, and love that characterize relations between people may be found in man's relation of prayer with God. Christian prayer carries its answer within: **we know that we have obtained the requests made of him.** Note that the KJV reads, **we know that we have the petitions that we desired of him.** The bold confidence of this high experi-

---

[2] *Tests of Life*, p. 189.

[3] *Johannine Epistles*, p. 102.

16 If any man see his brother sin a sin *which is* not unto death, he shall ask, and he shall give him life for them that sin not unto death. There is a sin unto death: I do not say that he shall pray for it.

17 All unrighteousness is sin: and there is a sin not unto death.

16 If any one sees his brother committing what is not a mortal sin, he will ask, and God[i] will give him life for those whose sin is not mortal. There is sin which is mortal; I do not say that one is to pray for that.

17 All wrongdoing is sin, but there is sin which is not mortal.

[i] Greek *he.*

16-17. The special case of intercessory prayer follows. The passage suggests the sense of intimate solidarity and responsibility which characterized the early Christians. Despite the ideal of vs. 18 and 3:6, 9, the elder knows that Christians sin (1:8–2:1). Those who walk in the light and see things as they are recognize their sin and are assured of forgiveness. But the crisis of the faith in the circumstances of the time made certain types of behavior fatal to the cause and drastic language is found for them, as by Jesus in an analogous situation, if the tradition is correct (Mark 3:28-29; Matt. 12:30-32; Luke 12:10; cf. Heb. 6:4-6; 12:16-17). **There is a sin which is mortal.** The Greek does not say **a sin** but speaks more generally, "There is sin unto death." It is understandable that with the growing need for concrete moral instruction, as the church became institutionalized, distinctions should be made in the gravity of offenses. Precedents in the Jewish synagogue of the time had an influence on this development. Later writings show

---

ence of prayer rebukes the skepticism of unbelievers and confirms the faith of believers in prayer. The outward obtaining of our requests is sometimes apparent, sometimes hidden; but when prayer is on the deep, dedicated, selfless level John describes, fulfillment "exists in the sphere of Divine Thought and Will, which is the sphere of reality, and only awaits manifestation."[4] Our imaginations and minds tend to define too narrowly the manner in which God enables us to obtain our requests. God answers prayer in ways we do not anticipate and often cannot realize. In any case, we may say that while God may not always seem to answer our prayers, he always answers true prayer.

The special case of intercessory prayer for one who has sinned (vs. 16) is doubtless lifted directly from the life of the early church, and illustrates once more the elder's unremitting concern for holiness of life: **If any one sees his brother committing what is not a mortal sin, he will ask, and God will give him life for those whose sin is not mortal.** The love that binds Christians together in fellowship ministers to moral and spiritual need as well as to physical need. It is one thing to share our goods with those in need (3:17); it is a better thing to share our prayers. So often we fail at precisely this point because we have not understood that one can do nothing more loving for another than to pray for him in the deep way John would have us pray. But effective intercessory prayer depends on the prior relation of mutuality as among brethren. Note the significance of

the word **brother.** The Christian must not be repelled by the sin of a fellow Christian; instead, he must hold him who sins in the relationship of brother and be willing to accept vicarious responsibility for sin and bear the guilt and punishment of it. This is perhaps the highest mark of genuine Christian fellowship and shows forth something of Jesus' spirit on the cross. The nature of God's answer to such intercessory prayer is important: **God will give him life;** not prosperity, or deliverance from trouble or temptation, or safety, but life. Intercession for one's brother in need is to participate in the great apostolate of prayer in the life of the church. When we pray we are not alone, but become members of an invisible society whose faith and love affect all. In Père Charles' "Prayer for All Times," the priest says to a soul that has been saved from some sin or danger:

How do you know whose prayer it is which has prevailed before God and won you this grace? Perhaps it is that old beggar at the church door, or the apple-woman in the market, or some sleepless sufferer, or some little child; who made with simplicity an offering of their prayer, and it was accepted for the purposes of God.[5]

16-17. *Different Degrees of Sin.*—The distinction in these verses between sin that is mortal and not mortal reflects the elder's moral realism, in that while he prefers to think in terms of black and white, he must yet acknowledge that life is sometimes too gray to be sharply judged.

[4] Law, *op. cit.,* p. 302.

[5] Quoted by Underhill, *Collected Papers,* p. 175.

18 We know that whosoever is born of God sinneth not; but he that is begotten of God keepeth himself, and that wicked one toucheth him not.

18 We know that any one born of God does not sin, but He who was born of God keeps him, and the evil one does not touch him.

its course. What surprises us here is not that some sin could be viewed as leading to spiritual death *if continued in,* but that the elder should write, **I do not say that one is to pray for that,** for this appears to contradict the deeper N.T. view that God's love persists to the utmost (Matt. 18:21-22) and "all things are possible with God" (Mark 10:27). Since, however, **all wrongdoing is sin,** and **there is sin which is not mortal,** there is a wide scope for confident intercession and God (or the interceder) **will give . . . life** to the brother in question. "The Will of God is pure, unchangeable, holy Love working for the highest good of every creature. It is the Will of God that the Eternal Life of Truth, Righteousness, and Love shall everywhere grow and multiply; and when we will this together with Him, nothing shall prevent its accomplishment." (Robert Law, *The Tests of Life* [Edinburgh: T. & T. Clark, 1914], p. 304.)

18. The epilogue closes, as Windisch notes, with three ringing affirmations, stressing sure knowledge as in vs. 13. Vs. 18*a* is from the source and repeats 3:9*a* almost exactly in the Greek: literally, "Everyone who is born of God does not sin." In 3:9 this general truth is used as a test of the children of God over against those of the devil. Here it is used to reinforce confidence, though an ethical appeal is implicit in either case, all the more so here because of the recognition of the presence of sin in the church in vss. 16-17. In 3:9 sinlessness is ascribed to the fact that God's "seed" abides in the believer; here to the fact that **He who was born of God** [i.e., Christ] **keeps him** (cf. John 17:12; note that the KJV follows a different reading, preferred by some: the child of God **keepeth himself**). **And the evil one does not touch him**—i.e., does not lay hold of him (cf. John 17:15). So Jesus had said of himself, "The ruler of this world . . . has no power over me" (John 14:30).

And despite the frequent corruption of this insight by institutional religion in elaborate classifications of mortal and venial sins, baptismal and postbaptismal sins, etc., it yet corresponds to the facts of the moral life. It is always true that **all wrongdoing is sin, but there is sin which is not mortal.** People have needlessly and fruitlessly long speculated about the nature of sin which is mortal, and often they have arrogated to themselves the judgment that belongs to God alone. The context of the epistle, together with N.T. teaching, would seem to mean that **mortal sin**—if one is to risk a definition—is the willful, knowing, persistent resistance to divine truth in Christ appealing to man's soul through the Holy Spirit (cf. Matt. 12:30-32; Mark 3:28-30; Luke 12:10; I Tim. 6:5; II Tim. 3:8). But note, the most the elder says about one who has committed even a mortal sin is that he is not an object of confident intercession; while he does not recommend, he also does not forbid prayer for a person who has so sinned.

18. *Jesus Defends from Sin.*—This verse resumes the familiar theme of the epistle that **one born of God does not sin** (cf. Expos. on 2:28–3:3; 3:4-10), but here an additional thought is introduced: **He** [Christ] **. . . keeps him, and the**

evil one does not touch him. In addition to his offices as Victor (vss. 4-5), Redeemer (1:7; 3:5, 8, 16; 4:10, 14), Advocate (2:1), Revealer (2:20; 5:6-8), Teacher (2:27), Jesus may be conceived as Defender or Keeper. The Christian man may be able in some ways to keep himself (cf. vs. 21), but in the last analysis the companionship of Jesus' spirit imparting moral strength and resolution of will, cleansing motive and disposition, exposing evil in both its subtle and gross forms, is the Christian's only safety. But the evil one attacks man in many ways, as the epistle abundantly shows, and we may also think of Jesus as our Defender from fear, from error, from barrenness and futility of living, from anxiety. The prayer of St. Patrick may well be the Chistian's daily prayer:

> I bind unto myself today
> The power of God to hold and lead,
> His eye to watch, his might to stay,
> His ear to hearken to my need,
> The wisdom of my God to teach,
> His hand to guide, his shield to ward,
> The word of God to give me speech,
> His heavenly host to be my guard.[6]

[6] "St. Patrick's Breastplate," tr. Mrs. Cecil Frances Alexander.

19 *And* we know that we are of God, and the whole world lieth in wickedness.

20 And we know that the Son of God is come, and hath given us an understanding, that we may know him that is true; and we are in him that is true, *even* in his Son Jesus Christ. This is the true God, and eternal life.

19 We know that we are of God, and the whole world is in the power of the evil one.

20 And we know that the Son of God has come and has given us understanding, to know him who is true; and we are in him who is true, in his Son Jesus Christ. This is the true God and eternal life.

---

19. The elder here applies to himself and his readers what is said generally in the third person in vs. 18: **We** [since we are "born of God"] **are of God** (cf. 4:4), and are safeguarded by him. But **the whole world** not only is not kept from the grasp of **the evil one** but lies passive—κεῖται; contrast μένει (3:14, 24)—in his power (cf. Luke 4:6).

20-21. The third affirmation is connected with the foregoing by an adversative conjunction. These bold and exclusive claims rest on our certainty that **the Son of God has come** [to abide with us] **and has given us understanding.** The term for **understanding** (διάνοιαν) is an unusual one, suggesting a "right reason" with respect to which the Gentiles are said to be "darkened" (Eph. 4:18). By it we are enabled to know **him who is true,** God as he truly is. Not only do we know God but **we are in him, . . . in his Son Jesus Christ;** i.e., it is because we are in the Son that we are in the Father. The KJV, by adding here the word **even,** implies that **him that is true** *now* refers to Christ. This leads to the view that the following words, **this is the true God,** refer also to Christ. This gives one of the most explicit statements in the N.T. of the deity of Christ. Theological controversy has long raged about this passage. But the natural sense of the passage and the characteristic thought of the epistle and the Gospel preclude this interpretation. It is through Christ that we are in God. This God so known **is the true God.** The thought centers in God from vs. 18 on, and the contrast with idols in the last verse confirms it. This God so known also means **eternal life.** Vs. 21, with its intimate appeal, **Little children, keep yourselves from idols,** merely states in a negative form the implicit charge

---

19b. A Final Warning.—The fundamental dualism between God and the world, and between God and evil (treated in Expos. on 2:15-17; cf. also Expos. on 3:12-13, 15; 4:4-6), appears once more in vs. 19. After striking again the note of confidence—**we know that we are of God**—the elder writes: **the whole world is in the power of the evil one.** The dreadfulness of these words may appall; yet only such bold language can gather up the essential tragedy of human existence. Life is woefully misread if it is not seen as grasped and possessed by evil so widespread and so powerful that only God can be trusted to deal with it. The picture of the world as lying passive in the grip of evil is true to reality. Not for nothing have generations of Christians prayed from century to century:

O God, who art the author of peace and lover of concord, in knowledge of whom standeth our eternal life, whose service is perfect freedom; Defend us thy humble servants in all assaults of our enemies; that we, surely trusting in thy defence, may not fear the power of any adversaries, through the might of Jesus Christ our Lord. Amen.[7]

[7] The Book of Common Prayer, A Collect for Peace, from the Order for Daily Morning Prayer.

20-21. The Final Truth.—The epistle closes with a final reference to the basis of the author's entire thought—the Incarnation: **the Son of God has come.** Here as elsewhere the Christian's confidence—**we know**—rests squarely on the historical fact of the coming of Christ (cf. Expos. on 1:1-2; 2:20-23; 3:4-10; 4:2, 7-12, 14-15; 5:6-12). But faith in the Incarnation means more than being able to secure the truth of one's religious conviction in an indubitable historical event. It means also appropriating the insight and understanding that Jesus gives: **the Son of God . . . has given us understanding, to know.** No one has understood life as Jesus understood it—fathomed its mystery and perceived its meaning, clarified its values or comprehended its destiny. And he who believes in Jesus Christ is heir to all this. His mind takes on something of the mind of Christ. He comes to know as Jesus knew. But most of all, through faith in the Son of God we come **to know him who is true, . . . the true God, and we are in him who is true.** These mystical words are John's way of describing the Christian experience of knowing ultimate Reality through faith in the historical Jesus and of sharing in the very

21 Little children, keep yourselves from idols. Amen.	21 Little children, keep yourselves from idols.

to abide **in him who is true.** For **idols** here refers to untrue, unreal objects of devotion: the delusions proffered by the "world" and the "spirit of error." Actual idol worship or acts indirectly involving it are hardly envisaged. Rather, the elder invokes the negative connotations of idolatry to enforce the heightened dualism which marks the entire epistle. Over against **the true God** can only be **idols,** and the readers are to abide in him with all that that means in conduct, and so to safeguard "the eternal life which was with the Father and was made manifest to us" (1:2).

life of God. Men have always sought final reality. Often they have stopped short, satisfied with substitutes for God—idols. In John's world idols signified paganism; but they are paralleled in our day by modern paganisms equally false, to which men mistakenly give their ultimate faith and loyalty—political ideas, popular cults, money, pleasure, the state. The Christian must ever beware of these. In contrast to such inferior realities and illusions stands the God revealed in Christ. He alone is the Real. In God alone man's soul finds its safety, its victory over sin and the world. In God alone the human spirit finds its destiny—**eternal life** both in this world and in the world to come. Richard Doddridge Blackmore describes the meaning of the reality of God to man's soul, when all else is taken from him in the crisis of death:

In the hour of death, after this life's whim,
When the heart beats low, and the eyes grow dim,
And pain has exhausted every limb—
    The lover of the Lord shall trust in Him.

When the will has forgotten the life-long aim,
And the mind can only disgrace its fame,
And a man is uncertain of his own name,
    The power of the Lord shall fill this frame.

When the last sigh is heaved and the last tear shed,
And the coffin is waiting beside the bed,
And the widow and child forsake the dead,
    The angel of the Lord shall lift this head.

For even the purest delight may pall,
And power must fail, and the pride must fall,
And the love of the dearest friends grow small—
    But the glory of the Lord is all in all.[8]

[8] *"Dominus Illuminatio Mea."*

II JOHN

TEXT, EXEGESIS, AND EXPOSITION

1 The elder unto the elect lady and her children, whom I love in the truth; and not I only, but also all they that have known the truth;	1 The elder to the elect lady and her children, whom I love in the truth, and not only I but also all who know the truth,

I. Address and Greeting to the Church (vss. 1-3)

For a general discussion of the two shorter epistles see the Intro., especially "Contents and Occasion" (pp. 209-10) and "Origin and Literary History" (pp. 215-16). In contrast

1-6. *Fellowship in the Church.*—Observe the author's anonymous designation of himself simply as **the elder.** What a man chooses to call himself reveals his character. The author does not speak of himself as "his eminence" or "right reverend"; he does not cite his academic or hon-

orary degrees; he does not refer his readers to a "Who's Who in Asia Minor." Nor does he permit his prestige to depend merely on length of tenure of office or on the impressiveness of his own personality. Rather, the elder assumes and asserts his authority as one who desires only

2 For the truth's sake, which dwelleth in us, and shall be with us for ever.

2 because of the truth which abides in us and will be with us for ever:

---

to the longer writing, both II and III John have an epistolary salutation and conclusion, and provide us therefore with some designation of the writer and the recipients.

1-2. The elder (πρεσβύτερος): This term, whether in pagan or Hellenistic Jewish usage, referred both to an elderly man (in the comparative degree) and to the office or dignity occupied by such. A number of elders commonly exercised functions of leadership in the local churches of this period (see note on "Elders" above, pp. 15-16). In the present instance the writer would hardly use the term in this sense since he assumes a larger authority and one over a general mission field. The author of I Peter, while he calls himself a "fellow elder" (I Pet. 5:1), also identifies himself at least pseudonymously as an apostle (I Pet. 1:1). **Elder** here, therefore, has the sense which it has in various post-apostolic writings where it refers to those intermediate figures, between the apostles and the later leaders, who could vouch for the original apostolic witness (cf. Eusebius *Church History* III. 39. 2-7; Irenaeus *Against Heresies* V. 5. 1; 33. 3) There are references also to a particular elder, identified as "the elder John" in Papias and later writers (Eusebius, *op. cit.* III. 39. 4-7, 14-15; V. 8. 8), though his identity with the "elder" of II and III John is not to be assumed. In the present case we have such a figure who is generally known in this area by this designation, and who profits by it to appeal to the authority of tradition of which he is, as an "elder," an accredited bearer.

The letter is ostensibly addressed to a devout matron (ἐκλεκτῇ κυρίᾳ) **and her children.** We have here a gracious personification of a particular church, as in vs. 13 of this epistle (cf. Baruch 4–5; Gal. 4:25). Our closest parallel is in I Pet. 5:13 where a local church is spoken of ἡ συνεκλεκτή: "She who is . . . likewise chosen, sends you greetings." Since the time of the early church it has been supposed by some that a certain individual, either the "elect Kyria" or the "lady Electa," is here addressed. But the contents of our letter exclude this view.

The term **truth** occurs five times in vss. 1-4, in close connection with the theme of **love.** We have seen that **truth** in these writings and in John refers to reality as known in the gospel. Where the article is used before it, reference is usually to the gospel message itself (see on III John 3-4 below). All those who have come to **know the truth,** in this sense, love every particular group of Christians. This solidarity of the universal church, a felicitous reminder of ecumenical responsibility, rests on the fact that **the**

---

that his word and life witness to the **truth** of the apostolic gospel. This is the only credential a true Christian needs. **To the elect lady and her children.** Does not this gracious phrase rebuke the want of dignity and good taste with which we so often speak of the church? A Christian fellowship is more than a charge, a parish, a congregation. These words are good, but compare them with the exalted language with which the N.T. speaks of the church: "Fellow citizens with the saints, and of the household of God" (Eph. 2:19); "A bride adorned for her husband" (Rev. 21:2); "The body of Christ" (I Cor. 12:27); "A glorious church, . . . holy and without blemish" (Eph. 5:27). Christianity makes large place for the use of beauty and imagery in conveying its meanings, and not least in regard to the church. Parenthetically, while one cannot press the metaphor too far, the figure of **lady and her children** implies motherhood, and tradition tells us that the church is called "mother" because of her power to bring forth new life.

Whom I love in the truth: The affection of ordinary friendship is raised to a holy level among Christians by the bond of mutual faith in the truth of the gospel. Comradeship in truth is always noble, but comradeship in Christian truth excels all else. Comradeship in seeking truth in the scientific laboratory is one thing; comradeship in truth in the Christian sanctuary is another. The former may be characterized by loyalty; the latter is characterized by love. **Also all who know the truth:** The truth of which the church is custodian unites all members in love, because as a "dynamic impulse" love begets those attitudes which alone can reconcile differences. Here lies the key to the problem of uniting Christendom. Differences of ecclesiastical tradition, theological viewpoint, cultural background, church government, cannot be reconciled by outward contrivance or adjustment.

3 Grace be with you, mercy, *and* peace, from God the Father, and from the Lord Jesus Christ, the Son of the Father, in truth and love.

4 I rejoiced greatly that I found of thy children walking in truth, as we have received a commandment from the Father.

5 And now I beseech thee, lady, not as though I wrote a new commandment unto thee, but that which we had from the beginning, that we love one another.

3 Grace, mercy, and peace will be with us, from God the Father and from Jesus Christ the Father's Son, in truth and love.

4 I rejoiced greatly to find some of your children following the truth, just as we have been commanded by the Father. 5 And now I beg you, lady, not as though I were writing you a new commandment, but the one we have had from the beginning, that

---

truth . . . abides in us as a dynamic impulse and **will be with us forever** (like the Paraclete, John 14:16).

3. The form of this promise **(will be with us)** is now borrowed for the customary expression of good wishes, here announced as **grace, mercy, and peace.** This assurance is grounded in the true confession with which we have become familiar in I John, especially in 2:22-24, and will be realized **in truth and love.** The form of the salutation anticipates the chief notes of the epistle.

II. Summons to Love (vss. 4-6)

4. Especially in the letters of Paul do we recognize the early Christian practice of beginning a message with an expression of joy. The precise formula used here is found in III John 3-4, a passage which also clarifies the circumstances under which the elder learned that some of the members of the church in question were **walking in truth.** The expression here (lacking the article before **truth**) has much the same sense as to "walk in the light" (I John 1:7). So to walk is the original charge (ἐντολή) of the gospel, going back to Christ himself, **just as we have been commanded by the Father.** What is in view is especially the commandment of love, as is soon to appear (cf. I John 3:23). Windisch (*Katholischen Briefe, ad. loc.*) well cites a saying assigned to Jesus in the apocryphal Gospel of the Hebrews: "Never," he said, "be joyful except when you are found in love with your brother" (fragment 25).

5. But it is implied that some others are not **walking in truth,** and the whole purpose of the little letter is summed up now in an appeal to all the members: **I beg you, lady, . . . that we love one another.** This appeal to a love that will override disaffection and schism is the chief practical aim of both I and II John. It is enforced here also by insistence that the commandment of love is both an old commandment **from the beginning** (cf. I John 2:7; 3:11 and John 13:34) and one that is the sum of all Christian instruction (vs. 6 and John 15:12).

True solidarity expressed in catholicity will come only through love—manifest in attitudes of humility, open-mindedness, brotherliness—that issues from unreserved devotion to the truth in Christ. Only by coming closer to Christ can Christians come closer to one another. **The truth . . . will be with us for ever:** Fellowship in love and truth among Christians transcends time and place, and partakes of eternity. Shared life in Christ has within it now intimations of immortality that will be fully consummated in the world to come.

Observe the loftiness of the sentiments in this salutation: **Grace, mercy, and peace . . . from God the Father and . . . Jesus Christ.**

Fellowship in Christian truth and love transforms everything, even conventional salutations and courtesies. No banal "Good luck" or "Cheerio" here! Life in its totality—even the ordinary writing of letters—is ennobled and sanctified by Christ.

The heart of a true pastor is revealed in the elder's joy that **some** of the congregation to whom he writes are growing in **following the truth.** He clearly realizes that they have not fully attained and that some have backslidden. His quiet realism, however, and his confidence in their perseverance serve as the strongest possible spur to faithfulness. The source of the elder's joy is thus at once the highest test of a

6 And this is love, that we walk after his commandments. This is the commandment, That, as ye have heard from the beginning, ye should walk in it.

7 For many deceivers are entered into the world, who confess not that Jesus Christ is come in the flesh. This is a deceiver and an antichrist.

we love one another. 6 And this is love, that we follow his commandments; this is the commandment, as you have heard from the beginning, that you follow love. 7 For many deceivers have gone out into the world, men who will not acknowledge the coming of Jesus Christ in the flesh; such a one is the deceiver and the antichrist.

---

6. In the first half of the verse love is defined. Its meaning, very concretely, is that **we follow his commandments** (so in I John 5:3 of the love of God). The context in both passages suggests that **commandments,** in the plural, refer particularly to such ways of life as distinguish the Christians from the "deceivers" and from those in the "world"— ways which may be thought of as "burdensome" (I John 5:3) and costly (Rev. 12:17; 14:12; John 14:15). In the second half of the verse the introductory phrase differs so that we do not here have a definition of **the commandment,** as we do of **love** in vs. 6a. The sense is: this is the commandment (i.e., of love) in which you should walk. **In it** refers to **the commandment;** the RSV paraphrases too freely.

III. Warning Against Error (vss. 7-11)

7. It is urgent to walk according to the old commandment (which also includes the true confession as in I John 3:23) **for many deceivers have gone out into the world** (cf. I John 2:18, 26; 4:1). The interpretation of vs. 6b in the RSV does not make the connection easily intelligible since the **deceivers** are not here actually accused of lovelessness. Probably not the exodus of the schismatics from the church (I John 2:19), but the emergence of false prophets in the world generally is pointed out. False gospels offer themselves, and it is a day of confusion. The believer, therefore, should walk in truth and follow the original message from the Father himself. For the deceivers **will not acknowledge the coming of Jesus Christ in the flesh.** The Incarnation is referred to here in the most general way (ἐρχόμενον; contrast ἐληλυθότα in I John 4:2). The elder has in view the Docetic denial of Christ's humanity and passion, which meant a failure to grasp the full love of the Father and the true basis for our quickening fellowship with the Son. **Such a one is the deceiver and the antichrist.** So I John 2:22 describes him as "the liar" and "the antichrist" (on this whole verse see Exeg. of I John 2:18-23 and 4:1-3; also Intro., pp. 213-14).

---

church's life and of a pastor's attitudes. Contrast the joy of growth in truth with the pride that a church's budget has been raised or its debt retired, a quota of new members received or the program humming.

Again the elder's heart and pen turn to "love" as the rule and spirit of Christian fellowship (vss. 5-6). He "begs" not that the congregation will raise the missionary apportionment or write their congressmen, but that first they grow in love. Significantly, this injunction to love precedes his condemnation of anti-Christian deceivers in the following verses. If there must be controversy, let it be within the atmosphere of love. Love can win where argument fails. Love in a controversial situation is respect for the sincerity of another's mind, the seeking of another's good at cost to oneself, forgiveness of erroneous opinions as well as wrong motives. Specifically, as in vs. 6, love is

the witness of Christian integrity in opposition to the ways of the world.

7-11. *Warning Against Deceivers; Summons to Faithfulness.*— (See Expos. on I John 2:18-19, 22; 4:1-3.) The menace of false gospels described in vs. 7 requires the warning **Look to yourselves.** These words remind us of the fatal readiness of human nature to judge others before one judges oneself (cf. Matt. 7:1-5), which takes the form of pride, condescension, making another the scapegoat, self-deception. Honest self-examination, on the other hand, is the gateway to salvation. Such self-examination need not be morbid, but it must be sincere. Paradoxically, only when we morally look to ourselves are we able harmoniously to live with ourselves and to become better selves. The success of psychological therapy, for example, often is found to lie in the fact that the only way to forget guilt and sin is first to suffer the pain of facing them. So the

8 Look to yourselves, that we lose not those things which we have wrought, but that we receive a full reward.

9 Whosoever transgresseth, and abideth not in the doctrine of Christ, hath not God. He that abideth in the doctrine of Christ, he hath both the Father and the Son.

10 If there come any unto you, and bring not this doctrine, receive him not into *your* house, neither bid him Godspeed:

8 Look to yourselves, that you may not lose what you*a* have worked for, but may win a full reward. 9 Any one who goes ahead and does not abide in the doctrine of Christ does not have God; he who abides in the doctrine of Christ has both the Father and the Son. 10 If any one comes to you and does not bring this doctrine, do not receive him into the house or give him any greet-

a Other ancient authorities read *we*.

8. Interpreters today prefer the textual readings which give the verbs here in the second person throughout as in the RSV (not as in the KJV). **Worked for** (RSV) or "earned" is preferable to **wrought** (KJV; cf. John 6:27: same construction). Yet the first person plural (**what we have worked for** [RSV mg.; cf. KJV]) may be original. In this case emphasis is placed on safeguarding the results of others' labors, including that of the elder (cf. John 4:36-38). **Full reward:** cf. I John 3:2 for present versus future satisfactions; also Matt. 5:12.

9. Progressivists are condemned so far as they do **not abide in the doctrine of Christ.** The errorists may have actually described themselves as those who "go ahead" (Greek: πᾶς ὁ προάγων; the KJV here follows an inferior reading, **whosoever transgresseth**). **The doctrine** (διδαχή) **of Christ** refers to the original teaching with regard to Christ and his coming assigned in John (cf. "my doctrine," John 7:16) to Jesus himself, to "the faith which was once for all delivered to the saints" (Jude 3). To abide in this instruction is to have **both the Father and the Son.** The verse reads like a summary of I John 2:23-24.

10-11. Itinerant evangelists and prophets are in view here, as often in the early writings. In this case, because of their false doctrine and spirit (cf. I John 4:5) they are not to receive the customary hospitality or even greeting (contrast Rom. 12:13; Heb. 13:2; I Tim. 3:2; Tit. 1:8). The Teaching of the Twelve Apostles (Didache), in its section dealing with traveling teachers, says: "If the teacher himself be perverted and teach another doctrine to destroy these things, do not listen to him" (Did. 11:2). Ignatius

church must look to itself before it undertakes to criticize others. Jesus criticized the church of his day—to which he himself belonged—more severely than any other institution. Denunciation of the social sins of greed, race prejudice, apathy, comes with poor grace if the church is unwilling to face these same sins in itself.

That you may not lose what you have worked for. The Christian life is falsely portrayed if it does not include plain, hard work (cf. III John 6*b*-8). The many analogies, parables, illustrations, which Jesus drew from the sphere of human toil (cf. Matt. 18:23-35; 20:1-16; 21:33-41; 25:14-30; Luke 20:9-16) underscore how vividly he conceived his ministry as work (cf. also John 4:34; 5:36; 9:3-4; 10:25, 37; 17:4) and how believers likewise are to conceive their discipleship as work (cf. Matt. 5:16). Love is more often work than emotion; faith requires labor of thought and will.

Our labor often is vain because it is undirected by awareness of the Christian's true rewards. Activity is not always work. A fanatic

has been described as one who redoubles his effort as he loses sight of the goal. The goal is to **win a full reward.** The place of reward in religion should not be underestimated. Rewards must be offered if the best in men is to be elicited. Jesus believed in rewards (cf. Matt. 5:12, 46; 6:1, 4, 6, 18, 20; 10:41-2), as did Paul (cf. I Cor. 3:8). The genius of Christianity is that it spiritualizes and ethicizes man's desire for rewards and offers the full rewards that alone are worth winning. The phrases of vs. 9, **have God, . . . has both the Father and the Son,** suggest that communion with God constitutes reward in the thought of this epistle, and the present tense of the verbs here implies that it is available now. The reward offered by Christianity in one sense is yet to be won; in another sense it is attained wherever men live the life of faith and love (cf. Expos. on I John 2:28–3:3).

9. *Two Kinds of Progressivism.*—This verse sets us the task of distinguishing between the right and wrong kinds of progressivism, and permits the inference that not all who go ahead

11 For he that biddeth him God-speed is partaker of his evil deeds.

12 Having many things to write unto you, I would not *write* with paper and ink: but I trust to come unto you, and speak face to face, that our joy may be full.

ing; **11** for he who greets him shares his wicked work.

12 Though I have much to write to you, I would rather not use paper and ink, but I hope to come to see you and talk with you face to face, so that our joy may be complete.

---

warns against even meeting such men or speaking of them (Ign. Smyr. 4:1; 7:2). Irenaeus tells us of how Polycarp once met the archheretic Marcion, and when the latter asked, "Dost thou know me?" replied, "I do know thee, the first-born of Satan." And Irenaeus adds, "Such was the horror which the apostles and their disciples had against holding even a verbal communication with any corrupters of the truth," then quoting Tit. 3:10 (*Against Heresies* III. 3. 4). A greeting, whether at meeting or parting in these days, had a kind of sacramental reality (cf. Matt. 10:12-13; Luke 10:5-6). The reader who is disturbed by the intransigence here may well ponder Jesus' words in Matt. 5:47. The counsel is perhaps best construed as a rule of excommunication on the part of the community (rather than a personal act), as also in Matt. 18:17; I Cor. 5:3-5; II Thess. 3:14, 15. The problems the church faced and its attitude are illuminated by Jude 23 and I Tim. 5:22.

IV. Conclusion (vss. 12-13)

12. The phrases closely resemble those in III John 13, with just enough difference to reassure us that no copyist or imitator is at work. **Paper** (i.e., papyrus) **and ink;** cf. "pen" (i.e., reed) and ink in III John 13. **Face to face** (literally, "mouth to mouth")

---

are to be condemned. Only the man who **does not abide in the doctrine of Christ** is condemned. As recently as in vs. 4 the elder has rejoiced in those who are "following the truth"; like all faithful interpreters of the gospel he conceives the Christian life to be movement and growth (cf. Expos. on I John 2:12-14). The sin of conservatism—failing to go ahead—is as common as the sin of spurious progressivism—not abiding in the doctrine of Christ. When is a progressive not progressive? When he parades his progressivism for its own sake, and falsely supposes that the new is always the best or that mere movement is progress. In theology and in Christian ethics, as in the everyday world of politics, art, and social reform, the new must be tested by the old. Jesus significantly describes the man who qualifies for the kingdom of heaven as one who brings forth from his treasure both "what is new and what is old" (Matt. 13:52). The false progressive also fails to test whatever truth he believes in or whatever ideal he seeks by the doctrine of Christ, i.e., the mind of Christ revealed in apostolic Christianity. Lesser standards are inadequate, e.g., literal quotation from the Bible, tradition for the sake of tradition, the contemporary mind, crystallized creeds.

10-11. *Warning Against Hospitality to False Prophets and Evangelists.*—The elder's warning may be interpreted figuratively rather than literally as a warning against false tolerance and promiscuous acceptance of popular gospels. Many minds pride themselves on receiving and greeting all doctrines; for these religion becomes a succession of fads. The popularity in our day of theosophical cults which mix elements of Oriental religions, insights of modern psychology, and fragments of the Christian gospel is a case in point. The mind of the Christian is an open mind in that it receives all truth; but it is a mind first possessed by the mind of Christ. These verses also set the problem of the right and wrong kinds of separatism, and require Christians to think through how far, if at all, alien religions and cultures can be accommodated to or must be absorbed by Christianity.

12-13. *Conclusion.*—Observe that the elder knows when to end a letter! He has accomplished his purpose to encourage his readers to follow truth, to walk in love, and to abide in the doctrine of Christ. Would that all letters and discourses were as complete and concise. Also the elder knows when not to write letters! Many matters, especially of a controversial nature, are better dealt with **face to face.** Note again the graciousness and charm of his concluding words to the Christian fellowship, **The children of your elect sister greet you.**

13 The children of thy elect sister greet thee. Amen.

13 The children of your elect sister greet you.

---

as in Num. 12:8 LXX, except for the preposition; cf. I Cor. 13:12. The elder's aim is that **our joy may be complete**, as in I John 1:4.

13. As we have noted in connection with 1:1, greetings are sent from the faithful in the church from which the elder writes.

III JOHN

TEXT, EXEGESIS, AND EXPOSITION

1 The elder unto the well-beloved Gaius, whom I love in the truth.

2 Beloved, I wish above all things that thou mayest prosper and be in health, even as thy soul prospereth.

1 The elder to the beloved Ga'ius, whom I love in the truth.

2 Beloved, I pray that all may go well with you and that you may be in health; I

I. Address and Greeting to Gaius (vss. 1-2)

1-2. We have in III John a clear example of a letter from one individual to another, as we do not in II John or even in the Epistle to Philemon. Our best parallel in the N.T. for the formula of address in such a letter is found in Acts 23:26, which includes the customary "greeting" (χαίρειν) absent here. The letter of Claudius Lysias, on the other hand, lacks the usual devout expression of good wishes or blessing found in a special form here in vs. 2. The salutations in the Pastoral epistles transform the conventional χαίρειν into "grace, mercy, and peace" (as in II John 3) or into "grace and peace" (Tit. 1:4). A Christian papyrus letter from a boy to his mother illustrates the usages of the time and those found in the opening of our present epistle: "Ammon to Kallinika, my lady mother: greeting. In the first place [πρὸ μὲν πάντων; so the text followed by KJV in vs. 2] I pray that you may be in health [ὑγιαίνειν; so here] in the Lord God . . ." (*Papyri Greci e Latini, Pubblicazioni della Societa Italiana* [Florence: 1912]; cited in *Hellenistic Greek Texts,* ed. Allen Wikgren with the collaboration of Ernest Cadman Colwell and Ralph Marcus [Chicago: University of Chicago Press. 1947], p. 130. The commentator's translation). Similarly, the elder writes here, **I pray that . . . you may keep well.**

For **the elder** see on II John 1. Gaius is a common name in this period, as indeed appears in the N.T. (cf. Acts 19:29; 20:4; Rom. 16:23; I Cor. 1:14). Unreliable tradition identifies the present Gaius with the first bishop of Pergamum. No title of office is assigned

---

1-2. Address and Greeting to Gaius.—Shared faith in the truth of Christ and shared experience of his life sanctify personal friendship as well as corporate fellowship (cf. II John 1), and establish human love in God as nothing else can. Contrast the friendship between David and Jonathan with the friendship Jesus shared with the disciples, and the disciples with one another (cf. John 15:12-17). The elder's spiritualization of conventional greetings, making religious well-

being the measure of good in other matters, rebukes our concern—if not obsession—with physical health and material prosperity as the maximum good in life, and causes us to rethink what we mean when we express the hope that **all may go well** and that one **may keep well.** Many people are healthy animals but desperately sick souls. Nevertheless, the elder declares that one can know without complacency that one's soul is **well** and find satisfaction therein,

3 For I rejoiced greatly, when the brethren came and testified of the truth that is in thee, even as thou walkest in the truth.

4 I have no greater joy than to hear that my children walk in truth.

5 Beloved, thou doest faithfully whatsoever thou doest to the brethren, and to strangers;

6 Which have borne witness of thy charity before the church: whom if thou bring

know that it is well with your soul. **3** For I greatly rejoiced when some of the brethren arrived and testified to the truth of your life, as indeed you do follow the truth. **4** No greater joy can I have than this, to hear that my children follow the truth.

5 Beloved, it is a loyal thing you do when you render any service to the brethren, especially to strangers, **6** who have testi-

---

to him here, though his activity and contacts are reflected in the note. Whether he was converted by the elder is uncertain (vs. 4).

The conventional epistolary terms for prosperity and good health are used (for the former cf. I Cor. 16:2, "as he may prosper"). Such external blessings are desired for Gaius; literally, "in all things," **even as thy soul prospereth** (KJV; RSV paraphrases here). The assured spiritual well-being is taken as the measure of good wishes in other matters.

II. Gaius and the Itinerant Missionaries (vss. 3-8)

3-4. The complimentary opening is continued with an expression of rejoicing (**I greatly rejoiced**; the same words in II John 4) over an aspect of Gaius' conduct which suggests the main theme of the letter. **Some of the brethren arrived and testified to the truth of your life**; the Greek participles indicate that numerous such reports had come in. There is frequent contact between the elder and his field. The testimony is to Gaius' **truth,** here in the sense of fidelity to the gospel; in what particular, vs. 5 will show. There is a shade of difference between the similar expressions in vss. 3b and 4. In the former case we have literally, "You walk in truth" (without article). In vs. 4 the article is present, "Walking in the truth." Both our English translations obscure the difference. But the elder, when he refers to *the* truth, commonly refers to the gospel message or revelation and its common apostolic formulation (cf. vss. 8, 12; also I John 2:21; 3:19; 5:7; II John 1b-2; the exceptions in I John 1:6, 8; etc., are due to special locutions). In vs. 3b emphasis falls on genuineness in the Christian life as against outward profession (cf. I John 3:18, "not . . . in word or speech but in deed and truth"; also II John 1a, 3-4, and vs. 1 above). **My children:** A special turn is given to the phrase in the Greek to indicate the peculiarly intimate relationship between the elder and followers like Gaius whom he had perhaps himself converted.

5. The "truth" of Gaius' life (vs. 3) has been reported to the elder in connection with his practice of caring for traveling missionaries in the area. He has aided such **brethren,** in many cases **strangers,** in accordance with the general practice of the early church (cf. Rom. 12:13; I Tim. 3:2; 5:10; Tit. 1:8; Heb. 13:2; I Pet. 4:9). In this he does a **loyal** (literally, "faithful") **thing.** Note J. B. Phillips' translation of Eph. 1:15: "Since, then, I heard of this *faith* of yours in the Lord Jesus and the practical way in which you are expressing it towards fellow-Christians . . ." (*Letters to Young Churches,* p. 101).

6-7. Such missioners in reporting their tours in meetings of the elder's own church (cf. Acts 14:27) have **testified** to Gaius' **love.** He is encouraged to renew this service now,

---

even though evil may still tempt (vs. 11; cf. Expos. on I John 3:19-24; 5:10a).

3-6a. *The Character of Gaius.*—The noble character of Gaius pictured here offers a high ideal for the churchman. Gaius, apparently a layman, follows **the truth** (vss. 3-4); his outward living corroborates his profession of faith. **Especially** does he minister **to strangers.** Above

all, he is **loyal.** He can be counted on. One commentator conjectures that Gaius was perhaps the one link that held this church in the Christian fold,[1] that without his loyalty it might have withdrawn from the apostolic communion and thus weakened the vital chain of Christian

[1] G. G. Findlay, *Fellowship in the Life Eternal* (London: Hodder & Stoughton, 1909), pp. 38-39.

forward on their journey after a godly sort, thou shalt do well:

7 Because that for his name's sake they went forth, taking nothing of the Gentiles.

8 We therefore ought to receive such, that we might be fellow helpers to the truth.

9 I wrote unto the church: but Diotrephes, who loveth to have the pre-eminence among them, receiveth us not.

fied to your love before the church. You will do well to send them on their journey as befits God's service. **7** For they have set out for his sake and have accepted nothing from the heathen. **8** So we ought to support such men, that we may be fellow workers in the truth.

9 I have written something to the church; but Di-ot're-phes, who likes to put himself first, does not acknowledge my authority.

---

and to speed the present deputation **on their journey** in a way "worthy of God." The verb used (προπέμψας) implies not only good wishes but material support. This is necessary because the evangelists have **set out** on their work according to the Christian practice without inviting or accepting gifts from the **heathen** (ἐθνικῶν, not ἔθνων, **Gentiles,** as in KJV), to whom they preached, lest their motives be misconstrued. For sensitiveness on this point cf. Ign. Trall. 8:2. In the Didache, in which there is detailed instruction with regard to hospitality and such visitations, there is warning against evangelists bent on exploitation (Did. 11:6), and the avariciousness of Hellenistic street preachers is documented in pagan literature. **For his name's sake,** cf. Ign., Eph. 7:1, "For there are some who make a practice of carrying about the Name with wicked guile, and do certain other things unworthy of God."

8. Support (RSV) follows a better text than **receive** (KJV), but both translations probably fail to give the true sense of the concluding phrase, "allies of the Truth" (Moffatt; in Jas. 2:22 we have a similar construction). **The truth** here refers to God's revelation and the life-giving message that makes it known.

III. Recalcitrance of Diotrephes (vss. 9-11)

9. The elder's appeal to Gaius to continue his practice of hospitality and support to traveling missionaries (vss. 5-8) has particular point in the light of the denial of such entertainment on the part of a certain Diotrephes. More responsibility of this kind is to fall on Gaius because of the shabby treatment accorded the deputations elsewhere, and perhaps with reference to one such particular band headed by Demetrius, who receives a word of recommendation (vs. 12).

When the elder writes, **I have written something to the church,** we naturally suppose that the reference is to that congregation of which both Gaius and Diotrephes

---

churches in Asia Minor. Such men save the day! How fine to be the man who is loyal!

6b-8. The Missionary Obligation.—While originally addressed to Gaius, these verses summon all laymen to imitate Gaius' spirit in furthering the work and growth of the gospel. Specifically these verses lay on the church the sacred obligation to **support** in every way, not merely with "good wishes" (Exeg. on vs. 6), the missionary outreach of the gospel (cf. Expos. on I John 4:14-15). The highest sanctions attach to this summons: such support is nothing less than **God's service,** and it unites Christians as "allies" (Moffatt) **in the truth.** The church must never hesitate to present the challenge of missions as fundamental to its purpose to save "the whole world" (I John 2:2). The laity must

understand that support of missions is correspondingly a first claim on their money and prayer and requires an intelligent comprehension of the world's need and of the gospel's truth. Appeals to support missions must consequently be pitched on the high plane of service to God and comradeship in working—even fighting—with him to conquer evil and falsehood, while the true motive for all missionary (and pastoral) work must be to **set out for his** [God's] **sake,** and to accept **nothing from the heathen.** Service offered in abandoned, joyful love to God and kept pure from worldly compromise, commercialism, flattery, and patronage, alone is worthy of Christ.

9-11. The Evil Character of Diotrephes.— Diotrephes may be taken as a character study in evil, as Gaius in goodness. Observe that in the

10 Wherefore, if I come, I will remember his deeds which he doeth, prating against us with malicious words: and not

10 So if I come, I will bring up what he is doing, prating against me with evil words.

---

are members. But Gaius could not in that case be ignorant of the details stated in vss. 9-10. The reference could be to a neighboring congregation with whose general situation Gaius was acquainted, but not with the most recent developments (so Dodd). More likely the elder has written to the large group of small conventicles or household churches in the district in which Gaius lives—all together making up "the church" of this area or of this city and its wider environs. In one of these "household churches" Diotrephes is in a position of power and rejects the instructions of the elder and excludes his delegation. Concerning this Gaius would need to be informed. The elder wishes to make sure that other leaders of this area do not act like Diotrephes (cf. vs. 11a), and that such emissaries as Demetrius should be well received. The elder's writing referred to in vs. 9 would then have been a letter addressed to the wider church of the area and to all its local conventicles recommending the deputation or deputations working in the region, and in that case could not have been either our first or second epistle.

The reason for Diotrephes' opposition is not clear. Explanation is sought in two directions: (a) In this period a new type of church organization was emerging which gave predominant local control to single individuals rather than to boards of elders or overseers. With this went an increasing local autonomy. The apostles had passed from the scene, and the second generation leaders of the wider church, appointed by the apostles and borrowing their authority, gave way more and more to the local leaders who in some areas soon took on the official status we associate with the term bishop. Diotrephes may represent this assertion of local authority and individual leadership. The process of decentralization and the emergence of local or native leadership is one with which we are familiar in the younger churches of the mission field. (b) But this opposition to the elder may have been motivated also or even primarily by theological differences. The evidence of our other two epistles and other sources shows that the churches of Asia at this time were beset by a wide variety of doctrines, and especially by Gnostic errors. III John has no specific reference to the false teachings opposed in I and II John; but the language used by the elder as he appeals to Gaius and commends Demetrius and the probabilities of the situation in letters so closely related as II and III John are persuasive. Diotrephes' radical intransigence was due not only to local independency and personal assertion (cf. I Pet. 5:3), but also to theological partisanship. He **does not acknowledge my authority.** The elder's letter will have been suppressed by Diotrephes.

10. The elder hopes to make a personal visit soon (cf. vss. 13-14; II John 12); at that time he **will bring up what** [Diotrephes] **is doing**—i.e., "bring to remembrance"

---

elder's thought all other defects in Diotrephes' character are made to issue from his desire **to put himself first.** Selfishness is the root sin, and with Diotrephes it takes the unlovely form of ecclesiastical ambition and domination. Findlay suggests that Diotrephes was "one of the first experiments in Episcopacy"![2] If a first experiment, he was not the last failure! The story of the church through the centuries is saddened by the spectacle of those who liked to put themselves first. Jesus' reversal of what constitutes being "first" and "last" (Matt. 19:30; Luke 22:24-27) forever judges the attitudes of pride and ambition that corrupt character in leaders

of the church as elsewhere. But John also describes Diotrephes as **prating against me with evil words.** A man is judged by those whom he attacks and by what he says of them, as well as by what he does. Is not Diotrephes' condemnation that he is known in Christian history only as the man who spoke evilly against the most revered and beloved figure of Christendom in his day? Note further that Diotrephes' selfish pride issued in outright insubordination (vs. 9b) and provoked schism in the church (vs. 10b).

The elder's injunction to **imitate good** reminds us that men need a living example more than verbal exhortation for noble living (cf. Expos. on I John 2:6), and that being a Chris-

2 *Ibid.,* p. 42.

THE INTERPRETER'S BIBLE

content therewith, neither doth he himself receive the brethren, and forbiddeth them that would, and casteth *them* out of the church.

11 Beloved, follow not that which is evil, but that which is good. He that doeth good is of God: but he that doeth evil hath not seen God.

12 Demetrius hath good report of all *men,* and of the truth itself: yea, and we *also* bear record; and ye know that our record is true.

And not content with that, he refuses himself to welcome the brethren, and also stops those who want to welcome them and puts them out of the church.

11 Beloved, do not imitate evil but imitate good. He who does good is of God; he who does evil has not seen God. 12 Deme'tri-us has testimony from every one, and from the truth itself; I testify to him too, and you know my testimony is true.

(the same word in John 14:26c). At the same time he will refute his empty and malicious charges. Diotrephes not only refuses to give hospitality to Christian **brethren** engaged in preaching the gospel, but he makes it a practice to excommunicate from the church (and not only from the local household fellowship where he reigns) any **who want to welcome them.** He thus arrogates to himself a power which later became legal for local bishops.

11. Gaius, who may have had pressure put on him in his own local church to take sides against the elder, is affectionately urged not to **imitate evil,** i.e., as exemplified by Diotrephes, but to **imitate good.** Appeal is then made to the central teachings and characteristic phrases of I John. **He who does good is of God,** i.e., in the present instance, he who practices love for the Christian brethren "is born of God" (I John 4:7). **He who does evil has not seen God;** Diotrephes is of those who, abiding in sin, have not either "seen him or known him" (I John 3:6). Whatever differences there may be between believers as to ecclesiastical ordering or theology, Christian charity is a test to which all must submit. How this theme of the elder is to be reconciled with his stern counsel in II John 10-11, where the situations are reversed, has been touched on at that point.

IV. Commendation of Demetrius (vs. 12)

12. This Demetrius (not the same one mentioned in Acts 19:24) is presumably an active figure in one of the deputations in view, either one hitherto unknown to Gaius, or one which has been subject to particular disparagement. The transition would be less abrupt if he had been one of those particularly assailed by Diotrephes and his party. He may be the bearer of the present letter. His good standing is vouched for by three testimonials: (*a*) **from every one** (cf. I Clem. 44:3, the same phrase); (*b*) from **the truth itself;** (*c*) from the elder. **The truth itself** speaks in his favor, i.e., God's revelation in the gospel exhibits itself in his life (cf. "doing" the truth, I John 1:6). Or the **truth itself** may refer to the interior witness of the Spirit. This phrase appears to be quoted

tian involves setting an example to others (cf. Matt. 5:14-15; John 13:15, 35). Daniel Webster once said that the strongest argument for God he knew was an aunt who lived in the hills of Vermont. However, verbal exhortation is sometimes necessary, as here; and people need to be reminded in plain language that there are such things as right and wrong, and that life with God in large part depends on simply doing good.

12. *Commendation of Demetrius.*—Ordinary prudence suggests that the three forms of testimony to Demetrius' character cited by the elder must be taken together if they are to provide a

reliable rule for commending people. **Testimony from every one** is good up to a point, but even *consensus omnium* can be wrong. Testimony from a trusted, Christian friend (**I testify . . . too**) is more reliable. **Testimony . . . from the truth itself,** i.e., the integrity of Christian character in which "the gospel exhibits itself in . . . life" (Exeg. on vs. 12), crowns all else. Whenever the truth of the gospel really possesses a man, his character inevitably manifests it in the attitudes of faith and love by which he habitually lives. These tests rebuke the facile ease with which we indiscriminately use the prestige of the Christian church to endorse candidates for office,

312

13 I had many things to write, but I will not with ink and pen write unto thee:

14 But I trust I shall shortly see thee, and we shall speak face to face. Peace *be* to thee. *Our* friends salute thee. Greet the friends by name.

13 I had much to write to you, but I would rather not write with pen and ink; 14 I hope to see you soon, and we will talk together face to face.

15 Peace be to you. The friends greet you. Greet the friends, every one of them.

by Papias; if so, it is one of the earliest evidences of the general circulation of these epistles (cf. Eusebius *Church History* III. 39. 3). Finally, the elder himself adds his own commendation, using an editorial **we. You** [singular, not **ye**, KJV] **know my testimony is true**; the similar phrase in John 19:35 and 21:24 suggests a close relationship between these epistles and the editor of the Fourth Gospel.

V. CONCLUSION (vss. 13-15)

13-15. The conclusion is in large part a word-for-word repetition of II John 12-13, but there are constant slight differences. Thus we have here **pen and ink** instead of "paper and ink" (II John 12). The **pen** is of course the reed. The epistolary conclusion follows the pattern of the time. The formula of greeting, **peace be to you**, came over into the church from Jewish usage (cf. I Pet. 5:14; Luke 10:5; John 20:19, 21, 26, and see the salutation in II John 3). Since this is a personal note, the greetings are more intimate than in II John 13. **Greet the friends, every one of them** (RSV); literally, **by name** (KJV), as in John 10:3. The term **friends** (in the plural a Johannine expression, John 15:13, 15; etc.) suggests those within the churches concerned who were favorable to the elder's authority.

commend people for employment or admission to schools, etc. The elder is called "the apostle of love," but his love was wise and discriminating. So let it be with us.

13-15. *Conclusion.*—Cf. Expos. on II John 12-13.

15. *Benediction and Salutation.*—The Christian benediction, **Peace be to you,** is more than a conventional literary form. In the deepest sense peace is the gift of God to those who through faith and love (the two fundamental themes of the Johannine epistles) live in the eternal life of God now. Such peace partakes of the ultimate reality and harmony of the universe, and derives from the eternal life which is "from the beginning" (I John 1:1). This is the peace which Jesus at the Last Supper, facing the agony of Gethsemane and the Cross, could yet bequeath to his friends as John invokes it here, "My peace I give to you" (John 14:27).

The Epistle of

JUDE

Introduction and Exegesis by ALBERT E. BARNETT
Exposition by ELMER G. HOMRIGHAUSEN

JUDE

INTRODUCTION

The modern reader of the New Testament may have difficulty in imagining how a letter so brief and apparently so remote from modern life achieved a place in the Christian canon. That it did so affords a significant insight into the process out of which the New Testament grew. The books of the New Testament were in most instances written to meet crises of one sort or another in the life of the early church. Their preservation was due to the importance of the issue they treated, and the esteem in which they came to be held in one or more of the principal churches.

Jude expressed the determined opposition of the Roman church to Docetism, a heretical doctrine of the person of Christ that denied his real humanity. The importance of the letter is shown by the fact that it was incorporated in the earliest official New Testament in the West. By the end of the second century it was in general circulation in the church, both East and West.

It has religious significance today not merely because of its clear perception of the tremendous ethical import of Jesus' humanity, but equally because it so forcefully emphasizes the relevance of sound theology for sound morality. Jude refutes the careless assumption that a man's beliefs are of little consequence. He insists that religious ideas are important in direct proportion to the seriousness with which they are believed. He urges that good religion deserves good theology, that un-thought-out religion has an insecure footing, and that the Christianity of apostolic days supplies sound norms for the guidance of later generations.

I. Authorship

Verbal resemblances between the doxologies of I Clem. 20:12 and 65:2 (A.D. 95) and that of Jude 25 (cf. Ecclus. 18:5) may represent literary indebtedness. They may, however, merely reflect common use of familiar liturgical formulas. Polycarp's reminder (A.D. 115) so to use Paul's letters as "to build yourselves up into the faith given you" (Polyc. Phil. 3:2) conceivably involves recollection of Jude 20. It more probably reveals that during the first half of the second century A.D. Christianity was increasingly understood in terms of authoritative teaching. The reference in Herm. Sim. V. 7. 2 (A.D. 130?) to the "defilement" of the body similarly does not require dependence on Jude 8.

Clearly, however, Jude was known to the author of II Peter. The latter incorporated it substantially as his ch. 2. His use of the letter (*ca.* A.D. 150) is the earliest evidence of its circulation in the church.

The Muratorian canon (*ca.* A.D. 190) includes Jude among the writings generally accepted by the church. It nevertheless reflects awareness of differences of opinion regarding its authorship in the statement, "The Epistle of Jude no doubt, and the two bearing the name of John, are accepted in the Catholic Church." Tertullian (A.D. 197) found in Jude 14-15 an argument for the scriptural status of the book of Enoch. He assures his readers that the latter possessed "a testimony in the Apostle Jude."[1] Clement of Alexandria (A.D. 190-202) quotes Jude 5-6 as by Jude.[2] A considerable portion of Clement's *Outlines,* containing expositions of I Peter, I and II John, and Jude, is preserved in Latin in Cassiodorus' *Adumbrations of Clement* (A.D. 560). There the Jude "who wrote the Catholic Epistle" is described as "the brother of the sons of Joseph," who though knowing "the near relationship of the Lord," refrained from saying that "he himself was his brother." Eusebius, however, entertains some doubt regarding Clement's judgment of the authenticity of Jude. He says that Clement in his *Miscellanies* "made use of testimonies from the disputed writings," and these Eusebius designates as "the book known as the Wisdom of Solomon, and the Wisdom of Jesus the Son of Sirach, and the Epistle

[1] *Apparel of Women* I. 3.
[2] *The Instructor* III. 8; cf. *Miscellanies* III. 2.

317

to the Hebrews, and those of Barnabas, and Clement, and Jude." [3] Origen (ca. A.D. 230) thinks the author was "the apostle Jude" listed in Mark 6:3 and Matt. 13:55 as a brother of Jesus.[4] Eusebius (ca. A.D. 324) lists the letter sometimes as "spurious" and elsewhere as "disputed." [5] Athanasius (A.D. 367) included Jude as the seventh in his full corpus of Catholic letters.[6] Jerome (ca. A.D. 392) similarly knew the letter as one of the seven Catholic epistles and described it as having been written by "Jude the brother of James." He refers to no dispute about its authorship, but mentions that some rejected it because it "quotes from the apocryphal book of Enoch." [7]

The letter itself designates its author as "Jude, a servant of Jesus Christ and brother of James." The phrase, "brother of James," may have been an editorial addition based on inference from gospel lists of Jesus' brothers, or it may represent the author's own employment of pseudonymity to gain an advantageous hearing for his message. Jude, the brother of Jesus and James, very probably died before A.D. 70, and could hardly have written our letter. This is implied by Hegesippus' story of the arraignment by Domitian (A.D. 93-96) of the grandsons of Jude as the surviving kinsmen of Jesus.[8] When Domitian saw their humble appearance and their poverty, he ordered them released as offering no threat to Roman security. They were mature men at the time, and Eusebius adds the note that they lived "until the time of Trajan" (A.D. 98-117). Their father was no longer alive at their arrest, and presumably their grandfather Jude had died even earlier.

Whatever his name, the author was a man who "believed passionately in a creed." [9] He was an advocate of old-fashioned Christianity. The apostles were the ideal figures of a sacred past (vs. 17), and any variation from doctrinal teaching traditionally emanating from them meant deterioration, not progress (vss. 3, 20). Orthodoxy and truth were synonyms. For the refutation of heresy it was enough to show its difference from "the faith which was once for all delivered to the saints" (vs. 3). Our author was, however, by no means a doctrinaire. His primary concern was with character, not orthodoxy. He saw an inviolable and indissoluble

[3] Church History VI. 13. 6; VI. 14. 1.
[4] Commentary on Matthew X. 17; XVII. 30; On First Principles III. 2. 1.
[5] Church History II. 23. 24-25; III. 25. 3; VI. 13. 6; VI. 14. 1.
[6] Festal Epistles XXXIX. 5.
[7] On Famous Men IV.
[8] Eusebius Church History III. 20. 1-2.
[9] Charles Bigg, A Critical and Exegetical Commentary on the Epistles of St. Peter and St. Jude (New York: Charles Scribner's Sons, 1901; "International Critical Commentary"), p. 325.

relationship between righteousness and correct belief. Sound ethics required sound doctrine as a foundation. Nonconformity with the teaching of the Scriptures and the authoritative principles of "the apostles of our Lord Jesus Christ" (vs. 17) would logically show men to be "grumblers, malcontents, following their own passions, loud-mouthed boasters, flattering people to gain advantage" (vs. 16).

II. Reading Public

The author of Jude designates his readers as "those who are called, beloved in God the Father and kept for Jesus Christ" (vs. 1). Any Greek-speaking Christian community would be covered by such a general salutation. The letter is clearly encyclical in character. Its message was for Christians wherever unity was endangered by the heretical teaching and the immoral practices of Docetism. Its warnings would be relevant in any locality where doctrinal and moral standards, traditionally Christian, were challenged.

Christian literature of the first several centuries supports no tradition of a particular locality or area to which the first readers of Jude belonged. The earliest evidences of acquaintance with the letter occur in the West in II Peter, the Muratorian canon, and the writings of Tertullian. It was thereafter about equally popular in the East and the West. The heresy at which its warnings are aimed corresponds in character with that refuted in the Fourth Gospel, I and II John, and the letters of Ignatius. It might have been written, therefore, especially for the churches of Asia Minor, or for Christendom in general.

III. Date and Place

That Jude was written before A.D. 150 is established by its incorporation in II Peter. The reverence with which its author regards the apostles appears in Christian writings from the closing decade of the first century onward (cf. Eph. 2:20; 3:5; Rev. 18:20; 21:14). The Fourth Gospel (ca. A.D. 95) and I and II John (ca. A.D. 110) represent orthodox hostility to Docetism. The Gospel of Peter (ca. A.D. 130) and the Acts of John (ca. A.D. 150), on the other hand, disclose friendliness toward Docetism on the part of some Christians. Jude's conception of Christianity in essentially creedal terms and its tendency to accord scriptural authority to the words of the apostles suggest the general period reflected in the earliest form of the Didache, the letter of Barnabas, and II Peter (A.D. 120-50). Such data combine to indicate for Jude a date of about A.D. 125.

The place of Jude's origin is about as uncer-

JUDE

tain as its destination. II Peter was very probably written at Rome. Its incorporation of Jude shows the popularity of the latter in the West around the middle of the second century, and conceivably points to Rome as the place of its composition. Its recognition as canonical by Tertullian and the author of the Muratorian canon also argues strongly for Roman origin. The letter's attitude of severity toward heresy, its definitely polemic character, and its exaltation of authority would make it a very natural expression of the point of view of Roman Christianity.

IV. Purpose and Message

A crisis caused the author of Jude to defer writing a treatise he had planned on "our common salvation," and in its stead to address an immediate appeal to the same public "to contend for the faith which was once for all delivered to the saints" (vs. 3). All else must wait because the very foundations of sound doctrine and sound morality are jeopardized. The crisis requiring attention was created by persons who secretly gained admission to the church and employed their status as members to popularize heretical ideas and immoral practices (vs. 4).

Shocked by the discovery of the success achieved by these propagandists, the author of Jude issues his manifesto. He takes for granted that his readers know the content of "the faith," and along with it the heretical teaching by which it is endangered. He offers no systematic exposition of either. He is more concerned to arouse than inform faithful church members. He therefore denounces heretical teachers instead of refuting their propaganda. In the interest of moral integrity and spiritual effectiveness, he pleads that his readers build themselves up on their "most holy faith" (vs. 20). They will thus most effectively "contend for the faith which was once for all delivered to the saints" (vs. 3).

The faith which Jude urges his readers to defend (vs. 3), and on which as a foundation he exhorts them to build themselves up (vs. 20), is a body of authoritative teaching. Its embodiment of the essentials of apostolic Christianity and its agreement with the Scriptures made it normative. It had the validity of revelation and supplied the indispensable foundation for Christian morality. Instead of criticizing or amending it, men ought to believe and regulate their lives by it.

Jude devotes his attention principally to certain "ungodly persons" whom he charges with proposing dangerous and deceptive substitutes for the faith generally accepted in the church. Their immorality is the product of their heresy. They endanger the church because they "per-

vert the grace of our God into licentiousness and deny our only Master and Lord, Jesus Christ" (vs. 4). Though claiming profound knowledge of the things of God, they are actually devoid of the Spirit (vs. 19). Their only knowledge is of "those things that they know by instinct as irrational animals do" (vs. 10).

The body of the letter (vss. 5-16) pictures the evil qualities of these interlopers and illustrates from the Scriptures and "the predictions of the apostles" the doom that awaits them. Toward the close of the letter, when the storm of his indignation has spent itself, Jude gives a brief but significant summary of Christian conduct in the presence of the disturbing situation (vss. 17-23). Established on the foundation of their "most holy faith," believers must "remember . . . the predictions of the apostles," "pray in the Holy Spirit," keep themselves "in the love of God," wait patiently for the blessings which will be theirs when Christ returns, maintain a consistently redemptive interest in those who are confused by heretical teaching, "snatching them out of the fire." On persons committed to heretical points of view, they will "have mercy with fear, hating even the garment spotted by the flesh."

V. Outline of Contents

I. The epistolary introduction (1-4)
   A. Salutation (1-2)
   B. Occasion of the letter (3-4)
II. Characteristics and doom of the heretical intruders (5-16)
   A. The Scriptures show that God invariably punishes sinners (5-7)
   B. Heretical teachers characterized and denounced (8-13)
      1. Their basic sin is irreverence (8-10)
      2. Jude passionately denounces them (11-13)
   C. Inspired prophecy warns of these intruders (14-16)
III. The most holy faith the true foundation (17-23)
   A. Apostolic teaching supplies elements in this foundation (17-19)
   B. Holy living the best witness to apostolic Christianity (20-23)
      1. Sound theology essential to the good life (20)
      2. This faith, holy in origin, produces holiness (21-23)
IV. The benediction (24-25)

VI. Selected Bibliography

BIGG, CHARLES. A Critical and Exegetical Commentary on the Epistles of St. Peter and St. Jude ("International Critical Commentary"). New York: Charles Scribner's Sons, 1901.
CASE, SHIRLEY JACKSON. "Jude," The Abingdon Bible Commentary, ed. F. C. Eiselen, Edwin Lewis, and D. G. Downey. New York and Nashville: Abingdon-Cokesbury Press, 1929.

MAYOR, J. B. *The Epistle of St. Jude and the Second Epistle of St. Peter.* London: Macmillan & Co., 1907.

MOFFATT, JAMES. *The General Epistles* ("Moffatt New Testament Commentary"). New York: Harper & Bros.; London: Hodder & Stoughton, 1928.

PLUMMER, ALFRED. *The General Epistles of St. James and St. Jude* ("Expositor's Bible"). New York: A. C. Armstrong & Son, 1891.

WAND, J. W. C. *The General Epistles of St. Peter and St. Jude* ("Westminster Commentaries"). London: Methuen & Co., 1934.

JUDE

TEXT, EXEGESIS, AND EXPOSITION

1 Jude, the servant of Jesus Christ, and brother of James, to them that are sanc-

1 Jude, a servant of Jesus Christ and brother of James,

I. INTRODUCTION (1-4)

A. SALUTATION (1-2)

The author introduces himself, designates his readers, and prays for the bestowal upon them of the blessings Christians most desire.

1. Jude or Judas was a popular name among Jews and early Christians. Judas Maccabaeus was one of the heroes of postexilic Judaism. Two of the disciples of Jesus had the name, "Judas the son of James, and Judas Iscariot" (Luke 6:16; cf. Acts 1:13; John 14:22). Others of this name in the N.T. are "Judas the Galilean" (Acts 5:37), Judas of Damascus (Acts 9:11), "Judas called Barsabbas" (Acts 15:22), and **Jude, . . . brother of James.**

"A slave," rather than **a servant of Jesus Christ,** would more accurately translate the Greek and more faithfully convey the author's conception of himself. The word δοῦλος describes one who is in bondage to another, being derived from a verb meaning "to bind." Jude employs it to express his utter devotion to Christ. No ulterior motives

---

1-25. *A Surprising Book.*—The Bible contains many surprising books. Esther, for instance, does not contain the word "God." Ecclesiastes sets forth the philosophy of a cynic who, though fed up with everything that life can offer, is represented as finally affirming that the fear of God and moral integrity are the highest obligations in life. The Revelation of John is a mysterious book containing many word pictures which are hard to understand.

The Epistle of Jude certainly presents more surprising phenomena than any other book of the New Testament. In style it is original and picturesque. In tone it is intense, vehement, denunciative. In its point of view, it is Judaeo-Christian. In structure it is Aramaic, abounding in triple arrangements.[1]

It has affinities with apocalyptic literature. Its aged writer fiercely denounces apostasy and idolatry. Its major content—with some significant omissions—is found in II Peter. It quotes from the uncanonical book of Enoch and the Assumption of Moses. It attributes the fall of angels to their sins with mortal women. It "identifies the pillar of fire with a manifestation of Jesus (verse 5)."[2] It is the last of the catholic letters of the N.T., and in a sense is the last admonition to Christians **to contend for the faith which was once for all delivered to the saints** (vs. 3). It closes with one of the most impressive and beautiful ascriptions or doxologies to be found in the Bible or for that matter in all literature.

The letter provides us with evidence regarding the heresies of doctrine and perversions of

[1] Frederick W. Farrar, *The Messages of the Books* (New York: E. P. Dutton & Co., 1909), p. 450.

[2] *Ibid.,* p. 458.

tified by God the Father, and preserved in Jesus Christ, *and* called:

To those who are called, beloved in God the Father and kept for Jesus Christ:

---

affect his message. He speaks for his Lord in a sense comparable to that in which the O.T. prophets spoke for Yahweh. The emphasis is on the absoluteness of his consecration, not the compulsory character of his service. He willingly regards himself as expendable in his Master's cause, entirely at the disposal of Jesus Christ.

Jude is the only writer in the N.T. who refers to his family ties to identify himself. **Brother of James** undoubtedly claims relationship for Jude to James, the famous head of the Jerusalem church. This claim may be understood in a variety of ways. Conceivably it is an indirect way of recording his relationship to Jesus, at the same time keeping uppermost the religious attitude expressed in the description of himself as **a servant of Jesus Christ**. Again, it could be an editorial addition by a later hand, with the intention of accentuating the authority of Jude's message. Most probably it is the author's own way of suggesting that he wrote in the spirit of the founding fathers. He calls himself the **brother of James**, not to establish his actual family status (see Intro., p. 318), but in effect to claim for his message continuity with the faith of the earliest Christians.

The readers are **those who are called, beloved in God the Father and kept for Jesus Christ**. In the Greek **called** is a noun and comes third in the series, but this order can scarcely be kept in the English translation. The letter is addressed to "the called," **beloved** and **kept** being attributive modifiers. By means of all that Christ did, by the preaching of missionaries, by the leading of the Holy Spirit, God had sought out his own (cf. Rom. 8:28; I Cor. 1:26-29). Their own part had been to respond to his search for them. They are his called. Because of this they are beloved in God and kept for Jesus Christ. He who calls men also keeps them, and does so because he loves them.

Beloved in God the Father may be rendered "beloved by **God the Father**" (Moffatt; cf. KJV). The issue turns on whether the Greek preposition has the local sense of "in," or means "by," in the sense of agency. The former would be its more usual meaning. It has been suggested, however, that the preposition originally belonged with **Jesus Christ** and that an error of an early scribe accounts for its present position (B. F. Westcott and F. J. A. Hort, *The New Testament in the Original Greek* [New York: The Macmillan Co., 1928], "List of Suspected Readings," p. 586). On that basis the reading would be "dear to God the Father and . . . kept through union with Jesus Christ" (Goodspeed). Taking the text as it stands, the phrase **in God** would be a "dative of person," meaning "in the presence of God" (cf. I Cor. 2:6; 14:11). As in the Pauline and Johannine writings

---

morality which not only confronted the early church, but which had surreptitiously made their way into the fellowship itself. The early church was not as united as we are often led to believe!

It alerts Christians to the diabolical dangers which face them within and without, and challenges them to pray and contend for that holy faith which has been bequeathed to them from their loyal ancestors. These heretical **men in their dreamings** were divorcing truth from life. "Humanity without divinity is bestiality." And a divinity without humanity is sheer gnosticism. Truth and morality belong together, the author contends. Certain judgment is to fall upon these deviates and corruptors of the faith and the life of the Christian community.

Christians are to meet this situation with a faith that is built up, or mature, with prayer in the Holy Spirit, with persistent reliance on the love of God, with a receptive and hopeful attitude toward the mercy of the Lord Jesus Christ, and with a solicitous evangelism which seeks to save some by pity and others by snatching them out of the fire even while hating the foul thing they have made of themselves.

1-2. *A Three-sided Salutation.*—There are three aspects of the salutation of this catholic letter.

First of all, the writer identifies himself by his given name, his close relationship to James the apostle, and his absolute servitude to Jesus Christ. If he was a relative of Jesus, he does not state it directly. Modesty prevented him from going that far. To be associated with James, the leader of the Jerusalem church, was quite enough. Most important, however, is the fact that he was a **servant** or "slave" of Jesus Christ.

2 Mercy unto you, and peace, and love, | 2 May mercy, peace, and love be multi-
be multiplied. | plied to you.

(cf. Rom. 3:24; 6:11, 23; 8:39; I Cor. 1:4; II Cor. 3:14; Gal. 2:4; 3:14, 26; John 14:20; 15:4; I John 2:24), it may also describe Christians as spiritually joined to God and subject to his power and influence, a relationship due to God's great love for them. The best index to the meaning is the author's exhortation, "Keep yourselves in the love of God" (vs. 21). J. B. Mayor thinks that **beloved** may be an equivalent for "brethren," and that the meaning is "beloved by us in God the Father" (*The Epistle of St. Jude and the Second Epistle of St. Peter* [New York: The Macmillan Co., 1907], p. 18). This view is almost certainly mistaken. The reference is to God's own love for his own.

If, as previously noted, the preposition ἐν goes with **Jesus Christ** rather than with **God,** the called are **kept** through being mystically united with Christ; i.e., enabled to overcome temptation. If, as is more probable, they are **kept for Jesus Christ,** God is represented as acting directly as their guardian. He watches over them protectively "for the sake of" ("at the request of") Christ (cf. John 17:11-12, 15; I Pet. 1:4; I John 5:18; Rev. 3:10); or else, in the futuristic sense of I Thess. 5:23, he keeps them "spirit and soul and body . . . sound and blameless" until "the coming of our Lord Jesus Christ." In either event, the kept are divinely sustained when tempted. Jude contrasts them in this respect with others who though also called, nevertheless succumbed to temptation and either left the church or remained to corrupt its life (cf. vss. 4, 22-23).

2. The address closes with the prayer, **May mercy, peace, and love be multiplied to you.** In Gal. 6:16 "peace and mercy" are invoked as blessings "upon the Israel of God," and in I Tim. 1:2 "grace, mercy, and peace" are blessings God bestows (cf. II Tim. 1:2; II John 3). Paul regularly closes the address of his letters with "grace to you and peace from God our Father." Jude substitutes **mercy** (ἔλεος) for grace (χάρις) in the Pauline formula.

All forms of God's help to men express **mercy.** Jesus' earthly life supremely embodied this quality in God (cf. John 1:14). **Peace** denotes the inner composure and the social harmony which follow when men are right with God. It is the antithesis of inward and outward turmoil. It belongs second in the series of blessings. Its subordination to grace or mercy emphasizes God as its source. It has its basis in God's mercy. Not only so, but God's **love** toward his "called" contributes to peace. They partake of his nature and demonstrate their sonship to him by being governed by a love for one another and for all men which qualitatively resembles his devotion to their welfare (cf. I John 4:7-19). Jude prays not simply that his readers shall be blessed with **mercy, peace, and love,** but that these gifts from God shall **be multiplied** to them. He shares Paul's conviction that God works through temptation and trials of every description to enrich the spirits of believers (cf. Rom. 5:3-5; 8:18, 28, 35-39; Phil. 4:11-20). The crisis which evokes his letter should have this outcome for them.

Christians are expendable in the cause of Christ. (See comment on "slave" in Expos. on II Pet. 1:1a.)

Second, he speaks of his readers as those who are **called, beloved in God the Father, and kept for Jesus Christ.** Though unknown and unnamed these Christians share with Christians of all time three great experiences—called, beloved, kept. All Christians are called; that is, they have been summoned from what they are to what they should become. Calls of many kinds come to everyone, but this call is unique, decisive, and prophetic. All Christians are recipi-

ents of the love of God the Father. All Christians are kept not only as they pass through the trials of this life, but they are kept for the future Day of Jesus Christ. God is the guardian and guarantor of the Christian's deliverance here and in the end.

Third, Jude prays that three graces may be multiplied in the lives of his readers—**mercy, peace, and love.** Mercy is the active and outgoing and continuous favor of God; peace is the deep blessedness that comes to those who are reconciled to God; love is the overarching and undergirding good will of God which is

3 Beloved, when I gave all diligence to write unto you of the common salvation, it was needful for me to write unto you, and exhort *you* that ye should earnestly contend for the faith which was once delivered unto the saints.

3 Beloved, being very eager to write to you of our common salvation, I found it necessary to write appealing to you to contend for the faith which was once for all

---

B. OCCASION OF THE LETTER (3-4)

While eagerly planning a treatise on the subject of **our common salvation,** Jude had been shocked by discovering an insidious threat to the soundness of the inner life of the church. Immediately he issued his appeal to believers **to contend for the faith which was once for all delivered to the saints.**

3. Three times Jude addresses his readers as **beloved** (vss. 3, 17, 20; cf. I Pet. 2:11; 4:12; Jas. 1:16; I John 2:7; 3:2, 21; 4:1, 7, 11). Paul uses the term frequently in connection with and as more or less a synonym for "brothers" (e.g., I Cor. 15:58; Phil. 4:1; Col. 4:7, 9; cf. Jas. 1:16, 19; 2:5). The word is used in three senses in the N.T.: (*a*) It describes Jesus as peculiarly the object of God's love in his role as Messiah (Matt. 3:17; 12:18; 17:5; Mark 1:11; 9:7; Luke 3:22). (*b*) It expresses God's attitude toward those who have been "reconciled" to him (Rom. 1:7; 11:28; cf. Col. 3:12; I Thess. 1:4). (*c*) It is used of the relationship Christians sustain toward one another (Rom. 12:19; I Cor. 4:14; Philem. 1; Heb. 6:9; Jas. 1:16; II Pet. 3:1).

In vs. 1 Jude used the perfect participle of the verb from which our noun is derived to indicate God's attitude toward Christians, "beloved in God." In vs. 3 he speaks of his own love for his brethren. Love describes the same essential disposition of disinterested devotion to the true well-being of its object, whether it is God's love or man's.

Ignatius described himself as having "been sent a prisoner from Syria for the sake of our common name and hope" (Ign. Eph. 1:2). Similarly, Titus is addressed as "my true child in a common faith" (Tit. 1:4). In these instances "common" (the Greek adjective κοινός) describes something commonly held and equally open to all. By **our common salvation** Jude meant the divine deliverance and preservation equally open to all who accepted the gospel, with reference to which none was especially privileged. The truths having to do with this salvation constituted for him **the faith which was once for all delivered to the saints.**

Although Jude did not get to write his exposition of these truths, it may be inferred that at the minimum they included such emphases as God's loving guardianship in the present, the glorious deliverance of believers "unto eternal life" at Christ's second coming (vss. 1, 21), and a vitally religious and socially redemptive ordering of life in the existing world (vss. 17-23). He is placed under the necessity of shifting from an exposition to the defense of these truths by the discovery that they are seriously jeopardized by the activities of heretical teachers. **The faith** requires neither repetition nor supplementation.

---

the context of "life's little day," and its future glory.

3-4. The Reason for the Letter.—Jude had intended to write about **our common salvation,** but he changed his mind. We wish we had his intended compendium of the faith, a statement of all things most surely believed by Christians of that time. But "new occasions teach new duties."[3] Many a preacher has changed his sermon because a new situation arose which demanded attention. Jude faced an emergency, a sudden danger. He was constrained by the cir-

cumstances to concentrate upon the defense of the faith instead of on the nature of it. In the history of the church, emphases have changed. Sometimes there has been need to interpret and formulate the faith, at other times there has been need to defend and contend for it. Both are always necessary, but one may at times be more necessary than the other.

The peril which confronted Jude and his fellow Christians was the existence and power within the church of **ungodly persons** who were making salvation by grace an occasion for **licentiousness** and were thereby **denying the only**

[3] James Russell Lowell, "The Present Crisis."

4 For there are certain men crept in unawares, who were before of old ordained
to this condemnation, ungodly men, turn-

delivered to the saints. 4 For admission has
been secretly gained by some who long ago
were designated for this condemnation,

It **was once for all delivered** to the founding fathers (for a similar use of ἅπαξ, **once for all,** see Heb. 6:4; 10:2; I Pet. 3:18). Successive generations have the duty to pass it on without innovation.

4. Against these errorists Jude brings a fourfold indictment: (a) They **secretly gained** admission into the church. They have no such credentials of membership as "those who are called" (vs. 1) and whom Jude addresses as **beloved** (vs. 3). Stealth, not divine vocation and an assumption of the obligations of brotherhood, accounts for their presence (cf. Matt. 7:15; John 10:7-18; Acts 20:29). They crept in unawares "by another way" instead of entering "the sheepfold by the door" (John 10:1). (b) They **long ago were designated for this condemnation. Long ago** refers both to the prophecy of Enoch (vs. 14) and to the predictions of the apostles (vss. 17-18). The author may have had in mind Enoch 81:8; 106:19; 108:7; and such N.T. passages as are cited under (a). Insofar as the context suggests the meaning, **this condemnation** refers back to vs. 3 to the determined opposition the errorists will meet from those who will **contend for the faith.** It includes also the coarsening and degradation of character and the eschatological penalties implied in vss. 5-16. Jude is much more interested in asserting the certainty of this condemnation, however, than in making its details explicit. The appearance of the errorists was foreseen and their punishment prearranged. Jude had been startled, but not God. However dangerous they appear, they cannot thwart God. God is abundantly able to deal with them and his truth will triumph in spite of them (cf. vs. 24). (c) They are irreverent. This is meant by the description of the errorists as **ungodly.** The same adjective is used in Rom. 4:5; 5:6; I Tim. 1:9; I Pet. 4:18; II Pet. 2:5-6. The corresponding noun is used in Rom. 1:18 and 11:26. Jude repeatedly so characterizes those whom he condemns (vss. 15, 18). Their irreverence expresses itself in a perversion of **the grace of our God into licentiousness.** The Greek word here translated **licentiousness** connotes lust and its unbridled expression in sexual intercourse. It pictures outbreaking and outrageous indecency, not merely impurity of heart. **The grace of our God** is practically synonymous with "the gospel." **Grace,** the distinctive element in the Christian message, describes the kindness which moves God to forgive sinners and through Christ offer them salvation and its attendant blessings (vss. 1-2, 17-25). The errorists apparently misinterpreted grace to mean that moral law no longer bound them and that as truly "spiritual" persons they could freely indulge their physical appetites (vss. 18-19). They thought of body and spirit as being independent of each other and of salvation as having to do exclusively with spirit. Their logic was precisely of the sort attributed to Paul by his critics and repudiated by him with utmost vigor (Rom. 3:5-8; 6:1-2, 15-23; I Cor. 6:12-15; 10:23;

Lord God, and our Lord Jesus Christ. This should have been no surprise, for their emergence was predicted long ago. They had gained entrance into the church quite silently and unobserved. Evidently their real nature had not been discerned and their influence had not at first been detected. Now they are exposed, and Jude is alarmed at their power. He sees these enemies of the faith entrenched; he sounds the trumpet of danger; he calls on Christians to wage a vigorous battle to preserve the **most holy faith** (vss. 3, 20).

To the writer the apostolic tradition is a body of revealed truth which is authoritative, valid

for all time, adequate, and final. It is normative. Paul referred to it as a "pattern of the sound words" (II Tim. 1:13-14). The **faith** in this case (vs. 3) is not a living attitude but a definite body of truth. It centers in Jesus Christ, the historical revelation of the Son of God. He reveals God's true character, and acceptance of the church's faith about and in him as well as obedience to him as Lord is a part of that faith.

And Jude is a vigorous defender of it. He is one in a long line of jealous and zealous people who have held "gospel truth" so dear as to **contend** for it. They have not stood silently by

ing the grace of our God into lascivious- | ungodly persons who pervert the grace of
ness, and denying the only Lord God, and | our God into licentiousness and deny our
our Lord Jesus Christ. | only Master and Lord, Jesus Christ.[a]

> [a] Or *the only Master and our Lord Jesus Christ.*

Gal. 5:13-24). (*d*) Most seriously, they **deny our only Master and Lord, Jesus Christ** (RSV). The MSS on which "the received text" rests insert "God" after **Master**. This warrants the translation, **denying the only Lord God, and our Lord Jesus Christ** (KJV). On similar textual basis Martin Luther translates the clause, "And they deny God, that he alone is Lord, and our Lord Jesus Christ" (*The Epistles of St. Peter and St. Jude* [tr. E. H. Gillett; New York: Anson D. F. Randolph, 1859], p. 321). The word translated **Master** usually refers to God (cf. Luke 2:29; Acts 4:24; Rev. 6:10). This fact may have suggested the insertion of "God" in the later MSS. Denial of "the Lord of Spirits," evidently God, is a sin condemned in the book of Enoch (cf. 38:2; 41:2; 45:2; 46:7; 48:10; etc.). Moreover, denial of Christ is associated with denial of God in the N.T. (Matt. 10:33; I Tim. 5:8; Tit. 1:16; I John 2:22). The RSV mg. says the proper reading may be **the only Master and our Lord Jesus Christ,** the word "God" being implied in the terminology but not actually present in the best MSS. There is no reason why **Master and Lord** may not both refer to **Jesus Christ**, as in RSV, ASV, ERV, Goodspeed, Moffatt, and the translation of the Vulg. by R. A. Knox. Confession of Jesus as Lord was the earliest Christian creed (Rom. 10:9; I Cor. 12:3; Phil. 2:11; cf. Col. 1:10-20). So to acknowledge him meant acceptance of Christian teaching about him as true and of his will as the law of life. To **deny** him involved disbelief of this teaching, which might take the form of acceptance of heretical theories of his person, and a corresponding moral lapse. Jude thinks that perversion of the grace of our God into licentiousness grows out of denial of Jesus Christ as our only Master and Lord. The issue in his time was the reality of Jesus' humanity. Ignatius, his younger contemporary, calls heretical teachers "beasts in the form of men" who regard Jesus' humanity and therefore his passion as "merely in semblance" (Ign. Smyr. 2:1; 4:1-2). Similarly, the author of II John brands as deceivers heretical leaders "who will not acknowledge the coming of Jesus Christ in the flesh" (II John 7). He regards the Antichrist as chief of such deceivers. For Jude, as for Ignatius and the author of II John, the idea that the divine Christ was only "seemingly" present in Jesus, or that Jesus was merely the earthward contact in a series of "aeons" through whom men came to God, was not only doctrinally unsound but tended to create the moral extremes of asceticism or licentiousness. He knew, as did John, that except as the "Word became flesh" (John 1:14) no effective salvation for men was possible. He agreed with the author of Hebrews that Christ "had to be made like his brethren in every respect" as the condition of becoming "a merciful and faithful high priest in the service of God" (Heb. 2:17). Only on the assumption that Jesus' humanity was actual could he dignify and redeem man's total life. Jude thus shares the general conviction of the N.T. that in the last analysis salvation is by incarnation (cf. II Cor. 3:18; Gal. 4:19; I John 3:2; etc.).

---

when Jesus Christ as interpreted by the apostles has been denied or perverted, or when new interpretations have made light of moral integrity. Jude illustrates the fact that the most subtle and alarming attacks upon Christianity have been made by those *within* the church. Regarding the gospel as "foolishness" or an "offense" these so-called enlightened Christians have sometimes tried to make the Christian faith something which can be easily adjusted to their pagan wishes.

Our author, however, does not believe that intellectual argument is the best defense of the gospel. While he centers the gospel in Jesus Christ, and in the essentials of the "faith," he insists that the best argument against a paganized or secularized Christianity is a holy life. He does not believe in employing the arm of the state to rid the church of these heretics. He is not pleading for their excommunication. Doubters may yet be convinced; others may be pitied; still others may be wrestled with and snatched from the fire. Above all, Christians must be mature, prayerful, God-loving, hopeful saints.

5 I will therefore put you in remembrance, though ye once knew this, how that the Lord, having saved the people out of the land of Egypt, afterward destroyed them that believed not.

5 Now I desire to remind you, though you were once for all fully informed, that he[b] who saved a people out of the land of Egypt, afterward destroyed those who did

[b] Ancient authorities read *Jesus* or *the Lord* or *God*.

II. CHARACTERISTICS AND DOOM OF THE HERETICAL INTRUDERS (5-16)

The principle emphasized through this section is that spiritual security demands unremitting spiritual discipline. Though saved, men may by unbelief fall into sin and be hopelessly lost (cf. Matt. 12:44-45; Luke 11:24-26; John 5:14; Heb. 6:4-8; 10:26-31; Herm. Mand. IV. 3. 1-7; Vis. II). The illustrations employed all show how people once spiritually privileged may make shipwreck of their lives. Jude wishes to warn Christians generally that profession of faith does not guarantee immunity from danger. The errorists, who serve as contemporary illustrations, are only indirectly his audience.

A. THE SCRIPTURES SHOW THAT GOD INVARIABLY PUNISHES SINNERS (5-7)

Three scriptural illustrations establish God's condemnation of persons once spiritually privileged who lapse into sin. They are (*a*) the unbelieving Israelites in the desert (Num. 14:11-35; cf. I Cor. 10:5-11; Heb. 3:16–4:2); (*b*) the fallen angels (Gen. 6:1-4; Deut. 32:8; Enoch 6–10; 18:14-16; 21:2; Justin *Apology* II. 5); (*c*) Sodom and Gomorrah (Gen. 19:23-25; Deut. 29:23; Wisd. Sol. 10:6).

5. The introductory clause, **I desire to remind you,** applies equally to each of the three illustrations. The lesson Jude emphasizes is no new thing. **Once for all** may be read with **fully informed,** or with **saved.** Moffatt translates, "The Lord once brought the People safe out of Egypt." Clement of Alexandria, among the early fathers, similarly understood the sense: " 'For I would have you know,' says Jude, 'that God, having once saved his people from the land of Egypt, afterward destroyed them that believed not' " (*The Instructor* III. 8). The critical Greek texts of Westcott and Hort, the eighth edition of Tischendorf, and Nestle favor the text translated in both KJV and RSV, and it is to be preferred. R. A. Knox reads, "Learn one lesson, and you know all." If this text is adopted, the emphasis is upon the thoroughness and finality of the knowledge given believers in "the faith which was once for all delivered." If the other, the reference is to "the creation of a people once for all" at the time of the Exodus, among whom, nevertheless, unbelievers appeared and were destroyed (Mayor, *Epistle of St. Jude and Second Epistle of St. Peter,* p. 29). The repetition of **you** shows that Jude is contrasting believers with the licentious errorists. A tragic deficiency of the latter is that they never acquainted themselves with authoritative Christian tradition. They lack the corrective which the recollection of a hallowed doctrinal foundation would have supplied.

The indisputable certainties about the Exodus are that God **saved a people out of the land of Egypt** and **afterward destroyed those who did not believe.** Errorists, and orthodox Christians as well, ought to learn from this that God always destroys those who

---

5-16. *The Nature and Destiny of False Christians.*—Jude realizes that Christians may know all about their "common salvation," and even know something about the enemies of the holy faith, yet not really understand any of it in a vital way. Like Peter, he desires to remind (vs. 5) his readers, to jar their knowledge into action about these matters. Memory here is not mere recollection; it is recollection with a view to discerning action (see Heb. 4:7 ff.; I Cor. 10:5).

It is not enough to be **once . . . fully informed** (vs. 5); Christians must be perennially reminded of some things. And they must be re-

minded of the fact that even after God has saved a people out of the bondage of Egypt some of those delivered people can suffer destruction because of disbelief. Being members of the saved community is no guarantee that they may not be subtly tempted to assume an attitude of skepticism toward God, even without knowing it. Or they may—like so many Christians of that and subsequent times—regard themselves as real Christians simply because they were baptized members of the Christian church. In virtue of their outward attachments they regarded themselves as safe from any peril. Such a false sense

6 And the angels which kept not their first estate, but left their own habitation, he hath reserved in everlasting chains under darkness unto the judgment of the great day.

7 Even as Sodom and Gomorrah, and the cities about them in like manner, giving themselves over to fornication, and going after strange flesh, are set forth for an example, suffering the vengeance of eternal fire.

not believe. 6 And the angels that did not keep their own position but left their proper dwelling have been kept by him in eternal chains in the nether gloom until the judgment of the great day; 7 just as Sodom and Go-mor'rah and the surrounding cities, which likewise acted immorally and indulged in unnatural lust, serve as an example by undergoing a punishment of eternal fire.

---

lapse into unbelief and disobedience. Induction into the Christian community does not guarantee people against being ultimately lost. Rigorous and continued spiritual discipline alone supplies a basis for assurance.

6. The original story of the disobedient angels occurs in Gen. 6:1-4. The highly embellished account of the book of Enoch, however, led Jude to use it (cf. I Pet. 3:19-20). Enoch gives an elaborate and dramatic account of these angels: (*a*) They were bound "hand and foot" and cast "into the darkness," with "rough and jagged rocks" piled upon them. They must suffer thus forever, or at least until "the day of the great judgment," when they "shall be cast into the fire" (10:4-6, 11-12). When they are cast "into the abyss of complete condemnation," they will be bound with "iron chains of immeasurable weight" (54:3-5). (*b*) The offense of the angels consisted in abandonment of their proper "domain" in heaven. They can expect "no peace nor forgiveness of sin." Never will they attain mercy and peace, even though they "make supplication unto eternity," because they "left the high heaven, the holy eternal place, and . . . defiled themselves with women" (12:4-6). (*c*) God did not give the angels wives because they were "holy, spiritual, living the eternal life . . . and immortal for all generations of the world" (15:4-6). The "position" for which the angels were responsible was that of "watchers." **Their proper dwelling** was the high heaven (cf. II Cor. 5:1-2). The story of their abandonment of these privileges to satisfy their lust reinforces Jude's warning of the possible loss by professing Christians of their privileged spiritual status and the punishment that must follow.

7. The destruction of **Sodom and Gomorrah and the surrounding cities** serves appropriately **as an example** in respect to **undergoing a punishment of eternal fire**. It is less clearly an illustration of backsliding. Jude's use of the story was probably dictated by the parallel between the angels' abandonment of **their own position** and the unnatural character of sensualism at Sodom and Gomorrah. These cities were thought of as continuing to burn eternally. To their wickedness, says Wisd. Sol. 10:7, "a smoking waste still witnesseth." The idea is comparable to the description of the angels in Enoch 67:4-13 as imprisoned in a valley underneath which subterranean fires burned. Jude regards

---

of security is dangerous, for it makes the Christian lax about his moral responsibilities (vs. 20).

The reader is also reminded of the tragic end of angels who in their desire for an unholy autonomy declared their independence from God, and like prodigals **left their proper dwelling**. These spiritual beings, whose proper abode was in the heavenly places, are supposed to have wandered into a lower plane of living and succumbed to an unholy lust for the women of earth. Whatever we may think of this quotation from Enoch, the truth is quite plain: angelic

beings accustomed to the higher things can and do yield to the temptation to live on the lower plane of a purely sensate life. The result is indeed what Jude says it is: They become enchained by an irrevocable law of judgment **in the nether gloom** of their chosen far country. Their bondage is tragic, and it is one that is kept until the final day of judgment.

A third illustration by which Jude seeks to shock his readers into creative remembrance is that of Sodom and Gomorrah and the cities that surrounded them. Unbelieving Israelites are guilty of skeptical disobedience, angels are

8 Likewise also these *filthy* dreamers defile the flesh, despise dominion, and speak evil of dignities.

8 Yet in like manner these men in their dreamings defile the flesh, reject authority,

---

these subterranean fires as a foretaste of the **punishment of eternal fire** (cf. Rev. 19:20; 20:10; 21:8). He regards the punishment of these cities as **an example**; i.e., their punishment is a specimen, a pattern, a warning. It warns all who face temptation of what they may expect if they succumb. In the spirit of the author of Hebrews, Jude reminds his readers that for those who "sin deliberately after receiving the knowledge of the truth, there . . . remains . . . a fearful prospect of judgment, and a fury of fire" (Heb. 10:26-27).

B. Heretical Teachers Characterized and Denounced (8-13)
1. Their Basic Sin Is Irreverence (8-10)

8. Dreamings may refer to "visions" as well as to dreams in the ordinary sense. This is somewhat obscured when the meaning of the term is restricted to lasciviousness, as in the rendering, **These filthy dreamers defile the flesh** (cf. Clement of Alexandria *Miscellanies* III. 2. 11). But here dreamings lead men not only to defile the flesh, but also to **reject authority, and revile the glorious ones.** Licentiousness is only one outcome of their dreamings. **Dreamings** probably refer here to vision experiences alleged to be the mediums of divine revelation. The Greek verb translated **dreamings** is used in Acts 2:17 (cf. Joel 3:1-5) to describe divine inspiration. Jude is charging that the vaunted "spirituality" of the errorists is spurious because it is empty of moral content (cf. vs. 19). They justify licentiousness, rejection of authority, scorn of the glorious ones, on the basis of revelation. True revelation, however, builds up character instead of degrading and demoralizing it. By that test, therefore, these errorists, like the false prophets of antiquity, "prophesy the delusions of their own minds" (Jer. 23:26 Amer. Trans.). Instead of the truth of God as contained in "the faith which was once for all delivered to the saints," the dreamings of these visionaries are a texture of lies (cf. Isa. 29:10; 56:10; Jer. 27:9).

Their dreamings cause these men also to **reject authority,** and in this second particular to follow the pattern illustrated by the people of Sodom and Gomorrah. **Authority** (κυριότητα) refers to such authority as angelic beings possess and may mean those beings themselves. The people of Sodom were guilty of disrespect for angels as well as sexual perversion. Lot's humility in the presence of "the two angels" who "arrived in Sodom in the evening" was in vivid contrast to the "depraved" irreverence of "the men of Sodom, from the youngest to the oldest" (Gen. 19:1-12 Amer. Trans.). The Docetists held all angels in contempt because they supposedly assisted God in creating the material universe and were thereby spiritually defiled. This attitude was of a piece with their denial of the reality of Jesus' humanity. Their view of matter as inherently evil encouraged a conception of "spirituality" having no relevance to life in the world. Because the body was physical, its appetites could be indulged without spiritual defilement. Their defilement of **the flesh,** and their rejection of angelic authority expressed this common principle.

---

guilty of vice, but Sodom and Gomorrah are guilty of homosexuality. The punishment is still evident in the residual ruins of those cities which may be seen to this day. The fires of that Gehenna are still burning.

Jude knows his religious history, for he also mentions **Korah,** that rebel against true authority in Israel who murmured against Moses, chafed at subordination, and dramatically perished by fire in an attempt to usurp the leadership that belonged only to God. False teachers and those who follow their doctrines are insubordinates who perish as did Korah. They are rejected as was Balaam who grasped **greedily** after rewards. Rushing after anything that promises gain, they relax all restraints and become less than human. They are also like Cain who, in his pride, animal appetitism, envy, and irreligiousness, was made an outlaw and outcast from society.

Enoch prophesied that God would deal with these **grumblers, malcontents, . . . loud-mouthed boasters** who follow their own passions, and kowtow to rich parishioners to receive gain (vs. 16). They are—and will be—judged by the Lord and his train of **holy myriads for their**

9 Yet Michael the archangel, when contending with the devil he disputed about the body of Moses, durst not bring against him a railing accusation, but said, The Lord rebuke thee.

and revile the glorious ones.[c] 9 But when the archangel Michael, contending with the devil, disputed about the body of Moses, he did not presume to pronounce a reviling judgment upon him, but said, "The Lord

[c] Greek *glories.*

Finally, **their dreamings** led them to **revile the glorious ones.** Philo thought the "glory of God" consists of the angels who surround him somewhat as the sun's rays compose its brightness. When God denied Moses' original request that he show himself to him, Philo reports a second supplication which Moses made: "I am persuaded by thy explanations that I should not have been able to receive the visible appearance of thy form. But I beseech thee that I may, at all events, behold the glory that is around thee. And I look upon thy glory to be the powers which attend thee as thy guards." (*On Monarchy* I. 5 and 6.) **The glorious ones** (δόξας) of whom Jude speaks are similarly supernatural beings. How they differed, if at all, from the angelic beings referred to in the preceding clause is not clear. Conceivably they were beings of equal dignity but different functions. They probably mediated God's presence in Christian services of worship. Paul had insisted that at church "a woman ought to have a veil on her head, because of the angels," presumably conceived to be present (I Cor. 11:10; cf. Matt. 18:20). The idea that supernatural beings could participate in such services and bring believers under their control (cf. Eph. 6:12, 18) appeared ludicrous to the heretics. Their insensibility to the divine presence made it possible for them to "boldly carouse together" at "love feasts" (vs. 12), and thus revile the glorious ones. In this they were like the men of Sodom.

9. Enoch names the seven archangels as Uriel, Raphael, Raguel, Michael, Saraqael, Gabriel, and Remiel. To each of them, he says, God assigned a province (Enoch 20:1-8). Michael is described as having been "set over the best part of mankind and over chaos." **Archangel** is used in the N.T. only here and in I Thess. 4:16.

According to Origen, Jude's allusion to **Michael, contending with the devil** over Moses' body was derived from the Assumption of Moses: "We have now to notice, agreeably to the statements of Scripture, how the opposing powers, or the devil himself, contends with the human race, inciting and instigating men to sin. And in the first place, in the book of Genesis, the serpent is described as having seduced Eve; regarding whom, in the work entitled *The Ascension of Moses* (a little treatise, of which the Apostle Jude makes mention in his epistle), the archangel Michael, when disputing with the devil regarding the body of Moses, says that the serpent, being inspired by the devil, was the cause of Adam and Eve's transgression." (*On First Principles* III. 2. 1.)

On the basis of extant Greek fragments, which he translates and publishes (see *The Apocrypha and Pseudepigrapha of the Old Testament in English* [Oxford: Clarendon Press, 1913], Vol. II), R. H. Charles summarizes the action of the original Assumption of Moses as follows: The devil sought to keep Michael from burying Moses on the twofold charge (*a*) that Moses' body belonged to him as lord of the material order, and (*b*) that

ungodliness and their **ungodly . . . deeds** which have been done in such **an ungodly way.** They will be judged for **all the harsh things** they have spoken against Enoch, and the Enochs of Christian history. This punishment is so certain that Jude can speak of it as accomplished, even though its fullness is yet to come.

But what is the nature of these false teachers and their teachings? Perhaps it was antinomianism, a heresy which has frequently arisen in the church and which believes that a Christian

is spiritual and that he need no longer be concerned about the body. Since his relation to God is the all-important matter, he pays no attention to his relation to nature and the neighbor. Stressing one aspect of religion out of all proportion to the rest, he perverts it. When salvation becomes only an activity of God's grace, and is dissociated from human response, there is danger that works will not only be neglected but distrusted. Neglected because they are not necessary to salvation; dis-

10 But these speak evil of those things which they know not: but what they know naturally, as brute beasts, in those things they corrupt themselves.

11 Woe unto them! for they have gone in the way of Cain, and ran greedily after the error of Balaam for reward, and perished in the gainsaying of Core.

rebuke you." 10 But these men revile whatever they do not understand, and by those things that they know by instinct as irrational animals do, they are destroyed. 11 Woe to them! For they walk in the way of Cain, and abandon themselves for the sake of gain to Ba'laam's error, and perish

---

Moses had committed murder. Michael leaves the second charge unrefuted but answers the first by insisting that God, not the devil, is Lord of the material world because his Spirit created the universe in its entirety. Michael then accuses the serpent of having seduced Adam and Eve. He successfully counters the devil's opposition, buries Moses' body in the mountains, and carries his spirit to heaven. (*The Assumption of Moses* [London: Adam & Charles Black, 1897], pp. 105-10.)

Jude's point is that although clear about the devil's duplicity (cf. I Cor. 6:3), Michael nevertheless showed him respect as a supernatural being, when with great restraint he merely said, **The Lord rebuke you** (cf. Zech. 3:2). Michael's restraint, even when dealing with the devil, puts to shame those "loud-mouthed boasters" (vs. 16) who, in a spirit of carousal (vs. 12), **revile the glorious ones** (vs. 8) who hallowed "love feasts" (vs. 12) by their presence and otherwise represented God in the existing world order (cf. Matt. 13:39, 49; 18:10; 25:31; 26:53; Luke 16:22; Acts 7:53; Gal. 3:19; Heb. 2:2).

10. Referring back to the claim of the errorists to superior religious knowledge, Jude remarks acidly that only as **they know by instinct as irrational animals do** have they any knowledge whatsoever, and by such knowledge **they are destroyed.** The senses are their only source of guidance. This explains their oblivion to the realities that must be "spiritually discerned" (I Cor. 2:14). Just as the rulers of this age have habitually destroyed themselves by their ignorance of the hidden wisdom of God, so the heretics are destroyed by the spuriousness of their dreamings (cf. I Cor. 2:6-16, where Paul works out fully the contrast implicit in Jude 10 between "the unspiritual" and those who "have received . . . the Spirit which is from God").

2. Jude Passionately Denounces Them (11-13)

11. Woe to them! is definitely an imprecation. Jude invokes the punishment of God on these ungodly persons (cf. I Cor. 9:16). The punishment of Cain, Balaam, and Korah, and God's reservation of **the nether gloom of darkness** for the **wandering stars** show what Jude wishes the fate of the errorists to be.

In Judaism and for the early Christian fathers, **Cain** typified treachery, lust, avarice, self-indulgence (cf. Wisd. Sol. 10:3; Jubilees 4:1-5; Apocalypse of Moses 3:2; Test. Twelve Patriarchs, Benjamin 7:3-5; Philo *On the Cherubim* XX; *Sacrifices of Abel and Cain* X, XIV; *Posterity and Exile of Cain* XV). Irenaeus says that certain Gnostic sects divided mankind into three classes, represented respectively by Cain, the physical or earthly man; Abel, the psychical man; and Seth, the spiritual man. Says Irenaeus, "They conceive . . . of three kinds of men, spiritual, material, and animal, represented by Cain, Abel, and

---

trusted because they may make a person rely upon his achievements in order to be pleasing to God. Such an extreme position may lead to an unchristian mysticism which ascribes creation to some power hostile to and lower than God and either despises man's bodily nature or regards anything done in the body as irrelevant to spiritual salvation.

This sort of "spiritual" interpretation of the world was prevalent in the days when the letter

of Jude was written. We cannot say for certain what these false teachers actually believed, because Jude has given us only a few fragments of their doctrines. Perhaps it was some aspect of the gnostic heresy, which placed the emphasis in salvation upon a peculiar kind of spiritual knowledge and repudiated the historical relationships of the Christian faith.

Hints are given here and there about the heresies of these errorists. They are given to

Seth. These three natures are no longer found in one person, but constitute various kinds of men." (*Against Heresies* I. 7. 5.) Discussing the doctrines of the Cainites, Irenaeus continues, "They also hold, like Carpocrates, that men cannot be saved until they have gone through all kinds of experience. An angel, they maintain, attends them in every one of their sinful and abominable actions, and urges them to venture on audacity and incur pollution. Whatever may be the nature of the action, they declare that they do it in the name of the angel. . . . And they maintain that this is 'perfect knowledge,' without shrinking to rush into such action as it is not lawful even to name." (*Ibid.*, I. 36. 2; cf. Eusebius *Church History* III. 29.) That Jude had errorists of this general type in mind in his reference to Cain is further suggested by the way in which Clement of Alexandria described the Cainites. He says they "adhere to impious words," that they "neither themselves enter into the kingdom of heaven, nor permit those whom they have deluded to attain the truth," that instead of entering the church properly "through the tradition of the Lord," they break in by "digging clandestinely through the wall of the Church" (*Miscellanies* VII. 17). Jude's characterization of his heretical opponents agrees in general outline and in many details with the allusions of Irenaeus and Clement.

Balaam's error was clearly covetousness. For the sake of a bribe from Balak, he perverted the youth of Israel in violation of his own conscience (Num. 22–24; 31:16; Neh. 13:2; Josephus *Antiquities* IV. 6. 5-9). Balaam represented for later Judaism the false teacher who misled youth. Says Pirke Aboth (5:21-22), "Every one that makes the many virtuous, sin comes not by his means; and every one that maketh the many to sin, they give him not the opportunity to repent. . . . Every one who has three things is one of the disciples of Abraham our father. And every one who has three other things is one of the disciples of Balaam the wicked. If he has a good eye, and a lowly soul and a humble spirit, he is of the disciples of Abraham our father. If he has an evil eye, and a boastful soul and a haughty spirit, he is of the disciples of Balaam the wicked. What is the difference between the disciples of Abraham . . . and the disciples of Balaam . . . ? The disciples of Balaam . . . inherit Gehenna and go down to the pit of destruction. . . . But the disciples of Abraham . . . inherit the world to come" (tr. R. Travers Herford, in Charles, *Apocrypha and Pseudepigrapha*, II, 709). Similarly, the author of Revelation condemns "the church in Pergamum" because they have some among them "who hold the teaching of Balaam" (Rev. 2:12, 14). The vigor of Jude's description is inescapable: The errorists **abandon themselves for the sake of gain to Balaam's error;** they "ran riotously in the error of Balaam for hire" (ERV); they "plunge into Balaam's error for gain" (Goodspeed). In spite of divine warnings, Balaam obdurately went ahead as Balak's partner. The errorists have likewise been warned, but they have been headstrong in continuing

---

dreamings or personal visions and revelations which evidently are attributed to divine origins. They abide by no apostolic authority. By these dreamings they **defile the flesh** or are indifferent altogether to immoral acts. Their spiritual visions being all-important, their earthly actions are insignificant. They think nothing of trying to combine high thinking with loose living. They **reject authority** and refuse to respect constituted powers. They are essentially libertines who prefer anarchy to any constituted authority. Having no concern for moral restraints they wish to abolish all order. This sort of spiritual anarchy has appeared again and again in Christian history. The Ranters were such and George Fox speaks of them as "lewd persons" who engaged in "wicked activities." There were medieval spiritualists who did not believe in moral **regulations** because they were not in harmony

with the free spirit of man, emancipated from the flesh. Luther had to contend against sectarians who would have wrecked the Reformation by their wild orgy of release from medieval restrictions.

These errorists denied **our only Master and Lord, Jesus Christ,** saying perhaps that Jesus was not the Son of God, or that there were other powers besides Jesus Christ in the hierarchy of heavenly beings. Some of them may even have regarded themselves better than Jesus Christ, as Irenaeus puts it. **Irrational animals** they are, writes Jude, who tell men contradictory things, obey their sensate urges, and live the "spiritual" life.

They are guilty, moreover, of reviling or scoffing at what they do not understand. Yet they obey their instinctual natures. Here understanding is set over against natural instincts.

12 These are spots in your feasts of charity, when they feast with you, feeding themselves without fear: clouds *they are* without water, carried about of winds; trees whose fruit withereth, without fruit, twice dead, plucked up by the roots;

12 These are blemishes[d] on your love feasts, as they boldly carouse together, looking after themselves; waterless clouds, carried along by winds; fruitless trees in late autumn, twice dead,

in Korah's rebellion.

[d] Or *reefs.*

---

their iniquitous course, "following their own passions, . . . flattering people to gain advantage" (vs. 16). By diluting the moral demands of religion on the authority of "their dreamings," they have apparently made money for themselves. They are well paid for convincing people that the immoral indulgence of their physical appetites does not violate the demands of religion.

Korah was the leader of a group of malcontents who "became arrogant and took their stand before Moses." They "gathered in a body against Moses and Aaron, and said to them, 'Enough of you; for all the community are holy, . . . since the LORD is in their midst; why then do you exalt yourselves above the LORD's assembly?'" Korah was able to gather "the whole community" against Moses, with the result that but for Moses' intercession the Lord would have consumed the community. Moses then induced Israel to move away from "the tents of these wicked men" and the ground under their tents "opened its mouth and swallowed them up, . . . and all the men who belonged to Korah. . . . So they . . . descended into Sheol alive . . . and they perished from the community" (Num. 16:1-34 *passim* Amer. Trans.; cf. Josephus *Antiquities* IV. 2. 1–4. 2).

The author of III John severely reproved the insubordination of one Diotrephes, who had rebelled against the authority of the elders (III John 9-10). The author of the Pastoral epistles notes the presence in the church of "many insubordinate men," their insubordination apparently consisting in their heretical teaching (Tit. 1:9-11). Bishops are charged with the duty of confuting these heretical contradictions of "sound doctrine" (Tit. 1:9; cf. I Tim. 1:19-20; 6:3-6; II Tim. 2:16-18, 23-25; 3:1-9; 4:14-15). Jude faces essentially the same problem. The conclusion he desires to drive home is that the outcome of heresy is utter destruction. Pride, greed, **rebellion,** are the trilogy of sins that constitute the iniquity of the "ungodly persons" who menace the spiritual health of the church. They bring annihilation in any age to those who practice them.

12-13. As though the three scriptural analogies were not enough, Jude employs five further metaphors to emphasize the iniquity of the errorists. (*a*) They **are blemishes on your love feasts. Blemishes** may be translated "hidden rocks" (ERV; cf. RSV mg.), the figure being that of **reefs** where ships and the lives of men are wrecked. This translation is in line with the later figure of **wild waves of the sea.** J. B. Lightfoot argues convincingly, however, against this rendering. He points out that the Greek word in the text of Jude (σπιλάς), while it also means "reef," is translated as if it were σπίλος ("spot") in all early versions, such as the O.L., the Vulg., both Egyptian versions, and the Philoxenian Syriac. In an Orphic poem (*Lithica* 614), written in the fourth century, the term has the sense of "spots." Lightfoot concludes also that **blemishes** fits better than "rocks" with **in your love feasts.** (*On a Fresh Revision of the English New Testament* [3rd ed.; London:

They are making fun of what is honorable; they condemn true Christianity which they do not understand. They might well heed the warning of the archangel who refused even to revile the devil for his insolence. Who then are these superior people that think lightly of the angels that do God's bidding? Claiming to possess superior insights in heavenly things, they do what comes **by instinct.** And it will prove their undoing. Like Cain, they look only after themselves and are not really concerned about peo-

ple; like Balaam they are interested only in using others for gain; like Korah they are intent only on usurping the holy authority that belongs to others and to God.

At the love feasts, those "charity suppers" (Moffatt) of the early church, Christians enjoyed a common meal in the spirit of love. The food was brought by the people themselves. On such occasions, in the Corinthian church, glaring immoralities took place (I Cor. 11:17-34). Greed and gluttony and irreverent gaiety, to say

13 Raging waves of the sea, foaming out their own shame; wandering stars, to whom is reserved the blackness of darkness for ever.

uprooted; 13 wild waves of the sea, casting up the foam of their own shame; wandering stars for whom the nether gloom of darkness has been reserved for ever.

Macmillan & Co., 1891], pp. 152-53.) So Goodspeed, Moffatt, KJV, and RSV. These men are blemishes because **they boldly carouse together** at love feasts, **looking after themselves.** The love feast was more than a symbol in the early church. It was a hearty meal whose cost was partly defrayed by the church. It demonstrated the family spirit of equality and community of goods (cf. Acts 4:34-35). For many humble members of the church it was their best meal of the week. Gluttony and clannishness contradicted the whole spirit of such occasions (cf. I Cor. 11:18-21). These qualities made the errorists blemishes on love feasts. **Looking after themselves** (ποιμαίνοντες) may be translated, "Shepherds that . . . feed themselves" (ERV). A shepherd who primarily looks after himself "is a hireling and cares nothing for the sheep," in contrast with "the good shepherd [who] lays down his life for the sheep" (John 10:11, 13; cf. Ezek. 34:8; Matt. 26:31; I Cor. 9:7; Heb. 13:20; I Pet. 2:25).

(b) Again, these men are **waterless clouds, carried along by winds.** Enoch 2–5 contrasts order among the phenomena of nature with unpredictability among men. The heavenly bodies "do not change their orbits . . . and transgress not against their appointed order." The seasons have accustomed characteristics. "In winter . . . the trees seem as though they had withered." In summer "the sun is above the earth over against it." "The sea and the rivers . . . accomplish and change not their tasks." But men "have not been steadfast, nor done the commandments of the Lord." Jude's analogies probably reflect the influence of Enoch. The present figure, however, is essentially that of Prov. 25:14:

> "Like clouds with wind that bring no rain,
> Is the man who boasts of gifts that are not given" (Amer. Trans.).

The point of the figure in Jude and Proverbs is that because clouds are waterless, they are carried along by winds and leave the earth parched. Similarly, these "loud-mouthed boasters" (vs. 16), prating of their spirituality but actually "devoid of the Spirit" (vs. 19), leave the lives of men unblessed and the church uninspired. They make no contribution to the church that justifies their membership in it.

(c) These men are **fruitless trees in late autumn, twice dead, uprooted.** Trees in late autumn, with winter just ahead, are understandably dry and leafless. To have borne no fruit at that time, however, indicates incapacity for producing fruit. Something more than a seasonal subsidence of vitality afflicts such trees. **Twice dead** violates the tree figure and denotes that Jude really has in mind the plight of apostate Christians (cf. Heb. 6:4-6; 10:26-27; Rev. 20:14-15; 21:8). Conceivably he includes in his thought persons never "born of water and the Spirit" (John 3:5; cf. Jude 10, 19; Col. 2:13). Clement of Alexandria interpreted **twice dead** as referring to the punishment after death: "Once, namely, when they sinned by transgressing, and a second time when delivered up to punishment according to the predestined judgments of God; inasmuch as it is to be reckoned death, even when each one does not forthwith deserve the inheritance" (Cassiodorus *Adumbrations,* or *Comments* I. 2). **Uprooted** probably refers to the spiritual

nothing of an easy-going relation between the sexes, spoiled the intention of the love feast. Lust blighted love. These false teachers with their false ideas are **spots** or **blemishes** on the pure fellowship of Christians. They are like hidden reefs or unseen rocks upon which the ship of Christian love would founder. And this is no old phenomenon!

They are **waterless clouds**—empty, unpromising shams, **carried along by winds;** lying trees in autumn whose looks betray their barrenness (**twice dead,** like Christians dead in sin before baptism, and dead still in sin as nominal members of the church); heaving waves which labor and strain only to bring forth a beach full of debris; **wandering,** erratic, aimless **stars**

14 And Enoch also, the seventh from Adam, prophesied of these, saying, Behold, the Lord cometh with ten thousands of his saints,

14 It was of these also that Enoch in the seventh generation from Adam prophesied, saying, "Behold, the Lord came with his

---

isolation of apostate Christians whose iniquity severs their vital connection with Christ's body even though they apparently remain members of it (cf. Matt. 13:28-30; 15:13; John 15:1-10). They will be ultimately and eternally excommunicated.

(d) These people are, to shift the figure, **wild waves of the sea, casting up the foam of their own shame.** Jude's analogy is essentially that of Isa. 57:20:

> "But the wicked are like the uptossed sea,
>   For it cannot rest,
>   But its waters toss up mire and filth.
> There is no peace," says my God, "for the wicked" (Amer. Trans.).

It is akin also to the thought of Jas. 1:6, "He who doubts is like a wave of the sea that is driven and tossed by the wind." The figure emphasizes both the filth cast up by the waves and their turmoil.

(e) Finally, they are **wandering stars for whom the nether gloom of darkness has been reserved for ever.** Jude is unmistakably indebted to the imagery of Enoch 18:12-16: "And beyond that abyss I saw a place which had no firmament of the heaven above, and no firmly founded earth beneath it: . . . it was a waste and horrible place. I saw there seven stars like great burning mountains, and to me, when I inquired regarding them, the angel said: 'This place is the end of heaven and earth: this has become a prison for the stars. . . . And the stars which roll over the fire are they which have transgressed the commandment of the Lord in the beginning of their rising, because they did not come forth at their appointed times.'" Instead of a place of fire as the "prison for the stars," Jude has **the nether gloom of darkness**—an alteration probably made under the influence of Isa. 14:9-15, where the king of Babylon is compared to "Lucifer, son of the dawn," who because of his pride was "brought down to Sheol . . . to the recesses of the Pit" (Amer. Trans.). He probably also recalls Paul's moving exhortation to Christians to "shine as lights in the world" (Phil. 2:14-15; cf. Matt. 5:14-16; 6:23; Luke 16:8; John 5:35). Instead of seeing a light to guide them to God, men who looked to the errorists found themselves in darkness and confusion. Jude's primary emphasis, however, is on the punishment of apostasy, as Clement of Alexandria's comment brings out. Jude means by **wandering stars**, says Clement, those "who err and are apostates." They are "of that kind of stars which fell from the seats of the angels,—'to whom,' for their apostasy, 'the blackness of darkness is reserved forever'" (Cassiodorus *Comments* II).

C. Inspired Prophecy Warns of These Intruders (14-16)

14-15. Jude's quotation draws upon a number of passages from Enoch: 1:9; 5:4; 27:2; 60:8; 93:2 (cf. Jubilees 7:38-39). Certain of the early fathers took Jude's quotation as a guarantee of the inspiration of Enoch. Later, the canonicity of Jude was itself questioned because of its quotation of an apocryphal book (Eusebius *Church History* II. 23. 24-25; VI. 14. 1; Jerome *On Famous Men* IV). For Jude, Enoch's prophecy about the Lord coming **to execute judgment** was conclusive. The doom of the errorists and their followers is settled. Enoch's words apply perpetually to such people. Whenever they appear and

---

that drop at last into **the nether gloom of darkness.**

They are **grumblers** who find fault with God's providential rule of things, **complainers** who are dissatisfied with their lot in life, secularists who live only by the law of sense satisfactions, loud-

mouthed and arrogant boasters who think they know it all. And yet they are cringing parasites who flatter people of wealth and prestige to enhance themselves.

They are divisive, for they separate Christian from Christian. They are sensual. And while

15 To execute judgment upon all, and to convince all that are ungodly among them of all their ungodly deeds which they have ungodly committed, and of all their hard *speeches* which ungodly sinners have spoken against him.

16 These are murmurers, complainers, walking after their own lusts; and their mouth speaketh great swelling *words,* having men's persons in admiration because of advantage.

holy myriads, 15 to execute judgment on all, and to convict all the ungodly of all their deeds of ungodliness which they have committed in such an ungodly way, and of all the harsh things which ungodly sinners have spoken against him." 16 These are grumblers, malcontents, following their own passions, loud-mouthed boasters, flattering people to gain advantage.

---

whoever they may be, the Lord will execute judgment on them and will **convict all the ungodly** of **their deeds of ungodliness** as well as of **the harsh things** they have said.

16. Jude has cited inspired prophecy to establish the certainty of the doom of the errorists. He now undertakes to demonstrate the justice of their fate by dwelling on the qualities of their evil character: (*a*) They are **grumblers.** The Greek noun for "grumbler" (γογγυστής) is used in the N.T. only here. It is used in the LXX in Exod. 16:8; Num. 11:1, 14-27, 29. The corresponding verb (γογγύζω) is used in Matt. 20:11; Luke 5:30; John 6:41-43; 7:32; I Cor. 10:10. The term describes the whispered expression of discontent or approval—more characteristically the former than the latter. Secrecy is the basic idea. The term is appropriately applied to heretical leaders who had "secretly" gained admission to the church (vs. 4) and had then insidiously used church membership as a screen for their numerous "deeds of ungodliness" (vs. 15). Stealth and conspiracy were their characteristic weapons.

(*b*) These people are **malcontents, following their own passions.** This second characterization and the third which follows it are reminiscent of passages from the Assumption of Moses: "And many in those times shall have respect unto desirable persons and receive gifts and pervert judgment" (5:5). "Destructive and impious men . . . shall stir up the poison of their minds, being treacherous men, self-pleasers, dissemblers . . . , devourers of the goods of the poor . . . , complainers, deceitful, concealing themselves lest they should be recognized, impious, filled with lawlessness and iniquity. . . And though their hands and their minds touch unclean things, yet their mouth shall speak great things, and they shall say furthermore: 'Do not touch me lest thou shouldst pollute me' " (7:4, 7, 9). The Greek word translated **malcontents** (μεμψίμοιρος) is a compound of μέμψις, censure or blame, and μοῖρα, meaning fate or lot. It designates people as querulous, as convinced that life has been unfair to them, as habitually complaining. Such people are self-centered. Service has no place in their view of life. Unlike the Son of man and his disciples, they desire "to be served," not "to serve" (cf. Matt. 20:28). The description of them as malcontents complements the preceding designation of them as grumblers and is itself illuminated by the further characterization of them as **following their own passions.** They are grumblers and malcontents because they are self-centered. They are for the same reason swayed entirely by their animal passions (cf. vss. 4, 8, 10, 18). They lack any trace of either humility or spirituality.

(*c*) They are **loud-mouthed boasters, flattering people to gain advantage.** Here, as in vs. 11, Jude denounces the avarice and cupidity of the errorists. The Greek word translated **boasters** literally means "overswollen." It describes the errorists as employing **great swelling words.** Although thoroughly arrogant in spirit, their self-centeredness causes them to be servile to people of power and wealth. They have no interest in their salvation; they merely desire to exploit them. Accordingly, they flatter them **to gain advantage** (cf. Jas. 2:1-7; 5:1-6). Humility would make them fearless and impartial in dealing with all sorts of men. Because they are arrogant, they tremble in the presence of the powerful and wealthy. Only after he had confronted God did Moses meet Pharaoh confidently, and so win the right to be described as "very modest, more so than all men

17 But, beloved, remember ye the words which were spoken before of the apostles of our Lord Jesus Christ;

18 How that they told you there should be mockers in the last time, who should walk after their own ungodly lusts.

17 But you must remember, beloved, the predictions of the apostles of our Lord Jesus Christ; 18 they said to you, "In the last time there will be scoffers, following their

---

upon the face of the earth" (Num. 12:3 Amer. Trans.). The heretics therefore combine the apparently contradictory qualities of boastfulness and servility. Were God in their thoughts, they would possess the meekness and courage of true spirituality. Because they are "devoid of the Spirit" (vs. 19), they are **loud-mouthed boasters, flattering people to gain advantage.**

III. THE MOST HOLY FAITH THE TRUE FOUNDATION (17-23)

A. APOSTOLIC TEACHING SUPPLIES ELEMENTS IN THIS FOUNDATION (17-19)

17. The letter of Jude is an urgent appeal to faithful church members "to contend for the faith" (vs. 3; cf. vs. 20). The **you** of vs. 17 is contrasted with the "these" of vs. 16. The call to remember **the predictions of the apostles** is a continuation of the exhortation of vs. 3. The words of the apostles embody "the faith which was once for all delivered." They are normative for Christians because they are inspired as the prophetic words of Enoch were inspired (vs. 14). That is the force of the complementary citations of the prophetic words of Enoch and of the apostles in vss. 14 and 17. The **scoffers** are effectively refuted and condemned when they are shown to be at variance with apostolic teaching. The predictions of the apostles represent the prophetic communication of God's saving truth to the church and constitute the "most holy faith" of its members (vs. 20). The Greek word ῥῆμα, here translated **predictions,** has that meaning in Rom. 10:8; Eph. 6:17; I Pet. 1:25 (cf. λόγοι in Rev. 17:17). This most holy faith is a body of authoritative teaching, whose divine origin is vouched for by the Scriptures and the predictions of the apostles. For Jude these predictions approximate in their authority the inspired contents of the Scriptures.

18. They said to you refers to the oral tradition of apostolic teaching that constituted the substance of early Christian preaching. Formalized oral summaries of this teaching were incorporated in the sermons of early heralds and in the instruction imparted to converts (cf. Acts 10:36-42; 20:28-31, 35; I Cor. 11:23; 15:3-7; I Tim. 4:6; 6:20; II Tim. 1:14; 3:1-7; Eusebius *Church History* III. 39. 4).

The last time means the end of the existing world order and the culminating judgment of the Messiah. The expectation of the Second Coming was for Jude a fundamental element in apostolic Christianity (cf. II Pet. 3:4). The point of **the predictions of the apostles** on which Jude focuses attention is that **in the last time there will be scoffers** who see no connection between spirituality and morality (vs. 4) and who ridicule the idea of an impending judgment. Those who are loyal to "old-fashioned Christianity," however, will take their scoffing both as a sign that the end is near and as a warning of the necessity of moral fitness on the part of any who hope to be favorably judged (cf. Matt. 25:1-13).

---

they claim the possession of the Spirit, their conduct makes all their pretentions to a Spirit-led life unconvincing. They could hardly claim the text, "your body is the temple of the Holy Spirit" (I Cor. 6:19; cf. Rom. 8).

17-23. *Meeting Heresy and Immorality.*—The preacher takes on a pastoral tone of voice when addressing his parishioners. He has been violent in his condemnation of these pseudo Christians. **Beloved,** says he, **remember.** Vehement language

may be fitting for these dangerous subversives who were denaturing the very substance of that **holy faith.** And it was **holy faith** because (a) it was divinely given, (b) it was a thing apart, and (c) its end was to make people holy or whole. But Christians ought to be addressed compassionately, pleadingly, winningly.

The letter in a real sense comes to its conclusion and climax in some final words of exhortation and counsel. One can feel the urgency of

19 These be they who separate themselves, sensual, having not the Spirit. | own ungodly passions." **19** It is these who set up divisions, worldly people, devoid of

---

19. Two further indictments are brought against those who hold God's moral demands in derision and make light of the idea of his approaching judgment: (a) they **set up divisions;** (b) they are **worldly people, devoid of the Spirit.**

In the first instance, the **scoffers** are conceivably described as "men who now keep themselves apart" (R. A. Knox), or as "those who by their wickedness separate themselves from the living fellowship of Christians" (J. H. Thayer, *A Greek-English Lexicon of the New Testament* [New York: Harper & Bros., 1886], *s.v.*). More probably Jude refers to the Gnostic division of humanity into three classes: the "spiritual," who by nature possess affinity for the unseen and divine order of life in independence of moral attainments; the "psychic" or "sensuous," who may by strenuous effort qualify for salvation; and the "somatic" or wholly "animalistic," who are by nature incapable of salvation. Irenaeus explains that certain heretics create a threefold classification of men on the ground that there are "three kinds of substances." Whatever is material "must of necessity perish, inasmuch as it is incapable of receiving any afflatus of incorruption." Animal existence is a "mean between the spiritual and the material" and may move one way or the other as its "inclination draws it." "Spiritual substance" is viewed as "having been sent forth for this end, . . . being here united with that which is animal" for the discipline of the latter. This "spiritual substance" is "the salt" and "the light of the world." The heretics regarded ordinary church members as "animal men" and themselves as "spiritual." They condescendingly told ordinary church members, says Irenaeus, that as "animal men, and as . . . being in the world" they must "practice continence and good works" in order to "attain at length to the intermediate habitation." Since they were themselves "spiritual and perfect," no such "course of conduct" was required. "For it is not conduct of any kind which leads into the Pleroma, but the seed sent forth thence in a feeble, immature state, and here brought to perfection." Thus, those who claim to be "the elect seed" possess grace "as their own special possession." This exempts them from the possibility of sinning and enables them to indulge freely their sexual desires. They reasoned that persons who are "of the world" seek intercourse with women "under the power of concupiscence," and they, accordingly, "shall not attain to the truth." But the "spiritual" who are merely "in this world" may without endangering attainment of truth and even as a means of attaining it "so love a woman as to obtain possession of her" (*Against Heresies* I. 6. 1-4 *passim;* cf. Clement of Alexandria *Miscellanies* IV; *Comments on Jude;* Tertullian *On Fasting* I). Such **divisions** were apparently the object of Jude's condemnation.

The **scoffers** naturally classified themselves as "spiritual" and on that basis felt that they were exempt from the demands of moral law. Jude, however, brands them as **worldly people** (ψυχικοί), **devoid of the Spirit.** He insists that people are properly differentiated as "worldly" and "spiritual" on the basis of character rather than nature. He thinks of God as having created all men capable of receiving his Spirit and becoming his children. Men disqualify themselves for their proper destiny only by becoming and

---

the preacher's plea. He does not denounce; he seeks to win and to save. The great objective of the gospel—as of its ambassadors—is to call men to be reconciled to God. "I came not to condemn but to fulfill" (cf. Matt. 5:17). Jude begins by urging his people to **remember.** Do not be taken off guard by what is happening. Be realistic! These things have happened before. It is time to grow up and become mature. Besides, when Christians face opposition it is an indication of the reality of the issue between

Christ and his enemies. Christian controversy can be creative. And the counsels are simple:

(a) A strong faith alone can make the infections of heresy sterile. Build up your lives! And use for your growth into that stature of maturity the things of our **holy faith.** Build on the foundation that has been laid. And inbuild into your mind and heart and will those truths, affections, and duties which will help you to ward off untruth. The uninformed mind is usually captured by dangerous propaganda. The

20 But ye, beloved, building up your- | the Spirit. 20 But you, beloved, build your-
selves on your most holy faith, praying in | selves up on your most holy faith; pray in
the Holy Ghost, | the Spirit.

---

remaining morally unfit. By electing sensuality do men remain "sensuous" or "animal-istic." The scoffers reveal that they are worldly people, devoid of the Spirit, when they refuse to acknowledge moral prerequisites to spirituality (cf. vss. 4, 8, 12, 16-17, 23). In the N.T. man's spirit represents his capacity for appropriating the invisible and eternal. Spirit is the aspect of his being through which the Holy Spirit captivates his entire life. When Jude describes the scoffers as devoid of the Spirit, he refers to the Holy Spirit, not to a lack of the element in human nature which supplies the basis for fellowship with God. Spirituality for Jude is definitely a moral achievement, not an inherited privilege of a favored few. Character, not natural endowment, separates the scoffers from the faithful church members to whom Jude addresses his letter.

B. Holy Living the Best Witness to Apostolic Christianity (20-23)
1. Sound Theology Essential to the Good Life (20)

20. You, beloved is a direct appeal to the faithful church members to whom Jude addresses his letter (cf. vs. 3). They are contrasted with the "scoffers" who follow "their own ungodly passions" (vs. 18; cf. vs. 4). They are urged to govern their lives by the lofty principles enunciated in vss. 20-23.

Build yourselves up on your most holy faith is an exhortation in which the erection of a building is used as an analogy for religious development (cf. Matt. 7:24-27; I Cor. 3:10-17; Eph. 2:20-22; Col. 1:23; 2:7; Heb. 3:1-6; I Pet. 2:4-10). The Greek verb translated **build yourselves up** contemplates the completion of a structure on a foundation already laid. That foundation is for Jude **your most holy faith.** Upon that foundation alone can the edifices of Christian character and the Christian fellowship be securely erected. For their foundation the scoffers have only their dreamings (vs. 8), instinct such as irrational animals possess (vs. 10), their own ungodly passions (vs. 18). **Faith** has the meaning given it in Polycarp's admonition to the Philippians: "From the study of [Paul's letters] you will be able to build yourselves up into the faith given you" (Polyc. Phil. 3:2). Faith is something given, "once for all delivered" (vs. 3), a deposit "entrusted to you" (I Tim. 6:20). It is the body of Christian belief indispensable to the proper development of Christian character and the progress of the church. It is holy in a twofold sense. It embodies the saving truth which originates with God, was revealed through Christ, and has been reported in the apostolic message (cf. vs. 17). Not only is this faith holy in its origin and transmission, however; it also produces holiness in its adherents. Abandonment of it produces "deeds of ungodliness" (vs. 15). Because the Spirit inspired this faith, genuine spirituality is its fruit. Scoffers who deride and invent substitutes for it are understandably "devoid of the Spirit" (vs. 19).

In the language of the N.T. to be **in the Holy Spirit** means to be inspired. Inspired persons are regarded as thinking, speaking, acting under the power and prompting of

---

uncommitted emotions are easily swayed. And without concentration upon some high purpose the will becomes enslaved to false masters.

(b) They are to **pray in the Holy Spirit,** for Spirit alone can teach men how and for what to pray. Calvin says that the Spirit "arouses" men to pray. The Spirit generates real ardor and fervency in prayer. The Holy Spirit is the inward teacher of the Christian. He helps our spirits to discern the deep things of God. He leads into all truth. He brings about that proper dependence upon God and communion with

God without which the Christian life has no foundation and no substance.

(c) They are to **keep** themselves in the love of God. To keep in that love involves strenuous activity. The consciousness of a love which will "never let us go" is a bulwark against despair and defeat; to believe in it is to know the soundness and the goodness of life; but it requires human effort if God's love and power are to be effective in us.

(d) They are to **wait** in quiet expectancy **for the mercy of our Lord Jesus Christ unto**

21 Keep yourselves in the love of God, looking for the mercy of our Lord Jesus Christ unto eternal life.

the Holy Spirit; 21 keep yourselves in the love of God; wait for the mercy of our Lord

---

the Spirit (cf. Rev. 1:10-11; 4:1-2), and here as praying in the Spirit. Paul, to whose letters the author of the letter of Jude is deeply indebted, thought of the Spirit as realistically aiding Christians when they attempted to pray. This had been his own experience, as he tells the Romans (8:15-16, 26-27; cf. Eph. 6:17-20). When Jude urged his readers to **pray in the Holy Spirit,** he meant that they should seek and follow the Spirit's guidance in prayer. He insists that they put their lives so unreservedly at God's disposal as to permit the Spirit to prompt their prayers. "Deeds of ungodliness" (vs. 15) are unimaginable for men who are so guided. The Spirit inspired the apostolic message, the **holy faith** which was once for all delivered (vs. 3). That faith embodies both the tradition and the continuing expectation of communion with God by means of prayer. Believers, without reference to time, become participants in a "communion of saints" when by the Spirit's aid they commune with God. In the light and strength so achieved they are enabled to rear a superstructure both of character and institutionalism appropriate to the foundation laid by the apostles. This holy faith alone establishes the lines within which the Spirit guides believers (cf. I Cor. 12:3). Guidance by the Spirit is thereby differentiated from the capriciousness inherent in the dreamings of the scoffers, who under the guise of spirituality follow their own passions.

2. This Faith, Holy in Origin, Produces Holiness (21-23)

21. Jude uses the passive voice of three verbs when in his salutation he describes his readers as "called, beloved in God the Father and kept for Jesus Christ" (vs. 1). The effect of this is to emphasize the initiative and power of God. The writer knows, however, the necessity of man's active co-operation. Without it, God's initiative is made ineffective (cf. John 15:9; Rom. 5:3-5; 8:37-39; Phil. 2:12-13; Jas. 1:26-27). There are two Greek verbs for "guard." One, τηρέω, seems to emphasize perseverance in the watchful care of something now possessed. The other, φυλάσσω, suggests keeping something safe from attack from without. Jude's use of τηρέω in both vss. 1 and 21 is appropriate. He shares Paul's confidence that no outward menace "will be able to separate us from the love of God in Christ Jesus our Lord" (Rom. 8:38-39). The relation which God's love makes possible between man and himself is invulnerable to attack from without. Man may himself, however, fail to appropriate God's blessings. He must **keep** himself **in the love of God.** God's assured attitude inspires and undergirds man's effort and saves it from futility. But for the outcome God desires he is dependent on man just as man is upon him. God's loving vigilance must be matched by man's vigilant effort.

Those who are "kept for Jesus Christ" (vs. 1) and who keep themselves **in the love of God** will be undismayed "in the last time" (vs. 18). With complete assurance they will **wait for the mercy of our Lord.** When others tremble at the prospect of eternal punishment (vss. 15, 23), faithful Christians will possess the guarantee of **eternal life.** The mercy of our Lord Jesus Christ is God's mercy expressed through Christ in his judicial capacity as Messiah "in the last time" (cf. Enoch 27:3-4; Matt. 5:7; I Pet. 1:3-7). Apostolic

---

eternal life. Humble they must be, for they deserve nothing. Expectant they must be, because such hope in the mercy of Christ Jesus is the final confidence of the Christian. Mercy will be shown them in fullest measure at the coming of Christ. That hope is our final sustenance and the one fair vision that keeps us from despair.

(e) They are to be compassionate to the poor victims who have succumbed to heresy. **Convince**

some, snatch some, but in all things **have mercy with fear,** and love the person while hating and loathing the manner of person he has become. These words from Jude 23 were the favorite words of Oliver Cromwell. The Christian is his brother's keeper; he is identified with all his brethren in sin and in salvation. For their sake he too must consecrate himself as did his Lord. He is not saved to glory in his religion; he is saved to serve. He is to "become all things

22 And of some have compassion, making a difference:

23 And others save with fear, pulling *them* out of the fire; hating even the garment spotted by the flesh.

Jesus Christ unto eternal life. 22 And convince some, who doubt; 23 save some, by snatching them out of the fire; on some have mercy with fear, hating even the garment spotted by the flesh.*

*The Greek text in this sentence is uncertain at several points.

Christianity involved for Jude this association of God's protective love and Christ's redeeming mercy (vss. 1, 21). To be able to wait joyously and expectantly (cf. Mark 15:43; Luke 2:25, 38; 23:51; Heb. 11:13; Tit. 2:13) for the mercy of our Lord Jesus Christ until eternal life, Christians must first have fulfilled the conditions Jude specifies in vss. 17, 20-21. This done, they will look forward to God's final scrutiny of their fitness for life in the kingdom without uncertainty or fear. In view of God's mercy, the conditions of eternal life lie within the power of all men, not simply a specially endowed few. Grammatically, so far as the Greek goes, **unto eternal life** may be read either with **keep yourselves in the love of God,** or with **wait for the mercy of our Lord Jesus Christ.** The punctuation of an English version expresses the preference of translators.

22-23. Christians are not concerned exclusively with their own salvation. They have a duty toward the misguided and the mistaken. The Greek text of these verses is confused. Such ancient versions of the verses as are presented by Clement of Alexandria, Jerome, the Codex Ephraemi Rescriptus (C), and the Philoxenian Syriac contain only two clauses. Moffatt regarded this as the best approximation of the original text and so reads the verses: "Snatch some from the fire, and have mercy on the waverers, trembling as you touch them, with loathing for the garment which the flesh has stained" (*The General Epistles* [New York: Harper & Bros.; London: Hodder & Stoughton, 1928; "Moffatt New Testament Commentary"], pp. 243-44). The great uncial MSS of the fourth and fifth centuries, Sinaiticus (א), Vaticanus (B), and Alexandrinus (A), however, contain three clauses. The RSV so translates the verses. There is the further textual uncertainty whether the verb in vs. 22 was originally ἐλέγχω, meaning "to chide" or "to confute," or ἐλεάω (or ἐλεέω), meaning "to pity" or "to succor." The RSV reads the former in vs. 22 and the latter in vs. 23, as is done in Alexandrinus and the critical texts of Lachmann, Tischendorf, and Tregelles. (Codices Sinaiticus and Vaticanus read ἐλεᾶτε in both instances, as does Nestle's critical Greek text.) **Some, who doubt** describes those who are the objects of the action of the verb in the opening clause of vs. 22. They have been confused by the pretentious intellectualism and moral sophistry of the heretics. Instead of despairing of them, church members must patiently and thoughtfully acquaint them with the faith (vs. 3), and by precept and example show how they may build themselves up on this most holy faith (vs. 20). Whether the verb is ἐλέγκετε or ἐλεᾶτε, the essential point is that church members will so handle the intellectual and moral problems of confused Christians as to hold them to the standards of apostolic Christianity.

The imagery of the first clause of vs. 23 is essentially that of Zech. 3:2-4, where Joshua is likened to "a brand snatched from the fire." In Amos 4:11-12 the reference of the imagery is to the wrath of God visited upon Sodom and Gomorrah, and in Num. 16:1-35 and Ps. 106:17-18 to the punishment of Korah. **The fire** from which Jude urges faithful church members to **save some** may refer figuratively to the indulgence of sexual passions encouraged by the heretical teachers. Clement of Alexandria so understood it. Much more probably it refers to punishment sent in the present to cause the wayward

to all men, that [he] might by all means save some" (I Cor. 9:22), and at the same time to be "in the world, yet not of it." God still beseeches men through other men.

The final word on heresy is not the condemnation of the deviate but redemption through

convincing argument, through identifying mercy, through vigorous encounter, through a strong exposure of error to the clear, penetrating, guiding light of truth about the one and only true God, and Jesus Christ, our Lord and Savior.

24 Now unto him that is able to keep you from falling, and to present *you* fault-

24 Now to him who is able to keep you

---

to repent and to the doom of the impenitent at the messianic judgment (cf. vss. 17-18; Enoch 21:1-10; 23:2-4; 27:1-5; etc.). Jude is of course aware that according to apostolic teaching, God alone can save men from the fire. Salvation is due to his mercy and is his gift. He knows with equal realism, however, that God works through the instrumentality of consecrated human lives. In urging upon his readers their responsibility to **save some, by snatching them out of the fire,** therefore, he calls upon them to permit God to reach the erring through their lives and efforts (cf. vs. 21; Jas. 5:20; I Pet. 4:10-11).

Martin Luther thought that in the two clauses of vs. 23 Jude distinguished between those whom one might save **by snatching them out of the fire** and those for whose salvation men could do nothing effective, but who would nevertheless excite the pity of Christians. He thus interprets Jude: "Let your life be so shaped that it shall allow you to have compassion on these who are wretched, blind and dumb; have no joy or pleasure over them, but let them go, keep from them and have nothing to do with them. But as to those others, whom ye can draw forth, save them by fear,—deal kindly and gently with them, as God has dealt with you." (*Epistles of St. Peter and St. Jude,* pp. 335-36.) This understanding of Jude accords neither with the meaning of the Greek verb (ἐλεάω) nor with the context. The verb expresses sympathy that transcends words and translates itself into deeds (cf. Jas. 2:14-17). It describes God's active and redemptive extension of opportunity and aid to men, unworthy though they may be (Rom. 9:15-16; 11:30-32; I Cor. 7:25; II Cor. 4:1; I Tim. 1:13, 16; I Pet. 2:10). In believers it connotes tenderness toward the sinner, the active attempt to succor the needy, the manifestation in human relations of Christ's mercy for which believers wait (vs. 21). But **mercy** takes account of moral distinctions. It does not treat evil as of no consequence. Christians **have mercy with fear, hating even the garment spotted by the flesh.** The **fear** that properly constitutes an aspect of sympathy toward sinners expresses an awareness on the Christian's part of his own weakness and a recognition of the danger of being understood to condone evil. "The faith which was once for all delivered" treats mercy and righteousness not as mutually exclusive, but as phases of a spiritual whole. The merciful man will, along with being merciful, cleanse himself "from every defilement of body and spirit, and make holiness perfect in the fear of God" (II Cor. 7:1; cf. I Thess. 5:23).

The influence of the imagery of Zech. 3:2-7 appears again in the reference to **the garment spotted by the flesh.** Likened to "a brand snatched from the fire," Joshua is also pictured as standing before the angel "dressed in dirty clothes." The angel orders attendants to "take away the dirty clothes from upon him" and then interprets the symbolism of their removal: "See! I have removed your guilt from upon you; and have clothed you with festal garments" (Amer. Trans.). Hatred of the garment spotted by the flesh, therefore, explains the fear with which the good man shows mercy. His mercy involves no condoning of sin. Jude insists, less eloquently but as clearly as does the prophet of Revelation, that "he who conquers" must not have soiled his garments, but must rather "be clad . . . in white garments" (Rev. 3:4-5). They alone "who wash their robes . . . have the right to the tree of life and . . . may enter the city by the gates" (Rev. 22:14).

IV. THE BENEDICTION (24-25)

The emphasis on righteousness as inclusive of mercy, with which the body of the letter concludes, is an appropriate climax to the thought of the letter in its entirety. The majestic benediction exalts the conception by making it characteristic of God.

---

24. The Final Word.—The last word in the letter is an ascription of praise to God. This is the final thing man can say. In all our prayers we begin and end with a doxology or ascription.

Nothing starts aright, nothing proceeds aright, nothing ends aright apart from God. Without his almighty saviorhood all our hoping and working and praying is in vain. "Except th⸗

less before the presence of his glory with exceeding joy,

from falling and to present you without blemish before the presence of his glory

---

24. Men "have mercy with fear" (vs. 23) ; but God exercises mercy with a confidence which his power warrants. He runs no risk of moral lapse. Not only so, but he actually communicates strength to men who would be merciful and who would otherwise be unequal to their responsibilities as sketched in vss. 20-23. **To him who is able** refers to God's competence for the responsibilities that are peculiarly his. His competence is due to the adequacy of the resources which reside in him (cf. Rom. 16:25-27; Eph. 3:20; Heb. 13:20-21).

Two effects significant for men are implicit in God's combination of mercy and power: he will **keep** [them] **from falling and present** [them] **without blemish before the presence of his glory with rejoicing.** The Greek verb φυλάσσω rather than τηρέω (vss. 1, 21) is used here. God is thought of as safeguarding the good man from all that might threaten him from without (cf. John 17:12; Rom. 8:38-39; Eph. 6:10-18). He also steadies the man himself. The Greek adjective represented by the phrase **from falling** usually refers to a horse and describes him as not stumbling, as standing firm, as sure-footed. Left to himself, man is prone to stumble. God is **able** to safeguard him at this point and, without isolating him from his equally frail fellow men, to keep him morally sure-footed (cf. John 17:15).

The figure of moral sure-footedness colors the description of the second effect of God's competence. **To present you** hardly does justice to the Greek infinitive στῆσαι. "To make you stand" (Goodspeed) is more accurate. Not only does God make the believer morally sure-footed in the midst of erring men, but he causes him to stand **without blemish** [or, better, "irreproachable" (Goodspeed)] **before the presence of his glory.** The reference is to the messianic judgment when, according to apostolic teaching, "the Son of man comes in his glory, and all the angels with him" (Matt. 25:31). God's mercy and power make security in that crucial hour possible for the believer, who is consequently "exultant" (Moffatt), "triumphant" (Goodspeed), **rejoicing** (cf. Rom. 5:6-11; 8:31-39).

Lord build the house, they labor in vain that build it" (Ps. 127:1).

Now to him. . . . God is a Person, not a process or a thing or even a Being, but the Person. The ultimate reality is personal; he may be more, but at least he is personal.

And he **is able.** His personal power is sufficient to accomplish what it purposes to do. God does not strive for position. He shares his throne of authority and power with no equal, although he does engage in the struggle with rebellious powers which have broken from his rule but not from his control. There is sure confidence here. He is able. The great men and women of the Bible believed that God was able. Jesus Christ's ministry was founded upon God's ability. The Christian movement through the ages has preached and taught and worked and died in the assurance that the God and Father of our Lord Jesus Christ was able. To falter in this confidence is to lose one's nerve, to recoil from suffering and opposition, to go down in the spirit of defeat, and to succumb to hopelessness.

And he is the one and **only God.** There is none other. This is a far cry from the heretical

propaganda of which Jude speaks, for these gnostics confused men's minds by teaching that there were all kinds of powers in heaven and earth. To them the God of creation was not the God of salvation. Their speculations spoke of the various powers, but their real heresy was their inability to get things together in the economy of one Deity. Their God was too small to satisfy the person who wanted a religion that embraced heaven and earth. Only a God of majesty, glory, dominion, and authority can do that.

But the God who is meaningful to the Christian is the one who has revealed himself as **Savior through Jesus Christ.** It is one thing to appropriate the light of truth which frees the mind from error, superstition, and dark powers. It is another thing to sense the majesty of the moral law as set forth in the Sermon on the Mount and as incarnated in the blameless life of Jesus. But truth and righteousness are tyrannical taskmasters, unless the forgiveness and the power of the Savior are vouchsafed to the despairing spirit. The power to **keep** the Christian from stumbling, and the power to **present** the Christian without blame before God is

25 To the only wise God our Saviour, *be* glory and majesty, dominion and power, both now and ever. Amen.

with rejoicing, 25 to the only God, our Savior through Jesus Christ our Lord, be glory, majesty, dominion, and authority, before all time and now and for ever. Amen.

25. **To the only God** expresses Jude's aversion to polytheism. No such distinction as Gnosticism drew between the God who created the world and the God who revealed himself in Christ is to be tolerated. The moral law flouted by the scoffers expresses the will not of some inferior deity, but of the God to whom **majesty** and **dominion** belong, **before all time and now and for ever.**

Seven times elsewhere in the N.T. God is called **Savior** (Luke 1:47; I Tim. 1:1; 2:3; 4:10; Tit. 1:3; 2:10; 3:4). Fifteen times Jesus is so designated. Salvation is regarded as God's gift, but the bestowal of the gift is accomplished **through Jesus Christ,** whom the church accordingly confesses and obeys as **Lord** (cf. Rom. 10:9; Phil. 2:11), since he alone effectively acts for God.

The combination of glowing ascriptions to God is a pattern frequently employed (cf. I Chr. 29:11; I Tim. 1:17; 6:16; I Pet. 4:11; 5:11; Rev. 1:6; 4:11; 5:13; 7:12; I Clem. 65:2; Martyrdom of Polycarp 20:2). It is the writer's prayer that the reverence and obedience accorded God in heaven may be found also on earth (cf. Matt. 6:10). His hope for mankind is based upon his faith in God's unity, righteousness, mercy, and power.

known only through the sacrificial act of Jesus Christ on the cross! Here is the supreme assurance that God is not only willing but able. His **glory, majesty, dominion, and authority** when seen through his loving heart are things about which to sing! Without the revelation of the reconciling love of God in the Cross, the glory, majesty, dominion, and authority would be forbidding and even threatening. But the God and Father of our Lord Jesus Christ can be trusted. "He that hath seen me hath seen the Father" (John 14:9). He is the "Father Almighty." The everlasting arms which sustain us and all men are "wonderfully kind." His **glory** (radiant magnificence), his **dominion** (spacious governance), his **majesty** (regal bearing, entourage, and presence), his **authority** (self-sufficient power), are the ultimate attributes of him in whom "we live, and move, and have our being" (Acts 17:28).

Only such a God can keep us from stumbling to a fall. In spite of our insufficiency and finitude and impotence and sinfulness he can and will present us on that Day **before the presence of his glory** without **blemish.** The keeping and the fulfilling and perfecting power of life are in the custody of a God who guards what is his own and finishes what he began. Christianity is adequate since it is meant for life at this present moment, for the whole pilgrimage of life, and for the consummation of life. And faith needs a keeper, since it so easily wanes in fervor.

Here is an ascription which is also a benediction. It not only affirms something about God, it also assures man of something about himself. It is a "good word" (*benedictum*). For that reason it is used at the end of a service of worship as Christians part from one another to go their several ways. They are to take with them the spirit of the church; they are to remember that God never forsakes them. He guards them and will **present** them before his presence without blame. Christians always live in the benediction of God.

The words are fairly saturated with joy and confidence and hope. In spite of all the troubles of the world and the church, Christians can sing. An ascription is an ejaculatory expression of exaltation. Who can keep from singing in the light of such a God, such a life, such a consummation! The future **rejoicing** (vs. 24) has its present anticipatory realization. The grand sweep of the Christian's confidence is rightly voiced: **To the only God, our Savior through Jesus Christ our Lord, be glory, majesty, dominion, and authority, before all time and now and for ever.** And to that, all Christians who share the author's faith will respond with a resounding **Amen!**

The

REVELATION

of St. John the Divine

Introduction and Exegesis by MARTIN RIST
Exposition by LYNN HAROLD HOUGH

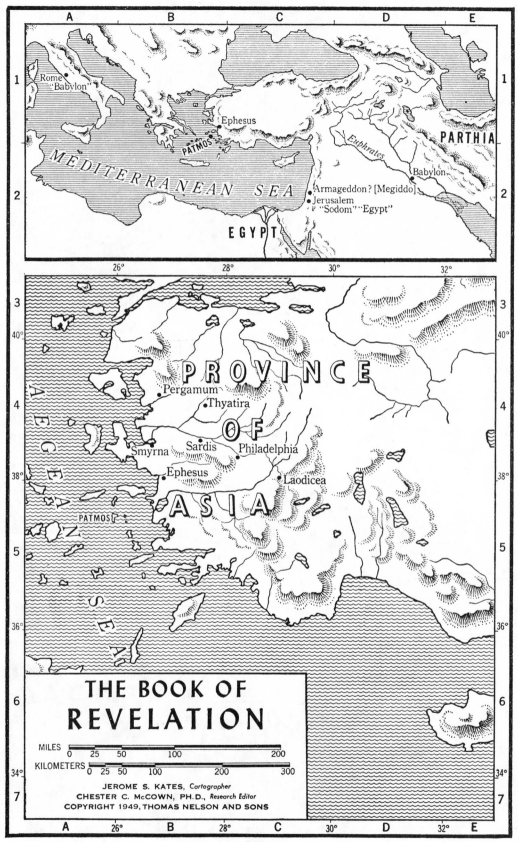

A   B   C   D   E

1

Rome
"Babylon"

Ephesus

PATMOS

MEDITERRANEAN   SEA

Euphrates

PARTHIA

Babylon

Armageddon? [Megiddo]
Jerusalem
"Sodom" "Egypt"

EGYPT

2

26°   28°   30°   32°

3

40°

PROVINCE

Pergamum
Thyatira

OF

38°

Smyrna

Sardis   Philadelphia

Ephesus

Laodicea

PATMOS

ASIA

36°

THE BOOK OF
REVELATION

MILES
0   25   50   100   200

KILOMETERS
0   25   50   100   200   300

34°

JEROME S. KATES, *Cartographer*
CHESTER C. McCOWN, PH.D., *Research Editor*
COPYRIGHT 1949, THOMAS NELSON AND SONS

A   26°   B   28°   C   30°   D   32°   E

REVELATION

INTRODUCTION

Revelation is by any criterion the finest example of an apocalypse in existence. What is an "apocalypse" and what are its distinguishing characteristics? This question is not readily answered, since the term has been defined so broadly and used so loosely that it has ceased to have a distinctive meaning, being applied to a variety of literary types ranging from prophecy to purported visions of the next world. To avoid confusion it seems best to restrict the designation to a specific type of literature, mainly Jewish and Christian (but also Persian and Mohammedan), which conforms to a distinctive and readily recognizable pattern of thought. According to this pattern, apocalypticism may be defined as the eschatological belief that the power of evil (Satan), who is now in control of this temporal and hopelessly evil age of human history in which the righteous are afflicted by his demonic and human agents, is soon to be overcome and his evil rule ended by the direct intervention of God, who is the power of good, and who thereupon will create an entirely new, perfect, and eternal age under his immediate control for the everlasting enjoyment of his righteous followers from among the living and the resurrected dead. This definition of the meaning of the term "apocalypticism" will be adopted throughout this discussion of Revelation.

I. The Meaning of "Apocalypse"

In elaboration of the definition, first of all it should be noted that apocalypticism is always eschatological, is always concerned with last things, with death and the end of this present age and with life in the age to come. This eschatological interest alone should be sufficient to differentiate apocalypticism from Old Testament prophecy, which is primarily if not exclusively concerned with this life and this age

of human history, rather than with the next life and the age to come. Accordingly, to avoid ambiguity the term "apocalypse" should never be used in connection with noneschatological books like Joel, Amos, Ezekiel, Zechariah, and Isaiah (save for Isa. 24–27), as is too frequently done. Likewise, this distinction should separate the concept of the kingdom of God (an outgrowth of Old Testament prophecy) as taught by the Pharisees and John the Baptist, as well as by Jesus, from apocalypticism; for the kingdom of God was to be established in this age and in this time of human history, not in an entirely new and different age to be created by God. Not even the resurrection and the judgment scenes as found in some depictions of the kingdom of God are sufficient to make it an apocalyptic concept, for the resurrection and judgment in these instances are to occur in this present age, which will continue after these events take place.

On the other hand, it should be emphasized that while all apocalypticism is eschatological, not all eschatology is apocalyptic. For example, the Orphic idea of immortality, in which the soul is finally separated from the body of flesh which had imprisoned and defiled it, is nonapocalyptic. Also, the so-called Apocalypse of Paul and similar works which are essentially purported visions of the place of the dead and their rewards and punishments are scarcely entitled to be classed as apocalypses along with Daniel, I Enoch, and Revelation.

Furthermore, not only is apocalypticism eschatological, it is also always dualistic. This dualism is not that of spirit and matter, of soul and flesh, as taught by Orphics and Gnostics, although Paul and the author of II Enoch combined this type with apocalyptic dualism. Instead, it is first of all a dualism of two opposing supernatural powers both personal and cosmic in character. In Persian apocalypticism—apparently the ultimate source of both Jewish and Christian apocalypticism—the dualism is most marked, for Ahriman, the evil god, and Ormazd, the good, are practically equal in power, like darkness and light. In both Jewish and Christian apocalypticism the force of evil, called Satan, or by some other name, is opposed to the righteous God; however, in these Jewish and Christian works God is clearly superior to his evil opponent, whom he permits to rule for a limited time; and in some Jewish sources the dualism is assumed rather than stated explicitly. While in Revelation this opposition between the cosmic forces of evil and good is more in evidence than is true of most apocalypses—Daniel, for instance—nevertheless it is basic to all writings in this category. This dualism is extended so that the supernatural and human followers of Satan and God are arrayed in opposing camps. For Satan has his angels, demons, and human agents who do his will, afflicting and persecuting the righteous; while God has his angels, and at times a Messiah, together with those who are his devoted worshipers and followers.

This opposition of two supernatural forces led to a belief in two distinct and separate ages. The present one, under the control of Satan, is of necessity evil, temporal, limited, and irredeemable in character; in direct contrast the one to come, under God's immediate direction, will be perfectly righteous, timeless, and eternal. It is either stated or assumed that in the beginning this age, created as it was by God, was initially good, as described in accounts of the Garden of Eden. However, for some reason, usually given as the sin of Adam or Eve or the intercourse of the sons of God with the daughters of men (Gen. 6:1-4), God abandoned this age to Satan and his evil supernatural and human followers, and is himself transcendent in heaven, far removed for the present from earth and men. Under Satan's rule this age has become progressively evil and corrupt, until by the time a given apocalypse is revealed to the world it has reached the very depths of evil and corruption, and can become no worse.

Intimately associated with this concept of two ages is that of two worlds, the present and the world to come. In fact, in the Greek the word αἰών may mean either "age" or "world," or both. The present world is the visible cosmos, the earth and the skies above and the underworld. It, like the present age, was originally good, since it too was the creation of God. However, under Satan's rule it has become so thoroughly permeated with evil that it will either be replaced with a perfect world (the "New Jerusalem") which has pre-existed in heaven, or in some cases will be thoroughly purged and renovated so as to be suitable for the new age.

This dualism of two ages and two worlds is not a characteristic either of prophecy or of the idea of the kingdom of God. For according to these views, while there are of course many evidences of evil in this age of human history and in this world, at the same time God has not for one moment relinquished his control, has not abdicated to Satan. In fact, he may be using certain aspects of evil as punishments for the sins of those who should be more faithful to him. For the prophets and the Pharisees, as well as Jesus, unlike the dualistic apocalypticists, shared the view of the psalmist that "the earth is the LORD's and the fulness thereof; the world, and they that dwell therein" (Ps. 24:1), a belief that is basic both to prophecy and to the doctrine of the kingdom of God.

It will be seen that apocalypticism attempts to explain the agelong existence of evil, especially in the form of the afflictions and sufferings of the righteous, and at the same time proposes a dramatic solution of the problem. As a result of God's temporary abdication he has left this age and this world to Satan and his evil agents, so that the righteous are oppressed, persecuted, and sometimes martyred by the unrighteous, that is, by the Gentiles or heathen (or in the case of Mohammedan apocalypses, by the Christian Crusaders).

Since overpowering forces of evil, both supernatural and human, are arrayed against them, there is little that the oppressed righteous can do of themselves to alleviate or improve their desperate situation. There is in fact but one course they can pursue, and that is to continue to be completely loyal and faithful to God, awaiting his divine intervention. In this connection it should be observed that in apocalypses (with the exception of II Enoch) righteousness is not primarily ethical and moral conduct, which in fact is seldom alluded to. This is not to say that apocalypticism and ethics are incompatible, for Paul combines both in his letters. But primarily apocalyptic righteousness consists in complete loyalty to God and to the cultic and ritualistic requirements of his religion. For example, in Daniel the test of righteousness is absolute conformity to the requirements of Torah, especially to the dietary laws and the commandments to worship God alone and to have nothing to do with idolatry. Similarly, in Revelation the criterion of righteous conduct is perfect loyalty and devotion to God and Christ, which is demonstrated by absolute refusal to worship the emperor or the state in any manner whatever, even though the death penalty might be invoked against the nonconformists. Accordingly, in Revelation there is a bare minimum of distinctly ethical and moral teaching. Indeed, the invoking of the vengeance and judgment of God against their persecutors by the martyrs might be considered to be unethical when judged by the highest Christian standards.

By contrast, the requirements of the kingdom of God as taught by Jesus consist in the highest type of ethical and moral conduct and behavior. By learning and doing God's will man may assist in bringing his kingdom into being, in this age and in this time. For the phrases "Thy kingdom come, thy will be done," as repeated in the Lord's Prayer, are interchangeable. When God's kingdom comes his will, of course, will be done by men; but at the same time, by learning and doing God's will, men will assist in bringing the kingdom into realization here and now.[1]

But to return to the plight of the righteous—desperate as their situation in this evil age under Satan's control actually is, they are not entirely bereft of all hope. For they are assured that God, now transcendent on his throne in heaven, will come to their rescue in the very near future. Trusting in his almighty power and justice—and, we must recognize, in his divine wrath and vengeance as well—they eagerly await the time when he will intervene on their behalf. Buoyed up and encouraged by this ardent hope of immediate help, they are enabled to endure their sufferings and afflictions, even the prospect of a cruel death, with sublime patience and fortitude. It is this confident expectation, with its prospects of glorious and immediate otherworldly rewards, that gives apocalypticism its tremendous hold upon people in times of oppression, affliction, distress, and persecution.

Accordingly, the righteous ardently expect that God with his forces will soon engage Satan and his hosts in a final cosmic struggle beginning in heaven and ending on earth. During this conflict the righteous will be interested spectators, save in Revelation, where the martyrs will comprise the armies of Christ (17:14; 19:14). After a terrific struggle, marked by cosmic disturbances and terrestrial disasters, God and his forces will overpower and subdue Satan and his human and supernatural followers, ending his power forever.

With his defeat Satan's rule, this present evil age, will be suddenly and dramatically terminated, making way for an entirely new and different age under God's direct control. In this new age there will be no evil, no corrup-

[1] But on this point see also Vol. VII, pp. 145-54.

tion, no wickedness, no suffering, no persecution, and no death; for Satan, the author of all of these ills affecting mankind, will no longer have any power to do harm. Instead, God in his perfect righteousness and justice will rule forever. Furthermore, this present world, corrupted through and through with evil, will either be renovated and restored to its original purity, or will be destroyed and replaced with a "new" and perfect world which has been made ready by God.

Furthermore, in this new age God will no longer be transcendent in heaven. Instead, in a sense heaven will come down to earth and God will be immanent in the world, directing and controlling it, and dwelling eternally with the righteous who have been devoted to him. Quite fittingly, in most of the apocalypses, but not all, the wicked will be eternally punished for their sins, including idolatry and the persecution of the righteous. Also, the righteous who survive the catastrophic end of this age, together with those who are resurrected from the dead, will receive their eternal reward of blessedness, peace, and joy in the new age under God upon the new or renewed earth.

Another striking feature of apocalypticism is its determinism. All that has happened or is to happen is the result of God's having willed it so. Moreover, there is a definite time schedule which God himself has predetermined. Also, as a rule, a certain limited number are foreordained to be among the righteous and the saved. Naturally enough, these are usually the author and his faithful coreligionists.

This, then, is the basic pattern of apocalypticism—a pattern unique and distinctive, differentiating this doctrine from prophecy, the belief in the kingdom of God, and from purported visions of the next world and the future life. Fundamentally it is a simple pattern, composed of elements that are more or less familiar. However, most apocalypses appear to be quite complex since their authors have usually interwoven a number of secondary elements into the basic pattern. These secondary features add variety, color, mystery, and vividness to the whole, but are not essential or distinctive: their inclusion does not modify the basic pattern and true apocalypses may lack any or all of them. Similarly, these secondary features are frequently found in works that are quite nonapocalyptic in nature. Some of these secondary elements occur in Revelation.

First of all, apocalypses are frequently represented as being visions of things to come, hence the name, for "apocalypse" is but the transliteration of a Greek word meaning "vision" or "revelation." But not all apocalypses are pur-

THE INTERPRETER'S BIBLE

ported visionary experiences. For example, one of the oldest if not the oldest extant Jewish apocalypse, Isa. 24–27, makes no pretense of being the result of a vision. Likewise, the apocalyptic ending of the seventh book of the *Divine Institutes* of Lactantius makes no claim to visionary authority.

The claim made in many apocalypses that the predictions came through visionary experiences is a literary device to give greater impressiveness to these writings. That this device is effective is shown by the ready acceptance of the claim by modern students of apocalypticism. For example, R. H. Charles, the greatest of all the modern students of this subject, wrote that the knowledge of both the prophet and the apocalyptic writer "came through visions, trances, and through spiritual, and yet not unconscious communion with God—the highest form of inspiration." [2] But do these purportedly divine visions correctly interpret the past and present and accurately predict the future? Are their depictions of the universe in which we live in conformity with our present astrophysical knowledge? Are their doctrines of God, of Satan, of Christ, of angels and demons, of two ages, of righteousness, and of rewards and punishments in harmony with our best Christian teaching? If our answers are in the negative, then the divine origin of these visions is subject to question.

Actually, the reality of these supposed visions may be tested on other grounds as well. For one, they frequently show dependence upon literary and traditional sources, as is so obviously true of Revelation. Furthermore, the books that contain these visions, and this is especially characteristic of Revelation, are usually conscious literary productions revealing considerable skill and artistry on the part of the authors. Moreover, the pseudonymous character of many of the apocalypses, as of Daniel, would almost preclude any belief that the visions were the experiences of their actual authors; for why would a true visionary ascribe these personal and striking experiences to someone other than himself if they had actually occurred?

Another secondary feature has just been mentioned, that of pseudonymity. This is an obvious literary artifice widely used in antiquity to gain authority for a given writing which it would not possess if issued under the name of its real author. Thus a number of the apocalypses are ascribed to patriarchs, prophets, and apostles to gain the prestige and authority of their names. But this is not true in all cases.

[2] *A Critical History of the Doctrine of a Future Life* (New York: A. & C. Black, 1913), p. 174.

Isa. 24–27 is an anonymous interpolation into Isaiah; the apocalyptic treatise by Hippolytus *On Christ and Antichrist* is written under his name, and Lactantius gave his to the apocalyptic section of his *Divine Institutes*. In this same connection it might be noted that Paul gives his apocalyptic utterances on his own authority. No one can be certain that Revelation is not a pseudepigraph, but a number of ancient and modern writers believe that the name of its author was actually John as the book itself claims.

Still another secondary feature of apocalypses is that of the Messiah. To be sure, the Messiah is present in all Christian apocalypses and in some Jewish ones. Indeed, in several Neo-Hebraic apocalypses there are two Messiahs. However, in some Jewish compositions that are undoubtedly to be classified as apocalypses, such as Isa. 24–27, Daniel, II Baruch 85, and the Assumption of Moses 10 (to mention but a few), there is no evidence whatever of a Messiah. Moreover, in certain others where the Messiah is present, his role is quite secondary and passive, as in II Esdras 7:28-30, and he could be eliminated without the apocalyptic scheme being materially affected. In fact, in several passages in Revelation itself angels, rather than the heavenly Christ, perform functions that more naturally might have been assigned to him, such as the defeat and expulsion of Satan from heaven in ch. 12 and his seizure and imprisonment in ch. 20.

Likewise, whereas the Antimessiah or Antichrist, the satanic counterpart of the Messiah, is prominent in Christian and some Jewish apocalypses, his secondary character is revealed by his absence from a number of Jewish writings which are unquestioned apocalypses. Also, even in works in which he is mentioned, is frequently merged with Satan, is at times the latter's alter ego, and performs no distinctive function.

Despite its presence in Revelation, the messianic reign is also a secondary feature of apocalypses, being absent from many of them. In Jewish apocalypses it is found in II Esdras (a period of four hundred years) and in the Neo-Hebraic Apocalypse of Elijah (an interval of forty years), but these examples are exceptional. Actually, it does not belong to apocalypticism, but has been engrafted from the non-apocalyptic expectation of a messianic kingdom in this present age. Other subsidiary elements, not essential constituents of the apocalyptic pattern but present in some apocalypses and missing from others, may be mentioned without discussion, such as elaborate angelology and demonology; strange and bizarre imagery, including animal symbolism; numerology; stereo-

350

typed lists of woes marking the end of this age; astrology; the Gog and Magog saga or its equivalent; a general resurrection of all the dead; a judgment scene in which the wicked are condemned and the righteous approved; heavenly books of life or books of doom; detailed descriptions of the punishments of the wicked and the rewards of the righteous in the next age; the conversion of the Gentiles; the New Jerusalem; the New Eden; the tree of life; and the river of life. Most of these features are present in Revelation, but this does not of necessity make them apocalyptic, for they are not found with any degree of uniformity in other apocalypses. On the other hand, they are often present in sources that are nonapocalyptic, indeed in sources that are noneschatological in character. Finally, unlike the primary elements, they may be added to or subtracted from an apocalypse without destroying its basic pattern.

There is a whole range of apocalyptic literature, both Jewish and Christian (as well as other noncanonical works), which is frequently referred to in the Exegesis. These writings are not always available to the reader who does not have access to a theological library. Some are found in publications which are difficult to obtain and a few have not been translated into English. However, the following publications in English are not too difficult to obtain and contain a representative number of the extant apocalypses:

Charles, R. H., ed. *The Apocrypha and Pseudepigrapha of the Old Testament*. Oxford: Clarendon Press, 1913. 2 vols.

James, Montague R. *The Apocryphal New Testament*. Oxford: Clarendon Press, 1924.

Charles, R. H. *The Ascension of Isaiah*. London: Society for Promoting Christian Knowledge, 1917.

Box, G. H. *The Apocalypse of Abraham*. London: Society for Promoting Christian Knowledge, 1918.

Roberts, Alexander, and Donaldson, James, eds. *The Ante-Nicene Fathers*. New York: The Christian Literature Company, 1890. 9 vols.

Buttenwieser, Moses. *Outline of the Neo-Hebraic Apocalyptic Literature*. Cincinnati: Jennings & Pye, 1901.

II. Early Circulation and Acceptance of Revelation

John expected not only that his book would be read aloud in the seven churches to which it was addressed (1:3), and possibly in other churches as well, but that it would also be accepted as a book of prophecy, possibly on a level with the prophetic books of the Old Testament (1:3; 19:10; 22:9-10, 18). Whether he provided a copy of his book for each of the seven churches, thereby expediting its circulation, or whether there was at first but a single copy which was taken from church to church, cannot be determined. However, it is certain that by the end of the second century Revelation was known and used throughout Christendom not only as a book of prophecy but also as a part of the canon of the New Testament, with the apostle John, the son of Zebedee, generally considered to be its author. At the same time, there were some who disputed both its canonical status and its apostolic authorship.

There may be some reflections of Revelation in Hermas, Ignatius, and Barnabas, but this cannot be stated definitely. More certainly, however, we are assured by Andreas in the prologue to his commentary that Papias of Hieropolis in Phrygia, who flourished before 150, knew Revelation and considered it to be inspired. Likewise, Justin Martyr, who lived in Ephesus around A.D. 135 before moving to Rome, writing about 155-60 states:

And, further, a man among us named John, one of the apostles of Christ, prophesied in a Revelation made to him that they who have believed our Christ will spend a thousand years in Jerusalem, and that afterwards the universal, and, in one word, eternal resurrection of all at once, will take place, and also the judgment.[3]

This is the earliest specific mention of Revelation extant and the first attestation of its supposed authorship by the apostle John. Whether Justin considered it to be scripture is difficult to decide, but the probabilities are against its canonical standing at this date.

Somewhat later, around 165, Melito, bishop of Sardis, one of the cities to which the apocalypse was originally addressed, wrote a treatise on Revelation which unfortunately is lost. Consequently it is impossible to determine what he thought about its scriptural status and its authorship. However, the very fact that he wrote a treatise about it is a testimony to the prestige it enjoyed in Sardis in his day.

One of his contemporaries, Theophilus, the sixth bishop of Antioch, wrote a polemic against a certain heretic named Hermogenes, in which he used testimonies or quotations from Revelation to refute the heretic and to advance his own arguments, thereby testifying to its circulation in Syria.

In Rome the book of Revelation was well received before the end of the second century, for Justin Martyr, no doubt, reflects Roman as

[3] *Dialogue with Trypho* 81.

well as Ephesian opinion concerning its character. Furthermore, the authoritative Muratorian Canon, which gives the list of Christian writings accepted as scripture in Rome around the year 200, states that Revelation was written by the apostle John to seven churches and includes it with the Apocalypse of Peter as scripture. There were those, however, who would not permit the latter to be read in the church, but this restriction did not apply to Revelation.

Furthermore, North Africa and Gaul, both greatly influenced by Roman belief and practice, accepted Revelation as canonical by this time. For Tertullian, the leading representative of North African Christianity at the end of the second century and the beginning of the third, frequently quoted from Revelation as scripture, as did his great successor Cyprian. Also, the Acts of Perpetua and Felicitas, which relates the martyr-deaths of Christians in Carthage in 202-3, shows the influence of Revelation and its imagery.

As for Gaul, in 177 a letter written from the Christians of Lyons and Vienna to the churches of Asia and Phrygia, relating their sufferings during a period of persecution, quoted Revelation several times and in one passage cited it as scripture. Moreover, Irenaeus, the influential bishop of Lyons from 177 to 202, frequently referred to Revelation, and considered it as a canonical work written by the apostle John.

Likewise, Clement of Alexandria, the head of the celebrated catechetical school, who flourished from about 190 to 210, knew and quoted Revelation, and considered it to be scripture coming from the hand of the apostle John, thus attesting its acceptance in Egypt.

In addition, the book was eagerly accepted by the chiliasts or millenarians of the second century, who looked forward to the enjoyment of material as well as spiritual goods in the promised millennium. Among them were the Montanists, a widespread heretical group which originated in Phrygia around the year 156 and eventually claimed Tertullian among its adherents.

At the same time, there were not a few who rejected Revelation for one reason or another. Among them was Marcion, a Gnostic heretic with a considerable following before the middle of the century, who discarded the Jewish scriptures and substituted for them the first-known Christian canon, a gospel and the letters of Paul. He was said to have rejected Revelation because of its Jewish character; moreover, he did not believe that its author was an apostle. However, there were other Gnostics, like the Marcosians, who apparently received Revelation as scriptural.

Another heretical group, the so-called Alogi, refused to accept the Logos doctrine as developed in the Gospel of John and in other writings. Accordingly, they would not receive the Fourth Gospel as scripture and at the same time refused to accept Revelation, since it was supposed to have been written by the author of the Gospel. Furthermore, they and others stated that Revelation was composed toward the end of the first century by a heretical Jewish Christian named Cerinthus, who wrote under the name of John to give his work apostolic sanction.

Likewise, some of the more orthodox who opposed the chiliasts, and especially the Montanists, were inclined to question both the canonicity and the apostolic authorship of Revelation. Among these was a certain Caius of Rome who, around the year 210, wrote an attack against the Montanists in which he rejected Revelation—but not, it would seem, the Fourth Gospel—because of its marvels and its allegedly materialistic doctrine of the millennium; like others he attributed the work to Cerinthus. This provoked a defense of Revelation in 215 by the great Christian leader Hippolytus, which was so vigorous that from this time on there were few in the West to question its canonicity and apostolic authorship. Accordingly, it was early included in the Old Latin canon and likewise in the Vulgate. Victorinus, who died as a martyr in 304, wrote a commentary on Revelation in Latin which later on was reworked by Jerome, even though the latter was somewhat dubious concerning the place of the apocalypse in the canon.

In the third century the situation in Alexandria, which with its school came to exert great influence, was somewhat different. Origen, who died in 254, accepted Revelation as a book of scripture written by the apostle John, but did so by means of an allegorical reinterpretation of its contents. A resolute opponent of chiliasm, he rejected the literal interpretation of the millennium by stating that while Christ would return, his Second Advent would be spiritual, not bodily, and that his kingdom would likewise be spiritual, not material. Origen also allegorized much of the imagery, so that the seven heads of the dragon became the seven deadly sins, the scroll with the seven seals the Scriptures, which Christ alone could interpret, and so on. This successful attempt to save Revelation as authoritative scripture by allegorical reinterpretation has been repeated with variations down to the present day.

A rather serious criticism of Revelation was made by Dionysius, the scholarly bishop of Alexandria from 247 to 264. He discovered that the Christians of Arsinoe had been attracted to the teaching of a certain Nepos, who in his book, *Refutation of the Allegorists,* maintained that the scripture, and especially Revelation, taught that "there would be a certain millennium of bodily luxury upon this earth." In his opposition to this materialistic chiliasm Dionysius wrote a two-volume work, *On Promises.* Assuming that the Gospel of John was from the apostle, he decided on the basis of its dissimilarity of style, grammar (which in places was barbarous), and ideas, that Revelation was not by the evangelist. He also observed that many did not accept Revelation as canonical, while some said that it was not by an apostle, but by Cerinthus. On the other hand, many held it in high esteem, and he himself would not discard it. However, he confessed that much it contains is obscure and should be taken figuratively, not literally, if one would discover its true meaning. But in effect, since he considered the book to be by a certain John of Ephesus of a later date, not by John the son of Zebedee, he cast considerable doubt upon its canonicity, for an essential condition of acceptance into the canon was apostolic origin.

As a result of a growing opposition, the canonical status of Revelation outside of the West came to be seriously questioned. Thus Eusebius, writing in 326 following the triumph of the church and its freedom from persecution, stated that Revelation may be accepted as scripture or rejected, "as may seem proper." He reflects a divided opinion concerning its place in the canon. The changed political situation, with the emperor now a supporter of Christianity, quite likely had a bearing upon the attitude of Eusebius, the friend and admirer of Constantine, toward this book which regarded both the Roman state and the emperor as satanic and prophesied their destruction, and this in turn no doubt influenced others.

At any rate, for one reason or another Revelation was not included in the canon of scripture approved by the Synod of Laodicea around the year 360. It was specifically rejected by the influential Cyril, bishop of Jerusalem until his death in 386, who forbade not only its reading in public but in private as well. The school of Antioch, second only in influence to that of Alexandria, was not favorably disposed toward Revelation, for it is not even mentioned by Chrysostom of Antioch and Constantinople (died in 407), nor by Theodore of Mopsuestia (died in 428). Furthermore, it was not included in the canon of the Syriac version called the Peshitta, which was authorized by the powerful Rabbula, bishop of Edessa from 411 to 435; nor was it included in the Armenian version. It is also possible that it was excluded from the earlier forms of the Coptic versions as well.

However, despite the widespread doubts concerning the scriptural and apostolic authority of Revelation in the East, Athanasius, the great and influential bishop of Alexandria, in his festal letter of 367, accepted it without question among the twenty-seven books of the New Testament, even though he must have been fully aware of the opposition toward Revelation. Quite likely this approval by Athanasius helped to maintain the scriptural standing of Revelation in the Greek church of the East; but even so, the relatively small number of Greek manuscripts containing Revelation is a testimony to lingering doubts concerning its right to be in the canon.

This brief survey of the stages by which Revelation came to be accepted as scripture and a part of the New Testament shows that from the middle of the second century, if not earlier, it was a mysterious and disputed book. On the other hand, there can be little question that its first readers, those persecuted Christians to whom it was originally addressed, experienced little difficulty in understanding and appreciating its message; for not only were they, like its author, steeped in apocalyptic thought and imagery, but the book was directed toward their own precarious situation. But when the time and situation for which it was written had passed, its acceptance as scripture created difficulties which persist to the present day. For by being canonized Revelation became a divinely inspired and therefore authoritative series of predictions of what was to occur at some time in the future, with the interpreter's, not the author's, time tending to be the point of departure. Likewise, as scripture its depiction of God and Christ, of Satan and Antichrist, of angels and demons and other supernatural powers commanded acceptance. In the same manner its portrayal of the universe in which we live, of heaven and hell, of the present age and the age to come, and of the millennium, with its philosophy of history, claimed the attention of believers. These distinctive ideas of the writer created difficulties which would scarcely have arisen had Revelation remained outside of the canon; for then it would have been understood and interpreted with reference to the historical situation which produced it and the purpose the author had in its composition. In other words, it would have been studied as objectively as uncanonical, nonscriptural apocalypses like I Enoch, II Baruch, the Apocalypse of Peter, or the Ascension of Isaiah are studied. Even though II Esdras is in the Old

Testament Apocrypha, its quasi-canonical status has made possible its being studied and interpreted quite objectively. But unfortunately, the canonical position of both Revelation and Daniel has been largely responsible for the artificial, subjective, and arbitrary manner in which they have been treated, not only by Christians in general but also by the majority of scholars down through the centuries.

III. Date and Occasion

It is obvious that Revelation was written in a time when the Christians of Asia Minor, and probably other places as well, were being persecuted by the Roman officials for their refusal to worship the emperors, both living and dead, as gods and to worship Roma, the personification of Rome, as a goddess. The cult of the ruler and of the state was established mainly as a political measure and served to inculcate political loyalty among the heterogeneous populations of the empire. To this end temples, shrines, altars, and statues were erected throughout the realm and an imperial priesthood was established to supervise the rites. Back of it all was the effective governmental and police power of Rome to encourage, and if necessary to coerce, all subjects of the state to show their loyalty by participating in the rites of the state cult. At first the emphasis was upon the worship of the dead emperors who had been apotheosized by the senate, along with that of Roma, although from an early period the living ruler had been accorded worship in the provinces. However, as time went on the worship of the living emperor was increasingly stressed for obvious political reasons.

The Jews alone were exempted from the requirements of the state cult in recognition that theirs was an ethnic religion which had by ancient custom strictly forbidden both the worship of any god save their own and the use of idols. Because of this unbending attitude of the Jews, who represented an important, cohesive minority group scattered throughout the empire, it was politic on the part of the Romans to grant them this as well as other concessions to their religious scruples. However, these concessions no doubt served to increase the feeling of anti-Semitism which had long been in evidence in the Greco-Roman world. At first Christians, as members of the Jewish race and comprising a sect of Judaism, shared in this exemption granted to the Jews; but by the end of the first century most Christians were non-Jewish in origin and Christianity itself had become a religion separate and distinct from Judaism. Hence Christians, even though they claimed

that they, not the Jews, were the true Israel, were expected to show their political loyalty by worshiping the state and its deified emperors, living and dead. Their reluctance to do so led to repression, persecution, and in some instances death. This compulsion by the government, coupled with the social pressure of family, friends, and neighbors, no doubt caused a number of Christians to seek some compromise whereby they might join in the rites of the state cult and at the same time maintain their membership in the church. When this was not permitted by the church, then no doubt a considerable number of Christians, confronted with the alternative of persecution and possible death, weakened and left Christianity, becoming apostates.

It was this situation which occasioned the writing of Revelation. A persecution of Christians of Asia Minor for their refusal to participate in the state cult had broken out. This had resulted in the martyr-death of at least one of the number. There were reasons to expect an intensification of the persecution, with the prospect that a number of the weaker and less devoted among the church's members would fall away. If left unchecked, this defection could result in such a weakening of Christianity that it might disintegrate and disappear. It was to meet this crisis in his times that the author of Revelation wrote his book. His purpose was to sharpen the alternatives open to the Christians, of worshiping either Caesar or God, of being completely loyal to the state or wholly devoted to Christianity. Furthermore, he endeavored to make martyrdom, with its eternal rewards, so attractive, and worship of the emperor, with its eternal punishments, so fearsome, that his readers would quite willingly accept death as martyrs rather than be disloyal to Almighty God and his Christ by worshiping Roma and the emperors.

But when did this persecution of the Christians of Asia Minor occur? Practically all of the early Christian writers place it toward the very end of the reign of Domitian, who died in A.D. 96, a date that is accepted by most modern students of the question. To be sure, some early and some modern authorities as well would date it earlier, particularly in the reign of Nero (A.D. 54-68), who is known to have been responsible for the death of a number of Christians, following the conflagration of Rome—but this was on the false charge of incendiarism, not because they had refused to worship him. Moreover, several unmistakable allusions in Revelation to the later development of the Nero redivivus legend, the belief that this infamous emperor would be restored to life and would lead an invading host into the empire from the East (cf. 13:3, 12, 14; 17:8, 11), preclude any date before his death. Furthermore, we know from other sources that the particular form of the Neronian myth that is reflected in Revelation was in circulation toward the close of Domitian's rule.

According to some, the sixth head of the beast (17:10), symbolizing the emperor who was ruling when Revelation was composed, should be identified with Vespasian. This identification is made by counting from Augustus as the first emperor and by omitting the three immediate predecessors of Vespasian—Galba, Otho, and Vitellius—whose rules were very brief. It is obvious that the basis for equating the sixth head with Vespasian is very unsubstantial. Furthermore, there is no evidence of any desire on the part of Vespasian to persecute Christians or anyone else for refusing to worship him as a deity. Tertullian, in fact, says explicitly that Vespasian did not persecute the Christians. Indeed, although for political reasons his worship was encouraged, this doughty soldier who apparently possessed a considerable amount of personal integrity did not take his divinity very seriously, and is reputed to have jested about it while on his deathbed.

In further support of an early dating attention is directed to the angelic command in 11:1 to measure the temple, which was destroyed in the year 70. However, there is no evidence in the rest of Revelation that the temple was still standing; and even here the author is probably referring to the temple figuratively, to symbolize the faithful Christians who are to be measured, and not to the actual temple of Jerusalem.

A date during the reign of Trajan (98-117) has also been suggested. That he ordered the persecution of Christians is certain. In fact, a rescript which he sent to Pliny the Younger, the governor of Bithynia, about 111-113, decrees that the Christians there were to be persecuted and put to death. Their offense, however, was not specifically stated as refusal to worship the state deities, but was simply the crime of being Christians. Apparently for the first time in the relations of the empire with the church, Christianity, which was neither an ethnic religion like Judaism nor a licit religion like that of the Great Mother, approved by the senate, was now considered illegal and adherence to it was a crime punishable by death. Revelation reflects an earlier situation, in which the sole offense for which Christians were persecuted and martyred was noncompliance with the requirement of the state cult that they show their political loyalty by worship of the rulers and Roma. It is also difficult to see how the sixth head of the beast in 17:10 could be identified with Trajan. Moreover, the persecution which occasioned Revelation could scarcely have occurred during the brief reign of Domitian's successor, Nerva (96-98), for he reputedly released those who had been imprisoned for religious offenses and recalled those who had been sent into exile.

Thus by the process of elimination the traditional date for Revelation, that of Domitian's reign, somewhere between the years 81-96, is rendered more likely. But there are more positive lines of evidence which not only point to this reign but also indicate a persecution in its closing years.

Of these indications we may note first that both for personal and political reasons Domitian was more concerned with the establishment of the imperial cult, especially as it pertained to the worship of the ruling emperor as god, than was any of his predecessors. A major factor in his attitude was a warped personality, doubtless the consequence of his thwarted desires as a youth when his older brother Titus was high in paternal and public favor. As a result of his frustration he was arrogant to the point of megalomania. Moreover, even though his father and brother had both been emperors before him, his family was quite plebeian in origin, and his ignoble heritage was both a social and a political handicap. Before coming to the throne his career had not been marked by any notable achievements, even though he had been given a number of high-sounding titles. Besides all this, his accession to the throne was not wholly regular. Actually, the imperial crown was not a hereditary right, but in theory was bestowed upon the best-qualified citizen. Vespasian had owed his elevation to the devotion of his victorious armies, and it was this same loyalty of the armies to his unworthy son, and this alone, that placed Domitian on the throne. Accordingly, he met with strenuous opposition from the Roman aristocrats, as well as from the Stoic philosophers, who had considerable influence.

As a result of these personal and political considerations Domitian was most zealous in stressing his claims to divinity. An important step in this direction was the development of the cult of the Flavian house in which the divine nature of his family was emphasized, so as to demonstrate that as the descendant of the divine Vespasian he had a divine parentage and was himself a divinity with an undeniable claim upon the loyalty, obedience, and worship of every citizen and subject of the empire. His divinity was emphasized and his worship enjoined, not only in the provinces where there was little opposition to the imperial cult, but even at Rome as far as this was possible. To promote his divinity he commanded public sacrifices to, as well as oaths by, his genius. Spectators who hissed his gladiators were executed on the grounds that they had despised his divine nature. He at one time called his bed the couch of a god. He ordered his household to call him "our Lord and God." The poets seeking royal favor referred to him as "most sacred emperor," as "god," and as "Jupiter." They also used such terms as his "sacred side," "sacred name," "sacred house," and "sacred banquets," and called the fish served at these banquets "sacred." [4]

Not only did he make these grandiose claims, but Domitian was ruthless in enforcing them. For example, for political reasons he persecuted the philosophers, banishing them from Rome together with the astrologers. Apparently Josephus, the friend and admirer of both Vespasian and Titus, feared a persecution of the Jews by Domitian for their refusal to accord him divine honors, and in A.D. 93 wrote his great historical apology, *Jewish Antiquities,* in anticipation of this threat to his people's religious liberty. Moreover, in A.D. 95 Domitian executed his cousin, the consul Clemens, together with others, for "atheism" and for adopting a Jewish mode of life, and for the same reason punished still others, including his niece Domitilla, the wife of Clemens, by confiscation of property and exile. It is generally conceded that those so punished were actually attracted to Christianity, and were considered atheists for refusing to worship the gods, including the imperial divinities—a contention supported by archaeological evidence. Both I Clement, written from Rome, and Hebrews, written to the Roman Christians, testify to a persecution of the Christians in the capital at about this same time. Furthermore, there is evidence that sporadic persecutions of the Christians, fortunately brief in duration, broke out in the eastern provinces in this same period. According to the accounts, there were a number of defections and not a few martyrdoms during these persecutions.

Unfortunately there is no unmistakable reference in Revelation to its date of composition. The sixth head of the beast in 17:10 might be equated with Domitian by counting only those of his predecessors who had been apotheosized by the senate, but by some other computation it might be identified with some other emperor. It is possible that the statement at the end of

[4] For these and other pertinent data see Donald McFayden, "The Occasion of the Domitianic Persecution," *American Journal of Theology,* XXIV (1920), 46-66.

6:6, "But do not harm oil and wine," is an allusion to an edict of Domitian's in the year 92, ordering half of the vineyards in Asia Minor and other provinces torn up, apparently to increase the acreage planted in grain and to help the winegrowers of Italy. This decree caused so much opposition, especially in Asia Minor, that it was revoked in the following year without being seriously enforced. While the edict did not mention oil, we should not expect the author to be too faithful to its exact wording. If this verse does contain an allusion to this order of Domitian's, then Revelation must be dated after the year 93, and probably shortly after, since it is unlikely that it was remembered for any considerable period of time.

One or two other indications of date may be mentioned. First, as noted above, there were some who stated that Cerinthus, a Jewish-Christian heretic from the end of the first century, was the actual author of Revelation. Whereas this statement concerning authorship must be greatly discounted if not discarded completely, it may still preserve a correct tradition concerning the time of composition. In addition, as noted above, the form of the Nero redivivus myth reflected in Revelation is known to have circulated during the reign of Domitian. It may also be observed that the author seems to show acquaintance with the Pauline corpus of letters to seven churches introduced by a covering or general letter. Unfortunately we do not know just when the Pauline corpus was collected and published. In fact, the traditional date of Revelation has been used as the *ad quem* date of the collection and publication of this corpus. But on other grounds it is doubtful that the collection was made or that Ephesians, the covering letter, was written much before the end of the first century. Consequently, the apparent dependence of the letter corpus of Revelation on the Pauline collection is another clue to the time of its composition.

Accordingly, since the negative evidence seems to preclude any date save the reign of Domitian, and the positive data seem to support this date, the tradition that Revelation was written during the rule of this last representative of the Flavian house, and more specifically in his last year or two, while not certain, must be accepted as highly probable.

IV. The Author

As previously observed, Justin Martyr, shortly after the middle of the second century, stated that Revelation was written by "John, one of the apostles of Christ," a view that came to be widely held by the early church, and is not without its supporters today.

One among many objections to this conclusion is the hesitancy on the part of certain Christians in the second and third century, when the New Testament canon was being formed, to accept Revelation as apostolic in origin. Indeed some went so far as to deny this ascription. The internal evidence of the work also fails to support the belief that it was by an apostle. In fact, while the author calls himself "John" in four verses (1:1, 4, 9; 22:8), at no time does he assert that he is an apostle or make any claims to apostolic authority. Indeed, in 21:14, where he states that the wall of the city had twelve foundations inscribed with the names of the twelve apostles, he seems to imply that the apostolic age was gone, and that he himself was not one of the twelve. In still another verse (18:20) he speaks of the apostles quite objectively and as if he were not one of this select company, but in this case he may have been using the term in its wider connotation, not in a special, limited sense. Moreover, nowhere in Revelation is there any indication that the author had seen Jesus in his lifetime, that he had ever been with him as a personal follower, or had ever heard him speak. On the contrary, almost everything that he has to say about Christ seems to be a denial that he had ever been associated with the earthly, human Jesus of Nazareth. In fact, his apocalyptic Christology is of a nature to make it highly unlikely, if not impossible, for him to have known Jesus in the flesh.

Furthermore, if the dating of Revelation toward the end of the first century is reasonably correct, it is doubtful that it could have been by John the son of Zebedee. For according to a statement attributed to Papias before the middle of the second century, which is supported by other evidence, John, like his brother James, was killed by the Jews before the year 70, while the temple was still standing. Their early death is apparently attested by what is usually regarded as a prophecy after the event in Mark 10:39, according to which Jesus says to them, "The cup that I drink you will drink; and with the baptism with which I am baptized, you will be baptized." To be sure, there is other evidence that John lived in Ephesus to a ripe old age, but the possible invention of this tradition is more readily explained than that of his early martyrdom. Obviously, if Papias is correct, then it would have been impossible for John the apostle to have been the author of Revelation toward the end of the first century.[5]

[5] For further discussion of this problem see Vol. VIII, pp. 440-41.

In this connection it is somewhat beside the point to contend with Dionysius that the great difference in style, grammar, and ideas between Revelation and the Fourth Gospel proves that the apostle did not write the former; for such an argument assumes the apostolic origin of the Gospel. One can agree with Dionysius, however, that the two books could not have been by the same author.

The belief maintained by some today that Revelation is pseudonymous was held as early as the second century, when the Alogi and possibly others maintained that it was written by Cerinthus toward the end of the first century in the name of the apostle John, so as to obtain "reputable authority for his fiction." Most, but not all, apocalypses are pseudonymous; but it is difficult to believe that Revelation is of this character, for it displays scarcely any of the characteristics of the art of pseudepigraphy. Certainly if the author were writing in the name of the apostle, one would have expected him to state explicitly that "John" was an apostle, one of the twelve, and an earthly companion of Jesus, and to have made attempts at verisimilitude. But since none of these characteristic traits is found in the book, it is probable that Revelation is not a pseudepigraph.

If the writing is not pseudonymous, then it follows that the author's name actually was John, even though he was not the apostle by that name. But which John? Some have suggested that he was the rather shadowy John the presbyter, who was first mentioned by Papias as living in Ephesus early in the second century.[6] Or he may have been quite a different John, for the name was not uncommon, who would be unknown to us save for Revelation. That he was connected with the Christianity of Asia Minor is quite obvious; that he was closely related to the church at Ephesus is not unlikely; that he had some official position in the church is another possibility; that he was a second- or even third-generation Christian is likely if the traditional date of Revelation is accepted.

He describes himself, in Pauline terminology, as a slave or servant of Christ (1:1). He also calls himself a brother of those Christians to whom he was writing, as if there were little distinction in position between himself and them (1:9; 19:10). He was, moreover, a confessor, that is, one who had testified that he was a Christian when brought before the Roman authorities, and as such had been exiled to Patmos (1:9). Although he does not say this, we may infer that he had not denied Christ and that he had refused to worship the image of the emperor—tests that were usually applied to

[6] See above, pp. 215-16.

Christians or suspected Christians in their trials. This status of confessor was one that doubtless gave him a considerable amount of prestige and authority. We need only recall that Ignatius, the bishop of Antioch, who was a confessor a few years later, was greeted with great reverence and acclaim, and was listened to with considerable respect by the Christians of Asia Minor while en route to Rome to be executed. It is possible, although this is purely a surmise, that John was permitted to return from exile during the lenient reign of Nerva, the successor of Domitian.

Furthermore, John claimed that his book was a prophecy and that he himself was a prophet writing with the authority of divine inspiration (1:3; 19:10: 22:7, 9, 18). A similar claim was made by his Roman contemporary, Hermas, whose book was widely received and was for a time accepted as a part of the New Testament canon in certain areas of the church. We also learn from the Didache, written around the year 100, that Christian prophets were highly esteemed. Justin Martyr, who had observed that John was an apostle, at the same time said that he was a prophet. Accordingly, as a confessor and a prophet he wrote with an authority which would have been respected by those Christians who first read his book.

Still other deductions concerning him may be made. He apparently knew some Hebrew as well as Greek, as is evidenced by the inclusion of Hebrew terms like Abaddon and Armageddon and the probable dependence of the cipher 666 upon the Hebrew. He seems to have used freely the Septuagint translation of the Old Testament, but at times he apparently used some other Greek translation, and on occasion he may have made his own translation from Hebrew into Greek. There are those who maintain that Revelation contains so many Semitisms that John must have been bilingual, writing in Greek but thinking in Hebrew or Aramaic. It is certain, as Dionysius observed, that Revelation is not written in good Greek; in fact, no other author of the New Testament so frequently disregards the canons of style, grammar, and syntax. Yet for the most part, strangely enough, this disregard has caused little or no loss of clarity and intelligibility. All this suggests that the writer was a Jewish Christian who was uneducated according to Greek standards; however, it does not of necessity follow that he was a native of Palestine, as some have suggested, for Jews were widely dispersed throughout the empire, with many in Asia Minor.

John was thoroughly acquainted with the Old Testament, and quotes or alludes to it throughout his book. It has been estimated that 278 verses out of a total of 404 contain references of one kind or another to the Old Testament. He makes frequent use, as might be expected, of the prophetic books, with Isaiah, Ezekiel, and Daniel among his favorites. He is also indebted to the Psalms and to the Pentateuch, especially to Genesis and Exodus, and uses a number of other books as well. No author of the New Testament, in fact, shows a more intimate acquaintance with the Old Testament than he, yet in no case does he specifically mention a book of the Jewish scripture, and seldom does he quote verbatim. As will be noted in the Exegesis, he usually reinterprets the passages he uses in the light of his apocalyptic interests.

While it cannot be demonstrated that he quoted any of the extracanonical Jewish writings, including the apocalypses known to modern scholarship, nevertheless he was thoroughly imbued with the apocalyptic tradition. Consequently, Revelation contains numerous parallels, more or less close, to the ideas, concepts, patterns, and symbols used in Jewish apocalypses such as I Enoch, II Esdras, II Baruch, the Apocalypse of Abraham, the Sibylline Oracles, and others, in addition to Daniel and Isa. 24–27. There are also striking similarities between Revelation and other Christian apocalypses and apocalyptic passages in other books which show that he represents an apocalyptic movement among the early Christians.

The author was acquainted, as noted before, with the Pauline corpus of letters to seven churches with its introductory or covering letters. However, save for a few phrases, he makes but little use of the contents of these letters. There are also some resemblances between the canonical Gospels and Revelation, but these similarities probably show the use of a common tradition rather than any literary dependence. John's disuse, for the most part, of the familiar teachings of Jesus, as well as his almost complete lack of interest in Jesus' earthly career, may indicate that he represents a circle of early Christian thinking and belief quite different from those out of which the several Gospels came.

A significant but somewhat neglected feature of Revelation is the relatively large amount of astrology that pervades the work from the first to the final chapter. Based upon the belief that the heavenly bodies controlled the destinies of mankind, astral speculation was widespread in the Mediterranean world, and was accepted by Jews as well as by non-Jews, by both the learned and the ignorant. Among its adherents was the emperor Domitian, who considered himself something of a student of this pseudo science. Among Jewish works it is particularly evident in the apocalypses. Although in certain instances John may not have been aware of the astrological significance of some of the sources he used, nevertheless his frequent use of astral concepts and symbols is rather clear evidence that for the most part he introduced them knowingly and deliberately.

There is not much in Revelation that can be termed characteristically Hellenistic. Apart from the adaptation of some pagan astral myth in the account of the woman clothed with the sun in ch. 12, the chief non-Jewish element in the apocalypse is its Christology, and even much of this is derived from Jewish teachings concerning the heavenly apocalyptic Messiah. This Christology in Revelation has some elements in common with Paul's, but is considerably less Hellenistic, showing far less contact with the so-called mystery religions than Paul's teachings reveal.

Finally, the author was an exceedingly practical person. As has been observed before, he was dealing with a very critical issue in the early church in its conflict with the empire concerning the cult of the ruler and the state. He was determined to oppose any temptation on the part of his readers to temporize and to make concessions in the mistaken belief that they could simultaneously worship both Caesar and God. At the same time, he strove to prevent defections from Christianity in the face of coercive measures and persecution, including the infliction of the death penalty, and earnestly endeavored to strengthen the faith of his readers by showing them that their death as martyrs would be infinitely better than apostasy. He and his fellow Christians were involved in a most serious life-and-death struggle. He had a vital message to give in his book. That he, in this grave situation, should clothe it in mysterious language and symbolism not easily understood is hard to believe. He, as an intelligent Christian leader, wrote that he might be readily understood, not misunderstood; it is unthinkable that he should have done otherwise. Therefore we are almost forced to conclude that the Christians in Asia Minor to whom his apocalypse was addressed were well acquainted with the apocalyptic ideas, concepts, symbols, and imagery which are so characteristic of Revelation, and that they understood and appreciated what John wrote. If the modern readers of Revelation had the same background of information as the first readers, there would be little difficulty in interpreting it, and no need, perhaps, for a commentary.

What, then, is the value of Revelation? For its own time and place it had tremendous value in that it enabled persecuted Christians to withstand the might and power of the Roman Empire and supplied them with the dynamic to remain loyal and faithful to the Christian religion. Consequently, it is a valuable monument from a historical crisis in the history of our faith, and a perpetual testimony to the undying courage and steadfastness of the pioneers of our religion in a desperate conflict with the forces of paganism and idolatry. We may only hope and pray that we may be as faithful in our day as they were in theirs.

V. The Text

The Greek text of Revelation is more uncertain in some respects than that of other books of the New Testament. For example, among the five main uncial manuscripts there are more than 1,650 variants, while those found in the cursive manuscripts and the versions are considerably more numerous. The Greek text upon which the King James Version was based, the so-called Textus Receptus, which goes back to the printed text of Erasmus in 1516, is especially corrupt. For, as is well known, Erasmus had but one Greek manuscript of Revelation, Codex 1, a cursive of the twelfth or thirteenth century that was often inaccurate and in some places defective. In order to supply missing passages, such as 22:16-21, Erasmus retranslated from the Latin back to the Greek. Some corrections were made in later editions of the Textus Receptus, but the text of Erasmus was substantially that used by the translators of the King James Version. The Revised Standard Version, on the other hand, was translated in the main from the seventeenth edition of Nestle's text, not too different from the critical texts of Westcott and Hort, Tischendorf, and Weiss; indeed, it is actually based upon the consensus, or if that is lacking, the majority opinion, of these three texts. This difference in texts used as the basis of translation accounts for many of the differences between the King James Version and the Revised Standard Version. While Nestle's text cannot be considered as final and definitive, nevertheless it is generally conceded to be far better than the Textus Receptus, and consequently is followed in this Exegesis.

On the other hand, although the variant readings between the texts used in our two versions are numerous, by far the greater number are minor in character, consisting in differences in word order; in the presence or omission of certain words such as articles and connectives; in the substitution of synonyms; and in "corrections" of the many grammatical errors made by the author. There is no apparent question of any major interpolations into the text, such as the resurrection narrative of Mark 16:9-20 or the story of the woman taken in adultery of John 7:53–8:11; indeed, there are relatively few certain instances of lesser corruptions, a sentence or even a phrase in length. In general, therefore, despite the numerous variations in the text of Revelation as it has come down to us, there is actually little uncertainty concerning the meaning of a given sentence or passage which a better text could clarify. It has been suggested by some commentators that there have been a number of dislocations or rearrangements of the original text. However, not only is this hypothesis without any manuscript support, but in addition it is based upon the unwarranted assumption that the author was always logical and consistent, so that any lack of logic and consistency should be attributed to redactors.

Apart from a few papyrus fragments, the earliest Greek manuscript containing Revelation is Codex ℵ (Sinaiticus) of the fourth century. Unfortunately Codex B (Vaticanus), from the same century, which is defective after Heb. 9:14, does not contain Revelation, nor is there any certainty that it ever did. Codex A (Alexandrinus) of the fifth century has Revelation in its entirety, and some believe that its text is the best to be found in any single manuscript. Codex C (Ephraemi), also from the fifth century, is defective, but much of Revelation has been preserved. These three uncial manuscripts represent a fairly uniform text supported by some of the fathers, by certain cursive manuscripts, and in part by the Latin. Also, the papyrus fragments, including the recently discovered p⁴⁷ or Chester Beatty Papyrus of Revelation from the third century, containing about a third of the book, in the main support the readings of the three uncials mentioned. Needless to say, it is the text of these uncials, which were unknown to the translators of the King James Version, which forms the basis of the modern critical texts, including that of Nestle. Even so, it should not be assumed that this text cannot be improved upon in many respects; indeed, there is every prospect that improvements will be made as the result of further investigations.

VI. Outline of Contents

As may be seen by referring to the detailed outline below, the literary structure of Revelation is somewhat involved, but in the main is comprised of groups of sevens. There is a brief preface (1:1-3) followed by the letter corpus (1:4–3:22), which is composed of a covering letter (1:4-20) and seven letters to

individual churches (2:1–3:22). These are followed by two introductory visions, one of God in his might and power (4:1-11) and the other of Christ the Lamb (5:1-14).

The main body of the book (6:1–21:4) is composed of seven groups of visions, each one of which comprises seven visions or tableaux, with a few interludes interrupting the scheme now and then. These groups of seven are (a) Seven Seal Visions (6:1–8:6); (b) Seven Trumpet Woes (8:7–11:15); (c) Seven Visions of the Dragon's Kingdom (12:1–13:18); (d) Seven Visions of Worshipers of the Lamb and Worshipers of the Beast (14:1-20); (e) Seven Visions of the Bowls of God's Wrath (15:1–16:21); (f) Seven Visions of the Fall of "Babylon" or Rome (17:1–19:10), and (g) Seven Visions of the End of Satan's Evil Age and the Beginning of God's Righteous Age (19:11–21:8). The nearest approach to this arrangement is to be found in II Esdras 3-14, which is professedly composed of seven visions (3:1–5:19; 5:20–6:34; 6:35–9:25; 9:26–10:59; 11:1–12:51; 13:1-58; and 14:1-48). However, none of these visions in II Esdras is sevenfold in character as in Revelation.

In Revelation the sevenfold division of the major sections is quite evident for the most part, but in one or two cases it is not so clear. Still, it must be evident that the author had this septiform pattern in mind, even if he did not follow it with exactness in every instance.

The next main division (21:9–22:5) consists of a supplementary scene in which the New Jerusalem and the New Eden are described in some detail. This scene is actually an extension or elaboration of the preceding vision (21:1-8). An epilogue (22:6-21) composed of warnings, exhortations, and promises completes the book.

In comparison with other apocalypses there is none that shows as careful a literary structure as does Revelation, nor is there any that is at the same time as complex yet as unified in its composition. Although John has used a variety of sources, nevertheless he has freely adapted them and skillfully woven them into a unified whole which shows his style, his thought, and his purpose from the beginning to the end.

According to Lohmeyer,[7] whom we follow here, the book may be outlined as follows:

[7] Ernst Lohmeyer, *Die Offenbarung des Johannes* (Tübingen: J. C. B. Mohr, "Handbuch zum Neuen Testament," 1926).

REVELATION

VII. Summary of Contents

Following a brief introductory assertion concerning its divine origin, Revelation continues with a general letter to the persecuted Christians of seven churches in Asia Minor. This letter represents Jesus Christ as the faithful martyr and witness, the supreme example for his followers to emulate, with a promise that he will return to earth very soon in all his might and power to rescue them from their persecutors. The author also identifies himself as a certain John who was exiled for his loyalty to God and Christ, that is, for his refusal to deny them and worship the emperors as divine. Chs. 2 and 3 contain separate letters to the seven churches, exhorting their members to be loyal to their religion and faithful unto death, with the assurance in each letter that even though they suffer as martyrs, they, like Christ, will be conquerors over death. Specific rewards are held out to the prospective martyrs: they will eat of the tree of life in Paradise; they will receive the crown of life; they will not be hurt by the second death, that is, by the fiery lake of eternal punishment; they will be given some of the hidden manna and a white stone inscribed with a new name; they will receive power over the nations to rule them with a rod of iron; they will receive the morning star; they will be clad in white garments; their names will not be erased from the book of life; Christ will confess them before God and the angels; they will be kept safe from the trials that are to come upon the world; they will become pillars in God's temple; and they will reign with Christ on his throne as he reigns with God. In short, they are promised that through their death as martyrs they will be assured of a blessed and glorious immortality.

Ch. 4 represents the almighty and majestic God on his throne in heaven surrounded by his heavenly court, removed for the time being from earth and the affairs of men which are now under the control of Satan. But the persecuted Christians as they read this passage are reminded of the might and power of God, the creator of the world and its inhabitants, and are made to see in this theophany a pledge that he will ultimately become victorious over all of the forces of evil and will soon terminate Satan's evil rule in which they, the righteous, suffer and are persecuted.

In ch. 5 there is a corresponding depiction of Christ the Lamb that was slain but is now alive, who is to be God's chief assistant in the divine plan for bringing Satan's power and age to an end. He alone is worthy to open the book of doom with its seven seals, thereby precipitating a series of disasters upon the earth and against its wicked inhabitants which are in part reminiscent of the plagues of Exodus. The readers are led to remember that as the blood of the Passover lamb protected the first-born of the Israelites from the plague of death, so the blood of Christ, the Lamb that was slain and yet lives, will protect the new Israel, the faithful Christians, and will ensure their eternal salvation.

With the breaking of the first four seals in ch. 6 a series of plagues, consisting of wars, famine, and pestilence, devastates the earth. The breaking of the fifth seal provides a glimpse of the martyrs under the altar in heaven crying out to God for justice and for vengeance upon their persecutors, but they are told to be quiet for a little while longer until their predetermined number is completed. By means of this scene the author assures his persecuted readers that they who persecute and kill them will be surely and quickly punished by God. This tableau is also a pledge that the souls of the martyrs go to heaven, not to Hades, there to await the first resurrection. This prospect, no doubt, was one of the most effective means of inducing persecuted Christians to choose death as martyrs in preference to the alternative of denying Christ and worshiping the emperor-gods. With the opening of the sixth seal a series of cosmic and terrestrial woes is unloosed as an omen of the terrible judgment of God upon the inhabitants of the earth.

Ch. 7 consists of two interludes. The first portrays the sealing of the entire body of martyrs (the new Israel), foreordained by God, who are symbolically numbered as 144,000, from the twelve tribes of Israel. Next, they are seen in heaven before God on his throne and before the Lamb. Here they serve God day and night; they will never hunger nor thirst any more, nor will the sun or any other scorching heat strike them. Thus once more the prospective martyrs are promised immediate and glorious heavenly rewards for their steadfastness.

The breaking of the seventh seal in 8:1 sets the stage for another series of plagues, the seven trumpet woes. Some of these are similar to the plagues inflicted upon Egypt, but others are more cosmic in character, indicating, perhaps, that the war in heaven between the forces of good and evil has begun. Among these seven woes are devastating invasions of the empire by hordes of demonic horsemen, described in ch. 9. Despite all these terrible evidences of God's avenging wrath, those who survive his anger are defiantly unrepentant of their idolatries and other sins. Accordingly, still greater punishments will be inflicted upon them.

This impending judgment of God is symbolized in ch. 10, where the author states that he was given a scroll, a prophetic book of doom, to eat. This tasted sweet in his mouth as he contemplated the approaching end of this evil age of Satan's, which would free Christians from suffering, persecution, and death; but it was bitter in his stomach as he considered the terrible punishments awaiting the heathen followers of Satan.

The first part of ch. 11 presents the dramatic episode of the two heavenly martyr-witnesses, who, though unnamed, are probably Elijah and Moses, represented as returning to earth from their heavenly abode to preach repentance to an unrepentant world. Upon finishing their testimony, they are killed by a satanic beast coming up from the abyss, but are soon restored to life and taken up again to heaven. Their appearance is to be taken as a presage of the coming of the end of this evil age, a token, probably, that God is about to intervene in a drastic way in fulfillment of a prophecy in Mal. 4:4-6. Moreover, it is a renewal of the pledge that those who are killed through the agency of Satan will be restored to life, like Elijah and Moses, and will be taken up to heaven. The blowing of the seventh trumpet, completing this chapter, provides the assurance that God is about to assert his power and assume control.

Accordingly, in ch. 12 the cosmic struggle between the forces of good and evil is brought out into the open. First, the celestial woman clothed in the sun who is about to bear a child appears, with the seven-headed dragon, Satan himself, standing by to devour her son as soon as he is born. However, Satan is foiled, for the child is saved from his evil designs and taken up to God. This astral-theological scene is a representation of the birth of the heavenly Messiah to his heavenly mother, which is the heavenly archetype of the birth of the earthly Jesus to his mother Mary. Toward the end of the chapter the symbolism changes, so that the celestial woman becomes the church whose other children are the faithful Christians who are persecuted at Satan's commands. Midway in this same chapter Michael (the guardian angel of the Christians, the true Israel) and his angels wage war with Satan and his angels. This heavenly conflict results in Satan's defeat and expulsion from heaven to earth to wreak his vengeance upon its inhabitants in the short time that remains to him to rule.

Up to now the ruler cult, the immediate cause of the irreconcilable and tragic impasse between empire and church, has been alluded to but not elaborated in specific detail; but in ch. 13 the entire situation which occasioned the persecution of the Christians is brought into focus. Two beasts appear, one symbolizing the emperors, the dead and the living, who are worshiped as divine, and the other the imperial priesthood that was in charge of the rites of the imperial cult. The first beast has seven heads; one of these with a mortal wound that had been healed is a definite reference to the Nero redivivus myth—the belief that Nero, though dead, would be restored to life to bring ruin upon the empire. It is because the Christians refuse to worship the emperors, symbolized by the first satanic beast and cryptically referred to by the number 666, that they are persecuted and put to death as martyrs.

The next series of scenes, in ch. 14, contrasts the worshipers of the beast, the Antichrist, with the faithful followers of the Lamb, the heavenly Christ. In a proleptic scene the martyrs, numbering 144,000, are shown with the Lamb on Mount Zion. The issue is clearly stated: Instead of worshiping the emperors, who are actually satanic, not divine, all peoples of the world are exhorted to worship God, the creator and judge of heaven and earth. For those who worship the beast will incur the judgment of God's wrath and will be tortured forever with fire and brimstone; moreover, Babylon—that is, Rome—will be destroyed. By contrast, the martyrs, those loyal Christians who die in the Lord, will be eternally blessed. The threat of divine punishment is emphasized by two scenes, one in which the wicked are harvested by the Son of man with his sickle, the other in which, like grapes, they are gathered by an angel and trodden in the winepress of God's wrath so that their blood flows like a river.

Ch. 15 serves as an introduction to another series of woes, the seven bowl plagues. The martyrs who have been victors in their resistance to the beast, representing the emperors, are seen in heaven on the shore of a sea of glass mixed with fire, which is the heavenly pattern of the Red Sea. In their rejoicing over their miraculous escape the martyrs, the new Israel, sing a new song of Moses and the Lamb. The chapter closes with a theophany which is an additional pledge of God's imminent intervention in their behalf.

In ch. 16 the seven bowls of God's wrath are emptied one after the other, thereby bringing upon the earth a new series of disasters, which are in part similar to some of the earlier woes and like them resemble the plagues of Exodus. The woe that is produced when the seventh bowl is emptied is a presage of the coming destruction of Babylon (Rome) which had been predicted in 14:8, the theme of the next series of seven visions.

Babylon the great (Rome) is depicted in the beginning of ch. 17 as a harlot, with the imperial beast as her paramour, who seduces the nations of the world, and is drunk with the blood of the saints and martyrs of Jesus. This harlot is not only the symbol of Rome, the supposedly eternal city, but more than likely she also signifies the goddess Roma, the divine personification of Rome and the empire, who was worshiped together with the emperors. According to dirges and songs of lament she is soon to be utterly destroyed, despite her great power and wealth, for she has been responsible for the death of the Christian martyrs. In dramatic contrast to Rome, the harlot, and her paramour, the satanic imperial beast, a preview is given in 19:6b-8 of the radiant and spotless Bride who is soon to be married to Christ the Lamb. The Bride is the church composed of faithful Christians.

The way is now prepared for a sequence of scenes portraying Satan's defeat and the end of his reign, followed by the beginning of God's eternal reign, with the millennium, the period of Christ's rule, as a messianic interregnum (19:11–21:8). First of all the heavenly Christ on a white horse, followed by his army of martyrs, comes from heaven to conquer. After a struggle with the two beasts and their followers, the kings of earth with their armies, Christ is completely victorious. All of the human followers of the beasts are killed by the sword from his mouth, and the beasts are thrown alive into the lake of fire and brimstone to be tortured forever. Next, an angel overpowers Satan and imprisons him in the bottomless pit for a thousand years, thus bringing his reign to an end, thereby making the millennium possible.

Accordingly, the souls of the martyrs who had been beheaded for their testimony to Jesus and their refusal to worship the emperors are restored to their bodies so that they may reign with Christ for a thousand years. This is the first resurrection, which no one, save the martyrs, is to experience. Those who share in this resurrection will not be liable to the second or general resurrection, the general judgment, and the second death, the fiery lake. In view of the attention it has commanded it is surprising that no detailed description of this messianic interval is given.

For some unexplained reason at the close of the millennium Satan is released and deceives all the nations of the earth (even though these had apparently all been destroyed with their kings in 19:21). These nations, personified as Gog and Magog, march against the saints, that is, the martyrs, in Jerusalem, the beloved city, but are soon consumed with fire from heaven. Then the devil himself, the author of all of the evil in this age (including, of course, the institution of the state religion which was the occasion for the persecution and the death of loyal Christians), is thrown into the lake of fire and brimstone to be tormented forever. With this event his evil age, his wicked rule, which had been temporarily interrupted when he was imprisoned in the bottomless pit, is ended forever. This episode, though described very briefly in a single verse (20:10), not only marks the culmination of this evil age but is the real climax of Revelation.

With the end of Satan's evil and temporal age God's new, perfect, and eternal age is inaugurated. Heaven and earth flee from the presence of God on his throne and are no more. Next, the second or general resurrection of all men save the martyrs takes place, and all are judged by God according to their deeds as these are recorded in the books of life. Death, the personification of the state of the dead, and Hades, the personification of their temporary underworld dwelling place, are cast into the lake of fire. Also, all those who are adjudged to have been idolaters and worshipers of the beast, including Christian apostates, are consigned to this same lake of fire with Satan, the two beasts, and Death and Hades for company, where they will be punished eternally for their sins. On the other hand, with all evil and all causes of evil forever eliminated, those who have been true and faithful to God, especially if not exclusively those Christians who suffered martyrdom, will be admitted to the New Jerusalem and the New Eden, which will take the place of the old heaven and the old earth of Satan's evil age. Moreover, as a supreme reward in this new age God and Christ will dwell with them forever.

Using all the rich symbolism and imagery at his command, the author next describes in some detail the glories and beauties of the New Jerusalem and the New Eden, the eternal home of the faithful Christians (21:9–22:5). In it there will be no suffering, persecution, or death, for Satan, the source of all these evils, is eternally shorn of his power to inflict evil upon the righteous. Furthermore, in this new age other rewards which had been promised to the prospective martyrs in earlier passages of Revelation will be bestowed.

The book of Revelation concludes with warnings, exhortations, and promises, with the repeated assurance that all that has been predicted concerning the second coming of Christ and God's new age, with its glorious and eternal rewards for the faithful, is to take place very soon. With this final word John completes his attempt to make a martyr's death for loyalty to Christ and God far more alluring and desirable than the freedom from persecution and physical death which could be obtained only by according worship to the Roman state and its rulers.

The diagram following will help to clarify the author's world view and apocalyptic scheme.

CHARLES, R. H. *A Critical and Exegetical Commentary on the Revelation of St. John* ("The International Critical Commentary"). New York: Charles Scribner's Sons, 1920. 2 vols.

KIDDLE, MARTIN. *The Revelation of St. John* ("The Moffatt New Testament Commentary") New York: Harper & Bros., 1940.

LOHMEYER, ERNST. *Die Offenbarung des Johannes* ("Handbuch zum Neuen Testament"). Tübingen: J. C. B. Mohr, 1926.

LOISY, ALFRED. *L'Apocalypse de Jean.* Paris: Èmile Nourry, 1923.

MOFFATT, JAMES. "The Revelation of St. John the Divine," in Bruce, A. B., ed. *The Expositor's Greek Testament.* London: Hodder & Stoughton, 1917. V, 279-494.

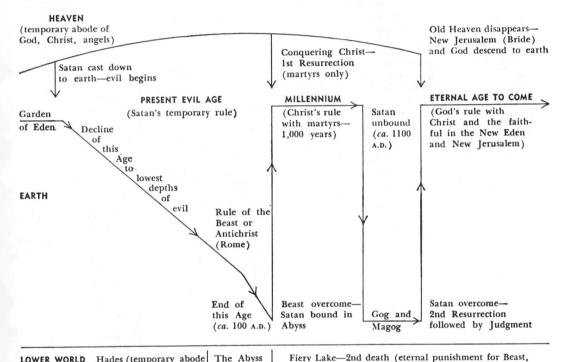

VIII. Selected Bibliography

The following are the most helpful of the commentaries on Revelation. While each has its special qualities, that by Charles is both the most comprehensive and in general the most useful.

BECKWITH, ISBON T. *The Apocalypse of John.* New York: The Macmillan Co., 1919.

BOUSSET, WILHELM. *Die Offenbarung Johannis* ("Meyer's Kommentar"). 6th ed. Göttingen: Vandenhoeck & Ruprecht, 1906.

CASE, SHIRLEY JACKSON. *The Revelation of John.* Chicago: University of Chicago Press, 1919.

SCOTT, C. A. ANDERSON. *Revelation* ("The Century Bible"). New York: Henry Frowde, n.d.

STRACK, HERMANN L., AND BILLERBECK, PAUL. *Kommentar zum Neuen Testament aus Talmud und Midrasch.* München: Oskar Beck, 1926. III, 788-857.

SWETE, HENRY BARCLAY. *The Apocalypse of St. John.* 3rd ed. London: Macmillan & Co., 1909.

WEISS, JOHANNES, AND HEITMÜLLER, WILHELM. "Die Offenbarung des Johannes," in Baumgarten, Bousset, & Gunkel, eds. *Die Schriften des Neuen Testaments.* 3rd ed. Göttingen: Vandenhoeck & Ruprecht, 1920. IV, 229-319.

REVELATION

TEXT, EXEGESIS, AND EXPOSITION

1 The Revelation of Jesus Christ, which God gave unto him, to show unto his servants things which must shortly come to pass; and he sent and signified *it* by his angel unto his servant John:

1 The revelation of Jesus Christ, which God gave him to show to his servants what must soon take place; and he made it known by sending his angel to his serv-

---

The title as given in the KJV, "The Revelation of St. John the Divine," is probably no earlier than the fourth century; it is obviously an attempt to identify the author with the apostle John, who was also presumably the author of the Fourth Gospel. The earliest certain title, dating from the second century, is ΑΠΟΚΑΛΥΨΙΣ ΙΩΑΝΝΟΥ. This is rendered in the ASV and in many of the commentaries as "The Revelation of John," but in the RSV as "The Revelation to John." The latter rendering is grammatically correct, but may have been induced by a desire to harmonize the title with the opening verses, in which John is definitely the recipient, not the author, of the purported revelation. The original title in all probability is lost, unless it is to be found in the first words of the book, "The revelation of Jesus Christ," just as, it has been suggested, the original title of the Gospel According to Mark may be found in the opening phrase, "The beginning of the gospel of Jesus Christ" (Mark 1:1).

I. The Preface (1:1-3)

1:1. The first three verses of Revelation constitute a kind of formal preface, such as is found at the beginning of certain of the prophetic books of the O.T. and of a number of the apocalyptic writings. Vs. 1 shows what the author wanted his readers to consider as the ultimate source of his book: it originated with God himself, and was transmitted by Christ to his **servant** (slave) John, here by an **angel**, but as we shall see, frequently without angelic mediation. We are reminded of those O.T. prophets whose oracles are given as the word of God, not their own, or of those apocalyptic writers who

---

1:1. *The Central Thought and the Central Person.*[1]—From beyond the silence and the mystery something of crucial importance has been brought to men. It comes with all the dramatic force and power of Revelation. It is **revelation.** This is the central thought of the book—and it is central in the Christian religion. Everything attains a new clarity, everything attains a new soundness, and life can be lived with a new assurance as we make this word of revelation our own.

But if the book has a central thought it also has a central person. This person is Jesus Christ. The word comes alive in him. He gives

it authenticity. He gives it reality. He gives it compulsion. Visible or invisible he is at the center of every vision and gives the **essence of** meaning to every proclamation.

The whole history of the fashion in which Christian men have managed to live **in the** world is full of the sense of the central person and of the truth which is made real to men because it is real in him. In "A Death in the Desert" Robert Browning makes the aged John responsible for the words:

I say, the acknowledgement of God in Christ
Accepted by thy reason, solves for thee
All questions in the earth and out of it,
And has so far advanced thee to be wise.

[1] Dr. Hough's general study of the book of Revelation is found on pp. 551-613. Editors.

2 Who bare record of the word of God, and of the testimony of Jesus Christ, and of all things that he saw.

3 Blessed *is* he that readeth, and they that hear the words of this prophecy, and keep those things which are written therein: for the time *is* at hand.

4 John to the seven churches which are in Asia: Grace *be* unto you, and peace,

ant John, **2** who bore witness to the word of God and to the testimony of Jesus Christ, even to all that he saw. **3** Blessed is he who reads aloud the words of the prophecy, and blessed are those who hear, and who keep what is written therein; for the time is near.

4 John to the seven churches that are in Asia:

claim merely to be channels of divine inspiration. In a number of apocalypses angels serve as mediums of revelation. The phraseology is reminiscent of a statement in Amos, "Surely the Lord Jehovah will do nothing, except he reveal his secret unto his servants the prophets" (Amos 3:7 ASV). It is essential to the author's purpose to stress the immediacy of the coming of the end of this age; what is going to happen **must soon take place,** the author's own times of course, not ours, being the point of reference.

2. John now gives his own guarantee of the validity of his book, for it contains that which he himself has seen or experienced, an attestation that is reaffirmed in 22:8, where he states that he has heard and seen all that he has reported. The identification of himself as one **who bore witness** (ἐμαρτύρησεν) **to the word of God and to the testimony** (μαρτυρίαν) **of Jesus Christ** may involve a play on words which is not reproducible in an English translation, for the word translated **testimony** may also mean "martyrdom," while **bore witness** is from a verb that may mean "to become a martyr." There is a close connection, for those who **bore witness** and gave **testimony** were candidates for martyrdom in the days of persecution.

3. This is the first of seven beatitudes in Revelation (cf. 14:13; 16:15; 19:9; 20:6; 22:7, 14). But it is far more than a beatitude, for by asserting that his book consists of **words** of **prophecy** (cf. 10:11; 19:10; 22:6-10, 18, 19) John places it on a level with a prophetic book in the O.T.; he presents it as inspired, revealed scripture. Indeed, he seemingly wants it read in church services along with the O.T., for he pronounces his blessing upon anyone who **reads aloud** from it and upon those who **hear** it read and pay heed to its message. This desire is reinforced in 22:7, "Blessed is he who keeps the words of the prophecy of this book." His book, then, is not to be a secret one such as Daniel purported to be, and to be kept sealed and unread until the end was actually at hand (Dan. 12:9). Instead, it was to be read at once, and preferably aloud in a church meeting so that as many as possible could become acquainted with its urgent message, for **the time** was short. It is unlikely that very many copies of Revelation were made and distributed to Christians soon after its composition; indeed, for a time there may have been but a single copy. But through its reading in public its author hoped to obtain a good hearing for his **prophecy.** Paradoxically, this work for which the author claimed so much, divine in origin and deserving to be read in church alongside the O.T. books, had difficulty in being accepted into the N.T. canon of scripture, and once having been accepted, continued to have difficulty in maintaining this position.

II. THE LETTER CORPUS (1:4–3:22)
A. COVERING LETTER (1:4-20)

E. J. Goodspeed has presented the attractive view that toward the end of the first century one of Paul's admirers collected letters and fragments of letters written by the apostle, edited them, and published them in a corpus (see Vol. IX, pp. 356-58). This collection consisted of letters to seven churches (with Philemon rightly considered as a letter to a church, not an individual), to which an introductory or covering letter (Ephesians) was written. According to this theory, this corpus of Paul's letters became so popular that it was imitated by the publication of similar collections. Among these imitations was the letter corpus in the first three chapters of Revelation, which consists of

from him which is, and which was, and which is to come; and from the seven Spirits which are before his throne;	Grace to you and peace from him who is and who was and who is to come, and from the seven spirits who are before his

letters to seven churches, prefaced by an introductory or encyclical letter to all the churches. The appearance in the letters of Revelation of certain characteristic Pauline words and phrases lends further credence to this theory (see Albert Barnett, *Paul Becomes a Literary Influence* [Chicago: University of Chicago Press, 1941], pp. 41 ff.) .

It is not to be thought that these were genuine letters which were actually sent to the separate churches named. Instead, they are artificial letters, literary compositions, which serve to introduce the rest of the book, giving the basic motif of the whole. This underlying theme, as expressed in the letters, is the rewards for the martyr who will patiently endure persecution, being faithful to God until death. He who is put to death for his refusal to deny Christ and worship the emperor is not vanquished by death; instead, he is a victor, a conqueror who will be richly and gloriously rewarded in the age to come. Specific rewards are promised to prospective martyrs in the letters, most of which find fulfillment in the rest of the book, particularly in the final chapters. These letters are not a later addition to Revelation, as some have maintained, nor are they loosely connected with the book as a whole; instead, they are integrally related to the chapters that follow, and summarize the author's message to persecuted Christians.

4. The covering letter, addressed to **the seven churches** in Asia Minor which are named later, gives the author's account of his vision of the heavenly Christ, who is represented as being the actual author of the seven letters to the individual churches. The opening verse of the encyclical follows the pattern of early Christian letters. First, there is the name of the author, next the mention of the recipients, followed by the greeting **Grace to you and peace.** There is nothing corresponding to the usual "thanksgiving" in Paul's letters (cf. I Cor. 1:4-8) .

It should be noted that whereas in apostolic or pseudoapostolic letters an emphasis is placed upon the author's apostolate, real or assumed, in the opening address (cf. Rom. 1:1; I Tim. 1:1; II Pet. 1:1) , in this case no such claim is made either in the beginning or elsewhere. Since the writer at no time claims that he is an apostle, we may doubt that he was one, or that he was writing in the name of one. While most apocalypses are pseudonymous, there are exceptions, and this may be one.

Seven churches . . . in Asia are addressed, not solely in imitation of the Pauline corpus of letters to seven churches, but also, in all likelihood, because seven, the author's favorite number, is sacred and signifies, among other concepts, completion. Consequently it may be that these seven churches are to be considered as symbolizing all the churches, thus making Revelation an open letter to all Christians. But why these seven churches in particular? There were other churches in Asia at that time. Could it be that these seven were under the author's special jurisdiction, or that he had some close relationship to them? Or was each of those named characterized by some aspect of the persecution that he wanted to emphasize? Still another possibility is suggested by the observation that when a line is traced on the map from Ephesus through the seven cities in the order named and back to Ephesus a rough circle is formed. Since a circle, like the number seven, is also a symbol of completeness, it may be that these churches were chosen in the order given for this reason.

Grace and **peace** are offered **from him who is and who was and who is to come.** This appellation for God, repeated in vs. 8 and 4:8, may have been an expansion of the phrase in Exod. 3:14 (LXX) , "I am he who is." According to a Targum, God told Moses, "I am he who is and who was and who will be, and there is no other God beside me" (Targ. Jer. I on Deut. 32:39) , a paraphrase that is paralleled in other rabbinical sources. However, similar designations of deity are found in the pagan world. Pausanias, an ancient Greek writer, mentions a song of doves at Dodona: "Zeus was, Zeus is, and Zeus shall be" (*Description of Greece* X. 12. 5) . Also, according to Plutarch, the shrine

5 And from Jesus Christ, *who is* the faithful witness, *and* the first-begotten of the dead, and the prince of the kings of the earth. Unto him that loved us, and washed us from our sins in his own blood,

throne, 5 and from Jesus Christ the faithful witness, the first-born of the dead, and the ruler of kings on earth.

To him who loves us and has freed us

---

of Minerva (identified with Isis) at Sais bore the inscription: "I am all that hath been and is and shall be" (*On Isis and Osiris* 9). In the Persian religion we read that "Ormazd and the region, religion, and time of Ormazd were and are and ever will be" (Bundahish 1:3). The terminology also reminds us of the designation in Heb. 13:8, "Jesus Christ is the same yesterday and today and forever." Obviously the title as applied here to God is a reference to his eternal and unchanging character. A minor grammatical item might be noted in passing. Although the participles are governed by a preposition, they are in the nominative case, contrary to good usage. However, the author may have done this deliberately to show the unchanging nature of God.

The greeting is also **from the seven spirits** who are before God's **throne.** Who are these seven spirits? They seem to represent a combination of astralism and angelology. They bear some relationship, if they are not identical, with the seven stars of vs. 16 and 2:1; with the seven golden lampstands of vss. 12 and 20; with the seven spirits, also called stars, of 3:1; with the seven torches or spirits of God before the throne in 4:5; with the seven eyes of the Lamb in 5:6, which are also called seven spirits; and with the seven angels who stand before God in 8:2. It is highly probable that they are related to the seven archangels of Jewish speculation (cf. Ezek. 9:2; Tob. 12:15; I Enoch 20:1-8; III Enoch 17:1-3; Test. Levi 8:2). These Jewish angels are probably the counterpart of the seven Amesha-Spentas of ancient Persian religion. But these seven spirits are also identified with the seven planets of Babylonian astral-theology, the sun, moon, and the five other heavenly bodies visible to the naked eye which apparently traverse the heavens in a regular manner. These heavenly bodies have a definite control over mankind, over his fate, and in general determine what is to happen on the earth. In popular thinking they became personified, and were regarded as divinities. In certain areas of Jewish thinking stars were specifically associated with angels (cf. I Enoch 82:8; 86:1-6; II Enoch 19:1-6; III Enoch 17:6). It was but another step to coalesce the seven archangels with the seven planets.

5. The third source of grace and peace is **Jesus Christ the faithful witness** who is also **the first-born of the dead.** The crux of this description is the Greek word μάρτυς, which is almost universally translated in this verse as "witness." True enough, the word here means **witness,** but it means this and more. No other translation than "martyr" is admissible in the context of the verse, as the phrase that is in apposition with it, **the first-born of the dead,** shows; indeed, no other rendering fits the context of the book as a whole. Here and throughout his work John urges his fellow Christians to accept martyrdom, if this is required of them for their Christian devotion. He cites Jesus as the

---

5. *A Dependable Message.*—The question "How can we be sure?" is one of the most anxious and searching and even terrible questions which men can ask. About the great matters we cannot afford to be deceived; and yet it is so easy to be deceived. The author of a very famous Persian poem declares that we come into the world knowing neither why nor whence.[2] Confusion of mind has settled with blighting and disintegrating power upon multitudes of men. Writing to people in the midst

[2] *The Rubáiyát of Omar Khayyám,* st. xxix.

of tragic experiences and of tragic fears the man of Patmos declared that he brings the word of **Jesus Christ the faithful witness.** That which he has seen, the conqueror of death and the ruler of kings faithfully declared to the churches. The word "witness" gives a certain quick and powerful sense of actuality. Not of shimmering dreams and of aspiring hopes is the message made. It is based on that which can be seen and reported. **The faithful witness** gives assurance of the dependableness of the message. In a sense Jesus is the divine reporter

6 And hath made us kings and priests
unto God and his Father; to him *be* glory
and dominion for ever and ever. Amen.

from our sins by his blood 6 and made us a
kingdom, priests to his God and Father, to
him be glory and dominion for ever and

---

protomartyr, the first one of their faith to give up his life, as well as the first one to be
born from the dead. He is their supreme example: as his devoted followers they are to
imitate him both in his dying and in his triumphant restoration to life. It is evident
that the usual translation **witness** is quite colorless and almost meaningless when placed
alongside the more meaningful "martyr." The promise that the martyrs, like their
example Jesus Christ, will be victors through their death for his sake, is one of the most
telling in the entire book. Jesus Christ is also designated as **the ruler of kings on earth.**
This is a presage of his ultimate victory over the temporal powers of the earth who are
responsible for the oppression and the persecution of his followers. The last two descriptions of Jesus may be a christological reinterpretation of Ps. 89:27,

> I will make him the first-born,
> the highest of the kings of the earth.

The martyred, risen, and sovereign Christ in his love for his followers **has freed us
from our sins by his blood.** This concept of the saving power of blood, its efficacy in
washing away sins, is found quite generally in the old sacrificial systems of religion.
The use of blood in the taurobolium or the criobolium in the Greco-Roman religions
of the time to effect salvation is well known. The author is probably using another source.
For according to him the Christians are the new Israel, the true Israel, who are to be
saved by God from their oppressors, the Romans, as the Jews were saved at an earlier
time from the cruel masters, the Egyptians. As will be noted from time to time, the
Exodus and its supernatural events are a prophetic prototype for the coming deliverance
of the Christians from their Roman persecutors. Accordingly, just as by the blood of
the Passover lamb the first-born of the Jews were saved from death, so the blood of
Jesus Christ, the new Passover Lamb that was slain, will preserve his first-born, the
faithful Christians, from final destruction and death. Further references to the saving
power of the blood of the Lamb are found in 7:14; 12:11; 22:14 (cf. Rom. 3:25; Heb.
9:14; I John 1:7; I Pet. 1:19).

6. Still another echo of the Exodus is found in this verse. In Exod. 19:6, God is
represented as promising Moses, following the miraculous deliverance from the Egyptians,
that the Israelites will be "a kingdom of priests, and a holy nation," i.e., they will become
a theocracy. Likewise, the new Israel, the Christians, when Christ has freed them, will
become **a kingdom, priests to his God and Father,** a promise that is recalled in connection
with the millennium in 20:6 (cf. 5:10; I Pet. 2:9). The phrase **to his God and Father** reveals that, as is the case in the Fourth Gospel, God is the Father of Jesus Christ in a peculiar and special way. In the later creeds the term Father as applied to God was not used to
denote a deity who was immanent and close at hand, but one who was transcendent

---

giving an account of that which is of infinite
concern to men.

5. The Love Which Will Not Let Us Go.—
Henry Vaughan once wrote of that which

> Hath no wings
> To raise it to the truth and light of things.[3]

The inaccessibility of the truth and light which
they so much need has been one of the heavy

[3] "I Walkt the Other Day."

and perplexing problems of men. It is the sense
of the love of God that gives men wings. The
churches are addressed as those loved by Christ,
as consisting of those whom he has made kings
and priests. And because they are Christians
all this is said not as something new but as a
glorious reminder of something which they already know. They may live in a world full of
evil. They may have sadly to confess that evil
has passed the portal and has entered into their
own life. But the great fact is that Christ has

7 Behold, he cometh with clouds; and every eye shall see him, and they *also* which pierced him: and all kindreds of the earth shall wail because of him. Even so, Amen.

8 I am Alpha and Omega, the beginning and the ending, saith the Lord, which

ever. Amen. 7 Behold, he is coming with the clouds, and every eye will see him, every one who pierced him; and all tribes of the earth will wail on account of him. Even so. Amen.

8 "I am the Alpha and the Omega," says

---

and remote. This is true in Revelation during the present age, but in the age to come God will be immanent, for his dwelling will be with men (21:3). The doxology **To him be glory and dominion, for ever and ever. Amen,** like the similar one in 5:13, is addressed to Christ, not to God (cf. II Pet. 3:18). The attribution of **dominion** to Christ is consonant with the title **ruler of kings on earth** (vs. 5), and is another pledge of his coming victory over the powerful forces of evil. The phraseology may have been suggested by Dan. 7:13-14, where glory and an everlasting dominion are to be given to the one like unto the Son of man (see vs. 7). This doxology is the first of many bits of liturgy which John has incorporated in his apocalypse.

7. John, anticipating the second coming of Christ, says quite dramatically, **Behold, he is coming with the clouds.** His use of the present tense instead of the future may be another indication that he expects the end to come very soon, that before long the conquering Christ will indeed establish his eternal dominion. The picture which he draws is reminiscent of Dan. 7:13, "Behold, one like the Son of man came with the clouds of heaven." However, in Daniel the words refer to the personification of the saints of Israel, the nation, which in the next verse is promised glory and an everlasting dominion over the nations that have oppressed it; they do not point to a personal Messiah at all, as they are made to do in this verse in Revelation. This is but one of many examples of the manner in which John reinterprets the O.T. and other sources, adapting them to his urgent message and ardent expectations.

In Zech. 12:10, Yahweh as the speaker says, "They shall look upon me whom they have pierced, and they shall mourn for him, as one mourneth for his only son." In some texts the word "me" is replaced by "him." In the one reading it is Yahweh who has been pierced, in the other some unknown Jewish martyr; but in neither case can the reference be to the Messiah. However, in predicting the mourning and wailing of the wicked when Christ who was **pierced** returns in his glory and power, John, in his characteristic fashion, finds an apocalyptic warning in this verse from Zechariah (cf. John 19:37). This dire warning is doubly attested, first in Greek, then in Hebrew, **Even so. Amen,** a further assurance that the end is drawing near.

8. God is the speaker in this verse, as also in 21:6, where again he calls himself **the Alpha and the Omega.** In 21:6 the title is quite naturally equated with "the beginning

---

loved them. He who has brought freedom from the chains of sin has for them all good things. In him they enter the realm of the light and truth of things. So it has been with men of the churches of every age. And so it may be with us.

7. *The Visible Lord.*—To the Christian the darkest hour of life is the hour when Christ becomes invisible. The man of Patmos announces the unmistakable presence of Christ. In a hostile world that may seem something beyond belief, but even hostile eyes at last will see the victorious king. The fact of Christ will bend all other facts to its power. Francis Thompson was impressed by the fact that

some have eyes, and will not see;
And some would see, and have not eyes.[4]

But eyes of awareness of the conquering Christ will be given to both friend and foe. There is no escaping the sight of his victory, but men may come to that sight as rapturous friends or as foes. And in the meantime the eyes of faith may see what at last even the faithless must apprehend.

8. *The Origin and the Conclusion of Everything.*—John Milton in the first book of *Para-*

[4] "Grace of the Way," from *Collected Works,* ed. Wilfred Meynell. Used by permission of Sir Francis Meynell and of Burns, Oates & Washbourne, publishers.

is, and which was, and which is to come, the Almighty.	the Lord God, who is and who was and who is to come, the Almighty.
9 I John, who also am your brother, and companion in tribulation, and in the kingdom and patience of Jesus Christ, was in the isle that is called Patmos, for the word of God, and for the testimony of Jesus Christ.	**9** I John, your brother, who share with you in Jesus the tribulation and the kingdom and the patient endurance, was on the island called Patmos on account of the word of God and the testimony of Jesus.

and the end"; in 22:13, where Jesus calls himself "the Alpha and the Omega," the title is synonymous with "the first and the last, the beginning and the end." In a Midrash an interesting variant is found. The seal of God was said to consist of the three Hebrew letters, *Aleph, Mem, Taw,* the first, the middle, and the last letters of the alphabet, for God had said in Isa. 44:6: "I am the first, and I am the last; and besides me there is no God" (Genesis Rabbah 81:2). Quite possibly more is meant in Revelation, for as God in the beginning created the heavens and the earth, soon he will bring all to an end, for he is **the Almighty,** the all-powerful.

9. Like certain of the prophets and apocalyptic writers, John now presents with circumstantial detail his claims to having a divine commission, his credentials as a prophet and seer. We have seen reasons for believing that Revelation is not the product of visionary experiences, but is to be considered a literary composition, the vision form being a frequent characteristic of this literary type (see above, pp. 349-50). Even if one could accept the belief, in the face of evidence to the contrary, that John actually experienced the visions he relates, it would be necessary to raise serious questions concerning their divine origin. But many, even among the most learned, would have it both ways: Revelation is the product of visions, and yet it shows many evidences of being a careful literary production in which a large number and variety of sources were used. Or, it is maintained, John's visions were real, and were of a divine origin, and yet his predictions were not fulfilled.

John begins by identifying himself as the **brother** of those to whom he is writing. Significantly, he does not state that he is an apostle, that he was one of the twelve. Since he is attempting to authenticate his work, this omission, as noted above, is significant. Neither does he represent himself as an official of the church, a bishop or an elder. He is, however, one who had shared a **tribulation,** i.e., a persecution with his Christian brothers to whom and for whom he is writing. Unfortunately for us, he gives few details of this persecution; he does not date it; he fails to give us the name of the reigning emperor; nor does he inform us concerning its extent and duration. All of this is a clear

---

dise Lost puts this request in the form of a prayer:

> What in me is dark,
> Illumine; what is low, raise and support;
> That to the height of this great argument
> I may assert eternal Providence,
> And justify the ways of God to men.

The man of Patmos must assert eternal Providence if his message is to have weight and authentic power. So it is declared that he represents the One who is **the Alpha and the Omega,** the Beginning and the End. It is the One who is the Origin and the Conclusion of everything who sends the message to the churches. Just this sense of finality must belong to the Christian message today. If it does

not come out of the very life of God it will not be effective in the life of men.

9. *The Individual Man.*—Dante's *Divine Comedy* opens in the first canto of the "Inferno" with the words:

> Midway upon the journey of our life
> I found myself within a forest dark,
> For the straightforward pathway had been lost.

All the vast interpretation of life which is found in the *Divine Comedy* is to come through the experience of an individual man. So it is, on a higher level, with the book of Revelation. The message is to be passed through the mind and the heart of John. In O.T. prophecy it is individual men who speak a word which God has given them. The power of the Christian reli-

10 I was in the Spirit on the Lord's day, and heard behind me a great voice, as of a trumpet,

10 I was in the Spirit on the Lord's day, and I heard behind me a loud voice like a

indication, if one were needed, that he was writing for his contemporaries who were already supplied with this information, and not for posterity. He has shared with them **the patient endurance** (ὑπομονῇ) with which they had met this **tribulation.** The Greek word soon came to be a common term in the accounts of the martyrs to denote their courageous patience and steadfastness in meeting their arrests, trials, imprisonments, indignities, tortures, and deaths. He hopes that by his words he will increase their patient endurance so that they may also share in the **kingdom** that is coming soon. Although he does not call himself an apostle or a church official, he does describe himself as one who in later persecutions was termed a confessor, i.e., when taken before the Roman authorities, he had not denied Christ and worshiped the emperor; instead, he had maintained the **word of God,** the Christian "message" (Goodspeed), and had given his **testimony,** his witness, that he was a Christian.

A description of the procedure is given by Pliny the Younger, then governor of Bithynia, in a letter to the Emperor Trajan written between 111 and 113. He had images of the gods, including the emperor, placed in the courtroom. He asked suspected persons if they were Christians. He asked those who "confessed" that they were Christians a second and a third time, threatening punishment. If they still persisted with their confession, they were led away for execution. Others, including some who admitted that they had been Christians, when questioned, cursed Christ and worshiped the statues of the gods and that of the emperor, things which those who are "really Christians" would not do (Pliny *Epistles* X. 96). Quite probably a similar process was used in the period and area of Revelation. John, however, was not executed for his confession; instead, he was exiled to the island of Patmos, off the coast of Asia Minor and about sixty miles southwest of Ephesus. According to the elder Pliny, it was used at times as a place of banishment (*Natural History* IV. 12. 23). Domitian banished his niece Domitilla to Pontia, another small island, and executed her husband, apparently because they had been attracted to the new religion (Eusebius *Church History* III. 18. 5). There is a cave or grotto on Patmos, now made into a chapel, which since the Middle Ages has been associated with John. Confessors enjoyed great prestige and influence in the early church. Ignatius, the bishop of Antioch who suffered the supreme penalty in Rome *ca.* 110, is an example of this. While en route from Antioch to Rome with his Roman guard he was received with great enthusiasm by the Christians of the cities through which he passed, and was listened to as an authority. This was not because he was the bishop of Antioch, but was due to his confession, to his testimony for Christ. Accordingly, it was because of his confession that John writes with a voice of authority. The past tense, **was on the island called Patmos,** might indicate that the book was composed after John was permitted to return from exile, but in view of his loose use of tenses this is by no means certain.

10. John continues that he was **in the Spirit** (cf. Ezek. 3:12), claiming that he was in a mystical ecstasy when he received his commission (cf. 4:2; 17:3; 21:10). Similar claims are made in other apocalyptic writings of the period. A good illustration is found in the vision of Isaiah. While he was in the presence of Hezekiah and others he received the Holy Spirit, "And as he was speaking in the Holy Spirit in the hearing of all, he became silent and his mind was taken up from him and he saw not the men that stood before him, though his eyes, indeed, were open. Moreover, his lips were silent and the mind of his body was taken up from him. But his breath was in him, for he was seeing a vision" (Ascension of Isaiah 6:10-12). John may have experienced similar trances, but his book is more the product of careful literary composition than a record of words he received in a trance. This experience, he asserts, occurred **on the Lord's day,** i.e., on

11 Saying, I am Alpha and Omega, the first and the last: and, What thou seest, write in a book, and send it unto the seven churches which are in Asia; unto Ephesus, and unto Smyrna, and unto Pergamos, and unto Thyatira, and unto Sardis, and unto Philadelphia, and unto Laodicea.

12 And I turned to see the voice that spake with me. And being turned, I saw seven golden candlesticks;

trumpet 11 saying, "Write what you see in a book and send it to the seven churches, to Ephesus and to Smyrna and to Per'ga-mum and to Thy-a-ti'ra and to Sardis and to Philadelphia and to La-od-i-ce'a."

12 Then I turned to see the voice that was speaking to me, and on turning I saw

---

Sunday. According to Ignatius, writing a few years later, the first day of the week was sacred to the followers of Jesus Christ because on this day "our life sprang up through him and his death" (Ign. Mag. 9:1). Thus it was but natural for Christians to call the first day of the week "the Lord's day." It is tempting to look for some implied contrast between this designation and that of the first day of the month as Sebaste's (Emperor's) day, with the opposition between the Lord Jesus and the Lord Caesar in mind; or possibly, since Sunday was the day of the sun god, the Lord Mithra, to reflect that the Christians may have borrowed their terminology from this source—but John used it probably without any symbolic intent. A **loud voice** or some other great noise frequently accompanies theophanies and christophanies; thus, Ezekiel writes, "Then the spirit took me up, and I heard behind me a voice of a great rushing" (Ezek. 3:12), a verse with which John may have been acquainted (cf. also Dan. 10:6). Travelers in Patmos are now shown a cleft in the roof of John's cave where the voice is said to have broken through the rock. This voice was like **a trumpet,** an instrument which is frequently mentioned in connection with apocalyptic expectations of the ending of this evil age and the glorious advent of Christ with power. Paul, our earliest Christian source, assures the Thessalonians, "For the Lord himself will descend from heaven with a cry of command, with the archangel's call, and with the sound of the trumpet of God" (I Thess. 4:16; cf. Matt. 24:31). To be sure, the trumpet in this verse in Revelation is not that of the end of this age and the second coming of Christ, but it does prefigure this joyous consummation, to be described toward the end of the book (19:11-16).

11. Christ's self-designation as found in the KJV, **I am Alpha and Omega, the first and the last,** is not found in the best texts and should be omitted. The voice, soon to be identified as Christ's, commissions John to **write** what he sees **in a book** and to send the book to **the seven churches** which are named. We are reminded of Habakkuk (2:2), who relates that Yahweh told him,

> Write the vision;
> make it plain upon tablets,
> so he may run who reads it.

Isaiah and Jeremiah received similar instructions (Isa. 8:1; 30:8; Jer. 36:2). The purpose of the command in Revelation is similar: the vision is to be written down and published so that all may read it as soon as possible. However, in some of the apocalypses the book is to be sealed and not opened until the proper time (II Esdras 12:37-38; Dan. 8:26; 12:4; I Enoch 82:1; Assumption of Moses 10:11). John is frequently told to write down what he sees and hears, save in the case of the seven thunders, when he is told not to write down what they have said, but to seal it up (10:4).

12. Turning at the sound of the voice, John sees first of all **seven golden lampstands.** In vs. 20 these lampstands are identified with the seven stars or planets, with the seven guardian angels of the seven churches, and with the seven churches themselves. Such protean changes in symbolism are characteristic of apocalyptic imagery, which is plastic and fluid, not set and fixed. This is especially true of the symbolism in Revelation.

13 And in the midst of the seven candlesticks *one* like unto the Son of man, clothed with a garment down to the foot, and girt about the paps with a golden girdle.

14 His head and *his* hairs *were* white like wool, as white as snow; and his eyes *were* as a flame of fire;

15 And his feet like unto fine brass, as if they burned in a furnace; and his voice as the sound of many waters.

seven golden lampstands, 13 and in the midst of the lampstands one like a son of man, clothed with a long robe and with a golden girdle round his breast; 14 his head and his hair were white as white wool, white as snow; his eyes were like a flame of fire, 15 his feet were like burnished bronze, refined as in a furnace, and his voice was like

13. John also sees **one like a son of man** amid the seven golden lampstands. This designation of the heavenly Christ is taken directly or indirectly from a description in Dan. 7:13, "One like the Son of man came with the clouds of heaven." As stated above (cf. vs. 7), in Daniel this personage is not the Messiah, but is an angelic personification of the saints of Israel. The earliest known use of this term as a title for the Messiah is in I Enoch, a pre-Christian compilation of apocalyptic and other sources. While in heaven, Enoch sees God, "One who had a head of days, and his head was white like wool," and with him was an angelic personage "whose countenance had the appearance of a man" (I Enoch 46:1). Enoch learns from an angel that this "Son of man," as he is now called, is actually the transcendent, heavenly Messiah (I Enoch 46:2-8). The dependence of I Enoch on Daniel is quite evident; the deviation which makes "Son of man" a title for the Messiah is an important development. There is no need to call attention to the frequent use of this phrase by Jesus, according to the Synoptic Gospels. Nor is this the place to inquire whether Jesus actually applied this title to himself, and if he did, whether in this messianic sense. Certainly, for John this is a fitting designation for the heavenly Christ although, strangely enough, he uses it in but one other place (14:14). He portrays him as **clothed with a long robe and with a golden girdle round his breast,** which recalls the angel in Dan. 10:5-6, "clothed in linen, whose loins were girded with fine gold of Uphaz: his body also was like the beryl, and his face as the appearance of lightning, and his eyes as lamps of fire, and his arms and his feet like in color to polished brass, and the voice of his words like the voice of a multitude." In a Coptic work, evidently of Jewish origin, a great angel is seen who has a golden girdle about his breast (Apocalypse of Zephaniah 9).

14. In Dan. 7:9 God, "the Ancient of days," is dressed in raiment "white as snow" and the hair of his head is "like the pure wool," while in I Enoch 46:1 (cf. 71:10) his head is "white like wool." John applies this description of God to the heavenly Christ, whose head and hair were **white as white wool, white as snow.** A similar transfer is seen in the description of the angel Jaoel, who guides Abraham through the various heavens: "The appearance of his body was like sapphire, and the look of his countenance like chrysolite, and the hair of his head like snow, and the turban on his head like the appearance of the rainbow, and the clothing of his garments like purple; and a golden scepter was in his right hand" (Apocalypse of Abraham 11). The Danielic angel may have been in John's mind when he states that Christ's eyes were like **a flame of fire.**

15. Still further dependence on the portrayal of the angel in Daniel may be observed in the statement that Christ's **feet were like burnished bronze** (like unto fine brass—

gion is always found in the spot where you meet one man aflame with God.

13. *The Divine Person.*—The human person meets the divine person. This divine person is clothed with humanity and yet is clothed with power. Within human life his voice, like many

waters, speaks the word of God. Everything depends upon a divine meaning entering into the very structure of human life. All other things fall into proper perspective if you can find the divine within humanity. Then human speech comes with all the authority and power

16 And he had in his right hand seven stars: and out of his mouth went a sharp two-edged sword: and his countenance *was* as the sun shineth in his strength.

the sound of many waters; 16 in his right hand he held seven stars, from his mouth issued a sharp two-edged sword, and his face was like the sun shining in full strength.

KJV), for the arms and legs of the Danielic angel were like "polished brass." In the Coptic Apocalypse of Zephaniah 9 the great angel who had a golden girdle also had feet like brass glowing in the fire. The voice of the angel in Daniel was "like the voice of a multitude," but that of Christ is like **the sound of many waters,** possibly a reminiscence of the sound of God's voice in Ezek. 43:2, which was also "like the sound of many waters."

16. A strikingly different element is now introduced, for **in his right hand** the heavenly Christ had **seven stars.** This is a vivid description of the power of Christ over the planets, which according to astral-theology had control over the fate and destiny of mankind. Apparently the author is thinking along lines suggested by Paul in his letter to the Colossians. The Gentile Christians in this church had been worshiping "the elemental spirits [στοιχεῖα] of the universe," a passage which might just as well be translated as "the astral spirits of the universe," and had personified them as angels (Col. 2:8-23). Paul corrects their error, for he informs them that Christ, the first-born of all creation, had created all things "in heaven and on earth, visible and invisible, whether thrones or dominions or principalities or authorities" (Col. 1:16); hence he controls these astral spirits of the universe. In I Enoch 82:7-8 the archangel Uriel is in control of the heavenly bodies, and in III Enoch 17:4-7 four subordinate angels have power over the sun, the moon, the constellations, and the planets; but in both of these works angels are merely the ministers of God.

One of the rival religions of early Christianity was Mithraism, in which the sun god Mithra was the central object of worship. A description of this powerful deity is presented in the so-called Mithraic Liturgy, ll. 691-705. He has a shining countenance and golden hair, wears a white robe and trousers, has a golden crown on his head, and in his right hand he bears the shoulder of a golden bull, which is stated to be the constellation of the bear. Lightning flashes from his eyes, and stars are emitted from his body. The Christ of Revelation could not be described in less magnificent symbolism; nor is he. Not only does his face shine **like the sun** (a characteristic also of certain angels; cf. II Enoch 1:5; Apocalypse of Zephaniah 9; Dan. 10:6), but a **sharp two-edged sword** projects from his mouth (cf. 2:12, 16; 19:15, 21), an ominous presage of his advent from heaven (ch. 19) as a mighty warrior who will slay his enemies with this sword and rule them with a rod of iron. It is possible that this double symbolism is derived from Isa. 11:4, where the Messiah "shall smite the earth with the rod of his mouth, and with the breath of his lips shall he slay the wicked." Analogous symbolism is to be found in other sources. In II Thess. 2:8 the Lord Jesus will destroy the lawless one "with the breath of his mouth"; in II Esdras 13:9-13 the Man from the sea (the Messiah) will destroy his enemies with the fiery stream from his mouth, the flaming breath from his lips, and the

---

of God. It was for this that Athanasius, the great bishop of Alexandria, contended in the fourth century. He knew that unless men met God when they met Christ the figure they met could not bear the weight of all that must he done for them. All this becomes structural in the book of Revelation.

16. Perfect Illumination.—Too many religious studies lose their insights in interlacing abstractions. In the book of Revelation every-

thing becomes gloriously concrete. You see the glory of the noonday sun caught in the splendor of a human face. There is perfect illumination in that shining countenance. And this is the face of Christ, so to shine in every age. It recalls to mind Robert Browning's words in "Epilogue":

That one Face, far from vanish, rather grows,
Or decomposes but to recompose,
Become my universe that feels and knows.

17 And when I saw him, I fell at his feet as dead. And he laid his right hand upon me, saying unto me, Fear not; I am the first and the last:

18 *I am* he that liveth, and was dead; and, behold, I am alive for evermore, Amen; and have the keys of hell and of death.

17 When I saw him, I fell at his feet as though dead. But he laid his right hand upon me, saying, "Fear not, I am the first and the last, **18** and the living one; I died, and behold I am alive for evermore, and I

---

storm of sparks from his tongue; while the Elect One (also the Messiah) of I Enoch 62:2 will slay all sinners with the word of his mouth.

It is readily seen that the portrayal of the heavenly Christ in vss. 13-16 is composite, made up of elements found in various representations of God, of angels, of the Messiah, and perhaps of a pagan deity as well. Like other passages in Revelation, it is highly syncretistic. That John actually saw such a celestial personage is difficult to believe. In trying to present the glorified, powerful Christ he has used the vivid pictorial language of his time and place. His readers understood this imagery, and were assured through it that the conquering, cosmic Christ would soon return to punish their enemies and to deliver them.

17. John heightens the impression he has sought to produce by writing that at this sight of Christ in all his glory and power he **fell at his feet** as if he were **dead**, but Christ, placing his **right hand** on him, told him not to fear. This reaction of fear at the sight of a supernatural being is to be expected; likewise, some word or act of reassurance by the heavenly personage is a natural sequence. This particular episode may be patterned after that which followed the vision of the mighty angel in Daniel which was mentioned above, especially since John shows evidence of some acquaintance with this passage. Daniel, we are informed, was greatly frightened and fell down in a trance, but the angel touched him, spoke reassuringly to him, and raised him up (Dan. 10:8-11). When Enoch saw the glorious angels in heaven, he fell on his face before the Lord of Spirits, but the angel Michael lifted him up by the right hand (I Enoch 71:1-3). Thus once again John is following a rather familiar pattern. It has been pointed out that Christ does not put the seven stars out of his right hand before placing it on John, but this is merely quibbling, for John is an apocalyptist, not a logician, and is not concerned with minor (or in places even major) inconsistencies. Christ calls himself **the first and the last**, a title similar to that given God, **the Alpha and the Omega**, in vs. 8—a further indication that for the author Christ is not greatly different from God himself in glory and power.

18. Christ also designates himself as **the living one**, emphasizing that though he was dead, he is **alive for evermore**. This is a pledge to the Christian that if he follows Jesus Christ to the death, he too, like his Lord, will be alive forever. In addition, Christ claims that he has **the keys of Death and Hades**. Hades, the Greek equivalent of the

---

17. *Perfect Reassurance.*—There is nothing so disintegrating as fear. Men fear all sorts of things for all sorts of reasons. They fear that which they know is hostile to their life and peace. They may cringe in the presence of the highest, fearing that it will crush them. Isaiah cries out: "Woe is me! For I am lost; for I am a man of unclean lips, and I dwell in the midst of a people of unclean lips; for my eyes have seen the King, the Lord of hosts!" (Isa. 6:5.) So the man of Patmos, when he sees the vision of one like the son of man, falls at his feet as though dead. But the right hand of the Master of life is laid upon him and he hears a voice

which says: "**Fear not.**" So he learns that the vision of the highest is to inspire and not to frighten; it is to reassure and not to crush. Once there was a preacher who made a whole village think new thoughts of God and Christ. Some of them never forgot a night when he was preaching on the awful glory of the son of God. "We think we could never feel at home with him," he said. "But this is the very one who, when we are almost lifeless with the awe of him, bends over us and says 'Fear not.' "

18. *The Argument of Life.*—There are arguments of words which sometimes leave us quite cold; there are arguments of facts which strike

19 Write the things which thou hast seen, and the things which are, and the things which shall be hereafter;

20 The mystery of the seven stars which thou sawest in my right hand, and the seven golden candlesticks. The seven stars

have the keys of Death and Hades. 19 Now write what you see, what is and what is to take place hereafter. 20 As for the mystery of the seven stars which you saw in my right hand, and the seven golden lamp-

---

Hebrew Sheol, was not for John a place of punishment, but was the temporary abode in the lower world of the souls of the dead, both good and evil, with the exception of the martyrs (whose souls went to heaven when they died), Moses and Elijah (11:3-12), and possibly the twelve apostles (21:14). The souls of the martyrs are to wait in heaven for the first resurrection (20:4-6), while the rest of the dead will remain in Hades until the second and general resurrection (20:12-13). In this context Hades is collocated with death, the one as the place of the dead, the second as the state or condition of death; or if personified as in 6:8 and 20:13, the former is the ruler of the dead, the latter the angel of death. Like the bottomless pit, a quite different place in the nether world, to which an angel had the key, Hades can be locked or unlocked. According to numerous rabbinical passages only God possessed the key of death. Elijah once asked for the keys for the raising of the dead, but was told that they belonged to God alone (Sanhedrin 113a; cf. Taanith 2b; Targ. Jer. II on Gen. 30:22; Targ. Jer. I on Deut. 28:12). But, as before, Christ assumes the power of God over Death and Hades. It has been suggested that there is a connection between this statement in Revelation and the doctrine of the *descensus ad infernos* (the descent to hell) of the creeds, according to which Jesus, following his death, went to Hades, where he preached to the dead there and released the righteous from the lower world. However, since it is John's ardent belief, as we shall see, that the martyrs go directly to heaven when they die, it is possible that he is implying that through his power over the keys Christ has closed Hades to them so that they cannot enter. On the other hand, the words may have been used metaphorically to suggest that Death and Hades, which had no power over Jesus Christ, and have been overcome by him, cannot control his faithful followers. If so, the thought is similar to Paul's apostrophe, "Death is swallowed up in victory. O death, where is thy victory? O death, where is thy sting?" (I Cor. 15:54-55.)

19. Christ's command to John is repeated (cf. vs. 11), with the added instruction that he is to write not merely what he has **seen** (the RSV seems to have missed the tense here) and what already exists, but more important, he is to write down that which is to occur, viz., the punishments of the wicked, which take up the greater share of the book, and the rewards of the righteous.

20. The smooth rendering of the RSV obscures the irregularity of the Greek of this verse, but makes the meaning clear. **The angels of the seven churches,** identified with **the seven stars,** are to be considered as the guardian angels of these churches. In Persian religion each individual had his fravashi, or guardian angel, a concept that passed over into Judaism and Christianity (cf. Tob. 5:21; Acts 12:15). It may also be recalled that

---

us down by their sheer weight. But for the greatness and goodness of life there is no argument like meeting someone who is triumphantly alive. The one who came back from death eternally **alive** brings convincing argument to all who are willing to feel the impact of his overwhelming vitality. It was this which completely mastered the man of Patmos. It is this which may completely master us. At a great church in the English Midlands they used to sing an Easter anthem every Sunday because the minis-

ter wanted perpetually to remind his people that Jesus Christ is alive. The minister of that church wrote a book called *The Living Christ and the Four Gospels* [5] which brought a new and happy faith to men all about the world. Its author, R. W. Dale, was a great thinker, and a great interpreter of living experience.

18. *The Unlocked Doors.*—To the man of Patmos it became clear that Jesus Christ was the Lord of death as well as the Master of life.

[5] New York: A. C. Armstrong, 1900.

are the angels of the seven churches: and the seven candlesticks which thou sawest are the seven churches.

2 Unto the angel of the church of Ephesus write; These things saith he that holdeth the seven stars in his right hand,

stands, the seven stars are the angels of the seven churches and the seven lampstands are the seven churches.

2 "To the angel of the church in Ephesus write: 'The words of him who holds the

---

in Daniel the separate nations had their guardian patrons or angels (Dan. 10:13, 20-21; cf. Deut. 32:8 LXX). The destinies of the nations and of their angelic guardians were intimately related: the nation was not punished until its supernatural patron was defeated. In the Ascension of Isaiah 3:15, a work contemporary with Revelation, there is the interesting statement that the angel of the Christian church will descend from heaven in the last days, a view that has some analogies to that in Revelation. In chs. 2–3 the relationship between each angel and his church is close: the letter to each church is addressed to its angel, and both share equally in the praise and the censure of Christ. The relationship is strengthened by the assertion that **the seven lampstands are the seven churches,** for the lampstands are probably a variation of the seven stars (cf. vs. 12). Accordingly, stars, lampstands, angels, and churches are interwoven with one another into an astral-angelic synthesis.

This covering letter, which serves as an introduction to each of the seven letters, explaining their occasion and purpose, does not have a conclusion, as do the genuine letters in the N.T.—another indication of its artificial character. Perhaps this has been saved for the end of the book, "The grace of the Lord Jesus be with all the saints. Amen" (22:21)—a variation of the formula customarily used by Paul. This epistolary conclusion to Revelation makes the entire work, from 1:4 to the very end, a kind of letter addressed to all the churches.

B. Letters to the Seven Churches (2:1–3:22)
1. Letter to Ephesus (2:1-7)

2:1. Ephesus, the chief city of Asia Minor and one of the leading cities in the empire, was a center of Christian life from the time of the founding of a church there by Paul, who used it as a headquarters. It was also the scene of much literary activity, both writing

---

There was literally no door which he could not open. Men had cowered in the presence of the last grim mystery of the disintegration of the body. There was a terrible finality about death. There was an awful inclusiveness about the grave. But Jesus had not only won the victory for himself, he had come back with the keys of death. For him there was no "point of no return." In one of his darkly pessimistic poems A. E. Housman pictured the human story as a tale of Adam's seed making tiny structures on the sand of the seashore.[6] These buildings made of sand do not last long; the inrushing ocean washes them all away. Over against that with quite another figure of speech you have the word of Jesus, **I have the keys of Death.**

2:1. *Christianity Confronts a Town.*—Will Durant in the volume of his *Story of Civilization,*[7] entitled "The Life of Greece," makes some interesting observations regarding **Ephesus.** It was the most famous city of Ionia; colonists

from Athens had founded it about 1000 B.C. Its second temple for Artemis (Diana) was regarded as one of the Seven Wonders of the World. The apostle Paul was intimately connected with the Christians at Ephesus. He had found disciples there and had led them into a deeper Christian life. Paul had been so successful in preaching at Ephesus that the trade in silver shrines of Artemis was endangered. At Ephesus he had found a door for effective work wide open and many who opposed him. On the journey to Jerusalem which led to his being sent in chains to Rome he called the elders of the Ephesian church to Miletus, and here he gave them a most touching and tender address. So the city where the great philosopher Heraclitus was born became the home of a distinctive and powerful Christian work. It is the first of the seven churches of the book of Revelation. The wise and the foolish, the good and the bad, the old and the new, lived together in this ancient town. It was the task of Christianity to do its selective work in this mixed environment.

[6] "Smooth Between Sea and Land."
[7] (New York: Simon & Schuster, 1939), Vol. II.

who walketh in the midst of the seven golden candlesticks;

2 I know thy works, and thy labor, and thy patience, and how thou canst not bear them which are evil: and thou hast tried them which say they are apostles, and are not, and hast found them liars:

3 And hast borne, and hast patience, and for my name's sake hast labored, and hast not fainted.

seven stars in his right hand, who walks among the seven golden lampstands.

2 " 'I know your works, your toil and your patient endurance, and how you cannot bear evil men but have tested those who call themselves apostles but are not, and found them to be false; 3 I know you are enduring patiently and bearing up for my name's sake, and you have not grown

---

and publication, by early Christians, and its influence was widespread. In 29 B.C. a temple was erected for the worship of the goddess Roma and the deified Julius Caesar, and from that time the imperial cult had been promoted there.

There is divided opinion concerning the extent to which each letter reflects the conditions in the church to which it was ostensibly addressed. Possibly because we know so little concerning these churches at this time, and desire to know more, we have been tempted to extract more specific information concerning them from these letters than is warranted.

That these are not true letters may be readily determined by comparing them with a letter of Paul's, such as Philemon, Galatians, or I Thessalonians. They lack both the customary beginning and ending of the letters of the time, and in other ways reveal that they are artificial letters, literary creations designed for a special purpose, viz., that of encouraging persecuted Christians to be loyal unto death if necessary, for by doing so they would triumph over both their enemies and death itself. They are hortatory, paraenetic from beginning to end. While Christ is presented as the speaker in these seven letters, the words are obviously those of John himself.

2-3. Apparently paraphrasing Paul's commendation of the church at Thessalonica (I Thess. 1:3), he praises the Ephesians for their **works, toil,** and **patient endurance,** or steadfastness, and for testing and refusing to be led astray by false and evil teachers who claimed to be **apostles,** i.e., itinerant prophets and missionaries. A few years later Ignatius of Antioch in writing to this same church commended its members for stopping their ears to false doctrine (Ign. 9:1). Even more to their credit, they were **enduring patiently** for Christ's **name's sake;** apparently in time of persecution they had not denied Christ, but had remained steadfastly loyal. As we have seen, Pliny the Younger, writing between 111 and 113, said that those who were really Christians could not be made to curse Christ and worship the emperor's statue (*Epistles* X. 96).

And so in various fashions it is in every modern town.

2. *The All-Seeing Eye.*—The power of Christ is symbolized by his holding of **the seven stars.** His relation to the truth to which the churches are to witness is symbolized by his walking **among the seven golden lampstands.** This master of heavenly destiny and of truth to be proclaimed on earth speaks to the church at Ephesus. Everywhere in the N.T. practical words are based on great and ultimate facts and truths. So it is here. All the life of the Christians at Ephesus is lived under the perfect scrutiny of the living Christ. **I know your works.** There is a quaint story of a little child who formed the habit of secretly taking pieces of pie and eating them with much relish hidden in a store-

room in the attic. There was an old picture of an eye in the attic. One day a bit of intruding light fell on this eye. The child was terrified and cut the eye out of the picture, but the next day in the open space in the picture where the eye had been there seemed to be a hidden eye ceaselessly watching. The sense of the child that there is an invisible eye ceaselessly watching is not without foundation.

3. *The Virtue of Endurance.*—The question "What makes people faithful?" has the quality of provoking manifold answers. One is given in the message to the church at Ephesus. Its members sharply discriminate between loyalty and disloyalty, goodness and evil, and truth and falsehood. The very sharpness of these discriminations produces their own faithfulness; so they

4 Nevertheless I have *somewhat* against thee, because thou hast left thy first love.

5 Remember therefore from whence thou art fallen, and repent, and do the first works; or else I will come unto thee quickly, and will remove thy candlestick out of his place, except thou repent.

6 But this thou hast, that thou hatest the deeds of the Nicolaitans, which I also hate.

7 He that hath an ear, let him hear what the Spirit saith unto the churches; To him that overcometh will I give to eat

weary. 4 But I have this against you, that you have abandoned the love you had at first. 5 Remember then from what you have fallen, repent and do the works you did at first. If not, I will come to you and remove your lampstand from its place, unless you repent. 6 Yet this you have, you hate the works of the Nic·o·la'i·tans, which I also hate. 7 He who has an ear, let him hear what the Spirit says to the churches. To

---

4. But lest they become too complacent, they are reproved for having left the **love** they once had shown. This might be a reference to a decrease in the brotherly love the members had shown toward one another, but more probably, in the light of the situation, it means that their devotion to Christ had to some extent weakened in a time of testing.

5. However this may be, unless they **repent** and return to their love, Christ will remove their **lampstand**, i.e., will disown them, either now or at his second coming.

6. Censure is changed to praise for their hatred of **the works of the Nicolaitans,** which Christ himself hates. The Nicolaitans may have been the false apostles of vs. 2, but precisely who they were is not clear. According to certain of the early church fathers, they were followers of Nicolaus, the proselyte of Antioch mentioned in Acts 6:5—a guess which does not afford any help in identifying them (see the discussion of the Nicolaitans and Balaamites, vss. 14-15).

7. The formula **He who has an ear, let him hear what the Spirit says to the churches** introduces the promises made to the conqueror in this and the next two letters, but comes after the promises of the last four letters. Since Christ is presumed to be the speaker, it is not surprising that the words echo the phraseology of certain passages in the Gospels (Mark 4:9, 23; 7:16; Matt. 11:15; 13:9, 43; Luke 8:8; 14:35). In Revelation

---

have not grown weary. When we lose our sense that good is good and evil is evil we are ready to become evil and faithless to a faith which has lost its power over us.

In William Langland's poem *The Vision of Piers Plowman* we see a man who says "Show me some skill to perceive falsehood." He is told to look on his left side and there he sees the maid Mede in marvelous apparel—the finest of furs, red rubies, dazzling diamonds. "Her raiment ravished me; its richness amazed me." He is told that she lies to the lords who have law in keeping. "She libels loyalty" and has a fickle tongue.[8] One must learn to look beyond the garments to find truth and falsehood. This is just what the members of the church at Ephesus have learned to do and this very act has enabled them to remain faithful and not to become weary.

4. *The Waning of Noble Emotion.*—The first fine rapture of the devotion of the members of the Ephesus church has waned. They

are loyal; but they have lost their spiritual glow. As their enthusiasm has waned their work itself has felt the lag of their devotion. It is a dangerous situation. They must learn the secret of renewing the vision splendid. In a brilliant book, *Convention and Revolt in Poetry,*[1] John Livingstone Lowes has a good deal to say about the waning of the creative spirit. It is an experience we meet in life in all sorts of ways. If it is in the spiritual life the matter of renewal is of the utmost importance. It is the problem of every church in every age.

7. *The Christian Victory.*—A man wins the Christian victory when hostile circumstances are unable to deflect him from his loyalty to Christ. There is a victory which consists in bending circumstances to your will so that you get what you want in spite of them. But this is not necessarily a Christian victory; indeed it may be a very unchristian victory. But when, although the hostile forces cannot be changed and may work tragic evil upon the devoted heads of those

---

[8] "The Vision of Lady Mede."

[1] Boston: Houghton Mifflin Co., 1930.

of the tree of life, which is in the midst | him who conquers I will grant to eat of the
of the paradise of God. | tree of life, which is in the paradise of God.'

---

the formula reinforces the author's previous assurance that those who hear his prophecy read aloud and observe it will be blessed (1:3), an admonition repeated in 22:7. The **Spirit** is not the Holy Spirit of the creeds, but is closely related to Christ, if not identical with him. An analogy is presented in the Ascension of Isaiah 9:33-36: Isaiah, while in the seventh heaven, saw the glorified Christ and another Glorious One who looked much like him. On inquiry he learned that this was the angel of the Holy Spirit, who speaks in Isaiah and in the rest of the righteous. Apparently, as in Revelation, the spirit of inspiration and prophecy is different from but intimately connected with Christ. By indirection John may be claiming the Spirit as his source of inspiration, since the promises he offers are made in the name of Christ and the Spirit.

To him who conquers is another formula, taken from military usage, found in the conclusion of each letter. The mighty cosmic conflict has begun between God and Christ and their forces of right on the one hand, and Satan and the Antichrist and their cohorts of evil on the other. The persecution of the Christians is an opening skirmish; they are the soldiers of Christ. The conqueror is the Christian who by his "patient endurance," his courageous steadfastness, his loyalty and devotion unto death, is an imitator of Christ himself. Just as Christ suffered a martyr's death, but overcame his enemies and death itself and is now triumphantly enthroned in heaven, so the Christian who takes up his cross and follows Jesus to a similar martyrdom will also triumph over his enemies, both human and supernatural, and will be a victor over death. So much emphasis is placed on this concept by the author that we are practically forced to conclude that for him "conqueror" and "martyr" are synonymous terms.

In this and in the other letters specific promises are made to the conqueror. In this case he is solemnly assured that he will **eat of the tree of life** which is in **the paradise of God.** Frequently in apocalypticism it is stated or assumed that the beginning of the new age will be similar to the beginning of this present age, that the new creation will reproduce the initial blessedness of the first creation, that the new paradise will be similar to the Garden of Eden. Accordingly, in Revelation it is supposed that the blessings and glories of the Garden of Eden will characterize the new age, and that in the paradise to come the martyr will eat of the tree of life, which is depicted in 22:2 with its twelve kinds of fruit. Although Adam lost paradise and immortality by eating of the tree in Eden, the martyr, by eating of its fruit, will live forever. This is but one of a series of glorious rewards which are held out to the prospective martyrs.

---

who are loyal to Christ, these evil forces, powerful as they are, cannot break the will or shatter the loyalty of the followers of Christ, this is indeed the Christian victory. A brilliant teacher used to tell a story of a terrible blizzard which imprisoned a group of men in the Far West. One of them risked his life to go through the storm to effect a rescue. He was successful and returned through the storm to a place of safety. He conquered the blizzard. But the teacher said, "If he had failed to make his way through the storm and had been frozen in the snow still he would have conquered the blizzard."

7. Satisfaction After Trial.—The Genesis story tells of a tree the fruit of which was forbidden. The message to the Ephesians tells of **a tree** of life of which Christian victors are allowed to eat. After trial comes satisfaction. There are some things which can be given safely to men only after they have been disciplined and, through firmness under the pressures of life, have attained genuine strength. The Christian learns to be more anxious to be worthy of satisfaction than to possess satisfaction. The Christian desires to meet the conditions for eating of the tree of life. That tree suggests noble discipline and not untutored lust of longing. Francis Thompson in a poem entitled "Her Portrait," speaks of

A sad musician . . .
Playing to alien ears—which did not prize
The uncomprehended music of the skies.[2]

[2] From *Collected Works*, ed. Wilfred Meynell. Used by permission of Sir Francis Meynell and of Burns, Oates & Washbourne, publishers.

8 And unto the angel of the church in Smyrna write; These things saith the first and the last, which was dead, and is alive;

9 I know thy works, and tribulation, and poverty, (but thou art rich) and *I know* the blasphemy of them which say they are Jews, and are not, but *are* the synagogue of Satan.

10 Fear none of those things which thou shalt suffer: behold, the devil shall cast *some* of you into prison, that ye may be tried; and ye shall have tribulation ten days: be thou faithful unto death, and I will give thee a crown of life.

8 "And to the angel of the church in Smyrna write: 'The words of the first and the last, who died and came to life.

9 "'I know your tribulation and your poverty (but you are rich) and the slander of those who say that they are Jews and are not, but are a synagogue of Satan. **10** Do not fear what you are about to suffer. Behold, the devil is about to throw some of you into prison, that you may be tested, and for ten days you will have tribulation. Be faithful unto death, and I will give you the

---

2. LETTER TO SMYRNA (2:8-11)

8. We do not know when the church at **Smyrna** was founded, but it is known that in the second century it became a church of some importance. While Rome and Carthage were disputing the mastery of the Mediterranean, Smyrna had erected a temple to the goddess Roma, and from the time of Tiberius, when permission was granted to found a temple to the emperor, it had been a center of the imperial cult. Reiterating the words of 1:17-18, John states that Christ is **the first and the last,** that though he had **died,** he now had come **to life.** The implication of this for the Christian who was wavering in his devotion and loyalty to Christ because of increasing pressure by the Roman authorities is evident.

9. Tribulation, or persecution, and **poverty** were the chief trials of the Christians of Smyrna, but they were also the common lot of most Christian churches of this and a later period. In view of the competition between synagogue and church, coupled with the Christians' claim that they were the true Israel, it is not surprising, even though regrettable, that Jews at Smyrna and elsewhere in the empire displayed hostility toward the Christians, slandered them, and at times were delators, giving the Roman authorities information against Christians who might otherwise have escaped investigation, arrest, and punishment. Nor is it surprising, though even more regrettable, that Christians returned this hostility and developed a considerable amount of anti-Semitism, so that the Jews of Smyrna are called a **synagogue of Satan.** We are reminded of a similar attitude in words no doubt mistakenly attributed to Jesus, "You are of your father the devil, and your will is to do your father's desires" (John 8:44). For the author of Revelation there can be no salvation for these Jews, who are on Satan's side in the conflict.

10. A persecution, lasting for **ten days,** in which some will be cast into prison, is predicted by John. Note that it will be caused by the devil, which is wholly consonant

---

It is a sobering thought that as the ear must be trained for the heavenly music, so the palate must be trained for heavenly food.

8. Foes Who Might Have Been Friends.— The city of **Smyrna** whose Turkish name is Izmir is a very ancient town. It is one of the cities which have claimed to be the birthplace of Homer. It has been destroyed by earthquake and sacked by hostile armies. It has been inhabited by people of various national and racial strains. There were many Jews in the city when Christianity was established there; some of them accepted it and became its ardent advocates, while others rejected it and became its very bitter foes. There Jews who might have become Christians are the foes who, if they had followed the deepest meaning of their own traditions, would have become its friends. In every age the church confronts the problem of those who are so very far away just because they are so near. Sometimes the boy with a strict Christian upbringing becomes the bitter antagonist of the church of his boyhood.

10. The Christian Mastery of Suffering.— Franklin Roosevelt once said that fear is always worse than the things of which you are afraid.

11 He that hath an ear, let him hear what the Spirit saith unto the churches; He that overcometh shall not be hurt of the second death.

crown of life. 11 He who has an ear, let him hear what the Spirit says to the churches. He who conquers shall not be hurt by the second death.'

---

with the view later developed in Revelation that the empire is satanic in character, with its rulers the very incarnation of evil. Why **ten days?** Why not three and a half years, as in 13:5? No answer to these queries is evident. John envisages that some may suffer martyrdom, for he exhorts them to **be faithful unto death.** If they are loyal and true, they will be given **the crown of life,** a sign not only of their final victory, but also of the eternal blessedness that awaits them. A crown of this type is mentioned in a number of Christian sources. In I Peter, likewise a product of a time of persecution, when Christ comes he will reward the faithful with a crown of glory (I Pet. 5:4). In the Ascension of Isaiah (9:13) the crowns will not be awarded to the saints in heaven until Christ descends for the Second Advent. But when Polycarp, the bishop of Smyrna, suffered martyrdom *ca.* 155-56, he received his crown of immortality immediately (Martyrdom of Polycarp 17:1; 19:2), as is the case in Revelation. A description of the crowning of the martyrs by Christ is given in II Esdras 2:43 ff. It is possible that this concept of an immortal crown was suggested by depictions of Greek gods with crowns of light or nimbi, such as the halo that later appeared on the heads of saints in Christian art.

11. The concluding formula of this letter introduces another significant reward for the martyr, for he will not be harmed by **the second death.** We learn from 20:14-15 that the second death, which follows the second resurrection and general judgment, consists in being cast into the lake of fire for an eternity of dreadful torture, along with Satan, the two beasts, and Death and Hades. The martyr, by reason of his martyrdom, escapes this terrible fate. Instead, upon his victorious death he will go to heaven to await the first resurrection, when he and his fellow martyrs—and they alone—will be resurrected to share in the blessings of the millennium while everyone else is in Hades. Also, they escape the necessity of the second resurrection, the final judgment, and any possibility of being thrown into the fiery lake for punishment. It is difficult to see how a more glorious, more compelling reward could have been offered to those who during persecution were tempted to participate in the rites of the imperial cult in order to avoid torture and death in this life.

There is something particularly shattering and disintegrating about fear. As the clouds, dark and black, descended upon the church at Smyrna the great command came: **Do not fear.** That strange man Søren Kierkegaard came to think of suffering as so essential to Christianity that you could almost say "agony is Christianity." There is not a trace of this eagerness for pain in the N.T. It is a tragic and evil thing which the Christian must meet in a world in which there are so many elements of hostility. And Christ will save the Christian from the fear of it and will enable him to triumph over it. "Fear not" is one of the most characteristic sentences to be found in the classical Christian documents.

10. The Christian Victory over Death.—The Christian church at Smyrna was to experience terrible days of persecution; the time came when Christians were subjected to fearful tor-

tures. Henry C. Sheldon's *History of the Christian Church* tells of the martyrdom of Christians at Smyrna. "Some were thrown to wild beasts, some burned at the stake. But, according to the memorial of the church, the grace given to the martyrs was equal to their sufferings. 'Not one of them let a sigh or groan escape them.' "[3] The *Ecclesiastical History* of Eusebius contains a full account of the martyrdom of Polycarp at Smyrna. When he was commanded to revile Christ he replied: "Eighty and six years have I served him, and he never did me wrong; and how can I now blaspheme my King that has saved me?"[4] So he met his death. It was to the church at Smyrna, in which these things were to happen as the years unfolded, that the message came: **Be faithful unto death, and I will give you the crown of life.**

[3] (New York: Thomas Y. Crowell, 1894), Vol. I, p. 146.
[4] IV. 15.

12 And to the angel of the church in Pergamos write; These things saith he which hath the sharp sword with two edges;

13 I know thy works, and where thou dwellest, *even* where Satan's seat *is:* and thou holdest fast my name, and hast not denied my faith, even in those days wherein Antipas *was* my faithful martyr, who was slain among you, where Satan dwelleth.

14 But I have a few things against thee, because thou hast there them that hold

12 "And to the angel of the church in Per'ga-mum write: 'The words of him who has the sharp two-edged sword.

13 "'I know where you dwell, where Satan's throne is; you hold fast my name and you did not deny my faith even in the days of An'ti-pas my witness, my faithful one, who was killed among you, where Satan dwells. **14** But I have a few things

---

3. LETTER TO PERGAMUM (2:12-17)

12. Pergamum, since 29 B.C. when a temple was dedicated to the goddess Roma and the emperor Augustus, had been active in the promotion of the imperial religion. With this temple and its powerful priesthood, Pergamum, the capital of the province of Asia, became the provincial center of the state religion as well. With this emphasis it was but natural that the Christians of Pergamum should undergo persecution for refusing to worship the emperor. As an omen of the retribution to the persecutors and the final victory of the saints, Christ is again represented with **the sharp two-edged sword.**

13. Some would see in the phrase **Satan's throne** an allusion to the great altar to Zeus Soter, which was erected on a huge base on the heights eight hundred feet above the city. John, however, was not especially concerned about Zeus, but he was vitally interested in the emperors, who in his opinion were the incarnation of Satan, and not divine as their worshipers supposed. Consequently, when he states that the throne of Satan is in Pergamum, he is castigating the city as the main seat of the imperial cult in the province of which it is the capital.

Persecution had previously broken out in Pergamum, but the members of the church there had been faithful, for they held fast to Christ's **name** and did not **deny** the faith. 'Αρνέομαι, translated as **deny,** like μάρτυς, became a technical term among the early Christians, being used to describe those Christians who denied the name and faith of Christ when confronted with the prospect of persecution. The Christians at Pergamum had remained loyal even though one of their number, a certain Antipas, had died as a **faithful martyr,** the only defensible rendering in this context. It is possible, in fact, that his fate had served to strengthen the faith of his fellow Christians. Unfortunately nothing else is known concerning this early martyr.

14. Despite their faithfulness as a whole, some were holding to the teaching of **Balaam,** who had caused Balak to induce the Israelites **to eat things sacrificed unto**

---

12. *A Cosmopolitan Town.*—Pergamum was famous for its statuary and was most famous for its library. It has been said that for fifty years it was the finest flower of Hellenic civilization. Here something came from everywhere, and these things were mixed together all too often without much criticism. The name **Balaam** had come to associate itself with the attempt to mix the purer life of Israel with paganism. And when Pergamum became a center of the imperial Roman cult the danger became the greater. The Christians were attempt-

ing to establish the throne of God in a place which too had something like a throne of Satan. The conflict was fierce and already there had been one Christian martyr. The attempt to combine things which do not belong together is a besetting sin of culturally advancing and sophisticated Christians. Sharp discrimination was and is the Christian requirement.

14. *The Tragedy of the Cosmopolitan.*— When, in spite of himself, Balaam prophesied for Jehovah, and the people who worshiped him, and against his own people he was not

the doctrine of Balaam, who taught Balak to cast a stumblingblock before the children of Israel, to eat things sacrificed unto idols, and to commit fornication.

15 So hast thou also them that hold the doctrine of the Nicolaitans, which thing I hate.

16 Repent; or else I will come unto thee quickly, and will fight against them with the sword of my mouth.

17 He that hath an ear, let him hear what the Spirit saith unto the churches; To him that overcometh will I give to eat of the hidden manna, and will give him a white stone, and in the stone a new name written, which no man knoweth saving he that receiveth it.

against you: you have some there who hold the teaching of Ba'laam, who taught Balak to put a stumbling block before the sons of Israel, that they might eat food sacrificed to idols and practice immorality. 15 So you also have some who hold the teaching of the Nic-o-la'i-tans. 16 Repent then. If not, I will come to you soon and war against them with the sword of my mouth. 17 He who has an ear, let him hear what the Spirit says to the churches. To him who conquers I will give some of the hidden manna, and I will give him a white stone, with a new name written on the stone which no one knows except him who receives it.'

---

idols, and to commit fornication. In Jewish tradition Balaam became the evil prototype of those who taught the Jews to engage in the worship of idols, which included the eating of food and sacred prostitution, or fornication (cf. Philo *Moses* I. 53-55; Josephus *Antiquities* IV. 6. 6; Sanhedrin 106a). **Fornication** (KJV) is not merely sexual **immorality** (RSV), but denotes idolatry, with special reference here to disloyalty to God and Christ through worship of the emperor, as in 19:2, where participation in the rites of the state religion is specifically called "fornication" in the RSV as well as in the KJV. John, it would seem, used Balaam to typify those who would induce Christians to desert their religion for idolatry, and especially to participate in the rites of the ruler cult, the most abhorrent form of idolatry known to him.

15. Apparently John classifies the Balaamites and the Nicolaitans of vs. 6 together, for by a popular etymology the one may be derived from the Hebrew for "consumer of the people," the other for "destroyer of the people."

16. According to Pirke Aboth 5:22, the followers of Balaam are destined to inherit Gehenna and to go down to the fire of destruction. Whether or not John had this tradition in mind cannot be decided, but he does warn the Christian Balaamites to **repent,** for if they do not, Christ, who is coming soon, will wage war against them with the **sword** that projects from his mouth. In his prediction of the destruction of those who engage in idolatry to any degree, John is in full accord with Paul, who told the Corinthians that if they dared to partake of the sacred meals of the pagans, God, who is a jealous God, would punish them most severely (I Cor. 10:14-22; 11:30).

17. For the third time the concluding formula precedes the promise to the martyr, which in this instance is twofold. In the first place, as the Israelites were fed manna

---

ready to become an out-and-out supporter of either. He wanted to combine the ways of Moab with the ways of Israel. The people of Israel were in danger of betraying their cause by unethical friendliness. It was easy to be a success in Pergamum if your mind became the home of a hospitality which made no critical distinctions, and your life included practices which morally did not belong together. Syncretism seemed a very broad-minded thing; but it would have meant the end of the Christian religion. Hinduism is a religion in which every sort of thing is given place, so all the permanent

distinctions soon begin to vanish. The cosmopolitan all too easily becomes a jellyfish. The modern follower of the teaching of Balaam has an air of fine urbanity, but he betrays the integrity of his own soul and the integrity of his religion.

17. *The Secret Glory of the Individual Life.*
—When Christianity is interpreted as a corporate experience it is easy to forget its significance as an individual experience. When we think of the Christian victory in social relations it is possible to forget its deep and mighty victory in the individual life. The classical pas-

18 And unto the angel of the church in Thyatira write; These things saith the Son of God, who hath his eyes like unto a flame of fire, and his feet *are* like fine brass;

19 I know thy works, and charity, and service, and faith, and thy patience, and thy works; and the last *to be* more than the first.

18 "And to the angel of the church in Thy-a-ti'ra write: 'The words of the Son of God, who has eyes like a flame of fire, and whose feet are like burnished bronze.

19 "'I know your works, your love and faith and service and patient endurance, and that your latter works exceed the first.

during their deliverance from Egypt, so the faithful Christian will receive spiritual **manna** in the next life following his liberation from death. This corresponds to the promise of II Baruch 29:8, that in the days of the Messiah manna will once more come down from heaven to earth as food for the righteous (cf. Ḥagigah 12b). In the second part of the reward Christ will give the martyr a **white stone** with **a new name written** on it, a name that will be known only to the one who receives it. The meaning is somewhat obscure, but possibly the reference is to a kind of phylactery or amulet with the secret name of Jesus, which the martyr has not denied, engraved on it so as to protect him in this life and to insure a blessed immortality in the next.

4. Letter to Thyatira (2:18-29)

18. The sun god Apollo Tyrimnaios was the tutelary divinity of this prosperous city, and his worship was joined with that of the emperors, who were identified as Apollo incarnate and each, like him, the son of Zeus. Possibly it was with this in mind that John represents the heavenly Christ, with **eyes like a flame of fire** and **feet** like **burnished bronze,** as the **Son of God.** Thus the celestial Christ, the **Son of God,** is set over against and above the emperor, who as the incarnate Apollo is the son of Zeus.

19. The members of this church are commended for their **patient endurance,** among other virtues, and for doing better than they had done at first.

sage in the N.T. about the individual is the promise of the **white stone, with a new name written on the stone which no one knows except him who receives it.** Each victorious Christian is to have an eternal secret with God. There is a central citadel in each personality which only God shares. God completely cleanses a man's life. So the stone he gives him is a **white stone.** The **new name** represents the individual personality achieved only through the grace of Christ. He is a new man; but he is not a new man just like every other new man. He is eternally something individual, and different, and eternally prized by God. Of course you cannot illustrate an unshared secret. But such a piece of writing as that great book *The Private Devotions of Lancelot Andrewes* [5] does suggest what is meant. Andrewes was a great figure at court; he had a notable fellowship with scholars. But his deepest life was lived alone with God.

18. *The Menace of a Corrupted Mind.*— Thyatira, on the site of the modern Akhisar, was famous for its purple dye. The interpretations ironically called **the deep things of Satan**

contended that the inner life might be so fully satisfying to God and man that outer conduct did not matter. This teaching is associated with a woman who had set up to be a **prophetess** and was given the biting and condemning name **Jezebel.** The suggestion of an inner life which makes conduct irrelevant provides a perfect escape from moral responsibility. This position has been repeatedly advocated in the history of religion. And it has always been repudiated by those possessing clear moral consciousness. A sect appeared in Germany in 1535 which was declared to hold the position that the moral law was not binding upon Christians who were under the law of grace. Historically the mood has been even more dangerous than the direct assertion.

19. *Onward and Upward.*—It is not enough for the Christian to maintain his position—he must advance. So there is great praise in the words **your latter works exceed the first.** In hours of strain men are likely very definitely to go backward or to go forward with equal energy. Stress and strain had led the Christians of Thyatira not to retreat but to go forward. It is a rich experience to meet a man after a few years' absence and to find that his touch upon

[5] Tr. John Henry Newman (New York and Nashville: Abingdon-Cokesbury Press, 1950).

20 Notwithstanding I have a few things against thee, because thou sufferest that woman Jezebel, which calleth herself a prophetess, to teach and to seduce my servants to commit fornication, and to eat things sacrificed unto idols.

21 And I gave her space to repent of her fornication; and she repented not.

22 Behold, I will cast her into a bed, and them that commit adultery with her into great tribulation, except they repent of their deeds.

23 And I will kill her children with death; and all the churches shall know that I am he which searcheth the reins and hearts: and I will give unto every one of you according to your works.

24 But unto you I say, and unto the rest in Thyatira, as many as have not this doctrine, and which have not known the

20 But I have this against you, that you tolerate the woman Jez′e-bel, who calls herself a prophetess and is teaching and beguiling my servants to practice immorality and to eat food sacrificed to idols. **21** I gave her time to repent, but she refuses to repent of her immorality. **22** Behold, I will throw her on a sickbed, and those who commit adultery with her I will throw into great tribulation, unless they repent of her doings; **23** and I will strike her children dead. And all the churches shall know that I am he who searches mind and heart, and I will give to each of you as your works deserve. **24** But to the rest of you in Thy-a-ti′ra, who do not hold this teaching, who have not

---

20. But praise is followed with blame for tolerating a woman named **Jezebel,** who called herself **a prophetess.** As Balaam was used as a type of the false prophet, his female counterpart, **Jezebel,** the immoral and idolatrous queen, is the type of the false prophetess who teaches the Christians **to commit fornication** and **to eat food sacrificed to idols.** As in vs. 14, **fornication** is not simply sexual immorality, but in a special way is equated with idolatry, particularly emperor worship.

21-23. This Jezebel, symbolic of Christian women who were leading members of the church into idolatry, and those Christians who sin with her are urged to **repent,** lest they be punished severely, even with death itself. Whereas the death of the martyrs guarantees their blessed immortality in the New Jerusalem, we learn that those who die as idolaters are to be cast into the lake of fire for an eternity of punishment (21:8). It is the Christ with the eyes of fire who **searches mind and heart** of all; no sinner can escape his searching look. This is probably a recollection of Jer. 11:20, where God tries "the heart and mind" and executes his righteous judgment, and is typical of the way in which the powers of God are assigned to Christ in Revelation.

24-25. Those who have refused to follow the teaching of this Jezebel, and do not as yet "know" what is called by some **the deep things of Satan,** are exhorted to continue

---

life is surer, his understanding deeper, and his actions finer. Matthew Arnold in "Rugby Chapel" wrote of spiritual leaders:

> Radiant with ardour divine!
> Beacons of hope, ye appear!
> Languour is not in your heart,
> Weakness is not in your word,
>
> .   .   .   .
>
> Ye fill up the gaps in our files,
> Strengthen the wavering line,
> Stablish, continue our march,
> On, to the bound of the waste,
> On, to the City of God.

It is the very genius of true Christians to go forward.

23. *The Searcher of Souls.*—In the book of Job there is a passage in which the unhappy sheik finds the perfect knowledge of God a tragic thing: "What do I do to thee, thou watcher of men?" (Job 7:20.) There is indeed something disconcerting as well as something very glorious about the thought of God's perfect knowledge of all our ways. He knows every thought we think, every emotion we feel. He is indeed the searcher of souls. Johannes Kepler was inspired by the idea that when he discovered the laws of planetary motion he was thinking God's thoughts after him. It is a strange and very significant inversion of this idea when we remember that God thinks our thoughts after us. But if it is a disconcerting thought it is

depths of Satan, as they speak; I will put upon you none other burden.

25 But that which ye have *already*, hold fast till I come.

26 And he that overcometh, and keepeth my works unto the end, to him will I give power over the nations:

27 And he shall rule them with a rod of iron; as the vessels of a potter shall they be broken to shivers: even as I received of my Father.

28 And I will give him the morning star.

29 He that hath an ear, let him hear what the Spirit saith unto the churches.

learned what some call the deep things of Satan, to you I say, I do not lay upon you any other burden; 25 only hold fast what you have, until I come. 26 He who conquers and who keeps my works until the end, I will give him power over the nations, 27 and he shall rule them with a rod of iron, as when earthen pots are broken in pieces, even as I myself have received power from my Father; 28 and I will give him the morning star. 29 He who has an ear, let him hear what the Spirit says to the churches.'

to **hold fast,** to be loyal and devoted until Christ himself shall come. It may be that the phrase **the deep things of Satan** is an ironical attack upon an incipient Gnosticism in which knowledge of the "deep things of God" is sought. It should be remembered, however, that it is the main concern of the author that Christians not participate in the worship of the ruler in any form. Such worship was thoroughly satanic in character, so that it was possible for him to speak of its devotees as having probed the very depths of Satan and all his works.

26-27. Two definite assurances of reward are now made to the conqueror who is faithful to Christ to the very end. For one, the glorified and conquering Christ, who has been empowered by his Father, will give the martyr **power over the nations, and he shall rule them with a rod of iron, as when earthen pots are broken in pieces.** This is a rather free quotation of Ps. 2:8-9, a psalm which presents the concept of a warrior-king, considered as Yahweh's anointed, or Messiah, who will vanquish the enemies of his people. This psalm was applied by John to the conquering Christ, who in 12:5 and especially in 19:15 will rule the conquered nations of the earth "with a rod of iron." But according to this promise, Christ will turn this power over to the martyr and his victorious companions in death. In harmonizing these views it should be observed that when Christ does come in power to smite the nations and rule them with an iron rod, he will be assisted by his army of martyrs, dressed in white linen and riding white horses (19:14; cf. 17:14).

28. The second promise is apparently quite different in character, for according to it the martyr is to be given **the morning star.** This takes us once again into the realm of astral speculation. The statement may mean that the martyr is to shine like a star in heaven, is to be given a kind of astral immortality, as in Dan. 12:3, where the resurrected saints will be "as the stars for ever and ever." This same concept of a glorious starry immortality for the righteous is presented in I Enoch 104:2; II Baruch 51:10; and II Esdras 7:97. But the belief in sidereal immortality was not confined to the Jews. It is well known that it had existed in the pagan world for a number of centuries. Certain heroes, among them Hercules and Perseus, had been changed into constellations as a reward for their virtuous deeds; but even ordinary people, if their lives had been pious,

one of infinite comfort too. "All instincts immature, all purposes unsure, this are we worth to God." [6] It is the living Christ who makes this tremendous claim in the message to Thyatira which is also a message to us.

28. The Heavenly Gift.—You have to go beyond the earth to find what God will give to the Christian of perpetual faithfulness. The

[6] Cf. Robert Browning, "Rabbi Ben Ezra," sts. xxiv, xxv.

morning star announces God's gift of the light of a new day, the symbol of Heaven's ministry to earth. In the hostile world men may live in darkness but God will give them the morning star that they may live in perpetual expectation and in perpetual hope. If a slave has a star in his mind he is no longer a slave; and if it is the morning star it foretells a freedom which is freedom indeed. It is one of the great-

3 And unto the angel of the church in Sardis write; These things saith he that hath the seven Spirits of God, and the seven stars; I know thy works, that thou hast a name that thou livest, and art dead.

3 "And to the angel of the church in Sardis write: 'The words of him who has the seven spirits of God and the seven stars.

" 'I know your works; you have the name

---

virtuous, and pure, could ascend to heaven, where they would be changed into stars. In consequence, John, on the basis of his undeniable acquaintance with astral speculation, may be promising a corresponding reward to those Christians who by their courageous lives and deaths are worthy of it.

But this theory ignores the emphasis on **the morning star.** Why is this particular star to be given the martyr? This question reminds some students of the astral belief that the goddess Ishtar, as the evening star setting at night, signified death, but as the morning star rising the next day, symbolized life and immortality. Accordingly, the gift of the morning star to the martyr is symbolic of the immortal life that he is to receive from Christ, who is himself identified with "the bright morning star" (22:16).

According to yet another view, the morning star was the symbol of world dominion. Consequently by giving the martyr the morning star, Christ is bestowing on him world dominion, which corresponds very closely to the previous promise that he was to have power over the nations and would rule them "with a rod of iron."

Which, if any, of these views would have been acceptable to John is impossible to determine. Since his symbolism, as well as that of astrology, was exceedingly fluid, it is possible that he entertained more than one of these ideas without any consciousness of incongruity or inconsistency. Or perhaps he held still another view, in which the morning star signified the Holy Spirit.

This letter, like the final three, ends with the familiar words of exhortation, **He who has an ear, let him hear what the Spirit says to the churches.**

5. Letter to Sardis (3:1-6)

3:1-3. Sardis, the capital of ancient Lydia, was another important city of Asia Minor. It had been greatly damaged by an earthquake in A.D. 17, but owing to the generosity of Tiberius it made a rapid recovery. The interest of the city in the imperial cult, which was stimulated no doubt by the emperor's gracious act, is shown by its competition with

---

est gifts of Christ to put the morning star into the hearts of men. There are some sad and brutal and pessimistic literatures which give men everything except a star. Whatever else may be said of them they do not represent that religion of hope which offers every man a star.

3:1. Outer Reputation and Inner Decay.— Eusebius in his *Ecclesiastical History* mentions **Sardis** three times. Each is in connection with the second-century bishop Melito, a famous man who wrote an "Apology" addressed to the Roman emperor. He lived entirely in the Spirit and lies buried at Sardis awaiting the heavenly call. Sardis was several times destroyed, the last time by Tamerlane at the beginning of the fifteenth century. On its site was built a village named Sart. Here at the time of the writing of the messages to the seven churches was found a church whose reputation outran its deserts. It is sharply called to reality by an unflinching description of its actual moral and spiritual situation. The process of decline had been so

subtle that it was actually unnoticed. The reader in a modern church will be apt to find something in the sharp words which comes home to his own mind and conscience. There is a sharp protest in respect of the difference between appearance and reality in the hot words of Hamlet to his mother:

> Seems, madam! nay, it is; I know not "seems."
> 'Tis not alone my inky cloak, good mother,
> Nor customary suits of solemn black,
>
> . . . .
> That can denote me truly: these indeed seem,
> . . . .
> But I have that within which passeth show;
> These but the trappings and the suits of woe.[7]

The difference between appearance and reality is of constant importance to the Christian.

1. Deceptive Appearance.—Superficial people evidently praised the church at **Sardis.** Seemingly there were visible signs of prosperity.

[7] Shakespeare, *Hamlet,* Act I, scene 2.

2 Be watchful, and strengthen the things which remain, that are ready to die: for I have not found thy works perfect before God.

3 Remember therefore how thou hast received and heard, and hold fast, and repent. If therefore thou shalt not watch, I will come on thee as a thief, and thou shalt not know what hour I will come upon thee.

4 Thou hast a few names even in Sardis which have not defiled their garments; and they shall walk with me in white: for they are worthy.

of being alive, and you are dead. 2 Awake, and strengthen what remains and is on the point of death, for I have not found your works perfect in the sight of my God. 3 Remember then what you received and heard; keep that, and repent. If you will not awake, I will come like a thief, and you will not know at what hour I will come upon you. 4 Yet you have still a few names in Sardis, people who have not soiled their garments; and they shall walk with me in

Smyrna for the privilege of representing the Asiatic cities by erecting a temple to Tiberius, an honor which went to its rival.

In the opening scene Christ is represented as having **the seven spirits of God,** which in 1:4 and 4:5 are before God's throne. For John, however, the distinction between God and Christ is not very marked. Christ also has **the seven stars** which he was holding in his right hand in 1:16. Possibly they and the seven spirits are to be considered as identical.

The exhortation of this letter is couched in rather general terms. The Christians in Sardis are described as being **dead** in their faith, for their **works** are far from **perfect.** They are warned to wake up, to heed the instructions they had previously received, and to repent. Just what their shortcomings have been is not stated definitely, but they are warned that if they do not **awake,** Christ will come unexpectedly like a **thief** to punish them (cf. 2:5).

4-5. Not all are guilty, however; there are some **who have not soiled their garments.** As a reward they will walk with Christ dressed **in white.** More specifically, the conqueror is to be dressed **in white garments**—a further indication that Revelation with its promises is primarily designed to encourage martyrdom. In a later document it is stated categorically that only those who in life "confessed" the name of Christ are to receive these garments (II Esdras 2:45-47). This concept of a special reward of this nature may have originated in Dan. 12:10, where we read that during the time of testing and persecution the faithful "shall purify themselves, and make themselves white."

From other sources we learn not only that the white garments are the symbol of righteousness and immortality, but that they replace the mortal body and constitute the immortal body of the saved. This is suggested in I Enoch 62:15-16, where they are called the garments of glory and life given by God; they will never grow old and their glory will never pass away. Paul longed for the day when "we would be further clothed, so that what is mortal may be swallowed up by life" (II Cor. 5:4; cf. I Cor. 15:53-54). According to the description in the Ascension of Isaiah 9:9, in the seventh heaven the saints, stripped of their fleshly garments, are given the garments of the upper world and are like angels in their glory (cf. II Baruch 51:5).

What met the eye could be interpreted in such a fashion as to call forth words of praise, but the one who looked beyond appearance to the heart found something very different. It was as if he heard the rattle of dead men's bones. The thought that you can be dead without knowing it is terrible enough. And this was what was necessary for the church at Sardis to learn. John Donne had a picture made of himself wrapped in winding sheets and placed in

a coffin. At this he looked daily to remind himself of the final adjudication of death. But that grim realist did not think of the fact that the startling picture might represent the possibility of a man's being dead while he was alive.

4. *Generous Praise.*—As we have seen, this letter to Sardis contains words of sharp and biting rebuke. It also contains words of generous praise. It might seem that nothing is less possible than to walk through this world with-

5 He that overcometh, the same shall be clothed in white raiment; and I will not blot out his name out of the book of life, but I will confess his name before my Father, and before his angels.

5 He who conquers shall be clad thus in white garments, and I will not blot his name out of the book of life; I will confess his name before my

White garments, heavenly and immortal bodies, are among the special and necessary rewards given to the conquerors, or martyrs, in Revelation. We are briefly told that while their souls are under the altar in heaven they are clothed with these white robes (6:11). Although garb of this type belongs to the angels (cf. I Enoch 71:1), the armies of heaven, clad in white, who accompany the conquering Christ on their white horses, are composed of martyrs, not angels (19:14; cf. 2:26-27).

As an additional incentive to complete loyalty, the name of the conqueror will not be blotted out of **the book of life**. To appreciate this statement with any degree of adequateness it is necessary to enter the realm of sidereal determinism and eschatology once more. In Babylonian thinking, since everything takes place in harmony with the movements of the stars, the seven heavenly bodies that move through the zodiac, viz., the sun, moon, and the five visible planets, are considered to be the interpreters of the divine will; they are the celestial scribes. The zodiac is the book or tablets upon which they write, an idea which accounts for horoscopes based on the signs of the zodiac, whereby the divine will may be discovered. The other constellations are, so to speak, the commentary on the margins of the book or tablets. As a whole, the stars are called the "writing of the heavens." Everything which each individual is to do during his life is inscribed on these tablets of destiny—a view which is wholly in keeping with the basic hypothesis that the stars, reflecting the divine will, control the lives and destinies of everyone. Likewise, the fate of nations and of the world itself is written in these tablets. The actual writer, the scribe of destinies, is the god Nebo.

Variations of these views are found in quite a number of Jewish and Christian sources, a few of which will be cited. Pure determinism is reflected in one of the psalms: "Thine eyes did see mine unformed substance; and in thy book they were all written, even the days that were ordained for me, when as yet there was none of them" (Ps. 139:16 ASV). A modified determinism is shown in Jubilees 30:20-22, where the deeds of the righteous will be recorded in a book of life, while those of the wicked will be written down in a book of destruction (cf. I Enoch 81:4; Ascension of Isaiah 9:22). Allied with this is the concept of a heavenly book of life, or register, in which the names, and presumably the deeds, of the righteous who are to be saved are recorded. Thus Enoch assures the righteous that the angels remember them for the good they have done and that their names are written before the glory of God (I Enoch 104:1). According to Luke 10:20, Jesus told the seventy to rejoice not because demons had been subject to them, but rather because their names were written in heaven. According to a Talmudic passage, one book listed the names of the righteous, another of the wicked, and a third of the undecided (Rosh Hashanah 1:49). Although a name might be written in the book of life, it could be removed if the individual turned to sin and wickedness, as in Jubilees 30:22, where those who become transgressors and impure will be removed from the book of life and placed in the book of destruction (cf. Ps. 69:28). Similarly, in the twelfth benediction in the Babylonian recension of the ancient Jewish daily liturgy, the Eighteen

out soiling one's garments. But precisely what is said about those who are praised in the church at Sardis is that they **have not soiled their garments.** How often we meet in churches everywhere people whose sheer goodness—a goodness of which they themselves are entirely unconscious—gives happiness and moral reassurance to all who know them. Sidney Lanier

wrote of "that beautiful Dinah Morris, you will remember in Adam Bede—solemn, fragile, strong . . . who would alone consecrate English literature if it had yielded no other gift to man."[8] In rare and beautiful books we have met these great Christians. Best of all, we have

[8] *The English Novel* (New York: Charles Scribner's Sons, 1883), p. 159.

6 He that hath an ear, let him hear what the Spirit saith unto the churches.

7 And to the angel of the church in Philadelphia write; These things saith he that is holy, he that is true, he that hath the key of David, he that openeth, and no man shutteth; and shutteth, and no man openeth;

Father and before his angels. 6 He who has an ear, let him hear what the Spirit says to the churches.'

7 "And to the angel of the church in Philadelphia write: 'The words of the holy one, the true one, who has the key of David, who opens and no one shall shut, who shuts and no one opens.

Benedictions, God is asked to remove the heretics (including Christians) from the book of the living.

It is against this background of thought that John assures the prospective martyr on the authority of Christ that his name will never be blotted out of **the book of life.** Apparently his martyrdom will be an absolute guarantee of immortality. Moreover, Christ himself will be his witness, and **will confess his name** before God and his angels. This pledge assures the Christian that if he will "confess" the name of Jesus, not "deny" it, when brought to trial before the Roman governor and his court, then Christ in turn will "confess," not "deny," his name before God and his heavenly court. Since the martyr is not to face the Last Judgment following the general resurrection, some earlier occasion for his acquittal, possibly soon after his death, was envisaged by John. It is quite possible that many a Christian, when confronted with the alternative of "denying" Christ and going free, or of "confessing" him and being sentenced to death, was strengthened to remain faithful to the end by this word of assurance.

6. The letter closes with the familiar exhortation to hear and heed the words which the Spirit has spoken (cf. 2:29).

6. Letter to Philadelphia (3:7-13)

7. Philadelphia was a newer and lesser city without any special distinction. Apparently a wine center, its chief deity was Dionysus. Damaged by the earthquake of A.D. 17, it too was aided in rebuilding by the generosity of Tiberius. In gratitude for the imperial assistance its name was changed to Neo-Caesarea, but the old name was restored during the reign of Nero. This letter is similar to that to Smyrna, since it contains no word of blame or censure; instead, the message is one of praise and encouragement. Christ is designated as **the holy one, the true one,** titles usually reserved for God himself. This, possibly, is to refute the Jews of Philadelphia, who may have ridiculed Christ as a false Messiah; more probably it is designed to show that as holy and true he will keep his promises.

He also has the **key of David, who opens and no one shall shut, who shuts and no one opens,** a quotation from Isa. 22:22. The reference is to a prediction of the succession of Eliakim to the office of governor of the palace. The key of David in that context is the symbol of his authority in this office. However, in keeping with his usual practice,

---

met them moving simply and quietly through the life of seemingly very ordinary churches.

7. *Victory as a Seed.*—The city of **Philadelphia** was on or near the site of the modern Alashehir. Though the name came from Attalus II Philadelphus of Pergamum it would have been a good name for a Christian city. The church here was more than a church which contained Christians—it was a Christian church. But the victories of loyalty and faithfulness it had won were more than achievements. They were seeds. The letter to this church tells what great things are to come out of its faithfulness.

As a matter of fact every thought is more than a thought; it is the seed of other thoughts. Every word is more than a word; it is the seed of other words. Every act is more than an act; it is the seed of other acts. The reward of goodness is always more goodness. The intelligence of fifth-century Athens planted seeds which grew up not only in that city but all about the world. The character of the Roman Republic planted seeds responsible for good growths yet found in many places. Every city which has been in any sense a Christian city has been a town where good seeds were planted.

8 I know thy works: behold, I have set before thee an open door, and no man can shut it: for thou hast a little strength, and hast kept my word, and hast not denied my name.

9 Behold, I will make them of the synagogue of Satan, which say they are Jews, and are not, but do lie; behold, I will make them to come and worship before thy feet, and to know that I have loved thee.

10 Because thou hast kept the word of my patience, I also will keep thee from

8 " 'I know your works. Behold, I have set before you an open door, which no one is able to shut; I know that you have but little power, and yet you have kept my word and have not denied my name. 9 Behold, I will make those of the synagogue of Satan who say that they are Jews and are not, but lie — behold, I will make them come and bow down before your feet, and learn that I have loved you. 10 Because you have kept

---

John takes this O.T. passage both messianically and eschatologically: as the messianic scion of David, Jesus Christ has his key with the power to open or shut the heavenly city of David, the New Jerusalem, to admit or to exclude as he wills. This concept may be both compared and contrasted with that in 1:18, where Christ possesses the keys of Death and Hades, and with Matt. 16:19, where Peter is given the keys of the kingdom of Heaven.

8. Christ knows the works of the Philadelphians; though they were weak with reference to this world, they had kept his **word** and had not **denied** his **name,** conduct that was expected of Christians. Since they have been faithful and true, he has set **an open door** before them which no one can **shut;** i.e., the door of the New Jerusalem, to which he has the key, is open to them, and no one is able to keep them out. This is but another variation of the theme of eternal reward awaiting Christians who endure patiently, with steadfast devotions, the temporary trials and persecutions of this world.

9. The **Jews,** who are really not Jews, are condemned again as **the synagogue of Satan,** as in 2:9. For the author the true Israel are the Christians, whom Paul considered the spiritual descendants of Abraham (Gal. 3:7), and not the Jews, a theme which John develops throughout his book. This came to be a familiar feature of Christian apologetic. The anti-Semitism of this letter is more marked, if possible, than that of the letter to Smyrna, for John adds that Christ will make the Jews **come and bow down** (RSV) or **worship** (KJV) at the feet of the Christians. In this context **bow down** is too weak a translation, and **worship** too strong; "do homage" (Moffatt) is better than either, but possibly "prostrate themselves" is the best rendering here. This concept of retribution may have been taken from Isa. 60:14, where the prediction is made that those who have afflicted and despised the Jews will bow themselves down at the soles of their feet (cf. Isa. 49:23). The homage that the Jews had expected from others in the messianic period they now will have to pay to the Christians, which will be a sign of Christ's love for his people. This promise is not fulfilled in the final episodes of Revelation.

10. Since the Philadelphians have kept the **word of patient endurance,** they are assured that Christ will keep them **from the hour of trial** that is to come upon the dwellers

---

8. *What Keeps Doors Open?*—If we ask the question "What keeps doors open?" the Christian answer may seem simple and immediate. God keeps doors open. He is the one who opens so that no one can shut. He is the one who shuts so that no one can open. But there is more to say. He opens because he sees that men can use open doors. He knew the works of the church at Philadelphia and they proved that these Christians could be trusted with more and larger opportunities. The men who lament the lack of open doors may well raise the question as to their capacity to use open doors. The doors

will be open for those who can use them. Gilbert Highet in his book *Man's Unconquerable Mind,*[1] written in connection with the celebration of the bicentennial of Columbia University, shows man entering almost endless open doors. You see the opportunity beyond these doors. You see the danger, the menace, of these doors. And you are not without a sense of the great mind overarching the human mind as man enters the open doors of life.

10. *Hours of Testing in Many Generations.*— The **hour of trial** referred to in the letter to

[1] New York: Columbia University Press, 1954.

the hour of temptation, which shall come upon all the world, to try them that dwell upon the earth.

11 Behold, I come quickly: hold that fast which thou hast, that no man take thy crown.

12 Him that overcometh will I make a pillar in the temple of my God, and he shall go no more out: and I will write upon him the name of my God, and the name of the city of my God, *which is* new Jerusalem, which cometh down out of heaven from my God: and *I will write upon him* my new name.

my word of patient endurance, I will keep you from the hour of trial which is coming on the whole world, to try those who dwell upon the earth. 11 I am coming soon; hold fast what you have, so that no one may seize your crown. 12 He who conquers, I will make him a pillar in the temple of my God; never shall he go out of it, and I will write on him the name of my God, and the name of the city of my God, the new Jerusalem which comes down from my God out

---

of earth. No doubt Christians wondered what would happen to them during the last days when God would be visiting the earth and its inhabitants with one calamity after another. Their anxieties are calmed by this pledge that those who remain firm and loyal will not be harmed.

11. Once more the statement is made that Christ is **coming soon.** This is a message of encouragement to the faithful, but a word of warning to the wavering, who are told to hold steady lest, through weakness and apostasy, they lose their **crown** and with it their prospects for eternal life. The force of John's message depended not solely on the expectation of glorious rewards to be given to the martyr, but also upon the belief in the immediacy of these rewards. Hence from time to time John emphasizes his conviction that the end is coming quickly.

12. John next guarantees that he who has the key of David will make the conqueror **a pillar in the temple** of God, and that he shall never leave it. The meaning is clear: Christ will admit the martyr to the **temple** of God in the New Jerusalem, where he will stay forever. At the end of the book, in the description of the New Jerusalem, John forgets this prophecy, for he says that there will be no temple in it, and God and the Lamb will take its place (21:22). This is but one of the numerous examples of the writer's indifference to consistency in details.

In developing his figure, John states that the names of **God** and of the **new Jerusalem,** coming down from heaven, and the **new name** of Christ will be inscribed on the martyr, who is now represented as a **pillar in the temple.** The significance of these names is difficult to determine. Logically they should not be a prophylactic against evil, for evil has all been eliminated by the time the New Jerusalem is to descend from heaven. Possibly they are a sign that the individual belongs to God and Christ, with the right to live in the New Jerusalem. This is in part the meaning of the sealing of the martyrs in 7:3, but only in part, for the sealing is also a protection against evil and danger. A

---

the church at Philadelphia has to do with one particular crisis in the history of the church and the world. This crisis may be said to be typical of many. The hour of testing has come again and again on a world-wide scale. When Christians confronted Islam there was such a trial between the church and the world without. In the days of the Protestant revolt there was such a trial between true Christianity and corrupting forces within. In our own time the spiritual dialectic of Christ confronts the dialectic of materialism. In every such hour of trial there

comes the reassurance that those of the true faith and the true life will be kept by God. They will have such inner strength that whatever evil forces may do they will not touch the central citadel of their lives.

12. *The Three Names.*—The symbolic picture of the Christian victor in this letter is of majestic sweep and of great importance. In the temple built of souls the Christian person is, of course, an essential support. And this victorious person is to bear the signature of God, the signature of the city of God among men,

13 He that hath an ear, let him hear what the Spirit saith unto the churches.

14 And unto the angel of the church of the Laodiceans write; These things saith the Amen, the faithful and true witness, the beginning of the creation of God;

of heaven, and my own new name. 13 He who has an ear, let him hear what the Spirit says to the churches.'

14 "And to the angel of the church in La-od-i-ce'a write: 'The words of the Amen, the faithful and true witness, the beginning of God's creation.

---

possible allusion to this passage, which may be of help in interpreting it, is seen in the letter of Ignatius to this same church at Philadelphia written a few years later. In warning against Jews and Judaizers, he says that unless they both speak of Jesus Christ, they are to him as tombstones and sepulchers of the dead on which only the names of men were written (Ign. Phila. 6:1). By contrast, the martyrs with the sacred names written on them are **pillars of the temple** of the living God.

The mention of Christ's **new name** is also puzzling, but it may be a reference to the name which Christ will bear at the time of his second advent (cf. 19:12, 16).

13. The customary formula also concludes this letter.

7. Letter to Laodicea (3:14-22)

14. Laodicea is the seventh of these commercial cities to which the letters in Revelation are directed. A church had been established there in the days of Paul, who requested that the Colossians and Laodiceans exchange the letters which he had written to them (Col. 4:15-16).

In the address Christ is given the unusual title **the Amen**, which may be an echo of Isa. 65:16 (Hebrew), where the phrase "the God of Amen" occurs. In 1:5 Christ is "the faithful witness [martyr], the first-born of the dead," which no doubt has in part suggested **the faithful and true witness** [martyr], **the beginning of God's creation**. Does John think of Christ as Paul did when he described him to the church of Colossae as "the first-born of all creation" (Col. 1:15), through whom all things were created in heaven and on earth? Or is he using the words in an eschatological sense to designate Christ as the creator of the new age, the new creation which is to replace the old? It could be that he has both ideas in mind, for they are complementary, not mutually exclusive.

---

and the signature of the living Christ. The very meaning of the life of God is to be alive in him. He is to bear the seal of the victory of God in history. The Christ who is God in human life and God above human life has put his signature upon him. Recently a theologian reporting the witness of one group at a great Christian conference described it in this fashion: "There is no hope for the world. What the world must hear is the Gospel. The Gospel is not hope for the world but judgment." This is different enough from our Lord's word, "God so loved the world" (John 3:16). And the picture in the letter to the church at Philadelphia of victorious Christians bearing the name of the city of God triumphant in this world, and the name of the Christ who having entered history reigns over history, and in this world where Christian victory has been achieved in their own lives bearing the very signature of the eternal God, strikes a note different enough

from the thought of a gospel which is only judgment.

14. The Church Which Has Lost the Sense of Meaning.—Søren Kierkegaard who was so often stormily egotistical and bitter and psychopathic sometimes wrote with singular penetration. When he discussed the failure of the church to make Christianity real he was raising an issue which the church in every age must face. The church at **Laodicea** had lost the power to make moral and spiritual distinctions. When it used great words it had lost their meanings. And because you cannot glow with enthusiasm for a truth of whose very existence you have ceased to be aware, the churchmen of this city were in the tragic position of those who have a flag but who have no country over which it is to wave. They were literally citizens of nowhere for they had lost that land of the spirit in which the home of the soul is to be found. What they needed was a recovery of the home of the soul.

15 I know thy works, that thou art neither cold nor hot: I would thou wert cold or hot.

16 So then because thou art lukewarm, and neither cold nor hot, I will spew thee out of my mouth.

17 Because thou sayest, I am rich, and increased with goods, and have need of nothing; and knowest not that thou art wretched, and miserable, and poor, and blind, and naked:

18 I counsel thee to buy of me gold tried in the fire, that thou mayest be rich; and white raiment, that thou mayest be clothed, and *that* the shame of thy nakedness do not appear; and anoint thine eyes with eyesalve, that thou mayest see.

19 As many as I love, I rebuke and chasten: be zealous therefore, and repent.

15 " 'I know your works; you are neither cold nor hot. Would that you were cold or hot! **16** So, because you are lukewarm, and neither cold nor hot, I will spew you out of my mouth. **17** For you say, I am rich, I have prospered, and I need nothing; not knowing that you are wretched, pitiable, poor, blind and naked. **18** Therefore I counsel you to buy from me gold refined by fire, that you may be rich, and white garments to clothe you and to keep the shame of your nakedness from being seen, and salve to anoint your eyes, that you may see. **19** Those whom I love, I reprove and chasten; so be

15-16. For John there was no middle ground between absolute faithfulness to Christ and participation in the rites of the emperor cult. The issue was as clear-cut as it was critical; there could be no compromise, no concessions. A Christian could not be **lukewarm;** he had to make a definite and decisive choice, either to be **cold** toward the claims of Christ, or burning **hot** in his adherence and loyalty to them. Those who seek to compromise, to trim, to follow a middle course, are detestable and nauseating, and like tepid, **lukewarm** water, will be utterly rejected. It was extremely fortunate for Christianity that there were leaders, among them Paul and the author of Revelation, who were uncompromising toward idolatry and were intolerant of its forms. Had this not been so, Christianity might have been assimilated to idolatrous polytheism instead of conquering and surviving it.

17-18. It is quite unlikely that there were even a few wealthy Christians in Laodicea. But the complacency of those who were relatively well off and in no apparent physical need is bitingly ridiculed. Actually, those who rely on their material prosperity are in dire need; they are indeed spiritually **wretched, pitiable, poor, blind and naked.** Instead of the riches of this world, they should purchase spiritual riches from Christ, such as **gold refined by fire,** the fire of trials and persecution; **white garments,** like those the martyrs will wear; and **salve** to anoint their eyes, so that their spiritual blindness may be cured. It is frequently stated that this advice contains an allusion to the three supposed main sources of wealth in Laodicea, banking, textiles, and a popular eye medicine called Phrygian powder; but the evidence for this suggestion is tenuous.

19. Just as God reproves those whom he loves (Prov. 3:12), so Christ reproves and chastens his beloved Laodiceans, urging them to **be zealous and repent** of their lukewarmness and complacency.

15. *The Wrong Temperature.*—The O.T. book of Zephaniah is sharp with indignation at the people

who are thickening upon their lees, those who say in their hearts, "The Lord will not do good, nor will he do ill" (Zeph. 1:12).

Of a city dominated by such people it may be said:

She listens to no voice, she accepts no correction. She does not trust in the Lord, she does not draw near to her God (Zeph. 3:2).

This is precisely the sort of religious indifference which characterized the church at Laodicea. As a result the moral and spiritual temperature of the church was all wrong. There was not the bitter cold of hard hostility to God; there was not the glowing heat of passion-

20 Behold, I stand at the door, and knock: if any man hear my voice, and open the door, I will come in to him, and will sup with him, and he with me.

zealous and repent. 20 Behold, I stand at the door and knock; if any one hears my voice and opens the door, I will come in to him and eat with him, and he with me.

---

20. They should repent immediately, for Christ is already here, saying, **Behold, I stand at the door and knock.** The tableau is largely, if not entirely, eschatological: the time for the consummation of this age is at hand, Christ in his second advent is about to make his appearance, he is already knocking at the door. The idea and the words are almost identical with the eschatological prediction in Mark 13:29, that certain signs will show that Jesus is near, is at the very doors (cf. Luke 12:36).

This eschatological interpretation is reinforced by the conclusion of the verse, in which it is said that if anyone hears him knocking and **opens the door,** Jesus will enter and will **eat with him.** The anticipation of a banquet which the Messiah and the faithful will enjoy together is frequently found in both messianic and apocalyptic expectations. According to certain prophecies concerning the day of the Lord, the righteous are to feast and be merry (cf. Isa. 65:13; Shabbath 153a). This concept was transferred to the day of the Messiah, which was not infrequently compared to a banquet (cf. II Baruch 29:1-8; I Enoch 62:14) and at times to a wedding feast (cf. 19:7). According to Mark 14:25 and parallels, Jesus makes the eschatological prediction that he will not drink again of the fruit of the vine until the day when he drinks it in the kingdom of God, apparently with his followers. In Luke 12:36 the disciples are warned to be ready for the second coming, so that when their master comes home from the wedding feast and knocks, they will be prepared. It can be seen from these illustrations that the hope expressed in vs. 20 was a common one. Other interpreters often find a noneschatological and mystical significance in this passage, especially since the words **if any man hear my voice, and open the door** involve initiative as well as receptiveness on the part of individual Christians here and now.

---

ate loyalty; there was only that **lukewarm** temperature which is about as distasteful as anything can be. The question is inevitable: "Had Christ died upon the Cross and suffered the great passion in order to produce such lukewarm disciples?" And the question answers itself in the words **I will spew you out of my mouth.**

20. *The Master of Life Asks Admittance.*—The contrast between the sharp rebuke and the loving outreach of friendliness is most impressive. And it comes to a climax in the picture of the Lord of all standing outside a human life and asking for admission. The proud and stubborn sinner is still a possible host of God. The one who is the judge waits as a humble suppliant outside the human door. This combination of sternness and tenderness is a central characteristic of the gospel. Neither is complete without the other; they must be seen together. Herbert H. Farmer in his appealing book *The Healing Cross* [2] attempts to set forth together the two aspects of God's dealing with men as he approaches them in Christ. The one who is severe is the one who is graciously good. The goodness is the tender side of a core of severity. The figure of the judge knocking as a suppliant

[2] New York: Charles Scribner's Sons, 1939.

at the door of a stubborn man is one of the most memorable in the N.T.

20. *Intimate Fellowship with the Living Christ.*—There is no picture of intimacy more striking than that of sitting at a common table and breaking bread together. This is the picture of the relation of the Christian to God as the Christian comes to him in Jesus Christ. There is nearness; there is sympathy; there is understanding; there is fellowship. In a sense, to a Christian, every meal can become a sacrament. All of this is expressed in a somewhat different figure by George Herbert:

All may of thee partake:
Nothing can be so mean,
Which with his tincture (for thy sake)
Will not grow bright and clean.

A servant with this clause
Makes drudgery divine:
Who sweeps a room, as for thy laws,
Makes that and the action fine.

This is the famous stone
That turneth all to gold:
For that which God doth touch and own
Cannot for lesse be told. [3]

[3] "The Elixir."

21 To him that overcometh will I grant to sit with me in my throne, even as I also overcame, and am set down with my Father in his throne.

22 He that hath an ear, let him hear what the Spirit saith unto the churches.

21 He who conquers, I will grant him to sit with me on my throne, as I myself conquered and sat down with my Father on his throne. 22 He who has an ear, let him hear what the Spirit says to the churches.' "

---

21. In a number of places in I Enoch, which has so much in common with Revelation, the Elect One, the Messiah, is to sit on a throne of glory (I Enoch 45:3; 51:3; 55:4; etc.). This, however, is the only pre-Christian source in which the Messiah is referred to as being honored in this way. But the Christians, in their elevation of the heavenly Christ, thought it but fitting that he should be enthroned in heaven (cf. Col. 3:1; Heb. 1:8; Phil. 2:9-11), or else be on a throne at his second advent (Matt. 19:28; 25:31; Luke 22:29). In Revelation, Christ is frequently depicted as being on a throne both in heaven and during his return to earth. More unusual is the promise to the victorious martyrs that just as Christ is seated with God on his throne, so they will sit on their thrones with Christ, but this is in keeping with the reward of a crown in 2:10. Once more a parallel is found in I Enoch, in which the righteous are assured that each of them is to be seated on a throne of honor (I Enoch 108:12, actually a fragment of the Book of Noah). In the Ascension of Isaiah thrones as well as crowns are reserved for the saints, but they will not receive these until the Beloved returns to earth (Ascension of Isaiah 9:13, 18). In Mark 10:35-45 (cf. Matt. 20:20-28), answering a request by James and John that they be allowed to sit at the right and left of him in his glory, Jesus replies that this is not in his power to grant. On the contrary, instead of ruling, they are to be like him, the "servant of all."

Quite a different view is presented in Matt. 19:28, as Jesus reportedly tells his disciples that when the Son of man sits on his glorious throne, those who have followed him "will also sit on twelve thrones, judging the twelve tribes of Israel." In the Lukan parallel to this (Luke 22:30) they are to dine with Christ at his table as well as to sit on thrones judging the twelve tribes, a joyous combination quite close to that provided by this verse in Revelation and the one preceding it. In Revelation the promise that the martyrs will rule is to find its glorious fulfillment in their millennial reign with Christ (20:4).

22. The same exhortation of the Spirit to **the churches** that concluded the previous letters is used here. The use of the plural "churches" in each case is perhaps significant, indicating that no letter actually is addressed to a single church, but is directed to all seven, and through the seven to all the churches everywhere. Thus the entire corpus becomes truly catholic in character, and might well be considered as an encyclical to the church as a whole.

In these letters the author clearly reveals his main purpose in writing his book; it is his obvious intention to encourage and strengthen the Christians who are faced with the prospect of persecution and death for their religious faith; to fortify them by promises of rewards beyond the imagination of man, coupled with warnings of punishment to the weak and the apostates, so that they would most willingly become martyrs rather than comply in the slightest degree with the demands of the Roman authorities that they show their loyalty to the empire by worshiping its rulers. All of the promises in the conclusion

---

21. The Coronation of the Christian.—The boundless generosity of the promises made to the man who is victorious through Christ flashes out in the amazing word, **I will grant him to sit with me on my throne.** There is not only felicity, there is authority and power. Christ does not allow his throne to put a distance between him and his loyal follower. He shares his throne with him who conquers. The limitless power of the divine grace is suggested by these words. A man is to be prepared to share the throne of Christ. Dante in the rose of love and fire in the *Divine Comedy* finds a great symbol for the Christian fulfillment. The picture of Christ sharing his throne surpasses all other symbols of the Christian hope.

4 After this I looked, and, behold, a door *was* opened in heaven: and the first voice which I heard *was* as it were of a trumpet talking with me; which said, Come up hither, and I will show thee things which must be hereafter.

2 And immediately I was in the Spirit:

4 After this I looked, and lo, in heaven an open door! And the first voice, which I had heard speaking to me like a trumpet, said, "Come up hither, and I will show you what must take place after this." 2 At once

---

of each letter are for the conqueror, i.e., for the prospective martyr; of this there can be no doubt. Moreover, most, if not all, of those made in the body of each of the letters are for this same group of Christians. For these and other reasons Revelation has been aptly called "a handbook for the training of martyrs." That these letters are to be treated as an integral part of the entire book is shown by the fact that most of the promises which they contain are later referred to as fulfilled, particularly in the final chapters.

III. Introductory Visions (4:1–5:14)
A. Adoration of God in Heaven (4:1-11)

The main body of Revelation is seemingly composed of seven series of purported eschatological visions, with seven visions in each of the series. As a fitting introduction to these series of apocalyptic scenes, two visions, one of God and the other of Christ, in all of their majesty, splendor, and power in heaven, are depicted. At present God and Christ are far removed from the earth and its inhabitants, who during this present evil age are under the domination of Satan and his demonic forces, both supernatural and human. But the Christian readers are assured that God and Christ are not unaware of their desperate plight, are not without deep concern about their sorrows and tribulations; nor are they powerless to rescue them from their enemies and to save them out of this age of evil and wickedness. On the contrary, these two scenes portraying them in all of their majestic might are a pledge that very soon they will intervene in the affairs of this world, will defeat and overpower Satan and his followers, will drastically terminate his dominion, his age, and then will institute a new age under their own control for the benefit of the faithful Christians.

4:1-2*a*. John writes that following his reception of the message to the seven churches, he looked up and saw **an open door** in heaven. Unlike certain of the apocalyptic writers who give elaborate descriptions concerning the upper world as well as the nether regions, he does not give us any detailed cosmology. But he does present enough information to

---

4:1. *The Summons from the Eternal World.* —It has been said that there are various possible views. There is a worm's-eye view; there is a bird's-eye view; there is a man's-eye view; and there is a God's-eye view. The need of the man of Patmos and of those he would help would not be satisfied by a crawling worm's view. It would not be satisfied by the merely physical loftiness of a bird. It would not be satisfied by the inquiring yet baffled eye of man. Only by seeing the universe with the eyes of God can he be satisfied. Then he is beyond bewilderment, beyond deception. Then he is secure. So he sees a door opening into the high world of the ultimate mystery and he hears a voice which calls him to that far height. So the quarry slave escapes into a world of freedom. So the man caught in the coils of time escapes into eternity.

2. *The Ultimate Ruler.*—In a poem of Robert Browning, Johannes Agricola says:

> There's heaven above, and night by night
> I look right through its gorgeous roof;
> No suns and moons though e'er so bright
> Avail to stop me; splendour-proof
> I keep the broods of stars aloof:
> For I intend to get to God,
> For 'tis to God I speed so fast,
> For in God's breast, my own abode,
> Those shoals of dazzling glory, passed,
> I lay my spirit down at last.[4]

It is only by getting to God that the sorely tried Christian can find peace and assurance and hope in a hostile world. There are rulers representing the emperor from whom the Christian can expect only oppression and persecution.

[4] "Johannes Agricola in Meditation."

| and, behold, a throne was set in heaven, and *one* sat on the throne. | I was in the Spirit, and lo, a throne stood in heaven, with one seated on the throne! |

indicate rather clearly that his universe is a three-storied one, consisting of the earth, with Hades, the bottomless pit, and the lake of fire below, and a single heaven above (cf. 5:3 for a summary statement). For many of the ancients there were seven heavens—one each, apparently, for the sun, the moon, and each of the five planets. Occasionally there were even a greater number. God dwelled, as a rule, in the highest heaven, but in certain Gnostic circles he was so transcendent, so remote, that he lived *above* the highest heaven. The belief in seven heavens is found in a number of sources, including I Enoch, II Enoch, III Enoch, III Baruch, the Ascension of Isaiah, the Apocalypse of Abraham, and in the Talmudic treatise Chagigah 12b. In most of these writings paradise is in the seventh heaven, but in II Enoch it is on the south side of the third heaven, with the place of punishment on the north side.

Evidences of a belief in a plurality of heavens are to be found in the O.T. (cf. Deut. 10:14; I Kings 8:27; Ps. 148:4). In the N.T. Paul speaks of his experience in paradise in the third heaven (II Cor. 12:2-3), and the plural is used in Heb. 4:14 and 7:26 (cf. Eph. 1:3, 20). However, John regularly speaks of a single heaven, save in 12:12 (οὐρανοί, as in KJV), where he is apparently influenced by Isa. 44:23. Furthermore, in conformity with a commonly held view, the heaven above him was a solid vault or firmament above the earth, with doors or windows that could be opened to permit passage between heaven and earth (cf. Ezek. 1:1; Test. Levi 5:1; II Baruch 22:1; Mark 1:10; Acts 7:56; 10:11; Ps. 78:23). Accordingly, it was not too difficult for him to think of an open door in heaven above him.

With this in mind, we note next that a voice **like a trumpet,** probably that of Christ as in 1:10, summoned John up into heaven that he might be shown **what must take place** in the near future. Accordingly, while **in the Spirit** he found himself in heaven. Others had made a similar ascent, and for much the same reason. In one account Enoch was borne upward by the winds into the outer court of God's palace (I Enoch 14:8-9); again, he was carried by two angels through the seven heavens (II Enoch 3–21); Levi entered through the gates that were opened (Test. Levi 5:1); Baruch went up as though borne by wings (III Baruch 2:2); Abraham ascended on the wings of a dove (Apocalypse of Abraham 15); and Isaiah was taken up by an angel (Ascension of Isaiah 7:3). Paul did not know how he was caught up to the third heaven, whether in the body or out of it (II Cor. 12:2-3). John simply says that he was **in the Spirit.**

Here he would be shown what was going to take place in the future. Since, according to astral theology, everything that was to happen on earth had already been predetermined in heaven, if a person could only visit heaven to learn its secrets through information provided by angels, or possibly by reading the heavenly tablets of destiny, he would have a preview of all that was to occur on earth. Indeed, the events that were to happen might even be re-enacted before his very eyes. Consequently, on his return to earth he would be able to predict with certainty what the future had in store. It was for this reason that Enoch, Abraham, Isaiah, and others were taken to the heavenly regions. It was for this same purpose that John ascended to the celestial realm. The future of the world and of all mankind is unrolled before him in one magnificent panorama after another. As a result of this preview he writes with authority. Also, he at times writes of events of the future as if they were occurring while he writes, or as if they had already happened, using future, present, and past tenses with almost complete indifference, as do other apocalyptic writers.

2b-3. When he reached heaven, John saw God seated on his **throne.** There is no need to cite any of the numerous passages in which God is said to be on his heavenly throne, for this was a commonplace in Jewish and Christian thought. In Revelation he is represented as being on his throne in every chapter, save ch. 15, where he is in the temple, and chs. 2, 9, and 10, where there is no occasion for any mention of the throne.

3 And he that sat was to look upon like a jasper and a sardine stone: and *there was* a rainbow round about the throne, in sight like unto an emerald.

4 And round about the throne *were* four and twenty seats: and upon the seats I saw four and twenty elders sitting, clothed in white raiment; and they had on their heads crowns of gold.

3 And he who sat there appeared like jasper and carnelian, and round the throne was a rainbow that looked like an emerald. 4 Round the throne were twenty-four thrones, and seated on the thrones were twenty-four elders, clad in white garments, with golden crowns upon their heads.

In the shaping of Jewish and consequently of Christian speculation concerning the appearance of God in heaven, the theophanies of Ezek. 1 and 3 and of Isa. 6:1-5 exerted a tremendous influence. Directly or indirectly, this chapter in Revelation has been molded by the symbolism of these O.T. writers. Accordingly, there is a minimum of anthropomorphic detail in this scene. Instead, God **appeared like jasper and carnelian, and round the throne was a rainbow that looked like an emerald,** imagery that is reminiscent of Ezek. 1:26-28 and 10:1. The rainbow is a symbol of God's glory; it may also signify that he has made a covenant with his people which he proposes to keep.

4. He is, of course, surrounded by his heavenly court. Around his throne are **twenty-four thrones,** upon which are seated **twenty-four elders, clad in white garments, with golden crowns upon their heads.** These elders constitute a puzzle, since their exact counterparts are not to be found in Jewish sources. It is possible that John obtained the suggestion for these elders, who sing God's praises, from a verse in the little apocalypse in Isaiah, "For the Lord shall reign in Zion and in Jerusalem and shall be glorified before the elders" (Isa. 24:23 LXX). It has also been proposed that they represent the twelve tribes (or patriarchs) combined with the twelve apostles, as in 21:12-14, where the names of the twelve tribes are inscribed on the twelve gates of the New Jerusalem with those of the twelve apostles on the twelve foundations. Another suggestion, posited on the priestly functions of the elders, is that they are a heavenly archetype of either the twenty-four courses of priests or the twenty-four courses of Levites in the temple of Jerusalem, just as the heavenly temple is the model of the earthly. Since they wear white garments and crowns, and sit on thrones, they have been identified with the heavenly company of martyrs. Another view is derived from a statement by a Greek writer that beyond the circle of the zodiac there were twenty-four other stars, twelve in the north and twelve in the south. Those that are visible are assigned to the world of the living, while those that are invisible, being adjacent to the dead, are considered to be the judges of the universe (Diodorus Siculus II. 31. 4). Since numerous evidences of astral speculation are to be seen in Revelation, it has been suggested by some that the twenty-four elders represent an appropriation and interpretation of the twenty-four stars outside the circle of the zodiac. These suggestions have been made, but none is wholly acceptable.

There is the ultimate Ruler on the ultimate throne from whom he can expect everything. When he gets to God everything is seen in a new light.

3. *The Promise in the Sky.*—In the thought of Israel the Flood brought vast destruction. But after the Flood the **rainbow.** After tragedy the great hope of a good future. The rainbow stands for a hope which tragedy cannot destroy. And the throne in the sky which is beyond the human sky has a rainbow about it. Here glorious expectation reigns. All the colors are required to express the manifold aspects of satisfaction represented by the reign of God. It means the

fruition of everything which is good and beautiful and true. The escape into eternity rectifies the false judgments of time; escape from slavery becomes the freedom of the reign of God. When he sees the rainbow round about the throne of God a man comes to have a rainbow in his own mind. Such a one can believe that in a larger sense than Robert Browning meant "the best is yet to be." [5] Many human thrones have been without rainbows. They were built upon human fears rather than upon human hopes. There is deathless, many-colored hope about the eternal throne.

[5] "Rabbi Ben Ezra," st. i.

5 And out of the throne proceeded lightnings and thunderings and voices: and *there were* seven lamps of fire burning before the throne, which are the seven Spirits of God.

6 And before the throne *there was* a sea of glass like unto crystal: and in the midst of the throne, and round about the throne, *were* four beasts full of eyes before and behind.

7 And the first beast *was* like a lion, and the second beast like a calf, and the third beast had a face as a man, and the fourth beast *was* like a flying eagle.

8 And the four beasts had each of them six wings about *him;* and *they were* full of eyes within: and they rest not day and

5 From the throne issue flashes of lightning, and voices and peals of thunder, and before the throne burn seven torches of fire, which are the seven spirits of God; 6 and before the throne there is as it were a sea of glass, like crystal.

And round the throne, on each side of the throne, are four living creatures, full of eyes in front and behind: 7 the first living creature like a lion, the second living creature like an ox, the third living creature with the face of a man, and the fourth living creature like a flying eagle. 8 And the four living creatures, each of them with six wings, are full of eyes all round and within, and day and night they never cease to sing,

---

5. Flashes of lightning, and voices and peals of thunder similar to the phenomena accompanying other theophanies (cf. Exod. 19:16; Ezek. 1:13; Apocalypse of Abraham 17; I Enoch 14:11, 17) issue from the throne, witnessing to the awesome majesty of God. These same ominous portents, with an earthquake added, follow the breaking of the seventh seal of the book of doom (8:5), the blowing of the seventh trumpet (11:19), and the emptying of the seventh bowl of wrath upon the peoples of the earth (16:18). They are a pledge to God's people that he soon will inflict dire punishments upon their persecutors. The **seven torches of fire,** which burn before the throne, specifically identified as the **seven spirits of God,** are the ones belonging to Christ in 3:1, and have been mentioned separately or together in other passages (cf. 1:4, 12, 16, 20; 2:1).

6*a*. According to Babylonian and Jewish cosmology, there was a sea above the vaulted firmament which separated heaven from earth. John saw a sea before God's throne, but it was different from the one immediately above the firmament, for it looked like **glass or crystal,** and appeared to be the floor or base supporting the throne. Since John has borrowed freely from Ezekiel, conceivably he has borrowed and adapted a scene described by the prophet, who saw four living creatures bearing a platform glittering like ice or crystal, which served as the support for God's throne (Ezek. 1:22-26; cf. 10:1-22). It was relatively easy to enlarge the platform into a sea.

6*b*-8. The **four living creatures** delineated in these verses are a combination of the living creatures or cherubim seen by Ezekiel and the seraphim observed by Isaiah. The cherubim as described by Ezekiel were four in number. Although somewhat human in form, each was four-headed, having the face of a man, a lion, an ox, and an eagle. Furthermore, they were winged, having four wings apiece. Their function was to carry the platform of God's throne, which was like a chariot. Beside each creature there was a double chariot wheel with its rim filled with eyes (Ezek. 1:3-25). These cherubim were of Babylonian origin, for the Babylonians had four-winged genii or guardians in the form of an ox, a lion, a man, and an eagle. These may have had some connection with

---

8. *Perpetual Music.*—Round the great throne are twenty-four thrones of delegated authority representing God's orderly reign through his servants. The **living creatures** with their endless eyes are graphic symbols of humanity united to do the will of God (but see Exeg.). And now the note of glad music which is so characteristic of the book of Revelation is struck. The living creatures **never cease to sing,** they make perpetual music. At a certain stage loyalty and love inevitably become lyrical, bursting into song. The heavenly fulfillment is rapturous with melody. There are many kinds of churches. But there is no church of perpetual silence. Every

night, saying, Holy, holy, holy, Lord God Almighty, which was, and is, and is to come.

"Holy, holy, holy, is the Lord God Almighty,
who was and is and is to come!"

---

four signs of the zodiac, the Bull, the Lion, the Scorpion (frequently depicted with a manlike face), and the Eagle (a nearby constellation substituted for Aquarius). They represented the four powers at the four ends of the earth, and were related to the four points of the compass and the four winds. Presumably they supported the firmament, the throne of the great god. John, however, was probably unaware of the Babylonian origin. As for the seraphim in Isa. 6:1-7, they were celestial beings, apparently human in form, but with six wings. They were stationed near the throne and sang, "Holy, holy, holy, is the LORD of hosts: the whole earth is full of his glory." In addition, they seem to have had something to do with the fire of the altar. Their origin is uncertain.

But whatever the origin of the cherubim and seraphim, they came to have importance in later Jewish thinking, and were often seen together. In one of his journeys to heaven Enoch saw the seraphim, the cherubim, and the ophannim (personifications of the eyes on the wheels), who sleep not and guard the throne of God (I Enoch 71:7; cf. 14:23). In another source we are told that Enoch saw the cherubim and seraphim standing before God's throne and singing, "Holy, holy, holy, Lord Ruler of Sabaoth, heavens and earth are full of thy glory" (II Enoch 21:1). In this passage the cherubim join with the seraphim in singing the *Tersanctus*. A further development is seen in the experience of Abraham in the seventh heaven. Around the throne were the all-seeing ones (the ophannim?) singing the song. Under the throne there were four living creatures who were also singing. They each had four faces like those of a lion, a man, an ox, and an eagle, and each had six wings, like the seraphim in Isaiah (Apocalypse of Abraham 18). In this Jewish work, approximately of the same date as Revelation, the cherubim and seraphim are merged with respect to appearance and function.

The **living creatures** of Revelation are to be seen as against this complex background. They are four in number, and are **full of eyes** all over their bodies, so that they could see everything. Thus the ophannim, the eye-bearing wheels, are now combined with the cherubim. Unlike the four-headed cherubim, these creatures have but a single head each, like the seraphim; but like the cherubim again, the head of one is like a **lion**, of another, like an **ox**, of the third like a **man**, and of the last, like an **eagle** flying. Finally, like the seraphim, they sing the "Thrice Holy." Accordingly, the cherubim, ophannim, and seraphim become merged into one type of heavenly being in Revelation—which represents still another stage in the history of their development. All of this serves to demonstrate that John is not original in his use of symbolism; indeed, that he may not be wholly original in his use of the O.T. On the contrary, it would appear that he was in the main stream of a growing apocalyptic tradition which greatly influenced the currents of his own thought.

John has modified the "Thrice Holy," changing the title of God to **Lord God Almighty.** He may have done this to break the force of a title assumed by Domitian, "Our Lord and God," or he may have wished to indicate that God is soon to display his almighty power in behalf of the suffering Christians. The concluding words of the song reiterate the designation given to God in 1:4.

---

church tries to echo the heavenly music. Shelley wrote in "To a Skylark":

> Hail to thee, blithe Spirit!
>   Bird thou never wert,
>   That from heaven or near it
>   Pourest thy full heart
> In profuse strains of unpremeditated art.

> Higher still and higher
>   From the earth thou springest,
> Like a cloud of fire;
>   The blue deep thou wingest,
> And singing still dost soar, and soaring ever singest.

As God has taught birds to sing, so he has put deathless melody in the hearts of Christians.

9 And when those beasts give glory and honor and thanks to him that sat on the throne, who liveth for ever and ever,

10 The four and twenty elders fall down before him that sat on the throne, and worship him that liveth for ever and ever, and cast their crowns before the throne, saying,

11 Thou art worthy, O Lord, to receive glory and honor and power: for thou hast created all things, and for thy pleasure they are and were created.

5 And I saw in the right hand of him that sat on the throne a book written within and on the back side, sealed with seven seals.

9 And whenever the living creatures give glory and honor and thanks to him who is seated on the throne, who lives for ever and ever, **10** the twenty-four elders fall down before him who is seated on the throne and worship him who lives for ever and ever; they cast their crowns before the throne, singing,

11 "Worthy art thou, our Lord and God,
to receive glory and honor and power,
for thou didst create all things,
and by thy will they existed and were created."

5 And I saw in the right hand of him who was seated on the throne a scroll written within and on the back, sealed with

9-11. When the **living creatures** sing their song of **glory and honor and thanks** to the ever-living God, the **twenty-four elders fall down** and **worship him,** casting **their crowns before the throne.** Then they sing an antiphonal to God the creator, by whose will everything was created. This song is further assurance that God can and does continue to exercise control over all of creation, and will soon make his great power evident to all. It also, perhaps, contains an intimation that he will do away with this present creation and produce a new and perfect one.

B. ADORATION OF THE LAMB OF GOD (5:1-14)

5:1. This scene of the adoration of God is a complement to the preceding one, in which God was the center of worship, and forms an integral part of it. John's attention was called to a **scroll,** written on both sides and **sealed with seven seals,** which God held in his **right hand.** This scroll is the book of destiny or doom for the earth and its unrighteous inhabitants, and contains a prophecy of the predetermined and inexorable judgments and calamities that are soon to be inflicted upon them. The scene is in part borrowed from the one in Ezekiel, where a book written on both sides with lamentations, mourning, and woe is given the prophet from the hand of God who is on his throne (Ezek. 2:9-10). The scroll which John saw was sealed with seven seals in such a way that

9. The God of Whom We Sing.—The One who sits on the throne is the ever-living Creator. All life raises to him a mighty song. On their knees the rulers answer with humble yet triumphant gladness. Here is a joy that is deeper than pride. Here is a joy in which pride dies. In the life of God all that lives rejoices. All the created sing to the Creator. In the will of God they find not only their peace but their joy. The thrones are thrones of obedience; life itself becomes a song of praise. John Dryden wrote in "A Song for St. Cecilia's Day":

From harmony, from heavenly harmony,
This universal frame began:
From harmony to harmony
Through all the compass of the notes it ran,
The diapason closing full in Man.

The music the man of Patmos heard in heaven had this perfection and completeness which is at best a wistful dream in the world below. But the man of Patmos well knew what we too may know—that the heavenly music can so sing in human hearts that all the world is changed. When the thought of God takes hold of us it changes all our songs.

5:1. The Book of Divine Administration.—The divine administration is a matter of the utmost significance to the Christian. His fundamental security is in his faith in the reign of God. This faith will be confirmed if he can be given some insight into the divine administration: he will have an inner security whatever desperate experiences may come to him. So the sight of the book of the divine administration

2 And I saw a strong angel proclaiming with a loud voice, Who is worthy to open the book, and to loose the seals thereof?

3 And no man in heaven, nor in earth, neither under the earth, was able to open the book, neither to look thereon.

4 And I wept much, because no man was found worthy to open and to read the book, neither to look thereon.

5 And one of the elders saith unto me, Weep not: behold, the Lion of the tribe of Juda, the Root of David, hath prevailed to open the book, and to loose the seven seals thereof.

seven seals; 2 and I saw a strong angel proclaiming with a loud voice, "Who is worthy to open the scroll and break its seals?" 3 And no one in heaven or on earth or under the earth was able to open the scroll or to look into it, 4 and I wept much that no one was found worthy to open the scroll or to look into it. 5 Then one of the elders said to me, "Weep not; lo, the Lion of the tribe of Judah, the Root of David, has conquered, so that he can open the scroll and its seven seals."

---

a portion of it could be unrolled at a time, thereby releasing a series of seven plagues, one after the other. In an analogous situation Enoch read from tablets of destiny which he had seen in heaven and predicted seven "weeks" of future events, some of them weeks of woe and fearful destruction (I Enoch 93). An angel handed Ezra a book of doom and was told to open it so that he might know what was to happen at the end of time (Syriac Apocalypse of Ezra 1). He did as commanded and a succession of terrible woes was revealed to him. Another writer saw a huge book of world destiny, sealed with seven seals, which was as thick as seven mountains and so long that no one could comprehend its length, so great are the seven series of woes it contains (Apocalypse of Pseudo-John 1).

2-5. As a prelude to the termination of Satan's reign, it is necessary to find someone who can open the book so as to release the seven plagues it contains. Therefore an angelic herald asked who was **worthy** to break the seven seals and **open the scroll**; who was able to precipitate its woes upon the earth. Apparently no one was to be found in heaven, on earth, or in the lower regions who was worthy to perform this essential task; whereupon John wept, since this meant a delay in the execution of God's fearful judgment. However, he was consoled by one of the elders who told him to weep no more, for **the Lion of the tribe of Judah, the Root of David,** is worthy to break the seals and unroll the scroll. The concept of the Davidic descent of the Messiah is a familiar one and needs no special comment. It is mentioned explicitly in one other place, Rev. 22:16, and is presupposed in 3:7. On the other hand, his descent from Judah is seldom stressed. His appellation as **the Lion of the tribe of Judah,** which is rare, may have been prompted by a messianic interpretation of Gen. 49:9, "Judah is a lion's whelp." In this connection the Messiah from the seed of David is symbolized as a lion who is victorious over an eagle representing

---

held in the right hand of the ultimate Ruler of all things is of central importance. It is a book **sealed with seven seals**. It is as secret as the inner counsels of God, yet it is of overwhelming importance to men. How men have longed to know that secret! Edward Fitzgerald in *The Rubáiyát of Omar Khayyám* voices this longing:

Would but the Desert of the Fountain yield
One glimpse—if dimly, yet indeed, reveal'd,
    To which the fainting Traveller might spring,
As springs the trampled herbage of the field!

Ah Love! could you and I with Him conspire
To grasp this sorry Scheme of Things entire.[6]

But the secret eludes the searching mind.

[6] Sts. xcvii, xcix.

2. The Interpreter of the Divine Mysteries.—The question, "Who has a right to speak for God?" is searching enough. We need, above everything, to know about the rule of God; but who can tell us? Especially under an imperfect and sometimes a malignantly evil rule, how shall men get beyond the confusion and the tragedy to the rule of God? In the vision of the man of Patmos no one in heaven or on the earth or under the earth was able to meet the test. Was the rule of God then to remain a mystery no one could apprehend? No wonder the man of Patmos wept. Confronted by this ultimate mystery the best human wisdom is silenced. When Socrates drank the fatal hemlock, with a strange and beautiful venture of faith he entered the unknown. He had found no

6 And I beheld, and, lo, in the midst of the throne and of the four beasts, and in the midst of the elders, stood a Lamb as it had been slain, having seven horns and seven eyes, which are the seven Spirits of God sent forth into all the earth.

6 And between the throne and the four living creatures and among the elders, I saw a Lamb standing, as though it had been slain, with seven horns and with seven eyes, which are the seven spirits of God sent out

the Roman Empire (II Esdras 12:31-32). In another source, the Test. Joseph 19:8, a lion, presumably from Judah, assists the Messiah, who is described as a lamb. The genealogical descent of the Christ, however, is not as important a qualification as the fact that he **has conquered.** It is because he is "the faithful witness, the first-born of the dead" (1:5), that he is worthy and able to open the seals which will bring death and destruction upon the wicked of this world and liberation and victory to his faithful adherents.

6. A quick and somewhat incongruous shift from one type of animal imagery to another is made, for Christ, the Lion of Judah, now is depicted as **a Lamb.** This incompatible collocation might be a survival of the tradition mentioned under vss. 2-5, in which a lion is the helper of the Messiah, who is a lamb. The Lamb in Revelation, however, is most unusual, for it looked **as though it had been slain** and had **seven horns and seven eyes.** Moreover, the Lamb is intimately associated with God, for it stands close to his throne. In fact, it is obvious that the traditional tableau of God on his throne in heaven surrounded by his court of supernatural beings, as depicted in ch. 4, has been thoroughly Christianized by the introduction of the glorified Christ, who now occupies the center of the stage.

This imagery of Christ as a slain but victorious **Lamb** is a favorite one with John, who uses it twenty-nine times in his book. It is not the same as the familiar figure in the Fourth Gospel, where, in fact, a different Greek word is used for lamb. We have already seen that in the Test. Joseph 19:8 the Messiah is a conquering lamb, indicating that the idea is not wholly original with John. The suggestion may have come in some measure from a messianic application of Isa. 53:7, "brought as a lamb to the slaughter," to Christ, as was done in Acts 8:32 and I Pet. 1:19. More likely, however, it was inspired by the account in Exodus of the Passover lamb whose blood saved the first-born of the Israelites from death. For John considers that God's miraculous deliverance of the Jews from their Egyptian oppressors after a series of devastating plagues was the prophetic prototype of the coming liberation of the Christians, the new Israel, from their Roman persecutors, after a series of similar destructive woes. In addition, the Passover lamb, which was instrumental in this deliverance, is considered as the archetype of Christ, through whose blood the Christians are to be saved. Paul had previously made this identification (I Cor. 5:7), but failed to develop the idea.

The **seven horns** of the Lamb testify to its great and complete power. In numerous O.T. passages horns are a symbol of power. More especially, the powerful fourth beast of Dan. 7:7, 20 had ten horns; the ram of Dan. 8:3 had two great horns; the he-goat of Dan. 8:5 had one large horn, replaced by four smaller horns, out of which a little

sure word to carry into the silence and the mystery.

6. The One Who Died the Judge of Life.—The one who opens the book is to adjudicate the judgments of God. It is as the crucified that the living Christ ascends the throne of judgment. The levitical system knew of lambs which were slain in sacrifice. But the idea that the Lord of life himself should be the sacrifice, that the Lion of the tribe of Judah should himself be the **Lamb** that was slain, was almost beyond

the imagination of man. In fact it was beyond the imagination of man, but it was not beyond the outreach of the love of God. And the Lord of all, who was the sufferer for all, was worthy to open the book of the reign of God. That famous painting of Salvador Dali, "The Christ of St. John of the Cross," which hangs in the Glasgow art gallery has many extraordinary characteristics. Perhaps the most outstanding is that the cross has been lifted right off the earth and seems to have begun an ascent into the

7 And he came and took the book out of the right hand of him that sat upon the throne.

8 And when he had taken the book, the four beasts and four *and* twenty elders fell down before the Lamb, having every one of them harps, and golden vials full of odors, which are the prayers of saints.

9 And they sung a new song, saying, Thou art worthy to take the book, and to open the seals thereof: for thou wast slain, and hast redeemed us to God by thy blood out of every kindred, and tongue, and people, and nation;

into all the earth; 7 and he went and took the scroll from the right hand of him who was seated on the throne. 8 And when he had taken the scroll, the four living creatures and the twenty-four elders fell down before the Lamb, each holding a harp, and with golden bowls full of incense, which are the prayers of the saints; 9 and they sang a new song, saying,

"Worthy art thou to take the scroll and
  to open its seals,
for thou wast slain and by thy blood
  didst ransom men for God
from every tribe and tongue and people
  and nation,

horn grew. Also, the victorious Maccabees are depicted in I Enoch 90:9 as lambs with horns; while in vs. 37 of the same chapter the Messiah is a white bull with large horns. From these examples it is seen that while there is no exact parallel to the seven-horned lamb in Revelation in earlier sources, nevertheless the symbolism in general has its antecedents.

The Lamb also is equipped with **seven eyes,** equated with **the seven spirits of God,** which are sent forth throughout the earth. The **seven spirits** were previously seen as seven torches before the throne of God (4:5), but here they are the eyes of the Lamb. We are reminded of the many eyes of the four living creatures (4:8), also of the little horn of Dan. 7:8 which had eyes like a man. But in this instance the imagery was probably prompted by the seven eyes of Yahweh in Zech. 4:10, "which run to and fro through the whole earth" seeing everything that occurs. As is his regular practice, John has freely adapted this passage so that Christ shares the omniscience of God as well as his omnipotence.

7-8. Since the Lamb was thoroughly qualified, he took the **scroll** from God. As he did so, **the twenty-four elders fell down** before him, as they had previously prostrated themselves before God (4:10). Each now has **a harp** in his hands and **golden bowls full of incense, which are the prayers of the saints.** Who are these saints whose prayers are ascending like incense before God? Are they the persecuted Christians on earth? If so, an interesting parallel is found in I Enoch 47:1, where the prayers of the righteous and their blood shall ascend to God in the last days, beseeching him to inaugurate his judgment. Or are these praying saints the martyrs in heaven as in 6:9 and 8:3? In either case, though the words of the prayer are not given, it may be assumed that it was a petition to God to initiate his work of punishment and judgment at once.

9-10. Accompanied by their harps, the elders sing **a new song.** In several of the psalms **a new song** is sung praising God and thanking him for his mercies, especially for his saving power (cf. Ps. 33:3; 40:3; 96:1; etc.). But in Isa. 42:10 the **new song** praises

sky. It has ceased to be merely an earthly event. It has become a cosmic event. The slain Lamb standing among the hosts of heaven expresses this eternal significance. The deed of the divine sufferer has repercussions which extend to the whole universe.

9. The Deed Which Gave a New World to Men.—The Lamb took the book of the rule of God. And the living creatures and the princely elders, harp and incense in hand, fell down before the Lamb. With glorious joy they sang

the new song of redemption. The great deed of death had given freedom to men who were slaves. It had given a new world of emancipation to men who now tasted a transcendent freedom. They became kings to reign under God, priests to represent God in their new world. So the Cross became that creative deed which remade the ways of human life. The one who wrought in this mighty fashion was worthy to open the book of God. In the words of ascription of praise to the doer of the mighty suffer-

10 And hast made us unto our God kings and priests: and we shall reign on the earth.

11 And I beheld, and I heard the voice of many angels round about the throne, and the beasts, and the elders: and the number of them was ten thousand times ten thousand, and thousands of thousands;

12 Saying with a loud voice, Worthy is the Lamb that was slain to receive power, and riches, and wisdom, and strength, and honor, and glory, and blessing.

13 And every creature which is in heaven, and on the earth, and under the earth, and such as are in the sea, and all that are in them, heard I saying, Blessing, and honor, and glory, and power, *be* unto him

10 and hast made them a kingdom and priests to our God, and they shall reign on earth."

11 Then I looked, and I heard around the throne and the living creatures and the elders the voice of many angels, numbering myriads of myriads and thousands of thousands, 12 saying with a loud voice, "Worthy is the Lamb who was slain, to receive power and wealth and wisdom and might and honor and glory and blessing!" 13 And I heard every creature in heaven and on earth and under the earth and in the sea, and all therein, saying, "To him who sits

Yahweh, who is soon to go forth as a mighty warrior to destroy his idolatrous foes, who are also the enemies of his people. It is possible that John obtained his idea of a new song from this passage in Isaiah. The song itself acclaims the slain Lamb as being worthy to open the seal of the scroll of doom, that his enemies might be punished and his people avenged and saved. The motif of the Passover lamb is repeated in this song, for it is through his **blood** that the Lamb that was slain is empowered to ransom and save his people. These, the new Israel, are from every race and nation, no doubt a true description of the constituency of Christianity by the end of the first century, for by then it had ceased to be a Jewish movement and was largely composed of the heterogeneous peoples of the Roman Empire. According to the song, they are to become **a kingdom and priests** to God, reigning on earth, a promise previously made in 1:6, which is to find glorious fulfillment in the millennium (20:6).

11-12. The **myriads of myriads and thousands of thousands** of angels surrounding the heavenly throne respond with a song of praise to the Lamb, quite liturgical in character, in which he is said to be wholly **worthy.** The number of angels as stated by John is probably derived from that given in Dan. 7:10 (cf. I Enoch 40:1). According to the angelology of the day, the angels were so numerous as to be beyond human calculations.

13-14. When the response of the angelic hosts was ended, every creature in the universe—in heaven, on earth and sea, and under the earth—joined in a doxology to God and the Lamb. The four living creatures concluded with the **Amen** and the twenty-four

ing deed of redemption there is a music of hope which has been heard in the world ever since. One hears it sing in words like those of Whittier:

> Ring, bells in unreared steeples,
> The joy of unborn peoples!
> Sound, trumpets far off blown.[7]

And so it has been sung by many a poet before and since. And so it has sung itself in human hearts.

13. *The Universal Song.*—The recognition of the crucified Lord is a matter of overwhelming importance in the book of Revelation. In his heavenly vision the man of Patmos hears count-

[7] "My Triumph."

less angels singing the praises of the Lamb that was slain. Then there is the mighty outburst of praise from all creatures in existence ascribing eternal **blessing and honor and glory and might** to the occupant of the throne and to the Lamb. There is no hostile minority; there are no angry and objecting voices. With complete unanimity the whole universe gives a place of ultimate loftiness to the Crucified. The Lamb deserves universal acclaim. He receives universal acclaim. Each picture in the N.T. Apocalypse has a certain completeness and finality. Each vision deals with one subject as if it is the only subject to consider. In later pictures the assertiveness of evil will be seen in the same uncompromising fashion. The contradictions

that sitteth upon the throne, and unto the Lamb for ever and ever.

14 And the four beasts said, Amen. And the four *and* twenty elders fell down and worshipped him that liveth for ever and ever.

6 And I saw when the Lamb opened one of the seals, and I heard, as it were the noise of thunder, one of the four beasts saying, Come and see.

upon the throne and to the Lamb be blessing and honor and glory and might for ever and ever!" 14 And the four living creatures said, "Amen!" and the elders fell down and worshiped.

6 Now I saw when the Lamb opened one of the seven seals, and I heard one of the four living creatures say, as with a

elders prostrated themselves in worship. (The words of the KJV, **him that liveth for ever and ever,** are not in the best texts.)

The liturgical features of Revelation, not only in chs. 4–5 but in ch. 7 and indeed throughout the book, have not been accorded the attention they deserve. Other apocalypses contain a considerable amount of liturgy, but none nearly so much as Revelation. Evelyn Underhill has observed that in this work we have a reflection of the worship services of the Christian churches of Asia Minor toward the end of the first century (*Worship* [New York: Harper & Bros., 1937], pp. 91-92). This is a logical conclusion, for where else would John have obtained the liturgy he used? Or what would have appealed more effectively to his readers than to be told that elements of their own familiar worship were used in heaven? It may be observed further that Revelation reflects an ordered and somewhat elaborate cultus. The worship itself is directed toward Christ the Redeemer as well as toward God the Creator. The Lamb that was slain shares equally with God himself in the adoration of the worshipers. Such accompaniments of worship as instrumental music, incense, and ritual movements are in evidence. Hymns, responses, doxologies, and prayers are heard, including the *Tersanctus,* which has played an important role in the liturgy of the church. The twenty-four elders constitute a kind of chorus or choir; everybody else participates in one way or another. To be sure, the author has undoubtedly idealized somewhat, and has adapted some of the liturgy to fit his special message and purpose. But even so, it is not unlikely that in Revelation we have echoes of the worship services of the writer's time and place.

IV. Seven Seal Visions (6:1–8:6)
A. First Seal: The White Horse and Its Rider (6:1-2)

6:1. Because he is worthy, and in compliance with the urgent requests and prayers, the Lamb opens the first seal, which releases the first of seven plagues from the book of doom upon the people of earth, who are to be punished for their wickedness and their oppression of the righteous. A similar scene is found in the Apocalypse of Pseudo-John 18–19. The author of that work is wondering about what is to occur before the end when

will be understood when we see that each theme is all-engrossing and excludes everything else while it is being considered. In this vision the One who has a right to reign receives universal homage. When we come to recalcitrant evil it must be seen against this background of the right of the living Lord to reign.

Does this picture give a far-off hope of change for the most evil men? Herbert H. Farmer in his rewarding book *Things Not Seen* writes:

"Was Caiaphas changed? Did Annas become a Christian?" Not in this life perhaps. But why confine the fruition of God's purposes . . . to this

life? . . . Somewhere, somewhen, we dare hope God will have his victory with Caiaphas—after much pain maybe both to God and Caiaphas.[8]

There are those who would carry the vision of the universal acclaim of Christ (of which, however, Farmer was not speaking in the words we have just quoted) as far as this. On the other hand there are those who would feel that such a position underestimates the possibility of finality in a human choice of evil. In any case there is no contesting the right of Christ to universal acceptance.

[8] London: Nisbet & Co., 1927, p. 34.

410

2 And I saw, and behold a white horse: and he that sat on him had a bow; and a crown was given unto him: and he went forth conquering, and to conquer.

voice of thunder, "Come!" 2 And I saw, and behold, a white horse, and its rider had a bow; and a crown was given to him, and he went out conquering and to conquer.

---

he sees a Lamb with seven eyes and seven horns. God informs him that he himself will ask who is going to open the book (the one as high as seven mountains and closed with seven seals), whereupon the angels will reply that it should be given to the Lamb. When the Lamb opens the book, seven catastrophic woes, one after another, will be released. Since these woes are not the same as the seven seal visions in Revelation, it is not certain that this account is based on the canonical book, especially since there are other marked differences. Instead, they both may be following a common tradition.

A common apocalyptic tradition may also account for most of the woes in Revelation, for similar patterns are presented in such diverse sources as Mark 13 and parallels in Matthew and Luke; Apocalypse of Abraham 30; Assumption of Moses 10:4-6; II Esdras 4:52–5:13; II Baruch 26–29; and Sibylline Oracles 3:796-808, to select but a few of the numerous examples that could be cited. In part these various lists of woes were suggested by the plagues of Exodus, in part by predictions of the O.T. prophets concerning the calamities that would usher in the day of the Lord, and in part by the apocalyptists' accounts of those that were to precede the coming of the Messiah. The presence in apocalypses of lists of dire calamities that are to precede the end of this age—indeed, that help to bring it to pass—may be due to a common desire to expand and make more explicit the prediction of Dan. 12:1 that before the end arrives "there shall be a time of trouble, such as never was since there was a nation."

But whatever the origin, direct or indirect, of the woes in Revelation, John freely changes and adapts his sources, and in certain instances devises some imagery of his own. This is especially true of the first four of this series, the four horses and their riders, which have been inspired by two descriptions from the O.T.—Zech. 1:7-17; 6:1-8. In the first passage the prophet depicts four horses of different colors with their riders, who go up and down the earth at God's command. These supernatural horses and horsemen are a presage of the restoration of the Jews to Jerusalem after seventy years of exile. In the second passage the prophet sees four chariots, the first drawn by chestnut horses, the second by black, the third by white, and the last by dappled. In some way these chariots are associated with the four winds of heaven, and ultimately may be related to Babylonian astral theology (cf. 4:6b-8). Their function is to patrol the earth for God and to execute his judgment upon the heathen nations.

By combining these two sources and ingeniously modifying them, John has produced some vivid imagery: four horses of different colors and their riders represent four apocalyptic woes, all concerned with warfare and its devastating results, a common feature of the various lists of woes.

6:2. *The Horseman of Victory.*—In a world where the Roman emperor claimed absolute rule the man of Patmos has seen the great vision of the reign of God. And he has seen that this is the reign of the living Christ. It is the Crucified who opens the seals of the book of the divine government. He opens **one of the seven seals.** The first of the mighty figures before the throne calls, **as with a voice of thunder, "Come!"** A fearful warrior, a bow in his hand, rides forth on **a white horse.** He receives **a crown** of power, then rides out on a career of triumph (but see Exeg.). Victory does not belong to the emperor upon his throne but to

the royal warrior sent forth by Christ. The horseman of victory is to bring reassurance to all oppressed and tortured saints. The last word does not belong to evil men or to evil kings. It belongs to the God whose face we see in the face of the living Christ. A. M. Fairbairn once published a book with the title *Christ in the Centuries.*[9] His sermons moved with a grand sweep. You saw the ways of the Christian in vast realms of thought and action. The book of Revelation has a cosmic sweep, and you get the very breath of it as you watch the crowned

[9] New York: E. P. Dutton & Co., 1893.

3 And when he had opened the second seal, I heard the second beast say, Come and see.

4 And there went out another horse *that was* red: and *power* was given to him that sat thereon to take peace from the earth, and that they should kill one another: and there was given unto him a great sword.

5 And when he had opened the third seal, I heard the third beast say, Come and see. And I beheld, and lo a black horse; and he that sat on him had a pair of balances in his hand.

3 When he opened the second seal, I heard the second living creature say, "Come!" 4 And out came another horse, bright red; its rider was permitted to take peace from the earth, so that men should slay one another; and he was given a great sword.

5 When he opened the third seal, I heard the third living creature say, "Come!" And I saw, and behold, a black horse, and its

When the Lamb opens the first seal, one of the four living creatures cries out with a thunderous voice, **Come!** (The additional words **and see** [KJV] are not well attested.) At this word of command **a white horse** appears, whose crowned rider, holding a **bow,** goes forth to conquer. This symbolizes a conquering invader, possibly the Parthians, adepts in the use of the bow from horseback, who were a constant threat to the peace and safety of the eastern borders of the empire.

B. SECOND SEAL: THE RED HORSE AND ITS RIDER (6:3-4)

3-4. When the second seal was opened, the second living creature gave the command **Come,** and another horse, **bright red** in color, whose rider was given **a great sword,** came into sight. This, too, typifies warfare, possibly civil war with its special horrors, although this cannot be stated with certainty.

C. THIRD SEAL: THE BLACK HORSE AND ITS RIDER (6:5-6)

5-6. The third horse which obeyed the command of the third living creature was **black** in color, and his rider had a **balance,** or scales, in his hand. A voice from the living creatures was heard to say, **A quart of wheat for a denarius, and three quarts of barley for a denarius.** A **denarius** was a small silver coin which was approximately equivalent to twenty cents, and was the ordinary wage for a day's labor, while a choenix, or **quart,** of wheat was a day's ration or allowance. The price for wheat, then, was quite exorbitant, probably eight to sixteen times normal; the price for barley was likewise far out of line. These were famine prices, in fact, which were a natural but regrettable result of war. The **balance** indicates that grain was so scarce and dear that it had to be weighed very carefully.

victor on the white horse riding forth **conquering and to conquer.**

4. *The Horseman of Man's Inhumanity to Man.*—The **second seal** of the book of divine government is opened by the Lord who came from the Cross. The second of the figures of might before the throne utters the command, **"Come!"** Now a horseman gallops forth on a **bright red** horse whose very color suggests the reign of blood. The first horseman came to rule, so he was given a crown. The second came to preside over terrible fights, so he is given **a sword.** He is to **take peace from the earth, so that men should slay one another.** He is to release the forces of destruction inherent in all evil. Allow evils to express their full nature and they will set about destroying each other.

Unwillingly wickedness holds its own judgment day and executes sentence upon itself. And all this is presided over by the rider on the red horse. Whenever evil men fight each other the second horseman of the Apocalypse appears. In this sense the day of judgment is not a time to come. It is almost always present somewhere in the world. The power of evil for self-destruction deserves our serious and repeated consideration. Although Robert Browning was but twenty years of age when he wrote "Pauline" he was already sensing the darker problems of life. And so we come upon the line: "I seemed the fate from which I fled." In a true sense evil men put a force into their lives which sends them forth to destroy others and to destroy themselves. The horseman of man's inhumanity to

6 And I heard a voice in the midst of the four beasts say, A measure of wheat for a penny, and three measures of barley for a penny; and *see* thou hurt not the oil and the wine.

7 And when he had opened the fourth seal, I heard the voice of the fourth beast say, Come and see.

8 And I looked, and behold a pale horse: and his name that sat on him was Death, and Hell followed with him. And power was given unto them over the fourth part of the earth, to kill with sword, and with hunger, and with death, and with the beasts of the earth.

rider had a balance in his hand; 6 and I heard what seemed to be a voice in the midst of the four living creatures saying, "A quart of wheat for a denarius,[a] and three quarts of barley for a denarius;[a] but do not harm oil and wine!"

7 When he opened the fourth seal, I heard the voice of the fourth living creature say, "Come!" 8 And I saw, and behold, a pale horse, and its rider's name was Death, and Hades followed him; and they were given power over a fourth of the earth, to kill with sword and with famine and with pestilence and by wild beasts of the earth.

[a] The denarius was worth about twenty cents.

The rest of the sentence, **do not harm oil and wine,** is indeed puzzling. The best explanation so far advanced is that it is an allusion to an edict of Domitian's in A.D. 92 in the interests of Italian winegrowers, ordering half of the vineyards in Asia Minor and other provinces to be uprooted (Suetonius *Domitian* 7 and 14). The opposition to this edict in Asia Minor was so strong that it was revoked before it was put into effect. This explanation does not take the reference to oil into account, but we would not expect John's allusion to the edict to be entirely accurate. If this interpretation is correct, then a Domitianic date for Revelation is given some additional substantiation.

D. FOURTH SEAL: THE PALE HORSE AND ITS RIDER (6:7-8)

7-8. At the order of the fourth living creature a **pale horse** was seen. The translation of the Greek as given here is supported by the ASV, but Goodspeed has "the color of ashes," while Moffatt has "livid." In view of the context, "livid," the bloodless color of a corpse, is the most descriptive rendering. The rider of this horse was **Death,** with **Hades** following him. More than likely the writer intended to place both on the horse, one behind the other. Death and Hades are together here, as in 1:18 (see Exeg., *ad loc.*) and

man overrules all this for the purposes of the administration of the divine justice.

6. *The Horseman of Famine.*—The sharp phrase, **a quart of wheat for a denarius,** indicates the presence of famine prices. Luxuries were accessible; necessities were coming to be beyond reach. The rider on a black horse, who came after the opening of **the third seal,** carried **a balance** which indicated not only the weighing of things to sell but the weighing of the people who bought and sold. Famine could bring commercial life to a standstill. And here famine is seen as part of the administration of divine justice. Bitter circumstances were not to be regarded as meaningless; they were to be seen in the light of the rule of God. The chaos which evil men and evil deeds let loose became itself a part of the rule of God. These things were to be sent forth in judgment of men who had flouted his will. The important principle at the heart of all this is that God's will so deeply reflects his own nature of perfect good-

ness and the requirement of the nature of man who was made for good that his judgments are never arbitrary. The horsemen are the overlords of a nature whose very processes work against evil and for good.

Arnulf Överland once wrote:

> Oppressor's ordered might
> Can not change wrong to right.[1]

That faith is deep in the heart of man. But there are great movements in life supported by God which justify this faith. The horsemen of the Apocalypse support such a faith. Each opened seal revealed a new action of God in history. Even famine bore the marks of the divine hand.

8. *Death Rides the Earth.*—The fourth horseman, who enters after the opening of the

[1] "We Shall Survive," Charles Wharton Stork. Quoted in *The Heart of Europe,* ed. Klaus Mann (New York: L. B. Fischer, 1943), p. 898. Used by permission of The American-Scandinavian Foundation.

9 And when he had opened the fifth seal, I saw under the altar the souls of them that were slain for the word of God, and for the testimony which they held:

10 And they cried with a loud voice, saying, How long, O Lord, holy and true, dost thou not judge and avenge our blood on them that dwell on the earth?

9 When he opened the fifth seal, I saw under the altar the souls of those who had been slain for the word of God and for the witness they had borne; 10 they cried out with a loud voice, "O Sovereign Lord, holy and true, how long before thou wilt judge and avenge our blood on those who dwell

in 20:13-14; and as in the second reference and probably in the first, they are personified. In this particular tableau they signify the sickness, pestilence, and death which are the inevitable results of wars and famine.

E. FIFTH SEAL: LAMENT OF THE MARTYRS (6:9-11)

9-11. Although the opening of the fifth seal does not immediately precipitate another woe, the depiction of the martyrs in heaven crying out for vengeance upon their persecutors is an ominous forecast of still greater calamities to come. Attention has previously been directed to the important promise made to the martyr-designate that he will go directly to heaven when he is slain, by-passing Hades, there to await the first resurrection (2:11). In this tableau the martyrs are represented as being under the altar, presumably the one in heaven which is mentioned in 8:3, 5; 9:13; 14:18; 16:7. Just as there was a heavenly temple, the archetype of the one in Jerusalem, so there was a heavenly altar of incense, the model of the earthly one, which, according to 8:3 and 9:13, is before God's throne. The bodies of the martyrs were slain on earth as a sacrifice, but their souls were sacrificed on the altar in heaven; just as the blood of sacrificial victims flows to the bases of the altar, so the souls of the martyrs are under the celestial one. This prospect of their souls ascending to the heavenly altar as a sacrifice to God no doubt was a compelling motive to accept martyrdom. This is shown in a prayer attributed to Polycarp, a second-century martyr, in which he gives thanks to God that he is to be accepted before him with other martyrs "as a rich and acceptable sacrifice" (Martyrdom of Polycarp 14:2).

In I Enoch 47:1-2 (cf. 97:3, 5; 99:3; 104:3; II Baruch 21:19-25) the prayers of the persecuted righteous, including the martyrs, praying for justice and vengeance, ascend to God. A similar plea by Christians for vengeance on their persecutors, the Romans, rises to God from their place beneath the altar, asking him how long it will be before he will judge and avenge their blood upon their persecutors, the dwellers on earth. This hope of persecuted Christians that God will avenge them is at least understandable, even though it may be regarded as far from commendable. Thus Polycarp warned the proconsul

fourth seal, is Death. He rides on a strange greenish yellow horse. He releases war and famine and pestilence and ravenous beasts for the destruction of men. The whole point is that he brings not meaningless destruction but destruction which serves the purposes of the justice of God. He is a part of the divine administration. A fourth of the earth feels his power that the rest may see and have the opportunity to repent. Not the power of Rome but the awful power of the Almighty is to be confronted with awe. The greater and nobler fear delivers from the lower and more ignoble dread. Some of the phrases of Joseph T. Shipley's translation of Paul Claudel's "Shadows" capture a mood similar to that of the words we are studying:

I feel a subtle wind, and my horror is released.
Flee from the danger of death, from the jaws of the beast!

Here once more the savor of death is between my teeth.
The travail, and the vomit, and the turning beneath.
. . . .
I must pray, for it is the hour of the Sovereign of the world.[2]

10. *The Impatience of the Dead Saints.*— The four horsemen have come and have gone to do their dread work. When the fifth seal is broken something quite different is seen—the

[2] *Modern French Poetry* (New York: Greenberg, 1926), pp. 72-73. Used by permission.

11 And white robes were given unto every one of them; and it was said unto them, that they should rest yet for a little season, until their fellow servants also and their brethren, that should be killed as they *were*, should be fulfilled.

12 And I beheld when he had opened the sixth seal, and, lo, there was a great earthquake; and the sun became black as

upon the earth?" 11 Then they were each given a white robe and told to rest a little longer, until the number of their fellow servants and their brethren should be complete, who were to be killed as they themselves had been.

12 When he opened the sixth seal, I looked, and behold, there was a great earth-

---

who was examining him of "the fire which awaits the wicked in the judgment to come and in everlasting punishment" (Martyrdom of Polycarp 11:2). This attitude, frequently encountered in the martyrologies and apologies, is quite different from that attributed to Jesus on the Cross, "Father, forgive them; for they know not what they do" (Luke 23:34), or to Stephen as he was dying, "Lord, do not hold this sin against them" (Acts 7:60).

The martyrs were each given a **white robe** (for the significance of this garb see Exeg. on 3:5). They were also told (by whom is not stated) to wait for a little while until the roll of the martyrs was completed. This is another instance of the determinism in Revelation, paralleled in other sources: the time for the liberation of the saints and the judgment upon their oppressors has been predetermined by God. In Dan. 12:6-7, e.g., the end is to come after three and a half years; according to another view, it will occur only after a predetermined number of souls are born (II Baruch 23:4-5; cf. Yebamoth 62a). A closer parallel is provided by a scene in Sheol related in II Esdras 4:35-37. To the question of the righteous souls in Sheol concerning the length of time they are to remain there before this age is to end and their resurrection is to occur, an angel replies that these things will not happen until the predestined number of saints like themselves have died. Even closer are the views expressed in I Enoch 47:4 and II Esdras 2:41 that all awaits the completion of the foreordained number of the righteous, particularly martyrs. Following a similar line of speculation, in Revelation the judgment of God will not be accomplished as an answer to the prayers of the martyrs for retribution until their foreordained number has been filled. This number was not revealed at the time, but in ch. 7 it is given symbolically as 144,000. Regardless of how many still remain to be martyred, the wait will not be long.

F. Sixth Seal: Cosmic Woes (6:12-17)

12-14. The opening of the sixth seal precipitates a series of ominous cosmic phenomena: first, **a great earthquake**; then **the sun became black**; the **full moon** turned to **blood**; the **stars** fell to earth like **figs** in a storm; the **sky vanished** as it was rolled up

---

souls of the martyrs kept safe under the **altar** appear. With a daring bordering upon audacity we are made aware of the impatience of the dead who have died for God. Why does the earth go on its dark and evil way unhindered with no avenging of the blood which has been poured out for God? The answer is in a way indirect. Each is given **a white robe** suggesting that the cleansing of the souls of the martyrs is more important than vengeance on their foes. There are others yet in the world whose faithfulness will lead to their death. The whole story of suffering for the faith must be told and then God can be trusted with the great adjudication. In the meantime they are to have God's great gift of **rest**. All the while we are seeing the rule of God in greater relations. In all his vast activi-

ties he never forgets the saints who have given their lives for the one who gave his life for them.

In one of his characteristically pessimistic poems A. E. Housman wrote:

> I promise nothing: friends will part;
>   All things may end, for all began;
> And truth and singleness of heart
>   Are mortal even as is man.[3]

Over against this you can put the everlasting faithfulness of God which is the hope of man.

[3] "I Promise Nothing: Friends Will Part," from *More Poems* (London: Jonathan Cape, 1936); and from *The Collected Poems of A. E. Housman* (New York: Henry Holt & Co., 1940). Used by permission of The Society of Authors as the Literary Representative of the Trustees of the Estate of A. E. Housman, and of the publishers.

sackcloth of hair, and the moon became as blood;

13 And the stars of heaven fell unto the earth, even as a fig tree casteth her untimely figs, when she is shaken of a mighty wind.

14 And the heaven departed as a scroll when it is rolled together; and every mountain and island were moved out of their places.

15 And the kings of the earth, and the great men, and the rich men, and the chief captains, and the mighty men, and every bondman, and every free man, hid themselves in the dens and in the rocks of the mountains;

16 And said to the mountains and rocks, Fall on us, and hide us from the face of him that sitteth on the throne, and from the wrath of the Lamb:

17 For the great day of his wrath is come; and who shall be able to stand?

quake; and the sun became black as sackcloth, the full moon became like blood, 13 and the stars of the sky fell to the earth as the fig tree sheds its winter fruit when shaken by a gale; 14 the sky vanished like a scroll that is rolled up, and every mountain and island was removed from its place. 15 Then the kings of the earth and the great men and the generals and the rich and the strong, and every one, slave and free, hid in the caves and among the rocks of the mountains, 16 calling to the mountains and rocks, "Fall on us and hide us from the face of him who is seated on the throne, and from the wrath of the Lamb; 17 for the great day of their wrath has come, and who can stand before it?"

like a scroll (cf. 21:1) and every mountain and island was moved from its position (cf. 16:18). Earthquakes were a common occurrence both in Asia Minor and in Revelation (cf. 8:5; 11:13, 19; 16:18). A number of these same omens precede the day of the Lord in Joel 2:10,

> "The earth quakes before them,
>   the heavens tremble.
> The sun and the moon are darkened,
>   and the stars withdraw their shining."

The falling of the stars like figs and the rolling up of the heavens like a scroll were predicted in Isa. 34:4. However, almost the same sequence as in vss. 12-14 is found in an apocalyptic source, the Assumption of Moses 10:4-6: An earthquake occurs; the sun is eclipsed; the moon turns to blood; the circle of the stars is disturbed; and the sea disappears and the rivers dry up. It is possible, therefore, that for his series of cosmic woes John has not drawn directly from the prophets mentioned, but has followed a traditional pattern. These cosmic disturbances, both celestial and terrestrial, are a sure sign that the end of this age is drawing close, that the martyrs will soon be avenged for their sufferings.

15-17. These terrible signs on earth and in heaven cause all people on earth, from the highest to the lowest, both free and slave, to be filled with great fear. In their fright they vainly seek safety by fleeing to the caves and rocks of the mountains, calling to the

17. *The Wrath of Love.*—The picture of destruction after the opening of the sixth seal is full of frightfulness. Men knew something of volcanoes, something of earthquakes. They had seen what they doubtless called falling stars. But at the summons of the justice of God these became the very order of life. Nature went mad and all its orderly life turned to chaos. But the disorder and the chaos were held in the firm hand of God. The Creator and the Redeemer

had set loose this cosmic storm. The world was united in the awful democracy of a terrible expectation of doom. Rank lost its meaning; social distinctions lost their meaning. Only the black dread held men together in a strange fellowship amid the destruction of worlds. And the hand that unleashed all this was a hand that had been nailed to the cross. The wrath is the wrath of the Lamb and it turns out to have a more final and awful menace than the wrath

7 And after these things I saw four angels standing on the four corners of the
earth, holding the four winds of the earth,
that the wind should not blow on the
earth, nor on the sea, nor on any tree.

2 And I saw another angel ascending
from the east, having the seal of the living
God: and he cried with a loud voice to
the four angels, to whom it was given to
hurt the earth and the sea,

7 After this I saw four angels standing at
the four corners of the earth, holding
back the four winds of the earth, that no
wind might blow on earth or sea or against
any tree. 2 Then I saw another angel ascend
from the rising of the sun, with the seal of
the living God, and he called with a loud
voice to the four angels who had been given

---

mountains to fall on them so as to hide them from the **face** of God and the **wrath of the Lamb.** They realize that **the great day of their wrath,** which no one can withstand or escape, has arrived.

G. Interlude: Sealing of the Martyrs (7:1-8)

7:1. Before the end of this age actually arrives, a great persecution will bring the number of the martyrs to the necessary total (cf. 6:11). Consequently there is a cessation of woes until those who are to become martyrs are sealed. For this reason **the four angels at the four corners of the earth** hold back **the four winds,** causing a temporary pause in the infliction of plagues on the peoples of the world.

According to a cosmology probably derived from the Babylonians, the earth was considered to be a square, with an angelic watcher of each of the four winds stationed at each corner. The idea of these four winds as destructive agents of God is found in a number of the apocalypses: e.g., in Dan. 7:2-3 the four winds of heaven broke upon the sea, causing the four fearful beasts of destruction to appear; in the Syriac Apocalypse of Peter, God warns that when he looses the four winds, brimstone will go before the sea wind, a flaming fire before the south wind, and mountains and rocks will be broken in two by the west wind (the effects of the fourth wind are not mentioned). According to the Apocalypse of Pseudo-John 15, God promises that he will permit four great winds to sweep the face of the earth from one end to the other so as to cleanse it from sin. In another source, the Questions of Bartholomew 4:31-34, four angels are set over the four winds to restrain them lest they destroy the earth. Nor should we forget that the archetypes of the four destroying horses with their riders in 6:1-8 are the four chariots of Zech. 6:1-8, which are identified with the four winds. The probable relationship of the four living creatures to the four winds should also be recalled (cf. 4:6).

2-3. While the winds are being restrained, another angel appears from **the rising of the sun,** bearing **the seal of the living God.** He orders the angels restraining the four winds not to permit them to do any harm until the **servants,** or slaves, of God have been **sealed** on their **foreheads.** This scene is similar to one in II Baruch 6:4–8:1. Four angels were about to set fire to the city of Jerusalem to keep it from falling into the idolatrous hands of the Babylonians (i.e., the Romans), when a fifth angel appeared and stayed their hands until the sacred objects of the temple were removed and safely hidden. When

---

of a lion. When love turns to white anger there is indeed something to fear.

Whittier was a mild and gentle Quaker poet, but when he felt that Daniel Webster had betrayed his country he wrote the poem "Ichabod" with words full of majestic irony and biting condemnation:

> he who might
> Have lighted up and led his age,
> Falls back in night.
>
> *   *   *   *   *   *   *   *

> Of all we loved and honored, naught
> Save power remains,—
> A fallen angel's pride of thought,
> Still strong in chains.

> All else is gone; from those great eyes
> The soul has fled:
> When faith is lost, when honor dies,
> The man is dead!

In these words of the gentle poet we get a suggestion of the wrath of the Lamb.

3 Saying, Hurt not the earth, neither the sea, nor the trees, till we have sealed the servants of our God in their foreheads.

power to harm earth and sea, **3** saying, "Do not harm the earth or the sea or the trees, till we have sealed the servants of our God

---

this had been accomplished, he ordered them to set fire to the city. However, in Revelation, even though we are led to believe from the statement in vs. 3 that the angels will be permitted to release the four destroying winds when the sealing is accomplished, this is not done (but cf. 9:15). This is but one of the several loose ends which are not caught and tied up by the author.

Neither the sealing nor the **seal** is described. However, some assistance in understanding this scene may be obtained from similar ones in other sources: e.g., we read in Isa. 44:5 that converts to Judaism will inscribe the name of Yahweh upon their hands as a sign that they are his. We are also reminded of the blood of the Passover lamb, which was sprinkled on the doorposts of the Jews so that their first-born would not be killed by the destroyer (Exod. 12). A brief statement in II Esdras 6:5 indicates that the faithful were sealed before creation to ensure their bliss in messianic times. A closer parallel is provided by the incident in Ezek. 9:1-8. Six men (angels) are prepared to destroy the inhabitants of Jerusalem for their sins, but before they begin their work of destruction, a seventh marks the foreheads of the righteous and the repentant with ink so that they will not be slain. Similarly, in Pss. Sol. 15:8 the righteous receive a mark on their foreheads to preserve them from the plagues of famine, sword, and pestilence, which God is to inflict upon the wicked who are also marked so that they can be identified. In a Talmudic version the righteous are to be marked with ink, the wicked with blood (Shabbath 55a). Also, according to II Esdras 2:38, the predetermined number of "confessors" had been sealed before the end.

It is possible that John was thinking along similar lines in connection with the sealing of the prospective martyrs, indicating that those who are sealed belong to God, that they are his slaves. Consequently this sealing acts as a phylactery, or supernatural protection, against the series of plagues which are to devastate the world, in conformity with the promise in 3:10. As an additional feature, not apparent in the parallels, it may serve to guard the faithful against the demonic forces (cf. 9:4), particularly during the reign of the Antichrist which is to come.

Does it have any connection with baptism, which was also called sealing? Certain resemblances are to be seen other than the use of the same term. Baptism not only marked the recipient as belonging to God, but it also protected him from Satan and his demons. In addition, as a sacrament it ensured immortality to the baptized, or at least it was a prerequisite to eternal life. It is quite probable that the sealing in Revelation, although it is not the same as baptism, performed this same important function. While it could not and did not keep the Christian from suffering or from a martyr's death, it would secure a blessed immortality for those who were sealed, i.e., for the martyrs-designate.

The **seal** itself may have been a sacred name, like that inscribed on the white stone which was to be given to the martyrs (2:17) or like those on the pillars in the temple

---

7:3. God's Care for His Servants.—The bitter thing about the worst storms of life is that men are likely to lose the thought of God in the storms. In the midst of all this swirling destruction how dare they believe that God keeps his eye upon those who are true to him and that whatever happens to them he gives them the inner victory of his presence? The cataclysm the man of Patmos is describing is likely to destroy the faith of the saints as well as the pride of

the sinners. So a mighty angel with the direct authority of God restrains the angels of destruction **till we have sealed the servants of our God upon their foreheads.** Every saint now bears upon his forehead the mark of God. So acknowledged by God they can go through any woe walking with triumphant feet.

It is only in the faith that they have been sealed by God that men can go through the worst days of testing without surrender and

4 And I heard the number of them which were sealed: *and there were* sealed a hundred *and* forty *and* four thousand of all the tribes of the children of Israel.

5 Of the tribe of Juda *were* sealed twelve thousand. Of the tribe of Reuben *were* sealed twelve thousand. Of the tribe of Gad *were* sealed twelve thousand.

6 Of the tribe of Aser *were* sealed twelve thousand. Of the tribe of Nephthalim *were* sealed twelve thousand. Of the tribe of Manasses *were* sealed twelve thousand.

7 Of the tribe of Simeon *were* sealed twelve thousand. Of the tribe of Levi *were* sealed twelve thousand. Of the tribe of Issachar *were* sealed twelve thousand.

8 Of the tribe of Zabulon *were* sealed twelve thousand. Of the tribe of Joseph *were* sealed twelve thousand. Of the tribe of Benjamin *were* sealed twelve thousand.

upon their foreheads." 4 And I heard the number of the sealed, a hundred and forty-four thousand sealed, out of every tribe of the sons of Israel, 5 twelve thousand sealed out of the tribe of Judah, twelve thousand of the tribe of Reuben, twelve thousand of the tribe of Gad, 6 twelve thousand of the tribe of Asher, twelve thousand of the tribe of Naph'ta-li, twelve thousand of the tribe of Ma-nas'seh, 7 twelve thousand of the tribe of Simeon, twelve thousand of the tribe of Levi, twelve thousand of the tribe of Is'sa-char, 8 twelve thousand of the tribe of Zeb'u-lun, twelve thousand of the tribe of Joseph, twelve thousand sealed out of the tribe of Benjamin.

---

which symbolize the martyrs (3:12). This surmise is reinforced by one of the final scenes in which the martyrs receive the divine name on their foreheads (22:4). To be sure, John represents the sealing as occurring in the present age, and the inscribing of the divine name on their foreheads in the next; but since John frequently is indifferent to the details of chronology, it could be that the former is thought of as being, in a sense, an anticipation of the latter.

4-8. The number of those sealed is given as **a hundred and forty-four thousand,** with **twelve thousand** from each of the twelve tribes of Israel. This is the total number of martyrs that must be completed before the prayers of those in heaven can be answered (cf. 6:11). More than likely John has used a Jewish source in which the saints are members of the Jewish nation from each of the twelve tribes. Whatever the source, he has allegorized the twelve tribes to signify the Christians, composed of every people and nation (cf. vs. 9; 5:9), who are the true Israel (cf. Jas. 1:1; I Pet. 1:1); more specifically, they symbolize the whole company of martyrs, as in 14:1, where the identification seems certain.

The exact order of the tribes in this list is not of great significance. In the O.T. there are at least nineteen different arrangements; that in Revelation does not agree with any one of them. There may be some symbolism involved in the heading of this roll by Judah, since the Christ was from this tribe (cf. 5:5). Although in all save possibly one of the O.T. lists the tribe of Dan is included, it is omitted from this one. Irenaeus, writing near the end of the second century, observed that this omission was due to the belief that the Antichrist was to come from the tribe of Dan (*Against Heresies* V. 30. 2). That such a tradition was current earlier is evident from a statement in Test. Dan 5:6 that Beliar, a form of the Antichrist, will come from this tribe. Furthermore, in Jewish tradition Dan came to be associated with that greatest of sins, idolatry, which was one of the marks of the Antichrist (cf. Judg. 18:30; Genesis Rabbah 43:2; Targ. Jer. I on Exod. 17:8).

---

with heads held high. The Covenanters in Scotland kept many great and good things alive through long and difficult days. They are conspicuous examples of the faith in God's sealing of those who are to meet terrible experiences.

They were sure that God had called them to a great work and that he would make them strong enough to do it whatever disaster came with the day and whatever tragedy came with the night.

9 After this I beheld, and, lo, a great multitude, which no man could number, of all nations, and kindreds, and people, and tongues, stood before the throne, and before the Lamb, clothed with white robes, and palms in their hands;

10 And cried with a loud voice, saying, Salvation to our God which sitteth upon the throne, and unto the Lamb.

9 After this I looked, and behold, a great multitude which no man could number, from every nation, from all tribes and peoples and tongues, standing before the throne and before the Lamb, clothed in white robes, with palm branches in their hands, 10 and crying out with a loud voice, "Salvation belongs to our God who sits

H. Interlude: The Glorified Martyrs in Heaven (7:9-17)

9-12. The scene shifts rapidly from the sealing of the martyrs to become a proleptic tableau of the entire company of the glorified and victorious martyrs in heaven, where they await the consummation soon to occur. They are not only from the twelve tribes of Israel, which have been used allegorically, but are from all nations and tongues (cf. 5:9). They are no longer under the altar, praying for vengeance, but are in the blessed presence of **God who sits upon the throne** and of **the Lamb.** They have their **white robes** of immortality which had been promised them (cf. 3:5); they carry **palm branches,** the symbol of victory and thanksgiving (cf. I Macc. 13:51; II Macc. 10:7; John 12:13; Leviticus Rabbah 30:2), and they sing a victorious song of praise. The scene is practically duplicated in II Esdras 2:42-48. Ezra is shown a multitude of confessors, who had previously been sealed in Mount Zion, the heavenly Jerusalem, before God and his Son. They were dressed in their garments of immortality, were given crowns and palms, and praised the Lord with songs. The song sung by the martyrs in Revelation is one of praise to God and the Lamb for the salvation and glorious victory which they are to enjoy soon. Whereupon the heavenly choir, consisting of the angels, the four living creatures, and the twenty-four elders, falling on their faces before the throne and worshiping God, respond with a highly liturgical sevenfold doxology beginning and ending with **Amen.**

---

9. *The Vast Assembly of the Redeemed.*—There is always something arresting and suggestive about a great crowd. To Jesus a multitude of people suggested a crowd of bewildered sheep having no shepherd. In the book of Revelation multitudes are sometimes seen as those committed to evil. We now see a vision of the innumerable **multitude** of the redeemed. If the book of Revelation were a purely literary work we would say that it is all done with great art. After scenes of tragic calamity and before others of equal terror we are carried forward to the ultimate felicity. It is an interlude which brings the greatest possible emotional and spiritual relief. From this vision men will come back to days of hard endurance with renewed fortitude and hope. The numberless multitude of victors comes **from every nation** and from every language. The salvation of God gathers up from every land and people those who have fought a good fight. As the O.T. prophet who thought that he was alone found that thousands had not bowed the knee to Baal, so the Christian finds that untold multitudes will share his endurance and his victory. In many a century Christians have dreamed of the great consummation. Bernard of Cluny in the twelfth century sang of

the "sweet and blessed Country." [4] In the nineteenth century Henry Alford wrote:

> The armies of the ransomed saints
> Throng up the steeps of light. [5]

Christianity has deep sources of joy in the great expectation.

10. *The Anthem of Redemption.*—All those from every nation and language who have entered into the happy consummation realize that they owe their felicity to the regnant God and to the Christ who died upon the Cross. So they sing the glorious song of the redeemed. These outbursts of song are characteristic of the book of Revelation. Indeed, in spite of all the tragedy which it describes, it may be said to be one of the very happiest books ever written. The music of eternity sends its triumphant joy back into the life of time. The justification of glorious Christian music in this world is always justification by faith—faith in the loving justice of the reign of God, faith in the achievement of the Cross, faith in the final fulfillment of eternity. The writings of Paul also have this

[4] "The Celestial Country."
[5] "Ten thousand times ten thousand."

11 And all the angels stood round about the throne, and *about* the elders and the four beasts, and fell before the throne on their faces, and worshipped God,

12 Saying, Amen: Blessing, and glory, and wisdom, and thanksgiving, and honor, and power, and might, *be* unto our God for ever and ever. Amen.

13 And one of the elders answered, saying unto me, What are these which are arrayed in white robes? and whence came they?

14 And I said unto him, Sir, thou knowest. And he said to me, These are they

upon the throne, and to the Lamb!" 11 And all the angels stood round the throne and round the elders and the four living creatures, and they fell on their faces before the throne and worshiped God, 12 saying, "Amen! Blessing and glory and wisdom and thanksgiving and honor and power and might be to our God for ever and ever! Amen."

13 Then one of the elders addressed me, saying, "Who are these, clothed in white robes, and whence have they come?" 14 I said to him, "Sir, you know." And he said to me, "These are they who have come out

The **power** and **might** which God possesses are now to be openly displayed. The Lamb is not specifically included in this doxology, but this is doubtless an unintentional omission, since for John God and the Lamb are essentially one in power.

13. Lest the reader fail to identify this glorious multitude in heaven before the throne, John introduces a dialogue. This is characteristic of apocalypses (cf. II Esdras 2:42-48 for a very similar situation). John writes that one of the elders asked him the identity of those who were **clothed in white robes.** When John professed ignorance, the elder replied in what may be termed a martyrological hymn of four strophes, or stanzas, each strophe consisting of one long and two shorter lines. In the RSV vss. 15-17 are arranged in poetic form in three stanzas of this character, but vs. 14 should have been treated by the typographer in the same fashion, for it is an integral part of the whole.

14. In this first stanza the elder identified this group as the persons who had come out of **the great tribulation,** i.e., here in an anticipatory presentation is the total group of martyrs whose predestined number is to be completed in the last and greatest persecution.

characteristic of bursting into song. You can judge an interpretation of the Christian religion by its capacity to set men singing. There is something wrong about a theology which does not create triumphant music.

12. *Angelic Praise.*—Over against the anthem of the redeemed is the praise of countless angels. They fling themselves **on their faces** in a mighty act of worship. In a rolling tide of praise they ascribe every imaginable **blessing** and **power** and **honor** to God. They represent heaven's answer to earth's praise. All the vast, unknown voices of the heavenly country are united in praise to God. When we attempt to go beyond any possible human knowledge we are in a precarious region. But there is something deeply satisfying in the thought of the heavenly voices and their rich and full ascription of praise to God. At the end of the War Between the States when men and women in many homes where there were empty chairs were casting their eyes eagerly toward the unknown country, Elizabeth Stuart Phelps Ward wrote *Beyond the Gates* [6] in an attempt to answer these cries of the human heart. It is

[6] Boston: Houghton, Mifflin & Co., 1883.

better, one suspects, not to try to fill out the details of the picture. The greatest word which has been uttered is probably Paul's "to depart and be with Christ, for that is far better" (Phil. 1:23). Then there are the wonderful pictures in the book of Revelation.

14. *Tribulation Not the Journey's End.*—We have here something more than pain recollected in tranquillity. We have pain recollected in triumph. The triumph is dazzling, but the memory of the pain is remembered in heaven. It is one of the mighty elders who has seen all from a throne in heaven who brings to mind the sufferings of the human beings who are a part of the heavenly host. The memory of their endurance is cherished in the bright land when, for themselves, agony has been lost in eternal joy. There is something very tender in this thought of heavenly memory of earthly pain. The lonely sense of being forgotten which has tempted many a man in hours of pain is corrected by the thought of the heavenly memory.

Once a group of martyrs arrived at the entrance of the beloved country. The guardian of the gate said to them: "God has given much to you. Have you brought any gift for Him?"

which came out of great tribulation, and have washed their robes, and made them white in the blood of the Lamb.

15 Therefore are they before the throne of God, to serve him day and night in his temple: and he that sitteth on the throne shall dwell among them.

of the great tribulation; they have washed their robes and made them white in blood of the Lamb.

15 Therefore are they before the throne of God,
    and serve him day and night within his temple;
    and he who sits upon the throne will shelter them with his presence.

John envisaged this final **tribulation** as occurring in the immediate future during the reign of the Antichrist.

These glorified saints are the faithful who **have washed their robes and made them white in the blood of the Lamb.** This statement is a reiteration of the theme that the salvation and victory of the martyrs are made possible because Christ, the first martyr, had been victorious through his death (cf. 1:5). It should also be remembered that the martyrs are saved to some degree by the shedding of their own blood—a baptism by blood, as it were.

15. Some of the eternal blessings which the martyrs are to enjoy are described in poetic language in the three remaining stanzas. They will be permitted to stand **before the throne of God** and will be a company of priests who **serve him day and night in his temple,** a repetition of an earlier promise in 1:6 and 5:10 that they would become priests. This is somewhat inconsistent with the later statement that there will be no temple in the New Jerusalem (21:22). God in turn **will shelter them with his presence;** i.e., his Shekinah, his divine presence, will overshadow and protect them (cf. Ezek. 37:27). This prospect reaches fulfillment in 21:3, when God makes his dwelling with men.

"Only our pain," said the martyrs, "and that is nothing compared with Christ's suffering for us." "Yet it is a good gift," said the guardian, "and you are doubly welcome as comrades of the cross."

14. Preparation for Heaven.—The triumphant saints represent change in character as well as change in circumstance. The change in circumstance sees the oppressed on earth enjoying the freedom and the victory of heaven. The change in character is represented by the washed robes. They wear their new character like a robe which has been washed until it is white and shining. Garments very often represent something very different from the character within. In this case the outer whiteness perfectly represents an inner whiteness. New men live in a new world. A good many social utopias rest on the idea that a new environment will produce a good and happy life. Even such a book as Martin Buber's *Paths in Utopia,*[7] in many ways a searching study of the difference between a utopia based on coercion and a utopia making room for freedom, never faces the problem of the making of individual men capable of living in utopia.

14. The Poured-Out Life and the New Men. —The book of Revelation is packed with the-

[7] Tr. R. F. C. Hull (London: Routledge & Kegan Paul, 1949).

ology. And it is already theology become warm and glowing Christian experience. It is an item of great significance that all this could be made the basis of assured appeal to everyday Christians at the time when the book of Revelation was written. The power of the deed on Calvary to remake men is a very important concern in the Christian religion. It is expressed in the powerful figure which speaks of **the blood of the Lamb.** The figure has been seized with great avidity by evangelistic piety. And we have vivid hymns about being washed in the blood. It is to be hoped that we will not allow the crude phraseology of some of these hymns to hide the truth which, sometimes quite inadequately, they so vigorously express. It is indeed true that the very life poured out on the Cross enters the lives of men to make them something different from what they were. The new man in Christ is far more than a figure of speech. There are many aspects to the thought of the blood of the Lamb. We shall need them all as we study the inner potency of the great redemption.

15. In the Divine Presence Serving God.— The new men are now in the very presence of God. What they are has become completely responsive to that divine light. In the very secret citadel of worship they serve God perpetually. The divine felicity is not merely enjoyment, but an opportunity to render service.

16 They shall hunger no more, neither thirst any more; neither shall the sun light on them, nor any heat.

16 They shall hunger no more, neither thirst any more;
the sun shall not strike them, nor any scorching heat.

16-17. The last two stanzas are largely an obvious adaptation of a prediction made in Isa. 49:10, "They shall not hunger nor thirst; neither shall the heat nor sun smite them: for he that hath mercy on them shall lead them, even by the springs of water shall he guide them," with an allusion made, perhaps, to Ps. 23. In keeping, therefore, with this alluring expectation in Isaiah, the martyrs will never **hunger** nor **thirst;** they will never be stricken again by the **sun,** nor with blazing **heat.** By a curious shift in symbolism, the **Lamb . . . will be their shepherd,** leading them **to springs of living water.** Finally, they shall have no more sorrow, for the elder (vs. 13), echoing Isa. 25:8, assures them that **God will wipe away every tear from their eyes.**

Even in heaven there is glorious work to do for God. And this work is done always under the divine Taskmaster's eye. That heavenly approval is one of the deepest joys of heaven. Even in the celestial country:

Our God is still the God of might
In deeds, in deeds he takes delight.

The difference between lovely literary expression of ideals and profound spiritual convictions is seen when we compare this picture of the heavenly felicity with some lines in Lowell's "Aladdin":

When I was a beggarly boy
And lived in a cellar damp,
I had not a friend nor a toy,
But I had Aladdin's lamp;
When I could not sleep for cold,
I had fire enough in my brain,
And builded, with roofs of gold,
My beautiful castles in Spain!

It is one thing to have the glow of a creative imagination. It is a richer and firmer thing to have full faith in the Christian consummation.

15. *Eternal Security.*—H. F. M. Prescott's brilliant story of early sixteenth-century England, *The Man on a Donkey,*[1] pictures the North-Country rebellion in the time of Henry VIII and has to do with the "Pilgrimage of Grace." The utter and tragic insecurity of those who dared to stand for justice is revealed on many a page. In the last war the underground movement in France is the tale of men and women who risked their lives day by day and hour by hour and whose insecurity was often turned to sudden death. History is full of such stories. They may be told of dauntless Christians living dangerously in many an age. Those for whom the book of Revelation was written knew all about such insecurity. It was for their

encouragement that the picture was painted of the victorious saints forever sheltered by the very presence of the living God. They lived in a time when a throne threatened them—they looked forward to a time when a throne would protect them.

16. *Deliverance from Unsatisfied Desire.*—The desires which are now considered are essentially legitimate. They are represented by **hunger** and **thirst.** They are the desire for food and the desire for that drink which is essential to the ongoing of life. Men have died of hunger and thirst rather than be false to convictions which were dearer to them than life. Hunger and thirst became starvation. Men were enduring just such privations when the book of Revelation was written. Lacking here that which is necessary to life, they are promised a time when there shall be no such lack. Hungry here, they are given the sight of a land where there will be no more hunger. Thirsty here, they are given sight of a land where there will be no unsatisfied thirst. There are good desires which are not physical—hungers for knowledge, thirsts for fellowship. There are desires for a life of the spirit which is life indeed. And all these desires will be satisfied in the great fulfillment.

Alexander Pope in his "Essay on Man" wrote:

Hope springs eternal in the human breast:
Man never is, but always to be blest:
The soul, uneasy, and confined from home,
Rests and expatiates on a life to come.[2]

The vague outreach in these charming lines is in sharp contrast to the glowing sense of reality which characterizes the picture of the life to come which we are now studying. In the book of Revelation hopes half-analyzed and scarcely understood have a way of coming to shine with clear reality.

[1] London: Eyre & Spottiswoode, 1952.

[2] Epistle I.

17 For the Lamb which is in the midst of the throne shall feed them, and shall lead them unto living fountains of waters: and God shall wipe away all tears from their eyes.	**17** For the Lamb in the midst of the throne will be their shepherd, and he will guide them to springs of living water; and God will wipe away every tear from their eyes."

It is known that the Christians at a somewhat later period composed and used martyrological hymns to indoctrinate prospective martyrs and prepare them for their ordeals of arrest, trial, sufferings, and death (cf. D. W. Riddle, *The Martyrs* [Chicago: University of Chicago Press, 1931], pp. 48-49, 155). One of this type may possibly have been preserved in II Tim. 2:11-13. John apparently had a somewhat similar purpose of indoctrination and preparation in mind in presenting this hymn which outlines the marvelous eternal blessings of the New Jerusalem awaiting those Christians who will accept death rather than betray their God and Christ. The glories of the New Jerusalem are given in greater detail in chs. 21–22, but the picture is basically that depicted in this hymn.

---

17. Intimate Personal Guidance.—In the book of Revelation sometimes we find something like sheer delight in complex figures. Here **the Lamb** which was the Sacrifice is **in the midst of the throne.** He has come to a place of supreme power; but by a sudden turn of thought he is also the **shepherd** of the victorious saints. He guides them with an intimacy like that of a shepherd for his flock of sheep. He is the Sacrifice and the Ruler and the Shepherd all in one. Sometimes scholars shy away from the richness of the N.T. revelation. Those who emphasize the great sacrifice of Christ do not always have much to say about his triumphant reign. And those who speak of the kingdom of God do not always have much to say about the tender and gracious intimacy of the divine guidance. Even when a mixed metaphor is involved, the book of Revelation insists on presenting the richness and the many-sidedness of God's relation to men. That the thought of the shepherd emerges with that of the sacrifice and the ruler gives one in a sudden vista a new sense of the intimate kindness of God. Coleridge once wrote a little poem about a dead child:

Thou in peace, in silence sleeping,
In some still world, unknown, remote,
The mighty parent's care hast found,
Without whose tender guardian thought,
No sparrow falleth to the ground.[3]

Stately interpretations of the Christian religion are strangely lacking if they have missed the sense of the tenderness of God.

17. Exhaustless Vitality.—With obvious reference to the twenty-third psalm we are told that **the Lamb** who is a **shepherd . . . will guide** the victorious saints **to springs of living water.** "He leadeth [them] beside the still waters" is changed to "he guides them to fountains of life." The exhaustless vitality of the Christian religion is one of its essential, characteristic qualities. Here this quality is projected into eternity. The saints shall ever be drinking of springs of living water. The great Guide knows sources of the water of life which will not fail. In time and in eternity these fountains flow without ceasing.

That fine poet Thomas S. Jones, Jr., wrote a sonnet dealing with David's longing for water to drink from the well of Bethlehem and then of his refusal to drink water for which brave men had risked their lives.

But he heeds not, in thirsting for the spring
That holds no taste of tears, whose waters sing
Sweeter than trumpets of all Israel.[4]

It is the springs that have no taste of tears to which the shepherd leads his willing followers in the great fulfillment.

17. The Land Where Tears Are Only a Memory.—The picture of men who have forgotten how to weep is full of comfort for those who dwell in our tear-drenched world. In heaven tears have no future, they have only a past. And the tears are wiped from the eyes which are to weep no more. God himself is the great comforter. Here again we have a picture in which the individual with his passion and pain comes to his own. No sorrowing heart is lost in the mighty movement of eternity. No tearful eye is forgotten in the glory of the great consummation. And the men who read these words would quickly see that the God who remembers the individual in eternity would not forget his

³ "Morienti Superstes,"

⁴ "David: II. The King's Well" from *Akhnaton and Other Sonnets* (Portland, Me.: Mosher Press, 1928), p. 22.

8 And when he had opened the seventh seal, there was silence in heaven about the space of half an hour.

2 And I saw the seven angels which stood before God; and to them were given seven trumpets.

8 When the Lamb opened the seventh seal, there was silence in heaven for about half an hour. 2 Then I saw the seven angels who stand before God, and seven

---

J. SEVENTH SEAL: PREPARATION FOR THE SEVEN TRUMPET WOES (8:1-6)

8:1. After these two interludes the Lamb now opens the seventh seal. The stage is set for the culminating act in the apocalyptic drama, for the reader might reasonably expect that the catastrophes following the opening of the first six seals would be followed immediately by the conquest of Satan, the end of this age, the resurrection, and final judgment. This is, in fact, the sequence of events in the Apocalypse of Pseudo-John 19–23. In that work, with the opening of the first seal the stars of heaven fall; of the second, the moon is hidden; of the third, the light of the sun is withheld; of the fourth, the heavens are dissolved; of the fifth, the earth is rent; of the sixth, half of the sea disappears; and of the seventh, Hades itself is uncovered. Then the end is at hand, the resurrection occurs, and the final judgment takes place. But not so in Revelation: the opening of the seventh seal is but the necessary prelude to a second series of woes, those of the seven trumpets.

When the seal is broken, there is a pregnant period of **silence in heaven for about half an hour.** Since the purpose of this silence is not stated, the explanation of it must be looked for elsewhere. In the Talmudic work, Hagigah 12ᵇ, the ministering angels sing praises by night, but are silent during the day so that the praises uttered by Israel may be heard. Consequently, it has been proposed that this **silence** is to permit God to hear the praise of the saints and their prayers for justice. Or perhaps its meaning is illustrated by a passage in II Esdras 7:30 in which a seven-day period of primeval silence, during which no man will be alive, intervenes between this age and the age to come, i.e., just as there were seven days for the creation of the first age, there is to be a corresponding period for the creation of the new. This parallel, however, does not explain the half-hour duration of the silence in Revelation. Possibly the most that can be definitely stated is that it is a dramatic pause preceding the new set of calamities that are to ensue.

2. When the silence ended, John saw **the seven angels who stand before God.** Strangely enough, these seven angels have not been mentioned before, unless, as is probable, they are the "seven spirits" before the throne of 1:4 and 4:5. In any event,

---

sorrowful way amid the tragedies of time. There are no tears which God does not see. There are no sorrowing hearts to which his compassion does not reach out. When we see that the reign of God is secure, all sorrow becomes temporary. "Weeping may endure for a night, but joy cometh in the morning" (Ps. 30:5). The sagas of Iceland are full of a courage which, in its own way, gives the lie to tragedy. The sagas of the Christian life also have their tales of moral and spiritual triumph in tragedy. But they press beyond tragedy to the tearless joy of God's own land. There is a shining glory in the Christian hope.

8:1. The Meanings of Silence.—From the vision of the ultimate felicity we come back to days of judgment. The Lamb opens **the seventh** and last **seal.** Before the terrific events which follow **there was silence in heaven for about half an hour.** Neither heaven nor earth is lost in the mere rush of overwhelming events. Times of quiet as well as times of action go to make up the reign of God. The silence of brooding apprehension, the silence of deep and meditative thought, the silence of the pursuit of understanding, the silence of the appropriation of the meaning of revelation, make up a significant part of life. That master of seminal silence Gaius Glenn Atkins is the author of a book with the title *Pilgrims of the Lonely Road.*[5] It tells of men who, whatever their activities, found time for the brooding silence out of which understanding comes. Something of the spiritual grace and loveliness of Atkins' own mind enters these studies. You see men in the deepest places of thought asking profound questions about life and its meaning and finding insights of ripe wisdom. Such books are fine

[5] New York and London: Fleming H. Revell, 1913.

3 And another angel came and stood at the altar, having a golden censer; and there was given unto him much incense, that he should offer *it* with the prayers of all saints upon the golden altar which was before the throne.

4 And the smoke of the incense, *which came* with the prayers of the saints, ascended up before God out of the angel's hand.

trumpets were given to them. 3 And another angel came and stood at the altar with a golden censer; and he was given much incense to mingle with the prayers of all the saints upon the golden altar before the throne; 4 and the smoke of the incense rose with the prayers of the saints from the

they are ministering angels carrying out God's will and commands. They are given **seven trumpets,** but by whom is not stated.

The trumpet, occasionally mentioned as heralding the day of the Lord or the messianic reign, came to have eschatological significance as well, i.e., in connection with the final judgment. In the Apocalypse of Abraham 31, following a series of ten woes, a trumpet sound will announce the coming of the Elect One to summon the righteous, and to burn the wicked who have insulted them and ruled them in this present age. According to another source, the appearance of a sword and trumpet will signify the coming of the final conflagration that will destroy this world (Sibylline Oracles 4:174). In still another account a trumpet sound, filling all men with fear, will announce the final judgment (II Esdras 6:23). We also read in a Christian work, the Book of John the Evangelist, that after the number of the righteous has been completed, an archangel will herald the coming of a series of dreadful plagues by blowing a trumpet. Likewise, in a variant text of the Apocalypse of Pseudo-John 28, the archangel Raguel will sound a trumpet to summon the angels of cold, snow, and ice to bring destruction upon the wicked. Similarly, when the seven trumpets of Revelation are blown in succession, they will produce additional plagues, one after the other, as God's judgment upon the world in answer to the prayers of the martyrs.

3-5. Before they are sounded, there is a scene similar to that of 5:8 prior to the breaking of the seven seals. In this earlier situation, when the Lamb had taken the scroll, the four living creatures and the twenty-four elders held "golden bowls full of incense," the "prayers of the saints," symbolizing the fact that the opening of the scroll of doom will be an answer to their petitions. This tableau is repeated, but with variations. An unidentified angel mingled **incense** with the **prayers of all the saints** in a **golden censer** which he placed on the **golden altar** which was **before the throne.** The smoke of this mixture of **incense** and **the prayers of all the saints** ascended as an offering to God. That these prayers are similar in content to those of the martyrs under the altar who besought God to "judge and avenge" their blood (6:10) must be assumed.

Although this angel is not specifically identified as an archangel—indeed he is probably not one of the seven—nevertheless it is important to observe that in Jewish

and stalwart foes of the hot and superficial action which stifles thought.

3. The Rich Splendor of Worship.—The vision of the seven seals is succeeded by the vision of the **seven trumpets.** The new series is inaugurated by the opening of the seventh seal. But there is another interlude while the angel of worship appears. Quantities of **incense** are mingled with the ascending **prayers of all the saints.** And what goes up from the earth as prayer returns as fire from heaven. Prayer sets the pace for mighty actions which are suggested by volcanoes and storms and earthquakes, but

first of all prayer and incense combine in glorious and magnificent worship. It is remarkable that in the midst of all the rushing movement of the book of Revelation there is always time to set each particular experience in rich and noble perspective. The hour of worship has its own rights amid all the heavenly events. Even God's judgments are not apart from the saints. They include the prayers of the saints. And the odor of the incense, like the fragrance of the alabaster box the woman broke in honor of Jesus, fills all heaven with the sweet awesomeness of worship. Indeed worship has its own

5 And the angel took the censer, and filled it with fire of the altar, and cast *it* into the earth: and there were voices, and thunderings, and lightnings, and an earthquake.

6 And the seven angels which had the seven trumpets prepared themselves to sound.

7 The first angel sounded, and there followed hail and fire mingled with blood, and they were cast upon the earth: and the third part of trees was burnt up, and all green grass was burnt up.

hand of the angel before God. 5 Then the angel took the censer and filled it with fire from the altar and threw it on the earth; and there were peals of thunder, loud noises, flashes of lightning, and an earthquake.

6 Now the seven angels who had the seven trumpets made ready to blow them.

7 The first angel blew his trumpet, and there followed hail and fire, mixed with blood, which fell on the earth; and a third of the earth was burnt up, and a third of the trees were burnt up, and all green grass was burnt up.

---

writings archangels are represented as intercessors for men with God, sometimes conveying their petitions to him. Thus Raphael is one of the seven holy angels who present the prayers of the saints to God (Tob. 12:15). In Test. Levi 3:5-6 the archangels make propitiation before the Lord "for all the sins of ignorance of the righteous, offering to the Lord a sweet-smelling savor" (cf. Test. Dan 6:2). On another occasion, when the martyrs were crying out to God for a cessation of the lawless deeds on earth, Michael, Uriel, Raphael, and Gabriel take their prayers to God (I Enoch 9:1-11; cf. 99:3). Finally, from III Baruch 11:1-9 we learn that Michael receives the prayers of men and takes them to God along with a large vessel containing the works and merits of the righteous. Clearly, it is from patterns of thought like these that John has obtained his concept of an angel who receives the prayers of the martyrs and presents them to God mingled with incense. The main difference between these verses and the passage in I Enoch 9:1-11 is that John's portrayal is far more colorful and dramatic.

5. After the prayers had ascended to God, the angel filled the censer with **fire from the altar** and **threw it on the earth**. Whereupon there occurred **peals of thunder, loud noises, flashes of lightning**, reminiscent of the theophanies of 4:5 and Exod. 19:16, giving assurance that God was there and had heard their earnest supplications. In addition, there was **an earthquake**, a token that their petitions would soon be answered.

6. **The seven angels** next prepared to **blow** their **trumpets**. Thus the woe of the seventh seal is sevenfold, for it produces the woes of the seven trumpets. By this ingenious device the author relates the two series of calamities to each other.

V. SEVEN TRUMPET WOES (8:7–11:15)

A. FIRST TRUMPET: HAIL AND FIRE (8:7)

7. With the sounding of the first trumpet, **hail and fire mingled with blood** rained down upon the earth, so that **a third of the earth** (wrongly omitted by the KJV), **a third of the trees**, and all the **green grass** were consumed by fire. This woe is ultimately

---

rights not to be forgotten in heaven or in earth. And the golden hour of worship has something to do both with the making and with the expression of Christian character.

Great enterprises have had a good beginning when their origin was associated with worship. The first book printed in America was the *Bay Psalm Book,* published in 1640. It was made for public worship. The colonists sang lustily

The heavens doe declare
the majesty of God.[6]

[6] Psalm 19.

The Lord reigns, cloth'd with majesty.[7]

Make yee a joyful noyse unto
Jehovah, all the earth.[8]

So in a setting of worship a new state was born.

7. *The Doomed Land.*—As the seven trumpets are blown terrible acts of doom come from the seat of judgment. As we follow the visions of these deeds of doom we realize how important it is to see them against the background of the picture of heavenly felicity which has preceded

[7] Psalm 93.
[8] Psalm 100.

8 And the second angel sounded, and as it were a great mountain burning with fire was cast into the sea: and the third part of the sea became blood;

8 The second angel blew his trumpet, and something like a great mountain, burn-

---

derived from the seventh of the ten plagues inflicted on the Egyptians, when a rain of fire and hail "smote every herb of the field, and brake every tree of the field," in addition to inflicting severe damage upon men and cattle (Exod. 9:13-26). According to a midrash on Ps. 2:9, a third of all the world's woes will come in the days of the Messiah, a view of partial destruction that may be reflected in this verse. We have noted several times (e.g., on 5:6) that the plagues of Exodus preceding the deliverance of the Israelites from their Egyptian oppressors served as a prototype for the plagues that are the precursors of the deliverance of the Christians, the true people of God, from their persecutors the Romans.

B. Second Trumpet: Burning Mountain Falls into Sea (8:8-9)

8-9. When the second trumpet sounded, what appeared to be **a great mountain, burning with fire,** was cast **into the sea** so that a third of it became **blood,** and a third of the **creatures** in the sea were killed, and a third **of the ships were destroyed.** This is a combination of the first Egyptian plague, in which the water in the river, streams, and wells was turned to blood, so that all the fish died and no one could drink the water (Exod. 7:14-25), with an astral phenomenon in which a huge star fell into the sea like a burning mountain. In I Enoch 18:13 seven stars like burning mountains fell into the sea; these are later identified as seven fallen angels who are to be punished for their disobedience to God (I Enoch 21:3 ff.; cf. 108:3-6). Another source relates that fiery swords (quite likely stars) will fall to earth, so that the fish in the sea, as well as all animals and men, will shudder, the sea itself will tremble, and the rocks will flow with blood (Sibylline Oracles 3:672-84). In this same work another great star will fall into the sea and destroy it, along with Babylon (Rome) and Italy, as a punishment for the oppression of the Jews by the Romans (Sibylline Oracles 5:158-61; cf. 512-31). On the basis of these

---

them. When **the first angel** blows **his trumpet** doom falls upon the lands where men dwell. Fire destroys the earth, the trees, and the green grass. It is **a third of the earth** to which this ruin comes. Men of bad hearts discover that ruin has come upon their world. Evil men cannot depend upon a good environment for a just God controls the environment. The doom is great enough to arouse their terror yet not conclusive enough to destroy their hope. Something is taken; but much is left. Opportunity remains in the midst of doom; but where doom strikes, the land becomes uninhabitable.

You get a sense of the sort of destruction involved in this vision when you think of the eruption of Vesuvius which overwhelmed the city of Pompeii and which is described in Bulwer-Lytton's *Last Days of Pompeii.* The vision extends this sort of doom to great sections of the earth.

8. The Doomed Sea.—We are not to think of the sea of which the man of Patmos speaks in the terms of modern oceans with mighty ships moving from continent to continent. Such a vision was beyond the range even of his far-traveling eye. But men of the sea did travel from port to port in that ancient world. And in a sense the sea became their partner in business. This partnership was to be dissolved. **The second angel blew his trumpet** and a fiery mountain fell **into the sea; and a third of the sea became blood.** Life in the parts of the sea so affected came to an end, and the ships in these regions were destroyed. The fishes and the ships represented two aspects of man's partnership with the sea. This partnership was broken. But again the doom was only in part; it did not yet affect the whole. Again opportunity remained in the midst of tragic destruction. It is made clear, however, that the power of God's judgment for destruction extends over far regions. The dark and turbulent and mysterious sea can be used as a vehicle for the action of his justice in dealing with recalcitrant men. If the power of Rome was sweeping over vast areas, the power of God extended over regions even more vast.

When we think of man's experience in dealing with the sea we are likely to think of the stories of Joseph Conrad who spent twenty years as sailor and officer and who knew the mystery and the fascination, the beauty and

9 And the third part of the creatures which were in the sea, and had life, died; and the third part of the ships were destroyed.

10 And the third angel sounded, and there fell a great star from heaven, burning as it were a lamp, and it fell upon the third part of the rivers, and upon the fountains of waters;

11 And the name of the star is called Wormwood: and the third part of the waters became wormwood; and many men died of the waters, because they were made bitter.

ing with fire, was thrown into the sea; 9 and a third of the sea became blood, a third of the living creatures in the sea died, and a third of the ships were destroyed.

10 The third angel blew his trumpet, and a great star fell from heaven, blazing like a torch, and it fell on a third of the rivers and on the fountains of water. 11 The name of the star is Wormwood. A third of the waters became wormwood, and many men died of the water, because it was made bitter.

passages it is conceivable that this heavenly body of Revelation like **a great mountain, burning,** which turned a third of the sea to blood, represents a fallen angel expelled from heaven to wreak destruction on the world.

C. Third Trumpet: Blazing Star Falls into Sea (8:10-11)

10-11. When the third angel blows his trumpet, a great blazing **star** (probably another fallen angel) falls **on a third of the rivers** and **on the fountains of water.** Its name was **Wormwood** (*Apsinthus*) and it caused the rivers and fountains to become **bitter** and poisonous, so that many people died, though actually wormwood, while bitter, is not poisonous. This scene, quite clearly, is a variant of the preceding one, and indicates that the object which looked like a burning mountain was actually a falling star. In both instances John has neglected to explain how a star can fall from a heaven that had been rolled up like a scroll, as was stated in 6:14. No star or fallen angel named Wormwood can be found in any other source. John may have obtained the inspiration for this name from Jeremiah, who warns that God will give his people wormwood and gall to drink to chastise them for turning to idolatry (Jer. 9:15; cf. 23:15) .

the tragedy, of the sea. Or we might think of Herman Melville's *Moby Dick.*[9] The man of Patmos sees the sea as subject to the judgment of God.

9. The Doomed Commerce.—When we have read many tales of brutal lawlessness at sea we are likely to be pursued by the thought, which sometimes comes to the men of the sea themselves, that somehow they live in a region which God has left beyond his control. Coleridge, in the *Rime of the Ancient Mariner,* has given immortal expression to the thought of God pursuing his purposes at sea. When the man of Patmos describes the destruction of **a third of the ships** he is saying that men's commerce at sea is under the control of God. They cannot pursue the ways of their merchandising as if God did not exist; or if they do, they will find that they have made a bitter mistake. The destruction of the ships is a parable of the justice of God at work among the men who do business in great waters.

10-11. The Doom of the Waterways.—The sounding of the **third . . . trumpet** brings the

[9] New York: The Modern Library, 1944.

falling of a fiery star. According to the meaning of its name this star called **Wormwood,** which **fell into a third of the rivers and on the fountains of water,** makes sweet water become bitter and poisonous. The men who drink the water die. The men who try to live without God find the very sources of ongoing life contaminated. When they have turned to wickedness they have tampered with something much more profound and powerful than they have known. They did not know that they were attacking the very water supply upon which their lives depended. How the star Wormwood accomplished its work of destruction we are not told. Enough that a heavenly power in fiery potency comes down from the heights to ruin the water upon which evil men depend for the very life which they are misusing. The ruin is tragic, but it is incomplete. There is still opportunity as well as doom. What we are being told is that there is nothing untouched by the power of God.

In every country as it passed from the first conquest of nature the waterways were the first highways. A great historian has spoken of this

12 And the fourth angel sounded, and the third part of the sun was smitten, and the third part of the moon, and the third part of the stars; so as the third part of them was darkened, and the day shone not for a third part of it, and the night likewise.

13 And I beheld, and heard an angel flying through the midst of heaven, saying with a loud voice, Woe, woe, woe, to the inhabiters of the earth by reason of the other voices of the trumpet of the three angels, which are yet to sound!

12 The fourth angel blew his trumpet, and a third of the sun was struck, and a third of the moon, and a third of the stars, so that a third of their light was darkened; a third of the day was kept from shining, and likewise a third of the night.

13 Then I looked, and I heard an eagle crying with a loud voice, as it flew in midheaven, "Woe, woe, woe to those who dwell on the earth, at the blasts of the other trumpets which the three angels are about to blow!"

D. Fourth Trumpet: Darkening of Sun, Moon, and Stars (8:12)

12. When the fourth angel sounded his trumpet, a third of the light of the sun, moon, and stars was darkened. Curiously enough, instead of diminishing the light throughout the day and night by one third, this calamity caused one third of the day and one third of the night to be without any light. This woe is a variation of that of the sixth seal (6:12-13), when the sun was totally eclipsed, the moon turned to blood, and the stars fell from heaven.

E. Interlude: The Eagle's Warning (8:13)

13. There is a pause as an **eagle** flying in midheaven pronounces a threefold **woe** upon the inhabitants of earth because of the calamities that are to follow the blowing of the next three trumpets. The incongruity of an eagle speaking in this manner may have caused the substitution of **angel** (KJV), an incorrect reading, even though in

situation in describing the untamed forest as king. But the rivers made it possible to travel through the untamed forest before roads were made, and rivers have remained highways even after the building of roads. Rivers and springs have had much to do with the life and the welfare of man. And these, says the man of Patmos, are subject to the reign of God.

12. *The Doom of the Stars.*—The reign of God includes the sun and the moon and the stars. It rises from the earth to include the heavens. When **the fourth angel blew his trumpet** the judgment of God struck the heavenly bodies. **A third of their light was darkened.** A third of the day became a starless night. And the night, for a third of it without moon or stars, became black indeed. The writer rushes on with his symbols without any regard for what we would call the realm of scientific fact. Of course our world of science did not exist for him, but he managed with his own symbols to characterize God's use of the heavenly bodies for his purposes in conducting the righteous rule of men. It is to be noted that in this picture the sun and the moon and the stars are seen only in relation to God's judgment of men. The question of other possible relationships is not raised. The book of Revelation always, for

the moment, sees each matter it is discussing as if it were the only matter in the world.

In the classical eighth psalm the sight of the heavenly bodies at first almost crushes man with a sense of his own insignificance. But soon the psalmist sees that man is created a little lower than God and crowned with glory and honor. He is over nature and under God. The book of Revelation preserves this sense of the dignity of man. The sun and the moon and the stars are used for the purpose of meting out justice to man. His wickedness involves the stars as instruments of punishment. The whole vast universe is one under the government of God. Men and stars are both a part of the divine rule.

A different note is struck by Matthew Arnold:

"Ah, once more," I cried, "Ye Stars, Ye Waters,
On my heart your mighty charm renew:
Still, still, let me, as I gaze upon you,
Feel my soul becoming vast like you!" [1]

The book of Revelation goes beyond the stars to the God of the stars.

13. *The Proclamation of Woe.*—The bird of doom flies through the sky. The **blasts of the remaining trumpets which the three angels are**

[1] "Self-Dependence."

9 And the fifth angel sounded, and I saw a star fall from heaven unto the earth: and to him was given the key of the bottomless pit.

9 And the fifth angel blew his trumpet, and I saw a star fallen from heaven to earth, and he was given the key of the shaft

---

14:6-7 it is an angel who utters a similar warning. That eagles could speak in apocalyptic writings is shown in II Esdras 11:7-9, where the eagle, symbolizing the Roman Empire, called out as it flew, though the voice came from its body, not from one of its three heads. Also, another eagle was chosen to deliver a letter of warning to the nine-and-a-half tribes (II Baruch 77:17-26). It is possible that this eagle in Revelation is the living creature with an eagle's head (cf. 4:7).

F. Fifth Trumpet: Plague of Demonic Locusts (9:1-12)

9:1. When the fifth trumpet was blown, another **star** fell from heaven to earth and was given **the key** to the opening of **the bottomless pit.** This star, quite evidently, stands for an angel, a concept that needs no further comment, since it has become a commonplace in Revelation. This falling star is not a fallen angel who has disobeyed God, as some have suggested, but is obviously an angel of God carrying out his divine will. More than likely he is the angel of 20:1, who has the key to this same **bottomless pit.** In I Enoch 19:1 and 20:2, Uriel is named as the archangel in control of the abyss.

This **bottomless pit** or abyss is not Hades or Sheol, the temporary dwelling of the spirits of the dead. Neither is it the place of final and eternal punishment, which in Revelation is the lake of fire, the equivalent of Hell or Gehenna. It is, however, underground, like these other localities, and has a narrow shaft or opening with a lid or door that can be closed and locked. Like Hell, Gehenna, and the lake of fire, it is a fiery place (vs. 2). Further, it is a region where evil spirits dwell under a ruler, or leader, called Abaddon or Apollyon (vs. 11). Moreover, Satan is to be consigned there for a thousand years before he is cast into the lake of fire. It is similar to the bottomless abyss, in which, according to I Enoch, fallen angels and others are kept for temporary punishment and which is described in I Enoch 18:12—21:7 as waterless, horrible, chaotic, and

---

about to blow will bring cumulative woe to the world. The hostile empire had brought woe to Christians. The hostile universe is to bring woe to the foes of the Christians in all their far-flung, wicked ways. The conclusive word is spoken not by Rome but by God, and that word is a word of terror to all who have enmeshed themselves in ways of evil. The eagle was used as an ensign of the Roman army. In a sense it was the symbol of the Roman power. But the **eagle . . . in midheaven** represents the power of God. It brings a judgment beyond the conception of any Roman emperor. The suffering caused by evil powers is answered by the coming of suffering upon those evil powers themselves.

The situation where men received encouragement from the thought of the woe which will fall upon vast evil powers has been strangely repeated in our own time. The tale of the inhumanity of totalitarian powers to man has never been completely told. It would fairly stagger the reason if it were put in one terrible book. But it gives the undercurrent of anxious fear to the life of our times. With such widespread and remorseless flaunting of justice can

justice itself survive? Apocalyptic injustices give men an ear for the proclamation of apocalyptic woes.

9:1. *The Underworld of Horror.*—The book of Revelation is very daring. It sees God not only as the King of heaven and earth, of stars and men, but it sees him as the Master of all those evil forces which, with all their malignant hatred of good, must unwillingly become the instruments of the divine will. There is nothing good or evil in the universe which escapes the will of God. There is a dark background to the thought of the most civilized men which comes from the long history of evil and deception and superstition in the world. This was particularly true at the time when the book of Revelation was written. John Buchan, in that strange book *Witch Wood,*[2] told of the dark forces invading the lives of men who would have called themselves civilized and Christian. The man of Patmos is not speaking in this passage as a critic of these things but as one who would bring help to human hearts. Whatever dark forces exist, he declares, are under the complete

[2] London: Hodder & Stoughton, 1927.

2 And he opened the bottomless pit; and there arose a smoke out of the pit, as the smoke of a great furnace; and the sun and the air were darkened by reason of the smoke of the pit.

3 And there came out of the smoke locusts upon the earth: and unto them was given power, as the scorpions of the earth have power.

4 And it was commanded them that they should not hurt the grass of the earth, neither any green thing, neither any tree; but only those men which have not the seal of God in their foreheads.

of the bottomless pit; 2 he opened the shaft of the bottomless pit, and from the shaft rose smoke like the smoke of a great furnace, and the sun and the air were darkened with the smoke from the shaft. 3 Then from the smoke came locusts on the earth, and they were given power like the power of scorpions of the earth; 4 they were told not to harm the grass of the earth or any green growth or any tree, but only those of mankind who have not the seal of God

---

fiery. S. J. Case has aptly suggested that the picture of this underground abyss may have been inspired by the thought of a volcano, with its crater leading down to the underworld, emitting smoke, fire, and sulphurous fumes. No more suitable place for evil spirits could be imagined (*The Revelation of John* [Chicago: University of Chicago Press, 1919], pp. 279-80).

2-3a. When the angel opened the shaft, smoke rose up in such dense clouds as to obscure the sun. Out of the clouds of smoke came swarms of **locusts upon the earth**. This plague of locusts is suggested in part by the eighth Egyptian plague in which locusts were so numerous as to cover the earth (Exod. 10:4-15), and in part by the devastating locust swarms of Joel 1:2-11; 2:1-11, which are precursors of the day of the Lord.

3b-6. But these are not ordinary locusts, like those of Exodus, for they possess a sting like **scorpions**. Moreover, whereas the locusts of Exodus destroyed all the vegetation (Exod. 10:15), as did those of Joel 2:3, these are forbidden to harm grass or trees or any other green plants. Instead, for a period of **five months** they are to sting and torture all

---

control of God. He holds **the key of the shaft of the bottomless pit**. Even the deep and dark and unanalyzed sources of fear and terror have no power to erupt and overthrow God. They are completely under his control. Indeed it is only those who have given themselves to evil whom they can harm.

3. *The Myth of the Malicious Locusts.*— We are now in the midst of a brilliant piece of mythological symbolism. Actual locusts represent a sort of impersonal destructiveness. These symbolical **locusts** with their golden **crowns** and their **human faces** and their feminine grace and their **lions' teeth** and their **breastplates** like warriors and their movement like the charge of war horses represent intentional personal malice with great power to destroy. **They have** stinging **tails like scorpions**, which they use with terrible effect. From the depths of concentrated evil they come to do their awful work. The power of imagination is pressed to the limit to describe these loathsome creatures of hate and malice. There is no tendency here to describe evil as a sort of confused and bewildered good. You would not try to have a peace congress with the locusts. You would not try by refined methods

of appeasement to win them over to your side. They are the very essence of malignant malice moving out on a career of destruction.

As you look at the locusts you are not tempted to say: "To understand all is to forgive all." You have a sense of evil stark and unrelieved. When such evil gets into human beings you have characters like Shakespeare's Iago and Browning's Count Guido Franceschini. The important thing is to remember that the locusts represent not a mere nightmare but something which, with dark and malignant purpose, manages to enter the world of men.

4. *The Immunity of the Saints.*—The description of the torturing of the wicked, **those of mankind who have not the seal of God upon their foreheads**, is, in its way, a tribute to the immunity of the saints and represents in an indirect way the safety of those who truly belong to God. The stinging tails can harm only those who have something in themselves which corresponds to the poison which the tails carry. Men of good will may have suffering enough, but there are some things which they never suffer. They are never torn by the dark suspicions of the treacherous who, being false them-

5 And to them it was given that they should not kill them, but that they should be tormented five months: and their torment *was* as the torment of a scorpion, when he striketh a man.

6 And in those days shall men seek death, and shall not find it; and shall desire to die, and death shall flee from them.

7 And the shapes of the locusts *were* like unto horses prepared unto battle; and on their heads *were* as it were crowns like gold, and their faces *were* as the faces of men.

8 And they had hair as the hair of women, and their teeth were as *the teeth* of lions.

upon their foreheads; 5 they were allowed to torture them for five months, but not to kill them, and their torture was like the torture of a scorpion, when it stings a man.

6 And in those days men will seek death and will not find it; they will long to die, and death flies from them.

7 In appearance the locusts were like horses arrayed for battle; on their heads were what looked like crowns of gold; their faces were like human faces, 8 their hair like women's hair, and their teeth like

---

mankind, i.e., all who do not have **the seal of God upon their foreheads** (cf. 7:3) ; they are to torture, but not to kill them. However, the torment will be so great that the victims will long to die. The faithful, who are sealed, will escape this dreadful and painful scourge. Why is it to last **five months?** No definite answer can be given. Perhaps this was to give the wicked time in which to repent, for contrary to the determinism of Revelation, in vs. 20 it is stated that this is the purpose of these plagues.

7-10. The locusts of Joel 1:2-11 are evidently to be considered as real locusts, but in ch. 2 the prophet changes them into a host of mythical monsters which look and act like supernatural cavalry in battle array. As they swarm over the land these harbingers of the terrible day of the Lord lay it waste as though with fire; the earth quakes, and sun, moon, and stars are darkened (Joel 2:1-12) . Elaborating upon the prophet's portrayal of doom, John likewise depicts his locusts as winged cavalry **horses** prepared for battle, with human faces, long hair like a woman's, lions' teeth (cf. Joel 1:6), **iron breastplates,** and stings in their scorpionlike tails possessing power to torture men for five months. As a sign of their conquering power they wear golden **crowns** on their heads. All this is

---

selves, expect falsehood in others. They are never shaken by the corrosive fears of the betrayers who, being ready to put their heel on the neck of others, bitterly anticipate the same treatment which they would give. Every evil enshrined in a human heart prepares the way for the reception of some new stinging poison. So what the locusts bring is really the self-destructiveness of evil released with torturing power. God's seal upon the forehead is the outer symbol of an inner rightness. The stinging locusts fly all about but they have no power over those fortified with inner good will. When Jesus was before Pilate the Roman governor had a curious sense that he could not reach the prisoner. He had a sense of hollowness and inner futility as he talked to Jesus of his power. The soul of Jesus was beyond the reach of imperial authority. In every age those really captured by the spirit of Jesus have given men this sense of an inner life beyond the reach of malignant attack. Again and again the lines of Richard Lovelace have been verified:

Stone walls do not a prison make,
Nor iron bars a cage.[3]

6. *The Longing for Extinction.*—The wish for death in the midst of agony is really a desire for extinction. It were better not to exist than to endure such pain. At a certain stage physical agony produces an end of thought. There is only a longing to have all this come to an end in the oblivion of nonexistence. That strange man Søren Kierkegaard in one of his curiously involved pieces of argument in *The Sickness Unto Death* wrote:

the torment of despair is precisely this, not to be able to die. . . . When death is the greatest danger, one hopes for life; but when one becomes acquainted with an even more dreadful danger, one hopes for death. So when the danger is so great that death has become one's hope, despair is the disconsolateness of not being able to die.[4]

[3] "To Althea from Prison."
[4] Tr. Walter Lowrie (Princeton: Princeton University Press, 1946), p. 25.

9 And they had breastplates, as it were breastplates of iron; and the sound of their wings *was* as the sound of chariots of many horses running to battle.

10 And they had tails like unto scorpions, and there were stings in their tails: and their power *was* to hurt men five months.

11 And they had a king over them, *which is* the angel of the bottomless pit, whose name in the Hebrew tongue *is* Abaddon, but in the Greek tongue hath *his* name Apollyon.

12 One woe is past; *and,* behold, there come two woes more hereafter.

lions' teeth; **9** they had scales like iron breastplates, and the noise of their wings was like the noise of many chariots with horses rushing into battle; **10** they have tails like scorpions, and stings, and their power of hurting men for five months lies in their tails. **11** They have as king over them the angel of the bottomless pit; his name in Hebrew is A-bad′don, and in Greek he is called A-pol′lyon.[b]

12 The first woe has passed; behold, two woes are still to come.

[b] Or *Destroyer.*

---

another interesting example of the way in which John not only appropriates but transforms his sources, adapting them to his own special interests and purposes.

11. These demonic locusts have a **king** over them who is designated as **the angel of the bottomless pit.** Is this the star-angel with the key who opened the pit to release them? (Vss. 1-2.) This is possible, for in I Enoch 19:1 and 20:2 an archangel, Uriel, is named as the archangel in control of the abyss. However, this identification is by no means a certain one, since the keeper of the pit and the king of the locusts need not be one and the same. He is given the Hebrew name **Abaddon** or the Greek equivalent **Apollyon.** The word **Abaddon** means "destruction" or "ruin" (Job 31:12); it is used as the equivalent for "death" in Job 28:22; for the "grave" in Ps. 88:11; for "Sheol," the temporary dwelling of the dead, in Job 26:6 and Prov. 15:11; 27:20; and for Gehenna, the region of the damned in Erubin 19a and Shabbath 89a. The transition whereby Abaddon becomes **the angel of the bottomless pit** and the ruler of the supernatural **locusts** is not a difficult one for John to make.

As for the Greek name **Apollyon,** in the LXX Abaddon is regularly rendered as Ἀπώλεια, "destruction," so that Apollyon (Ἀπολλύων) is essentially the Greek equivalent of the Hebrew. Because of the similarity, some see in this a slighting reference to the god Apollo and through him to the claims of the emperors to divine status, since Augustus considered himself to be under the protection of Apollo, even calling himself his son, and successors of Augustus thought of themselves as being closely related to the sun god. **Abaddon,** however, is an angel not of Satan but of God, performing his work of destruction at God's bidding.

12. The phrase **the first woe has passed** is puzzling if considered in connection with the entire series of trumpet woes, but if related to the eagle's warning of three to come (cf. 8:13), it should present no special difficulty. The first of these is now over, but two more are to come.

The book of Revelation is more direct. Agony can produce such a state that only the longing for nonexistence remains, and that longing is not satisfied. The suffering lasts for a clearly defined period. With its cessation there is the possibility of honest thought and repentance.

11. *The Angel of Destruction.*—The malicious locusts are seen under the dominion of **the angel of the bottomless pit** whose name both in Hebrew and in Greek signifies "one who destroys." It seems just a little odd that the name does not appear in Latin as that vast

empire is always in the background of thought in the book of Revelation. In any event the thought of these particular malignant forces is seen as going beyond the realm dominated by Hebrew thought and including that larger world of understanding which came into existence when the conquests of Alexander carried Greek culture everywhere. It is notable that though the name of the angel is **Destroyer** the locusts cannot destroy. They can only hurt. The activities of the angel of destruction are held firmly in the control of one higher than himself.

13 And the sixth angel sounded, and I heard a voice from the four horns of the golden altar which is before God,

14 Saying to the sixth angel which had the trumpet, Loose the four angels which are bound in the great river Euphrates.

15 And the four angels were loosed, which were prepared for an hour, and a day, and a month, and a year, for to slay the third part of men.

16 And the number of the army of the horsemen *were* two hundred thousand thousand: and I heard the number of them.

13 Then the sixth angel blew his trumpet, and I heard a voice from the four horns of the golden altar before God, 14 saying to the sixth angel who had the trumpet, "Release the four angels who are bound at the great river Eu·phra′tes." 15 So the four angels were released, who had been held ready for the hour, the day, the month, and the year, to kill a third of mankind. 16 The number of the troops of cavalry was twice ten thousand times ten thousand; I heard

G. Sixth Trumpet: Destroying Horsemen from the Euphrates (9:13-21)

13-14. The sixth trumpet plague seems to be a variation of the fifth, especially of the second scene of the latter (vss. 7-11), and may have some connection with the four horses and their riders of 6:1-8. When the sixth angel blew his trumpet, a **voice** from the **altar** before God ordered him to release **the four angels** who were bound at **the great river Euphrates.** This order may be in response to the prayers of the martyrs in 8:3 before the sounding of the first trumpet. A similar situation is depicted in 14:18, when the angel of the altar commanded another to use his sickle, whereas in 16:7 the altar itself speaks, commending God for his judgments.

15. In compliance with this order the **four angels** who had been bound at the Euphrates for this specific time were released. Once more the determinism of the apocalyptic drama comes into evidence. Are these the four angels at the four corners of the earth who were told to hold back the four devastating winds of heaven until the faithful had been sealed? (7:1-3.) This could well be, for a small detail such as the change in locality to the Euphrates would present no difficulties to John. Also, there may be some connection with the four horses and riders of 6:1-8. Whatever these relationships may be, now that the faithful have been sealed, these four angels are unbound that they might **kill a third of mankind.**

16-19. They are the leaders of a vast host of supernatural cavalry, **twice ten thousand times ten thousand** in number. It is the **horses,** not their richly caparisoned riders, that

John Kelman's brilliant interpretation of Bunyan's *Pilgrim's Progress* [5] contains an important chapter, "The Battle with Apollyon." Bunyan's Christian does not meet the locusts but he fights their king. Kelman puts much ripe wisdom into his account of the fight with Apollyon and the victory of Christian. Beyond all symbols it is important always to keep in mind the stark reality of the battle of good and evil in the human heart.

15.2. *More Forces of Destruction.*—The blowing of the **trumpet** by the **sixth angel** is the signal for the release of more forces of destruction. Beyond an actual invasion is seen the more terrible invasion of angels of destruction leading millions of troops and horses of fearful destruction. And now **a third of mankind** meets death. The locusts had been able

only to cause suffering—the new forces of destruction execute a sentence of death. Terror upon terror mounts in the description of the death of a third of mankind. In the most unmistakable fashion the man of Patmos is saying to hard-pressed Christians: "You should fear the justice of God who controls the universe and not Rome whose strength is weakness compared with the strength of God." In a way the whole passage is a study in the direction of the proper kind of fear. There are, we may say in the terms of our own life, hard and inescapable facts beyond that merely psychological peace of mind which so many of our contemporary restless men and women seek. The final way to deal with a feeling is to confront it by a fact. If all of a man's loyalties are wrong the fact of the reign of God will increase his fear and not decrease his anxiety. The ultimate facts of life are moral facts having to do with the rule of God. They are not political facts having to

[5] *The Road: A Study of John Bunyan's Pilgrim's Progress* (Edinburgh and London: Oliphant, Anderson, & Ferrier, 1912).

17 And thus I saw the horses in the vision, and them that sat on them, having breastplates of fire, and of jacinth, and brimstone: and the heads of the horses *were* as the heads of lions; and out of their mouths issued fire and smoke and brimstone.

18 By these three was the third part of men killed, by the fire, and by the smoke, and by the brimstone, which issued out of their mouths.

19 For their power is in their mouth, and in their tails: for their tails *were* like unto serpents, and had heads, and with them they do hurt.

20 And the rest of the men which were not killed by these plagues yet repented not of the works of their hands, that they should not worship devils, and idols of

their number. 17 And this was how I saw the horses in my vision: the riders wore breastplates the color of fire and of sapphire[c] and of sulphur, and the heads of the horses were like lions' heads, and fire and smoke and sulphur issued from their mouths. 18 By these three plagues a third of mankind was killed, by the fire and smoke and sulphur issuing from their mouths. 19 For the power of the horses is in their mouths and in their tails; their tails are like serpents, with heads, and by means of them they wound.

20 The rest of mankind, who were not killed by these plagues, did not repent of

[c] Greek *hyacinth.*

---

are deadly. They have lions' heads (cf. the lions' teeth of vs. 8) , and they kill their quota of men by the **fire and smoke and sulphur** which belch out of their mouths. The colors of the **breastplates** of the riders match those of the **fire, smoke, and sulphur** coming from the mouths of their mounts. (**Jacinth**—KJV—is a rather meaningless transliteration of the Greek.) Similar to the locusts with the scorpionlike tails, these **horses** had the power to **wound,** but not to kill, with their snakelike **tails.**

Like the composer who presents variations of the same motif in his symphony, so John delights in variations of the same theme, as is evidenced in this chapter. An additional example may be seen in 16:12-16, when another demonic invasion crosses the Euphrates.

20. Following the destruction and devastation in the wake of the locusts, Joel presents an appeal from God for sinners to repent (Joel 2:12-14) . It may be more than

---

do with any far-flung government among men. The tyrants of our own time become insignificant seen against the background of the justice of God. Much has been written about the power of the United States in our time. The inescapable question is this: "Will that power be exercised on the side of the justice of God?" The vision of the destruction let loose by the righteousness of God dwarfs the thought of any selfish human purposes among men or states.

18. The Study of Fractions in Moral History. —Again and again one deals with fractions in the book of Revelation. The fraction is always a symbol of the mercy of God. The calamity is not universal but always leaves those who can learn from tragic events. The picture is never one which attempts to deal with every aspect of the moral situation. These can be left to the ampler activity of God's administration. Indeed sometimes they are dealt with in later pictures of the rule of God. Here we see God striking and using instruments which are under his complete control. And after the tragedy

there are left multitudes who can benefit from its contemplation if they will. The reader of that vast work *A Study of History,*[6] by Arnold J. Toynbee, may often be confused by the march and countermarch of nations and civilizations, the rise and the fall of great powers, the relation of events to ideas and of actions to moral and spiritual principles. If he will he may see it as an attempted study on a large scale of what is really the administration of God. In a sense history is the tale of the rule of God. One always sees in fractions, but the fractions always have large significance for the whole. Toynbee's judgment may not always be wise but he is asking the great questions and he makes it easier to find dependable answers. When destruction comes to the fraction there are always left behind those who, if they will, may think and study and understand.

20. Men Who Will Not Learn from Experience.—"That man is quite impervious to the impact of facts," it was once said of a man

[6] (London: Oxford University Press, 1935-54), 10 vols.

gold, and silver, and brass, and stone, and of wood; which neither can see, nor hear, nor walk:

21 Neither repented they of their murders, nor of their sorceries, nor of their fornication, nor of their thefts.

the works of their hands nor give up worshiping demons and idols of gold and silver and bronze and stone and wood, which cannot either see or hear or walk; 21 nor did they repent of their murders or their sorceries or their immorality or their thefts.

---

coincidence, especially in view of the evident dependence of John upon Joel for his imagery of the locust-horses, that he too mentions repentance in these closing verses of the chapter. However, despite the manifestation of God's wrath, those who remained alive **did not repent** of their sins, chief of which was idolatry, the worship of **demons and idols of gold and silver and bronze and stone and wood, which cannot either see or hear or walk.** This is a conventional Jewish-Christian ridicule of idolatry based almost verbally, in this instance, on Dan. 5:23 (cf. I Enoch 99:6-7). John is not merely attacking idolatry in general, but specifically the imperial cult, with a warning of the punishments awaiting those who continue in its idolatrous practices. These idolaters indulge in murder, magic, theft, and fornication. We are later told (21:8) that the second death, the lake of fire, awaits those who persist in idolatry and its accompanying sins and vices.

---

who seemed never to be influenced by events, however important they were. The mass of mankind, according to the man of Patmos, was quite uninfluenced by the death of a third of the human race. To them applied the truth of the word that "there is none so blind as they that won't see." The O.T. prophets are all the while rebuking their people for failing to see what God was saying to them in events whose meaning should have been perfectly clear. The destruction of Jerusalem, for instance, left many of the people with old illusions and old confused ways of thinking undestroyed. Events which were tragic enough spoke with terrible insistence. But they were blind to the meaning of events. In the many volumes which he devoted to the study of men and women Gamaliel Bradford is deeply interested in their moral experiences. He is especially interested in those "Damaged Souls" who, in spite of many good characteristics, were deeply soiled by the evil of life.[7] It is remarkable how rarely he describes a man facing the meaning of his own moral experience and learning from it. Century after century men have confronted life with unseeing eyes and unhearing ears. It seems sometimes that loud speakers are shouting forth the meaning of events but that men refuse to listen to their words.

20. Helpless Images.—It must have greatly disconcerted Jeremiah when, after the destruction of Jerusalem (Jer. 44:15-25), he was with a remnant of his people in Egypt to discover that the women, aided and abetted by their husbands, were burning incense to alien gods. And they were quite ready to attempt to justify their worship of the queen of heaven. They

belonged to that great company of people who carry their illusions right through events which bring an almost overwhelming revelation. The man of Patmos scornfully catalogues the materials used in the making of the idols from which men refused to turn. From **gold and silver** to **stone and wood,** every sort of material was used; but there was no power in any of the idols. Perhaps men liked to worship them because they themselves had made them. There is a not too obscure fascination in making a god in your own image or at least a god created out of your own thoughts. And men chose to worship these helpless, lifeless creatures instead of the living God. It was unbelievable and yet it was true. Sometimes the prophet is reduced to awed bewilderment when he is confronted by men's blindness to that which stands clearly revealed before their eyes. Then he is reduced to utter humiliation as he finds traces of that same blindness in his own soul. The reign of things has replaced the reign of God.

21. Bad Deeds Follow Bad Worship.—Murder, black magic, every sort of sexual vice, and theft made up the practices of those in whose lives the God of goodness had no place. Every sort of evil grows in the soil of godlessness. And when great acts of judgment fall upon the world the people, enmeshed in their own evil ways, do not repent. They are likely to try some new magic, some new idolatry, instead of turning to the living God. All this is the consummation of a dark process which may be described in this fashion. At first men do evil deeds and the deeds are theirs; there is something in them which can sit in judgment upon the deeds of wickedness. But at last they become one—the men and their evil deeds are synonymous. They

[7] *Damaged Souls* (Boston: Houghton Mifflin Co., 1923).

10 And I saw another mighty angel come down from heaven, clothed with a cloud: and a rainbow *was* upon his head, and his face *was* as it were the sun, and his feet as pillars of fire:

10 Then I saw another mighty angel coming down from heaven, wrapped in a cloud, with a rainbow over his head, and his face was like the sun, and his legs

H. INTERLUDE: JOHN EATS THE SCROLL OF DOOM (10:1-11)

As the opening of the seventh seal was delayed by two scenes in ch. 7, so the blowing of the seventh trumpet must wait upon the scenes in 10:1-11:14. The tableau in ch. 10 is largely a rewriting of certain striking scenes in Ezek. 1-3. Accordingly, these O.T. passages will be briefly summarized.

Ezekiel relates that he saw the heavens opened, and a great cloud driven by a high wind came from the north flashing with light and glowing with an inner fire. As it drew near, the cloud was resolved into the throne of Yahweh. Yahweh himself was something like a man, but far more glorious. From the loins up he appeared like fiery amber, and from the loins downward like fire, with brightness all around him like a rainbow. After this marvelous theophany, God commissioned Ezekiel to prophesy against the rebellious children of Israel, and commanded him to eat a little scroll which he extended to him. The scroll, written on both sides, contained lamentations, mourning, and woe. Ezekiel did as he was told, and found the scroll sweet as honey in his mouth (Ezek. 2:8-3:3). By eating it he became possessed of its prophecies, so that his book is actually a reproduction of the heavenly one. It was sweet as honey in his mouth because he found its prophecies of doom against the wicked most acceptable. John's earlier dependence upon this section of Ezekiel has been noted before.

10:1. With this before us, as it was before the author, let us turn to his portrayal. Since 4:1 he has been writing as though he were in heaven, but apparently his position

do not repent. The practical evil is accepted without hesitation. No human life is safe if it cuts across a man's desire. He is ready to use lawless means for any desired end. A flash of gratification seems worth more than an eternal value. What belongs to other men is taken from them without a moment's hesitation. Walt Whitman indulged in the making of many catalogues which he delighted to roll from his lips. He never made a catalogue representing the grim realism of Rev. 9:21. The situation described may seem hopeless, but God allowed these people to survive. It must have meant that he was not without hope.

10:1. The Angel of Shining Glory.—The book of Revelation is a work of mighty interludes. We have seen a series of pictures representing progressive judgments. Now the note of the great consummation is sounded. The angel of shining glory is the announcer of the final victorious judgment of God. Over against the horror of the scenes through which we have passed is put a sudden vision of heaven's resplendent beauty and wonder. The colors of the rainbow surround a face full of eternal sunlight. The very limbs of the angel blaze with fiery magnificence. All this reflects the splendor of that celestial region of ultimate glory. There are writers who seem obsessed by the terrors of the book of Revelation and who have no eye for its immortal beauty. In a sense one finds what one brings in the book of Revelation. If one brings a mind of psychopathic pessimism one finds only judgment and horror. If one comes with an uncorrupted imagination one passes with joy from scenes of darkness to scenes of heavenly light. The book of Revelation is no product of a diseased imagination. It faces evil and ugly facts with unparalleled honesty. Then it passes into realms of light and song. And in between its darkest pictures are pictures shining with heavenly light. The poet William Blake, like the man of Patmos, always thought with his eyes. Pictures became golden ideas. He could write:

> Bring me my bow of burning gold!
> Bring me my arrows of desire.
> Bring me my spear! O clouds, unfold!
> Bring me my chariot of fire! [8]

He could also write:

> Father, O father! what do we here
> In this land of unbelief and fear?
> The Land of Dreams is better far,
> Above the light of the morning star. [1]

[8] "Milton."
[1] "The Land of Dreams."

2 And he had in his hand a little book open: and he set his right foot upon the sea, and *his* left *foot* on the earth,

3 And cried with a loud voice, as *when* a lion roareth: and when he had cried, seven thunders uttered their voices.

like pillars of fire. **2** He had a little scroll open in his hand. And he set his right foot on the sea, and his left foot on the land, **3** and called out with a loud voice, like a lion roaring; when he called out, the seven

---

has now shifted to earth, for he writes that he **saw another mighty angel** descending **from heaven.** This angel arrived in a **cloud,** as Yahweh did in Ezek. 1:4, but not as dramatically; and his appearance was reminiscent of that of Yahweh in Ezek. 1:27-28, for he had **a rainbow** on his head, **his face** shone **like the sun,** and **his legs** were **like pillars of fire** (cf. also Dan. 10:5-6; Apocalypse of Abraham 11).

2a. Like Yahweh in Ezek. 2:9, **he had a little scroll open in his hand,** which contained a prophecy of doom (cf. 5:1 and Exeg., *ad loc.*).

2b-3a. **He set his right foot on the sea, and his left foot on the land,** possibly to symbolize his mastery over all of the world, both **sea** and **land.** It was but to be expected that he should speak with **a loud voice;** but it is also said that he sounded like a **lion roaring.** The Messiah, according to II Esdras 11:37, roars like a lion; while in Amos 3:8 the voice of God himself was like that of a roaring lion, filling all people with fear and forecasting his divine punishment upon the sinful. This may be the significance of the lionlike voice of the angel.

3b-4. **When he called out, the seven thunders sounded**—which brings to mind that in the incident related in John 12:28-29, the voice of God sounded like thunder to some of the bystanders. However, a closer resemblance is to be found in Ps. 29:3-9, where the

---

The book of Revelation is always taking us above the light of the morning star.

2. *The Angel of Victorious Mastery.*—The angel of light and glory brings heavenly power for the mastery of land and sea. Heaven does business with earth. It comes in victorious splendor to master the world of men. This world is not apart from the heavenly light; it is suffused with the heavenly light. There is a kind of imperial majesty about the picture of the shining angel with **his right foot on the sea, and his foot on the land.** Rome may seek to bestride the earth, but it is heaven whose power really overtops the world. Time shrivels up in the presence of eternity. Rome shrivels up in the presence of the heavenly power.

The reader of that powerful book *Fire in the Ashes,*[2] by Theodore H. White, sees Europe in mid-century with anxious and sometimes with greatly startled eyes. In so many ways it is a world of burning tragedy. That tragedy affects all of mankind. America cannot live apart from it. The thoughtful reader, as he ponders it all, may chance to think of the angel with one foot on the sea and one foot on the land. And he will realize that this sense of a good and noble Lordship above the tragedies of this world is greatly needed in our time.

3. *The Wisdom of Heaven.*—The **seven thunders** are not merely sounds. They are voices representing the wisdom of heaven. Here

are words for which the man of Patmos has been waiting. There is so much that is temporary about the ripest words which men can hear. Something in all of us longs for words of utter finality. We would like to hear the speech beyond which there is no speech. We would like to look at the period at the end of the last great sentence in the universe. The very thought of the seven thunders of God causes something to vibrate in our own souls.

The most bitter thought of a complete skepticism is that there is no final wisdom. This ultimate skeptic presents us with a picture of the heavens not only silent but empty. "There are no voices," he says, "because there is no meaning." Sound is never more than sound; thunder is never more than thunder. Matthew Arnold knew how to express the mood of skepticism in haunting and sadly beautiful words:

The Sea of Faith
Was once, too, at the full, a round earth's shore
Lay like the folds of a bright girdle furl'd.
But now I only hear
Its melancholy, long, withdrawing roar,
Retreating, to the breath
Of the night-wind, down the vast edges drear
And naked shingles of the world.[3]

Utterly foreign to all this is the mood we find in the book of Revelation. The universe is full of meaning, a meaning great and glorious. It

[2] New York: Sloane, 1953.

[3] "Dover Beach."

4 And when the seven thunders had uttered their voices, I was about to write: and I heard a voice from heaven saying unto me, Seal up those things which the seven thunders uttered, and write them not.

5 And the angel which I saw stand upon the sea and upon the earth lifted up his hand to heaven,

thunders sounded. 4 And when the seven thunders had sounded, I was about to write, but I heard a voice from heaven saying, "Seal up what the seven thunders have said, and do not write it down." 5 And the angel whom I saw standing on sea and land lifted

---

sevenfold voice of God, which seemed like thunder, had powerful effects on both sea and land. More than likely we are to consider that these **seven thunders** are the voice of God proclaiming the doom of the world. John was about to transcribe what the **seven thunders** had revealed, but for some reason he is ordered to **seal up** what he had heard and not to **write it down.** This is somewhat strange, for up to now John has been more than willing to relate what he has seen and heard. Possibly he considered the **seven thunders** as prophecies of doom which should not be revealed to mankind until later (as in Dan. 12:9); but they are not set forth later in this book.

5-7. In Dan. 12:6, when the angel who was above "the waters of the river" was asked how long it would be before the end arrived, he held up both his right and left hands to heaven and "sware by him that liveth for ever" that it would come in a "time, times, and a half." With this as an exemplar, John writes that the mighty angel raised **his right hand to heaven and swore by him who lives for ever and ever,** and by the creator of heaven, earth, and sea, and all that were in them, that **there should be no more delay.**

---

gets itself expressed. To one who understands, the seven thunders are luminous speech.

4. *The Urge to Communicate.*—The man of Patmos understood the seven thunders. He fairly tingled with a sense of their meaning; and he **was about to write.** One of the greatest things about mankind is this deep urge to find expression for that which is clear and sure within. We were not meant to be Robinson Crusoes of the mind in lonely isolation, cherishing thoughts which are never expressed. We are not meant to live on lonely islands having no true commerce of the mind with other men. Not idly has the book of the man of Patmos been called the book of Revelation. His deepest desire is to communicate all that he has learned of the truth of God and of the ways of God with men. So the moment he becomes possessed of a new insight he desires to write it down for the perusal of others.

As men grow older they often lose this eager desire to communicate. The eager outreach for fellowship with other minds somehow ceases. Too often age builds its own walls of isolation, incomprehensible to youth. In this sense, at least, the Christian who amply and continuously experiences the true quality of his own religion has found the fountain of perpetual youth. He is always eager to communicate.

4. *The Inarticulate.*—The startling command comes to **seal up what the seven thunders have said.** They are as yet heavenly secrets. Men are

not ready to hear them. The insights of the book of Revelation are very profound. The Christian must have faith in that which is beyond his present insight and understanding. His belief in the character of God leads him to believe that the ultimate word of harmony will be spoken, but men are not prepared for it now. The words of the seven thunders however were heard by the man of Patmos. They were heard and they were understood. But they were not to be shared with men. No doubt all men of profound Christian experience would say that they have received more than they can ever tell. About some of the deepest matters which have become compelling to them they cannot speak. They are sure and yet they are inarticulate.

> Souls to souls can never teach
> What unto themselves was taught.[4]

Life is actually richer than speech. You cannot capture some insights in a net of words. Another aspect of the situation can be expressed in the words of Oliver Wendell Holmes:

> Alas for those that never sing,
> But die with all their music in them![5]

But it is not all sadness. It would be more tragic to have nothing to say than to have that which is beyond expression.

[4] Christopher Pearse Cranch, "Gnosis," st. 1.
[5] "The Voiceless."

6 And sware by him that liveth for ever and ever, who created heaven, and the things that therein are, and the earth, and the things that therein are, and the sea, and the things which are therein, that there should be time no longer:

7 But in the days of the voice of the seventh angel, when he shall begin to sound, the mystery of God should be finished, as he hath declared to his servants the prophets.

up his right hand to heaven 6 and swore by him who lives for ever and ever, who created heaven and what is in it, the earth and what is in it, and the sea and what is in it, that there should be no more delay, 7 but that in the days of the trumpet call to be sounded by the seventh angel, the mystery of God, as he announced to his servants the prophets, should be fulfilled.

Bound by this oath, even more solemn than the one in Daniel, the angel gives his assurance that **the mystery of God** will be fulfilled—i.e., the end of this age which has been predicted will surely arrive—following the blowing of the trumpet by **the seventh angel.** This is a departure from the source in Daniel, where it is stated that the end will come after three and a half years of persecution of the Jews by the Syrians, but in 11:2 John returns to the Danielic scheme by allowing a period of forty-two months in which the "nations," i.e., the Romans, will trample the Holy City.

But despite the solemn promise by the angel, the end does not come after the seventh trumpet is blown (11:15); indeed, much is yet to happen. Even so, this pledge that the end was actually in sight must have been most reassuring to the first readers of the book when they reached this section.

8-11. In these verses John returns to the scene in Ezek. 2:8–3:3. The **voice** from **heaven** which he had heard in vs. 3 spoke to him again and ordered him to take the open **scroll** from the angel. The angel, giving him the scroll, told him to **eat it,** and warned him that it would be **bitter** in his stomach but **sweet as honey** in his mouth. So it proved to be. It was sweet in his mouth, no doubt, because the prophecies it contained were most agreeable to him. On second thought, however, it became bitter because he

6. *The End of an Epoch.*—The shining angel standing athwart the world raised **his right hand** for a mighty oath and **swore** it in the name of the Everlasting, the Creator of heaven and all that it contains, of the earth and everything in it, and of the sea and all that is a part of it. Thus the angel swears a mighty oath. And this is the oath. The moment of consummation has come. **There should be no more delay.** No time is left for anything that belongs to the old epoch; or, in picturesque words near to the Greek, "time shall be no more." With the sounding of the **trumpet call . . . by the seventh angel** history will end. It will have been completed.

There is an interpretation of the Christian religion which has been called the theology of crisis. Without committing ourselves to any theological fashion we may say that deep in the Christian religion is the sense of the rounding out of human history under the administration of God. The crisis may be considered as the perfecting of the meaning of history. At any precise moment the threads of human existence may seem to be in hopeless confusion but they are being woven into a tapestry which,

at the command of God, will be revealed to be complete. Seen in this light the crisis will be a great fulfillment. So in a great oath the shining angel swears that the consummation is at hand.

7. *The Completion of Prophecy.*—The great fulfillment is to gather up the meaning of prophecy. The prophets were men who set forth the will of God and interpreted the purpose of God to their own people. So the divine mystery became the divine revelation. Elijah had seen the triumph of Jehovah over a pretentious false worship. Amos had declared a God who was righteousness alive. Hosea had proclaimed a God who was love alive. Micah had declared that God requires humble and gracious service of human need and offers fellowship to those who will turn from ways of pride. Isaiah had seen the highway of holiness and the highway of friendliness. The great prophet of the Exile had seen the suffering Servant. Ezekiel had seen productive waters flowing from the place of worship. All this and much more was to be gathered up in the fulfillment which made into harmony the various elements of the revelation of God.

8 And the voice which I heard from heaven spake unto me again, and said, Go *and* take the little book which is open in the hand of the angel which standeth upon the sea and upon the earth.

9 And I went unto the angel, and said unto him, Give me the little book. And he said unto me, Take *it,* and eat it up; and it shall make thy belly bitter, but it shall be in thy mouth sweet as honey.

10 And I took the little book out of the angel's hand, and ate it up; and it was in my mouth sweet as honey: and as soon as I had eaten it, my belly was bitter.

11 And he said unto me, Thou must prophesy again before many peoples, and nations, and tongues, and kings.

8 Then the voice which I had heard from heaven spoke to me again, saying, "Go, take the scroll which is open in the hand of the angel who is standing on the sea and on the land." 9 So I went to the angel and told him to give me the little scroll; and he said to me, "Take it and eat; it will be bitter to your stomach, but sweet as honey in your mouth." 10 And I took the little scroll from the hand of the angel and ate it; it was sweet as honey in my mouth, but when I had eaten it my stomach was made bitter. 11 And I was told, "You must again prophesy about many peoples and nations and tongues and kings."

---

realized the sufferings that many Christians would have to undergo before their final deliverance. Unlike Ezra, who is appalled by the doom awaiting the wicked and vainly intercedes for them with God (II Esdras 7:17-25, 102 ff.), this does not grieve John. Indeed, later on (in ch. 18) he actually exults over the prospect of the destruction of Rome with all of its inhabitants.

Ezekiel was commissioned to prophesy to the rebellious Jews on the basis of the lamentations, mournings, and woes in the book he was to eat; similarly, John, after eating the scroll, is told that he must **prophesy** once more **about many peoples and nations and tongues and kings.** Neither the scroll nor the woes it contains are specifically mentioned again in Revelation, although there may be a direct connection between them and ch. 11 which follows.

An interesting parallel is provided by the way in which the prophet Hermas, writing a few years later than John, obtained material for his book of prophecy. He writes that a supernatural Lady (identified as the heavenly church) appeared to him

---

9. *The Little Roll of Papyrus.*—The little roll of papyrus naturally turns our minds back to the book of the seven seals, which had been a book of the divine administration. The little **scroll** is a book of man seen in the light of God. There is glory in it which comes like honey to the mouth of the reader. There is moral and spiritual tragedy which is bitterness to his stomach. But so deeply concerned is the man of Patmos with the book and its message that he must make it a part of his very organism. Its essence must enter into his life.

There is great need of reading the book of man seen in the light of God. In our own time these materials may be found in many books. Usually they are books of men and we must bring to them from the Christian interpretation of life the principles by whose use we see the divine meaning. It is still true that the studies of Sainte-Beuve are an amazing introduction to the study of man. In America the many books of Gamaliel Bradford represent something very much like the dissection of human personality.

W. Robertson Nicoll used to make a remark to the effect that he never read a biography without learning something from it. And every biography has something special to bring to every man who comes to it with a Christian mind. The three volumes on the evangelical succession edited by Alexander Whyte see men especially in their relation to the Christian message.

11. *The Message to the World.*—The time perspective is always shifting in the book of Revelation. If we realize this it will make a good many things simpler. We have just been hearing of the final consummation of history. But as the man of Patmos makes the book of man seen in the light of God his own he is instantly back in the world of men, where he actually lives, with a message of world-wide significance. He must summon men to see their lives in the light of the rule of God.

This commission the man of Patmos handed on to all who followed him in speaking for God to men. It is always of the utmost importance

11 And there was given me a reed like unto a rod: and the angel stood, saying, Rise, and measure the temple of God, and the altar, and them that worship therein.

11 Then I was given a measuring rod like a staff, and I was told: "Rise and measure the temple of God and the altar

---

and read to him out of a heavenly book of prophecy. The last part pleased him, for it dealt with the fate of the righteous; but the first part he found hard and difficult, because it was concerned with the heathen and the apostates (Herm. Vis. I. 3–4). Later on he was permitted to copy from this book rather than depend on his memory (Herm. Vis. II. 1).

This entire ch. 10 is illustrative of the manner in which John uses his sources, interweaving, modifying, and adapting them for his eschatological drama. That he is an artist in this respect is quite evident when comparisons are made.

J. INTERLUDE: THE TWO HEAVENLY WITNESSES (11:1-14)

11:1-2. In this second interlude before the seventh trumpet is blown John once more develops his basic theme, the coming victory of the martyrs. In doing so he has, as is his custom, used a variety of sources, O.T. and others, constructing another scene which gives a practical message of hope and assurance to persecuted Christians resisting the ruthless might of Rome.

The tableau opens with the measuring of the temple. John was given a **rod** (RSV) or **reed** (KJV) by someone who is not identified—probably an angel is to be understood —and was told to **measure the temple of God,** including the altar and the worshipers. The scene, like the one in ch. 10, is ultimately derived from Ezekiel, who describes the careful measurement of the temple and all of its parts by a heaven-sent messenger who used a linen cord and a reed (Ezek. 40:3–42:20; 47:1-12). This was done in Ezekiel (also in

---

that men should see their lives in the light of the rule of God. And a great succession of men have undertaken this task. Edgar DeWitt Jones in his book *The Royalty of the Pulpit* [6] tells the tale of what many leaders have thought of this task as they have discussed it in the Lyman Beecher Lectures on Preaching, given at Yale. E. D. Jarvis of Glasgow in that meaty little book *If Any Man Minister,* [7] the 1950 Warrack Lectures on Preaching, gives an interpretation of intimate and outstanding quality. The task is endless. The good words said about it are endless too. And they merit our deep consideration.

11:1. The Importance of Standards.—The man of Patmos is given **a measuring rod.** The book of God and man has become a part of his very life and now he is ready to receive a standard of measurement. The man who understands the ways of God with men is inevitably the master of standards which can be applied to the profoundest matters of worship and action. A standardless life is a chaotic life. Such a life is lived by numberless people in the modern world. Jean Jacques Rousseau used all his power to put impulse in the place of principle in the life of man and he must bear his share of responsibility for the confusion in modern

society. It is easy for what may be called an instrumental view of life to leave no place for those standards without which civilization would perish. We must have standards. It is the insight of the book of Revelation that when the measuring rod is given by God it has a depth and an adequacy and a power to be found in no other way.

1. The Christian Church Must Be Judged by the Standards by Which It Judges.—We may see in the temple a symbol of the Christian church. And the temple itself is to be measured. The church must first of all submit itself to the rod of measurement. Søren Kierkegaard's famous *Attack Upon "Christendom"* [8] was an attempt to judge the church. While it contained much shrewd criticism it was defaced by personal malice. And his conception that the church existed simply to be in agony was far from the N.T. view that the Christian must be prepared for suffering without idealizing agony as if it is the essence of religion. The judgment of the church requires fairness and understanding as well as fiery indignation against the evils which have entered the church.

1. The Christian Judgment of Christians.— Socrates conducted a school of judgment; in a far more penetrating way Jesus conducted a

[6] New York: Harper & Bros., 1951.
[7] London: Hodder & Stoughton, 1951.

[8] Tr. Walter Lowrie (Princeton: Princeton University Press, 1944).

2 But the court which is without the temple leave out, and measure it not; for it is given unto the Gentiles: and the holy city shall they tread under foot forty *and* two months.

3 And I will give *power* unto my two witnesses, and they shall prophesy a

and those who worship there, 2 but do not measure the court outside the temple; leave that out, for it is given over to the nations, and they will trample over the holy city for forty-two months. 3 And I will grant my two witnesses power to

---

Zech. 1:16; 2:2-8 and Jer. 31:39) as preparatory to the restoration and rebuilding of the temple. For Ezekiel envisions a restored temple, on a larger and grander scale than the old, which would become the dwelling of Yahweh among his people. In other O.T. books measurements of this type signified destruction, as in II Kings 21:13, where Jerusalem, measured by a line and plummet, is destined for destruction (cf. also Amos 7:7-9; Lam. 2:8). In Isa. 34:11 it is Edom which is measured for destruction. In an interesting incident in I Enoch 61:1-5, angels with cords measure the righteous and the faithful so that they may never be destroyed before the Lord of Spirits.

It may be that John is conscious of these various concepts as he writes, but using figurative language he stresses the last one in his portrayal. The physical temple had been burned, and according to his view it will never be rebuilt; so probably he is thinking of the temple as symbolizing the holy and righteous among the Christians, particularly the martyrs-to-be. These have been "measured" by God's commands as they had previously been "sealed" (7:3). As a result of this measurement, although their physical lives and bodies will be destroyed, they will be protected, as in I Enoch 61:1-5, against all spiritual and supernatural dangers. Since their souls will not be destroyed, they will dwell with God and Christ in the New Jerusalem. The scene in which the New Jerusalem is measured (21:16-17) may well be a sequel to this, even though here it is the temple, not the city, that is involved.

There is, however, to be a period of physical destruction, for since the outer court of the temple is not to be measured, it will be **given over to the nations** (Romans) who will **trample** the Holy City for **forty-two months,** or three and a half years. This is the mystic number of years, according to Daniel (9:27; 12:7), during which the Syrians under Antiochus IV Epiphanes, a kind of Antichrist, would desecrate the temple and persecute the Jews; afterward the end would come. We may also recall the prediction of Luke 21:24 that "Jerusalem will be trodden down by the Gentiles, until the times of the Gentiles are fulfilled," although no specific time is given. According to the Ascension of Isaiah 4:12-14, the Antichrist is to persecute the Christians for 1,335 days (following the chronology of Dan. 12:12), which is somewhat more than three and a half years. Rabbinical speculation concerning the significance of this period was prolix and varied (cf. Strack and Billerbeck), and frequently was concerned with determining when the Messiah was to come.

It is evident that for John the reign of the Antichrist, which will be the final period of persecution of the Christians by the Romans, is to last this traditional period of years, a belief which is stated specifically in 13:5-6.

3. This brief episode prepares the way for the appearance of the **two witnesses,** appropriately clothed in **sackcloth,** the garb of sorrow and lamentation, who will **prophesy for one thousand two hundred and sixty days,** the three and a half years

---

school of judgment. In every age the Christian church must be judged by its capacity for self-judgment. The rod of measurement must perpetually be applied to Christians. From within their experience as Christians standards arise which they must apply to their own lives. Christian autobiography is full of this process. *The Confessions of Augustine* is, in a sense,

a school of judgment which he conducts upon his own life.

3. *The Law and the Prophets in the Modern Church.*—The **two witnesses** make Moses and Elijah contemporary. The advancement of religion gathers up and makes applicable to the present all of God's dealing with men in the past. The law gives regulations. Prophecy puts

thousand two hundred *and* threescore days, clothed in sackcloth.

4 These are the two olive trees, and the two candlesticks standing before the God of the earth.

5 And if any man will hurt them, fire proceedeth out of their mouth, and devoureth their enemies: and if any man will hurt them, he must in this manner be killed.

6 These have power to shut heaven, that it rain not in the days of their prophecy: and have power over waters to turn them to blood, and to smite the earth with all plagues, as often as they will.

prophesy for one thousand two hundred and sixty days, clothed in sackcloth."

4 These are the two olive trees and the two lampstands which stand before the Lord of the earth. 5 And if any one would harm them, fire pours from their mouth and consumes their foes; if any one would harm them, thus he is doomed to be killed. 6 They have power to shut the sky, that no rain may fall during the days of their prophesying, and they have power over the waters to turn them into blood, and to smite the earth with every plague, as often

---

during which the Romans will be permitted to continue their evil rule, the period of the Antichrist.

4. These witnesses are **the two olive trees and the two lampstands** which are before God. The symbolism is borrowed from Zech. 4:1-14, where the prophet sees a seven-branched candlestick and two olive trees. The septiform candlestick is identified as the eyes of God going to and fro about the earth (cf. Rev. 5:6), and the trees are quite probably Joshua and Zerubbabel, the anointed religious and civil leaders. John changes the seven-branched candlestick to **two lampstands** and completely discards the meaning of the symbols for Zechariah. For him **the two lampstands** and **the two olive trees** are the two witnesses who are to prophesy.

5-6. These two witnesses are not named, but from their description they may be readily identified. They have the power to destroy their enemies with **fire** from their mouths; to keep the **rain** from falling; to turn water into **blood**; and to inflict every type of **plague** upon the earth. Following these clues, it has usually been considered that these witnesses are Elijah and Moses returned to earth. For it was Elijah who called fire down from heaven to consume the messengers of King Ahaziah (II Kings 1:9-16). To be sure, this was not with fire from his mouth, but this transition was easily made, as in Ecclus. 48:1, "Also there arose Elijah the prophet as fire, and his word burneth like a torch." Moreover, Moses was associated with destructive fire, for the seventh plague consisted of hail mingled with fire (Exod. 9:23). Furthermore, Elijah was responsible for a drought (I Kings 17:1) which lasted three and a half years, according to Luke 4:25 and Jas. 5:17. Moses was God's agent in turning water into blood in the first Egyptian plague (Exod. 7:17); indeed, on reading Exodus one might easily assume that he was able to smite with every kind of plague he desired. Without too much difficulty John ascribes all these powers to both witnesses equally.

But why these two? First of all, Jews and, later, Christians held that both were residents in heaven along with Enoch. The ascension of Elijah to heaven is described in II Kings 2:11; that of Enoch is deduced from Gen. 5:24, "Enoch walked with God: and

---

a soul into the regulations. So the two witnesses are always needed. There is a continuity of evil in the world. But there is also a continuity of good in the world. The wise men of the law and the men of glowing minds who are prophets are needed in every age. In the study of the life of Alfred the Great (and the Good) it is noteworthy to observe the fashion in which he sought to make available the best of the Christian past for that present of which he was a

part. The two witnesses may be seen as fit symbols of that long story of legal sanction and glowing speech by which God has dealt with men, as it is brought to the living church.

6. *The Forces of Nature and the Forces of God.*—The picture suggested by the words, **they have power to shut the sky,** comes from the story of Elijah in which the closed heavens made a memorable part. The man of Patmos is saying that the forces of nature are not apart

7 And when they shall have finished their testimony, the beast that ascendeth out of the bottomless pit shall make war against them, and shall overcome them, and kill them.

as they desire. **7** And when they have finished their testimony, the beast that ascends from the bottomless pit will make war upon them and conquer them and kill them,

---

he was not; for God took him." As for Moses, a Jewish tradition, embodied in the apocryphal Assumption of Moses, stated that he had likewise been taken up into heaven.

The belief in the heavenly residence of Elijah led to the expectation that God would cause him to reappear shortly before the great and dreadful day of the Lord to "turn the heart of the fathers to the children, and the heart of the children to their fathers," lest God himself "come and smite the earth with a curse" (Mal. 4:4-6; cf. 3:1). Also, according to Jewish anticipations (cf. Strack and Billerbeck) which were taken over by the Christians, Elijah was to be the forerunner of the Messiah on his return to earth. The prediction of Deut. 18:15 that God would raise up a prophet like unto Moses was interpreted to mean that Moses would also come back to earth. The Samaritans, in fact, taught that their Taheb (Messiah) would be Moses *redivivus.* Similarly, Enoch's return was also anticipated.

As residents of heaven they were in a position to learn what was going to happen to the earth and its inhabitants; to discover when and how God was going to destroy this world and this age. Consequently, there was a development of a belief that one or more would reappear to prophesy; to warn their fellow men of the calamities that were to come; and to urge them to repent of their sins and turn to righteousness. In some sources Elijah was to appear alone, in others, in company with Enoch, and in still others, possibly because of their collocation in Mal. 4:4-6, with Moses.

This helps to explain why Jesus could have been mistaken for Elijah (Mark 6:15), or why he said that Elijah must come first "to restore all things." This expectation also accounts for the appearance of Moses and Elijah during the transfiguration scene (Mark 9:2-8).

7. Accordingly, Elijah and Moses appear as prophets and preachers of repentance. They are "witnesses," but they are also "martyrs," since the Greek may be translated either way (cf. 1:5). For a demonic **beast** appears from **the bottomless pit,** and he **will make war** against the witnesses and **kill them.** This **beast** is the first of four of his kind in Revelation: the others are the dragon or Satan (12:3); the beast with ten horns and seven heads (13:1); and the beast with two horns who spoke like a dragon (13:11). These beasts are different, and yet they are all incarnations in one form or another of Satan, and all are the determined enemies of God, Christ, and the Christians. Further, those in ch. 13 are identified with the deified emperors, and with the dead Nero, who will come back to life to slay the faithful. The **beast** in this chapter partakes of the character of these and for convenience may be termed the Antichrist. The Antichrist,

---

from the administration of God. They are part of the divine rule of men. Obviously we are here moving in the realm of faith, a realm where it is precarious to make detailed statements about concrete situations. But it is an important matter to feel that under God the whole order of nature works with the man of abiding Christian faith and not against him.

7. When Evil Conquers.—The man of Patmos is always realistic. Law and prophecy speak their great word and do their great work. Then the force of evil becomes articulate and mighty. From the dark underworld a **beast** comes forth which **will make war upon them and conquer**

them and kill them. With all the triumphant outbursts of evil in our own time the words seem particularly contemporary. The time in the last century when almost everyone felt that by sure processes of evolution the world was getting better and better seems curiously remote. We get a suggestion of the situation in one country in the book *Now I Can Tell* [9] by the Chinese Christian bishop, Quentin K. Y. Huang, who was imprisoned by the Chinese Communists. Just where the witness of law and prophecy had been heard, it has been overthrown.

[9] New York: Morehouse-Gorham, 1954.

8 And their dead bodies *shall lie* in the street of the great city, which spiritually is called Sodom and Egypt, where also our Lord was crucified.

9 And they of the people and kindreds and tongues and nations shall see their dead bodies three days and a half, and shall not suffer their dead bodies to be put in graves.

10 And they that dwell upon the earth shall rejoice over them, and make merry, and shall send gifts one to another; because these two prophets tormented them that dwelt on the earth.

8 and their dead bodies will lie in the street of the great city which is allegorically[d] called Sodom and Egypt, where their Lord was crucified. 9 For three days and a half men from the peoples and tribes and tongues and nations gaze at their dead bodies and refuse to let them be placed in a tomb, 10 and those who dwell on the earth will rejoice over them and make merry and exchange presents, because these two prophets had been a torment to those

[d] Greek *spiritually.*

---

quite naturally, played a greater role in Christian apocalypses than in Jewish, but is not absent from the latter. Not always is he depicted as a beast; frequently he is a human being of monstrous appearance.

Although the two martyr-witnesses have deadly supernatural fire at their disposal, with which they are supposed to kill their opponents (vs. 5), they will be overcome and killed by the Antichrist. In most instances this is the outcome, but in the account of the Akhmim Apocalypse of Elijah 42-43, Elijah and Enoch kill the Antichrist.

8. Their dead bodies lay unburied for the mystical number of three and a half days **in the street of the great city . . . allegorically called Sodom and Egypt, where their Lord was crucified.** Were it not for this last clause, **Sodom and Egypt** would certainly be taken to mean Rome. Kiddle, it would seem, has solved the difficulty by suggesting that **Sodom and Egypt** are not a single city, but constitute the evil "great city" of this world order, the earthly and temporal in contrast to the heavenly and the eternal. It was in this "great city" that Jesus was crucified; it is here that his followers are persecuted and martyred; and it is here that Elijah and Moses in their reincarnation are killed by the Antichrist.

9-12. Thus the two "witnesses" in their reincarnation became "martyrs." The whole non-Christian world rejoiced at their death, for its people had been tormented by the **prophets.** Conceivably, this might be a reference to the miraculous punitive powers they were said to possess (vss. 5-6). But there is no indication that they actually exercised

---

8. The Ignominy of Defeated Good.—Again and again there is an awful publicity about the triumph of evil. In the ancient world to be deprived of honorable funeral rites was a bitter infamy. The symbolic figures representing the will of God are left dead upon the street. Goodness lies dead upon the street. It is not only slain; it is insulted and scorned. The situation is all the more cruel because the good had just been dramatically triumphant. The debauchery of the Restoration in England was all the more tragic seen against the background of the overwhelming moral earnestness of the period of Cromwell. In such times the testimony of the lawless streets seems to be the most powerful thing in the world.

8. The City of Transcendent Crime.—In a striking figure of speech the evils of the cities are gathered up into one symbolic town. There is unnatural vice like that of **Sodom.** There is sophisticated wickedness like that of **Egypt.** There is murderous disloyalty to a tradition of good like that of the city of God which became the city **where their Lord was crucified.** The truth is that the lawless evil of any modern town is a consummation. It gathers up many bad things from the cities of the past. Books with such titles as *The Shame of the Cities* tell the tale in dramatic fashion. In its darkest hours many a modern town becomes a city where goodness has been slain.

10. The Carnival of Evil.—With a curious but dramatic and effective inconsistency all the world comes to the city of sin to see the dead bodies lying in the street. The awful light of the triumph of evil shines in numberless eyes. It is a matter of unabashed pleasure to **peoples and tribes and tongues and nations** that the

11 And after three days and a half the Spirit of life from God entered into them, and they stood upon their feet; and great fear fell upon them which saw them.

12 And they heard a great voice from heaven saying unto them, Come up hither. And they ascended up to heaven in a cloud; and their enemies beheld them.

who dwell on the earth. 11 But after the three and a half days a breath of life from God entered them, and they stood up on their feet, and great fear fell on those who saw them. 12 Then they heard a loud voice from heaven saying to them, "Come up hither!" And in the sight of their foes they

---

these powers in their second appearance on earth. It has been suggested that possibly the **torment** consisted in the pricking of the consciences of the wicked by their testimony and by their preaching of repentance. The deaths of these martyr-witnesses were celebrated with great festivities by those who hated them; ironically enough, festivals in honor of martyrs, commemorating the dates of their martyrdom, were instituted later on in the church. As a sign of dishonor their bodies were left unburied for **three and a half days.** Then when they were restored to life by God, all who saw them were filled with great fear. Next, in obedience to a heavenly voice which summoned them, they reascended to heaven on **a cloud** (as Jesus had done in Acts 1:9) in the sight of their enemies.

This great triumph over their foes and over death by the two martyr-witnesses, Elijah and Moses, is another sure pledge that Christians who suffer and die for their testimony to Christ, enduring all kinds of taunts and insults as well, will likewise triumph over death and be vindicated in the sight of their persecutors by being taken to heaven when they die. Thus Elijah and Moses, like Jesus in 1:5, become exemplars of the victorious martyr. Not a few of the Christian martyrs were women. This may account for a variant tradition that Tabitha, who was resurrected in Acts 9:36-43, will appear to accuse the Antichrist. He will succeed in killing her, but she is to be resurrected again and will inform him that while he can kill the body he cannot destroy the soul (Sahidic Apocalypse of Elijah 6–7).

Despite their great prominence in this scene, Elijah and Moses do not reappear in Revelation, not even at the consummation of this age, as might reasonably be expected, nor are they mentioned in connection with the new age. Nor is this particular beast mentioned again, save as he is merged with the other three that follow. Apparently John

---

voices of restraint and order and moral control have been silenced. Mad chaos holds festival with merriment and gifts. You know a great deal about people if you know what makes them happy. Those who celebrate the death of goodness are the darkest blight upon the life of mankind. Is the picture overdrawn? The darkest days of the French Revolution and many another bitter day in the history of the world will give the grim reply.

11. The Last Word Is the Best Word.—There is an inevitable change. Evil never has the last word. **A breath . . . from God** gives life to the dead. **A loud voice from heaven** speaks, while the dead stand **on their feet.** The truth is there are some things you cannot slay. The carnival of wicked joy had come too soon. It is always a mistake to rejoice when goodness lies dead in the streets. It is the Hitlers and the Mussolinis who have the sentence of death upon them even when they seem most powerful. And

the breath of life is already on the way to those who suffer and die for that which is good.

11. The Fear Which Is Itself a Doom.—A notable leader once said that fear is always worse than that of which you are afraid. This is often true. But it is not true of the fear with which evil men behold the triumph of that which is good. There is no peace of mind which can alleviate this trembling agony. The fear of the liar whose falsehood has been detected, the fear of the murderer whose vicious deed has been discovered, the fear of dethroned evil at the presence of triumphant good, represent an ultimate reality which no clever psychologist can turn into serenity. This fear is itself a part of the doom of wickedness, a part of the punishment which settles heavily upon their souls.

12. The Story of Earth Is Completed by Heaven.—The last chapter is always written in **heaven.** Earth asks questions which only heaven can answer and sets going processes which only

13 And the same hour was there a great earthquake, and the tenth part of the city fell, and in the earthquake were slain of men seven thousand: and the remnant were affrighted, and gave glory to the God of heaven.

14 The second woe is past; *and,* behold, the third woe cometh quickly.

went up to heaven in a cloud. 13 And at that hour there was a great earthquake, and a tenth of the city fell; seven thousand people were killed in the earthquake, and the rest were terrified and gave glory to the God of heaven.

14 The second woe has passed; behold, the third woe is soon to come.

---

has inserted an apocalyptic tradition which he has not thoroughly integrated and harmonized with what is to follow.

13. Subsequent to the assumption of Elijah and Moses **a great earthquake** occurred as a sign of God's displeasure and wrath, destroying **a tenth of the city** and killing **seven thousand people.** These figures are but a token of the total annihilation which is to occur. Those who were left alive were filled with dread and **gave glory to the God of heaven,** but despite this there is no sign that they repented, nor did John expect that they would. Unlike the apologists of the second and third centuries who worked for, and rather expected, a change of attitude on the part of the heathen and the Roman authorities toward Christianity, John was convinced that no such transformation would occur; consequently Rome must and will be destroyed.

14. This earthquake is probably the **second woe** proclaimed by the eagle in 8:13; the **third** will follow before long. Although not specifically identified as such, the **third woe** is probably the terrifying phenomenon described in vs. 19 following the blowing of the seventh trumpet. John has not stated explicitly that this scene of the two martyr-witnesses was contained in the little book which he wrote, but it is probable that this was his intent; certainly while their death would be bitter to contemplate, their triumph coupled with the certain destruction of their enemies would be very sweet indeed. For their death and triumph symbolize the death and triumph of the martyrs, and the partial destruction of the great city is the promise of its final annihilation.

---

heaven can complete. The heavenly voice called. The two witnesses to the truth of God were no longer lying dead upon the streets. Their foes saw them in the very act of entering the felicity and the triumph of the heavenly life. They beheld a vision of a happiness which they could not share. The carnival of evil is succeeded by a great consummation which could be apprehended in its true meaning only by the upward look. The upward journey told the story of the complete finality of the victory of good. Heaven had spoken and heaven had acted. "Behold, I see the heavens opened" (Acts 7:56), cried Stephen, the first Christian martyr, as he died.

13. The Trembling World.—An earthquake somehow suggests that the foundations of life have become precarious. It was, however, the foundations of a life which could be turned to evil purposes which were revealed to be unstable as the two witnesses vanished into the heights. What men actually felt as the earth trembled was the instability of life apart from God. The sense of the uncertainty of the ground on which we tread is so dreadful that there is a certain city subject to earthquakes where the

word is never mentioned. If fire follows the earthquake they refer to the fire. In the same fashion men try to hide from themselves the true meaning of the tremor beneath their feet when they defy God by defying his laws. But there you have it. The only way to find stability in human experience is through faith in God.

13. The Obeisance of the Frightened.—Death struck fiercely. In a panic of fear those left alive gave tokens of reverence and respect for God. The acknowledgment which came only from fear was, of course, not very deep or noble or true. In Robert Browning's famous poem "Caliban Upon Setebos" the creature Caliban, who has been talking rather freely about his god Setebos, becomes thoroughly frightened when a great storm comes. He sees in it all evidence of the anger of his god:

His thunder follows! Fool to gibe at Him!
Lo! 'Lieth flat and loveth Setebos!
'Maketh his teeth meet through his upper lip,
Will let those quails fly, will not eat this month
One little mess of whelks, so he may 'scape!

The religion of groveling fear is not worth much.

15 And the seventh angel sounded; and there were great voices in heaven, saying, The kingdoms of this world are become *the kingdoms* of our Lord, and of his Christ; and he shall reign for ever and ever.

16 And the four and twenty elders, which sat before God on their seats, fell upon their faces, and worshipped God,

17 Saying, We give thee thanks, O Lord God Almighty, which art, and wast, and art to come; because thou hast taken to thee thy great power, and hast reigned.

15 Then the seventh angel blew his trumpet, and there were loud voices in heaven, saying, "The kingdom of the world has become the kingdom of our Lord and of his Christ, and he shall reign for ever and ever." 16 And the twenty-four elders who sit on their thrones before God fell on their faces and worshiped God, 17 saying,

"We give thanks to thee, Lord God almighty, who art and who wast,
    that thou hast taken thy great power
        and begun to reign.

K. Seventh Trumpet: God's Impending Assumption of Power (11:15-19)

15. The blowing of the seventh **trumpet** has been delayed by the interludes portrayed in 10:1–11:14. The entire scene is a duplication, with variations of course, of 4:8-11. In the earlier tableau the four living creatures acclaim God with the "Thrice Holy" and assert his almighty power, past, present, and future. In response the twenty-four elders fall down before God on his throne and sing a hymn praising God the creator. A similar scene is presented in 7:10-12.

In this instance, following the sounding of the trumpet, loud **voices in heaven** were heard singing a song proclaiming that **the kingdom of the world,** i.e., the rule of Satan, exemplified by the Roman Empire, has now been ended, and will soon be replaced by the eternal **kingdom of our Lord and of his Christ.** Here, in a brief liturgical sentence, is the main outline of Revelation, expressing the apocalyptic hope of the author and his readers. The words of this hymn are similar to the prediction of Dan. 7:27.

16. Upon hearing this liturgical proclamation, **the twenty-four elders,** leaving their thrones and prostrating themselves, **worshiped God** in a liturgical response.

17-18. In the first stanza of this hymn **thanks** is accorded God, who is the **Almighty,** not only because he is and was always God, but also because he has now begun to show his **great power,** has now **begun to reign.** (The inclusion of **and art to come**—KJV—is probably a harmonistic gloss.) The second stanza is somewhat more explicit concerning God's assumption of power. Although **the nations raged**—an allusion to their final onslaught against the saints (cf. 20:8-9)—they were unable to withstand God's **wrath.** **The dead** have been **judged,** the **saints** have been rewarded, those who feared the name of God, **both small and great** (cf. Ps. 115:13), and **the destroyers of the earth** have

---

15. The Royal Continuity.—The time for the third woe is soon to come. **The seventh angel blew his trumpet.** Then comes one of those quick turns which give such fascinating surprise to the book of Revelation. Before the woe unfolds its meaning there is a glorious picture of the ultimate victory of Christ. This of course means woe to the evil, but it means something very glorious to those who have accepted the will of God. And it has the most impressive continuity with the good in history. The book of Revelation always states each principle absolutely. The qualifications are left for some other symbolic picture. So here it is said with complete finality: **The kingdom of the**

world has become the kingdom of our Lord and of his Christ.

From the time of the Greeks there have been many books telling the tale of an ideal state made real in human life. The book of Revelation reminds us that such hopes can only become real as a part of the kingdom of God. All utopias lack the last quality of reality unless they express the will of Christ. But the man of Patmos reminds us that in spite of all the evil there is something in history which leads forward to Christ's glorious reign. There is a good in the kingdom of this world which can find its fulfillment only in the kingdom of Christ.

18 And the nations were angry, and thy wrath is come, and the time of the dead, that they should be judged, and that thou shouldest give reward unto thy servants the prophets, and to the saints, and them that fear thy name, small and great; and shouldest destroy them which destroy the earth.

19 And the temple of God was opened in heaven, and there was seen in his temple the ark of his testament: and there were lightnings, and voices, and thunderings, and an earthquake, and great hail.

18 The nations raged, but thy wrath came,
    and the time for the dead to be judged,
  for rewarding thy servants, the prophets and saints,
    and those who fear thy name, both small and great,
  and for destroying the destroyers of the earth."

19 Then God's temple in heaven was opened, and the ark of his covenant was seen within his temple; and there were flashes of lightning, loud noises, peals of thunder, an earthquake, and heavy hail.

---

themselves been destroyed. All this is a preview of what the writer ardently expects is soon to happen. He is so certain that he stands on the very threshold of these eschatological events that he uses the past tense instead of the future—the "prophetic past," as it has been termed. Revelation as a whole is but an amplification of the two liturgical songs in this scene that follows the blowing of the seventh trumpet.

19. After the singing of this apocalyptic hymn the heavenly **temple** of God **opened** so that **the ark of his covenant** was visible within. The **ark** had long been lost, probably at the time of the capture of Jerusalem by the Babylonians in 586 B.C.; certainly it was not in the second temple. However, there was a Jewish belief that it had been safely hidden (cf. II Macc. 2:4-8; II Baruch 6:7-10) and would be brought to light with the restoration of Israel. The ark that is now disclosed, however, is the heavenly archetype, not the earthly copy. As the earthly ark was a sign of God's protecting presence with his people Israel, so the heavenly ark signified that God was with the Christians, that he would guard and protect them from all the forces of evil. This theophany was accompanied by the usual phenomena—lightning, thunder, earthquake, and hail—a sign of the coming display of God's power. Although not designated as such, this is probably the third woe predicted by the eagle (8:13).

---

18. *The Destruction of Destruction.*—The mighty **elders** kneel before the throne. Their adoration is full of the joy of the reign of God, full of judgment, gracious with reward. And one sees the meaning of the presence of woe in the glory of God's reign as they announce the **destroying** [of] **the destroyers of the earth.** In the reign of God the forces of destruction are themselves to be destroyed. Only that which has no right to live must die. Only that which has no right to exist must be brought to an end. But this must happen with conclusiveness and finality. There is no suggestion of the moral inconclusiveness of the words:

> There is so much good in the worst of us,
> And so much bad in the best of us,
> That it hardly behooves any of us
> To talk about the rest of us.[1]

[1] Attributed to Edward Wallis Hoch. First printed in *The Marion (Kansas) Record.*

Rather the good is searched out and honored, the evil searched out and destroyed.

19. *The Ancient Agreement.*—The book of Revelation is always related to the deepest moral and spiritual experiences of Israel. So in the midst of the glorious vision of final things we are reminded of the ancient covenant. There the ark of the covenant stands in the midst of the temple. God's ancient promises are not forgotten. But all of God's promises have moral conditions which were all too often repudiated. So the promises are terrible as well as glorious things. And so **the ark of his covenant was seen within his temple,** surrounded by flashes of lightning; and the earth itself trembles. The idea of the covenant has had an important place in Christian history. When the Covenanters plighted their faith to one another they did it in the name of the plighted faith of God. It is the divine covenant which gives the deepest meaning and the fullest promise to all noble human pledges.

12 And there appeared a great wonder in heaven; a woman clothed with the sun, and the moon under her feet, and upon her head a crown of twelve stars:

12 And a great portent appeared in heaven, a woman clothed with the sun, with the moon under her feet, and on

VI. Seven Visions of the Dragon's Kingdom (12:1–13:18)

Before God's reign actually is to begin, Satan and his minions are to be allowed a brief period, three and a half years, of rule. This is depicted in chs. 12–13, and according to the scheme followed here, it is divided into seven episodes. Admittedly, this sevenfold division may seem somewhat arbitrary, but since other main sections in Revelation are sevenfold it is not likely that John has departed from this pattern here.

A. First Vision: Heavenly Mother and Birth of Heavenly Messiah (12:1-6)

This is probably one of the most puzzling episodes in Revelation, and requires special treatment. Accordingly, a brief summary is in order. A celestial woman who is about to bear a child appears in heaven. A red, seven-headed dragon stands over her in order to devour the babe when it is born. She gives birth to a male child, destined to rule the nations with a rod of iron, who is taken up in safety out of the dragon's reach to God's throne. The mother flees in safety to a wilderness which has been prepared for her and where she will remain for 1,260 days.

It has long been recognized that this scene, which is not derived from any known Jewish source, must be based upon a rather widespread myth of the divine child whose destruction is sought by those whose power he threatens, this myth being coupled with some astral speculation. The Greek story of the birth of Apollo has been cited in this connection, although it has few astral features. The goddess Leto, with child by Zeus, was pursued by the dragon Python, who sought to kill her because of a prophecy that the child, if born, would live to vanquish him. However, at the order of Zeus, Boreas, the god of the North, took Leto to Poseidon, who provided her a refuge on an island where she gave birth to Apollo. The thwarted dragon withdrew to Parnassus, where four days later Apollo fulfilled the prediction and killed him.

A second myth, even closer since it combines the astral motif, is that of the birth of Horus. Isis, the Egyptian goddess, is identified with Virgo, a constellation of the zodiac. Her consort is Osiris, the sun god. Set-Typhon, frequently depicted as a red crocodile of the Nile, is identified with the constellation Hydra or Dragon. He kills Osiris, and then pursues Isis and her child Horus, the son of Osiris. They escape in a papyrus boat to an island; according to a variant account, Isis uses wings in her flight. Horus later avenges his father by vanquishing Set-Typhon, but Isis orders him released.

Some variation of this myth of the birth of the sacred babe interwoven with astrology lies at the base of John's account. Since according to astral thinking everything occurring on earth has previously happened in heaven, this is not an allegorical depiction of the earthly birth of Jesus to Mary. Instead, it relates the birth of the heavenly Messiah to a

12:1. *The Emergence of Woman.*—The symbol of the **woman clothed with the sun** and wearing **a crown of twelve stars** suggests the emergence of woman into a new place of significance. Christianity has certainly given woman a place which she never had in the ancient world and the same may be said of the world so far as it has been affected by Christianity. Gamaliel Bradford, the American biographical essayist, painted a series of brilliant portraits of women. They are found in such of his books as *Portraits of Women,*[2] *Portraits of American Women,*[3] *Elizabethan Women,*[4] and *Wives.*[5] It is easy for the reader of such keen and bright contemporary essays to fail to realize that the Christian religion has created the society where such women are possible. The far-off hint of a world in which women can come

[2] Boston: Houghton Mifflin Co., 1916.
[3] Boston: Houghton Mifflin Co., 1919.
[4] Boston: Houghton Mifflin Co., 1936.
[5] New York and London: Harper & Bros., 1925.

2 And she being with child cried, travailing in birth, and pained to be delivered.

3 And there appeared another wonder in heaven; and behold a great red dragon, having seven heads and ten horns, and seven crowns upon his heads.

her head a crown of twelve stars; 2 she was with child and she cried out in her pangs of birth, in anguish for delivery. 3 And another portent appeared in heaven; behold a great red dragon, with seven heads and ten horns, and seven diadems upon his

---

celestial mother, possibly before creation began. The enmity of the dragon, Satan, toward the child prefigured that which was later to exist between them. The woman is not only the mother of the Messiah, but she is also, by one of those characteristic shifts in symbolism, the church, which is persecuted by Satan for 1,260 days. In passing, the astral motif in the Matthaean story of the birth of Jesus, with its astrologers (magi) and star, might be noted. The account of Ignatius of Antioch, according to which the birth of Jesus was hidden from the prince of this world (Satan), with the sun, moon, and other stars gathered in a chorus around Jesus' star, is more significant, for this would indicate a heavenly birth, hidden from Satan, which preceded the earthly one (Ign. Eph. 19:1-2).

12:1-2. The woman is a great portent, or sign, in that her appearance has significance for the Christians undergoing persecution. Frequently when John tells about a future event, he speaks as though it were present or past. Here the situation is reversed; for he is relating an event that occurred in the past, possibly before creation, but writes as though it were just happening. The woman is clothed with the sun, with the moon under her feet, and on her head a crown of twelve stars. She is, therefore, no earthly being, but a glorious astral, celestial being, a veritable Queen of Heaven. Her apparel may be compared with that of the goddess Isis, who was considered the Queen of Heaven, as described by Apuleius. Above her forehead Isis had a shining circle that resembled the moon; stars were to be seen on the surface of the garment which she wore, with the moon in the middle of them shining like a flame of fire in midmonth (*Metamorphoses* 11:3-4). In some depictions she wore a star in her hair. The crown composed of the twelve constellations of the zodiac which the woman wore, symbolizing her power over the destinies of mankind, recalls that Christ held the seven planetary stars in his right hand (cf. 1:16). She is, it should be noticed, about to bear a child.

3. A second and ominous portent was the appearance of a great red dragon, with seven heads. The portrayal of an evil force as a serpent, crocodile, or dragon, sometimes with more than one head, was widespread. The Greeks had Python and the nine-headed Hydra; the Egyptians depicted Set-Typhon as a red crocodile; for the Persians, Azhi

---

to their own is found in the picture in the book of Revelation of the woman clothed with the sun.

2. *Motherhood Is Self-Sacrifice Alive.*—The great question about the symbols in the book of Revelation is not their origin, interesting as that question is. In truth these symbols were found in all sorts of places. But the important matter is the Christian use to which they are put. If the story of the radiant woman turns the tale of the birth of Christ into a graphic myth, perhaps by the aid of an existing myth, the great thing is what the finished product meant to the man of Patmos. Of course at the very least he is saying that the birth of Christ has cosmic significance. It is plain to see that the suffering of motherhood in giving new life to the world came well within his ken. And he lifts the pain of childbirth into vast and

noble relations. The one who suffers to give new life to the world is a very important person. The story of the devotion of men of high distinction to their mothers is a long and beautiful narrative. One thinks of Lord Haldane and Lord Balfour as conspicuous examples. Something new had happened in the world when motherhood ceased to be taken for granted.

3. *Evil and Personal Intention.*—The man of Patmos sees clearly that the core of evil is malignant will. The hard center of personal commitment to evil is the darkest of all moral problems. This sort of evil is never misunderstood good. It is not good intention in confusion. It is stark, complete devotion to evil just because it is evil. All this is symbolized by the great red dragon. It is an aspiring, ambitious passion of wickedness which sweeps across the

4 And his tail drew the third part of the stars of heaven, and did cast them to the earth: and the dragon stood before the woman which was ready to be delivered, for to devour her child as soon as it was born.

5 And she brought forth a man child, who was to rule all nations with a rod of iron: and her child was caught up unto God, and *to* his throne.

heads. 4 His tail swept down a third of the stars in heaven, and cast them to the earth. And the dragon stood before the woman who was about to bear a child, that he might devour her child when she brought it forth; 5 she brought forth a male child, one who is to rule all the nations with a rod of iron, but her child was caught up to

---

Dahaka was a three-headed monster, two of his heads being serpents growing out of his shoulders; the ancient Canaanites, according to the Ras Shamra tablets, believed in a great sinuous serpent with seven heads which may have been the forerunner of Leviathan, the swift serpent, and Leviathan, the crooked serpent, of Isa. 27:1. An Accadian seal from the twenty-fifth century B.C. depicts a seven-headed monster being killed by two gods, an indication of the antiquity of the concept (cf. Cyrus H. Gordon, *The Living Past* [New York: John Day Co., 1941], seal 14, facing p. 124). In time, of course, the serpent that tempted Eve came to be identified with Satan. The **seven diadems** on his head are a sign of his dominion over this world, and should be compared and perhaps contrasted with the many diadems worn by the conquering Christ, the King of kings and Lord of lords (19:12). The **ten horns** are doubtless a reflection of the ten horns of the terrible one-headed beast of Dan. 7:7 with its ten horns, and are signs of the dragon's power. This dragon, then, is a composite creature made up of special aspects of various earlier models. He is, of course, the devil or Satan (vs. 9).

4a. The Danielic beast with ten horns also had a little horn, symbolizing the persecutor Antiochus IV Epiphanes, a semidemonic personage who exalted himself to the skies and cast some of the stars down to the ground and trampled upon them (Dan. 7:7). These stars, quite likely, are the righteous Jews who are persecuted and slain by him, and are restored to their heavenly places as stars following the resurrection and judgment (Dan. 12:3). The dragon swept **one third of the stars of heaven** down to the earth with his tail; whether these represent the righteous whom he persecutes, or whether they are fallen angels who will assist him in his nefarious plans, is not clear.

4b-5. Like Python trying to destroy Apollo before he was to be born, lest in time he should be vanquished by him, the dragon stood near the heavenly mother to **devour her child** as soon as he was born, and probably for a very similar reason. For the child was a son, the pre-existent Messiah, who is **to rule all the nations with a rod of iron.** This prediction, taken from Ps. 2:9 and previously applied to the martyrs (2:27), is fulfilled in 19:15-21, when the conquering Christ with the martyrs vanquishes Satan's two chief minions, the two beasts of ch. 13, along with the nations of the earth. It is this prediction that accounts for the deadly hostility of the dragon, and his desire to kill the

---

sky. It is the very nature of this malignant will not only to desire a throne but to desire an unshared throne. It would possess even the throne of God. And there can be no appeasement here. The desire to hold peace congresses with that which must be overthrown is recurrent in history.

Milton's great epic *Paradise Lost* strikes the very note of ultimate opposition between the divine intention for good and that which contradicts it which we find in this passage. The symbol of the great red dragon is repulsive

and evil enough, but it represents something which cannot safely be ignored.

5. *The Promise of Birth.*—Birth represents the future. It is full of the promise of days to come. Evil fears every birth which threatens its own supremacy. Herod killed many children hoping to kill one. In a sense red dragons of evil are always ready to slay goodness at its birth. And infant good always seems extremely helpless. But the infant king **was caught up to God and to his throne.** God himself is on the side of all new births of good. It is a far call

6 And the woman fled into the wilderness, where she hath a place prepared of God, that they should feed her there a thousand two hundred *and* threescore days.

God and to his throne, 6 and the woman fled into the wilderness, where she has a place prepared by God, in which to be nourished for one thousand two hundred and sixty days.

child. But this was not to be, for the **child was caught up to God** on his throne. The term **caught up** is not a prediction of the ascension of Jesus into heaven, as some have thought, since the birth itself took place in heaven and the child was already there. Instead, he is taken from one place in heaven to the presence of God and was there enthroned, was recognized as God's Son. Ps. 2, which John has just loosely quoted, depicts the enthronement upon Mount Zion of the anointed king, who is to break the nation with a rod of iron (Ps. 2:6). This may have suggested the recognition and enthronement of the pre-existent heavenly Messiah. This scene is the archetype of the earthly history of the Christ: just as the pre-existent Messiah was enthroned at God's side following his escape from Satan, so Jesus Christ, after his escape from the prince of this world and the powers of darkness through his death and resurrection, is to be glorified and placed at God's right hand in heaven (cf. 3:21; 5:6; 7:10; 22:1, 3).

6. The mother now flees **into the wilderness** to a place that God has prepared for her; here she will be **nourished for one thousand two hundred and sixty days,** or about three and a half years. Apparently, by one of those quick shifts in symbolism which has been observed in other connections, the woman becomes the heavenly personification of the church. This kind of personification is not without parallel. In II Esdras 9:38–10:59 both the heavenly and the earthly Jerusalem are represented by a woman. Paul, in his allegory, says that "the Jerusalem above is free, and she is our mother" (Gal. 4:26). Hermas, a contemporary of John, on several occasions saw a supernatural woman who was identified as the church (cf. Herm. Vis. I. 2; Vis. II. 1; Vis. III. 1). Also, by a change in metaphor John represents the church as the heavenly bride of Christ (21:2). Apparently, therefore, the heavenly mother of the pre-existent Messiah is also the heavenly mother of the Christians, i.e., she is the pre-existent church, a conclusion supported by vs. 17, where the persecuted Christians are considered her offspring. Although her children are to be persecuted for three and a half years by the dragon, she herself will be unharmed, will be **nourished** in a place of safety. This, of course, is a sign of the ultimate safety of her children.

It is tempting to find other explanations of this verse, such as an allusion to the wanderings of the Jews in the wilderness for forty years, to the escape of the holy family to Egypt as narrated in Matt. 2:13-14, or to the escape of the Jewish Christians from the siege of Jerusalem to Pella beyond the Jordan; but none of these takes into consideration the very evident astral theology which is so conspicuous in this chapter.

from Lincoln's Kentucky cabin to the White House. But there is a power which watches over births of promise. A purpose which includes infants in its vast designs presides over the ways of men.

6. *A Place Prepared by God.*—The woman clothed with the sun is not left helpless. God himself has prepared a place for her security. In all this involved mythology certain central ideas appear clearly enough. There is no waste suffering to secure the purposes of God. The book of Revelation never gets far from its purpose of bringing comfort and assurance to those who are enduring the birth pangs of a new life in

the world. There is a great deal in the statement that it is essentially a book of comfort for hard-pressed Christians. Of course it is more than that. But the intention of bringing comfort and hope is very near to the heart of the book. It is said that John Watson, whose pen name was Ian Maclaren, said near the end of his career that if he had to live his life over again he would preach more sermons the central thought of which was to bring comfort to the hearers. So the great British preacher sensed more deeply as years went on the need of those who sat in the pew for the comfort of the gospel.

7 And there was war in heaven: Michael and his angels fought against the dragon; and the dragon fought and his angels,

7 Now war arose in heaven, Michael and his angels fighting against the dragon;

B. Second Vision: Michael's Victory over the Dragon (12:7-9)

7. The preceding section has prepared us for a conflict between Christ and the dragon. However, the struggle that now takes place is between **Michael and his angels and the dragon and his angels.** This conflict is a prelude to the final cosmic contest in which Satan and his cohorts are completely overthrown and his reign terminated, so that God's new and perfect age may be ushered in. These eschatological struggles are not as different as one might suppose from those which so frequently characterize creation myths, such as the one in the Babylonian story of Marduk and Tiâmat, for the new age is a new creation which can arrive only after a contest in which the old is destroyed. Nevertheless, there is a closer relationship to the Persian belief of a series of conflicts between forces of good and evil culminating in the final defeat of Ahriman, the god of evil, with his hordes. Also, there is some connection with the brief statement in Isa. 27:1, that in the last days the Lord with his great sword will kill Leviathan, the swift serpent, and Leviathan, the crooked serpent, and the monster in the sea. These three heavenly enemies of God have been tentatively identified with three more or less serpentine constellations, Serpens, Draco, and Hydra (George B. Bray, *A Critical and Exegetical Commentary on the Book of Isaiah I-XXXIX* [New York: Charles Scribner's Sons, 1912, "The International Critical Commentary"], pp. 449-52). Also, the defeat and overthrow of the various beasts in Daniel come to mind.

In this situation, however, it is **Michael and his angels** who act as the champion of God and of his afflicted people in waging war with Satan and his angels. This choice is not without reason. For one thing, his very name, which may mean "he who is like God," could lead to his selection. More definitely, however, he had previously been designated as the guardian angel of Israel and had fought in her behalf against the guardian angels of the other nations (Dan. 10:13, 21; cf. Dan. 12:1). It is probably Michael, the unnamed "chief" of the angels in the Assumption of Moses 10:2, who plays a leading part in the final overthrow of Satan. Likewise, along with Gabriel, Raphael, and Phanuel, he will cast the fallen angels into the burning furnace, since they have become subject to Satan and have led astray those who dwelt on earth (I Enoch 54:6). The presence of the dragon in heaven may be an occasion for surprise unless the astral features of the entire account beginning with vs. 1 are taken into consideration. Besides, there are other sources which place his residence in heaven, sometimes in a lower heaven (cf. Luke 10:18; Eph. 6:10-12; I Enoch 40:7; II Enoch 7 and 18; Ascension of Isaiah 7:9; 10:29). It is not necessary to assume that Satan has left the lower regions to assault heaven, as is sometimes suggested.

It may be somewhat unusual, considering the normative Christian usage, that the dragon's forces should be called **angels,** instead of "demons." However, the word was frequently applied to both good and evil supernatural beings. Thus, in Test. Asher 6:4 the phrase "the angels of the Lord and of Satan" is found (cf. II Enoch 29:5). Also, in Matt. 25:41 reference is made to the eternal fire prepared for "the devil and his angels." Mention has already been made of the fallen angels who having come under Satan's control lead men astray (I Enoch 54:6).

---

7. The Cosmic Conflict.—The Greeks were accustomed to tales of cosmic battles, as those between Cronus and Uranus, Jupiter and Cronus, and Jupiter and the giants. The task of early Christian leaders was to make Christian the minds of Greeks and Romans who accepted the new religion. Their own mythology was filled with a moral and spiritual meaning quite new to their world. The battle in heaven was not seen as mere brute conflict for power. In cosmic conflict the forces of evil came defiantly against the forces of good. The moral perceptions which had come to the little church had a heavenly as well as an earthly reference. Once moral and spiritual distinctions are seen they have a universal meaning. So the struggles on earth were

8 And prevailed not; neither was their place found any more in heaven.

9 And the great dragon was cast out, that old serpent, called the Devil, and Satan, which deceiveth the whole world: he was cast out into the earth, and his angels were cast out with him.

10 And I heard a loud voice saying in heaven, Now is come salvation, and strength, and the kingdom of our God, and the power of his Christ: for the accuser of our brethren is cast down, which accused them before our God day and night.

and the dragon and his angels fought, 8 but they were defeated and there was no longer any place for them in heaven. 9 And the great dragon was thrown down, that ancient serpent, who is called the Devil and Satan, the deceiver of the whole world — he was thrown down to the earth, and his angels were thrown down with him. 10 And I heard a loud voice in heaven, saying, "Now the salvation and the power and the kingdom of our God and the authority of his Christ have come, for the accuser of our brethren has been thrown down, who accuses them day and night before our God.

8-9. Right triumphs over wrong; the dragon and his angels are defeated and cast out of heaven. It is strange that the battle itself is not described. Now, for the first time, the dragon is specifically identified as **the Devil and Satan,** the one who deceives **the whole world.** The first word is Διάβολος, meaning "slanderer," regularly used in the LXX for the Hebrew Satan, which means "adversary" or "accuser." In the O.T. Satan is found as a proper name in but three books, Zech. 3:1; Job *passim;* and I Chr. 21:1. In the first two instances Satan is clearly subordinate to God, is, in fact, his agent; but in the third he acquires a limited independence of God and tempts David to take a census of the people. A later development in Judaism, which is most clearly marked in the apocalyptic writings, tended toward an increasing dualism in which Satan is the chief supernatural agent of evil, and is not only the deceiver, tempter, and enemy of men, but becomes the adversary and opponent of God as well. This may have been due to the influence of Persian theology, in which Ormazd and Ahriman were as much opposed to each other as light is to darkness. However, in no Jewish or Christian apocalypse, not even in Revelation, is the dualism as thoroughgoing as in Persian thinking. Outside the O.T., Satan is given a variety of names in Jewish and Christian sources, including Beliar or Belial, Azazel, Sammael, Mastema, Asmodeus, and Beelzebub or Beelzebul.

The result of this conflict in which Satan and his cohorts of angels are thrown out of heaven is by no means final; for they are not overthrown and destroyed at this time. We are reminded of the statement accredited to Jesus after the seventy reported that even the demons had been subject to them in his name; he replied, "I saw Satan fall like lightning from heaven" (Luke 10:18). In Revelation this fall to earth of Satan with his forces may explain why he, not God, is in immediate control of the world and the people of the world, why he is the ruler of this present age, and why both this world and this age are irretrievably evil and corrupt; but it also assures his final complete doom.

C. THIRD VISION: SONG OF WOE AND REJOICING (12:10-12)

10. **A loud voice** is now heard from **heaven;** it is the singing of a song of mingled woe and rejoicing. The singers (plural, since the first person plural is used) are not identified; however, since reference is made to **our brethren,** i.e., the martyrs, who are accused day and night by Satan, it may be that the singers are martyrs (cf. 6:10), not angels. More important, however, is the content of the song, which is martyrological in

seen as a part of a mighty cosmic struggle. Heaven itself was ready to fight for the kind of goodness which had been revealed to men in Jesus Christ.

10. *The Cosmic Victory.*—The fight between **Michael and his angels** and **the dragon and his angels** was fought to a finish. The evil leader and his hosts were vanquished and cast out of heaven. The salvation of saints is made secure. With a sudden turn the myth becomes Christian theology: the victory was won **by the blood of the Lamb.** Even the sacrifice of the martyrs had somehow had its share in making possible the heavenly triumph. So the foes who

11 And they overcame him by the blood of the Lamb, and by the word of their testimony; and they loved not their lives unto the death.

12 Therefore rejoice, *ye* heavens, and ye that dwell in them. Woe to the inhabiters of the earth and of the sea! for the devil is come down unto you, having great wrath, because he knoweth that he hath but a short time.

13 And when the dragon saw that he was cast unto the earth, he persecuted the woman which brought forth the man *child*.

14 And to the woman were given two wings of a great eagle, that she might fly into the wilderness, into her place, where

11 And they have conquered him by the blood of the Lamb and by the word of their testimony, for they loved not their lives even unto death. 12 Rejoice then, O heaven and you that dwell therein! But woe to you, O earth and sea, for the devil has come down to you in great wrath, because he knows that his time is short!"

13 And when the dragon saw that he had been thrown down to the earth, he pursued the woman who had borne the male child. 14 But the woman was given the two wings of the great eagle that she might

---

character. With this initial defeat of Satan the power and authority of God and Christ come into evidence, and the salvation of the righteous, whom Satan in exercising one of his functions has accused before God, is closer at hand.

11. Satan is to be **conquered** not only **by the blood of the Lamb** (cf. 1:5), but also by reason of the **testimony** of the martyrs, who preferred death to disloyalty to God and Christ. Thus the theme that the martyrs through their deaths are to be conquerors is repeated. The phrase **for they loved not their lives even unto death** resembles John 12:25, "He who loves his life loses it, and he who hates his life in this world will keep it for eternal life" (cf. Mark 8:35).

12. Like the scroll of doom and destiny which John ate (cf. 10:10), the coming events were to be both sweet and bitter to the martyrs: sweet because Satan's **time is short;** bitter because in his wrath during the time that remains he will bring **woe** upon the people of the earth.

D. FOURTH VISION: THE WOMAN AND HER OTHER CHILDREN (12:13-17)

13-16. This scene is likewise based on mythological elements. When the dragon was cast down to earth, he resumed his pursuit of the **woman,** who is now apparently on earth. However, she was given **two wings of a great eagle** and escaped again to a **wilderness** where she was taken care of for three and a half years, being protected from the dragon's wrath. This appears to be a duplication of vs. 6, save that in this case the action is staged on the earth, not in heaven as formerly. However, the serpent-dragon now **poured water like a river out of his mouth** to engulf her, but the friendly **earth** came to her rescue and **opened its mouth and swallowed the river.**

---

were cast out of heaven saw a complete end of a hope of felicity of which they were unworthy. They were cast on the earth. And here they set about doing all the wicked deeds they could. But they had the mark of destruction upon them. They were already defeated in heaven. The thought that all their foes are defeated foes brings great comfort to good men. So the heavens are telling not only the glory of God but the hope of all men of good will. It is not a part of the richness of the deeper thought of our age that there is so little consideration of the heavenly reference. We may think it a part of the quality of a scientific age to deplete our spiritual imagination. But it is only through a

misunderstanding both of the nature of science and of spiritual reality that we allow a knowledge of the orderly ways of nature to clip the wings of our spiritual apprehension. No sophisticated knowledge should be allowed to blind the eyes of the spirit.

12. *The Mortality of Wickedness.*—Evil belongs to time; goodness belongs to eternity. The victories of wickedness are temporary and deceptive. In our own time we have seen great evils come and go. Hitler came upon the world in great wrath; but his time was short. There are evil forces unleashed upon the earth today whose immoral fury seems unappeasable. But whatever their temporary victories, their time

she is nourished for a time, and times, and half a time, from the face of the serpent.

15 And the serpent cast out of his mouth water as a flood after the woman, that he might cause her to be carried away of the flood.

16 And the earth helped the woman; and the earth opened her mouth, and swallowed up the flood which the dragon cast out of his mouth.

17 And the dragon was wroth with the woman, and went to make war with the remnant of her seed, which keep the commandments of God, and have the testimony of Jesus Christ.

fly from the serpent into the wilderness, to the place where she is to be nourished for a time, and times, and half a time. **15** The serpent poured water like a river out of his mouth after the woman, to sweep her away with the flood. **16** But the earth came to the help of the woman, and the earth opened its mouth and swallowed the river which the dragon had poured from his mouth. **17** Then the dragon was angry with the woman, and went off to make war on the rest of her offspring, on those who keep the commandments of God and bear testimony to Jesus. And he stood[e] on the sand of the sea.

[e] Other ancient authorities read *And I stood*, connecting the sentence with 13. 1.

Isis, according to one account, escaped Set-Typhon by flying. However, John, considering the woman as the church, the true Israel, may have been thinking of the words of God to the Israelites in the wilderness, "Ye have seen what I did unto the Egyptians, and how I bare you on eagles' wings and brought you unto myself" (Exod. 19:4).

The episode of the flood coming from the serpent's mouth has no parallels in Jewish sources. Since, however, several references are found to the dragon or his equivalent as a water monster (Ezek. 29:3; 32:2-3; Ps. 74:13; Isa. 27.1; Test. Asher 7:3), conceivably such a flood might reasonably be expected to issue from his mouth. Again, in an Egyptian tradition, the evil Set-Typhon, the crocodile who in this instance is identified with the Nile, attempted to engulf Isis with a flood (the annual overflow of the Nile), but the thirsty earth saved her by swallowing the water.

Possible origins, however, are of little significance unless they throw some light on the meaning of John's symbolism. In this case they are of little assistance. Even so, the meaning is probably clear enough: the **woman** now is the earthly church which is persecuted by Satan, but is providentially saved from his onslaughts.

17a. The dragon next turned his attention to the **offspring** of the woman, described as those who have kept **the commandments of God and bear testimony to Jesus.** Her **offspring** are without any question the loyal and faithful Christians who are yet to be persecuted and martyred in order that the number of martyrs may be completed (cf. 6:11); just as unmistakably the heavenly mother of the pre-existent Messiah is now the church, the mother of the faithful. The church will be spared, for it is eternal; her children, however, are to suffer for a while, but despite their sufferings and deaths, we know that they too will escape their persecutor, Satan, and live in triumph forever. Regardless of her striking appearance and evident significance, this woman does not appear in the rest of the book; her place is taken toward the end by the bride of Christ.

17b. And he stood on the sand of the sea (RSV) has the support of the best texts, including the third-century Chester Beatty Papyrus p[47]. A later text, "and I stood," followed by the KJV, Moffatt, and Goodspeed, at first sight seems to make a smoother connection with the scenes to follow. However, when we realize that the dragon is summoning help from the sea and is going to give his authority to the beast that comes out of its depths, the reading followed by the RSV is as logical as it is well attested.

will be short. They will go the way of all evil earthly things.

16. *The Earth Is on the Side of Goodness.* —Again we have vivid mythology whose ways of suggestion were easier for the first readers

of the book of Revelation than for us. But a glorious insight emerges from the heart of it. The very earthly system is on the side of goodness and not on the side of evil. When the serpent would have destroyed the woman the

13 And I stood upon the sand of the sea, and saw a beast rise up out of the sea, having seven heads and ten horns, and upon his horns ten crowns, and upon his heads the name of blasphemy.

2 And the beast which I saw was like unto a leopard, and his feet were as *the feet* of a bear, and his mouth as the mouth of a lion: and the dragon gave him his power, and his seat, and great authority.

13 And I saw a beast rising out of the sea, with ten horns and seven heads, with ten diadems upon its horns and a blasphemous name upon its heads. 2 And the beast that I saw was like a leopard, its feet were like a bear's, and its mouth was like a lion's mouth. And to it the dragon gave his power and his throne and great author-

---

E. Fifth Vision: The Beast from the Sea (13:1-4)

13:1. The **beast** which John saw **rising out of the sea** was similar in appearance to the dragon: like the dragon it had **seven heads** and **ten horns,** but unlike the dragon, who had diadems on its heads, this beast had them on its ten horns. In Dan. 7:6 the four heads of the leopard representing Persia symbolize the kings of Persia (cf. Dan. 11:2); likewise, the three heads of the eagle that stands for the Roman Empire in II Esdras 12:22-28 signify Roman emperors. Following a similar pattern of picture language, the seven heads of this beast in Revelation are symbolic of the Roman emperors, an identification which is made specific in 17:10. In addition, it had a **blasphemous name upon its heads** (RSV). Nestle's text, usually followed by the RSV, has the plural "names," which agrees with the parallel section in 17:3. However, the singular is supported by the Chester Beatty Papyrus and other good MSS, and is probably correct. What this name was is difficult to determine. Since the beast symbolizes the line of divine Roman emperors, it might be one of the divine titles, such as *divus* or *augustus* (σεβαστός), which they had assumed. Whatever the name was, it was blasphemous from the author's standpoint, and was in direct opposition to that of the conquering Christ (19:13).

2a. There are other differences as well, for this beast is not serpentine in appearance. Instead, it combines features of the four beasts of Dan. 7. The author of Daniel writes that he saw four beasts coming out of the sea: the first was like a lion; the second like a bear; the third like a four-headed leopard; and the fourth a terrible, fierce beast with ten horns. Three of these horns were plucked out, and a little horn with eyes like a man, and speaking great things, took its place. This little horn made war on the saints (Dan. 7:21; cf. 7:8 LXX). These four beasts represent respectively the kingdoms of Babylon, Media, Persia, and the Greco-Syrian Empire. The little horn is Antiochus IV, whose surname, Epiphanes (God manifest), was blasphemous according to Jewish standards. It was he who persecuted the Jews, precipitating the Maccabean revolt and occasioning the writing of Daniel. The death of the persecutor and the end of this evil age were promised after three and a half years of persecution. The apocalyptic prediction of Daniel was not fulfilled, for obviously the age of human history was not terminated; but Antiochus did die soon afterward, and the Jews gained their independence and re-established the theocracy.

However, in 63 B.C. they were conquered by the Romans under Pompey. As a result, the fourth beast of Daniel was reinterpreted to apply to Rome, or its ruler, or both. This identification is explicitly made in the Talmudic treatise Abodah Zarah 2ᵇ (cf. II Esdras 12:11). Likewise, the concept of four world empires, the last one Rome, as depicted in II Baruch 36–40, is probably another reinterpretation of Dan. 7, even though the symbolism used, the forest, the vine, the fountain, and the cedar, is quite different. Accordingly, it is not surprising that John has made a similar reinterpretation, but in his grandiose manner has combined all four beasts into a single one, with seven heads, to signify the deified emperors and through them the empire.

2b. The dragon gave this beast **his power and his throne and great authority,** signifying that the beast is satanic in character, is almost Satan incarnate. This is possibly a satire on the Roman belief that the empire and the emperors were divine

3 And I saw one of his heads as it were wounded to death; and his deadly wound was healed: and all the world wondered after the beast.

ity. 3 One of its heads seemed to have a mortal wound, but its mortal wound was healed, and the whole earth followed the

in origin and character. This view differs greatly from that expressed by Paul, who wrote to the church at Rome that the empire is of God and those in office are God's ministers (Rom. 13:1-7). For Paul the empire and its rulers are inherently good, though not divine, because they are under the direct control of God himself, not of Satan, as in Revelation. Similarly, I Peter, like Revelation written in a time of persecution, probably during Trajan's reign a few years later, commends the Christians for the Lord's sake to be subject to the emperor and his governors; they are to fear God and honor the emperor (I Pet. 2:13-16). However, for John there is nothing good about either the empire or the emperors; the rulers are not ordained by God, but are the agents of Satan himself, who has invested them with his own authority.

3. Not only is the beast symbolic of the emperors, but in a special way it is associated with Nero, the notorious matricide, in whose reign a number of Christians, probably including Peter and Paul, suffered and died as martyrs. In July, 68, Nero, condemned to death by the senate for his misrule and crimes, fled to a villa where he committed suicide by stabbing himself in the throat. Due both to certain mysterious circumstances connected with his death and to the character of his rule which was the first to give the Roman citizens and subjects the feeling that the imperial authority, which could be awesome and terrible, as well as beneficent, was above law, the belief developed that Nero had not died as reported. Instead, it was rumored, he had gone into hiding in the East, and would return with a Parthian host to invade and devastate the empire he had once ruled. In keeping with this rumor several impostors arose who had brief careers during which they created disaffection and disturbances in the eastern portions of the empire. The myth concerning a later emperor, Frederick II, who died in 1250, is comparable; for more than a century after his death it was believed that he was alive, and several impostors impersonated him.

The original rumor developed into the belief that Nero had really died, but that in due time he would be restored to life to lead an army, presumably from Parthia, to ravage the empire (cf. Sibylline Oracles 5:361-67; 4:119-27, 137-39). A further stage was the identification of this Nero *redivivus* with the Antichrist, who is to be destroyed along with his invading armies by the king (the Messiah) sent from heaven by God (Sibylline Oracles 5:106-10; cf. 5:33-34). In the Christian Ascension of Isaiah 4:1-14 he is the incarnation of Beliar (i.e., Satan), the Antichrist who will persecute the church. In a second-century Christian source Nero *redivivus* is portrayed as a purple dragon and a great beast (Sibylline Oracles 8:88-157).

This somewhat detailed presentation helps to explain the otherwise unintelligible statement that one of the heads of the beast **seemed to have a mortal wound, but its mortal wound was healed.** The seven heads represent the emperors as a whole, as noted under vs. 1. As for the head with a **mortal wound** which had been healed, this is evidently an allusion to the myth that Nero, who had died of a wound in his throat, would return to life to plague the empire and as the Antichrist to persecute the Christians. Quite naturally, the marvelous restoration of Nero to life will fill all the world with wonder (cf. 17:8).

earth destroyed the destructive forces which he released. This world may have become the dwelling place of all sorts of evil but it was not made for such a situation. It was made to be the home of goodness. And in its very structure it is the friend of embattled goodness. It

is only a misuse of the earth and its forces which turns them to evil. In an atomic age it is a severe faith that the tremendous forces extorted from nature will at last be turned against those who would misuse them. But it is a faith worth maintaining.

4 And they worshipped the dragon which gave power unto the beast: and they worshipped the beast, saying, Who *is* like unto the beast? who is able to make war with him?

5 And there was given unto him a mouth speaking great things and blasphemies; and power was given unto him to continue forty *and* two months.

6 And he opened his mouth in blasphemy against God, to blaspheme his name, and his tabernacle, and them that dwell in heaven.

7 And it was given unto him to make war with the saints, and to overcome them: and power was given him over all kindreds, and tongues, and nations.

beast with wonder. 4 Men worshiped the dragon, for he had given his authority to the beast, and they worshiped the beast, saying, "Who is like the beast, and who can fight against it?"

5 And the beast was given a mouth uttering haughty and blasphemous words, and it was allowed to exercise authority for forty-two months; 6 it opened its mouth to utter blasphemies against God, blaspheming his name and his dwelling, that is, those who dwell in heaven. 7 Also it was allowed to make war on the saints and to conquer them.*f* And authority was given it over every tribe and people and tongue and na-

f Other ancient authorities omit this sentence.

4. Instead of worshiping God, people **worshiped the dragon**, i.e., Satan, who had given some of his authority to this beast; they also **worshiped the beast**, i.e., the allegedly divine rulers of Rome, who are actually demonic and satanic. This is the most explicit reference to the imperial cult, which for John was so evil an institution that Satan alone could have devised it. Awed by the power of the beast, i.e., by the unprecedented extent, might, and power of the Roman rule, people asked the question: **Who is like the beast, and who can fight against it?** For the Christian the answer is obvious, since the Lamb that was slain is far more powerful than the slain emperor who returns as the Antichrist and persecutor of the Christians. The Lamb will shortly overpower and destroy him.

F. Sixth Vision: The Beast Exercises His Authority (13:5-10)

5-7. Not only does the **beast** wear a name of blasphemy, but he also has been **given a mouth speaking great things,** blaspheming God, **his name** and **dwelling,** and those who reside **in heaven.** Both the phraseology and the idea are taken from the description of an earlier Antichrist, Antiochus IV Epiphanes, who had "a mouth speaking great things" (Dan. 7:8) with which he would speak "words against the Most High" (Dan. 7:25). That John had Daniel before him is supported by the statements in vss. 5 and 7 that the beast would exercise authority **for forty-two months** and **was allowed to make war on the saints and to conquer them.** It was for this same period of time that Antiochus was permitted to "wear out the saints of the Most High" (Dan. 7:25); i.e., during this time he "made war with the saints, and prevailed against them" (Dan. 7:21). Furthermore, just as the fourth Danielic beast "shall devour the whole earth, and shall tread it down, and break it in pieces" (Dan. 7:23), so the beast symbolizing Rome was given authority **over every tribe and people and tongue and nation.**

13:4. *Giving a Bad State the Place Which Belongs to God.*—We now come straight into the heart of the question of what to do when the civil power becomes the expression of evil. So the man of Patmos saw Rome. But the problem has emerged in many a century. The Soviet ambition to conquer and rule a godless world gives the form of the problem in our own time. Such power is so massive and mighty that there is the greatest temptation to make terms with it in such a fashion as to surrender our own faith and the integrity of our moral and spir-

itual and political insights and true loyalties. Too many books are being published in our time which suggest that all standards are relative and therefore life is simply a form of expediency. There is something not quite unlike a cult of the relativity of all the moral judgments of history. If this is not the worship of **the beast,** it easily prepares for the worship of the beast. Whenever we allow political considerations to replace the authority of moral and spiritual judgments the day of political idolatry has arrived.

8 And all that dwell upon the earth shall worship him, whose names are not written in the book of life of the Lamb slain from the foundation of the world.

9 If any man have an ear, let him hear.

10 He that leadeth into captivity shall go into captivity: he that killeth with the sword must be killed with the sword. Here is the patience and the faith of the saints.

11 And I beheld another beast coming up out of the earth; and he had two horns like a lamb, and he spake as a dragon.

tion, **8** and all who dwell on earth will worship it, every one whose name has not been written before the foundation of the world in the book of life of the Lamb that was slain. **9** If any one has an ear, let him hear:

10 If any one is to be taken captive,
    to captivity he goes;
  if any one slays with the sword,
    with the sword must he be slain.

Here is a call for the endurance and faith of the saints.

11 Then I saw another beast which rose out of the earth; it had two horns like a

8. The observation that all dwellers on the earth would worship the beast is perhaps a justifiable hyperbole in view of the widespread and general acceptance of the imperial cult throughout the empire. For all subjects of the Roman Empire worshiped the emperors, save the Jews, whom the author ignores, and the Christians, who were foreordained before **the foundation of the world** to have their names written **in the book of life of the Lamb that was slain.** (The word order of the KJV, which has followed the Greek too literally, is somewhat ambiguous.) The view expressed here is highly deterministic (cf. also 6:11 and 7:4). Only those whose names are in "the Lamb's book of life" are to be permitted to enter the New Jerusalem (21:27).

9-10. If any one has an ear, let him hear is a reiteration of the exhortation which either precedes or follows the glowing promises to the martyrs in the conclusions of the seven letters in chs. 2–3. Here it serves to preface a warning, almost like a chant, which is apparently a paraphrase of Jeremiah's dire prediction that those who are destined for death will go to death; for the sword, to the sword; for famine, to the famine; and for captivity, to captivity (Jer. 15:2; cf. Matt. 26:52). As used by John, the words are a reminder to the Christians that if they are destined for captivity, they will go into captivity, i.e., if they are destined to be persecuted and martyred, this will be their fate, for they have been chosen for the Lamb's book of life before the world was established. On the other hand, the persecutors are warned that those who slay Christians by the sword will themselves be killed by the sword, presumably by the two-edged sword projecting from the mouth of the conquering Christ with which he slays the nations in 19:15. The period of persecution that lies ahead, in which Christians will be slain, calls for **endurance and faith,** two necessary prerequisites for martyrdom, for without patient steadfastness in a time of persecution and death, coupled with a sublime faith in the final outcome, few would become martyrs.

G. Seventh Vision: The Beast from the Earth (13:11-18)

11. The first beast came from the sea, the second comes **out of the earth.** This may be a survival of a tradition preserved in II Baruch 29:4 and II Esdras 6:49-52 of two beasts, one, Leviathan, from the sea, and the other, Behemoth, from the earth. He may be the same beast that ascended from the "bottomless pit" to persecute the two heavenly witnesses. Not only is he a "false prophet," as he is called in 16:13; 19:20; and 20:10, but he is also another representation of the Antichrist, or more specifically, of the pseudo Christ. This dual character may be a reflection of the tradition in the Marcan

10. Tragedy as a Challenge.—The most desperate situations are a summons not to surrender but to courageous faith and action. History has many a story of the courage of men who held truth and liberty and faith dearer than life. The principle is one of large and

varied applications. When Patrick Henry cried "Give me liberty or give me death" he was not indulging in idle rhetoric. The deepest story of this sort of loyalty has to do with religion. One meets it in the O.T., in the N.T., and all through Christian history. Out of such courage

12 And he exerciseth all the power of the first beast before him, and causeth the earth and them which dwell therein to worship the first beast, whose deadly wound was healed.

13 And he doeth great wonders, so that he maketh fire come down from heaven on the earth in the sight of men,

14 And deceiveth them that dwell on the earth by *the means of* those miracles which he had power to do in the sight of the beast; saying to them that dwell on the earth, that they should make an image to the beast, which had the wound by a sword, and did live.

lamb and it spoke like a dragon. 12 It exercises all the authority of the first beast in its presence, and makes the earth and its inhabitants worship the first beast, whose mortal wound was healed. 13 It works great signs, even making fire come down from heaven to earth in the sight of men; 14 and by the signs which it is allowed to work in the presence of the beast, it deceives those who dwell on earth, bidding them make an image for the beast which was wounded by the sword and yet lived; 15 and it was allowed to give breath to the image of the

"little apocalypse": "False Christs and false prophets will arise and show signs and wonders, to lead astray, if possible, the elect" (Mark 13:22). In his deceptive impersonation of the Christ—but one that should not mislead the discerning—he had **two horns like a lamb;** but despite his Christlike appearance, he was actually satanic, since he **spoke like a dragon.** The possession of **two horns** may have been suggested by the Danielic ram with two horns (Dan. 8:3). A different but quite popular description of the Antichrist and false prophet is given in the Apocalypse of Pseudo-John 7: "The appearance of his face is dusky; the hairs of his head are sharp, like darts; his eyebrows are like a wild beast's; his right eye like the star that rises in the morning and the other like a lion's; his mouth about one cubit long; his teeth span long; his fingers like scythes; the print of his feet two spans; and on his face an inscription, Antichrist."

12. Invested with **the authority of the first beast,** he also acts as a priest of the imperial cult, causing all people to **worship the first beast,** the one whose fatal wound was now healed. The part is equal to the whole; the single head representing Nero redivivus now becomes the symbol for the entire line of Caesars who are worshiped as gods. As a priest, the second beast symbolizes the priesthood of the imperial cultus which organized and supervised the worship of the emperor gods.

13-14. As predicted in Mark 13:22, this false Christ deceives people by working miracles. Similarly, in other early Christian sources he would be a miracle worker (cf. II Thess. 2:9-10; Did. 16:4; Ascension of Isaiah 4:4-5). This belief that the false prophet, or pseudo Christ, was to be a worker of miracles may have been an apocalyptic reinterpretation of Deut. 13:1-3, which is, in effect, a warning about the false prophets who by their signs and wonders would entice people to worship other gods than Yahweh. This is precisely the case here, for the beast deludes people so that at his bidding they make an image of the first beast, **which was wounded by the sword and yet lived.** This is a derisive parody of the description of the slain Lamb who died and yet lives evermore (1:18; 2:8). In the contemporaneous account in the Ascension of Isaiah 4:6-11, Beliar, the Neronic Antichrist, will set up images of himself in every city, and the people of the world will believe in him and sacrifice to him, saying that he is god. A considerable number of Christians, even, will turn aside and worship him.

came the great word: "The blood of martyrs is the seed of the Church." [6]

14. *World-Wide Surrender to Evil Power.*—The Roman Empire has become the implacable foe of the true religion and its evil power is seen as centered in a particular emperor. He becomes the deceiver of mankind. His reign is

based upon a surrender which involves the world-wide acceptance of moral deception. The throne of the world becomes the corrupter of mankind. Such processes are often slow and subtle and confusing. The spread of secularism in the modern world is, in its own way, a tragic example of what we mean. Joseph Wood Krutch, who has often been confused bv his

[6] Tertullian *Apologeticus* ch. 50.

15 And he had power to give life unto the image of the beast, that the image of the beast should both speak, and cause that as many as would not worship the image of the beast should be killed.

16 And he causeth all, both small and great, rich and poor, free and bond, to receive a mark in their right hand, or in their foreheads:

17 And that no man might buy or sell, save he that had the mark, or the name of the beast, or the number of his name.

beast so that the image of the beast should even speak, and to cause those who will not worship the image of the beast to be slain. 16 Also it causes all, both small and great, both rich and poor, both free and slave, to be marked on the right hand or the forehead, 17 so that no one can buy or sell unless he has the mark, that is, the name of the beast or the number of its

---

15. Among the miracles attributed to the false Christ is that of giving life to the image of the first beast, enabling it to speak. This may be an allusion to some priestly deception involving ventriloquism; more likely it is a reference to the fact that the image is that of a human being, a living person. Invested as he is with imperial power, the second beast causes all who do not worship the first beast **to be slain.** This, of course, was the crux of the entire situation for the Christians: there were but two alternatives, one was to deny Christ and worship the emperor, the other was to confess Christ and refuse to worship the ruler. The first course led to temporal safety and security but to eternal damnation and punishment; the second led to persecution by the state and to death, but to a triumphant death and a glorious immortality.

16-17a. We have seen that the faithful, those designated to become martyrs, were symbolically sealed on their foreheads (7:3). Quite probably as a counterpart to this act of the sealing of the faithful, John writes that the beast causes all classes of mankind **to be marked on the right hand or the forehead.** Those who do not have this **mark** (χάραγμα), the technical term for the imperial stamp on official documents, would not be able to **buy or sell,** to engage in business. Some think of this as a visible mark, such as the ivy-leaved symbol of Dionysus, which Ptolemy Philopator I is said to have had placed on those Jews who refused to sacrifice to the pagan deity (III Macc. 2:29). More probably it was as invisible as the seal placed on the faithful. We are reminded again of the parallel in Pss. Sol. 15:8-10, where the mark of God is placed on the righteous so that they may be saved, while the mark of destruction is placed on the wicked so that they may inherit destruction and darkness. Accordingly, in Revelation those who have the mark of the beast will be destroyed in the last days (19:20).

It is also unlikely that there was an official ban to prevent Christians from engaging in business. That there was an unofficial social boycott, however, in numerous instances is quite probable; e.g., the letter from the church at Lyons, written after a persecution in

---

materials, in *The Measure of Man* [7] deals with human values in a way which raises many of the vital questions which face the age caught in coils of self-betrayal.

15. *Living in an Unreal World.*—The picture the man of Patmos paints is fairly fantastic in its evil confusion. The true God is ignored. The beast is worshiped. The lifeless image breathes and speaks words of wicked power. A phantasmagoria of evil has taken the place of the reign of good. The false vitality of wickedness masters the state. What seems real to men is actually unreal to them. What for the moment seems unreal to them is the eternal rule of

[7] Indianapolis: Bobbs-Merrill, 1954.

God. In the world in which we live the tyranny of habits of thought which contradict the true meaning of life and history is all too obviously present. The deceptive vitality of intellectual fashions which betray the minds of men in its own odd way gives **breath to the image of the beast.** In a secular and materialistic age the spirit of the time all too easily contradicts the spirit of God. The war with our favorite obsessions is one of the real battles of our time. Bertrand Russell has often assumed that he represented the breath of intelligence when he only represented the breath of intellectual decadence.

17. *The Passport to Success in a Wicked World.*—You can be sealed with the mark of

18 Here is wisdom. Let him that hath understanding count the number of the beast: for it is the number of a man; and his number *is* Six hundred threescore *and* six.

name. 18 This calls for wisdom: let him who has understanding reckon the number of the beast, for it is a human number, its number is six hundred and sixty-six.[g]

[g] Other ancient authorities read *six hundred and sixteen.*

A.D. 177, states that the Devil "endeavored in every manner to practice and exercise his servants against the servants of God, not only shutting us out from houses and baths and markets, but forbidding us to be seen in any place whatever" (Eusebius *Church History* V. 1. 5).

17*b*-18. Although the mark was invisible, John conceived of it as being the **name of the beast or the number of its name.** This is an introduction to one of the most celebrated and controversial symbols in Revelation, the number **six hundred and sixty-six,** as it is given in most texts including the third-century Chester Beatty Papyrus p[47]. However, a variant number, 616, found in the fifth-century Codex C (Ephraemi), was known to Irenaeus, who wrote toward the end of the second century. The verse in which it is found, but one of a total of more than four hundred in Revelation, has been given far more attention in popular thinking than it deserves. Indeed, for many people Revelation is chiefly thought of as the book containing this mysterious number. Unfortunately, John intended it to be something of an enigma; as he says, it calls for **wisdom,** and only he who has **understanding** can discover its significance.

In contrast to our modern usage, neither the Hebrews nor the Greeks had special numerical symbols; instead, they used the letters of the alphabet as numbers. Accordingly, following the clue of 17*b*, **the number of its name,** 666, has generally been considered a cipher which can be resolved into letters spelling a name. An example of this is seen in the Sibylline Oracles 1:324 ff., where by equating letters and number, 'Ιησοῦς (Jesus) equals 888 as follows: $I(10)+H(8)+\Sigma(200)+O(70)+Y(400)+\Sigma(200)=888$.

It is thought that the cipher 666 was formed in an identical manner. But what name lies behind it? According to John it is **a human number** (RSV), or **the number of a man** (KJV), which may mean that the hidden name is personal and historical. This, however, is not certain, since in apocalypticism human beings often symbolize angels, just as animals symbolize human beings. But on the assumption that the name is personal, since the number is that of the beast symbolizing the imperial line, it should be the name or title of an emperor. This rules out suggestions like Λατεῖνος (i.e., the Roman Empire) and Τεῖταν (Titan) in Greek, or the Hebrew equivalent of Primitive Chaos (Tiamat; a proposal of Gunkel). The search being narrowed to an emperor, the notorious Γαῖος Καῖσαρ (Gaius Caesar) has been proposed. The letters of his name do add up to 616, the variant noted by Irenaeus, but this fails to account for the much better attested 666.

The connection of the beast with Nero *redivivus* has led others to find the solution in his name. This may be done by transliterating the Greek Νέρων Καῖσαρ (Neron Caesar) into Hebrew letters and giving them their numerical equivalents in the following manner: (200)ר+(60)ס+(100)ק+(50)נ+(6)ו+(200)ר+(50)נ. These sums, when added up, total 666. Furthermore, if the proper name is written without the final "n," according to the Latin form, the sum is 616, the variant reading already noted.

If this identification is correct, it fits very well into the practically certain belief that the beast is closely related to the satanic Nero, returned to life. It quite fittingly

God. You can be sealed with the mark of the devil. So in blunt words we can put what the man of Patmos is saying. Commercial life can become so involved in current idolatry that one cannot succeed in business without **the mark . . . of the beast.** We need only to stop long

enough with the number of the beast to remark that the author is playing with the numerical value of letters so combined that they express the very opposite of perfection. And we must remember that we are dealing with a time when a name was supposed to express the **very char-**

14 And I looked, and, lo, a Lamb stood on the mount Sion, and with him a hundred forty *and* four thousand, having his Father's name written in their foreheads.

14 Then I looked, and lo, on Mount Zion stood the Lamb, and with him a hundred and forty-four thousand who had his name and his Father's name written on

---

bears his name, just as the scarlet woman in 17:3-5 quite properly has the name Babylon (symbolizing Rome) on her forehead. Furthermore, as Nero *redivivus,* the Antichrist is compared and contrasted with Christ; thus the number 666 may be compared and contrasted with his number, 888.

Lohmeyer in his commentary proposes a wholly different solution (*Die Offenbarung des Johannes* [Tübingen: J. C. B. Mohr, 1926; "Handbuch zum Neuen Testament"], pp. 115-16). He states that according to Pythagorean numerology, 666 is a so-called triangular number, being the sum of the numbers from 1 through 36 inclusive; further, 36 is itself the sum of the numbers from 1 through 8. Accordingly, 666 is resolved into 8, a number which has special significance in 17:11, "As for the beast that was and is not, it is an eighth but it belongs to the seven, and it goes to perdition." Accordingly, so Lohmeyer observes, the number 8 designates the fearful, demonic Antichrist whose end is at hand. The number 666, then, is **a human number** which is a cipher for the demonic number 8. Thus by coincidence Lohmeyer arrives at practically the same conclusion: the number is that of the Antichrist who in 17:11 is also Nero *redivivus.*

With the appearance of these two beasts in ch. 13, the leading characters of the apocalyptic drama have now come on the stage, save for the scarlet woman, the bride of Christ, and Gog and Magog, who make their entrance later. On the one side, the evil side, are Satan, the beasts representing the demonic Roman emperors and the Antichrist, the angels of Satan, the pagans who are generally grouped as enemies and persecutors of the Christians, as well as Jews and apostate Christians, who are also on Satan's side. On the other, the good side, are God, Christ, the archangels and angels, the two heavenly witnesses, the four living creatures, the twenty-four elders, and the faithful Christians, especially the martyrs. The forces of Satan and God are in battle array; the two sides of evil and good are about evenly balanced; and the cosmic war is reaching its dramatic and inevitable conclusion. The struggle will be a desperate one to determine whether righteousness or evil is to rule. Through it all, however, the reader is made conscious of the author's belief that God is more powerful than Satan, indeed, that he is all-powerful; and he is assured that despite temporary evidences to the contrary, God will overcome Satan and bring his evil reign to an end.

VII. Seven Visions: Worshipers of the Lamb and Worshipers of the Beast (14:1-20)

A. First Vision: The Martyrs and the Lamb on Mount Zion (14:1-5)

14:1. Continuing with his dramatic use of contrasts, John now turns from a depiction of the beast and his worshipers to a portrayal of the Lamb and his followers. This is somewhat anticipatory—a preview of the near future, after the three and a half years of persecution, when the martyrs will receive their reward. The scene is on **Mount Zion,** which is in accordance with a common Jewish expectation. Micah, for one, prophesied that following the judgment of his day of wrath, God would summon the faithful

---

acter of the wearer of the name. The corrupting power of unethical customs in business requires constant scrutiny. There have been times when men could do business in certain places only by paying a bribe. Men try to shrug these things off, but when business wears the mark of the beast it means the corruption of society.

14:1. *The Mark of Redemption.*—The picture of the stainless saints is put over against the picture of the soiled merchants. In the grim and bitter age in which he lived it was nothing less than perfection which captured the imagination of the man of Patmos. But it is a particular kind of perfection of which he speaks. It

2 And I heard a voice from heaven, as the voice of many waters, and as the voice of a great thunder: and I heard the voice of harpers harping with their harps:

their foreheads. 2 And I heard a voice from heaven like the sound of many waters and like the sound of loud thunder; the voice I heard was like the sound of harpers play-

---

remnant to Mount Zion, where he would reign over them forever (Mic. 4:6-8). Others prophesied in a similar vein (cf. Joel 2:32; Isa. 11:9-12; 40:1–46:13). In some cases it is the Messiah who is to assemble the faithful Israelites in the holy mount. Thus, in II Esdras 13:32-39 the Messiah will be revealed on Mount Zion, and after punishing the nations he will summon a peaceable multitude, metaphorically called the ten tribes, to himself. Likewise, in Pss. Sol. 17:26-28 the Messiah will gather at Jerusalem a holy people, whom he will govern in righteousness.

In Christian sources, as might be expected, it is usually the Christ, not God, who will perform this role. An early example is provided by Mark 13:27, which predicts that at his second advent Christ will gather his elect from "the ends of the earth to the ends of heaven." According to Heb. 12:22, this ingathering is to take place on Mount Zion in the presence of the angels. A close parallel to the scene in Revelation is provided by a later Christian source, II Esdras 2:42-48, which was also written in a time of persecution. It represents Ezra as seeing a great multitude arrayed in their immortal garments on Mount Zion, praising the Lord with songs. A tall young man, the Son of God, was seen placing crowns on their heads and giving them palms to carry. In answer to his query, Ezra is informed that this multitude consists of those who had confessed the Son of God in this world, i.e., they were martyrs who were now receiving their rewards from Christ. The close resemblance to the tableau in Revelation is quite evident.

But where is Mount Zion located in this scene? Is it in heaven or on earth? Probably in both places. While in a sense the **hundred and forty-four thousand** are in heaven, as in ch. 7, John is also envisaging the time when the Messiah will establish his kingdom on the earthly Zion. In view of the fluid nature of his symbolism, which flows without difficulty along the channels of his changing thoughts, it is easy to understand how for him this gathering occurred both in heaven and on earth at the same time.

A second problem is the identity of the **hundred and forty-four thousand**. Although they are not distributed among the twelve tribes, they most probably are the 144,000 martyrs-to-be who were sealed in 7:3. For one thing, it is not likely that John would have introduced a quite different group of 144,000 people without differentiating them more specifically than by the statement in 4a. Furthermore, in both scenes the company were sealed on their foreheads; but whereas in the earlier scene the nature of the seal was not indicated, now we learn that it consisted of the names of the Lamb and his Father. The 144,000 are also the same as the great multitude of 7:9-17, who came out of the great tribulation. The names of the Lamb and of his Father which they bear on their foreheads are in direct contrast to the name, or the number of the name, of the beast which was placed on the right hand or forehead of his worshipers (13:16-17).

2-3. A **voice** sounding like **many waters** and **loud thunder** was heard from heaven, **like the sound of harpers playing on their harps.** Also, **a new song** was being sung **before the throne** and before **the living creatures** and the **elders.** The singers are not identified, but if John thinks of the martyrs as being both in the heavenly and earthly

---

is a perfection which has been made possible by the death of Christ. Of this he speaks under the figure of **the Lamb.** The mark of the Lamb is the mark of redemption. The rather mixed metaphor of the father of the Lamb indicated that God is the father of the one who achieved redemption. The thought of the redemptive death of Christ is never far from the mind of

the author of the book of Revelation. Sometimes it seems to be peering around every corner. We are reminded of the words in Thomas Tiplady's hymn:

Above the hills of time the cross is gleaming,
Fair as the sun when night has turned to day;
And from it love's pure light is richly streaming,
To cleanse the heart and banish sin away.

3 And they sung as it were a new song before the throne, and before the four beasts, and the elders: and no man could learn that song but the hundred *and* forty *and* four thousand, which were redeemed from the earth.

4 These are they which were not defiled with women; for they are virgins. These are they which follow the Lamb whithersoever he goeth. These were redeemed from among men, *being* the firstfruits unto God and to the Lamb.

5 And in their mouth was found no guile: for they are without fault before the throne of God.

ing on their harps, 3 and they sing a new song before the throne and before the four living creatures and before the elders. No one could learn that song except the hundred and forty-four thousand who had been redeemed from the earth. 4 It is these who have not defiled themselves with women, for they are chaste;[h] it is these who follow the Lamb wherever he goes; these have been redeemed from mankind as first fruits for God and the Lamb, 5 and in their mouth no lie was found, for they are spotless.

[h] Greek *virgins.*

Zion in this scene, he could readily visualize them as the singers, as in the parallel passages in 7:10 and II Esdras 2:42. The words of the song are not given. As in 5:9, it is called **a new song,** and is probably to be understood as a song of praise and thanksgiving, possibly like the one in 15:3-4. Since it could be learned only by the **hundred and forty-four thousand,** this is another indication that they are the singers.

4-5. The one distinctive description of the 144,000 is that they are celibates, **who have not defiled themselves with women, for they are chaste.** If taken literally, this description might distinguish them from the earlier groups in ch. 7. Consequently, Charles would eliminate the words as a monkish interpolation, even though they are supported by the earliest textual evidence. More probably, the statement is to be considered metaphorically as a symbol of the "spotless" character of the martyrs who had not participated in idolatry, which is frequently compared with immorality and fornication. They are those **who follow the Lamb wherever he goes,** even unto death. Like their brother martyrs under the altar in 6:9, they are **first fruits for God and the Lamb.** Since they had not denied Christ, **no lie** was found in their mouths; they are indeed **spotless.**

3. *The Beatific Chorus.*—The heavenly music is characterized by the most utter loveliness. From stainless souls come sounds of stainless beauty. There is a lascivious music hot with all lawless lust. Not such is the heavenly music sung by the redeemed. It is born in the passion of a great victory and not in the madness of impetuous surrender. The character of the saints makes the song. There is a contemporary poetry which is only the echo of vivid vices. There is a strange poetry which follows the depletion and frustration of consummated lust. Lord Byron knew how to sing the song of the sated in many a key. There is always a smell of death about this poetry of the exhausted body and the empty soul. There is a poetry which, like the song of the serene saints, has the taste of immortality in it.

5. *The Deathlessness of Truth.*—Lies always get found out. And when the last lie is revealed in its own true nature there will be no more lies to tell. You can sing about a lie only while

you suppose it is not a lie. The eternal music is shot through with truth. In fact it is truth crystallized into music. So the serene saints, because truth has become the very quality of their being, can sing the deathless song. So with Keats's words: "A thing of beauty is a joy forever" [8] we must also put the other words: "Without truth there is no eternal beauty." The last evil thing to be cast out of a man is some lie that sticketh closer than a brother, some bit of self-deception by means of which a man persuades himself that he is better or more important than he is. Søren Kierkegaard told the bitter truth about many things and so confused truth and falsehood that what he called truth was a lie. But he never faced the falsehood told to him by his own ingrowing egotism. The serene saints had cast the last lie from their souls. And so they could sing the song which cannot die.

[8] "Endymion," Book i.

469

6 And I saw another angel fly in the midst of heaven, having the everlasting gospel to preach unto them that dwell on the earth, and to every nation, and kindred, and tongue, and people,

7 Saying with a loud voice, Fear God, and give glory to him; for the hour of his judgment is come: and worship him that made heaven, and earth, and the sea, and the fountains of waters.

8 And there followed another angel, saying, Babylon is fallen, is fallen, that

6 Then I saw another angel flying in midheaven, with an eternal gospel to proclaim to those who dwell on earth, to every nation and tribe and tongue and people; 7 and he said with a loud voice, "Fear God and give him glory, for the hour of his judgment has come; and worship him who made heaven and earth, the sea and the fountains of water."

8 Another angel, a second, followed, say-

B. Second Vision: Angelic Admonition to Worship God (14:6-7)

6-7. The description of this prospect of marvelous reward for the martyrs is followed by the first of three angelic proclamations. This tableau is to some extent reminiscent of the eagle described in 8:13 as flying in midheaven and crying out a threefold woe upon the inhabitants of the earth. Like the eagle, this first angel was **flying in midheaven** and proclaimed **an eternal gospel** to those **who dwell on earth.** While "gospel" means "good news," in this case it is a stern warning in answer to the question raised by the worshipers of the beast in 13:4, "Who is like the beast, and who can fight against it?" The angel, in answer, strictly admonishes that all should **fear God and give him glory, for the hour of his judgment has come.** He, the Creator, should be worshiped, and not the emperor. In content this warning, which is similar to the doxology of the twenty-four elders in 4:11, was along the lines of early Christian preaching against idolatry; e.g., we are told in Acts 14:15 that when Paul and Barnabas were about to be worshiped as gods, Paul cried out, "We also are men, of like nature with you, and bring you good news, that you should turn from these vain things to a living God who made the heaven and the earth and the sea and all that is in them."

C. Third Vision: Angel Pronounces Doom of Babylon (14:8)

8. A second **angel,** who apparently was also in heaven, followed the first and uttered a woe over Babylon (Rome), which is amplified in the dirge of ch. 18, beginning, **Fallen,**

---

6. *Invitation and Judgment.*—The author of the book of Revelation does not forget that the gospel comes as a great invitation to mankind. So in the midst of pictures representing the great fulfillment and terrible judgment there comes the picture of an **angel flying in midheaven, with an eternal gospel** offered **to every nation and tribe and tongue and people.** The hymns of invitation in countless number echo this call. In the eighteenth century Gerhard Tersteegen wrote: "God calling yet? Shall I not hear?" Anna L. Barbauld, whose long life crossed the line of the eighteenth and nineteenth centuries, wrote:

> Come, said Jesus' sacred voice,
> Come, and make my path your choice.

The great proclamation is the supreme task of the church in every age.

7. *Sentimentality Transcended.*—The Christian invitation is often given in fashions of luscious sentimentality. All this is transcended in the summons to **fear God and give . . . glory** to **him who made heaven and earth.** There is something awesome about approaching this great God. There is a noble fear which is a part of worship. The Redeemer is also the Creator and the Judge. The solemn grandeur of the Christian religion must not be lost in the proclamation of its tenderness, true and profound as that tenderness is. The greatest proclaimers of the Christian message have always given the sense of echoing the awesomeness of eternity. The French lords of the pulpit of the court of France did not forget that they were speaking for the King of kings. One can still hear the words of one of their great preachers: "Only God is great."

8. *The Doom of the Imperial City.*—The city of evil men can only be a city of destruction. The name **Babylon** of course means Rome. It

great city, because she made all nations drink of the wine of the wrath of her fornication.

9 And the third angel followed them, saying with a loud voice, If any man wor-

ing, "Fallen, fallen is Babylon the great, she who made all nations drink the wine of her impure passion."

9 And another angel, a third, followed, saying with a loud voice, "If any one wor-

---

fallen is Babylon the great. The phrase, save for the last two words, is probably an echo of Isa. 21:9*b*, which reads, "Fallen, fallen is Babylon; and all the graven images of her gods he hath broken unto the ground." For John, Rome, the new Babylon, was to be destroyed because of her idolatrous ways. The added words **the great** are probably a reflection of Dan. 4:30, "Is not this great Babylon . . . ?" In subsequent passages in Revelation, Babylon (Rome) is always called **the great,** possibly as an acknowledgment of her great power, which, however, was not great enough to stand against the might of God.

It has been assumed that Babylon has been used as a designation for Rome. In a similar manner the Jews came to call their conqueror Rome by the name of their ancient enemy Edom, a usage which is quite common in the Talmud. Occasionally they also designated Rome as Babylon, their earlier idolatrous conqueror; e.g., in a description of the capture of Jerusalem and the destruction of the temple in A.D. 70 the Romans are called Chaldeans and their capital is given as Babylon (II Baruch 6–8; cf. 11:1; 67:7). In another source the prediction is made that a great star falling into the Mediterranean will consume the sea and Babylon and Italy with fire (Sibylline Oracles 5:158-61; cf. 143). Obviously in this passage Babylon stands for Rome, the capital of Italy. No reader of these statements would have been misled by this obvious comparison; nor should any reader of Revelation (or I Pet. 5:13) seek to find any mystical or hidden meaning in the use of the name Babylon other than Rome, the persecutor of the true Israel as Babylon had been of the Jews. Previously in Revelation Egypt, by allusion, is the prototype of Rome, but from now on, save for chs. 15 and 16, Babylon takes her place.

The rest of the verse is probably a free rendering of the condemnation of Babylon in Jer. 51:7, "Babylon hath been a golden cup in the Lord's hand, that made all the earth drunken: the nations have drunken her wine; therefore the nations are mad." Consequently, thinking of Rome as the new Babylon, the idolatrous conqueror of many nations which had been intoxicated and seduced by the imperial cult, John writes, **she who made all nations drink the wine of her impure passion** (RSV), or better perhaps, **of the wrath of her fornication** (KJV), with **fornication** signifying idolatry as in 2:20. In an elaboration of this theme in 17:2 Rome is depicted as the great harlot who made all nations drunk with the wine of her "fornication." Furthermore, the angel's words are reiterated in the dirge over Babylon in 18:2-3.

D. FOURTH VISION: ANGELIC CONDEMNATION OF WORSHIPERS OF THE BEAST (14:9-12)

9. A third **angel,** following the other two, now appeared, and with **a loud voice** cried out a condemnation of anyone who might be tempted to worship **the beast and its image,** or permitted his **mark** to be placed upon his **forehead** or **hand.** While ostensibly directed against the pagan worshipers of the beast, it may have been especially intended as a warning to those Christians who had been tempted almost beyond their strength to deny Christ and worship the emperor and his image. That apostasy did occur is certain; that it was on a larger scale than we might care to admit is highly probable, for

---

is a Rome which has set itself against the will of Christ and so it must meet doom. Once and again Rome was to be captured. The long tale has been told by Gibbon in stately language. But we do well to see in Babylon any city in so far as the forces of evil come to control its

life. Like the tolling of a bell ring the words: **Fallen, fallen is Babylon the great.** And it would be well if their meaning could be understood amid the proud evils of the modern towns where the will of God is flouted in haughty pride.

ship the beast and his image, and receive *his* mark in his forehead, or in his hand,

10 The same shall drink of the wine of the wrath of God, which is poured out without mixture into the cup of his indignation; and he shall be tormented with fire and brimstone in the presence of the holy angels, and in the presence of the Lamb:

11 And the smoke of their torment ascendeth up for ever and ever: and they have no rest day nor night, who worship the beast and his image, and whosoever receiveth the mark of his name.

ships the beast and its image, and receives a mark on his forehead or on his hand, 10 he also shall drink the wine of God's wrath, poured unmixed into the cup of his anger, and he shall be tormented with fire and brimstone in the presence of the holy angels and in the presence of the Lamb. 11 And the smoke of their torment goes up for ever and ever; and they have no rest, day or night, these worshipers of the beast and its image, and whoever receives the mark of its name."

---

at times the pressure exerted by the Roman authorities was almost irresistible, to say nothing of the social pressure of friends, neighbors, and families. In any adequate understanding of Revelation it is necessary to remember that John was engaged in a counterpressure, resorting to all of the supernatural sanctions of both reward and punishment that he could think of or imagine, in order to encourage Christians to be faithful against tremendous odds.

10. The first part of this warning to worshipers of the beast is apparently a loose quotation of Jer. 25:15, "Take from my hand this cup of the wine of wrath, and make all nations to whom I send you drink it." As adapted by John, it is probably a prediction of the plagues of "the seven bowls of the wrath of God" (16:1) which are to be poured out upon the earth in the very near future. Furthermore, possibly in recollection of the destruction of Sodom and Gomorrah by "brimstone and fire" (Gen. 19:24), the idolaters are to be tortured with **fire and brimstone,** a prediction of "the lake that burns with fire and brimstone, . . . the second death," into which they will be cast (21:8). **The holy angels** and **the Lamb** will witness their torture, the thought apparently being that the faithless will thus be eternally shamed before the face of him whom they have denied. A somewhat different concept is presented in I Enoch 48:9, for according to this passage, one of the privileges of the elect will be to witness the fiery tortures of the damned in Gehenna.

11. The destruction of Edom with brimstone and burning pitch is prophesied in Isa. 34:8-9, with the additional prediction that the fire "shall not be quenched night nor day; the smoke thereof shall go up for ever" (Isa. 34:10*a*). A recollection of this prophecy may have inspired John to adapt it to an eschatological warning to the worshipers of the emperor, predicting that **the smoke of their torment goes up for ever and ever; and they have no rest, day or night.** The author's acquaintance with and his use of the O.T. are evidenced in the angel's denunciation of the worshipers of the beast, for it is largely a catena of O.T. phrases and recollections.

---

10. *The Wine of God's Wrath.*—The man who accepts the mark of the beast courts the wrath of God. This wrath is described in speech edged about with terror. The cup of God's anger receives this unmixed wine of wrath, and the **worshipers of the beast** must drink it. Hard words like **torment** are used with unflinching and unhesitating energy. Agony and restlessness are to be the lot of those who turned

their backs upon goodness and upon God. You have to go to Dante for pictures which accept this forecast and amplify its meaning. At the heart of it all is the eternal principle that character determines destiny. An evil man cannot have a good fate; a good man cannot have an evil fate. The words about the wine of God's wrath present a grim picture but it is a picture not unrelated to reality.

12 Here is the patience of the saints: here *are* they that keep the commandments of God, and the faith of Jesus.

13 And I heard a voice from heaven saying unto me, Write, Blessed *are* the dead which die in the Lord from henceforth: Yea, saith the Spirit, that they may rest from their labors; and their works do follow them.

12 Here is a call for the endurance of the saints, those who keep the commandments of God and the faith of Jesus.

13 And I heard a voice from heaven saying, "Write this: Blessed are the dead who die in the Lord henceforth." "Blessed indeed," says the Spirit, "that they may rest from their labors, for their deeds follow them!"

12. The oracle in 13:10, which concludes with a solemn warning that the persecutors will be punished, is followed by words of assurance to the faithful Christians, "Here is a call for the endurance and faith of the saints." Almost the same fortifying statement is repeated here after further predictions of the tortures awaiting idolaters, **Here is a call for the endurance of the saints,** who are identified as those **who keep the commandments of God and the faith of Jesus.** For those who are faithful will escape the eternal torments of fire and brimstone; they will not be subject to the second death.

E. FIFTH VISION: HEAVENLY BENEDICTION OF THE MARTYRS (14:13)

13. In direct contrast to the eternal damnation of the worshipers of the beast a voice from heaven, whose speaker is not named, tells John to write, **Blessed are the dead who die in the Lord henceforth.** This, the second of seven beatitudes (cf. 1:3), is to comfort and strengthen those who are facing the prospect of dying as martyrs because they have confessed their Lord. This beatitude is solemnly affirmed by the Spirit, doubtless the same Spirit closely related to the glorified Christ, who pledged eternal rewards to the conquerors in the letters to the seven churches (cf. chs. 2–3). Unlike the worshipers of the emperor, who will be tortured forever in the lake of fire and brimstone, the martyrs will **rest from their labors**—which probably includes far more than cessation of physical work and toil. More than likely it signifies their final release from the sufferings, tortures, and death which they had undergone for their Lord. Furthermore, the Spirit pledges the martyrs that their **deeds** (RSV) or **works** (KJV) will **follow them.** Despite the thorough-

12. *Inner Victory.*—Really present in the thought of the author of the book of Revelation all the while is the desire to rouse men to courage and to give them strength for **endurance.** The book is more than a book of consolation. It is a book for the giving of strength. The ultimate victory of the good and the overthrow and punishment of the evil when once understood and accepted by faith give a firm basis for endurance. Jesus himself first had this faith, and faith in him gives a new strength of loyalty to the commandments of God. Even after his complete breakdown in health Woodrow Wilson never lost his faith in the ultimate triumph of the things for which he stood. His inner endurance in those days when the world seemed to have repudiated his ideals and his own strength was gone has been duplicated again and again as men have, like him, fought for something which they really found in their Christian heritage.

13. *The Light on the Face of Death.*—It is everywhere evident in the book of Revelation

that the glorious hope which it maintains transcends and transforms all the darkness of death. **The dead who die in the Lord** are to be congratulated. They are to be counted happy. After the hard toil of the day of life they have found rest. And their deeds of goodness do not die; they follow them into another good day which lies beyond. Year after year the Ingersoll Lectures at Harvard University have discussed the subject of immortality. The first was given by George A. Gordon. Such men as William James, John Fiske, and William Osler have contributed. After all wise words it remains true that the experience of "dying in the Lord" is most compelling. Those who die in the Lord cannot conceive extinction to be possible.

13. *One Life Here and Hereafter.*—There are not really two worlds, one before death and one after death; there is really one world over which the Lord reigns. So past experience is not lost after death. The new life is one into which old deeds follow. This principle of the continuity of life here and there comes to Christians as a

14 And I looked, and behold a white cloud, and upon the cloud *one* sat like unto the Son of man, having on his head a golden crown, and in his hand a sharp sickle.

15 And another angel came out of the temple, crying with a loud voice to him that sat on the cloud, Thrust in thy sickle, and reap: for the time is come for thee to reap; for the harvest of the earth is ripe.

14 Then I looked, and lo, a white cloud, and seated on the cloud one like a son of man, with a golden crown on his head, and a sharp sickle in his hand. 15 And another angel came out of the temple, calling with a loud voice to him who sat upon the cloud, "Put in your sickle, and reap, for the hour to reap has come, for the harvest of the

---

going determinism that is so evident in Revelation, the doctrine of works is also given a very prominent place. This is a basic inconsistency which does not seem to have disturbed John, if he was aware of it at all.

The doctrine of works was stated explicitly in 2:23, "I will give to each of you as your works deserve," and is re-emphasized in 20:12-13 and 22:12. In fact, the main purpose in writing Revelation was to convince the Christian that his loyalty, devotion, steadfastness, suffering, and death are not in vain, and that he is thus assured of a blessed immortality.

Similar concepts of the efficacy of works are found in a number of our sources. Those which are usually cited from the O.T. are somewhat beside the point, since for the most part they have to do with rewards in this life, not the next. However, after Judaism accepted a belief in punishments and rewards beyond the grave, this reliance on the efficacy of good works was given eschatological significance. The view was characteristically stated by Rabbi Jose ben Kisma (*ca.* A.D. 110), who taught that when a man departed this life for the next "neither silver nor gold nor jewels nor pearls go with him, but only his knowledge of Torah and good works" (Pirke Aboth 6:10). In general, the apocalyptic literature, like Revelation, stressed both predestination and good deeds. Both concepts are combined in I Enoch 38:2, where it is stated that when the Righteous One (the Messiah) appears before the righteous, "their elect works hang upon the Lord of Spirits." However, in another passage in this composite work, when Enoch was in heaven, he saw how men's actions were "weighed in the balance" (I Enoch 41:1), and he is told later on by an angel that the Elect One (the Messiah) will judge the deeds of men and weigh their works (I Enoch 61:8). In II Esdras 8:33 the belief in a treasury of works laid up in heaven is stated explicitly, as is true in II Baruch 14:12, where the observation is made that "the righteous justly hope for the end, and without fear depart from this habitation, because they have with thee a store of works preserved in treasuries."

F. Sixth Vision: The Son of Man and the Harvest (14:14-16)

14. Were it not that he is called **one like a son of man**, the heavenly being **seated on the cloud** would scarcely be identified as the heavenly Christ in his second advent, but would be considered as an angel, for his function here differs but little from that of the angel in the next scene. However, since in 1:13 Christ is termed "one like a son of man," even though the description is substantially different, it is probable that John is now anticipating the second advent of the conquering Christ, which is given in its proper place in greater detail in 19:11-21.

His appearance on **a white cloud** with **a golden crown on his head** (which should be contrasted with his appearance on a white horse with many diadems on his head in 19:11-12) resembles his advent in the Apocalypse of Peter 6, where he is to come "upon a cloud of brightness," with God placing a "crown" on his head. The use of **a sharp sickle** by the Messiah as a weapon of punishment is unusual; elsewhere in Revelation he is to use the sharp sword that projects from his mouth or a rod of iron.

15. After the appearance of the Son of man **another angel came out of the temple.** The word **another** should not be taken as indicating that the "one like a son of man" is

16 And he that sat on the cloud thrust in his sickle on the earth; and the earth was reaped.

17 And another angel came out of the temple which is in heaven, he also having a sharp sickle.

earth is fully ripe." 16 So he who sat upon the cloud swung his sickle on the earth, and the earth was reaped.

17 And another angel came out of the temple in heaven, and he too had a sharp

---

also an angel; instead, as in vs. 6, it is the equivalent of "an." This angel commanded the Son of man to **reap** with his **sickle,** for the **hour,** or **time,** had come, and **the harvest of the earth** was **ripe.** It seems somewhat strange that the angel should give orders to the heavenly Christ to begin his punitive work of harvest, until we realize that he is merely a messenger bringing a command from God himself, who is in his temple. This is quite in harmony with the statement in Matt. 24:36 that no one, not even the angels nor the Son, knows the day or the hour of the end, save the Father himself.

The tableau recalls the eschatological explanation (probably editorial) of a parable in Matt. 13:37-43. The field is the world in which the Son of man sowed wheat, the sons of the kingdom; whereas the Devil sowed weeds, the sons of the evil one. The harvest is to come at the end of this age, when the Son of man will send his angels to reap the weeds, the evildoers, and throw them into the fiery furnace, while the righteous will shine like the sun. An interesting parallel is provided by II Esdras 4:28-32, where two harvests are depicted: the first, in this age, will be that of the wicked; the second, to occur in the age to come, will be the ingathering of the righteous. While the resemblances to these scenes are striking, it is probable that in these verses in Revelation the reaping, which is immediately followed by the vintage, may have been inspired by the dual picture of harvest and vintage in Joel 3:13, "Put ye in the sickle; for the harvest is ripe: come, tread ye; for the winepress is full, the vats overflow; for their wickedness is great" (ASV). John's ability to transform noneschatological imagery into apocalyptic symbolism, which has been noted before, is evident in his reinterpretation of the verse from Joel in this scene of the apocalyptic harvest. It is tempting to think of this episode as representing the harvest of the righteous by the Son of man, with the vintage representing the punishment of the wicked; but there is no evidence to support this suggestion, save the parallel in Matthew, where the harvest of wheat is the ingathering of the righteous. Apparently, as in Joel, the harvest is the harvest of the wicked who are to be punished.

G. Seventh Vision: The Angel and the Vintage (14:17-20)

17. This episode of the vintage is a doublet of the preceding one of the harvest, and like it was probably suggested by Joel 3:13. In this case it is an **angel,** not the Son of man, who appears with **a sharp sickle,** but their functions are very similar. This angel came out of the heavenly **temple,** showing that he too is an agent of God's wrath.

---

truth shining with inspiration. The new life which had no relation to the present world would seem very strange and baffling. There would be nothing to seize with a firm and eager grasp. But if life is one continued story and the first chapter and the first chapter here we can truly say, as is said in the serial magazines, "to be continued in our next." Everything good in our experience here is to be gathered up in the life of fulfillment beyond.

16. *The Ripe Earth.*—Human life is not merely a series of scattered items; it is a process. It involves growth and ripening. Some of the things which ripen are good; some of the things which ripen are bad. Each, however, comes to

the full expression of its essential quality. Then it is truly ripe. So the angel proclaims that the earth is ripe and ready to be harvested. The harvester wears a crown and sits triumphantly upon a cloud. The swung sickle is an act of judgment as well as an act of harvesting or, rather, the harvesting is judgment. The great dramas of the world—especially the great tragedies—usually tell the tale of a human harvest. In *King Lear* you see the harvesttime of all the weak and dangerous qualities of the king. In *Macbeth* you see the harvesttime of a lawless ambition in murder. In Greek tragedy sometimes it is the harvest coming after a long series of events. But every human life as well as those interpreted in great drama is slowly ripening

18 And another angel came out from the altar, which had power over fire; and cried with a loud cry to him that had the sharp sickle, saying, Thrust in thy sharp sickle, and gather the clusters of the vine of the earth; for her grapes are fully ripe.

19 And the angel thrust in his sickle into the earth, and gathered the vine of the earth, and cast it into the great winepress of the wrath of God.

20 And the winepress was trodden without the city, and blood came out of the winepress, even unto the horse bridles, by the space of a thousand and six hundred furlongs.

sickle. 18 Then another angel came out from the altar, the angel who has power over fire, and he called with a loud voice to him who had the sharp sickle, "Put in your sickle, and gather the clusters of the vine of the earth, for its grapes are ripe." 19 So the angel swung his sickle on the earth and gathered the vintage of the earth, and threw it into the great wine press of the wrath of God; 20 and the wine press was trodden outside the city, and blood flowed from the wine press, as high as a horse's bridle, for one thousand six hundred stadia.[i]

[i] About two hundred miles.

---

18. In the harvest scene an angel told the Son of man that the time had come for him to use his sickle. Maintaining the parallelism, another angel, **from the altar,** who had **power over fire,** told the angel with the sickle to use it **to gather the clusters of the vine of the earth,** for the **grapes** were **ripe.** According to the angelology of the time, angels presided over the various forces of nature. The angels of the four winds appeared in 7:1; the angel of the water will make his entrance in 16:5. It was but natural that there should be an angel of fire. The Zoroastrians considered the archangel Asha Vahishta as the guardian of the fire. In Jubilees 2:2 the angels "of the spirit of fire" are among those in charge of the natural elements. In the O.T. the cherub who took fire from the wheels of God's chariot-throne in Ezek. 10:7 may be comparable to an angel of fire. But this angel of fire in Revelation has a special significance, for he is **from the altar.** Indeed, he may be the same angel who filled the censer with fire from the altar (8:5) just before the seven trumpet plagues. In any event, his appearance is ominous, for it is followed by the vintage; and before long the seven bowls of God's wrath are to be poured out.

19. In obedience to the heavenly command **the angel swung his sickle on the earth and gathered the vintage,** which he cast **into the great wine press of the wrath of God.**

20. The wine press was trodden outside the city. What city is meant? Probably Jerusalem, since there was a belief, not as common as might be expected, that God's judgment on the nations of the earth will take place in the neighborhood of Jerusalem (cf. Zech. 14:1-5; Dan. 11:45; Ezek. 39:1-10). The symbolism of the treading of the grapes may be derived from Isa. 63:1-6, which depicts God as a mighty warrior who will in his righteous wrath trample in the wine press the nations which oppressed Israel, pouring their lifeblood upon the earth. John has transformed this into an apocalyptic scene anticipatory of the time when the conquering Christ, not God, "will tread the wine press of the fury of the wrath of God the Almighty" (19:15).

The prediction of Isa. 63:6 that the lifeblood of the nations will be poured out over the earth is elaborated by John, who states that the blood flowing from the wine press

---

for a harvest which is at once a reaping and a judgment.

19. The Vintage of Wickedness.—Now the grapes of wickedness are seen apart from all good growth—it is now the grapes of evil which are ripe. They are gathered in and flung **into the great wine press of the wrath of God.** And when they are pressed great quantities of blood come forth. The picture is lurid enough with the blood rising over a vast area to the height of **a horse's bridle.** Wickedness has thrived on

bloodthirsty deeds; now its own blood is shed. Here we have stark and unmitigated judgment. The sentimental dreamer often shuts out every evil thing in order that he may paint the lovely pictures of his imagination. The poet sometimes sings as if there were no tragedy in the world of his bright melody. But the man of Patmos always fully faces the ugly and bitterly malignant nature of wickedness even as he sings the song of the triumph of the good. The great satirists of Rome sternly faced all the loath-

15 And I saw another sign in heaven, great and marvelous, seven angels having the seven last plagues; for in them is filled up the wrath of God.

2 And I saw as it were a sea of glass mingled with fire: and them that had gotten the victory over the beast, and over his image, and over his mark, *and* over the

15 Then I saw another portent in heaven, great and wonderful, seven angels with seven plagues, which are the last, for with them the wrath of God is ended.

2 And I saw what appeared to be a sea of glass mingled with fire, and those who had conquered the beast and its image and

---

will be **as high as a horse's bridle, for one thousand six hundred stadia,** making a river about two hundred miles in length. The symbolism of the number sixteen hundred, if any was intended, is obscure. A similar symbolical hyperbole is found in I Enoch 100:1-3: after the slaughter of the wicked by each other, streams will flow with their blood up to the breasts of horses and so deep as to submerge chariots. Also, the author of a later Christian passage, II Esdras 15:35-36, anticipates that the destruction of Babylon (Rome) will be preceded by conflicts in which blood will flow up to a horse's belly, a man's thigh, or a camel's hocks (cf. Sibylline Oracles 3:682-84).

It would appear that the harvest and vintage in which the nations are destroyed would precipitate the end of this age; but this is not to be, for another series of apocalyptic catastrophes must take place before this is to happen. Further, it should be emphasized that ch. 14 is anticipatory of the final punishments for the wicked and rewards for the righteous.

VIII. Seven Visions of the Bowls of God's Wrath (15:1–16:21)

A. Introduction: Preparation for the Seven Bowl Plagues (15:1–16:1)

Another series of calamities, the seven plagues of the bowls of God's wrath, is about to ravage the earth. These are similar in character and purpose to the plagues of the seven seals (6:1–8:6) and of the seven trumpets (8:7–11:19), especially the latter. A period of preparation preceded each of these series. In the first we have the acclamation of the Lamb as worthy to break the seal on the book of doom (5:1-14). In the second the opening of the seventh seal (8:1-6) prepares the way for the blowing of the seven trumpets. Seven angels, it may be recalled, stood before God and were given seven trumpets. Then another angel stood at the altar and mixed incense with the prayers of the saints in a golden censer. After the incense and prayers had ascended to God, the angel filled the censer with fire from the altar and threw it upon the earth, causing a number of celestial and terrestrial disturbances. Following this preparation the seven angels proceeded to blow their trumpets. In some ways the preparation for the seven bowl plagues is a doublet of that for the seven trumpet plagues.

15:1. First, another wonderful **portent in heaven** is seen, **seven angels with seven plagues.** These are to be the **last** plagues, for with them the **wrath** of God will reach its culmination. It is true that this will be the last series of seven typical woes, but a number of additional woes must take place before this age of evil is terminated. These **seven angels** of punishment may be the seven archangels who perform a number of roles for God.

2. In the prelude to the seven trumpet woes prayers of the martyrs ascended to God; this is paralleled by the song of triumph which the martyrs sing before the throne. John

---

some evils around them. When you have faced with Juvenal the moral obliquity of Rome you are ready for the picture of the vintage of wickedness.

15:2. *The God of Music.*—There is an implicit contrast here between the degradation of the worship of the beast and the noble and

gracious glory of the life with God. There is no lofty music in the ritual of the beast. To worship the beast is to journey downward; to worship God is to journey upward. And the lofty life with God is graciously expressed in the figure of the **harps of God.** He is the God of noble music or, as we might say, he is the

number of his name, stand on the sea of glass, having the harps of God.

3 And they sing the song of Moses the servant of God, and the song of the Lamb, saying, Great and marvelous *are* thy works, Lord God Almighty; just and true *are* thy ways, thou King of saints.

the number of its name, standing beside the sea of glass with harps of God in their hands. 3 And they sing the song of Moses, the servant of God, and the song of the Lamb, saying,

"Great and wonderful are thy deeds,
　O Lord God the Almighty!
Just and true are thy ways,
　O King of the ages!*j*

j Other ancient authorities read *the nations.*

---

writes that he saw what seemed to be **a sea of glass mingled with fire.** This is the same sea of glass before the throne described in 4:6. However, it now has an added feature, for it is fiery red in color, which helps to identify it as the heavenly Red Sea. **Those who had conquered the beast,** who had refused to worship his **image** or to have the **number of his name** on their foreheads, i.e., the martyrs, have crossed it in safety. (The phrase **and over his mark** [KJV] is a later but understandable interpolation into the text.) Just as the Israelites with God's aid had earlier passed through the Red Sea to escape Pharaoh and his oppression, now the Christian martyrs have made their escape over the heavenly Red Sea from their persecutor, the satanic Roman emperor, and stand before the throne holding **harps of God,** i.e., harps for the service of God.

3a. There is a marked contrast between this tableau and the one in 6:9-11, when the martyrs under the altar in heaven cried out for vengeance upon their persecutors, and then were told to rest until their number was completed (cf. 8:3-4). For in the scene before us the number of martyrs is complete; all have crossed the symbolic Red Sea to a place of safety in heaven, and their enemies are about to be overwhelmed by God in his wrath. Consequently, instead of praying for divine vengeance as before, they now sing a song of praise to God for their liberation. This is called **the song of Moses, the servant of God,** in recollection of the song sung by Moses and the children of Israel following their victorious passage of the Red Sea (Exod. 15:1). It is also called **the song of the Lamb,** for it was through him that they have been saved.

3b-4. The song itself, despite its name, bears little resemblance to the words of the song of Moses in Exod. 15. Like certain other songs in Revelation, it is largely a catena of O.T. phraseology (cf. Ps. 11:2; 139:14; Amos 4:13 LXX; Deut. 32:4; Ps. 86:9; Mal. 1:11; Ps. 144:17 LXX; Ps. 98:2). Obviously the author, whoever he was, was thoroughly imbued with O.T. phrases, which came readily and naturally to his pen as he wrote. Furthermore, its arrangement in parallel lines of thought reflects the poetic form of the O.T.

God of a noble fulfillment of art. Homer began his song of the Trojan War by appealing to the goddess to sing the wrath of Achilles. There was to be a divine source for his music. In a loftier sense the man of Patmos sees that it is the harps of God the victorious saints are to use. But the picture of the harps of God has vast and varied implications as we think of the fulfillment of all harmony in that which is associated with the divine. If he only understands it every artist is called upon to learn to use heavenly instruments.

3. The Law and the Gospel Turned into Music.—As the people of Israel had stood beside the sea after their deliverance through the destruction of the Egyptians, so the author of

the book of Revelation pictures the victorious saints standing beside a sea of glass and fire. The law and the gospel have now become one and they are merged in a glorious song of triumph. They sing of the deeds of God which have brought to them truth and salvation. The whole story of the ways of God with men becomes a revelation of his high and lonely holiness. The thought of God is the goal of all their experience. The great redemption is consummated in song. And this song gathers up all the meaning of that ancient law through which men were led to an apprehension of the character of God. When we think of the many books about the Christian religion which simply tell of some one of its aspects we are ready to turn

4 Who shall not fear thee, O Lord, and glorify thy name? for *thou* only *art* holy: for all nations shall come and worship before thee; for thy judgments are made manifest.

5 And after that I looked, and, behold, the temple of the tabernacle of the testimony in heaven was opened:

6 And the seven angels came out of the temple, having the seven plagues, clothed in pure and white linen, and having their breasts girded with golden girdles.

4 Who shall not fear and glorify thy name, O Lord?
For thou alone art holy.
All nations shall come and worship thee,
for thy judgments have been revealed."

5 After this I looked, and the temple of the tent of witness in heaven was opened, **6** and out of the temple came the seven angels with the seven plagues, robed in pure bright linen, and their breasts girded with

Like other liturgical passages in Revelation it praises God for his power and might, for his justice and truth, for his name and his holiness, and for his coming judgment. One line, **All nations shall come and worship thee,** is thoroughly out of harmony with the belief rather consistently expressed throughout the rest of Revelation that the nations will stubbornly refuse to repent, but will go on their reckless, idolatrous, persecuting way to destruction. It could be that John used a current Christian hymn without changing this line concerning the ultimate repentance and conversion of the heathen, an outcome to which a number of Christians, including Paul, looked forward. On the other hand, his consistency may be preserved by supposing that this worship did not involve the conversion of the nations, but signified the homage that they would pay to God in acknowledgment of his awful might and power. But perhaps John is not consistent here (see 22:2).

The hymn presents a slight textual problem. Some authorities read, **O King of the nations** in vs. 3, but the Chester Beatty Papyrus supports the reading which is followed here. **Thou King of saints** (KJV) is a corrupt reading without any ancient support.

5. Following the singing of the song of triumph, the **temple of the tent of witness in heaven was opened.** The collocation of **temple** with **tent of witness** is unusual. Furthermore, the phrase **tent of witness** is found in but one other place in the N.T. (Acts 7:44), and there it is used without reference to the temple. In 13:6 and 21:3 σκηνή, translated "dwelling" or "tabernacle," occurs without the qualification "of witness." However, the exact phrase, tent of witness, is found in a number of places in the Greek translation of the O.T., especially in Exod. 40. Its significance in Revelation is far from clear. Could this "tent of witness" associated with the Exodus be an allusion to the new exodus, in which the new Israel, comprised of witnesses and martyrs who have been liberated from Egypt, is traveling through the wilderness to the eternal promised land, i.e., to God's temple in heaven? This is farfetched, perhaps, but no better solution has been offered.

6. The seven angels having the seven plagues, first seen in vs. 1, now came out of the temple. They are garbed in pure **linen.** A slight textual difficulty is presented here, for in some texts the reading is "stone" (λίθον) instead of "linen" (λίνον), so that in the ASV the rendering is "arrayed with precious stone." However, once more the Chester

with new appreciation to the fashion in which whole streams of experience of men with God and of God with men are brought together in the song of the victorious saints beside the sea of glass and fire.

4. The Universal Acclaim.—The book of Revelation always makes its pictures thoroughgoing and complete. When it speaks of evil there is complete destruction. When it speaks of the glory of the good God there is complete

triumph. So now we hear the anthem declaring **all nations shall come and worship thee.** The contradiction is only on the surface. The evil in the nations shall be destroyed; the good in the nations shall be gathered up and made a part of an eternal worship. Even among the grimmest pictures of the judgment of evil the vision of the universal acclaim of God is present too. The difference between Carlyle and Emerson lay in the moral wrath of one and the

7 And one of the four beasts gave unto the seven angels seven golden vials full of the wrath of God, who liveth for ever and ever.

8 And the temple was filled with smoke from the glory of God, and from his power; and no man was able to enter into the temple, till the seven plagues of the seven angels were fulfilled.

golden girdles. 7 And one of the four living creatures gave the seven angels seven golden bowls full of the wrath of God who lives for ever and ever; 8 and the temple was filled with smoke from the glory of God and from his power, and no one could enter the temple until the seven plagues of the seven angels were ended.

Beatty Papyrus supports the reading adopted here with λινοῦν, "a garment made of flax." Like the heavenly Christ in 1:13, these angels have **golden girdles** about their breasts. An angel in the Coptic Apocalypse of Zephaniah 9 wore a golden girdle similar to these.

7. One of the **living creatures** appeared and gave the seven angels of punishment **seven golden bowls full of the wrath of God.** The word φιάλας, translated **bowls** (RSV), or **vials** (KJV), designated a broad, shallow vessel used for drinking purposes, as well as for libations, as in 5:8, where the golden bowls held by the twenty-four elders were filled with incense, i.e., with "the prayers of the saints." Moreover, this same word also signified a funerary urn which served as a receptacle for the ashes of the dead. John may have been thinking of these various meanings in using the word here. He may have considered these bowls as drinking vessels, "cups of anger," from which the worshipers of the beast, as in 14:9-10, are to drink the wine of God's wrath. Certainly, following the emptying of the seventh bowl it is stated that God had made Babylon the great "drain the cup of the fury of his wrath" (16:19). Also, like the censer in 8:5, filled with fire from the altar, which caused thunder, lightning, and an earthquake when cast upon the earth, these bowls may have contained a burning incense which would cause destruction and death when poured upon the earth. It is also possible that John may have been thinking of the use of the word for receptacles for the ashes of the dead in connection with the death-dealing contents of these bowls of wrath.

8. Mention has been made of the occurrence of the phrase "tent of witness" in the Greek version of Exod. 40. Toward the end of this chapter in Exodus it is stated that a cloud covered the tent of witness, for it was filled with the glory of God, so that Moses was not permitted to enter it (Exod. 40:34-35). It is quite possible that John was aware of this description when he wrote that **the temple** [i.e., "the temple of the tent of witness" in vs. 5] **was filled with smoke from the glory of God and from his power** so that **no one could enter** it until the seven bowl plagues were ended. This is another indication that for John the exodus of the Jews from Egypt through the aid of God is a prototype of the divine deliverance of the loyal Christians from the power of the satanic beast representing the rule of the Roman state and from Satan himself. It may be, as suggested in the Exeg., vs. 5, that this gives the explanation for his use of the unusual phrase, "the temple of the tent of witness."

---

serene optimism of the other. Both notes are needed in an understanding of life and both are found in the book of Revelation.

7. The Moral Beauty of Judgment.—And now we come to a conception which is difficult enough but the importance of which we can scarcely deny. The **seven angels with the seven plagues** are clad in **pure bright linen**; they wear **golden girdles.** The bowls of wrath are made of gold. There is an austere beauty in their acts of judgment. The picture suggests one reminder at least worthy of our thought. The reformer

gets down into difficult situations and tries to do something about them. And all too often his garments are more or less soiled by the materials in which he works. In the midst of the fight he scarcely thinks of giving moral and spiritual distinction to his very campaign of hostility. When one studies the noble and useful career of Jane Addams he sometimes feels that there is more evidence of the bitterness of the conflict than of the serene beauty of the goal. It is difficult to wear shining garments and girdles of gold in the fight with wickedness.

16 And I heard a great voice out of the temple saying to the seven angels, Go your ways, and pour out the vials of the wrath of God upon the earth.

2 And the first went, and poured out his vial upon the earth; and there fell a noisome and grievous sore upon the men which had the mark of the beast, and *upon* them which worshipped his image.

3 And the second angel poured out his vial upon the sea; and it became as the

16 Then I heard a loud voice from the temple telling the seven angels, "Go and pour out on the earth the seven bowls of the wrath of God."

2 So the first angel went and poured his bowl on the earth, and foul and evil sores came upon the men who bore the mark of the beast and worshiped its image.

3 The second angel poured his bowl into the sea, and it became like the blood of a

---

16:1. When the preparations for the seven trumpet woes had been completed, the seven angels "made ready to blow" their trumpets. Corresponding to this scene, now that the seven bowl plagues have been prepared, **a loud voice from the temple** ordered the **seven angels** to empty **the seven bowls of the wrath of God** upon **the earth.** The speaker is not named, but since it has just been announced that no one but God was to be in the temple until the seven bowl plagues were ended (15:8), the speaker giving the command can be none other than God himself, who now is to take personal charge of this last series of seven woes. The plagues that follow are patterned in part after those preceding the exodus from Egypt. However, in his dependence upon the account of the exodus, John has reversed the sequence of events, in which the safe passage of the Red Sea, celebrated by the triumphant song of Moses, comes after the plagues; in Revelation the crossing of the heavenly Red Sea by the martyrs, who then sing the victorious song of Moses and of the Lamb, comes before the sequence of seven plagues. However, prosaic considerations of this nature seldom deter the author. In this case he desires to show that the martyrs will be safe in heaven, out of harm's way when the seven bowl plagues are poured out.

B. First Bowl: Plague of Ulcers (16:2)

2. In partial fulfillment of the warning of the angel in 14:9-10 that worshipers of the beast and his image, who bore his mark on their forehead, would be made to drink the wine of God's wrath from his cup of anger, the first of the seven angels **poured his bowl on the earth.** As a result, **foul and evil sores** appeared on the bodies of those who **had the mark of the beast,** of those who **worshiped its image.** This plague of ulcers is a retelling of the sixth Egyptian plague of boils. According to the familiar narrative in Exod. 9:8-12, Moses and Aaron threw ashes into the air which covered the land of Egypt and caused grievous boils and sores to break out on all men and beasts.

C. Second Bowl: The Sea Turned to Blood (16:3)

3. The second bowl plague, like that of the second trumpet (cf. 8:8-9), is derived from the first Egyptian plague, in which the water of the Nile was turned to blood, making

---

16:2. *When the Whole Organism Is Corrupt.* —The pouring of the contents of the first bowl is the occasion for the breaking out of that inner corruption which is of the very nature of evil. Those **who bore the mark of the beast** had become beastly. Those who worshiped its image had experienced a process of inner decay. The **evil sores** bring the inner putrefaction to an ugly appearance on the surface. Oscar Wilde once wrote a tale entitled *The Picture of Dorian Gray* [9] which told of a man whose inner life and

[9] New York: The Modern Library, 1926.

whose deeds were completely evil but whose face for a time preserved a deceptive appearance of moral nobility. But at last the face came to express the very ugly quality of the inner rottenness. So the quality of the inner life is bound to reach the surface at last.

3. *When Nature Refuses to Be the Friend of Man.* —Nature has many mysteries and many tragedies. But on the whole it is fitted for the life of man and offers to him a certain inarticulate co-operation. But nature refuses to be the friend of evil beings. When the contents of the

blood of a dead *man:* and every living soul died in the sea.

4 And the third angel poured out his vial upon the rivers and fountains of waters; and they became blood.

5 And I heard the angel of the waters say, Thou art righteous, O Lord, which art, and wast, and shalt be, because thou hast judged thus.

6 For they have shed the blood of saints and prophets, and thou hast given them blood to drink; for they are worthy.

7 And I heard another out of the altar say, Even so, Lord God Almighty, true and righteous *are* thy judgments.

dead man, and every living thing died that was in the sea.

4 The third angel poured his bowl into the rivers and the fountains of water, and they became blood. **5** And I heard the angel of water say,

"Just art thou in these thy judgments,
  thou who art and wast, O Holy One.
6 For men have shed the blood of saints
    and prophets,
  and thou hast given them blood to
    drink.
  It is their due!"

7 And I heard the altar cry,
  "Yea, Lord God the Almighty,
    true and just are thy judgments!"

the water foul and killing all the fish (Exod. 7:14-25). The blowing of the second trumpet affected the sea, rather than the Nile, so that a third of it became blood, thereby killing a third of the fish. The effects of the second bowl were even more disastrous, for when it was emptied upon the **sea,** it **became like the blood of a dead man,** foul and coagulated, killing all life that was in it.

D. THIRD BOWL: RIVERS AND SPRINGS TURNED TO BLOOD (16:4-7)

4. As an additional result of the first Egyptian plague, water in all the streams, pools, and ponds throughout the land became filled with blood, as well as the water in household utensils (Exod. 7:19). A variant of this theme is seen in the second trumpet woe, which caused a third of the water in "the rivers and the fountains of water" to turn to blood.

5-6. Just as there were angels over the winds (7:1) and an angel of fire (14:18), so there was also an angel guardian over the **water.** It might be expected that he would resent this deadly pollution of the water which is under his care; instead, in a liturgical utterance, which echoes phrases of the song of Moses and of the Lamb (15:3-4), he avers that these **judgments** of God are **just.** The reading **O Holy One** (RSV) is much to be preferred to the weakly attested **O Lord** (KJV). The **judgments** are **just** because those who are now being punished **shed the blood** of the Christian martyrs, who are described as **saints and prophets;** consequently, it is only right that they should be given **blood to drink.** Once more the *lex talionis,* the law of retribution, which permeates all of Revelation, is given vivid expression.

7. The **altar** cried out a brief antiphon in response to the angel's song, reaffirming that the **judgments,** the punishments inflicted by God on the persecutors, are **true and just.** In the account of 14:18 the angel of the fire, who had some relationship to the

second bowl are poured into the sea **every living thing died that was in the sea.** This is a symbol of the end of the partnership between nature and life. Because of evil men the sea becomes a place of death. The book of Revelation is saying that we take for granted the fact that nature was made for man and man was made for nature. We have no right to this easy and casual faith. Nature itself will become a tragic place for a man who has no right to a home in nature. The ten thousand Greeks shouted with joy when they beheld the sea. But the sea of

death which the man of Patmos pictures gives no reason for gladness. If the sailor is full of moral decay the sea without will answer to the death within.

5. *The Fatal Draft.*—Jesus had turned water into wine. The woe of the third bowl turns **the rivers and the fountains of water into blood.** Rivers and fountains offer men death instead of life. And by a quick turn of fancy the very angel of water praises God's just judgments. Dealers in **the blood of saints and prophets** find that their transactions have not come to an

8 And the fourth angel poured out his vial upon the sun; and power was given unto him to scorch men with fire.

9 And men were scorched with great heat, and blasphemed the name of God, which hath power over these plagues: and they repented not to give him glory.

8 The fourth angel poured his bowl on the sun, and it was allowed to scorch men with fire; 9 men were scorched by the fierce heat, and they cursed the name of God who had power over these plagues, and they did not repent and give him glory.

---

altar, gave an order to the angel with the sickle to gather the earth's vintage. In this case, since according to 15:8 no one but God is to be in the temple, the altar itself speaks. No other translation of the Greek, such as **And I heard another out of the altar say** (KJV), is permissible. That an altar should speak is not surprising in a book where an eagle, the dragon, the beasts from the sea and land, and other nonhuman creatures are given the power of speech. The words coming from the altar represent the fulfillment of the prayer of the martyrs under the altar in 6:10, beseeching God to avenge their blood on the peoples of the earth who have persecuted and slain them. Now that his judgment has arrived, the altar speaking for the martyrs affirms that it is just.

E. Fourth Bowl: Scorching Heat of the Sun (16:8-9)

8-9. When the fourth trumpet was sounded, a third of the sun, moon, and stars was darkened (8:12). The plague that follows upon the emptying of the fourth bowl is similar in that the sun is affected; but the similarity ends there. For in this instance, when the fourth bowl was emptied on the sun, its power was greatly increased so that **men were scorched** with its **great heat.** In some areas of apocalyptic speculation the world is to be destroyed by an all-consuming fire, as in II Pet. 3:10, where we read the prediction that "the elements will be dissolved with fire, and the earth and the works that are upon it will be burned up." In the Apocalypse of Peter 5, written at the time of II Peter, *ca.* the middle of the second century, the prophecy is made that floods of consuming fire, which men will try in vain to escape, will be the means of ending this age of evil (cf. Apocalypse of Pseudo-John 14; Sibylline Oracles 2:196-200; 4:162-78; 8:225-38). But these examples are scarcely parallel to the prediction of this verse; for the purpose of the increased heat of the sun will be to scorch and torture the wicked, not to consume them and the world with fire. A much closer parallel is provided by Lactantius, who warns that God will cause the sun to stand still for three days so that it will catch on fire; whereupon the impious and hostile people of the earth will be punished by its excessive heat and burning (*Divine Institutes* VII. 26).

As a result of the torment of this scorching heat, the wicked **blasphemed the name of God,** as the first beast had previously done, according to 13:6. (The RSV is somewhat inconsistent in translating the Greek verb as "blaspheme" in 13:6 and as "curse" in this verse and in vss. 11 and 21.) However, despite their painful burns, just as the wicked were unrepentant following the first six trumpet plagues (9:20-21), so now **they did not repent and give him glory.** In a striking passage the Sibyl calls upon the wicked to repent lest God complete the punishments he has already begun by sending an all-consuming fire upon them (Sibylline Oracles 4:162-78). Just as we may wonder why it took ten disastrous plagues to make Pharaoh and the Egyptians relent and permit the Israelites

---

end with the death of their victims. Blood they have shed; blood they must drink. Men cannot attack the friends of God and expect God's world to be their friend. Its very fountains will become fountains of death. The book of Revelation is expressing in another fashion the doom of those who make evil their good. In Appian's *Roman History* the account of the civil wars makes very emphatic the sense that Romans had become the worst foes of Rome. Inner decay is always worse than outer assault.

8. The Sun Becomes a Foe.—In no end of ways the sun is a promoter of life. But the contents of the fourth bowl turn the **sun** into man's enemy; it **was allowed to scorch men with fire.** Life-giving heat becomes torturing heat. Men whose burning passions had been their moral undoing burn with a fire which brings

10 And the fifth angel poured out his vial upon the seat of the beast; and his kingdom was full of darkness; and they gnawed their tongues for pain,

11 And blasphemed the God of heaven because of their pains and their sores, and repented not of their deeds.

12 And the sixth angel poured out his vial upon the great river Euphrates; and the water thereof was dried up, that the way of the kings of the east might be prepared.

10 The fifth angel poured his bowl on the throne of the beast, and its kingdom was in darkness; men gnawed their tongues in anguish 11 and cursed the God of heaven for their pain and sores, and did not repent of their deeds.

12 The sixth angel poured his bowl on the great river Eu-phra′tes, and its water was dried up, to prepare the way for the

to leave, so we may also be amazed that these series of apocalyptic woes in Revelation will have little or no effect upon the attitude and behavior of the idolatrous Romans toward the Christians.

F. Fifth Bowl: Darkness of the Beast's Kingdom (16:10-11)

10a. When the fifth trumpet was blown, the sun and the air were darkened by a cloud of smoke ascending from the bottomless pit which contained a huge swarm of locusts (9:1-12). The resemblance of this scourge to the eighth Egyptian plague (Exod. 10:4-15) has already been noted. However, the fifth bowl plague is much closer to the ninth Egyptian plague of darkness for a period of three days over all of Egypt, which almost caused Pharaoh to repent (Exod. 10:21-29). Consequently, when the fifth bowl was emptied **on the throne of the beast,** a pall of **darkness** enveloped his **kingdom.** The plagues of Exodus were inflicted upon Pharaoh as well as upon his kingdom. Now for the first time when the bowl is poured out **on the throne of the beast,** the emperor himself becomes a direct target of God's terrible wrath. This is an omen of his coming defeat and destruction.

10b-11. This enveloping darkness, coupled with the **pain** from the scorching sun and the **sores,** caused men to gnaw their **tongues in anguish,** but still they refused to **repent of their deeds.**

G. Sixth Bowl: Kings of the East Assembled for Armageddon (16:12-16)

12. The plague of the sixth bowl is apparently a combination of the second Egyptian plague (Exod. 8:1-15) and the sixth trumpet woe (9:13-19), with added features from other sources. The result is a strange and confusing scene, concluding with the mysterious word **Armageddon.** The second scourge inflicted on the Egyptians was that of the innumerable frogs which swarmed everywhere throughout the land. The story grew with the passage of time, so that in Ps. 78:45 it was stated that the frogs had destroyed the Egyptians. As for the sounding of the sixth trumpet, it produced an invasion of 200,000,000 locustlike horses with their riders from across the Euphrates into the empire, where they killed a third of mankind (9:13-19). In this connection should be remembered

the acutest agony. Over larger and larger areas the forces of nature turn against man. He who has made God his foe has no friend in the universe. The scorching sun shines upon men who have become so evil that they have no thought of repentance. With furious hatred **they cursed the name of God.** The truth is that the universe can never be a friend to men whose purposes have become evil. A powerful French story told the tale of a young man who

was guilty of the grossest act of betrayal during the period of German occupation. The center of the tragedy of the tale comes when, after the war was over, it is evident that he is completely incapable of seeing the moral quality of what he has done. The good which has died in him has made him incapable of repentance.

10. *The Curse of Darkness.*—The contents of the fifth bowl are poured upon the very throne of evil. There is now complete **darkness**

13 And I saw three unclean spirits like frogs *come* out of the mouth of the dragon, and out of the mouth of the beast, and out of the mouth of the false prophet.

14 For they are the spirits of devils, working miracles, *which* go forth unto the kings of the earth and of the whole world, to gather them to the battle of that great day of God Almighty.

kings from the east. 13 And I saw, issuing from the mouth of the dragon and from the mouth of the beast and from the mouth of the false prophet, three foul spirits like frogs; 14 for they are demonic spirits, performing signs, who go abroad to the kings of the whole world, to assemble them for battle on the great day of God the Almighty.

the myth that Nero would return to life to lead an invading army of the unsubdued Parthians with their satraps over the Euphrates to ravage the empire which he had once ruled (see on 13:3), and to wage war with the saints and the Lamb (cf. 17:12-14).

Accordingly, when the bowl of the sixth angel was emptied out on **the great river Euphrates, it was dried up** to make it easy for the **kings from the east,** i.e., the satraps of Parthia, to invade the kingdom of the beast. This drying up of the Euphrates to facilitate an invasion may be modeled after the story of the miraculous way in which a dry passage through the bed of the Jordan was provided for Joshua to expedite his invasion of Canaan (Josh. 3:14-17). There was also a current tradition to the effect that God would stay the springs of the Euphrates to aid the ten tribes on their return for the messianic ingathering (II Esdras 13:47; cf. Zech. 10:11). Centuries earlier Herodotus had related that the Euphrates became dry to permit Cyrus to capture Babylon (*History* I. 191). Accordingly, wholly apart from the rolling back of the Red Sea during the exodus, there was plenty of precedent for such an event as this.

13. The satanic character of this coming invasion, similar in character to that of 9:13-19 is evidenced by the appearance of **three foul spirits like frogs,** one each from **the mouth of the dragon,** the **beast,** and the **false prophet.** Unlike the swarms of frogs in the plague of Exodus, there are but three this time; but their small number is more than compensated for by their demonic nature. These demonic frogs have a partial parallel in Zoroastrianism. According to belief all animals were in two categories, good and evil, and as such were related to or identified with Ormazd or Ahriman. Ahriman (as well as Ormazd) could change his shape at will and at times became a frog, his most natural animal form. He also spread the frog (sometimes described as an aquatic lizard) and other demonic, noxious animals throughout the world to cause blight, pain, disease, pollution, and the like (cf. Bundahish 3:9, 15; 18:2-6; 28:1; Fargard 5:36; 14:5; Plutarch *de Iside et Osiride* 46). In Dinkard 9:10 there is a warning against killing the three-headed demonic spirit Azhi Dahaka by cutting lest he fill the earth with serpents, toads, scorpions, lizards, tortoises, and frogs. Instead he was chained for a period of time (cf. Rev. 20:1-3). Nor is the manner of the appearance unexampled, for Hermas, a Christian prophet who lived and wrote at about the same time as John, related that he once saw the great beast Leviathan (evidently Satan) with fiery locusts coming out of his mouth, a sign of the persecution which was soon to come (Herm. Vis. IV. 1.6). So these satanic frogs represent the last attack of the nations of the earth against the people of God.

14. These three demonic froglike **spirits** have powers similar to those of the pseudo Christ, for like him they performed **signs** (RSV) or **miracles** (KJV, cf. 13:14), apparently to deceive those who dwell on the earth. At any rate, they succeeded in assembling

over the whole empire of wickedness. None of the activities of life can go on. Nothing is left but suffering. In one of the most terrible pictures in the book of Revelation we see men in the dark cursing God. The awful condemnation tolls on like a bell of doom. They **did not repent.** All of these pictures are saying that to live at all you have to have seas and fountains

and sunshine and health and when all these turn against you life has become hopeless. But still it is possible to preserve grimly an unrepentant heart. Once and again as we go through the dooms of the book of Revelation we remember Byron's poem "Darkness" when the sun has gone out and the last fire in the world ceases to burn. Figures crouch by the

15 Behold, I come as a thief. Blessed *is* he that watcheth, and keepeth his garments, lest he walk naked, and they see his shame.

16 And he gathered them together into a place called in the Hebrew tongue Armageddon.

15 ("Lo, I am coming like a thief! Blessed is he who is awake, keeping his garments that he may not go naked and be seen exposed!") 16 And they assembled them at the place which is called in Hebrew Ar-ma-ged'don.

---

the kings of the whole world, not merely those of the East, for the great battle that will occur **on the great day of God the Almighty**—the apocalyptic conflict in which the forces of evil are to be finally defeated and destroyed. The words **of the earth** (KJV) are an interpolation into the text.

15. This third beatitude is frequently considered a displacement from another chapter (from 3:3 or before 3:18), or else a scribal interpolation, since it apparently breaks the smooth flow of the narration of coming events. But this was probably John's intent: the end is at hand, the final conflict is about to begin. Consequently, in order to warn his followers to be on their guard, and at the same time to give them fresh assurance concerning the outcome, the heavenly Christ dramatically interjects himself into the scene. He announces that he is **coming** suddenly **like a thief,** and pronounces his blessing upon the Christian **who is awake** with his **garments** of immortality ready lest he be **naked** and others **see his shame.** Thus the warnings of the heavenly Christ in 3:3 and 3:18 are reiterated for emphasis; there is no need to suppose either a displacement or an interpolation.

16. The kings of the world are assembled for this final struggle at a place called by the Hebrew name **Armageddon** or "Har-Magedon" (ASV). This mouth-filling word, like the number 666, has been magnified in popular thinking out of all proportion to its significance. John mentions it but once, and even then he does not take the trouble to give its Greek equivalent, as he previously did for Abaddon, another Hebrew term (cf. 9:11).

This strange name makes its first appearance in literature in this verse. Like the number 666, its meaning is obscure, but several solutions have been proposed. It has been suggested that it is a corruption of the Hebrew for "his fruitful mountain," Mount Zion, since according to Dan. 11:45, the final battle in which Antiochus IV Epiphanes was to be vanquished was to be "between the sea and the glorious holy mountain." Or, since this last conflict was to occur in the neighborhood of Jerusalem, a second proposal is that the term is a corruption of the Hebrew for "the desirable city."

There is more agreement with the suggestion that the phrase is associated with the ancient city of Megiddo and means "the mountains of Megiddo." Megiddo was a stronghold at the head of the Plain of Esdraelon, called the Plain of Megiddo by Jerome. It was here that Barak and Deborah, with the stars fighting on their side, defeated Sisera and the Canaanites (Judg. 5:19-20). The plain was the scene of frequent and decisive battles in antiquity. Hence, by association the name Armageddon was used by John to symbolize the site of the eschatological conflict between the cohorts of God and Satan. A major difficulty, the fact that there were no mountains of Megiddo, may be removed if it is considered that the term refers to the mountains in the neighborhood of Megiddo.

---

expiring embers. In the picture in the book of Revelation there are no expiring embers—all is darkness.

16. *Preparing for the Greatest Battle.*— Theodore Roosevelt with his gift for appropriating striking phrases called his last great political battle an **Armageddon.** The word was of course much too large. Yet whenever men are fighting for what they believe to be completely good and against that which they conceive to be completely wicked they are likely to think of it. The previous pictures of the dooms of the bowls are characteristically forgotten while in the new picture not only evil but loathsome and repulsive evil is painted. **Spirits like frogs** assemble the wicked forces of the world for the battle against God. In a telling figure it is said that they come **from the mouth of the dragon**

17 And the seventh angel poured out his vial into the air; and there came a great voice out of the temple of heaven, from the throne, saying, It is done.

18 And there were voices, and thunders, and lightnings; and there was a great earthquake, such as was not since men were upon the earth, so mighty an earthquake, *and* so great.

19 And the great city was divided into three parts, and the cities of the nations fell: and great Babylon came in remembrance before God, to give unto her the cup of the wine of the fierceness of his wrath.

17 The seventh angel poured his bowl into the air, and a great voice came out of the temple, from the throne, saying, "It is done!" **18** And there were flashes of lightning, loud noises, peals of thunder, and a great earthquake such as had never been since men were on the earth, so great was that earthquake. **19** The great city was split into three parts, and the cities of the nations fell, and God remembered great Babylon, to make her drain the cup of the fury

But why was not the phrase "Plain of Megiddo" used, thereby avoiding the difficulty in the first place? Possibly because according to Ezekiel's account, which John seems to follow in a later description of this battle, the conflict was to take place on "the mountains of Israel" (cf. Ezek. 38:8, 21; 39:2, 4, 17). The derivation, however, is not as important as the fact that John has chosen this memorable name to signify the final battle between the forces of good and evil, a battle in which the latter will be overthrown and destroyed.

H. Seventh Bowl: Impending Destruction of Babylon (16:17-21)

17. While John has maintained a certain parallelism between the bowl visions and the earlier trumpet visions, there were certain incidents between the sixth and the seventh trumpets which are not duplicated in the bowl sequence (cf. 10:1–11:14). On the other hand, certain events following upon the sounding of the last trumpet are paralleled by episodes in the seventh bowl scene. When the last and seventh bowl was poured out into the air, **a great voice** from **the temple** and **from the throne**, which no doubt is the awful voice of God himself, exclaims: **"It is done!"** This corresponds to the loud voices from heaven which were heard after the seventh trumpet blast, saying that "the kingdom of the world has become the kingdom of our Lord and of his Christ." The end, however, was even closer than when the seventh trumpet was sounded; God himself had said that the plagues were finished, that everything was ready for the consummation of the apocalyptic drama. A very similar divine exclamation is repeated in 21:6 after the first heaven and earth have passed away, the new heaven and the new earth have been created, and the New Jerusalem has come down from heaven to earth.

18. There is no antiphonal by the twenty-four elders as in 11:16-18, but the phenomena following the vision of the ark when the temple in heaven was opened—**lightning, loud noises, peals of thunder, earthquake,** and hail (11:19)—are all repeated, save for the hail, in those that occur after God's voice was heard announcing the end (but cf. vs. 21 for the hail). On the other hand, the earthquake that happened this time was the greatest in the history of mankind.

19. Immediately before the seventh trumpet, just after the two witnesses had ascended into heaven, an earthquake destroyed one tenth of the great city and killed seven

and from the mouth of the beast and from the mouth of the false prophet. Evil words always prepare for evil deeds.

19. *The City God Did Not Forget.*—It really seemed that in the midst of its cruel and wicked power Rome had no need to fear. It seemed that God had turned his face away; it seemed that God had forgotten Rome. But in

the very consummation of the dooms of the bowls, as the word of mighty finality, **It is done,** is spoken, God remembers Rome. It is called by the symbolic name, **Babylon,** for that ancient city had brought evil to God's people. So had Nineveh, but Babylon is chosen as the name of the great contemporary city which, destroying, was itself to find destruction. Bad cities always

20 And every island fled away, and the mountains were not found.

21 And there fell upon men a great hail out of heaven, *every stone* about the weight of a talent: and men blasphemed God because of the plague of the hail; for the plague thereof was exceeding great.

17 And there came one of the seven angels which had the seven vials, and talked with me, saying unto me, Come hither; I will show unto thee the judgment

of his wrath. 20 And every island fled away, and no mountains were to be found; 21 and great hailstones, heavy as a hundredweight, dropped on men from heaven, till men cursed God for the plague of the hail, so fearful was that plague.

17 Then one of the seven angels who had the seven bowls came and said

thousand people (cf. 11:13). This greatest of earthquakes, however, split **the great city** into three parts and destroyed **the cities of the nations** as well. This **great city** is identified as **great Babylon,** i.e., Rome and the Roman Empire, as the following words show: **God remembered great Babylon, to make her drain the cup** [of the wine] **of the fury of his wrath.** (The words in brackets, unaccountably omitted from the RSV, are in Nestle's Greek text, used by the translators.) Thus the predictions of 14:8 and 10, that Babylon the great would fall, and that the worshipers of the beast "shall drink the wine of God's wrath, poured unmixed into the cup of his anger" reach fulfillment. The other cities that were destroyed are probably those of the pagan world outside the empire.

20. Another astounding result of this great earthquake was that **every island fled away, and no mountains were to be found,** doubly astounding since this had already occurred as far back as 6:14b as one result of the opening of the sixth seal. This repetition is just one of the indications that the different series of plagues are not actually to be considered as following one upon the other, but are probably to be regarded as differing versions of the same series of eschatological woes preparing the way for the end of this world and age.

21. The "heavy hail" which concluded the list of phenomena resulting from the seventh trumpet blast is magnified in this scene, where it consists of **great hailstones,** each one **about the weight of a talent** (KJV). The talent, which varied in value, weighed approximately a hundred pounds. Although Pharaoh had given some evidence of repentance during the plague of hail (Exod. 9:27), these dreadful hailstones of supernatural origin and size which fell on the Roman persecutors served only to cause them to blaspheme God, as in vss. 9 and 11.

With these hailstones the seven bowl plagues are completed; the end is at hand. Christ had signified this when he exclaimed in vs. 15, "Lo, I am coming like a thief," and God had reaffirmed it when he proclaimed in vs. 17, **"It is done!"** We are on the threshold of the consummation; but a number of events are yet to occur before the final act of this cosmic drama is staged.

IX. SEVEN VISIONS OF THE FALL OF "BABYLON" OR ROME (17:1–19:10)

A. FIRST VISION: THE HARLOT, BABYLON THE GREAT (17:1-6a)

When the city of Rome first began to be a political force, the development of the cult of Roma, the deified personification of Rome, occurred. This cult did not originate

overestimate their own power. But as they follow ancient vices and invent new vices of their own the searching eye of God is upon them. It is well to remember that the tale is contemporary. A brilliant Congregational preacher had this in mind when he called a book about New York *A Prophet in Babylon.*[1]

[1] William J. Dawson (New York: Fleming H. Revell Co., 1907).

20-21. No Language but a Blasphemous Cry. —The very islands and mountains flee away from Rome. Nature repudiates the wicked city; **great hailstones** fall **from heaven** upon the evil town. At last there is nothing left but a wild voice. And the voice is a curse. The final expression of God's just will in the dooms of the seven bowls leaves men unrepentant. The whole chapter is a picture of the recalcitrant

of the great whore that sitteth upon many | to me, "Come, I will show you the judg-
waters; | ment of the great harlot who is seated upon

in Rome itself, but with the Italian cities which were allied with Rome and the Greek cities which had become more and more dependent upon her. The citizens of these municipalities recognized a divine element in the increasingly significant city of Rome, which they personified and worshiped as the goddess Roma. When Rome extended her sway to Asia and the East, this worship of Roma was soon introduced in these areas. Apparently there was little opposition to this state cult; in fact, the Smyrnians boasted that they had erected a temple to Roma before Carthage had fallen to Roman power, and the goddess became the tutelary divinity of this city. It was only natural that the cult of Roma should become connected with that of the ruler. Thus, in 29 B.C. temples were erected by Octavian to *Dea Roma* and *Divus Julius* at Ephesus and Nicaea for the benefit of Roman citizens in these cities, and to Roma and himself in Pergamum and Nicomedia for the provincials of Asia and Bithynia. The remains of the one at Pergamum are still to be seen; it may have been "Satan's throne" referred to in the letter to Pergamum (2:13). More frequently, it seems, the cult of Roma was associated with the worship of the dead emperors, not the living, and in this form became established quite generally throughout the empire. Along with this concept of *Dea Roma,* the provincials, both to flatter and honor the conquering city and state, developed the belief in *Roma aeterna,* eternal Rome, a political dogma that gained wide acceptance. Save for Lohmeyer, who mentions it, commentators have tended to ignore the significance of the worship of Roma, along with that of the emperors, as well as her supposedly eternal character in their interpretation of this chapter. Evidently, the harlot is not only Rome and the empire, but *Dea Roma* herself, who with the emperors, the seven-headed beast, is accorded divine worship. Moreover, although she is considered eternal by her deluded subjects and their leaders, actually like the beast she is temporal and is soon to be destroyed.

17:1. One of the seven angels, acting as a guide and interpreter in conformity to a familiar apocalyptic pattern (cf. 7:13), now offered to show John the coming **judgment** which is to be inflicted upon **the great harlot.** This judgment, of course, is the impending destruction of Rome for her idolatry and for her persecution of the saints. The depiction of the goddess Roma as a harlot corresponds to the previous portrayal of the emperors as a horrendous, satanic beast, and is in keeping with her enticement of the nations into idolatrous practices, designated as "fornication" in vs. 4. Moreover, there was in the prophets good precedent for this figure. John may have been aware that Nahum called Nineveh a harlot for seducing the nations and had pronounced a terrible and bloody doom upon her (Nah. 3:1-4). In quite a similar manner and for similar reasons another prophet had applied the same opprobrious epithet to Tyre and predicted her ruin (Isa. 23:15). In several other passages Jerusalem was named as a seductive harlot who had been disloyal to the Lord by turning away to idolatry (Isa. 1:21; Ezek. 16:15; cf. Hos. 2:5). Similar imagery is used by the Sibyl who prophesies Rome's destruction in the following words, "O Rome, pampered offspring of Latium! thou virgin oft intoxicated by many suitors in marriage, as a slave girl [i.e., prostitute] thou shalt be wedded without ceremony" (Sibylline Oracles 3:356-58). John's dramatic love for contrast has been noticed before. Now he is evidently preparing the way for the contrast between this

---

nature of wickedness. Its stubborn defiance is unconquerable. And Rome is the very symbol of its essence. Vast quantities of modern books take the opposite view. There are always qualifying elements in the situation; there is confused thinking; there are bewildered minds; to understand all is to forgive all. When the elements of truth in all these interpretations have | been admitted, it still must be said that there is a hard core of wickedness in the world whose only voice is a mad defiance of the good. The book of Revelation speaks a stern word, but it is a word which must be heard. When we have considered these things we are not surprised at the appearance of such a man as Savonarola of Florence. We are surprised that more such

2 With whom the kings of the earth have committed fornication, and the inhabitants of the earth have been made drunk with the wine of her fornication.	many waters, 2 with whom the kings of the earth have committed fornication, and with the wine of whose fornication the dwellers on earth have become drunk."
3 So he carried me away in the spirit into the wilderness: and I saw a woman sit upon a scarlet-colored beast, full of names of blasphemy, having seven heads and ten horns.	3 And he carried me away in the Spirit into a wilderness, and I saw a woman sitting on a scarlet beast which was full of blasphemous names, and it had seven heads and

wicked harlot and the bride of Christ in all her radiance and purity, and that between the harlot's bestial consort and Christ the bridegroom.

The harlot is depicted as sitting **upon many waters.** This is not a true picture of Rome, but it was of Babylon, the prototype of Rome, which is correctly portrayed by Jeremiah, in prophesying her approaching doom, as dwelling "upon many waters" with all her rich treasures (Jer. 51:13; cf. Rev. 17:15).

2. As Nineveh and Tyre had led other peoples astray and forced them to commit idolatry, so now Rome, the mistress of the Mediterranean, had seduced the **kings of the earth** whom she had conquered along with their subjects and had made **drunk** with **the wine** of her **fornication** (cf. 14:8 for very similar words); i.e., she had enticed them into the idolatrous worship of herself and her consort, the beast, which is represented by John as "fornication" (cf. 2:21; 9:21; 14:8).

3. Following this introductory explanation, John while **in the Spirit** (as in 1:10 and 4:2) was carried away by the angel **into a wilderness** where the harlot was shown to him. John will also be **in the Spirit** when this same angel carries him to a high mountain to see the bride, the New Jerusalem, descending from heaven (21:10). Thus the contrast between the two cities, between the earthly and the heavenly, the idolatrous and the faithful, the wicked and the righteous, the temporal and the eternal, is to be vividly drawn. While the glorious view of the bride is to be seen from a mountaintop, the sordid scene of the harlot will be shown in a **wilderness,** possibly to suggest the coming desolation of the city.

The basic relationship of the worship of the goddess Roma with that of the emperor gods is shown in the portrayal of the harlot being carried by her consort, the seven-headed beast with ten horns. This beast had "a blasphemous name" on its heads in 13:1; but now its body is **full of blasphemous names.** Previously it had diadems on its ten horns (13:1); but now these are not mentioned. In the earlier passage the color of the beast was not stated (although the dragon was described as red in color); he now is **scarlet** hued. This, however, may refer not to the color of the beast but to his apparel; it matches that worn by the harlot.

The inconsistency between this picture of the woman sitting on the beast with that in vs. 1, where she is sitting "upon many waters," is not uncharacteristic of John and other apocalyptic writers; for picture language is not much concerned with logic, consistency, and precision.

The emperor gods are satirized as a demonic beast; the goddess Roma, the personification of the divine state, is held up to scorn as a harlot who is his mistress, sharing in

prophets have not appeared in bad towns. If the prophet simply talks of peace of mind he is crying peace when there is no peace. **17:3. The Lawless City of Law.**—The Roman system of order was being applied all about the world. Rome was the giver of law, but the man of Patmos bitterly describes Rome as the great violator of law. And with grim irony he de-	scribes the great city as a harlot deriving her strength from a passionate and powerful beast. Plato described the good life which consists in participating in the reality of the great and eternal Ideas. From above and beyond life comes this great power. But Rome receives from the subhuman the power to misuse the human. A clever writer once wrote a story about a man

4 And the woman was arrayed in purple and scarlet color, and decked with gold and precious stones and pearls, having a golden cup in her hand full of abominations and filthiness of her fornication:

5 And upon her forehead *was* a name written, MYSTERY, BABYLON THE GREAT, THE MOTHER OF HARLOTS AND ABOMINATIONS OF THE EARTH.

ten horns. 4 The woman was arrayed in purple and scarlet, and bedecked with gold and jewels and pearls, holding in her hand a golden cup full of abominations and the impurities of her fornication; 5 and on her forehead was written a name of mystery: "Babylon the great, mother of harlots and

---

all his satanic wickedness. Far from being divine, they are everything that is wicked, debauched, and degraded. This is the compelling message which John is preaching to his readers with his symbolic language, dramatically warning those who might be seduced into worshiping the state and its ruler.

4. This prostitute was arrayed in costly raiment of **purple and scarlet,** symbolic of her imperial status, and was adorned with **gold and precious stones,** indicative of the wealth of the empire. She held a **golden cup** in her hand, a detail that may be a reworking of the description in Jer. 51:7 of Babylon as a "golden cup" in God's hands filled with wine which has made the nations drunk and mad (cf. 14:10). Varying the figure of vss. 2 and 14:8, John represents the cup, in contrast to the luxurious apparel of the harlot, as **full of abominations and the impurities** [**filthiness** KJV] **of her fornication.** The Greek word translated **abominations** is the almost unpronounceable βδέλυγμα, and in the LXX is frequently used to denote moral and ceremonial impurity, especially that incurred in connection with idolatrous rites. More especially it was used in the phrase "the abomination that maketh desolate" (Dan. 11:31; 12:11; cf. Dan. 9:27) with reference to the desecration of the holy temple by the impious Antiochus IV Epiphanes as an insulting climax to his persecution of the Jews (cf. I Macc. 1:54). The prediction was made in Dan. 9:27 that this desolater would himself be desolated for his abominations at the consummation of this age. A similar correlation of the "abomination of desolation" with the impending apocalyptic doom and destruction is seen in the "little apocalypse" (Mark 13:14). Possibly the presence of **abominations** in the golden cup that the woman in scarlet was holding implies that she too will be made desolate because of the abominations she has committed. The cup also contained **the impurities of her fornication,** synonymous with "abominations," since for John "fornication" signifies idolatry, especially the imperial cult.

5. The body of the beast was "full of blasphemous names," while in an earlier passage (13:1) the same beast had "a blasphemous name upon its heads." Corresponding with this description of her consort is the statement that the woman had a **name** on her **forehead.** The blasphemous name or names of the beast are not given by John, but that of the harlot is quite evident. It was **Babylon the great, mother of harlots and of earth's abominations. Babylon the great,** of course, means Rome and *Dea Roma.* The **name** is one of **mystery,** i.e., it is to be understood allegorically, not literally. The title **mother** was assigned to a number of goddesses, especially to the *Magna Mater,* the Great Mother of the Gods, a pure and chaste goddess of Asia Minor, who since 204 B.C. had also been domiciled in Rome, where she was greatly revered. Possibly John is drawing a comparison between this chaste goddess, who is the Mother of the Gods, and the impure wanton Roma, who is the mother of nothing but **harlots** and **abominations.** Such a comparison would be recognized and appreciated by his readers, especially those who lived in Asia Minor and Phrygia.

---

who lived a double life. He was a member of the body which made the laws, and he was also a successful and secret violator of the laws. The book was called *Lawmaker and Lawbreaker.*

When the great lawmaker for the world is also the great breaker of all good laws the situation is one of deep and woeful tragedy. So Rome had become the lawless city of law.

6 And I saw the woman drunken with the blood of the saints, and with the blood of the martyrs of Jesus: and when I saw her, I wondered with great admiration.

7 And the angel said unto me, Wherefore didst thou marvel? I will tell thee the mystery of the woman, and of the beast that carrieth her, which hath the seven heads and ten horns.

8 The beast that thou sawest was, and is not; and shall ascend out of the bottomless pit, and go into perdition: and they that dwell on the earth shall wonder, whose names were not written in the book of life from the foundation of the world, when they behold the beast that was, and is not, and yet is.

of earth's abominations." 6 And I saw the woman, drunk with the blood of the saints and the blood of the martyrs of Jesus.

When I saw her I marveled greatly. 7 But the angel said to me, "Why marvel? I will tell you the mystery of the woman, and of the beast with seven heads and ten horns that carries her. 8 The beast that you saw was, and is not, and is to ascend from the bottomless pit and go to perdition; and the dwellers on earth whose names have not been written in the book of life from the foundation of the world, will marvel to behold the beast, because it was and is not and

---

6a. For John by far the greatest "abomination" of all that had been perpetrated, the heinous sin for which Rome, her rulers, and her people would be punished and destroyed by God, is the shedding of the blood of Christians who steadfastly refused to deny their God and Christ and worship the goddess Roma and the emperors. This conviction comes to the forefront in this verse, for Roma, the consort of the imperial Antichrist, was **drunk with the blood of the saints,** i.e., **of the martyrs of Jesus** (cf. 16:6). This bloodguiltiness is the unforgivable sin which soon is to be requited by the wrath and vengeance of God.

B. Second Vision: Interpretation of the Harlot and the Beast
(17:6b-18)

6b-7. When John saw this **woman** carried by the **beast,** he was greatly puzzled and **marveled greatly.** His angel-interpreter assured him that he would explain this strange sight for him. But the angelic interpretation, which is concerned more with the beast than with the woman, is actually more perplexing than the scene which had mystified John.

8. Earlier the beast was satirized as "the beast which was wounded by the sword and yet lived" (13:14), in contrast to the slain Lamb that died and yet lives evermore (cf. 1:18; 2:8). According to the angelic explanation, the beast that puzzled John **was, and is not, and is to ascend from the bottomless pit and go to perdition.** This description is an ironical parody of the title given to God in 1:4, "Who is and who was and who is to come" (cf. 4:8). It refers to the Nero *redivivus* expectation, for the beast like the demonic Nero had died, but is to return to life. It will not descend from heaven, as the slain Lamb is to do in his second advent, but will **ascend from the bottomless pit.** Its demonic nature is shown by its appearance from the bottomless pit, like the beast that waged war with the two heavenly witnesses (11:7), instead of from the sea, as in 13:1. This

---

6. *The Intoxication of Cruel Power.*—"O Rome, Rome, thou hast been a tender nurse to me!" said the gladiator Spartacus in a supposed speech full of irony, which young orators used to declaim sixty years ago. Many had felt the hard heel of Rome upon their necks. But the book of Revelation is full of hot and intense indignation at the thought of Rome's persecution of the Christians. The imperial power is literally **drunk with the blood of the saints.**

It has found a sadistic satisfaction in cruelty. Its real supremacy is in cruel lust and not in law. This is the power which is to be judged by the righteous God. The persecution of Christians is a long and terrible story. One aspect of it has been told with unflinching graphic power in Foxe's *Book of Martyrs.* The whole, long story caused one preacher to say: "The Christian church has been paid for, not cash down, but blood down."

9 And here *is* the mind which hath wisdom. The seven heads are seven mountains, on which the woman sitteth.

10 And there are seven kings: five are fallen, and one is, *and* the other is not yet come; and when he cometh, he must continue a short space.

is to come. **9** This calls for a mind with wisdom: the seven heads are seven hills on which the woman is seated; **10** they are also seven kings, five of whom have fallen, one is, the other has not yet come, and when he comes he must remain only a little while.

---

may not be as inconsistent as appears on the surface, for the abyss (translated as **the bottomless pit**) was at times considered to be a bottomless watery deep. Despite the beast's exaltation of itself as God, it was destined to **go to perdition,** a fate that will be dramatically fulfilled in 19:20, when it will be thrown into the lake of fire, along with the false prophet. When this Neronic beast first appeared all people worshiped it, save those whose names were in the Lamb's book of life from the foundation of the world (13:8). These words are repeated in this context, for those **whose names have not been written in the book of life from the foundation of the world** will look upon this beast with amazement. This will be because **it was and is not and is to come,** which repeats the irony of the first words of this verse.

9a. So far the angel's interpretation is clear, following in the main the theme underlying 13:1-10. The rest, however, requires **wisdom** if it is to be understood, as was also the case with the mystic number 666 in 13:18.

9b. The **seven heads** signify **seven hills on which the woman is seated**—which clearly means Rome, for according to classical tradition, it was built upon seven hills. Although in this chapter it is the woman who is equated with Rome, the plastic nature of his symbolism now allows John to identify the heads of the beast with the imperial capital.

10-11. These two verses are among the most obscure in Revelation, though the general sense is quite clear. The seven heads, which were seven hills in the preceding verse, now shift in meaning and represent Roman emperors. Furthermore, one of them is related to Nero, who died and yet lived. All this is in conformity with the general sense of 13:1-4. The difficulty centers in discovering just which seven emperors are meant, and the precise relationship of Nero *redivivus* to the group.

The discussion may be helped if it is prefaced with a consideration of symbolism of a similar character. The earliest examples of this type are to be found in Daniel, which John has used as a main source for his own book.

One of the exemplars for the beast in Revelation is the four-headed leopard of Dan. 7:6. It is obvious that this animal signifies the kingdom of Persia, and later the four heads are said to stand for four kings (Dan. 11:2). One head is probably Cyrus, the fourth Xerxes, but it is impossible to identify the other two with any certainty at all. Another model for the beast of Revelation is the fourth one in Daniel with its ten horns, with an additional little horn growing out where three others, plucked out by the roots, had been (Dan. 7:7-8). The beast itself is the Greco-Syrian kingdom, one of the divisions of Alexander's empire following his death. The little horn is undoubtedly Antiochus IV Epiphanes, the persecutor of the Jews, who was the special concern of the author. The ten horns are said to represent ten kings (Dan. 7:24), but again, no one can determine just which ten are meant. Prior to Antiochus there were but six kings in the Seleucid line, or if Alexander is included, but seven. This leaves either four or three to be accounted for to make up the ten. It is possible, therefore, that in Daniel the numbers four and ten are used symbolically to represent the kings of Persia and the kings of Syria respectively, and not historically with reference to four or ten specific kings.

Another illustration, important because it is practically contemporary with Revelation, is provided by the eagle vision in II Esdras 11–12. "Ezra" saw a strange eagle rising from the sea with three heads and twelve large wings, with eight smaller wings growing out of the larger ones. The eagle has power for a while, but with the coming of a conquering lion it is destroyed. Ezra is puzzled and disturbed by this sight, but God interprets it for him. However, the divine explanation is almost as mystifying as the vision was, although in general the meaning is clear. The eagle is the Roman Empire, the oppressor of the Jews. The three heads are three emperors, one the current ruler, Domitian, the others his brother Titus and his father Vespasian. The lion is the Messiah, who soon is to bring about the destruction of the empire and its evil emperor. The twelve large wings are twelve imperial predecessors of these three from the Flavian house. If two wings are counted to an emperor and only the Julian line is considered, this solution is reached; but it seems quite arbitrary to omit Galba, Otho, and Vitellius. On the other hand, if one wing is assigned to an emperor, three very obscure pretenders must be added to make a total of twelve, and this too is arbitrary. Apparently twelve is to be taken as a symbolic number to indicate those emperors preceding the Flavian line, without any attempt at a more specific identification. As for the eight smaller wings which are dependent upon the others, these are clearly lesser rulers or governors, but any further attempts to identify them are sheer guesswork. The author, actually, is not interested in these or in the twelve larger wings—his main concern is with the Flavian line, whose last representative was the infamous Domitian.

With this background in mind it may be easier to examine the interpretation of the beast with seven heads and ten horns. The beast, as we have seen before, represents the empire and the imperial line, and is also a symbol of the Antichrist. But now the seven heads are said by the angel to be **seven kings,** no doubt seven Roman emperors. **Five** of these have died; **one,** the sixth, is now ruling; the seventh **has not yet come,** and when he does, he will **remain only a little while.** Also, and somewhat less cryptically, **the beast** itself **that was and is not** is said to be an **eighth,** i.e., he is an eighth emperor, who at the same time is one of **the seven;** moreover, he is to go to **perdition.** This explanation is most confusing, although the second part, vs. 11, presents fewer difficulties than vs. 10. The beast is said to be an **eighth** emperor who also was one of **the seven,** a rather definite identification of the beast with the emperor Nero, who had died and yet was expected to return to life (see on 13:3 and 18). Furthermore, this Neronic beast, which previously has been related to the Antichrist, is going to destruction, a prediction that has been made before. However, there seems to be a discrepancy, for if this eighth is also the seventh of vs. 10 who is yet to come, it would mean that the Antichrist, who according to ch. 13 has already appeared, actually is not to come until sometime in the future, after the ruling emperor has died, and then is to have a brief reign. This is not in harmony with the repeated assurances of the author that the end is to come very soon, for apparently the rule of the sixth or present ruler is indefinite in length.

Also, who are the five emperors who have died? The answer depends upon a number of variables. First, should the computation begin with Julius Caesar or with Augustus? Second, should Galba, Otto, and Vitellius be omitted from consideration by reason of the brevity of their reigns, or should they be counted among the five who had fallen? Depending upon the formula used, the sixth, or current, ruler, could be Nero, Galba, or Vespasian. Nero should be excluded as the ruling emperor, for it is impossible to see how the Nero *redivivus* belief could have originated prior to his death. The reign of Galba, it is thought, was too brief and uneventful to cause him to merit consideration. But by beginning with Augustus, and eliminating Galba, Otho, and Vitellius from consideration, Vespasian becomes the sixth emperor.

Consequently, it has been proposed that this passage was originally a Jewish oracle written soon after A.D. 70, and was directed against Vespasian, who initiated the siege against Jerusalem. His probable successor, the seventh, would be his son Titus, who completed the siege and was blamed for the destruction of the temple. According to this view, the eighth and last would be the infamous Nero returned to life, whose brief reign would terminate with his destruction and with the end of this age. According to this theory, John incorporated this Vespasianic oracle into his work, bringing it up to date by considering Domitian as the sixth and ruling emperor, with the anticipation

11 And the beast that was, and is not, even he is the eighth, and is of the seven, and goeth into perdition.

12 And the ten horns which thou sawest are ten kings, which have received no kingdom as yet; but receive power as kings one hour with the beast.

13 These have one mind, and shall give their power and strength unto the beast.

11 As for the beast that was and is not, it is an eighth but it belongs to the seven, and it goes to perdition. 12 And the ten horns that you saw are ten kings who have not yet received royal power, but they are to receive authority as kings for one hour, together with the beast. 13 These are of one mind and give over their power and author-

---

that he would soon be replaced by the Neronic Antichrist. A variation of this theory would be to suppose that Domitian not only was the sixth emperor, but that he also was the reincarnation of the seventh, the revived Nero. This gains some support when it is realized that Domitian was considered another Nero by some of his subjects (cf. Juvenal *Satires* IV. 37, 38; Martial *Epigrams* XI. 33).

Another solution—proposed now, it is believed, for the first time—is based upon the observation that only those dead rulers who had been apotheosized by the senate were worshiped. Consequently, it is possible that the first five heads of the beast that is worshiped are the first five rulers to be so honored—Caesar, Augustus, Claudius, Vespasian, and Titus. If this is true, Domitian, who demanded worship while living, would be the sixth and ruling emperor, while the seventh and last, the Neronic Antichrist, who at the same time might be considered as reincarnated in the person of Domitian, was still to come.

But it is possible that none of these interesting conjectures is correct. In Daniel the four heads and the ten horns were used symbolically, not historically, and the same is true of the twelve eagle wings in II Esdras. Accordingly, it is conceivable that the beast had seven heads because of John's partiality for this number, or because in his sources there was a beast with seven heads, just as there was one with ten horns. One of the heads represents the present ruler, another the Antichrist who is to come; as for the other five, they may represent the imperial predecessors as a group, and not five specific individuals. Indeed, it has been suggested that John would probably have been unable to name the rulers of the century or more preceding the date of Revelation.

12-13. The ten horns without the crowns they wore in 13:1 remain to be explained. In the light of the belief that Nero would return from the East with a Parthian army of invasion, it is possible that these ten horns represent the Parthian satraps, uncrowned governors, who will be Nero's allies and generals. The fact that there were supposedly fourteen of these satraps at a given time presents no difficulty, for the ten horns, derived from Dan. 7:7, symbolize the entire group. When Nero has his brief renewal of imperial power they will **receive authority as kings.** Apparently at this time they will receive the diadems that are mentioned in 13:1. However, they will be completely under the control of the Antichrist, ceding him all of their own **power and authority.**

---

12. *The Kaleidoscope of Thrones.*—The impressiveness of a throne is found in the continuity of its power. Rome is to lack just this. Kings with beastly connections are to come and go with dizzy rapidity. A kaleidoscope at the center of the world is a matter for scorn rather than for awe and high honor. We are being led to see that kings and thrones may perish but God remains constant. There is a throne which is not subject to dizzy change. With the death of Queen Anne the hopes of a whole circle of brilliant men came suddenly to an end. Passing thrones have a way of defeating the hopes of

men. Like a word of doom the man of Patmos sounds out over evil kings the judgment **but . . . for an hour.**

13. *The Evil Unity of Malignant Power.*—Once and again the book of Revelation emphasized the fact that there are seeds of disintegration in evil powers. Soon this principle is to be called in again. But in the meantime we are reminded that there is sometimes an evil unity in malignant power and that God uses this for his own long purposes of judgment. Kings whose only line of continuity comes from their devotion to the beast seem, and indeed are,

14 These shall make war with the Lamb, and the Lamb shall overcome them: for he is Lord of lords, and King of kings: and they that are with him *are* called, and chosen, and faithful.

15 And he saith unto me, The waters which thou sawest, where the whore sitteth, are people, and multitudes, and nations, and tongues.

16 And the ten horns which thou sawest upon the beast, these shall hate the whore, and shall make her desolate and naked, and shall eat her flesh, and burn her with fire.

ity to the beast; 14 they will make war on the Lamb, and the Lamb will conquer them, for he is Lord of lords and King of kings, and those with him are called and chosen and faithful."

15 And he said to me, "The waters that you saw, where the harlot is seated, are peoples and multitudes and nations and tongues. 16 And the ten horns that you saw, they and the beast will hate the harlot; they will make her desolate and naked, and devour her flesh and burn her up with fire,

---

14. Evidently they are among the kings from the East whom the Antichrist is to assemble against the **Lamb** and his saints at the battle of Armageddon (cf. 16:12-16). The Lamb is now given the honorific title of **Lord of lords and King of kings,** one which is repeated in reverse order in 19:16. Similar titles were assigned to Babylonian, Persian, and Roman rulers, reflecting not only their conquering might but their divine character. This same appellation was also accorded to God, who is called "Lord of lords, God of gods, and King of kings" by the four archangels in I Enoch 9:4, as they pray to him in behalf of the souls of the martyrs for justice. Similarly, in Dan. 2:47, when Daniel told Nebuchadrezzar that God would destroy the kings and kingdoms of the earth and would set up his own eternal kingdom, the frightened king acknowledged God as "God of gods, and Lord of kings" (cf. Dan. 11:36; Deut. 10:17). Now this title is most fittingly given to the Lamb, who with his army is to vanquish the Antichrist (who considers himself both god and king) and his cohorts under the ten kings from the East. The Lamb's army is not composed of angels, but in conformity with the promise of 2:27 and 12:11 it consists of martyrs, those who **are called and chosen and faithful.** The word **chosen** is used nowhere else in Revelation. In I Enoch 1:3, 8; 41:2; 48:1; 51:5, *et passim,* its equivalent, the "elect," denotes the righteous who are to share in the rewards of the future. This coming battle is a preview of the last and final conflict before the millennium which is described in 19:11-21.

15. Continuing with his interpretation, the angel informs John that the **waters** upon which the harlot was seated (cf. vs. 1, "many waters") signify **peoples and multitudes and nations and tongues.** These are the dwellers of the earth who, according to vs. 2, had become "drunk with the wine of her fornication," those who were subject to the woman and the beast and worshiped them as gods. This symbolism of the **waters** may have been suggested by its use in Isa. 8:7 and Jer. 47:2 to represent the armies of the Assyrians, but the connection is not too close.

16. Before their disastrous war against the Lamb, the **beast** with the assistance of the **ten horns** will turn on his paramour, **the harlot,** whom they now **hate.** In the fury of their hate **they will make her desolate and naked,** will feast on her **flesh,** and will

---

the very essence of evil. But they do not have the last word.

14. *Thrice Told Tales.*—The story of the battle between evil and good is repeated again and again in the book of Revelation. Sometimes the battle is in heaven, sometimes on earth. Always the arrogant forces of wickedness are conquered. Here in this world the forces of **the Lamb** are now seen overcoming the forces of the beast. No details are given but the **called**

and chosen and faithful have a share in the victory. When, under Constantine, the empire became Christian the persecuted suddenly became the powerful. At an earlier period the man of Patmos looks forward to the time when faithful Christians will be victors even in the political realm.

14. *From Death to Conquest.*—The book of Revelation is constructed by one who is always ready to burst out in adoration of the living

17 For God hath put in their hearts to fulfil his will, and to agree, and give their kingdom unto the beast, until the words of God shall be fulfilled.

18 And the woman which thou sawest is that great city, which reigneth over the kings of the earth.

18 And after these things I saw another angel come down from heaven, having great power; and the earth was lightened with his glory.

17 for God has put it into their hearts to carry out his purpose by being of one mind and giving over their royal power to the beast, until the words of God shall be fulfilled. **18** And the woman that you saw is the great city which has dominion over the kings of the earth."

18 After this I saw another angel coming down from heaven, having great authority; and the earth was made bright

consume her with **fire.** Thus Roma will be destroyed by those whom she has seduced and made drunk with the wine of her fornication. This scene is to be understood against the background of the belief that Nero would invade the empire with an army of Parthians to ravage and destroy the realm he once ruled. A prediction of the Sibyl is pertinent: the matricide (Nero), returning from the ends of the world and seizing the sovereignty for which he had perished, would ruin all the earth, slaying and burning men as no one had ever done before (Sibylline Oracles 5:363-69; cf. Exeg. on 13:3). The account in Revelation of this same eschatological scene may have been colored by Ezekiel's prediction of the destruction of idolatrous Jerusalem, the harlot, whose lovers will uncover her nakedness, stone her, and burn her houses in carrying out God's wrathful judgment against her (cf. Ezek. 16:35-43). Also, there may be an allusion to the charge that in A.D. 64 Nero had deliberately set fire to Rome, a crime which he attributed to the Christians, causing their persecution.

17. It is noteworthy that the dualism of Revelation is toned down in this passage, for in their destruction of the woman these kings have been carrying out God's own **purpose.** Since they had given **their royal power to the beast,** and presumably were acting under his orders, it follows that the beast, the Antichrist who is the incarnation of Satan, has been an agent of God in this punishment of Rome. This may have been suggested also by Ezekiel's prophecy of the destruction of the harlot Jerusalem by her lovers, for they too will be acting at the direction of God (Ezek. 16:37).

18. The original readers of this book hardly needed to be told that this **woman,** this imperial harlot, is the **great city** who has sovereignty **over the kings of the earth,** the personification of Rome, *Dea Roma* herself.

C. THIRD VISION: ANGELIC PROCLAMATION OF ROME'S FALL (18:1-3)

18:1. Following this description of the coming fall of Rome, John saw still **another angel** descending **from heaven.** He was a powerful and magnificent angel, resembling the mighty angel of 10:1, so that **the earth was made bright with his splendor** (RSV) or **glory** (KJV). A similar effect was noted in the theophany of Ezek. 43:2, when the earth shone with God's glory.

Christ, the Lamb which was slain. He had tasted death; he is to reign in life; **he is Lord of lords and King of kings.** The poet Keats wrote words which indicated that those who know as much about the bitter fruits of life as old men know have a right to go mad. The book of Revelation contains darker pictures than Keats could paint with words but always there is the basis of the eternal hope. There is always the triumph of goodness through the Lamb which was slain.

17. God's Use of Evil Men.—Here we see battles in this world in which the very kings turn against the harlot city and set it on fire. The figure is rather mixed but the meaning is plain enough. And in a flashing aside it is indicated that God himself has confirmed the evil kings in a false unity for the very purpose of the destruction of the city. The imperial tyranny indeed contains seeds of destruction which God uses for his own purposes of judgment. It is a sobering and yet an inspiring thought that God bends evil men to his own purposes as a part of his great reign. The tragedy of A. E. Housman's pessimistic poetry is that he found a call

2 And he cried mightily with a strong voice, saying, Babylon the great is fallen, is fallen, and is become the habitation of devils, and the hold of every foul spirit, and a cage of every unclean and hateful bird.

3 For all nations have drunk of the wine of the wrath of her fornication, and the kings of the earth have committed fornication with her, and the merchants of the earth are waxed rich through the abundance of her delicacies.

with his splendor. 2 And he called out with a mighty voice,

"Fallen, fallen is Babylon the great!
It has become a dwelling place of demons,
a haunt of every foul spirit,
a haunt of every foul and hateful bird;
3 for all nations have drunk[k] the wine of her impure passion,
and the kings of the earth have committed fornication with her,
and the merchants of the earth have grown rich with the wealth of her wantonness."

[k] Other ancient authorities read *fallen by.*

2-3. This angel, direct from heaven, sang a taunting, exultant dirge over Rome as if it were already a destroyed and dead city. This is an amplification of the woe upon Babylon pronounced by the angel of 14:8 and begins with the same ominous words, **Fallen, fallen is Babylon the great!** (Cf. Isa. 21:9*b*.) This once great city, the capital of the mighty empire, is now the haunt of **demons,** of **every foul spirit,** and of **every foul and hateful bird.** This picture may have been prompted by Isaiah's portrayal of the coming destruction of Babylon, which will be inhabited only by wild (and possibly demonic) beasts and by ostriches, a bird of the desert places whose night cries were terrifying and almost devilish (cf. Jer. 50:39).

The reasons for her ruin and desolation are briefly stated. In line with previous predictions, it is because the nations of the world had **drunk the wine of her impure passion** (RSV) or **fornication** (KJV; cf. 14:8) and their **kings** had **committed fornication with her** (cf. 17:2). Because Rome had seduced the peoples under her sway with the idolatrous worship of the state and its rulers, she would be destroyed; it also follows that those who were seduced would share in her ruin.

Another cause, mentioned here for the first time, is that the **merchants of the world** had become **rich** by sharing in **the wealth of her wantonness.** The Roman imperium, with its unified and relatively peaceful rule over the Mediterranean world, a natural political and economic unit of extensive size, had produced trade and commerce and, with these, prosperity and wealth to a degree that was unprecedented in the ancient world. Rome, the capital, was no doubt the wealthiest and most magnificent city of antiquity. There was of necessity a close relationship between the merchants and the government, so that it was only natural that the author, a member of a poor and weak religious group being persecuted for its beliefs, should associate the merchants with the oppressors of the Christians.

for meaning in his own thoughts to which he found no answer in the world. The man of Patmos finds all good meanings at last in the reign of God and that, he clearly sees, involves the judgment of the harlot city.

18:2. The Doom of the Proud City.—Will Durant's *Story of Civilization,*[2] monumental in size and varied in scope, gives one volume to Rome. Significantly enough it bears the title "Caesar and Christ." The title would give great surprise to the followers of the imperial cult.

[2] (New York: Simon & Schuster, 1944), Vol. III.

But in truth the most significant hour in the life of Rome was the hour when it met Christ as judge. The taunt song beginning with the words **Fallen, fallen is Babylon the great** is spoken by an angel whose authority is vast and who brings a splendor of brightness which suffused the earth with the very light of heaven's power. Whenever immoral power sits on the throne of the world men long for and sometimes possess the faith which can announce the doom of a particular evil force just when it seems most secure. Faith is able to **cry fallen is Babylon** before the event.

4 And I heard another voice from heaven, saying, Come out of her, my people, that ye be not partakers of her sins, and that ye receive not of her plagues.

5 For her sins have reached unto heaven, and God hath remembered her iniquities.

6 Reward her even as she rewarded you, and double unto her double according to her works: in the cup which she hath filled, fill to her double.

4 Then I heard another voice from heaven saying,

"Come out of her, my people,
lest you take part in her sins,
lest you share in her plagues;
5 for her sins are heaped high as heaven,
and God has remembered her iniquities.
6 Render to her as she herself has rendered,
and repay her double for her deeds;
mix a double draught for her in the cup she mixed.

D. Fourth Vision: Exultation and Mourning over the Fall of Rome (18:4-20)

This vision has two main divisions: the first is a paean of rejoicing over the fall of the city, representing the views of the persecuted Christians (vss. 4-8); the remainder (vss. 9-20) is composed mainly of the mourning of kings, merchants, and shipmasters.

4. In response to the angelic proclamation **another voice from heaven** exulting over the city's fall and ruin is heard. The speaker is not identified; he might be Christ or possibly God himself (cf. 16:1). Overlooking the picture of the utter desertion of Rome by all human inhabitants, as depicted in vs. 2, the heavenly speaker exhorts his people, the Christians, to leave the city lest they share in **her sins** or be harmed by **her plagues.** The warning may be a reinterpretation of God's exhortation to the Jews in doomed Babylon as reported in Jer. 51:45, "My people, go ye out of the midst of her, and save yourselves every man from the fierce anger of Jehovah" (ASV; cf. Jer. 50:8; 51:6, 9; Isa. 48:20; Mark 13:14; II Baruch 2:1).

5. Just as in Jer. 51:9*b* Babylon's judgment "reacheth unto heaven, and is lifted up even to the skies," so the **sins** of Rome **have reached unto heaven** and **God has remembered her iniquities.**

6. In fact, God will invoke the *lex talionis,* the law of revenge. The idea is in part taken from Jer. 50:29, where the archers arrayed against Babylon are told to "recompense her according to her work." This is also in harmony with Ps. 137:8, which reflects the exile's longing for home and ardent desire for Babylon's destruction, "O daughter of Babylon, who art to be destroyed, happy shall he be, that rewardeth thee as thou hast served us." However, John goes even beyond the psalmist's revenge, for Rome is to be repaid **double for her deeds;** in a reaffirmation of 17:4 (cf. 14:8), she is to have a **double** portion of the deadly **cup** she had mixed for others, a cup which, according to the earlier passage, was filled with the "abominations and the impurities of her fornication."

---

4. *The Way of Escape.*—There are two ways in which to deal with an evil environment. One is to fight for its transformation from within, the other is to flee from it and so to escape its contamination. Here the people of God are commanded to take the way of escape. They are to go away for two reasons: first, so that they shall escape the ugly fascination of Rome's sins; and secondly, so that they shall escape the plagues which God is about to send upon the wicked city. The whole story of monasticism represents the acceptance of this solution on a large scale. The situation is rather more complicated than the words **Come out of**

her indicate, for when men flee from the city of destruction they carry something in their hearts which they must fight. It is the tragedy of life that every man carries a little city of destruction in his own soul. The coming out of that city must mean an inner transformation.

5. *The Shame of the City.*—The publication of Gilbert Highet's *Juvenal the Satirist* [3] after twenty years of research is a major event of achievement in technical scholarship. It is also a matter with its own significance for the student of the N.T. and especially of those parts of the book of Revelation which have to do

[3] New York: Oxford University Press, 1954.

7 How much she hath glorified herself, and lived deliciously, so much torment and sorrow give her: for she saith in her heart, I sit a queen, and am no widow, and shall see no sorrow.

8 Therefore shall her plagues come in one day, death, and mourning, and famine; and she shall be utterly burned with fire: for strong *is* the Lord God who judgeth her.

9 And the kings of the earth, who have committed fornication and lived deliciously with her, shall bewail her, and lament for her, when they shall see the smoke of her burning,

7 As she glorified herself and played the wanton,
    so give her a like measure of torment and mourning.
    Since in her heart she says, 'A queen I sit,
    I am no widow, mourning I shall never see,'
8 so shall her plagues come in a single day,
    pestilence and mourning and famine,
    and she shall be burned with fire;
    for mighty is the Lord God who judges her."

9 And the kings of the earth, who committed fornication and were wanton with her, will weep and wail over her when they

---

7. In an oracle against Babylon in Isa. 47:8-11, that city is pictured as sitting in pleasure and security saying, "I shall not sit as a widow, neither shall I know the loss of children." However, in a day she will become a widow and lose her children. Doubtless with this in mind John represents Rome as saying complacently, **A queen I sit, I am no widow, mourning I shall never see.** In a close parallel the Sibyl warns Rome, "Woe unto thee all unclean city of Latin land, frenzied and poison-loving, in widowhood shalt thou sit beside thy banks; and river Tiber shall mourn for thee, his wife, that hadst a bloodthirsty heart and a godless mind" (Sibylline Oracles 5:168-71).

8. Despite her assurance, God will punish her with a variety of plagues **in a day,** which will consist in the **mourning** she was sure she would never experience, and for good measure **death** and **famine** and **fire.** All this is inescapable, because the **Lord God** has the power to carry out his judgment upon her.

9-10. Three groups are next represented as mourning the fall of Rome. The first are **the kings of the earth** who, as in 17:2, had **committed fornication** with her. Just as the princes of the sea came down from their thrones, according to Ezek. 26:15-17, and

---

with Rome. For the city whose vices Juvenal castigates with something like brilliant ferocity is essentially the city of which the book of Revelation speaks. Highet reminds us that Tacitus confirms the picture for he felt that in its essential being the empire was corrupt; it all comes to life with singular clarity in his book. You come to feel what it was like to live in the city of which the N.T. Apocalypse says: **God has remembered her iniquities.**

7. The Blindness of Pride.—Such pride as that of Rome is incapable of self-analysis. There are plenty of signs ready for the understanding eye. But in disdainful confidence Rome ignores them all. As in Paris before the Revolution it is easier to cherish a blind sense of security than to face the tragically disturbing facts. Moral blindness is often the last quality of the doomed man and the doomed town. The sharp instrument strikes and the faces of the doomed are full of startled surprise. One of the most

subtle tasks of the man who speaks to other men for God is to shock them out of a false and unjustified sense of security. The psychology which offers peace at the very entrance of the house of doom is a strange phenomenon.

8. The Discovery of Genuine Might.—That which seems powerful is often revealed to be impotent; that which seems impotent is often revealed to be full of power. The voice from heaven turns the thoughts of suffering Christians from the power which is a pretense to the power which is real and permanent. We are not for long allowed to forget that the book of Revelation is a book of the acts of God. Now it is said that his greatness is adequate in respect of any demands which can be made upon it. If there is impotent evil, there is also impotent good. There are good men whose understanding pronounces judgments which they are not able to enforce. But God is not impotent goodness; he is almighty goodness. H. G. Wells once

10 Standing afar off for the fear of her torment, saying, Alas, alas, that great city Babylon, that mighty city! for in one hour is thy judgment come.

11 And the merchants of the earth shall weep and mourn over her; for no man buyeth their merchandise any more:

12 The merchandise of gold, and silver, and precious stones, and of pearls, and fine linen, and purple, and silk, and scarlet, and all thyine wood, and all manner vessels of ivory, and all manner vessels of most precious wood, and of brass, and iron, and marble,

13 And cinnamon, and odors, and ointments, and frankincense, and wine, and oil, and fine flour, and wheat, and beasts, and sheep, and horses, and chariots, and slaves, and souls of men.

see the smoke of her burning; 10 they will stand far off, in fear of her torment, and say,

"Alas! alas! thou great city,
     thou mighty city, Babylon!
  In one hour has thy judgment come."

11 And the merchants of the earth weep and mourn for her, since no one buys their cargo any more, 12 cargo of gold, silver, jewels and pearls, fine linen, purple, silk and scarlet, all kinds of scented wood, all articles of ivory, all articles of costly wood, bronze, iron and marble, 13 cinnamon, spice, incense, myrrh, frankincense, wine, oil, fine flour and wheat, cattle and sheep, horses and chariots, and slaves, that is, human souls.

---

lamented the downfall of Tyre, so these kings and puppet rulers dependent on Rome mourn her destruction. The words of their lament are familiar by now: in a single hour the judgment of God has come upon great and mighty Babylon (Rome).

11. In Ezek. 27:36 the merchants (apparently of rival cities) hiss in scorn at ruined Tyre, whose power has been broken forever. But in the case of Rome **the merchants of the earth,** who have been so dependent upon her, **weep and mourn** at her downfall, **since no one buys their cargo any more.**

12-13. The description of the rich and varied merchandise which constituted Rome's great trade is comparable with the description of the trade of Tyre as portrayed in Ezek. 27:1-24, save that the latter passage is far more detailed.

---

played with the idea of a finite God fighting with us against an evil which is rather too much for him as it is entirely too much for us. Such is not the idea of the book of Revelation. God is completely in possession of the power necessary for acts of righteous judgment.

10. *The Sinful Sorrow.*—Henryk Sienkiewicz, the Polish writer, gained world-wide fame when he wrote *Quo Vadis.*[4] It brought to many people in many lands a sense of living in Rome in the days of Nero. The city which the book of Revelation condemns became a real place to them. In the words we are now considering, the kings who had shared in the evil ways of the proud city wail as they witness its destruction. The sorrow itself is an evil sorrow for the kings regret that which itself belongs to an evil order of life. They really love the sins whose punishment they cannot deny.

11. *The Commercial Standard of Judgment.* —Napoleon once, however unjustly, called the English a nation of shopkeepers. They have

certainly been something more than that, and they have been something far more glorious than that. But it can scarcely be denied that when a nation becomes a center of world-wide trade the temptation is always near to substitute commercial standards for permanent standards. To the great merchants the fall of Rome meant the end of trade. The words describing the manifold materials in which they dealt fall with a certain bitter music from their lips. All this vast empire of trade has come to an end. They weep bitterly. When business has come to an end they have nothing left to love. The words have their own challenging significance for those who belong to the many-sided organization of business in the United States.

13. *Buying and Selling Persons.*—Unethical commerce sooner or later inevitably comes to the offering of personality itself for sale. It is not merely that human slavery is a selling of the souls of men as well as their bodies, though of course that is tragically true; it is that, in a world of trade which has no higher standards than commercial success, inevitably character

[4] Boston: Little, Brown & Co., 1896.

14 And the fruits that thy soul lusted after are departed from thee, and all things which were dainty and goodly are departed from thee, and thou shalt find them no more at all.

15 The merchants of these things, which were made rich by her, shall stand afar off for the fear of her torment, weeping and wailing,

16 And saying, Alas, alas, that great city, that was clothed in fine linen, and purple, and scarlet, and decked with gold, and precious stones, and pearls!

17 For in one hour so great riches is come to nought. And every shipmaster, and all the company in ships, and sailors, and as many as trade by sea, stood afar off,

18 And cried when they saw the smoke of her burning, saying, What *city is* like unto this great city!

14 "The fruit for which thy soul longed
　　has gone from thee,
　and all thy dainties and thy splendor
　　are lost to thee, never to be found
　　again!"

15 The merchants of these wares, who gained wealth from her, will stand far off, in fear of her torment, weeping and mourning aloud,

16 "Alas, alas, for the great city
　　that was clothed in fine linen, in
　　　purple and scarlet,
　　bedecked with gold, with jewels, and
　　　with pearls!

17 In one hour all this wealth has been
　　laid waste."

And all shipmasters and seafaring men, sailors and all whose trade is on the sea, stood far off 18 and cried out as they saw the smoke of her burning,
　　"What city was like the great city?"

---

14. It has been suggested by some that this couplet is out of place and properly belongs after vs. 21 or vs. 23. However, it seems to come quite appropriately immediately following the enumeration of the costly articles of merchandise which flowed into Rome. The luxuries and dainties for which the Romans longed are no longer theirs now that the city itself is gone.

15-17a. The merchants continue their wailing and lamentations. In this brief dirge the city is personified, and is represented as being garbed **in purple and scarlet** and adorned **with gold, with jewels, and with pearls,** as was the harlot in 17:4 (cf. also Hiram, of doomed Tyre, covered with gems, Ezek. 28:13). In addition, in this scene her purple and scarlet garments are said to be made of **fine linen.** But **in one hour,** so the merchants lament, **all this wealth has been laid waste.**

17b-18. Among the mourners of Tyre were the seafarers (Ezek. 27:25-34) who threw dust upon their heads and cried out, "Who is there like Tyre, like her that is brought to silence in the midst of the sea?" (Ezek. 27:32 ASV.) In a duplication of this scene the navigators who carried goods to and from Rome mourned as they saw the smoke of the burning city and cried out, **What city was like the great city?**

---

itself is put on the scales and is sold. When Henry Ward Beecher sold a slave from the pulpit of Plymouth Church in Brooklyn to secure the freedom of the victim of an evil system, he illustrated graphically enough the quality of the business which deals in human beings. But the end of this sort of slavery does not mean the end of the commerce in men. Many a man has confronted the test which came when he knew that by selling himself he could make his fortune.

17. The Transient Treasure.—Men looking at the heaps of rubble after the destruction of Berlin and thinking of all the pompous splendor of that great city beheld a visible evidence of the transient quality of material human

treasures. Not merely the fine linen and purple and scarlet but everything which these signify in the way of visible magnificence belonged to a wealth which, so long in the gaining, could be quickly destroyed. The question What is there which is not subject to the destructive power of the bursting bomb? has made certain passages, like the one we are now considering, strangely contemporary. Anthony Trollope in *Dr. Thorne* paints a terrible picture of a man of vast wealth who had ruined his body through drunkenness coming to the hour when as far as he is personally concerned his wealth has ceased to exist. The contrast between transient and permanent treasures is one of the fundamental contrasts of human life.

19 And they cast dust on their heads, and cried, weeping and wailing, saying, Alas, alas, that great city, wherein were made rich all that had ships in the sea by reason of her costliness! for in one hour is she made desolate.

20 Rejoice over her, *thou* heaven, and *ye* holy apostles and prophets; for God hath avenged you on her.

21 And a mighty angel took up a stone like a great millstone, and cast *it* into the sea, saying, Thus with violence shall that great city Babylon be thrown down, and shall be found no more at all.

19 And they threw dust on their heads, as they wept and mourned, crying out,
"Alas, alas, for the great city
    where all who had ships at sea grew
        rich by her wealth!
In one hour she has been laid waste.
20 Rejoice over her, O heaven,
    O saints and apostles and prophets,
    for God has given judgment for you
        against her!"

21 Then a mighty angel took up a stone like a great millstone and threw it into the sea, saying,
"So shall Babylon the great city be
    thrown down with violence,
    and shall be found no more;

---

19. Like the sailors who lamented for Tyre, **they threw dust on their heads** and cried out, **Alas, alas, for the great city,** which had made them wealthy, for in a brief period of time she had **been laid waste.** The similarities of these dirges of the kings, merchants, and seafarers are obvious.

20. This paean of joy, an amplification of 12:12a (cf. Isa. 44:23; Jer. 51:48), is in contrast to the laments of the mourners. Indeed, it represents the rejoicing of heaven and of the martyrs resident there over God's **judgment,** which now has been visited upon Rome in retribution for her manifold sins. Some believe that it is misplaced and belongs after vs. 24; but its present position is not inappropriate, since it provides a dramatic and striking contrast to the dirges of the mourners, forming a delayed conclusion, as it were, to the exultation of the heavenly voice in vss. 4-8.

E. Fifth Vision: Millstone Thrown into the Sea and Final Dirge over the City (18:21-24)

21a. In Revelation angels play a great part, not only in the preliminaries of the apocalyptic drama, but also in its concluding events. For the most part Christ, like God, does not intervene directly. Accordingly, in this symbolic scene of the actual destruction of Rome, it was another **mighty angel** who **took up a stone like a great millstone** which he threw **into the sea,** pronouncing doom upon the city as he did so, a theme which John never tires of repeating. The scene is obviously patterned after the symbolic act related in the oracle against Babylon, taken from an interpolation into the prophecies of Jeremiah (Jer. 50–51), which John has previously used. Jeremiah is represented as uttering an oracle against Babylon, accusing her of wickedness and of tyrannical oppression of the Jews, and prophesying her destruction by powerful enemies as a judgment of God. He then instructs a certain Seraiah, who was traveling to Babylon, to take a scroll of this prophecy with him and to read it on his arrival in the city, at the same time recalling God's promise to punish Babylon. Having done this, he is to throw this scroll, weighted

---

19. *Moral Values and the Ships at Sea.*—The sight of noble ships sailing in and out of one of the great ports of the world has its own great beauty and its own qualities of inspiration. But what if these ships are involved in some evil business? The story of the ships which carried slaves to distant markets is one of the darkest stories in the world. Men like Wilberforce saw that the slave ship was placed squarely upon the conscience of England. It was a great

night in the House of Commons when the wretched and tragic business was brought to an end. Over the world the battle had to be fought until the ships carrying slaves vanished from the sea. But though the issues may not seem so dramatic it is always true that the carrying trade over vast ocean spaces has moral responsibilities which must be faced.

20. *The Heavenly Judgment and Earthly Minds.*—In the words of vs. 20 the shipmasters

22 And the voice of harpers, and musicians, and of pipers, and trumpeters, shall be heard no more at all in thee; and no craftsman, of whatsoever craft *he be,* shall be found any more in thee; and the sound of a millstone shall be heard no more at all in thee;	22 and the sound of harpers and minstrels, of flute players and trumpeters, shall be heard in thee no more; and a craftsman of any craft shall be found in thee no more; and the sound of the millstone shall be heard in thee no more;

with a stone, into the river Euphrates. As it sinks into the water he is to prophesy that Babylon herself will sink in a similar way as a result of God's judgment and will never rise up (Jer. 51:59-64).

In John's adaptation and rewriting of this prophetic symbolism Seraiah becomes a mighty angel; the scroll weighted with a stone is a large stone like a millstone; the Euphrates becomes the sea; Babylon becomes Rome; and Seraiah's prophetic prediction of the fall of Babylon becomes an angelic pronouncement of the apocalyptic doom of Rome. This scene is another enlightening illustration of John's literary skill in adapting and reinterpreting a prophetic, noneschatological source to create an apocalyptic scene. Also, this demonstration of his use of a written source provides additional support for the conviction that Revelation is a carefully composed literary work, and not the mere record of visionary experiences.

21b. The threnody of the angelic counterpart of Seraiah which is contained in vss. 21b-24 is one of the finest examples of poetic writing in Revelation. Like other passages in the book, particularly the liturgical, it is replete with recollections of O.T. phraseology. The opening words, quite naturally, are an echo of those ascribed to Seraiah the traveler, "Thus shall Babylon sink, and shall not rise from the evil that I will bring upon her" (Jer. 51:64). Thus, the angel predicts, **So shall Babylon the great city be thrown down with violence, and shall be found no more,** maintaining the parallelism (cf. also Ezek. 26:21).

22a,b. In Ezekiel's oracle against Tyre, God warns, "I will cause the noise of thy songs to cease; and the sound of thy harps shall be no more heard" (Ezek. 26:13; cf. Isa. 24:8). Amplifying this, John through the angel predicts that the sound of musicians of various kinds will no longer **be heard** in the city, and that no **craftsman** will ever **be found** there again.

22c-23b. As may be seen by comparing them, these lines are a free rendering of a verse from Jeremiah's prediction of the destruction of Judah and her neighbors by the

of a world-wide trade are seen to acknowledge the justice of the judgment of God. For a flashing moment they cease to think of their own loss and see the destruction of the vile city with the eyes of heaven. These men who travel about the seas have not been entirely ignorant of the moral and spiritual history of the lands whose shores they have visited. They have heard of the **saints and apostles and prophets** and they know now they must **rejoice** when evil is overthrown. They see the Roman view of life and the saints' view of life set over against each other and they see that the saints have conquered through the acts of God. There was a conscience which was not inactive among these men of the sea. They had seen the far-off stars from the decks of ships and they had heard good words which in the midst of their wild life at sea they could not quite forget. They remembered them when Rome fell. The

great societies for the aid of seamen remind us that the men who sail the seas have moral and spiritual needs which ought not to be forgotten. Some of them may seem to many persons merely a wild lot. But there come to them thoughts of destiny and God.

22. The End of Music.—The earthly dirges had lamented the loss of voluptuous experience and bountiful markets and all the splendor of magnificent array and the give-and-take of world-wide trade. The heavenly dirge begins with the end of music. The varied instruments of harmonious sound fall upon silence. Rome had possessed some harmony of sound. It had no harmony of life, and so even the harmony of sound faded away. Lovely sounds cannot go on when people have no music in them. The very sources of music have completely decayed. Orpheus, in the myth, brought music to the dark and unlovely underworld. But you cannot

23 And the light of a candle shall shine no more at all in thee; and the voice of the bridegroom and of the bride shall be heard no more at all in thee: for thy merchants were the great men of the earth; for by thy sorceries were all nations deceived.

24 And in her was found the blood of prophets, and of saints, and of all that were slain upon the earth.

23 and the light of a lamp
    shall shine in thee no more;
and the voice of bridegroom and bride
    shall be heard in thee no more;
for thy merchants were the great men
    of the earth,
and all nations were deceived by thy
    sorcery.
24 And in her was found the blood of
    prophets and of saints,
and of all who have been slain on
    earth."

Babylonians as God's agents of punishment, "Moreover I will take from them the voice of mirth, and the voice of gladness, the voice of the bridegroom, and the voice of the bride, the sound of the millstones, and the light of the candle" (Jer. 25:10). John turns this oracle against Rome, rearranging the sequence, so that he predicts that the **sound of the millstone** will no longer be heard in the city, that a **lamp** (RSV), or **candle** (KJV), will no longer **shine** there, and that **the voice of bridegroom and bride** will never be heard there again.

23c-24. The causes of Rome's destruction and desolation are given once more. One reason is the wealth and power of her merchants (cf. vs. 3). A second is given as the deception of all peoples by her **sorcery.** The word **sorcery** is neither defined nor explained, but since in other passages it is used in conjunction with gross sins like idolatry, fornication, and murder (9:21; 21:8; 22:15), no doubt it is used here with the same associations in mind. However, the main cause of Rome's impending doom is her responsibility for shedding **the blood of prophets and of saints,** i.e., for the death of the Christian martyrs. Her bloodguiltiness, the outgrowth of her idolatry and sorcery, makes her doom inevitable. This was to happen so soon that John writes as if it had already occurred. The doctrine of divine retribution for one's enemies, which is found in certain areas of the O.T., including parts of the prophets and the psalms, has been developed by John into an eschatological, apocalyptic triumph of the righteous over their enemies and persecutors.

bring music to a life in which the sources of music have dried up.

22. When the Wheels of Industry Are Silent. —The **millstone** is the symbol of all productive toil. When great evil is destroyed something which might have been good is destroyed with it. Bad character at length corrupts even good toil. The wheels of industry shall slow down and stop when the wells of soundness and good character have dried up. There is something ominous in the complete silence to be found in a factory town in the days of a great strike. There is a ghostlike quality in the town where all the wheels of industry are still. The strike may be settled and the wheels begin to move again, but there is a stillness which is final and complete. The quietness of complete moral futility has no promise for future motion of the wheels.

23. The End of Illumination.—A **lamp** makes a little bit of day in the midst of the night. But deeds of darkness can put out all the lights. There are men who go about the world lighting lights everywhere; there are men who go about the world putting out lights everywhere. Rome had been full of extinguishers of light. So there will be no more little lights shining like "good deeds in a naughty world." [5] Complete darkness is complete impotence; and that is precisely what Rome leaves behind. But what about big modern towns? What happens when the extinguishers of lights go about their streets? When you are dealing with moral principles you are not having to do with something which comes to an end with the completion of an age or the fall of a city.

23. The End of Joyous Weddings.—Wedding feasts appealed greatly to the imagination of Jesus. How many vivid tales told in many a century have ended in a wedding! And they have so ended precisely because they promised happy beginnings. But there can come tragedy so complete that it brings to an utter end the stately and beautiful rhythm of family life. The

[5] Shakespeare, *The Merchant of Venice,* Act V, scene 1.

19 And after these things I heard a great voice of much people in heaven, saying, Alleluia; Salvation, and glory, and honor, and power, unto the Lord our God:

2 For true and righteous *are* his judgments; for he hath judged the great whore, which did corrupt the earth with her fornication, and hath avenged the blood of his servants at her hand.

3 And again they said, Alleluia. And her smoke rose up for ever and ever.

19 After this I heard what seemed to be the mighty voice of a great multitude in heaven, crying,

"Hallelujah! Salvation and glory and power belong to our God,
2 for his judgments are true and just;
he has judged the great harlot who corrupted the earth with her fornication, .
and he has avenged on her the blood of his servants."
3 Once more they cried,
"Hallelujah! The smoke from her goes up for ever and ever."

F. Sixth Vision: Hymns of Praise to God (19:1-5)

19:1-2. In contrast to the laments over Rome a heavenly host now sings the first of several songs of praise to God for his righteous judgment (vss. 1*b*-2). The scene is in heaven, with God seated on his throne surrounded by the four living creatures and the twenty-four elders, as in ch. 4. The singers of the song, a **great multitude in heaven,** may possibly be the angelic host of "many angels, numbering myriads of myriads and thousands of thousands" who are around the throne in 5:11. The first word, **Hallelujah** (**Alleluia**—KJV), is the Hebrew for "Praise ye the Lord," and in the N.T. is found only here and in vss. 3, 4, and 6, with a Greek translation in vs. 5. This briefest of doxologies is used in certain of the psalms: at the beginning in two (Pss. 111; 112) as in Revelation; in others at the close (Pss. 104; 105; 115; 116); and in still others at both beginning and end (Pss. 106; 113; 117; 135; 146–150). Most of these psalms deal with God's might and power; some of them praise him for the deliverance of his people from their enemies and oppressors. These same emphases characterize this praise-song of the multitude. Save for the **Hallelujah** it is composed of phrases and ideas from earlier parts of Revelation. The first line echoes words uttered by the voice from heaven in 12:10, "Now the salvation and the power and the kingdom of our God and the authority of his Christ have come." The second repeats the cry from the altar in 16:7, "True and just are thy judgments." The next is a reiteration of the angelic words in 17:1, "Come, I will show you the judgment of the great harlot who is seated upon many waters." While the last line is almost identical with a promise from the song of Moses, "For he will avenge the blood of his servants" (Deut. 32:43*b*), it is actually an answer to the prayer of the martyrs in 6:10 for vengeance for the shedding of their blood and is a fulfillment of the prediction in 18:24 that the harlot will be requited for her bloodguiltiness.

3. The heavenly host sing another brief **Hallelujah** song, whose one-line refrain is probably a quotation from the description of the burning of Tyre in Isa. 34:10*b*, "The smoke thereof shall go up for ever." This prediction that the **smoke** of burning Rome will rise **for ever and ever** should not be taken too literally, for according to John's ardent anticipation, not even the earth on which Rome is situated is to last very much longer, but is soon to disappear (cf. 20:11; 21:1).

story of Tobit in the Apocrypha is full of odd bits of mythology but it is saturated with a sense of the ongoing of family life. The wedding is a sacred experience and the coming of children a consummation in the gifts of God. The wedding feasts of Tobias the son of Tobit have profound symbolic significance. There is no more searching suggestion of the end of human hopes than the word that **the voice of bridegroom and bride shall be heard . . . no more.** Happy experiences which have no moral foundation already have the sentence of death upon them. The death of goodness is the death of all human hopes.

19:1. *The Hallelujah Chorus.*—Handel's great oratorio *The Messiah* was produced in

4 And the four and twenty elders and the four beasts fell down and worshipped God that sat on the throne, saying, Amen; Alleluia.

5 And a voice came out of the throne, saying, Praise our God, all ye his servants, and ye that fear him, both small and great.

6 And I heard as it were the voice of a great multitude, and as the voice of many waters, and as the voice of mighty thunderings, saying, Alleluia: for the Lord God omnipotent reigneth.

4 And the twenty-four elders and the four living creatures fell down and worshiped God who is seated on the throne, saying, "Amen, Hallelujah!" 5 And from the throne came a voice crying,

"Praise our God, all you his servants,
    you who fear him, small and great."

6 Then I heard what seemed to be the voice of a great multitude, like the sound of many waters and like the sound of mighty thunderpeals, crying,

"Hallelujah! For the Lord our God the
    Almighty reigns.

4. Neither **the twenty-four elders** nor **the four living creatures** have been seen since their mention in 14:3, although one of the latter did appear briefly to give the seven bowls to the seven angels in 15:7. Moreover, this is the last time they are to be seen in Revelation, for, strangely enough, despite their prominence in earlier sections of the apocalypse, they play no part in the concluding scenes. Here, in their last appearance, both the **elders** and the **living creatures fell down** before the throne (cf. 4:10 and 5:8) and **worshiped God,** uttering a brief but solemn ratification of his awful judgment, **Amen. Hallelujah!** (Cf. 5:14, where the four living creatures give their assent with a simple "Amen!")

5. **A voice** from the throne is heard urging, **Praise our God, all you his servants, you who fear him, small and great.** The first phrase of this heavenly exhortation is a translation of the Hebrew "Hallelujah"; much of the rest may have been suggested by a verse in one of the hallelujah psalms, "He will bless them that fear the LORD, both small and great" (Ps. 115:13). There is probably some connection between this song and that sung by the twenty-four elders following the sounding of the seventh trumpet in 11:17-18, which quotes this same verse from Ps. 115. Since this voice came **from the throne,** it may be that of God, despite the opening phrase, **Praise our God,** or it may be the voice of the Lamb.

G. SEVENTH VISION: MARRIAGE HYMN TO THE LAMB AND HIS BRIDE (19:6-10)

6a. John next heard **the voice of a great multitude** which is not specifically identified. Their singing was **like the sound of many waters and like the sound of mighty thunderpeals,** a description which is almost the same as that of the singing by the 144,000 martyrs in 14:2.

6b. The song that follows (vss. 6b-8), presumably by the martyrs, is the fourth in this series to begin with "hallelujah" or its equivalent. In words similar to those sung by the twenty-four elders in 11:17, they assert that **the Lord our God the Almighty reigns.** This may be an allusion to the title which Domitian conferred upon himself, "Our Lord and God" (Suetonius *Domitian* 13); if so, the hymn suggests that it is the **Almighty,** not this blasphemous Roman emperor, who is now in sovereign control of the affairs of this world.

Dublin in 1742. It attained a place all its own among oratorios and the "Hallelujah Chorus" became very famous. The custom of audiences to stand while it is rendered is a tribute to the wonder of the attempt to suggest the music of heaven. In its setting in the book of Revelation this outburst of song is the expression of the heavenly joy over the destruction of that supremely wicked city, Rome. In a sense Rome had become the symbol of the ultimate evil in the world. The chorus may be considered heaven's rejoicing at the victory over the final expression of evil among men. The curtain is down on the city of destruction. It is raised on

7 Let us be glad and rejoice, and give honor to him: for the marriage of the Lamb is come, and his wife hath made herself ready.

8 And to her was granted that she should be arrayed in fine linen, clean and white: for the fine linen is the righteousness of saints.

7 Let us rejoice and exult and give him the glory,
　　for the marriage of the Lamb has come,
　　and his Bride has made herself ready;
8 it was granted her to be clothed with fine linen, bright and pure" —
for the fine linen is the righteous deeds of the saints.

---

7. Rejoicing and exultation and the glorification of God are now in order **for the marriage of the Lamb has come, and his Bride has made herself ready.** This symbolic concept of a divine marriage is found in a number of places in the O.T., where Israel is the bride of the Lord (cf. Isa. 54:5-6; 62:5; Ezek. 16:6-14; Hos. 2:19-20). Furthermore, through allegorical interpretation the Song of Songs was considered by the rabbis to be a depiction of God as the bridegroom and the congregation of Israel as the bride, and on this basis was included in the canon of scripture (cf. Song of Songs Rabbah 4:10). With the development of the belief in the Messiah, the figure was changed by some so that the day of the Messiah was compared to a wedding feast, it being implied that he was the bridegroom and Israel the bride (Leviticus Rabbah 11:2; Exodus Rabbah 15:31; Jer. Shebuoth 4:25). In the Hellenistic mystery religions, far removed from any Jewish messianic hope, the initiation was frequently considered a sacred marriage uniting the believer with the savior-God. The form of such conceptions, both Jewish and Hellenistic, may have some original connection with ancient fertility cult rites.

The Christian symbolism in which Christ became the bridegroom and the believers the bride may well have been influenced by both Jewish and Hellenistic patterns of thought. The parable of the five wise and five foolish virgins was intended to teach that the kingdom of heaven would be like a wedding feast, presumably with the Messiah as the bridegroom (Matt. 25:1-13; cf. Matt. 22:1-14). Christians, of course, interpreted this parable as teaching that Jesus would be the bridegroom with the church as his bride. In Mark 2:19-20 and parallels, Jesus speaks of himself as the bridegroom, with his disciples as the wedding guests, while according to John 3:29 the Baptist refers to Jesus as the bridegroom. Paul used the figure both mystically and eschatologically when he told the Corinthian Christians that he had betrothed them to Christ and hoped to present them as a pure bride to him, their one husband, presumably at his second coming (II Cor. 11:2); this symbolism was elaborated in what is probably the post-Pauline Epistle to the Ephesians (Eph. 5:22-27).

Using the marital figure in an eschatological sense, as Paul did in II Cor. 11:2, John now speaks of the joyous time, at the Second Advent, when the marriage of Christ, the Lamb, with his bride is to be celebrated. The symbolism of the bride is somewhat mixed. She is, no doubt, the New Jerusalem coming down from heaven as described in 21:9-10. She is also the church, the congregation of the faithful. Furthermore, she may be in some special sense closely related to the martyrs, as we shall see. This marriage of the Lamb with his pure bride is in sharp and vivid contrast to the impure relations between the imperial beast and his wanton paramour, the harlot, as depicted in ch. 17. Further, the apparel of the bride, **fine linen, bright and pure,** is probably designedly different from the purple and scarlet garb of the harlot who is also bedecked with jewels (cf. 17:4; 18:16; but see 21:19-21). Thus the eternal city, the church of Christ, is placed over against the temporal city, Rome, mistakenly considered as *Roma aeterna.*

---

the heaven glory, and from that glory come multitudes of voices praising God.

7. The Nuptials in Heaven.—Over against the picture of the destruction of the city of per-

petual adultery is put the picture of a perfect marriage. With a sure instinct the author of the book of Revelation realizes that lust must not be allowed to have the last word, even if

9 And he saith unto me, Write, Blessed *are* they which are called unto the marriage supper of the Lamb. And he saith unto me, These are the true sayings of God.

9 And the angel said[l] to me, "Write this: Blessed are those who are invited to the marriage supper of the Lamb." And he said to me, "These are true words of God."

[l] Greek *he said.*

The bride's linen costume is described as **the righteous deeds of the saints.** Some are inclined to regard this statement as a later interpolation into the text. However, it is quite in harmony with views previously expressed by the writer. The white garments are like those the martyrs themselves are to wear (3:4, 18; 6:11; 7:9, 14). Moreover, their good works, which had accompanied the martyrs to heaven (cf. 14:13; 20:12; 22:12), could quite appropriately be symbolized by the bride's pure white garb. It may be that by this symbolism John intended to show a special relationship between the martyrs and the bride, and through her to her husband, the Lamb, so that they in particular are considered to be his bride.

9. Just as the beatitude of 14:13 is introduced by a voice from heaven commanding, "Write this," so now the same formula is used to preface the fourth beatitude. The speaker is not named, but is probably the same angel who has been acting as John's mentor since 17:1, as is indicated by the explanatory gloss **the angel** in the RSV. The words spoken are a blessing upon those who are summoned to **the marriage supper of the Lamb.**

As mentioned above (cf. vs. 7), certain of the rabbis taught that the day of the Messiah would be like a wedding banquet. According to an account in II Baruch 29:4, at the messianic banquet (not, however, a wedding feast) which is to precede the resurrection the two mythical monsters, Behemoth and Leviathan, will be eaten—a view that was popularly accepted. Also, the earth is to be marvelously productive, yielding ten thousandfold, so that no one will hunger (II Baruch 29:5-6). Likewise, we read in III Enoch 48:10 that Israel is to enjoy a banquet in Jerusalem with the Messiah. We note also two Gospel parables in which the kingdom of heaven is compared with a wedding feast (Matt. 22:1-14; 25:1-13; cf. Luke 12:35-38).

The same concept of a sacred meal was transferred from messianic to apocalyptic thinking, so that according to I Enoch 62:14, the righteous and elect are to eat with the Son of man during the age to come. Even closer, perhaps, is the picture in the neo-Hebraic Apocalypse of Elijah. Here, as in Revelation, there is to be a messianic interregnum between this age and the age to come. During this period, which in this case is to last forty years, the righteous are to rejoice and eat with the Messiah. Everything in the way of food will be had in abundance; e.g., a measure of wheat will produce nine hundred measures, and the same will be true of wine and oil, while the trees will be loaded with the finest fruits.

John, then, is referring to an eschatological feast, similar to those in I Enoch and the Apocalypse of Elijah. It is to occur only when the forces of evil are overcome and the Messiah has established his rule, and is to be a fulfillment of the promise made to prospective martyrs in 3:20*b*, "I will come in to him and eat with him, and he with me" (cf. also the "hidden manna" in 2:17). If, as seems probable, the martyrs are peculiarly the bride of Christ, their invitation to the wedding feast as guests is something of an anomaly, until we recall the fluidity of apocalyptic imagery whereby Christ can be both

---

that is a word of destruction. The last word belongs to the marriage in heaven. **The Lamb** victorious after his sacrificial death is the bridegroom. The church made stainless by the great Redemption is the **Bride.** There is a great supper. And now the thought of fulfillment and not the thought of destruction fills the mind and heart. In Wisd. Sol. 8:2, in the Apocrypha,

we are told how the author of the book longed for wisdom.

> Her I loved and sought out from my youth.
> And I sought to take her for my bride.
> And I became enamoured of her beauty.

The deepest spiritual union is the very goal of life.

10 And I fell at his feet to worship him. And he said unto me, See *thou do it* not: I am thy fellow servant, and of thy brethren that have the testimony of Jesus: worship God: for the testimony of Jesus is the spirit of prophecy.

10 Then I fell down at his feet to worship him, but he said to me, "You must not do that! I am a fellow servant with you and your brethren who hold the testimony of Jesus. Worship God." For the testimony of Jesus is the spirit of prophecy.

Lamb and shepherd in a single verse (7:17). As in 14:13, where the Spirit affirms the validity of the beatitude spoken by a voice from heaven, so now the angel pledges that these words of blessing are the **true words of God** (cf. 21:5; 22:6).

10a. This verse introduces an entirely new element into Revelation (repeated in 22:8-9), viz., the repudiation of the worship of angels. When we consider the splendor and might of these supernatural beings, according to both Jewish and Christian angelology, the temptation to worship them must sometimes have been irresistible. Since Christians in many cases came from a polytheistic background, their temptation was presumably greater than that of the Jews. That even the Jews were susceptible, however, is seen from an incident in the Coptic Apocalypse of Zephaniah 9–10, in which is portrayed a mighty angel whose face shone like the sun. Being mistaken for God, he is worshiped, until he informs the seer that this must not be, that he is an angel, not God.

As for the Christians, we discover that Paul found it necessary to warn the Gentile Christian community at Colossae against a religious syncretism which included angel worship (Col. 2:18). His argument in part was that the Creator (i.e., the pre-existent Christ) and not the creature, the angels, should be worshiped. Further, in another place, he states that the Christians are to judge the angels (I Cor. 6:3).

The view is dramatized in the Ascension of Isaiah 7:21. Isaiah, while in the second heaven, fell down to worship his angelic guide and interpreter, whereupon the latter told him to worship neither any throne nor any angel in the first six heavens. Later on, in the sixth heaven he addresses this guide as "My Lord"; accordingly, the angel reprovingly tells him that he is not his lord but his fellow servant (Ascension of Isaiah 8:4-5). The seer is further informed that when he reaches the seventh heaven he will be given his heavenly garments, becoming the equal of the angels there (Ascension of Isaiah 8:14-15; cf. 9:9).

In a scene similar to those in the Apocalypse of Zephaniah and the Ascension of Isaiah, John prostrated himself at the feet of his angelic mentor **to worship him.** As he did so, the angel reproved him and said that he was his **fellow servant** along with his **brethren,** those who have held to **the testimony of Jesus,** i.e., the faithful confessors and martyrs. Accordingly, as in the Ascension of Isaiah, the martyrs are to become like angels. Consequently, they are to **worship God,** not angels, with whom they are to be equal. Essentially this same incident is repeated in 22:8-9.

10b. The sentence, **For the testimony of Jesus is the spirit of prophecy,** is a back reference to 1:9-11, where John explained that while he was in Patmos for his preaching and for his "testimony of Jesus" he "was in the Spirit" and received his commission to write his prophecy. Here again he presents his authority not only for the particular beatitude in vs. 9, but for his entire book of "prophecy."

---

10. When the Good Becomes the Foe of the Best.—There is an idolatry which consists in the worship of the evil. There is an idolatry which consists in the worship of the good put in the place of the worship of the best. When the man of Patmos would have worshiped the glorious angel he was in danger of the second sort of idolatry. It was and always is a very subtle sort of temptation. When a thing is good we are likely to surrender to it without scruple. But what if the best summons us to a higher allegiance? All our relation to the good must be through our relation to the best; it must not be made a substitute for the best. Jerome felt that his fascinated interest in classical studies was becoming a danger to his supreme loyalty. No doubt one can think of these things with a nervous self-consciousness which is not fully Christian. We have a right to remember Paul's word "All things are yours" (I Cor. 3:21). **But**

11 And I saw heaven opened, and be- hold a white horse; and he that sat upon	11 Then I saw heaven opened, and be-

X. Seven Visions of the End of Satan's Evil Age and the Beginning of God's Righteous Age (19:11–21:4)

The six series of seven visions each have ended. They have presented, with a good deal of repetition, a depiction of the evils and wickedness of this idolatrous age under the control of Satan, culminating in the persecution and death of the faithful Christians who refused to worship his depraved creatures, the Roman state and its rulers. These six series have also portrayed the unprecedented woes and plagues, calamities and catastrophes, which God will visit upon the earth and its inhabitants as a sign of his divine wrath. Furthermore, the eschatological conflicts between the supernatural forces of evil have also been described. In addition, vivid prophecies of the imminent ruin and destruction of Rome and the empire have been proclaimed. Nevertheless, despite these predictions of terrible punishments, which will be climaxed by eternal torture in the lake of fire and brimstone, the wicked and the idolatrous have remained stubborn and unrepentant. On the other hand, promises of glorious eternal rewards from God have encouraged the Christians to remain loyal to him, and to continue in their determination not to worship the state and the emperors even though death will be the penalty. The time, then, has come for God to enter into the stage of human history to fulfill his promises of punishment and reward. Accordingly, in this seventh series of seven visions the climax of the apocalyptic drama is reached, and Satan, with his demonic forces and idolatrous human followers, will be completely overthrown and his power will be destroyed forever. With his downfall this world will cease and this satanic age will be terminated. Then there will be a new earth—heaven itself will come down to earth—and God will create a new and eternal age for the righteous, which will be under his direct control forever.

There are a number of difficulties involved in the interpretation of this culminating series of visions. These may in part be dispelled if it is realized that the first six series are to a considerable degree anticipatory as well as repetitious, e.g., the conflicts portrayed in these preliminary series are to be considered as dramatic previews or vivid prophecies of the climactic apocalyptic struggles between right and wrong which are to culminate in the complete defeat and final overthrow of Satan.

Additional assistance may be gained through a brief summary of the eschatological pattern presented in this new series of visions. First, the conquering Christ will come from heaven with his heavenly army and will defeat the Antichrist, who with the false prophet will be cast into the lake of fire, thus ending his rule forever; and Christ will also annihilate the Antichrist forces composed of the peoples of the earth. Following this defeat of his demonic agents, Satan himself will be bound by an angel and locked in the bottomless pit for a thousand years, his rule being thus suspended. With Satan and the beasts safely out of the way, the martyrs will be restored to life, and they, and they alone, will reign with Christ for a thousand years. At the end of this blessed millennium Satan will be unbound and will instigate two new evil personifications, Gog and Magog, to gather the four nations from the corners of the earth against the saints in the holy city—this despite the previous annihilation of all peoples in the battle preceding the millennium. However, fire from heaven will destroy them, and Satan himself will be cast into the fiery lake to be company for the two beasts; thus will his age, his rule, end forever. Also, the earth over which he reigned will disappear, along with heaven. Then the second

there is no doubt as to where the supreme loyalty belongs. And our Lord himself spoke stern words about confusion at that point.

11. The Lord of Battles.—An entirely new picture flashes before our eyes. The figure on

the **white horse** is our Lord himself. From heaven he comes to fight the battles of earth. Because he is **Faithful** he cannot let his people fight alone. Because he is **True** he must bring truth to victory. The white armies of heaven

him *was* called Faithful and True, and in righteousness he doth judge and make war.

hold, a white horse! He who sat upon it is called Faithful and True, and in righteous-

---

and general resurrection will occur, and the general judgment of all the dead, save the martyrs, will take place before God on his throne. Death and Hades will be consigned to the fiery lake, the second death, as well as those men whose deeds were evil. Next, a new heaven and a new earth will be created, the New Jerusalem will come down to earth, and God's perfect and eternal age will begin. God himself will descend to earth, and with Christ will dwell among the saints in the New Jerusalem for an eternity of joy and bliss.

It has been maintained quite generally that this particular sequence of events originated with John. It should be noted, however, in that connection that the main outline is to be found also in the neo-Hebraic Apocalypse of Elijah. According to this work, the Messiah (named Winon) will appear from heaven with his angels to wage war with the Antichrist, and will destroy him and his armies and slay the rest of the heathen. Then Israel will enjoy the bliss of a messianic period of forty years, which will end when Gog and Magog will assemble the heathen against the Jews in Jerusalem. With God's help the Messiah will annihilate these enemies of his people and will destroy all the cities of the heathen. There will be a period of doom lasting forty days, after which the general resurrection and judgment will take place. The wicked will be consigned to a fiery hell, but the righteous will live eternally in a veritable paradise. The New Jerusalem will come down from heaven, and peace and knowledge of the law will prevail. There is no first resurrection in this work, nor is there any Satan who must be eliminated; but otherwise the eschatological pattern is essentially that of Revelation from 19:11 on. This apocalypse was written about A.D. 261, and so is considerably later than Revelation. However, there is no evidence of any dependence upon the earlier work. More probably, both have drawn upon a common apocalyptic tradition in which this pattern had been developed.

A. First Vision: The Conquering Christ (19:11-16)

Before the marriage of the Lamb can take place, he must vanquish the enemies of himself and of his people. The conflict that now is to take place, with the Christ at the head of his forces and the Antichrist leading the nations of the earth, has been adumbrated in many earlier passages. It is, in part, the fulfillment of the harvest and the vintage of 14:14-20; it is, in addition, the battle of Armageddon (16:12-16); it is also the conflict between the beast assisted by the ten kings from the East and the Lamb aided by the martyrs, as described in 17:12-14; it is likewise the realization of the prediction that the martyrs (2:27) and the pre-existent Christ child (12:5) will rule the nations with an iron rod. In fact, this is the conflict which will end the reign of the satanic, Neronic Antichrist, symbolic of all the power and might of the Roman Empire which has persecuted and slain the saints.

11. As on previous occasions (cf. 4:1; 11:19; 15:5), John saw **heaven opened,** just as the heavens once opened for Ezekiel (Ezek. 1:1), and the heavenly Christ appeared riding **a white horse.** We are reminded of the white horse and its rider in 6:2; but the only resemblance is that in both cases the riders are conquerors. Christ is given the title of **Faithful and True,** a designation which had previously been accorded him in 3:14 (cf. 1:5; 3:7). Like the Messiah of Isa. 11:3-4, who will judge with righteousness, the conquering Christ **judges and makes war.** We are also reminded again that God's judgments are just and true (vs. 2; 15:3; 16:5).

---

share in the battle of the Lord. When Abraham Lincoln died Walt Whitman wrote "O Captain! My Captain!" in tribute to the greathearted leader. There is a greater Captain who comes

in stainless splendor to share the struggles of men. The vision of that invisible army and its glorious leader gives the taste of victory in the midst of the battle.

12 His eyes *were* as a flame of fire, and on his head *were* many crowns; and he had a name written, that no man knew, but he himself.

13 And he *was* clothed with a vesture dipped in blood: and his name is called The Word of God.

ness he judges and makes war. 12 His eyes are like a flame of fire, and on his head are many diadems; and he has a name inscribed which no one knows but himself. 13 He is clad in a robe dipped in[m] blood, and the name by which he is called is The

[m] Other ancient authorities read *sprinkled with.*

---

12. In harmony with the descriptions in 1:14 and 2:18, Christ's **eyes are like a flame of fire.** The dragon had diadems on its seven heads (12:3); and the beast had diadems on its ten horns (13:1); also, the one like a Son of man who reaped the harvest of the earth had a gold crown on his head. Now the conquering Christ wears **diadems** as insignia of his royal power. This crowning may have been a sequel to the enthronement of the pre-existent Christ child who was to rule the nations with a rod of iron (12:5). The **name inscribed which no one knows but himself,** the fourth mention of Christ's secret name (cf. 2:17; 3:12; 14:1), is difficult to identify. It could be one of the three in this chapter (vss. 11, 13, and 16), but such inclusion here seems a bit too obvious; besides, how could one choose one from the three? Apparently the name is one of some potency. It is well known that among the early Christians the name "Jesus" was by far the most powerful for, as Paul asserted, "at the name of Jesus every knee should bow, in heaven and on earth and under the earth" (Phil. 2:10). There is plenty of evidence that the name "Jesus" was frequently invoked to heal diseases, to overpower demons, and to thwart Satan himself. The name, of course, was no secret; but this did not deter a contemporary of John from stating that "Jesus" was the name of the pre-existent heavenly Christ which "none of the heavens" could learn, but which would be revealed when he descended from heaven (Ascension of Isaiah 9:5; 8:7). Conceivably it was by a similar process of reasoning that John thought of the powerful name "Jesus" as the secret name of the heavenly Christ even though it actually was no secret. Also, as one with an interest in cryptography, he might have been aware that the name "Jesus" added up to 888, and as such would be a perfect foil to the secret name of the bestial Antichrist which added up to 666. Indeed, in 14:1 the secret name of Christ seems to be placed in direct contrast to that of the beast in the preceding verse (13:18). Moreover, the name "Jesus" either by itself or more frequently in combination with "Christ" or "Lord" occurs but fourteen times in Revelation. It is found in the opening and in the concluding verses of the book. In ten other instances it is used with μάρτυς (martyr or witness) or a word from the same root. In the two remaining cases it is associated in some way with "patient endurance," which has martyrological meaning. Thus it would seem that John regularly uses the name "Jesus" in connection with his martyr motif. It may also be significant that all four references to the secret name have a similar connection. In 2:17 it is to be inscribed on the stone to be given each martyr; in 3:12 and 14:1 it is to be written on the martyrs; in 19:12 it is to be written on the conquering Christ as he leads his armies composed of martyrs to victory. The problem is perplexing, but the evidence seems to support the conclusion that the secret name is "Jesus."

13a. As noted in the discussion of 14:20, the scene of the treading of the wine press is a rewriting of Isa. 63:1-6, where it is an avenging warrior, God, not Christ, who will

---

12. *The Secrets Which Belong to God.*—The book of Revelation has its noble references to that which has not been revealed. There is something about the living Christ which belongs to the ultimate mystery of the life of God. What to us is his nameless majesty to him is a perfect name. All that we do not know of the perfection and splendor of the divine life belongs to that name which is his own eternal secret. All the good which our minds cannot think, all the beauty which our minds cannot understand, all the harmony of God's beatific perfection, belong to that hidden name. In vision we can see his many crowns. But in his heart is the invisible crown of the eternal God.

13. *The Speech of God in Christ.*—But we are not allowed, even in the midst of the thought of the eternal secrets of God, to forget

14 And the armies *which were* in heaven followed him upon white horses, clothed in fine linen, white and clean.

15 And out of his mouth goeth a sharp sword, that with it he should smite the

Word of God. 14 And the armies of heaven, arrayed in fine linen, white and pure, followed him on white horses. 15 From his

---

trample in his wine press the nations who oppressed his people so that their blood is spilled out upon the earth. While doing this, their lifeblood also is sprinkled upon his garments and stains them. Showing still further dependence upon this O.T. passage, John makes another transfer of symbolism to the conquering Christ, whose outer garment is **dipped in blood.** This is not his own blood, that of the Lamb that was slain, which has redeeming power (cf. 1:5; 5:9; 7:14; 12:11), but is the blood of his foes. A very similar picture of the Messiah victorious over his enemies and sprinkled with their blood is presented in Targ. Jer. I on Gen. 49:11, "The mountains became red with the blood of their slain; his garments, dipped in blood, are like the outpressed juice of grapes."

13b. The conquering Christ is now called **The Word of God.** Although the diction is similar to that of the prologue to the Fourth Gospel, the meaning is quite different. It bears some similarity to the metaphor in Heb. 4:12, in which the word of God is sharper than any two-edged sword, although here it is not used allegorically. Much closer is the picture of the militant Messiah in Wisd. Sol. 18:15-16, who is described as God's word leaping from the royal throne in heaven as a stern warrior and bearing God's commandment like a sharp sword with which he fills everything with death.

14. The heavenly **armies** of Christ **followed him on white horses.** Enoch saw armed soldiers serving God in the fourth heaven (II Enoch 17:1). With more pertinence to the scene before us, Levi, while in the third heaven, saw the armies which on the Day of Judgment would execute God's judgment on the deceitful spirits and on Beliar, the Antichrist (Test. Levi 3:3). Also, according to the Ascension of Isaiah 4:14, in the final conflict with Beliar and his forces Christ will come "with his angels and with the armies of the holy ones." Here the "holy ones" are probably angels, not ascended saints and martyrs. Moreover, in the heavenly war Michael had the help of his angels in casting Satan out of heaven (Rev. 12:7). We are also told in Matt. 26:53 that Jesus had "more than twelve legions of angels" at his disposal, should he care to use them.

However, these armies of the avenging Word of God, dressed in **fine linen** which is **white and pure,** are probably not angels, but the martyrs in their heavenly garments (6:11; cf. 3:5); the promise that they were to have power over the nations and rule them with an iron rod (2:26-27) is now being fulfilled. It is they who "follow the Lamb wherever he goes" (14:4) and it is they who were with Christ in the proleptic battle, mentioned in 17:14, in which the beast and the ten kings were defeated. Now their hour of personal triumph over the beast and their persecutors has come; they will have a part in exacting the vengeance for their blood for which they prayed while under the altar in heaven just before receiving their white robes (6:10). This is to be one of the rewards for their faithfulness.

15. This verse is compiled from earlier statements about the heavenly Christ. The **sharp sword** projecting from his mouth is the "sharp two-edged sword" described in 1:16;

---

that our Lord represents not God retreating into the mystery of his own life but God marching manward. He represents God's speech to men. He is called **The Word of God.** In Christ God has become articulate in words which we can understand. It is not by chance that this thought is connected with the **robe dipped in blood.** It is in his death that Christ speaks the word of suffering, which everyone who is

morally lonely and spiritually hungry can understand. Charles Wesley wrote:

O Love divine, what hast Thou done!
Th' incarnate God hath died for me!
The Father's coeternal Son
Bore all my sins upon the tree!
The Son of God for me hath died:
My Lord, my Love, is crucified.

nations; and he shall rule them with a rod of iron: and he treadeth the winepress of the fierceness and wrath of Almighty God.

16 And he hath on *his* vesture and on his thigh a name written, KING OF KINGS, AND LORD OF LORDS.

17 And I saw an angel standing in the sun; and he cried with a loud voice, saying to all the fowls that fly in the midst of heaven, Come and gather yourselves together unto the supper of the great God;

18 That ye may eat the flesh of kings, and the flesh of captains, and the flesh of mighty men, and the flesh of horses, and of them that sit on them, and the flesh of all *men, both* free and bond, both small and great.

mouth issues a sharp sword with which to smite the nations, and he will rule them with a rod of iron; he will tread the wine press of the fury of the wrath of God the Almighty. 16 On his robe and on his thigh he has a name inscribed, King of kings and Lord of lords.

17 Then I saw an angel standing in the sun, and with a loud voice he called to all the birds that fly in midheaven, "Come, gather for the great supper of God, 18 to eat the flesh of kings, the flesh of captains, the flesh of mighty men, the flesh of horses and their riders, and the flesh of all men, both free and slave, both small and great."

his use of the **rod of iron** to **rule** over his enemies (inspired by Ps. 2:9) was predicted in 12:5 (cf. 2:27); the figure of the **wine press** of the **wrath of God** was presented in 14:19-20. There is no need to discuss these further, save to point out that the concluding chapters are to some extent a fulfillment of the earlier ones. Thus we see again that, unlike a number of apocalypses, Revelation is a literary unit, despite the variety of sources used.

16. The name inscribed on his robe and thigh, **King of kings and Lord of lords,** is the same, save for the order of the phrases, as that of 17:14, in the anticipatory battle of Christ and his martyrs against the beast and the ten kings.

B. SECOND VISION: VICTORY OF CHRIST OVER THE BEAST, THE ANTICHRIST (19:17-21)

17-18. The description of the conflict is in part dependent upon the narration of the destruction of Gog and Magog in Ezek. 39:1-20 (see also on 20:8-9). God commands the prophet to summon every bird and beast to feast upon the bodies of Gog and his hordes who are to be slain (Ezek. 39:4, 17-20). With this gruesome picture before him, John depicts **an angel standing in the sun** and summoning all of the birds to come to **the great supper of God** to gorge themselves on the flesh of the peoples of the nations who comprised the armies of the Antichrist (cf. vs. 21). This angel in the sun recalls the eagle flying in midheaven who pronounced a threefold woe upon the people of the earth (8:13) and the angel in midheaven in 14:6 who, with two others who followed him, pronounced the judgment of God upon Babylon and those who worshiped the beast. Thus once again earlier scenes are retold in this climactic section.

On the Cross our Lord became completely the speech of God.

16. Supreme over Men.—If one were writing a book about the N.T. Apocalypse it might well bear the title **King of kings and Lord of lords.** For everything in the book begins and continues and ends in Christ. The man of Patmos had doubtless heard of Alexander the Great. He knew all too much for his own comfort about Roman emperors. We have a larger perspective. We know of many kings and many kingdoms; the names of Tamerlane and Napoleon fall easily from our lips; the name of Hitler once

held the evil place in our thought which an emperor who wanted to be a god held in the mind of the author of the book of Revelation. It is still true that all the evil lordships stand on one side and the **King of kings and Lord of lords** stands on the other. Again and again men have tried to forget him. Stout skeptics have talked glibly of the end of his power. But like the Captain on the white horse he rides forth whenever the battle between the evil and the good is fiercely waged. We judge him only to discover that he has a mightier word than we can utter. And at last it dawns upon us that we

19 And I saw the beast, and the kings of the earth, and their armies, gathered together to make war against him that sat on the horse, and against his army.

20 And the beast was taken, and with him the false prophet that wrought miracles before him, with which he deceived them that had received the mark of the beast, and them that worshipped his image. These both were cast alive into a lake of fire burning with brimstone.

19 And I saw the beast and the kings of the earth with their armies gathered to make war against him who sits upon the horse and against his army. 20 And the beast was captured, and with it the false prophet who in its presence had worked the signs by which he deceived those who had received the mark of the beast and those who worshiped its image. These two were thrown alive into the lake of fire that burns

19-21. As in 17:14, the beast with his armies made war on Christ and his army of martyrs. However, both he and the **false prophet** (the pseudo Christ, whose latest appearance was in 16:13, just prior to the battle of Armageddon) were **captured** and **thrown alive into the lake of fire that burns with brimstone.** As for the armies of the beast, all **were slain by the sword** which projected from the mouth of Christ, and the **birds** that had been summoned by the angel **were gorged with their flesh.**

Thus the reign of the Antichrist, of the satanic Roman emperors and empire, will come to an end. The Antichrist and his colleague, symbolizing the priesthood of the imperial cult, will be tortured in **the lake of fire** forever. This fiery lake is not to be confused either with Hades (Sheol) or with the bottomless pit. Instead, it is a place of eternal damnation and punishment for the wicked, the opponents of God and of the righteous, similar to the Jewish Gehenna or the Greek Hell. In one form or another this fiery place of everlasting punishment is depicted in many Jewish and Christian writings (cf. I Enoch 21:7-10; 54:1-2; 90:26-27; II Esdras 7:36; II Baruch 85:13; Sibylline Oracles 2:196-200, 252-53, 286; Mark 9:43; Matt. 5:22; II Enoch 10:2; Apocalypse of Peter 8; Mekhilta on Exod. 14:21; Hagigah 13b). Those nations of the earth who worshiped the beast and bore his name will be restored to life in the second or general resurrection (20:13) and following the judgment, in accord with the warning of 14:9-10, they too will be consigned to the fiery lake for an eternity of torment (20:15; 21:8).

That John has been using current traditions concerning the final victory over the Antichrist and his followers may be seen by reference to other sources. According to Dan. 7:11, the fourth beast, representing the Greco-Syrian kingdom, with the little horn

are under his authority even when we deny his reign.

19. Final Antagonisms.—There is a philosophy which sees the final consummation in a unity in which the distinction between being and nonbeing, between truth and error, and between good and evil is forever lost. The whole position of the N.T. is the opposite of all this. The great distinctions are eternal. There is no marriage between heaven and hell. The evil forces must be fought—they must be conquered. The man who understands and accepts the Christian religion can have no commerce with pantheistic monism. So we watch the Captain on the white horse and his mighty army in white. And we watch the forces of wickedness— kings commanded by a beast—gathered for battle. We watch the vampires too. Clearly the man of Patmos does not regard evil as good somehow misunderstood. He understands its malignant quality and its grim destiny.

20. The Defeat of the Subhuman.—The forces of beastliness are arrayed against God and right properly they are led by a beast. All the dark and lawless motives below the level of the human and remorselessly hostile to the divine are unleashed for conflict. But the beast and the false prophet were captured and all the men with the beastly mark were slain. And the birds of prey have their way with bodies which have ceased to have even a subhuman vitality. One word from the Captain on the white horse came like a sword, and all the human foes were silent in death. If the spirit of beastliness is still alive, it is alive only as a captured foe. There is a burning fire for the beast and the false prophet who had burned with lust against God. In an inverted fashion their evil passion finds a dark equivalent of the bush which is burning but not consumed. Wickedness is so real to the man of Patmos that only terribly vivid words can describe its fate. It is a matter of more than

21 And the remnant were slain with the sword of him that sat upon the horse, which *sword* proceeded out of his mouth: and all the fowls were filled with their flesh.

20 And I saw an angel come down from heaven, having the key of the bottomless pit and a great chain in his hand.

2 And he laid hold on the dragon, that old serpent, which is the Devil, and Satan, and bound him a thousand years,

with brimstone. 21 And the rest were slain by the sword of him who sits upon the horse, the sword that issues from his mouth; and all the birds were gorged with their flesh.

20 Then I saw an angel coming down from heaven, holding in his hand the key of the bottomless pit and a great chain. 2 And he seized the dragon, that ancient serpent, who is the Devil and Satan, and

symbolizing Antiochus IV Epiphanes, was slain and its body burned. Further on in Daniel it is predicted that Antiochus will attack the saints in the last days, but will come to his end "between the sea and the glorious holy mountain" (Dan. 11:44-45). As for the wicked and the persecutors, they will be raised to "shame and everlasting contempt" (Dan. 12:2); apparently Gehenna is meant here. We read in II Thess. 2:8-10 that the "lawless one" will be destroyed by the breath of the mouth of the Lord Jesus, and that those who are deceived by him are destined to perish. In a Jewish apocalypse the armies of the Antichrist will be destroyed by the sword, while he himself will be bound and taken before the Messiah, who will convict him and put him to death (II Baruch 40:1-4). The Sibyl predicts that Beliar and the overweening men who have been deceived by him will be burned up by a world-wide conflagration (Sibylline Oracles 3:68-73). Finally, from the Ascension of Isaiah 4:14 we learn that Christ with his armies will defeat Beliar, the Antichrist, and his forces and will drag them into Gehenna. Later on the godless will be totally consumed with fire (Ascension of Isaiah 4:18). It is from this stream of apocalyptic tradition, coupled with an eschatological reinterpretation of Ezek. 39:17-20, that John has developed his pattern of thought concerning the conquest and eternal punishment of the Antichrist and the deluded people of earth who became his followers and worshipers.

The gruesome feast of the birds on the flesh of the slain (cf. vs. 17) should be contrasted with "the marriage supper of the Lamb," to which the martyrs are invited (vs. 9). A similar feast, likewise showing dependence, direct or indirect, upon Ezek. 39:17-20, is found in other sources; e.g., in the Sibylline Oracles 3:697 the beasts will eat their fill from the flesh of those who perished in the last days. Also, according to the neo-Hebraic Apocalypse of Elijah, subsequent to the defeat of Gog and Magog and their armies after the messianic interim, the birds of the heaven and the beasts of the field will eat the flesh and drink the blood of the fallen.

C. Third Vision: Satan Bound and His Rule Suspended for a Thousand Years (20:1-3)

20:1-3. The reign of the Antichrist and of idolatrous Rome ended forever when the beast was hurled into the lake of fire. Satan, who had endowed them with all his power and still remained as the ruler of the world and of this age, is to meet a similar fate. For John saw **an angel** descending **from heaven** holding **the key of the bottomless pit**

ordinary concern to those capable of serious thought that so much of current literature contains the mark of the beast. In the name of art the beast seems to have received the freedom of the world. What will become of the minds of those who continually read books of uncensored beastliness? And what will be their fate?

20:2. *Evil as Personal.*—There is no end of impersonal evils in nature. Storms and earthquakes and volcanic eruptions and all natural phenomena which bring tragedy to men belong to this order of events. Diseases like the Black Death which swept over Europe in the fourteenth century belong to the same class. But

3 And cast him into the bottomless pit, and shut him up, and set a seal upon him, that he should deceive the nations no more, till the thousand years should be fulfilled: and after that he must be loosed a little season.

4 And I saw thrones, and they sat upon them, and judgment was given unto them:

bound him for a thousand years, 3 and threw him into the pit, and shut it and sealed it over him, that he should deceive the nations no more, till the thousand years were ended. After that he must be loosed for a little while.

4 Then I saw thrones, and seated on them were those to whom judgment was

---

and a great chain. He is probably the star-angel of 9:1 who fell from heaven and unlocked the bottomless pit with this same key so as to release the scourge of demonic locusts. This time he had an infinitely more important task, that of overpowering Satan and bringing his evil age to an end. We are not given the details of the conflict, but are simply told that he succeeded in capturing Satan, and after binding him with the chain, cast him into the **bottomless pit,** which he **shut** and **sealed** and presumably locked with the key. Here Satan was to be kept securely **for a thousand years,** after which **he must be loosed** for a short period of time.

Thus Satan's career is interrupted for a millennium, and his rule over this world and this age is suspended. Why this all-important role was assigned to an unnamed angel rather than to Christ or to Michael, who had previously forced Satan from heaven (12:7-9), is a puzzle; why Satan was not immediately cast into the fiery lake, along with the two beasts, his power ended forever, is a still greater mystery.

This brief but significant episode, like the expulsion of Satan from heaven, has a mythological base. Reference has previously been made to the cosmological myth of the conflict between the god Marduk and Tiâmat, the monster of chaos (cf. 12:7), as well as to the ancient account of the struggle between the serpentine Leviathan and the gods (cf. 12:3). We may also recall that after Horus had overcome the evil Set-Typhon, for some reason Isis relented and ordered him released. To turn to a Jewish source, in I Enoch 10:4-6 and 54:5-6 the fallen angels are to be bound until the Day of Judgment, a view that is repeated in Jude 6.

But none of these is a true parallel. Perhaps the closest analogy is to be found in the Iranian eschatological story of the demonic Azhi Dahaka, with two serpent heads growing out between his shoulders, who traced his lineage to Ahriman. His thousand years of evil rule over the earth ended when Fredun overcame him and chained him beneath Mount Damavand, since he was not able to put him to death. At the end of the world, however, he will be released, only to be put to death finally by Sama, who will be miraculously restored for this purpose (cf. Bundahish 29:7-9; 31:7; Bahman Yast 3:58-62; 9:7-8). In a similar fashion the power that Satan exercised over the world was checked when he was bound and imprisoned in the bottomless pit.

D. Fourth Vision: The Reign of Christ—the Millennium (20:4-6)

Apart from a few allusions these verses are all that the writer has devoted to the millennium. Despite this neglect on his part, the concept of the thousand years

---

the most tragic evils in the world have their source directly in deliberate wicked intention. And in religious thinking the conception has arisen of a mighty and bad personal will associated with the black blight of sin in the world. It appears in the story of the garden of Eden; it appears in a slightly different form in the book of Job; and it is woven into the texture of the book of Revelation. Our own sense of willfully doing what we know is not right belongs to a long tradition of the consciousness of sin. Out of this long experience has arisen

the conception of a great and wicked master of wrong. The man of Patmos sees this **dragon** of sinning, this **Devil** of demoniac inspiration, this **Satan** of dire power to tempt, seized and held bound and helpless for a long period of time. At the heart of the picture of the bound devil is the conviction that God is stronger than the mightiest forces of wickedness which seek to do evil in the world.

4. The Enthronement of the Martyrs.—The imprisonment of the devil is followed by the reign of the saints. Those who had died as

and *I saw* the souls of them that were be- | committed. Also I saw the souls of those
headed for the witness of Jesus, and for | who had been beheaded for their testimony

---

of Christ's reign on earth, either taken literally or allegorized in some fashion or other, has been the center of a great deal of attention by Christians from early times to the present. The doctrine itself is an outgrowth of the prophetic view of the day of the Lord, when the enemies of the Jews would be defeated and the righteous theocracy of Israel as God's people would be re-established here on earth in this present age of human history, a belief that developed into the expectation of the kingdom of God. With the increasing importance of the Messiah in some areas, this blessed period came more and more to be related to him. As for its duration, the messianic period might be limited definitely, or it might last indefinitely or even eternally. According to some beliefs, Jerusalem would be restored, the temple would be rebuilt, and the earth renewed so that it would be miraculously productive. There were also those who taught that there would be no death; further, an expectation that the dead would be resurrected—the righteous to share in the joys of this blessed time, and the wicked to be consigned to Gehenna—was gradually embodied in the messianic hope. It cannot be emphasized too strongly that despite variations, the beliefs in the day of the Lord, the kingdom of God, or the messianic period were all this-worldly, attaching to this present age. They were based on the fundamentally optimistic view that this world and age, despite the evil, could and would be improved so that God's reign would be actually realized in it.

Apocalypticism, however, is basically a belief in two totally distinct and different ages: this present age is temporal and irretrievably evil because it is under the control of the author of evil; whereas the new age will be eternal and perfectly righteous because it will be under the direct governance of God. The early Jewish apocalypses, like Daniel and Isa. 24–27, gave no place to the Messiah or to a messianic kingdom. It was but natural, however, that as the Messiah became more important in apocalyptic thinking, a temporal kingdom should be assigned to him. So also, according to Zoroastrian eschatology, the last millennium of the twelve of world history would be the millennium of the third and most important Saoshyant, a kind of savior or messiah.

A somewhat similar combination of messianism and apocalypticism in Judaism is provided by II Esdras 7:26-30. At the end of a series of messianic woes the Messiah will appear with the patriarchs, who had ascended to heaven, to establish his kingdom for the righteous who survived the woes. This temporal and terrestrial kingdom will last for four hundred years, after which the Messiah and all who draw human breath will die. Following a seven-day period of primeval silence, the resurrection and judgment will take place and God's new age will be established. Likewise, according to II Baruch 39–40, the Messiah will establish his kingdom, after the Antichrist is destroyed, and his kingdom will endure as long as this world of corruption endures. A somewhat similar pattern is outlined by Paul in I Cor. 15:23-28. At the second coming of Christ the Christians will be resurrected and Christ will establish his kingdom on earth. Then after destroying every supernatural rule and power, including the last enemy, death, he will turn his kingdom over to God.

In some respects, however, the closest analogy to the pattern in Revelation is that of the neo-Hebraic Apocalypse of Elijah, in which a messianic kingdom of forty years comes after the destruction of the Antichrist and before the destruction of Gog and Magog. Only after this will this age end and God's age begin.

---

martyrs are at the center of the picture. They had been cast away like human refuse; now they sit on **thrones . . . with Christ.** There is a long period when goodness is enthroned. The man of Patmos is not afraid of the idea of reward. Any world in which the death of the martyrs is the end of the last chapter of the last book would be a world of moral confusion. To the Christian martyr the hour of death has always been an hour of hope. The book of Revelation declares that this hope is to be followed by a great fulfillment. There is to be a long period when the security and power of goodness represent the very essence of the life of men. But

the word of God, and which had not worshipped the beast, neither his image, neither had received *his* mark upon their foreheads, or in their hands; and they lived and reigned with Christ a thousand years.

5 But the rest of the dead lived not again until the thousand years were finished. This *is* the first resurrection.

to Jesus and for the word of God, and who had not worshiped the beast or its image and had not received its mark on their foreheads or their hands. They came to life again, and reigned with Christ a thousand years. 5 The rest of the dead did not come to life again until the thousand years were ended. This is the first resurrection.

---

4. The way has been prepared for the messianic reign by the elimination of the two beasts and the imprisonment of the dragon. John says that he saw **thrones,** and seated upon them those to whom **judgment** had been given. The scene was inspired by Dan. 7:9, 27, where thrones are mentioned in connection with the dominion given to the saints. These **thrones** in Revelation are probably occupied by the martyrs, a realization of the promises of 3:21 that the conqueror would sit on a throne with Christ, and of the prediction by the four living creatures and the twenty-four elders that they would reign with Christ (5:10). Furthermore, it is explicitly stated that the millennium is for but one group of people, viz., the martyrs, **those who had been beheaded** because of their **testimony** (RSV; μαρτυρίαν) or **witness** (KJV) of Jesus, and **the word of God** (the causes of John's exile to Patmos; cf. 1:9), those who had died because they **had not worshiped the beast or its image,** and did not have its **mark on their foreheads** or **hands** (cf. 13:15-16; 14:9). These martyrs, whose souls went to heaven upon their death (cf. 6:9), **came to life again,** descending from heaven to earth as Elijah and Moses had done, so that they might share Christ's reign for **a thousand years.** This reign of theirs may be considered a fulfillment of the promise that they would rule the nations with a rod of iron (2:26-27), even though the nations have all been destroyed. The duration of the messianic reign for a thousand years may be a survival of the Zoroastrian belief that the reign of the Saoshyant would be during the last millennium of world history. Or it may come from another source which stated that the duration of the world would be a world-week of seven days of one thousand years each, with the last day a millennium of rest and blessedness preceding the end of this age, a view presented in II Enoch 32:2–33:2.

5a. That the martyrs, and they only, are to share in the joys of the millennium is emphasized by the statement that **the rest of the dead,** Christians as well as pagans, righteous as well as wicked, will not be restored to life at this time; instead they must await the general resurrection. Nothing in Revelation can be more certain than the teaching that the millennium is for no one but the martyrs; yet perhaps no passage in the Bible has been subjected to more misinterpretation than these three verses. Another problem connected with the millennium, however, is more difficult: What of Christians *alive* at the time of the second advent of Christ? Paul's teaching alluded both to the Christians who were alive and to those who would be resurrected in Christ's kingdom; neither would have any advantage over the other, save that the resurrected would be the first to greet Christ coming through the clouds to earth (I Thess. 4:16-17). But in Revelation no notice is taken of the living. Possibly the author considered that no Christians would be left alive after the final great persecution which he anticipated; that in order for the number of martyrs to be completed, all Christians would need to suffer martyrdom.

5b-6. The restoration of the martyrs to life is called the **first resurrection.** Whether it is a physical resurrection in which their flesh-and-blood bodies are raised, or whether

---

even great victories are not necessarily final victories. The reign of the martyrs is to be followed by new eruptions of the dark forces of wickedness. When the venerable Bede wrote his great

history there was a profound sense of the great place of martyrs in the history of the church. Their utter devotion was the crowning glory of the Christian life. Do we think too little

6 Blessed and holy *is* he that hath part in the first resurrection: on such the second death hath no power, but they shall be priests of God and of Christ, and shall reign with him a thousand years.

7 And when the thousand years are expired, Satan shall be loosed out of his prison,

8 And shall go out to deceive the nations which are in the four quarters of the earth, Gog and Magog, to gather them together to battle: the number of whom *is* as the sand of the sea.

6 Blessed and holy is he who shares in the first resurrection! Over such the second death has no power, but they shall be priests of God and of Christ, and they shall reign with him a thousand years.

7 And when the thousand years are ended, Satan will be loosed from his prison 8 and will come out to deceive the nations which are at the four corners of the earth, that is, Gog and Ma'gog, to gather them for battle; their number is like the sand of

---

they are still wearing their heavenly bodies which were given them in 6:11, is not stated. The fifth beatitude affirms that **he who shares in the first resurrection** is **blessed and holy.** Among his blessings will be his automatic exemption as a martyr from the **second death,** the eternal punishment in the fiery lake, a promise made in 2:11. That the period of the millennium is to be a most blessed interlude may be inferred from the permanent elimination of the beasts from the world and the imprisonment of Satan, the author of the martyrs' sufferings, in the bottomless pit. The martyrs are **holy** because, as stated previously in 1:6 and 5:10, they shall be **priests of God and of Christ.**

Apart from stating that the martyrs will reign with Christ and will be priests to him and God, John fails to inform us about the nature of their life during the thousand years. He has avoided the gross materialism of some pictures, both Jewish and Christian, of the messianic reign; but he has failed to put anything in its place. Had he done so, some of the crassness that characterized the Christian chiliasm of the early centuries might have been forestalled; e.g., Lactantius said that throughout the millennium the stars, sun, and moon will give more light; a rain of blessing will descend morning and evening; the earth will produce crops without man's labor; honey will drip from rocks; wine and milk will flow from fountains; and all birds and beasts will live in peace with one another (*Epitome* 72).

E. Fifth Vision: Gog and Magog Defeated and Satan Cast into the Lake of Fire, Ending His Age (20:7-10)

7. The bliss of the millennium is brought to an end after **the thousand years** when **Satan,** according to plan, is released from his imprisonment (cf. vs. 3). This release is the beginning of an episode which marks his final and complete elimination from the scene and the termination of this evil and corrupt age of human history.

8-9. This episode of Gog and Magog is based upon a popular saga that makes its earliest known appearance in a strange prophecy in Ezek. 38–39. According to it, God

---

today of the price the supreme human sufferers paid for the survival of the Christian fellowship in the world?

6. The Insight of the Martyrs.—Søren Kierkegaard sometimes declared that only martyrs are true Christians. This was, of course, to put an emphasis upon martyrdom which does not belong to classical Christianity. The psychopathic Dane was quite wrong in asserting that Bishop Mynster, the saintly Christian leader of Denmark, could not be a witness to the truth because he did not suffer a martyr's death. The

man who puts Christ first can be a witness to the truth even though he is not called upon to make the supreme sacrifice. But the vision of the martyrs as priests does serve to emphasize the fact that the man of divided mind cannot be a true priest of God. Ambivalence is not a characteristic of the authentic priest. The martyrs were the most dramatic illustration of that finality in loyalty to Christ which gave a man the right to be a priest.

8. The Final Battle.—In a variety of ways the final fight has been pictured in the book of

9 And they went up on the breadth of the earth, and compassed the camp of the saints about, and the beloved city: and fire came down from God out of heaven, and devoured them.

the sea. 9 And they marched up over the broad earth and surrounded the camp of the saints and the beloved city; but fire came down from heaven[n] and consumed

[n] Other ancient authorities read *from God, out of heaven,* or *out of heaven from God.*

will entice Gog of the land of Magog to attack and plunder the seemingly defenseless Israelites dwelling in their cities in peace and prosperity. Gog with his armies will come upon the mountains of Israel and cover the land like a cloud. But God in his wrath against these heathen people will destroy them with hailstones, fire, and brimstone. Birds and wild beasts will gorge themselves on the flesh of the slain, and their bones will be buried east of the Jordan so that the Holy Land may not be defiled.

This prediction, frequently with Gog of Magog changed to Gog and Magog, and at times without these mouth-filling names, was soon adapted, with variations, to messianic and apocalyptic expectations (cf. Strack and Billerbeck). In some sources Gog and Magog would make their appearance before the messianic reign; in others, during it; and in still others, as in Revelation, following the kingdom of the Messiah. (For the last type cf. Abodah Zarah 3b; Hebrew Apocalypse of Elijah; Lactantius *Divine Institutes* VII. 26; *Epitome* 72; cf. Syriac Apocalypse of Ezra 12–13 and I Enoch 56:5-8.)

In line with this stream of tradition John writes that when he was released, Satan (not God, as in Ezekiel) deceived **Gog and Magog,** personifications of the **nations . . . at the four corners of the earth,** inducing them to besiege **the camp of the saints and the beloved city,** i.e., of the martyrs with Christ in Jerusalem. This gathering of the **nations** quite obviously overlooks their previous destruction by Christ, along with the two beasts preceding the millennium (cf. 19:11-21). Evidently this account of Gog and Magog is a retelling of the story of the earlier battle, which also showed some dependence upon the prophecy in Ezekiel.

Revelation. Now for the last time we see the forces of evil gathered like **the sand of the sea.** The golden period of the triumph of goodness is succeeded by a last eruption of the forces of moral and spiritual destruction. It is all the more terrible because it follows the happy period of prosperous goodness. Actually there are many periods when goodness achieves a partial victory. But it is a tragedy to confuse the partial with the complete. In the picture of the final conflict the man of Patmos brings from the prophet Ezekiel the name Gog (Ezek. 38:2 "of the land of Magog") and the sense of mighty forces arrayed against God. Now all the flashing, forward looks to the final fight are gathered together. We face the ultimate conflict. Again and again men have gathered from these pictures in the book of Revelation that which has suggested that the fight of their own time was the final fight of the world. In any event the great fight of any period of world-wide stress between good and evil seems the final fight for those alive in that period. There is this great truth in the words we are now considering: the fights will not go on forever. The war to end war entered into with such devotion by many idealists may prove to be but one

among many. But the cyclical conception of history is a false conception. Perpetual recurrence would be utter moral confusion. Because we believe in the final conflict our own struggles are seen in an entirely different light.

9. *The City of God Is Besieged.*—In the midst of the world of men stands the city of God. It is **the beloved city,** the city of man's noblest devotions and of his loftiest dreams. Now it is surrounded by forces of wickedness gathered from all the world. But there it stands, in the midst of time a witness to eternity. There it stands, a city of God built in this very world. In the Boxer rebellion in China when, under the leadership of a missionary, the city of Peking was being defended it must have seemed that the cause of God was at stake. The defense was successful. Darker days have since that time come to China and to the world. But the human cause is still the cause of God. And to the eyes of faith the city of God is still the citadel of all high hopes. Vast forces gather against it. But there it stands with the eye of God upon it.

9. *The Victory Is God's.*—In the deepest sense the N.T. Apocalypse is a book of divinity. It is a book about God; it is a book about the

10 And the devil that deceived them was cast into the lake of fire and brimstone, where the beast and the false prophet *are*, and shall be tormented day and night for ever and ever.	them, 10 and the devil who had deceived them was thrown into the lake of fire and brimstone where the beast and the false prophet were, and they will be tormented day and night for ever and ever.

Strangely enough, the Messiah does not destroy Gog and Magog with the sword from his mouth, as he slew his enemies in 19:21; instead, in harmony with Ezek. 38:22, **fire came down from heaven and consumed them** (for the diction cf. II Kings 1:10). The phrase **from God** (KJV), while it may be a gloss, gives the sense, for apparently God is now actively engaged in the decisive affairs climaxing the end of this age.

10. As the beast and the false prophet had been captured and thrown into the lake of fire after their defeat by the conquering Christ, so now the **devil,** following the destruction of Gog and Magog whom he had deceived, **was thrown into the lake of fire and brimstone** alongside his two chief agents, there to be tortured forever. This is the consummation of all of the woes, plagues, celestial and terrestrial phenomena, and conflicts between supernatural foes which had begun with the breaking of the first seal by the Lamb in 6:1. Save for the millennium, Satan had been in control. He had deceived the Roman emperors and their subjects, and the kings of the nations and their subjects, so that all of the heathen had been destroyed by the wrath of God. The harlot and the beasts, his chief agents, had been eliminated. Except for Death and Hades, he was the only enemy of God, Christ, and the faithful Christians that remained. He now is shorn of his power, and the age of world history, his age, which had become increasingly debased and corrupt, comes to an end with him. This is the climax to which John has been building up; but even so, despite his skill for vivid and dramatic portrayal, he has given us only a brief (one verse) and exceedingly colorless account of the final downfall of Satan, the source and symbol of all of the evil the world and the Christians had suffered during his reign.

As a result, the denouement is somewhat disappointing, and the great contrast between Satan's age and the age to come is somewhat blurred. We are not even told who cast the beasts and Satan into the fiery lake. For dramatic effect Christ should have been depicted throwing his special enemies into this place of eternal torment, and God should have been shown making final disposal of Satan, his archenemy. Perhaps this is what John intended to convey; his failure to name any angels of punishment in the final scenes of the beasts and Satan might imply this. At any rate, despite its brevity and lack of dramatic color, this verse marks the climax of Revelation and the consummation of the age of evil, for the devil has been cast into the everlasting fire which had been prepared for him (cf. Matt. 25:41).

That the powers of evil had to be overthrown and destroyed or made powerless before the new age began was recognized in what is perhaps the earliest extant Jewish apocalypse, Isa. 24–27. In it we read that the Lord himself will punish the hosts on high, as well as the kings of the earth, who will be gathered like prisoners in the pit and shut up in prison (Isa. 24:21-22). One may note also the conquest of Ahriman and his evil hordes and the burning of the serpent in molten metal before Ormazd renovates the world in the new age (Bundahish 30).

acts of God. So the final defeat of the forces of evil is a divine act. **Fire came down from heaven and consumed them.** The dwellers in the beloved city find that God has made their cause his own. They have no weapons mighty enough for this conclusive battle. But God provides the destructive fire from heaven. In one of his poems Robert Browning suggests that the lone man speaking for God may have an audience too. The divine listener to the words of men is always aware. The divine watcher of the deeds of men is always understands. And now the divine listener and the divine watcher becomes the doer of divine deeds. The fire comes

11 And I saw a great white throne, and him that sat on it, from whose face the earth and the heaven fled away; and there was found no place for them.

12 And I saw the dead, small and great, stand before God; and the books were opened: and another book was opened, which is *the book* of life: and the dead

11 Then I saw a great white throne and him who sat upon it; from his presence earth and sky fled away, and no place was found for them. 12 And I saw the dead, great and small, standing before the throne,

---

F. Sixth Vision: Disappearance of Heaven and Earth, Second Resurrection, and General Judgment (20:11-15)

11. John now sees God on **a great white throne.** This could be a different throne from that seen in ch. 4, but there is no evidence one way or another. Either through accident or design the four living creatures, the twenty-four elders, and the angelic hosts are missing from the scene. Even more strange than their absence is the lack of any reference to the presence of Christ.

John next relates that both **earth and sky** [or **the earth and the heaven**—KJV] **fled away, and no place was found for them.** The translation of οὐρανός as "sky" in Moffatt, Goodspeed, and the RSV is linguistically correct, even though the term is usually rendered in Revelation as "heaven," as it is in this case in the KJV. Furthermore, the translation "sky" avoids the apparent difficulty of the heaven passing away and vanishing along with the earth which had been polluted and corrupted to such an extent that it could not be purified and renovated. Was heaven also so polluted that it too must disappear? Furthermore, with heaven still remaining, a place is left for God's throne and the final judgment. These are cogent arguments, but they seem to miss the point developed in Revelation that the new age is a completely new creation and that heaven as well as the earth must vanish in order to provide a place for it. Although the method employed by God in II Peter is to be fire, the result will be the same, for "the heavens will pass away with a loud noise, and the elements will be dissolved with fire, and the earth and the works that are upon it will be burned up," so as to prepare the way for the "new heavens and a new earth" (II Pet. 3:10, 13). As for a place for God's throne, perhaps this problem is answered by a Talmudic belief that God's throne existed before the first creation of heaven and earth (Genesis Rabbah 1:4); consequently, it may be that John considered God's **great white throne** as existing before the second creation.

12-13. In vs. 12 the resurrection, described in vs. 13, is assumed. That the resurrection is for all humans, save the martyrs, has been noted (cf. vs. 5a). This second or

---

down from heaven. The last sure hope of men of God is in divine acts.

11. The Authority of God.—A great nineteenth-century egotist is said to have declared: "I cannot believe in God. For if there were a God I should have to be God." There you have a definitive expression of that bloated selfishness which is unable to look up. It is incapable of recognizing an authority above itself. It never sees in vision **a great white throne.** It has lost the sense of reverence; it has lost the sense of awe; it has become incapable of noble obedience. But the great white throne still stands, and he who sits upon it is the ruler of the universe. The man who has no place in his thoughts for a noble and lofty throne has already begun to lose the sense of the

meaning of life. And one day he must confront the throne though now it has completely vanished from his thought.

12. The Glorious and Tragic Gift of Immortality.—It is not surprising if certain men dislike the thought of immortality. They have no thoughts worthy of being immortal. They have no hopes requiring immortality. Everything they care about has a very definite and limited range. To them immortality at its best would be infinite boredom and at its worst something which vaguely disturbs them but which they do not understand. It might not merely be dull; it might be terrible. But immortality must be seen in the perspective of eternity. It must be seen with the eyes of God and not with the eyes of men who have repudiated their human-

were judged out of those things which were written in the books, according to their works.

13 And the sea gave up the dead which were in it; and death and hell delivered up the dead which were in them: and they

and books were opened. Also another book was opened, which is the book of life. And the dead were judged by what was written in the books, by what they had done. 13 And the sea gave up the dead in it, Death and

---

general resurrection is apparently physical, i.e., the souls of both the righteous and the wicked which went to Hades (Sheol) at death are now reunited with their earthly bodies. This seems to be implied by the statement that **the sea,** which inconsistently remains even though the earth is gone, gave up those that had been drowned. Also, it may be inferred that without a physical body the saved could not enjoy the blessings of eternal life on earth nor could the wicked be suitably punished in the fiery lake.

Orthodox, i.e., rabbinical Jewish teaching of the time insisted upon the physical resurrection as certain (cf. Berakoth 60^b and the parable in Sanhedrin 91^a), a belief that had earlier been acquired from Persian eschatology. The Greeks, on the other hand, frequently considered the body as thoroughly evil, as the prison of the soul; consequently, for them immortality consisted of the complete liberation of the soul from the corrupting body of flesh. Paul, both a Jew and a Hellenist, attempted a compromise, according to which there would be a body at the resurrection, but it would be a spiritual body, not the physical, for "flesh and blood cannot inherit the kingdom of God" (I Cor. 15:50).

The belief in a physical resurrection, however, was in the main accepted in the apocalypses. Thus in the Zoroastrian work, Bundahish 30:7, it is stated that the "bones" of all mankind are to be "roused up." According to II Baruch 49–51, the resurrection will be physical, but the bodies of the righteous will be in time like those of the angels, while those of the wicked will waste away. In I Enoch 51:1 the earth will give up the body and Sheol will give up the spirit of the dead so that both may be united for the judgment (cf. I Enoch 61:5). However, a later transformation of the bodies of the righteous into "spiritual" bodies is indicated in I Enoch 62:15-16. Similarly, according to II Esdras 7:32, the earth and the dust give up the bodies of the dead while the "treasuries," the inter-

---

ity. The man of Patmos sees all living creatures **standing before the throne.** Some will discover how much they have gained, some will discover how much they have lost.

12. Character Becomes Destiny.—Literature is full of the account of the fashion in which character becomes destiny. The most many-sided treatment of the subject is found in Dante's *Divine Comedy.* Here men are seen permanently fastened to the central meaning which they have given to their lives. The more one studies this great work the more one wonders at its subtle insights. Shakespeare's great tragedies are a masterful exposition of the fashion in which, even in this world, character becomes destiny. The sense in which a man's life history becomes the prophecy of his future as well as the tale of his past is indicated in the symbol of the opening of the books. Men spend a good deal of their time hiding from their true selves. When the books are opened they must face just what they are. They must see just what they have made of themselves. This is the basis of judgment.

12. The Good Story.—Sometimes it seems that modern realistic novels combine to make a vast collection of books of death. They tell the story of the moral decay of the race; they are the apotheosis of the unlovely; they give a full account of that which is of bad report. Some of them soil the minds of those who read them. They must have soiled the minds of those who wrote them. The book of Revelation is the most realistic of books. It frankly faces the whole evil of human life but it is also realistic about the good. It does not falsify the story for the sake of brilliant castigation. **The book of life** is the whole story of human good. Here simple and humble souls will face fine aspects of their lives which they themselves had forgotten. The instincts immature which reached out after God, the purposes unsure which sought for goodness, the wise words spoken and the good deeds done—all are here. The book of life is God's own generous memorial of the best of human life.

13. The Deeds Which Turn to Judgments.— Here we find the final tribute to the moral

were judged every man according to their works.

Hades gave up the dead in them, and all were judged by what they had done.

---

mediate place of the dead, will restore the souls to the bodies. In the neo-Hebraic Apocalypse of Elijah, where the eschatology is so similar to that of Revelation, the resurrected dead are to have the same earthly forms they had in life, for an angel will open the graves to make this possible. A more detailed depiction of the fleshly resurrection is given in the Apocalypse of Peter 4.

The second resurrection was to be general, i.e., all of the dead, both righteous and unrighteous, were to be raised, save for the martyrs who had previously been restored to life. This belief in a general resurrection was maintained in Zoroastrianism and in the main was the Jewish belief as well. However, in the apocalypse of Isa. 24–27, the resurrection, which is physical, is limited to the Israelites, and apparently only the righteous among them will be raised (Isa. 26:19). Also, it is highly probable that the resurrection in Dan. 12:2 is confined to the very good, that they might be rewarded, and to the very wicked, that they might be punished.

In this verse God is on his "great white throne" to judge all who have been raised from the dead, save the martyrs who are automatically exempt. The judgment scene is probably derived from Dan. 7:9-10, where the books are opened before God, the Ancient of Days, who is seated on his throne. An almost identical picture is provided in I Enoch 47:3, where the books of the living are opened before the Head of Days seated on his throne of glory and surrounded by his heavenly hosts (cf. 90:20-27, where angels and apostates are judged). Also, in II Esdras 7:33, after the resurrection, the Most High on his throne of judgment executes his sentences without compassion. This scene in which God acts as judge is in harmony with earlier statements in Revelation (6:10; 16:7; 19:2). It should be noted that according to John 5:22 it is the Son who is to be the judge. Paul seems to refer to both God and Christ as the judge: in Rom. 14:10 he writes that all will "stand before the judgment seat of God" ("of Christ" [KJV] is weakly attested), whereas in II Cor. 5:10 he states that all will "appear before the judgment seat of Christ." Also in two scenes in I Enoch the Messiah is depicted on his throne of glory judging the sinners (I Enoch 45:3; 69:27-29; cf. II Baruch 72:2-6). But in Revelation, while Christ and various angels execute God's judgment on the living, it is God himself who judges the resurrected dead (cf. 22:12).

The judgment itself is represented as the opening and reading of the books in which the records of men's deeds on earth have been kept. In the judgment scene in Dan. 7:9-10 (cf. 12:1), which directly or indirectly was the exemplar for this tableau in Revelation, the books are opened before God on his throne of judgment. This motif is also found in I Enoch 47:3; 90:20; II Baruch 24:1; II Esdras 6:20.

The concept of the "books" has been discussed (see Exeg., 3:5; cf. 13:8), but a few additional observations are in order. Some books contain only the deeds of the wicked, others the deeds of the righteous, while still others (as in Daniel) are inscribed with the acts of both classes. In Revelation there seems to be a distinction, with a book of life for the righteous who had not worshiped the beast (cf. 13:8) and other books for the wicked and idolatrous. All are to be judged according to their works while on earth (cf. 14:13), but the principal, if not the determining, criterion, of course, will be whether or not they have participated in the state cult.

---

dignity of man. He is lord of his own destiny in the sense that he is the master of his own deeds. God has given him the grace of existence, the grace of opportunity, the grace of freedom, the grace of the free hours of choice. Everything comes from God in all these matters. But now there is something which comes from man.

There is something which he creates. This is the choice which comes forth in the deeds which determine destiny. So, in a sense other than the author of "Invictus" [6] meant, man is the master of his fate. So, under the grace of God, man is the captain of his soul.

[6] William Ernest Henley.

14 And death and hell were cast into the lake of fire. This is the second death.

15 And whosoever was not found written in the book of life was cast into the lake of fire.

14 Then Death and Hades were thrown into the lake of fire. This is the second death, the lake of fire; 15 and if anyone's name was not found written in the book of life, he was thrown into the lake of fire.

---

14. Now that their function is over and the dead have been raised, Death and Hades will be thrown into the lake of fire. Thus the chief supernatural enemies of mankind, Satan, the two beasts, Death and Hades, are finally disposed of. Certain supernatural agents of Satan, however, such as his angels, the harlot, and Gog and Magog are unaccounted for. The ultimate destiny of Death as depicted by John is perhaps a dramatization of a sentence in Isa. 25:8 (quoted by Paul in I Cor. 15:54*b*) that Yahweh had "swallowed up death for ever" (ASV). There is also a close parallel in II Esdras 8:53 which affirms that with the passing of the first and evil age, Death is hidden and Hades and Corruption have fled away. A curious belief is found in Zoroastrianism to the effect that after the resurrection and judgment, hell, the temporary place of punishment for the wicked, would be purified, presumably by molten metal, for use in the new age (Bundahish 30:32). This consignment of Death and Hades to the fiery lake is called **the second death.** Inasmuch as they were not humans and consequently had not died, this description is hardly logical. On that account, some propose that it is an interpolation, or else displaced material which belongs after vs. 15; but these suggestions do not seem necessary, since lack of precise and logical statement is characteristic of the writer.

15. The warning had previously been given that those who worshiped the beast would be tortured forever with fire and brimstone (14:9-11). This prediction is now fulfilled, for those whose names were not **in the book of life,** who by definition in 13:8 had worshiped the beast, are the next to be thrown **into the lake of fire,** where, of course, they will be tortured for an eternity of time. Here they will dwell with Satan and the beasts whom they followed and worshiped.

A similar punishment for the wicked is forecast in other sources. In I Enoch 48:9 they are to be burned like straw; in II Esdras 7:36 the pit of torment, the furnace of Gehenna, is reserved for those whom God condemns, as over against the place of refreshment and paradise of delight for the righteous; according to II Enoch 10:2, a Gehenna of fire is provided for all the wicked. An interesting description of the punishments for those who are condemned at the judgment is found in the neo-Hebraic Apocalypse of Elijah: they are imprisoned in a large pit where they are showered with fire and brimstone coming down from heaven. The fiery pit as a place of torture for the wicked is mentioned in Mark 9:43 and Matt. 5:22 among Christian sources. A more detailed picture of this lake of fire and the torments of the damned is given in the Apocalypse of Peter 8–14, the Sibylline Oracles 2:190-338, and the Apocalypse of Paul 31–43. It is from such Christian sources as these last three, which were probably influenced by Orphic views, that the popular Christian concept of hell has arisen.

A somewhat different concept of the ultimate fate of the unrighteous is presented in Zoroastrian eschatology. Upon their death their souls go to hell, where they are punished,

---

15. The Utter Destruction of Evil.—After the judgment of those who have made evil their good comes the second death. After this judgment comes **the lake of fire.** That which has no right to be is thrown into the midst of the burning flames which will destroy its very existence. Are there questions which are left unasked and unanswered in this picture of fiery destruction? In any event the man of Patmos sees that to become one with evil is to lose the right to exist and he expresses this insight with terrible finality. Jonathan Edwards' famous sermon on "Sinners in the Hands of an Angry God" seems to be at times an utterance of condensed terror. The moral earnestness is all to the good. But there is also the love of God which is broader than the measure of man's mind. The book of Revelation sees the awful finality of evil choice, but it is also in a very noble sense the book of the Lamb that was slain.

21 And I saw a new heaven and a new earth: for the first heaven and the first earth were passed away; and there was no more sea.

2 And I John saw the holy city, new Jerusalem, coming down from God out of

21 Then I saw a new heaven and a new earth; for the first heaven and the first earth had passed away, and the sea was no more. 2 And I saw the holy city, new

---

while those of the righteous go to heaven to await the resurrection. After the general resurrection all are to walk through a stream of white-hot molten metal. To the righteous this will be like warm milk, but to the wicked it will be a terrible ordeal, which, however, will purify them of all their sins so that everyone will enjoy the new age. John would not have approved of this view of ultimate universal redemption.

G. Seventh Vision: The New Creation and God's Eternal Age (21:1-8)

21:1. According to the Iranian eschatology, by the divine will of Ormazd the universe, including hell, will be purified or renovated in the new age and will last forever (Bundahish 30:32). This view of renovation of the old world, rather than an entirely new creation, is also found in Jewish sources; e.g., despite the phrase "I create new heavens and a new earth" in Isa. 65:17 (cf. 66:22), the concept is actually that of a transformation of the present heaven and earth, not a new creation; for the writer of the passage in which this is found was not thinking in terms of two distinct ages; his view was prophetic, not apocalyptic. In an apocalyptic section in II Baruch the present world is considered evil and corrupt; however, it will be renovated or transformed (II Baruch 32:6), will be everlasting and undying (II Baruch 48:50; 51:3), and will be incorruptible (II Baruch 44:12). Similarly, from I Enoch 45:4-5 we learn that the heaven and the earth are to be transformed in the new age to be an eternal blessing.

On the other hand, a distinctly new creation for the coming age is mentioned in I Enoch 72:1. Likewise, in the so-called Apocalypse of Weeks, found in this same book, we are told that after the destruction of the world and the judgment, the first heaven will pass away and a new heaven will appear in its place (I Enoch 91:16). According to the apocalyptic section in II Esdras, after the destruction of this world and the end of this age there is to be a seven-day period of "primeval silence," like the seven days of creation in Genesis, for the creation of the new world in the new age (II Esdras 7:30, 75). In Christian writings a reference to an eschatological regeneration is made in Matt. 19:28, but without elaboration, so that it is difficult to know whether a renovation or a new creation is meant. In II Pet. 3:10, 13 (see also Exeg. on 20:11) there can be no doubt: the first heavens and earth are to be annihilated by fire, and according to promise, new heavens and a new earth are to be created. This, quite definitely, is the view of John as he writes, **Then I saw a new heaven and a new earth.**

2a. Among the blessings of the messianic reign the prospect of a restored Jerusalem with its temple was a natural expectation (cf. Isa. 54–55; Ezek. 40–48; Sibylline Oracles 5:423-26; II Baruch 6:9). In at least one messianic prediction both Eden and Jerusalem

---

21:1. The Creative Spirit.—One of the glorious things about the book of Revelation is its full appreciation of the creative spirit. In the most patient way it connects itself with great and notable things in the past but it never becomes hard and rigidly conventional. The spirit of creativity is as rich and manifold as the life of God himself. So as we come to the climax there is **a new heaven and a new earth.** Religion is often thought of as conventional but it is questionable if, apart from the rich

energies of noble religion, the creative spirit can be kept alive in the world. Decadence, decay, and death belong to unethical religion. All the splendor of rich creativity belongs to ethical religion as it comes to a climax of fulfillment and inspiration in Jesus Christ. The decadent prose and poetry of our own time find their distinctive lack at the point of the creative inspiration of religion.

2. The Holy City of God Among Men.—Many literary men have found the thought of

heaven, prepared as a bride adorned for her husband.

3 And I heard a great voice out of heaven saying, Behold, the tabernacle of God *is* with men, and he will dwell with them, and they shall be his people, and God himself shall be with them, *and be their God.*

Jerusalem, coming down out of heaven from God, prepared as a bride adorned for her husband; 3 and I heard a great voice from the throne saying, "Behold, the dwelling of God is with men. He will dwell with them, and they shall be his people,ᵒ and God himself will be with

ᵒ Other ancient authorities read *peoples.*

---

would be restored (Test. Dan. 5:12). In some instances it was thought that a pre-existent heavenly Jerusalem would come to earth in the days of the Messiah (II Esdras 13:36; II Baruch 4:2-7). In a highly figurative messianic prophecy a disconsolate woman was seen mourning for her son; she was the earthly Jerusalem and her son was its inhabitants who were slaughtered or captured by the Romans. Suddenly the woman's aspect changed, and she became bright and shining. Then the earth shook and the woman disappeared, leaving a city, the heavenly Jerusalem which she personified, in her place (II Esdras 9:38–10:59).

It was to be expected that this symbolism would be taken over into apocalypticism. Accordingly, in the concluding section of the apocalyptic dream visions incorporated into I Enoch, in the new age God will build a new Jerusalem to take the place of the earthly city (I Enoch 90:28-29). Also in II Esdras 7:26*b*, when the new age is established, the invisible heavenly city, Jerusalem, will appear along with the land, apparently Eden, that had been concealed (cf. II Esdras 8:52; I Enoch 24:3–26:3). In view of the similarity of the eschatological pattern of the neo-Hebraic Apocalypse of Elijah to that of Revelation, it is of more than passing interest that the new age there will be characterized by a heavenly Eden and a new Jerusalem which will come down from heaven. So also John writes that he **saw the holy city, new Jerusalem, coming down out of heaven from God.**

2b. The New Jerusalem is the **bride** of Christ, mentioned in 19:7-10, **adorned for her husband.** The heavenly city was personified by Paul as the mother of the true Israel (Gal. 4:26), while in the involved allegory of II Esdras 9:38–10:59 it was the prototype of the earthly Jerusalem as well as the mother of the slain and captured Jews. Now as the new and eternal dwelling of the redeemed Christians, it is personified as the bride of Christ (see further on 19:7-10; also 12:6). A more complete account of her descent and appearance is given in vss. 9 ff. The contrast between the temporal city personified by the harlot (cf. ch. 17) and the eternal city of God symbolized by the bride of Christ is as obvious as it is dramatic.

3-4. A **voice** is now heard **from the throne,** as in 19:5, uttering a brief chant, summarizing the blessings that the inhabitants of the eternal city will enjoy, which should

---

great cities full of fascination and importance. Émile Zola wrote a famous trilogy about the great cities of Lourdes, Rome, and Paris. Hugh Walpole's *Fortitude* [7] is among other things a subtle interpretation of the city of London. Many years ago a book was written to put in literary form the sense of New York. It is quite forgotten now. But at the time of its publication it commanded a full-page review in the literary supplement of the *New York Times.* These studies of cities do not have to do with **the holy city.** That city has qualities which are determined by the character of the living God. Augustine found in the conception mate-

[7] New York: George H. Doran Co., 1913.

rials for a Christian exposition which he put into his great work *De Civitate Dei* (*The City of God*). The city of God is still Jerusalem, for God's own city can be connected with men only if it has some sort of continuity with their own lives.

3. *The Glorious Fellowship.*—With amazing daring it is declared that **the dwelling of God is with men.** In order that there may be no mistake the words are repeated: **He will dwell with them.** Then the thought is expressed in a veritable climax of hope: **They shall be his people.** Then there is another eager repetition: **God himself will be with them.** For fullness and propulsion of utterance this series of state-

4 And God shall wipe away all tears from their eyes; and there shall be no more death, neither sorrow, nor crying, neither shall there be any more pain: for the former things are passed away.

them;[p] 4 he will wipe away every tear from their eyes, and death shall be no more, neither shall there be mourning nor crying nor pain any more, for the former things have passed away."

[p] Other ancient authorities add *and be their God.*

---

be contrasted with the dirge over Rome and her unhappy, doomed inhabitants sung by the angel who threw the millstone into the sea (18:21-24). Like the earlier hymn, it is largely based on O.T. phraseology. The first part is an apocalyptic restatement of a messianic prophecy in Ezek. 37:27, "My tabernacle also shall be with them; yea, I will be their God, and they shall be my people." In fulfillment of this prophecy the authoritative voice from the throne promises that God's **dwelling** (RSV) or **tabernacle** (KJV) will be with **his people** forever. No longer will he be transcendent in heaven, far removed from his worshipers, as he was in the previous age; instead, in this new age he will be immanent, leaving heaven for earth where his Shekinah or divine presence will be eternally with them in the New Jerusalem (cf. I Enoch 105:2).

According to Isa. 25:8, in the new age, after swallowing up death forever, God "will wipe away tears from off all faces." Similarly, now that **death** has been eliminated forever (cf. 20:14) the martyrs are told, as in 7:17, that God **will wipe away every tear from their eyes.** Further, since **the former things,** the first age with all of its causes of evil, **have passed away,** there will now be **neither . . . mourning nor crying nor pain.** Thus

---

ments has scarcely a parallel in the Scriptures. Here we have the ultimate contrast between Christianity and pantheism. In pantheism men are at last seen as one in essence with the divine. In Christianity they are seen in moral and spiritual fellowship with the divine. The two conceptions belong to two worlds which can never live together in harmony. In pantheism moral distinctions vanish; in Christianity they are seen as gloriously permanent. Moral and spiritual fellowship is the very characteristic of the heavenly fulfillment.

4. The End of Weeping.—Vergil, with his profound human sympathy, saw the tears in things. The strange, low accompaniment of tragedy which, like a sad song, follows the activities of men spoke to something very deep in the mind and, we may say, in the heart of the poet. Indeed tears have fallen like rain through all the centuries. But in the holy city of God among men there are to be no tears. The last heartbreak has been experienced, the last tear has fallen, for human tears fall upon the heart of God and make a sadness there. And this sadness must be turned into a serenity which becomes a gift for men and leaves no place for tears. James Whitcomb Riley once wrote a tender little poem containing the words: "There, little girl, don't cry." In a simple, human way the words echo the voice of a greater compassion.

4. The End of Death.—The words, **death shall be no more,** must always be read with these great words of Paul clearly and deeply in

mind: "This mortal nature must put on immortality. . . . Death is swallowed up in victory." (I Cor. 15:53-54.) In the temporal city death is the end of so many sentences. But in the city of God among men death simply ceases to be. The divine fellowship is exhaustless. It cannot be thought of as coming to an end. Once man has an experience capable of immortal meaning, immortality is secure. The man who in a desperate illness cried out, "I want my heavenly father," was calling for this fellowship. The longing for something which death cannot touch was implicit in the words. The beasts of the field do not feel such restless desires. So man is given a destiny which is not offered to them.

4. The End of Parting and Pain.—Goethe put into the mouth of Faust the words:

No wing material lifts our mortal clay.
But 'tis our inborn impulse, deep and strong,
Upward and onward still to urge our flight.

Wagner a student replies:

the measures of the mind,
Bear us from book to book, from page to page!
. . . .
and ah! when we unroll
Some old and precious parchment, at the sight
All heaven itself descends upon the soul.[8]

There is an old and precious parchment at whose voice all heaven does descend upon the soul. When we listen to the words which tell us

[8] *Faust,* Part I, scene ii.

5 And he that sat upon the throne said, Behold, I make all things new. And he said unto me, Write: for these words are true and faithful.

6 And he said unto me, It is done. I am Alpha and Omega, the beginning and the

5 And he who sat upon the throne said, "Behold, I make all things new." Also he said, "Write this, for these words are trustworthy and true." 6 And he said to me, "It is done! I am the Alpha and the Omega,

---

some of the promises of the hymn sung by the twenty-four elders in 7:15-17 are realized (cf. also 3:12). The Lamb is not mentioned by name in this scene; but we should probably assume that he was present as the groom awaiting his bride, the New Jerusalem, adorned for her husband and descending from heaven (vs. 2; cf. vss. 22-23 and 22:3).

5a. God, seated on his **throne** in the New Jerusalem, ratifies all that has happened with the statement, **Behold, I make all things new.** The old age of Satan has vanished forever, along with Satan himself; God's new age has now been firmly established. The sinners have been fittingly punished by being cast into the fiery lake forever, while the redeemed are to enjoy an eternity of blessedness in the New Jerusalem with God and the Lamb. It is strange that Elijah and Moses, the woman clothed with the sun, the four living creatures, the twenty-four elders, and the hosts of angels (save for one angel guide and twelve angelic guards over the gates) do not appear to share in the felicities of the new age. Apparently their roles are finished, and in these final scenes of the great drama they have been overlooked.

5b. God next commands John to **write** down what he has heard, for the words, like Christ himself, are **true and faithful** (the rendering **trustworthy** [RSV] obscures the parallelism with 3:14 and 19:11). While this divine order referred specifically to the words just spoken, it no doubt was intended also to include the entire book of prophecy. Similar commands were given by Christ (1:11), by a voice from heaven (14:13), and by an angel (19:9). This, of course, is a means whereby the author authenticates his predictions. Here, as in 1:1, their ultimate source is God himself.

6. In 16:17, after the last of the series of plagues had been emptied from its bowl, a voice from the throne approvingly said, "It is done!" Now that the final acts of the consummation have occurred, God approves them by affirming, "They are come to pass"

---

that the mourning which comes from parting will be no more—and that pain shall cease to do its torturing work—we find ourselves in a world of moral and spiritual and social expectation where gloom and despair are changed to joyous expectation.

5. That Which Is Eternally New.—The consummation of Dante's *Divine Comedy* is the eternal newness of the rose of love and fire. There is the perfection of bloom. There is beauty beyond the powers of speech. There is ceaseless thought luminous with beauty. There is ceaseless action suffused with meaning God himself makes possible. Obedience is free felicity. There is a new integration of time and eternity in which God's will is indeed man's peace. And all is bound together by that love which has the secret of the movement of the sun and all the other stars. Here centuries of Christian meditation amplify the meaning of the glorious words: **Behold, I make all things new.**

6. The Alphabet of God.—In the Greek myth Prometheus was fastened to the bleak crag

Caucasus for his kindness to mankind. Aeschylus was fascinated by the old tale. In *Prometheus Bound* we see many aspects of the myth. We hear Prometheus himself say:

> mercy's now denied
> To him whose crime was mercy to mankind:
> And here I lie, in cunning torment stretched.

Again we hear his words:

> Of human kind,
> My great offence in aiding them, in teaching
> The art of speech, and rousing torpid mind
> To sense and reason.

In the Scriptures it is the supreme and only God who shows mercy to mankind. His words bring every good hope to mankind. There is a divine alphabet which spells out in conclusive words the ultimate meaning of things. This the God who himself is **the Alpha and the Omega, the beginning and the end,** of all the words which spell out meaning has brought as a great gift to mankind. God is not the enemy of man.

end. I will give unto him that is athirst of the fountain of the water of life freely.

7 He that overcometh shall inherit all things; and I will be his God, and he shall be my son.

8 But the fearful, and unbelieving, and the abominable, and murderers, and whoremongers, and sorcerers, and idolaters, and all liars, shall have their part in the lake which burneth with fire and brimstone: which is the second death.

the beginning and the end. To the thirsty I will give water without price from the fountain of the water of life. 7 He who conquers shall have this heritage, and I will be his God and he shall be my son. 8 But as for the cowardly, the faithless, the polluted, as for murderers, fornicators, sorcerers, idolaters, and all liars, their lot shall be in the lake that burns with fire and brimstone, which is the second death."

(ASV) —less literally, "They have been accomplished," or It is done. Repeating his words of 1:8, God again identifies himself as the Alpha and the Omega, adding, the beginning and the end. Both of these titles are assumed by Christ in 22:13, along with "the first and the last," an appellation announced by him in 1:17 and 2:8.

The martyrs were promised in 7:17 that they would be guided "to springs of living water"—an assurance that is given here and is to be repeated again in 22:17. The symbolism, perhaps, needs no further explanation at this time.

7. The martyrological motif is emphasized again in this utterance by God, who says that these rewards are to be the **heritage** of the one **who conquers**, the special designation for the martyr used in the conclusions of the letters to the seven churches in chs. 2–3 in connection with the promises of reward made to them then. Moreover, God now promises that he will be **his God** and the martyr will be his **son**, a concept of divine sonship that Paul had earlier developed (cf. Gal. 4:7; Rom. 8:17). Although the martyr is God's son, God is not called his Father; for in Revelation, as in the Fourth Gospel (except for 20:17), he is the "Father" of Jesus only.

8. In contrast to those who will be permitted to inherit the eternal blessings of the New Jerusalem as sons of God, are Satan's followers, whose inheritance will be the **lake** of fire and brimstone, i.e., **the second death.** These condemned persons are characterized by vices similar to those listed in Rom. 1:28-32 and II Enoch 10:4-6. However, in this case the vices are all related in one way or another to the worship of the state and the emperors. **The cowardly** and **the faithless** are those who in fear of their lives became apostates; **the polluted** (RSV) or **the abominable** (KJV) are those who partook of the "abominations" of the harlot (17:4); the **murderers** are the persecutors of the Christians who put them to death; the **fornicators** and **sorcerers** are the same as **idolaters**; while the

---

He is man's great friend. And the language which he brings to men is the language of supreme hope and high expectation. Men who share that hope learn the alphabet of God. So in the final book of the N.T. the man of Patmos declares that God gives the best of hope and fruition to man.

6. The Thirst for Eternity.—Every appetite is an indication of a legitimate satisfaction and for these satisfactions the God who made the appetite has provided. They represent an ascending scale. Some appetites will perish with time and do not reach out into eternity; but in the deepest sense of all God has put the passion for eternity in man's heart and then has given to him a thirst which only eternity can satisfy. This thirst the one on the throne declares he will satisfy freely **from the fountain**

of the water of life. The drink of the heights belongs to the man who is destined for the heights. In *Thus Spake Zarathustra*, Friedrich Nietzsche cries out: "In the mountains the shortest way is from peak to peak." [9] The words are true in a much more profound sense than the writer about the superman ever knew. God summons men to leave the lowland of confusion and evil and by his grace to move from peak to peak. It is so that he gives them a thirst which can be satisfied only by water from the very fountain of life.

8. The Catalogue of Evildoers.—With one of the quick changes so characteristic of the book of Revelation we are gazing at a great picture of evildoers of all sorts. They have no

[9] Part I, ch. vii, "Reading and Writing."

9 And there came unto me one of the seven angels which had the seven vials full of the seven last plagues, and talked with me, saying, Come hither, I will show thee the bride, the Lamb's wife.	9 Then came one of the seven angels who had the seven bowls full of the seven last plagues, and spoke to me, saying, "Come, I will show you the Bride, the wife of the Lamb." 10 And in the Spirit he carried me away to a great, high mountain, and showed me the holy city Jerusalem coming down out of heaven from God,
10 And he carried me away in the spirit to a great and high mountain, and showed me that great city, the holy Jerusalem, descending out of heaven from God,	

liars are those who denied Christ. By their conduct they are completely different from the martyrs and deserve the fate that has overtaken them.

With this scene and verse the apocalypse itself is virtually ended; that which, remains is a picture of the New Jerusalem (21:9–22:5) and an epilogue (22:6-21) consisting of sundry promises and exhortations.

XI. SUPPLEMENTARY SCENE: DESCRIPTION OF THE NEW JERUSALEM (21:9–22:5)

This section of twenty-four verses, practically the length of a chapter, is a somewhat detailed and not wholly consistent description of the New Jerusalem. The belief in a heavenly city is rooted in astral speculations, according to which there was a perfect, heavenly model for everything on earth, including cities and temples. Thus there was a heavenly Babylon; also a heavenly temple of Marduk, which came to be identified with the city. The heavenly city quite naturally took on astral features. The sun and moon became the chief deities, while the twelve constellations of the zodiac symbolized lesser deities. The twelve portals through which these constellations were thought to pass became gates of the square city, with its sides facing the four winds of heaven. Also, it was thought that the Milky Way was a broad street or river through the city. The city itself had a certain cosmic significance in that it symbolized or came to be identified with the universe itself. That the Jews took over this concept and adapted it has been shown above (cf. 21:2a).

A. EXTERNAL APPEARANCE OF THE CITY (21:9-14)

9. One of the seven angels of the bowl plagues, presumably the one that had been John's mentor since 17:1, offered to show him **the Bride, the wife of the Lamb.** The same words, **Come, I will show you,** were used by this angel before he took John "in the Spirit" to a wilderness to see the great harlot. Accordingly, as John was **in the Spirit** once more, the angel took him **to a great, high mountain** and showed him **the holy city Jerusalem**

place in the great consummation which has just been described. There is no blurring of moral or spiritual issues in the book of Revelation. It is the farthest removed from Nietzsche's ugly falsehood: "There is an old illusion—it is called good and evil." [1] Henrik Ibsen's *An Enemy of the People* with a certain hard frankness portrays the savage and ugly selfishness of which a little town is capable. In many a century bitterly angry men have gone back to Juvenal to find corrosive phrases in which to castigate the wickedness of their own time. The distinction between good and evil will not go down. Good words must always face the bad facts or they become false and sentimental.

The book of Revelation meets this demand triumphantly.

10. Eternity Invading Time.—Lewis Mumford in *The Culture of Cities* [2] discusses many things which do not come within the ken of the man of Patmos. But these bustling cities with their vast organization and their manifold life need, far more than the author of this thoughtful volume realized, the vision of the book of Revelation of the **city . . . coming down out of heaven from God.** Only in the immortal can you find the real secrets of mortal life. Only when eternity invades time do you find the real meaning of life in time. Indeed clever men are all the while saying every word but the

[1] *Ibid.*, Part III, ch. lvi, "Old and New Tables."

[2] New York: Harcourt, Brace & Co., 1938.

11 Having the glory of God: and her light *was* like unto a stone most precious, even like a jasper stone, clear as crystal;

12 And had a wall great and high, *and* had twelve gates, and at the gates twelve angels, and names written thereon, which are *the names* of the twelve tribes of the children of Israel:

13 On the east three gates; on the north three gates; on the south three gates; and on the west three gates.

11 having the glory of God, its radiance like a most rare jewel, like a jasper, clear as crystal. 12 It had a great, high wall, with twelve gates, and at the gates twelve angels, and on the gates the names of the twelve tribes of the sons of Israel were inscribed; 13 on the east three gates, on the north three gates, on the south three gates, and on the

---

coming down out of heaven from God. The contrast between the wilderness and the mountain is as marked as that between the two cities. The scene itself, however, is a rewriting of Ezek. 40:2, "In the visions of God brought he me into the land of Israel, and set me upon a very high mountain"; thence Ezekiel was able to see the new temple of a restored Israel, like a city in size, on a near-by mountain. Ezra, according to II Esdras 9:26, sat in a meadow of flowers when he had a vision of the heavenly city.

11. When God was in his temple in 15:8, it was filled with the smoke of his "glory" or divine presence. Now, as the holy city descends, it is seen to possess **the glory of God.** Furthermore, as God himself had the appearance of "jasper and carnelian" in the theophany of 4:3, so now its **radiance is like a most rare jewel, like a jasper, clear as crystal.** Since φωστήρ, translated as **radiance** (RSV), **light** (KJV), and "luminary" (ASV mg.), could also mean "star," its use here may reflect the astral origins of this way of describing the heavenly city. At any rate, the imagery used shows its divine nature; it is indeed a fitting residence for God and Christ and their people. In quite similar language the New Jerusalem is described in the Sibylline Oracles 5:420-27: it was "more radiant than the stars and the sun and the moon," and was set "as the jewel of the world"; likewise, those who saw its temple towering to the clouds would be seeing "the glory of the invisible God, the vision of delight."

12-13. The city had a **high wall, with twelve gates,** with **three gates** to a side—east, north, south, and west. Each gate was inscribed with the name of one of the **twelve tribes** of Israel, and an angel guardian was at each gate. This picture is derived from Ezek. 48:31-34, which describes the city as having twelve gates, three on each side (cf. Ezek. 42:16-19) with each one bearing the name of one of the twelve tribes. The twelve angels at the gates are a feature added by John. Quite fittingly, in Ezekiel this city is called "The LORD is there," a name that would also be very appropriate for the New Jerusalem in Revelation. Since in 7:1-8 the twelve tribes symbolize the whole company of

---

most important word and they continually fail to see that their own useful words gain both in meaning and in clarity when they are shot through with something which comes from eternity. The deepest lesson of human life is that you must find beyond time the secrets of living truly in time. If the city coming down from God is in a man's heart he will have new power for the lifting of his own town in this world to higher levels.

12. The Old and the New.—The extraordinary poise and balance of what we may call the fundamental thinking of the book of Revelation is now happily illustrated. We are seeing the fashion in which all things are made new. And

at once the past appears. The great walls of the city have **twelve gates, and on the gates the names of the twelve tribes of . . . Israel.** You cannot enter the holy city without being reminded of the revelation of God which came through Israel. The O.T., we may say, is seen at every entrance to the sacred city. You can enter the city from the east or the north or the south or the west, there is a road from any point at which a man finds himself to the city of God. In the series "American Literature: A Period Anthology" Robert Spiller edits the volume *The Roots of National Culture*.[3] The

3 New York: Macmillan Co., 1933.

14 And the wall of the city had twelve foundations, and in them the names of the twelve apostles of the Lamb.

15 And he that talked with me had a golden reed to measure the city, and the gates thereof, and the wall thereof.

16 And the city lieth foursquare, and the length is as large as the breadth: and he measured the city with the reed, twelve thousand furlongs. The length and the breadth and the height of it are equal.

17 And he measured the wall thereof, a hundred *and* forty *and* four cubits, *according to* the measure of a man, that is, of the angel.

west three gates. 14 And the wall of the city had twelve foundations, and on them the twelve names of the twelve apostles of the Lamb.

15 And he who talked to me had a measuring rod of gold to measure the city and its gates and walls. 16 The city lies foursquare, its length the same as its breadth; and he measured the city with his rod, twelve thousand stadia;*q* its length and breadth and height are equal. 17 He also measured its wall, a hundred and forty-four cubits by a man's measure, that is, an an-

q About fifteen hundred miles.

Christian martyrs, John no doubt considers that these twelve gates bearing the names of the twelve tribes signify these same martyrs, who are the new Israel.

14. It is allegorically stated in Eph. 2:19-22 that the household of God will be like a temple "built upon the foundations of the apostles and prophets," with Christ Jesus as the cornerstone (cf. Heb. 11:10; I Pet. 2:5; Matt. 16:18). Part of this understanding is presented somewhat realistically in the portrayal of the city **wall** resting upon **twelve foundations** bearing the **names of the twelve apostles.** This is the only specific reference to the twelve apostles in Revelation, indicating perhaps that they did not greatly concern the author. That he had twelve specific names in mind may be questioned. If so, there is no way of knowing precisely which twelve. More than likely he was thinking of **the twelve apostles** under an institutional aspect as symbolizing the community of the faithful in much the same manner as the twelve tribes did.

B. Measurement of the City (21:15-17)

15-17. In an earlier passage John was given a reed with which to measure the temple (11:1-2). As suggested in the Exeg. of this scene, it probably symbolized the measurement of those who were destined to be martyrs. This second scene of the measurement of the New Jerusalem, which is so closely related to the martyrs, is most likely a sequel to the first, and probably indicates that those who had been "measured" to be martyrs are now being "measured" for everlasting security, peace, and blessedness in the New Jerusalem. In their imagery both episodes have been influenced by the measurement of the temple as related in Ezek. 40:3 ff. The city, as measured, was an immense cube, each side **twelve thousand stadia (about fifteen hundred miles)** in length. Its size was not unexampled, for the new temple to be built by God, which was envisioned in the Sibylline Oracles 5:418-27, would have a tower that touched the clouds; whereas the holy city seen descending by Elijah, according to the Hebrew apocalypse bearing his name, had

---

various and many-sided quotations show how manifold are the sources which had a share in making that new thing, the American outlook on the world. There is a large outlook with even more manifold sources. It is the mind of the city of God.

14. Building on the Past.—The high wall of the city has **twelve foundations, and on them the twelve names of the twelve apostles.** These new things which God is doing are solidly based on the foundation of the Christian revelation.

The great act of Redemption is kept in view, for the apostles are called the **apostles of the Lamb.** You must keep the Cross in your thought as you think of the foundations of the Christian future. The only complete new thing is anarchy. The nobly new always has its roots in the past. And since it is the Christian religion which gives a clue to the meaning of the past and the possibilities of the future the basis of the life of new days must be found in old days when Christ was made known. The new city

18 And the building of the wall of it was *of* jasper: and the city *was* pure gold, like unto clear glass.

19 And the foundations of the wall of the city *were* garnished with all manner of precious stones. The first foundation *was*

gel's. 18 The wall was built of jasper, while the city was pure gold, clear as glass. 19 The foundations of the wall of the city were

---

3,000 towers on its walls, some 500,000 yards apart (cf. Baba Bathra 75b) . Why was the city cube-shaped? This feature may have been suggested by the fact that the holy of holies, an earlier dwelling of God, was a cube (I Kings 6:20) .

The measurement given for the wall is somewhat ambiguous, for its measurement of **a hundred and forty-four cubits** (about 216 feet) could be either its height or its thickness. If the latter, this was all out of proportion to the height of the city. More important, however, may be the fact that the measurement is twelve times twelve cubits, for in the description of the city twelve is obviously a significant number. The observation that this is **by a man's measure, that is, an angel's,** is puzzling but not too important. It may be intended to show, as in 19:10 and 22:9, that men and angels were on an equality.

C. Composition of the City (21:18-21)

18. The harlot was dressed in "purple and scarlet" and was adorned with "gold and jewels and pearls" (cf. 17:4) . The bride was even more gloriously adorned; indeed, to change the figure, the city was actually composed of gold and all kinds of precious stones with single pearls for gates (cf. 19:8) . The concept, a rather natural one, is earlier seen in Isa. 54:11-12, where Yahweh figuratively promises the Jews: "I will set thy stones in fair colors, and lay thy foundations with sapphires. And I will make thy pinnacles of rubies, and thy gates of carbuncles, and all thy border of precious stones" (ASV) . Similarly, according to Tob. 13:16-17, the following assurance is given: "For Jerusalem shall be builded with sapphires and emeralds and precious stones; thy walls and towers and battlements with pure gold, and the streets of Jerusalem shall be paved with beryl and carbuncle and stones of Ophir." Apparently following the same tradition as that found in Isa. 54:11-12, the writer of the Hebrew Apocalypse of Elijah states that the three thousand turrets of the city were composed of emerald, precious stones, and pearls. Similar imagery is now used in John's depiction of the heavenly Jerusalem come down to earth. Its walls were made of **jasper** (cf. vs. 11) and the city itself was **pure gold,** as **clear as glass.**

19-20. The best and most learned interpretation of these verses is given by Charles (*Revelation of St. John,* II, 165-69). It is obvious that the twelve different precious

---

is firmly founded on that which comes from the N.T. and the O.T. Williston Walker's rich and rewarding book *Great Men of the Christian Church* [4] reminds us that the Christian foundation for the future not only has elements which come from the apostolic age but also elements which come from every century since. The great men of many ages of Christian thought and life in the world contribute something to that new future which we associate with the presence of the city of God.

18. *The Material and the City of God.*—We are more and more impressed by the daring with which the book of Revelation builds up its great synthesis. The holy city is to be a city of gold. The material is to be glorified and is

[4] Chicago: University of Chicago Press, 1908.

to become a part of the sacred city. Gold has been used in so many evil ways that sometimes the very word seems to be associated with that which is of bad report. But gold can be nobly used, and so used it is not cast from God's perfect town. On the contrary this perfect city is **of pure gold, clear as glass.** There is a bad materialism and there is a good materialism. When the material is used as the instrument of the spiritual it becomes a part of that nobility by which it is used. The greatest age of Roman writing was called the golden age. It is a sound instinct which uses the most valuable metal to express that which alone can give to the material a permanent meaning.

19. *The Shining Jewels.*—Corresponding to the twelve apostles who give spiritual meaning

jasper; the second, sapphire; the third, a chalcedony; the fourth, an emerald;

20 The fifth, sardonyx; the sixth, sardius; the seventh, chrysolite; the eighth, beryl; the ninth, a topaz; the tenth, a chrysoprasus; the eleventh, a jacinth; the twelfth, an amethyst.

21 And the twelve gates *were* twelve pearls; every several gate was of one pearl: and the street of the city *was* pure gold, as it were transparent glass.

adorned with every jewel; the first was jasper, the second sapphire, the third agate, the fourth emerald, **20** the fifth onyx, the sixth carnelian, the seventh chrysolite, the eighth beryl, the ninth topaz, the tenth chrysoprase, the eleventh jacinth, the twelfth amethyst. **21** And the twelve gates were twelve pearls, each of the gates made of a single pearl, and the street of the city was pure gold, transparent as glass.

---

stones with which **the foundations of the wall of the city were adorned** were substantially the same as those that composed the breastplate of the high priest as given in Exod. 28:17-21 and 39:10-14, allowances being made for differences between the Hebrew and Greek nomenclature. (In the LXX these twelve stones also adorn the dress of the king of Tyre, according to Ezek. 28:13, while in the Hebrew text but nine are listed.) In the Exodus passages each stone was engraved with the name of one of the twelve tribes.

According to the ancient Jewish writers Philo (*On Monarchy* II. 5; *Moses* III. 14) and Josephus (*Antiquities* III. 7. 7), these twelve stones on the high priest's breastplate are to be equated with the twelve signs of the zodiac. Other evidence may be cited to support this interpretation. Charles further points out that the stones are in the reverse order of the normal sequence of the zodiacal signs, and suggests that John has done this in order to Christianize the concept.

More significant, perhaps, is the observation that whereas in Exodus the stones are engraved with the names of the twelve tribes, in Revelation they adorn the twelve foundations and are inscribed with the names of the twelve apostles (vs. 14); the twelve gates symbolize the twelve tribes. John is attempting to show once more that the faithful Christians are the true Israel (cf. 7:1-8). Furthermore, if he is acquainted with the siderial significance of these twelve stones—and in view of his use of astral symbolism elsewhere this is quite possible—he may be suggesting that, as in Dan. 12:3, the saints, i.e., the martyrs, are to be "as the stars for ever and ever."

A comparison of the various translations will show some discrepancy in the English equivalents given for the third, fifth, and sixth stones, but this is due to the difficulty of making precise identifications.

21. Since **the gates** are not to be made of the twelve precious stones of the high priest's breastplate, they are each composed **of a single pearl**, a statement that almost surpasses the imagination and no doubt was intended to. This idea may have been originally suggested by the predictions in Isa. 54:12, that the gates of Jerusalem would be made of "carbuncles." However, it is more in line with the tradition preserved in the Talmud, professedly based on the verse in Isaiah, that the gates of the New Jerusalem would be composed of single precious stones and pearls each thirty cubits—about forty-five feet—square (cf. Baba Bathra 75a; Sanhedrin 100a). **The street of the city**, like the city itself, was made of **pure gold** which was **transparent as glass.** The reference to a

---

to the foundation of the city are the twelve jewels which give sparkling loveliness and radiant beauty. The man of Patmos goes to the farthest length in making the material the servant of the spiritual. The sacred city has a right to all the shining and colorful brightness of rare jewels as a part of its own beauty. When the evil has been destroyed the good will remain in the cleansed and glorious beauty of the new and perfect world. When one thinks of the

fashion in which priceless jewels have been a characteristic part of the vanity and of the pretentious pomp and circumstance of the world the daring of this picture of the jewels on the wall of the holy city is all the more striking. Nothing but the evil is to be shut out of the glory of God's perfect town. It is said that when a famous architect was planning one of the loveliest churches in New York City he said: "This is not the spot for a monument. I

22 And I saw no temple therein: for the Lord God Almighty and the Lamb are the temple of it.

23 And the city had no need of the sun, neither of the moon, to shine in it: for the glory of God did lighten it, and the Lamb *is* the light thereof.

22 And I saw no temple in the city, for its temple is the Lord God the Almighty and the Lamb. 23 And the city has no need of sun or moon to shine upon it, for the glory of God is its light, and its lamp is the

single street may reflect the early belief that the Milky Way was a street running through the heavenly city.

D. Divine Glory of the City (21:22-27)

22. The exemplars of the heavenly city, both Jewish and Gentile, call for a temple; in fact, from the Jewish point of view the new temple was the main object; there would be no use for such a city unless it possessed one. In earlier passages of Revelation this same expectation has been reflected, in places stated quite explicitly, as in 3:12, "I will make him a pillar in the temple of my God," and in 7:15, where the martyrs will "serve him day and night within his temple." But despite such anticipations it is now stated explicitly that there was **no temple** in the New Jerusalem (**in the city** [RSV] is an explanatory addition), for **the Lord God the Almighty and the Lamb** would constitute the **temple.** The absence of the temple is wholly in keeping with the Christian view expressed in Heb. 9:23-28, that the sacrifice of Christ, made once and for all, has done away with all other sacrifice. This view is also reflected in Revelation, where Christ is spoken of as the slain Passover lamb by whose sacrificial blood the martyrs are redeemed (cf. 1:5; 5:9). Consequently, by a characteristic straining of the imagery God and the Lamb become a spiritual temple.

23. According to a prayer in the Apocalypse of Abraham 17, no light is needed in the heavenly dwelling places other than "the unspeakable splendour from the light of Thy countenance." Similarly, we learn from II Esdras 7:40-43 that in the day of judgment in the new age there will be no sun, moon, or stars, or any other light save "the splendor of the glory of the Most High." These passages may be based on the description of the glorified city in Isa. 60:1, 19, according to which Yahweh will be the glory and the light of the city overpowering the light of both sun and moon (cf. Isa. 24:23). Thus, in Revelation also there will be no sun or moon in the New Jerusalem, for **the glory of God is its light, and its lamp is the Lamb.** It may be that John has in mind here the contemporary astral theology and is affirming that the solar and lunar deities are now displaced by God and Christ. In any event, the city has divine significance; likewise, it has cosmic meaning as well, as did the heavenly cities in astro-religious

will make a jewel." The Christian use of beauty is a deep and noble theme.

22. The Temple of the Divine Presence.— With characteristic balance after glowing tribute to the material as an element in the city of perfection the man of Patmos goes on to say that there is no material temple, for the divine presence makes a material place of worship unnecessary. At the very center of worship the spiritual not only transcends the material but makes it unnecessary. Not even the most noble and beautiful temple stands between the soul and God. The members of the Society of Friends are so much impressed by this that even in the present world they build their worship about the invisible presence.

23. The Illumination of the Divine Presence. —The light of the divine presence makes the city radiant. With his characteristic and constant emphasis on the Lamb that was slain the man of Patmos tells us that the city's **lamp is the Lamb.** A light shines from the Cross which gives final illumination to the redeemed. A brilliant theologian who is overfond of abstractions has confessed annoyance with associating the power of Christianity with a particular time or place. Classical Christianity—and the book of Revelation expresses its insight—takes the contrary position. The eternal city itself receives an illumination which comes from the green hill far away. From the Cross the radiance gleaming adds more luster to the day.

24 And the nations of them which are saved shall walk in the light of it: and the kings of the earth do bring their glory and honor into it.

Lamb. 24 By its light shall the nations walk; and the kings of the earth shall bring their

thought, for apart from the lake of fire it embraces the entire cosmos; it is indeed the divine, perfect, eternal universe, combining both the new heaven and the new earth.

24-26. Among the characteristic views both of Jewish messianism and apocalypticism was the belief that the Gentiles would in time become converts to Judaism and worship Yahweh. This expectation is stated in I Enoch 10:21 as follows, "And all the children of men shall become righteous, and all nations shall offer adoration and shall praise me and shall worship me" (cf. Zech. 2:11; 8:23; Test. Levi 18:9; Test. Naph. 8:4; Test. Jud. 25:5). The opposing concept, viz., that the wicked would be punished forever, was more characteristic of apocalyptic literature, much of which came out of periods of dire oppression and persecution. It is the latter belief that has been so pronounced in Revelation up to this point: the nations had all been destroyed from the face of the earth, both before and following the millennium, and after the judgment they were sent to the fiery lake as idolaters for everlasting punishment there. But now, seemingly, the **nations** will appear and **walk** by the **light** of the city, and **the kings of the earth** will **bring their glory** into it, since its **gates** will not be **shut** during the **day;** which means that they will always be open, for there will be **no night there.** Also through these open gates they will bring **the glory and the honor of the nations.**

In order to avoid the inconsistency which this scene presents, the KJV has followed a poorly attested gloss, **And the nations of them which are saved,** but obviously this is no solution of the problem. How, then, may this glaring inconsistency, for such it is, be accounted for? Apparently it is due to a rather careless adaptation by John, either directly or indirectly through some apocalyptic source he may have been using, of Isa. 60:3, 11, verses from a chapter of Isaiah which is also reflected in vs. 23 (cf. Isa. 60:1, 19). The first verse, Isa. 60:3, reads,

> And nations shall come to your light,
>   and kings to the brightness of your rising,

while the second, Isa. 60:11, promises,

> Your gates shall be open continually;
>   day and night they shall not be shut;
> that men may bring to you the wealth of the nations,
>   with their kings led in procession.

The dependence of vss. 24-27, directly or indirectly, upon these two in Isaiah is quite evident; that John has failed to modify them to suit his own severe and unrelenting

---

24. The Far-Flung Illumination.—The picture now widens to include vast perspectives. We have had a picture of the destruction of evil nations; now we have a picture of good nations walking in the light of the Lord. There is no narrow exclusiveness which sees only a few individuals rescued from universal chaos. In the vision of the renewed world there is the picture of the cleansed and glorious nations; only as they are allied to wickedness are the nations destroyed. As the willing servants of the good God they are to walk in the divine light. Now we come to a picture which replaces

the dark and bitter gloom of the satirists of the world. In the place of the corrosive pessimism of Juvenal and his followers in many centuries we have the vision of the obedient nations walking in God's own light.

24. There Shall Be No Lost Good.—In one terrible picture after another we have seen the fate of wicked men and wicked states. Now that matter has been disposed of definitively and thoroughly. The man of Patmos tells us with great joy that **the kings of the earth shall bring their glory** into the city of perfection. All their good thoughts and good words and good deeds

25 And the gates of it shall not be shut at all by day: for there shall be no night there.

26 And they shall bring the glory and honor of the nations into it.

27 And there shall in no wise enter into it any thing that defileth, neither *whatsoever* worketh abomination, or *maketh* a lie; but they which are written in the Lamb's book of life.

glory into it, 25 and its gates shall never be shut by day — and there shall be no night there; 26 they shall bring into it the glory and the honor of the nations. 27 But nothing unclean shall enter it, nor any one who practices abomination or falsehood, but only those who are written in the Lamb's book of life.

views concerning the fate of the nations, presented throughout the rest of the book until now, is also apparent. Thus we are accorded another insight into the literary methods of the author. This also may serve to explain the otherwise difficult statement that the nations **bring their glory** into the city, instead of walking in its glory as well as by its light.

27. Still carrying out the contrast with harlot Babylon, whose cup was filled with "abominations and the impurities of her fornication" (17:4), **nothing unclean** can enter the New Jerusalem, nor can **any one who practices abomination or falsehood** (cf. Isa. 35:8; 52:1 LXX; Ezek. 44:9). Those who practiced these sins, of course, are by now in the lake of fire (cf. 21:8). As stated in the judgment scene and elsewhere only those

shall be gathered up and made a part of God's city. There shall be no lost good. Stringfellow Barr's book *The Pilgrimage of Western Man* [5] contains much that is wise and some rather definite foolishness. In moving over many centuries he does see a stream of good hope which must not be lost in the sand. The book of Revelation has a word of confirmation regarding the heritage of good pilgrims who would march toward the city of God.

25. The Hospitality of the Holy City.—There is a rich and warmhearted quality to the picture of the city of the open gates. It offers the gift of open doors to all pilgrims of the light. Whenever men have seen stars of hope in the night sky and have been willing to journey toward the birthplace of expectation they have belonged to the company of those who are welcomed with open gates to the city of light. Even the O.T. law is full of tenderness for the stranger; he is to be treated as the homeborn. In the perfect city there are no strangers; all who are willing to welcome the light belong to its life. One of the nobler characteristics of our time is a certain quality of understanding sympathy. Arthur F. Grimble's book *We Chose the Islands* [6] brings this quality to primitive people. When there are open gates to the city of light there is new hope for the world.

26. The Goal of Civilization.—We are still dealing with the positive side of the story. Nations have a glory which deserves to be made part of the golden city. Nations have an honor

which has a place in the city of God. Oswald Spengler presented some of the elements of the negative side of the great tale in *The Decline of the West.* [7] Ralph Tyler Flewelling attempted a brief reply in *The Survival of Western Culture.* [8] Toynbee has made a massive analysis in *A Study of History,* [9] raising many questions. Every age of course confronts the possibility of saying "Yes" to the good of life or of saying "No" to civilization. The book of Revelation sees the alternatives in the light of the will of God. And it visualizes a future in which civilization will have become one with the purposes of God, and the nations will bring every good gift they possess into the holy city.

27. The Great Exclusion.—Again the man of Patmos makes his perspective complete. The hospitality of the holy city is by no means to be a matter of gregarious and unethical friendliness. Those who have refused the divine cleansing are to be shut out; those whose very life is built on falsehood are to be excluded. The centuries as they passed had developed manifold and disintegrating abominations— those who practice them shall be shut out. The mighty voice of moral discrimination is never allowed to be silent. There is a terrible and unforgettable phrase about those who have sinned themselves away from God. That phrase applies here. God's verdict of exclusion is the

[5] New York: Harcourt, Brace & Co., 1949.
[6] New York: William Morrow, 1952.

[7] Tr. C. F. Atkinson (New York: Alfred A. Knopf, 1926-28).
[8] New York and London: Harper & Bros., 1943.
[9] London: Oxford University Press, 1935-54, 10 vols.

22 And he showed me a pure river of water of life, clear as crystal, proceeding out of the throne of God and of the Lamb.

22 Then he showed me the river of the water of life, bright as crystal, flowing from the throne of God and of the

---

whose names are **in the Lamb's book of life** will be permitted to go into the city to enjoy its glory and its blessings (cf. 3:5; 13:8; 17:8; 20:12, 15).

E. THE NEW GARDEN OF EDEN WITH THE RIVER AND TREE OF LIFE (22:1-5)

22:1-2. It was to be expected that the account in Genesis of the Garden of Eden, with its river divided into four streams, and its two trees, particularly the tree of life (Gen. 2:8-13; 3:22), should form the basis for both prophetic and apocalyptic expectations. Accordingly, we are not surprised to find predictions that the Garden of Eden would be reconstituted either in the messianic period of the prophets or in the new age of apocalyptic speculation. It was peculiarly adapted to the latter, for apocalypticism in positing a new age frequently taught that it would reproduce the newly created beginnings of the first. At times this view of a new Eden merged with that of a new Jerusalem (see Exeg. on 21:2a), but in other sources it was presented by itself, as in the Apocalypse of Abraham 21; II Enoch 8:1-8; Test. Levi 18:11; Apocalypse of Peter 16; II Esdras 2:12.

One of the earliest passages in which these two views are combined is Ezekiel's prophecy of the new temple in Ezek. 47:1-12. Evidently drawing upon the familiar story of Genesis, the prophet writes that he saw a great river with healing waters that originated under the altar in the temple. This river, in which multitudes of fish of great size lived, flowed to the Dead Sea, which it made fresh. On both banks were many trees, with leaves that never withered and fruit which was borne every month, because the trees were watered with the healing waters from the temple. The fruit of the trees was for food and the leaves were for healing.

It was from this prophetic picture of a restored Jerusalem that John derived his eschatological conception of a new Garden of Eden in the new age, and in the New Jerusalem. The river which he envisaged came **from the throne of God and of the**

---

confirmation of a verdict which they have already pronounced upon themselves. In Robert Browning's "Pippa Passes" one of the characters after a cruel murder talks of being "magnificent in sin." That illusion of satisfaction in evil clouds the very thoughts of wicked men. The man of Patmos cannot allow us to forget what happens to those who make evil their good.

27. The Cross and the Promise of Life.—There is the profoundest meaning in the fact that the book of human destiny is **the Lamb's book of life.** That is, it is the book of one who loved men enough to die for them. Sometimes we are asked to judge with eyes which have seen the Cross. The final judgment is the verdict of one whose eyes looked out upon humanity from the Cross. Only those who say "No" to the love which speaks from the Cross are refused a place in the Lamb's book of life. It is a book of infinite compassion, of the tenderest love. Love must have died in the man who says "No" to the cross. The desire for goodness must have perished in one who makes the great

refusal. The desire to be forgiven must have come to an end in the man who can look unmoved at Calvary. So it comes about that the Lamb's book of life, the book of the last judgment, is the tenderest book in all the world. Unless there is the great refusal, in "the heart you only keep your oxen in, the great love finds a place to sleep, and enters in."

22:1. The Life-Giving River.—Rivers have a way of flowing through history. In the old, old world the Euphrates and the Nile; then much later the Danube and the Rhine. The Euphrates, the Nile, and very especially the Jordan, appear in the Scriptures. Then there are symbolic rivers, e.g., in Ezekiel there is the river which flows from the temple and sweetens the Dead Sea. Now at the end of the book of Revelation we have the life-giving river which flows **through the . . . city.** It is very beautiful, shining like crystal. It flows **from the throne of God.** The very streets of the city are transformed by this life-giving loveliness. Much of the book of Revelation has had to do with

2 In the midst of the street of it, and on either side of the river, *was there* the tree of life, which bare twelve *manner of* fruits, *and* yielded her fruit every month: and the leaves of the tree *were* for the healing of the nations.

3 And there shall be no more curse: but the throne of God and of the Lamb shall be in it; and his servants shall serve him:

Lamb [2] through the middle of the street of the city; also, on either side of the river, the tree of life [r] with its twelve kinds of fruit, yielding its fruit each month; and the leaves of the tree were for the healing of the nations. [3] There shall no more be anything accursed, but the throne of God and of the Lamb shall be in it, and his servants shall

[r] Or *the Lamb. In the midst of the street of the city, and on either side of the river, was the tree of life, etc.*

Lamb, not from the altar in the temple, for of course there was no longer a temple (cf. 21:22). In either case, however, the source was divine. This river, which flowed down **the middle of the street of the city** (like the Milky Way?) contained **the water of life,** a concept similar to that of the healing stream that came from the altar in Ezekiel. This religious symbolism of life-giving water is too widespread to need comment. In Revelation it had earlier been promised that the Lamb would guide the martyrs "to springs of living water" (7:17), a prospect that is reaffirmed by God himself in his speech from the throne (21:6). Now the supernatural river of living water itself is seen as it flows from the throne.

The religious figure of a tree of life is also a very common one. According to the description of the tree of life in II Enoch 8:3-4, it is ineffably good and fragrant, is adorned more than any other living thing, is golden, vermilion, and fiery in appearance, and covers everything. The promise was made to the martyr in the letter to the church at Ephesus that Christ would permit him "to eat of the tree of life" in the coming paradise (2:7). In a realization of this promised reward **the tree of life** (apparently used collectively to include a number of trees) was seen on both sides **of the river.** It bore **twelve kinds of fruit,** and like the trees in Ezekiel, it yielded fruit monthly. Whether all kinds were produced each month, or a different fruit for each, cannot be determined. Also, as in Ezekiel, its **leaves** had healing properties, for they were **for the healing of the nations.** The word **nations** in this context causes some difficulty unless it is taken to mean the martyrs who are described in 7:9 as coming from every nation, tribe, people, and tongue. Otherwise the inconsistency of 21:26 is repeated.

3. Nothing **accursed,** i.e., no execrable person or thing under the anathema or ban of God, will be permitted in the city (cf. Zech. 14:11). There will be no desecration of any

---

death and destruction, now the very words pulsate with life.

2. *The Tree of Exhaustless Productiveness.*— In Norse mythology the Igdrasil is the tree of the universe. In the Genesis story the garden of Eden contained trees for food and the tree of life whose fruit was forbidden. In the holy city the fruit of **the tree of life** is accessible to everyone. It produces its fruit twelve times a year, and on the branches of the same tree are **twelve kinds of fruit.** The picture is one of rich variety and constant productivity. There are no prohibitions in the holy city, for the minds of the dwellers in that sacred town have become one with the mind and the will of God. Their very desires have been lifted to the level of the divine purpose.

2. *The Work of Healing.*—The taking of the Hippocratic oath by those receiving the Doctor of Medicine degree reminds us that the profession of healing is a very ancient one with a very ancient code. In the book of Revelation the healing leaves as well as the nourishing food are taken straight from the book of Ezekiel. Men's work of healing is often inadequate because of lack of knowledge; it has performed great services but there are limits to its power. In the perfect city the work of healing is to be complete. There is no human need to which the ministry of the golden city will not be adequate.

3-4. *Life in the Perfect City.*—We are now in a region to which the words, "Eye hath not seen, nor ear heard, . . . the things which God hath prepared" (I Cor. 2:9), must be kept in mind. Even words of revelation can only suggest the richness and the amplitude of the great fulfillment. It is enough to know that it will

4 And they shall see his face; and his name *shall be* in their foreheads.

5 And there shall be no night there; and they need no candle, neither light of the sun; for the Lord God giveth them light: and they shall reign for ever and ever.

worship him; 4 they shall see his face, and his name shall be on their foreheads. 5 And night shall be no more; they need no light of lamp or sun, for the Lord God will be their light, and they shall reign for ever and ever.

---

kind allowed, for the holy **throne of God and of the Lamb** will be there. A proleptic view of the martyrs before God's throne serving or worshiping him night and day was given in 7:15; this prospect of reward now finds its fulfillment in the new age.

4. In the first age no one could see God's face, for he was too holy for mere mortal to look at and live (Exod. 33:20). But in the new age the situation is changed. Thus, in II Esdras 7:98 it is stated that the seventh and highest reward for the righteous following the judgment will be the joy of beholding "the face of him whom in their lifetime they served." So in Revelation, the *summum bonum* is the beatific vision of God which his servants will experience. Another earlier assurance, that God's name would be inscribed on the martyrs to show that they are his (cf. 3:12), is reaffirmed in the second part of this verse.

5. This verse is a rephrasing, for the most part, of statements previously made in 21:23, 25; with God in the city there will be no need of the **sun**; there will be **light** day and night. However, no mention is made here of the Lamb as a "lamp" as in 21:23. The brief statement that the servants of God are to **reign for ever and ever** is a further assurance of their eternal bliss in the New Jerusalem, and may have been intended to suggest that while their reign in the millennium was but for a thousand years (cf. 20:6), their reign with God and Christ in the new age will be forever. Both the limited and the eternal reign are fulfillments of a promise made to the martyrs in the first part of Revelation (3:21; cf. 1:6; 5:10). An almost identical promise that the saints will dwell with God and Christ eternally is found in I Enoch 105:2, "For I and my Son will be united with them forever in the paths of uprightness in their lives; and ye shall have peace: rejoice, ye children of uprightness. Amen."

The entire apocalyptic concept of the new Eden and Zion in the age to come is summarized in II Esdras 8:52-58 in a way that bears repeating: "For unto you Paradise is opened, the tree of life is planted, the future age is prepared, plenty is provided, a city is built, a rest is appointed, good works perfected, and wisdom perfected beforehand. The root of evil is sealed up for you, infirmity is extinct, and death is hidden; Hades and corruption have fled away into oblivion, sorrows have passed away, and finally the treasure of immortality is displayed. Therefore, do not inquire any more concerning the multitude of those who perish; for though they had received liberty they despised the Most High and had contempt for his Law and forsook his ways. Moreover, they have

---

all be as satisfying as the endless and exhaustless resources of God. There will be perfect worship flowering out into perfect service. The old conception was that no man could see God and live; in the city of perfection the very sight of the face of God will be life giving. In sentence after sentence the limitations of time are transcended in the fulfillment of eternity. The N.T. nobly expresses the transforming power of the vision of God: "We shall be like him, for we shall see him as he is" (I John 3:2).

5. *No More Invading Darkness.*—Perhaps man's oldest fear is the fear of what may happen in the dark. The story of warfare is full of surprise attacks in the night, the famous story

of the geese who saved Rome from attack in the night being one of a thousand. Foes plan to do their deadly work in the blackness of the night. In the perfect city there is no succession of light and darkness—there is perpetual light, and that light is as unchangeable as God himself for **the Lord God will be their light.** There are no deeds of darkness for there is no darkness in which such deeds can be done. And even more deeply there are no dark minds which would plan dark deeds for God's light has completely conquered the mind of man.

5. *Serving and Reigning.*—The glorious eighth psalm pictures man under God but having dominion over all the works of the divine

6 And he said unto me, These sayings *are* faithful and true: and the Lord God of the holy prophets sent his angel to show unto his servants the things which must shortly be done.

7 Behold, I come quickly: blessed *is* he that keepeth the sayings of the prophecy of this book.

6 And he said to me, "These words are trustworthy and true. And the Lord, the God of the spirits of the prophets, has sent his angel to show his servants what must soon take place. 7 And behold, I am coming soon."

Blessed is he who keeps the words of the prophecy of this book.

---

trodden his saints under foot, and said in their heart that there is no God, even though they knew that they must die." Here in a single paragraph is substantially a Jewish outline of the same eschatological pattern seen in Revelation, written at or about the same time—another indication that John was representative of the apocalyptic thinking of his day.

XII. Epilogue (22:6-21)

The epilogue is a somewhat disjointed section, largely composed of final assurances and exhortations. In some places it is difficult to determine just who the speaker is supposed to be. Consequently various rearrangements of the text have been suggested in order to make it more coherent. Thus, in his translation Moffatt has worked out the following sequence of verses: 8-9, 6-7, 10-11, 14-16, 13, 12, 17-21. This does provide a better connection of thought, but is based on a presupposition that John originally wrote these verses in an orderly sequence which some careless scribe or editor has disrupted. Charles was of the opinion that from 20:4 to the end there was a great deal of dislocation, causing incoherence and self-contradiction, which he attributed to the untimely death of the author, either through natural causes or as a martyr, before he had completed his book. However, he had left notes and other materials which a zealous but unintelligent disciple had used in finishing his master's work. Consequently, in his commentary Charles has done a good deal of rearranging in the concluding chapters (*Revelation of St. John*, II, 144-54). Probably the difficulty is traceable to another cause, viz., that throughout the epilogue the writer has not always been as careful as he might have been in assigning his words to the different dramatis personae. Accordingly, the discussion will follow the order of the verses as given in the text.

6. The speaker of this verse is not identified: he may be Christ, as in the next verse, or he may be the angelic guide. The verse as a whole is a guarantee of the divine inspiration of the book. The first part, **These words are trustworthy and true,** repeats the words of assurance spoken by God from his throne in 21:5. The second part refers to the opening verse of Revelation, "The revelation of Jesus Christ, which God gave him to show to his servants what must soon take place; and he made it known by sending his angel to his servant John" (1:1). The claim was also made in the opening verse of I Enoch that the book was a vision of the Holy One in the heavens which angels had revealed to Enoch. Emphasis is placed upon the immediacy of the coming consummation of this age as well as upon the divine origin of the apocalyptic predictions.

7. If the angel is the speaker in the preceding verse, then Jesus interrupts to emphasize that the time is short by exclaiming, **And behold, I am coming soon.** The belief that his second advent was near at hand, or imminent, was an important factor in strengthening Christians in times of trouble and persecution. The next sentence, the sixth beatitude in Revelation, is a reiteration of the first beatitude which promises that "he who reads aloud

---

hand. In the picture of man in the perfect city he is seen serving and reigning forever, a king under the King of kings, a lord under the Lord of lords. No sour pessimism invades the final picture of the dignity of man. He owes

everything to God; but in the perfect city what he very especially owes to God is a throne. All this is under the authority of the Lamb that was slain, who by his death has made possible the final royalty of man. He is restored to that

8 And I John saw these things, and heard *them*. And when I had heard and seen, I fell down to worship before the feet of the angel which showed me these things.

9 Then saith he unto me, See *thou do it* not: for I am thy fellow servant, and of thy brethren the prophets, and of them which keep the sayings of this book: worship God.

10 And he saith unto me, Seal not the sayings of the prophecy of this book: for the time is at hand.

11 He that is unjust, let him be unjust still: and he which is filthy, let him be filthy still: and he that is righteous, let him

8 I John am he who heard and saw these things. And when I heard and saw them, I fell down to worship at the feet of the angel who showed them to me; 9 but he said to me, "You must not do that! I am a fellow servant with you and your brethren the prophets, and with those who keep the words of this book. Worship God."

10 And he said to me, "Do not seal up the words of the prophecy of this book, for the time is near. 11 Let the evildoer still do evil, and the filthy still be filthy, and the

---

the words of the prophecy," and those who hear them read, "and who keep what is written therein" are blessed (1:3). By these means John wishes his reading and listening public to believe that what he has written is practically scriptural in its authority.

8-9. As in 1:9, the author identifies himself by name as a certain **John,** to whom these various revelations which comprise his book were made. Unfortunately he does not add to the scanty information concerning himself which he gave in ch. 1. The brief scene that follows, in which John is reproved by his angel mentor for attempting to worship him since they are fellow servants, is a duplication of the episode related in 19:10, as is the adjuration, **Worship God.**

10. When an apocalypse is a pseudepigraph in which the author takes the name of someone who lived years before his time, a natural reaction of the reader would be to wonder why the book had not been known earlier. To anticipate such questions the author might resort to the device of claiming that the ancient seer had been ordered to seal up his book so that it would not be read until the proper time, which might be centuries later. Thus, we find "Daniel" must seal his book up to "the time of the end" (Dan. 12:4, 9; cf. 8:26). For much the same reason "Enoch" states that what he had learned about the future from the angels was not for his generation, but for a remote time that was to come (I Enoch 1:2; cf. 104:13). According to the prologue, the Apocalypse of Paul, purporting to relate what Paul saw and heard while in the third heaven, but could not reveal at the time (II Cor. 12:2-4), was supposedly hidden by the apostle in the foundations of his house at Tarsus. It was not discovered and published until the end of the fourth century, when at the direction of an angel the man who at that time lived in Paul's dwelling dug it up and gave it to the emperor Theodosius. But this was not true of Revelation; although John could not write what he heard the seven thunders say (10:4), he was commanded to make the rest of what he saw and heard known at once, **for the time is near**—further evidence of the urgency of his message.

11. The obdurate, unrepentant attitude of the **evildoer** and the **filthy,** which had been noted before (cf. 2:21; 9:20; 16:9, 11), is mentioned once more. On the other hand,

---

for which God made him, by the mighty act of Redemption. And even this restoration is transcended in the glory of the golden city.

9. *Only the Highest to Receive Adoration.*— Once more we are reminded that only God is to be met with a bended knee. Even the high must not be given the place of the highest—even the good must not be given the place of the

best. The tragedy of mistaken loyalties is one of the great tragedies of the world. Too late Wolsey realized that he had given to his king, Henry VIII, what belonged only to God.

11. *The Challenge of Finality.*—In the O.T. the darkest prophecies of doom are meant to startle men into repentance. So the words hurled at men about the finality of their choice

be righteous still: and he that is holy, let him be holy still.

12 And, behold, I come quickly; and my reward *is* with me, to give every man according as his work shall be.

13 I am Alpha and Omega, the beginning and the end, the first and the last.

14 Blessed *are* they that do his commandments, that they may have right to the tree of life, and may enter in through the gates into the city.

righteous still do right, and the holy still be holy."

12 "Behold, I am coming soon, bringing my recompense, to repay every one for what he has done. **13** I am the Alpha and the Omega, the first and the last, the beginning and the end."

14 Blessed are those who wash their robes,*s* that they may have the right to the tree of life and that they may enter the city

s Other ancient authorities read *do his commandments.*

---

while determinism is basic to John's apocalyptic thinking, and the saved are chosen or elected, there is still the possibility that their names may be erased from the book of life (cf. 3:5); hence this exhortation to **the righteous** and **the holy** to continue in the way of righteousness and holiness.

12a. Christ again enters the scene to announce that he is **coming soon.** It cannot be emphasized too strongly that John expected the establishment of Christ's millennial reign to occur very shortly in his own lifetime. He had no expectation that this age of human history would last even a generation, to say nothing of centuries. The immediacy of the Second Coming is the burden of his exhortation from the very beginning to the end of the book.

12b. It was stated in connection with the judgment scene (cf. 20:12) that for John it is God, not Christ, who is to be the final judge. In the admonition given now by Christ that he will **repay every one** according to his deeds (for the doctrine of works see Exeg. on 14:13), it would seem that he has assumed the function of judging, just as he takes the title of God in the next verse. However, despite the seeming implications of this statement, there can be no doubt that for John it is God, not Christ, who is to be the final judge of all mankind.

13. Christ now claims the title which God used with reference to himself in 21:6, with the addition of a designation, **the first and the last,** which he had used in his first appearance to John in 1:17 (cf. 2:8): in the new age the distinction between Christ and God will not be important or even clear.

14. This seventh and last beatitude presents a difficult textual problem. Some ancient authorities read **that do his commandments** (KJV) while others have **who wash their robes** (RSV). Either is quite in harmony with the rest of Revelation. As for the former, according to 14:12-13 (cf. 12:17), the saints who are to be rewarded for their good works are "those who keep the commandments of God." On the other hand, in 7:14-17 (cf. 3:4) we are told that those who "have washed their robes and made them white in the blood of the Lamb," i.e., the martyrs, are to be before God's throne, serving him day and

---

are meant to rouse torpid minds and to provide a last opportunity for repentance. The picture remains true of the final choices. And it gives one more moment of probation on the edge of finality. Great evangelists have well understood the secret of painting the picture of the land of no return in such a way that men set about returning at once.

12-13. The Great Presence.—The man of Patmos is now back in the world from which he had been caught up for his overwhelming visions. Clearly enough he sees now that this world does not belong to Rome or to the Ro-

man emperor. Its master is the one who is **the Alpha and the Omega, the first and the last, the beginning and the end.** That great master of life promises to enter the world where men dwell in such moral and spiritual confusion in the very fullness of power. The Deists thought that God had made the world and then had left it to spin in its own fashion—they built their view of life on the absent God. The book of Revelation sees not the great absence but the great Presence.

14. Cleansing.—The soiled life has no place in the stainless city. But the great act of cleans-

15 For without *are* dogs, and sorcerers, and whoremongers, and murderers, and idolaters, and whosoever loveth and maketh a lie.

16 I Jesus have sent mine angel to testify unto you these things in the churches. I am the root and the offspring of David, *and* the bright and morning star.

by the gates. 15 Outside are the dogs and sorcerers and fornicators and murderers and idolaters, and every one who loves and practices falsehood.

16 "I Jesus have sent my angel to you with this testimony for the churches. I am the root and the offspring of David, the bright morning star."

---

night, and will receive other rewards which are realized in the final scenes. But no matter which reading is followed—and the correct decision is difficult if not impossible—the martyrs are the objects of this seventh beatitude.

They are also the ones who by reason of their martyrdom **have the right to the tree of life.** This is in keeping with promises in other sources that only the elect, the faithful, the righteous, may eat from this tree of life (cf. I Enoch 25:4-5; II Esdras 8:52; Test. Levi 18:11) and reinforces the prospect of reward offered to the conqueror or martyr in the first letter to the churches (2:7; cf. 22:2). Likewise, as in 21:27, only those whose names are in the book of life have access to the city, so here only the martyrs have the right to **enter the city by the gates.**

15. It has frequently been assumed from this verse that those who are described as **dogs and sorcerers and fornicators and murderers and idolaters,** and those who love and practice **falsehood,** are just outside the city gates vainly seeking admission. This, however, is to overlook 21:8, where these same individuals (**dogs** is the only new epithet) were consigned to the fiery lake for everlasting torment and punishment for their sins. **Outside,** therefore, involves a reference to the lake of fire.

16. Looking back again to the beginning of the book, particularly to the letters to the churches in chs. 2–3, John writes that Jesus has once more given his guarantee to this book, **this testimony for the churches,** which he has mediated through his angel (cf. vs. 6; 1:1); although, strictly speaking, there have been other means of mediation as well. By this allusion to the letter corpus John indicates that the book as a whole is in the nature of a letter.

The Lamb was described in 5:5 as "the Lion of the tribe of Judah, the Root of David," who had conquered, a designation which is echoed in part in this verse. It must be recognized, however, that apart from his sacrificial yet conquering death, the earthly, human Jesus is not of paramount interest to this writer; attention is centered mainly

---

ing will prepare men to walk the streets of the perfect city and to partake of its food. It is something God does. And yet in a sense it is something man does, for man himself must plunge into the waters of cleansing. There had been many inadequate views of a sacred bath. The cult of Mithra had given such an idea to many a Roman soldier. What the ethnic cults had failed to give, Christianity offered in abundance.

15. *Not Included.*—There is one final picture of wicked and foul souls **outside** the city gates. Nothing has been sacred to them, they have misused everything which they touched. They are no longer human; they are subhuman. They are no longer men; they are **dogs.** They not only tell **falsehoods;** they are living lies. So the moral distinctions are seen with clarity to the very end. The almost unreadable ac-

counts of the cruelties practiced in the concentration camps bring all this home. But we must not forget that the book of Revelation is speaking of men's cruelty to their own minds and to their own bodies and to their own souls as well as to their fellow men.

16. *The Star of Joyous Expectation.*—William Wordsworth in one of his sonnets paid a memorable tribute to John Milton:

Thy soul was like a Star, and dwelt apart:
Thou hadst a voice whose sound was like the sea:
Pure as the naked heavens, majestic, free,
So didst thou travel on life's common way,
In cheerful godliness; and yet thy heart
The lowliest duties on herself did lay.[1]

These are noble and gracious words, spoken of a great man. But we appreciate the lonely

---
[1] "Milton! thou shouldst be living at this hour."

17 And the Spirit and the bride say, Come. And let him that heareth say, Come. And let him that is athirst come. And whosoever will, let him take the water of life freely.

17 The Spirit and the Bride say, "Come." And let him who hears say, "Come." And let him who is thirsty come, let him who desires take the water of life without price.

---

on the transcendent, glorified, heavenly Christ conceived of in terms of the imagery found in I Enoch and other apocalyptic sources.

The final promise to the church at Thyatira was that Christ would give the conqueror, the martyr, "the morning star" (2:28), which was a symbol of a new day and of immortality. Now, in a realization of this promise, Christ identifies himself as **the bright morning star** which the faithful will see in the new age. Save for the explicit identity of the morning star with Christ, the imagery is not too different from that used later in II Pet. 1:19b, "You will do well to pay attention to this as to a lamp shining in a dark place, until the day dawns and the morning star rises in your hearts."

17. Turning now from the picture of the future age to the plight of his fellow Christians, who like himself are oppressed and persecuted, John writes, **The Spirit and the Bride say, "Come."** The Spirit is that divine manifestation different from, but intimately related to, Christ mentioned in the close of each of the seven letters in connection with the promises to the martyrs, as in 2:7, "He who has an ear, let him hear what the Spirit says to the churches." Now that the preparations for the end have been made, with everything in readiness for the marriage between the Lamb and his bride, the Spirit and the bride call upon Christ to make his appearance. Also, echoing a phrase in the formula concluding each letter to the churches, "He who has an ear, let him hear," they add, **And let him who hears say, "Come."** Apparently, as in the letters, this is an appeal to the martyrs-designate. In concluding their exhortation they invite **him who is thirsty** to partake freely of **the water of life,** which is another fulfillment of the reward offered the martyr in 7:17 (cf. 21:6; 22:1).

---

splendor of our Lord's position all the more when we see how far these words about a star which dwelt apart fall short of describing him. He did not dwell apart; he came to be the promise of a new day for men. The future belonged to him, and it was to be a glorious and radiant future. Like the morning star he announced the shining brightness of a day to be. Only Christianity fills the future with light.

17. The Glorious Invitation.—The eighth-century Chinese poet Tu Fu, writing of the sacred mountain Tai Shan, said:

I open my breast toward widening clouds,
And I strain my sight after birds flying home . . . .
When shall I climb to the top and hold
All mountains in a single glance!

In a sense the book of Revelation can be said to view all mountains in a single glance. They are mountains of eternity and not merely mountains of time. The man of Patmos from the perspective of eternity has seen the meaning of eternity and of time. From beyond the world of choices he has viewed the results of choices; now he is back in his own world again. It is a world where men are still choosing. With a

great thrill he realizes that it is still possible to say "Yes" to God. So he breaks out with the great invitation. It is the climax of the N.T. and of the Holy Scriptures. **The Spirit and the Bride say "Come."** God himself invites men and the Church joyously extends the invitation. Like glorious bells of joy the invitation rings out.

17. Passing On the Invitation.—Everyone who hears of the glad tidings is asked to spread the news. We have a sense of numberless human voices repeating: "God has invited men! God has invited men!" The spreading of news is one of the most fascinating things in the world. The spreading of the best news of all is the story of a vast contagion of goodness. It is said that in early days traveling salesmen with the packs on their backs used to display their wares to interested little circles and then, after the sales were made, to pour into fascinated ears the tale of how Christ had come to call men to God. Everyone with a tongue could be a divine courier.

17. Unfulfilled Longing.—If everyone who thirsts is invited it means that all are invited, for every human being thirsts for that which only God can supply. God writes no instincts

18 For I testify unto every man that heareth the words of the prophecy of this book, If any man shall add unto these things, God shall add unto him the plagues that are written in this book:

19 And if any man shall take away from the words of the book of this prophecy, God shall take away his part out of the book of life, and out of the holy city, and *from* the things which are written in this book.

18 I warn every one who hears the words of the prophecy of this book: if any one adds to them, God will add to him the plagues described in this book, 19 and if any one takes away from the words of the book of this prophecy, God will take away his share in the tree of life and in the holy city, which are described in this book.

Possibly it may be charged that the rewards for the martyr have been overemphasized in the interpretation of the book as a whole, and in the picture of the New Jerusalem and the new Eden in particular. However, it is not the interpreter who has provided this emphasis, but John himself. He apparently has paid little attention, perhaps none at all, to the fate of those Christians who were neither apostates nor martyrs. By linking these final chapters with the letters to the churches, which contain promise of reward to the martyrs, he has shown that the new age, as well as the millennium, is for those who are to die as Christian martyrs for their refusal to worship the Roman emperor and the empire. In this his eschatology is similar to that of Daniel, which apparently teaches eternal rewards to the very righteous, the martyrs, and eternal punishments for the wicked, the apostates and persecutors, without any provision for those who come in between these two categories (Dan. 12:2-3; cf. I Enoch 90:33; II Macc. 7:9, 14, 23).

18-19. The speaker of this cursing colophon may be Christ, as some maintain, but more probably the words are intended to be taken as those of the author. A warning or curse to prevent any alterations in a book was not uncommon in ancient times. Irenaeus, toward the end of the second century, appended such a curse to a book he had written against heretics, adjuring copyists to make no changes "by our Lord Jesus Christ, by his glorious advent when he comes to judge the living and the dead" (Eusebius *Church History* V. 20. 2). Ironically enough, the curse is about all that remains of this particular book. The author of Deuteronomy, a work that purports to be the revelation of God to Moses, includes two solemn warnings against any additions or omissions (Deut. 4:2; 12:32). According to the apocryphal account of the translation of the LXX, the assembly of Jews pronounced a curse upon anyone who altered it in any way (Letter of Aristeas 310-11). A strict warning, but not a curse, given with the knowledge that it would be disregarded, was written in the conclusion of I Enoch (104:9-13). In a much stronger statement the author of II Enoch pronounces a terrible judgment upon him who rejects his book, but a blessing on him who accepts it, for he will be released on the Day of Judgment (48:6-9). A similar view is found in II Pet. 3:16, where it is said that certain heretics have twisted Paul's letters, as they did the other scriptures, to "their own destruction."

---

in human beings without providing for their satisfaction. For the deepest desire of all—the thirst for God—he has provided the deepest satisfaction. So the eager and joyous hymn,

Send the proclamation over vale and hill; . . .
Whosoever will may come,[2]

exactly expresses the climactic word of the N.T.

[2] "Whosoever Will."

17. The Free Gift.—Whoever chooses to do so, let him **take the water of life without price.** The Pope in the great poem, "The Ring and the Book," which is the noblest achievement of Robert Browning, sums everything up by saying: "Life's business being just the terrible choice." It is a terrible choice; great stakes are involved. It is a free choice; it is a universal choice; the way is open to all human feet. And there stands the fountain of life like a waiting friend. "Whosoever!"

20 He which testifieth these things saith, Surely I come quickly: Amen. Even so, come, Lord Jesus.

21 The grace of our Lord Jesus Christ *be* with you all. Amen.

20 He who testifies to these things says, "Surely I am coming soon." Amen. Come, Lord Jesus!

21 The grace of the Lord Jesus be with all the saints[t]. Amen.

[t] Other ancient authorities omit *all;* others omit *the saints.*

It has been noted before that John not only wants his book to be considered a divinely revealed prophecy, but that he also would like to have it placed on a par with the books of the O.T. (cf. 1:3). Accordingly, the first and last of the beatitudes are pronounced on those who consider it as such and who are controlled by its teachings (1:3; 22:7). If, in contrast to these, anyone takes the prophecy lightly and **adds** anything to it, God himself **will add to him the plagues** that are written in it; further, if anyone **takes away** any of its words, God will deprive him of **his share in the tree of life and in the holy city** as these have been depicted. Surely, it would take a foolhardy soul to disregard these dire warnings; yet no book of the N.T. has suffered more alterations at the hands of scribes and more misinterpretations and distortions than Revelation.

20. For the third time in this final chapter Christ gives his solemn assurance that he is **coming soon** (cf. vss. 7 and 12). The rest of the verse, like so many of the passages in Revelation, suggests a liturgical origin. Paul, in the conclusion of one of his letters, uses what may have been a cultic ejaculation, "If any man love not the Lord Jesus Christ, let him be Anathema. Maranatha" (I Cor. 16:22). The Aramaic phrase, which has a sound similar to that of the Greek "anathema" means "Our Lord, come!" Its liturgical usage in the early church is attested by the Didache, a church manual that was composed not long after Revelation, if it was not contemporary with it. In this work, in connection with directions for the celebration of the Lord's Supper, appears a Eucharistic prayer which concludes with an invitation: "If any man be holy, let him come! if any man be not, let him repent: Maranatha, Amen" (Did. 10:6). This same liturgical phrase, with the "Amen" first and the Aramaic "Maranatha" translated into Greek, is now used by John in a purely eschatological sense to express the ardent hope of the author and his first readers that the Lord would soon come. Only here and in the next verse in Revelation is Jesus called **Lord Jesus.**

21. In ending his letters Paul used a characteristic epistolary formula, e.g., immediately after writing "Maranatha," Paul concluded I Corinthians as follows: "The grace of the Lord Jesus be with you. My love be with you all in Christ Jesus. Amen" (I Cor. 16:23-24). Neither the individual letters in the first part of Revelation nor the letter corpus as a whole has what might be termed an epistolary conclusion. The suggestion has been made that this omission may have been due to the author's desire that his entire book of prophecy be considered a letter to the churches, and that in line with this expectation he saved the epistolary conclusion for the end of the book. Accordingly, in

---

20. *The Insatiable Longing.*—Everything is included in the triumphant presence of the living Christ. That, to the man of Patmos, means the fulfillment of all hope, the realization of all aspirations, the amplitude of blessedness, the possession of eternal joy. God had said "Come" to men. In the man of Patmos a voice from humanity full of wistful longing says "Come" to Christ. We leave the lonely figure with eternity in his heart and high expectation filling his mind.

> Jesus, the very thought of Thee
> With sweetness fills my breast,
> But sweeter far Thy face to see,
> And in Thy presence rest!

> Jesus, our only joy be Thou
> As Thou our prize wilt be:
> Jesus, be Thou our glory now,
> And through eternity.[3]

So from the man of Patmos we move to the eager expectation of Bernard of Clairvaux. Then we look into our own hearts.

21. *The Religion of Grace.*—So the curtain falls. And if we ask in deep concern what is the deep and central meaning of it all the answer comes in the last golden words: **The grace of the Lord Jesus.** Toward this the O.T. moves;

[3] Hymn, "Jesus, the very thought of Thee."

this final verse there is a conclusion which, despite some minor variations in the text, is essentially an abbreviated form of the one used in the end of I Corinthians, **The grace of the Lord Jesus be with all the saints. Amen.**

this the N.T. proclaims. And with this word the book of Revelation ends. *The Private Devotions of Lancelot Andrewes,*[4] unsurpassed as the expression of the human soul in its meeting with God, may be said to be a little book of the grace of God. On the last birthday of his life Samuel Johnson, seventy-five years of age and with less than three months to live, wrote

[4] Tr. John Henry Newman (New York and Nashville: Abingdon-Cokesbury Press, 1950).

a revealing prayer whose characteristic words are "O my gracious God." None of his brilliant achievements in the world of men are in his mind. The man stands alone with God and with deep and humble joy finds God to be a God of grace. In all ages the deepest word in Christian devotion is the grace of Christ. In all hours of awakening the greatest inspiration to action is that grace which speaks to us from both a cross and a throne.

THE MESSAGE OF THE BOOK OF REVELATION

There are many possible approaches to the study and the interpretation of Revelation. It has the profoundest kinships with various writings of the same type within the Christian and the Jewish traditions and beyond. Many scholars of competence with regard to a vast body of such material have written with much skill of assured and of possible connections. The student of the book will be in debt to them constantly and in many ways.

There are a number of questions involved in another and quite different approach. Revelation came right out of the heart of the Christian community. It spoke so deeply to Christian consciousness that, though not without difficulty, it obtained its secure place in the N.T. canon. It has spoken a living Christian word to every generation of Christians since it was written. What are the qualities, we may ask, which make it a Christian book? What are the methods by which it turns its manifold and sometimes bizarre materials to Christian uses? How are even the mythological elements turned to a Christian purpose? In just what fashion do the truths and sanctions of classical Christianity master the rich and opulent symbolism? What principles emerge of such significance that they are relevant not only to the century when the book was written but to every century since? How does it speak to men today, warming the heart, quickening the imagination, sharpening the moral and spiritual judgment, and bringing comfort and inspiration to the quiet reader wherever he may be found? It is such questions as these which we shall try to answer.

Numbers of men of varied religions and races and nations and cultures had listened to a new and compelling word, and had become Christians. Their experience with the new faith was

to make new men of them. That faith was to go through their lives with transforming power. But they did not come under its influence with empty minds or with empty lives. Their whole past spoke to them in a thousand ways. Their minds were full of pictures which came from old religions. Their hearts were full of passions which came from old ways of living. Some of these the new faith could make its own and could completely appropriate. Some it must utterly cast out. Old forms of thinking and of using the imagination, such as those represented by apocalypse, were familiar to many. How very familiar they were is illustrated by the fact that they could be used for conveying the subtle and overwhelming message of Revelation. The apocalyptic mood must have captured the mind of multitudes of Christians before this book could ever have been written. The apocalyptic mind had given them an alphabet by which the words in the last book of the N.T. could be spelled out. If we could understand the minds of those who first read these pages, it would at once become easier for us to understand what is written here. But if old apocalyptic thoughts and writings provided the mental framework, they must not be supposed to contribute the definitive and essential meaning. It was the astonishing power of the new religion to take over the old thoughts and writings and make them the vehicle of its mighty message. This it did in the most masterful fashion, and the result is often the complete transforming of the material. One of the most fascinating tasks of N.T. study is just the investigation of the fashion in which Christianity by a mighty act of eminent domain turned old thoughts and conceptions and images to its own uses.

By the time Revelation was written, Christianity itself had become a living tradition, working its way through the texture of the lives of its votaries. Certain facts and truths were not only accepted; they were glorified by the richness of a great adoration. At the very thought of them Christians were ready to burst into song. We find this mood in the apostle Paul. It becomes commanding in Revelation. There is much tragedy. There is more glory. We are constantly hearing bursts of heavenly music. It is this rapture which changes old materials and makes them into something new. The new religion has given to Christians the environment in which they live. They can retreat into this environment of the mind and the spirit, and so can escape the threatening and evil environment of the world. They believe with all their minds and hearts in one great God of perfect goodness and perfect truth and perfect strength. He has come to the world in Jesus Christ, who has all the authority of God and all the power of God. The Son of God has suffered the fierce onslaught of the whole evil of the world. It has done to him the very worst it could do. It has nailed him to the Cross. And from the Cross he has come forth completely triumphant, alive, and powerful forevermore. His throne is the ultimate throne of the universe. His great deed upon the Cross is a mighty deed of rescue. In his death men find life, as in his life they find life forevermore. He is not only Savior. He is Judge. And his judgment is the final word in the destiny of men and of nations. All other authorities and powers dissolve and disintegrate. His authority and his power are eternal. Men are either on his side or against him. And if they are against him, however powerful they seem to be, the death sentence has already been pronounced upon the proud and evil life in which they seem to be so secure. Those who are for him have all the security of his own glorious and triumphant destiny. All this, alive in Christian consciousness, was the very substance of the life of the church and of its members. And all this alive in the mind and conscience of the author of Revelation masters his materials, bends them to its own purposes, and makes them the vehicle of its own great message.

When Revelation was written, the world had settled into hostility to everything which Christians believed and to everything for which they stood. The worship of the emperor set Rome against the Christian religion. Christ must occupy an unshared throne. The Christian could not worship the emperor. Indeed, to the Christian, Christ was the judge both of the emperor and of the empire. And this position, of course, the proud imperial cult could not accept. So the great empire and the little church met in battle array. And the Christian witnessed to his faith by dying for it. The martyr became the triumphant soldier of Christ. It was a terrible test, and there were many who could not meet it. For the encouragement and the strengthening of Christians in these grim days Revelation was written. Its very vocabulary of brilliant and amazing symbolism made it a book which the Christian could understand, but which was completely bewildering to a hostile Roman. So it did its great work. It was fairly saturated with the splendid sense of complete and ultimate Christian victory. What ought to be not only had a right to be. It was already triumphant in the invisible reign of God. It was Rome which was passing. The reign of Christ was eternal. The Rome which attempted to judge Christ must accept the judgment of Christ. The martyr was completely victorious in the very hour of his seeming defeat. Those who were loyal to Christ, and they alone, had complete and dependable security in a universe where Christ reigned. The very timeless splendor of this faith made it potent not only in the period when it was written but in every succeeding age. For this faith is the faith of the Christian in every generation and in every land. And never has it been expressed with more commanding authenticity and more ineffable glory than in Revelation. It is with all this in mind that we must approach the detailed inspection of the contents of the book.

1:1-3. The Man Who Received the Message.— In his famous Yale Lectures Phillips Brooks defined preaching as "truth given through personality." The first thing to say about Revelation is that its message is given through a person. We meet this person—John—at the very beginning of the book. All that follows has been passed through his mind. It has become warm in his heart. It has glowed in living symbol in his imagination. It comes to the Christians of his age from one of their own number. Their own experience becomes articulate in him. Their own hopes and fears are expressed in his thoughts and in his words. The truth comes not in impersonal formulas or in abstract discussion. It is warm with the blood of life. In a sense it is the spiritual autobiography of the author. In a sense it is the spiritual biography of the greatest Christians of his time.

But if the word is essentially John's word, coming through his own personality, it is very especially God's word entrusted to John. This divine sanction is of overwhelming importance. Men are in too tragic and critical a situation to have time for other men's interesting thoughts about their experience. If they are to go through these bitter days, they must have a word straight from God himself. What John has to say is as certain as the truth of God. It is as dependable as the character of God. He sets forth something which God has given to him. And everything which John has to say centers in Jesus Christ. He is at the beginning of the book. He is at the end of the book. He is the central and dominant figure in the book. Its whole meaning lies in the fact that it is a living word of the living Christ. It comes from the heart of a man to whom Christ is all in all. It is written to a community to whom Christ is all in all. Christ is a witness to the truth of God. John is a witness to the truth of Christ.

Happy is the man who takes the message of the book seriously, for it is immediately relevant. As it comes right out of contemporary life, so it is of the utmost importance at the moment and in the hour at which it is uttered. It has the very stuff of history in it.

4-8. The Living Christ.—But if the message of Revelation is concrete because it comes from the living God and the living Christ through the living John, it also gains in concreteness because, first of all, there are letters to seven churches in the Roman province of Asia. Actual people in actual situations are brought vividly to mind. There is first a general greeting to the seven churches, literally packed with phrases indicating the glory and the power of God and Christ. Over against the proud visibilities of the Roman Empire is put the realm of God and Christ, and there is a flashing sense of heavenly creatures concerned with the life of churches in the world. At the heart of this mighty realm of God is the one who died for men and who calls men to be ready to die for him. He is not only their king, but he is the one who has solved their moral problems in a deed of divine agony; and he, the great king, gives them a kingdom, and he, the great priest, makes them priests of God. They seem despised and rejected now: but their future is bound up with the one who is to come in clouds of glory, pierced and yet victorious; and they who have suffered in his name are to be pierced and victorious too. They belong to the one who is **Alpha and Omega.** So the past and the future belong to them and not to the empire whose position now seems to be entirely impregnable. The little churches are set against the background of eternity. They move through the world surrounded by an invisible glory in which they are to find their true life. The great Emancipator has given them citizenship in the kingdom of his own glory. They are released from their sins and they are incorporated in the stainless kingdom of Christ. All these quick and penetrating references show that John is writing to men whose minds are literally saturated with the positions which later became associated with classical Christianity. He does not have to ex-

plain. He makes a dramatic reference and passes on. The word of Christ is the word of God. Everything which has been and everything which is and everything which is to be finds its ground and its meaning in the God who authenticates all the words of Christ.

9-20. The Master of the Heavenly Glory.—General principles come to life in quite a new way when they are associated with actual persons in actual places at an actual time. Revelation has all this tremendous concreteness. John is suffering for Christ in the little island of Patmos. Every day is like every other day in its quarries. But to John every day is not like every other day. He does not forget **the Lord's day** when it comes around. This is the day when Jesus rose from the dead. This is the day in which the Christian finds security for all of his hopes. And on the Lord's day John's spiritual environment makes his physical environment irrelevant. A voice speaks in the silence of his soul, which is mightier than the voice of any cruel overseer driving men to work in the quarries. The little Christian communities in the province of Asia are much in John's mind. To seven of them, typical of the situation of the Christian religion in the world, he is given a message, and through them a message is given for the whole church. And now John's experience is set forth in terms which come to the eye and the ear with all the force of present reality. The living Christ himself is seen standing gloriously in the midst of seven lampstands of gold. He is garbed in royal splendor, and under his white and shining hair his eyes gleam like flashes of fire. Even his feet are like the refined product of some fiercely blazing furnace. And his voice has the exhaustless richness and rhythm of the throbbing waves of the sea. A supernal meaning is expressed in his very presence. Seven stars, as it were plucked from the sky, are in his hand. And the cutting finality of his speech is seen in the double sharpness of the sword which comes out of his mouth. His very countenance is like the rising of another sun in another and more glorious sky. What can Rome do to overthrow the new religion when its votaries see such glorious visions and dream such imperial dreams? A man's true environment is in his mind. And quite obviously the cruel power of Rome has not captured the mind of John.

Indeed, his fear is quite another fear. Not a visible tyranny but an invisible spiritual splendor overwhelms John. It is the figure alive in his imagination which overwhelms him. The experience is so real that he seems to fall at the feet of the mighty figure like one dead. But at once there comes a great word and a great act of reassurance. The right hand of the living Christ is laid upon him and the voice like many waters is heard saying, **Fear not.** The mighty Christ is the beginning of everything. He is the end of everything. He is the very actuality of life. He met death only to conquer it. And now he is alive with a quenchless and final vitality. The fact of death and all that follows death are under his control. He has the keys which unlock all these dark mysteries. He has appeared to John not to frighten him, but to give him a commission. The man of Patmos is to write what he has seen. For these great symbolic pictures which have become compelling in his mind have in them the inner meaning of the present and of the future. The seven stars indicate the heavenly connections of the little churches. They are not merely collections of men about merely human matters. There is heavenly observance of them. There is a heavenly life of which they are an earthly expression. When one says that every church below has its angel in the heights, one is giving the most dramatic expression to this assurance of a divine reference. The seven lampstands indicate the sense of the churches as the earthly basis for a heavenly light. In every way the church is lifted out of the depths of an immediate tragedy into the glory of a heavenly reality which is the fulfillment of its very life.

In a sense ch. 1 of Revelation is a great prologue to the rest of the book. The principles and facts and doctrines set forth with brilliant imagery and powerful statement represent the warp and woof of the Christian position. In just as much as they believed these things, in just as much as these things had come to triumphant life in their experience, the members of the little churches of Asia and of Christian communities everywhere were ready for any later experience which might come to them. And what was true of the first century has been true of every century since. Just the convictions and thoughts and beliefs which girded these early Christians have been the buttress of Christians in every century. It was against this background that preaching became effective in the apostolic age. And just this background is essential if the proclamation of the Christian message is to be powerful and transforming in the world and generation in which we live. On one side the Christian religion is a series of syllogisms based upon great and decisive premises. And the setting forth of the conclusions without the premises has been the great weakness of much clever and adroit preaching in our time. The first chapter of Revelation presents a series of premises always decisive for the Christian message. And so it has a perpetual importance. It must be a part of the living tissue of the conviction of the hearer if he is to receive the Christian word with **understanding.** And it must be a part of the very life of the preacher if he is to speak the word with authenticity and compulsion.

The author of Revelation believes tremendously in the living God. He believes so tremendously that he assumes the belief even more than he declares it. But the assumption is so interwoven with everything which he says that there is no mistaking it. Take away the belief in the living God who has made and sustains the world and men and who guides them to the fulfillment of his own purposes, and the very essence of what John has to say begins to evaporate. The fashion in which the living God tends to disappear and to be replaced by abstract principles or impersonal ideals in modern preaching accounts for much of its lack of vitality and power. Christianity becomes the vaguest of sentimentalities when it is not based upon a masterful conviction of the reality of the living God. We read what is said and we find it full of kindness and altruism, but somehow lacking in power to grip the mind or to command the conscience. And soon we see that it is fruitless because it is rootless. It has no basis in the ultimate reality of the universe. And without that basis religion at last becomes little more than the fabric of an idealistic dream. God is always just back of every assertion made in Revelation. And he is just back of every authentic utterance made by the Christian preacher. This perpetual sense of the presence of God makes thinking and worship and living come to new dimensions of reality and of power. Much brooding meditation over Revelation will be justified if this sense of the presence of the God who is alive passes from the book to the mind and heart of the reader.

The consciousness that Jesus Christ speaks as God in human life and as God on the throne of the universe pervades the whole of Revelation. And if we are inclined to be deeply impressed by the difficulty of such a conception for modern men, we ought at once to see that one of the most extraordinary things about the people addressed in the N.T. writings, and particularly in Revelation, is that this sort of conception was of the very greatest difficulty for them. It did not belong to any familiar categories of thought. It transformed all of these. Yet revolutionary as it was, it had not only entered their minds, it had come fully to possess their minds. It had become so much a part of their thinking and feeling about life that it was decisive for all their living relationships. Christianity had come not to be modified by men's familiar fashions of thought. It had come to master their mind as well as to dominate their conscience, and, as we shall amply see, to satisfy their heart. This is precisely what classical Christianity always does. It comes not to be modified by the *Zeitgeist*. It comes to master the *Zeitgeist* in every century and in every generation. No end of elements in contemporary thought were accepted and used by the Christian religion. But first of all it made its own imperial assertions and moved to the throne of thought with complete mastery. The fact that a conception was difficult for the contemporary mind molded by Roman and Greek ways of thinking was never of determining significance. The Christian never went to Rome to learn what he must think about Jesus. He never went to Athens to learn what he was to think about the central matters of his faith. As years went on, he was to learn how deep and how satisfying were certain connections between his own living faith and the thoughts of the greatest Greeks. But his religion stood in its own right. From his first appearance in Revelation, Jesus speaks from the ultimate throne of the universe. He comes not to be judged but to judge.

This sense of the finality and decisiveness of the Christian position, which is so characteristic not only of ch. 1, but of all Revelation, is always found in the great periods of the Christian faith. And it is of the utmost importance that the church of our time should recover it where it has been lost, and maintain it where it is present. The contemporary world is in a process of complete breakdown, and it is not to be allowed to speak from its ruins to tell the church what to believe and what to say. The world waits for a voice of moral and spiritual mastery. Its needs will not be satisfied by holding a mirror before it which reflects its own helplessness and trying to find in the reflected confusion the way of the future. For us, as for the first century, the imperial figure of Jesus Christ must be on the throne. Any confusion at this point will lead to frustration and futility on the part of the church. The mighty figure standing among the golden candlesticks is the one figure to which the eyes of men in our time can be turned with any moral hope or with any spiritual or social expectation.

Every sentence in ch. 1 is based upon a profound conviction that the living Christ has spoken a word which must be brought to the attention of men. John is to write what he has seen and we quickly come to understand that what he writes is important not only for the seven churches, it is important for all the churches. It is important for all the world. Christianity is a religion of revelation. It is not merely a religion of men's thoughts about life. It is the religion of God's word about life. And that word is expressed in the message which **John** brings to the churches and to the world.

When one asks whether the characteristic preaching of the contemporary church is characterized by this sense of a commanding message from the living Christ to men, one is raising for consideration a searching and significant question. The truth is that too often the uncertainty of the church answers in antiphonal fashion to the confusion of the world. John was able to provide men with inner certainty in the midst of outer confusion. So we can account for the bursts of beatific song which, as we shall see, are always breaking in upon the processes of thought and of declaration in the book. This does more than suggest the fashion in which in the midst of our tragic age men may be set to singing. The belief that God has spoken, and that the church declares his word, is at the very heart of the church's commission.

Even in ch. 1 we begin to see what will become much more clear as we go on, viz., that from whatever wide regions John secured the materials which went into the form of his symbolic utterance, all of this was passed through his own mind and mastered by his own conscience, even as his mind and conscience were mastered by the sense that he had an authentic message from the living Christ. And that living mastery of the varied materials is of the utmost importance for our understanding of the book. This document came to life in the Christian community, whose very blood pulsed with the quality of vital Christian experience. Only so should Revelation be approached. Only so can it be understood.

2:1-7. *The Message to Ephesus.*—Ephesus is an imperial city. It is the center of the Roman government in the province of Asia. But it is subject to an even loftier authority. And its little Christian church represents an authority higher than that of the Caesars. But the church itself must be judged by a judgment as stern as that which God applies to the world. And in this, as in all the letters to the Christian communities of Asia, the church itself comes to judgment. As in the case of the other communities, the message is addressed to **the angel of the church.** The judgment is not from the standpoint of the relativities of time. It is a heavenly judgment. It is a judgment from the standpoint of eternity. There is a flashing vision symbolically representing the living Christ with divine authority walking in the midst of the churches. Then his word to Ephesus is set forth. The Master of the church finds that the community of Ephesus is a church of loyal living and patient endurance. It has maintained the integrity of its own life by inspecting falsehood and pretense and by seeing them for just what they are and casting them out. When men have pretended to be apostles who were not, their pretensions have been challenged, and the church at Ephesus has refused to have traffic with them. It has endured the burden of Christians in a hostile world with genuine faithfulness and without that weariness which slackens the very sinews of loyalty. This it has done for the very sake of Christ. But under all the stress of tension and outer frustration, the church at Ephesus has lost its first fine rapture. It is loyal. But its living enthusiasm has waned. And this is not to be taken lightly, for it might easily be the beginning of a real disintegration of purpose. The time to repent is in the incipiency of what may become a great evil. Let the church repent, for it is its very place among the churches of God which is at stake. When enthusiasm begins to lag, loyalty itself may soon follow. But the church has this memorably good quality. Instinctively it rejects with horror that interpretation of the Christian position which would surrender Christian character in the name of false freedom. The proclamation of a Christian freedom which would come in effect to mean freedom from goodness is hateful to the living Christ as it is to the little church at Ephesus. The word to Ephesus is a word to Christians everywhere. Let all Christians take the word seriously. And they who hear and conquer shall enter a garden lovelier than Eden and shall eat of a tree which is **the tree of life** indeed.

8-11. The Message to Smyrna.—Smyrna, a very prosperous city, well situated for commerce and a center of the royal cult, is in the midst of a period of stress and strain, indeed, of profound suffering of the sort where loyalty may involve the giving of life. So the message begins with the assertion that the living Christ from whom it comes was dead but is alive. He has been loyal unto death as they are asked to be loyal unto death. And death has not been the last word for him, even as it would not be the last word for them. The one who sends them the message is **the first and the last,** and it is he who gives to them their true dignity, even though they find themselves in such bitter circumstances. They seem to exist only to be trampled under foot. But the one who is eternal gives them high and glorious position. The Jews who have not accepted the new religion have become the very bitter foes of the little church, and are only too ready to aid the hordes of persecution. But such Jews are not true Jews. The true Jews are those who have recognized in Christ the Messiah and have accepted him. The Jews who are persecuting the little church in Smyrna with such malignant hostility are **a synagogue of Satan.** It was a strange enough alliance when Jews aided members of the imperial cult in hounding the Christians. So the members of the **church** at Smyrna could expect imprisonment

and even death. For the church the tribulation would be brief (indicated by the **ten days**). But for individual members the call to **be faithful unto death** was a very practical demand. But death for Christ meant triumphant life. The **crown** he offered was not a crown of golden memory. It was a crown of living triumph. It was the amazing achievement of Christian faith that it made death incidental. The message belonged not only to Christians in Smyrna. It belonged to all who had ears of understanding. There was a death which men should fear, after the death of the body. But that gust of destruction, which came from God himself, had no terrors for the man who had won the Christian victory.

12-17. The Message to Pergamum.—In Pergamum the conflict between the worship of the Roman emperor and the worship of Christ had already sharpened to very tragic issues. So the living Christ presented himself to them as the Christ of the **sharp two-edged sword.** With grim finality this city of the imperial cult is described as the city of the throne of Satan. To live in such a town was dangerous business if one ventured to criticize the worship of the emperor. For the Christians who believed that Christ must sit upon an unshared throne, to live in Pergamum was to live under the constant menace of death. And the church had not flinched even when one of its members, Antipas, had met his death because he would not give to the emperor that supreme loyalty which belonged only to Christ. So there are words of praise. But there is also sharp criticism of those whose practical life was leading them to become dangerously involved in the practices of idolatrous cults, and for those who were interpreting the freedom in Christ as if it meant emancipation from the observance of important moral demands. Christian liberty did not mean the liberty to indulge in immoral practices. And idolatry itself was in a sense the most definite fornication of all. Some who strayed from the path were likened to those ancient people of the chosen race who were betrayed by Balaam into a mixed loyalty which actually became disloyalty. Others there were who held to the teaching of the Nicolaitans, already condemned in the message to the church at Ephesus. Uncompromising loyalty is demanded on the part of the men of Christ in the world. Those who in difficult circumstances have fallen into moral confusion are commanded to repent. They are to change their minds or the living Christ will make war against them with words which will smite like swords. Let whoever hears heed this word wherever men are tempted to be betrayed by confused loyalties. The one who overcomes in this subtle warfare may seem for a while like a man going through the wilderness without food. But God has **hidden manna** for his sustenance. Actually, Christ's relationship to his followers is a most individual matter. Every Christian has an experience with his Lord which can only be described as a secret which he shares with no other man. It is as if he carried a stone, whitened from all stain, upon which his own new name as a Christian is written. There is much which he possesses in common with others; but what is done for him is done for him alone. The subtle integrity of the individual life is forever safe with Christ. And in this experience there is a final security in the midst of great danger. So an imperial cult which rides down and crushes the individual is contrasted with a faith where each individual has a life of his own at the center of a deathless and absolute loyalty.

18-29. The Message to Thyatira.—To men who lived in a town where Apollo was worshiped, the Christ of the burning eyes and shining feet, the true Son of God, is speaking. The little Christian community is vigorously praised. It has the eagerness of **love,** the insight of **faith,** the quality of effective activity, and the strength of steadfast **endurance.** The passing of time has actually witnessed the improvement of its Christian life. But there was another side to the picture. In a commercial community, where there were many prosperous guilds in whose membership all men of business shared, the problem of relating the life with God and the life with men became acute. The food at the feasts had been offered to pagan deities, and the feasts themselves often came to a climax of completely lawless indulgence. It was easy to say that the idols were nothing, but the whole atmosphere was one which led to the grossest immorality. Oddly enough, it was a woman, of such powerful personality that she is likened to Jezebel, who from within the church led men to what she might have called the new freedom, to enter into the intimacy of the feasts and even to participate in their excesses. Here we get a hint of the particularly menacing idea of an inner life so secure that outer deeds do not matter. The woman who used the church to debauch churchmen had been given an opportunity to face the true moral quality of her position. But there had been no repentance. So instead of a bed of indulgence she is to have a bed of pain. And those who had followed her into lawless ways, unless they stop short and turn about, will be thrown into bitter tribulation. She is really responsible for what will become a process of evil from generation to generation, a sort of genealogical succession in wickedness. Such a growing evil is to receive summary treatment. **I will strike her children dead.** All such evil ways and evil deeds, of course, have their source in the invisible regions of men's minds and the far hidden places where motives are born and purposes are determined. The living Christ will bring all these things to light, and as he acts with conclusive and terrible finality, the churches will come to understand the fashion in which he searches the inner life and the evenhanded justice which he applies to each individual. All this is terrible enough, and a gentler note immediately follows. To those who have remained free from this disloyalty and the subtlety of supposing that they can be masters both of the deep things of Satan and of the deep things of God, the living Christ speaks tenderly. They have a sincere simplicity which is its own protection. **I do not lay upon you any other burden.** Hold tenaciously your Christian position. I am invisible now but I will be visible in all potent strength. He who does the will of Christ unto the end, and so becomes a moral victor, will also be made a ruler. As Christ has received power from his Father to break down what does not deserve to survive, so the triumphant Christian will become the instrument of judgment. He who has been a maintainer of that which is good will be a destroyer of that which is evil. Then there is a sudden vista of glorious expectation. **I will give him the morning star.** In ethnic religions sometimes a hero was depicted as being caught up into heaven and becoming a star. But by contrast like that between the shining Apollo of men's dreams and the burning-eyed Christ, the true Son of God, the Christian in his hour of triumph is seen as the possessor of the brightness and glory happily symbolized by the morning star. And here again what is said to one church is meant for all who have ears of understanding.

Already it is easy to see that in Revelation particular situations are treated so profoundly that principles emerge which are applicable in every situation. The modern reader following the account of the struggle of members of the early churches, with their temptations to disloyalty and loss of the rapture of a great faith, feels that all this has significance not only for them but for him. The situation may be different, but there is a similarity more significant than the difference. In the cruel days through which generations have lived, many Christians in many parts of the world have felt that Revelation has spoken to their own immediate situation. The saga of the loyal church in a hostile world goes on age after age. There is always a tendency to believe that the church must be judged by the world and that the church must accept the world's judgment. All the while the church is holding peace congresses with those who deny its very essential position. So the call for loyalty must be sounded with a clarion note. It is the business of the church to express the judgment of God. And sometimes the very virtue of humility, and the necessary repentance of the church for its own sins, are so set forth as to compromise the clarity of its witness to the truth which it is set in the world to speak. The sharp analysis of the situation in the churches which we have already discussed comes with a sort of antiseptic vigor to the Christian who lives in the midst of the complexities of the modern world. And it calls attention to something which is very important for the modern pulpit. The note of moral authority is readily lost and sweet reasonableness may easily be made a substitute for unhesitating loyalty in the proclamation of a message which, even when expressed most quietly, has moral judgment at the heart of it.

It is important to realize that past loyalty is never a substitute for present faithfulness. There is a picture of St. George standing in such utter weariness and lassitude beside the dragon which he has just slain that one wonders what would happen if another dragon were suddenly to appear. The first vigor is easily lost in the tense strain of the conflict. When the driving power of the vigorous passion of devotion begins to wane, a most dangerous process sets to work. Insights tend to become conventions. And conventions tend to become forms of words uttered without inner conviction or the sense of moral responsibility. And if the process is not arrested, what had been the most real and compelling thing in all the world at last becomes quite unreal and without power to command the mind or stir the imagination or strengthen the will. The problem of the waning enthusiasm in the community at Ephesus is a perpetual problem in the Christian church.

There is always a terrific shock when men come to realize that they have committed themselves to one position and the most powerful forces in their world are committed to a position which is quite the opposite. The early church found its world against it. The influence of Christianity has been so great that during the latter part of the nineteenth century in many parts of the world men felt that the essential Christian principles for living were scarcely subject to attack. People might be disloyal. But they gave at least lip service to the very principles which they betrayed. But once more we have come to a time when it is the very fundamental elements of the Christian position which are under attack. There has been a vast reversion to a code which Christianity can only condemn with the utmost sternness. Men once more know what it is to wake up and find that

they are on one side and their world is on another. Views of life and conduct which in their inner essence are completely incompatible are contending. And there is no way of reconciling these contradictions in a higher unity. In this conflict the very moral and spiritual nature of its own life puts Christianity on one side. The words "loyal unto death" have come to possess a meaning which is strangely contemporary. Revelation does not bring us a map of the future. But it treats certain situations with such finality of understanding that whenever similar situations emerge its word is not only relevant but determining for Christian understanding and action. The experiences of certain little churches in a Roman province thus come to men of other centuries and other continents with masterful significance.

But another sort of problem has become insistent. The church must be on its guard against corruption from without. But what about corruption from within? Already men and women are thinking about Christian freedom in terms which would produce moral decay. They are ready to say "All things are yours" in a sense which Paul would have repudiated with intense indignation. They are giving an interpretation of conduct which disintegrates the very laws of right living. No wonder the words of judgment have a ring of something not unlike moral ferocity. Inner spirituality must never be made an excuse for outer lawlessness. The same battle has come again and again century after century. And the very integrity of the church is at stake whenever men are tempted to say that a right heart can go with an irresponsible hand. The church which is to conquer the world must watch its own inner life with ceaseless and completely honest scrutiny.

3:1-6. The Message to Sardis.—Sardis, as the center of a pagan cult, a wealthy, voluptuous town, with memories of a shattering earthquake from whose devastation the generosity of the emperor had saved the people, was a particularly difficult town for the new and clean religion which was making its way in the world. **The church in Sardis** had a good reputation rather than a good character. It had the appearance of Christian virtue but was suffering from a process of inner decay. The living Christ speaks as one with an amplitude of inner spiritual vitality and of heavenly power. The words come with a sharp, cutting edge: You seem to be alive; actually you are dead. None of the beginnings of Christian living and achievement have come to any sort of fruition. The situation is critical. Let the church go back to its beginnings and rescue those good things which it is losing and recover that which has been lost. A sharp and clear change is required if the church is to be saved from the tragedy which hovers over it. It is not the visibilities of the city overlooking the Hermus Valley or of the great empire which should master the minds and dominate the lives of those men and women who have professed the Christian faith. **Like a thief** in the night, the great Master of cities and empires will come, and then they will see to whom their loyalty should have been given. But in this city, famous for garment making, there are a few who **have not defiled their garments;** they shall be given garments of a stainless beauty, in complete contrast to all that a town famous for the dyeing of wool could do. He who overcomes and confesses Christ in all the vicissitudes of this dangerous life will be confessed by Christ in the presence of God in the glory of the ultimate kingdom. And to all who are tempted to trust an outer reputation as an inner character is slipping, to all who are tempted to give to a secondary loyalty what only belongs to the great ultimate loyalty, the message comes.

7-13. The Message to Philadelphia.—Philadelphia was founded in the second century B.C. and bore the name of its founder. The most important cult of the city had to do with the worship of the god of wine. But it was Jews who were defiant in their rejection of the religion of Christ that made a particular problem for the church in Philadelphia. The living Christ speaks to the church as the one who has full authority, coming out of and transcending the ancient religious life of Israel. He has **the key of David.** He is the fulfillment of that holiness and truth which had come to have so deep a place in the consciousness of Israel. He knows the works of the members of the church in Philadelphia and he approves them. In spite of bitter opposition, they are to go on proclaiming and representing the claims of Christ. The power they have may be small but it has been used in full loyalty. The Jews who oppose them because they have rejected Christ have departed from the deepest movement of their own life. It is a **synagogue of Satan** which opposes Christ. The true Jews in the true line of their own tradition accept him. Someday this will become clear to these opposing Jews now false to their own tradition, and at the feet of the Christians they will acknowledge the truth of the faith which they have failed to understand. They will see that the men they are now opposing are beloved by the God whose final word is spoken by Christ. But the Christians must face something deeper and more far-reaching than opposition in their own city. They have kept the word of steady endurance in the trials which have come upon them. The living Christ will keep them in the fierce **hour of trial** which is to

come to all who dwell upon the earth. These words sound a deeper note of tragedy than any to be found up to this point in the letters to the churches. In the vicissitudes of life he may seem the absent Christ. But he is coming soon in imperial power. He commands his followers to hold fast until he comes. For the conqueror he who has the keys of the divine temple will not only make room, but he will make him a pillar with its own supporting place in the center of divine worship. Actually, only those who are loyal under the utmost strain and pressure can offer to God a worship which is finally authentic. They are indeed pillars in the temple of worship. And since that living relationship to the living God which is expressed in the deepest acts of worship is an ultimate Christian experience, it may be truly said that they shall go out no more. So profound is this relationship that they may be said to have written upon them the name of God, the name of the city of divine fulfillment, and the name which expresses the work of Christ in his ultimate revelation.

14-22. The Message to Laodicea.—Laodicea was a happily located and particularly prosperous city. Evidently the members of the Christian community shared in the prosperity of the town in which they lived. And they had felt the softening and subtly corrupting influence of their comfortable conditions. The easy acceptance of the standards of their community is challenged at once by setting over against its busy self-satisfied life the eternal Creator and Truth-teller who judges time by that which is beyond time. From the vantage ground of perfect knowledge and perfect character he surveys and estimates the members of the church at Laodicea. He finds them spineless and without vigor or virility. They are not good enough to be called good. They are not bad enough to be called bad. And so they are in a situation which is very evil indeed. **Neither cold nor hot,** they are an offense to the lips, and so are to be cast forth with complete distaste. They are like food offered at a banquet which is so completely unpalatable that the guest is forced to leave the table. The utter lack of character is really bad character. And worst of all, these people, so colorless morally, are completely and self-consciously complacent. They think of themselves as rich and altogether to be envied. And they think proudly of their pursuit of gain which has been so amply rewarded. It is their own achievement. As a result, they are full of smug contentment. They have everything they want. They are in need of nothing. And now the voice of the living Christ comes with the utmost severity. Actually, they are miserable and wretched enough. If only they could see themselves truly, they would know that they were living in utter poverty, without sight and without clothing. And these naked, blind people had the audacity to call their poverty wealth, their blindness sight, and, naked as they were, to suppose that they were sumptuously clothed. They had counted as treasure that which was not treasure, and thus had become of all men most miserable. But there was a **gold refined by fire** they could have if they really desired it. There were clean and **white garments** held by Christ and ready for their possession. There was a healing for sightless eyes which could be applied to their blindness. And now the fierce castigation turns to a wondrous tenderness. Those whom Christ loves he disciplines and chastens. His reproof is an evidence of his affection. He is at the very door of their lives, knocking and waiting for the door to be opened. And when it is opened, he will come in for the most hearty and intimate fellowship. They shall eat with him in deep affection and mutual trust. And those who choose the path of hard and demanding loyalty and carry on with complete faithfulness will join with their Master in the great company of victors. As he overcame and sat down with his Father on his throne, so they shall overcome and sit with Christ upon his throne. The issues are tremendous. The reward is infinitely glorious. So the people in danger of being cast out as utterly unprofitable are shown a way to immortal victory. And what is said to them is said to everyone who is capable of hearing and understanding.

The modern man reading the words addressed to Sardis and Philadelphia and Laodicea may well have the startled feeling that they are addressed to him. He too knows all too well the dullness which comes with the loss of the first fine rapture. A principle capable of very general application is involved. John Livingston Lowes, of Harvard University, in his brilliant volume of critical analysis, *Convention and Revolt in Poetry*,[1] has shown how periods of creative power in thought and expression are followed by periods when the creative energy departs and gradually a hard and lifeless conventionality takes its place. Then come revolt and the vigor of a new creative vitality. And these, in turn, are followed by times of waning power. Of course there is nothing inevitable about the process either in literature or in life. But the danger is always present. In times when men are most alive they may actually be digging their own graves. And in life as well as in letters, moral decision and moral courage are likely to have the secret of permanent vitality in them. It is when insight ceases to be costly that it

[1] Boston: Houghton Mifflin Co., 1930.

becomes conventional. Really there is no more painless way to die, either intellectually or morally or spiritually, than just by surrendering to that invasion of dullness under whose influence apprehension becomes less and less clear until at last the very sense of meaning vanishes. And the very painlessness of the process makes it all the more dangerous. We are conscious of no sudden crisis. The change is so subtle that we are not even aware of its various stages. First comes sleep. Then comes death. No wonder the word to the men of the church of Sardis is sharp and stern.

There is a social side to the waning of the first glowing and potent energy. Ages of tremendous tang and achievement are likely to be followed by ages when the very sources of flaming energy seem to have dried up. A post-Reformation period is likely to be a period of dull scholasticism. To set an age on the way of a renewed vitality at the very point where it has sunk into lifeless convention is a task which is difficult enough. But it is a task which the Christian church must accept and which it must perform. Of all institutions, that church can least accept the doctrine of inevitably recurring cycles about which nothing can be done. The age which is sinking into intellectual or moral or spiritual sleep can be roused. The lost vitality can be recovered. And a new vitality can be discovered. There are always words of life waiting to be spoken to decadent ages.

But in the profoundest sense it is in the individual that the great things happen. Even social processes move out from the lives of significant individuals. It is really the individual who loses the first fine rapture. And it is the individual who must recover it. When a man stops growing he begins to die. And this strange process of inner decadence and decay is one of the most tragic facts of the individual life. In the great matters of the moral and spiritual life the process can be detected. It can be arrested. And it is a part of the very mission of the Christian religion to detect and to arrest that heavy dullness which is the precursor of death.

The church at Philadelphia is discovering the glorious way of the open door. It has been loyal when Jews set themselves in utter hostility against its whole message and mission. And this very loyalty has prepared it for the greater test when the whole world will be set against it. Little loyalties prepare for the exercise of great loyalties. Little disloyalties make men incapable of great loyalties when the day of testing comes. Being faithful when the area of struggle is small prepares men to be faithful when the struggle widens to the limits of the world. To be loyal in increasingly large areas of moral and spiritual demand is to have a great door opened which no one can shut. But more than this. The person who achieves triumphant loyalty to Christ has been enabled to enter a sanctuary of inner security which is as permanent as the character of God. He becomes a pillar in God's temple—a part of the very structure of the ultimate spiritual security of true worshipers. Having found his place in an eternal citadel, he never comes back to the insecurity of a godless man. Once incorporated in the very structure of the temple, never shall he go out of it. If this is a vision of the ultimate blessedness, it is something more. For even in this life the Christian victor can have inner security in the midst of outer tragedy. His soul can dwell in the eternal temple at the very time when his body moves among the vicissitudes of this baffling and tragic world. It is ultimate matters with which he deals. The very quality of the character of God is to be written into his character. He is to be a living expression of the quality of God's perfect city. And he is to be the possessor of that which gives definitive meaning to the ultimate reign of Christ. The ultimate perfections are to be made real to him and in him. So from a little Greek city our minds are lifted to the glories of the ultimate universe.

The church at Laodicea, with its internal poverty and its external pretense, its combination of arrogant complacency with intellectual, moral, and spiritual destitution, seems strangely contemporary to the modern reader. We too know all too well the tragedy of having the form without the essence, of combining glittering externality with inner impotence. Too many of us are incapable of moral and spiritual enthusiasm. And we are incapable of that shuddering sense of cold which comes with the authentic awareness that the fires of life are going out. Too many of us live in a middle country, incapable either of great hopes or of great despair. If such as we have been prepared for the festive board of God, he can look at us only with supreme distaste. The incapacity for decisive experience is the characteristic of a decadent age and of a decadent church. Like the Laodiceans, many of us are incapable of decisive moral and spiritual experience. And this very apathy is accompanied by an amazing pride. We too think of our ignorance as knowledge, of our poverty as wealth, and of our nakedness as if we were clothed with the most sumptuous garments. But for us too the analysis and the corrosive condemnation prepare the way for a marvelously friendly offer of that which we do not yet understand that we really need. But we must confront the actual situation with complete honesty and utter moral candor before we are ready for the friendly word. The complacent man who assumes the right to judge

the judgment which confronts him has put himself beyond the reach of the very help which he so deeply needs. Modern literature has much to offer in the way of setting forth the contemporary destitution. T. S. Eliot's *The Waste Land* [2] may stand for a vast body of writing in which modern men see themselves as morally and spiritually naked and destitute. If we consider such writing not as the end of the journey but as a preparation for the divine invitation, it may render great service. However it may be when human pessimists express their sense of decadence in dark and dreary words, when the living Christ comes with castigation it is the voice of love preparing men to hear his offer of utter friendliness. He is at the door of every human life knocking. The door must be opened from within. There is no way to open it from the outside. But when Christ is welcomed, he comes with a wealth of intimate fellowship which solves all problems and satisfies all needs. There is a great cosmic coming. But this intimate individual coming is of the very essence of Christianity as a gospel. The words are among the tenderest in Revelation—indeed, in the whole N.T. It is a far call from castaway people, unfit for the banquet of God, to triumphant sharers of the throne of Christ. But these are the exact alternatives. Christ has overcome. And he is the creator of the great order of overcomers. That which is unfit may be made gloriously fit. There is a possible journey from the refuse heap to the throne. And if we as modern men find the thoughts about God's throne and the throne of Christ so high that they seem beyond our impoverished imagination, we must frankly face our situation, and patiently begin to study the alphabet of moral and spiritual understanding. So will we be buying true gold. So will we be finding white garments. So will we be given that anointing which changes the very power of the eyes to see. If we once see moral destitution for what it is, we can understand the offer of spiritual wealth.

Clearly the messages to the seven churches in the province of Asia are of ecumenical range and of ecumenical significance. They belong to every age. They belong to every place. They belong to the Christian church always and everywhere. No Christian can read them without finding words which speak directly to his own mind and heart. Somewhere in one of these letters his own secret is told. His own need is probed. And a cure is offered which fits his own disease. So the moral analysis and the spiritual promise speak to us today.

4:1-11. *The World's Maker and Ruler.*—From the earth and its tribulations we are now trans-

[2] New York: Boni & Liveright, 1922.

ported to the heavenly glory. From the relativities and tragedies of time we are taken to the absolute finality of eternity. The prisoner of Patmos is transported to the freedom of the life which is without beginning or end. In order that he may see that the timeless reign of God is to express itself in full victory in the life of men, he is given a vision of that absolute reign in a region beyond the touch of human wickedness and human fear. He is to see the life of time with the eyes of eternity. He is to see the crumbling pretensions of men in the light of the permanent powers of God. So he is to be able to take men out of the regions of shuddering fear to the experience of a confidence which cannot be shaken. The inexpressible is, of course, set forth in a rich and complex symbolism. The author gets his material from all sorts of places, but the important matter is to see how he turns it to Christian uses. There is nothing more important in the study of Revelation than to realize that its author is never the slave of his sources. He is always their master. It is his use of the materials and not their own curious and baffling complexity which the student of the book must keep in mind. They speak to the eye rather than to the analytic reason. But there is nothing unreasonable about their essential message. In heaven he finds a throne. The ultimate Master sits upon it. There is ineffable splendor in the spectacle. One feels that the author is trying to express in words all too inadequate the ultimate power and the ultimate reign of the universe. There is a rainbow about the throne. For this reign makes all true and good hopes secure. It represents triumph over tragedy, not submergence in tragedy. All other powers derive from this one final authority. There are twenty-four thrones about the throne of the ultimate ruler. All this delegated authority has been cleansed from evil like the white garments which the four and twenty wear, and has a golden magnificence which is the gift of God himself. There are great flashes of lightning from the central throne, and there is the roll of vast and resounding thunder. For the reign of God breaks forth like a terrible tempest against evil, even as it is a rainbow of promise for that which is good. Fiery lamps blaze before the throne to tell the tale of the amplitude of spiritual resources with which God confronts the universe. There is a sweeping beauty before the throne like the tossing of the sea. And the perfect knowledge and energy at God's constant disposal are expressed in the living creatures, all eyes and with qualities suggested by the mighty lion, the gentle calf, the light of intelligence in a human face, and the flying far movement of an eagle. Their very wings are full of eyes. They go everywhere.

They see everything. All knowledge and all power are perpetually at the disposal of God. They sing forever of the majesty of God. He is thrice holy, the last and perfect reality of holiness. He has the whole mighty power of the universe held in his own grasp. Always he has been. Everywhere he is. Always he will be. All who have true power and glory in the universe reflect their glory and power back upon the God who has given it, and ascribe to him every ultimate perfection. And in the midst of this outburst of heavenly praise the four and twenty elders fall in worship before the one sitting on the throne and sing their own beatific chorus. God is worthy to receive every glory, and every honor, and all power. Everything comes from him. In his mind and will creation was conceived. And through his power all that is came to have existence. So all creation belongs to him even as he gives glory to all creation (cf. p. 565). Earth may be full of shattering uncertainty and of bitter tragedy. But in heaven the reign of God is perfectly secure already. So men may always appeal from the tragedies of time to the perfection of eternity. The prisoner of Patmos is a prisoner no more. He has experienced the emancipation which comes from an authentic vision of the reign of God. And it is this which he is to share with those to whom he writes.

This vision of ultimate reality involves truths of the utmost importance for men of every country and of every century. First, there is a genuine relationship between earth and heaven. Time and eternity have very real connections. Men find life becoming so hard as to be almost impossible if there is no bond which binds this tragic world to a world which answers to the deepest necessities of the moral and spiritual life. The deists of the eighteenth century declared that doubtless God made the world but that, once having made it, he left it to run itself. God was at the source of life, but he had nothing to do with its ongoing. Men of every age have felt under the stress of grave and baffling circumstance that the Great Avenger seemed to be very careless indeed. This is precisely what the author of Revelation denies. And the door opened in heaven is the symbol of the denial. Just because there is this perfection in heaven it must be accessible to men. God's servant is summoned to come up to the divine heights, where he can see the fashion in which the character of eternity must impress itself upon the history of men in time. The whole contention is that human history is not a thing apart from God. It is a process to be shot through and mastered by his perfection and his power. But to understand what God will do among men we have first of all to see what he is in himself. And so there comes the vision of the divine character and the divine glory. And this vision of divine perfection must always be seen in contrast to human imperfection. It is because the life in heaven is so perfectly right that it can be brought in to right the wrongs of time. And in this vision the prisoner of Patmos becomes the freeman of God.

The immediate point of central importance in the heavenly vision is the sight of a throne. The universe is not a chaos with mutually contradictory forces endlessly contending. There is a central and final authority. There is one ultimate throne. And as we shall see, every other throne has a derivative authority. And the one sitting on the throne is the eternal expression of perfect harmony as well as of final power. The perfections of God are seen in the vision of complete and glorious beauty. There is not only rightness. There is eternal loveliness. Over against the intolerable ugliness which defaces human life is seen the perfect beauty of the life of God. It is the glowing union of all that gives a root to goodness and nobility and truth. Something of this is assumed here. But it is soon made explicit and it is asserted again and again. The deepest instincts of men find satisfaction in the vision of God. To paraphrase a sentence of Horace Bushnell: He is all that he ought to be. And this satisfaction in the character of God is basic to everything else in Revelation. All that God does comes from what he is. And so the vision of his perfection gives the key to everything else in the book. There is a rainbow about the throne. The rainbow was the well-understood symbol of the promise of good hope after tragedy. After the worst that man had done came the best that God would do. This is of the utmost importance. For the very perfections of God might crush man beyond the possibility of hope. But quite the contrary is the truth. It is in God's perfections that man is to find his hope. The reign of God always involves promise of good to men. There is always a rainbow about this throne. Of course, as we shall see in no end of ways in the whole book, evil-minded men can defeat God's purpose of good. But even that defeat he will turn to victory if men allow him to do it. His reign is the very enthronement of the best of human hopes. All pessimisms regarding the ultimate nature of the universe are overthrown in the vision of the rainbow about the throne. There is no rainbow about the throne of the Caesars. When Paul made his great journeys, Roman citizenship was a protection, a thing of which a man could be proud. But the Rome which had rendered such great service to men was settling into hard hostility to the reign of God. To the Christian there was moral and spiritual darkness about that throne. So the vision of the throne surrounded by a rainbow meant that men could appeal from a throne of darkness to a throne of light. The good hopes which were blighted here were held securely by the one who sat on the eternal throne. Rome had not had the first word. It would not have the last word. The first and the last words belonged to God. And these words were abounding in beatific hope. Indeed, you could not see the throne without the rainbow. To see the throne at all was to be bathed in the beauty of high and dauntless expectation.

There were other thrones. There is reference to four and twenty of them. They represent mighty powers. But they do not represent power apart from God. They represent power received from God, as they joyously and eagerly admit. Their loyalty is expressed in acts of worship. It is expressed in words of praise. There is not merely obedience. There is joyous obedience. All this is of the utmost practical importance. If the thrones of the world exist in a state of mutual antagonism and bitter hostility, and at last in desperate warfare, the world is in a state of moral confusion. And when one of the human thrones becomes supreme, in the very act of achieving supremacy it becomes the throne of a tyrant. It is only as all the human centers of power gladly receive their authority from a moral power which is far above them that there is any sort of moral safety for the world. All human authority is delegated authority, and whenever the divine authority is forgotten or repudiated there is chaos indeed. So all forms of human society, whether tribal or kingly or imperial or feudal or democratic, have met their ultimate judgment at the point of their relation to the authority of God. All human judges are in perpetual process of being judged by divine standards. All human kings are perpetually subject to the judgment of the King of kings. The understanding of all this made the world over for the Christians who confronted an empire which had no place for their faith or for their loyalties. They could appeal from the usurping throne to the ultimate throne of the universe. And this same experience has come in every age to Christians who in the midst of tragic circumstances caught an authentic vision of the reign of God.

In every time of dissolving human authorities and mounting human aggressions the whole situation is clarified when we come to have the vision of the throne to which all other thrones are subservient. Often enough the existing human authorities do not seem much like the four and twenty elders occupying their thrones in full loyalty to the one who sits upon the throne of final authority. But this simply means that they are subject to a judgment which will not falter and which cannot fail. This is the faith which the Christian must proclaim. This is the faith which the church must proclaim. Without it the church becomes involved in endless compromises with authorities which have no genuine basis for their pretensions, and powers which have no right to the allegiance of men. So there come endless peace conferences with the vices and endless subtle adjustments with that which contradicts the very character and the very purpose of God. The church is never on more precarious ground than when it claims the authority of divine sanctions to validate all too human judgments. The church in the catacombs has both moral and spiritual dignity. The church which sits upon a throne of power which it has purchased by disloyalty to the will of the very God whom it professes to worship has reached the depths of moral confusion. The vision of the four and twenty elders reigning by a perpetual series of acts of moral obedience comes with fresh authority to every age when men renew their allegiance to the one who sits upon the ultimate throne. Democracy itself comes to particularly definite judgment at this point. For democracy is the equal right of every man to discover and to do the will of God. It is not the right of every man to flout and to disobey the will of God. In a democracy, in a sense, every man is a king. But he sits upon a delegated throne. He is a man under authority as well as a man exercising authority. Demos rightly upholds his head against tyrants. But Demos himself must be judged by the rightness of God. Our escape from moral anarchy is not in tyranny. It is in the character of God. And so when democracy becomes secular and godless, it enters upon particularly bad days. It is like a ship without a rudder. It is like a traveler without a map. And if it is swept into the fashion of following its own lawless desires with no chart for measurement and no standard for judgment, it becomes one of the worst tyrannies of all. Even social idealism becomes a corrupting thing if it is not mastered and guided by the authority of the good God. A materialistic socialism always sinks to a level where the doctrine that the end justifies the means is complacently accepted. Lies and treachery and even murder are recognized as instruments for securing what is conceived as a good social end. And so in the name of something good, evil is set upon the throne. Such dark and wicked folly is of course impossible to those who have a perpetual sense of the overlordship of the good God. You cannot contradict the character of God as a part of the endeavor to get the will of God done. So social passion is cleansed and purified by a perpetual reference to the character of the one who sits on the throne of ultimate lordship.

One other characteristic of the heavenly reign deserves our closest attention. It is found in the outbursts of triumphant praise and worship. There is a sense of the sort of creative gladness which inevitably bursts forth into song. The highest thrones under God exist for the sake of singing obedience as well as for the exercise of authority. The ruler under God is like the choirmaster of a heavenly chorus. And so the prisoner of Patmos comes back from his vision with a song in his heart. He knows the secret of setting captives everywhere to singing. He knows the secret of giving to the prisoners of Rome a heart of victory. Christianity possesses the secret of putting music in the heart of prisons. And indeed nothing disconcerts tyrants like hearing the songs of the oppressed. In truth, a part of the very secret of Christianity is to be found in its capacity to bring singing gladness out of eternity into time. When the church loses its capacity to sing, it has begun to lose its power. And great revivals with good promise for the future in them are sure not only to have sermons but also to have songs. Luther preached and wrote *Ein' Feste Burg*. The hymns of Charles Wesley do not have an accidental relationship to the great eighteenth-century revival. They are a part of its genius and a part of its power. You can test the creative power of preaching by the presence or the absence of the singing note. Men go away from hearing great sermons with gladness singing in their hearts. They may be plunged into gloom by the moral incisiveness of the sermon, but the last word is always the triumphant hymn of the forgiven. You can test a theology by its power to set men singing. Psychopathic theologies of cosmic gloom simply fail to capture the really Christian note. Christianity comes bringing a message of triumph over tragedy. It does not come with a message of submergence in tragedy. And the reign of God, by its very inherent quality, inspires men to sing. The vast organizing activities which the church inspires and conducts sometimes get out of hand. And when they do, the very activity of the church becomes mechanical. You can test the quality of the church in a machine age by asking if it still knows how to make men sing. The vast activities of the church must be conducted in an atmosphere of triumphant praise. Otherwise there is a terrible sound of grinding wheels and at last the machinery itself becomes impotent. All of this may be admitted in such a fashion that there is intellectual assent to the idea, but no really joyous and creative moral and spiritual fervor. The result is like a picture of a singing church without any music.

It is at this point that inner experience becomes outer power. If the members of the church really have the music of the heavenly kingdom in their hearts, all their activities are set to this music. And if hard and tragic days come, the music remains. The great ideas which are so central and so conclusively important to the Christian religion must meet the same test. It is only when theology is shot through with music that it is able to do its real work. It is not unimportant that when Paul concludes an argument he breaks forth into a doxology. The echo of the heavenly music must be present in all earthly experiences if they are to be truly Christian. The lift of the mind and the lift of the heart and the lyrical gladness change the very quality of life. And so the service of worship is the instrument of a glad and awful dignity in the sense that it is always an attempt to remind men of the heavenly music. To go back to the sources of power is to go back to the sources of gladness. And in just this sense all Christian prisoners become prisoners of hope and not prisoners of despair. Like the man of Patmos we must be in the spirit, and so capture a sense of heavenly praise and heavenly worship and heavenly gladness if we are to suffuse the deeds of the body with heavenly light.

5:1-14. The World's Redeemer and Lord.— The vision of the world's Maker and Ruler is followed by the vision of the world's Redeemer and Lord. The two really belong together and make one great picture of the authority of the Maker and the authority of the Redeemer of the world. The Maker of the world holds in his hand the book of the divine reign. It is closely written and **sealed with seven seals. Who,** the question is asked, **is worthy to open the book,** who is worthy to be the instrument of the divine reign? No one in the heights or in the depths or upon the earth is found to meet the test. The man of Patmos weeps bitterly. The plight of those caught in the tragedy of the world, and waiting for the faithful judgment of God, is indeed desperate if the book of the divine reign is to remain unopened. One of the enthroned elders speaks to him words of encouragement. There is a victor who has won the right to open the book of God. He comes like a lion in strength. The Davidic tradition has its root and its fulfillment in him. He stands in the presence of the divine glory, the living emblem of tragic sacrifice fully achieved, both the Lamb which was slain and the sevenfold power and perfect knowledge of God. The one who has died is to be the very instrument of the reign of God. He takes the book of the reign of God, and as he performs this mighty act the living creatures and the enthroned elders fall down before him, as they had fallen down be-

fore the Maker and Ruler of all. Each has a harp and they carry golden bowls whose incense is the prayers of the troubled saints of God. They bring the prayers of men to him for the divine answer. The acceptance of the Redeemer to be the instrument of the divine reign inspires a new song. With his blood he has bought men of every human group for God. He has made men into a kingdom of God. He has made them kings and priests. They are the real rulers of the world. There is a sudden sense of the heavenly glory in all of its amplitude as the man of Patmos hears innumerable multitudes of angels singing the praises of **the Lamb that was slain.** Words are piled upon each other in rapturous tribute. He is **worthy** to exercise power. He is worthy to possess all wealth. He is the possessor of all wisdom. He is worthy to exercise the control of all the military power of God. He is worthy to receive all honor. He is worthy to possess the ultimate glory. All that brings blessing belongs to him. It is very clear that everything which can be said of God is said of the Lamb. And everything is brought together at last in a rich and glowing song of rapturous praise addressed to God and to the living Christ, as the one **that sitteth upon the throne** and **the Lamb.** All blessing and all honor and all that is glorious and all regnant might belong to God and to the living Christ forever and forever. The **living creatures** shout a mighty **Amen** to the great ascription of praise and the enthroned elders fall down and worship (cf. 11:16). The last word of joyous submission to the one sitting on the throne and to the Lamb is represented as coming from every created being **in heaven, on the earth,** and **under the earth,** and on the sea and **in the sea.** It is the universal acclaim of all creation to God and to Christ.

The whole of the fifth chapter of Revelation has tremendous significance in showing the place which was already given to the one who had been crucified. Already it is felt to be fitting to ascribe to him everything which would be ascribed to God. It is clear enough that his death is not a merely human death. It is a divine deed wrought in human life. He has paid in blood for the life of men. His acts are all divine acts. Who but God could be a providence establishing a human kingdom? Who but God could make men not only kings but priests? It is the very doer of these divine deeds who has the right to open the book of the reign of God. For he himself is the divine master of the seals. By every sort of pictorial symbol the preeminence of the one who has come from the cross to the throne of power is expressed. Seven horns represent his power. Seven eyes **represent** his control of the very spirits of God sent forth into all the earth. The eyes of God are his eyes. The living creatures fall down before him. The enthroned elders acknowledge his lordship in utter submission. There are harps to add to the music of his praise. And the very prayers of men are brought to him for answer. The heavenly host fairly exhaust the powers of speech in offering him honor. He is the doer of the deeds of God. He is all that God is to men. It does not require much imagination to see that the true power of the living Christ is being set over against the false assertion of power of the Roman emperor. The Roman emperor thinks he is God. But men actually meet God in Christ.

As we read all this tribute to the living Christ, we see how deeply it speaks to the very classical form of Christian experience as we encounter it century after century. Already in the early church Christian experience had come to possess the quality which made it possible to use all these words of glorious tribute. And precisely here we find a secret of the vitality which made it possible for the book to win its hard fight for a place in the N.T. canon. It is not the quality of the symbolism, though this has its own interest, which makes us sure that the book speaks in the deepest fashion to the Christian mind and heart. It is the central insight in respect of the pre-eminence of Christ. This expresses the very genius of the Christian church. And it is important to see that the secure confidence in the lofty place given to Christ comes precisely from the fact that he does for Christians things which only God can do. His mighty enthronement in the Christian mind and heart does not come as a result of an abstract argument or even of a concrete argument, significant as these indeed prove themselves to be. He appears in the experience of men at the precise point where the need of God is greatest, and with complete masterfulness he meets that need. So he comes securely to the throne room of the human soul. We do not use our reason in order to give to him a high place. We use our reason to interpret and explain a high place which we have already given to him. And so we come to see that life has no goal without him. History is meaningless without him. The book of the reign of God remains closed without him.

Here we come upon matters which speak very deeply to the minds of Christians of every century. Men must find secure and dependable meaning in life if they are to be saved from being completely broken by its vicissitudes. They can endure tragedy. They cannot endure meaningless tragedy. And it is an understanding of the significance of one pre-eminent figure which saves life from dark confusion and gives to it rich and abiding meaning. The vision of the Master of the rolls of the book of God dries the bitter tears of the man of Patmos and sends him back with a message of victory to those who seem to be called to endure the worst that life can do. Even heaven would be a lonely place without Christ. And the confusion of the world would be complete and final. Even the great cultures of the world, with all their contribution to human life, come to the place where they must find their fulfillment and their completion in him or they will lose the meaning which they already possess. The stately humanisms of the world remain human only as they are completed by the divine. And it is as the divine becomes human in Jesus Christ that humanity finds its true place and its real significance. The book of the human story, as well as the book of the divine reign, is closed and sealed until he breaks the seals. The mechanistic and mathematical frame in which our life is lived is like a machine without a driver until he masters it for his own purposes. Even science gives us instruments without meaning until the Master of meaning comes to infuse them with mighty purposes. So the book of science is sealed until the Master of the rolls comes to break the seals. Meanings tend to become half meanings and at last to lose their significance unless they are confirmed by him. The individual life with its glimmerings of truth tends to become lost unless it can find truth looking out of human eyes and speaking with a human voice. And all this it finds in the human life divine. So the mighty symbols of the pre-eminence of Christ in Revelation speak to something in men which comes to have the widest and the deepest significance. We, too, weep in the presence of the books which are closed and sealed. We, too, have weeping turned to joy when the Master of the seals appears.

But there is one act which stands out in the claim of the living Lord to authority in respect of the book of the reign of God. And this is expressed in the figure of the Lamb which was slain. This obviously and without question refers to the death of Christ. And it says very clearly to all who have ears to hear that in his death our Lord did for men what they could never do for themselves. He opened doors which would otherwise be closed. In a brilliant figure it is declared that his blood is the currency with which he bought men for God. His death was a deed of universal significance. It affected the destiny of men of every nation and of every race. There is no speech which is not to tell the tale of its meaning, for it has to do with men of every language. By his death he has made it possible for men to become citizens of God's kingdom. They are not only to be citizens. They are to be priests. They represent God in worship and they reign in his name in the world. It is as the one who has died that the living Christ comes to power and riches and wisdom and might and honor and glory. So he reigns as the instrument of redemption. All these figures and symbols attest the place which the thought of the death of Christ had won for itself in the minds of very early Christians. And all of it of course completely fits in with the attitudes expressed in the other books of the N.T. In fact, it expresses an essential position of classical Christianity (cf. Expos., ch. 7).

That it has special significance for an age when men are called to express their loyalty to their faith by martyrdom is surely true. They are asked to die. Yes, but they are asked to die for one who has already died for them. He went to the Cross to save them. They must be willing to give their lives in loyalty to him. There could be no profounder basis for the summons to martyrdom. The Christians are never nearer to Christ than when, in antiphonal response to his great deed of suffering death for them, they give their lives for him. And it must be said that this appeal has its force precisely because the death of Christ is the pivotal deed in the Christian religion. It is not a deed given particular emphasis in order to inspire martyrs to meet their fate with unflinching loyalty. It inspires men to martyrdom because it is the very central and definitive matter in the Christian religion. So it speaks to men in every age and in every circumstance. Here they find their entrance into a new and happy and creative relationship to God through Christ. This has been expressed in manifold hymns, some of them rich in high dignity and glowing with spiritual splendor, some of them managing to keep near to a great insight in spite of a certain crassness of expression. The death which gives life to men is perpetually remembered in the defining act of Christian worship, the sacrament of the Lord's Supper. It gives the most inspiring and compelling element to Christian preaching. It is more than a principle of universal application. It is a divine deed of universal relevance.

But it also sets a pattern for living, even as it offers a basis for faith. When a preacher, addressing for the first time the congregation of a church of which he had become pastor, asked them to look upon him with eyes which had seen the Cross, he was addressing them in the language of the deepest Christian understanding. Bunyan's Pilgrim, losing his burden at the Cross, is an immortal because a typical figure. And if these things do not burn in our minds with a sort of living fire, we do well to find the blame in ourselves and not in the posi-

tions to which we fail to respond. The Cross is in the world not to be judged by men. It is in the world to judge men as well as to save them. It was an event in history. But it has a timeless significance. All this is implicit in the symbolic scenes and the figurative actions in ch. 5. In this chapter the deepest and most characteristic quality of Christian devotion comes to vital and commanding expression.

Theology becomes particularly commanding when it enters so deeply into human experience that it finds for itself dramatic symbol and vivid imagery. And this book is full of theology. Moreover, its theology is crystallized into that figurative expression which has the very genius of vital experience. When the Cross has once mastered the mind, enfranchised the conscience, energized the will, and captured the heart of Christendom, it speaks to men in language of singing devotion to the Lamb which was slain. The final acts of praise and allegiance described here unite the one who sits on the throne and the Lamb as objects of devotion. The Maker and Sustainer of the world and the Redeemer and Ruler of the world together receive the ultimate loyalty, the supreme devotion and the final praise. This symbolic picture throws its own light on the process by which Christ is seen to ascend to the ultimate position of power and authority. He has done for men what only God could do; therefore he must be addressed as God is addressed. The life of the Deity must be rich enough to include all that is meant by God the Creator and Christ the Redeemer. There is no formal statement of doctrine. But we see the doctrine in the very process of becoming necessary.

The vision of all creation uniting in the ascription of every grace and authority and glory to God and Christ deserves very special attention. Revelation is largely concerned with those who refused to accept and obey the authority of God and Christ, and with the fashion in which God deals with them. But here in cumulative and inclusive inscription every creature in heaven, on the earth, under the earth, on the sea, and in the sea, combines in the acknowledgment and acceptance of the final power and glory and authority of the Maker and the Redeemer of the world. All creation is seen in the terms of divine purpose in making everything which exists. Every creature is seen accepting and declaring the authority and the glory belonging to the one who has made and the one who has saved mankind. Is there a suggestion that after the terrible and tragic judgment to be described in succeeding chapters every creature is at last to accept and return to the true allegiance? Rather, perhaps, there is an account of what God meant and what could be if men would have it so. In any event, in this golden passage the vote is unanimous. Every creature exhausts the power of language to express a complete and final devotion to him that sitteth upon the throne and to the Lamb. And the great delegated authorities join in the acclamation. The four living creatures shout Amen. And the enthroned elders fall down and worship. The ultimate authority receives universal and eternal allegiance.

6:1-2. The First Seal.—The Book of the Reign of God is fastened with **seven seals**. The living Christ, seen in symbol as the Lamb that had been slain, royally opens the seven seals. Ch. 6 describes the opening of six of these seals.

The Lamb opens the first of the seven seals. One of the four mighty living creatures calls in a voice resounding like thunder, **Come.** At once **a white horse** comes plunging on the scene. The rider has a bow. He has received a crown. He rides forth on a career of continuous conquest. He is the first of the Four Horsemen of the Apocalypse. He is the veritable incarnation of war. He is to be used as an instrument of God for the overthrowing of that which is against the divine will. A power rising to master Rome may well be in mind. But the man of Patmos is announcing a profound principle of wide application. The forces of evil which go forth to conquer the earth will have released against them a force which under the hand of God will effect their overthrow. The fierce horseman has an invisible Master who will determine the outcome of all his battling and bend it to the purposes of his own will.

3-4. The Second Seal.—The Lamb opens the **second seal**. The second of the mighty living creatures shouts, **Come.** A red horse breaks forth, carrying a rider who is to bring civil war. He receives **a great sword.** It is the symbol of the force men are to use against each other. For the forces of evil are not only to be attacked from without. They are to destroy each other. There is an inherent principle of self-destruction in evil. The second horseman sets into action those inner energies of disintegration by whose means evil men become their own worst foes. When the tale of wrong is told to the finish, it means destruction in every way. Foes without and foes within betray those who are the foes of God.

5-6. The Third Seal.—The Lamb opens the **third seal**. The third of the living creatures cries out, **Come.** And the third of the Four Horsemen of the Apocalypse appears. A **black horse** comes forth. His rider has **a balance in his hand.** A cry of destitution is heard. Wheat and barley are to be sold at prices presaging terrible hardship. The necessities of life are almost beyond reach. And by a hard irony, only superfluous things like **oil and wine** can be easily obtained. This utter social and economic maladjustment is produced by the one who carries the scales. This third horseman is Famine. Those who survive civil war and attack from without are to confront starvation. It is an evil society reaping the product of the seeds of its own planting. Divine judgment is the making secure and final of that fate which is already enshrined in the very heart of evil.

7-8. The Fourth Seal.—As the Lamb opens the **fourth seal** the voice of the fourth living creature shouts, **Come.** A greenish yellow horse appears. The name of his rider is **Death. Hades,** a personification of that which follows death, comes after him. The picture is somewhat confused here and may indicate a confusion in the text. As they stand, the sentences describe the coming of death and of the tragedy following death. The fourth horseman kills men with the sword and famine and pestilence and by means of **wild beasts.** A fourth part of the world is subject to his attack. So the horses of destruction ride on and do their terrible work. The picture is not entirely coherent, but it is characterized by a massive terror. It is not Rome which is to be feared. It is the one who controls the activities of these awful horsemen. Over against the terror of political injustice is put the terror of the justice of God.

9-11. The Fifth Seal.—When the Lamb opens the **fifth seal**, one might expect a fifth horse to ride forth. But the symbol of the horses has been brought to completion. An entirely different scene appears. Under the altar are seen the souls of those who had given their lives in loyalty to **the word of God.** They cry with a loud voice that the world cannot be left merely a place of the martyrdom of the faithful. It must be a place of the punishment of their murderers. How long will the one who is completely holy and perfectly true allow the present cruel situation to go on? When will the world see the spectacle of a vast judgment whose mighty vengeance will set all moral values clearly before the minds of men? The cry for vengeance is a cry for a world where justice is not defeated and injustice does not sit upon the throne. Each martyr is given a white robe. They are to wear the garments of ultimate purity. Gently they are told that for a time they are to rest secure in the protection of God until they are joined by others who pay the same price for their loyalty. The Great Avenger is not careless, but he holds his times of action in his own hands. And in hands of gentleness he holds the martyrs too.

12-17. The Sixth Seal.—The Lamb opens the **sixth seal**. There follows a vast cataclysm in which the universe itself is seen in process of disintegration. There is the awful shaking of a terrible **earthquake.** The sun becomes black and loses its capacity to give light. In place of the silvery glory of the full moon there appears something like a splotch of blood. The stars fall like **untimely figs** in a storm. The sky disappears as if it were a scroll to be rolled up. The mountains and islands in a kind of insane movement change their places. It is the complete breakdown of everything upon which men had depended. The proud **kings of the earth** try to find a place to hide. The princes forget their lofty station in their mad quest for safety. Military leaders flee to seek security. The rich forget their possessions. The strong forget their might. Slaves and freemen, held for a moment in the community of a great fear, seek a common safety. Caves and rocks of the mountains provide only a momentary refuge in a crumbling world. And more dreadful than the awful breaking apart of the universe is the sense that the one on the ultimate throne and the Lamb who had been slain have come at last in a terrible judgment. The great and the small of earth call upon the mountains and the rocks to fall upon them. Any fate is better than the confronting of the fury of the wrath of God. Who could stand in an hour when everything begins to fall apart the very moment it is touched? The Great Avenger has come to his day at last.

This chapter is first of all a document of the divine overlordship. Men were afraid of the Roman power. There was a power far mightier than Rome which ought to inspire real fear. It is the judgment of God rather than the misjudgment of Rome which is the final, and for evil-minded men the terrible, fact of life. There can be no true reign of God without conclusive judgment of evil. And so as the seals are opened, one by one, mighty acts of judgment are set forth in vivid symbol. War, disintegrating civil disturbance, pestilence, and death are instruments in the hands of God for acts of judgment whose awful finality no one can dispute. Of course the evil in the hearts of wicked men and the evil expressed in their deeds have the seed of every sort of practical tragedy in them. Men themselves produce the tragedies which destroy them. God has made life so that evil is in its very nature self-destructive. But more than this, he presides over the tragedy which comes as the judgment of evil men. He sends forth the Four Horsemen of the Apocalypse. The awful unfolding of tragedy in a world full of wickedness is not a lawless and uncontrolled process. God sends the horseman of war. God sends the horseman who sets bad men at each other's throats. God sends famine. God sends death.

When the world defies God, he uses that very defiance for the forging of his instruments of judgment.

The fashion in which the one who is perfectly good uses that which is evil to work out its own destruction involves some of the subtlest problems of what may be called the ethics which determine the relations of God with men. It is in the perfection of his own nature that God finds the source of the moral demands which even he obeys. His sovereignty is his complete obedience to the behests of the perfection which he finds in his own nature. That he uses the evil which men produce to work out its own destruction is a part of the very strategy of the divine rule. And in a way the perfection of God is revealed in the fashion in which moral imperfection shows itself for what it is, as its acts express its true genius and its inevitable disintegration. There is a great moral virility in this point of view which is definitive for Revelation. Before this cosmic picture of the reign of God, the rule of Rome becomes something petty and passing. And Rome itself will at last appear not as a judge but as a power subject to judgment.

There is a subtle apologetic for this whole position in the episode of the souls of the martyrs under the altar. These are the good men for whom an evil world had no place. Because they were loyal to goodness and to God, their lives were snuffed out. They cry out for an act in history which will vindicate their loyalty and the power and the finality of that to which they were loyal. They are asking for precisely what was set forth in symbol as occurring in the episodes of the four horsemen. If the last word history has to say about martyrs is that they were slain, then morally history comes to a dead end. No wonder the martyrs call for acts in history which will conclusively set forth the finality of the moral reign of God. The reply sets the whole matter in larger relations. A white robe is given to each of them. The utter and complete purification of good men is more important than the destruction of bad men. The inner felicity of the men who have attained the beauty of whitened lives has an even greater significance than the outer processes by which goodness is vindicated in history. They are to have rest with God while the preliminary processes of human life go on. There are others who must pay the great and terrible price which they have paid. But the acts of judgment in history are sure. In God's own good time the mighty acts of vindication for which the martyrs call will come in the very world and in the very life of men.

There is something graciously significant about this tale of the fashion in which restless saints were taught to accept the rest of God. They had a right to ask for that for which they cried out. But deeper than the justification in history which they so painfully and eagerly desired was that life with God in which was perfect peace and perfect rest. The gift of the white garments meant that there were men whose complete loyalty answered to the very purpose of God in making men. If evil had been effectively punished with no triumphant good remaining, what a tragedy that would have been. For the goal of history is seen not in the judgment of the evil, important and necessary as that is, but in the triumph of the good. The picture of the saints at rest under the altar has a peaceful and quiet beauty of its own. To put this picture of inner felicity between one series of pictures of explosive judgment and another picture of terrible doom is more than a work of art. The artist has his justification in the fact that what he says corresponds to the truth of things. There is the outer tragedy. And there is also the inner peace. And one day, as in time we shall see, the inner peace shall come forth to dwell in a world where there is no tragedy. To have attained the white flower of a blameless life is to have fulfilled the very purpose of creation.

When the sixth seal is opened, the ultimate cataclysm seems to have come. And we must not allow to escape from us the fact that in the symbolic picture all this comes to pass as a result of the action of the Lamb that was slain. The Cross was to save men from judgment. But inevitably it became the central fact in judgment. It is to the world in which Christ died that all these woeful happenings come. They come to a world which has rejected the Cross. Life is lived in constant dependence upon the stability of the cosmic environment. The sun giving heat and light, the moon shining with silvery grace at night, the stars piercing the darkened sky with points of light, are symbols and more than symbols of the stability of that nature in relation to which we live our life. The sky and the mountains and the islands keep constant appointments with men. And in the frame of this stability man can live his life. But the wickedness of men has robbed them of the right to the co-operation of nature as they live their lives. So in magnificent and terrible symbol the sun turns black, the moon becomes a token of blood in the night, the stars drop down like fruit dislodged from lifeless branches by fierce blasts of wind. The sky vanishes like a curtain raised at the beginning of a tragedy. The mountains and the islands become a part of the general dance of death. The friendly universe turns ferocious and hostile. Proud men suddenly realize that their world has turned against them. The mighty leaders of men find their authority gone, their power dissipated, the distinctions of their proud life without meaning, and the very bases of existence disintegrating. Caves and rocks furnish no real refuge where every physical object is in process of coming apart. They can only hope that the refuse of a disintegrating universe will fall upon them and protect them, if only through annihilation, from the wrath of God. The implicit contract between man and nature is in the hands of God, and when he wills it, will come to an end.

The whole conception has something tremendous and overwhelming about it. Not only is God stronger than all human powers. He is stronger than all natural forces. Indeed, he is the very energy of all natural energies. It is only through him that they exist and carry on their activities. They are not only the products of his creative activity; they are the servants of his will. Nature ceases to be the willing servant of men who defy God.

But it is no mere general theism which is being expressed in these powerful symbols. It is the God who has come to the world in Jesus Christ, who has made and controls the world. It is the God that in Jesus Christ met death upon the Cross who is the awful Master of nature. The wrath men fear is the wrath of the Lamb. The one who died to save men is the very one whose judgment they must confront when they deny and defy him. Nature is the servant of the one who died upon the Cross. The world has complete moral and spiritual coherence in respect of its ultimate control. There is not one moral world, and another spiritual world, and another world of physical facts and forces. Sun and stars and mountains and islands and the mind and heart and conscience of man belong to one universe controlled by the God whose face we see in the face of Jesus Christ.

7:1-8. The Sealing of the Saints.—After the vision of the breakdown of the orderly life of the universe in a kind of cosmic chaos, the very thought of which may well make the hearts of devout men congeal with terror, there is a sudden change and we come upon a great vision for the reassurance of believers who have felt the clutch of the most shattering fear. The heavenly bringers of tragic events are to be restrained until a powerful angel puts **the seal of the living God** upon the foreheads of the saints. With that seal they can pass through the very disintegration of the foundations of life unafraid. The angels holding **the four winds** have at their disposal mighty forces which may be used to bring devastating tragedy upon men. From every direction evils are ready to be let loose upon mankind. But God has not forgotten the faithful, and there comes blazing from the rising sun a mighty angel whose masterful voice restrains the angels who control the forces of evil until **the servants of God** have the divine imprint placed upon them. A symbolic number, conveying a sense of vastness and completeness, is given to represent the multitude who receive the seal of God. As twelve tribes of Israel had represented God's ancient people, so twelve tribes become a symbol of the greater Israel of God's people in the world. A certain stiffness and oddity in the form may be due to the fact that the author is using old materials incompletely focused for his present purpose. A symbolic number of twelve thousand is sealed from each of the tribes of this greater Israel.

9-17. The Heavenly Fulfillment.—More is needed for the reassurance of the troubled saints than the vision of the sealing of the faithful. And now the scene enlarges and the glory of the ultimate universe of Christian fulfillment is revealed. Now it is a multitude which no man can number which shares in the Christian victory. They come from every nation. They bear the marks of every tribe. They have the characteristics of every one of the diverse peoples in the world. They speak every language which has ever been spoken by men. And they stand before the throne of God's final victory. This ultimate fulfillment is in the terms of redemption. They stand before the Lamb which was slain, even as they stand before the throne. For the throne is really his throne. Their garments are shining white, and they carry palms, even as those who welcomed Jesus on his day of triumphal entrance into Jerusalem took branches of palm trees as they went to meet him. The vast multitude of Christian victors lift a great shout of singing. It is a glorious ascription of salvation to God who sits upon the throne and to the Lamb. Their final experience of joyous triumph has come through Christ and his Cross. The figure of the Lamb is always rich with memories of Calvary. Perfect and complete felicity is the gift of the Cross. And now joined to the voices of the redeemed there are heard the voices of the elders and the voices of the four living creatures. Of one accord they fall before the throne of power and redemption. And they lift their voices with a great Amen to the song of triumph of the redeemed. They ascribe blessing to the God who has given such blessing. They exult in God's glory. Their words vibrate with the wonder of his wisdom. They give thanks to the one who is the source of all thanksgiving. They see in God the very omnipotence of honor. They see in him the very essence of power. They behold in him the living presence of unshakable might. And all these glories they ascribe to God not for time but for all eternity. And then there swells another vast Amen.

It is all so overwhelming that somehow it must be made near and human. So we hear the man of Patmos addressed by **one of the elders** who asks him to tell who these are who are arrayed in white. In all humility the man of Patmos replies that the lordly being addressing him knows the answer to his own question. Then comes the description of the numberless host as consisting of those who came out of great suffering. It is **the blood of the Lamb** which has whitened their garments. Their very standing before the throne of God comes from the great redemption. So they are able to give tireless and acceptable service to the living God day and night. They shall be in the very dwelling place of the one who sits upon the throne, and so their security will be complete. They, many of whom had known such bitter hunger, shall hunger no more. They who had panted with such awful thirst shall thirst no more. No heat of the sun and no vicissitude of life shall any more menace their perfect safety from harm and from pain. The Lamb shall be their safety and their security. And that there may be no possible mistake about his ultimate authority, it is stated that he is **in the midst of the throne** of ultimate power. Then there is a sudden and gracious turn of thought. The Lamb upon the throne is not only to be their king. He is to be their shepherd. He is to guide them to waters of eternal vitality. They have known burdens and buffeting and tears. But now **God will wipe away every tear from their eyes.** After the thought of a **shepherd** guiding his sheep, there is just the suggestion of a mother wiping away the tears of little children. So the passage ends with all the wonder of the tenderness and the gentleness of God.

All the forces of the universe are subject to the power and the authority of God. The angels of destruction are his angels and do his will. The great angel of sealing is his servant and carries out his behests. The symbolic picture is one of infinite comfort to hard-pressed men. Events may seem wild and lawless but God is their master. His control is absolute. And at his will they feel the restraint of his hand. There is an ultimate power. There is an ultimate authority. And this authority and this power are found in the God who made and sustains the universe. It is a high view of the sovereignty of God, and in days of desperate moral tragedy it can be maintained only by those capable of great faith. It is the aim of Revelation to create and to maintain just such faith. It comes home with special relevance to those who have to take account of concentration camps and of the unbelievable cruelty of mass murder as they build their houses of faith. Some have tried to solve the problem by conceiving that God is as much a victim as are we in the presence of deeds of terrible cruelty. He hates them but they come in spite of him. Really, though, such problems are not solved by dethroning God. It is precisely because he is on the throne that we may look for light beyond the darkness. A finite God would need a mightier deity to protect his own moral interests. The author of Revelation has no hesitation here. He himself and the people to whom he writes are the victims of unethical power. But he never doubts that the God of perfect righteousness is on the throne and will turn all things to purposes of good at last. It is this which the prisoner on Patmos has in mind as he tells of the sealing of the saints. They are to pass through the fire of tragedy, but they have inner security because they have been sealed as those who belong to God.

There is no detailed symbolic picture of the process of sealing. The main matter is that God has not forgotten his own. He has come to them in intimate strength to prepare them for what they must endure. The consciousness of the divine seal upon their foreheads prepares them for every vicissitude. Marked as his own by the very God of the universe, the bitter tragedies of time cannot break their courage or sap their strength. Drop the symbolism, and we know at once that we are talking about something which Christians of every century have experienced. In one way we can almost define a Christian as one who has found an inner security which cannot be touched by outer tragedy. Christian heroism has always been buttressed by this very potent faith. Out of eternity a power has come to make a man who must live in the midst of time invincible. The tribes of the living Christian Israel are joined in a great fellowship through this experience of the victorious touch of God upon each separate life. To go back to the symbol, the sealing of the saints is a perpetual act in every generation.

But what is an inner experience, giving strength in the individual life, is to become a mighty cosmic event of outer fulfillment. So the author of Revelation anticipates the final beatific vision at the end of the book. He lifts the curtain and there is revealed a glorious scene of utter felicity and triumph. There is no attempt to use even a symbolic number for those who stand shining in the glory of the ultimate triumph of redemption. All ages and all places make their contribution. All languages and every political organization find representation in the great host. The vicissitudes of human life are over. Faith has become sight. Hope has become realization. The inner security has become an outer stability as firm as the eternal hills of God. The white and shining garments are the outer expression of an inner purity. The saints are cleansed as well as victorious. And their palms of triumph express an inner conquest as well as an outer victory. Their soaring song of redemption is joined by the anthem of all heavenly beings lifting high the deathless music of immortal praise. Our author clearly believed that strugglers in time have the right to the encouragement which comes from the full vision of the eternal splendor. There is an old French proverb to the effect that to understand earth you must have known heaven. There are, to be sure, those who fear that if you believe in heaven, you will become impotent upon earth. As a matter of fact, it is just because a man believes in the ultimate triumph of all that is good that he is driven to new energy in the pursuit of goodness here and now. His life in time is transformed by his faith in eternity. There is a moral and spiritual lift about faith in an eternal consummation which quite transforms a man's thoughts of this world and its experiences and its responsibilities. He is to live in time as a citizen of eternity. We need not be afraid of the heavenly vision. In fact, it is only those who possess the heavenly vision who can live with full courage and power in this present world.

James Denney used to say, "The death of Christ—that is Christianity." One may well remember these words as he sees in the great vision of Revelation the place given to the Lamb which was slain. It is very clear that by the time this book was written the thought of the death of our Lord had become central for all Christian thinking. And it had become central for Christian thinking because it had already become central in Christian experience. The figure of the robes washed and made white in the blood of the Lamb expressed something which was at the very heart of the life of the Christian. That the Cross has completely captured the imagination of Christendom is clear to anyone who studies the history of Christian experience. The cathedral built in the form of a cross is only one of many examples of the way in which the deed on Calvary has twined itself about the thought and the life of Christian men. It is very significant that the place which was given to the Cross after centuries of Christian living was already secure at the time when Revelation was written (see Expos., ch. 5). No scholastic or formal exercise relating the shedding of blood on Calvary to the system of O.T. sacrifice can tell the whole truth about it. Indeed, that system and Christian beliefs about the Cross sprang from a common root, all of it coming to a climax in the thought of the suffering God, himself the victim in the great sacrificial rite. The distillation of the deepest experiences of untold numbers of Christian men came to the conviction that in Christ the very God who is the judge of men had died for them in order that the judgment of the Cross might become a great act of redemption. What Christ had done for them upon the Cross was to become a power for the transforming of their lives. To say that they washed their robes and made them white in the blood of the Lamb was to use a figure so vital and so true that it dripped with the very quality of living experience. One may readily see how all this at once became a practical power in the days of persecution. It was the very one who had died for men who was to maintain their lot when all the powers of the world turned against them. His death for them made it possible for them to die for him. So the Cross created courage and maintained a deathless hope.

But the Cross has not only a past reference to the moral tragedies which it solves, and a present reference in respect of the dauntless courage which it inspires. It also has a future reference. The figure of the Lamb is suddenly changed to the figure of the Shepherd. And the Shepherd who died for the sheep is seen as the Shepherd who is to guide the sheep in all the felicity of the life of perfect fulfillment. He is the Lord of the blood which removes stains. But he is also the Lord of the fountains of exhaustless vitality. He is the Shepherd guiding the sheep to the waters of life. In this whole passage the word God and the word Lamb are used interchangeably. God is to put his tabernacle over those who are to be protected from all burdensome and destructive heat. The Lamb is to be the Shepherd. God is to wipe every tear from eyes which have been wet with suffering. The Lamb exercises divine powers. The ultimate authority belongs to God and to the Lamb. The dwellers in the tearless land meet God as the one who suffered for them on the Cross.

As we have already seen, the blessing, the honor, the majesty, given to Christ come not as the result of an argument, though arguments may be very well in their own way. They come as the result of a vivid and a vital experience. Christ has done for men what only God can do. Therefore he shares the ultimate throne. Because he has the place of God in their lives, he receives the place of God in their thought. And this, it must be said, has been true of Christians in every century. Brilliant arguments and profound processes of dialectic might have left them acquiescent but not profoundly

moved. But at the very heart of their experience Christ has met them as the one who satisfied their deepest need. Everything that God could do for them he did. Therefore he holds in their hearts and in their minds the place which only God can hold. If the time were to come when men ceased to receive from Christ what only God can give, the words ascribing to him a place in the divine life would have ceased to have any meaning. As long as he captures in their lives a place which can be given rightly only to God, the position which classical Christianity has given to him will be secure.

In every age men need the illumination of eternity if they are to have full faith for the living of the life in time. By this living faith the tearless land must be the possession of those who live in the land of many tears.

8:1-6. The Seventh Seal.—The **seventh seal** of the Book of the Reign of God is opened by the Lamb. We are now to move rapidly from one set of symbols to another. From the seals we are to move to the trumpets. And the transition is achieved by means of the seventh seal. When it is opened, there is a mighty and seminal **silence in heaven.** So tremendous have been the issues, and so dramatic the symbols, that there must be quiet for their understanding and for the appropriation of their meaning. Then the great pageant goes on. Each of the seven great angels of the Presence receives a trumpet. The seven seals had represented divine decision. The seven trumpets represent divine action. But before the sounding of the first trumpet there is another episode having to do with **the prayers of the saints.** An angel with a great censer appears. And to him is given much incense. This is added to the prayers of the saints, and prayers and incense go up in a mighty glory of worship from the hand of the angel to the most high God. The saints are never forgotten in the unfolding of the events of the reign of God. They are always a part of the vast ritual of the kingdom. The censer which had been filled with the rich incense of a glorious worship is now filled with destructive fire. And the angel casts the fire upon the earth. There follow staggering portents of rolling thunders and awe-inspiring voices and flashing lightning and the shaking of the earth. And in the midst of all this the seven trumpeters prepare to sound their trumpets.

7. The First Trumpet.—When the first trumpet sounds, we see that the trumpets are to call for the action of vast and destructive forces. Sometimes they suggest the plagues of Egypt. And sometimes they suggest the action of tremendous volcanic energies. Always they signalize the deeds of judgment of the great God of moral action. After the sounding of the first trumpet there is **hail** and there is **fire mingled with blood** and these are **cast upon the earth.** **A third** of the earth is destroyed by burning. **A third of the trees** become a blazing conflagration. **All green grass** is devoured by fire. It is becoming increasingly clear that the good and orderly life of the world cannot continue if men turn in wickedness from the right will of God. That at first the destruction is incomplete and partial indicates that an opportunity for moral consideration and change of mind and change of life is being given to men. Later symbols, as the book goes on, will make it clear how utterly men failed to respond to this opportunity.

8-9. *The Second Trumpet.*—The **second angel** blows a great blast upon his trumpet. And the judgment which had come to the land now comes to the sea. What looks like a blazing **mountain** is **cast into the sea.** The man of Patmos was doubtless familiar with volcanic eruptions and here he found his figure. **A third part of the sea became blood. A third of the living creatures** in the sea died. And **a third of the ships** sailing on the sea met destruction. The power of God embraces the sea as well as the land. His acts for the destruction of that which is evil will move out over the great deep. But here again the operation of the terrible forces set in motion by God will be gradual, giving opportunity for the changed mind and the changed life.

10-11. *The Third Trumpet.*—The **third angel** blows his trumpet and a **star burning like a torch** falls from heaven. **A third part of the rivers** and **the fountains of waters** used by thirsty men are touched by the blight of the falling star. It is bitter and destructive and it bears the name of Wormwood. A third of the waters become wormwood and many men die as they quench their thirst. The very sources of the ongoing of life are contaminated. The men whose misdeeds had brought bitter and evil quality to their character find that forces from the sky are so changing nature that it is bringing bitterness to them.

12. *The Fourth Trumpet.*—The **fourth angel** blows his trumpet and the blight which had come to land and sea and the waters men drink reaches the sun and the moon and the stars. **A third of the sun** is blackened. **A third of the moon** turns to darkness. And **a third of the stars** cease to shine. And according to the symbolic picture, **a third of the day** and **a third of the night** there is no light. The mighty heavenly bodies are the instruments of the righteous acts of God, though here once more the gradual quality of the action gives time for moral response.

13. *The Flying Eagle.*—At this point there is a terrific portent in midheaven. A great eagle flies in these vast spaces and shouts with a mighty voice a threefold and cumulative woe to fall upon the earth dwellers as the three remaining trumpets speak forth their release of tragic destiny. Always the anticipation carries implicitly within it the call to repentance. While the deeds are in the future it is possible to avert them.

The mighty apocalyptic catastrophes with their vast symbolism are so overwhelming that they dazzle the imagination and tend to reduce the mind to something not unlike terrified stupor. So there comes the silent time when all these tremendous impressions may be sorted out and some clear sense of their meaning can come to the mind. The time of silence for the sake of dependable apprehension and true understanding brings suggestions of very great importance. Times of action all too easily become times of thoughtlessness. The rush of tremendous deeds takes away the sense of meaning. And yet without meaning there is only chaos. Of course silence itself brings no assurance of thought. But the silence of heaven suggests a lofty perspective when the mind is lifted above the dark and heavy experiences far below and comes to see things as they really are. A certain meaning can be seen by an evil mind. A certain meaning can be seen by a confused mind. A certain meaning can be seen by an acute and able mind. But the real meaning is the meaning as God sees it, and that is the meaning the man of Patmos would bring within the reach of those for whom he writes. The heavenly silence may be a silence in which the mind of God becomes clear to the minds which he has created. If there is a silence of vacuousness, there is also a silence of understanding.

But the great action is to go on. The seven angels of the Presence receive seven trumpets. The trumpet is for proclamation. And proclamation is in part an announcement of meaning. The drama of the action of God is to be announced for the understanding of men. And as the angels stand ready for the blowing of their trumpets, we are aware that we are to witness not only action but revelation.

The interlude of the angel of the golden censer is a vivid symbol of God's care for the hard-pressed saints and of the destruction which is to be released. The same censer contains the incense to go up with the prayers of the saints and the fire whose awful burning is to be cast upon the earth. God's judgment never causes him to forget his kindness. The very people whom the world treats with cruelty and then forgets are forever in the mind of God. And the poignant cries of the saints for the help of God go up in a perfect cloud of incense, magnificent with all the glory of worship. The moral order of the universe is the expression of the very character of God. And this comes forth in the preservation of all that is good and in the destruction of all that is evil.

The mind and the imagination are carried along by the symbolic picture as the seven angels prepare to sound their trumpets. In a sense the revelation is given line upon line, and precept upon precept, and there is much inevitable repetition. The same picture is seen from different points of view, and the same facts and truths are expressed by means of different symbols. When the first angel sounds his trumpet, destructive forces symbolized by hail and fire and blood are cast upon the earth. The destruction which follows consumes a third of that which grows upon the land. The picture is made graphic by the special reference to the trees and the green grass. The earth with all its productivity is not to be taken for granted by man. It is the gift of God, and God can at any time take it away. To snatch from man the very environment in which he lives his life is indeed to leave him completely undone. The partnership between man and God is dissolved. The friendliness of the good earth has turned to hostility. Man's bad use of that which was given him for good use has robbed him of the very gift which he has neither understood nor appreciated. The law of the destruction of that which is misused is seen in action by multitudes of men while there is yet time to mend their ways. Those who live on the two thirds of the earth untouched by destruction are yet in the land of moral opportunity. Of course the mathematical symbol is not to be taken too seriously. The truth at the heart of the symbol is this: We may see the mighty movement of God for the destruction of evil in action before it touches us individually. And we can determine our action by what we see.

The blowing of the trumpet of the second angel is the announcement of the application to a third of the sea of the same destructive activity which has already been applied to the land. Death comes to a third part of all the creatures living in the sea. And a third of the ships upon the sea come to destruction. The mighty deep is subject to God's government even as is the far-spread land. It has always been easy for men to be tempted to think that God is not in the wide stretches of the sea. But God is there. And he is there in all the full meaning of the character which makes him a God of justice and truth. The rule of God is to be vindicated upon the sea as upon the land.

If we insist upon living in the moral depths, destruction will fall upon us from the heights. This is the truth involved in the symbol of the falling of the star called Wormwood. Men of evil lives can find only bitterness in their contacts with the divine rule as long as they continue in their evil ways. The men who make evil their good always find the reign of goodness bitter. The very stars in their courses fight against bad men. And a star will break away from its place in the sky and become a blazing torch bringing destruction. If the force of Rome is used against good men and for evil men, the process is reversed when the heavenly forces come into action. And this is made more emphatic with the vision of the darkening of a third part of the sun and a third part of the moon and a third part of the stars. The contract between earth and heaven is breaking up. Men felt as if they could depend upon the sun and the moon and the shining stars with complete and constant assurance. But the God who gave men light by means of the sun, and made the night bright with the moon and the stars, is on the throne. He has made no contract to give light to bad men. There is of course no astronomy in the symbol. The day and the night will each lose light for a third of its continuance when a third of the sun and a third of the moon and a third of the stars are darkened. The writer is an apocalyptic seer and the age of the technical study of the heavenly bodies is far away. Indeed, it is probable that if he had lived in a scientific age he would still have used his symbol. William Blake was not too much affected by the findings of mathematical science. The man of Patmos is interested in saying that the present order represents a kind of contract between God and men for the ongoing of the world. And if they break their part of the contract, it will come to an end. The sun will no more give dependable light. The moon will no more give the accustomed illumination. The stars which shine at the behest of God will become the foes and not the friends of men. But even this process will come slowly. For God is more interested in the moral transformation than in the destruction of evil men. You live in a precarious world, says the man of Patmos. You think the order of nature is safe. Actually the sun and the moon and all the stars are your foes if you become the foes of God.

The drama heightens with the vision of the mighty eagle flying in the midst of the sky and crying with a terrible voice. The reiterated woe breaks forth like the doom of the universe itself. The three remaining trumpets will bring evils and terrors of incredible dimensions. All of this desperation of horror is intended to rouse men from their moral apathy. They are so sunk into the torpitude of indifference, and something worse than indifference, that no ordinary proclamation of their tragic plight will rouse them. Only the awful sword thrust of sheer terror will stab them awake. Christina Rossetti once wrote a grim little poem about sailors asleep at sea as the tempest approached.[3] The sleepers have been held for years by dreams which have caused them to forget the real sorrows, the real fears, and the real hopes. Stainless spirits try in vain to awake them until at last the spirits' voices become silent as they see that their word is useless. They go sadly away and are replaced by other spirits. Upon the sails can be seen their shadows, like stains of blood. The modern poet is dealing with the same problem that confronted the man of Patmos long ago, the utter lassitude into which evil beguiles men.

The flying eagle has also another message. There are always plenty of men who are ready to declare that goodness represents a lovely world of ideas and ideals, but that the facts are on the side of realistic and selfish men who go their way without moral scruples or spiritual hesitations. But this is simply not true. It is the selfish cynics who refuse to face relevant facts. It is cynicism which offers to men a dreamworld. Goodness is not merely an idea. It is a power. Rightness is not merely an ideal. It is an enthroned authority. And in the very world of action goodness has the last word. It is not only a last word. It is a terrible word to those who have committed themselves with final decisiveness to an evil allegiance. If a man declares that as a practical man he must make moral short cuts and do evil things in order to get on, the reply is that moral short cuts are the most impractical things in all the world. In the long run the good facts are always stronger than the bad facts. Goodness appears as a friend with an outstretched hand. But if that hand is refused, goodness will appear at last as a moral executioner with a sharp and terrible sword. At last, the moral law has the facts as well as the values upon its side. If only men had eyes to see and ears to hear, there is always an eagle in the midst of the sky crying forth these truths which have in them the very safety of our souls.

9:1-12. The Fifth Trumpet.—At the sound of the first four trumpets terrific forces of nature had been used in fearful acts of destruction. God uses nature itself for the punishment of evil men. Now the fifth trumpet sounds and we come upon the beginning of the symbolic drama of the divine use of malignant spiritual forces for his own great ends. Moral evil, which is really a defiance of God, becomes the instru-

[3] "Sleep at Sea."

ment of God in working out his own purposes. Like a star of light falling from the sky, an angel descends to the earth and stands at the entrance of the abyss where the dark spirits of evil are confined. The key to this region of horror is given to the angel, and he opens the strange prison. Awful fiery smoke comes forth, darkening everything under the sun. Out of this great cloud emerge monstrous locusts. They are free from their prison, but they are under the complete and constant mastery of God. They are not allowed to hurt the green grass or the trees or any growing thing. But like scorpions, they are to sting the men who do not bear the mark of the **seal of God.** The sting is not fatal but its effect is such excruciating torture that men long to die. They try to find death. But death eludes them. For nearly half a year the agony continues. The monster locusts are described in words calculated to arouse intense feelings of terror. They seem to wear crowns, as kings of destruction. Men's faces look out under heads of hair like the hair of women, and their fierce teeth suggest the teeth of lions. Their wings make a sound like masses of chariots drawn by multitudes of horses in the full fury of battle. But the scorpionlike tails of the monsters, with their power to sting, do the bitter work they have come to do. They have a demonic king whose name is given in Hebrew and in Greek. In awful solemnity we hear a voice saying that the first of the three woes of which the eagle in midheaven had spoken is passed. Two more are yet to come.

13-21. The Sixth Trumpet.—The sixth trumpet sounds. And from **the horns of the golden altar,** which stands before God, there comes a divine command: **Release the four angels who are bound at the great river Euphrates.** A great army of two hundred million horsemen comes forth. The horsemen have fiery breastplates and the heads of the horses are like the heads of lions. Fire and smoke and brimstone come furiously from their mouths, dealing death everywhere. Their tails, serpentlike, have heads, and these have their own destructive power. A third of the men in the world are killed. The earth is full of the woe of the awful tragedy. But those who remain alive do not repent. Demon worship still holds them. Golden idols still capture their imagination. Silver idols still enslave them. Brass idols still command their worship. Stone idols still rule them. And even idols of wood receive their homage. None of these can see or hear or walk. But to such as these they give their devotion. There is no moral power in such make-believe deities. And so men's fierce impulses unrestrained lead to murder, to sexual vice, even in abnormal forms, which their religion sanctifies, and to such widespread theft that there is nothing which a man can securely call his own. All values disintegrate in a worship which has no intellectual or moral force and no spiritual loftiness. The men caught in the malignant fascination of these practices are quite unmoved as they watch the release of the mighty forces of destruction let loose at the command of God. They do not repent.

In these symbolic pictures we have seen the very forces of evil turned by God to the destruction of evil. And we have seen the men caught on the edges of this tragedy with no moral understanding of its meaning and no turning to God in repentance and no repudiating of their evil ways. The moral tragedy within matches the moral tragedy without. The man of Patmos is saying to those who are willing to listen that there is no power which is not under the control of God. Everything on the earth and in the heavens moves according to his behest. So those who are against God find that everything which goes to make up the pattern of their lives is against them. The world has only destruction for those who would destroy the will of God. All the spiritual beings in the universe are the servants of God. If they accept his lordship, they are glad and willing servants, joyously doing his will. If they try to defy him, they find that they are impotent in their opposition. Their very rebellion is turned to his purposes. They are unwilling servants, but they are servants still. It is not hard to see the fashion in which the tremendous symbolic pictures, through which the man of Patmos gives his message, make it clear to hard-pressed and persecuted men that it is really the persecutors who are impotent. The men who are loyal to God as he has spoken to them in Christ have the very mark of God upon their foreheads. So whatever they may have to suffer as the days pass, in the ultimate sense they are immune. The God they worship is truly on the throne. And he will never forget his own.

The author of Revelation has no end of materials of diverse kind passing through his mind. When he uses them in his masterful fashion, it is to express his own message. They form the raw material for the most astonishing symbolic pictures. But they are always used in such a fashion as to express with clear finality some great Christian position. In ch. 9 we are introduced to a vast underworld of wicked and lawless spirits. The men who read the book had many such pictures in their own minds. The man who wrote the book goes right to the heart of the matter. His great insistence is clear: God is seated in full power upon an unshared throne. He is the ultimate master of all forces.

He is the ultimate master of all spirits, good and evil. He imprisons the spirits who might work in devastating fashion against his will. And when he releases them, it is only to carry out his own design of moral judgment. They have no power to hurt anything except according to his will. They appear in full panoply of terror. But it is a terror under the complete command of God. There is no force in the universe which God does not control. There is no creature in the universe which God does not control.

This sense of God as sovereign in spite of all the dark and evil things which men must face is of the utmost significance. Two matters are of great importance in our thought about the Deity. One has to do with the character of God. The other has to do with the power of God. The author of Revelation finds his conception of the character of God by contemplating the Lamb which was slain. He now sets forth his conception of the power of God by asserting his complete mastery even of that realm of moral evil which is the darkest fact of life. Over against the sovereignty of Rome he puts the sovereignty of God. At its worst, as we shall see later on, Rome is the very incarnation of the spirit of evil. God is the living presence of eternal good. No earthly power can stand against the reign of God. And no spiritual evil in high places or in low places has any capacity to withstand the will of the Almighty Ruler of the universe. This sense that the God of all goodness is securely seated upon the throne of the universe is the very basal conviction of the Christian religion. In times of persecution and of widespread moral tragedy it is a faith maintained at the very point of the sword. Life itself seems to contradict it, but it must be held if existence itself is not to fall into utter moral chaos. Those for whom the man of Patmos wrote lived in such a time. So the vision of the good God in absolute control of the universe is as important as anything to be found in the whole book.

The men whose foreheads bore the seal of God had already chosen the will of God as over against everything which contradicted it. And now God holds them in the safety of his own guardianship. But there are those who have chosen not God's way but the way other than God's. Upon them the forces of destruction are unleashed. The period of their torture is limited. And even when they want to die, their lives are preserved. All this is in the hope of their repentance. The true nature of the evil with which they have allied themselves is revealed in agony in order that they may turn from it. The thought of redemption is implicit in all the tale of terror. But the thing from which they must turn has the very quality of disintegration at its heart. The king of the demonic host bears a name which means destruction. It is of the very nature of moral evil to break apart and to decay. And the forces of malignant evil can be used in divine judgment precisely because it is of the very genius of evil to be its own undoing. If we give our allegiance to the god of destruction, we must not be surprised if we are destroyed.

But it is after the sixth angel has blown his trumpet that torture becomes death. More angels of destruction are released and hundreds of millions of riders go forth on horses of death to do their deadly work. The symbolic picture becomes one of unmitigated horror as the fire and smoke and sulphur issuing from the mouths of the horses, and the stings of the horses' tails with their biting heads of fury, bring death to a third of mankind. If the author uses a Parthian invasion to give dramatic color to his picture, it is something more than any human invasion which he has in mind. Men's own cherished evils turn against them and the ultimate power of darkness uses their own evil character to destroy them. Because the destiny which approaches from without corresponds to the character within, its destructive power cannot be resisted.

All of this had no effect upon the portion of mankind which remained alive. So deeply had they become one with their evil loyalties that even the shock of the most terrible circumstances left them untouched. It is a profound principle that bad choices go on from being acts and become the very character of those who perpetrate them. And when bad deeds have solidified into bad character, there is tragedy indeed. The presentation and analysis of this dark and evil process, as exemplified in the history of bad men, are meant to inspire the very repentance to which the evil men of the description did not come. Indeed, all the threats of the scripture are meant to produce a change in the hearers which will prevent the fulfillment of the threats. It was this which so angered the Jonah of the O.T. parable that instead of going to Nineveh, he started to go to the other end of the world. If he told the people of Nineveh that for their wickedness they would be destroyed, they would repent, and then they would not be destroyed. So he did not want to announce a threat which had a hope at the heart of it. He came to realize that God would save, and he wanted to destroy. One terrible passage after another in Revelation has the same hope at the heart of it. But men may crush that hope. They may refuse to repent. And this possibility the man of Patmos sets before his readers with a kind of stark realism.

The wicked men of whom Revelation speaks are really worshiping not the Spirit of Good but the spirits of evil. Their worship is really demon worship. But it is also idolatry. It puts things in the place which belongs only to their Creator. Gold makes men forget the Creator of gold. Silver makes men forget the Creator of silver. Brass makes men forget the Creator of brass. And even wood makes men forget the Creator of all the forests. With a scorn which is quite characteristic of O.T. prophecy, the man of Patmos reminds his readers that these lifeless images can neither see nor hear nor walk. How can they answer petitions when they cannot hear? How can they do anything important when they cannot even move? (Cf. Isa. 44:12-17.) Men themselves are mightier than these products of their own hands. Their religion has become a process of complete self-deception. And it is for this sort of prostration before the impotent that they have turned from the living God. Perhaps there is a certain subconscious satisfaction in worshiping gods who cannot see your misdeeds and cannot hear your evil words. But gods who are impotent to punish are impotent to bless. And for the living to resort to the lifeless is the most abject of human debasements. Along such lines religion becomes incapable of intellectual insight and moral discipline and lofty spiritual satisfaction. Worship itself becomes a corrupting influence upon the life of mankind. Bad religion comes out at last in bad morals.

And so we have a typical list of the evil deeds of which men did not repent. They had no sense of the sacredness of human life. They were murderers and their lifeless gods confronted murder with no power of moral rebuke. How can the lifeless inspire a sense of the sacredness of life? The worship of the subhuman tends to reduce human experience to subhuman quality. And so idolatry lifts a curtain and we behold a world where man has no responsible relationship to his fellow man. Tooth and knife take the place of moral standards. The very conceptions which give gracious beauty to human life are without root and begin to wither and to die away. To kill another man before he kills you becomes the law of life.

Neither has the world of idolatry any power to preside over the rush and energy of the senses and turn them to high uses. These steeds of hot desire require a masterful driver, and in the world of idolatry men simply surrender to their impetuous energies. The sorceries to which reference is made seem to point in the direction of abnormal vice. And of course in a world of idolatry there is no real restraint to the burning heat of sexual lust; rather there is a surrender to its lawless demands. Men and women are bound together by ties of sensation and not by moral and spiritual fellowship, and the life of the senses, which can be so happy and gracious a part of an experience of noble companionship, loses all its loftier connections. In a world where intellectual and moral and spiritual values are forgotten the conscious life becomes an intense biological experience without the hand of high discipline upon it. Desire takes the place of principle. The world of idolatry offers no stable basis for economic life. Theft becomes the very principle of its practical existence. There are no rights of possession such as those which are necessary for a civilized social order. It may seem rather pleasant to a man if other men have no rights of possession in property which he wants to take from them. But if he himself has no rights of possession, he suddenly discovers that the situation is not so agreeable. Economic life begins to fall apart. The thief turns out to be his own foe as well as the foe of the men from whom he steals. The world of idolatry is not only a world of spiritual confusion. It is a world of moral disintegration. That men should choose to live in such a world rather than in the world provided by a great Person of perfect character, ruling the universe and the life of men with perfect goodness and righteousness, reveals something very evil at the heart of their lives. And when with the unfolding of events their evil world falls completely apart, they are confronted by its true nature in a way which it would seem they must understand. But men can hold to purposes of evil even in the presence of a distintegrating world. They can cling to their murderous and licentious and thieving ways as the storms of moral judgment burst all about them. The principle involved is very clear. Tragedy offers the opportunity of an experience of the moral meaning of events. But it does not make that experience inevitable. The destructive forces released by evil deeds may be so surveyed as to produce repentance. But there is nothing about the process which makes repentance inevitable. So the words "nor did they repent" go to the heart of that strange inverted dignity of freedom by which man can refuse to be taught by history. The man of Patmos may be using strange symbols. But he is dealing with matters of perpetual significance.

10:1-4. *The Mighty Angel and the Seven Thunders.*—Before the sounding of the seventh trumpet there are interludes which have to do with the **mighty angel** and the little book and the measuring of the temple and the two witnesses. The mighty angel descended from heaven wearing a cloud as if it were a garment, the colors of the rainbow shining around his head, his face dazzling **as the sun** and his feet like two burning pillars. He held in his hand a small open book, and he placed his right foot upon the rolling sea and his left upon the solid earth. Then he cried out with a resounding voice like the roaring of a lion. The seven thunders spoke in echoing voices. The man of Patmos understood the words spoken by the seven thunders, and he was about to write them down when a heavenly voice commanded him to hold the words secret and not to write them. The real control of events, the readers are being assured, comes from the heights, not from the depths. It is all clear in heaven and its meaning is thundered forth in heavenly voices, but the time has not come when the whole meaning is to be revealed to men. Some things are said to men in glorious symbols. Some are left to the silence of faith.

5-7. *The Mighty Angel and the Mighty Oath.*—With a tremendous gesture the great angel **lifted up his right hand to heaven** as he stood upon the land and upon the sea. He registered a mighty oath by him who lives eternally, by him who made the heavens and all that they contain, by him who made the earth and all that it contains, and the sea and all that moves in its vast life. And this was the oath: There is no more time for the tentative. The great finalities are to appear. When the seventh angel has sounded, the mighty mystery of events is to come to a conclusion, and the good tidings which have been proclaimed by the prophets are to be fulfilled. If time is taken to mean the period of the relative before the great and final action, then we may well say that the angel declared that time shall be no more. All things are to come to a vast clarification with the great consummation. The good tidings which had been spoken to men of good will are to come to conclusive and final fulfillment.

8-11. *The Mighty Angel and the Little Book.*—But could tidings so inevitably involved in the wickedness of men, the tragedy of the suffering of the good, and the awful cataclysms to burst upon a wicked world, be good tidings? The mighty angel, as we have seen, holds an open book. The analysis of the meaning of human experience, the essence of prophecy, and the vast reach of judgment are declared in that book. It is as vast as human life and divine appraisal. The man of Patmos is told to **take the little book** from the hand of the angel. And the angel tells him to eat it, to assimilate it, and make it a very part of himself. It would be like honey in his mouth, but it would turn to bitterness in his belly. The great and conclusive qualities of prophecy are indeed both sweet and bitter. There is a glory of good tidings. But there are also tidings which are full of tragedy. **In the little book** the past meets the future.

And as the man of Patmos makes its meaning his own, in a sense he experiences a renewal of his mission. The word he has been making so deeply his own has to do with **many peoples and nations and tongues and kings.** For them all he has a mission. And he is commissioned to be in a sense a universal prophet. In truth, he is to become an incarnation of the tragedy and the glory of the divine message. But we are not allowed, and his first readers were not allowed, to forget the glory in the tragedy. The sweetness of honey remains even when the bitterness is present too. In the last analysis, the tidings are good tidings of the victory of God.

It must never be forgotten that the man of Patmos wrote to Christians who dwelt in a world which seemed the contradiction of all their beliefs and of all their hopes. They were in danger of being morally and spiritually crushed by the hard and relentless pressure of their environment. They must be made to understand that they have a secure place in the universe even if their situation is precarious in the little world in which they dwell. They must be assured that eternity is on their side even if time seems to be against them. The mighty angel in full panoply of splendor, claiming the land and the sea for the divine rule, and speaking in a voice in comparison with which the greatest human voices are weak and impotent, meets the deepest need of the hard-pressed men to whom Revelation is addressed. This glorious symbol takes them out of the tragedies of time into the very glory of eternity. They cease thinking of the reign of Caesar and begin really to think of the reign of God.

It may well be said that one of the greatest needs of the men of our own time is some spiritual equivalent of the vision of the angel astride land and sea. The very frame of the contemporary mind is curiously hard and secular. The bitter tragedies which darken the life of our world are clear enough. But men do not know how to lift their eyes to regions where they will behold deathless realities beyond the bitter world in which they dwell, yet having the most tremendous relevance to the ongoing of its life. One of the outstanding characteristics of the literature of our time is the absence of any compelling sense of "the light that never was, on sea or land," which is yet the true illumination of those who live upon the land and sail upon the sea. Men have lost the compelling sense of the eternal frame of reference. And so the moral life has lost the very basis of its demanding sanctions. The spiritual life has become weak and anemic. And even the practical everyday life has lost that quality of security which comes to even the simplest experiences when

there are great convictions about the moral and spiritual nature of the universe behind them. It is only beyond time that we can find the motives for life in time. Without the great sanctions which come from eternity, men tend to abdicate their manhood and to become beasts or merely things. The invasion of the subhuman is a perpetual threat to humanity. The invasion of the divine is the perpetual security of a true humanity. John Milton was a great scholar and a great thinker. It has been said that all the knowledge within the reach of any man in the seventeenth century was alive in his mind. But his belief in the great Taskmaster made all the difference. His sonnet "On His Blindness" comes to a deep and rich peace because of its eternal reference. And so, century by century, men have met the vicissitudes of time strong in a faith which came to them from eternity. It is idle to say that within time men may find resources for the life of time. It is indeed this attempt more than anything else which has led to the twentieth-century debacle in the life of men. If we are to recover the basis for true stability, we must see the vision of the angel clothed with a cloud, glorious with all heavenly majesty and radiance, astride the land and the sea. To drop the figure, we must realize the mastery of the spiritual in the very realm of the temporal. We need—how we need—books written in our own time, glorious with the very wonder of the confidence of a vision which comes out of eternity. In the meantime, we must feed our spirits upon mighty books written in ages when faith was glorious with a light which was brighter than the sun.

The voice of the seven thunders represents the complete and final pronouncements about the reign of God. But this word is not yet for us. It is good, however, to know that the universe itself is echoing with a testimony to the reign of God, whose meaning we are not yet able to make our own. There is a sense in which those who come to compelling experiences of spiritual reality always have a little experience of what the man of Patmos felt as he listened to the thunders. The message is majestic and compelling. But the mind of the age is too secular, too much held in chains of its own limitations, to be ready for the word which would bring such radiant understanding. One of the strangest aspects of the life of men complacent in their own limited use of their intelligence is the fashion in which they assume that what lies beyond their present understanding has no real meaning and no permanent importance. We with our estranged faces all too often miss the meaning of the many-splendored thing. The frank recognition that there is truth which cannot yet be translated into the contemporary vernacular makes for good humility and opens the way to intellectual and moral and spiritual growth. We sometimes say that a thing is "dated," meaning that it shares the intellectual limitations of a particular period. It is a sobering thought that we are all "dated," and that many a great truth pauses at the threshold of our minds because we are not yet capable of receiving it.

The mighty angel swears a great oath. With the utmost solemnity he calls to witness the one who fills the whole life of eternity and who gave existence to the heavens and the land and the sea. To the men whose faith is in danger of being shattered, who are fairly overwhelmed by what seems to be the august strength of that imperial power which has appeared in the temporal order, he declares that this order itself, with all that it contains, is about to come to an end. It is time which is really weak and impotent, not eternity. It is time which has the seal of death upon it. The institutions of time all smell of death. If the empire seems the very contradiction of the good tidings which the prophets have proclaimed, it cannot be said too emphatically that it is the empire which is to go down. There were truths beyond the reach of the Christians to whom the man of Patmos wrote. The one great truth which was gloriously within their reach was this: that which God had given to them in the Christian faith was indestructible. Empires came and went. Christian truth remained. The good tidings which proclaimed the victory of God would be gloriously and completely realized.

The symbol of the little book opens fascinating areas for serious thought. The book of the seven seals had been a book of divine sanctions. The little book is a book of human experience with divine meanings. It is a book of the expression of divine meanings in history. And rightly enough, the great angel who announced the completion and the consummation of history has this book in his hand. But this little book is of the most tremendous significance to the man of Patmos. All past prophecy is alive in it. And it contains everything which gives his message moral and spiritual continuity. So, in a vivid and somewhat stark figure, he is commanded to eat the book and to make its contents a part of his very organism. The first effect is rich and joyous. In this deep and far-reaching fashion God has been present in history. It is not something which can be seen and understood without him. It is something which can be understood only by means of him. And this sense of companionship with God is a happy and glorious thing. It is like honey to the mouth. But it is a stern and austere matter to do business with God. To see human character in the light of the divine character is a devastating experience. And to confront the announcement of God's judgments in history is a heavy and terrible matter. It is like bitterness in the belly. History is in the hands of the living God. And that is no light or easy matter to contemplate. But awe-inspiring and fearful as it is, without it there could be no sure hope and there could be no permanent joy. So the sweet and the bitter always combine in the book of God.

One of the important disciplines to which men should turn their attention is the study of history in the light of divine meanings. The popular reception of the one-volume condensation of Arnold J. Toynbee's monumental work *A Study of History* [4] made very clear men's wistful desire to find genuine and secure meaning in history. But a much profounder and more sure-footed guide than Toynbee is needed to travel these difficult ways. It is all to the good that he is not without consciousness of the deeper moral and spiritual meanings. But really to see history in the light of the lordship of Christ demands a mind with sterner clarity of thought and the suffusing presence of a more completely Christian quality of apprehension. No end of studies of history and biography contain elements which must be a part of the book of Christ in history, and to read widely, always looking for the clues to Christian meaning, is a most rewarding experience. In a sense every serious Christian student and reader must construct his own little book of Christ in history. But in another sense that book comes from the great angel of Christian understanding astride the land and the sea, proclaiming the victory of God. This book will always be both sweet and bitter. Looking at Dante, after he had published his great work, observers used to say, "There goes the man who has been in hell." But they might also have said after the publication of the *Paradiso*, "There goes the man who has been in heaven." Life on the human level can be understood only by one who knows the meaning both of the abysmal depths and of the divine heights. There are always the bitter and the sweet.

Life must continually be interpreted in the light of these profound insights. And so when the man of Patmos has eaten the book and made its contents a part of his very life, he hears the great commission to be a prophet not only to the small group of hard-pressed Christians but to many peoples and nations, and to those who speak many languages, and to many rulers of men. There is a breath-taking hour when we realize the universal relevance of the

[4] New York: Oxford University Press, 1947.

Christian message. Revelation is in one way a book engrossed with the great Christian consummations. But it is also a book about that which must be done before its words of finality have been fulfilled. It is particularly significant that the very passage (vss. 5-11) containing the impressive and imperial proclamation of the great conclusion should also contain the commission of the man of Patmos to be a prophet to those who dwell in time before time has been resolved into eternity. It is of the very nature of Revelation to flash with insights which really supplement each other, though at first they may seem to be paradoxical if not contradictory. The slides of the picture move swiftly, and it requires a mind of great agility and moral and spiritual energy to follow their kaleidoscopic changes. The reader of the book of Christ in history cannot escape the responsibility of telling its meaning to his fellow men.

11:1-2. The Measuring of the Temple.—A symbolic instrument of measurement is given to the man of Patmos. The description of the vision puts him in **the temple of God** at Jerusalem (actually no longer existing), with orders to **measure the temple** and **the altar** and the worshipers. The outer court is not to be measured, for it is seen as subject to the lawless nations who overcome the city and tread it underfoot. The whole picture is meant to convey the assurance that God does not forget his people in the midst of calamity. The true meaning of their worship, the death which was the prelude to deathlessness, and the loyalty of those whose worship and character have been responsive to the very truth of God are held perpetually in the divine mind. So much lies back of the symbol of the measuring of the temple, the altar, and those who worship there. The true worshipers are not to be saved from calamity. But they are to be preserved and to find the fulfillment of their hopes beyond the calamity. There are those who are not true worshipers. They will meet the coming tragedy without the security which God will give. Their fate is symbolized by the unmeasured outer court. Whatever earlier materials the man of Patmos uses, the fashion in which he turns them to a Christian purpose is not too difficult to see.

3-13. The Two Witnesses.—This passage is full of quality rich with O.T. memories. We see in picture the word of God proclaimed to men all too little inclined to be responsive, and all too much inclined to settle into wicked ways. The **two witnesses** inevitably suggest Moses and Elijah. The plagues and the fire from heaven are all the while in the background of the reader's mind. The law and the prophets are to become vocal, and law itself is to become masterful prophecy. Too powerful to be si-

lenced, the representatives of God are to speak out their full word. They hold at their disposal the lives of those to whom they speak, and the forces of nature upon which men depend for existence. So their word must be heard. So their word is heard. But when their testimony has been given, from the very abode of ultimate evil a diabolical creature comes who contends with them and slays them. Their death is to be a part of their witness. And in the symbolic picture, the Jerusalem which had rejected so many prophets is seen as the place where they, like their Lord, meet death. Their **dead bodies** were treated with ignominy. There were no funeral rites. Their bodies were not laid in the tomb. Men from all about the world came to gaze upon them. There was a general sense of relief, as if the silencing of voices of condemnation blotted out the tragic moral situation. Men held celebrations and sent each other presents to signalize their joy. The prophets whose words had **tormented them** spoke no more. But after a period the **breath of life** returned to them. In full vitality **they stood up on their feet.** The men who had celebrated now trembled with fright. A mighty voice called the resurrected prophets from the heights to come to the heavenly regions. And while their enemies looked on in tense and agonizing fear, **they ascended** in a cloud. The earth shook. Everywhere there was the sound of falling buildings. A multitude of people met death. Mastered by fear, the rest gave glory to the God whose voice they had despised.

14-19. The Seventh Trumpet.—The second of the woes proclaimed by the eagle in the sky is past. And it is announced that the third woe is to come at once. **The seventh angel blew his trumpet.** The woe which brings evil to wrongdoers is a glorious thing to those who maintain the right. So in lofty symbol we behold the rejoicing of heaven over the triumph of God. Great voices are heard declaring that **the kingdom of the world is become the kingdom of our Lord and of his Christ,** and that his kingdom is to continue unto the ages of the ages. **The four and twenty elders** once more leave their thrones and fall upon their faces. They thank God, existing forever, for asserting his complete power and making his reign absolute. The nations were wickedly angry, but they had to meet the righteous anger of God. The time for the judgment of the dead has come. The prophets and the saints and those fearing God are seen receiving their reward. All are kept in the mind of God, the small as well as the great. And **the destroyers of the earth** are now themselves destroyed. The perfect fulfillment is symbolized by a vision of **God's temple in heaven.** God's covenant does not end with death, and so **the**

ark of his covenant is seen in the heavenly temple, secure in eternity as in time. The lightnings flash. The thunders roar. The ground shakes. The hard hail falls. But the security of the covenant ratified in the heavenly temple remains.

In the symbol of the measuring of the temple the man of Patmos is declaring that order is at work in the midst of what seems like moral chaos. There is more than mere counting. There is estimate. And this estimate is made at the command of God and according to his standards. There is more than a hint that though the temple has been destroyed, the values for which it stands are to be permanent. The altar is the place of sacrifice. And in the measurement of the altar there is more than a hint of the value of that great sacrifice the meaning of which is so near to the deepest thoughts and the deepest emotions of the author of Revelation. And in the measuring of the worshipers there is a clear symbolic statement that loyal men truly worshiping God are not ignored and are not forgotten. There loyal worship is measured with the sharpest sense of its value. And all this measurement is for the preservation of that which belongs to the will of God and of those who do the will of God when so much will be destroyed. The outer court, which is not measured, belongs to the company of those who are irresponsive to divine truth and hostile to its commands. The lawless shall tread down the law-abiding. But the period of lawlessness will have limits. And through the calamity those who have chosen the will of God in good loyalty will come to triumph at last.

The sense of order at the heart of chaos is an ever-present need in history. In many nations right and orderly ways are trampled down. The lawbreaker appears among the lawmakers for the moral confusion of the world. And sometimes in the midst of all this it seems as if our temple, too, has been destroyed, and the great sacrifice kept at the heart of Christendom for so many centuries has been forgotten. But the divine measuring rod is at work. And all that belongs to the will of God, and all who belong to the will of God, will come to glad and glorious victory, even though passing through experiences of tragic bitterness.

The power of the two witnesses deserves the closest inspection. They represent the law and the prophets made articulate in contemporary speech. The very stuff of reality is in their words. Under God, life itself is mastered by the principles which they proclaim. The words which come from their mouths turn to fire for the destruction of those who oppose them. Indeed, Christianity is always winning negative victories over those who repudiate that for which it stands. Men try to organize a world upon principles which contradict the very principles for which the Christian religion stands. And their world comes crashing to ruin at their feet. While the victory of those who accept Christianity is not always visible over vast areas, the defeat of those who deny Christian sanctions is always in process of being worked out. Those who deny the moral truths upon which Christianity stands have the sentence of death passed upon them from the moment of their denial. The disintegration of institutions which repudiate the values upheld by the Christian religion can be seen upon every page of history.

But while the truth which the witnesses declare has this awful power, the witnesses themselves must be prepared to suffer for their loyalty. They are slain and their bodies lie unburied on the streets of the world's cities. There is not even a tomb of dignity for those who have dared to speak for God. Indeed, the death of the witnesses is regarded as the destruction of all for which they stand. In sheer relief wicked men celebrate their deliverance from the cruel behests of the moral law. They have gala days and send each other presents. The moral voice will torment them no longer. The moral voice is dead. Conscience lies lifeless and dishonored upon the street. The death of conscience is a spectacle for the world. The death pangs of goodness have been the joy of the lawless. And somehow from all nations men are imagined as coming quickly to view the lifeless forms of the witnesses who have given voice to that conscience which has made cowards of all mankind. A distinguished English poet once declared that when men who have fought evil die, there is a dreadful light upon the faces of their foes. The joy in the death of goodness is the most horrible joy in all the world. But no one can really say the last word over the dead body of conscience. Goodness will not stay dead. It rises and stands immortal in its strength. So it was with the two witnesses. And so the men who had so darkly rejoiced found their gladness turned to shattering fear. There were no more presents. There was no more celebration. The men of the moral voice stood stark and menacing before the men who had despised them. They were recalled to the heaven where all perfections dwell. And as they moved toward the heights in triumph, the startled and fearful eyes of their enemies were fastened upon them. Tragic events came to the city which had become a city of destruction, and those who remained alive after the cataclysm gave fearful glory to the God whom they had despised and whose ways they had dared to repudiate. In time and in eternity the last word belongs to goodness. In time and in eternity the last word belongs to God.

The third woe begins by being a great joy. This paradox is resolved when we realize that the defeat of the evil is always the gladness of the good. The end of the destruction of that which is against God is the beginning of the visible triumph of God everywhere. So for the reign of the world we have the reign of God. Not Caesar but Christ is on the throne. And his rule is an endless and perpetual reign. The vision of the rule of Christ, before the rule of Caesar has come to an end, is a great act of faith. And in every age when there is an outburst of completely unethical power, this faith becomes both more difficult and more necessary. To change noble ideas and high ideals into historic facts is the perpetual task of Christians. And the kingdom of the world has a way of appearing as the deadly and remorseless foe of this whole process. To believe that the visible kingdom is unreal, and that the invisible kingdom is real, is the supreme act of faith. To this faith the kingdom of the world has already become the kingdom of our Lord and of his Christ.

But this faith must be the reflection of an inner fact. Only the man in whose heart Christ reigns can believe in his reign in the world. The kingdom of the world is the external master of unconquered hearts. That kingdom which masters men's hearts already has a power which the glittering kingdom of this world may envy but cannot possess. It is the task of the Christian church to produce this kingdom of inner loyalty. Every time a heart is won to the great allegiance, the kingdom of this world is depleted. One of Edith Wharton's novels tells the tale of an Italian duke who awoke to the consciousness that he had lost the hearts of his people. They were looking at him with alien eyes. And before long he had lost the ducal throne as well. The messenger of God is able to say to every man to whom he speaks: The kingdom of God comes first of all in you. Each man has a throne in his soul which he can give to Christ. And so to men and women, one by one, the new kingdom comes. It is a fact in men's hearts before the powerful political leaders of the world realize what has happened. They live in a realm of externals. They do not realize the awful power of those forces which work within. The realization of the lack of inner vitality which characterizes great external powers comes at last. The seventh trumpet is sounded and what only seems goes down and what really is remains. And just because it does not depend upon environment or external actions, the inner victory is an eternal victory.

A man does not give his heart to Christ for a day or for a year. It is not an act belonging only to time. It is an act which belongs to eternity. The revelation of the power of this inner kingdom is the recurring miracle of history.

In secular ages men are all the while afraid of the eternal reference. But to the author of Revelation it is clear that perpetually man must be fortified for the life in time by the vision of eternity. So at the consummation of history we see the four and twenty elders on their faces before God, as heaven rejoices at the triumph of Christ (cf. 5:8 ff.). Not the anger of the nations but the anger of God has proved the really important matter. The great act of judgment is a supreme act of moral clarification. Death may seem to leave everything in utter confusion. But that great moral act which gathers up all the dead will make all things plain. Something has to be said to the prophets. Something has to be done about the prophets. Something has to be said to the saints. Something has to be done about the saints. The author of Revelation is not afraid of the great word "reward." There is a vast democracy in the final adjudication. It includes the small as well as the great. No virtue unnoticed by men escapes the eye of God. The smallest flower of goodness in time is given a place in eternity. But it must also be said that nothing evil escapes the all-seeing eye. The sons of destruction shall inherit the destruction which they thought to inflict upon others but to escape themselves. The poison which the destroyer pours forth turns inward to do its deadly work upon the man himself. God is pledged to the complete achievement of the moral order. The covenant is not merely for time. It belongs to the deathless ages held in the hand of God. So, in symbol, the ark of the covenant is visible in heaven. The question as to whether a vision of the victory of goodness in eternity unfits men for the life in time must be faced. And we need not fear to face it. There is no danger that we will believe less in goodness here when we have learned that it is seated there upon an eternal throne.

12:1-6. The Woman and the Dragon.—Here we have a piece of sheer mythology turned to Christian purposes. The man of Patmos, we must remember, was writing for people whose mind was crowded with materials coming from no end of mythological sources, and whose imagination was colored by endless images coming from these same sources. With no little daring the author of Revelation bends a part of what he finds to his own uses. He is so secure in his Christian position that he does not hesitate to go to pagan sources for symbols and images. A glorious **woman** appears to whom the sun has given a shining garment, with stars on her head as a crown and the silver moon under her feet. She is about to give birth to a son and she cries out in agony. Not, however, in birth pangs do we find the tragic center of the situation, but in an ugly **red dragon,** with seven richly crowned heads, powerful enough with a swing of his tail to sweep multitudes of the stars from the sky, which waits to pounce upon the child and devour it as soon as it is born. A son is brought forth who is destined to be a stern and mighty ruler on earth, so he is caught up to the throne of God to save him from the dragon. The woman of the shining garment and the star-crowned head flees into a vast desert, where she is cared for during a long period of rest. The moral issues in the life of men represent issues of tragic importance in heaven.

7-12. *The Battle in Heaven.*—The conflict is joined between the hosts of God and the hosts of the dragon. The armies of God are led by Michael, and the war goes on with furious intensity. But with all their ferocity the forces of the dragon are utterly unable to prevail. There is no description of the fighting, but there is one terrible sentence of doom regarding the minions of the dragon, **Neither was their place found any more in heaven.** The dragon—assimilated in a fierce passage with the **old serpent, the Devil, Satan**—the universal deceiver, is cast down to the earth, and his angels are thrown from the heights with him. A far-sweeping voice of victory is heard in heaven. The salvation of God is secure. The power of God is triumphant. The kingdom of God is firmly established. The authority of Christ is vindicated. The evil which threatened day and night is thrown out of heaven. The symbolic picture wears thin, but the meaning is perfectly clear when it is said that this victory is due to the death of Christ. And in a phrase of unutterable encouragement it is declared that those who were willing to die for Christ have had a significant share in the achievement of the victory. The heavens and all who dwell in the heights are called upon to rejoice. But woe is approaching the dwellers on the earth and those sailing upon the sea. Here **the devil has come.** He realizes that essentially he is defeated, though he has a short time to rage in the world. And so his rage is frantic. Worst of all, perhaps, those who suffer his tortures can know that they are being persecuted by a defeated foe.

13-17. *The Fierce Dragon Persecutes the Woman on Earth.*—The dragon finds the woman of the shining garment and the star-crowned head, and sets about persecuting her. From his mouth comes a great rushing river of water hurled in the direction of the woman to carry her away. But the friendly earth drinks up the vast flood before it reaches her. The dragon comes to a climax of wrath and bitter frustration. He leaves the woman whom he cannot destroy, and makes **war** with the rest of her children, who are faithful to the law of God and the message which Jesus has brought. He towers upon **the sand of the sea,** a mighty figure of persecution, though bearing the scars of his defeat in heaven. In the *camera obscura* of the imagery, where the changes are easy and rapid, the woman has somehow become the symbol of the church, and the dragon the symbol of the persecuting empire. We are moving rapidly to the part of the book where Rome stands out with clear and terrible distinctness as the desperate foe of the Christian faith. In the meantime, the sense is clear that ultimate antagonisms are involved as the religion of Christ fights its foes.

Interpreters have frankly found ch. 12 of Revelation the source of many difficulties. It is best to keep to clear indications of a central meaning, and not to be beguiled by the temptation to microscopic analysis of details. Indeed, this is the method which is being followed by this Expos. all through the book. The feeling was bound to come, even to men and women of great moral and spiritual earnestness, that they were caught in the confusions of an experience of nothing less than ethical anarchy. The man of Patmos is determined to have them see that their struggle is part of a great pattern which belongs to heaven as well as to earth. There is a divine reference to the struggles of the most humble Christians. Their fight has reality in heaven as well as on earth. To a Christian everything was changed by the birth of a child who had brought God to men as he had never come before. Very well, the author declares, you must understand that this too is a divine fact with a glorious heavenly reference. There is therefore the vivid picture of a desperate attempt of the forces of wickedness to overthrow the will of God in heaven itself. The heavenly babe is to be destroyed at birth if this can be accomplished. The dragon stands ready to devour the child whose very existence is a threat to every evil thing. But God frustrates his evil design. The child finds its security on the very throne of the universe. There are no cosmic forces that can defy the good will of the one who sits there. The Christian religion enters the world in the full glory of heavenly victory.

The man of Patmos is not recounting celestial history. He is using the most powerful and graphic symbols to express the finality of the power of Christ. Goodness always has humble beginnings. It must be born in the minds of men and it must grow and mature. Always it finds foes which would destroy it at its very birth. But really, it is as strong as the throne of God. It is as strong as the one who sits upon the throne. In time and in eternity there is always a Power which is ready to snatch it away from the destroyer. There is a heavenly source for all those good births which bring wisdom and righteousness and the power to make righteousness triumphant in effective life. The figure of the woman of heavenly radiance is not pressed unduly. There is a sense of the pain of the moral process. There is a sense of the dark forces which hound the path of goodness. There is a sense of the overarching protection of heaven. There is a sense that all goodness is secure at last on the throne of God. The battle on earth is suddenly seen in a vast heavenly setting. Those who are caught in grim and hard and confining places of suffering are suddenly offered the glory of heavenly vistas. Men do not leave old patterns of thought quickly or easily. The author of Revelation uses their imagination as he finds them and turns the imagery of their mythology to Christian uses.

It is easy to see that the Christian insight will remain long after the vivid image coming from the old way of thought has ceased to have meaning. When men have come to the place where they are a little puzzled by the symbol of the woman who wears a dozen stars as a crown, it is yet not hard for them to see that unless the will of God is secure against all evil forces, the very good meaning of life has disappeared. There is that which would oppose goodness and destroy it at its very birth. But it has no real power against the goodness which it would destroy. Just when it seems victorious, frustration comes upon it. And this happens because the goodness which must triumph in time has already been made secure in eternity. It is this sense of an eternal security which the man of Patmos would bring home to his hearers with unforgettable power. And after the suffering which brings goodness to birth, heaven itself provides nourishment and rest. The picture of the woman of heavenly radiance coming to a time of glorious and quiet rest, after the pain of giving birth to the child of destiny, would come with its own meaning to men and women to whom it seemed that the birth of goodness in the world required a price greater than they could pay. An agile and easy-moving imagination was one of the happy gifts of men who lived in the world which was ruled by Rome, but which had received its gift of an understanding use of the fancy from Greece.

That the desperate struggle on earth has the most significant meaning in the ultimate universe is expressed in the symbolic tale of the battle in heaven. Heaven has already fought and won the very conflict in which we are now contending. On the vast fields of eternity the victory has been won for which we are contending in time. This is the meaning the man of Patmos would extort from the account of the fight in heaven. The dragon is utterly routed, and with all his followers is cast down to the earth. But all his rage cannot hide the fact that he has been defeated in heaven. When men fight evil in this world, they are fighting something which has already been overthrown. It has no secret of inner vitality. Indeed, the sentence of death has been passed upon it. Once more it must be said that this is not celestial history. It is the expression in glorious symbol of the fact that when we are fighting anything which is evil, we are fighting something which has already been defeated because God is on his throne. In the midst of time Revelation would give to men the perspective of eternity. And when we view wickedness from the vantage point of eternity, we can see it only as something completely overthrown. That we who are in the world greatly need the perspective of eternity as we fight the battles of time ought to be abundantly clear. Whatever we may do in our own struggle with evil, on the broad fields of eternity the battle has already been settled. Again and again great leaders in human conflicts have gained immeasurable assurance from their profound conviction that the issue in which they are engaged has already been decided in the eternal world. The harder the fight and the more bitter the situation, the more this inner conviction makes just the final and decisive difference. When one has once moved from the symbol to the thing signified, the meaning is not only clear, but it is seen to be of the utmost importance to struggling men in every century.

The voice full of satisfaction in the victory of God and Christ takes us into the region of deathless realities. Without help of symbol, but with stark realism, we are told that the victory won in heaven was made possible by the death of Christ. And we are told that all those who have died rather than surrender their loyalty to Christ have had a share in making this victory possible. Evil can never suffer unselfishly either in time or in eternity. It is the suffering God who is always sure to conquer the malignantly selfish evil which arrays itself against him. And every expression of selfless loyalty is a part of that timeless nobility which sits secure upon the throne of the world. The martyr expresses something which he has received from the very character of God. And so while he may be trampled upon by the evil forces of time, he belongs to the very central force which in the character of God controls the universe. That heaven itself would be incomplete without that vicarious love which is expressed in the death of Christ is a high and august principle which may well occupy our most earnest meditation and arouse our adoring awe. The ultimate universe, we are being told, is built along the lines of unselfish love. God himself has the right and even the power of victory because of an eternal selflessness which lives forever in his deepest life. The Cross is the expression in time of that which God is in eternity. This very unselfishness which seems so impotent in the midst of the cruel events of this strange world is on the very throne of the universe. And it is secure on that throne because of its very quality of moral perfection. In time and in eternity when the world of fact and the world of character meet, the character is victorious. The thought that the martyrs make a contribution to the heavenly victory of God is at first staggering. But the more we think of it, the more we see that they are a part of that perfect achievement of God in which the very essence of his victory lies. So, inevitably they make their own contribution to the music of heavenly triumph. The very transcendent splendor of such conceptions girds with unconquerable strength men who must prepare for martyrdom.

We return from these high matters to the struggle upon the earth. And here the radiant woman has become the church. And the dragon has become the Roman Empire, set about to destroy it. The symbols are still used but the meaning is coming through more and more clearly. The empire is so strong that it can send forth a mighty and destructive stream which, it seems, must wash away the church so that it will be no more. Perhaps in spite of the wings of heavenly idealism, the church will be completely overthrown. But here there is a sudden and surprising change in the symbolic picture. The very earth, the friend of that which the dragon would destroy, swallows up the rushing stream, and so ends its destructive career. Rome represents a man-made tyranny. The earth represents a divinely established order. The very system of things, as God has made them, fights for the church as it battles with the lawless cruelty of the empire which men have made. There is something in the very laws of life, as God has established them, which fights the wickedness of men. And so, when the God who established the world establishes the church, the two belong to one order of life. The very world which God has made is the friend of those who would do his will. The church may be driven to the desert but the church will survive. The mighty empire will find itself impo-

tent when the church becomes an invisible presence which baffles pursuit and which, indeed, cannot be reached. But if the institution cannot be overwhelmed, individual men and women can yet be treated with the utmost savagery. So it is that the seed of the woman feel the full cruel power of the dragon. The members of the church feel the full wrath of the empire which bestrides land and sea in awful power. Gradually we have approached the awful climax of understanding. The organized life of the world has become the foe of God. Many people in many centuries have had an experience which to greater or less degree has corresponded to the experience of the Christian church when the Roman Empire set itself against her. And always the message that God is not on the side— indeed, cannot be on the side—of the secular power which would assert its authority, but is on the side of the persecuted minority, comes home with deep and commanding reassurance and comfort and strength-giving force. Evil powers may dominate land and sea. But the sentence of death has already been passed upon them.

13:1-10. The Beast from the Sea.—A powerful beast comes up from the sea. His ten horns have upon them ten crowns. His seven heads bear names of blasphemy. Here in symbol the Roman Empire stands clearly before us. The reference is sharpened to point to particular emperors. And the blasphemous inscriptions borne upon the heads as clearly refer to claims to supernatural dignity made by the emperors, claims which in their very nature involved a blasphemy which was vividly seen as over against the true divinity of the Lord of all that exists. All beastly powers were united in the empire. It was like a leopard. It was like a bear. It was like a lion. All this power was not good power. It came from the ultimate source of evil in the universe. One of the symbolic heads was marked as if it had received a fatal wound but had been restored to life. The whole world was overcome by a lust of loyalty to the empire, which had now become almost the incarnation of evil. Its power was so great that men worshiped the evil source of its strength even as they worshiped its imperial energy. "Who is like this imperial power?" they cried. Who would dare to **make war** against it? But its capacity to speak resounding words and to do terrible deeds against the saints and to win what seemed easy victories over them was not its own. That capacity was given to it. Its worldwide dominion was limited by an authority greater than itself. There were limits to its usurpation. In the meantime, only those held safe by the timeless strength of God resisted its tyranny. The book of the one who had met and conquered death was the record of a divine purpose which could not be defeated. Captivity and death might seem to seal the final victory of the empire. But the **patience and the faith** of those who endured reached beyond present tragedy to the unconquerable purpose of God. The book of the Lamb that was slain contained the last words.

11-18. The Beast from the Earth.—Up **out of the earth** comes **another beast**. It has the appearance of a lamb but it speaks with a dragon's voice. Here we may see a symbol of the priestly organization which conducts the worship of the emperor. And the symbol of the dead beast restored to life can perhaps best be regarded as referring to the dead Nero alive again to do more mischief. The cult was promoted by fire which seemed to have a supernatural origin, and by voices which seemed to make an image alive. It exercised a profound and deadly pressure. One might indeed say that there was a mark of the beast even as there was a mark of God. The very business of the world was so tied up with the imperial cult that without its acceptance men could neither buy nor sell. It was all a travesty of true worship, putting the beast which had been slain in the place of the Lamb which had been slain. The number of the beast—**six hundred and sixty-six**—was a studied imperfection, always falling short of that perfection symbolized by the number seven, to which the author of Revelation pays so much attention. Various expedients have been resorted to for the purpose of connecting the number of the beast with the Emperor Nero. It is clear enough, at least, that the number is the symbol of utter wickedness impersonated in an emperor seated upon a throne of power which controls the world. The author of Revelation is saying that the empire itself had become satanic. The imperial cult was the vehicle of a devilish power let loose upon the world. The emperors claiming the place of God, and persecuting his true servants, are seen in quite a different light from that which characterizes the writings of the apostle Paul. And it is different enough from that which emerged when the empire itself became Christian. The empire which the man of Patmos confronted seemed to have made itself one with the very ultimate evil of the universe.

In one way Revelation is a brilliant and deadly attack upon the Roman Empire as it sets itself to destroy the Christian faith. It is a book of life and power for a persecuted church. It is a kind of symbolic state document of an eternal kingdom dealing with a temporal power which made claims to an eternal authority. The kingdom of time seemed to be stronger than the kingdom of eternity. But it was not so. And with a faith which must have seemed to reach the limits of audacity, the man of Patmos sets about judging the Roman Empire. He is all the while giving the mind of victors to men who were meeting every kind of earthly defeat. He is giving to them a secure sense that the invisible empire of their hearts' loyalty is really the ruler of the world. The Roman Empire has become a kingdom not of gods but of devils. They have no real power against the eternal God. Their assertive pride is to meet a terrible doom. And at the very moment of their seeming triumph it is possible for the citizens of God's true empire to see the real character of this empire of falseness and evil and to stand stalwart while it does its worst to them. There is no attempt at all to make a map of events which are to unfold with the passage of dim and unknown centuries. Revelation is concerned with an immediate problem. Such historic references as are caught in the symbols are meant to have contemporary relevance. But the picture is foreshortened because the historic process is to be far longer than the man of Patmos dreams. And the principles expressed are so deeply true that they will reveal their meaning in many centuries of which the author has no thought at all. It is simply impossible for persecuted men in any century when the foes of God seem to be winning complete triumph over the purposes of God not to feel that the stinging and powerful symbols of Revelation speak directly to their own minds and to their own hearts. And if the man of Patmos could have foreseen the actual processes of history, no doubt he would have been glad to have it so.

In truth, the kingdom of man and the kingdom of the beast are in perpetual conflict century after century. The kingdom of man is the kingdom of God's purpose and the kingdom of the beast is the kingdom of whatever contradicts and defies the purpose of God. Sometimes the conflict loses its sharpness and it almost seems that the beast has been tamed. Then the awful energies of evil burst forth again and the beast claims the thrones of the visible world. The latter part of the nineteenth century, when democratic forms of government were receiving at least lip service all about the world, and when liberal ways of good will captured the imagination of multitudes of men and women, seemed to make the harsher symbols of Revelation completely irrelevant. But the middle of the twentieth century came to men who had listened once again to the beast's wild cries and who had seen evil claim its right to the throne of the world. The Christians meeting tragedy in the days of persecution in the Roman Empire seemed strangely near to hard-pressed men and women in Europe. And if truth is still what the man of Patmos believed it to be, and if righteousness can still be conceived as he conceived it, and if God is as he believed truly upon the throne of might, then his powerful symbols spoke directly to the mind and the conscience of an age which he did not foresee.

The sharpness of the insight of Revelation at once begins to clarify our own vision in respect of some very important matters. The sentimental view of the worst evil as representing merely a confused judgment, and not a dark and bitterly wicked intent, meets with short shrift from one who has viewed wickedness with the awful clarity of this book. No doubt there is evil which has its root in a confused mind rather than in a bad heart. But there is also a wickedness bitterly malignant and a wickedness characterized by a hard clarity of evil purpose. This the man of Patmos sees clearly and he expresses his insight in the symbol of the kingdom of the beast. There is something here which belongs to the darkest depths of moral turpitude. It is bad, and wholly and completely bad. It is not a misguided friend. It is a final and uncompromising foe. It must be met not with any suggestion of compromise, but with unhesitating and permanent hostility. Sometimes wickedness knows its foes better than goodness recognizes its enemies. The empire which tried to crush the Christian faith knew what it was about. Only an empire which found new standards and new loyalties could be the friend of Christ.

But wickedness is not an abstract matter. Indeed, it is most concrete. It associates itself with definite persons who are responsible for its dark deeds. So the movement from the empire to particular emperors is as true as it is inevitable. And the movement from emperors to one emperor who is seen as the very embodiment of dark and bad ways is inevitable too. And the sense that the kingdom of evil is in a fashion a travesty of the kingdom of good, as the men who would not worship the Figure who spoke from the Cross were ready to worship the beast which had been slain, has its own most startling insight. To be sure, it would be silly merely to say that the man of Patmos had in mind the darker and more sinister and villainous figures who appeared in later centuries. But it is not at all silly to say that he is dealing with principles so profound that they have their relevance whenever wicked men come to places of power.

The imperial cult is the very living expression of the worship of the emperor. And so it is the very center of that deadly blasphemy which fills the author of Revelation with a kind of moral horror. We have a picture of the very ways in which an evil cult holds its power over men's minds. Supernatural fire and speaking images tell an old, old story. We are confronting the sort of situation which arises when worship itself becomes allied with falsehood and evil. Both Hitler's Germany and Communist Russia have illustrated the fashion in which an evil state tends to become an autocratic religion. To multitudes of Nazi men and women Hitler took the place of God, and their devotion to him became in a very actual sense a religious devotion. To numberless Communists the materialistic dialectic of Karl Marx has become not merely a substitute for religion but itself a very actual religion. The instinct for worship is so deep a thing in men's souls that if they do not worship that which is true, they are sure to worship that which is false. The ethical and spiritual majesty of the Christian religion has always worked against the influences which would turn the church itself into the devotee of a false cult bearing a Christian name. But it must be confessed that again and again the state church has been tempted to put the state in a place which belongs only to God, and to claim Christian sanctions for the temporary interests of the state. Without being false to its own deepest meaning, the Christian church can never be the instrument of anything where the real source of compulsion is beyond the area of the inspiration which comes from the God whose face we see in the face of Jesus Christ. Instead of standing for social principles because they express the will of Jesus Christ, it is possible to maintain an interest in the Christian church because it can be used for the furtherance of social positions. The politically minded church is always in danger of being corrupted by the politics which so easily become a major rather than a secondary interest. This does not mean that the church must lose its interest in practical problems. It does mean that it must be constantly alive to the temptations which arise in connection with these immediate interests. The imperial cult is not always as far from us as we may think.

When religion itself becomes an evil thing, then there is evil indeed let loose among men. The author of Revelation sees the very commercial life of the empire so entangled with the imperial cult that only those who worshiped the emperor could have any possible hope of success in business. A very practical ostracism confronted those who did not bend to the purposes of the cult that made emperor worship a power in the world. It was the subtlest sort of opposition and it seemed to leave no room for Christians in the world. There is no more unhappy experience than to become aware that one is the object of invisible and yet very potent social pressures which make real freedom of choice and of action almost unbelievably difficult. The good life is killed at its very source if men submit to such pressures, for in the most literal sense they are unable to call their souls their own. It is indeed the mark of the beast which would seal them to a permanent surrender of that personal loyalty to the highest without which life loses all noble meaning. No more searching question confronts powerful church leaders than the question as to whether or not they are using their authority to compel men's allegiance to that which does not belong to the will of Christ. Perhaps there ought to be added to the litany of every communion a petition that the church may itself be delivered from the mark of the beast. To claim divine sanctions for very human positions is the constant temptation and the deep humiliation of the church. It is, of course, when the state becomes an autocratic and unchristian church that the situation is most darkly tragic. But this ought not to hide from us the fact that the Christian church itself may all too easily be tempted to exercise pressures which are entirely unchristian.

It is characteristic of the deep quality of insight which we find again and again in Revelation that the tragedy of unethical pressure is at last associated with a particular person. The number of the beast is the number of a particular man. The immediate historical reference is much less important than the fact that a bad social situation can always be traced to some particular individual with whom responsibility finally may be seen to rest. This sharp sense of individual obligation has never been more important than it is today. Men try to hide behind all sorts of elements in the general situation and so try to escape from the real demand involved in their position of power. But they must not be allowed to do this. The mark of the beast is always the mark of a particular man. Who is responsible for this evil thing? we must ask. Who could change this evil thing if he would? we must inquire with all sober insistence. By holding our leaders to their true responsibility, and by choosing them in the light of the fashion in which they themselves choose their loyalties, we shall be doing our own duty in a difficult world. The Roman Empire was not a democracy. Fortunately we have better ways to deal with those who prostitute their leadership.

14:1-5. The Lamb and the Triumphant Host. —Suddenly turning from the mark of the beast to the mark of the Lamb, we behold a great multitude of victorious saints standing in the presence of **the Lamb on Mount Zion.** Each person in the great multitude bears upon his forehead the name of the Lamb and (dropping the figure) the name of his Father. There is a mighty voice like the roar of many waters and the reverberations of thunder. And there is glorious music like many harpers who, as they play their instruments, **sing a new song,** in the very presence of the divine court. No one can learn the song but those who have been purchased **from among men** to be **the firstfruits** for the heavenly kingdom. They are utterly stainless, free from sensuality and free from falsehood.

6-7. The Angel of Good Tidings.—With another change in the pattern of the picture, quick as a kaleidoscope, the author of the book turns our attention from judgment to the proclamation of the great evangel. An **angel flying in midheaven** calls upon all mankind to **fear God and give him glory.** He made all things and **the hour of his judgment** is near.

8. The Fall of Rome.—Swiftly the picture of the angel of good tidings is changed to the picture of an angel of judgment who proclaims the fall of the great **Babylon** whose world-wide rule has corrupted all of the nations. This Babylon is, of course, Rome. In the midst of Rome's power its fall is proclaimed as if it has already occurred.

9-11. The Doom of the Worshipers of the Beast.—In bitterly terrible words the doom of the **worshipers** of the **beast and his image** is proclaimed. They shall carry the mark of the beast into regions of fiery and endless agony. Without rest and in intolerable torture those who have drunk of the wine of Rome's falseness and fornication **shall drink of the wine of the wrath of God.** The figures become fairly cluttered in the passionate picture of final doom.

12-13. Steadfastness and Its Reward.—In the midst of the awful issues involved in these quickly succeeding pictures, the saints are to remain steadfast, loyal to God's commands and **the faith of Jesus.**

14-16. The Harvest of the Earth.—Another flashing picture reveals a **cloud** of whiteness upon which sits a glorious crowned figure **like a son of man.** In his hand he holds **a sharp sickle.** He receives the message that the hour of harvesting has come. He casts his sickle upon the earth and it becomes a vast harvest field.

17-20. The Wine Press of Blood.—There is another flashing picture of another angel with **a sharp sickle.** Now the vines of wickedness are reaped and put into the **wine press,** which is outside the city. The blood which comes from the wine press reaches to the bridles of horses, over an area of **two hundred miles.** No evil growth escapes the sickle of God.

The moral and spiritual imagination of the reader is tested as he follows these swift-moving and amazing pictures. It is not too hard, however, to get at their central meanings. Over against those who bear the mark of the beast are seen those who bear the mark of the Lamb. At last the mark of the beast means destruction. And the mark of the Lamb means triumph. The mighty army of the stainless victors, radiant and lyrical upon Mount Zion, is set before the reader in a fashion which cannot be forgotten. There is an apparent blurring of the distinction between the improper use of the natural processes and their right use. The group of triumphant saints are described as if the freedom from all sexual experience is a virtue. This, of course, is not a Christian position, and if Charles is wrong in thinking that the reference is a gloss, one can only say that in an age of bitter persecution the perspective of the one writing to the persecuted was blurred in a way which is not hard to understand. The real point of the picture is that the triumphant saints have been freed by the Lamb from every sort of stain. Truth has become the very essence of their lives. And the spirit has triumphed over the body. Their salvation from everything which destroys goodness is complete.

The general position of Revelation, which regards men in the light of final moral and spiritual decisions already made, is once and again replaced by sudden views of men called to decision. Such is the picture of the angel of good tidings. In the very hour when judgment is imminent, the great opportunity for good decision is held before all who dwell upon the earth, unto every nation, and kindred, and people, and tongue. In the proclamation of the angelic messenger the mighty Creator calls for the loyal worship of all his children. This calling to mind of the great invitation in the very midst of the announcement of judgment is profoundly characteristic of classical Christianity. And it has very great significance for our understanding of the Christian faith.

In Revelation, Rome is always in the background as the great foe of true religion. The sense of the finality of this view centers in the cult of emperor worship which gives to an earthly ruler a place which belongs only to God. But it involves all sorts of corrupt ideas and corrupting practices with the result that the Imperial City increasingly moves into the foreground for the most terrific condemnation. The great angel who announces the fall of Rome under the name of Babylon sees the moral and spiritual lawlessness of that vast corrupter of the world meeting its inevitable doom. Like the ringing of a terrible bell of destiny, one hears the refrain, "Fallen, fallen is Babylon the great." It is easy to be wise after the event. But in the midst of the far-flung grandeur of Rome, to see it as already disintegrating under the mighty hand of God requires courage of the highest type. Even good men are sorely tempted to hold peace congresses with evil when it sits upon the throne. Surely it is a mistake to be violent in one's opposition. There must be much misunderstanding. There must be much good mixed up with the evil. By all means let the representatives of the opposing forces talk together and see if they do not have much in common. The author of Revelation will have none of this. There is not a drop of moral or spiritual appeasement in his blood. The forces which set themselves against Christ and his complete reign, however powerful they are, must be seen in their true nature and unhesitatingly condemned. Their doom is sure and that doom must be declared without any sort of moral qualification. Age after age the situation is in greater or lesser measure repeated. And only the bravest of men dare to declare the doom of Babylon while Babylon sits grandly upon the throne.

With another quick change we see a picture which takes us back to those who bear the mark of the beast. The human city of moral destruction is to fall. But we are not allowed to forget that every question is at last an individual question. If there is in very fact a kingdom of the beast, there are individual citizens of that kingdom. And what is to be their destiny? In words which stand out even among the awful words of Revelation, the fate of those who have repudiated the worship of God and have turned to the worship of the beast is set forth. They are to drink of the wine of God's wrath. They are to suffer incredible and final torment. Besides the fury of the fire which burns them, they are to suffer from an incurable internal restlessness. For the sake of security in a baffling world many of them have chosen the worship of the beast and have quaffed the wine of the kingdom of the beast. But they will find no security. Rather, their world will fall apart in burning ruin, and their hearts will be the prey of a restlessness which cannot be assuaged. Obviously the man of Patmos is seeking symbols to express the final destruction of those who make evil their good. They have found lawless pleasure in the physical world. That is to turn to burning agony. They have sought rest in accepting a false allegiance. That is to turn to an inner tempest which has no hope of rest. The principles involved are not too hard to find. The very world of nature betrays all who seek physical satisfaction at the expense of those moral and spiritual standards which give meaning to life. The rest that comes from the acquiescence in evil turns out to be the greatest unrest of all. Those who seek burning passion will find a burning which has become torture and which has no pleasure in it at all. A surprising amount of brilliant literature comes from the pens of those who think only of sensations and have lost all sense of ideas and ideals and values and deathless truths. And not too strangely the doom of this sort of thing is written in that literature itself. There is an awful and gnawing restlessness. There is a burning pain which has ceased to have any hint of joy. You do not have to go beyond this world to see the doom of those who worship the beast.

Over against all this the picture of the stainless saints singing a new song, which only they can learn, stands out with startling clarity. Their deathless music is the product of a character which God himself has made to express the meaning of perfect goodness and perfect truth. They have the mark of the Lamb, which is the mark of redemption. The sense of Christ's sacrifice and what it has meant to men is never far from the thought of the author of Revelation. The work of Christ is consummated in the perfection of those in whom it becomes complete. God is actually engaged in making perfect men and women, and when redemption has reached its full fruition, their song will be a song of realized perfection. Nothing less than the passionate pursuit of perfection is good enough for the Christian man. The contrasts of Revelation are stark and clear. Perhaps it is not too much to say that the blurring of these eternal distinctions is the characteristic vice of all idolatry and worldliness. Here, as so often elsewhere, the great N.T. apocalypse speaks to the very point of our need.

The man of Patmos is always, to use our own form of words, a pastor responsible for hard-pressed men and women. He is a shepherd caring for sheep caught in the terrible tempest of life. And so when he has painted the great pictures of eternal contrasts, he reminds those to whom and for whom he writes that their steadfastness, their keeping of the behests of God and of that great and trustful belief which centers in Christ, are the matters of constant and never-to-be-forgotten importance. These truths belong not to one century but to every century. The man responsible for the cure of souls today must keep them in his mind just as they were kept in mind by the author of Revelation. And these truths belong not merely to the leader but also to the people whom he leads. It is upon this rock of steadfastness and loyalty that the Christian church stands.

The vision of the harvesting of the earth takes us again from immediate responsibilities to eternal issues. The one sitting on the white cloud bears symbols that his power and his authority come from Christ. The golden crown is the symbol of an authority which comes from God himself. The sickle is the symbol of that conclusive hour when the growths of time are brought in for the judgment of eternity. This great event is set forth in the tremendous phrase "the earth was reaped." In a way the vision seems incomplete. It does not go on to picture the good grain which is reaped nor the tares which feel the cut of the sickle too. Perhaps our Lord's parable of the harvest was so much in the minds of the readers that this was unnecessary. Perhaps the terrible finality of the phrase "the earth was reaped" was enough. To the thoughtful Christian mind the suggestion was compelling. Every white cloud in a sunlit sky brought to mind the angel of the sickle and God's harvest of the growth of life.

But men almost overwhelmingly impressed by the present triumph of deadly evil must be made aware of its ultimate doom in another overwhelming symbolic picture. So we see another angel with another sickle. From the very center of heavenly worship this angel, with his power over the destructive forces symbolized by fire, comes forth. The clusters of evil are growing lusciously on the vines of men all about the world. Wickedness itself has come to its final ripeness. The vines of the earth with their great clusters of wrong are gathered and thrown into a great wine press outside the city where evil has no place. There it is trodden, and the wine which comes forth is blood which rises higher and higher over a vast area, coming up to the very bridles of horses. The vitality which is poured out, never to be potent again, is the vitality of evil. The stream of red blood gradually soaked into the ground and vanishing is all that is left of the wickedness which threatened the very existence of goodness in the world. Imperial evil seemed powerful enough now. By and by it would be harvested and put into the wine press of God. There would be the power of trampling feet. There would be the rush of red blood, like an inland sea of death. Then there would be only a stain on the good earth. Then the stain itself would disappear. And the world would be as if the clusters of evil grapes had never appeared upon the branches of its vines.

The minds of simple-minded men must be mastered by the thought of the utter destruction of evil. But more than that, their imagination must be completely possessed by the vision of wickedness meeting its doom. The man of Patmos is speaking to the mind and conscience through the eye. In fact, he is always doing that. But never with more breath-taking and terrible vividness than in the picture of the inland sea of blood pressed from the grapes of wickedness. Good and evil, triumph and tragedy, hope and fear, how they jostle each other in the minds of those who behold these flashing pictures—pictures that have to do, it is clear enough, not with matters which belong to one passing age, but with perennial matters in the story of that strange creature man. As long as man is man and God is God and righteousness is righteousness they will speak first to the eyes and then to the very souls of men.

15:1. Seven Angels and Seven Last Plagues.— The sky is suddenly bright with the vision of **seven angels** having **seven plagues** which will complete the expression of **the wrath of God.** The author of Revelation has just been describing the terrible wine press of blood. Now he is reminded, and his hearers are reminded, that terrible earthly events of judgment have a heavenly source.

2-4. The Victorious Saints by the Fiery Sea.— The great O.T. deliverance is now in the mind of the man of Patmos as he describes the final deliverance of the saints of God. They stand triumphant by the **sea of glass mingled with fire,** as the Israelites had stood with a sense of awe looking back on the waters of the Red Sea. There is continuity in moral and spiritual history, and the song of victory which they sing is described as **the song of Moses . . . and . . . the Lamb.** The harps they hold are **the harps of God.** In every way we are witnessing a scene of divine consummation. These victorious saints have maintained their loyalty in spite of the beast and his image. They have refused to be marked with the terrible number of blasphemy. When the human world of facts was against them, they maintained their loyalty to the invisible kingdom of the eternal God. Now the facts are all on their side. In the glory of complete deliverance they sing their song of victory by the fiery sea. Praise and adoration are ascribed to God for his mighty works. His power is the expression of eternal righteousness and perpetual truth. With awe and worshipful homage men approach the Holy One. There is a sudden rift in the clouds of judgment, and **all nations** are seen coming to worship him. What had been discerned in dark days only by means of the insight of faith has now been made clear for all to apprehend. The character of God has been made manifest in righteous acts.

5-8. The Seven Shining Angels and the Seven Bowls of Judgment.—From the great consummation we move back quickly to the world of process. It must always be remembered that this darting from one period to another is characteristic of Revelation. Once and again there are the symbols which represent the perspective of eternity. Then there is a quick return to the events of the time order. And this again sweeps into completions which lie beyond the borders

of time. Out of that center, which represents the full witness of God's truth in his dealings with men, come seven glorious angels. Their very garments are bright and shining and they wear girdles of glittering gold. Each receives a golden bowl full to the brim **of the wrath of God.** It is the Eternal One who releases his hot hostility against the wickedness of time. The temple is full of the dreadful smoke of his powerful enmity. Even worship itself, we are told in a graphic figure, must wait upon the consummation of the awful judgments of God.

The man of Patmos is constantly thinking of those whom he would guide and strengthen and reassure. The pictures of terrible doom are always relieved by pictures of glorious felicity. And the moral meaning of the consummation is always kept clear through the sense of the judgment which must precede it. There is a kind of mighty rhythm between the final judgments and the glorious fulfillment. So the moral and spiritual perspective of the writer and the readers is kept stable. The preliminary vision of the angels of the plagues in the sky is a part of this whole movement. The modern interpreters of the Christian religion can learn much from the sense of moral proportion which is found in Revelation. It is the perpetual temptation of the Christian thinker, the Christian leader, the member of the church, engrossed with all sorts of practical activities, to become preoccupied with some particular aspect of Christian truth and Christian life and to ignore all the rest. The more one studies Revelation the more he is impressed by its amplitude and by the fashion in which the many-faceted lights of Christian truth are kept in mind. The book is as many-sided as the manifold character of the moral and spiritual life. So it comes to pass that the very startling suddenness with which we are swept on from one picture to another, transcending the time sequence again and again, contributes to the fullness and adequacy of the Christian witness of the book. The vision of the wine press of blood, quickly succeeded by the vision of the sky occupied by the angels of the final judgments, and this in turn as suddenly followed by the vision of the saints by the fiery sea, give us first the sense of earthly judgment, then the sense of the heavenly reign from which this judgment comes, and then the sense of perfect deliverance and final victory. Long ago a great French writer declared that you cannot understand earth unless you have known heaven. This the man of Patmos profoundly believes, and as deeply he believes that you cannot understand time unless you have known eternity. This large perspective is one of the great needs of all who would be witnesses to the gospel of Christ. Many idealistic pronouncements give one the feeling of being strangely circumscribed. Revelation is constantly giving out vistas of eternity. And the right sort of interpretation must do just that.

Ravishing visions of final felicity were needed badly enough by hard-pressed men feeling the heel of Rome upon their necks. Working like slaves in cruel quarries, they came to apprehend that actually they were a part of a great movement which could look back to the deliverance under Moses, and forward to the company standing beyond the burning sea of human misery and singing in happy satisfaction the song of the praise of God. The isolated sense of lonely agony was replaced by the glorious participation in an anticipated triumph. The victors have met the full impact of the beast. They have felt the awful power of a false image to master the mind and the imagination of untold multitudes of people. They have seen the evil mark of a false allegiance become the very symbol of security and success. And in spite of all this they have maintained their loyalty to the God who made them and to the one who died for them. Now hands once marked by slavish toil for an evil taskmaster happily hold the harps of the heavenly kingdom while they sing their song of deliverance and triumph. And the heart of their happiness is this: God is not only eternal might. He is goodness alive and on the throne. He is truth regnant. All moral hopes are safe in his hands. All the interests of justice and truth are secure in his judgments. The final meaning of the adventure of living is the complete manifestation of the righteousness of God.

And here there is a totally unexpected sentence describing a worshiping world secure in its loyalty to the God of perfect goodness and perfect truth. When judgment is described, it is delineated in terms which seem almost to indicate the annihilation of the nations. When the victory of God is described, one sees a worldwide vision of nations worshiping. Each picture tells its most important story. As far as organized human life is against God, all the storms of judgment are let loose. As far as organized human life is made the vehicle of the will of God, it is included in the final consummation. The vision of a world of nations worshiping comes with living power from Revelation. Of course there is always the business of the terrible choice. And this the man of Patmos remembers, as we have seen again and again, though he is so deeply occupied with the results of choices already made.

Everything is seen by the singing saints in the light of a vision of the holy God. Nothing can be truly apprehended without him. Everything is sure to be misunderstood without him. All things fall into final and proper perspective when seen at last in that glorious light. The thought of God is the most overwhelming thought which can take possession of the minds of men. Constantly we should ask ourselves if our thinking and our living have that at their center. We should never be beguiled by the efficient energy of the ungodly church.

But we miss the very heart of the meaning of the vision of the victorious saints if we do not understand that the man of Patmos wants to do more than to describe the ultimate music of victory. He wants to put a song into the hearts of men still oppressed by the heavy and wearisome and tragic burdens of this world. By their faith he desires those who are setting the steel-like firmness of their decision against the power of Rome to meet their foes with such music in their souls as shall give them an irresistible strength. It is one of the most amazing characteristics of the Christian religion that it sets life to music. The eighteenth-century revival was accompanied by a great outburst of sacred song. Already in this world the true experience of the Christian religion enables men to sing the song of the victory beyond the fiery sea.

The reader is likely to feel that there is a good deal of repetition in Revelation. The seven seals and the seven trumpets and the seven bowls may seem to tell the same story in slightly different symbols. And there are elements of truth in this way of looking at the matter. The thing the man of Patmos has to say must be said again and again with different pictures to make it graphic, and different methods of expression to bring it home to the mind and to the conscience. The truly great interpreter always knows how to say the same thing in many different ways. His originality consists in the vast variety which he is able to give to the expression of a few fundamental realities. He is always seeing the light fall upon those realities, first from one angle, then from another. The truth is one. But his experiences with that truth are manifold. And his expression of that truth is characterized by a manifoldness and variety wonderful to contemplate.

But Revelation is not merely a magnificent book for the interpreters of the Christian faith, though it is precisely that. It is essentially a seminal and inspiring book for all Christians. The fact is that while the Christian must receive all he can from others, in a sense he should carry on his adventure of understanding as if there were no others. He must learn for himself to find different symbols for the same great realities. He must learn to apply principles to the most manifold relationships and the most varied experiences. In all of this Revelation will come finely to his assistance. A thing is not said once and for all. It is said and then it is said again. And all this variety of approach and exposition makes it more and more compelling.

While it is true that the same things are said in many different fashions in Revelation, it is also true that there is genuine progress as the book moves along. until we come at last to the great climax. The pictures of the seven bowls of judgment have a certain finality which gives one a sense of the advance that has been made. The angels who are the instruments of this final judgment are gloriously attired. They are clothed with the very glory and stainless beauty of God. They have a bitter and terrible work to do, but they do it with a royal movement and with a royal gesture. There is, if one will look for it, a subtle meaning behind this symbolism. A good many things come to men in the way of duty as the responsible administrators of justice which it is almost impossible to accomplish with dignity and nobility. Sometimes the application of justice seems to stain the judge. Sometimes the methods by which men seek good ends are themselves utterly unworthy. But the angels of judgment never lose their stainless loftiness. And those who would work for good ends and represent the administration of justice must make their methods worthy of the high purposes they have in mind. The instruments of justice must themselves be just.

The bowls are full of the wrath of God. There are those who picture the Deity as so remote from all the moral vicissitudes of human life, so far removed from the very issues which tear human lives asunder, that his beatific existence can be conceived only as an eternal tranquillity untouched even by noble passion. This is very definitely not the view of Revelation. And it is not the view of the Scriptures. It is the very one who liveth forever and ever who is full of a holy passion of wrath against wickedness. It is the very indignation of the eternal which is released with destructive force against evil. There is a kind of overrefinement among men which becomes incapable of moral indignation. It maintains a sophisticated serenity in situations which call for all the awful splendor of the voice of righteous wrath. The truth is that moral distinctions begin to have a precarious hold when we become incapable of expressing them with holy passion. The proclamation of the Christian gospel which loses the sense of the bowls of wrath will suffer from an inevitable process of devitalization.

The place of worship is so filled with the smoke of the glory and the power of God that it becomes a mighty portent. Men gaze at it in awe. But they cannot enter it until the completion of the great acts of judgment. There is a sentimental and dilettante type of worship which is quite ready to turn from any responsible sense of the tragedy of the world to what becomes almost an immoral type of ecstasy. With a terrible bluntness which reminds us of the moral energy of Thomas Carlyle, the man of Patmos declares that even worship must wait on the moral acts of God.

16:1. The Seven Bowls of the Wrath of God: The Divine Command.—From within the temple, full to overflowing with the wrath of God and the terrible glory of his mighty anger, comes the voice commanding the seven angels to **pour out** their bowls of divine indignation.

2. The First Bowl.—The contents of the first bowl are poured **upon the earth.** The men who are marked as the possession of the beast, and who worship the very image of evil, find ugly and painful ulcers breaking out upon their bodies. Here, as once and again while we follow the figure of the seven bowls, we will be reminded of the Egyptian plagues. There is a continuity in the punishment of evil, even as there is continuity in the felicity into which goodness flowers.

3. The Second Bowl.—The second bowl is poured **into the sea,** which at once is turned into blood. All living things in the sea perish. The foes of the true faith had shed the blood of its adherents. Their lifeblood had ebbed away while they maintained their loyalty unto death. Now blood becomes the very vehicle of judgment. It has ceased to be the sign of the death of the saints. It has become the sign of the judgments of God.

4-7. The Third Bowl.—The third bowl is poured **into the rivers and the fountains of waters.** All the waters turn to blood. The men who thirsted for the blood of the saints now find blood the deadly drink which they must take. The very angel of the waters bursts forth in words of deep satisfaction in this evidence of the justice of God. The wicked at last are receiving their just reward, what is their due. And the altar, so long symbolic of the worship of helpless saints, speaks forth words ascribing praise to the Almighty God, whose judgments so perfectly vindicate truth and righteousness.

8-9. The Fourth Bowl.—The contents of the fourth bowl are poured out **upon the sun.** Its heat is terrifically increased and it scorches the wicked men who had scorned the will of God. They burst out into words of blasphemy against the power which plagues them. Not even the desperate nature of their sufferings leads them to repent. They are fixed in their allegiance to wickedness.

10-11. The Fifth Bowl.—The contents of the fifth bowl are poured upon the very **throne of the beast.** His kingdom is suffused in darkness. And in that darkness men gnaw their tongues as they suffer terrible agony. And they lift up their voices in awful blasphemy of the God of the heights who has given them the pains and the sores which they feel in the very climax of torture. Now they are beyond the capacity to be taught by even the most overwhelming events. They do not repent.

12-16. The Sixth Bowl.—The contents of the sixth bowl are poured out **on the . . . river Euphrates.** So the way is prepared for a great invasion of **the kings of the east. From the mouth of the dragon** and of the beast and of the false prophet **unclean spirits like frogs** come forth. They are the unholy messengers of unholy powers to gather together the kings of the world to fight against God. There is an interlude in which we hear the living Christ speak. True, the wicked kings are coming, but he himself will come unexpectedly and those who have not learned to keep the watch of Christ will be revealed utterly naked, defenseless, and helpless. The hosts of wickedness gather together. As many a decisive combat has been fought out in the Plains of Esdraelon, so the final battle is to take place in the Mount of Megiddo, overlooking that plain. The final struggle is to be the consummation of many an ancient fight.

17-21. The Seventh Bowl.—The contents of the seventh bowl are poured out. From within the temple full of the billows of the anger of God the divine voice itself is heard declaring, **It is done!** The whole scene is saturated with the sense of utter finality. Lightnings flash. Great voices reverberate. Thunders roar. The earth is shaken as it has never been shaken before. The city of men's wicked power is broken apart. The cities of the nations fall. But most of all that great city of evil called Babylon, which is Rome itself, which has been the source of such wrath against the will of God, is now to **drink the wine of the fierceness of his wrath.** That tale will be told in terrible symbolic pictures. But immediately the very earth is changed. The islands move away suddenly as if fleeing from the anger of God. The mountains disappear. And mighty hailstones, such as have never been known, fall upon men. But only the blasphemy of tortured human voices is heard. The greater their suffering, the greater their helpless defiance. They are beyond the reach of the regenerating forces which turn men from evil to good.

Always the man of Patmos keeps before the minds of his readers the conviction that these great and ultimate events are the product of the will of God and occur at his command. This sense of the divine overlordship is one of the very most profound elements in the book. In a world which often seems to have no purpose,

and all too often seems to have an evil purpose, it is of the utmost importance for good men to realize that a divine purpose is regnant in the affairs of men and ultimately will be amply vindicated. In a sense the whole book is an endeavor to see history from the perspective of the throne of God. The implicit contrast is always that between the throne of God and the throne of the Caesars. The one is proud, opulent, imperious, and utterly confident. The other is secure and majestic and utterly powerful and will be potent when Rome is only a dim memory of ancient oppression. The contrast between the throne of God and evil earthly thrones is one which recurs century after century. The little day of pre-eminent energy seems terribly conclusive while it lasts. But it has the secret of decay and death and destruction in it. Already it is judged by the God of eternal goodness and eternal righteousness and eternal truth. The bowls of wrath do not belong alone to one century or to one epoch.

The Egyptian plagues become world-wide in the visions of the seven bowls. And plagues vaster and more bitterly tragic are brought about. That ancient land suffered deeply because it had defied the will of God. The world which has defied his will is now to suffer no less desperately. The man of Patmos lives in a time when the very ethical ties which bind life together appear to be falling apart, and it seems that there is no moral continuity in history. So the judgment which he sets forth is connected with an ancient judgment. The God of the present is the God of the past as well as the God of the future. History comes to a climax in the judgments of the seven bowls. That life is organic is one of its deepest lessons. Karl Marx attempted to interpret this quality by means of a materialistic dialectic. The Christian who understands his faith always thinks in the terms of a moral and spiritual dialectic which does justice to all the events of this tortured and troubled and stubborn world.

Revelation does not picture bad men as without religion. It pictures them as the worshipers of the image which is the very symbol of wickedness, and as the bearers of the mark of the beast which seals their loyalty to the black blight of that which is utterly bad. Religion in their experience has become the servant of all that is unlovely and of bad report. When idealism turns sour and becomes the servant of moral and spiritual disintegration, there ensues a situation which is terrible enough. It indicates the prostitution of the very meaning of life. Religion itself becomes a sacrament of evil. The last form of the expression of wickedness always takes the form of a pseudo religion. Many a German youth gave to Hitler a place which belonged only to Christ. Even the soapbox orator who speaks in the name of a materialistic dialectic has all the passion of a pseudo prophet. Whenever men give to evil a loyalty which belongs only to the good, one can see the mark of the beast. Revelation deals with principles so profound that one can see them at work all through history. It is not a book of magical formulas. It is a book of moral and spiritual insights. The real quality of these insights is apprehended more adequately when it is seen that they may be applied to the past as well as to the future. Wherever kingdoms and empires moving madly in their proud and lawless way have come upon destruction, the symbol of the bowls of wrath against rampant evil becomes relevant. To read history in the light of moral and spiritual meanings is to read it with understanding.

The man of Patmos is sure that wickedness is always preparing for its own retribution. When blood is shed unjustly, there is created a situation of moral confusion which will react upon the doers of the deed. The blood which has been shed will return as a terrible plague. Those who give men blood to drink will come at last to the place where there is nothing else for their own tortured lips. The God who maintains the vast scales of the universe turns evil back upon itself. The doers of evil are transgressors against the health of the community. But they are also the foes of their own health. The sores which break out upon their bodies are the product of their own character. The divine will maintains the moral stability of human life. Those who defy the moral structure of the universe will find every element of its vast life fighting against them. So when the waters turn into blood, it is the angel of the waters who expresses profound satisfaction. In a vivid figure the moral order of the universe is seen giving glory to God. And from the altar comes a voice of praise that life itself, as it is ruled by God, vindicates those who have suffered for goodness, and satisfies every need of the soul for noble worship.

When the wrath of God is poured upon the throne of the beast there is utter darkness; it follows the scorching when the sun, which has given the heat of health, sends forth the heat of destruction. As the power which is beneficent for the good man becomes hostile for the bad man, and nature itself is revealed as the foe of the foes of God, so false religion becomes the vehicle of a darkness in which men are utterly confused. That which should have given illumination becomes a blackout of all true understanding, and those men who have no standards of moral discrimination cry aloud in blasphemous agony. But the very moral confusion becomes the vehicle of more deception. The three unclean spirits like frogs, gathering the nations together to fight against God, become the very symbol of a world of false religion in which moral and spiritual confusion reigns. Events all over the earth furnish the best sort of commentary upon these insights.

With quicksilverlike movement Revelation applies its principles now to the finalities of eternity and now to the movements of history. The drying of the Euphrates for the feet of armies from the East is the symbol of the use of events in time for the furtherance of the principles which rule in eternity. There is actual providential clearing of the way for the organization of the forces which would mobilize to fight against God. The tactics of small campaigns are to be replaced by a world-wide strategy. And God himself helps to bring the conflict to a head in a great movement which will bring every earthly opposition clearly against him in order that this vast mobilization of wickedness may be entirely overthrown.

But good men are not to think with fear of the coming of the vast forces of evil. Rather are they to watch and wear the clean garments of right living for the time when the Prince of Righteousness shall come. The mobilization of the forces of evil is always an indication of the coming of the living Christ, who does not desert his own, and does not leave the world to the lawless sovereignty of evil. Armageddon is only incidentally a geographical term. It is any place where after many incidental conflicts the embattled hosts of wickedness gather to hurl defiance against all the forces of goodness and of God.

In the fabric which the man of Patmos is weaving the shuttle moves to the very end and back again with breath-taking rapidity. And an understanding of these quick changes is of the greatest importance to the reader. After the pouring out of the seventh bowl of wrath, the mighty voice of God is heard saying, "It is done." This might be the last word at the end of the last chapter of the book. But the shuttle turns and soon we will be engrossed with symbolic events still to take place. The real meaning of this for the reader is that to the eyes of faith the consummation is so sure that in a sense it may be said to have been reached before it is actually accomplished. The men who hear the voice of God saying "It is done," when the final battles are yet to be fought, find infinite reassurance in the experience. This faith, to which all that has a right to be but is not is more real than all that has no right to be but is, constitutes one of the greatest spiritual forces of the world. At every stage of the fight the Christian is conscious of the final victory.

Again and again, as the tale of the seven bowls is recounted, we are told of the wicked that do not repent. If there is a gate to hell beside the final gate to heaven, the reverse is true, and there is a gate to heaven just beside the final gate to hell. Repentance is always within reach as the final plagues do their deadly work among men. But there is a moral determinism for which the wicked themselves are responsible. The final tragedy of bad men is not that God sets himself against them with a hard fatality. It is that they themselves become incapable of responding to the moral opportunities which God still holds before them. The willingness of God to receive those who repent is never exhausted. But we may grow so completely one with the evil which we have chosen that we become incapable of moral response. There is infinite sadness and all the strange wonder of a divine regret in the refrain of ch. 16, "They repented not."

17:1-6. The Woman Seated on the Beast in the Wilderness.—One of the angels of the seven bowls carries the man of Patmos in vision into a great wilderness where he sees a woman sitting **upon a scarlet-colored beast** with **seven heads and ten horns.** She is the great harlot and she is magnificently arrayed in costly garments and decked with jewels. The very golden cup which she carries is full of the drink of lawlessness. She wears a mysterious name written on her forehead, **Babylon the great, mother of harlots and of earth's abominations.** She is drunk with **the blood of the saints and . . . the martyrs of Jesus.** The great series of powerful symbols in which the wicked glory of Rome and its complete destruction are to be set forth begin to appear. With bitter irony the lawgiver of the world is pictured as the world's supreme harlot. Not law but lawlessness is the living force of the great empire. And when those appear who represent the will of God for men, she slays them and in fierce joy in her wickedness appears **drunk with the blood of the saints.** The dragon which bears her is a somewhat shifting symbol. First, it would seem to be the empire carrying in heads and horns symbols of particular rulers.

7-13. The Explanation of the Angel.—Seeing the bewilderment of the man of Patmos as he gazes upon these complicated symbols, the angel who has carried him to the wilderness offers to explain their meaning. Because there is much dangerous reference to contemporary events, the explanation itself must be guarded almost to the point of making it utterly unintelligible to those who are hostile to the persecuted faith. The result is that it comes very near to being unintelligible to those who are to hear it. The fact that old materials are incorporated without being thoroughly fitted into the immediate situa-

tion may add complications to the whole body of symbols and to their explanation. Some things emerge, however, with sufficient clearness. The harlot is Rome. The heads of the beast are Rome's **seven hills.** But by a quick turn of symbolism they are also **seven kings,** whose coming and going is expressed in words full of mystery. Somehow the belief that Nero, restored to life, would work incredible havoc moves through the symbolism. And by another swift transition the beast itself seems to become a demonic Nero.

14-18. The War and the Victory.—The angel continues speaking as he moves through rather complicated figures to describe the war of the forces of the Lamb with the forces of wickedness. Powerful kings with one mind give their authority to the beast. They turn against the woman seated upon many waters, which symbolize the vast masses of people under the rule of Rome. The very forces of wickedness which Rome has created become the instrument of its own destruction. The beast becomes the foe of its own queen of lawlessness. She is hated and made naked and desolate. Her foes **eat her flesh, and burn her with fire.** The words flame with the most bitter hatred and fury. But the great fight is not really that between Rome and hostile forces in the empire. It is the war between the armies of the Lamb and the embattled imperial forces of wickedness. The saints fight on the side of the Lamb in this great war. And the one who is truly **Lord of lords and King of kings** wins the final victory. The Cross has become a sword to conquer the forces of evil. The queen who reigned over the kings of the earth is overthrown. The evil forces of the empire are utterly defeated.

We must always keep in mind the fact that in this Expos. we are seeking for those insights which have permanent significance for the Christian religion. This makes it possible for us to escape the struggle with details of confused and complicated symbolism which had a contemporary reference. The thoughts of the man of Patmos about a Nero restored to life and doing desperate deeds have long lost any relevance to the ongoing experience of the Christian church. But the picture of a world organized without any fundamental loyalty to the God of righteousness, and of kings without moral purpose or spiritual understanding, coming and going, themselves the victims of lawless impulses, the source and meaning of which they do not really understand, expresses something which is worthy of the thought of men of every age.

The attack upon Rome involves some of the most terrible and magnificent rhetoric to be found in Revelation. And every word is related to intolerably bitter experience and to personal grapple with the most terrible problems. The situation is tragic enough when the controlling forces in one's environment are against everything which gives life moral meaning and spiritual nobility. The belief that the world is ruled by a God who is righteousness alive is the most important conviction which can be held in the mind of man. The belief that the God who is living righteousness is also the God of suffering love has in it the power to make all things new. These two beliefs were the precious inheritance of the man of Patmos. The sense of the God of justice lies under everything which is said in the book. And the repeated references to the Lamb that was slain show how the idea of the suffering love of God had become a very part of the warp and the woof of the author's thought. The joyous acceptance of the lordship of Christ, which expresses the very meaning of the divine character and makes the divine will real in the world of men, throbs like a perpetual music on every page. And it is these things which are set at nought by the proud power of Rome. More than that, she has marshaled herself with defiant energy against them, so that she has become an organized attack against the moral and spiritual meaning of life. The city which is supposed to be the center from which law goes forth has become the center of lawlessness. The government to which men must look for the upholding of virtue has become the very apotheosis of vice. The figure of Rome as the great harlot is unsurpassed for bitter irony in the literature of the world.

Men who live in the twentieth century do not need to be reminded of the terrible relevancy of the picture of immoral power seated in the place of judgment. Not since the days of the decadent Roman Empire have these things expressed themselves in history as they have among us. To keep the moral sense of the eternal alive in a time when voices of the most tremendous power have been denying that existence has any moral meaning at all has been the supreme task of those who would uphold the traditions of moral religion. The coming and going of turbulent powers described in ch. 17 has its own deep meaning for the moral vicissitudes of modern governments. The man of Patmos tells us that all temporarily triumphant evil powers come from the abyss. The beastly order whose potencies they reflect is doomed. The sentence of the beast to perdition includes everything for which a civilization below human meanings and below divine sanctions stands. In the very nature of a universe supported by a righteous God the beastly powers cannot permanently control the thrones of the world. Temporarily the situation is con-

fusing enough. Only those who belong to the company of the book of life have any sort of safety. The evil powers in their own wicked and persuasive way can capture the intelligence, master the imagination, and control the purposes of mankind. This desperate danger that men and women will be corrupted by the forces of triumphant wickedness is perpetually before the mind of the man of Patmos. Indeed, it may be said that one of his purposes in writing is to clarify and to maintain the power of the voice of a Christian conscience. No words can be too fierce and cutting, no figures can be too dramatic, and no symbols can be too vivid to express the great truths it is his purpose to convey. And he writes with a desperate sense of urgency precisely because of the perpetual danger that the souls of men may be stolen by the allurements of the beast. As one meditates about all this in the light of the modern moral and spiritual debacle, it becomes evident that the very intensity of his passion has a special meaning for us. Urbanity may itself become the foe of moral insight and of spiritual loyalty. There is a realm of ethical urgency beyond the power of sweet reasonableness. This is made clear not only in Revelation. In the Gospels the voice of our Lord becomes biting and explosive in his great hours of mighty castigation. There come times when the Christian message must flash like lightning and burst with the clap of thunder. The issues are overwhelming. The moral clarification of the human mind cannot be accomplished without words which bite with terrible intensity.

We must always remind ourselves that in a democracy where the people really control the policies of the nation the problem of the corruption of the public conscience becomes immediate and compelling. If the beast comes to the place of power, we ourselves are responsible for the authority which we have so tragically misplaced. The literature of moral and spiritual guidance is of the greatest importance in a republic. Where every man is a king, the debate about public questions comes to have a new meaning. And all questions in principle turn out to be religious questions at last. It is only minds mastered by the moral imperatives of the Christian religion which can approach the great problems of state with the fullest promise of character and wisdom. In a country where men of various religious convictions can hold citizenship it becomes particularly imperative that the power of the Christian religion to enlighten the public conscience shall be completely felt.

Once and again in Revelation we come across symbols of the final struggle and the final victory. In ch. 17 the battle between the forces of the Lamb and the forces of his foes is seen for the first time as taking place upon the earth. In this very world the conflict takes place. In this very world the victory is won. In this very world the Lamb that was slain becomes Lord of lords and King of kings. Later we shall hear more of a Christian victory in history. The proponents of the Christian religion are often accused of otherworldliness. Extreme left propaganda has been particularly coarse and raucous in its satirical attack upon a view of life which satisfies men with good hopes of a heavenly future ("pie, in the sky, when you die"). It is at least clear that the man of Patmos is sure there will be a victory of the Christian religion and of all for which it stands in this world. Faithful followers of the Lamb will have a share in the fight and a share in the victory. Here is a clear picture of the saints fighting against the evils of our present life and overthrowing them. When the great R. W. Dale was attacked as lacking in heavenly-mindedness because he fought with the evils of his day in Birmingham and in England, his reply was to the effect that there were no wrongs to right in heaven, but that if there were, it would be necessary to fight them. Real heavenly-mindedness consists partly in struggling to make the life of this world conform to that good life which is secure in heaven. The evangelical Christian is sometimes put on one side and the Christian of practical moral and social passion on the other. Those who feel that they owe everything to the Lamb that was slain are pictured in Revelation as going forth in this world to fight against all which is contrary to his will. The last bitter days of Woodrow Wilson were given serenity and assurance because he profoundly believed that the things for which he stood would ultimately be victorious in the very world where he had battled for them.

There is the profoundest moral insight in the symbols which reveal the beast and the kings turning upon the harlot with utter hatred and making her desolate and naked. The angry figures become confused and distorted. They shall eat her flesh. They shall utterly burn her with fire. The wicked empire, in other words, contains the seeds of its own destruction. The empire will destroy Rome. When a world-wide empire is established upon falseness and cruelty and the refusal to acknowledge the God of moral love, already it has signed its own death warrant. A power founded upon injustice ultimately will be hated by the very instruments which it has created. The beast represents the spirit of disintegration, not the spirit of construction. So the empire which has built a capital of oppression will become the greatest foe of this very capital. Bad organization is always in the long run ineffective organization. The

little human kings will turn against the great human kings when the force which holds them together is the force of cruelty and oppression. The tyrant always lies awake at night anxiously suspecting the human instruments of his tyranny. And the servants of the tyrants never feel safe and are always ready to turn against him in order to save themselves. When evil men come to be of one mind against the organization of which they are a part, then there is a disintegration indeed. Tyranny is always killing its own offspring. And the offspring of tyranny are always killing the tyrant. But because there is no principle of justice or truth or honesty on either side, the result is anarchy rather than moral progress. But to see the self-defeating quality of evil is to come upon a very great insight. The proud forces of unrighteousness are always preparing their own doom.

And all of this the man of Patmos sees as a part of the government of God. For God himself presides over the processes by which evil forces accomplish their own suicide. Providence uses men's evil hands and evil purposes to accomplish their complete defeat. He uses their own wicked minds to realize ends other than their own. There is a divine will which uses the worst thoughts and the worst purposes of the worst men to bring about their final overthrow. They are held to that dark loyalty to their own bad character which becomes the instrument of their own fate. All these are high and terrible matters. But, moving through the terror which they describe, there is a vast reassurance for those who have chosen good and not evil for their ultimate loyalty, those who have learned that goodness is saved from being a powerless abstraction when it is securely associated with the character of the living God.

18:1-3. *The Shining Angel of Prophetic Doom.*—This chapter of Revelation contains a series of dirges over the fallen city of Rome. They are all uttered while the city is in the full splendor of its power. So they are the dirges of faith that the city will be utterly destroyed. They come with heavenly authority. They anticipate the lamentations of kings and merchants and men of the sea. In a fashion they have the quality of taunting songs. Yet they are not without pity and regret for a splendor which, seen by the eyes of faith, has completely vanished. In a way the pity is a part of the terrible irony.

An **angel** appears, of such vivid light that the earth is illuminated by his brightness. The destruction of Rome is pronounced as if it had already occurred. And again Rome is given the name of **Babylon.** Like the toll of a terrible bell, the words of rhythmic doom roll out. The city which had been so great has vanished. Hateful birds and spirits of foulness haunt the place once full of all the sights and sounds of a magnificent metropolis. The city whose very quality of life violated every law of noble living, the corrupter of kings, and the betrayer of merchants whose very wealth came from sharing in her lawlessness, is no more.

4-8. The Heavenly Warning and the Heavenly Sentence.—Another voice from heaven speaks. Swiftly returning to the day when Rome is still great, people of good will are commanded to leave the city which is condemned to destruction, lest sharing in her sins they share in her destruction. Then in stern words the doom of the wicked city is pronounced. Her evil is to come back upon herself in double intensity. She is to drink **a double draught** of her own poison. For her pride and wantonness she is to receive torture and weeping. She says in proud self-consciousness that she is no widow and shall never know grief. So pestilence and famine and bitter cries shall come upon her. She shall be destroyed in a furious conflagration. Not Rome but the **God who judges her** exercises true might.

9-10. The Weeping Kings.—The kings whose very prosperity and power were the gift of Rome's lawlessness shall stand in the distance in the day of her destruction, and as they watch **the smoke of her burning** shall cry aloud bewailing the mighty city whose judgment has come.

11-16. The Weeping Merchants.—The **merchants** whose busy commerce and great wealth Rome had made possible will bewail her fall. In fear of a destruction which may engulf them, they will recount bitterly the objects of their trade, the vast variety of the things which they bought and sold, ministering to every necessity and impulse of luxury, and at last including the very bodies and souls of men. All these things are lost never again to be found. They remember the city clothed magnificently and adorned with the most precious stones. All this wealth has been laid waste forever.

17-20. The Weeping Men of the Sea.—The ships which carry the commerce of Rome about the world are manned by shipmasters and sailors who join in the terrible chorus of lamentation. They throw **dust on their heads** as they watch the smoke of the burning city, and cry aloud that never was there a city like it which sent ships of treasure to every port around the sea. She is laid waste. And they acknowledge that in the destruction of Rome God has given his judgment in favor of the saints and apostles and prophets whom she has destroyed.

21-24. Nevermore.—A mighty angel throws a great **stone into the sea**, announcing that like its swift falling shall be the violent end of Rome. Then like a stately funeral march of

words comes the long-drawn song of nevermore. All sounds of music shall be heard no more. The busy work of craftsmen shall be found no more. The grinding of the millstone shall never be heard again. The lamps shall go out, never to be relighted. Happy voices of bridegrooms and brides are silenced forever. And in the vast, dark stillness the great merchant princes and the nations deceived by the false lordliness of Rome are remembered as belonging to an era completely passed. The obdurate foe of the good and the godly has been brought to utter destruction at last.

The faith which can project itself into the time when evil which is now triumphant shall become evil which has been destroyed is the most vital kind of faith. The principle involved is that since God is on the throne, righteousness will inevitably triumph in history. That which has no right to be but is, will be brought to an end. That which is not but has a right to be, will come to have secure and victorious being. So thoroughly is the man of Patmos able to project himself into the future when that which is now defeated will be triumphant that he does more than declare it. He does more than proclaim it. He sings a series of songs about it. He makes the future the present, and looks back upon the present from that future of triumph. This power in a bad present to live in a good future makes the world a different place for the person who possesses it. And this is just the power which the author of Revelation would give to his readers.

Most men, far more than they know, are creatures of their environment. They are molded by their surroundings. H. A. Taine believed that if one understood the climate of England, he would know something of the forms which English literature must inevitably take. Writers untouched by higher tradition are likely to write of human life as completely submerged in circumstances. It is one of the deepest lessons of history that men do not need to be the slaves of their surroundings. They can master them. Every exodus in the history of mankind has been led by a Moses who was stronger than his environment. The man of Patmos deliberately sets out to make men so much stronger than Rome that they can laugh at the claims of the Imperial City. He sets forth the sources of this strength. God is stronger than Rome and therefore his loyal followers are also mightier than the proud and arrogant city. And God has remembered the iniquities of Rome. He is not a passive spectator of the pageant of history. He is its supreme actor. And his action against Rome will be final and conclusive. The future is already in the past to one who has sufficient faith in God. The very site of Rome is seen as a place of utter desolation. The real light of the world comes not from the false glory of time but from the true glory of eternity. The angel who proclaims the doom of Rome is all-shining with eternal light. If we have only the light of Rome, we are on the way to darkness. If we have the heavenly light in our hearts, we have the beginning of an eternal illumination. When the Imperial City has become a jungle of wild beasts, the light of God will still be shining upon his true servants.

Naturalistic writers are always ready to sing the dirge of the Christian religion. Christ is dead to rise no more. His character has no significance for us. His principles are irrelevant. The world will go its way and forget that he has ever been. But in the very hour when they proclaim the destruction of Christianity, the naturalists declare their own despair. It becomes clear to the discerning reader that when Christ dies, hope dies. When his influence comes to an end, all high ideals become lifeless. With his departure the soul of happiness has gone from the world. The naturalists have no one to give us in the place of Christ. They have nothing to give us instead of his kingdom. The extinction of Christ is the extinction of the very meaning of life. So we turn from the gospel of despair to the gospel of the angel of shining light. It is the cities of moral lawlessness which are to be destroyed. It is the empires of wickedness for which dirges are to be sung. It is the corrupters who are to come upon corruption. It is the fabric of falseness which is to fall. It is the fabric of truth which is to remain forever.

The warning not to have fellowship with the evils of the city of destruction has meaning for every age. That men may be citizens of the city of God, though their feet press the streets of the city condemned to death, is one of the great facts of the moral life of man and one of the great facts of history. They do not have to accept the moral evasions which corrupt the soul. They do not have to accept the compromises which deface the character. If the city of God is in a man's heart, the city of evil cannot corrupt his hand. Evil has no power over him until it masters the citadel of the inner life. To use a figure of a great seventeenth-century Christian, it may attack at the eye-gate, and it may attack at the ear-gate, but it is helpless unless the gate is opened from within. That Christians have something priceless to maintain against all attacking foes is very clear in the mind of the author of Revelation. They belong not to the city of Rome but to the city of God. If they maintain their loyalty to their own city, they will have inner safety even if their world falls apart.

One of the subtlest and most difficult prob-lems of history is involved in the story of the weeping kings and the weeping merchants and the weeping men of the sea. They who owe their prosperity to evil institutions are likely to be the most ardent defenders of these institutions. If the institution goes, their prosperity goes. So they rise in full armor for its defense. When Paul's preaching endangered the trade of certain men of Ephesus, they set all the city crying, "Great is Diana of the Ephesians" (Acts 19:28). So it has been in every century before and since. It is always difficult to have any question considered on its merits when financial interests become involved. Political leaders and manufacturers and controllers of transportation are tempted to unite in the defense of all those institutions in which the successful prosecution of their activities is involved. One of the greatest achievements of the Christian religion is the production of men who will stand by great principles when such loyalty may wreck their business. Their kind of loyalty demands a heroism which deserves very high praise. The prophet who has no personal stake in the things which he condemns sometimes does not realize the full severity of the demand he is making upon those who have quite failed to understand how much their prosperity is dependent upon that which is evil. They have accepted the standards in which they have grown up and are very much disconcerted when they find themselves the object of moral castigation. Of course the word of the prophet must be uttered. And if he did not utter it, the very processes of a life with moral meaning at the heart of it would bring disintegration to that which is ethically unsound. But the plight of a man caught in the coils of an evil system can be understood even if it may not be condoned.

The situation becomes more complicated when it is understood that much good becomes involved in the ongoing of institutions which have a heart of evil. It is always harder to fight a tyranny when the alternative seems to be anarchy. So many of the good processes of everyday life fall with its fall. The author of Revelation realizes this. And with a certain wistfulness we hear of the going out of all the lamps, the silencing of the voices of the bridegroom and the bride, the end of all music, and the complete disruption of all the crafts by means of which the life of men is carried on. But even with this understanding, he does not hesitate. When an institution has become evil at its heart, it must go down whatever goes down with it. Institutions like human slavery have in various nations become so deeply involved in the very ongoing of life that no end of good and gracious things seemed to depend upon them for very existence. It is possible to paint a picture of some aspects of social life in the days of slavery which is not without a charm and allurement of its own. But the corrupting power of the institution was of such a nature that it had to go.

The weeping singers of the dirge of Rome bewail the loss of many things which in themselves are good. But before the end of the book we shall confront a type of life so good in essence that all things will be saturated with its own noble quality. The things bewailed by the kings and merchants and seamen, in so far as they are good things, can and will have their place in a life whose institutions are sound and righteous. The music will return in a nobler society. The craftsmen will do their work in the terms of a better life. The voices of the bridegroom and the bride will once again be heard in a society which is not rotten at the core.

Here in the hour when the doom of a city essentially evil is being faced, the fairer picture is left beyond immediate vision. There must be no compromise with that which is morally destructive and spiritually disintegrating. So the grim irony is greater than the pity in the dirges of the doom of Rome. There is really no basis for the good life in a society the very central meaning of whose existence is poisoned by processes of moral decay. So it is for the sake of the ultimate triumph of goodness that the conclusive word is pronounced.

To the man of Patmos the opposition to the reign of God and to the doing of his will, together with the persecution of the saints and the prophets and the shedding of their blood, is the final wickedness of Rome. Though those who represent the good will of the good God may seem to be in a hopeless minority, the future really belongs to them, and to that for which they stand. To many a Roman official the followers of the religion of Jesus Christ must have seemed to be quite beneath contempt. He thought he was judging them. But really he was being judged by them. It is in the name of the moral and spiritual order of the world that Revelation pronounces the doom of that which opposes the divine will. The form which evil takes may be imposing. Its structure may seem impregnable. But its fate is sure.

19:1-5. *The Song of Heavenly Triumph over Rome.*—A mighty chorus is heard from heaven ascribing all honor and glory to God who has judged Rome and **avenged the blood** of his saints. There is a flashing sense of a great heavenly scene with the four and twenty elders and the four living creatures bent in worship of God upon his throne, and a voice as if the throne itself has become articulate, calling upon all God's servants who worship him with noble fear to give him praise.

6-10. *The Song of the Marriage of the Lamb and the Refusal of the Angel to Accept Worship.*—A vast and joyous chorus rejoices in the reign of God and **the marriage of the Lamb.** The church, spotless at last, is offered as the bride. And blessed are those who are invited to the hymeneal feast. The man of Patmos would worship the glorious angel who announces these things, but he is forbidden: **Worship God.** Jesus himself is put at the heart of the divine life in the declaration that it is the very genius of true prophecy to testify of him.

11-16. *The Warrior on the White Horse and His Mighty Army.*—There is a quick change and we behold quite another picture. Now the living Christ is seen as a fierce warrior upon **a white horse.** He is **Faithful and True** and he battles for righteousness. His garment is sprinkled with blood, which reminds us of his suffering. He is **The Word of God** in judgment and in battle. A white army follows him, for heaven itself joins in his battle and his victory. A cutting sword leaps from his lips. He is to smite the nations and to rule them with the stern strength of iron. He is the very instrument of the moral anger of God treading **the wine press** of his righteous **wrath.** He comes as a figure of mystery. His many crowns can be seen, but no one knows his secret name. He belongs to the very hidden and uncomprehended wonder of the life of God. But all can see that he is **King of kings and Lord of lords.**

17-18. *The Summons to the Vultures.*—Grim matters are being dealt with and grim words are used to tell the tale of them. An angel bright with the light of the sun calls to all birds of prey to come and feed upon the flesh of the mighty who are to be slaughtered because they have allied themselves with that which is utterly evil. **Kings** and **captains** and fighting **men** and the war **horses** upon which they have ridden proudly are to lie dead, waiting for the fierce and ravenous vultures who are summoned for this awful feast.

19-21. *The Defeat of the Beast and the Kings and Their Armies.*—The **beast** and the **false prophet** and the **kings** and their great **armies** advance and are utterly defeated. The beast and the prophet are cast into the fiery lake which burns with brimstone. The sword from the mouth of the great leader of the army in white slays the rest. And the vultures come to their hideous feast.

We must always be prepared in Revelation for intense and vital words of repetition. The same picture is presented from many points of view. The same truth is driven home in a great variety of ways. The book becomes a kind of rhapsody of fear and joy, of wrath and judgment, of battle and victory. With all the quick changes, the reversals and the movements forward, there is a wonderful artistic unity. And everything moves toward the grand climax of the final and complete victory of God. The ringing choruses of "Alleluia" join the glorious praise of the O.T. with the singing gladness of the N.T. As the Psalter moves to its conclusion with a great burst of alleluias, so the victory of God is sung in the final book of the N.T. with the echoing majesty of the same ascription. This note of utter joy in God has something conclusive about it. And at the same time it has about it something gloriously creative. That the slave on Patmos, by the anticipation of faith, can participate fully in this music of singing joy, and can share his triumph with his fellow sufferers under the heel of Rome, reveals the deathless quality of the religion for which men are called to suffer.

It is an essential quality of ethical religion that it is joyously creative. Philosophy is contented with clear and cogent statement. At its best it convinces the mind; it may leave the heart quite unmoved. But truth must be set on fire before it becomes really creative. It must arouse the emotions and kindle the imagination and become a burning passion of quickened energy. Revelation is best understood when it is inspected in the light of this necessity that the whole life must be inspired by triumphant gladness if the greatest words are to be said and the greatest deeds are to be done. This book survives because to the fullest extent it possesses that quality of being morally and spiritually creative. Its heavenly music represents more than a hope for the future. Its rapture and its song are an immediate and present inspiration.

There are many important questions which may be asked about the religious life of any period. Is it morally sound? Is it intellectually clear and firm? Does it have a deep and true spirituality? Does it release energies which have every potency of creative action? In respect of each of these questions it is possible to say that the Christian religion as interpreted by the man of Patmos meets every essential need. The moral soundness of what he writes is such as to uphold every sanction of righteous living. He is not a philosopher, but the more we go back of his images and pictures the more we see the presence of clear and compelling intelligence. He is at every moment aware of all the spiritual values. The unseen becomes visible in noble symbol. The spiritual suffuses every word and every phrase. And more than anything else, his book simply surges with vital energy. The heavenly chorus is the rich expression of that triumphant vitality. And we miss the whole point of it if we do not see that those who listen to the heavenly music at once approach the earthly experience of living and all its vicissitudes in a completely new fashion. Human eyes now shine with a happy light. Human hearts beat with a joyous rhythm. Human wills achieve living strength. The rapture which is joy in the heart becomes might in the hand. The foretaste of heavenly music becomes earthly power.

All of this has a particular meaning for the music of the church. At its best the worship of music in a Christian church always means the capture of a heavenly gladness for earthly inspiration. The environment of heaven becomes available for the strengthening of men who walk the ways of earth. The church expresses its true character when its life is set to heavenly music. And the rapturous outbursts of Revelation have done more to make this possible than is often realized.

The presentation of the stainless church to be the bride of the living Christ involves a memorable and inspiring figure. Christ is seen as the Lamb who was offered in sacrifice. Now the happiest of human consummations is used to express his union with the perfected church. The one who died, now alive forevermore, is seen in eternal and happy intimacy with those whom he has redeemed. A Christian is a man who is in training for perfection. The Christian church is an institution destined for perfection. This is the high calling of which men and churches must begin to be worthy now. This is the ultimate fulfillment of the Christian church in the light of which present responsibilities must be seen. The haunting vision of the spotless church should be with Christian leaders and with those who follow as they go about their daily tasks. The searching and demanding quality of this vision will change many things if it is kept before the mind.

The quick aside in which the man of Patmos is commanded not to worship a radiant angel, but to worship only God, has a perpetual relevance. We are all the while tempted to give a final allegiance to that which, though good, is secondary. Only the highest is good enough to command our complete devotion. It is perhaps our most constant temptation to become so engrossed with secondary matters that we fail to keep in constant mind the ultimate devotions. There are so many good things Christians may be doing that it is easy for them to lose sight of the greatest thing of all. And that which commands our constant attention of course possesses our real worship. The radiant angels of opportunity are to be received and welcomed. But beyond them the eye must be constantly searching for the ultimate authority. It is a hard lesson to learn, but the welfare of the church depends upon our learning it well.

For it is made clear at once that the living Christ dwells in this region of ultimate authority. In his word the ultimate word of God is found, and he himself is the living presence of the final spirit of prophecy. There is nothing which belongs to God which does not belong to him.

The power which controls eternity watches the struggles in the temporal order and invades the life of time for purposes of good. This is the meaning of the symbol of the warrior on the white horse and his heavenly army. The moral decisiveness of heaven is to be made real and final in the life of time. The living Christ who once entered the world to die for men again enters the world for the final conflict with evil. The battle against evil may seem to be a losing struggle. But the mighty armies of heaven are gathering, and of the outcome of the struggle there can be no doubt. The one whose blood was shed now wears many diadems and his very word is a flashing sword for the destruction of evil. Pretentious earthly kingdoms fall apart. His reign is eternal. He is veritably King of kings and Lord of lords. But the very setting forth of the symbol of the warrior on the white horse suggests a perpetual conflict with evil, as well as a final battle and a final victory. The thought is not far away that a heavenly army like that seen by the prophet and his servant in the olden time is always near the beleaguered servants of God.

Life must be lived, then, in the light of the larger environment. Only because our eyes are dull do we fail to see the heavenly reinforcements which are already at our side. The secular man is aware only of the hard material forces. The Christian goes forth to his daily struggles with a constant awareness of the nearness of the armies of God. There is no more important task than that of giving men such an awareness. Strugglers for a better social life are all the while fighting those elements in the environment which contradict every nobler aspect of life. It is a good fight in which they are engaged, and it surely has the blessing of God. But there is a subtler battle in respect of the environment of the mind. And the symbols of Revelation indicate a mental environment which gives our life in time the very deathless qualities of eternity. To provide men with deathless thoughts is to transform at last every aspect of their lives. The Christian interpreter is the perpetual purveyor of divine thoughts in the midst of human life. He gives men the freedom of a city of the mind where God reigns and the living Christ is already victorious. The N.T. is full of these ideas. Repentance is a change of mind. We are to have the mind in us which was in Christ Jesus. The first step in the transformation of human life is the claiming of the minds of men for God.

Nothing is clearer to the reader of Revelation than the fact that the heavenly army is to master every hard and grim fact. The summons of the vultures may seem to belong to a very different realm from that of the stainless beauty of the thoughts which belong to the kingdom of heaven. But the forces of evil are to be defeated in this very hard and material world. The picture of the birds of prey eating the flesh of the slaughtered foes of Christ is a symbol of the utter disintegration of unethical materialism even in the regions in which it is most sure of itself. The very world of flesh and blood in which it feels so confident is to witness its complete and bitter defeat. If we believe only in a world of vultures, the vultures will destroy us at last. And if we believe only in a world of flesh unillumined by spirit, the vultures quite agree with us in that they make no distinction between the flesh of horses and the flesh of kings.

The beast and the false prophet are taken. The beast is the symbol of evil power. The prophet is the symbol of evil speech. False interpretations of life corrupt men's minds. False and evil governments corrupt every one of their practical relationships. These inspirers and actors in a drama of physical and mental and moral and spiritual disintegration are captured and hurled into the fiery lake. They produced conflagration in the world. Their own fate is conflagration. It is always hard for bad men to see that their doom is already implicit in their own thoughts. It is always hard for them to see that their doom is already present in their own action. What we are becomes our destiny.

Out of the mouth of the warrior on the white horse comes the sword which slays the embattled hosts of wickedness. His word is mightier than all their deeds. Perhaps Luther had this in mind when in his great hymn *Ein' Feste Burg* he wrote, "One little word shall fell him." The principle is a profound one. For words have a way of becoming deeds. And the power of words is one of the greatest of all the powers we know. The betraying word corrupts men. The good word redeems men. And the word of moral judgment is a word of destiny.

Mortality is a sad enough business if it is not suffused by an immortal hope. If the physical organism tells the whole story, the vultures indeed have the last word.

20:1-3. The Binding of the Devil.—A powerful **angel from heaven** unlocks and opens the abyss, captures the devil, binds him and hurls him into the abyss, seals the entrance, and so leaves him for a thousand years of captivity.

4-7. The Thousand Years of Blessedness.— There is a vision of many **thrones.** Upon them are seated those who had remained loyal to Christ under the greatest pressure of persecution. They have been recalled from death to share in the reign of Christ for **a thousand years.** They are **priests** and judges and the utmost felicity is given to them.

7-10. The Defeat of the Forces from the Ends of the Earth.— The devil is released, and from the ends of the earth gathers a multitude like the sands of the sea for the final conflict. They surround the beloved city, but fire comes down from heaven to destroy them. They are devoured by its furious burning, and the devil is thrown **into the lake of fire, . . . where the beast and the false prophet** are already suffering. Together they confront an eternity of torment.

11-15. Resurrection and Judgment Before the Great White Throne.— The very physical environment of the ages when wickedness flourished vanishes. The **great white throne** rests secure, and the **dead** stand for judgment before the face of God. The mighty **books,** the records, are opened. And the dead are judged **according to their works.** The lake of fire receives everything that is subject to destruction, and those whose names are **not found . . . in the book of life** are cast into that lake.

The man of Patmos is firmly convinced that those who have suffered most must receive conspicuous reward. He is also convinced that there must be a triumph of Christ in this very world which has seen so many moral tragedies. So he pictures the thousand years of splendor when these faithful dead are recalled to sit on thrones with the regnant Christ. The very world which had spurned the saints is to be ruled by them. This sense of what may be called a victory of good in history has haunted the imagination of earnest men century after century. In a way it has pervaded the fascinating but sometimes uncritical writing which has been the expression of utopian thought. It has played about and given color to what has often been called "the American dream." It has been the inspiration of many a fantasy regarding the "Land of Heart's Desire." It has felt the influence of every nostalgic memory and of every evasive hope. It has sung itself in poetry and it has reasoned itself in prose. And the ethical elements have failed to receive due place in that world of irresponsible dreaming. It is the essential characteristic of the thousand years of the triumph of goodness and of the good in Revelation that every moral value is firmly maintained. Those who have been treated with miserable and bitter injustice on the field of history are brought back for triumph where they had experienced only defeat. The happy futures to which men look have a sad way of ignoring those who perished on the road. Here is a vision of felicity which takes full account of those who have given their lives for a truth their age denied. There is here expressed a principle which must be a part of the Christian witness. The "choir invisible" must come back to sing. Its music must not be merely a matter of memory. The picture here in this chapter has often been misunderstood. It has been turned to curious and fanatical purposes. But it will always strike a responsive chord when men think of a justice whose faith is brave enough and secure enough to include the dead.

It has been made amply clear as we have moved through the book that to the author the dark and bitter and malignant evil of the world is of such a nature that it must be associated with a power greater than that wielded by men, a power which works for their moral undoing. This dramatizing of the most bald and brutal badness which afflicts human life is done again and again with great energy. It is seen always over against the greater power of the eternal goodness, and finally as subject to defeat of the most conclusive fashion at God's hands. Such a view can be so set forth as to represent rather an evasion than a clear acceptance of human responsibility. "The serpent beguiled me, and I did eat," says the woman in the Genesis story. But the man of Patmos has two profound convictions regarding the supernatural evil in which he believes. First, it can tempt men, but it cannot coerce them. Men do not have to listen to evil voices from whatever source they come. They can refuse to worship the beast. And the repeated words, "They repented not," are sharp with a sense of their personal responsibility. Men are the masters of their decisions under whatever pressure of temptation they may live their lives. Second, it is evident that God is the master and controller of whatever supernatural evil exists. So the devil is pictured as bound and imprisoned for a thousand years, and finally as subjected to utter defeat and to an existence which is only torture. The reign of God is not finally threatened by the forces of evil. The truth which comes out of all this varied and graphic symbolism in respect of supernatural wickedness is that there is no dark power in the world or beyond it which is not at last completely subject to the will and the power of God. When evil comes upon men, so dark and so terrible that it seems to indicate that the very ultimate powers of the universe have made an alliance with wickedness, it remains true that God is on the throne. The triumph of the powers of darkness is temporary. God's word will be the last word. And it will compass the complete defeat of everything which is contrary to his own purpose of good.

Through all the symbolism of Revelation there runs a shrewd and practical realism which sometimes fills the reader with surprise. In this torn and difficult world the victories of goodness are often temporary. There are glad hours of victory when it seems that blatant wickedness has been put to flight. But after a while the evil thing reappears, sometimes with another name and wearing other garments. And so the whole battle has to be fought once more. It is very important that men should not think that a relative triumph is a final triumph. Once and again after some great victory the forces of goodness fold their arms and settle to the enjoyment of what they think is a complete achievement. In the latter part of the nineteenth century the liberal and progressive editor of a famous New York magazine used to say that some moral victories had been won by man for all time. The tooth and the nail would never appear with devastating power in human life again. To a real degree civilization had conquered the beast. This complacent gentleman did not live long enough to witness the resurgence of barbarous cruelty over great areas in the twentieth century. In a way, it is easy now to look back on the Victorian period with its assured optimism as a kind of millennium before another terrible unloosing of devilish power. It is important to see that Revelation, with all the glory of its ultimate assurance, never surrenders to uncritical hopes. Its words make clear enough that the man of Patmos knew how often the victory of good would be a relative victory. There is always a power ready to break loose and threaten the reign of the saints even when they seem most secure. The implicit threat of evil belongs to the life of time.

We must not treat the symbolic pictures of this book as if they represent an ordered and chronological record of the events which are destined to unfold. Each picture presents some insight and some principle with complete and secure sharpness. There is a deep inner harmony. But often there is contradiction enough on the surface, it we try to treat symbolic pictures as records of chronological sequence. Literal-minded scholars have been perplexed by the picture of the saints sitting on thrones of judgment after the destruction of the armies of evil, and of another gathering of evil forces after the King of kings and Lord of lords has ridden forth upon his white horse to glorious victory. There is really no need for perplexity.

The writer moves forward and backward in the easiest fashion. We see the end, and then for the sake of emphasis we are taken back to an earlier period. There is a final climactic movement, but there is many a backward flash. One important matter, however, in the picture of the saints as judges and priests must not be passed by casually. The faithful are to come upon great felicity and unmeasured happiness. But they are also to receive high and noble responsibility. The judge ministers in political justice. The priest ministers in spiritual things. Both types of responsibility are to be borne by the triumphant saints. There is to be a full exercise of every lofty power as well as the attainment of glorious happiness.

We have become accustomed to the fact that in Revelation there is a recurrent presentation of finalities. In the concluding picture in ch. 20 the dead stand in the presence of the great white throne. There is no description of the figure seated on the throne, but this reserve makes his presence all the more impressive. Every limited and opposing element fades away. There is the throne in blazing whiteness. There sits the mighty ruler, truly imperial when Rome has ceased to be. There are the dead. And there are the books. There are the books of record which tell what men have done. There is the book of life with its promise for the future. All sorts of things have been destroyed. But men cannot escape their own past. There in the books of record and the book of hope it stands waiting to meet them in the great adjudication.

Human life is not a series of unrelated events. It does not consist of separate fragments having no connection with each other. It is all of a piece. The present is woven from the past and the future is woven from the past and the present. Men's deeds are adhesive. They cannot be torn away from the men who perform them. To use the figure of the author, they are recorded in indestructible books. When earth and sky have faded away, the books remain. This principle of the moral continuity of life is embedded in the very depths of the Revelation of the man of Patmos. Here it emerges as the final principle of judgment. The dead who stand before the throne have an organic relation to the books, if one may put it so. Each bears implicit in his own life that which the records make explicit. The books are, in fact, photographs of human souls. Each man comes trailing his own destiny in that which he himself has become. Each himself is heaven or hell.

But what is psychology is also history. There in the books is the record. And in the description of themselves the men who have made bad choices face what they would like to hide from all eyes, human and divine. There is the book of life. The story of the soul's adventure with goodness and with God may seem so subtle and inward a thing that it is impossible to make it the subject of record. But there is no movement of the individual spirit toward God which has not been marked and entered. All that

the world's coarse thumb
And finger failed to plumb [5]

is here clearly set forth. Thoughts which have not yet been packed into the sharp concreteness of an act are fully apprehended. This is what men are worth to God. The making objective of the very secrets of the soul in the books of record and the book of hope gives the basis for an understanding completely searching and completely adequate. Once and again men feel that no one cares and no one understands what is really going on in their lives. But the great white throne is revealed as more than understanding, though as we look at it we cannot say that to understand all is to forgive all. To understand all is to apprehend all. And a part of what is seen is finally and conclusively evil. When evil thoughts and evil deeds have crystallized into an evil character so that a man has become completely one with his worst self, there is only one verdict which is possible. The death of goodness always precedes the death of hope.

So when the majestic potencies of glittering evil environment have disappeared, and each naked soul confronts the books of destiny, the ultimate moral values are vindicated. The forgotten is remembered. The invisible becomes visible. The motive is revealed in the act. The character which has been built up by means of great numbers of deeds, each sealing and expressing a deep and definite purpose, stands forth before the face of God. For at last revelation makes clear not only what God is. It also makes clear what man is. And the final revelation of what a man is becomes itself a conclusive act of judgment.

It is to be remembered too that there has to be good to record before there can be a book of life. The tale of men is not merely a tale of folly and frustration and wickedness. By the grace of God it can be, indeed it has been and is, a tale of eyes seeking for the vision of God, of hearts yearning for the love of God, and of the divine answer to the human yearning and the human outreach. The life of God in the souls of men and in the deeds of men is the most real thing in the world. And its record is found in the book of life. So another picture of the great consummation tells its story. The moral continuity of each human life comes to complete expression as it confronts the books

[5] Browning, "Rabbi Ben Ezra."

of destiny in the presence of the great white throne. Thoughts become purposes. Purposes become deeds. Deeds become destiny.

Inevitably one compares the various pictures of judgment in Revelation with the picture of the great adjudication which Jesus himself painted in memorable words. Here too those on the right and those on the left are judged by deeds which have expressed the very inner meaning of their lives. "Inasmuch as ye have done it . . ." and "Inasmuch as ye did it not . . ." become words of destiny.

21:1-8. *The City of Happiness.*—Now the words of the man of Patmos are filled with the wonder of the great consummation. The evil and the incomplete are no more. Perfection descends from heaven, a rapturous city for the dwelling of men. The tearless town becomes their possession. Their very felicity is found in the fact that God dwells with them, abolishing everything which brings pain or wailing, and giving to life the fullness and amplitude of his own perfections. God's voice is heard proclaiming that he makes **all things new.** He is the first and last letter of the eternal alphabet. In him are the origin and the conclusion of every experience. Whoever truly thirsts will receive from him access to the very **water of life.** Those who contradict the thoughts and ways of goodness and of God will come upon fiery destruction. The new and glorious city is not for them.

9-27. *The Triumphant Church Returns as a Great and Magnificent City.*—One of the angels of tragedy becomes an angel of good hope as he carries the man of Patmos in vision to a **high mountain** for the sight of the descending city of God, which is the victorious church visible in the splendor of an eternal town. The figure is complex as well as vivid. For the city is not only a church. It is a radiant bride. The Lamb that was slain is the Lord of the city, and the church is his happy bride. The city of the harlot has vanished, and the city of the living church is the bride of the living Christ. In every way tragedy has been replaced by glory.

The city, new creation as it is, has defining relations with the past. It has profound relations with the ancient life of God's chosen people, and its **twelve gates** bear the names of the **twelve tribes.** It is profoundly related to the witness of the disciples of Jesus, and its **twelve foundations** bear the names of the **twelve apostles.** Its very measurement sees the meeting of the human and the celestial. **The measure of a man** and the measure of an angel represent the same standard. Every beauty of physical adornment is exhausted to express a splendor in which the physical has become the instrument of the spiritual. The living Christ who was once the slain victim is the illumination of the city, which needs no light of sun or moon. There is **no temple,** for the divine Presence brings the reality of which all temples are symbols. As we have already seen, the pictures in Revelation have a fascinating independence of each other. While there is forward movement, there is no strict chronological succession. So we are not surprised, after all the pictures of destruction, to see the **kings of the earth** bringing **their glory** to the immortal town. Nothing evil or unclean shall enter the city. But in a world of perpetual day the gates of the town of light are forever open for those who desire to find the way of goodness and obedience to God.

If the N.T. apocalypse is a book of tragedy, it is even more characteristically a book of abounding happiness. If it is a book where we confront the very menace of the most blighting fears, it is essentially a book of the most serene and glittering hopes. And as the book comes to a climax, these hopes are completely regnant. The city of God's perpetual presence is a city of eternal joy. The dwelling place of God is with men. And in this sentence we come upon one of the most tremendous utterances in the whole book. Indeed, it is one of the most overwhelming sentences in the N.T. The man of Patmos is fully aware that he has come to a veritable splendor of climax. And so we hear the very voice of God himself saying that he makes all things new. But this is a newness which gathers into itself the true meaning of things from the beginning to the end. For it is in God that the beginning and the end meet together. It cannot be said too strongly that Christianity is the religion of the divine Presence. It is the tale of men's adventures with God, and of God's adventures with men. And its consummation comes with God's perpetual dwelling with men.

The consummation is a combination of creation and fulfillment. All things are made new by the one who is both the beginning and the end. This combination of originality and continuity is of very far-reaching meaning and application. Aristotle saw in great writing eternal principles applied to new and ever-changing situations. So the writing was as stable as deathless truths and had all the freshness of the new situations in which the principles were seen in action. Mere continuity would harden into conventionality. Mere originality would break down into lawless anarchy. But the application of permanent principles to constantly new and different situations combined stability and creative energy. The great consummation in Revelation does not represent a kind of divine anarchy. It gathers up the whole spiritual past of the old covenant. The very gates bear the names of the twelve tribes of Israel. They gather up the whole Christian past. The twelve foundations of the wall of the city bear the names of the twelve apostles of Jesus. They are called the apostles of the Lamb, and so the connection with the great sacrifice which is at the heart of the Christian religion is clearly made. The God who produces the consummation is the God of the beginning, and the figure of Alpha and Omega suggests perpetually new meanings spelled out by means of letters belonging to a divine alphabet. The changeless letters give continuity to all the newness of adventurous speech. The principles involved play in and out of all biography and all history. The conservative is busy with the tasks of maintaining. The adventurer is busy with the fresh wonder of finding and creating the new. The true radical goes down to the roots in order that he may conform to dependable meanings. True originality is always related to those defining origins which give real meaning to things.

The leader in the Christian church needs to keep these principles constantly in mind. He is full of the vision of a great consummation. He is joyously looking forward to a more perfect life dominated by the will and the spirit of Christ. It is easy for him to forget the great matters of continuity as he occupies himself with the thought of making all things new. On the other hand, he may be so eagerly possessed by the sense of the glories of an ancient Christian tradition that he forgets the perpetual Christian task of transformation. So loyalty and adventure must combine in his leadership. But it is also true that Christianity is so vast and many-sided a thing that being in loyalty to some part of it a man may be false to the whole of it. Every rich contribution of the law, the prophets, and the apostles must find a place in the structure which he is building.

But the matter cannot be fully expressed by symbols related to architecture and building. In Revelation another aspect is expressed by the symbol of the water of life. Every legitimate thirst of man is to be satisfied freely by the fountain of life. God regards human longings. In fact, he has created the very forms of life which make these longings inevitable. So the one who has created thirst will satisfy the thirst which he has created. God has not made men for frustration but for satisfaction. And the satisfaction is to be as rich and many-sided as the legitimate desires of men. It must be confessed that there is a type of preaching and teaching which does not suggest the offer of sparkling water to thirsty men. It is only when we have come to see that in the deepest sense Christianity does not represent denial, but fulfillment, that we will really understand it.

There are no denials in the Christian religion which are not in the name of life and of health. It forbids only in the name of the very life which it would bring to full completion and satisfaction. The very presence of thirst is an implicit promise of access to the fountain. The battle is with that which destroys. The victory is over that which would disintegrate life itself. And the victor inherits a richness of life so ample that it is beyond the imagination of man. The fullness of it all is expressed in one great sentence, "I will be his God and he shall be my son." The man who, according to Genesis, was made in the divine image, will come to the consummation of his experience as a son of God.

In the city of the divine Presence there are to be no more tears. There is to be no more pain. There is to be no more mourning. There is to be no more weeping. There is to be no more death. All the while, subtly present, is the contrast between the city of Rome and the eternal city of divine fulfillment. There had been tears enough in Rome. And that city of imperial pretension had produced tears all about the world. There had been mourning and weeping enough in Rome. And she had produced mourning and weeping wherever her power had been felt. There had been all the agony of death in Rome. And she had brought death to just men all over the empire. All this was to cease. Not only unjust death but death itself was to come to an end. The city of tears was to be replaced by the city of endless joy.

Yet the great moral and spiritual distinctions are never lost to sight. We are told of no consummation in the terms of unethical gregariousness. And so, right after the description of the tearless city, there is a grim and biting catalogue of those who will not have access to its splendors or its joys. These lawless spirits represent a kind of incarnate and restless unhappiness. And they are creators of unhappiness in the world. Once more there is a flashing picture of the lake of burning fire and the second death. The triumph of joy is secure only with the destruction of the destroyers of joy. Idealism easily takes the form of a gregarious and sentimental friendliness in which all ethical and spiritual distinctions are done away. Neither here nor in our thought of the future should we forget that moral finalities do not vanish in the great picture of the city of joy. In fact, it is a city of gladness just because of the complete triumph of righteousness and truth, and the complete destruction of all that opposes goodness. God is the living actuality of all moral perfection, and the city of his perpetual presence will be pervaded by his own quality. What else then can be said but that it is the business of Christians by the grace of God to make real in time that which is to be completely triumphant in the life of eternity?

Some people without much spiritual imagination have been offended by the material splendor ascribed to the perfect city. If they were to read with any sort of understanding the great medieval hymn, "Jerusalem the golden," they would come to see how perfectly material figures can be used to express spiritual meanings. The most magnificent and priceless things of the material world are used to express the exhaustless glory of the city of moral and spiritual perfection. The author of Revelation is quite free from that sort of ascetic dualism which sees the material as essentially evil. He has no hesitation at all about using gold and precious stones as symbols of the glowing beauty of the final city. But more than this, the perfection of which he speaks is no ghostly and ethereal splendor unrelated to the warm realities of life. There is adumbration of the same view in the N.T. teaching about the resurrection of the body. It is implicit in the account of the ascension of Jesus. The material is not the foe of the spiritual. It is made to be the instrument of the spiritual. A human face may shine with a celestial light. The physical is meant to wear the livery of the spiritual. So the perfect city is pictured with gold and precious stones, all of them serviceable materials in the fashioning of moral and spiritual triumph.

But the writer is thoroughly aware that the spiritual must have the last word. So he represents the city as a place having no need of shining sun because it is perfectly illuminated by the moral splendor of the character of God. A day in this world when the sun is full of burning brightness may be very black to a man who has just experienced the bitterness of human treachery. A dark night may be full of gentle and beautiful light to a man who has just experienced the costly loyalty of a faithful friend. It is the moral and spiritual light which is final.

The nations are to walk in this light. And now, by one of the quick and happy transitions of the book, we are gazing not upon wicked nations destroyed, but upon faithful nations living in the light of God. We are gazing not upon wicked kings fearfully bearing the moral wrath of God, but faithful kings bringing their glory to the city of perfect light. A great O.T. scholar used to say that all prophecy is psychologically mediated. And its great alternatives are often presented side by side in the O.T.—a picture of utter destruction and then a picture of utter felicity. Back of the seeming contradiction lies the summons to the terrible choice. Either of the two pictures may come to actual fulfillment. The men and the nations who make the choices of destiny determine which it shall be. The man of Patmos sees pictures of nations destroyed and pictures of obedient nations worshiping. Only in the light of both can the great choice be made. These things, however, are sure: That which is against goodness and God will be destroyed. That which is loyal to God and to goodness will be glorified. So are we once more reminded that the doers of the deeds of night shall not enter the city of eternal day.

Jesus in the days of his flesh was troubled by those who worshiped places instead of worshiping the God who gave to places memorable meaning. The worship of the symbol, and the forgetting of that for which it stands, have been sadly present in religion in every age. The conclusion of the whole matter is happily expressed by the man of Patmos. The city of the divine Presence will need no temple. The symbol will vanish with the coming of the reality. So is the city of God set in perfect contrast to the city of the harlot, who prostitutes every good meaning of life. Even in this world, when men's true citizenship is in the city not made with hands, they have found a security of which they cannot be robbed.

22:1-5. *The River of Life and the Ineffable Future.*—The biblical account of human life begins with a garden. It ends with a city. But the city is to have all the characteristics of the garden. In a sense it is to be a garden city. **From the throne of God and the Lamb** a river of water of life is to flow. And **the tree of life** is to have **twelve kinds of fruit,** and each month is to see its branches freshly full of the fruit which it produces. Its very leaves are to be **for the healing of the nations.** Moreover, the garden city is to be free from curse. God's throne is to be there, and is to be itself also the throne of the crucified Christ. And God's **servants shall serve him.** At last **they shall see his face.** His very name shall be inscribed upon their foreheads. His divine Presence will give them perfect illumination. And the reign of his triumphant servants shall last forever.

6-9. *The True Words, the High Event, and the True Object of Worship.*—And now the vast succession of pictures has been presented. The words about them have been spoken. Next we hear the pronouncement that these words are **faithful and true,** that **the Lord God of the holy prophets** has **sent his angel** to open the door of the future to his people. The angelic messenger speaking for Christ says, **Behold, I come quickly.** A blessing is pronounced upon those who take the message of the book with the utmost seriousness. The man of Patmos, overawed, falls down to worship the angel, but he is commanded to desist. Not an angelic fellow servant, but God, is the true object of worship.

10-15. *Words of Finality.*—Still the great events move on apace. The words of the book are to be scattered about among men and are not to be sealed. Let every man now be committed to his own way, the evil to evil, the good to good. The reward of all whose good deeds have been the product of a good purpose is imminent. **The Alpha and the Omega** pronounces his blessing upon **those who wash their robes** and have the right to **enter the city** and come to the **tree of life.** Without are the unholy and the evil, with all those who have misused their bodies, and have taken human life, and have perverted their minds to falsehood.

16. *The Pre-eminence of Jesus.*—The living Christ speaks, declaring that he is the fulfillment of the old dispensation, **the root and the off-spring of David,** and the promise of the future, **the bright and morning star.**

17. *The Great Invitation.*—Back from the great finalities, the author once more comes to the world of immediate destiny where decisions are yet made. Using the figure of **the water of life,** he proclaims the great invitation. **The Spirit and the bride say, Come. Let him that heareth say, Come.** Let all who are thirsty, and all who will, drink of **the water of life freely.**

18-19. *Words of Warning.*—But the book must not be treated lightly. It is a part of the very message of God to men. Sharp and terrible words are spoken of any who shall add to or take from its words.

20-21. *The Last Word of Hope and the Last Word of Blessing.*—All expectation for time and for eternity centers in the manifestation of the living Christ in the very life of men. He promises to come quickly. The man of Patmos devoutly prays, **Amen. Even so, come, Lord Jesus.** Then the benediction of grace upon those who belong to Christ brings all to an end.

The first and the last books of the Bible and the prophecy of Ezekiel are happily connected in the picture of the garden city and the river of the water of life. The author is saying that the very perfection of fulfillment is to bring ultimate joy to the loyal servants of the living Christ. Everything that belongs to a perfect garden and everything that belongs to a perfect city will be united in the great consummation. There is a glorious amplitude about the satisfactions of the perfect life. A few artistic touches indicate their richness. The tree of life, which bears twelve kinds of fruit and offers a new harvest every month, stands for many things. The leaves, with all their power of bringing health to the nations, open vistas of happy expectations. The dull and plodding mind is likely to suggest painfully that the nations are all gone. It cannot be said too often that we are not dealing with chronology but with a great series of pictures, each expressing an insight with rich finality. We may love our human city, but how much there is in it which we cannot love. The perfect city is to be free of every curse coming from evil. It is to be the visible center of the reign of God, enriched by his very presence. His servants shall serve him in a fashion beginning with worship and going out in all good deeds. The people of the old covenant, with an awful reverence, had feared the very thought of seeing the divine Person. But in the great fulfillment the servants of God will see his face. And his name and the quality of his life shall be written so deeply in their character that it will shine on their foreheads. The light of the divine Perfection, visibly present, will be their sun. Their life will be more than one of perfect felicity. It will be one of high authority under God. And this reign of saints will have no end. So for a moment the curtain is drawn aside and we see the great future as one of perfect fellowship, perfect service, and noble command. To understand this is to be able to live in time in the light of eternity. It is to be able to find motives in eternity for the life of time. The narrowing vision of a secularity which makes it difficult, if not impossible, for many good people to draw upon the motives which come from the richest spiritual vision is an element in contemporary life which deserves close examination. It is a part of what may be described in the words of Matthew Arnold as "this strange disease of modern life." Revelation contains much medicine for that disease.

The man of Patmos is profoundly moved by the thought of the truth of all that he has been saying, and he hears happily, through an angel's voice, a divine pronouncement on the validity of his message, on its consummation in a high event, and on the blessedness of those who take it with the most serious faithfulness. In utter and glad humility he casts himself before the angelic messenger, only to be reminded gravely that God alone is to be the object of worship. The highest of all creatures are but fellow servants of the men who seek to do the divine will. The story of misplaced worship is a long tale in the life of man. The church needs perpetually to be on its guard against giving to the instruments of the divine truth that devotion which belongs only to God himself.

The words of this book are not to be held as a great secret. They are to be sent forth wherever there are men who will read them. And the stern challenge which says in effect, "If you love evil, continue to be devoted to it; if you love good, give it your utmost loyalty," like such desperately earnest sentences of the O.T., is an implicit summons to repentance as well as a demand for faithfulness. That which is implicit in character is to be made explicit in judgment. Deeds determine destiny. But there is the washing of soiled garments and there is the cleansing of soiled lives. The tree of life and the joy of the garden city are for the cleansed and the forgiven. Without the city of fulfillment are those who belong to the way that is not the way of God. Their positive doom has been indicated elsewhere. Here there is a swift and tragic awareness of what they have lost. The sorcerers who would misuse the divine, the evil brood of those who prostitute the body in all sorts of ways, the dark company of those to whom human life has no sacredness, the worshipers who have made gods of that which is not divine, the grim company of those who have taken the mind which was meant for truth and have turned it to purposes of falsehood—all these have put themselves forever beyond the good purposes of God. They are without. In a sense they have descended below the human level. They are dogs. They are no more men. With all the singing gladness of the book, there is no room for gregarious altruism, and there is no room for sentimental and uncritical hopefulness. The writer is a stern realist. His good hopes have survived the fire of the severest testing. It is necessary to ask whether a good deal of our modern Christian witness has not become soft. Are the hard facts evaded or ignored? Is utopia the premature promise of uncritical hopes? Is there a tendency to announce the Christian promises without the Christian discipline? Is there a tendency to declare the Christian fulfillment without the Christian judgment? For all such tendencies Revelation offers ample corrective. Its hopes are never buttressed by the smallest amount of intellectual or moral evasiveness or dishonesty. It is a book of ethical truth as well as a book of spiritual life. And because it is a book of truth as well as a book of life, it has all the more power to command unshakable confidence. Apocalypse, like prophecy, always sees the truth in foreshortened fashion. There are stretches of time and fashions of manifold historical circumstance about which the man of Patmos did not know. But about the ultimate moral and spiritual concerns he speaks with an assurance which we may well make our own. In these central matters we have a right to feel that his message is not merely from man or from a high celestial messenger, but that it is the very word to us of the living Christ.

The past and the future meet in the triumphant Lord. Everything of deep and noble meaning in the old dispensation is gathered up in him. He is both the root and the fulfillment of the Davidic tradition. But all glorious and happy experience in a future as new and wonderful as the resources of God belongs to him too. He is the morning star of a new and unending day. So, to the Christian, loyalty and adventure are always present. Deathless memories continually enrich his life. Unexpected vistas are ever opening out before him. If the evening of memory lives in his mind, the morning of hope is perpetually shining in his heart. He comes at the end of old experience. And behold a gleam of shining light flashes over the future. He follows the gleam.

Marvelous journeys the man of Patmos has taken. And he has given to the church a vast gallery with tremendous pictures full of insight into eternal principles and their expression in action. He has written a book of finalities. Now he comes back to the world in which the gospel is still being proclaimed and choices are still being made. In the light of all the vistas he has opened before our eyes, surely we have every reason for high and noble decision. So comes the eager invitation which brings the moral and spiritual message of the book to its climax. Much has been written in the light and the shadow of decisions already made. But there is still time. The hour waits upon men. The Spirit says, "Come." The church cries, "Come." Let everyone who hears the true word join in the great invitation and cry, "Come." Let everyone who thirsts for goodness and for God, come. Let everyone who will, come and drink freely of the water of life. The whole offer of salvation is focused upon these climactic words. They are a commission to the Christian church for its work of evangelism. They are a commission to all Christian men to sound forth the words of eager welcome to the kingdom of God. All exclusiveness and all narrowness vanish before the endless outreach of this summons. The doors are all open. Whosoever will may come. So the profoundest spiritual understanding meets the simplest spirit of sharing in the words of welcome to all who will hear and heed. There is a tendency—and it must be watched with critical thoroughness—so to pronounce the ultimate issues that the word of invitation is muted or silenced. But the very genius of Christianity is misunderstood if it does not lead to the great invitation. The face of the prophet has been dark with the gravity of the word of judgment against evil. Now it is all alight again. We are still living in the world. New directions can be taken. The present moment is full of glorious opportunity. And the insistent word "Come" rings like the call of many bells in many churches. It rings with a heavenly welcome. It sounds down the ages and is heard in our very streets.

These words come to us with the high claim that they are God's words. To read them in such a fashion as to find in them not what is really there, but what we want to find, is all too human a temptation and all too frequently a fact. The caution about meddling with the message probably has had profound influence in maintaining the integrity of the text of Revelation. But it has meaning for us as well. As we open this book and the other books of the N.T. and of the O.T. do we really try, with every earnestness of striving and every honesty of purpose, to apprehend the full meaning of what is said without hesitation and without evasion? There is an exposition which is emasculation, and nothing but the desperate earnestness and entire honesty of the reader can save him from seeing the thing as the eye likes the look.

And now the Christ who has triumphed in the heart must be the Christ who triumphs in events. The living Lord has promised to make himself felt completely and with utter victory in the very world where men dwell. And the man of Patmos utters a deep Amen, adding the simple and moving words, "Come, Lord Jesus."

It is indeed fitting that the final benediction should be a prayer for the grace of the Lord Jesus upon all those who bear his name. The whole book is Christocentric. In completest harmony with the deepest movement of all its thought it sees what Christ has done for us become a power in us, what he promises to achieve on our behalf surging up as an inner energy of transforming potency. So the last word of the N.T. is the first word of our deepest need: the grace of the Lord Jesus.

SUPPLEMENTARY
GENERAL ARTICLES

THE TRANSMISSION OF THE NEW TESTAMENT

by KENNETH W. CLARK

I. The Manuscript Evidence
II. From A.D. 200 to 1450
III. The Received Text

IV. Toward a Critical Text
V. The Critical Text
VI. Work to Be Done

I. The Manuscript Evidence

It is a well-known fact that no original autograph of any New Testament writing is known to have survived. The original strips of papyrus upon which Paul wrote his letters have apparently perished. The original scrolls employed by the evangelists and all other New Testament authors have disappeared, leaving only copies and copies of copies, most of them several times removed, for the earliest *copies* have themselves perished, leaving gaps of different lengths for the various New Testament documents. The letters of Paul were written about A.D. 50-62; about A.D. 95 they were revised as parts of a collection. But the oldest copy of them extant today, discovered as recently as 1929, was made in Egypt in the first half of the third century. Since this ancient manuscript (the Beatty-Michigan papyrus in Dublin and Ann Arbor) is amazingly well preserved it provides the text of Paul's letters, largely complete, in a copy made about 180 years after the death of Paul or 150 years after the editing of the Pauline corpus. An interval of approximately 180 years applies also to the Gospels, Acts, and Revelation, except that the extant third-century copies of these are fragmentary; so for most of the text the true interval is about 280 years.[1] Even prior to the third century copies of individual books, or of groups such as the four Gospels or the letters of Paul, must have been produced; but all of them have disappeared. However, we are not without grounds for confident conjecture as to how the scribes dealt with the text in this early period for, when extant copies from the third and fourth centuries can be consulted, we find that the text of each book has by that time acquired numerous variant readings which point to scribal changes or even to different recensions.

When comparison is made between New Testament and Old Testament as regards transmission, the textual situation of the former is found to be the more favorable. Between most of the ancient Hebrew prophets and the earliest extant record of their preaching lies a period of sixteen centuries, and for the Torah (the Pentateuch) the interval is about thirteen centuries. If, however, the Greek translation of these Hebrew writings is taken into account, substantial extant texts make possible our subtracting seven centuries from these intervals. For the books of Isaiah and Habakkuk and fragments of others, the discovery, since 1947, of Hebrew copies from about 100 B.C. reduces the interval to from four to six centuries.

If comparison is made with the works of classical authors, again the New Testament is found to have an advantage. Most of the classics survive in manuscripts no earlier than twelve to sixteen centuries later than their authors. The interval is shorter for Lucretius, Horace, and Terence, and shortest of all for Vergil, for whom there is a gap of just less than four hundred years (but for one fragment a gap of less than three centuries).

The earliest survivals of Greek New Testament manuscripts come from the third century, although these are extremely few. There are but eighteen such items, mostly fragmentary. They all come from Egyptian Christian communities, and together they contain much of the Pauline corpus, portions of the four Gospels and the book of Acts, and approximately one third of the Apocalypse in mutilated state. These fragments rarely overlap to provide two witnesses for the same passage. There is not even one witness in that century for nine of the

[1] A most startling datum is the identification, in 1935, of a fragment of the Gospel of John (18:31-38) copied in Egypt about A.D. 150 or earlier, within a generation of the original composition, but the fragment (Rylands Papyrus 457) is so tiny that it offers no textual assistance.

books (I and II Timothy, Philemon, and the general epistles except James). But when we come to the fourth century we are on firmer ground, for here we find the earliest surviving *complete* copy of the Greek New Testament (Codex Sinaiticus, in the British Museum). There is also a sister codex containing all except Hebrews 9:14 to the end, the Pastoral epistles, and the Revelation of John (Codex Vaticanus, in Rome). There is a third copy of the Gospels (Freer Gospels, in Washington), besides about thirty fragments on papyrus and parchment.

From the period 400-900 somewhat more numerous copies have survived, and later centuries yield increasing numbers, rising to a peak about 1300. Although Greek culture was at a low ebb in western Europe before the fifteenth century the Eastern Church continued to produce vast numbers of copies of the New Testament text in its original Greek language, from which a rich heritage has been preserved for present-day textual studies. Such source materials did begin to flow westward as early as the twelfth century and by 1500 had come to exert considerable influence upon the traditional use of the Latin Vulgate by Western Christians.

Altogether, witnesses to the text of the Greek New Testament have survived to the number of about 4,500, ranging between the third and the eighteenth centuries. In comparison it may be noted that Hebrew Old Testament manuscripts number perhaps half as many (unless we count also the numerous modern copies still prepared for use in the synagogues). But the text of these Hebrew manuscripts is much more uniform than is that exhibited by the copies of the Greek New Testament. Classical authors are preserved in quite limited numbers of copies, these usually falling into two or three main textual types for each work.

Although the Greek New Testament text is preserved in thousands of witnessing manuscripts, this does not mean that the whole text is so fully attested or that every part is equally attested. Rarely was the New Testament copied entire in one book (fewer than 4 per cent of the surviving manuscripts contain the whole of it). The four Gospels, usually together, were copied more than any other part and are found in about half of the surviving manuscripts. Copies of the epistles, usually with the Acts, are only one third as numerous. Least often copied, and frequently alone, was the Revelation of John, which survives today in fewer than 250 manuscript copies.

The abundant attestation of the text of the New Testament is often emphasized as a boon to critical studies on the sacred text; and so it is. Yet at the same time it creates for the textual

scholar a far more complex and difficult task than falls to the textual critic of any other writing. Because the New Testament has been in constant use, and has been repeatedly copied with variation through eighteen hundred years, its text has experienced a more intricate history of transmission than any other known work. In the centuries before the invention of the printing press, any two copies of New Testament text contained many differences, the result both of scribal error and of editorial emendation. Therefore the numerous copies known in our time display a complex network of variation, through which the original text must be sought. The fortunate discovery of a more ancient witness does not mean the complete solution of the problem, for the earlier copy does not disqualify the testimony of the later. Even when two very ancient witnesses are available, they are found to differ from each other, often in quite striking ways.

The primary purpose of textual criticism in biblical research is the recovery of the lost original text. It is true that the church has never been without the text of the Bible, but that very text in its multiple variations now serves to obscure the original form and its historical vicissitudes. Furthermore the Western Church employed a Latin translation for a thousand years, and it was to this version that any textual labors were applied while the original Hebrew and Greek forms were disregarded. The reversal of this position came upon the wave of the New Learning, and with it came a fresh critical search for the authentic biblical text. Therefore the biblical study known as "textual criticism," like other branches of critical biblical study, has matured only in later centuries. It seeks to apply scientific method to the objective of reconstructing the original text and its history.

II. From A.D. 200 to 1450

The early Christian churches were mostly Greek-speaking and their sacred literature was in Greek. From Hellenistic Jews they acquired a Greek version of the Old Testament to which were later added the Greek works composed by New Testament writers. But as early as 200 the Christian Scriptures had been put into two additional languages—Syriac and Latin. From this time on, chiefly Syriac and Greek texts served Eastern Christians while those in the West increasingly employed the Latin version and gradually excluded the original Greek. By about 400 these three versions had become largely stereotyped. Of the Syriac, the later Peshitta version (late fourth century) completely eclipsed the "Old Syriac" and almost all surviving manuscripts preserve the stereotyped Peshitta form, the most important exceptions being two rare and ancient codices discovered only in the nineteenth century (the Cureton and Sinai codices).

The Greek New Testament also developed a typical Byzantine text which, though substantially different from earlier recensions, was generally received and was usually followed in the copies of medieval scribes. Therefore today copies reflecting earlier types of text are quite rare. In the Eastern Orthodox Church the Byzantine form has remained in use to the present day, chiefly in the traditional lections of its liturgy, and there has been little interest within the Eastern Church in recovering the earliest form of the text.

The New Testament in Latin was deliberately revised by Jerome in 382 at the instigation of Pope Damasus. Out of numerous discordant manuscript copies there was produced the Latin Vulgate text which was to serve Western Christianity until the sixteenth century and Roman Catholic Christianity in particular even to the present. Roman Catholic scholars over the centuries have applied considerable effort to improving the Vulgate text but until quite modern times have paid little attention to the Hebrew and Greek witnesses. Thus it was that Western Christianity lost sight of the New Testament in its original Greek form, and Western learning virtually forgot the Greek language.

For a thousand years the Vulgate reigned in the West without challenge and all learning was mediated in the Latin language. Yet through these centuries this Latin text was subject to persistent corruption and repeated correction. For example, Jerome's version was revised in 540 by Cassiodorus. In 801 the Emperor Charlemagne received his crown and a corrected Vulgate Bible prepared by the scholarly Alcuin. Another contemporary, Haimo of Auxerre, compiled an index of textual differences in Latin manuscript copies, thus producing a primitive *apparatus criticus*. The early revival of learning in the twelfth and thirteenth centuries produced numerous textual critics who applied themselves to the correction of the scriptural text, as they found it in manuscripts of the Latin Vulgate. The twelfth century saw two editions produced by Cistercians: in 1109 by one of the founders of the order, Abbot Stephen Harding; and again, in 1150, by Cardinal Nicholas of Manjacoria. The Victorines of Paris [2] and later the Dominican and Franciscan scholars interwove with their exegetical studies emendations of the Vulgate text, the current copies of which Roger Bacon in 1268 condemned as untrustworthy. In the fifteenth century Lorenzo Valla

[2] This school was the source of the modern chapter divisions, first applied to the Latin version in the early thirteenth century.

produced a revised Vulgate. This was followed in the sixteenth century by the printed editions of Cardinal Jiménez (1514-17), Erasmus (1527), Pagninus (1527), Münster (1535), Stephanus (1538-40), John Hentenius (1547), and finally by the great Clementine edition of 1592, which became the standard text. But all these efforts were expended on the Latin Vulgate translation, officially adopted by the Council of Trent in 1546, rather than on the original Hebrew and Greek texts.

The learning and literature of the East had begun to creep back westward in the early medieval period, thus preparing the way for the recovery, long afterward, of the original biblical text. Without a knowledge of Hebrew and Greek, and without manuscript witnesses in these languages, it would have been impossible to make any progress toward recovering the original text. And without a commitment to free inquiry and experiment, which came with the New Learning, there would have been no disposition even to seek it. These essential factors came to be provided in the course of the medieval centuries.

It was a Greek, Theodore of Tarsus, Archbishop of Canterbury after 668, who, with his associates from the East, Benedict Biscop and Hadrian, established the first English center of Greek learning (where Aldhelm and Bede studied). Theodore brought with him a number of Greek texts, probably including the Greco-Latin copy of the Acts written about 600 which is now in the Bodleian Library in Oxford (Codex Laudianus). This is the earliest known acquisition of a Greek New Testament manuscript in England. On the Continent, some interest in and knowledge of Greek continued in the south, whence we have acquired two early Greco-Latin codices, a fifth-century copy of the Gospels and Acts (Codex Bezae, now in Cambridge University) and a sixth-century copy of the Pauline epistles (Codex Claromontanus, now in the National Library in Paris). While such Greek texts were not to affect the critical search for the original New Testament until the sixteenth century they illustrate an early motivation and interest never entirely lost. There soon also arose a new interest in the works of the Greek Fathers, although for several centuries they could be consulted only in Latin translation. Resort to the original Greek text itself is illustrated in the episode of Emperor Charles the Bald (grandson of Charlemagne) who about 850 assigned to John the Scot the task of translating into Latin the original Greek work of "Dionysius the Areopagite," a Neoplatonist. As early as the twelfth century, scholars who knew no Greek or Hebrew were consulting contemporary Jews with reference to the meaning and accuracy of the Old Testament text, as determined by the Hebrew original.

But a fundamental change occurred when the interest in refining the biblical text was joined to a direct knowledge of Hebrew and Greek, for this opened the way for application of textual criticism to the original language of the biblical text. The case of Hebrew was different from that of Greek in that the knowledge of Hebrew had not been confined to the East. In the twelfth century Jews from France settled in England in great numbers, with the result that teachers of Hebrew were readily found there. A century later Roger Bacon observed that it was difficult to find a Greek from whom to learn his language whereas "Jews are to be found everywhere." [3] Nevertheless it remains true that it was as necessary for Christian scholarship during the Renaissance to *recover* the knowledge of the Hebrew Scriptures as of the Greek New Testament. It is recorded that Abelard, in the twelfth century, advised his Benedictine sisters to learn Hebrew and Greek if they would understand the Scriptures. Roger Bacon also insisted that it was "impossible to obtain a perfect knowledge of the Scriptures without knowing Hebrew and Greek." [4] One of the first medieval scholars to learn both languages was Robert Grosseteste who was taught by Nicholas the Greek at Paris in the early thirteenth century. In turn, Grosseteste taught Greek to Roger Bacon who produced the first Greek grammar in the West; in this manner informal instruction in Greek reached numerous scholars in Italy, France, and England.

Well before the fall of the Byzantine Empire the study of Greek was well established in western Europe. Although formal courses in Greek would come much later, even in the thirteenth century there were centers of Greek learning. A group of Franciscans at Oxford gathered about Robert Grosseteste (1175-1253) who later, as Bishop of Lincoln, developed there a second center. Nicholas the Greek, Roger Bacon, Edmund Rich, Adam Marsh, John of Garland, and John of Basingstoke were included in this group. Basingstoke studied also in Paris and journeyed to Greece, where he was tutored by Constantina, the daughter of the Archbishop of Athens. John of Garland, Grosseteste, and Bacon studied Greek also in Paris, as did another contemporary, Alexander of Hales. Peter of Abano (1250-1318) learned Greek in Constantinople and taught it at Padua. William of Moerbeke (*ca.* 1280) translated works of Aristotle from Greek into Latin for Thomas Aquinas. All these are but examples of the increasing number of students of Greek.

The fourteenth century brought a further extension of the knowledge of Greek. Pope Clement V (1305-14) proposed the establishment of a school of Greek at Rome and the installation of professors of Greek at Oxford. The Council of Vienna in 1311 recommended the appointment of two Greek teachers in each important city of Italy. These pioneering efforts did not materialize, but the official attitude reflects the new interest in Greek in the West. By 1325 formal instruction in Greek was established at the University of Paris. Such instruction in Italy was promoted by Petrarch (1304-74), who had learned Greek from Barlaam, a Calabrian returned from Constantinople (1339). Petrarch came to be called "the first Hellenist in modern Europe" and stimulated a larger circle of disciples in the humanist tradition and in the study of the Greek language. Under the patronage of the Medici family, Florence became a center of Greek learning after Leontius Pilatus (*ca.* 1360) came from Byzantium as the first Greek professor at the University of Florence. He also studied Greek under Barlaam and in turn taught it to Boccaccio (1313-1375) in whose house he stayed and for whom he translated the Iliad. Probably the first Greek scholar of high ability in the West was Manuel Chrysoloras (1355?-1415), who taught in Florence and other Italian cities. In the first half of the fifteenth century Greek learning flowered luxuriantly in the West and was prepared to exploit the opportunity to the full when the scholarly migration from Constantinople occurred at the mid-century.

As early as the thirteenth century Greek manuscripts were acquired in the West in great numbers, as when Grosseteste sent his agents abroad or John of Basingstoke brought copies from Greece. Even a dealer, John Arretinus, dispatched his own scribes about 1400 to copy manuscripts in Eastern monasteries. In 1422, Giovanni Aurispa brought back 238 manuscripts from Constantinople. Other notable Italian collectors were Bracciolini and Filelfo; and contemporary English collectors included Humphrey Duke of Gloucester, Free, Grey, Gunthorpe, and Tiptoft. Western scholars were very active in translating Greek works into Latin for their fellow humanists who knew no Greek.

The earliest manual for the study of Greek was the *Summa Grammaticae* prepared by

[3] Quoted by Charles Singer in *The Legacy of Israel*, ed. E. R. Bevan and Charles Singer (Oxford: Clarendon Press, 1927), p. 299; also quoted by J. W. Adamson in *The Legacy of the Middle Ages*, ed. C. G. Crump and E. F. Jacob (Oxford: Clarendon Press, 1926), p. 271.
[4] *Opus Majus*, ed. Samuel Jebb (1733), p. 44; quoted by J. E. Sandys, *A History of Classical Scholarship* (3rd ed.; Cambridge: Cambridge University Press, 1921), I, 590-91; also quoted in L. Magnus, *History of European Literature* (London: Nicholson, 1934), p. 19.

Roger Bacon (never printed until the 1902 edition of the Cambridge Press). The *Erotemata* of Chrysoloras (1396) had wider usefulness, especially when printed a century later in Florence and Paris. It was used at both Cambridge and Oxford, and notably by Erasmus and Linacre. Such linguistic activities across Italy, France, and England prepared the way for the recovery of the New Testament in Greek in the West. Important steps forward in the recovery of the authentic Greek text were now to be expected under the combined impetus of the humanistic inquiry, concern for true exegesis, knowledge of Greek, and possession of new manuscript sources. The force of these factors was greatly intensified in the mid-fifteenth century, when Byzantium's fall increased the westward stream of Greek culture, and the invention of the printing press provided a marvelous device for reproducing the text.

III. The Received Text

The fifteenth century brought stirring changes to the Old World. Indeed, it brought the peak of the Renaissance, which was to remain for the historian a Great Divide of human events. It was marked by the incredible defeat of great Byzantium, a momentous event which has ever since divided history into medieval and modern, and the world into East and West. It was a remarkable coincidence that about the same time the German printer, Gutenberg, perfected a printing press the operation of which was to aggravate and accelerate the rapid revolution affecting the human spirit. But it was more than coincidence that William Grocyn was appointed, in 1491, to a chair of Greek at Oxford, the first in English history. The fifteenth century prepared the way for discoveries and researches affecting both Christianity and its Bible. "The 'discovery of the Bible' was one of the firstfruits of the humanist movement, and the diffusion of knowledge of the Bible was made possible, in the first instance, by the publication of the original texts." [5]

When Gutenberg printed the first book at Mainz, about 1455, it was the Bible; more exactly, it was the traditional Latin Vulgate, which looked back over a thousand years. At Soncino in 1488, a Jewish press first printed the traditional Hebrew Old Testament, derived from the Masoretes six centuries earlier. But the press was soon to serve the purposes of the new age. In 1500, Jiménez, the Archbishop of Toledo, to honor the birth of a grandson to Ferdinand and Isabella of Spain during that year, proposed the printing of a great polyglot Bible. This project, with the aid of eight associates, he accomplished by 1517. Besides being a most noteworthy printing achievement, it was the first Christian printing of the Old Testament in Hebrew and the first printing ever of the New Testament in the original Greek. [6] The cultural revolution of the fifteenth century had broken a millennium of Vulgate monopoly and directed scholars of the West again to the original biblical tongues. But in this polyglot the Latin Vulgate still appears alongside the Greek New Testament; and in the Old Testament the Vulgate occupies the central column between the Hebrew and the Greek. Today we perceive that this noble Complutensian Polyglot of Cardinal Jiménez unwittingly inaugurated a new era for the Christian Bible.

The next important episode has to do with the New Testament only, and reveals the basis for the King James Version. This was the printing in 1516 of the Greek New Testament prepared by the humanist scholar and monk, Erasmus. His printer in Basel had learned of the preparation of the Spanish polyglot and engaged Erasmus to provide him with a Greek Text of the New Testament to be published in advance of the Polyglot. Erasmus completed the task promptly, in 1516, and in the same year his bilingual New Testament in Greek and Latin was issued. This was one year before Luther delivered his Theses at Wittenberg; it provided also the Greek base which Luther translated into German (1522). The third edition of Erasmus appeared in 1522 and was used for the Tyndale translation in 1525. Because Tyndale's phrases largely remain in the King James Bible it is important to evaluate the Greek base with which Erasmus provided him.

It is obvious that the text had to be secured from manuscript copies. Erasmus and Jiménez did not use the same manuscripts. Besides borrowing a few copies from the Vatican, the Cardinal spent 4,000 ducats to buy Greek New Testament manuscripts which still remain in the Madrid library. Erasmus found manuscripts already in the library at Basel. The Cardinal with his staff of eight spent fifteen years at the task, whereas Erasmus worked ten months with two incompetent assistants and confessed that his work was "made hastily rather than edited." But the Cardinal and Erasmus did use the same textual type of Greek manuscript, for by this time European libraries had been flooded with manuscript copies of the standard Byzantine revision which had all but destroyed the record of the older textual forms. Erasmus used five

---

[5] G. H. Box in *The Legacy of Israel*, ed. E. R. Bevan and Charles Singer (Oxford: Clarendon Press, 1927), p. 347.

[6] It also contained the first printing of the Old Testament in Greek translation (the "Septuagint"), preceding the Aldus Bible of 1518.

such manuscripts in Basel, only one of which was a complete New Testament. They added up to two witnesses for the Gospels, three for Acts, four for Paul, and only one for the Apocalypse, even this incomplete at the end. To fill this lacuna he made his own translation of the Latin Vulgate into Greek. All of his sources were late copies and the latest of them all, a manuscript less than 100 years old, he used as printer's copy to facilitate his hasty work. But it was the edition of Erasmus that was used by Luther and Zwingli and Tyndale. This was an improvement upon earlier translations into German, Swiss, and English in that these sixteenth-century versions were based upon the Greek original rather than upon the Latin translation; nevertheless, time would expose the inferior quality of these pioneer translations and their Greek base.

The controversy of Erasmus with Lopez de Stunica, the editor for the rival Polyglot, is well known, and it illustrates well the inadequate methods then applied to the biblical text. The debate was over I John 5:7, where all the Greek manuscripts read: "For there are three that bear record, the Spirit, and the water, and the blood; and these three agree in one." But Stunica argued for the authenticity of the longer passage in the Latin Vulgate: "For there are three that bear record in heaven, the Father, the Word, and the Holy Ghost: and these three are one. And there are three that bear witness in earth, the Spirit, and the water, and the blood: and these three agree in one." Erasmus disputed the point but agreed to the interpolation if shown a Greek witness containing it. Such a manuscript witness soon appeared, written within a generation—some have charged that it was prepared for the occasion—and true to his word Erasmus introduced the passage into his third edition of 1522. Five years later it was exscinded again from the fourth edition. But the third edition had already been used by Tyndale, whose English translation is still embedded in the King James Version, and this spurious passage was to remain for centuries.

Erasmus could not have realized the far-reaching effect of his admittedly careless work. His first two editions of 1516 and 1519 sold 3,300 copies. His third edition was reprinted with minor changes by the Paris printer, Stephanus, and was thus circulated in still larger numbers through 140 editions between 1546 and 1644.[7] Theodore Beza issued ten similar editions from 1565 to 1598. The Elzevir brothers in Holland put out eight editions from 1624 to 1678. Many other printers picked up the text and reprinted it throughout Europe and England, with manifold uncontrolled revision. The hundreds of late and corrupt manuscript copies containing that traditional Byzantine text standardized in the fourth century, which had been acquired from the East for Western libraries, were now far exceeded by the thousands of printed copies disseminating a similar text. It seems reasonable enough that in 1633 the Elzevir brothers proclaimed in their preface: "You now have the text received by everyone . . . ," and their claim actually bestowed a name upon the well-nigh universal form: the Received Text.

By way of comparison, it may be noted that the Hebrew Old Testament had a similar, though much simpler, development. The Masoretic text, first printed by Jews in Soncino in 1488, passed through periodic revision, chiefly in a series of famous sets of noble proportions: the six-volume Complutensian Polyglot in Spain; the Jewish Bomberg Bible in Venice (not a polyglot), of which the second edition in 1524-25 established the text for all subsequent publications; the ten-volume Paris Polyglot of 1628-45; and the six-volume Walton Polyglot in London in 1657. By this time the Greek language was more widely known than the Hebrew and the demand for the Greek New Testament was by far the greater.

The printing press had done its work. It had emancipated Western Christianity from the dominance of the Latin Vulgate, a translation rather than an original tongue. The press had succeeded in disseminating the Bible widely in its original languages. What is more, it had reversed the process of increasing manuscript variation and had produced a printed stereotype "received by everyone." Yet this very unanimity created a false sense of authenticity. It determined the form of the Scriptures in all the modern language versions first printed in the sixteenth century. In English, all the versions from Tyndale in 1525 to the King James in 1611 were based on this uncritical printed stereotype. The Received Text was edited by Bishop Lloyd (1827) and again by William Sanday (1889) for the Oxford Press, whose continuous printings of it even into the twentieth century were adopted by the British and Foreign Bible Society as the base for its many translations. But long before it became displaced, modern discoveries had opened a new chapter for the Christian Bible.

IV. Toward a Critical Text

The new King James Bible was still making its way with some difficulty when a manuscript gift was dispatched to King James from the

---

[7] The third edition of 1550, called the Royal Edition, became the standard Greek text in England. The fourth edition of 1551 was the first to receive the modern verse numbers, and these first appeared in an English version in 1557 (the Geneva New Testament).

East. In 1621 the Greek Patriarch of Alexandria, Cyril Lucar, promoted to the see of Constantinople, carried with him there a large and old Greek Bible. To honor the royal patron of the new English version he presented this Bible through the English ambassador, Sir Thomas Roe. It arrived in England after the death of James, was accepted by King Charles I for the royal library, and still remains today in the British Museum. In its time this discovery was as sensational as the discovery of the Dead Sea Scrolls. Codex Alexandrinus, as it came to be called, was written in the fifth century, a thousand years earlier than the manuscript on which Erasmus chiefly relied. Study of this ancient copy revealed substantial differences from the traditional text. It gave the first public warning that the Received Text held many errors. Its variants were first published in the London Polyglot by Brian Walton in 1657.

Before the Codex Alexandrinus came to England in 1627 there were only a few really ancient manuscripts in the West. The Dominicans in Basel had received a manuscript from Constantinople as early as 1431 (Codex Basiliensis). It contained the four Gospels only and, though written in the eighth century, exhibited the common Received Text. The Royal Library in Paris also held an eighth-century copy of the Gospels (Codex Regius) which was only slightly used by Stephanus in 1546 but which contained many original readings which he overlooked. Strangest of all were two manuscripts which had been acquired by Theodore Beza out of French monasteries, with Greek and Latin text written in the fifth and sixth centuries (Codex Bezae of the Gospels and Codex Claromontanus of the Pauline epistles). Because their texts contained so many strange readings Beza himself hesitated to use these manuscripts for his printed editions. In Codex Bezae at Luke 6:5, for example, an otherwise unrecorded saying of Jesus is interpolated: "On that day, seeing a certain man working on the Sabbath, he said to him, 'Man, if you know what you are doing, blessed are you. But if not, cursed are you and a transgressor of the law.'" But none of these manuscripts affected the traditional use of the Received Text, and it awaited the arrival of Codex Alexandrinus to stimulate the modern search for the original biblical text. Before the excitement of interest began to subside, still another old manuscript came to light in England, in 1636, when Archbishop Laud presented to the Bodleian Library a Greco-Latin text of Acts written about 600. We now know that it had been in England for almost a thousand years, though little used since the days of the Venerable Bede. Its text was of a character similar to that of the strange Codex Claromontanus acquired by Beza. It is the earliest manuscript to include the confession of the eunuch in Acts 8:37 (found in the KJV, omitted in the RSV): "I believe that Jesus Christ is the Son of God." The Codex Laudianus was made available in published form by Hearne in 1715.

Almost with the close of the seventeenth century came another important discovery—a copy of the Greek Bible from the fifth century. This discovery is romantically linked with the Florentine center where the Greek scholars Pilatus and Chrysoloras first had taught under the patronage of the Medici family. A copy of the Commentary of Ephrem Syrus (a fourth-century Church Father) which had been prepared in the twelfth century was acquired for the Medici library about 1500. When Catherine de Médicis became queen of France this Codex Ephrem Syrus was among the books she brought to Paris. So it happened that a young scholar, Peter Allix, there examined it and discovered that the twelfth-century scribe had reused the parchment of a fifth-century book. The original text was a Greek Bible and was still extensively legible. Its ancient witness to the Greek text of the New Testament was immediately taken into account in the work of Küster (1710) and Wettstein (1716).

By the beginning of the eighteenth century, three essential factors of constructive criticism were present—advanced knowledge of the Greek language, possession of numerous manuscript witnesses reaching back to the fifth century, and a commitment to recover the original form of the text. The principle was being debated among English divines whether or not it was proper to subject the text of the Bible to the same critical scrutiny and emendation applied to the text of classical writings. An opponent of this proposition urged that

. . . it is agreeable to Reason to suppose that He who has established the Scriptures as the sole Rule of the Church for all time has had regard for this rule in such a way that it should never be inadequate or unsuitable for securing this end. For neither can infinite wisdom ever fail in its intention, nor can highest goodness, not to say justice, demand that the Christians should under gravest penalty order their life according to a standard which is insufficient for the purpose owing to corruptions that have become mixed with it.[8]

A proponent of the proposition argued:

We begin to be convinc'd from what *Capellus* has done upon the Old Testament, and what all the great *Criticks* have done upon the *Classicks*, that the *Scriptures* can never be rightly understood,

[8] Daniel Whitby, *Examen variantium lectionum Johannis Millii* (1727), Preface §1; quoted by Adam Fox, *John Mill and Richard Bentley* (Oxford: Blackwell, 1954), p. 106.

or an Edition of them be made to all the Advantage, it might, till the same Rules of *Critick* be here follow'd and observ'd, that have so successfully been us'd in explaining and correcting other antient Books.[9]

The issue was to go unresolved for more than a century but, in the end, the affirmative position prevailed and became a cornerstone of critical studies upon the text. John Fell, Dean of Christ Church College in Oxford, was the first to publish (1675) an edition of the Greek New Testament text with a critical apparatus for reporting all the variant readings found through comparing more than a hundred manuscript copies. He in turn inspired John Mill, a fellow of Queen's College, to continue these studies. After thirty years at the task, during which Fell died, Mill published his edition in 1707, only two weeks before his own death. In it he reported 30,000 variants in the Greek New Testament text as a result of the accumulating discoveries and researches.

For two centuries, from 1627 to 1830, biblical scholars sought to learn more and more of the meaning of the evidence that was piling up. The clear indication of this evidence was that the Received Text did not adequately report the original text. But the theologians engaged in heated controversies over proposed corrections. Whitby publicly charged John Mill with undermining the authority of the Scriptures. A later defender of Mill, Samuel Tregelles, commented:

If Mill could be thus charged with *making* the text of Scripture *precarious*, by those who professed to reverence its authority, simply because he presented to their view *thirty thousand* various readings, it is no cause for surprise that enemies of revelation, who knew . . . that Mill did not *make* the variations, but only stated the previously existing *fact*, should have taken up the assertion, and declared that the text of Scripture *is* precarious on this very ground.[10]

Anthony Collins also attacked Mill in 1713 in a published "Discourse of Free Thinking." He in turn was answered by Richard Bentley of Oxford, who assumed the role of a Leipzig scholar adjudicating a British debate and who called himself Phileleutherus Lipsiensis. He pointed out that manuscript copies of any document contain textual differences, that the New Testament is the more fortunate in the large

number of copies, and that the larger the number of textual variants the better a lost original may be reconstructed. Bentley was applauded by Bishop Hare in the tract, "A Clergyman's Thanks to Phileleutherus," and the groundwork by Mill was extolled by Wettstein: "This learned man alone did more, in the labour of thirty years, than all those who had preceded him." [11]

These early textual studies on the Greek New Testament were all conducted by English scholars, stimulated by the Codex Alexandrinus. They were extended further by a group of German scholars through the next century. Johann Albert Bengel (1687-1752) of Tübingen was the first to classify the types of text witnessed by the manuscripts. He adopted the view of Richard Bentley that agreement of the earliest Greek and Latin witnesses must point to original readings. He therefore classified Codex Alexandrinus and the Old Latin manuscripts as the ancient text (the "African *natio*"). The great mass of Byzantine manuscripts were classified as the recent text (the "Asiatic *natio*"). This principle of classification assumed the validity of another principle, that a few ancient witnesses would outweigh the great mass of recent witnesses akin to the Received Text. Bengel also proposed the criterion that a difficult reading is to be preferred to an easier reading because the latter is more likely, a priori, to be a spurious emendation. Such principles illustrate the first groping toward objective procedure in restoring the true text. Bengel published in 1734 an edition of the Greek New Testament, but as yet there was little change from the Received Text. A contemporary of Bengel was Johann Jacob Wettstein (1693-1754) of Basel, who rejected Bengel's principles. Wettstein still adhered to the principle of numerical preponderance and therefore followed no classification of witnesses. He was assiduous in collating manuscript texts and collecting variant readings. The results of his labors appeared in his two-volume edition of 1751-52, although the New Testament text he printed agrees generally with the Elzevir edition of 1624. The contributions of Wettstein consist of fresh collations of about 100 manuscripts and the first formal listing of Greek New Testament manuscripts in accessible collections (approximately 225).

Johann Salomo Semler (1725-1791) of Halle developed the principles of Bengel. He accepted the principle of weighted value and further refined the classification of manuscripts. His classes were called Oriental (Antioch and Constantinople), Occidental (the mass of later

---

[9] Francis Hare, *The Clergyman's Thanks to Phileleutherus* (1713); quoted by Adam Fox, *op. cit.*, p. 117.

[10] Samuel P. Tregelles, *An Account of the Printed Text of the Greek New Testament* (London: Samuel Bagster & Sons, 1854), p. 48. Here he repeats the argument of Richard Bentley (*Remarks upon a Late Discourse of Free-thinking* [1713]) addressed to Bishop Francis Hare. Bentley's original statement is quoted by Tregelles, p. 50, and by Adam Fox, *op. cit.*, pp. 113-14.

[11] Quoted by Tregelles, *op. cit.*, p. 43.

copies), and Alexandrian (Egyptian). The last of these was considered the most primitive type while the Occidental was considered the least valuable. Semler's greatest contribution was really the training of a brilliant disciple, Johann Jacob Griesbach (1745-1812). Before he was thirty Griesbach published a three-volume edition of the Greek New Testament (1774-75) and in his late years issued mature revisions of this work. He early followed the classifications of Semler and identified specific witnesses of each. He emphasized comparison of *recensions* rather than of individual manuscripts in order to determine a primitive reading. He supported the theories of Bengel and Semler against those of Wettstein, a judgment which has since been confirmed as true. From Mill to Griesbach was the important century of transition from the medieval text transmitted by the Eastern Church to a critically reconstructed text derived from the early Church. In the West, the Latin Vulgate predominated from Jerome to Erasmus. Among Western Protestants the Greek Received Text held the field from Erasmus to the early nineteenth century. But two centuries after the Codex Alexandrinus came to the West, the "text received by all" was at last discredited and repudiated, and the way was prepared for the acceptance of a different text in its place.

V. The Critical Text

The new text was created by Karl Lachmann, the professor of Classical Philology at the University of Berlin. Earlier textual critics had been clerics and theologians, but it was left to a philologian to act boldly in applying the canons of criticism which had been affirmed. Whereas the past two centuries had attacked the textual problem on the eclectic principle of emending the traditional Received Text at points, Lachmann applied an opposite technique. He set aside the printed Received Text and disregarded the mass of late manuscript witnesses. In their place he reconstructed an objectively critical text based upon the earliest authorities. Chief of these authorities was Codex Alexandrinus. He had partial knowledge of a still older copy, from the fourth century, in the Vatican library (Codex Vaticanus). He had a collation made by Wettstein in 1716 of the Paris manuscript whose twelfth-century commentary had been written over a fifth-century Greek Bible. And he consulted the biblical quotations of Origen, the Alexandrian Father of the early third century. Relying upon the few and select authorities he claimed thus to have recovered "the oldest attainable text," reaching back to the fourth century. Quite properly he has been described as "the first creator of a text." It was based upon the principles of manuscript classi-

fication and the supremacy of the "Oriental" type. His small edition of 1831 was followed by a two-volume expansion in 1842 and 1850. It would have been too much to expect that Lachmann's new text should be universally accepted in place of a text so long in use, and some decried this "wholesale innovation" and the "want of reverence for Holy Scripture." One year after the publication of his final edition Lachmann died. There is pathos in the appeal of his preface: "I may be allowed to hope that my object, undertaken with diligence and with confidence of Divine aid, and brought to a completion to the best of my ability, will be approved by posterity from the utility being known, more than has been the case from this age."

"Posterity" did begin to approve almost immediately, especially in the person of Samuel Tregelles who, three years later, recognized the new text to be "the first Greek Testament, since the invention of printing, edited wholly on ancient authority, irrespective of modern traditions." [12] The most effective kind of approval was to come when his successors built upon his work, first the fabulous Tischendorf and then the respected British team of Westcott and Hort. But in the meantime two other sensational discoveries occurred to confirm the Lachmann text. Lachmann's first article in 1830 inspired the fifteen-year-old Konstantin von Tischendorf (1815-74) to textual studies, which he actually began at twenty-two. At twenty-five his searching for old Bible manuscripts took him to the desert of Sinai and to the ancient Monastery of Saint Catherine. There he found an accumulation of old manuscripts and returned with a parchment fragment of forty-three leaves containing Septuagint text from the fourth century, "the pearl of all my researches." When, after two more journeys to Sinai in 1853 and 1859, he discovered the entire manuscript (Sinaiticus) he writes of "the transport of joy which I felt [for] I knew that I held in my hand the most precious Biblical treasure in existence." [13] It was also owing to Tischendorf that a fourth-century Greek Bible in the Vatican (Vaticanus) at last revealed its witness. It had actually been in the Vatican four hundred years but had remained largely inaccessible. It may therefore be considered a "discovery" in 1867 when Tischendorf published its text.

These two great codices, Sinaiticus and Vaticanus, are co-witnesses to the fourth-century Greek Bible of Egyptian Christians. They reach back a century nearer to the original than

[12] Tregelles, *op. cit.*, p. 113.
[13] "The Discovery of the Sinaitic Manuscript" in *When Were Our Gospels Written?* (New York: American Tract Society, 1866), pp. 35, 43-44.

Codex Alexandrinus. Fundamentally, they confirm the 1850 text of Lachmann and have made possible the improved revisions of Tischendorf who began his series of editions in 1841. In the course of thirty years he collated the texts of twenty-three manuscripts, published the texts of seventeen important codices, and issued twenty editions of the Greek Testament with continuous improvement. Not long before his death the two volumes of the Editio Maior were completed (1869-72), the chief feature of which was the extensive and precise *apparatus criticus*. This remains today the most valuable reference work presenting the weight of attestation for and against various readings in the manuscripts. His New Testament text rests largely upon the fourth-century codices Sinaiticus and Vaticanus, which became accessible less than a century ago.

After Tischendorf, textual leadership again passed to England with the researches of several contemporaries of stature: Tregelles, Scrivener, Burgon, Westcott, and Hort. It was the last two, however, who in partnership built upon the structure reared by Lachmann and Tischendorf. Brooke Foss Westcott (1825-1901), Regius Professor of Divinity at Cambridge and afterward Bishop of Durham (1890-1901), and F. J. A. Hort (1828-92), Hulsean Professor of Divinity at Cambridge, united in textual studies and for twenty-nine years labored together on the task of restoring the original Greek of the New Testament. They worked with the mass of data already gathered by predecessors and accepted the basic principles of Lachmann and Griesbach. They went further, however, and constructed a history of the early text which postulated that the first-century apostolic text moved down in three lines of descent. One was preserved especially in Alexandria and its second-century form ("Neutral") was represented by Vaticanus and Sinaiticus, but by the third century it had been revised and polished. Another ("Western") was preserved especially in the West from the second century, a "rewrought" text influenced particularly by the Latin version. The third was revised in Syria and accommodated to both the others, and by the fourth century had assumed the form which the mass of Byzantine manuscripts followed. Granting the truth of this history, it was necessary to reverse the process in order to isolate the apostolic text, and this was the method employed. The resultant text published in 1881 was called the Neutral text, implying its primitive state and freedom from corruption. It has been widely accepted as the most authentic Greek text available to Christians since the early centuries and has become the basis of modern translation and interpretation. This text of Westcott and Hort is the product of the critical process begun in the sixteenth century.

Although the Neutral text still remains the best critical text available today, any claim to have recovered a primitive apostolic form is not seriously held. It is essentially the text of Codex Vaticanus, believed to have been in use in the fourth century in Egypt—perhaps in Alexandria. Yet practically every critical text published since 1881 has been essentially the same. Just as the Byzantine text of Erasmus continued with little revision to be republished for more than three centuries, so now the Westcott-Hort text is frequently republished with but a few eclectic emendations; for example, Weymouth 1886, Brandscheid 1893, Hetzenauer 1893, Weiss 1894-1900, Blass 1895-1902, Nestle 1898, Bodin 1911, Colombo 1932, Merk 1933, and Bover 1943. The Eberhard Nestle editions, begun in 1898, have been carried on by his son Erwin into the twenty-first edition of 1952. The two Jesuit scholars August Merk and Joseph Bover have published ten editions from 1933 to 1953.

The Neutral text holds its pre-eminence while further discoveries and researches continue. Agnes Lewis of Cambridge went to Saint Catherine's Monastery in Sinai in 1892 and found a fifth-century Syriac text of the Gospels underlying another eighth-century text. This (the so-called Sinaiticus Syriac manuscript) has given us another witness to the Old Syriac translation, made from the original Greek earlier than any other Greek witness we now have. It was this text that Moffatt accepted at Matt. 1:16: ". . . and Joseph (to whom the virgin was betrothed) the father of Jesus, who is called 'Christ.'" In 1897 the British scholars Grenfell and Hunt brought home additional papyrus treasures from middle Egypt, including a fragment from Matthew from the third century (the oldest biblical witness then known). In 1906 Charles Lang Freer of Detroit purchased near the Pyramids fifth- and sixth-century manuscripts of the Gospels and letters of Paul (now in the Freer Gallery in Washington). In 1910 the Pierpont Morgan Library acquired a biblical collection in Coptic, the primitive Egyptian version. Really sensational was the purchase in 1931 by A. Chester Beatty, a copper magnate of Dublin, of a papyrus collection of eleven Greek manuscripts. Three of the Beatty manuscripts contain extensive portions of the New Testament text—the Gospels, Acts, the Pauline letters, and the Apocalypse. They all belong to the third century, one century nearer to their origins than we have previously come. The manuscript of Paul is nearly complete if we include a section of thirty leaves acquired by the University of Michigan. These latest major acquisitions are our oldest known witnesses to the Greek New Testament, except for the tiny papyrus fragment of John 18 in the John Rylands Library.

VI. Work to Be Done

Do we dare hope that new discoveries will bring us any closer to the original text? Before we answer such a question we must consider what we seek in an original text. Do we expect to recover a letter as Paul wrote it to the Thessalonians in A.D. 50? Or do we hope to recover the original manuscript of the Pauline corpus of about A.D. 95? Or shall we be content with the complete New Testament after A.D. 150? Or must we first reconstruct the variant local texts of Christian communities like Antioch, Alexandria, Caesarea, and Rome? Manuscript discoveries and textual researches go hand in hand. Along with the discovery of additional important witnesses there have proceeded also the investigations of particular textual problems. Since Westcott and Hort another early recension, the Caesarean, especially related to the third-century Eastern Father, Origen, has been defined. Also, special "families" of Byzantine manuscripts bearing a textual resemblance have been isolated. Furthermore, numerous studies have been made on the lectionaries of the Eastern Church, exploring the conservative text as fixed by liturgical practice. Such researches supply pieces of the textual puzzle to be held in reserve until all may fall into place.

A particular problem of authority remains for those who must read the Bible in translation rather than in the original language. The synagogue still retains its Hebrew Scriptures and the Eastern Church still reads the New Testament in Greek, but the Eastern Church reads the Old Testament in Greek translation and the Roman Church has long used the Latin translation. It seems obvious that even the best translation removes the reader somewhat from the original sense of the word and therefore from the authentic truth of the initial concept. Furthermore, while a single translation suffers loss, a double translation is completely unreliable. This is true of the Latin Vulgate in the Psalter, which is a translation from the Greek which is a translation from Hebrew. It was true of the first English Bible, such as Wycliffe's version, which was translated from the Latin which was in part a translation from the Greek and, in the case of the Old Testament, a further translation from Hebrew. Wycliffe's Psalter was therefore three translations removed from the Hebrew! But this was still true for most of the first printed English Bible, the Coverdale of 1535, and for the Roman Catholic Douay Bible of 1609, which came directly from the Latin. These historical examples illustrate the need to restore to Christianity the original Hebrew-Greek Bible.

But almost all Christians rely upon the modern translations of the Bible, and here it becomes necessary to exercise intelligent choice. There have been literally hundreds of English translations since the King James Bible appeared in 1611. A considerable number of them are well known but they are not all of equal authority. Not only does this depend upon the translator, but even more upon the basic text he selected to translate. Among recent English translations of the New Testament we may note that Weymouth (1903) used his own Resultant Greek Text, Bell (1923) and Ballantine (1923) used Nestle, Montgomery (1924) and C. K. Williams (1952) used Souter's text, Moffatt (1913) used Von Soden, Kleist (1932) used Vogel's text, while the Twentieth Century (1904) and Goodspeed (1923) used Westcott-Hort. The Revised Standard Version, reflecting the present eclectic stage of criticism, used both Westcott-Hort and Nestle and occasionally emended these.

The progress of textual criticism is made through separate stages which form successive cycles: discovery of manuscript sources, collection of data from these manuscripts, and reconstruction of the text through the application of the data. Although the three activities overlap, their successive stages of emphasis have been evident. One cycle reached completion with the Westcott-Hort text in 1881. Since then the stages of discovery and collection have recurred, and criticism today may be said to stand between the era of collection and that of application. Certainly abundant data have been accumulating in the last thirty or forty years, and the culmination of this stage may be attained in the project known as the International Greek New Testament. Begun in 1948 as a joint Anglo-American task (with the aid of Continental scholars), the objective is to publish a thorough *apparatus criticus* to replace the old one of Tischendorf (1869-72) and to include data from all discoveries that have intervened. Advances in method and form are proposed also, with a view to providing the textual critic with an instrument by which to illumine the history and form of the New Testament text. The logic of the situation encourages the hope that the final stage of the cycle—the stage of application—may now be opening, the end of which should be a critical text approaching more closely than any earlier text to what the original manuscripts of the New Testament contained.[14]

[14] For a related article, with a selected bibliography, see "Text and Ancient Versions of the New Testament" by Ernest C. Colwell, Vol. I, pp. 72-83. Editors.

ILLUSTRATED HISTORY OF THE BIBLICAL TEXT

by JOHN C. TREVER

The following pages of color plates are intended to help the student visualize the historical development of the biblical text. Plates 1-19 illustrate the history of the Old Testament text, while Plates 20-27 illustrate the history of the New Testament text. Such manuscripts as the Codex Sinaiticus (Plate 15) and the Codex Vaticanus (Plate 24), however, include both.

The early stages of the writing of the Old Testament, unfortunately, cannot be illustrated, for no manuscripts from that period have been discovered. That a written literature existed among the Hebrews as early as the tenth century B.C. is possibly indicated by the references in II Sam. 8:16-17 to a "recorder" (mazkîr—literally, "one who causes to remember") and a "secretary" (sôphēr—literally, "one who enumerates") in the court of David (cf. II Sam. 20:24-25). Since the earliest evidences for a Hebrew-Phoenician alphabet come from the sixteenth century B.C., and a standardized script emerges only about the tenth century B.C., it is unlikely that any written literature in Hebrew existed in extensive form prior to the time of David (see "The Literature of the Old Testament," Vol. I, pp. 175-84).

The references in Num. 21:14 to the "Book of the Wars of the LORD" and in Josh. 10:13 (cf. II Sam. 1:18) to the "Book of Jashar" suggest that collections of poetry may have existed in writing even earlier than the tenth century B.C., but nothing from such early documents is extant except as quoted in later writings. The Ten Commandments and some other early laws, of course, are said to have been written down (Exod. 24:4; 34:28), but no epigraphic evidence of them has been found.

Although the Gezer Calendar, the stele of Mesha (the Moabite stone), the few inscribed potsherds (ostraca) from Samaria, and the Siloam inscription [1] might have been used to illustrate the development of the Old Testament text from the late tenth century to the late eighth century B.C., this series of color plates begins with the Lachish Letters, which were written about 588 B.C., at the time when the idea of a canonized Scripture had just arisen. Furthermore, in their contents and language the Lachish Letters are quasi-biblical, supplementing with dramatic vigor the stories recorded in II Kings 24–25 and the narratives in Jeremiah. (For a more detailed treatment, see "The Canon of the Old Testament" and "Text and Ancient Versions of the Old Testament," Vol. I, pp. 32-62.)

The inclusion of the little-known letter of 'Arsham, written on leather, illustrates several developments in the fifth century B.C. The tendency to adopt the Aramaic language in Judah, along with its "square" script, probably began about that time. The use of leather, more abundant in Palestine and probably more economical than papyrus, was standard for Hebrew Scripture. The formal script of these official letters indicates the early development of the "book hand" for sacred Scripture, now seen to be fully developed in the Dead Sea Scrolls.

The Dead Sea Scrolls dominate this series. Their importance to the story here portrayed is obvious, since they now fill in what have been large gaps in our previous knowledge. The several illustrations from these discoveries provide opportunities for comparison of a number of characteristics. A few scenes relating to this discovery have also been included. The absence of Aramaic documents from the first century A.D., previous to the Dead Sea Scrolls, makes imperative the inclusion of the fragment from the Aramaic "Scroll of the Patriarchs," dating from the very period of the "oral gospel."

To complete the story, we must take note of the versions. In addition to the Greek Old Testament, the Syriac has been selected to represent them, with an example from each testament. (For a detailed treatment, see "Text and Ancient Versions of the Old Testament," Vol. I, pp. 59-60, and "The Canon of the New Testament," Vol. I, pp. 67-68.)

[1] See *Bulletin of the American Schools of Oriental Research*, 92 (Dec., 1943), pp. 16-26; J. B. Pritchard, ed., *Ancient Near Eastern Texts Relating to the Old Testament* (Princeton: Princeton Univerity Press, 1950), pp. 320-21; and Jack Finegan, *Light from the Ancient Past* (Princeton: Princeton University Press, 1946; London: Oxford University Press, 1947).

1. THE LACHISH LETTERS—6th cent. B.C.

Among the earliest evidences relating to the writing of the Bible are the twenty-one letters, inscribed in archaic Hebrew on broken pieces of pottery (ostraca), found in a guard room behind the outer gate at Tell ed-Duweir, biblical Lachish. They were written by Hosha'yahu, a military commander during the invasion of Nebuchadrezzar in 588 B.C.

2. LETTER FROM 'ARSHAM—5th cent. B.C.

The square Aramaic script was gradually adopted by the Jews after the Exile (586-538 B.C.). No biblical documents copied as early as the fifth century are known, but this letter of 'Arsham on leather (about 410 B.C.) found in Egypt illustrates how such a manuscript would look. The upper strip shows the address of the letter on the outside of the folded document and reads, "From 'Arsham to Nehtihur, the officer who is in Lower Egypt."

3. FRAGMENTS OF I SAMUEL
(4QSam^b) —*ca.* 200 B.C.

Probably the earliest biblical fragments in any language have been found in Cave IV (Plate 11) near Khirbet Qumrân, among thousands of other fragments. Some were from a manuscript of I Samuel, like these three showing portions of I Sam. 23:9-16. Affinities in script to Plate 2 are apparent, suggesting a date before the second century B.C.

4. QUMRÂN EXODUS SCROLL IN ARCHAIC HEBREW (4QEx^a) —2nd-1st cent. B.C.

Also from Cave IV has come a large group of fragments from twenty-four columns of an Exodus scroll written in archaic Hebrew, similar to that on the Lachish Letters, but probably a Maccabean revival from the second or first century B.C. Shown here is the broken column containing Exod. 30:10-30. Affinities with the Samaritan text are seen in the first two lines.

6. EARLY GREEK DEUTERONOMY FRAGMENT—2nd cent. B.C.

This fragment from a papyrus scroll of Deuteronomy (20:12-14) in Cairo is one of a few pre-Christian **Greek** biblical fragments. They use Hebrew letters for the sacred name, YHWH, as in the third line of this slightly enlarged example.

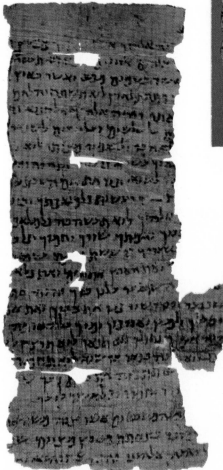

5 NASH PAPYRUS (Or 233—natural size) — 2nd-1st cent. B.C.

Until the discovery of the Dead Sea Scrolls in 1947, this small sheet of papyrus was our earliest biblical Hebrew document. It contains the Ten Commandments and the Shema' (Deut. 6:4).

7. RYLANDS GREEK FRAGMENTS (Papyrus 458)—2nd cent. B.C.

These fragments of a Greek scroll of Deuteronomy were gathered from Egyptian mummy wrappings and contain parts of Deut. 23–25. These and the Cairo fragments were our earliest biblical manuscript evidences until 1947.

Photo by John C. Trever

8. ISAIAH "A" SCROLL FROM DEAD SEA CAVE (1QIsaa) —1st cent. B.C.

Now our earliest known extensive biblical document, this Hebrew scroll of Isaiah made from seventeen pieces of sheepskin reveals the nature of a first-century-B.C. biblical manuscript. Here are shown the first three columns, which include Isa. 1:1–3:23.

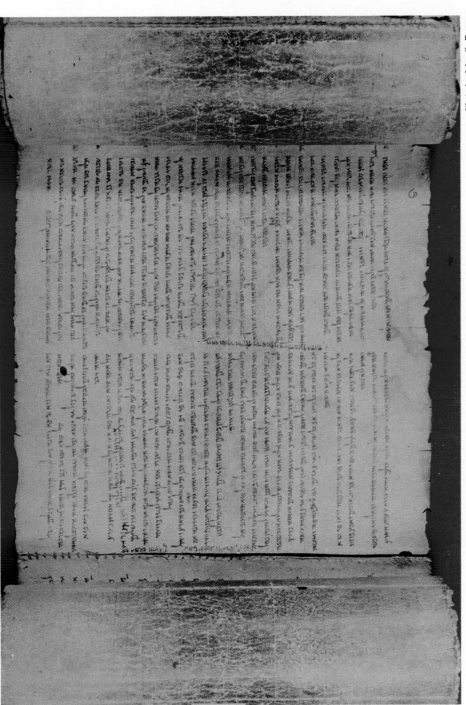

9. ISAIAH SCROLL OPENED TO CHAPTER 40 (1QIsaa)

Opened here to columns 32 and 33, the scroll shows Isa. 38:8—40:28. A symbol in the margin by the last line on the right indicates the beginning of ch. 40. Three insertions by later hands to correct omissions by the first scribe can clearly be seen on the two columns. Except for a few minor breaks, the twenty-four-foot scroll includes the entire sixty-six chapters of Isaiah in its fifty-four columns. Its height is ten inches, with an average of thirty lines per column of text.

10. KHIRBET QUMRÂN BY THE DEAD SEA

The excavated community center overlooks the Dead Sea about eight miles south of Jericho. The northwest corner defense tower dominates the picture. The center was occupied by Essenes from about 110 B.C. to A.D. 68.

Photo by David J. Wieand

Photo by David J. Wieand

11. QUMRÂN CAVE IV

High above Wãdi Qumrân, just a few hundred feet north of the khirbet, Cave IV in 1952 yielded thousands of fragments from some 330 manuscripts. Ninety are biblical.

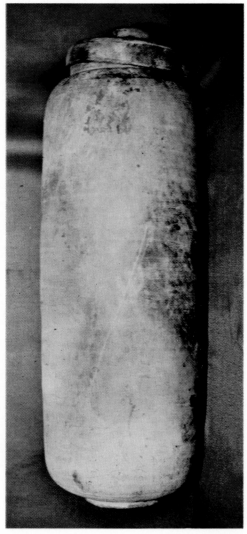

12. SCROLL JAR WITH COVER

Only two of about fifty jars originally in Cave I were recovered whole. Each had a closely fitting bowl cover to seal the linen-wrapped scrolls stored inside. Caves near by yielded similar jars, and one was found in the khirbet.

Photo by Yigael Yadin, courtesy of the Hebrew University, Jerusalem

Photo by Yigael Yadin, courtesy of the Hebrew University, Jerusalem

13. QUMRÂN SCROLL OF ISAIAH "B" (1QIsa^b) —1st cent. A.D.

This badly disintegrated scroll of Isaiah was secured by the Hebrew University from the Bedouin who made the original find in Cave I. Here are portions of four columns from Isa. 44:21–51:10. Parts of twelve columns, covering Isa. 35:12–66:24, have been recovered, plus a number of fragments. The script shows that the scroll was copied perhaps a century after Isaiah "A."

Photo by John C. Trever, courtesy of the Jordan Department of Antiquities

14. FRAGMENTS FROM A SCROLL OF DANIEL (1QDan) —1st cent. A.D.

These fragments of Daniel from Cave I are from one of the last scrolls copied at Qumrân before its destruction. Parts of Dan. 1:10–2:6 are included. In 2:4 the Aramaic portion of Daniel begins, as seen here on the left, the fourth line down.

15. CODEX SINAITICUS (Codex ℵ) —4th cent. A.D.

Among the early Greek manuscripts of the Bible the Codex Sinaiticus is most widely known, because of the dramatic story of its discovery in St. Catherine's Monastery at Mount Sinai by Konstantin von Tischendorf. Here we see the beautiful vellum codex opened to Isa. 41:26b–44:2.

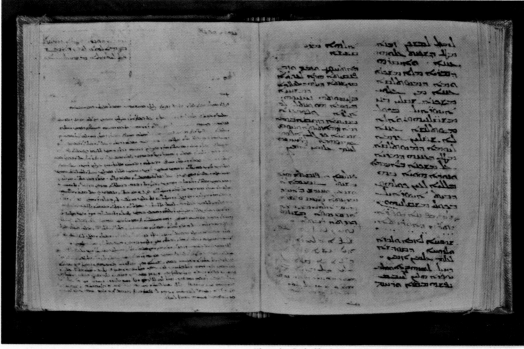

16. SYRIAC PESHITTA CODEX (Add. 14,425) —A.D. 464

The Old Testament was translated into Syriac in the second or third century A.D. for the benefit of Syrian Christians. This Syriac Peshitta ("simple") is the oldest dated biblical manuscript in existence, copied in A.D. 464 according to the notes at the end of Exodus shown here. The last few verses of Exod. 40 appear on the right column. The rest is the colophon and scribal notes.

17. FRAGMENT OF EZEKIEL SCROLL (T.S. 20:59)—6th cent. A.D.

Among a large collection of manuscript fragments from the "Cairo Genizah," now in the Cambridge Library, several fragments of biblical scrolls have been identified. Here is a large fragment of a parchment scroll of Ezekiel which may well date from the sixth or seventh century A.D. On it an early type of Palestinian vocalization is found. Ezek. 13:11–16:31 is included.

18. BRITISH MUSEUM TORAH CODEX (Or 4445)—9th cent. A.D.

This huge parchment codex of the Torah is one of the earliest known examples of the standardized Hebrew text of the Masoretes. Prior to the discovery of the Qumrân scrolls, it was the oldest Hebrew Bible. It dates from about A.D. 900. It is opened here to Exod. 29:39b–30:24a. Masoretic comments occupy the margins.

Photo by John C. Trever

19. SCROLL OF THE PATRIARCHS (1QLamech) — 1st cent. A.D.

This fragment is from a large scroll belonging to the original find at Qumrân Cave I. When removed in 1949, it was identified as an Aramaic scroll of Lamech, who in this fragment speaks in the first person. The whole scroll proved to be an Aramaic paraphrase of Genesis.

20. SAYINGS OF JESUS (Papyrus 1531 verso) — 2nd cent. A.D.

The second of two fragments from codices of "sayings of Jesus" not in the Gospels, this piece of papyrus was found in 1903 at Oxyrhynchus in Egypt. It illustrates an early stage in the growth of the Gospels.

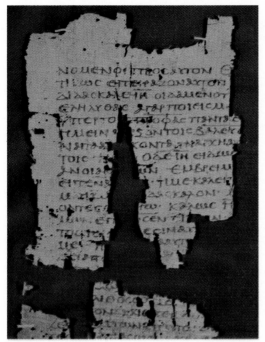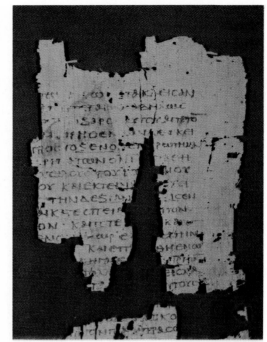

RECTO   VERSO

21. THE UNKNOWN GOSPELS (Egerton 2 Papyrus) —2nd cent. A.D.

This leaf, found in Egypt, is from a papyrus codex of a gospel not found in the New Testament. It illustrates the development of gospels in the early church, as suggested by Luke 1:1-4.

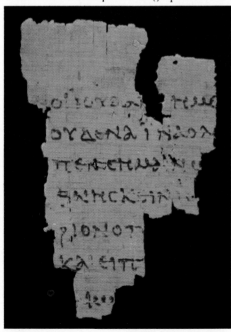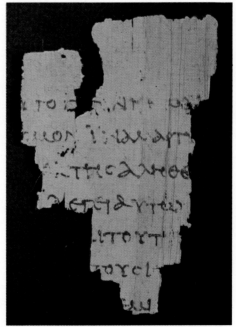

RECTO   VERSO

22. EARLY FRAGMENT OF JOHN (Rylands Papyrus 457) —2nd cent. A.D.

This scrap of papyrus is the oldest witness to the New Testament text known. Only 2½ by 3½ inches in size, it contains parts of John 18:31-33, 37, 38. Dated in the early second century A.D., it has the distinction of being the earliest extant fragment of a codex.

ρμθ

ΕΝ ϹΑΡΓΑΝΗ ΕΧΑΛΑϹΘΗΝ ΔΙΑ ΤΟΥ ΤΕΙΧΟΥϹ
ΚΑΙ ΕΞΕΦΥΓΟΝ ΤΑϹ ΧΕΙΡΑϹ ΑΥΤΟΥ ΚΑΥΧΑϹ
ΘΑΙ ΔΕΙ ΟΥ ϹΥΜΦΕΡΟΝ ΜΕΝ ΕΛΕΥϹΟΜΑΙ ΔΕ
ΕΙϹ ΟΠΤΑϹΙΑϹ ΚΑΙ ΑΠΟΚΑΛΥΨΕΙϹ ΚΥ ΟΙΔΑ
ΑΝΘΡΩΠΟΝ ΕΝ ΧΩ ΠΡΟ ΕΤΩΝ ΔΕΚΑΤΕϹϹΑΡΩΝ
ΕΙΤΕ ΕΝ ϹΩΜΑΤΙ ΟΥΚ ΟΙΔΑ ΕΙΤΕ ΕΚΤΟϹ ΤΟΥ ϹΩ
ΜΑΤΟϹ ΟΥΚ ΟΙΔΑ Ο ΘϹ ΟΙΔΕΝ ΑΡΠΑΓΕΝΤΑ ΤΟΝ
ΤΟΙ ΟΥΤΟΝ ΕΩϹ ΤΡΙΤΟΥ ΟΥΡΑΝΟΥ ΚΑΙ ΟΙΔΑ ΤΟΝ
ΤΟΙΟΥΤΟΝ ΑΝΘΡΩΠΟΝ ΕΙΤΕ ΕΝ ϹΩΜΑΤΙ ΕΙΤΕ
ΧΩΡΙϹ ΤΟΥ ϹΩΜΑΤΟϹ ΟΥΚ ΟΙΔΑ Ο ΘϹ ΟΙΔΕΝ ΟΤΙ
ΗΡΠΑΓΗ ΕΙϹ ΤΟΝ ΠΑΡΑΔΕΙϹΟΝ ΚΑΙ ΗΚΟΥϹΕΝ
ΑΡΡΗΤΑ ΡΗΜΑΤΑ Α ΟΥΚ ΕΞΟΝ ΑΝΘΡΩΠΩ ΛΑ
ΛΗϹΑΙ ΥΠΕΡ ΤΟΥ ΤΟΙ ΟΥΤΟΥ ΚΑΥΧΗϹΟΜΑΙ ΥΠΕΡ
ΔΕ ΕΜΑΥΤΟΥ ΟΥΔΕΝ ΚΑΥΧΗϹΟΜΑΙ ΕΙ ΜΗ ΕΝ ΤΑΙϹ
ΑϹΘΕΝΕΙΑΙϹ ΕΑΝ ΓΑΡ ΘΕΛΩ ΚΑΥΧΗϹΟΜΑΙ
ΟΥΚ ΕϹΟΜΑΙ ΑΦΡΩΝ ΑΛΗΘΕΙΑΝ ΓΑΡ ΕΡΩ
ΦΕΙΔΟΜΑΙ ΔΕ ΜΗ ΤΙϹ ΕΙϹ ΕΜΕ ΛΟΓΙϹΗΤΑΙ ΥΠΕΡ
Ο ΒΛΕΠΕΙ ΜΕ Η ΑΚΟΥΕΙ ΤΙ ΕΞ ΕΜΟΥ ΚΑΙ ΤΗ
ΥΠΕΡΒΟΛΗ ΤΩΝ ΑΠΟΚΑΛΥΨΕΩΝ Ι ΝΑ ΜΗ
ΥΠΕΡΑΙΡΩΜΑΙ ΕΔΟΘΗ ΜΟΙ ϹΚΟΛΟΨ ΤΗ ϹΑΡΚΙ
ΑΓΓΕΛΟϹ ϹΑΤΑΝΑ Ι ΝΑ ΜΕ ΚΟΛΑΦΙΖΗ Ι ΝΑ
ΥΠΕΡ ΑΙΡΩΜΑΙ ΥΠΕΡ ΤΟΥ ΤΟΥ ΤΡΙϹ
ΠΑΡΕΚΑΛΕϹΑ Ι ΝΑ ΑΠΟϹΤΗ ΑΠ ΕΜ
ΒΗ ΚΕ ΜΟΙ ΑΡΚΕΙ ϹΟΙ Η ΧΑ ΡΙϹ
ΔΥ ΝΑΜ

Courtesy of the Kelsey Museum of Archaeology, University of Michigan

23. EARLIEST CODEX OF PAULINE EPISTLES (Papyrus 46)—3rd cent. A.D.

This papyrus leaf, which includes II Cor. 11:33–12:9, is from an early-third-century codex of Paul's letters. More than three fourths of the original codex was recovered in the early thirties, partly by Mr. A. Chester Beatty and partly by the University of Michigan. It is the earliest substantial New Testament manuscript known to exist.

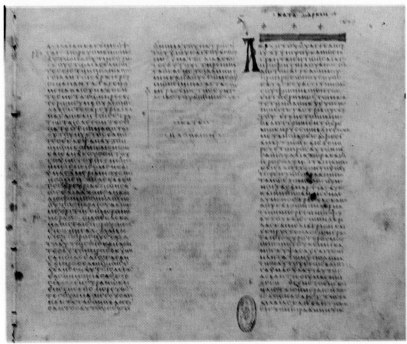

24. CODEX VATICANUS (Codex B) —4th cent. A.D.

As the oldest extant almost-complete Bible, this codex supplies a Greek text of basic authority for both Old and New Testaments, particularly the latter. It is written in a graceful uncial character on 759 leaves of fine vellum measuring 10 by 10½ inches. Shown here are Matt. 1:1-26 (above) and Matt. 28:10–Mark 1:9 (below). The paragraphing of the genealogy contrasts with the usual solid columns. Illustrating both ancient abbreviations and textual variations, the second line of Mark begins ΙΥΧΥΥΙΟΥΘΥ ("Jesus Christ, the Son of God") where Codex Sinaiticus (Plate 15) has only the first two words. The titles, initials, decorations, and oval Vatican seals are later additions.

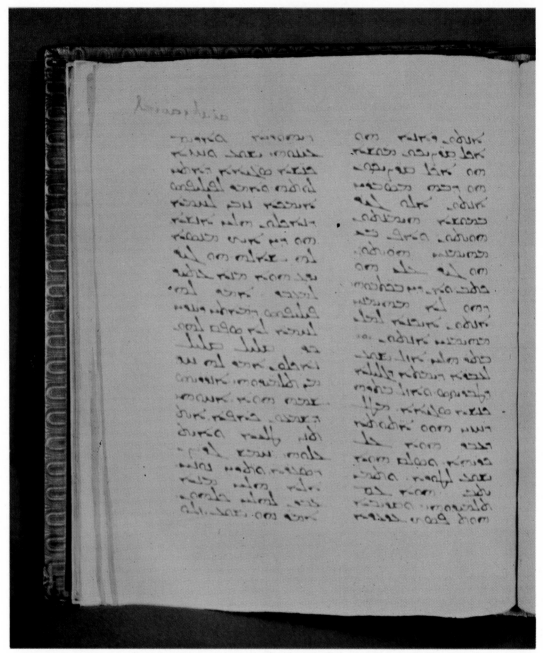

25. OLD SYRIAC GOSPELS (Add. 14,451) —5th cent. A.D.

The Old Syriac translation was made from an early Greek New Testament, and thus is one of the most important versions for textual studies. Only two representatives of it are known: the Sinaitic Syriac, discovered in 1892 in the St. Catherine's Monastery at Mount Sinai; and the Curetonian Syriac, discovered by Dr. Cureton among a group of Syriac books secured in 1842 by the British Museum. These Syriac texts, including only the Gospels, represent an earlier translation of the Greek than the Peshitta (Plate 16). Both were copied probably in the fifth century, however. The page from the Curetonian Manuscript shown here includes John 5:45–6:10.

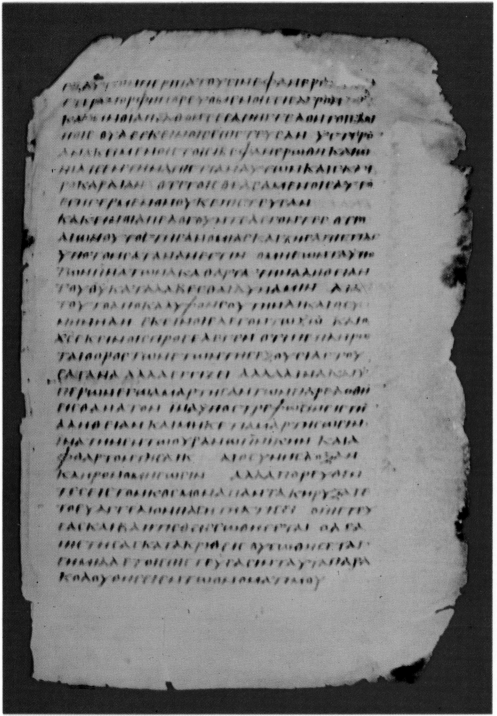

26. FREER GOSPELS (Codex W) —5th-cent. Greek uncial

Among the great uncial manuscripts of the New Testament, the Freer Gospels, or Codex Washingtonianus, is one of the most interesting. A composite of several different texts, it includes some notable variations, like the long interpolation after Mark 16:14 shown here in lines 9-24. The order of the Gospels in this manuscript is like that of Western manuscripts: Matthew, John, Luke, and Mark.

27. ROCKEFELLER-McCORMICK NEW TESTAMENT—13th-cent. minuscule

The uncial Greek characters gave way to the minuscule style during the tenth century. This New Testament, copied about A.D. 1265, is a beautiful example with its ninety-one miniatures. Illustrated here is the Transfiguration, with text including Matt. 17:1–18:8.

THE DEAD SEA SCROLLS

by FRANK MOORE CROSS, JR.

In the spring of 1947 seven antique scrolls of leather were found by shepherds in the Judean desert bordering the northwestern shore of the Dead Sea. The discovery set off a series of finds which are without precedent or parallel in the history of modern archaeology. Again and again the lonely precincts of the wilderness have been invaded successfully by treasure hunters—clandestine Bedouin diggers and accredited Western scientists. The most important and best known of the series of finds come from the Wâdī Qumrân, some seven or eight miles south of modern Jericho. But other districts have yielded precious groups of documents as by-products of the intense search of the desert: Wâdī Murabba'ât, twelve miles southwest of Qumrân; an unknown place perhaps farther south along the Dead Sea; and the ancient ruins of Khirbet Mird, inland on the western flank of the Judean Buqei'ah.

Eleven caves in the vicinity of Qumrân have now produced manuscripts or manuscript fragments. These eleven include the cave of the initial discovery (Qumrân I) and a cave found in January, 1956 (Qumrân XI). Today in the museums of Palestine there are more than four hundred manuscripts—a few well preserved, most extremely fragmentary—from these Qumrân caves alone.

I. Discovery of the Qumrân Caves

The complete story of the discovery of the first cave has not yet been told, though it is now clear in its essentials. In the spring (or early summer) of 1947 two shepherd lads of the semi-sedentary Ta'âmireh tribe were tending their mixed flocks of goats and sheep at the foot of the crumbling cliffs that border the Dead Sea in the vicinity of Qumrân. According to their account, one of their animals strayed. In the

search for it one of the shepherds, Muhammed edh-Dhîb by name, tossed a stone into a small circular opening in the rock. Instead of the expected smack of rock against rock, he heard a sound of shattering. He was frightened and fled. Later he and his companion 'Ahmed Muhammed returned and crept into the cave, where they found decaying rolls of leather in one of a number of strange, elongated jars embedded in the floor of the cave. These were the original "Dead Sea Scrolls."

In the year between the Bedouin discovery and the first press releases announcing the discovery to the world, there were confusion, blundering, and intrigue such as are often associated, unfortunately, with spectacular chance finds. At least one, and probably several, clandestine excavations ravaged the cave site; additional materials came to light; no doubt some precious material was destroyed in the process. The details of this part of the history of the scrolls of Cave I cannot be certainly established. In any case, after some of the scrolls had passed about in the tents of tribesmen, they were brought to Bethlehem and fell into the hands of antiquities dealers. At some point they were joined by a portion of the manuscript materials from clandestine excavations. Ultimately one lot was purchased by the Syrian Orthodox metropolitan of Jerusalem, another by the Hebrew University through the agency of the late E. L. Sukenik.[1]

[1]Accounts of the early history of the scrolls as told by principals may be found in the following: G. Lankester Harding in *Qumran Cave I*, vol. I of *Discoveries in the Judaean Desert*, by D. Barthélemy, J. T. Milik, *et al.* (Oxford: Clarendon Press, 1955), pp. 1-7 (cf. *idem*, "The Dead Sea Scrolls, *PEQ*, 81 [1949], pp. 112-16); Burrows, *The Dead Sea Scrolls*, pp. 3-28; E. L. Sukenik, אוצר המגילות הגנוזות (Jerusalem: Bialik Institute, 1954), pp. 13-20; A. Y. Samuel, "The Purchase of the Jerusalem Scrolls," *BA*, 12:2 (1949), pp. 26-31; John C. Trever, "The Discovery of the Scrolls," *BA*, 11 (1948), pp. 46-68. The enormous secondary literature on the early dis-

A key to the abbreviation of journal titles used in the footnotes appears on p. 667.

The first announcement to the world of the discovery of ancient manuscripts was made by the American School of Oriental Research in Jerusalem in April, 1948.[2] The Arab-Israeli fighting already had begun to disturb Palestine so much that attempts to locate and excavate the site of the extraordinary finds were frustrated until the spring of 1949. Nevertheless, scientific excavations were carried out successfully (February 15–March 5, 1949); and some seventy documents, including fragments of some of the original seven manuscripts, were found, more or less *in situ.* Thus the provenience of the purchased lots was established; further, sufficient archaeological data were recovered to date the deposit roughly, confirming earlier paleographical results.[3]

The fantastic episode seemed closed. For nearly two years the cliffs were left undisturbed. It was generally assumed that by a stroke of fortune an isolated cache had been found. Apparently it occurred to no one that Cave I was other than a chance hiding place chosen by some odd but happy quirk of an ancient mind.

In the winter of 1951 G. Lankester Harding, director of antiquities in Jordan, and Père Roland de Vaux, director of the École Biblique et Archéologique Française in Jerusalem, proposed to make soundings at an ancient ruin to the south of Cave I on the Wâdī Qumrân. The ruin was by no means unknown. De Saulcy in the nineteenth century had identified it as biblical Gomorrah; and soberer scientists in the modern period of archaeology had noted evidence of its Roman date. The excavations at the cave brought the curious ruin to immediate attention.

Excavations at Qumrân initiated a series of five campaigns between 1951 and the spring of 1956. The first soundings yielded enough evidence to permit the tentative suggestion that the site was an ancient community center of the Essenes.[4] Already the internal evidence of certain of the sectarian manuscripts had led

coveries is recorded by Rowley, *The Zadokite Fragments . . . ,* pp. 3-6. Newer developments have wholly antiquated the early discussion, though it retains some human interest.

[2] Burrows released word of the Syrian lot of scrolls on April 11, 1948. Announcement of the lot belonging to the Hebrew University followed hastily on April 26. Cf. G. Ernest Wright, "A Phenomenal Discovery," *BA,* 11 (1948), pp. 21-23; W. F. Albright, "Notes from the President's Desk," *BASOR,* 110 (April, 1948), pp. 2-3.

[3] *Discoveries in the Judean Desert, I,* 6-38. Cf. Harding, "The Dead Sea Scrolls"; R. de Vaux, "La grotte des manuscrits hébreux," *RB,* 56 (1949), pp. 586-609; O. R. Sellers, "Excavation of the 'Manuscript Cave,'" *BASOR,* 114 (Apr., 1949), pp. 5-9. Note that the cave is a little over half a mile north of Khirbet Qumrân.

[4] See De Vaux, "Fouille au Khirbet Qumrân," *RB,* 60 (1953), pp. 83-106, especially p. 105, and note 65.

scholars to assign them an Essene authorship.[5] Slowly a new pattern began to emerge: the scrolls belonged to an ancient people who had occupied the caves north and south of Khirbet Qumrân; the ruin was their community center; and this was precisely the Essene desert retreat remarked by the Roman historian Pliny.[6] However, in 1952 this interpretation of the origin of the scrolls and the site on the Wâdī Qumrân was yet to be established securely.

In February, 1952, Ta'âmireh tribesmen found fragmentary remains of manuscripts in a new cave hard by Cave I. Cave II was not an impressive find. However, the various archaeological schools in Jerusalem were galvanized. They mounted an expedition to explore systematically all the caves of the high rocky bluffs north and south of Khirbet Qumrân on a line some five miles long. The exploration was carried out during the month of March, 1952.[7] Soundings were made in more than two hundred caves. In twenty-five the pottery recovered proved to come from the same potteries which had served the building complex at Khirbet Qumrân. However, only one new cave produced inscribed materials. This was Cave III, to the north of Cave I, from which was dug the "Copper Scrolls," actually a single work. The document, preserved in two oxidized rolls of beaten copper, was at length cut into small strips at the Manchester School of Technology and successfully deciphered. The first announcement of its contents was made on June 1, 1956. Its twelve columns of writing contain a curious list of treasures and their hiding places.[8] The amounts of gold and silver involved and the nature of their hiding places certify the folkloristic character of the list; presumably the document records the national and/or priestly treasures which popular imagination assigned to old Israel and supposed had survived in caches distributed over Palestine. Actually the document is interesting largely for the Mishnaic dialect in which it is written, of which it is the earliest exemplar (*ca.* A.D. 50).

[5] See especially Dupont-Sommer, *Aperçus préliminaires . . . ,* pp. 105-17.

[6] *Naturalis historia* V. xv. 73. Cf. *Dio apud Synesium* 39 (ed. Migne).

[7] See De Vaux, "Exploration de la région de Qumrân," *RB,* 60 (1953), pp. 540-56; W. L. Reed, "The Qumrân Caves Expedition of March, 1952," *BASOR,* 135 (Oct., 1954), pp. 8-13.

[8] See J. T. Milik, "The Copper Document from Cave IV, Qumran," *BA,* 19 (1956), pp. 60-64. K. G. Kuhn in a provisional study, "Les rouleaux de cuivre de Qumrân," *RB,* 61 (1954), pp. 193-205, anticipated in part the contents of the document from what could be read in reverse on the outside of the rolls. However, his natural supposition that the treasures were actual Essene hoards buried in the neighborhood of Qumrân has proved incorrect.

The attrition of heat, malaria, and simple fatigue ground the expedition to a halt at the end of March. It had succeeded in investigating most of the natural caves of the sandstone cliffs. On the other hand, it had ignored the artificial caves and clefts in the marl terrace at the foot of the cliffs. Time and funds were short, and logical Western minds, noting that the caves which had yielded manuscripts all were located in the upper level, concluded that exploration of the marl terrace was to no purpose. So the archaeologists retired from the desert of Qumrân. The Bedouins continued the search. Being less logical, and perhaps less energetic, they attacked the marl caves in the terrace supporting Khirbet Qumrân. In the summer of 1952 they discovered a cave some two hundred yards from the Essene center, and three or four feet beneath the floor of the cave they came upon the matted and decayed remains of manuscripts.

The clandestine diggings of the Ta'âmireh were halted, fortunately, before the cave was exhausted. In the month of September (22-29), 1952, controlled excavations were undertaken in the remaining untouched levels of the cave, now known as Qumrân Cave IV. Caves V and VI were both found in conjunction with the discovery of Cave IV—Cave VI by Bedouins in the late summer, Cave V by scientists in September.[9] Both V and VI are significant but minor finds. In the spring of 1955, during the fourth campaign at Khirbet Qumrân, four additional new caves were located: VII-X. Like IV and V, these latter were found in the marl terrace near Khirbet Qumrân, carved out in antiquity for human use. Unlike the other caves, they had collapsed in ancient times as a result of erosion. Only a handful of fragments was recovered from all of them combined—enough to prove, only, that manuscripts had been deposited in them.[10]

In January, 1956, Bedouins detected another cave between Caves I and III, a little over a mile north of Khirbet Qumrân. Its entrance had collapsed, but by Herculean efforts the cave was opened and excavated. Their labors were thorough; when archaeologists halted the unauthorized digging, little more than Iron Age and Chalcolithic levels remained intact. Two splendidly preserved scrolls were found by Bedouins, and significant fragments of at least five other works by Bedouins and archaeologists. Cave XI thus rivals I and IV in importance.

In the meanwhile excavations at Khirbet Qumrân proceeded.[11] Both the chronology and the function of the site have been securely established. The people of the scrolls, no doubt the well-known Jewish party of the Essenes,[12] founded the settlement no later than the beginning of the first century B.C., probably in the reign of the Hasmonaean priest-king Alexander Jannaeus (103-76 B.C.). It flourished until the days of Herod the Great, when an earthquake, probably that of 31 B.C. recorded by Josephus, laid the community in ruins. After an apparent gap of some years, the community was re-established and prospered until the terrible days of the first Jewish revolt against Rome (A.D. 66-70). Actually the Essene center seems to have suffered violent destruction at the hands of the Tenth Roman Legion (Fretensis) in A.D. 68. After this date the Essenes disappear, leaving as witnesses to their life and faith only the ruins of their desert retreat, a few laconic notes in classical authors, and the litterings of manuscripts on the floors of caves.

II. The Qumrân Manuscripts

Of all the caves found to date, Caves I, IV, and XI are most significant. The remaining caves have each produced only some few ill-preserved fragments.[13]

From Cave I come the original seven manuscripts. These include the great Isaiah scroll (1QIsa^a), a commentary (pésher) on Habakkuk, and a Rule of the Community (1QS), all three published by the American Schools of Oriental Research in 1950-51.[14] Another group of three, published in 1954 by Hebrew University scholars, includes a second, fragmentary copy of Isaiah (1QIsa^b); a sectarian collection of psalms (hôdhāyôth); and an odd document called the War Between the Children of Light and the Children of Darkness (1QM)—a liturgy of Armageddon, so to speak.[15] A seventh scroll remains unpublished—the recently opened "Roll of the Patriarchs," an elaboration of

---

[9] A brief and handy chronology of the cave finds may be found in P. Benoit's introduction in "Le travail d'édition des fragments manuscrits de Qumrân," RB, 63 (1956), pp. 49 ff.

[10] See provisionally De Vaux, RB, 63 (1956), p. 74.

[11] See De Vaux, "Fouille au Khirbet Qumrân," RB, 60 (1953), pp. 83-106; Harding, "Khirbet Qumran and Wadi Murabba'at," PEQ, 84 (1952), pp. 104-9; De Vaux, "Fouilles au Kh. Qumrân. Rapport préliminaire sur la deuxième campagne," RB, 61 (1954), pp. 206-36; "Chronique archéologique: Khirbet Qumrân," RB, 61 (1954), pp. 567 f.; RB, 63 (1956), pp. 73 f.; E. Vogt, "Effossiones in Khirbet Qumrân," Biblica, 36 (1955), pp. 562-64 (with a diagram of ruins). Cf. J. A. Kelso, "The Archaeology of Qumran," JBL, 74 (1955), pp. 141-46; A. Parrot, "Les manuscrits de la Mer Morte: Le point de vue archéologique," RHPR, 35 (1955), pp. 61-67, etc.

[12] This will be discussed in more detail later, especially in note 69.

[13] See "Le travail d'édition des fragments . . . ," pp. 54-56.

[14] Burrows, Trever, Brownlee, eds., The Dead Sea Scrolls of St. Mark's Monastery; Vol. I, The Isaiah Manuscript and the Habakkuk Commentary (New Haven: American Schools of Oriental Research, 1950); Vol. II:2, Plates and Transcription of the Manual of Discipline (New Haven: American Schools of Oriental Research, 1951).

[15] Sukenik, op. cit.

Genesis in Aramaic.[16] In addition Cave I has produced fragments of some seventy documents, biblical and nonbiblical, published in 1955 in the first volume of *Discoveries in the Judean Desert*.

From Cave IV have come literally tens of thousands of fragments. It is by far the largest of the discoveries, and in many ways the most significant. Unlike the several documents of Caves I and XI, which are preserved relatively intact, the manuscripts of Cave IV are in an advanced state of decay. Many fragments are so brittle or friable that they can scarcely be cleaned with a camel's-hair brush. Most are warped, crinkled or shrunken, crusted with filth or soil chemicals, blackened by moisture and age. The problems of cleaning, flattening, and identifying them are formidable.[17] A single fragment may require many hours of a scholar's time before it receives initial identification and is placed in position in a slowly growing column of a manuscript. This is the ultimate in jigsaw puzzles.

A somewhat detailed sketch of the contents of Cave IV may be useful for the discussion to follow.[18] At the end of three years' labor, more than 330 manuscripts have been identified from this cave. This number can change. Thousands of fragments are still awaiting initial identification. Most of these belong, however, to known documents and presently will be read and fitted in place. Of the manuscripts identified thus far, more than ninety—slightly less than one third of the total—are biblical. All the books of the Hebrew canon are extant with the exception of the book of Esther.

The best preserved of the biblical lot, and in some ways the most important biblical document of all the finds, is a manuscript of Samuel designated as 4QSam[a].[19] The secret of its relatively good state of preservation is a backing of papyrus applied in antiquity, probably some half century or so after its copying. As is expected, both books of Samuel are copied on a single scroll. A total of forty-seven of the fifty-

seven columns of the original manuscript are preserved in fragmentary form. The importance of the document lies less in its bulk than in the unusual text it records. As we shall see, it belongs to a textual family known hitherto only in the old Greek translation, the so-called Septuagint. Even more extraordinary, in passages where Samuel and Chronicles overlap, this manuscript preserves a text much closer to the text of Samuel used by the author of Chronicles than to the traditional text of Samuel surviving from the Middle Ages.

At the other extreme is our single copy of the book of Chronicles from Qumrân. It is found on a three-inch strip of leather. Parts of six lines, two columns, are preserved, but only four complete words are legible!

A special category among the biblical documents is a group written in Paleo-Hebrew script.[20] These include five Pentateuchal manuscripts and some fragments of Job. Especially interesting is a superb specimen of Exodus which presents a text type related to the Samaritan recension of Exodus.[21]

The biblical scrolls from Qumrân span in date nearly three centuries. Our earliest scrolls can be dated no later than about 200 B.C. No doubt these were master scrolls imported into the community at its founding. The heavy majority, however (including all the sectarian scrolls), date to the first centuries before and after the beginning of the Christian Era, the series terminating with the death of the community center in A.D. 68.[22]

[16] This roll had been given preliminary identification as the Apocalypse of Lamech (cf. Trever, "Identification of the Aramaic Fourth Scroll from 'Ain Feshkha," *BASOR*, 115 [Oct., 1949], pp. 8-10; and *Discoveries in the Judaean Desert*, I, 86 f.). The announcement of the preliminary decipherment of the roll was made on Feb. 7, 1956. Cf. *BA*, 19 (1956), pp. 22-24.

[17] Cf. the description of the process of editing the fragments in "Le travail d'édition . . . ," pp. 52 ff.

[18] See Cross, "A Report on the Biblical Fragments of Cave Four in Wâdī Qumrân," *BASOR*, 141 (Feb., 1956), pp. 9-13; "Le travail d'édition . . . ," pp. 56-67.

[19] Fragments of this MS recovered in the controlled excavation of Cave IV by Harding and De Vaux have been given preliminary publication in Cross, "A New Qumran Biblical Fragment Related to the Original Hebrew Underlying the Septuagint," *BASOR*, 132 (Dec., 1953), pp. 15-26.

[20] This script, sometimes incorrectly called "Phoenician" or "Samaritan," derives from the old pre-Exilic Hebrew script. Apparently it survived as a book hand and enjoyed a renascence in the period of Maccabean nationalism and archaism. In any case, at Qumrân it appears in documents contemporary with the Jewish hand, a derivative of the official Aramaic cursive of the late Persian Empire. The Samaritan character is a descendant of the Paleo-Hebrew script of the Hasmonaean period.

[21] See P. W. Skehan, "Exodus in the Samaritan Recension from Qumran," *JBL*, 74 (1955), pp. 182-87.

[22] See Cross, "The Oldest Manuscripts from Qumran," *JBL*, 74 (1955), pp. 147-72, where references may be found to literature on the paleography of the Jewish script in the period in question. The broad lines of Jewish paleography were securely established by W. F. Albright as early as 1937. Since the discovery of the Qumrân, Murabba'ât, and related documents, scholars have had a repletion of data with which to reconstruct an extremely accurate typological sequence of the Hebrew scripts. Thanks to MSS in other scripts (notably Greek) found in several series of caves, including Cave IV, and documents of the first two centuries A.D. with date formulas affixed, as well as closely dated new and old funerary inscriptions, ostraca, and the like, the absolute chronology of the sequence datings has become quite precise. Paleography has been and remains the most precise means of dating the Qumrân scrolls; its dates in no case can be more than a century off, and dates within fifty years are regularly possible.

At the same time other lines of evidence for dating the scrolls have strengthened and become sure with the

Another large portion of Cave IV documents belongs to the category of Apocryphal and Pseudepigraphical works in Hebrew and Aramaic: Tobit (and Ecclesiasticus, 2Q), Jubilees, the Psalms of Joshua, a pseudo-Jeremianic work, sources of the Testaments of the Twelve Patriarchs,[23] and Enoch are examples. There is another lot of specifically sectarian works, though this category overlaps with the former. In this group fall the various recensions of the Rule of the Community, best known from Cave I; the Damascus Document (CDC); and various books too numerous to list in detail, containing laws, liturgies, prayers, hymns, and wisdom of the Essenes.[24] Three categories of this group have

special interest and may be singled out. There are the biblical "commentaries," including works on Isaiah, Hosea, Psalms, and Nahum (cf. Micah and Habakkuk, 1Q). The commentary on Nahum (4QpNah) is remarkable because of its direct historical allusions to known historical figures,[25] the first such allusions among the many documents from Qumrân. The second category is composed of the documents in two cryptic scripts whose existence at Qumrân recalls the various traditions of the esoteric character of Essene teaching. One script ("A") was readily deciphered by J. T. Milik in the summer of 1954; the other should occasion no difficulty if ever sufficient connected text comes to hand. The contents are not startling, but belong to well-known categories of literature at Qumrân. One cryptic work is named, for example, the "Exposition [*midhrash*] of the Book of Moses."

Finally there is a series of most intriguing calendrical works found at Qumrân, relating to the Zodiac, to the calculation of feast days, the courses (*mishmārôth*) of the priests, and so on. Already the calendrical materials found in published sectarian works have enabled scholars to solve a number of long-standing problems related to the solar calendar used in Jubilees and Enoch; it now appears that this calendar was at home among the Essenes and that it is reflected in certain of the primitive Christian traditions.[26]

III. Other Discoveries

Before turning to the bearing of the discoveries at Qumrân on biblical studies, brief mention needs to be made of other series of finds in the southern desert of Judah. While the latter discoveries are of later date for the most part, stemming from Jewish fugitives unrelated to the quasi-monastic Essenes, they complement the finds at Qumrân, especially in furnishing data for the history of the Old Testament text and versions.

In the winter of 1951 and the early spring of 1952, a group of gargantuan caves in the Wâdī Murabbaʿât were located and excavated, at first by the indefatigable Taʿâmireh tribesmen, later by archaeologists.[27] Among the most important

development of the finds and their study. The archaeological data from both the caves and the community center have become unambiguous. There is no question of separating the deposit in the caves which cluster around the ruin from the Essene occupation of the site itself. Internal data, while not as clear cut as dating criteria in detail, since subjective elements enter more easily into their analysis, nevertheless are extremely strong in their cumulative effect. Certain of the sectarian works belonging to the genre of commentaries (*pᵉshārîm*) are for the most part autographs (see Cross, "Qumran Cave I," *JBL*, 75 [1956], pp. 121-25), and characteristically allude to events contemporary with the community as fulfillment of ancient prophecy. Most of these allusions best fit the first century B.C., and a few transparently so (cf. 4QpNah in J. M. Allegro, "Further Light on the History of the Qumran Sect," *JBL*, 75 [1956], pp. 89-95, where "[Deme]trius, king of Greece" [i.e., Demetrius III, *Eukairos*] is named, and the wholesale crucifixion of Jews by Alexander Jannaeus is mentioned). Again, the variety of Hebrew textual traditions at home at Qumrân is without witness after the first century A.D.; the *wholesale* survival of such texts after the fixing of the authoritative proto-M.T., including those in the condemned Paleo-Hebrew script, is scarcely plausible. Again, Qumrân is producing a variety of lost or condemned works: sources of Enoch and the Testaments of the Twelve Patriarchs, a source of Daniel, and so on. In such variety they must stem from pre-Christian times. Coincidental survival as an explanation becomes less plausible with each new work of this kind. All this is not to mention the theological structure and *Weltbild* of the sectarian scrolls; these have no real parallels in Judaism after primitive Christian times. Nor is it to remark the post-biblical, pre-rabbinic position of the Hebrew and Aramaic dialects in which most of the sectarian documents are written (cf. S. Lieberman, "Light on the Cave Scrolls from Rabbinic Sources," *PAAJR*, 20 [1951], p. 404). Only one document at Qumrân anticipates a developed Mishnaic morphology and idiom; the Aramaic at Qumrân, like that of Daniel, is closely affiliated with the older Empire Aramaic rather than with later Palestinian Aramaic. The orthography of the documents, in many ways unusual, nevertheless conforms to the predictions made by specialists in Semitic epigraphy before the discovery.

Each set of data, paleographical, archaeological, internal, is sufficient to establish independently the early date of the scrolls. In combination they fix the late pre-Christian date of the Qumrân corpus with certainty.

[23] See Milik, "Le Testament de Lévi en araméen. Fragment de la grotte 4 de Qumrân," *RB*, 62 (1955), pp. 398-406.

[24] A relatively complete catalogue of the documents of Cave IV, together with brief descriptive notices, may be

found in the reports of the international staff members, "Le travail d'édition des fragments . . . ," pp. 56-67.

[25] Cf. note 22.

[26] Barthélemy, "Notes en marge de publications récentes sur les manuscrits de Qumran," *RB*, 59 (1952), pp. 187-218, especially pp. 200 ff.; A. Jaubert, "Le calendrier des Jubilés et de la secte de Qumran. Ses origines bibliques," *VT*, 3 (1953), pp. 250-64; J. Morgenstern, "The Calendar of the Book of Jubilees, Its Origin and Character," *VT*, 5 (1955), pp. 34-76; Jaubert, "La date de la dernière Cène," *RHR*, 146 (1954), pp. 140-73. Cf. Vogt, "Antiquum kalendarium sacerdotale," *Biblica*, 36 (1955), pp. 403-8; "Dies ultimae coenae Domini," *ibid.*, pp. 408-13.

[27] For details of the discovery and excavation, and a partial catalogue of the finds, see De Vaux, "Les grottes

of the documents recovered was a series of biblical fragments from the late first and early second centuries A.D. from a cache belonging, apparently, to fleeing remnants of the army of Bar Cocheba, the pseudo Messiah who led second Jewish revolt (A.D. 132-35). Actually the most important of the Murabba'ât finds, a magnificent scroll of the minor prophets from the second century A.D., came to light in 1955. The preserved portion of the manuscript extends from the middle of Joel to the beginning of Zechariah, including (in the traditional order) Amos, Obadiah, Jonah, Micah, Nahum, Habakkuk, Zephaniah, and Haggai. Four columns are preserved almost intact.

A second group of documents comes from an undesignated provenience. Like Murabba'ât, the bulk of its documents must be attributed to the era between the two Jewish revolts against Rome.[28] The most important of these, for our purposes at least, is a manuscript of the minor prophets in Greek, a lost recension of the Septuagint. When combined with three "standard" Septuagint manuscripts from Cave IV, Qumrân,[29] this newly found recension will place textual critics in a much improved position to solve certain problems of the history of the text of the Septuagint.[30]

[de Murabba'at et leurs documents," *RB*, 60 (1953), pp. 245-67; Harding, "Khirbet Qumran and Wady Murabba'at," *PEQ*, 84 (1952), pp 104-9; Cross, "The Manuscripts of the Dead Sea Caves," *BA*, 17 (1954), pp. 8-12. Several texts have been given preliminary publication: De Vaux, "Quelques textes hébreux de Murabba'at," *RB*, 60 (1953), pp. 268-75; Milik, "Une lettre de Siméon Bar Kokheba," *ibid.*, pp. 276-94. For recent literature on the last-mentioned text, see Cross, "La lettre de Siméon Ben Kosba," *RB*, 63 (1956), pp. 45-48. The reports of the excavation in Wâdî Murabba'ât, together with the publication of the texts, compose the second volume of *Discoveries in the Judaean Desert*.

[28] The documents were purchased from Bedouins in August, 1952. Presumably the caves from which they came were discovered during the summer of that year. Several of the texts of the find have been published together with brief notices on the find as a whole: Barthélemy, "Redécouverte d'un chaînon manquant de l'histoire de la Septante," *RB*, 60 (1953), pp. 18-29; J. Starcky, "Un contrat nabatéen sur papyrus," *RB*, 60 (1953), pp. 11-181; Milik, "Un contrat juif de l'an 134 après J.-C," *RB*, 60 (1953), pp. 182-90.

[29] Qumrân IV has produced leather fragments of two MSS of the LXX—one of Leviticus, the other of Numbers. A third MS, represented by papyrus fragments, is a second exemplar of Leviticus. These documents are probably to be dated in the first century B.C. paleographically; in any case, none can be later than the early first century of our era. There is no doubt that they belong to the common LXX tradition. This is noteworthy inasmuch as they derive from a Jewish community in Palestine. Otherwise only two fragmentary papyri of comparable age are known, both of Egyptian provenience. I am indebted to Patrick W. Skehan for permitting me to read in manuscript his treatment of the Qumrân LXX fragments, and to draw upon it here.

[30] In addition to Barthélemy's preliminary publication (see note 28), cf. Vogt, "Fragmenta prophetarum mino-

IV. Contributions to Old Testament Studies

The most direct and obvious contribution of the Qumrân manuscripts is to the field of Old Testament textual studies.

At the outset it may be noted that the new scrolls give evidence of the antiquity of the type of textual tradition which has survived in the form of the traditional Hebrew Bible.[31] Again, the scrolls preserve many new readings, some of which will appear in any future biblical translation produced by serious scholars. Nevertheless, the textual scholar finds the chief interest of the scrolls neither in their testimony to the age of our received text nor in their individual readings as such. The real importance of the biblical scrolls lies in the data they yield for the reconstruction of the textual history of the Old Testament.

To make this point clear, perhaps it will be useful to glance backward at the state of textual studies before the coming of the Qumrân and Murabba'ât scrolls.

A. The Search for the Pre-Rabbinic Text.—The eighteenth and nineteenth centuries witnessed the assiduous collection and study of extant Hebrew manuscripts, together with the ancient versions into which the Hebrew had been translated. These studies led to the first systematic reconstructions of the history of the Old Testament text. The culmination of this stage of study is found in the works of Paul de Lagarde, who stated categorically that all medieval Hebrew manuscripts were descended from a common ancestor, a single master scroll. This official text, according to Lagarde, could be dated no later than the first century of the

[rum Deserti Iuda," *Biblica*, 34 (1953), pp. 423-26; J. W. Wevers, "Septuaginta-Forschungen I," *Theologische Rundschau*, 22 (1954), pp. 136-38; K. Stendahl, *The School of Matthew* (Copenhagen: Einar Munksgaard Forlag, 1954), pp. 177-80; Cross, "The Manuscripts . . . ," pp. 12 f.; P. Kahle, "Der gegenwärtige Stand der Erforschung der in Palästina neu gefundenen hebräischen Handschriften. 27. Die im August 1952 entdeckte Lederrolle mit dem griechische Text der kleinen Propheten und das Problem der Septuaginta," *TLZ*, 79 (1954), pp. 82-94; P. Katz, "Septuagintal Studies in the Mid-Century," in *The Background of the New Testament and Its Eschatology*, W. D. Davies and D. Daube, eds. (Cambridge: Cambridge University Press, 1956), pp. 206-8.

Mention might be made also of the late Byzantine and early Arabic finds from the cisterns of Khirbet Mird (ancient Hyrcania) by Bedouins in the summer of 1952. For references to the discoveries and the subsequent expedition of the Mission Archéologique Belge de Louvain in the spring of 1953, see Milik, "Une inscription et une lettre en araméen christo-palestinien," *RB*, 60 (1953), pp. 526-39, especially pp. 526 f.; De Vaux, "Fouille au Khirbet Qumrân," *ibid.*, p. 85; and Cross, "The Manuscripts . . . ," *BA*, 17 (1954), p. 12.

[31] That is to say, a proto-Masoretic recension for certain books is present at Qumrân. As we shall see, this tradition was chosen by the rabbis, who after further recensional activity established the base of the *textus receptus*, the traditional consonantal text.

Christian Era. That is, these studies seemed to establish that about A.D. 100, in the days of Akiba, the rabbis had fixed an authoritative Hebrew text, chosen arbitrarily from the more or less fluid textual traditions alive in the pre-Christian period, and that this official text in effect destroyed all variant lines of tradition in normative Judaism.[32] Old Testament textual criticism found itself at an impasse.

There were only a few crevices in the recen-

[32] See Lagarde, *Anmerkungen zur griechischen Übersetzung der Proverbien* (Leipzig, 1863). Cf. Reider, *Prolegomena to a Greek-Hebrew and Hebrew-Greek Index to Aquila* (Philadelphia: Dropsie College, 1916), pp. 81 ff.; H. M. Orlinsky, *On the Present State of Proto-Septuagint Studies* (New Haven: American Oriental Society, 1941), pp. 81-91, especially p. 84 and references; R. H. Pfeiffer, *Introduction to the Old Testament* (New York: Harper & Bros., 1941), pp. 78-79; B. J. Roberts, *The Old Testament Text and Versions* (Cardiff: University of Wales Press, 1951), pp. 23-29.

Attacks on Lagarde's position show at most that he overstates his case. All medieval MSS stem from a single, narrow, recensional base. This is evidenced not only by the early, pre-Tiberian MSS from the Cairo Geniza, but decisively now by the appearance of the Murabba'ât fragments, especially the great minor prophets scroll (not to be confused with Barthélemy's *Greek* recension). Medieval variants, whether in biblical MSS or in rabbinic texts (see Aptowitzer, *Das Schriftwort in der Rabbinischen Literature* [*Sitzungsberichte der Kais. Akad. der Wiss. in Wien*. Phil.-Hist. Klasse Bd. 153:6, 1906; 160:7, 1908], and H. L. Strack, *Prolegomena critica in Vetus Testamentum hebraicum* [Leipzig: J. C. Hinrichs, 1873]), are for the most part merely orthographic, or secondary, a witness to subsequent development of variant readings which for a number of reasons may coincide with older witnesses, the LXX, etc. In the Targums, Aquila, and Jerome, some genuine survivals of readings which predate the official recension of *ca.* A.D. 100 are expected, since in each case older materials were used alongside the new standard text.

Part of the difficulty arises from differing presuppositions as to the state of the Hebrew text in the pre-Christian period. For those who presume an extremely conservative development of the Hebrew textual tradition, the variants of the post-Akiba period loom large. For those who suppose that the pre-Christian period was marked by a Hebrew text which exhibited widely different recensional traditions, the medieval variants appear to be negligible. As we shall see, the pre-Christian Hebrew text exhibits *recensional* variation which differs *toto caelo* from the variation exhibited after the promulgation of the official Hebrew (consonantal) text.

The general reaction against Lagardian positions, therefore, represented today especially by the Kahle-Sperber school (cf. Kahle, "Untersuchungen zur Geschichte des Pentateuchtextes," *TSK* 88 [1915], pp. 432-39), has gone much too far. The text established about A.D. 100 appears to be the culmination of rabbinic recensional activity which began perhaps a century or more earlier, to judge from the Qumran texts (cf. Cross, "A New Qumran Biblical Fragment Related to the Original Hebrew underlying the Septuagint," *BASOR*, 132 [Dec., 1953], p. 24, note 36). Barthélemy's Greek recension of the LXX is evidence of this early trend. There is no doubt that our copy dates at the latest from the first century A.D., and preferably about the turn of the Christian Era, and represents an early attempt *to revise the LXX* into conformity with proto-M.T. (On the dating see Barthélemy, *op. cit.*, p. 19; and C. H. Roberts quoted

sional wall constructed by the promulgation of a standard text. The Pentateuch of the Samaritans, having been transmitted along different channels, preserved an alternate form of the text for the Torah.[33] Actually, however, the Samaritan provided little help toward reconstructing the early history of the Hebrew text. This was due not only to its restricted scope, but also to certain confusions which attended its early study. Generally it was presumed to be an extremely early branch of tradition separating from the main Jewish line at the time of the early Samaritan rift. In fact, its text is a relatively late branch, going back at earliest to Hasmonaean times.[34] That this was the case has long been likely on historical grounds. It is now clear both on paleographical grounds—the Samaritan script is a derivative of the Paleo-Hebrew script which was revived or became resurgent in the Maccabean era of nationalistic archaism—and on orthographic grounds.[35] The text type found in the Samaritan is difficult to categorize. On the one hand, it stands very close to the proto-Masoretic text. Yet it has a large number of readings in agreement with the Septuagint. Again, it is replete with inferior readings —expansion, transposition, insertion of parallels from other passages or books, readings of a type which must have been introduced at a fairly early date when the text was relatively fluid. They are not, in all probability, the result

by Kahle, ". . . Die im August 1952 entdeckte Lederrolle . . . ," *TLZ*, 79 [1954], col. 81). It may be noted that in his article devoted precisely to this new recension, Kahle fails to deal with this point, that the scroll is a Jewish revision, *not* translation, which takes the pre-Christian LXX as its base. This is most curious, since this is easily the most significant characteristic of this text, as well as most damaging evidence against Kahle's theories of LXX origins.

The Murabba'ât texts certify that the consonantal base of the *textus receptus* had been fixed finally by the days of the second revolt, and that Lagarde was, after all, right in principle. Indeed, the evidence from Murabba'ât indicates that even the *principles* of orthographic practice (use of vowel letters, *matres lectionis*) became fixed at this time. While minor orthographic variations appear, as well as a few variants of other types, they are no more significant than variants in Tiberian Masoretic MSS. The relatively fluid orthographic practice of the Hasmonaean and Herodian periods known from Qumrân has vanished, once for all.

[33] A non-M.T. type also appears in some of the Apocryphal and Pseudepigraphical works, which, being rejected by rabbinic Judaism, did not undergo revision. Cf. Kahle, "Untersuchungen . . . ," and *The Cairo Geniza* (London: Oxford University Press, 1947), pp. 147-48.

[34] Cf. Cross, "A Report on the Biblical Fragments of Cave Four . . . ," p. 12, note 5a. Contrast Kahle, "Untersuchungen . . ." and Roberts, *The Old Testament Text and Versions*, pp. 188-96.

[35] That is, Samaritan orthography reflects neither the restricted use of *matres lectionis* characteristic of the third century B.C. and earlier, nor the revised spelling principles of the rabbinic text. Rather, it exhibits the char-

of specifically Samaritan recensional activity.[36] In any case, the Samaritan Pentateuch has been only of limited use in the task of recovering a more primitive form of the Hebrew text of the Old Testament.

The best hope for a break-through into the unknown era before the promulgation of the official textual recension of the rabbis lay in the Septuagint, the standard Greek Old Testament of the early church, which, according to tradition, traced its lineage to an Alexandrian translation of the third–second centuries B.C. By reconstructing the Hebrew underlying this antique version, the textual critic might perhaps gain detailed knowledge of the development of the early text, enabling him thereby to reconstruct a more nearly original form of the Hebrew Bible.

This was not an easy path to the pre-rabbinic Bible. Two difficult and complex problems required resolution before the Septuagint could be used confidently to reconstruct an old Hebrew text type. In the first place, Septuagint scholars had to establish the original form of the Old Greek translation (the proto-Septuagint) out of a maze of manuscripts belonging to its Christian recensions, and out of its daughter versions. This required first of all the grouping of the manuscripts, the versions, and citations in ancient authors into families and then the establishment of the text types belonging to the recensions of the Septuagint known, especially, from Jerome: the Hesychian (Egyptian), Lucianic (Syrian), and Hexaplaric (Palestinian), as well as unknown recensions to be detected by inductive critical procedures. The task was further involved by the presence of contamination in the transmission of the Septuagint by later Jewish Greek texts which had been successively revised back into conformity with the developing Hebrew text. Such recensions include the Barthélemy text, probably identical with the Quinta of the Hexapla, which revises the Septuagint by a late pre-Christian Hebrew text (closely allied with the proto-Masoretic tradition), and especially the texts of Theodotion and Aquila, both of which appear to be based on the earlier Jewish recension, revising it to conform to the authoritative Hebrew text, which emerged about A.D. 100.[37]

The task of supplying the materials from which the proto-Septuagint text can be recovered is by no means completed. Progress has been made in the years since Lagarde initiated his program, despite pauses to solve unexpected complexities, and occasional loss of faith by some in the very existence of a proto-Septuagint which consisted of more than a congeries of distinct and competing Greek translations. The still incomplete edition of the Larger Cambridge Septuagint, the continuing publication of the great Göttingen edition of the Septuagint, and the publication of individual studies of which Margolis' *The Book of Joshua in Greek* is the outstanding example, are major advances. Nevertheless, the determination of the text of the Septuagint in a given Old Testament passage is one of the most exacting tasks of the biblical scholar, and in some portions of the Old Testament, fortunately decreasing steadily in extent, it remains a precarious task at best.

If we can presume that we know what the text of the Septuagint is, a second formidable difficulty appears when the Septuagint comes to be used as a witness to the archaic Hebrew text. Does the Septuagint in a given passage witness to an ancient Hebrew text at variance with the *textus receptus,* or are its divergent readings to be explained away as due to translation procedures? Does the Septuagint reflect in distorted form the *Hebraica veritas* as assumed by Origen and Jerome as well as ancient Jewish scholars, or does it often testify in faithful fashion to a different Hebrew text from the one we know?

These questions gave rise to sharp debate in the nineteenth century. The issue was joined between supporters of the antiquity and fidelity of the Masoretic tradition who would explain away the apparently divergent readings of the

acteristic full orthography of the Maccabean and especially the Hasmonaean eras. Cf. Cross, "The Oldest Manuscripts from Qumran," p. 165.

[36] Cf. Kahle, "Untersuchungen . . . ."

[37] The above description is, of course, oversimple. The number of Jewish revisions of the LXX may be larger than the present evidence suggests, and the detailed relationships between such and the "Three" (Theodotion, Aquila, and Symmachus) may be more complex than is suggested by first study. The problems of proto-Lucian, proto-Theodotion, Rahlfs and Katz's "R" recension, etc., will require complete re-examination in light of the new

Greek data from Qumrân, and the "undesignated provenience," as well as the new Hebrew texts from these finds and from Murabbaʿât.

All the new evidence seems to suggest that these problems will be solved in the general framework of the proto-LXX hypothesis formulated by Lagarde and developed by Rahlfs, Montgomery, Margolis, and in the present generation by Orlinsky, Katz, and especially Ziegler. That is to say, the remnants of Greek texts at variance with the standard LXX, which appear to be pre-Hexaplaric in date, are now most easily explained as surviving from Jewish revision(s) of the LXX. Not only do we now possess such a recension, but we possess the various Hebrew text types reflected by it, by the "Three," and, indeed, by the proto-LXX itself.

For recent discussions of the proto-LXX question, see Orlinsky, *op. cit.* (cf. "The Septuagint—Its Use in Textual Criticism," *BA,* 9 [1946], pp. 21-34); "Current Progress and Problems in Septuagint Research," in *The Study of the Bible Today and Tomorrow,* ed. H. R. Willoughby (Chicago: University of Chicago Press, 1947); Katz, "Septuagintal Studies in the Mid-Century . . ."; "Das Problem des Urtextes der Septuaginta," *ThZ,* 5 (1949), pp. 1-24; Wevers, "Septuaginta Forschungen . . ."; Kahle, *The Cairo Geniza,* chap. ii:2; Roberts, *Old Testament Text . . .* , pp. 104-19.

Septuagint, and those who insisted on laying their Septuagint side by side with the traditional Hebrew Bible—as if the two were variant manuscripts which by comparison could be forced to yield a text superior to both. On the side of the medieval Hebrew text stood such figures as Fränkel and Löhr; in support of the importance of the Old Greek for textual criticism stood Thenius, Lagarde, and the master, Julius Wellhausen. The debate persists into the twentieth century. Indeed, the polemic against the trustworthiness of the Septuagint translators and the usefulness of their version as a witness to the pre-Masoretic text had come close to winning the day. How can the critic be sure, said this school of thought, that when the Greek translator departs radically from the received text, the Hebrew manuscript from which he translated also deviates? Could not these deviations be caused by bad translation techniques? Was the Greek a literal and faithful translation of its *Vorlage*? Or was it full of error, paraphrasing, and arbitrary changes? Increasingly scholars have looked upon the Septuagint with a jaundiced eye, and following the lead especially of H. S. Nyberg, a new conservative respect for the medieval Hebrew text has gained sway.[38]

B. Textual Traditions at Qumrân.—Then with the discovery of the Qumrân scrolls we were suddenly catapulted over the alleged barrier into the forbidden land. The great Isaiah scroll of Cave I was published first. It proved rather an anticlimax. While it conserved thousands of variant readings, few of its readings were significant, and even fewer superior to the traditional readings. It seemed that the defenders of the traditional Hebrew Bible were vindicated, and that the work of the rabbis in preparing the official text current in the second century A.D. had had negligible effect on the history of textual transmission. Certainly it was true that the text of Isaiah preserved in the Masorah was based on an extremely early textual type, already at home in Palestine in the late second century B.C.[39]

[38] Cf. Nyberg, "Das textkritische Problem des Alten Testaments am Hoseabuche demonstriert," *ZAW*, 52 (1934), pp. 241-54; *Studien zum Hoseabuche* (Uppsala: Almqvist & Wiksells, 1935); P. A. H. de Boer, *Research into the Text of 1 Samuel I-XVI* (Amsterdam: H. J. Paris, 1938), and sequent studies in *Oudtestamentische Studiën*, I (1942) and VI (1949). Cf. the literature, especially that of the German school discussed by Wevers, "Septuaginta-Forschungen. II. Die Septuaginta als Übersetzungsurkunde," *Theologische Rundschau*, 22 (1954), pp. 171-90.

[39] The literature on the Isaiah scroll (1QIsaᵃ) is quite extensive. The most recent discussion of the text of Isaiah at Qumrân is that of Skehan, "The Text of Isaias at Qumran," *CBQ*, 8 (1955), pp. 38-43. A general discussion may be found in Burrows, *The Dead Sea Scrolls*, pp. 301-15, and full bibliographical notes for textual studies of the early finds may be found in his bibliography, pp.

There was one ambiguity in this construction of the evidence. Isaiah in the Septuagint is not one of those books where traditional renderings and those of the Greek translation clash. Isaiah in Greek appears to have been translated from a manuscript quite close to the proto-Masoretic tradition. However, it was difficult to be certain, since the translation of Isaiah is among the poorest in the Greek Bible.[40] What was needed was a group of manuscripts from other biblical books where the Septuagint translation was good, where in places it was extremely literal when it agreed with Masoretic readings, but where it branched radically from this later standard text. This was the case, for example, in the historical books, especially in Joshua and Samuel. It is also true of Jeremiah, where the Septuagint omits or changes the order of large sections of material. Ideally, of course, the scholar needs samplings from the whole Old Testament in order to reconstruct a valid history of its transmission.

The recovery of nearly a hundred biblical scrolls from Cave IV came, therefore, as incredibly good fortune. Here at last was the basis for sampling the textual types extant in virtually every book of the Old Testament. Here was a substantial basis for the establishment of the archaic, pre-Masoretic history of the Hebrew Bible. Moreover, thanks to the Murabba'ât texts, which extend the series from Qumrân down into the second century B.C., we have direct evidence for the first time as to just what happened to the text in the crucial era before, during, and after the time when the official text was fixed.

The results were surprising. We were suddenly in a new world in which sharply differing textual traditions lived side by side.

Initial study was directed to the historical books, especially to Samuel.[41] The text of Samuel contained in the three scrolls from Cave IV is widely at variance with that of the traditional Masoretic Bible; it follows systematically the rendering of the Septuagint of Samuel.[42] For example, in the few published fragments of the archaic Samuel text (4QSamᵇ), there are some thirteen readings in which the Qumrân text agrees with the Greek against the readings of

420-35. Of the older studies, noteworthy are the contributions of Baumgartner, Beegle, Hempel, Kahle, Loewinger, Milik, and Orlinsky. More recent text-critical studies of Qumrân materials will be noted below.

[40] See J. Ziegler, *Untersuchungen zur Septuaginta des Buches Isaias* (Münster i. W.: Aschendorffs, 1934).

[41] Cross, "A New Qumran Biblical Fragment . . . ," pp. 15-26; "The Oldest Manuscripts from Qumran," pp. 165-72.

[42] The older Samuel MS (4QSamᵇ) often preserves a text superior to both the LXX and Hebrew *textus receptus*. A translation of one such passage may be found in Cross, "The Oldest Manuscripts from Qumran," p. 171.

the received text, four readings in which the Qumrân text agrees with the traditional text against the Septuagint. The ratio of readings in agreement with the Septuagint against the Masoretic text is even higher in the large Samuel manuscript (4QSam[a]).[43]

Other historical books (Joshua and Kings) follow suit, insofar as they are preserved, in presenting the tradition of the Septuagint. It now becomes clear, at least in these books, that the Septuagint's divergent text was due less to "translation idiosyncrasies" than to the type of text which it translated. These manuscripts establish once for all that in the historical books the Septuagint translators faithfully and with extreme literalness reproduce their Hebrew *Vorlage*.[44] And this means that the Septuagint of the historical books must be resurrected as a primary tool of the Old Testament critic. This is a repudiation of much of the textual theory and method developed and applied to the Hebrew text of Samuel during the last generation.[45]

All this does not mean that the Septuagint in the historical books presents a text which is *necessarily* superior to the Masoretic text. The question of which witness is superior is another problem to be decided in individual readings. It does mean that the Septuagint reflects accurately a Hebrew textual tradition at home in Egypt in the third–second centuries B.C., and that, thanks to the Qumrân manuscripts, we have the means to control its evidence.[46]

[43] Cf. Cross, "A New Qumran Biblical Fragment . . . ," *passim;* and Vogt, "Textus praemasoreticus ex Qumran," *Biblica,* 35 (1954), pp. 263-66.

[44] The literalness of the LXX of Samuel is not, of course, the mechanical and tortured literalness of Aquila. However, in his translation the translator systematically reflects shifts of tense, the presence or absence of the article, and so on, so far as Greek idiom permits, and often when it does not. Study of the method of the translator over against the Qumrân text soon teaches one his technique, so that from his translation his *Vorlage* can be predicted with high accuracy. Save for a very few poetic passages (e.g., the Song of Hannah) where the Greek text probably had a prehistory, paraphrasing is virtually absent from the LXX of Samuel, and no evidence is to be found of conscious changes made by the translator on theological or otherwise tendentious grounds.

[45] Among the studies of the text of Samuel, for example, that which needs least revision in light of the new evidence is Wellhausen's *Der Text der Bücher Samuelis,* published in 1871!

[46] In fact, comparative studies of the text of Samuel are tending to indicate that the M.T. here is based on an extremely narrow, and often inferior, textual recension. Its text is often defective as the result of systematic revision. Textual scholars are accustomed to the fact that a *textus receptus* is normally a conflate text. The reverse is true of Samuel; it is a text characterized by frequent and extensive haplography. On the other hand, the Hebrew underlying the LXX is a full text, sometimes conflate, frequently original. That the two texts stand at opposite poles in their textual develop-

The state of the text in other books of the Old Testament is a more complicated one. Among no fewer than thirty Pentateuchal manuscripts from Cave IV, Qumrân, at least three sharply defined textual traditions persist.[47] The majority of the texts are allied closely with the proto-Masoretic tradition. However, the text type underlying the Septuagint is well represented. For example, there is the Deuteronomy manuscript of which fragments of Deuteronomy 32 were published by Skehan. It preserves a text derivative from the Hebrew recension underlying the Septuagint in a passage where the *textus receptus* is defective, so that by comparison of the three texts, a text superior to any one of the witnesses may be reconstructed.[48]

ment is a most fortunate circumstance for the critic who wishes to reconstruct their common ancestor and thereby press back to an extremely early form of the Hebrew text.

[47] Cf. Cross, "A Report on the Biblical Fragments of Cave Four . . . ," p. 12; "Le travail d'édition . . . ," p. 56.

[48] Skehan, "A Fragment of the 'Song of Moses' (Deut. 32) from Qumran," *BASOR,* 136 (Dec., 1954), pp. 12-15; cf. Albright, "New Light on Early Recensions of the Hebrew Bible," *BASOR,* 140 (Dec., 1955), p. 32, note 27.

The textual history of Deut. 32:32 in 4Q, the LXX, and the M.T. can be diagramed as follows, the reconstructed portions being indicated by square brackets:

ORIGINAL TEXT

הרנינו שמים עמו	והבו עוז (?) לו בני אלהים
כי דם בניו יקום	וכפר אדמת עמו

Shout for joy, O heavens, before him;
    And ascribe might to him, O sons of God;
For he avenges the blood of his children,
    And purges the people's land.

PROTO-M.T.

הרנינו [שמים עמו	והבו עוז (?) לו בני אלהים
הרנינו] גוים עמו	כי דם { עבדיו } יקום
Etc.	

Shout for joy, [O heavens, before him,
    And ascribe might to him, O sons of God;
Shout for joy], O nations, { for his people };
    For he avenges the blood of his { servants, }
Etc.

PROTO-4Q DEUTERONOMY

הרנינו שמים עמו	[והבו עוז (?) לו בני אלהים
הרנינו גוים עמו]	והשתחוו לו כל אלהים
כי דם בניו יקום	Etc.

Shout for joy, O heavens, before him,
    [And ascribe might to him, O sons of God;
Shout for joy, O nations, before him,]
    And bow down to him, all ye divine ones;
For he avenges the blood of his children,
Etc.

The following points may be observed in vs. 43a. The corruption of the M.T. is best explained on the basis of a text in which one doublet, הרנינו שמים עמו (Shout for joy, O heavens, before him) and הרנינו גוים עמו (Shout for joy, O nations, { for his people }), but only this doublet appears. As pointed out to me by John Strugnell, the LXX μετὰ τοῦ λαοῦ αυτοῦ is merely a double rendering of

One Exodus manuscript (4QExᵃ) belongs systematically to the Egyptian textual tradition reflected in the Septuagint, though at points it offers a more consistent form of this tradition than the Septuagint itself. For example, in the first five verses of this manuscript no fewer than eight variants are found. Five agree with the Septuagint; three point to an Egyptian text form of the same tradition as the Septuagint, but probably superior to that used by the translator; none agrees with the Masoretic text against the Septuagint.[49]

There are also manuscripts from Cave IV which ally themselves with that line of tradition of which the Samaritan is a collateral witness. One of these is a Paleo-Hebrew Exodus published by Skehan.[50] Another unpublished example is a Numbers manuscript in Jewish ("square") script (4QNumᵇ).[51] This latter manuscript, however, is by no means a simple or consistent witness to the Samaritan recension, or even to the proto-Samaritan recension. While it contains expansions characteristic of this recension,[52] and regularly follows less striking

Samaritan variants, its contacts with the Septuagint tradition are even more striking. To be sure, the standard Samaritan text frequently agrees with the text underlying the Greek; however, in this manuscript the agreement is far more extensive, and often its text sides with the Septuagint over against both the *textus receptus* and the Samaritan.[53]

The text of Jeremiah is of particular interest. In the recension underlying the Septuagint text it is one-eighth shorter than in the Hebrew Bible. Scholars have suggested that the translators simply abbreviated their text for their own reasons. Other scholars have maintained that two ancient recensions are responsible for the differences.[54] From Qumrân comes a Hebrew manuscript which follows the short text of Jeremiah found hitherto only in Greek. In ch. 10, for example, the Septuagint omits no fewer than four verses, and shifts the order of a fifth. The Qumrân Jeremiah (4QJerᵇ) omits the four verses and shifts the order in identical fashion. The longer recension is present also at Qumrân.

As for the remaining books of the Old Testament, a number of books are preserved in texts which belong to the proto-Masoretic family: Isaiah, as we have seen; Ezekiel; and the Book of the Twelve (minor prophets). It is still premature to discuss the text of the Hagiographa at Qumrân. Study has not proceeded far enough, and some manuscripts appear to present complicated textual problems.[55]

C. The Early History of the Text.—Sufficient materials are available now to permit first attempts to reconstruct in outline the early Hebrew recensions of the Pentateuch, the historical books, and perhaps Isaiah and Jeremiah. An excellent beginning has been made by Albright in his programmatic study, "New Light on Early Recensions of the Hebrew Bible."[56] However, as Albright is the first to admit, the ground is not yet sure, and many missteps will be taken before sure results can be hoped for. The following suggestions, therefore, are provisional; they attempt to comprehend the evidence as presented above.

First of all, we may inquire into the history of the Hebrew recension which underlies the Septuagint of Samuel. As in the case of the

---

עמו (a familiar phenomenon in the LXX). The shifts to גוים (nations) here and to עבדיו (servants) in the next bicolon are secondary, though perhaps early, variants which modernize the primitive diction of the passage. In both cases, therefore, the LXX and 4Q are superior to the M.T.

The text of 4Q presumes a double conflation. Not only is there the doublet underlying the haplography of the M.T., but a second doublet appears: וחשתחוו לו כל אלהים (And bow down to him, all ye divine ones), taken from Ps. 97:7 (or its source), no doubt because of its strong resemblance to the original והבו עוז לו בני אלהים (And ascribe might to him, O sons of God; cf. Ps. 29). On the Greek rendering ἄγγελοι Θεοῦ for בני אלהים, cf. Deut. 32:8 LXX, and the text referred to by Skehan, p. 12.

The doubly conflate text presumed by the reconstruction above actually appears, though in a slightly different order, in the LXX.

In vs. 43b the loss of ולמשנאיו ישלם is best explained as a haplography in a (hemi-)stichometric manuscript. However, the entire bicolon ונקם ישיב לצריו ולמשנאיו ישלם is intrusive from vs. 41, two verses earlier, where it is surely original. Here it constitutes, not poetic parallelism, but mere tautology. Its introduction may have been occasioned by the combination יקום ונקם, as suggested by John Strugnell.

[49] For example, in Exod. 1:5, 4QExᵃ reads as follows: [חמש ושבעים נפש וימת[
". . . seventy-five persons. And [Joseph] died . . ."
The reading "seventy-five" persons rather than 'seventy" (M.T.) is striking (cf. Gen. 46:27 [LXX], Deut. 10:10 [LXX], and Acts 7:14). It gives the *coup de grâce* to lingering theories that the LXX translators inserted their own (recalculated) chronologies or numbers into their translation in defiance of their Hebrew *Vorlage*.
[50] "Exodus in the Samaritan Recension from Qumran," *JBL*, 74 (1955), pp. 182-87.
[51] "Le travail d'édition . . . ," p. 56.
[52] For example, Deut. 3:21 is inserted after Num. 27:23, a reading otherwise with witness only in the Samaritan and the *Samareitikon*. And after Num. 20:13, Deut.

3:23-24 is inserted; the Samaritan is likewise expanded here by the addition of Deut. 3:24.
[53] The following are chosen at random: in Num. 35:21, 4Q and LXX add מות ימות הרוצח after הוא (θανάτῳ θανατούσθω ὁ φονεύων); Num. 26:33 in 4Q and LXX reads שמות בנות ואלה (καὶ ταῦτα τὰ ὀνόματα τῶν θυγατέρων) *versus* M.T. and Samaritan ושם בנות.
[54] Cf. Orlinsky, *On the Present State of Proto-Septuagint Studies*, p. 85; Albright, "New Light on Early Recensions . . . ," p. 28 and references.
[55] For brief comments on the Daniel MSS, see Cross, "Le travail d'édition . . . ," p. 58.
[56] See note 48.

Pentateuch, so no doubt in the case of Samuel, the text type was present in Egypt in the early Ptolemaic period when the Septuagint began to be translated. Albright has argued that behind the translators' Hebrew text stands a recension edited sometime in the fifth–fourth centuries B.C. in Egypt.

There is, however, other strong evidence which ties this old recension to Palestine. For example, examination of the passages of the large Samuel manuscript (4QSam[a]) which are paralleled in Chronicles gives direct evidence that the Chronicler utilized an edition of Samuel much closer to the tradition of the Cave IV scroll than to that which survived in the Masoretic recension. This suggests that the text type underlying the Septuagint, which is closely allied to that used by the Chronicler not long after 400 B.C. in Palestine, is derived from an Old Palestinian recension. Again, the archaic Samuel manuscript (4QSam[b]) obviously reflects at many points a text which antedates both the proto-Masoretic recension and that underlying the Septuagint,[57] though its affinities are clearly with the latter. Since the manuscript itself dates from the end of the third century, and there is no strong reason to suppose that several texts imported from Egypt came to Qumrân,[58] we must conclude that it is a witness to a collateral line of tradition that persists in Palestine from a time antedating the divergence of the Chronicler's Palestinian text of Samuel and the Hebrew textual tradition surviving in Egypt. Perhaps it is easiest to suppose that this Old Palestinian text type derives from the fifth-century Jewish community in Palestine, and that the ancestral Egyptian textual tradition diverged from the Old Palestinian text no earlier than the fourth century, not later than the early third century, B.C.[59]

We are left with the problem of the origin of the proto-Masoretic recension of Samuel. No exemplars of its text are found at Qumrân, but there is no reason to suppose that it did not exist in the pre-Christian period. The analogy of other books—Isaiah, Jeremiah, the Pentateuch—warns us that the proto-Masoretic tradition is sometimes old, and not merely the crea-

tion of the recensional activities of the rabbis, and that the appearance of one recension at Qumrân does not exclude the presence of another. Moreover, the proto-Masoretic text of Samuel is clearly the result of systematic revision.[60] Can we suppose it to be a late Palestinian recension which ousted the Old Palestinian surviving both in Egypt and at Qumrân? The radical divergence of its text, as well as its frequently inferior readings, speaks against such a conclusion. A recension in Palestine should have produced both a better text and a text closer to the Egypto-Palestinian family. We can hardly suppose the proto-Masoretic recension to be a "standard" text while a text superior in many ways, and certainly standard in the day of the Chronicler, is reckoned a vulgar text. If, then, Egypt and Palestine are eliminated as possible localities for the development of the proto-Masoretic text, we may look to Babylon. It is not impossible that the ancestral proto-Masoretic tradition developed independently in Babylon and was reintroduced into Palestine in the Hellenistic period or later.[61]

The evidence for reconstructing the history of the local recensions of the Pentateuch is rapidly accumulating. However, the problems are more complicated, and the recensional distinctions less clear cut than in the case of Samuel.

The Paleo-Hebrew text of Exodus, and especially the Numbers scroll described above, furnish materials for reconstructing the prehistory of the Samaritan recension. As we have seen, the Samaritan recension proper branches off in the early Hasmonaean period.[62] It differs from the "proto-Samaritan" text at Qumrân only slightly. The differences would include, no doubt, the specifically Samaritan readings—by chance the passages in question are not extant at Qumrân—and closer affinities to the proto-Masoretic tradition.[63] There is not the slightest

---

[57] So Albright, "New Light on Early Recensions . . . ," p. 33. Cf. Cross, "The Earliest Manuscripts from Qumrân," p. 172.

[58] It is not impossible, of course, that a number of the Qumrân texts came from Egypt. There are a number of lines of potential connection between the Essenes and Alexandrian Jewry. The presence of Greek LXX MSS at Qumrân as well as the MSS under consideration could be explained by such contacts.

[59] Albright's evidence for Egyptian influence on the Hebrew tradition used by the Greek translators is most convincing in the Pentateuch. The question as to whether or not the historical books underwent recensional work in Egypt, and when, perhaps should be left open.

[60] For example, in II Sam. 4:1-2 the M.T. reads היו בן שאול . . . וישמע בן שאול . . . The latter phrase makes no sense whatever; the former is not happy. In both the LXX and 4QSam[a] the reading is וישמע מפיבשת בן שאול . . . היו למפיבשת בן שאול, which grammatically makes perfect sense. However, "Mephibosheth" is an obvious blunder. Beyond question, "Ishbosheth" is meant in both instances. The reviser of the text did not replace the erroneous reading with the correct one; rather, he excised the mistake and left the text standing. In the case of היו למפיבשת בן שאול, he cut out not only מפיבשת but also ל, and forgot to replace it before בן שאול, leaving nonsense. Precisely the same phenomenon, the excising of a mistake and thereby the creation of a defective (and senseless) text, appears in II Sam. 3:7. Here again the LXX and (in part) 4Q preserve the full, but corrupt, text to which the M.T. is secondary.

[61] Albright has proposed such an origin for the great Isaiah scroll (1QIsa[a]) on the basis of correct vocalizations of Babylonian names in its text.

[62] See above, notes 34 and 35.

[63] See note 53.

reason to suppose that the "proto-Samaritan" is in any sense a sectarian recension. In its textual characteristics it stands between the proto-Masoretic recension and the Egyptian recension preserved in the Septuagint as well as at Qumrân. Contrary to both the Egyptian and the proto-Masoretic traditions, however, it is characterized by free expansion, "modernizing" revisions, insertion of parallel passages, and the like, most of its changes being transparently secondary. Such a process must have taken some time; these peculiarities are the product of traditional growth, not recensional endeavor.

Similarly, if Albright is correct, the Egyptian influence reflected in the Hebrew underlying the Septuagint suggest that the old Egyptian recension was made no later than the fourth century.[64] Probably the Egyptian textual tradition and the proto-Masoretic tradition separated as early as the fifth century, and the "proto-Samaritan" probably did not diverge much later.

There can be no doubt that the proto-Samaritan text is Palestinian. If for no other reason, this can be argued from the fact that the Paleo-Hebrew script survives thanks to its transmission in texts of this type. The origin of the proto-Masoretic tradition is less than clear. Possibly it was a text in use in official circles from the fifth century onward in Palestine, being transmitted independently though side by side with the developing vulgar text represented in the proto-Samaritan. On the other hand, it may be that it is a type which developed outside Palestine in the fourth and third centuries (presumably in Babylon), later being reintroduced —though in no case later than the Maccabean period. This would explain the repudiation of the traditional Paleo-Hebrew script in the rabbinic period (an unexpected development), as well as the influence of the proto-Masoretic text on the Samaritan (stricto sensu) recension.

These details are enough to indicate that the biblical scrolls from Qumrân begin a new period in the study of the text of the Old Testament. Perhaps it is not too much to hope that, in proper time, Old Testament scholars will be able to establish a genuinely critical or eclectic text of the Old Testament which would reconstruct a pre-Christian state of the Old Testament. At all events, the discoveries will chart new courses by which progress will be made toward a more accurate, more intelligible Old Testament.[65]

[64] Albright, "New Light on Early Recensions . . . ," p. 30.

[65] For the contribution of the scrolls to our knowledge of the development of the Hebrew canon, see Cross, "Qumran Cave I."

Their bearing on other aspects of O.T. study should be mentioned—their data for the history of the Hebrew language and orthography, and their contribution to

V. Contributions to New Testament Studies

If the biblical scrolls from Qumrân are important for the study of the text of the Old Testament, the nonbiblical scrolls are even more important for the study of Christian origins. While none of these documents contains allusions to Christian figures, or indeed to Christianity, they provide us nevertheless with a library from the days shortly before the rise of Christianity.[66] Moreover, this library derives from a Jewish sect which in many ways anticipates Christianity.[67]

We have remarked that the people of the scrolls were Essenes, an apocalyptic sect within Judaism. They are known to us from Pliny, who tells us of their community between Jericho and 'En Gedi; from Philo of Alexandria; and especially from Josephus, who seems to have had a flirtation with the sect in his idealistic youth.[68] There is no longer any solid argument

the field of form and literary criticism. Attention may be called to one instance in which the Qumrân MSS promise to throw direct light on the literary or oral sources lying behind the fixed editions of the O.T.—an Aramaic document, identified by Milik, which appears to present an earlier form of one of the folkloristic tales of the first section of Daniel.

[66] To be sure, there have been premature attempts to relate the scrolls to Jewish-Christian groups, notably by J. L. Teicher in a series of articles in JJS beginning in 1951. For references and more balanced discussions, see O. Cullmann, "Die neuentdeckten Qumran Texte und das Judenchristentum der Pseudoklementinen," in Neutestamentliche Studien für Rudolph Bultmann (Berlin: A. Töpelmann, 1951), pp. 35-51; J. A. Fitzmeyer, "The Qumran Scrolls, the Ebionites and Their Literature," Theological Studies, 16 (1955), pp. 335-72.

In fact, we must now attribute the composition of a large portion of the specifically sectarian works to the first century B.C. See above, note 22.

[67] Among the many general studies of the Qumrân MSS and the N.T. we may select the following for special reference: K. G. Kuhn, "Die in Palästina gefundenen hedräischen Texte und das Neue Testament," ZTK, 47 (1950), pp. 192-211; W. Grossouw, "The Dead Sea Scrolls and the New Testament. A Preliminary Survey," Studia Catholica, 26 (1951), pp. 289-99; 27 (1952), pp. 1-8; Kuhn, "πειραμός-ἁμαρτία-σάρξ im Neuen Testament und die damit zusammenhängenden Vorstellungen," ZTK, 49 (1952), pp. 200-222; J. Coppens, "Les documents du Désert de Juda et les origines du Christianisme," Analecta Lovaniensia, II:41 (1953); F.-M. Braun, "L'arrière-fond judaïque du quatrième évangile et la Communauté de l'Alliance," RB, 62 (1955), pp. 5-44 (broader than its title indicates); O. Cullmann, "The Significance of the Qumran Texts for Research into the Beginnings of Christianity," JBL, 74 (1955), pp. 213-26; A. Metzinger, "Die Handschriftenfunde am Toten Meer und das Neue Testament," Biblica, 36 (1955), pp. 457-81; Cross, "The Scrolls from the Judean Desert," Archaeology, 9:1 (Spring, 1956), pp. 41-53, especially 48-53; Burrows, The Dead Sea Scrolls, ch. xv (pp. 326-45).

[68] Philo Judaeus Quod omnis probus liber sit (Loeb edition XI) xii-xiii (75-91), quoted in full by Eusebius Praep. evang. viii. 12; Hypothetica (Apologia pro Iudaeis), quoted by Eusebius Praep. evang. viii. 11 (cf. Loeb edition, XI, 437-43, [11, 1]); Josephus Vita 2; War II. viii. 2-13 (119-61); Antiquities XIII. v. 9 (171-73);

against the identification.[69] If the covenanters

XV. x. 5; XVIII. i. 5 (18-20); Pliny *Naturalis historia* V. xv. 73; cf. *Dio apud Synesium* 39 (ed. Migne).

[69] As Khirbet Qumrân (biblical '*ir ham-mêlaḥ*, "City of [the Sea of] Salt") has revealed its communal facilities —its enormous system of cisterns, its scriptorium and banquet hall, its stores, ovens, and domestic equipment, and in turn the size and nature of the community which occupied its environs including the large installations at 'Ên Feshkha—the possibility that it could be identified with aught else than the Essene "city in the wilderness" has grown so unlikely as to be almost inconceivable. Similarly, the evidence of the texts has grown, and will swell irresistibly, in my opinion, when the texts of Cave IV, especially new liturgical and legal material, are fully published. When one analyzes afresh the classical sources, especially Josephus, in light of the Qumrân materials, there are no discrepancies which are not easily explained by the exterior view of the classical source. Indeed, most of the discrepancies exist, not between the sources and the texts, but between former scholarly interpretations of the sources and the texts! For example, one may cite the spurious distinction drawn between the Essene attitude toward sacrifice and that of the "Covenanters" of the Zadokite document—see the discussions of J. M. Baumgarten, "Sacrifice Among the Jewish Sectarians of the Dead Sea (Qumrân) Scrolls," *HTR*, 46 (1953), pp. 141-59; and R. Marcus, "Pharisees, Essenes, and Gnostics," *JBL*, 73 (1954), pp. 157-61, especially p. 158; cf. R. North, "The Qumran 'Sadducees,'" *CBQ*, 17 (1955), pp. 164-88, especially pp. 177 ff.

The only plausible grounds for hesitation in making a definite identification of the sect with the Essenes—once the date and provenience of the scrolls were established and the life of the Qumrân settlement was reconstructed —have been (1) parallels between the sect and the Pharisaic *ḥᵃbhûrôth*, and (2) the argument that since Palestine "swarmed" with obscure sects in the first century B.C., one must exercise caution in assigning our sect to a known group (cf. S. Lieberman, "The Discipline of the So-called Dead Sea Manual of Discipline," *JBL*, 71 [1952], pp. 199-206). As for the first point, it is to be observed that there is no question whatever of identifying the people of the scroll with the main body of Pharisees. The issue is, rather, Do some parallels to Pharisaism in the practice of the sect constitute an *objection* to the Essene identification? On the contrary, some such parallels to Pharisaism are to be expected in Essenism and would be troubling only if *absent*. For the Essenes must be counted close relatives of the Pharisees, having a common origin in the Hasidic movement (cf. Marcus, *op. cit.*). The second point has only apparent relevance to our problem. When the Damascus Document alone was known, one could well suppose that an obscure or unknown sect was responsible for its composition. Now that a library of more than four hundred manuscripts is known, the perspective has changed. The "Qumrân" sect was not an ephemeral group. Its substantial commmunity at Qumrân persisted some two centuries. Moreover, it was not restricted to Qumrân, but, as we know from its documents, counted its camps and settlements in the villages of Judah (and perhaps as far away as Damascus), as did the Essenes, according to Philo and Josephus. Its own sectarian literature was enormous, and of profound and direct influence on Jewish Christian and Christian movements of the first century A.D. and later.

The enumeration of various minor divisions and ephemeral groups which allegedly proliferated in Judaism is no longer pertinent, therefore, to the discussion. Our task is to identify a major sect in Judaism. And to suppose that a major group in Judaism in this period goes unnoticed in our sources is simply incredible. The people of the scrolls belong to the Essene party.

of Qumrân were not the Essenes, then they were a similar sect living in the same center at the same date, holding common beliefs and practicing a like discipline, and reading, if not composing, the same books.

A. The History of the Essenes.—The Essenes had their origins in the party of the Pious, the *ḥᵃsîdhîm* of the national revival in the Maccabean era (*ca.* 175-135 B.C.) . The Essenes appear first under the early Hasmonaeans, and probably crystallized into their normative structure as a separatist party toward the beginning of the first century B.C. This was the era when the center at Qumrân was constructed. And it was probably in the early decades of the first century B.C. that the priest called the "Teacher of Righteousness" flourished. No doubt the teacher played an important role in fixing the direction and faith of the community. He was believed to be in possession of the Spirit of Truth, thus an inspired interpreter of the ancient Scriptures, one who "spoke with authority."

A new text from Cave IV, the *pésher* Nahum ("Commentary" on Nahum) ,[70] seems to support the view widely held on the basis of published material, that certain events crucial to the sect took place in the days of Alexander Jannaeus (103-76 B.C.) , and it follows most probably that the career of the Teacher of Righteousness roughly coincides with the reign of this priest-king. In this case Jannaeus himself would be the "Wicked Priest" of the commentaries, who persecuted the Teacher—whether to the point of martyrdom is a moot question.[71]

For less than two centuries the Essenes lived their humble, disciplined lives in the villages of Judah, and in their desert retreat at Qumrân. After the Roman war of A.D. 66-70 they disappeared.

As a matter of fact, the Essenes go without mention in the New Testament. This is extraordinary, since there is impressive evidence of Essene survivals in Christian literature or Christian editions of older Jewish literature which has passed through Essene editions. An example is the Essene material which forms the

[70] See note 22.

[71] Dupont-Sommer, the most articulate advocate of a martyr death, has defended his position systematically in "Le maître de justice fut-il mis à mort?" *VT*, 1 (1951), pp. 200-215; and more recently in "Quelques remarques sur le *Commentaire d'Habacuc*, à propos d'un livre récent," *VT*, 5 (1955), pp. 113-29, a review and answer to K. Elliger's careful study, *Studien zum Habakuk-Kommentar vom Toten Meer*.

There is in the scrolls no unambiguous reference to the manner of his death, an extraordinary circumstance if in fact he suffered violent death at the hands of the Wicked Priest. On the contrary, there is at least one unpublished reference which suggests that he was delivered from persecution at some time or other, to add to the references in which it is said merely that he was "gathered (to his ancestors)."

nucleus of the Testaments of the Twelve Patriarchs.[72] Again, the Essene or proto-Essene Enoch literature is quoted in the New Testament, and survives in Christian editions.[73] The doctrine of the "Two Ways" found in the Rule of the Community is implicit in the Gospel of John,[74] and this and like Essene formulations found in the Didache (Teaching of the Twelve Apostles), the Epistle of Barnabas, and elsewhere,[75] together with many features of the Jewish-Christian sect of the Ebionites,[76] make clear that direct use of Essene themes and materials was made in Christian compositions. There is also some evidence that the Essene sectaries were a fruitful field of evangelism, and that they in turn had influence on the formation of institutions of the apostolic and sub-apostolic church.[77] Perhaps we must suppose that the absence of mention of the Essenes in the New Testament arises, not from ignorance, but from lack of antipathy; we hear of the other Jewish parties largely in polemical passages.

B. Parallels of Word and Concept.—The contribution of the literature of the Essenes to our understanding of the New Testament and the origins of Christianity is many-sided. Their library presents a literature in its original Semitic garb for an era when our Hebrew and Aramaic sources are almost non-existent. Their sectarian works speak a religious language held in common with the primitive church. And it is quite clear that the people of the scrolls and early Christianity drank from a common source of theological ideas, chose or rejected institutions belonging to a common environment, and responded with new solutions to common problems of faith. We cannot deal exhaustively with each or any one of these aspects of scroll research. At best, illustrations can be given to indicate the directions in which our rich new data point research.

[72] On the (Judeo-)Christian origin of the Testaments, see now M. De Jonge, *The Testaments of the Twelve Patriarchs: A Study of Their Text, Composition and Origin* (Manchester: Manchester University Press, 1954); Milik's review of De Jonge, *RB*, 62 (1955), pp. 297-98; and "Le Testament de Lévi en araméen," *ibid.*, pp. 398-406, especially pp. 405-6. Cf. Braun's discussion and citation of older literature, *op. cit.*, p. 5, note 4. Milik has now identified a second source of the Christian edition of the Testaments, a Testament of Naphtali, which adds weight to his analysis (and De Jonge's).

[73] On the Qumrân Enoch literature, see provisionally Milik's remarks in "Le travail d'édition . . . ," p. 60. Kuhn, in "Les rouleaux de cuivre . . . ," p. 203, note 1, has gone so far as to suggest that II Cor. 6:14–7:1 is cited (freely) by Paul from an Essene source.

[74] Braun, *op. cit.*, p. 18.

[75] See J.-P. Audet, "Affinités littéraires et doctrinales du 'Manuel de Discipline,' " *RB*, 59 (1952), pp. 219-38; 60 (1953), pp. 41-82.

[76] Cf. the literature cited in note 66.

[77] See the remarks of Cullmann, "The Significance of the Qumran Texts . . . ," pp. 217-26.

One of the most complicated and delicate problems in exegesis of the New Testament arises from the fact that the New Testament writings rest on a Semitic, dominantly Aramaic, substructure, but are written in Greek. One need not accept the extreme position that large sections of the New Testament are translated from Aramaic, or even the moderate position that some of the primitive documents used by New Testament authors were Aramaic, to recognize that the idiom of the New Testament is essentially Semitic, and that this fact has serious consequences for New Testament interpretation.[78] There can be no doubt that the primitive oral tradition underlying the Gospels was Aramaic (sometimes Hebrew), and that even such writers as Paul, who composed freely in Greek, were forced to use rough Greek equivalents of Semitic concepts and theological language. To recover, therefore, the precise nuances of the theological idiom of the New Testament, it is not enough to know Greek well; one is forced back to Aramaic and Hebrew. Heretofore, owing to the lack of a contemporary literature, scholars have been obliged to reconstruct as best they could a theoretical Aramaic and Hebrew of this period from earlier and later sources. Now the Qumrân scrolls, with their rich linguistic resources, provide a new basis from which the New Testament philologist can attack these problems.

As illustrations we may cite one or two instances of New Testament expressions, long obscured by Greek dress, which are illuminated by the language of our new documents.

In Luke 2:14 there is the familiar expression, no doubt quoted from a Hebrew hymn:

> Glory to God in the highest
> And on earth peace, good will to men.

It is now generally recognized that the text above, found in the *textus receptus,* is inferior to the readings of the great uncials: ". . . [peace] among men with whom he is pleased." [79] The latter reading is obscure, however, and conceals a Hebrew idiom. Our new texts now present the idiom in its original form and, what is better, in unambiguous contexts.[80] It must be translated "men of [God's] favor"—that is, the community of the elect in the new age.[81]

[78] For the older literature on "Aramaic origins," and a judicious discussion of the present state of research in this field, see M. Black, *An Aramaic Approach to the Gospels and Acts,* 2nd ed. (Oxford: Clarendon Press, 1954), especially pp. 1-12.

[79] ἐν ἀνθρώποις εὐδοκίας for ἐν ἀνθρώποις εὐδοκία.

[80] 1QH [*ôdhāyôth*] 4:32-33 (Sukenik, *op. cit.*, p. 40). Cf. 1QS 8:6.

[81] See C.-H. Hunzinger, "Neues Licht auf Lc 2:14 ἄνθρωποι εὐδοκίας," *ZNW*, 44 (1952-53), pp. 85-90. Cf. the précis of Vogt, " 'Pax hominibus bonae voluntatis,' Lc 2, 14," *Biblica*, 34 (1955), pp. 427-29.

Again, the expression "poor in spirit" (πτωχοὶ τῷ πνεύματι) in the first beatitude receives light from the scrolls. The Greek does not give a proper meaning, and the parallel in Luke 6:20 reads only, "[Blessed are you] poor." Is the Matthaean version of the saying (Matt. 5:3) merely a spiritualizing of the Hebrew *'ebhyôn*, "needy," which is probably reflected in the Greek of Luke? Or is the Lukan form an "Essene" or "Ebionite" variant of the saying which is original in Matthew? Both positions have been defended. Actually, *both* expressions appear in our new documents. "Poor," *'ebhyôn*, is especially frequent; but the phrase "poor in spirit," *'anwê rûaḥ*, also occurs. In the War scroll (1QM 14:7) it is found in a fairly clear context. Here it stands in antithesis to "hard-hearted," in formal parallelism with "those perfect in the Way." The expression follows a series which includes the "frightened," "dumb," "powerless," "weak-kneed," and "smitten." Perhaps "meek" is the best English equivalent for the Hebrew expression.

Linguistic and conceptual contacts between the scrolls and the New Testament are nowhere more in evidence than in the Gospel of John.[82] Such phrases as "the spirit of truth and the spirit of deceit" (I John 4:6),[83] "the light of life" (John 8:12),[84] "to do the truth" (John 3:21),[85] "sons of light" (John 12:36),[86] "eternal life" (John 3:15, 16; *et passim*),[87] familiar elements in the Johannine vocabulary, are also characteristic of the diction of the sectarian writings. More important are the repeatedly contrasted themes which sound a kind of counterpoint in both Johannine and Essene literature: light and darkness, truth and error or lying, spirit and flesh, love and hate, death and life. As in the scrolls, religious "knowing" has a special flavor and wide usage in John. However, "knowledge" as a revealed, especially eschatological knowledge, which belongs properly to the community of the saved—its most striking usage in the Essene literature—has its best

parallels in Paul and Matthew.[88] In both John and the scrolls juridical language is strong, and in both may be found a tendency to treat the inner teaching or sacraments of the community as esoteric.[89] The gift of salvation is not known by "flesh," but through the "spirit." "Unless one is born of water and the Spirit, he cannot enter the kingdom of God" (John 3:5) ; "then God in his faithfulness [or by his truth] will purify all the works of man, and cleanse for himself the body of man, in order to consume every wicked spirit from the midst of his flesh, and to make him pure with [a] holy spirit from every wicked deed; and he will sprinkle on him [a] spirit of truth like water for impurity . . . so as to give the righteous understanding in the knowledge of the Most High" (1QS 4:20-22).[90]

In both the Essene literature and the Johannine writings there is the strongest emphasis on unity and community. The Essenes call themselves the "Community,"[91] literally the "Unity." This oneness is a sign of the Kingdom, which

[82] Already an extensive literature has sprung up in this field. In addition to the discussions to be found in the general articles cited in note 67, the following articles which deal primarily with Johannine parallels may be noted: L. Mowry, "The Dead Sea Scrolls and the Gospel of John," *BA*, 17 (1954), pp. 78-97; R. E. Brown, "The Qumran Scrolls and the Johannine Gospel and Epistles," *CBQ*, 17 (1955), pp. 403-19, 559-74; Dupont-Sommer, "La mère du Messie et la mère de l'Aspic dans un hymne de Qoumrân," *RHR*, 147 (1955), pp. 174-88 (parallels to Rev. 12); and Albright, "Recent Discoveries in Palestine and the Gospel of St. John," in *The Background of the New Testament and Its Eschatology*, pp. 153-71.

[83] רוחי אמת ועול (1QS 4:23). רוח אמת and רוח עול also appear standing alone often in Qumrân literature.

[84] באור החיים (1QS 3:7).

[85] לעשות אמת (1QS 1:5, etc.).

[86] בני אור (1QS 1:9, and especially 1QM *passim*).

[87] חיי נצח (1QS 4:7, etc.).

[88] Typical of Johannine usage is John 17:3: "And this is eternal life, that they know thee the only true God, and Jesus Christ whom thou hast sent (cf. I John 4:7 ff.). Compare 1QS 2:2-3: "May he bless you with every good thing and keep you from all evil, and illuminate your heart with the wisdom of life, and favor you with eternal knowledge." On the Johannine use, see Bultmann, "γινώσκω γνῶσις, etc.," *Theologisches Wörterbuch zum Neuen Testament*, ed. G. Kittel, Band I (Stuttgart: W. Kohlhammer, 1933), pp. 711-13.

On the usage of "knowledge" in the scrolls and elsewhere in the New Testament, and the relationships to Gnostic usage, see especially Kuhn, "Die Sektenschrift und die iranische Religion," *ZTK*, 49 (1952), pp. 296-316; W. D. Davies, "'Knowledge' in the Dead Sea Scrolls and Mt. 11:25-30," *HTR*, 46 (1953), pp. 113-39; and F. Nötscher, *Zur theologischen Terminologie der Qumran-Texte, ad loc.*

[89] On the juridical language of John, see Théo Preiss, *Life in Christ* (London: Student Christian Movement Press, 1954; from *La Vie en Christ* [Neuchâtel: Delachaux et Niestlé, 1951]). Preiss remarks of the Johannine literature: "In a style of grandiose monotony, it develops a few unchanging themes." No better description could be given of the theological sections of the sectarian document. There can be little doubt that the origins of the Johannine style must be sought after in Essene circles.

On the esoteric elements in John, especially in connection with the Eucharist, see J. Jeremias, *Die Abendmahlsworte Jesu*, 2nd ed. (Göttingen: Vandenhoeck & Ruprecht, 1949), pp. 58-62.

[90] Cf. Y. Yadin, "A Note on DSD IV:2:20," *JBL*, 74 (1955), pp. 40-43.

[91] היחד, "unity" or "togetherness." The translation "community" is poor in English, since it permits secular connotations or the wide English usage to blur its narrow meaning. Moreover, the term in our texts has specific theological overtones; it applies to the "eschatological" community or *Heilsgemeinschaft*, or to its activities "in common" (ביחד, etc.). A good number of the passages in published texts are collected by Habermann, עדה ועדות Jerusalem: Maḥbārôt le-Sifrût, 1952), pp. 136-37. Note such phrases as ביחד אל, ביחד אמת(ו), ביחד עצתו, ליחד קודש, ברית היחד, לברית יחד עולמים, ליחד ברית עולם, where the normal theological connotations are made explicit.

is dawning and to which they belong, and is a gift of the Spirit. The Johannine phrases, "that they may be one," "become perfectly one" (John 17:11, 21, 23), use typical Essene diction.[92]

The quality of life in the true community is to be marked by love of the brethren. This is a basic theme of Essene discipline, and, of course, the repeated motive of the Johannine writings, especially I John. The Essene Rule also requires that one "hate all the children of darkness," even as he must "love all children of light."[93] The note of hate is not characteristic of the New Testament ethic of disinterested love; however, as has often been remarked, the Johannine emphasis, unlike that of the New Testament in general, is almost exclusively on love within the "little flock"; and a note of hostility toward the "world" occasionally appears,[94] which, while milder than the Essene exhortation "to hate," is nevertheless reminiscent of it.

According to Essene doctrine, the world is in the grip of two warring spirits, created by God from the beginning: the Spirit of Truth and the Spirit of Wickedness or Perversity. The Spirit of Wickedness is none other than Belial, the "Prince of Darkness," Satan. The Spirit of Truth is otherwise called the holy spirit (not identical with the Holy Spirit, though often hard to distinguish), the "Prince of Lights," the "Angel of Truth." All men have their "lot" in one of these spirits, and thus are children of light or darkness.[95] These two powers are locked in a titanic warfare, a struggle which mounts to a climax in the last times (compare Revelation and the War scroll). The war is waged not only between the opposing arrays of spirits and their human hosts, but also within the heart of each "son of light."[96] For the people of the scrolls the end of the war is in sight. God is about to destroy forever the rule of the Spirit of Perversion, and bring an end to all darkness and wickedness. In the Johannine literature, however, although the struggle persists, and a final Armageddon is to be fought, yet the crisis

of the battle is past, Jesus the Christ has "overcome the world" (i.e., the domain of the Prince of Darkness).[97]

The "Prince of Light" or "Spirit of Truth" is appointed, according to the Essenes, as a *helper* to all children of light.[98] The figure of the Paraclete or Advocate of John (John 14:17; 15:26; 16:13; I John 5:6-8[99]) is derived from this complex of ideas. His function, described as "to witness," "to intercede," "to speak," yet "not on his own authority," has always been puzzling, for it does not fit the expected description of the Holy Spirit. And the origin and meaning of the term "Paraclete" as an appellation of the Spirit of Truth has been much in dispute.[100] In the light of the new Essene parallels, we now understand the title and vocation of the Advocate–Spirit of Truth for the first time with some clarity.

The origins of the concept are found in the heavenly court of Yahweh in the Old Testament, where in scenes of judgment Satan as prosecuting attorney stands over against the Angel of the Lord as advocate or witness.[101] In the elaborate angelology and dualism of the

---

[92] Note the Semitic and presumably "Essene" form of the following: ὦσιν . . . εἰς ἕν (John 17:23); להיות ליחד (1QS 5:2); συναγάγῃ εἰς ἕν (John 11:52); בהאספם ליחד (1QS 5:7).

[93] 1QS 1:9-10. Cf. Matt. 5:43-44, which seems to be a reaction against such an emphasis.

[94] E.g., I John 2:15; 3:13. See the discussion of Braun, *op. cit.*, pp. 19-20; and especially Brown, *op. cit.*, pp. 561-64.

[95] Cf. John 8:42-47; I John 4:1-6; 5:19 (as well as II Cor. 6:14–7:11), etc.; and especially 1QS 3:13–4:26.

[96] 1QS 4:23-26. It is in this framework that the N.T. concepts of temptation, predestination, and justification must be understood (as well as corresponding ideas in the scrolls). See Kuhn's admirable analysis, "πειρασμός-ἁμαρτία-σάρξ im Neuen Testament . . . ." On the scrolls and "justification" see also S. E. Johnson, "Paul and the Manual of Discipline," *HTR*, 48 (1955), pp. 157-65.

[97] See Brown's discussion, pp. 410-12. On the *Kampfsituation* in the thought of Jesus see Kuhn, pp. 219 ff., who draws attention to the pertinent passages Matt. 10:34; 12:28 f. and parallels.

[98] Cf. 1QM 13:10 שר מאור מאז פקדתה לעוזרנו; and 1QS 3:24-25 ואל ישראל ומלאך אמתו עזר לכול בני אור.

[99] Often in the Johannine material the functions of the Spirit of Truth as (1) bearer of light, (2) leader of the armies of God, and (3) advocate or witness are shifted to the Christ. Cf. (1) John 9:5; 12:46; (2) Rev. 12:7-12 parallel to 19:11-21; and (3) I John 2:1.

[100] As early as 1933 S. Mowinckel, on the basis chiefly of Essene material in the Testaments of the Twelve Patriarchs, was able to reconstruct much of the O.T. and Jewish background of the Paraclete figure. See his studies, "Die Vorstellungen der Spätjudentums von heiligen Geist als Fürsprecher und der johanneische Paraklet," *ZNW*, 32 (1933), pp. 97-130; and "Hiobs *gō'ēl* und Zeuge im Himmel," in *Vom Alten Testament* (Marti Festschrift), ed. K. Budde (Giessen: A. Töpelmann, 1925), pp. 207-12. Cf. N. Johansson, *Parakletoi* (Lund: C. W. K. Gleerup, 1940); and especially Théo Preiss, *The Life in Christ*.

However, Mowinckel's work has been widely ignored, especially by members of the Bultmann school in Germany. This is unfortunate, since the new texts (e.g., those quoted in note 98) directly support Mowinckel. The opinion of Bultmann himself has been expressed most recently in his *Theology of the New Testament*, I (New York: Charles Scribner's Sons, 1954), 88n. For the present state (pre-Qumrân!) of the discussion, see W. Michaelis, "Zur Herkunft des johanneische Paraklet-Titels," in *Coniectanea Neotestamentica*, XI (Lund: C. W. K. Gleerup, 1947), 147-62; G. Bornkamm, "Der Paraklet in Johannesevangelium," in *Festschrift Rudolph Bultmann* (Stuttgart: W. Kohlhammer, 1949), pp. 12-35.

[101] See especially I Kings 22:19-24; Zech. 3; and Job, especially 16:19 and 19:25, where the "Heavenly Witness" is to be identified with the "Angel of the Lord," as first pointed out by Mowinckel (see above, note 100; called to my attention by G. Ernest Wright). The function of the angel, or divine messenger, as witness in heavenly court scenes is found already in ancient Canaanite mythology (as I have been reminded by G. E. Mendenhall).

Essenes, partly under Iranian influence, its Old Testament origins are blurred and transmuted so that the two angels become the two opposing principles or spirits of truth and error, light and darkness. In the cosmic struggle the heavenly accuser becomes the diabolical tempter of the sons of light, the Prince of Darkness who is at war with the Prince of Lights. The Heavenly Advocate becomes the Spirit of Truth, a holy spirit who testifies to truth in the heart of those in the "inheritance" of truth, as well as the accuser of the children of darkness.[102] In John the Essene dualism is partly resolved, but reflections of the Essene structure of thought still survive. This is especially clear in the Johannine Advocate, but also to a lesser degree in the special function of the Spirit in Acts and in Paul.

These Essene parallels to John and the Johannine epistles will come as a surprise only to those students of John who have attempted to read John as a work under strong Greek influence. It now turns out—as a small group of scholars has long maintained—that John has its strongest affinities, not with the Greek world, or Philonic Judaism, but with Palestinian Judaism. Its concepts of truth, knowledge, spirit, and even the Word [103] must be seen, not as rooted in Greek thought, but as concepts emerging precisely out of sectarian Judaism. So that rather than being the most Hellenistic of the Gospels, John now proves to be in many ways the most Jewish.

Ultimately these conclusions will bear on critical theories in regard to the origin of John.[104] We must look for a *Sitz im Leben* for the development of Johannine tradition where Jewish Christianity was dominant, and where Essene influences persisted. Some have suggested that John may no longer be regarded as the latest and most evolved of the Gospels, but as the most primitive, and that the formative locus of its tradition was Jerusalem before its destruction. This is not to suggest that the present form of the book has not had an elaborate literary history. The point is that John preserves authentic historical material which first took form in an Aramaic or Hebrew milieu where Essene currents still ran strong.

C. Essene and Christian Eschatology.—Several broad theological themes in Essenism and primitive Christianity may be fruitfully compared. Perhaps it will be most instructive, however, to choose one of the most striking of these, the eschatological structure of the thought and practice of the two communities—their doctrines of history's end, their messianism, their understanding of their communities as the anticipation of the kingdom of God.

Both the Essenes and the primitive church believed that the new age was imminent. Indeed, they were living in the last times; they were the last generation. In some sense the new age had dawned; at least its signs were discernible in the events of their day. History had reached its crisis. The powers of darkness and light were poised for the final, decisive struggle. The church was exhorted to "put on the full armor of God, . . . to stand against the wiles of the devil, . . . to be able to withstand the evil day, and having done so to stand" (Eph. 6:10-17). The Essenes divided their little community into battle divisions, and drew up a liturgy of Armageddon; they were a former-day salvation army!

In the prophecies of the Old Testament the Essenes saw predicted the events of their own day. Where the prophets spoke of the last days and their signs (and even where they did not!), the sectarian commentators discovered fulfillment in the history of their own times or in the inner life of their sect. Those with "knowledge" should now recognize that the final war had begun. They must "decide," understanding by faith and the spirit the fulfillment of prophecy, expectant of the full consummation of history.

Of themselves the Essenes wrote, quoting Isaiah: "When these things come to pass in Israel to the Community, . . . they will separate themselves from the midst of the abode of perverse men to go into the desert to prepare there the way of the Lord according as it is written, 'In the desert prepare ye the Way [of the Lord], make straight in the wilderness a highway for our God'" (1QS 8:12-14).

Thus these people understood themselves to be in the situation of John the Baptist, of whom the New Testament quotes the identical passage of Isaiah.[105] Jesus' early teachings are in

---

[102] Cf. Test. Judah 20. Preiss comments on this passage: "Similarly in John 16:7 ff. the Spirit of Truth will convict the world of sin. . . . It plays the part of accuser before the world. . . . But as soon as man has received the truth in faith the roles are reversed: the Satanic Spirit of Error will seek to accuse him . . . while the Spirit of Truth as Paraclete will witness to him of the certainty of the love of God."

[103] Actually, no equivalent of ὁ λόγος in the Johannine sense can be documented in the scrolls. However, intimate parallels to the Prologue of John, in style, content, and vocabulary, appear in the new documents. Cf. Braun, *op. cit.*, pp. 15-16; 1QS 11:11; 1QS 3:15-17.

[104] See especially Albright, "Recent Discoveries in Palestine . . . ."

[105] On John the Baptist's relationship to the Essenes, see Braun, "L'arrière-fond judaïque . . . ," pp. 41 f.; Metzinger, pp. 472-77; Brownlee, "John the Baptist in the New Light of Ancient Scrolls," *Interpretation*, 9 (1955), pp. 71-90 (cf. "A Comparison of the Covenanters of the Dead Sea Scrolls with Pre-Christian Jewish Sects," *BA*, 13 [1950], pp. 49-72). Older literature may be found in Carl H. Kraeling, *John the Baptist* (New York: Charles Scribner's Sons, 1951).

much the same eschatological framework.[106] The man in the early church lives in a "later" moment, as it were. He believes that the Messiah has come. Yet he lives in a like tension. The kingdom delays; the "world" remains. He must partake of life in the kingdom to come proleptically, anticipating the coming day when ambiguity will end, the world be transformed, an end be brought to all wicked flesh, and the kingdom of God fulfilled.

The Essenes therefore searched the Scriptures and interpreted their prophecies eschatologically. As several scholars have pointed out, Essene exegesis has no real parallel either in Pharisaic Judaism or in Philonic Judaism.[107] Their interpretation is neither legalistic nor allegorical. But it falls precisely into the pattern of the New Testament's use of the Old Testament. In both, exegesis is "historical" (i.e., eschatological) and pneumatic.

The Essenes believed themselves to be the people of the New Covenant. They yearly celebrated the renewing of this new or "eternal" covenant,[108] no doubt recalling Jeremiah's prediction of a new covenant (Jer. 31:31). They understood this "New Covenant" to be at once the "renewed [old] covenant" and the "eternal covenant" to be established at the end of days—i.e., precisely in the New Testament sense.

The Essenes had a most developed messianism. They expected an eschatological prophet recalling Deut. 18:15-18.[109] This figure has a counterpart in the New Testament in John the Baptist. However, it is interesting that in John's Gospel the Baptist denies that he is Elijah, and also that he is the expected prophet, implying that Jesus is the prophet to come.[110] And in Acts 3:22 Jesus is identified in Peter's sermon precisely with the prophet of Deut. 18:15-18.

A second eschatological figure is the Anointed Priest. He is the faithful priest of prophecy, the Messiah of Aaron.[111] In the Testament of Joseph[112] he is called the Lamb, who takes precedence over the Lion of Judah, the royal Messiah. There is no precise counterpart of the priestly Messiah in New Testament thought, though reminiscences of like categories may be recognized in the militant Lamb of Revelation,[113] and especially in Jesus' role as the heavenly high priest in the Epistle to the Hebrews.[114] Here Jesus is the combined priestly and royal Anointed in the type of Melchizedek, the priest-king of Salem in the days of Abraham.

The Essenes also expected the coming of the Davidic or royal Messiah. They quote various proof texts of the Old Testament, some of which are used of Jesus in the New Testament. Of course the identification of Jesus as the Davidic Christ or Messiah of Israel dominates New Testament confessions.

The question may be raised as to the role of the "Teacher of Righteousness" in the eschatology of the Essenes. Is he an eschatological figure? Is he one of the three, prophet, priest, or king?

Apparently the Teacher is to appear in the last days. So we are told in the Damascus Document.[115] In itself this is an ambiguous datum, since the community lives in the last days. The fall of Jerusalem in 63 B.C. (1QpHab 6:4-7), the persecution of the Wicked Priest, presumably Jannaeus, and so on, are eschatological events inasmuch as they are signs of the end of the age. In another text is the phrase, "from the day the Teacher of the Community died until the Messiahs from Aaron and Israel arise";[116] on the surface at least this seems to draw a clear distinction between the Teacher and either Messiah.

It has been plausibly suggested that the Teacher of Righteousness was identified by his sect as the priestly Messiah. Certainly he acted as chief priest in the community, and was of

[106] Cf. James M. Robinson, "Jesus' Understanding of History," *JBR*, 23 (1955), pp. 17-24.

[107] Cf. L. Mowry, *op. cit.*, pp. 93 f. G. Vermès in his article, "À propos des commentaires bibliques découverts à Qumrân," *RHPR*, 35 (1955), pp. 95-102, after distinguishing the Qumrân *peshārim* from both the midrash and Philonic exegesis, attempts to find parallels in the Targumim, but without notable success cf. C. Rabin, "Notes on the Habakkuk Scroll and the Zadokite Documents," *VT*, 5 [1955], pp. 148-62).

[108] Milik in an oral communication indicates that on the basis of new data, including a reading in an unpublished text, he can establish that the festival of the New Covenant among the sectarians fell on Pentecost (i.e., at the traditional time when the law was given at Sinai). This suggests intriguing possibilities for interpreting the setting of the event of Pentecost in the N.T.

[109] Cf. 1QS 9:11. The Deuteronomy passage is cited also in a "Testimonia" list published by Allegro in a fall, 1956, issue of *JBL*; see also *Discoveries in the Judaean Desert* I, 121, where Milik describes the list, including the "star" passage from Num. 24:15-17 and Levi's blessing in Deut. 33:8-11.

[110] John 1:21, 25; 6:14; 7:40.

[111] In addition to Milik's study just cited (note 109), see Kuhn, "Die beiden Messias Aarons und Israel," *NTS*, I (1955), pp. 168-79; Burrows, "The Messiahs of Aaron and Israel," *ATR*, 1952, pp. 203-6. Literature predating the publication of 1QSa (*Discoveries in the Judaean Desert*, I, 105-18) and the 4Q Testimonia is now antiquated.

[112] Ch. 19. To be sure, there is a Christian hand visible in the chapter, and any attempt to analyze the elements into older and later strands is bound to be partly subjective.

[113] Rev. 17·14; cf. Test. Joseph 19:8! Cf. R. H. Charles, *The Revelation of St. John* (International Critical Commentary), I (New York: Charles Scribner's Sons, 1920), pp. cxiii f., especially note 2.

[114] Cf. Braun, *op. cit.*, pp. 35-38.

[115] 6:10-11 עד עמד יורה הצדק באחרית הימים. Cf. 1:11.

[116] CDC 19:35(=8:21)–20:1 (ed. Rabin): מיום האסף (with Kuhn, Milik, *et al.*) מורה היח[י]ד עד עמד משיח(י) מאהרן ומישראל.

Zadokite blood. However, nowhere is there explicit identification of the Teacher with the Messiah-Priest.[117]

These problems are complicated. All hypotheses are tentative until the full literature is published and thoroughly digested by scholars.

The scroll materials are especially rich in materials which illuminate the origins of the organizational structure of the early church, especially the church in Acts.[118] Throughout the history of Christianity there have been debates concerning the nature of church government in apostolic times. Some have contended that the order had a democratic government without stated offices; others that it was presbyterian, following the practice of the synagogue; still others that its form of government was monarchic, governed by bishops. Actually elements of each of these types of organization appear in the New Testament. Scholars have increasingly attempted to fit them into an evolution moving from the free and congregational order to a more rigid monarchic structure.

The Essenes are a priestly and lay community, governed by hereditary priests in cultic and ritual affairs, by laymen in their common religious and "secular" life. There is, of course, no precise counterpart in Christianity to the dominance of the Levitic office. The organization of the Essenes is most instructive, however, once this qualification is made.

The ruling assembly of the Essenes, made up of all the mature members of the covenanted community, is called the *Rabbîm*—literally,

"the Many." It is a technical term in Hebrew which appears in literal translation in the New Testament with similar technical meaning.[119] The Jerusalem council is so designated in Acts 15:12; the assembly which chooses the seven and places them before the apostles is so named in Acts 6:2, 5; Silas and Judas, together with Paul and Barnabas, assemble the "Many" of the church at Antioch to hear the report of the "Many" in Jerusalem (Acts 15:30).

Within the "Many" was a higher judicatory consisting of twelve laymen and three priests. These were the types of the twelve princes of the tribal assembly in the Mosaic era, together with three priests representing the princes of the three clans of Levi,[120] as seems clear from the role and number of the princes in the War scroll. The circle of the twelve in the early church in part parallels the Essene twelve. For example, the Essene inner circle, according to the Rule of the Community, when it is established in Israel (in the last days), will be "an eternal planting [Isa. 60:21; 61:3], a holy temple for Israel, . . . faithful witnesses in judgment, the Elect of [God's] favor to atone for the earth, and to mete out punishment to the wicked. It [the inner circle] is the tried [foundation] wall [misquoting Isa. 28:16], the precious corner whose foundations shall not be shaken." [121] Rev. 21:14 (cf. Eph. 2:20; Heb. 11:10) alludes to the same passage (Isa. 28:16; cf. Ezek. 48:31), recording that the wall of the New Jerusalem "had twelve foundations, and on them the twelve names of the twelve apostles of the Lamb." In Luke 22:28-30, Jesus addresses the twelve: "You are those who have continued with me in my trials; as my Father appointed a kingdom for me, so do I appoint for you that you may eat and drink at my table in my kingdom, and sit on thrones *judging the twelve tribes* of Israel." Here again is the theme of the twelve "judges" of the *eschaton* after the pattern of the old princes in the tribal assembly of Israel.[122]

Finally, to mount another stage, the highest office of the Essene community was called *mebhaqqēr*, "overseer." He was president of the session of the "Many," fiscal agent of the community, and director of labors, religious and

---

[117] One indirect line has been suggested. There is yet another title applied to the priestly Messiah—דורש התורה, the "Expositor of the Law." This is clear from CDC 7:18-20; and the following text published by Allegro: וחוא יחיח לי לבן הואה צמח דויד העומד עם דורש התורה, "And he shall become a son to me; he is the shoot of David who shall stand with the Expositor of the Torah." In another context the Expositor appears to be a figure of past history (CDC 6:7-10). Hence it follows that the Expositor must be the priestly Messiah, and his forerunner presumably the Teacher of Righteousness.

This is not impossible. However, another explanation conforms much more easily to the data. The "historical" Expositor seems to be a figure of history long past, early in, or even before, the "epoch of wrath," who is to guide Israel "until there shall arise one who teaches righteousness at the end of days" (CDC 6:10). One could therefore identify him as David's priest Zadok, the ancestor of the priestly Essenes, the "sons of Zadok." In CDC 5:5 we read: "It [the Torah] was hidden [and not] revealed until Zadok arose" as an explanation why David's sins were overlooked. The typology in the sect's messianic doctrine thus would be: the royal Messiah= David *redivivus;* the priestly Messiah=Zadok *redivivus.*

[118] See especially S. E. Johnson, "The Dead Sea Scrolls and the Jerusalem Church of Acts," *ZAW,* 66 (1954), pp. 106-20; B. Reicke, "Die Verfassung der Urgemeinde im. Lichte jüdischer Dokumente," *ThZ,* 10 (1954), pp. 95-112; Cross, "The Scrolls and the New Testament," *Christian Century,* Aug. 24, 1955, pp. 968-71; J. Daniélou, "La communauté de Qumrân et l'organisation de l'Eglise ancienne," *RHPR,* 35 (1955), pp. 104-15.

[119] The same term may be applied in nonsectarian Judaism with reference to members of a synagogue or ḥabhûrāh. In this case it does not, apparently, carry the technical meaning of a body with democratic powers.

[120] This was first called to my attention by Milik.

[121] 1QS 8:5-8.

[122] Compare also the more general application of Isa. 28:16 to the church in I Pet. 2:4-5. The two figures, the "planting" and the "building," used in the Essene text are also combined in application to the church in I Cor. 3:9. Of course the description of the church in the figure of a holy temple is a familiar motif in Pauline writings (I Cor. 3:16; II Cor. 6:16).

secular. He was to act as shepherd (CDC 13:7-9 [ed. Rabin]). Scholars have long recognized here a parallel to the Christian shepherd, the bishop or ἐπίσκοπος, a term applied to Jesus in I Pet. 2:25 (together with the designation "shepherd"), but usually to leaders in the early church. Yet the parallel left something to be desired, since the terms ἐπίσκοπος and *mebhaqqēr* are *not* linguistic equivalents. However, even this difficulty is resolved in Qumrân material. In one passage (1QS 6:12-14), the *mebhaqqēr* is called the *pāqîdh* "at the head of the *Rabbîm*"—that is, the "bishop of the Many." *Pāqîdh* is the precise linguistic equivalent of ἐπίσκοπος.[123]

Thus a democratic assembly, a council of twelve, and an episcopal overseer all belong to the pattern of community organization among the Essenes. It would appear that the early church appropriated and modified offices and institutions belonging to its Jewish environment in developing its own organizational structure.

The central "sacraments" of the Essene community appear to be baptism and its communion meal. The baptism of the Essenes, like that of John, was on repentance of sins into the eschatological community of God.[124] Contrary to early Christian usage, the Essenes seem to have practiced continual lustrations as well as baptism on entrance into the New Covenant of the community.

In the recently published liturgy of the common meal of the Essenes, we discover material of the first importance for understanding certain elements in the Eucharistic practice of the early church.[125] Here are excerpts:

This is the order of the session of the "Men of the Name Who Are [Invited] to the Feast"[126] for the counsel of the Community (when [God] sends[127] the Messiah[128] to be with them):

[The Priest][129] shall enter [at][130] the head of all the congregation of Israel and all the fa[thers of] the Aaronids, ... and they shall sit be[fore him each] according to his rank.

Next[131] the [Messi]ah of Israel [shall enter], and the heads of the tho[usands of Israel] shall sit before him [ea]ch according to his rank. ...

[And][132] they shall sit before the (two) of them, each according to his rank. ...

W[hen th]ey solemnly meet together[133] [at a tab]le of communion[134] [or to drink the w]ine, and the common table is arranged [and the] wine [is mixed] for drinking, one [shall not stretch out] his hand to the first portion of bread or [of the wine] before the Priest; for [he shall b]less the first portion of the bread and the wi[ne and shall stretch out] his hand to the bread first of all.[135] Nex[t] the Messiah of Israel shall [str]etch out his hand to the bread. [Next] all the congregation of the Community [shall give tha]nks (and partake), each according to his rank.

And they shall act according to this prescription whenever (the meal) [is arr]anged[136] when as many as ten solemnly meet together.

The common meal of the Essenes is here clearly set forth as a liturgical anticipation of the messianic banquet. This is clear on the one hand from the roles of the Priest[137] and the Messiah of Israel in the protocol. But it is especially clear when the final rubric (11:21-22) is compared with the elaborate protocol. That is, in the "taking of seats" at the meal, the whole of (true) Israel is arranged before the two messianic figures, the priestly class before the Priest, the laity before the Messiah; in the rubric, however, we are told that this prescription is to be carried out *whenever* the meal is arranged, when as many as *ten men* meet together. Obviously this applies to the current practice of the sect.

The anticipation of the messianic banquet is a very strong element also in the New Testament accounts of the Lord's Supper and in the later Eucharistic practice of the Palestinian church. In the Marcan account we read, "Truly, I say to you, I shall not drink again of the fruit of the vine until that day when I drink it new in the kingdom of God" (14:25); in the Lukan version it is even stronger, especially if one follows the shorter text (22:14-19a); and it appears as well in the Pauline and later formulas: "For as often as you eat this bread and drink the cup, you proclaim the Lord's death *until he comes*" (I Cor. 11:26); "*maranatha*, Come, our Lord," and "the holy vine of

---

[123] Cf. Cross, "Qumran Cave I."

[124] 1QS 5:13-15. Cf. 3:4-7 (where baptism is connected not only with repentance and covenant, but also with the gift of the spirit); 4:20-22; etc.

[125] 1QSa 11:11-22 (*Discoveries in the Judaean Desert,* I, 108-18). On the brief notice in 1QS 6:4-6, cf. Kuhn, "Über den ursprünglichen Sinn des Abendmahles und sein Verhältniss zu den Gemeinshaftsmahlen der Sektenschrift," *ETh,* 10 (1950-51), pp. 508-27.

[126] Recalling Num. 16:2.

[127] Reading (ר)יולי for יוליד (cf. Cross, "Qumran Cave I").

[128] I.e., the royal Messiah.

[129] Restoring [הכוהן] as in l. 19.

[130] Restoring [ב]רוא[ש].

[131] Text: ואהר.

[132] Restoring [ו]ישבו.

[133] Text: [ו]יועד.

[134] Text: [לשול[חן יחד. The translation "communion" is technically correct, though it may carry too many connotations in English. Cf. the next line, where I translate השולחן היחד "the common table," which errs in the other direction, since "common" carries too few religious connotations.

[135] Text: לפנים.

[136] Text: [לכול מע]רכת.

[137] I.e., the priestly Messiah to come; no doubt the chief priest of the community in fact played this role.

David thy servant which was made known to us through Jesus" (Didache 9:2; 10:6) .[138]

The early church (Acts 2:46, etc.) ate common meals regularly, "partaking of the food in joy." Indeed, these banquets of joyous anticipation led to the excesses referred to in Jude 12 and I Cor. 11, and to the later reforms which in turn led to the separation of the Eucharist proper from the regular common meals of the faithful.

What is the background of the institution of common meals of the entire community, eaten in anticipation of the messianic banquet? The Passover, the other element in the background of the Lord's Supper, can give no suitable context.[139] It is a yearly feast of memorial, eaten in private in families, and is not, properly, an eschatological festival. The Essene meal gives the first suitable answer.

This is not to suggest that the church merely took over an Essene meal. Within the Lord's Supper are notable original elements: the formulas which transform the old Passover into the feast of the New Covenant memorialize the sacrifice of the body and blood of the victim, the pledge of the covenant.[140] And there is no reason, I think, to suppose that the combination of the two elements, the memorial of the sacrifice and the anticipation of the messianic banquet, does not exist already in the most primitive traditions of the Jerusalem Christian community.

The extreme emphasis on rank at the Essene

banquet is noteworthy. It seems hardly by chance that in the Gospels of Luke (22:24-30) and John (13:12-16) , teaching which repudiates the desire for rank among the disciples is placed in discourses at the Last Supper. Elsewhere we also hear Jesus condemning those who seek places of rank in his kingdom. Moreover, in the parable of the banquet in Luke 14:15-24 (cf. Matt. 22:1-14) , which in its present context is told in reply to one who says, "Blessed is he who shall eat bread in the kingdom of God," we find the remarkable expression, "For I tell you, none of those men who were invited shall taste my banquet"; while the feast of the Essenes is for "the Men of the Name Who Are Invited to the Feast." [141]

We have noted that the life of the sect is understood as life in anticipation of the kingdom of God. This eschatological community is made concrete not only in the common meal of the Messiah, but also in the sharing of goods. Entry into the Essene community meant giving up all private property. In the New Testament church, especially in Palestine, a similar practice obtains: "Now the congregation of believers were of one heart and soul, and no one said that any of the things he possessed were his own, but they had everything in common" (Acts 4:32; cf. 4:32–5:11) ; "and all who believed were together and had all things in common. . . . And day by day, attending the temple together and breaking bread together [in common meals] in their homes. they partook of food with glad and generous hearts" (Acts 2:44-46) .

Again, many (though not all) Essenes eschewed marriage. We have learned that they were soldiers already mustered and prepared for the Holy War of the End Time. Being engaged in the war of God, they took up the ancient ritual prescriptions of the Old Testament for holy war, keeping the "purity of their camps." They refrained from sexual intercourse and marriage, which disqualified one for war, kept the stringent sanitary regulations of holy war, and all the rest. Theirs was not a genuine asceticism, but an eschatological asceticism. They did not, it seems, reject marriage as such, but marriage in the present circumstances.

Compare this structure of thought with the following passage from Paul:

I mean, brethren, the appointed time has grown

[138] Many other allusions to the messianic banquet appear which occur in Eucharistic contexts, or which seem to be shaped by liturgical usage in the early church —e.g., Rev. 19:9: "Blessed are those who are invited to the marriage supper of the Lamb." In Luke 22:30 we read: "that you may eat and drink at my table in my kingdom." This saying is placed in the context of a dispute over rank at the Lord's Supper. The account of the miracle at Cana has frequently been held to have Eucharistic overtones. In any case Jesus' reply to his mother when told that the wine has failed is obscure: "O woman, what have you to do with me? My hour has not yet come." Normally in John "the hour" refers to Jesus' passion and death. Why does Jesus refuse (at least at first) to provide the wine at the feast because his "hour" has not come? Perhaps Jesus is portrayed here as alluding to the day when he properly will provide wine as host at the messianic feast.

[139] For recent attempts to equate the Lord's Supper with the Passover, see J. Jeremias, *op. cit.;* and A. J. B. Higgins, *The Lord's Supper in the New Testament* (Chicago: Henry Regnery Co.; London: Student Christian Movement Press, 1952).

A. Jaubert (see note 26) has argued with no little weight that the Gospel accounts are best understood if Jesus celebrated his Last Supper on the date of Passover in the Essene (and old religious) calendar, while the Crucifixion took place on the eve of the official Jewish Passover.

[140] The rite of the renewal of the covenant among the Essenes is not, so far as we can tell, directly related to their communion meals, the former being an annual affair.

[141] Milik and Barthélemy (*Discovery in the Judaean Desert*, I, 117) have called attention to this parable of the banquet in connection with the list of rules which prohibited men who were maimed, unclean, blind, etc., from entering into the inner councils and cultus of the Essene community. Jesus, in absolute contrast, asserts that "the poor and maimed and blind and lame" will be brought in to the banquet (Luke 14:21)! It is difficult to suppose that the parable is not in conscious reaction to sectarian doctrine.

very short; from now on, let those who have wives live as though they had none, and those who mourn as though they were not mourning, and those who rejoice as though they were not rejoicing, and those who buy as though they had no goods, and those who deal with the world as though they had no dealings with it. For the form of this world is passing away. (I Cor. 7:29-31.)

In the new Essene texts we are in the conceptual world of the New Testament. The New Testament writers draw on common resources of language, theological themes, and concepts; they share common religious institutions. They breathe the same atmosphere, confront the same problems. We can now enter into this rich, variegated world of sectarian Judaism in the first century A.D. with new boldness and understanding. The strange world of the New Testament becomes less baffling, less exotic.

VI. Selected Bibliography

BURROWS, MILLAR. *The Dead Sea Scrolls*. New York: Viking Press, 1955.

DUPONT-SOMMER, A. *Aperçus préliminaires sur les Manuscrits de la Mer Morte*. Paris: A. Maisonneuve, 1950. (*The Dead Sea Scrolls*, tr. E. Margaret Rowley. Oxford: Basil Blackwell & Mott, Ltd.; New York: The Macmillan Co., 1952.)

———. *Nouveaux aperçus sur les Manuscrits de la Mer Morte*. Paris: A. Maisonneuve, 1953. (*The Jewish Sect of Qumran and the Essenes*. London: Vallentine, Mitchell & Co., Ltd., 1954.)

ELLIGER, K. *Studien zum Habakuk-Kommentar vom Toten Meer*. Tübingen: J. C. B. Mohr, 1953.

GASTER, T. H. *The Dead Sea Scriptures*. Garden City: Doubleday & Co., 1956.

KAHLE, P. *Die hebräischen Handschriften aus der Höhle*. Stuttgart: W. Kohlhammer, 1951.

MICHEL, A. *Le Maître de Justice*. Avignon: Aubanel, 1954.

NÖTSCHER, F. *Zur theologischen Terminologie der Qumran-Texte*. Bonn: Peter Hanstein, 1956.

RABIN, H. *The Zadokite Documents*. Oxford: Clarendon Press, 1954.

ROWLEY, H. H. *The Zadokite Fragments and the Dead Sea Scrolls*. Oxford: Basil Blackwell & Mott, Ltd., 1952; New York: The Macmillan Co., 1953.

YADIN, Y. מגילת מלחמת בני אור בבני חושך ממגילות מדבר יהודה. Jerusalem: Bialik Institute, 1955.

ABBREVIATIONS

ATR	Anglican Theological Review
BA	Biblical Archaeologist
BASOR	Bulletin of the American Schools of Oriental Research
CBQ	Catholic Biblical Quarterly
ETh	Evangelische Theologie
HTR	Harvard Theological Review
JBL	Journal of Biblical Literature
JBR	Journal of Bible and Religion
JJS	Journal of Jewish Studies
NTS	New Testament Studies
PAAJR	Proceedings of the American Academy of Jewish Research
PEQ	Palestine Exploration Quarterly
RB	Revue biblique
RHPR	Revue d'histoire et de philosophie religieuses
RHR	Revue de l'histoire des religions
TLZ	Theologische Literaturzeitung
TSK	Theologische Studien und Kritiken
ThZ	Theologische Zeitschrift
VT	Vetus Testamentum
ZAW	Zeitschrift für die alttestamentliche Wissenschaft
ZNW	Zeitschrift für die neutestamentliche Wissenschaft
ZTK	Zeitschrift für Theologie und Kirche

LITERARY CHRONOLOGY

THE OLD TESTAMENT, APOCRYPHA, AND PSEUDEPIGRAPHA

by Samuel Terrien

THE NEW TESTAMENT

by John Knox

The tables presented here show in broad outline the probable chronology of the literature making up the Old Testament, the Apocrypha and other religious writings of Judaism at the dawn of Christianity, and the New Testament and other early Christian writings. They necessarily represent an extreme simplification of the complex relationships inherent in the growth of this literature.

For convenient comparison, a column showing major historical events has been included in each table. Further details about matters of political, cultural, and social development may be found in the tables of the article "Chronology, Metrology, Etc.," Vol. I, pp. 142-64, and in the articles "The History of Israel," Vol. I, pp. 272-91, and "New Testament Times," Vol. VII, pp. 75-113.

I. The Old Testament

The threefold division in Table I—The Law, The Prophets, The Hagiographa—follows the three canons of the Hebrew Bible (see article, "The Canon of the Old Testament," Vol. I, pp. 32-45). In all cases the suggested dates are approximate.

The documentary hypothesis of Pentateuchal composition is indicated in its general outline. For details about the various strata of the main documents, J, E, D, P, see the article "The Growth of the Hexateuch," Vol. I, pp. 185-200. Many scholars are unwilling to offer a precise analysis or dating of these documents, since large blocks of the oral tradition were perhaps as firmly "fixed" as if they had been preserved in written form. It is today increasingly recognized that not only the earlier documents,

such as the Yahwist (J) and the Elohist (E), but also the later documents, such as the Deuteronomist (D) and the Priestly Code (P), incorporate considerable material which goes back to the highest antiquity of Hebrew history.

The literary growth of the other divisions involves similar complexities. As is well known, all the prophetic books have been compiled and edited by several generations of the prophets' disciples. Some indication of this development appears here in the differentiation of parts of Isaiah and Zechariah. Also, various anthologies of proverbs and psalms preceded the canonical forms in which these collections have been finally preserved. The possibility of oral traditions springing from various sources is indicated for these and for the Song of Songs, Ruth, Chronicles, and Daniel; and the relationship between Samuel-Kings and Chronicles is also noted. For further details, the reader is referred to the introductions of the respective books of the Old Testament.

II. The Apocrypha and Pseudepigrapha

Table II includes both the Apocrypha and the Pseudepigrapha, the Apocrypha being distinguished by being printed in *italics*. In addition, the larger documents belonging to the Dead Sea Scrolls have been listed. Attempt has been made in the arrangement to distinguish the main literary genres or types (*Gattungen*). It goes almost without saying that such a division is in many cases arbitrary, since a number of these writings belong to more than one genre and include both prose and poetry. In Table II, as well as in Table I, the conjectural character of the dating must be kept

TABLE I. GROWTH OF THE OLD TESTAMENT

B.C.	HISTORICAL EVENTS	THE LAW	FORMER PROPHETS	LATTER PROPHETS	WISDOM POETRY	LYRICAL POETRY	PROSE
1500		Oral tradition					
1400							
1300	The Exodus						
1200			Oral tradition				
1100			Oral				
1050	Founding of the monarchy—Saul		tradition				
1000	David	J		Memoirs		Oral tradition	Oral tradition?
950	Solomon			& archives			
	Schism of Israel and Judah, 922 B.C.				Oral tradition		
900		E		Oral			
	Jehu's revolution,			tradition			
850	842 B.C.						
800		JE					
750	Fall of Samaria, 722 B.C.			Amos Hosea			
700	Hezekiah			I Isaiah Micah			
650	Reform of Josiah (621 B.C.)	D		Zephaniah Nahum			
600		JED		Kings Habakkuk Samuel Jeremiah	Job		
	Fall of Jerusalem, 586(7) B.C.		Judges Ezekiel Joshua			Lamentations	
550	Return of exiles, 538(9) B.C.	P		II Isaiah Haggai			Oral tradition?
500	Persian rule			I Zechariah III Isaiah			
450		Pentateuch		Obadiah Joel Malachi		Psalms Song of Songs	Ruth Jonah
	Nehemiah						
400				Isaiah 24–27			
350	Alexander the Great conquers Palestine, ca. 332 B.C.				Proverbs	Ezra- Nehemiah Chronicles Esther	
300							
250						Ecclesiastes	
200							
150	Maccabees			II & III Zechariah			Daniel

in mind. For further details the reader is referred to the following articles: "The Literature and Religion of the Apocrypha," Vol. I, pp. 391-419; "The Literature and Religion of the Pseudepigrapha," Vol. I, pp. 421-36; "The Dead Sea Scrolls," Vol. XII, pp. 645-67.

III. The New Testament

For the New Testament, as for the Old, no chronological scheme can be comprehensive and at the same time precise and certain at every point. The table proposed by Clarence T. Craig [1] and presented here in condensed form comes as near perhaps to representing prevailing opinion as any which could be devised. The opinion of the writer of this note would differ at a number of points.

There will be little dispute among scholars as to the dates set forth in the first column,

[1] *The Beginning of Christianity* (New York and Nashville: Abingdon-Cokesbury Press, 1943), pp. 338-41. Used by permission.

TABLE II. GROWTH OF THE APOCRYPHA AND PSEUDEPIGRAPHA

B.C.	HISTORICAL EVENTS	LITERATURE				
		STORY & LEGEND	APOCALYPSE	SERMON & ESSAY	WISDOM	PSALMODY
250	Palestine under Ptolemies (Egypt)	Ahikar (?) *Tobit, ca.* 220? B.C.				
200	Palestine under Seleucids (Syria), from 198 B.C.	*Additions to Esther, ca.* 181-145 B.C.				
	Antiochus IV desecrates temple, 167 B.C.; Judas Maccabaeus purifies, 164 B.C.	*Judith,* 180-100? B.C.		Testaments of the Twelve Patriarchs *I Baruch,* 150? B.C.	*Wisdom of Jesus ben Sirach* [Ecclesiasticus], *ca.* 180 B.C.	
150	Hasmonaean dynasty	*I Esdras* [in Vulg. III Esdras], before 100 B.C.	I Enoch [Ethiopic Enoch], 183-80 B.C.	Manual of Discipline, *ca.* 100? B.C.		
100		*I Maccabees,* 105-63? B.C.		Zadoqite Fragments		*Song of the Three Children*
	Pompey takes Jerusalem, 63 B.C.	*II Maccabees,* 100 B.C.–A.D. 70?	War of the Sons of Light with Sons of Darkness	Sibylline Oracles III Epistle of Jeremy		Psalms of Qumran Sect
		Susanna, 80-50 B.C.		Letter of Aristeas		
50		*Bel and the Dragon,* 80-50 B.C.		Commentary on Habakkuk 1-2		Psalms of Solomon
	Herod the Great, 40-4 B.C.	The Lives of the Prophets			*Wisdom of Solomon,*	
A.D. 1		Assumption of Moses, 4 B.C.–A.D. 28	IV Maccabees, 50 B.C.–A.D. 70	50 B.C.–A.D. 10	Prayer of Manasseh	
	Judea under Roman procurators	III Maccabees, 50 B.C.–A.D. 50 Martyrdom of Isaiah Paralipomena of Jeremiah Life of Adam and Eve [Apocalypse of Moses]			Sayings of the Fathers [Pirke Aboth], *ca.* A.D. 10-100?	
50			II Baruch [Syriac Baruch]			
	Jewish war begins. A.D. 66 Fall of Jerusalem, A.D. 70		II Enoch [Slavonic Enoch, or Secrets of Enoch]			
100			II Esdras [in Vulg. IV Esdras], A.D. 88-117 Apocalypse of Abraham III Baruch [Greek Baruch]			

TABLE III. GROWTH OF THE NEW TESTAMENT AND OTHER EARLY CHRISTIAN LITERATURE

B.C.	GENERAL HISTORY	NEW TESTAMENT HISTORY	LITERATURE
50 A.D.	Herod the Great, 40-4 B.C.	Birth of Jesus, 8-4 B.C.	
1	Augustus Caesar, 27 B.C.–A.D. 14 Tiberius, A.D. 14-37 Pontius Pilate procurator, A.D. 26-36	Preaching of John, A.D. 28 Crucifixion of Jesus, A.D. 30 Expansion of the church Conversion of Paul, between A.D. 32 and 39	
	Gaius Caligula, A.D. 37-41 Claudius, A.D. 41-54	Evangelization of South Galatia (Acts 13–14), A.D. 45-46 or 47-48	
	Famine in Palestine, A.D. 46	Jerusalem Council (Acts 11:30; 15:2; Gal. 2:1), A.D. 46-47 Incident at Antioch (Gal. 2: 11 ff.), A.D. 48	
50	Expulsion of Jews from Rome under Claudius, A.D. 49 Gallio proconsul of Achaia, A.D. 51-52 Felix procurator, A.D. 52-58 Nero, A.D. 54-68 Festus procurator, A.D. 58-62	Paul in Galatia and Macedonia (Acts 16–17), A.D. 49 Arrival at Corinth (Acts 18), A.D. 50 Paul in Ephesus and Asia (Acts 19), A.D. 52-55 Paul in Macedonia and Greece (Acts 20:1-6; 21:17), A.D. 55-56 Paul arrives in Jerusalem, A.D. 56 Paul reaches Rome (Acts 28: 16), A.D. 59 End of Acts story, A.D. 61	I Thessalonians, A.D. 50 II Thessalonians, A.D. 50-51 I Corinthians, A.D. 54-55 Galatians, A.D. 54-55 II Corinthians, A.D. 55 Romans, A.D. 56 Colossians, A.D. 59-61 Philemon, A.D. 59-61 Philippians, A.D. 59-61
	Neronian persecution, A.D. 64	Death of Paul, A.D. 61-64 Outbreak of Jewish revolt; Christians flee to Pella, A.D. 66	
	Galba, Otho, Vitellius, A.D. 68-69 Vespasian, A.D. 69-79 Titus, A.D. 79-81 Pompeii destroyed, A.D. 79	Fall of Jerusalem, A.D. 70	Mark, A.D. 65-75 Approximate order but exact dates uncertain: James (?) Hebrews Luke-Acts Ephesians Matthew
100	Domitian, A.D. 81-96 Nerva, A.D. 96-98 Trajan, A.D. 98-117 Pliny persecutes Christians, A.D. 112 Ignatius martyred at Rome, A.D. 115		Revelation of John I Peter (?) I Clement The Gospel of John The Letters of John Jude I & II Timothy, Titus Letters of Ignatius Didache
150			II Peter, ca. A.D. 150

although there are some who would put the martyrdom of Ignatius somewhat earlier in Trajan's reign and others who would place the date of Festus' accession as procurator of Judea in 55 rather than in 58. Again, some would date the expulsion of the Jews from Rome earlier in Claudius' reign than 49. But the dates for the "New Testament History" can for the most part be only approximate, and even then they presuppose a general conception of the movement of events in the New Testament period which not every scholar would share. Note that a rather wide range of possible dates is indicated for the birth of Jesus and for the conversion of Paul. Some would hold that the date of the crucifixion of Jesus should be put down as 29-30, although 30 is undoubtedly the generally preferred date. The dates in the second column beginning with the "Evangelization of South Galatia" and ending with the "Death of Paul" rest almost entirely upon the two assumptions that Acts has given us the correct order of events and that Paul's missionary work began in the year 45. Many would feel that the Acts order cannot be trusted so implicitly and that there are good reasons for thinking Paul's missionary activities began somewhat earlier. This is not the place to present an alternative chronological scheme—such a scheme would be open to the same objections as this one—but it is important that the reader recognize the hypothetical nature of these dates in many cases and that he be prepared for differences of opinion about them within this Commentary.

The same caution needs to be observed when it comes to the third column. The dates given for the several letters of Paul depend of course upon the chronological scheme of Paul's life which one adopts. A scholar who favored a different scheme from Craig's would propose somewhat different dates for the letters. Even the order of the letters cannot be regarded as established. Craig is properly very cautious about proposing any date at all for the rest of the New Testament books, allowing a range of ten years for Mark, and simply putting the other documents in a certain order without any attempt at precise dating. Obviously he thinks of all of them as falling between about 75 and 150, when II Peter is dated. Question marks are placed after James and I Peter because many scholars believe that both of these books are earlier than 75. But there can be no real certainty even as to the order of the books in this list. Many, for example, would take Matthew before Luke-Acts.

Such an exhibit as this one is useful in setting a picture before us with approximate accuracy. For precise information, where it is available, the reader is referred to the respective introductions.

INDEXES

Prepared by CHARLES L. WALLIS

INDEX OF SCRIPTURE

EZRA cont'd	NEHEMIAH cont'd	ESTHER cont'd	JOB cont'd
3:10 ....4:10b	8:18 ....2:116	9:24 ....3:825b	13:15 ...3:1124; 4:473b; 6:
4:2 ....3:283	9:7 ....9:201	9:27 ....3:825a, 827b	695b
4:6-24 ....3:558b	9:11 ....3:749	10:2-3 ....3:840b	13:16 ....3:1097; 11:33b
4:7-24 ....3:561a, 561b	9:18 ....3:750	10:4-13 ....3:830a	13:21 ....3:1081
4:8-16 ....3:716	9:26 ....3:127	13:7 ....3:828b	13:24 ....5:943b
4:10 ....3:283	10:1 ....3:586		13:26 ....3:909b
4:12 ....3:612	10:2 ....6:368	**JOB**	14:1-2 ....4:489b
5:13-15 ....3:614	10:6 ....3:563b; 6:367	1 ....2:831b	14:7-9 ....3:1038
5:16 ....3:55	10:15 ....3:578	1:1 ...3:898b, 998, 1105; 5:	14:12 ....4:489; 8:419b
5:17 ....3:673	10:23 ....6:367	802b	14:13 ....3:901a
6:2 ....3:724; 6:433, 469	10:28-30 ....3:658	1:3 ....3:49, 886b	14:14 ....8:419b; 11:693b
6:3-5 ....3:571	10:32 ....1:1054	1:5 ....3:886a	14:14-15 ....3:901a
6:14 ....3:606	11:10 ff. 3:563b	1:6 ....6:403	14:15 ....3:887b
7:1-5 ....3:559b	11:12 ....3:583	1:8 ....3:887b	14:16-17 ....3:909b
7:8 ....3:554a	11:12-14 ....3:776	1:9 ...3:1024a, 1067, 1192a;	14:17 ....6:712b
7:9 ....4:638	11:16 ...3:559b, 562b, 642	6:1140a	15:7-8 ....3:899b
7:10 ....6:605b	11:17 ....4:9a	1:10 ....3:887b	15:11 ...3:949b, 1064, 1064b
7:14 ....1:35a, 354b; 3:837	11:23 ....3:758	1:12 ....3:1116a	15:13 ....3:1131
7:15 ....3:606	11:31 ....3:581	1:15-18 ....3:886b	15:15 ....3:1069
7:21 ....3:674	12:23 ....3:674	1:16 ....3:1064a	15:30 ....3:1038
7:25 ....1:35a; 3:734	12:24 ....3:589; 4:10b	1:20 ....3:646	16:2 ....3:1064
7:25-26 ....1:354b	12:27 ....4:5b	2:6 ....11:395	16:4-5 ....3:933b
8:1-20 ....3:562b	12:36 .....3:560b, 589; 4:10b	2:9 ..1:800b; 4:474a; 6:695b	16:15 ....3:743
8:2 ....3:563b; 6:367	12:39 ....3:684, 685	2:10 ....2:838b	16:19 ....3:901a, 1052
8:20 ....3:559a	12:45-46 ....4:10b	2:11 ....5:604	16:21 ....3:901a, 1052
8:21 ....3:562b	13 ....3:565b	3:1-26 ....5:975b	17:4 ....3:1078
8:22 ....3:624	13:10 ....3:578	3:4 ....1:1081a	17:5 ....3:1057
8:31 ....3:624	13:10-11 ....3:563a	3:8 ....4:397, 556	17:11 ....7:720a
8:33 ....3:562b, 721	13:11 ....3:769	3:13-19 ....2:884	17:13-16 ....3:996b
8:34 ....3:562b	13:13 ....3:562b	3:13-22 ....3:880a	18:5 ....3:1068
8:36 ....3:674, 731	13:15-22 ....5:959	3:17 ....5:54b	18:12 ....3:1068
9:1 ....3:744	13:16 ....3:684	3:17-19 ....6:241	18:14 ....1:504
9:2 ....5:213	13:19-22 ....6:321	3:23 ....5:904b; 6:579a	19:6 ....2:838
9:3 ....3:816	13:23-24 ....3:563a	3:26 ....5:939a	19:8 ....6:579a
9:5-15 ....3:668	13:23-25 ....2:830a	4:2-11 ....3:895	19:10 ....3:641
9:6-15 ....3:666a, 667b	13:24 ....1:223b	4:9 ....3:1131	19:14 ....3:620
9:7 ....3:652, 668b	13:25 ....1:678b	4:14-15 ....5:802a	19:18 ....1:62a
9:13 ....3:652	13:28 ....1:35b; 3:563a	4:17 ....3:976a	19:21 ....2:838
9:14 ....3:556b	13:28-29 ....5:759	4:18 ....3:1005, 1069	19:22 ....4:146a
9:15 ....3:652	13:31 ....3:765, 766	4:21 ....3:641	19:23-24 ....2:490a
10:8 ....10:62b		5:1-7 ....3:895	19:24 ....1:48a
10:9-12 ....3:745a	**ESTHER**	5:2-3 ....3:934a	19:25 ....3:1026; 5:1129a
10:10 ....10:79	1 ....6:421	5:8-27 ....3:896	19:25-27 .....3:901b, 928a,
	1:8 ....6:409	5:17-18 ....4:802b	996b
NEHEMIAH	1:11 ....3:839a	5:21 ....4:68b	19:27 ....3:915a
1:1 ....6:469	1:12 ....3:888b	5:26 ....5:84b	19:28 ....3:1072a
1:3 ....3:1172; 6:929	1:14 ....3:627	6:4 ....3:1131; 5:917b, 939a	21:7 ....5:917b
1:4-5 ....3:572	2:7 ....3:846b; 6:368	6:18 ....1:225a	21:22 ....3:1072
1:11 ....3:631	2:10 ....3:842b	7:1-6 ....4:540	22:2-3 ....3:899b
2:4 ....3:572	2:12 ....5:138a	7:2 ....3:1162	22:14 ....5:441
2:8 ....6:531	2:15 ....3:842b	7:8 ....3:1057	22:22 ....3:631
2:11 ....3:641	3:2 ....3:647	7:11 ....3:1131; 5:939a	23:3 ....10:191a
2:20 ....3:572	3:7 ....3:824b, 825b	7:12 ....4:397	23:3-4 ....11:747b
3:1 ....3:654	3:8 ...3:827b, 828b, 848a,	7:16 ....10:611b	23:3-5 ....11:636a
3:4 ....3:562b, 642	867	7:17 ......3:887b; 10:611b	23:10 ...5:446a, 867a, 917b
3:5 ....3:418b	3:9 ....3:848b	7:20 ...1:61b; 3:987a, 1040b,	23:11-12 ....3:1151a
3:10 ....3:562b	3:12-15 ....3:827b	1041; 12:388b	24:18-24 ....3:1089
3:14 ....1:1062	3:13 ....3:834b, 865	7:21 ....3:900b, 1007	24:20 ....3:1098b
3:21 ....3:562b, 642	3:15 ....6:150b	8:3 ....3:976a, 1043	26:4 ....3:1030
3:25 ....3:797	4:1 ....3:841a	8:13 ....3:1006	26:11 ....2:885
3:27 ....3:214	4:2 ....4:78a	8:16-19 ....3:1038	26:12 ....3:964
3:31 ....3:187; 6:305	4:8 ....3:842b	8:20 ....3:992a	26:12-13 ....4:397
3:32 ....3:551b	4:11 ....3:843a; 6:383	9:6 ....2:885; 4:400	26:13 ....3:1131
4:1-4 ....5:665a	4:13-14 ......3:841a, 843b	9:9 ....1:117a	26:14 ....1:949a
5:2 ....1:994	4:14 ....3:829b	9:13-14 ....4:397	27:13-23 ....3:1089
5:14 ....3:612	4:16 ....3:844a, 844b, 845a;	9:22 ....3:1185	28 ....4:592b; 5:18b
6:11 ....1:555b, 801a	6:486	9:23 ....3:1123a	28:1-11 ....4:793
7:2 ....6:531	5:10 ....3:860	9:24 ....3:976a, 1156a	28:2 ....3:63
7:3 ....3:813	5:14 ....3:860	9:34 ....3:1081	28:12 ....5:274b
7:5 ....3:554b, 555a, 577	6:1-11 ....3:846	10:8-13 ....4:374	28:14 ....3:964
7:7 ....3:559a, 576	6:9 ....3:655	10:21-22 ....6:241	28:20-23 ....4:773b
7:15 ....3:579	6:11 ....3:655	11:5 ff. 3:1069	28:21 ....4:594b
7:25 ....3:579	6:13 ....6:484	11:7 ....3:1099; 10:530a	28:23 ....4:594b
7:43 ....3:593	7:8 ....3:708	11:19 ....6:489	28:27-28 ....4:773b
8 ....2:315b	7:10 ....3:850b; 6:402	11:20 ....3:1057	28:28 ....4:594b
8:1 ....3:627	8:1 ....3:850	12:6 ....3:900a	29:3 ....4:146
8:4 ....6:368	8:11 ....3:835a	12:7 ....3:1035; 4:818	29:7-25 ....4:770a
8:6 ....4:151	8:13 ....3:835b	12:9 ....9:398b	29:14 ....11:219
8:8 ....1:57b; 3:604	8:17 ....3:827b	12:11 ....3:1141b	29:15 ....3:934b, 1112
8:9 ....3:560b, 586	9:19 ....3:824b, 825b	12:12-21 ....3:895	30:25 ....3:934b
8:10 ....6:673a; 8:254a	9:20-32 ....3:824b	12:14 ....5:904b	31:10 ....5:545
8:16 ....3:685	9:22 ....3:825b	12:14-15 ....3:1005	31:11 ....3:1033
		13:4 ....3:1014	31:16-17 ....3:934b

689

MATTHEW cont'd

7:13 .....6:579a; 7:485a; 12: 241b
7:13-14 ....4:634a
7:14 ...3:930b; 6:648a; 10: 522a; 11:272a; 12:180
7:14-23 ....9:613a
7:16 3:471b, 937a; 6:679a; 7:828b; 10:297a, 580b; 11: 550b, 655b
7:16-20 .....6:363b; 10:149a
7:17 ....11:532a
7:20 . 6:611a, 655a, 666b, 698b; 10:380a, 648b; 11: 532a
7:21 1:402a; 2:774a; 4: 648a; 8:210b; 10:469a; 11: 493a; 12:231a
7:21-23 ....10:148
7:22 ....8:696a
7:24 .....4:781b; 12:231a
7:24-27 ....3:157b; 9:411b; 10:398b
7:25 ....11:492a
7:26 ....12:231a
7:26-27 ....2:927a
7:27 ....2:1056b
7:28 ....7:156a
7:28-29 ...2:774b; 6:704b; 7:155b
7:29 ....10:385b
8:4 ....2:7a, 70
8:8 ....5:135a
8:9 ....9:380a
8:10 ....6:80b, 666b; 7:789b
8:11 ....6:722b
8:16-17 ....6:200a
8:17 ....5:413b, 622
8:20 ....1:122a; 2:795a; 7: 405a
8:22 ....2:554a; 6:830a
8:28 ....10:501b
9:2 ....3:958b, 1111b
9:6 .....7:339a; 9:392b
9:8 ....9:392b
9:11 ...2:251b; 7:170a, 517a
9:13 ......6:595a, 628b
9:20 .....3:1095a; 9:255
9:21 ....8:781a
9:22 ....8:41a
9:29 ....8:41a
9:35-38 ....8:533
9:36 ....12:150b
9:40 ....2:407b
10:2 .....7:687b; 10:276
10:5 ....8:7a
10:8 ....7:672a, 730a, 877b; 10:102
10:10 ....10:102
10:12-13 ....7:53a
10:14 ....1:915
10:16 ...2:562a, 844b, 1068b; 3:1159a; 8:283, 735a; 10: 712b
10:16-39 ....3:937a
10:19 ......3:674a; 11:566a
10:19-20 ....3:138b
10:22 ...6:623a; 8:735a; 10: 185a
10:23 ....7:182b
10:24 ....6:641a; 11:259a
10:25 ......3:189; 7:865
10:28 ...3:935b; 4:295b; 6: 600a
10:29 ....6:592b; 8:223a
10:29-30 ....2:501a
10:30 ....7:53a
10:35 ....2:929b
10:36 ....2:735a, 1091b, 1155a; 5:915a; 7:215b
10:37 ...3:181a; 6:830a; 7: 451b
10:37-38 ....9:590b
10:37-39 ....3:453a

MATTHEW cont'd

10:39 ......3:946a, 948b; 5: 1103b; 7:874b; 9:82b; 11: 568a
10:40 ....8:188
10:40-42 ....7:790
10:42 ...10:18a, 171b, 348a
11:2-6 ......3:993b; 5:716b
11:3 ....7:826b; 8:363a
11:3-4 ....3:1170b
11:4 .....8:346b; 10:469a
11:4-5 .....8:648, 721a
11:5 ......2:29b; 5:359b; 7: 891a; 9:56a
11:6 ....7:150b; 8:470b
11:7-8 ....11:291a
11:7-14 ....7:14b
11:9 ....4:268a
11:11 ....7:15a, 735a, 735b; 515a
11:12 ....5:716b
11:15 ......4:212b, 793b
11:19 ...8:69a; 10:702b, 714a
11:21 ....3:1061a
11:21-24 ....6:660a
11:25 ...6:595a; 10:33, 585a; 12:250b
11:26 ....8:760a
11:27 .....7:13a; 12:295
11:28 ...2:1060b; 4:715b; 5: 533b; 6:684a; 7:13a, 722a, 829b, 885b; 8:357a; 10: 498b; 11:631a
11:28-29 ...5:864b; 6:724a; 11:657a
11:28-30 ....3:174a; 5:647a; 11:447a
11:29 . 2:202b; 5:99b, 862, 8:497a; 10:312b; 11:643a
11:29-30 ...... 6:676b
11:30 ....7:529b; 12:291
12:3-4 ....2:996b
12:4 ....1:1025
12:7 ....6:628b
12:13 ....1:74a
12:15-21 ....5:413b
12:20 ....6:690b
12:25 ....3:155b, 969b
12:28 ....9:71
12:30 .....2:511a; 3:969b; 7: 16a
12:33-34 ....11:663a
12:34 ....3:1041b
12:34-37 ....4:641b
12:36 ...2:896; 3:934a; 10: 399b, 701a; 12:136
12:37 .....10:348a; 12:49a
12:39-40 ....7:760
12:42 .....4:778a; 11:288a
12:43-45 ...10:416a, 528a
12:49-50 ....8:794b
12:50 ...1:986a; 4:882b; 10: 355a
13:3 ....1:496a
13:12 ....5:885a
13:13-17 ....7:17a
13:15 ....2:502b
13:16-17 .....7:15b; 8:139a
13:17 ....9:383a
13:19 ....10:315b
13:21 ....10:419b
13:24-30 ....3:176a
13:25 ....6:659b
13:31 ....1:496a
13:31-33 ....7:148a
13:32 ....6:722b
13:33 ...1:922a; 7:166b
13:35 ....7:489a, 494b
13:38 ....10:46
13:38-39 ....12:259
13:44 .....4:793; 7:697b
13:47 ....10:612a
13:47-50 ....7:151a
13:58 ....5:367a; 6:608a,

MATTHEW cont'd

631b; 7:729a; 9:183b; 10: 498a, 573b
14:25 ....2:742
14:27 .....3:958b, 1111b
14:36 ......3:1095a; 9:255
15:11 ....2:56a
15:14 .....4:61b; 9:414b
15:19 ...5:688, 699a; 6:710a; 7:305a
15:21-28 ....3:1044b
15:22-28 ....5:718a
15:24 ...7:130a, 142b; 8:7a
15:28 ....11:721a
15:34 ....6:695b
16:3 .....1:539b; 2:1075b
16:6 ....1:920b
16:15 .....10:393b; 12:245b
16:16 ......9:126; 11:275b
16:17 ....1:22a
16:17-18 ....2:838a
16:17-19 ....1:121a; 10:461
16:18 ....4:676b; 5:491b, 697a; 7:53a, 151b, 723b; 9:33; 10:47, 218
16:22 ......7:130b; 8:136b, 174b
16:23 ......8:497a; 9:624a
16:24 ...3:948b; 6:684a; 7: 375a; 8:809; 10:554b; 11: 175b; 12:62a
16:25 ......6:877b; 12:27a
16:26 ....10:621a
16:27 ....10:331
17:1-7 ....1:1080
17:1-8 ....5:413b; 10:547a
17:1-21 ....10:43a
17:5 .....1:1018; 5:464
17:8 ....4:130a
17:17 ....7:584a
17:20 ....2:384b; 6:1073b; 10:170
17:21 ....1:850a
17:24-27 ....1:1054
17:27 ....1:95a
18:3 ...2:461b; 3:946a; 8: 506; 11:291b, 296b; 12: 106a
18:3-4 ....7:152a
18:6 ...3:1023b; 4:152b; 6: 25b; 10:403a
18:7 ...2:1044a, 1152b; 9: 624a
18:8 ....4:821a
18:10 ....5:135a
18:11 ....7:342b; 11:567a
18:14 .....6:570a, 586a; 8: 139b, 161b
18:15-17 ...10:63, 353b
18:17 ....7:151b
18:19 ....8:797
18:20 ...2:340b, 415b; 8: 798b; 10:465a, 575a, 585a, 677a, 745b
18:22 .....2:119b, 906b; 3: 1106a; 4:428b
18:28 ....9:606a
19:6 ....4:236b
19:8 ....2:450b, 474b
19:9 ....10:79
19:17 ...2:7a; 7:401b; 8:313; 10:656b
19:18 ....2:93b
19:20 .....7:801; 8:312b
19:21 ....6:684a
19:23 ....2:520b
19:27 ...3:1150a, 1192a; 6: 628b; 7:489b
19:27-30 ....3:914a
19:28 .....11:544; 12:399
20:1-15 ....10:46
20:1-16 ....3:32b
20:16 .....3:946a; 10:56
20:21 ....2:1056a

MATTHEW cont'd

20:22 ....7:579a
20:25-26 ....11:290b
20:25-28 ...3:103a; 6:690b
20:26-27 ....2:1073b
20:26-28 ....3:934b
20:27 ....3:946a
20:28 ......6:602a; 8:124a, 619a; 11:285a; 12:126a
21:1-17 ....7:137b
21:5 ....6:591a
21:9 ....4:620
21:12-13 ....3:804
21:13 ....5:872, 872b
21:19 ....5:884b
21:22 ....11:195a
21:30 ....1:576a
21:31 ...3:105b; 6:666b; 7: 354a; 8:145b; 10:702b
21:33 ....8:346b
21:33-42 ....4:434
21:41-44 ....4:26b
21:42 ....4:620
21:43 ....6:1129a
21:44 ....6:703b
22:2-10 ....4:835
22:10 ....10:725b
22:14 ....10:16
22:21 ....9:604b
22:23-28 ....10:223b
22:37 ....1:794b
22:37-38 ....10:730
22:37-40 ....4:195a
22:41-46 ....4:588
22:42 ....8:356a
23 ....5:965; 7:851
23:4 ....12:291
23:8 .....1:793a; 6:878a; 8: 216b; 10:445; 11:295b, 547b
23:8-11 ....11:229b
23:12 ....5:135a
23:14 ....6:666b
23:15 ....8:497b
23:16 ....9:414b
23:17-19 ....2:44b
23:23 ...3:768; 4:265; 6: 661b; 11:662b
23:24 ....1:95a; 7:53a
23:27 ......8:497b; 9:298
23:27-28 ....6:132a
23:33 ......6:688a; 8:497b
23:35 ....3:509b
23:37 ...2:311b; 5:480a, 888b; 6:630a, 660a, 678a, 702b, 937b; 8:633b; 10: 343a
23:37-39 ....7:137a
23:38 ......6:572a; 8:782b
23:39 ....4:620
24:2 ....6:688a
24:3 ....7:856
24:6 ....6:500
24:10-12 ....12:243
24:12 ....12:257
24:15 ....6:476
24:15-16 ....1:74b
24:23-24 ....12:244
24:35 ....6:1063b
24:36 .....1:75a; 7:584b
24:38-39 ....1:539a
24:41 ....5:545
24:44 ....7:557b
25:13 .....2:724a; 8:232a
25:14 ....10:365b
25:14-29 ....10:581a
25:14-30 ....8:327
25:21 ...4:821b; 9:380a; 11: 512a; 12:96
25:23 ...2:350b; 12:96b
25:24 ....8:277a
25:29 ....4:837a
25:31 ....12:342
25:31 ff. 5:676
25:31-32 ...6:253; 10:331

INDEX OF SUBJECTS

A

À Kempis, Thomas: on cross bearing, 5:925a f
on love, 5:143a
on spiritual lukewarmness, 6:1129b
on waiting upon God, 6: 1132a
Aaron: death of, 2:240 f, 241a f
genealogy of, 1:891 f
as Moses' spokesman, 1: 878 f
rod of, 2:227 f, 227a f
sons of, 2:152 f
stories about, 4:688b f
Aaronic priesthood: consecration of, 2:42 f
in Ezekiel, 6:55b
genealogy of, 3:366
"Abaddon," meaning of, 12: 434
"Abba," meaning of, 9:517
Abbé de Saint-Cyran, spiritual independence of, 5: 1009a f
Abbott, Lyman, on immortality, 11:469b
Abdon the Pirathonite, 2:775
Abel: Cain and, 1:517 f; see also Cain
faith of, 11:722, 722a
sacrifice of, 11:722a
Abelard, Peter, on Jerusalem, 6:760b
Abiathar: banishment of, 3: 35
identification of, 3:22
"Abiding," meaning of, 12: 250a
Abigail, David and, 2:1011 f
Abihu, Nadab and, 2:49 f, 49a f
Abijah (Jeroboam's son), death of, 3:125 f
Abijah (wife of Ahaz), 3: 287b f
Abijah (or Abijam) of Judah: battle of Zemaraim and, 3:478 f
reign of, 3:132 f, 478 f
Ability, conspicuous, 3:378b f
Abimelech (Genesis): Abraham and, 1:640 f
deception of, 1:670 f
Abimelech (Judges): ambition of, 2:751a f
Shechemite quarrel with, 2:755 f
story of, 2:751 f
Abiram, revolt of, 2:222 f
Abner: death of, 2:1060 f
Ishbaal and, 2:1055 f
Joab and, 2:1155b
Abominations, in Revelation, 12:491 f
Abraham: call of, 1:440b, 570 f
character of, 1:566a f
children of, 8:604a
covenant with, 1:598 f, 608 f; 10:512a f
descendants of, 11:617b

dispute with Abimelech, 1:640 f.
divine promises made to, 1:372a
in Egypt, 1:579 f
example of, 9:448b f
faith of, 11:61b f, 724b f; 12:41 f
faith of (Hebrews), 11: 657b f, 658, 724 f
faith of (Pauline), 9:446 f, 446b f; 10:501 f, 501b f; 11:658
as friend of God, 12:44
genealogy of, 1:567 f
Hagar and, 1:604 f
hospitality of, 1:617 f
Isaac and, 1:633 f, 636a f
justification of (Pauline), 9:439 f, 439a f
leaves Hebron, 1:633 f
Lot and, 1:583 f
Melchizedek and, 11:661 f
as name, 1:609 f
obedience of, 11:724b f, 728 f
primacy of, 1:442b
promise to, 3:747; 5:411a; 11:656, 712a
sacrifice of Isaac by, 1: 642 f, 642a f; 11:61a f, 728 f, 728b f
Second Isaiah reference to, 5:590 f
self-renunciation of, 11:61a
settles in Hebron, 1:588 f
testing of, 1:642 f; 11: 728b f
tradition of, 1:442a
Abrahams, Israel, on Jewish home life, 3:396b
Absalom: defeat and death of, 2:1138 f
flight and return of, 2: 1114 f
rebellion of, 2:1122 f
revolt of, against David, 2:1108 f, 1108a f
Absolution, right of, 8:106
Abstinence: marital, 10:77b f
Pastoral teaching on, 11: 425 f
Abyssinian Church, canon and, 1:42a
Accent of Peter, 2:773b f
"According to the scriptures," 1:11a
Acedia, as medieval sin, 1: 552a f
Achaia, identification of, 10: 374
Achan, sin of, 2:583, 583b f
Achievement: partial, 1:569b
persistence and, 9:160b f
pride of, 4:41a
Achish, David's vassalage to, 2:1021 f
Acquaintance, friend and, 6: 908a
Acquisitive instinct, 6:699b f
Acquisitiveness, Ecclesiastes teaching on, 5:58 f

Acrocorinth, identification of, 10:3b
Acropolis, description of, 7: 89b
Acrostic Dialogue on Theodicy, 3:882a f
Acrostic poem, 4:954a f
Acrostic psalm, 4:135, 135a f, 592, 592a, 622
"Act of God," 7:312a, 761a
Action: appeal for, 4:59b, 711a f
faith and, 5:215b f; 6:394b
need for, 5:80 f
thought and, 9:578a f; 12: 47b f
word and, 12:47b f
Activism, 3:173a f
Acton, John, on power, 1: 588b, 1154b f; 3:977a; 5: 70b; 6:912a
Acts, as literary form, 7:38a f
Acts (book of): abrupt ending of, 9:351 f
apologetic purpose of, 9: 12b f
authorship of, 8:3a f, 9a f
Catholic epistles and, 9: 4b f
composition of, 9:15b f
criticism of, 9:12a f
date of, 8:9a f; 9:11b f, 14b
Greek text of, 9:a f
as history, 9:a, 12b f
importance of, 9:3a f
Josephus and, 9:11b f
literary contacts of, 9:10b f
literary form of, 7:38a f; 8:3a f
Luke and, 7:38a f; 8:3a f
map concerning, 10:428
"Neutral" text of, 9:9a f
outline of, 8:5a; 9:22b f
Pauline epistles and, 9: 4b f, 10b f
political motive of, 9:12b, 14a
preface of, 9:23 f
purpose of, 9:352
sources of, 9:15b f
style of, 8:3b f
title of, 9:5a
"we sections" of, 9:16a f
"Western" text of, 9:9a f
Acts 1-12, map concerning, 9:2
Acts 2, 6, 7, map concerning, 9:2
Acts of Paul, 7:38b, 188a
Acts of Solomon: identification of, 3:4b f
as source of Kings, 3:4b f
Actual, ideal and, 6:686b f
Adam: deception of, 11:406
descendants of, 1:527 f, 527a f
legend about, 7:372b
sin of, 1:501 f, 501b f
sin of (Pauline), 1:501b f; 9:462 f, 518 f
Adams, Charles Francis, on religion of John Quincy Adams, 5:664a

Adams, Harry, on meaning in life, 1:515b
Adams family, moral energy of, 5:519b
Addams, Jane, work of, 6: 1070a
Adder, charming of, 5:885a f
Addison, Joseph, on Sabbath keeping, 5:655a
Adequacy, sense of, 10:446b f
Adler, Felix, on character of sin, 4:790b; 6:582b
Administration, justice in, 6: 916
Admiration, loss of, 4:803b
"Admonish," in Pauline usage, 11:312
Admonitions, for life, 4:192 f
Admonitions of an Egyptian Sage, on life's paradoxes, 5:16a
Adolescence, description of, 7:705b
Adolescents, drift of, 11:106b
Adoni-bezek, identification of, 2:690
Adonijah: death of, 3:34
proclaimed as king, 3:20 f
Adonis, identification of, 5: 81
Adonis cult (Isaiah), 5:273 f
"Adoption," in Pauline usage, 7:24b; 9:516
Adrammelech, identification of, 3:285
Adrian, biblical interpretation of, 1:114a
Adullam: cave of, 6:909
identification of, 3:782
Adult, obligations of, 2:998b
Adulteress, Proverbs warnings against, 4:821 f
Adultery: Christ's teachings on, 7:297a f
Deuteronomic decalogue on, 2:367b f
Jewish law on, 7:297
Levitical code on, 2:101b f
O.T. punishment of, 2: 166 f; 8:592 f
prohibition against, 1:986, 986b f; 2:367b f
woman taken in, 8:591 f, 591b f
Advance, retreat and, 6: 829a f
Advent: of God, 4:262; 5: 426a f, 597b
Second, 7:6a f
Adventure: faith as, 1:568a; 10:549b f
life as, 6:374a
Adversary, God as (Joban), 3:1114b f
Adversity: as blessing, 8:735a
character and, 3:225a f
facing of, 9:333a f
integrity and, 3:897b f
power of, 9:530b f
security from, 4:62a f
uses of, 3:1155b f
Advertisement of Christianity, 7:684a

in church, 12:24a
denial and, 12:274b f
disbelief and, 5:420b, 748a
doubt and, 5:912a
faith as, 10:491a f
I John teaching on, 12:
  289
in God; see God
hesitancy in, 8:424b
hilarity and, 5:510b
importance of, 7:405a
Johannine concept of, 12:
  270 f
love and, 12:270a f
in luck, 2:99a f
in man, 1:625b
meaning of, 10:491a
momentousness of, 8:511a f
nature of, 2:921a
obstacle to, 9:193a f
"Believe": as commandment,
  12:270a f
etymology of, 1:231b
as Johannine concept, 8:
  442b
will to, 3:1142b
Believer: complacent, 5:
  554b f
half, 11:417b
priesthood of, 1:972a f; 2:
  17a f; 11:619b f
unbeliever and, 12:112 f
Believing, seeing and, 9:
  119b f
Bell, church, 4:693b
Bell, Clive, on religious
  spirit, 2:973b
Bell, W. Cosby, on meaning
  of death, 3:1010a
Beloved, Christ as, 10:617
"Beloved": as Christian
  term, 12:112a
in N.T. usage, 12:323
Beloved community, 7:250b,
  310a
Belshazzar: feast of, 6:346b,
  418 f
identification of, 6:422
as name, 6:420
sin of, 6:431
Ben Shetach, Simeon, writings of, 1:36b
Ben Sirach, Jesus: identification of, 5:4a
writings of, 1:35b f
Benedict, biblical interpretation of, 1:115b f
Benedict, George, on Judaism and Christianity, 12:
  19b
Benediction: appreciation of,
  2:173a f
Christian use of, 11:460b
Benedictus, of Zechariah, 8:
  45, 47a f
Benét, Stephen Vincent: on
  Lincoln and will of God,
  6:879a f
on patience of Lincoln, 3:
  963b
Benevolence: example of, 4:
  598b f
shallow, 9:587b
Bengel, Johann Albert, biblical study of, 12:624b
Ben-hadad: death of, 3:226 f
defeated by Ahab, 3:165 f
identification of, 3:135
Benjamin: birth of, 1:741 f
cities of, 3:782 f
genealogy of, 3:372 f
Benjamin Gate, 5:970, 1071
Bennett, John C.: on appeal
  of Communism, 6:584a

on limits of evil, 2:909a
on wealth, 4:843a
Bennett, W. H., on Christian
  freedom, 12:115
Bentley, Richard, on textual
  criticism, 12:624a f
Bequest, enduring, 5:39b f
Berdyaev, Nicholas: on
  Christian responsibility,
  12:37b
on Christianity, 6:878b
on Dostoevski, 5:817b
on hope, 11:711b
on spiritual freedom, 5:
  818a
Bereavement, nature of, 1:
  814b
Berenice, daughter of Ptolemy II Philadelphus, 6:
  515
Berggrav, Eivind J., Christian witness of, 11:483a
Bergson, Henri L., on spiritual progress, 2:916a
Bernadotte, Count, on God's
  help, 2:723a
Bernard of Clairvaux: biblical interpretation of, 1:
  120b f
on Christ, 12:550a f
humility of, 11:291b
on love of Christ, 5:108a
on myrrh, 5:138a
on Song of Songs, 5:107a,
  125b
spirit of, 5:101b f
on sufficiency of love, 5:
  102a, 113b f
on virtue of love, 5:130b
on wealth of church, 12:
  65a
Bernard of Cluny, on beauty
  of Zion, 5:639a
Beroea, identification of, 9:
  229
Bertholet, Alfred, on Ezekiel,
  6:43b f, 51b
"Beseech," in N.T. usage,
  11:293
Best: good and, 12:510a f
perversion of, 6:708b f
Bethany, identification of,
  7:507a; 8:335
Beth-aven: as Bethel, 6:564b
calf of, 6:672, 672b f
Beth-eden, identification of,
  6:779
Bethel: Amos oracle on, 6:
  798 f
calf of, 6:668 f
Jacob at, 1:688 f, 738 f,
  738a f; 6:696, 696b
shrine at, 6:1082a f
Bethel (deity), worship of,
  5:1113 f
Bethesda, identification of,
  8:539 f
Beth-haccherem, identification of, 3:689; 5:857
Beth-haggan, identification
  of, 3:235
Beth-jeshimoth, identification of, 6:202
Bethlehem, identification of,
  6:931; 7:256 f
inn at, 6:617b
meaning of, 2:837; 8:50a f
Micah reference to, 6:
  930b f, 931
significance of, 2:833a f; 6:
  931
well of, 12:424b
Beth-pelet, identification of,
  3:781

Beth-shemesh, identification
  of, 5:1096
Beth-togarmah, identifica-
  tion of, 6:213 f
Beth-zur, identification of, 3:
  690
Betrothal, Jewish custom of,
  7:254
Better, worst and, 6:814b
Better times, Haggai promise of, 6:1043 f
Bevan, Edwyn, on light as
  symbol, 10:709a
Beveridge, Albert J., on Ten
  Commandments, 12:230b
Bewkes, Eugene G., on divination, 2:886a
Bezalel and Oholiab, ap-
  pointment of, 1:1059 f,
  1084 f
Bèze, Théodore de: on
  church, 4:676b
Greek text of, 8:20a
Bias, defense of, 5:706a; 11:
  75a
Bible: achievement of, 1:460b
allegorical interpretation
  of, 1:107a f, 109b f,
  113a f, 116a f, 117b f,
  124a; 5:104b
appeal of, 1:465b; 3:485a
appreciation of 1:870b
archaeological study of, 1:
  135a f
authority of, 1:3 f, 13a f,
  24a f; 10:486b f
as basis for teaching, 1:
  31a f
as best seller, 11:111b
Bishops', 1:91b f
"bleeding" of, 9:230a f
Breeches, 1:91b f
chronological tables of, 1:
  142 f
church and, 1:293b f
Complutension Polyglot
  text of, 12:621b
conversion and, 7:165b
of Cranmer, 1:89b f
critical study of, 12:623b
critical text of, 12:622b f
criticism of, 1:127b f,
  168b f; 7:484b, 585a
developing revelation of,
  1:27a
distribution of, 1:90a
as earthly book, 11:675a f
English; see English Bible
exposition of, 1:458a f
Geneva, 1:90b f
Great (1539), 1:89b f
Greek, 7:97a f
Greek influence in, 7:97a
Hebrew, 12:655b f
Hellenistic, 1:35a f
historical exegesis of, 1:
  118b f
historical interpretation
  of, 1:120b f
as history book, 1:166a f
history of interpretation
  of (ancient), 1:106a f
history of interpretation
  of (medieval), 1:115 f
history of interpretation
  of (modern), 1:127 f
history of interpretation
  (Reformation), 1:123a f
honesty of, 2:582b f
inerrancy of, 1:16b, 29b,
  124b f, 166b f; 11:29a
influence of, 5:539a; 11:
  310a
inspiration of, 1:4a, 129a,

166b f, 453a, 891b f; 11:
  507a
interpretation of, 5:103a f;
  11:352a, 630b
interpretation handbooks
  of, 1:113a f
interpretation principles
  of, 1:26a f, 460b, 464b f
interpretation rules of, 9:
  38a
King James Version: see
  King James Version
knowledge of, 11:432a
knowledge of God and, 10:
  629a f
literal interpretation of, 1:
  106b f, 110b, 126b,
  167a f
literary analysis of, 1:
  130a f; 5:104a
as literature, 1:166a; 6:
  745a
as love story, 5:141a f
Masoretic, 12:653b f
memorizing of, 4:623a f;
  11:391a f, 462b f
metrology of, 1:153b f
mistakes of, 1:849b
modern methods of inter-
  pretation of, 1:135b f
neglect of, 4:749a f; 11:
  309a f
need of, 11:309b f
normative function in
  church of, 1:12b f
numismatics of, 1:157a f
objectivity of, 5:455b f
pessimism of, 10:641a
philological research of, 1:
  128a f
picturesque language of,
  11:43a
printing of, 12:621a f
promises of, 11:712a f
purpose of, 1:165b f
rationalistic principle of
  interpretation of, 1:
  128b f
reading of, 1:87a, 170b f,
  293a f, 645a f, 971a f; 2:
  450b f; 4:51a, 159b, 493b,
  707b; 5:538b f; 7:165b,
  289a, 456b, 495b, 513b;
  8:581b, 600b f
rediscovery of, 3:317a f
Reims-Douay Version, 1:
  92b f
as revelation, 1:3a; 11:
  25a f
Revised Standard Version;
  see English Bible
Revised Version; see Eng-
  lish Bible
scholarly study of, 1:17a f
scholarship dilemma of, 1:
  169b f
as scientific book, 1:166a f
scientific research and, 1:
  26b
significance of, 1:3 f
study of, 1:165 f, 883a; 5:
  883b f
study barriers of, 1:165a f
study rewards of, 1:168a f
"surprising books" of, 12:
  320a f
symbols in, 11:29a
Taverner, 1:89b
teaching of, 11:461b f
textual classification of,
  12:624b f
textual criticism of, 12:
  618b

Bowen, George, on insignificance, 5:421b

Bowie, Walter Russell, on city of God, 11:217b

"Bowls," in Revelation usage, 12:480

Bowls of God's wrath, Revelation vision of, 4:751a

Bowman, W. D., on significance of names, 2:908b

Bowring, John, on cross, 6:685b

Box, G. H., on Bible in the Renaissance, 12:621a

Boy: "boily," 7:705b
disobedience of, 3:1029b f

Bradford, Gamaliel: on knowledge of God, 5:532a
on moral experience, 12:437a
on thirst for God, 4:411b

Bradford, William: on hardships of Pilgrims, 5:572a
on sustenance of God, 5:539b

Bradley, F. H., on nature of God, 1:869b

Bradley, Omar, on war, 1:592a f

Brainerd, David, faith of, 4:544a

"Branch," as messianic term, 5: 787a, 988 f; 6:1070

Bravery: basis of, 3:160b f
contagion of, 11:743a

Bread: breaking of, 8:379b; 9:51
cast on waters, 5:81
"our daily," 7:312b f
"house" of, 8:50a f
of life, 2:386a f
need of, 7:271b
staff of, 4:560
as sacrament, 7:430b f
as symbol, 1:1025b f; 2:19b, 118a f

Bread of Life, Christ as, 8:167a f, 552 f, 566, 567a, 572, 572b f

Bread of the presence, 2:117b f, 160a f

Breasted, James Henry, on conscience, 1:755a

Breastpiece, description of, 1:1040 f

Breath, ancient concept of, 6:1042

"Breathless life," 7:738b

Breeches Bible, 1:91a

Brethren: consciousness of, 10:573a
in Hebrew usage, 3:663
meaning of, 11:148, 259

Bride: as Revelation symbol of, 12:508 f
simile of, 5:812b

Bridegroom, Christ as, 7:354b f; 10:727 f

Bridgebuilder, 10:551a

Bridges, Robert, on increase in love, 5:137a

Briggs, Le Baron R., on work, 1:512b

Bright, John, social concern of, 3:1107a; 6:604b

Britain: Christianizing of, 1:84a
monarchy of, 4:590b f

British Commonwealth, traditions of, 1:816a f

Brittain, Vera, on defeat, 5:619a f

Broadness, Hebrew concept of, 4:809

Broglie, Louis de, on law of probability, 2:907a

Broken bottle, parable of, 5:966b f, 967 f

Brokenhearted, God's healing of, 4:751a

Brontë, Charlotte: on lack of sympathy, 5:733a f
on looking forward, 5:443a f
on Psalms, 4:507b
religion of, 5:685b

Bronze serpent: Hezekiah destroys, 3:289 f
identification of, 3:290
story of, 2:242 f, 243a f

Brooke, Rupert, on peace in death, 5:307a

Brooke, Stopford: on abiding, 12:250a
on God as Father, 12:255a

Brooks, Frederick, death of, 9:274a f

Brooks, Phillips: eloquence of, 6:810b
on fatherhood of God, 6:1125a
good cheer of, 3:958b
pastoral affection of, 11:282b f
on perfection of Christ, 11:220a
personality of, 8:28b
prayer of, 3:670b
preaching of, 9:177a
on preaching, 12:552b
on visions on goodness, 1:777a f, 922 f

Brooks, Van Wyck, on despair, 12:267b

Broom tree, description of, 3:161; 4:642

Brother: Christ as, 7:764a; 11:615a f
in Pauline usage, 10:445

Brother's keeper, 6:83a f; 11:571b

Brother Lawrence, 2:18b f; 8:493a, 648b

Brotherhood: basis of, 2:428a f; 6:1134a f; 8:404a f
bond of, 7:530b f
in Christ, 10:650a f; 11:149a f, 217a f, 460a f
Christian, 11:744a f
Christ's teaching on, 7:530b f
covenant of, 6:781 f
deeds of, 7:674a
Malachi teaching on, 6:1120a f, 1134
of man, 4:468a f; 6:878a
necessity of, 1:884b
origin of, 11:460a
Pauline teaching on, 11:291b f
rejection of, 1:519a
religion of, 5:452a f
Stoic teaching on, 7:84a, 86b
universal (Stoicism), 7:84a

Brotherly affection, II Peter teaching on, 12:177

Brotherly love; see Love

Brown, Charles R., on brotherhood, 11:571b

Brown, John: on death of mother, 3:918b
on human perfection, 11:277a

violence of, 1:863a f; 8:586a f

Brown, John Mason, on peace, 6:1081a f

Brown, S. L.: on Hosea, 6:575b, 630a
on sin of Israel, 6:674b f, 705b, 714b

Brown, Thomas Edward, on smug complacency, 5:639b

Brown, William Adams, on work of church, 6:651a f

Browne, Thomas: on diaries, 4:546a
on God's mercies, 4:498a
on God's will, 5:762a f

Browning, Elizabeth Barrett: on benefits of love, 5:101b
on greatness of God, 3:1198b
on love, 5:100b, 113b
on married love, 1:660a f
on nature, 5:101b
on opposing force in nature, 3:912b
on patience of God, 5:557a

Browning, Robert: on access to God, 12:400b
on activity of God, 5:428a
on anger of God, 12:449b
on bad bargains, 5:76a
on belief, 11:623b
on being born too soon, 6:1040a f
on cheerful disposition, 4:514a f
on choice, 4:835a; 12:549b
on Christian love, 10:92b
on Dante, 5:725a
on death, 1:596a; 3:1012a
on death of John, 12:209a
on disbelief, 5:748a
on dread of death, 11:616b
on duty, 3:930a; 6:1088b
on face of Christ, 12:376b
on finger of God, 1:1062a f
on God, 10:409b
on God in Christ, 11:289a, 600a; 12:366b
on guidance of God, 2:1164b
on hell, 11:741b
on humiliation of Athens, 4:250a
on love, 5:106b; 10:167a
on love of God, 11:708b
on need of Christianity, 10:417a
on old age, 4:901a f; 6:9a; 11:536a
on poets, 5:845b
on praise, 11:738b
on presence of God, 5:561a
on profit and loss, 11:745a
on recognition of God, 5:735b
on roaring tides, 4:242b
on submission to God, 5:763a
on true worship, 5:761a
on voice of God, 11:626a
on Wordsworth, 11:513b
on work, 11:722b
on worship of power, 11:681a

Brownlee, William H., on Habakkuk, 6:974b

Bruce, Robert: divine companionship of, 5:738a f
on silence in church, 5:660b

Brunner, Emil: on accessibility of God, 5:799a
on election, 5:849a
on encounter with God, 5:798b
on knowing God, 2:1087a f
on love and marriage, 5:123a
on means and ends, 11:426b
on pharisaism, 5:883b
on responsibility, 11:749a f
on surrender to God, 11:537a f
on thankfulness, 11:750b
on turning from God, 5:952b f

Bryce, James, on religion and nation, 5:444a

Buber, Martin: on Hosea, 6:591, 718
on love of God, 6:562a
on responsibility for life, 5:863a
on word of God, 5:805a

Buchan, John: on Bible training in home, 11:461a f
on Christian civilization, 11:415a f
on conversion, 11:464b
on courage, 9:455b
on human effort, 5:421a
on thinking, 4:20b
on war, 1:913b f

Buck, Pearl S., on giving, 4:801a f

Budde, Karl, Hexateuch study of, 1:191a f

Buddhism, Ecclesiastes and, 5:23a

Building, world as, 11:621b

Bull, image of, 3:117 f

Bultmann, Rudolf: on I John, 12:212b
on love, 12:281

Bunam, Rabbi, on unrepentance, 5:831b

Bunyan, John: on attractiveness of Christians, 5:704a f
on byway to hell, 1:1064a
on care of God, 1:1074a f
on Christian graces, 5:574b f
courage and fear of, 4:598a
on difficulty, 4:497b
on faith and action, 6:394b
on God's guidance, 1:801a; 5:927a
on God's promises, 3:1087b
imprisonment of, 5:1042b f
on opposition, 5:466b
on overconfidence, 5:944b f
on Paul, 10:411a
on prayer, 6:641a f
on religious differences, 1:586a
on sin, 4:656a
on swearing, 1:983b
strength and weakness of, 10:409b

Burden: bearing of, 6:1070a f; 8:637b; 10:576b f; 12:147b
etymology of, 5:995
kinds of, 10:577a f
of life, 1:578b; 5:53b f
necessity of, 7:391a
sharing of, 2:196a f
of white man, 8:404b

as revelation of God, 8:
54b; 11:400b; *see also*
Christ, God revealed in
as revelation of righteousness, 9:429a f
reverence toward, 10:717;
12:129b
revolutionary teaching of,
7:279a
as Revolutionist, 7:787a
righteousness of, 12:169
as Risen Lord, 8:789 f,
792a f; 12:91 f
risks taken by, 8:349b f
rivals of, 11:596a f
role in creation of, 11:
599a f, 607a
rule of, 12:584a
sacrifice of, 2:13 f, 772a f;
7:18b f, 758a; 10:138b,
145a, 335b f, 701a f
sacrifice of (Hebrews), 10:
577b f, 678 f, 693 f, 706 f
sacrifice of (Pauline), 11:
52
sacrifice of (uniqueness
of), 10:281b f
sacrificial death of, 9:370b;
10:606b
salvation through, 9:
368b f; 10:615 f; 11:
196b f, 671a f
Samaritan woman and, 8:
519 f
as Sanctifier, 11:615
as Savior; *see* Savior
saviorhood of, 10:229a f;
12:229a
as scandal, 8:348b f
scourging of, 8:771a f; 12:
120
scribes and; *see* Scribes
search for, 8:322a f, 587a f
Second Advent of, 7:6a f,
543, 556a; *see also*
Christ, return of
Second Coming of (delay
of), 8:328
Second Coming of (I
John), 12:252 f, 252b f
Second Coming of (He-
brews), 11:696 f
Second Coming of (Jude),
12:336
Second Coming of (predic-
tion of), 7:136a
Second Coming of (rein-
terpretation of), 12:
252b f
Second Coming of (Reve-
lation), 12:371, 546
Second Coming of (II
Peter), 12:165a, 183 f,
196a f, 203 f
as Second Man, 9:370b
secrecy of, 7:120a f, 644a f,
767
secret name of, 12:513
seeking man, 8:486b
as "seen by angels," 11:422
self-consciousness of, 11:
643a f
self-emptying of, 11:48b f
selflessness of, 8:691b f; 11:
643a f
self-revelation of, 8:490 f
self-witness of, 8:594 f
sense of failure of, 7:17a
"separated unto," 7:293b
serenity of, 8:741b
as Servant, 5:631b f; 7:15a;
11:48b f, 49 f; 12:320 f
Servant of the Lord and,
5:413b f

serving, 8:493a, 663b,
804b f
shame of, 11:757a f
sharing of, 8:486a; 11:625b
as Shepherd, 11:760 f,
761b; 12:120, 149, 424a,
571b, 573a; *see also*
Christ Jesus, as Chief
Shepherd, as Good
Shepherd
significance of, 11:164b;
12:566b
silence of, 7:18a, 335b,
396a f, 442b f, 889,
890a f; 8:396a f, 399b
simplicity of, 6:830b; 8:
54b, 378b
as sin offering, 1:226a f
sin-bearing of, 2:84a f
sinlessness of, 7:267b,
597b; 8:78a, 605b f; 9:
477; 10:343b f; 11:639;
12:258
sin's removal and, 8:483 f,
483a f
slave of, 7:203b f; 9:379 f,
379b f; 11:15, 15a f; 12:
167b f
sleep in, 11:302 f
social gospel of, 8:553b f
soldier of, 11:69, 479 f
solitude of, 6:830a f
as Son of David; *see* Son
of David
as Son of God; *see* Son of
God
as Son of Man; *see* Son of
Man
sonship of, 10:279a f; 11:
162, 164a
sorrow of, 2:1128b
as source and center of the
world, 11:212a f
sovereignty of, 7:332a; 8:
38a f
spirit of, 9:511 f, 513b f
spiritual struggle of, 7:19a
"stoneship of," 12:108
as storyteller, 7:407b f
as Stranger, 8:422a f
subordination to God of,
7:31a; 10:279a f; 11:207a
suffering of, 8:628a, 705a;
10:274a, 281a f; 11:
645a f, 669b, 742a; 12:
144a f
suffering of (I Peter), 12:
98 f, 118 f, 130b f, 131
suffering of (necessity of),
8:424b
suffering of (Pauline), 10:
510 f; 11:141b
suffering of (perfected
through), 11:614a f
suffering of (and Psalm-
ist's suffering) 4:115 f
suffering of (sharing), 12:
142 f
as Suffering Servant, 7:18b,
129b f, 149b f; 9:115; 12:
118 f
sufficiency of, 10:431a; 11:
178b
as superior to angels, 11:
600, 602b f
as superior to Moses, 11:
619 f
superiority of, 11:674
supremacy of, 8:566a f; 11:
51b f, 449b, 598 f; 12:
515a f
supremacy of (Pauline),
10:431a; 11:261b f

as surety of God's promise,
11:669b f
surrender of, 11:62b
sympathy of, 8:556b, 609b;
11:640
Synagogue and; *see* Synagogue
Syrophoenician woman
and, 7:441a f
table talk of, 8:15a
tardiness of, 8:639a f
as Teacher, 11:269b f
teaching of 7:145 f, 277b f;
8:146 f, 552b f
teaching of (authenticity
of), 10:463b
teaching of (Catholic concept of), 8:713a
teaching of (interpreta-
tion of), 1:29a; 8:228b,
544a
teaching of (and Lucan
emphases), 8:12b
teaching of (moral significance of), 7:155b f
teaching of (use of para-
bles in); *see* Parables of
Christ
teaching of (significance
of), 7:153a f
teaching of (verification
of), 7:874a f
"templehood" of, 2:8b
temptation of, 1:110a; 3:
719a f; 7:15b, 116a f,
269 f, 269a f, 654 f,
654a f; 8:83 f, 83a f; 11:
618b, 639
thankfulness for, 12:92a
as theodicy of God, 3:
1173b f
throne of, 12:399
timelessness of, 12:229a
as title, 7:23b, 56a f, 251;
11:150
titles of, 11:164a f
tomb of, 8:414 f
tormenting of, 8:157b f
touch of, 8:117b f
tradition and, 7:436b f,
746 f, 746b f
transfiguration of, 7:17b,
130b f, 458 f, 458a f,
774 f, 774b f; 8:173 f,
173a f; 10:547a f; *see
also* Transfiguration
trial of, 7:140b f, 585 f,
586b f, 593a f, 887,
887a f, 893 f, 893b f; 8:
395 f, 395a f, 759 f; *see
also* Caiaphas, Herod,
Pilate, Sanhedrin
tribute to, 9:492a; 12:
565b f
triumph of, 8:349b, 664b;
11:607a f, 706b f
triumphal entry of, 4:
936b f; 6:591a; 7:137b f,
500 f, 502a f, 823a f, 824;
8:334 f, 334a f, 657 f,
657a f
trustworthiness of, 11:486,
595a f
as Truth, 1:232a; 7:253a;
8:595b, 701; 10:544b f
turning away from, 11:
652a f
as unchanging, 11:606b f
understanding of, 7:765a;
9:26a f; 11:123a
as unincarnate, 9:190a
union with, 11:207b
union with (Christianity),
11:207b

union with (Johannine),
8:445a f, 573, 709 f, 717 f
union with (Pauline), 5:
129b f; 9:475a f; 10:141b
uniqueness of, 8:169a,
564b f; 11:261b f, 274a f,
287b f, 382a f, 401b; 12:
245b
unity in, 9:38b f, 300b,
584b f, 611b f; 10:654a f;
11:208a f
unity in (Ephesians), 10:
605b f, 626 f, 654, 654a f
unity of (Ephesians), 10:
685f
unity with God of, 8:545 f,
709 f
universal acclaim of, 12:
409a f
universal appeal of, 12:
229a
universality of, 8:82a; 9:
26a f, 139a f
as unrecognized, 7:513b
unselfish love of, 10:178a f
as unwanted, 7:348a f
as "very God of very
God," 7:250a; 8:78b f
vicarious suffering of, 7:
25b; 10:182b
victory of, 8:79b f, 343b;
10:39a; 11:187 f; 196b f
victory over beast of
(Revelation), 12:515 f
as vindicated in Spirit, 11:
421 f
virgin birth of; *see* Virgin
Birth
as visible Lord, 12:371a f
as Way, 5:869a; 8:700 f;
11:710b
weakness of, 7:765b
weariness of, 8:520b f
weeping of, 8:645b f, 646 f
welcome of, 12:561b
wisdom of, 4:423a f,
595a f; 7:339a, 841b
wisdom identified with, 4:
774b, 778a f
as Witness, 12:369 f
witness of, 8:548a f, 656a f,
727b f; 9:28a f
witness of (eyewitness), 8:
27b f
witnessing for, 12:295b
woman and; *see* Woman
woman taken in adultery
and, 8:591 f, 591b f
as wonder-worker, 8:146 f
as Word of God, 1:30a f,
388a; 7:30a f; 12:513b f,
514; *see also* Word of
God
as Word made flesh, 7:4a,
30a; 8:472 f
words of, 7:551a f; 8:
130a f; 11:221
words of (relevancy of),
8:172a f
work of, 8:612b f, 745 f
work of (Hebrews), 11:
583a f
work of (Pauline), 9:370b
world peace and, 7:257b
worship of, 7:258b, 621,
621a f; 9:619; 12:253b
worship of (by the magi),
7:258b
yearning for, 8:524a
yoke of, 3:174a f; 6:677a;
7:390, 390b; 11:447a
"Christ of the Andes," 7:
257b

universal mission of, **11:**
182*b* f
universality of, **10:**470*b* f;
11:154*a*
usage of word, **9:**78 f
as vine, **4:**673*b*
visible and invisible, **8:**
603*b* f
vitality of, **12:**276*b*
war and, **12:**265*a*
warning to, **4:**125*a*
wealth of, **5:**700*b* f; **12:**65*a*
witness of, **5:**489*a* f
woman and, **9:**217*b*; **10:**
123*b* f, 212*a* f; **11:**404*a* f,
406*a* f
woman's silence in (I
Timothy), **11:**405
wonder of, **10:**670*b* f
world and, **11:**541*b* f; **12:**
111*a*, 252*a*, 557*b* f
youth and, **12:**152*b*
Church (early): achievement
of, **11:**430*b*
apocalyptic hope of, **8:**
302*a*
baptism and, **7:**180*a*; **8:**
445*a*; **9:**112; **11:**545
baptismal creed of, **9:**116
behavior of Christians in,
5:715*b*; **11:**415
beliefs of, **7:**179*b* f
bishops in, **11:**345*b* f
characteristic features of,
9:50 f, 72 f
common meal in, **12:**
665*b* f
communal life in, **9:**50 f,
50*b* f, 69 f, 72*b* f
deacons in, **11:**345*b* f
difficulties of, **11:**261*a*
elders in, **11:**345*b* f
expulsion of Hellenists
from, **7:**182*b* f
fellowship in, **9:**50 f
Gospel in, **7:**4*b* f
government of, **12:**664*a* f
growth of, **11:**153*a* f
history of, **7:**176 f
hospitality in, **9:**590 f; **11:**
412, 437 f
Last Supper and, **7:**180*a*
liturgical confession of, **11:**
421
meeting places of, **11:**
562*b* f
mission of, **7:**7*a*; **8:**11*a*
missionary motive of, **8:**
11*a*
organization of, **7:**179*b* f;
11:345*b* f
persecution of, **7:**181*a* f;
276*a* f; **12:**142*b*
Pharisees and, **8:**214
prayer in, **8:**8*a* f
preaching in, **8:**11*a*
professional opportunity
of women in, **11:**349*b* f,
406 f
prophets in, **9:**165; **10:**
163 f
Psalms in, **4:**16*a* f
role of women in, **11:**
349*b* f, 403 f, 404*b* f
separation from Judaism
of, **7:**181*a*
slavery and, **11:**446 f
state and, **5:**646*a*
supersedes synagogue, **8:**
6*b* f
task of, **11:**274*b* f
teacher in, **9:**165; **10:**164
variety of action and
thought in, **11:**138*a*

women in, **8:**8*b*
worship in, **7:**179*b* f; **8:**
630*b*; **10:**11*a*; **11:**222; **12:**
31*a* f
Church, Richard William:
indignation of, **4:**491*b*
on reverence, **5:**599*a*
"Churchianity," Christianity
and, **5:**503*b*
Churchill, Winston: on appeasement, **4:**643*b*
on decisions, **11:**103*a*
on divine plan, **5:**521*b*
on duty, **4:**138*a*
faith of, **4:**658*b* f
on God's providence, **4:**
658*a* f
on national courage, **1:**
800*b*
on national danger, **1:**
589*b*
on "their finest hour," **11:**
277*b*
Churching of woman, **2:**61*a* f
Churchmanship, principles
of, **11:**510*a* f
Circle, love as, **8:**690*b*; **11:**
161*a*
Circumambulation, ritual of,
3:794 f
Circumcision: ancient practice of, **1:**882
Antiochian dispute about,
7:194*a* f
of Christ, **8:**59 f, 59*b* f; **9:**
199*b* f
covenant of, **1:**608 f
as covenant seal, **5:**833*a*
Mosaic law and, **8:**584
Moses and, **1:**882 f
origin of, **1:**882*b* f; **2:**60 f
Pauline teaching on, **7:**
21*b*, 22*a*, 194*a* f; **9:**
413*a* f, 418*a*, 442*b* f; **11:**
74 f, 74*a*
as sign, **1:**613 f, 613*a* f
significance of, **2:**60 f,
60*a* f, 574*a* f
spiritual (Pauline), **11:**
141*b*, 192 f
as symbol, **11:**74*a*
of Timothy, **9:**210 f, 211*b*
of Titus, **10:**470 f
Circumcision party: identification of, **11:**529 f
opposing Peter, **9:**142*a* f
Circumstance: conscience
and, **3:**332*a* f
extenuating, **4:**307*a* f
mitigating, **2:**649*b* f
victim of, **3:**964*a* f; **6:**158*a* f
working under difficult, **9:**
185*a* f
Cistern: broken, **5:**815*a* f
of Jerusalem, **5:**1075
well and, **5:**858*b*
Cities of Refuge, **2:**303 f,
303*a* f, 360, 360*b* f, 451 f,
648 f, 648*a* f
Citizen, Christian as, **2:**28*a* f;
9:598*a* f; **11:**223*b*
Citizenship: Christian, **11:**39;
12:113*b* f
good, **9:**605*a* f
in heaven, **4:**628*a* f; **11:**101,
101*a* f
Pauline teaching on, **9:**
599*a* f
in Zion, **4:**78 f, 470 f
City: character of, **6:**630*a* f
children of, **6:**1086*b* f
fallen, **5:**603*a*
function of, **6:**1086*a*
growth of, **4:**253*b* f

interpretation of, **12:**529*a*
holy; *see* Holy City
life in, **3:**433*a*; **7:**387*a*
lure of, **6:**185*a* f
need of, **6:**186*a* f
noise of, **11:**298*a*
significance of, **6:**1085*a* f
City of David, identification
of, **3:**690
City of God, **4:**242 f; **5:**700*b*;
11:217*b*; **12:**602*a*
among men, **12:**528*b* f
exclusion from, **12:**540*b* f,
547*a* f
hope of, **11:**513*b*
hospitality of **12:**540*a* f
Jerusalem as, **4:**469; **6:**
336*b* f
life in, **12:**542*b* f
Revelation vision of, **12:**
528 f, 528*b* f, 608*b* f
song of, **5:**306*a* f
City of God (Augustine),
writing of, **11:**750*b*
Civil obedience, Pauline
teaching on, **9:**604*b* f
Civilization: beginnings of,
1:516 f
Christian basis of, **11:**
415*a* f
conquest and, **6:**993*a* f
criticism of modern, **8:**
428*b*; **9:**46*b* f; **12:**53*b*
"cut-flower," **6:**667*b*
as disease, **6:**789*a*
goal of, **12:**540*a* f
maturity of, **4:**431*b*
placidity of, **5:**728*a*
progress of, **5:**461*b*
saving of, **11:**104*a*
sins of, **6:**822*b* f
technical, **6:**224*b*
Clarke, William Newton, on
traditionalism, **1:**462*b*
Class, leisure, **5:**682*b*
Class conflict, **6:**253*b* f
Class consciousness, **4:**654*b* f
Class privilege, **6:**321*a* f
Class war, **1:**987*b*
Claudel, Paul: on death, **12:**
414*a* f
on suffering, **5:**902*a*
Claudia Procla, **7:**596*a*
Claudius, **7:**107*b* f
Clay: feet of, **6:**386*a* f
potter and, **5:**518*a*
"Clean," in N.T. usage, **7:**
285*a*
Clean and unclean animals,
Hebrew law of, **2:**56 f
Clean and unclean food,
Deuteronomic teachings
on, **2:**422 f
Cleanliness, ceremonial, **7:**
536, 536*b* f, 667*b*
Cleanness, moral and spirit-
ual, **2:**335*a* f
Cleansing: act of, **3:**808; **12:**
546*b* f
procedure and rules for
(Numbers), **2:**235 f
of self, **10:**355*a* f
spiritual, **5:**1049*b* f
Cleanthes, on following God,
6:889*b*
Clear conscience, Pauline
teaching on, **11:**461
Clemency, plea for, **11:**556*b* f
Clement of Alexandria, **1:**
65*a* f; **7:**224*b* f
on authorship of Hebrews,
11:581*b*
on the church, **10:**638*a*
on fear of God, **12:**116*a*

on Jude, **12:**317*b*
on new song, **5:**766*a* f
on presence of God, **5:**
698*b* f
on Revelation, **12:**352*a*
on II Peter, **12:**163*a* f
on use of possessions, **12:**
64*b*
on work of Christ, **5:**529*b*
Clement of Philippi, **11:**108
Cleopatra, **6:**521 f, 527; **7:**
79*b* f
Cleopatra's Needle, **5:**1096
Clergy: laity and, **6:**607*b* f
mercenary, **3:**506*b* f
moral decadence of, **6:**
604*a* f
remuneration for, **1:**
1045*a* f
sins of, **8:**217*a* f
vestment of, **10:**532*b* f
see also Minister, Pastor,
Preacher
Clericalism: curse of, **2:**
886*b* f
evils of, **1:**1037*b* f
Clermont Manuscript, **1:**67*a*
Cleverness: idealism and, **11:**
35*a* f
weakness of, **4:**106*a*
wisdom and, **12:**49*b* f
Climate of Palestine, **4:**645*a*
Cloak, description of, **11:**516
Clock, as symbol, **11:**36*a* f
"Close of the age," **7:**21*a*
Closed mind, church with,
9:232*b* f; *see also* Mind
Cloud: presence of God in,
3:70 f
waterless (Jude metaphor),
12:333
of witnesses, **11:**737*b* f
Cloud of Unknowing, on sufficiency of God, **4:**391*a*
Clough, Arthur Hugh: on
adoration of God, **5:**
647*b*
on truth, **11:**509*b*
Coarse meal, identification
of, **3:**767
Cobden, Richard, social concern of, **3:**1107*a*; **6:**604*b*
Cocteau, Jean, on choice of
Barabbas, **5:**855*a*
Code: crystallization of, **2:**
351*b* f
of Hammurabi; *see* Ham-
murabi
Holiness; *see* Holiness Code
of Lipit-Ishtar, **1:**250*b*
moral, **4:**106*b*
Codex, description of, **7:**34*a*;
8:19*a*
Codex Alexandrinus, **12:**
623*a* f
Codex Basiliensis, **12:**623*a*
Codex Bezae, **8:**19*b* f; **12:**
619*b*, 623*a*
Codex Claramontanus, **12:**
619*b*, 623*a* f
Codex Ephrem Syrus, **12:**
623*b*
Codex Laudianus, **12:**619*b*
Codex Regius, **12:**623*a*
Codex Sinaiticus, **1:**67*b*; **8:**
19*b*; **12:**618*a*, 625*b* f,
Plate 15
Codex Syriac Peshitta, **12:**
Plate 16
Codex Vaticanus, **1:**67*b*; **8:**
19*a* f; **12:**618*a*, 625*a* f,
Plate 24
Codex Washingtonianus, **12:**
Plate 26

of sin, 5:741*a* f, 931; **6:** 718*b* f; 12:223*a* f
sin and, 2:166*a* f, 588*b* f; **4:** 170*b* f, 565*a* f, 679*a* f, 939*a* f; 8:275*a* f; 10:471*a*
value of, 4:939*a* f
Confessional: Protestant use of, 11:638*a* f
Roman Catholic concept of, 6:719*b* f
Confessor, identification of, 12:357*b*, 373
Confidence: of Christian, **12:** 266*a* f
of faith, 4:492*b*
false, 6:248*b* f; 7:495*b*, 577*b* f
I John teaching on, **12:** 251, 266 f, 282 f, 282*a* f
foundation of, 6:919*a* f
ladder of, 7:328*a* f
meaning of, 11:622*b*
mutual, 4:746*b* f
nature of, 4:492*a*
need of, 11:622*b* f
of Psalmist, 4:167*b* f, 377*a* f
religious, 4:110*a* f
undismayed, 9:390*a* f
Confinement, reaction to, **5:** 1042*a* f
Conflict: class, 6:253*b* f
cosmic, 12:456*a* f
inner, 12:54*a*
international, 6:622*b* f
meaningless, 7:750*a*
problem of, 3:1105*b*
response to, 4:289*a* f
Confusion: faith and, **4:** 390*b* f
modern, 11:30*b* f
Congregation: minister and, 5:664*a* f; 6:607*b* f; **11:** 281*b* f
preaching to intellectual, 9:233*a* f
responsibility of, 9:182*b* f
segregated, 5:657*a* f
Congreve, William, on charm of music, 3:201*a*
Connelly, Marc: and *The Green Pastures*, 3:982*b*
on mercy of God, 2:763*a* f
Conqueror, death as, **11:** 612*a*
Conquest, civilization and, 6:993*a* f
Conquest (period of), **1:** 305*a* f
division of land in, 2:617 f
historical background of, 1:305*b* f
history of, 2:615 f, 615*a* f
Joshua account of, 2:546*a* f
literature of, 1:177*a* f
moral standards of, **1:** 310*a* f
religion of, 1:307*a* f
sources of, 1:305*a* f
Conscience: action of, 4:106*b*
awakening of, 4:212*a* f; **7:** 569*a*; 11:425*a* f
beginnings of, 1:497*b* f, 755*a*
Christian, 12:599*b*
circumstance and, 3:332*a* f
clear, 3:390*a*; 11:461
corrupting of, 12:599*b*
cowards and, 3:1037*b* f
death of, 3:498*b* f; **11:** 424*b* f; 12:583*b*
decline of, 6:824*b* f
democracy and, 12:599*b*
discipline of, 10:589*b*

domestication of, 11:295*a* f
dulled, 11:424*b* f
faith and, 11:417*a* f, 424*b* f
free, 7:324*a*; 12:68*a*
good, 1:611*b*; 11:394*b* f
of individual, 2:1024*b* f
instinct and, 6:602*b*
lamp of, 4:899*a* f
light of, 8:266*b*
meaning of, 4:899*b* f; **6:** 649*a*, 824*b* f
money and, 8:359*b*
obedience to, 4:900*a*
in Pastoral usage, 11:385
Pauline teaching on, 9:297, 412*a* f, 493*a* f, 612 f; **10:** 95; 11:385
protecting, 11:78*b* f
recalcitrant, 8:77*b* f
religious, 3:238*b* f
scriptural concept of, **4:** 141*a* f
sensitive, 2:451*b* f; 12:32*a*
significance of, 9:619*b* f
social, 5:711*a*
Stoic concept of, 7:86*b* f; 9:411
twisted, 7:592*b*
weakening of, 3:213*b*
Conscientiousness, social, **5:** 681*b* f
Consciousness, prophetic; *see* Prophetic consciousness
Conscript, reluctant, 7:902*a*
Consecration: "entire," **11:** 224*a*
Hebrews teaching on, **11:** 743*b*
James teaching one, 12:70
need of, 11:314*b*
need for (Ephesians), **10:** 682 f
Consequences, 11:103*a*
truth and, 6:1059*b* f
Consent, compulsion and, **11:** 568*b* f
Conservation, need of, **1:** 473*b* f
Conservatism: contribution of, 9:197*a* f, 205*b*
progress and, 8:218*a* f
religious, 8:218*a* f
true, 1:673*a* f
Conservative, liberal and, **9:** 200*b*
Consideration, need of, **5:** 644*a*
Consistency, foolish, 4:296*a* f
Consolation: of Israel, **5:** 598 f, 632 f; 7:281; 8:60
ministry of, 3:923*a* f
need of, 3:1064 f, 1064*b* f; 10:205*a* f
religion and, 6:837*a*
"Conspiracy," in Isaianic usage, 5:226
Constitutional Convention, 5:706*b*
Consummation, final, **10:** 236*b* f
Contempt, sin of, 7:470*b* f
Contented Christian, Pastoral teaching on, 11:450 f
Contention, reasons for, **4:** 931*a*f
Contentment: of life, **11:** 117*b*, 754*a* f
shallow, 11:741*b*
Contribution, identification of, 3:769
Contribution and tithe, Nehemiah reforms concerning, 3:767 f
Control, kinds of, 10:479*b*

Controversy: charitable, **9:** 553*b* f
Christian, 11:189*b*
good and bad, 11:495*a* f
necessity of, 8:519*a* f; **11:** 543*a* f
Pastoral teaching on, **11:** 542, 547
result of, 9:617*b* f
solution of, 7:436*b*
Convenience, appeal to, **3:** 117*b* f
Conventionalized religion, failure of, 11:53*b*
Conversion: of Augustine, 11:702*a*
Bible reading and, 7:165*b*
in Church, 11:272*b* f
of Cornelius, 9:131 f, 131*b* f
essence of, 10:418*b*
false, 8:540*b* f
growth and, 12:236*a*
meaning of, 8:273*b*
of Paul: *see* Paul
repentance and, 6:625*b*
result of, 8:535*a*; 10:338*b* f
Conviction: arriving at, **3:** 1131*b* f
conflict of, 9:612*b* f
differences of, 5:764*a* f; **9:** 617*b* f
living by, 11:486*b*
moral, 6:437*a* f
religious, 4:130*a* f
weakening of, 11:647*a* f
Conwell, Russell, 8:423*a* f
Cooke, G. A., on Ezekiel, **6:** 44*b*
Coolidge, Calvin, on Job, **3:** 1194*b*
Co-operation, 1:585*b*
basis of, 11:15*a* f
competition and, 5:54 f; 11:442*a*
international, 4:707*b*
Coponius, as procurator, **7:** 105*a*
Coptic church, canon and, **1:** 42*a* f
Coptic N.T., 1:67*a* f
Corban controversy, 7:437 f
Corinth: church at ("Christ party" of), 10:21 f
church at (emancipation tendency of), 10:7*b*
church at (factions in), 10:7*b* f, 20 f, 43 f, 43*a* f
church at (false leaders of), 10:391 f
church at (founding of), 10:4*b* f
church at (membership of), 10:16*b* f, 32 f, 32*b* f
church at (pagan cults in), 10:214*b* f
church at (Paul and), **9:** 238 f, 238*b* f; 10:265*b* f, 284 f, 350 f
church at (problems of), 10:265*b* f
identification of, 7:77*b*, 196*a*; 9:238*b*; 10:3*a* f
in Pauline times, 10:3*a* f
Pauline visit to, 10:4*b* f, 415 f
Corinthian Letters, Galatians and, 10:440*a* f
Corinthians, repentance of, 10:357 f
Corn Laws, 6:604*b*
Cornelius: baptism of, 9:141
conversion of, 9:131 f, 131*b* f

Peter and, 9:131 f, 131*b* f, 133*b* f
Cornerstone: chief, 4:620
Christ as, 4:620; 10:661 f; 12:107 f
Cornhill, C. H., on Jonah, 6:875*a*
Corporate personality, Samuel teaching on, 2:872*a* f
Corporate responsibility, Hebrew doctrine of, 6:49*b*
Correction, accepting and refusing, 4:836*b* f
Corruption: moral, 6:824*a* f
political, 4:306*a* f
Cosmic destruction, 5:841*b*
Cosmic woes, of Revelation, 12:415 f
Cosmology, of Revelation, 12:400 f
Cosmopolitan, tragedy of, 12:385*b* f
Cosmos: Babylonian concept of, 5:518*b*
philosophy of, 4:550
Cost, counting of, 3:677*a* f
Cotton, John, on authority of church member, 11:95*a*
Coulton, G. G., on celibacy, 4:673*b*
Council of Jerusalem, **9:** 195 f, 195*b* f
Council of the Lord, 5:992 f
Counsel, wise, 4:783
Counselor (Paraclete), **8:** 707 f, 707*b* f, 711 f, 727, 730; *see also* Paraclete
Counselors: multitude of, **4:** 848*a* f
wise, 2:1026*b*
Countenance of faith, 4:224*a*
Country, town and, 3:433*a* f
Countryman, reverence of, **4:** 103*a*
Courage: accomplishment of, 3:263*b* f
through Christ, 7:577*a*
as Christian virtue, **11:** 254*a* f
example of, 11:254*b*
faith and, 11:254*a* f
I Peter as epistle of, 12:77*a*
meaning of, 3:160*b*; **10:** 479*a* f
moral, 1:768*a*; 7:428*a*, 469*a*, 591*a*; 9:455*b*
moral and physical, **6:** 648*b*
of psalmist, 4:144 f
as religious virtue, 7:735*a*
renewal of, 5:673*a*
self-reliance and, 3:160*b* f
test of, 5:869*b*
Court of the Gentiles, 8:497
Court of law, in Hebraic tradition, 5:448
Court of Susa, 3:834 f
Courtesy: as Christian virtue, 10:674*a* f; 11:542
example of, 11:570*b* f
Courts of heaven, 4:24*b* f
Courtship, marriage and, **9:** 253*a* f
Covenant: baptism and, **10:** 518*b* f
book of, 1:990*b* f
breaking of, 1:319*b* f; **6:** 644*a*
ceremonies of, 1:354*b* f
of David, 5:405*a* f, 644 f
with death (Isaiah), **5:** 313*b* f, 317 f

Roman practice of, 7:83*a*, 600 f
  see also Christ Jesus
Cruelty: doom of, 5:546*b* f
  Habakkuk teaching on, 6:992 f
  limits of, 1:856*a* f
  prophets' teaching on, 6:965
Cullman, Oscar: on Eternal God, 5:672*a*
  on progressive reduction, 6:607*a*
Cult: function of, 1:340*b* f
  history and, 1:341*a* f
  holiness of God and, 1:341*b*
  modern, 6:133*a* f
  necessity of, 1:341*b* f
  religious, 5:667*a* f
Cultic sins: Malachi teaching on, 6:1119*b*
  Second Isaiah teaching on, 5:747 f
Cultural isolation of Jews, 7:98*b*
Culture: of ancient Near East, 1:175*a* f
  church and, 10:158*b* f
  godly wisdom and, 5:894*a*
  religion and, 5:1059
  senate, 12:240*a*
Cultus: Amos rejection of, 6:818 f
  Jeremiah teaching on, 5:867 f
  P's ordinances for, 1:1020 f
  in Psalms, 4:13*a* f
Cunliffe-Jones, Herbert: on Deuteronomic law, 5:868*b*
  on love of God, 6:563*a*
Cup: divining, 1:793*b* f
  of God, 6:989*b* f
  God's wrath as, 4:401; 5:860*b* f, 998*b* f, 1001*b*, 1002; 6:192
  overflowing, 4:129 f, 129*a*
  of salvation, 4:613
  of suffering, 6:85*b* f
  as symbol of prophetic eschatology, 5:603 f
Cupbearer: identification of, 3:670 f
  Nehemiah as, 3:670
Cure of souls, 6:244*b* f; 11:182 f
Curetonian Manuscript, 12: Plate 25
Curie, Madame: on scientific spirit, 2:1148*b* f
  transfiguration of, 9:96*b*
Curiosity: definition of, 1:491*a*
  intellectual, 9:235*a* f
  virtue of, 2:911*a* f
Curse: ancient concept of, 6:1075*a*
  of darkness, 12:484*b* f
  on day of birth, 5:974 f
  Deuteronomic use of, 2:493 f
  Hebrew concept of, 2:491*a* f; 3:175 f; 4:703 f; 10:509
  by incarnation, 4:304*b* f
  of law (Pauline), 10:505 f
  meaning of, 1:998*a*
  power of, 2:491*a* f
  work as, 1:511*a* f
Curse and blessing, Hebrew concept of, 3:38
Curses, twelve (Deuteronomy), 2:490 f

Custom, change of, 9:280*b* f
Cuthah, identification of, 3:283
Cybele, myth of, 7:92*b*; 10:496
Cymbal, use of, 3:793
Cynicism: cause of, 2:1027*a*
  faith and, 7:464*a*
  modern, 5:606*a*
  pride and, 8:206*b*
Cyrus (seventh century B.C.), 1:269*a* f
Cyrus (sixth century B.C.): anointing of, 5:516 f, 516*a* f
  Babylonian conquest of, 5:522*a* f, 1124; 6:1038*a* f
  commission of, 5:521 f
  conquests of, 1:287*a* f; 5:396*a*
  Danielic reference to, 6:500
  edict of, 3:570 f, 613 f
  God's purpose fulfilled in, 5:516 f, 520*b* f
  mission of, 5:559 f
  return of temple vessels by, 3:574 f
  Second Isaiah reference to, 5:449 f, 462, 466, 516*a* f, 520*a* f
Cyrus Cylinder, Second Isaiah and, 5:396*b*

D

Dagon, identification of, 2:796 f
Dale, R. W., on living Christ, 12:378*b*
Dalmatia, identification of, 11:514
Damascus: Amos oracle against, 6:779 f
  identification of, 6:779
  Isaiah oracle on, 5:272, 272*b* f
  Jeremiah oracle against, 5:1120 f
  Paul's escape from, 10:403 f, 404*b* f
  significance of, 3:212
Damon, S. Foster, on charity of Job, 3:1116*a* f
Dampier, William: on Leonardo da Vinci and the church, 2:911*a*
  on science and church, 2:912*a* f
Dan, sanctuary at, 2:798 f
Dance, in O.T. worship, 1:946*a*
Dancing (social), attitude toward, 1:1065*a* f
Danel, Ezekiel allusion to, 6:217 f
Danger: facing, 4:495*a* f; 7:771*a*
  prayer in, 4:296 f
  security in, 4:210*b*
Daniel: courage of, 6:362*a*
  at court, 6:360 f
  dream of, 6:449 f
  as dream interpreter, 6:370, 380 f, 408 f, 427 f
  faith of, 6:356*a* f
  hymn of praise of, 6:381 f
  in lion's den, 6:346*b*, 434 f
  loyalty of to God, 6:356*b* f
  as name, 6:367
  in Nebuchadrezzar's court, 6:346*a*
  plot against, 6:442 f
  prayer of, 6:443

as symbolic name, 6:344*b* f
  testing of, 6:438 f
Daniel (book of): angels in, 6:351*a*
  as apocalyptic, 6:350*a* f
  as apocryph, 6:345*a* f
  chronological table of, 6:352 f
  composition of, 6:348*b* f
  conception of history in, 6:351*b*
  date of, 6:348*b* f, 355*a*
  Dead Sea Scroll of, 12: Plate 14
  epilogue of, 6:545 f
  eschatology of, 6:351*a*
  Ezekiel reference to, 6:137, 217 f
  four-empire theory in, 6:373 f, 450
  historical background of, 6:341*a* f
  "historical blunders" in, 6:345*b* f
  historicity of, 6:345*b* f
  introducing readers to, 6:355*a* f
  literary genre of, 6:345*a* f
  misunderstanding of, 6:355*a* f
  origin of, 6:344*a* f
  relevance of, 6:355*b* f
  religious significance of, 6:355*a* f
  stories in, 6:346*a* f
  structure of, 6:346*a* f
  teaching of God in, 6:351*a* f
  teaching of man in, 6:351*a* f
  text of, 6:351*b* f
  theme of, 6:356*a* f
  Theodotion's version of, 6:351*b* f
  theology of, 6:351*a* f
  visions in, 6:346*b* f, 449 f, 468 f
Danites, spies of, 2:802 f
Dante, love and indignation of, 5:725*a*
Darius, 1:270*a*; 6:433 f, 484
  Alexander's defeat of, 6:1092
  building the temple under, 3:588 f, 606 f, 619 f
  decree of, 6:440 f, 447 f
  as name, 6:434
  reconstruction of altar under, 3:588 f
  re-establishment of sacrifices under, 3:588 f
  reign of, 3:606 f
  report of Tattenai to, 3:609 f
  revolts under, 6:1039*a*
Dark Ages, church in, 10:655*a* f
Darkness: curse of, 12:484*b* f
  of day of the Lord, 6:743
  fear of, 12:543*a* f
  light and, 4:42*b* f, 317*b* f; 5:81*b* f, 691*a* f, 697*a* f; 6:382*a* f, 637*b* f, 1061*a*; 7:289*b*; 8:213*b* f, 672*b* f, 789*a* f; 10:709*a* f; 12:222*a* f
  light and (Johannine), 8:445*b* f, 466 f
  plague of, 1:910, 910*a* f
  treasures of, 5:523*a* f
  walking in, 12:223*b* f
Darrow, Clarence, on meaning of life, 1:578*b*

Darwin, Charles: on cruelty of nature, 5:436*a*
  evolution theory of, 1:462*a* f
  limitation of, 8:259*a*
  on missions, 5:715*b* f
  on universe, 4:833*a*
Dathan, revolt of, 2:222 f
Davey, Noel, on I–III John, 12:213*b* f
David: Abigail and, 2:1011 f
  Absalom's revolt against, 2:1108 f, 1108*a* f
  achievement of, 1:280*a* f, 312*a* f
  aims of, 3:72*a* f
  anointing of, 2:965 f
  arrogance of, 3:415*a* f
  Asaph and, 3:801
  Bathsheba and, 2:1097 f, 1097*a* f; 3:23 f; 4:268*a*
  capture of Jerusalem by, 2:1069 f
  census of, 2:1171 f, 1171*b* f; 3:413 f
  character of, 1:312*b*
  city of, 3:690
  court of, 2:1108 f
  at court of Saul, 2:969 f, 969*b* f
  Covenant of, 5:405*a* f, 644 f
  death of, 3:433*b* f
  defeat of Philistines by, 2:1074 f, 1074*a* f
  desire of to build temple, 3:404 f
  dirge of on Saul and Jonathan, 2:1045 f
  dismissal of, 2:1030 f
  election of, 5:645
  escape of, 28:986 f
  exploits of warriors of, 2:1160 f, 1167 f
  failure of to bring the Ark to Zion, 3:392 f
  farewell of, 3:434 f, 437*b* f
  flight of from Jerusalem, 2:1124 f, 1124*b* f
  flight of to Ramah and Gath, 2:864*a* f, 999 f
  genealogy of, 3:357 f
  God's promises to, 4:482 f, 483*a* f
  Goliath and, 2:970 f, 970*b* f; 3:412 f, 412*a* f
  house of, 2:1055*a* f, 1091*a* f
  impotency of, 3:20
  incapacity of, 3:19 f
  Joab and, 2:1052 f
  Jonathan and, 2:980*b* f, 989 f; 4:288*a* f
  key of (Revelation), 12:393 f
  as king at Jerusalem, 2:1068 f
  as king of Judah, 2:1049 f
  last days of, 3:18 f
  last words of, 3:30 f
  legacy of evil of, 3:32 f
  magnanimity of, toward Saul, 2:1009*b* f, 1017 f
  "madness" of, 4:273*a* f
  marriage of to Michal, 2:981 f
  Meribbaal and, 2:1092 f
  military and civil administration of, 3:430 f
  military organization of, 1:281*a* f
  at Nob, 2:995 f
  personal life of, 2:1092 f
  personality of, 4:267*a*
  plague of, 3:413 f, 415*a* f
  polygamy of, 3:396*a*

preparations for temple of, 3:418 f
promises to, 5:645
as rebel, 4:282a
reign of, 2:1088 f; 3:381 f
return of to Jerusalem, 2: 1145 f
as a revolutionist, 4:272b f
rise of, 2:958 f
rivals for throne of, 3:19 f
rule of, 1:313a
Saul and, 2:985 f, 993b f, 995 f; 4:272b f, 288b f
sepulchres of, 3:690 f
song of deliverance of, 2: 1161 f, 1161b f
sorrows of, 2:1128a f
spoils of, 3:409a
supremacy of, 5:645
as symbol of mankind, 4: 483a f
takes ark to Zion, 3:396 f
testament of, 2:1166 f, 1166b f
thanksgiving of, 3:401b f, 439a
tomb of, 9:47
tower of, 5:122
triumphs of, 3:385 f, 408 f
vassalage of to Achish, 2: 1021 f
war of against Ammon, 2: 1094 f
weakness of, 3:19b f
Davidic kingship, 5:1051 f
in Ezekiel, 6:53a f
future (Haggai), 6:1049
restoration of (Amos), 6: 850 f
Davidic Messiah, Servant of the Lord and, 5:412b f
Davidman, Joy, on conversion from Communism to Christianity, 11:545a f
Davidson, A. B.: on Ezekiel, 6:42a, 82b
on Habakkuk, 6:977b, 987
on one God, 1:981b
on Second Isaiah, 5:466a
Davies, D. R., on sin, 1: 503b; 4:568a f
Davies, William Henry: on harmonies of nature, 4: 763a
on money and friends, 4: 842a
on praise, 4:580b
on song of the robin, 4: 612b
Dawn, false, 7:548a
Dawson, William J., on God's plan for man, 5: 673b
Day: "evil," 10:739
journey of, 4:124b f
of judgment; see Judgment day
last; see Last day
new, 5:28b
seizing the, 5:74b f
summer, 5:707a
uneventful, 3:1164b f
of wrath (Second Isaiah), 5:725b
Day, Beth, on speech, 12:49b
Day, Clarence, on sense of unworthiness, 6:419b
Day and night, creation of, 1:470 f; 3:1176
Day of Atonement; see Atonement
Day of Christ, Philippians concept of, 11:13a, 22 f, 27

"Day of eternity," in II Peter usage, 12:206
Day of judgment, 5:255b f
I John teaching on, 12: 285, 285a f
Day of the Lord, 1:372a; 7: 13b, 26b, 30a
Amos concept of, 6:791a, 817 f, 817b f
darkness of, 6:743
Ezekiel concept of, 6:229
I Thessalonians concept of, 11:249b f
interpretation of, 5:842a
Isaiah concept of, 5:182 f
Jeremiah concept of, 5: 1023 f
Jerusalem and, 6:1017
Joel concept of, 6:735a, 741
Obadiah concept of, 6: 857b, 865 f
Pauline concept of, 11: 308 f, 325 f
as prophetic theme, 5:610
Zephaniah concept of, 6: 1009b, 1013a f, 1016 f
Day of the Messiah, 7:146a, 251
"Day of small things," 6: 1073b f
Day Star, identification of, 5:261 f
Day of vengeance, Second Isaiah concept of, 5: 727 f, 727b f
Days, special (observance of), 9:619a f
Day's activities, preview of, 3:176a f
Days of old, wonders of (Second Isaiah), 5:733 f, 733b f
Daysman, as Joban theme, 3:900b f
Deacon: character of (I Timothy), 11:415 f
derivation of, 7:497
as ecclesiastical term, 11: 17a f
function of in early church, 11:345b f
N.T. concept of, 10:690a f
Philippians reference to, 11:16
wives of (Pastoral), 11: 417 f
Deaconess, N.T. reference to, 9:655
Dead: Christ's raising of; see Miracles of Christ
life from, 6:266b f
N.T. prayers for, 11:477
prayers for, 10:240b f
quick and, 12:136
raising of; see Miracles
resurrection of; see Resurrection
tribute to, 4:512b
"twice," 12:333
usefulness of, 8:811b
Dead Sea Scrolls, 12:645a f, Plates 3, 4, 8-14, 19
calendrical materials of, 12:649b
Chronicles manuscript of, 12:648b
copper scrolls of, 12:646b
dates of, 12:648b f
Deuteronomy manuscript of, 12:654b
discovery of, 12:645a
Essene authorship of, 12: 646a f

Essenes and, 12:657b f
Exodus manuscript of, 12: 655a
Isaiah manuscript of, 5: 161a; 12:653a f
Jeremiah manuscript of, 12:655b
John (Gospel) and, 12: 660a f
Nahum manuscript of, 12: 649b, 658b
N.T. and, 12:659a f
N.T. studies and, 12: 657b f
O.T. and, 12:650b
O.T. studies and, 12:650b f
Paleo-Hebrew script of, 12:648b
Pentateuch manuscript of, 12:654b
proto-Samaritan text of, 12:656b f
Samuel manuscript of, 12: 648a f
scroll jar, 12: Plate 12
textual revelations of, 12: 653a f
"Dead works," meaning of, 11:650 f
Deafness: moral, 8:263b f
as theme of Second Isaiah, 5:475 f
Dearmer, Percy, on pain, 12: 29b
Death: as act of God, 6: 1015a
appointment with, 3: 1037a f
approach of, 3:420a f
attitude toward, 1:595b f, 813a f; 3:954b f, 1010b; 7:724a; 10:625a; 11: 306a f
beneficence of, 4:476a f
of child; see Child
Christian, 1:596a f; 5: 264a f; 8:278a; 12:302b, 473a f
Christian victory over, 12: 384a f
Christ's acceptance of, 3: 1082a f
Christ's power over, 12:378
Christ's teaching on, 8: 354b f; 11:617a
as common experience, 3: 962b; 5:72 f
as conqueror, 11:612a
covenant with (Isaiah), 5:313b f, 317 f
dance of, 4:258 f
description of, 3:880a
despair over, 5:264a f
dispensation of, 10:307b f
dread of, 11:307a f, 613b, 616b
Ecclesiastes concept of, 5: 10a, 16a f, 18b, 72 f
end of (Revelation), 12: 530a f
as enemy, 4:56b; 10:237b
facing, 6:1015a
fact of, 6:237a f
fear of, 1:529b; 7:618a f; 8:417b; 11:616b f, 693b f; 12:285a f
fearlessness in, 1:827b
finality of, 3:1010b f; 5: 38b f; 9:472a
of first-born (plague), 1: 911 f, 911a f
gates of, 4:58, 58b
of godly, 4:71a f

Hebrew concept of, 3: 954b f
hope in, 1:828a f
horseman of (Revelation), 12:413 f, 413b f
indifference to, 11:693a f
inevitability of, 1:528b f, 827a f
Joban concept of, 3:1010 f
key of, 12:378
as leveler, 5:263b; 8:662a; 10:325b
life and (I John), 12:251 f
life out of, 4:58b; 8:369b f
longing for, 3:929a f
manner of, 11:755a
meaning of, 3:1010a; 8: 420a, 668b; 10:51b f
meeting, 2:241a f; 5:374a
metaphors for, 11:510b f
of mother, 3:918b
O.T. concept of, 5:264a
Pauline teaching on, 9: 514b f; 10:237, 326 f, 326a f, 638b; 11:306a f
peace in, 5:307a
power of, 11:613a f
preparing for, 1:679b f; 8: 781b f
problem of, 1:370a f
Psalter concept of, 4:13b
as reaper, 5:892b f
reunion after, 10:230b f
scene of, 4:128a
serenity in, 1:827b f
as shepherd, 4:258b
sin and, 9:462 f, 464b, 510; 10:638a f; 11:617a
as sleep, 6:542; 11:302
solemnity of, 1:743a f
of son, 2:349b; 3:924b f, 1023a, 1107a; 6:199a
Stoic attitude toward, 10: 237b
as taboo topic, 11:694a
unafraid of, 8:700b
universality of, 1:528b f
valley of, 4:127, 127b f
violent, 6:1015a
as warrior, 7:602b
of wife; see Wife
of youth, 4:113b
"Death wish," 3:929a f
Deborah: Barak and, 2:711 f
character of, 2:713b f
identification of, 2:712 f
Joan of Arc and, 2:713b f
song of, 1:177a f, 278b, 441b f; 2:717 f, 717a f; 11:321b f
Debs, Eugene V., philosophy of, 6:1070a
Debt: credit and, 2:973a
Pauline concept of, 7:57a
payment of, 10:277a, 368b
responsibility for, 4:817b f
Debts, forgiveness of (Christ's teaching on), 7:313, 313b f
Decadence, modern, 6:1057b
Decalogue, 1:842a f, 979 f, 979b f; see also Ten Commandments
covenant and, 1:843a f; 2: 353 f
Elohistic, 1:303a f
forms of, 1:850b
Mosaic authorship of, 1: 843b
non-Mosaic origin of, 1: 981, 984
ritual, 1:1076 f
Decapolis, identification of, 7:278; 8:10a

Decatur, Stephen, on nationalism, 1:505b
Deceiver, warning against (II John), 12:305b f
Decency, meaning of, 8:389a
Deception, political, 6:928b f
Decision: deferred, 3:156a f
great, 1:592b f
by lot, 2:688 f; 4:788; 6:179a, 881 f
making of, 11:75a
necessity of, 11:103a f; 12:238a
power of, 3:156b f
quality of, 1:782a f
responsibility of, 7:896a
valley of, 6:756b f, 758
Dedan: identification of, 6:203
Isaiah oracle about, 5:288 f
Dedication: compromising of, 6:434b f
courageous, 1:595a
feast of; see Feast
Dedication of first-born, meaning of, 1:915, 927 f
Deed: creed and, 6:666a f
idea and, 7:680b
irrevocable, 11:745a
Johannine concept of, 12:261 f
vision and, 1:575b f
word and, 1:875b; 3:662a f, 934a; 4:70a f, 504b; 5:626a; 6:801b, 810b; 8:433b; 11:533a f; 12:48b
worship and, 12:437b f
Defeat: deliverance from, 1:767b f
excuse for, 1:764b
lesson of, 9:532a
overcoming,   1:603a f, 767b f
persistence in spite of, 7:732b
result of, 5:619a f
spiritual victory in, 7:719a
victory and, 3:1051a f; 4:115b f; 11:503b
Defeatism, 1:507a
causes of, 1:535a f
Defender,   Christ   as,   12:300a f
Defense, national, 4:670a
Defense mechanism, 3:1041b
Defilement, inner, 7:439a
Definition,   inadequacy   of, 10:29a
Deissmann, Adolf: on ancient infanticide, 6:144a f
on biblical faith, 4:648b
on Colossians, 5:1043a f
on types of religion, 4:505a f
Delight: eternal, 11:112b
Hebrew meaning of, 4:20
Delilah: identification of, 2:792
Samson and, 2:792 f
Delitzsch, Franz: on Ecclesiastes, 5:12b
on self-sacrifice, 2:16a
Deliverance: psalmist's cry for, 4:148 f, 162 f, 204b, 361 f
reaction to, 5:305b f
significance of, 3:1138b
song of, 4:92a f
temptation and, 10:111a f
Deliverer, Christ as, 7:346a; 10:228a; 11:265
Delphic Oracle, 7:91b f
Demagogue,   danger   of,   2:1151a f

Demand, Christian, 12:62b
Demant, Charles, on affirmations, 12:244a
Demas: desertion   of,   11:513 f, 513a f
identification of, 11:238
Demeter, myth of, 7:90b
Demetrius (bishop), 7:225a
Demetrius (son of Seleucus), 6:524
Demetrius (III John), commendation of, 12:312 f, 312a f
Demetrius   of   Ephesus,   9:258b f
Demiurge, belief in, 7:85b
Democracy: of Christ, 11:572a f
Christian foundation of, 10:735a f
conscience and, 12:599b
definition of, 11:77b
despotism and, 4:325a f
devotion to, 2:1062a
dictatorship and, 11:124a
God and, 12:564a
Lincoln's concept of, 11:15b
nature of, 12:564a
neglect of, 11:96b
present condition of, 4:327a f
as religious faith, 7:394a f; 11:561a
responsibility in, 6:670b f
of Roman Empire, 7:80b
spirit of, 9:101b f, 143b f
Demon: angel and, 12:456
Christ's power over; see Miracles of Christ
exorcism of, 8:205 f; see also Miracles
O.T. references to, 1:376a
pagan belief in, 1:375a f
Demon possession,   7:404, 660b f, 661; 8:96 f, 156b f; see also Miracles of Christ
N.T. concept of, 1:29b
Demoniac: Christian concept of, 12:272a f
doctrine of (I Timothy), 11:424 f
modern concept of, 10:737b f
Demoniac and his relapse, parable of; see Parables of Christ
Demonology: Israel's rejection of, 1:375b f
N.T. concept of, 7:346a f, 396b f
Demosthenes, on candle and sun, 5:916b
Denarius, identification of, 12:412
Denial, belief and, 12:274b f
Denny, James: on grace, 12:91
on minister's character, 10:302b
on priesthood of Christ, 11:705b
Denominational competition, 10:390a f
Denominationalism, 4:689b f
self-centered, 7:678b
"Deny," meaning of, 7:770a
"Deposit of faith," 11:471 f
Depravity, total, 3:84
Depression,   shadow   of,   4:230b f
Deprivation: appreciation and, 6:597b f

lessons from, 7:426a
Derision, chapel and, 7:900b
Desert: Isaiah knowledge of, 5:342b f
streams in (Second Isaiah), 5:496 f
as symbol, 5:145b
Desire: commandment and, 9:494b f
contradictory, 2:989a f
duty and, 11:567b f
evil, 11:213
false and true, 1:573b f
frustration of, 5:61 f
instinct and, 5:219a
limitless, 11:23a
satisfaction and, 6:608a f
self-defeating, 12:54a f
Stoic concept of, 11:451
unsatisfied, 12:423b
wrongful (James), 12:52 f
Desire of Nations, Christ as, 7:257b
Desolation, hope born in, 4:541b f
Despair: anatomy   of,   3:925b f
cause of, 5:26a
faith and, 5:839b
hope and, 1:552a f; 3:1003b f; 8:369a; 10:652a f
meaning of, 3:924
modern, 12:267b
overcoming of, 9:502b f
sin and, 4:340a
unreasonableness of, 8:325a
Desperation, act of, 3:518b f
Despotism, democracy and, 4:325a f
Destiny: character and, 12:525a f
divine, 1:594b
human, 1:559b
makers of, 6:159a f
problem of, 5:810a
romance of, 10:324b
Destruction: cosmic, 5:841b
forces of, 12:435a f
in Pauline usage, 11:320 f
Detachment, attachment and, 11:123a f
Determination: example of, 2:920b
result of, 7:707a
Determinism: in apocalypticism, 12:349b
astrological, 11:192a
as creed, 2:923a; 11:100b
personal   responsibility and, 12:27b
of Revelation, 12:415
Detour: God's purpose and, 7:720a
value of, 3:1160b
Deuteronomic law, 5:868b
Deuteronomic reforms: Jeremiah and, 5:779a f
Jeremiah teaching on, 5:905 f, 906a f
Deuteronomy (book of): aim of, 2:324a
character of, 2:311b f
characteristic words and expressions of, 2:318a f
Christ's quotations from, 2:311b
code of, 1:324b f; 3:733; 5:908b f
date of, 2:323b f
Dead Sea Scroll of, 12:654b
defects of, 1:326b

E and, 2:319b f
early Greek scroll of, 12:Plate 6
greatness of, 2:331a f
H and, 2:325a
Hezekiah reform and, 2:323b f
humanitarianism   of,   2:328b f,   332a,   415a, 425b f, 427 f, 477a
idolatry and, 2:324a
Jeremiah and, 2:319a f; 5:882 f
Jeremiah as author of, 5:788b
Kings and, 3:4a f, 7a f
as law book, 2:311b f
literary character of, 1:181b f
moral logic of, 1:326a f
Mosaic authorship of, 2:332a
N.T. and, 2:311b
origin of, 1:197b f; 2:323a f
outline of, 2:329b f
prophetic element in, 2:332a
purpose of, 1:197b f; 2:316b
significance of, 2:311b f
structure of, 2:314b f
style of, 1:181b f; 2:318a f
theme of, 2:311a f
theology of, 2:326b f
title of, 2:311b f
"Developing revelation," 7:110a
Development, personal, 10:120a
Devil: belief in, 10:737b f
child of (I John), 12:251 f
Christ vanquishes, 11:616 f
disguise of, 8:358a
Hebrew meaning of, 3:475b f
meaning of, 12:457
in N.T. usage, 7:270
O.T. concept of, 7:269a; 8:84
in Pastoral usage, 11:414
Pauline concept of, 8:84
personal, 3:1024a
snare of, 11:414b f
strategy of, 6:582b
wiles of (early Christian concept), 10:737
Devotion: daily, 4:498b f
evening, 4:499a
fixedness of, 5:466b
to God, 7:870b
importance of, 4:498a f
methods of, 4:499a
morning, 4:36b f
naturalness of, 11:105b f
necessity of, 6:439a
private, 11:423a f, 429a
religion as, 11:106a
unlimited, 1:645a f
Devotional life, 11:230a
Devout, discouragement of, 5:568a f
Devoutness, element of, 5:678a f
Dew, as O.T. symbol, 6:706, 721
Dewey, Orville, on love of man, 12:263b
Diaconate, examination for in early church, 11:417
Diagnosis, correct, 6:621b f
Dialogue of the Man Weary of Life with His Soul, 3:879b f
Diamond, valueless, 7:271b

Pauline teaching on, 9: 543*a* f; 11:259 f
problem of, 1:353*a* f
uniqueness of (Amos), 6: 791 f
Election love, Hosea teaching on, 6:681 f
Elemental spirits: doctrine of, 11:140*a* f
Pauline teaching on, 11: 191 f, 192*a* f
"Elementary doctrines of Christ," 11:650
Elephantine, temple at, 5: 281
Eleusinian Mysteries, 7:90*a* f
Eli, fall of house of, 2: 862*b* f, 889 f
Eliakim, identification of, 5: 293*b* f
Eliashib the priest, identification of, 3:805
Elihu: anger of, 3:1130 f
discourse of, 3:1127 f, 1127*b* f, 1169
intervention of, 3:1130 f
as name, 3:1129
Elijah narrative (Kings), 3: 12*b* f
Elijah the Tishbite: achievement of, 1:316*a* f
Ahab and, 3:143 f
at Carmel, 3:148 f
compared with John the Baptist, 7:263, 263*b*, 384, 461*b*, 462, 778; 8: 137
courage of, 3:160*a* f
Elisha succeeds, 3:192 f, 203*a* f
energy of, 3:190*b* f
feeding of, 3:145 f
at Horeb, 3:160 f
James reference to, 12:72
Jezebel and, 3:159 f
legends about, 3:194
Malachi reference to, 6: 1143 f
mantle of, 3:193
as martyr-witness (Revelation), 12:445 f
as name, 3:145
prophets of Baal and, 3: 154 f
reviving of widow's son by, 3:147 f
Transfiguration and, 8: 174, 174*b* f
translation of, 3:192*b* f
vision of, 11:157*b*
Eliot, Charles William: on controversy, 11:495*b*
on loss of faith, 11:468*b*
tribute to, 1:546*a*
Eliot, George: on affection of God, 5:574*a*
on anguish, 5:620*b*
on comprising, 5:66*a*
on family prayers, 5:655*b*
on happiness, 1:604*a*
on receptiveness, 5:583*a*
on self-centeredness, 10: 178*a*
on sin, 4:681*a*; 5:737*b*
on skill of man, 5:209*b*
on true greatness, 12:56*a* f
Eliot, T. S.: on fear of God, 5:796*a*
on fool, 5:814*b*
on hollow men, 5:899*a* f
on humility, 5:606*b*
on iniquity, 5:847*a*
on justice of God, 5:931*a*
on man's hope, 5:773*b*

on test of poet, 5:830*b*
theme of, 4:321*a*
on Word of God, 5:932*a*
Eliphaz the Temanite: discourse of, 3:932 f, 932*b* f, 1015 f, 1016*b* f, 1071 f, 1072*a* f
identification of, 3:922, 923*b* f
Elisha, 1:317*b*
arrow of victory and, 3: 255 f
capture of Syrian army and, 3:216 f
character of, 3:196*a*, 203*a* f
Christ compared with, 3: 203*b* f
cleanses spring at Jericho, 3:196
curses jeering boys, 3:197
Gehazi the leper and, 3: 214 f, 214*a* f
Hazael and, 3:226 f
healing of Naaman the Syrian by, 3:209 f
miraculous feeding of hungry men by, 3:209
narratives in Kings of, 3: 13*a* f
needy woman and, 3:203 f
poisoned pottage and, 3: 208 f
Shunemmite woman and, 3:204 f, 204*b* f, 224 f, 224*b* f
siege of Samaria and, 3: 218 f
tomb of, 3:255 f
vessels of oil and, 3:203 f
wonder stories about, 3: 196, 203 f, 255 f
Elishah, identification of, 6: 211 f
Elkanah: Hannah and, 2: 879 f
Peninnah and, 2:879 f
Elkosh, identification of, 6: 957 f
Ellicott, on emotion, 4:111*b*
Elmslie, W. A. L., on death of David, 3:434*a* f
Elohim, God as, 1:726*b*; 4: 7*b*; 5:17*a*
Elohistic Decalogue, 1:303*a* f
Elon, identification of, 2:775
Eloquence: gift of, 10:169*a* f
true, 10:28*a* f, 169*a* f
El Shaddai, God as, 1:889
Elymas the magician, 9:171, 171*a* f
Elyot, Thomas, on deceit, 4: 322
Emancipation Proclamation, 5:599*a* f
Emancipation tendency, in Corinthian church, 10: 7*b*
Emancipator, Christ as, 8: 601*b* f
Emerson, Ralph Waldo: on acceptance of duty, 3: 1164*a*
on conventional behavior, 5:567*b*
on Daniel Webster, 5:479*b*
disinterestedness of, 3: 1110*b* f
on evil, 11:81*b*
on foolish consistency, 4: 296*a* f
on friendship, 2:981*a* f; 3: 960*a*
on God in nature, 5:481*a*

on guidance of God, 5: 521*a*
on handicap, 10:409*a*
on influence of the faithful, 5:592*a* f
on presence of God, 2:808*a*
on scriptures, 5:1058*b* f
on slavery, 5:1056*a*
on social order, 5:711*a*
on solitude of soul, 5:941*b*
on trifles, 4:782*a*
"Emmanuel": derivation of, 7:255
Christ as, 7:253*b*
Emmaus: identification of, 8:421
road to; *see* Resurrection
Emotion: control of, 9:160*a*
evil use of, 1:681*b* f
freedom from, 8:693*b* f
heart as seat of, 4:811*b* f
importance of, 8:90*b*
instinctive, 4:306*b* f
music and, 4:762*b*
noble, 12:381*a* f
outburst of, 4:878*a* f
pity as, 6:893*a* f
religion and, 1:779*a* f; 11: 262*b* f
religious significance of, 10:155*a* f
restraining of, 4:111*b*
Stoic concept of, 7:86*b*; 8: 693*b* f
training of, 6:663*b*
uncontrolled, 9:288*a* f; 10: 581*b* f
Emperor worship, 7:80*b*, 94*a*; 11:245*b*; 12:589*a* f
Christians and, 12:354*a* f, 552*a* f
Revelation teaching on, 12:354*a* f, 388 f, 471 f
Emphasis, distorted, 1: 1006*b* f
Empire, ephemeral character of, 2:1088*b* f
Emptiness, danger of, 8:209*b*
"Encourage," in N.T. usage, 11:312
Encouragement, 4:69*b*
meaning of, 9:635*b* f
need of, 11:713*a* f
End: Christ as, 11:166*a*, 167
Daniel concept of, 6:549
Daniel date of, 6:548
means and, 2:49*a* f, 1064*a* f; 6:803*a* f, 928*b*; 7:273*a*, 792*b*; 8:401*a*; 9: 555*a* f; 11:426*b*; 12: 50*b* f, 564*a*
O.T. concept of, 6:478 f
Revelation visions of, 12: 511 f
End of age: Christ's teaching on, 7:541; 8:360 f
signs of, 7:543*a* f, 549
"Ends of the earth," meaning of, 4:318, 382
En-dor, identification of, 4: 450
Endurance: faith and, 7: 860*b*
lesson of, 9:55*a*
test of, 7:545*b* f
virtue of, 12:380*b* f
En-eglaim, identification of, 6:328
Enelow, H. G., on Christian and Jew, 12:19*b*
Enemy: attitude toward, 2: 727*b*; 9:595*b* f
of Christian, 12:156*a* f
compassion for, 4:927*a*

of Cross, 11:97 f
dealing with, 3:1122*b* f
death as last, 4:56*b*; 10: 237*b*
deliverance from (Psalms), 4:72 f
description of (Psalms), 4:335 f, 335*b* f
extermination of, 1:939*a* f
forgiving of, 4:587*a* f
God as, 10:340*a* f
internal, 2:299*a* f
love of, 4:332*a*, 927*a* f; 7: 58*b*; 8:193*b* f, 765*a*; 9: 153*a* f
love of (Christ's teaching on), 6:596*a*; 7:58*b*, 302 f, 302*b* f; 8:193*b* f
love of (Pauline), 9:591 f
maledictions on (Psalms), 4:183 f, 289 f
of man, 11:325*a* f
number one, 11:325*a* f
praying for, 9:105*a* f
pride of, 4:400*b*
redemption of, 4:452*a* f
self as, 8:386*b* f
treatment of, 2:457*b* f; 4: 587*a* f, 926*a* f
Energy, increase and decrease of, 12:560*a* f
En-gedi, identification of, 6: 328
English Bible, 1:84 f
Miles Coverdale and, 1: 88*a* f
early translation of, 1:84*a* f
first authorized revision of, 1:89*b* f
first licensed translation of, 1:89*a* f
first publication of, 1:88*a* f
first Roman Catholic, 1: 92*b* f
Jewish versions of, 1:99*b* f
George Joye and, 1:88*a*
modern speech versions of, 1:98*a* f
printing of, 1:86*b* f
Revised Standard Version of, 1:100*a* f
Revised Version of, 1:95*b* f
Roman Catholic versions of, 1:99*b* f
second authorized version of, 1:91*b* f
Richard Taverner and, 1: 89*b*
third authorized version of, 1:94*b*
William Tyndale and, 1: 86*b* f
versions of (table of comparative readings), 1: 101*a* f
John Wycliffe and, 1:85*b* f
Enlightenment, mental, 4: 84*a*
Enoch: faith of, 11:723*a* f
Hebrews and, 11:588*a*
Jude reference to, 12:324, 327, 334 f
translation of, 11:723
walks with God, 1:530*a* f
Enthronement ceremony, Egyptian, 11:423
Enthusiasm: meaning of, 10: 715*a*
religious, 3:399*a* f; 9:382*a*
spontaneous, 7:826*a*
uncontrolled, 10:148*a* f
Entrance of Hamath, identification of, 3:89

deliverance of (Psalms), 4:26 f, 40 f
demand of, 4:739a; 6:422b, 939b f; 11:486a
demand and succour of, 10:381a
democracy and, 12:564a
demonstration of, 6:96b f
denial of, 4:75a, 278a f, 371b, 747a f; 6:574a f; 12:325
departure of, 2:793b f
departure of glory of (Ezekiel), 6:114 f
dependableness of, 5:454b; 7:704a; 11:656 f
dependence on, 2:399a f, 665a f; 4:668 f, 668b f; 5:579b f; 6:582a; 8:364a, 394b; 9:374a, 551b; 11:22a f
derision of, 4:309a f
desire of, 4:263b f
as destroyer of Ephraim (Hosea), 6:708 f
Deuteronomic concept of, 2:326b
developing concept of, 2:354b f; 3:394a
devotion to, 8:808a
direction of, 5:820b
direction of in history, 2:327a f
disapproval of, 6:1093a f
disciplines of, 5:476b f
discourse of (Joban), 3:1170 f
disinterestedness of, 5:32
disobedience to, 1:501 f; 2:705a f; 8:510a; 11:627b f
as Disturber, 11:78b f
doctrine of (I Corinthians), 10:9a f
doing of, 3:407b f
doubt of (Deuteronomic), 2:337 f
drawn by, 8:571b f
dread of, 1:884b
dwelling of among men, 11:171
dwelling place of, 4:148a; 5:671 f
elect of, 11:259b f
election by, 5:800a f
Elijah concept of, 11:597b
Eliphaz concept of, 3:941, 941a f
as Elohim, 1:726b; 4:7b; 5:17a
as El Shaddai, 1:889
elusiveness of (Joban), 3:1082 f
encounter between man and, 5:798b
as enemy, 10:340a f
enemy of (Isaiah), 5:354 f
enlarged ideas of, 1:477a; 3:161b
enmity of (Joban), 3:1044 f
enmity toward, 4:451b
enthronement of, 4:247; 6:47a
equity of, 4:352a
escape from, 5:803a; 11:635a f
eschatological titles of (Second Isaiah), 5:399b f, 492a f
estrangement from, 10:340a
as eternal, 4:253b, 479b f; 5:402a f, 672a

as Eternal Paradox, 3:1166a f
eternal purpose of, 7:13b; 10:522b f
eternity of, 4:487 f, 488b f
eternity of (Psalms), 1:337a
evading, 11:683b f
everlasting arms of, 5:538b
everlasting mercy of, 6:890b f
everlastingness of, 5:444 f, 445a f; 6:458a f
as ever-present, 6:69b f
as ever-present help, 4:240 f
evidence of, 7:651a f
exaltation of, 5:440b f
exaltation of (Isaiah), 5:164b
excellent name of, 4:48b f
exclusive love toward, 12:238b f
exclusive worship of, 12:604b
existence of, 4:370b f
expectation of, 3:1149b f
experience of, 5:378a f
eye of, 3:609, 967a; 6:1018; 7:517a
Ezekiel concept of, 6:69b f, 169a f
face of, 4:222; 5:687; 12:543
faith in, 2:209a f; 3:844a f; 7:831b f; 11:628a f, 659a f, 721b f
faithfulness of, 1:544a f; 2:487a f; 3:1143b f; 4:165a, 480 f; 11:484b f, 720b f, 727a f; 12:224b
falling away from, 11:624a f
false, 4:609a
false concept of, 6:611b, 647b
fame of, 4:543a f
family of, 10:529a f, 674b f, 676
as father of Christ (Revelation), 12:370 f
fatherhood of, 1:727a f, 869b f; 3:356a f, 406a f; 4:126a, 468a f, 548; 5:166, 166a f, 736 f; 6:1125a f; 8:388a, 604a f, 738b f; 10:447, 606a, 676; 12:225a f, 247a
fatherhood of (Christ's teaching on), 7:12a f, 256a, 304a f, 309b f, 531b; 8:81a f, 200 f, 200b f, 604a f, 701b f, 738 f, 738b f; 10:447; 11:332a
fatherly love of, 12:254b f
of fathers, 1:816a f
favor of, 4:58; 6:749a f; 8:37a f
favoritism of, 4:426b f, 429b f
fear of, 1:785b f, 989 f; 2:399 f; 3:286a f, 710, 1169 f; 4:595, 784b, 784b f; 5:763b; 6:599a f, 882; 11:59a f; 12:103b, 116a
fellow worker of, 10:345a
fellowship with, 5:818b; 11:275a f, 396b f; 12:221 f, 224a f
fidelity of, 5:571a

figurative descriptions of (Second Isaiah), 5:388a f
finding of, 2:396a f; 3:1080 f, 1080a f; 5:746a f, 1018a f; 6:586b f; 8:67a, 199b
finding of in church, 8:55b
finger of, 1:1062a f; 8:207
fire of, 3:158; 5:351a f
as first and last (Second Isaiah), 5:558, 558b f
I Peter concept of, 12:83b f
fleeing from, 4:715a
fleeing in emergency to, 3:256a
flock of, 12:84b f, 149a
following, 6:889b
foolishness of (Pauline), 10:25 f
forbearance of, 3:105
foreknowledge of, 3:990b; 6:1102b f
forgetfulness of, 3:1086b; 4:394a f; 5:549b f
forgetting of, 2:521b f; 3:973b f; 4:565b f, 620b f; 5:598b f
forgiveness of, 3:458b; 968; 5:497b f; 7:350b, 477b; 8:145a, 277b, 669b f; 9:573b; 10:296a f, 645a f; 11:389b f; 12:229
forgiveness of (availability of), 8:146b
forgiveness of (I John), 12:224b f
forgiveness of (Kings), 3:16a
forgiveness of; see also Forgiveness
forgiveness and justice of, 11:487
forgiveness toward, 5:580b f
forsaken by, 5:686b f
forsaking of, 5:956b
as fortress, 4:493 f
foundation of, 11:492a f
as fountain of living waters (Jeremiah), 5:784a, 815, 815a f
as Friend, 4:84b f
fulfillment and, 11:727b
fullness of, 4:352b f; 10:680
future of, 5:597a
generosity of, 8:638a
as gentleman, 5:427a f
gentleness of, 2:1165a f; 4:99b f, 315a f, 408a
gift of, 3:1151 f; 5:458b f; 8:479a, 704b
as giver (Ecclesiastes), 5:16b
glorifying, 2:15b; 4:102a f, 606 f; 8:564a; 9:447b, 620 f; 10:531b; 11:322
glorifying (Pauline), 10:378 f, 466
glory of, 3:70a f; 4:460; 5:986a; 8:475; 10:449; 11:601, 601a f; 12:172a f
glory of (evidences of), 2:47a f; 9:138b f
glory of (Philo), 12:329
glory of (Second Isaiah), 5:697 f
glory of in heavens, 4:101 f
glory of in the law, 4:101 f, 104b f
glory of in nature, 3:

1163 f; 4:49 f, 101 f, 102a f, 555b f
glory of in the sun, 4:102 f
glory of in the world, 4:101 f
glory of reflected in Christ, 11:601, 601a f
Gnostic concept of, 11:355b f
of Gods, 6:534
good tidings of, 5:708b
goodness of, 2:366b f; 3:1093b f; 4:460 f, 499b f, 699 f; 5:962b; 6:569b f; 8:313a f
goodness of (Psalms), 4:123 f, 177 f, 189b f, 337b, 387
goodness and severity of (Isaiah), 5:339b f
gospel of (Pauline), 11:268
governance of, 4:326b f; 6:1072b
grace of, 5:480a f, 558a, 642 f; 8:477b f, 632b f; 10:368a f; 11:55b f, 521b f, 538, 551b, 743b f; see also Grace
grace of (forms of), 12:141a
grace of (Second Isaiah), 5:669 f
graciousness of, 4:343 f, 352, 547b f; 5:729a f
as Grand Inquisitor, 3:1174a f
gratitude to, 3:1172b; 4:265a f; 8:299a, 631a f; 9:386a f
as Great Architect, 5:805b
greatness of, 2:518b f; 3:1090 f, 1135a f, 1198b; 4:370a f, 695 f; 5:434b f, 438a, 602a, 986b; 6:690b; 11:331a f, 539 f; 12:268a
guidance of, 1:659a, 669b f, 807a; 2:187a f, 1164b; 3:140a f; 4:346 f, 663b; 5:521a f, 597a, 734 f, 927a; 9:214a f
hallowed name of, 6:262a f
hand of, 3:159; 4:170b, 525b f, 656b f, 805; 5:942; 6:167a f, 894a; 8:718b f; 12:154a f
handiwork of, 4:101 f, 101a f
happiness in, 8:513a
harmony with, 4:34
haste of, 4:34b f
healing of, 4:369a f
as heavenly Father, 8:604b
heirs of, 9:517a f
help of, 2:723a f, 930b f; 4:474b f, 495b f; 5:501b, 596b; 11:320a f
help of (appeal for), 4:29 f, 29b f, 582 f
help of (psalmist's assurance of), 4:110 f, 110a f, 150 f, 181 f, 199 f, 659 f
as hidden, 3:454b f; 5:1080a f, 1173a f; 5:530a f, 768a f
history and, 2:341a, 383b; 4:431a f; 6:373b f, 997b f
in history, 2:140a, 1085b f; 3:570b f, 1153a f; 4:431a f, 548b f, 554b f, 603a f; 5:524a f; 11:15b f, 168b f; 12:581a f

love of (understanding), 3:1070a f
love of (universality of), 7:28a
love of Christ and, 11:401a
love and justice of, 3: 955b f
love toward, 7:523b f, 847b; 8:582b
love toward (I John), 12: 235 f, 278 f, 278a f
love toward (motive of), 12:290a
love toward (ways of), 12: 289a f
as loving creator, 11:90a f
lovingkindness of, 3:33 f; 4:329b f
loyalty to, 4:232; 6:356b f, 436a; 8:210a, 286a f
magnificence of, 11:331b
magnifying of, 4:177
majesty of, 3:1094a f, 1168b f; 4:48 f, 405b f; 6:74b, 690a f, 847; 8: 409b
as Maker, 4:715b f; 5:526 f, 526a f, 962b
mammon and, 4:61a; 7: 319b f
man and, 1:367b f; 3: 406a f, 909a f, 1035b f, 1135a f; 4:425b f, 478b f; see also Man
man of, 3:297b f
man challenges, 3:1148a f; 6:986a f
manifestation of, 4:338b f; 7:440a
as manifested in nature, 4: 155, 342a f, 555b f, 646a f; 5:481a
as manifested in storm, 4: 156 f
man-made, 5:451a f; 6: 646b f
man's acceptance with (Pauline), 10:430b f
man's co-operation with, 2:555b f
man's gift from, 11:611a f
man's relationship to, 2: 487b f, 1087a f; 3:994a f; 4:137 f; 5:900b f; 9:67a
man's security in, 4:240b f
mastery of, 1:881a f
mediation of, 3:1026b
mediation between man and, 3:942b f
mediator of (Joban), 3: 1137 f
meeting with, 6:696b f, 804a f
menial service of, 5:427b
mental image of, 12:248a
mercy of, 1:625b; 2:507b f, 702a f, 763a f; 4:527a f, 547b f, 698b f; 6:571a f, 1094b f; 8:257b f, 393b; 9:436b, 563b f; 11:759a
mercy of (everlasting), 5: 334a
mercy of (Joban), 3:1154 f
mercy of (limiting), 6: 891 f
mercy of (Pauline), 9: 547b f, 579 f
mercy of (prayer for), 4: 491b f
messenger of, 3:137a f; 5: 731 f; 6:1137 f
metaphysical approach to, 4:370b f
might of, 5:442b f

mighty acts of, 4:741, 742b f
military figure to describe, 5:472
mills of, 3:983b f; 5:72a; 6:783a
mind of, 3:983b f
misrepresentation of, 10: 227a f
misunderstanding of, 4: 947b
modern concepts of, 4: 354a f
Mohammedan doctrine of, 4:506a
and monotheism; see Monotheism
moral approach to, 4: 370b f
moral demands of, 7:13b
moral love of, 12:231a
moral nature of, 6:1021a f; 8:685a
moral will of, 12:230a f
as Most High, 4:246
as murderer (Joban), 3: 1003 f, 1025 f
music of, 12:477a f
mysterious ways of, 3: 145a f; 6:1061b f; 11: 569a f
mystery of, 1:977a f; 3: 1174b f; 4:61b, 948b f; 6: 483a f; 10:191b f; 11: 185 f
Nahum concept of, 6:953a, 958
as Name, 2:118; 3:79 f
name of, 1:363b f, 726a f; 2:780a; 4:281 f; 5:469; 6: 382, 1031; 7:310b f; 8: 338a f; 10:403b f; 11: 689a f
name of (ineffable), 2: 366a f
name of (reverence for), 4:672b
nation and, 4:175a f
nation under, 3:471a f
nation's trust in (Psalms), 4:229 f
nature and, 5:436a f; 6: 1098b f; 12:445b f
nature of, 2:212a f, 707b, 953b f; 3:76a f, 363b f, 986a f; 4:407a f; 6: 486b f; 7:171a; 8:701b; 9:374b f; 12:278b f
nature of (Greek), 8: 684b f
nature of (Johannine), 8: 443a
in nature, 11:605b
nearness of, 3:455b f, 969b, 1164a f; 4:221b f, 391 f, 493a, 602a; 6:903b f; 8: 54a, 600a f; 12:57a f
need of, 3:1072 f; 4:229a f
new age of, 1:371a f
new order of, 11:610b f
oath of, 11:656 f, 670a
obedience to, 1:369a, 571b f, 576b; 2:402 f, 406a f; 3:1012a; 4:738a f; 5:851b; 6:358a f; 7:372a; 8:38a, 393a, 628b; 11: 377a f, 754b; 12:101b f, 226 f, 241b f
obscuring of, 10:193a f
observation of, 11:507b f
O.T. concept of, 1:8b, 362a f; 4:527b f; 10:447
omnipotence of, 3:976b f,

978 f, 1093 f; 4:343 f, 601a f; 5:641; 9:545b
omnipresence of, 3:78, 78a; 4:327b f, 714 f, 714b f
omniscience of, 3:982b f, 1145 f, 1145b f; 4:510a f, 713 f, 713a f
oneness of, 5:524; 11:399a f
oneness with, 7:388b; 8: 705a
oracle of, 4:315a f
of "orthodox," 3:941a f
otherness of, 6:689b f; 11: 75b
overlordship of, 12:569a f, 596a f
ownership of, 3:406b f
partaker of nature of, 12: 174 f, 174a f
participation of, 5:726a f
partisanship of, 4:229a f, 429b f
past deeds of (Psalms), 4: 229
Pastoral concept of, 11: 357a
patience before, 6:945b f
patience of, 2:211b; 3: 258b f; 5:557a; 8:241a f; 10:173a f; 11:319a, 653b f
patience of with man, 3: 968a f
patronizing attitude toward, 6:689b
Pauline teaching on, 9: 188b f; 10:273a f; 11: 271a f
peace of, 7:57b; 9:664b; 11:114 f, 114b f, 761a
peace with, 9:450 f, 450b f
people of (Israel), 5:404b
perfect knowledge of, 12: 388b f
perplexity of, 3:982b f
as person, 5:166b f; 6:101b; 10:458a f, 640a f, 678b f, 1087a f; 11:629a
persuasion of, 5:832a; 6: 398b
as persuasive element, 1: 979b
philanthropy of, 11:544
philosophical belief in, 10: 613b f
as physician, 4:751a
pity of, 8:667a
plan of, 5:339a; 6:356a f, 373b; 8:371b f
pleading of, 5:725a
pleading with, 5:720b f
pledge of (Christ), 11: 670a f
possessed by, 2:736a f
possessing of, 4:329b
as potter, 5:518a, 743, 784a, 960 f, 960b f
power of, 2:733a f; 3: 976b f; 4:315a f, 736b f; 5:448b, 809a f; 6:558a; 8:410a, 739a f; 9:392a f; 10:348a, 418a f; 11:707b f
power of (categories of), 4:345a
power of (Ephesians), 10: 632
power of (evidences of), 4:243a f, 345b f
power of (Isaiah), 5:334 f
power of (Joban), 3:1093 f
power of (in nature), 5: 851 f
power of (Psalms), 4:187 f, 326b f
praise of, 1:338a f; 4:

300a f, 345a f, 438, 578a f, 602b, 694 f, 759 f, 760b f
praise of (reason for), 4: 761, 761b f
praise to, 4:159 f, 173, 173a f, 177b f, 223b f, 549a f, 592 f; 8:320a, 745a; 9:623a; 10:208a f
praised by, 8:674b f
presence of, 1:366b, 958b f, 1016a f, 1098a f; 2:339b f, 556a f, 808a; 3:985b f; 4: 493a, 714b f; 5:560b f, 698b f, 738a f; 8:474a; 10:530a
presence of (awareness of), 2:733b f; 5:482a f
presence of (in cloud), 3: 70 f
presence of (evidences of), 10:190a f
presence of (in holy places), 2:1123
presence of (Joban), 3: 1107 f
presence of (unexpected), 1:690a f
pride toward, 4:946a
primacy of, 6:902b
priority of, 1:465b f, 609b; 3:172b f; 5:521b f; 8: 55a f, 336a f
promise of, 3:1087b f; 7:22b; 8:433b f; 11:656b f, 712a f
promise of (Hebrews), 11: 656 f
promise of (Pauline), 10: 288a f
promise of (Second Isaiah), 5:682a f
prophetic concept of, 11: 597b f
as prosecutor (Micah), 6: 937 f
protection of, 1:937b; 4: 663b, 739b; 5:341b
protection of (metaphors), 6:759
as protector of Zion, 4: 242 f, 249
protests of, 5:821b f
providence of, 1:481b f; 710a f; 2:387 f, 871b f; 4:459b f, 575b f, 658a f; 5:574a; 7:322a; 8:758b f, 9:214b f; 10:377a f
providence of (Christ's teaching on), 8:227 f
providential care of, 4: 743b f
provincial concept of, 7: 843b
provision of, 12:171a f
Psalms concept of, 4:12a, 354b, 696a f
punishment by, 8:718b; 11:330
purpose of, 3:313b; 4: 211b f; 5:277b, 644a; 6: 879a; 7:322b; 10:324a f; 11:103b f, 147b
purpose of (in Christ), 10:673; 11:468a f
purpose of (fulfilling), 11: 467a f
purpose of (Joban), 3: 1139 f
purpose of (Pauline), 7: 207b
purpose of (rejection of), 8:139b f
purpose of (resisting), 11: 466b f

essentials for, 4:147*b*
Greek and Jewish concepts of, 4:499*b*
Good man: characteristics of, 4:79 f, 79*b* f, 498*a*
Jewish concept of, 4:17*a*
Good news, of the Gospel, 7:3*b*, 250*a*, 647*b*; 9:178*a* f; 10:667*b*; 11:523*b*, 629
Good report, Pauline teaching on, 11:119
Good Samaritan, parable of; *see* Parables of Christ
Good Shepherd, Christ as; *see* Christ Jesus
Good will: charity and, 9:590*b* f
importance of, 7:401*b*
source of, 10:553*b*
triumph of, 1:869*b*
Good works, 7:290*b*
Ephesians teaching on, 10:645 f
Goodall, Norman, confession of faith of, 11:508*a*
"Good-by," derivation of, 8:713*b*
Goodness: Christ's teaching on, 8:148*a* f
completion of, 11:23*a* f
creative, 11:94*b*
death of, 12:583*b*
dullness and, 11:540*a* f
Greek concept of, 4:499*b*
growth of, 12:585*b* f
Jewish concept of, 4:499*b*
man's natural, 11:23*b* f
meaning of, 3:1119*a*; 8:148*a* f, 313*b*, 628*a* f, 721*a*; 11:543
monopoly of, 11:83*a* f
motives for, 10:647*b* f
nature of, 1:893*a*, 922*b*; 4:497*b* f; 8:468*b*, 606*a* f, 735*a* f; 9:597*a*; 12:26*b* f
origin of, 12:28*b* f
patronizing of, 11:94*b*
of people, 1:488*a*
power of, 11:264*a* f; 12:576*a*
reasons for, 3:1118*a* f
recognition of, 8:206*b*
reward of, 3:106*a*
standard of, 11:83*a* f
transitoriness of, 6:627*a* f
triumph of, 12:586*a*
way of, 11:94*b*
Goodspeed, Edgar J.: on Ephesians, 10:602*b* f
on origins of Pastorals, 11:368*b*
on Paul, 10:461*a*
on Romans, 9:367*a*
Gordon, Charles ("Chinese"): character of, 5:716*a*
on God's will, 5:762*b*
Gordon, T. Crouther: on Hebrew poetry, 5:836*b* f
on Jeremiah, 5:813*b*
on Jeremiah character, 5:914*a* f
on Jeremiah elegy, 5:886*b*
on Jeremiah and Hamlet, 5:975*a*
on Jeremiah prophecy, 5:1105*a* f
on prophetic consciousness, 5:804*a*
on statesmanship of Jeremiah, 5:1009*b* f
Gore, Charles: on good life, 4:596*a*

on sacrifice, 9:643*b*
on sin, 9:400*b*
on victory of God, 4:601*b*
Goshen, identification of, 1:807
Gospel: accommodating of, 11:466*a*
according to man (Pauline), 10:454
accustomed to, 5:212*b* f
appeal of to youth, 12:153*a*
ashamed of, 8:794*b*
bearing witness to, 10:746*b* f
certainty of (Pauline), 11:29*b* f
of Christ, 7:3*b*, 21*b*
"concentrated," 8:566*b*
in early church, 7:4*b* f
essence of, 8:675*b* f; 10:642*b* f
false, 11:201*a* f
foolishness of, 3:984*a* f
formidableness of, 8:62*a* f
glory of, 11:270*b*
of God (Pauline), 11:268
as good news, 7:3*b* 250*a*, 647*b*; 9:178*a* f; 10:667*b*; 11:523*b*, 629
of grace, 11:609*a* f
as hidden mystery, 10:669*b* f
human wisdom and, 10:25*a* f, 28*b* f
individual, 11:260*b*
interpretation of, 11:432*a*
as invitation, 12:470*a*
Jewish rejection of (Pauline), 9:535
law and, 8:287 f, 287*b* f
as literary form, 7:36*a*
meaning of, 1:30*a*; 7:3*a*, 3*a* f, 641*a*; 9:390
as mystery (Pauline), 11:85*b*, 179*b* f, 180 f
as mystery revealed, 10:665*b* f
nature of, 7:648*b*
necessity of, 10:416*b* f
novelty of, 10:667*a* f
oral tradition and, 7:73*a* f
in Pastoral usage, 11:387
Paul and, 7:21*a* f
personal character of, 11:629*a*
perversion of, 11:32*b*
preaching of, 3:223*b* f; 8:574*b*; 11:508*b*
propagation of (Pauline), 11:179 f
of redemption, 4:585*b* f; 5:509*a* f
rediscovery of, 11:449*b*
of repentance, 5:647*a* f
response to, 8:479*a*
as sacred trust, 11:387*b* f
of service, 10:690*b*
"simple," 12:63*a*
social, 2:449*b*; 6:376*a*; 11:224*b* f; 12:63*a*
social implications of, 11:224*b* f
social reform and, 10:732*b* f
of success, 3:30*b* f
uniqueness of, 8:433*a*
universalism of, 11:539*a*
universality of, 9:436*a* f; 11:153*a* f, 236*b* f, 683*a*
of wealth, 11:80*b*, 124*a*
witness of, 11:153*a*
Gospel According to Egyptians, 7:225*a*

Gospel of Peter, 7:218*a*
Gospels: as biographies, 9:8*b*, 269*a*
as faith documents, 1:18*b* f
final redaction of, 7:74*b*
form criticism of, 7:69*a* f
growth of, 7:60*b* f
language of (Aramaic), 7:67*b*
modern study of, 7:61*b*
oral tradition and, 7:61*b*, 73*a* f
origin of (records of), 7:61*a* f
sources of, 7:62*a* f, 66*b* f
sources of (critical study of), 7:62*a*
sources of (fragments of), 7:69*a*
sources of (Marcan), 7:62*b* f
sources of (two-document theory of), 7:62*b*
theme of, 7:4*a*, 5*b*
tradition of (authenticity of), 7:71*b*, 73*b*
tradition of (collections of), 7:73*b*
tradition of (controls of), 7:71*b*
tradition of (eyewitness account of), 7:71*b*, 73*b*
tradition of (Luke), 10*a* f, 15*b* f
tradition of (Mark), 8:15*a* f
tradition of (Matthew), 8:15*b*
tradition of (migration of), 7:60*b* f
tradition of ("outside"), 7:72*b* f
tradition of (preservation of), 8:10*a* f
tradition of (records of), 7:61*a* f
tradition of (sources of), 7:73*b*
translation of, 7:62*a*
trustworthiness of, 1:17*b* f
varieties in, 11:260*b*
Gosse, Edmund: on indifferent Christians, 5:554*a*
on ministers, 5:662*b* f
Gossip: danger of, 10:181*a*, 573*a* f
nature of, 5:682*b*
sin of, 11:438*b* f
test of, 4:78 f, 889*b*; 10:181*a*
unkind, 4:889*a* f
Gossip, Arthur John, on Thomas Chalmers, 11:290*a*
Gothic cathedral, 5:671*b*; 12:110*b*
Gourd, identification of, 6:893
Government: attitude toward, 4:379*a* f
Christian attitude toward, 11:541*b* f
concept of, 11:65*a* f
control in, 11:66*a*
control of, 11:80*b*
fear of, 11:65*a*
purpose of, 12:114 f
religion and, 1:968*b*; 6:1072*b* f
respect for, 9:605*a* f
responsibility for, 6:670*a* f
righteous, 4:56*b* f
sins of, 5:626*a* f
sound, 4: 536*b* f

totalitarian, 5:441*b*
world, 9:94*a* f
"Governor," as title, 3:608, 643
Grace: before meal, 2:15*a*; 3:225*b* f, 387*a* f; 5:722*a* f; 8:557*a* f
costingness of, 10:617*b* f
dangerousness of, 8:512*b* f
disgrace and, 10:617*a*
doctrine of, 10:645*a* f
experience of, 11:56*a*
faith and, 9:445*a* f
falling from, 11:161*b*
free, 9:566*b*
of God, 11:55*b* f, 743*b* f
of God (Second Isaiah), 5:669 f
godliness as, 12:177*a* f
gospel of, 11:609*a* f
as great conserver, 10:547*a* f
growth in, 12:170*b* f
growth in (II Peter), 12:205
Johannine concept of, 8:442*b*, 473
justice and, 11:522*b*
knowledge and, 12:205 f
law and, 4:19*b*, 424*b*; 5:1039*b*; 8:478*a*; 10:546 f
of life, 12:124
meaning of, 5:480*a* f, 716*b*; 7:57*a*; 10:18*b*, 277*b* f, 456*b* f; 11:55*b*, 390*a* f, 521*b* f, 572*b* f; 12:91
meaning of (N.T.), 7:57*a*; 10:367*b* f, 612
medical, 7:704*a*
mercy, peace, and, 11:379 f, 380*b* f
past and future, 11:538*b* f
Pastoral teaching on, 11:367*a* f
Pauline teaching on, 7:57*a*; 8:331*b*, 442*b*; 9:431, 453, 453*a* f, 468*a* f; 10:277 f, 277*b* f, 446 f, 446*a* f, 456*b* f, 547*a* f; 11:158*b* f, 367*a* f, 380
peace and, 10:278*a* f, 612*b* f; 12:91*a* f
practice of, 11:236*b*
prevenient, 4:38*a*; 11:56*b* f, 83*a*
pride, and, 6:121*b*
redemption by (Second Isaiah), 5:552*b* f
religion of, 12:550*b* f
stewardship of, 10:664*b* f
stewardship of (Pauline), 10:664*b* f, 665
sufficiency of (Joban), 3:902*a* f
throne of, 11:639*b*
work of, 8:469*b*
works and, 10:645*a*, 646*b* f
see also Christ Jesus
"Grace of our Lord Jesus Christ," 3:76*b*
Graciousness of Christian, 11:233*a*
Graf, Karl H., Hexateuch study of, 1:189*a* f
Graf-Wellhausen hypothesis, 1:189*a* f, 193*b* f, 200*a*
Graf-Wellhausen school of O.T. criticism, 1:134*a* f
Grain, grinding of, 5:545
Grant, Robert, on changeless decree of God, 3:1084*a*
Gratitude: as basis for faith, 5:730*a*
character of, 11:564*a*

Christ's teaching on, 8: 297 f, 297b f
definition of, 10:617a
habit of, 4:744a
importance of, 4:498a
inadequate, 4:514b
nature of, 10:368b
sense of, 4:495a, 579a; 5: 852b
for simple things, 4:709a f
Grave: flowers on, 2:10
Palestinian, 4:38 f
Gravestone, finality of, 7: 910b
Gravity, law of, 3:138b; 8: 345a
Gray, George Buchanan: on Isaiah, 5:157b
on P, 2:138a
Gray, Herbert, on belief in God, 11:468a
Gray, Thomas, "Elegy" of, 4:705b
Great Bible of 1539, 1:89b f
Great cedar, Ezekiel oracle of, 6:233 f
Great Commandment, 7: 846 f, 846a f; 8:691 f, 692b f
Great commission, 7:621, 622b f
Great dragon, identification of, 6:224
Great feast, parable of, 8: 255a f
Great Hallel, 4:700b
Great Mother Cult, in Greek religion, 7:92b f
Great promise, 7:624b f
Great Stone Face, 3:1087b
Greatness: admiration of, 11: 16b
bigness and, 6:1064a
Christ's teaching on, 7: 496a f, 785 f, 811b f; 8: 179, 381 f, 381b f
essentials of, 1:588a f; 7: 786a f
inner and outer, 3:910a f
seeking its own, 5:1082b f
source of, 1:820b f
test of, 2:744b f
true, 7:811b f; 8:33a, 381b f; 12:56a f
Greco-Roman world, 7:75 f
dualism of, 11:425
morality of, 7:80b f
philosophy of, 7:84b f
religion of, 7:88a f; 8: 454a f
Greece: geography of, 7:77b f
history of, 7:77b f
influence of, 7:75b
Greed, as sin, 12:240a
Greek art, influence of, 7: 98a f
Greek Baruch, contents of, 1:436a f
Greek Bible, 7:97a f
Greek Christianity, in post-apostolic age, 7:223a f
Greek drama (theater of Dionysus), 7:90b
Greek Ezra; see I Esdras
Greek games, 7:91a f
Greek influence on Judaism, 7:97b
Greek language: Byzantine, 7:46a
Christ's use of, 8:10b
classical, 7:44a f
history of, 7:43a f
history of (periods of), 7: 44a

"koine"; see Koine
modern, 7:46a
N.T., 1:58a; 7:78b
Renaissance recovery of, 12:620a
study of, 12:620a f
Greek letters: form of, 11: 255 f
salutations in, 11:149
Greek N.T., 12:617b f
Greek philosophy: Aristotle, 7:85b f
Epicureanism, 7:86a f
Plato, 7:85a f
Stoicism, 7:86b f
Greek religion: cult of Dionysus, 7:90b f
Delphi Oracle, 7:91b f
Eleusinian mysteries, 7: 90a f
Great Mother Cult, 7:92b f
polytheism, 7:88b f
Greek Uncial Codices, 1:67b
Greeley, Horace, on class war, 1:987b
Green, as color, 4:125b
Greene, Theodore M., on faith, 11:416b
Gregory the Great, biblical interpretation of, 1: 116a f
Gregory of Nazianzen, on discouragement, 5:568b
Grenfell, Wilfred, on service, 4:801b
Gressmann, Hugo: on Exodus, 1:834b f
Hexateuch study of, 1: 191b
on Hosea's marriage, 6: 560a
on Kenite hypothesis, 1: 839b f
on Second Isaiah, 5:385a
Grey, Sir Edward, on past, 1:744b
Grey, Viscount, on order in nature, 5:28a
Grey of Fallodon, hymn appreciation of, 4:580a
Grief, commonness of, 4:409a
effect of, 4:166a f
expression of, 1:649a f
fellowship of, 2:243a f
godly and worldly, 10: 359a f
manifestation of, 3:924b f
"neurotic," 4:166b
poignancy of, 4:160a f; 8: 636b
public and private, 6: 197a f
selfish, 8:646b
Griesbach, Johann Jacob, biblical study of, 12: 625a
Grievance: imaginary, 8:697b
sense of, 10:278a
Grigg, James, on Churchill's faith, 4:658b f
Group, individual and, 1: 650a f; 2:476a f, 872b
Group responsibility, concept of (Ezra), 3:652
Growth: Christian, 11:216a f, 648a f; 12:106b f, 200a f
conversion and, 12:236a
as evidence of life, 5:503a
meaning of, 2:928b
miracle of, 1:496a f
nature of, 7:705a
need of, 2:928a f; 6:393a f, 645a

process of, 1:715a; 2:917a; 8:429b
religious, 12:236a f
spiritual, 5:503a; 8:729a f
Grudge, character of, 6:713b
Grumbler: chronic, 5:526a f
Jude concept of, 12:335
Guests who made excuses, parable of; see Parables of Christ
Guidance: definition of, 9: 216b
personal, 12:424a
prayer for, 1:653b f
Guide: blind, 8:124b f
Christ as, 4:641a; 11:756a
spiritual, 5:861b f
Guillaume, Alfred, on Jeremiah, 5:841a
Guilt: acceptance of, 2:585b
accumulating, 8:219a f
acknowledgment of, 1: 519a f
common, 6:739a f
communal, 7:792a
of community, 2:459a f, 462b f
confession of, 4:939a f; 5: 624a, 741 f; 7:590a
consciousness of, 1:502b; 7: 372a
enormity of, 4:139a
feeling of, 3:1038a f
hereditary (Joban), 3: 1069 f
hidden, 1:786b
of Israel, 6:554a, 804 f
Joban concept of, 3:975 f
meaning of, 5:1049b
national, 5:623b
revulsion of, 2:1113b f
sense of, 10:341a f
significance of, 12:258b
social, 2:459a f
solidarity of, 2:223b f
sorrowing over, 11:118b
unresolved, 11:109b
in war, 2:690b f; 5:623a
weight of, 10:229b
Guilt offering, Leviticus law on, 2:30 f, 30a
Guilty bystander, 6:863a f
Gunkel, Hermann: on Bible, 1:870b
biblical study of, 1:136a f, 191a f
classification of Psalter by, 4:6b f
Gutenberg, Johann, printing of Bible by, 12:621a
Guyon, Madame, on absence of God, 5:143b

H

H document, Deuteronomy and, 2:325a
Habakkuk: despair of, 6: 979a f
as name, 6:979
Habakkuk (book of): complaints of, 6:975b
date of, 6:975a f
diversity of material in, 6:973a f
integrity of, 6:975a f
origin of, 6:975a f
prayer of, 6:977b
problem of, 1:327a f
psalm of, 6:973a f, 977a f, 995 f
religious teaching of, 6: 977b f
woes of, 6:973a f, 977b, 989 f, 990b f

Habit: abandoning of, 4:89a
influence of, 5:785b; 8: 602b, 741a
Hadad the "atmospheric high god," identification of, 3:135
Hadad of Edom, revolt of, 3:105 f
Hades: Christ's descent into, 10:689 f; 12:132 f
Christ's power over, 12:378
as Ephesians doctrine, 10: 600a
identification of, 7:89b f; 12:377 f
vision of, 6:241a f
Hadrach, identification of, 6: 1093
Hagar: Abraham and, 1: 604 f
in desert, 1:605 f
expulsion of, 1:638 f
God's promise to, 1:639 f
Ishmael and, 1:604b f, 637 f
as mother of slaves, 10: 539 f
Hagedorn, Hermann, on doors, 3:965b
Haggai: as name, 6:1037a
O.T. references to, 6:1037a
as prophet, 6:1037a
Zechariah and, 6:1053a f
Haggai (book of): authorship of, 6:1037a f
composition of, 6:1037a f
historical background of, 6:1038a f
message of, 6:1040a f
messianism in, 6:1039a
opposition of to Samaritans, 6:1039b, 1046
rebuilding of the Temple in, 6:1038b f, 1040 f, 1045b f
relevance of, 6:1040a f
significance of, 6:1039a f
style of, 6:1044a f, 1047
text of, 6:1037b f
Hagiographa, canonization of, 1:43a f
Hail, plague of, 1:903 f
Hailstones, Revelation reference to, 12:488
Hair: offerings of, 2:172
of Samson, 2:794 f
Halah, identification of, 3: 279
Haldane, J. B. S.: on satisfaction in life, 1:808b
on serving a cause, 1: 801b f
Hale, Matthew, self-control of, 5:624b
Half-believer, 11:417b
Half-gods, 6:95a f
Half-truth, 6:613b
Hall, Charles Cuthbert, on understanding Christ, 11:123a
Hallel: Egyptian, 4:600a
Hebrew, 4:599b f
"Hallelujah," biblical use of, 12:506
Hallelujah Chorus, 12:506b f
Halyburton, Thomas, on thankfulness, 5:730a
Haman: Antiochus identified as, 3:827b
anti-Semitism of, 3:847a f
downfall of, 3:861 f
humiliation of, 3:858 f
Mordecai and, 3:858 f
plot of, 3:849 f

Revelation teaching on, 12:437, 437a f, 578b
Second Isaiah teaching on, 6:936
sin of, 4:523b f; 6:943a f
of Solomon, 3:101 f
types of, 6:646b f
vanity of, 4:697 f
weakness of, 10:735b
"Ifs," of Bible, 11:175b
Ignatian letters, early church revealed in, 11:347a
Ignatius: bishopric of, 11:347b
on church, 10:386b
as confessor, 12:358a, 373
on disbelief in Christ, 12:260
on heretical teachers, 12:325
on joy, 12:220
letters of, 7:219a
Pastorals and, 11:369a
prayer of, 11:408a
on serving God, 2:50b f
on silence of God, 5:740b
Ignorance: awareness of, 4:946b f
danger of, 4:781a f
intelligent, 3:102a
invincible, 8:125a
justifiable, 11:390a
knowledge and, 6:606b
mystery and, 4:948b
sin and, 6:581b f
sins of, 11:389b
unbelief and, 11:389
IHS, as Christian symbol, 7:254b
Illness, recovery from, 4:158a f; see also Sickness
Illustration, sermon, 1:954a
Illyricum: identification of, 11:247b
Pauline visit to, 11:247b f
Images, prohibition of, 1:981 f, 982a
Imagination: of Christ, 7:759a
inspired, 1:594b f
Imitation, 10:703a f
criticism of, 8:685b
Immanuel: Christ as, 5:218a f
as Isaiah sign, 5:217 f
messianic interpretation of, 5:218 f
Immaturity, evidence of, 8:563b
Immigrant, contribution of, 1:713b f
Immorality: in Greco-Roman world, 7:80b f
heresy and, 12:336a f
sexual (Greco-Roman world), 7:81a f
at Thessalonica, 11:294a f
Immortality: anticipation of, 11:469b
argument for, 7:843a f
assurance of, 1:828b; 8:644b
of believer, 4:667b
character of, 12:241b f
Christ and, 11:469a f
as Christian doctrine, 1:230b f
communal, 4:122a f
credibility of, 11:469b f
crown as symbol of, 11:512
disbelief in, 1:650a
faith in, 5:47a f, 374b f
"four pillars of," 7:74b
gift of, 12:524b f

Greek concept of, 7:90b; 10:251; 11:490 f
Hebrew concept of, 4:478a; 5:374b
hint of, 4:85b f
hope in, 7:617a f; 10:194a, 231a f
indifference to, 11:693a f
in Isis cult, 7:93b
judgment and, 10:638b f
life and, 11:468b f
Mesopotamian concept of, 5:52
O.T. concept of, 5:304b f
pagan concept of, 10:652 f
Pauline teaching on, 11:294 f
personal, 10:245b f
Platonic concept of, 7:85b; 10:251a f; 11:490
proof of, 5:375a f
question of, 4:476a f
reasons for, 10:251a f
resurrection and, 10:253a f
sidereal, 12:389 f
Stoic concept of, 7:88a
wisdom as source of, 4:774a
Impalement, as Assyrian punishment, 3:613
Impatience: faith and, 4:372a f
as sin, 4:372a f
Imperatives, Second Isaiah use of, 5:389a, 391b f
Imperfection, sense of, 5:692b
Impetuosity, experience and, 2:1053b f
"Impossible," in Hebrews usage, 11:653a
Impossibility, "possible," 7:487b
"Impostor," meaning of, 11:504
Impression, first, 9:191a f
Impulse: acting on, 2:28b f
first, 7:800b
two (Jewish doctrine), 10:561
Impurity, sin of, 11:213b, 294b f
"In God we trust," as motto, 5:325b
Inadequacy, feeling of, 2:732a f
Inanna, identification of, 6:108
Inarticulate, witness of, 8:339a f
Inattention, danger of, 8:94a f
Inattention and neglect, Hebrews teaching on, 11:608 f
Incantation, curse by, 4:304b f
Incarnation: as appearing of Christ, 11:469 f
as central Christian belief, 1:5b f
Christian confessions of, 12:245b f
etymology of, 1:12a
evidence for, 12:292b
faith in, 12:301b f
Hebrews teaching on, 11:614
Johannine concept of, 7:29b f, 472 f, 472b f
meaning of, 4:734b; 7:79a, 169b; 8:686b; 10:536b f; 11:87a f, 290b; 12:115b
message of, 8:62a f

mystery of, 6:690b f; 11:43b f
necessity of, 1:13b f; 5:219a f
oversimplification of, 11:44b
paradox of, 8:54a f
Pauline teaching on, 9:457b
significance of, 12:246b
Incense: manufacture of, 3:466b f
use of in worship, 1:1058a f; 2:215a f; 3:67; 8:31a
Incense altars, identification of, 6:96
Incentive, adequate, 9:611b f
Incest, Pauline teaching on, 10:59 f
Increase, law of, 7:561a f
Incunabula, meaning of, 8:20a
Indecisiveness, peril of, 11:103b
Indebtedness, confession of, 4:665b f
Indians, injustice toward, 1:941a f
Indifference: attitude of, 4:865a f; 7:791b
tolerance and, 3:155a f; 6:357a
Indifferent, fate of (Zephaniah), 6:1017 f
Indignation: Christlike, 10:403a
easy, 7:869b
power of, 5:728b
Individual: Christ's concern for, 7:819a; 8:502b f
church and, 3:97a f
community and, 6:8af, 138a f
in contemporary schools of early church, 11:139a
dealing with, 11:233b
in family, 11:534b f
glory of, 12:386b f
group and, 1:650a f; 2:476a f, 872b
importance of, 1:702a; 2:1084b f
inconspicuous, 3:575b f, 726a f
Jeremiah concept of, 5:785a f
liberty of, 1:702a f
religion and, 12:107a f
significance of, 2:788b f; 6:567b f; 8:503a; 11:447b; 12:372b f
society and, 2:348a f
state and, 2:1059a f; 9:602a f
worth of, 1:623b, 811b f; 8:266b f, 502b; 11:447a f
worth of in God's sight, 8:222 f, 223a f
Individual responsibility, doctrine of (Ezekiel) 6:48b f, 157 f, 246, 576a f
Individualism: collectivism and, 11:34a f
Hellenistic concept of, 7:76a
universalism and, 4:469a
Indo-Europeans, identification of, 1:240a f
Indolence: danger of, 4:818b
Proverbs warnings against, 4:818 f, 818a
Industrial relationships, 12:52b

Industry: Christianizing of, 3:99a
example of, 11:300b
exploitation of, 11:80b
mechanism of, 5:209a f, 253b
obligation of, 11:442a
Inequality: human, 4:751b f
social function of, 10:717b f
Inertia, spiritual, 5:308a f
Inevitable, co-operating with, 6:407b
Infallibility, papal, 5:515a
Infancy, significance of, 1:612a f
Infanticide, ancient practice of, 6:144a f
Inferiority complex, 7:371b; 8:267a
cause of, 7:424b f; 10:176a
of church, 5:570b f
result of, 1:570b
Infidelity, 4:785b
Influence: Christian, 3:152a; 11:234b f, 265a
of Christianity, 3:150b
conscious and unconscious, 10:65a f
degradation of, 11:94b
of man, 9:106b f
of mother; see Mother
Ingathering, feast of; see Feast of Ingathering
Inge, William Ralph: on bereavement, 1:814b
on broad and narrow way, 4:638b
on cherished values, 4:803a f
on civilization, 6:789a
on law and gospel, 4:634a f
on love, 12:287b
on mysticism, 4:699a
on persecution of Jews, 4:677a
on prayer, 12:72a f
on private devotions, 11:429a
on shallow optimism, 5:675a f
on worldliness, 12:34b
Ingelow, Jean, on kinsman, 12:228a
Ingemann, B. S., on hymn of praise, 4:549a
Ingratitude, 3:508a f; 8:297b f
sin of, 6:141b f
spiritual, 6:823b f
Inheritance: attitude toward, 3:86a f
Christian, 11:393a f
eternal, 11:698b f
in I Peter usage, 12:163a
insecurity of, 5:39b
meaning of, 12:94a
national, 1:725a
spiritual, 2:504b f
undefiled, 12:94a f
Inheritance (female,) Israelite law on, 2:271 f
Inheritance rites, Deuteronomic law on, 2:461 f
Iniquity: etymology of, 1:226a
mystery of, 4:567b; 5:847a
plowing of, 3:937a f
sin of, 5:328b
Initiative, futility of, 5:27a
Injustice: anodyne for, 4:386a f
God and, 8:417a f

622b f; 10:52 f, 330 f; 11: 19b f
perspective and, 6:1059b
of Pharisees, 7:293b
present, 5:588a
righteous, 9:422b f; 11: 319 f
salvation and, 1:373a
scales of, 1:818a f
Second Isaiah teaching on, 5:479 f, 744 f
Second Zechariah teaching on, 6:1105a f
standard of, 10:188a f
universal (Obadiah), 6:865
universal (Zephaniah), 6: 1020 f
value of, 4:803b
vision of (Amos), 6:828a f
Judgment books, Revelation concept of, 12:526
Judgment Day, 7:563a; 8: 304a f, 780a f, 794b
Judicial system: Israelite, 2: 436 f; 3:494
sacredness of, 1:988
Judith, contents of, 1:402b f
Jung, Carl G.: on confrontation of self, 5:869b
on inner voice, 5:806b
on limitation of man, 11: 613a
on meaning of life, 5:803b, 903a f
on religion and the unconscious, 12:275b
on symbol of fire, 5:808a
Junilius Africanus, biblical interpretation of, 1: 114a f
Jupiter Capitolinus, Zeus Olympius and, 6:536
"Just," Pauline teaching on, 11:119
Just man, unjust and, 4: 662 f, 662a f
Just One, Christ as, 9:124
Justice: Amos teaching on, 6:820, 827
basis of, 4:283b
confidence in, 4:283b f
covenant law and, 1:1009 f
definition of, 4:511b
divine, 3:45b f
economic, 4:902a f
"even-handed," 3:937a
of God; see God
grace and, 11:522b
Hebrew concept of, 3: 494b f; 5:894b
ideal of, 2:436b f
in life, 6:158b
love and, 2:120a; 5:895a
meaning of, 4:901b f; 5: 894b f
mercy and, 3:46b f; 7:478a
nature of, 2:649b f
O. T. meaning of, 4:782
perversion of, 5:201b f
plea for, 4:225a
primacy of, 4:538b
prostitution of, 5:328b f
redemption through (Isaiah), 5:179b
righteousness and (Isaiah), 5:176
of rulers (Isaiah), 5:342 f
Solon's concept of, 5:894b f
symbol of, 2:1019a f; 3: 44b f, 1168a
wisdom and, 3:43b f; 5: 895a
Justification: consequences of, 9:435a f

doctrine of, 10:549b
forgiveness and, 9:450
interpretation of, 11:76a f
James teaching on, 12:9a, 41 f
meaning of, 10:483
old covenant and (Pauline), 9:437 f, 437b f
Pauline teaching on, 9: 428 f, 431b f; 10:483 f; 12:41 f
sanctification and, 10:485
of ungodly (Pauline), 9: 441a f
Justification by faith, 10: 644b f; 12:43b f
justification by works and, 9:375b f; 10:483 f
Pauline teaching on, 7: 24a f; 9:180a f, 375a f, 428 f; 10:483 f; 11:81 f
Justification by works: Pastoral concept of, 11:468
Pauline teaching on, 9: 409; 10:483 f
Justin Martyr: martyrdom of, 7:226a f
on Revelation, 12:351b
Justinian, on justice, 4:902a
Juvenile rebellion, 2:462 f

K

Kadesh: Israelite sojourn at, 2:237 f
wilderness of, 4:157
Kafka, Franz: on doubt and belief, 5:912a
on growth, 5:917a
on guilt, 3:976a
Kagawa, Toyohiko, 3:956b; 8:42b
devotions of, 4:498b f
on return to God, 5:882a
on will of God, 4:506b f
Kaiwan, identification of, 6: 821 f
Kant, Immanuel: on human relationships, 4:909a
on reason, 10:37b, 157a
on stars and moral law, 1: 477a; 4:101b
Karma, doctrine of, 8:611a f
Karnaim, identification of, 6:827
Keats, John: on beauty and truth, 12:469b
on love, 5:100b
on poetic calling, 5:629a
on thrill of discovery, 3: 984b
Keble, John, on Passion of Christ, 3:924
Kedar: identification of, 4: 643; 5:814, 1121
Isaiah oracle about, 5: 288 f
Jeremiah oracle against, 5: 1121 f
Keeping, giving and, 9:54a f
Keil, C. F., and Franz Delitzsch, on self-sacrifice, 2:16a
Keilah, relief of, 2:1004 f
Kelly, Thomas R., on manner of prayer, 1:695b
Kelman, John, on suffering, 4:40b
Kenite hypothesis, 1:839b f
Kenites, identification of, 2: 262, 693 f
Kennedy, A. R. S., on sources of Samuel, 2: 857b, 860a

Kennedy, Charles Rann, on living church, 12:90a
Kennedy, Gerald, on judging others, 11:440a
Kennedy, H. A., on influence of Christ, 11:287b
Kerioth, identification of, 6: 784
Kerr, Hugh T.: on coming of God, 5:143b
on meaning of love, 5: 109a
Key of David, Revelation reference to, 12:393 f
"Keys of the Kingdom," 7: 453
Khirbet Mird, identification of, 12:645a
Khirbet Qumrân, 12: Plate 10
communal facilities at, 12: 658a
excavation of, 12:646b f
Kidd, Benjamin, on institutions, 5:766b
Kidnaping, covenant law and, 1:998, 998a
Kidron Valley, identification of, 3:134; 8:755 f
Kierkegaard, Soren: on being known by God, 5: 803a
on Christ as friend of sinners, 12:262
on Christ as pattern, 11: 84b
on Christian demand, 12: 62b
on cursing God, 4:975b
on disorder, 6:421a
on dread, 1:990b
existentialism of, 11:107a
on genius and apostle, 5: 810b
on guilt, 11:118b
Hegel compared with, 3: 994b f
on hope, 11:35b
on immortality and judgment, 10:639b
on Job, 3:899b
on martyrdom, 12:521a
on meaning of Christianity, 3:995a
on paradox of faith, 4:410a
on prayer, 12:269b
on redemption, 11:17a
on self-consciousness, 1: 1055b
self-renunciation of, 11: 61b f
on suffering, 6:87b f; 12: 384a
on way of life, 5:863b
Killing, prohibition against, 1:986a f
Kindness: Christ's teaching on, 11:564b f
compelled, 11:568b
evidence of, 3:218a f; 9: 342a; 10:174a f
importance of, 10:347b
law of, 2:463b f
meaning of, 6:599
patience and, 10:173b f
spirit of, 11:752a f
unrecorded, 11:564b f
virtue of, 4:527b
King: allegiance to, 6:435b
anointing of, 3:26
Christ as, 3:1006b; 7:13b, 142b, 501a, 604b f, 605a, 823a f, 904a; 8:559b f; 658b f; 11:455a f

compassion of, 4:380 f
death of, 5:1142b
divine right of, 6:414
duties of (Deuteronomic law on), 2:441
friends of, 4:77b f
Hebrew concept of, 5:231
ideal (Isaiah), 5:247b f
ideal (Psalms), 4:587b f
justice of, 4:380 f, 380b f
marriage of, 4:234 f, 234a f
meaning of, 4:537a
as Messiah, 5:522
moral ideals of, 4:536 f
psalm for, 4:112 f, 536 f
psalmist's prayer for, 4: 107 f, 109a f, 320 f, 320a f, 379 f, 478 f
rightful (Psalms), 4:22 f, 22b f
rights of, 2:920 f
as sacred person (O.T.), 3:239
spiritual guardsmen of, 4: 321b f
subject and, 4:873b f
King James Version, 1:93a f; 8:20a f
as literature, 5:25b
revisions of, 1:95a f
"King of kings," as title, 11: 455, 455a f
King preparing for war, parable of; see Parables of Christ
Kingdom: theocracy and, 2: 923a f
yoke of, 7:275
Kingdom of Christ; see Christ Jesus
Kingdom of God, 6:386b f; 7:15b, 117b
Christ's teaching on, 7: 13b, 117b f, 145 f, 275, 656b; 8:172b f, 207b f
Christ's teaching on admission to, 8:245 f, 246a f
Christ's teaching on advent of, 8:299 f, 299b f
Christ's teaching on inwardness of, 7:148a
Christ's teaching on present realization of, 7:148b
church and, 7:151a f; 8: 229b f
coming of in Christ, 8: 299b f
commitment to, 11:284a f
demands of, 8:182b f
as God's act, 8:244a
imminence of, 8:164b f, 172b f, 246b f
interpretations of, 7:152a f
inwardness of, 7:148a; 12: 584a
meaning of, 7:145a
mission of, 7:365a f
mystery of, 7:17a
nature of, 9:626b f
need of, 10:325b
Obadiah teaching on, 6: 859b
O.T. concept of, 1:355b; 7:13b, 145a f, 274
Pauline teaching on, 7: 27a f; 9:626 f, 626b f
preaching on, 8:164a f, 184b f
primacy of, 8:153b
priority of, 7:323a f
II Peter teaching on, 12: 181
secrets of, 8:148b f

Monica, as mother of Augustine, 6:83b f

Monism, ethical, 4:442b f

Monogamy, Proverbs concept of, 4:796

Monotheism: definition of, 1:361a f
development of, 2:356a f; 3:76; 4:443a f
dualistic, 8:455a
ethical, 1:357b f
Israelite concept of, 1:302a, 359b f; 2:359 f
of Jeremiah, 5:784b f
Kings teaching on, 3:15b f
Platonic concept of, 7:85a
polytheism and, 7:847a
Second Isaiah teaching on, 5:403b f
universalistic (Malachi), 6:1120a

Montague, William Pepperell, on religious yearning, 2:935b

Montanism, 7:222a f

Montanus, 7:222a f

Montefiore, C. G., on compassion of Christ, 4:655b

Montgomery, James, on prayer, 4:581b; 6:641a

Moods, cycle of, 4:223b f

Moody, Dwight L.: on Christian fellowship, 11:713a
Christian witness of, 9:116a f
concern of for people, 11:151a
humility of, 3:266b
on repentance, 6:717a
on sowing and reaping, 6:12a

Moon festival, 6:584

Moore, G. F., on Babylonian religion, 5:550a

Moorehead, William, on II Peter, 12:200b f

Moral action, consequences of, 2:494b f; 5:1003b f

Moral ambiguity, 11:734b

Moral arrogance, 11:96a

Moral behavior, 6:981b f

Moral blindness, 12:437a
of church, 11:700b

Moral code, cautionary character of, 4:106b

Moral collapse, 6:600a f

Moral commandment, 12:232a f

Moral compacency, 12:607a

Moral confusion, 11:100a f
of church, 12:564a

Moral consistency: need of, 11:92b f
Pauline teaching on, 11:92 f, 92b f

Moral conviction, 6:437a f

Moral corruption, 6:824a f

Moral courage, 1:768a; 7:428a, 469a, 591a; 9:455b

Moral decay, Christianity and, 10:705b f

Moral defilement, ceremonial uncleanness and, 11:697b f

Moral discipline, 11:82a f; 12:230b

Moral effort, 5:567b

Moral evil, 4:386a f

Moral history, fractions of, 12:436a f

Moral ideals, evolution of, 3:191b

Moral indignation, 2:938b f

Moral integrity, basis of, 1:764a f

Moral isolation, 3:151a f

Moral judgment, 6:995b f
relativity of, 12:462b

Moral law, 4:212a; 6:957a; 7:750b
ceremonial law and, 2:995b f
Israelite concept of, 1:381b
Jewish contribution of, 1:381b
nation and, 6:1119b
respect for, 11:661b f
violations of, 11:213b f

Moral laxity, 2:1113a f

Moral life, stages of, 9:495b

Moral living, Thessalonians teaching on, 11:252b f

Moral murder, 1:517b f

Moral necessity, 6:586a

Moral obedience, 12:230b f
Jeremiah teaching on, 5:874 f, 875a

Moral order, 3:1034b f; 4:379b; 12:230a f
basis of, 4:382b f
Chronicles teaching on, 3:341a, 471b
prophets and, 5:841a

Moral perversion, 3:245a f

Moral problem, dealing with, 9:471a f

Moral rectitude, 4:386a f

Moral relations, 4:707a

Moral responsibility, 1:625a; 10:118b f

Moral retribution, 3:106a f, 230a f

Moral salvation, through Christ, 11:196b

Moral security, 4:383a f

Moral standard: of church, 11:526b f
lowering of, 6:1126b f
Pauline teaching on, 11:119 f

Moral strength, 6:81a f

Moral unity, 4:707a

Moral universe, 6:579b, 1060a f; 11:321b f; 12:258a

Moral value, Malachi teaching on, 6:1124 f

Morale: importance of, 4:111a; 6:927b f
national, 5:169a
public, 5:912b f, 927b f
in war, 4:111a

Moralism: gospel of, 10:496a f
helplessness of, 11:80a
perverted, 2:931a f
self-deceit of, 11:80a
theology and, 11:158b

Morality: Christian; see Christian morality
Christian and non-Christian, 10:701b f
Christian and pagan (Ephesians), 10:696 f
Christianity and, 6:602b; 10:419b f
faith and, 11:294a f
feminine, 5:191
in Greco-Roman world, 7:80b f, 84a
of homosexuality, 7:81b
national, 6:994a
open and closed, 11:87b
pagan, 7:80b f
politics and, 4:335a f; 6:646a

prosperity and, 11:81a
prudential, 8:384b
as quest, 6:393a f
reasons for, 8:734b
relative, 11:100a f
religion and, 1:580b, 581b; 4:389b, 516b f; 5:678a f; 6:602b f; 11:705b f
sexual (Greco-Roman world), 7:81a f
of universe, 12:230a f
utility and, 6:697b
welfare and, 5:347a

Moralizing, weakness of, 11:105a

Morals, sufficiency of, 3:1162b f

Mordecai: advancement of, 3:863 f
character of, 3:840a f
dream of, 1:405a f
Esther and, 3:840 f
greatness of, 3:873 f
Haman and, 3:847 f
plan of, 3:852 f

More, Paul Elmer: on confession of sins, 12:223a
on goodness of God, 5:962b

Morgan, Charles, on responsibility for wrong, 11:389b

Morgan, G. Campbell: on demands of God, 4:739a
on protection of God, 4:739b

Morgan, William, on results of sin, 4:501b f

Morgenstern, Julian, on separatism of Jews, 3:852b

Morley, John: on Gladstone, 4:707b
on influence of wealth, 5:545b f
on right and wrong, 12:232b

Morning, wings of, 4:714 f

Morning cloud, figure of, 6:627a f

Morning devotions, 4:36b f

Morning sacrifice, psalmist's prayer at, 4:35 f, 35a f

Morning star: Christ as, 12:548
as Revelation symbol, 12:389 f

Morrison, George H., on gentleness of God, 2:1165a f

Morrison, Robert, on God's work, 4:506b

Morrison, S. E., on mission of Columbus, 11:111b

Morrow, Dwight L., on responsibility, 6:908a f

Morton, H. V., on city life, 3:433a

Moses: addresses of (Deuteronomy), 2:314b f
adoption of, 1:861, 861a f
anger of, 2:289 f
assumption of, 12:329 f
as author of Deuteronomy, 2:332a
as bearer of people's sin, 2:349 f
birth of, 1:857 f
blessing of, 2:527 f, 529b f
breaks tables of testimony, 1:1067 f, 1067b f
call of, 1:866 f, 866a f
call of (E), 1:867b f
call of (J), 1:867a f
call of (JE), 1:870b

call of (P), 1:868a f, 888 f
character of, 1:862
Christ and, 11:621a f, 731, 731b f
circumcision of, 1:882 f
complaint of against Miriam and Aaron, 2:200 f, 200b f
death of, 2:511, 526 f, 535 f
departure of from Midian, 1:880 f
devotion of, 2:395a f
divine charge to, 2:513 f
education of, 1:861a
Egyptian influence on, 1:298a f
exile of, 1:864 f, 864a f
faithfulness of, 11:621b f, 730 f, 730a f
father-in-law of, 2:191a f, 192 f
flight of from Egypt, 11:732, 732b
genealogy of, 1:891 f
God's revelation to, 1:1073 f
greatness of, 2:272a f, 449b f, 536a f, 537
inadequacy of, 1:890
intercession of, 1:1066, 1069 f; 2:395 f
Jethro and, 1:963b f, 967 f, 967a f
as judge, 1:966, 966b f
killing of Egyptian taskmaster by, 1:862, 862a f
as legislator, 1:842a f
Lincoln and, 1:929b f
meekness of, 2:201 f, 201b f
as martyr-witness, 12:445 f
in Midian, 11:732b
"murmuring" against, 1:947, 957 f
as name, 1:298a, 861, 861b
parting words of, 2:511 f
pity shown by, 4:865a
as priest, 4:531
as prophet, 1:871, 1067 f; 2:449b f
as servant of the Lord, 2:553; 11:621b f
significance of, 1:1063
sin of, 2:238a f
song of, 1:940 f, 940b f; 2:514 f
song of (Revelation), 12:478 f
tent of meeting of, 1:1071 f
transfiguration of, 1:1080 f
Transfiguration and, 8:174, 174b f
use of magician's craft by, 1:877 f, 894
vision of, 1:871 f, 871b f; 11:157a f

Moses: age of (historical background of), 1:298a
age of (sources of), 1:297b f
"Most High," God as, 4:246

Mother: death of, 3:918b
forgiveness of, 3:1029b f
influence of, 1:937b f; 3:287a f, 504a f, 665a; 7:286b, 328b; 8:555b f; 11:55a
love of, 2:728a f, 1159b f; 4:217a; 5:133b f; 8:246b; 11:87a
reward of, 1:986a
tragedy of, 2:727a f
tribute to, 4:786b

on words, 6:1022a
Pfeiffer, Robert H.: on achievements of Nehemiah, 3:663b
on Ezra, 3:565b
on Hosea's marriage, 6:561a
on Nahum, 6:960b
on Nehemiah as autobiographer, 3:662a
on Priestly Code, 1:528a; 3:345b
on Purim, 3:825a
on source of Samuel, 2:861b
Pharisaism: characteristics of, 5:883b; 9:442a f
Christ's condemnation of, 7:527b f, 761, 761b f; 8:357 f, 357b f
criticism of, 10:475a
danger of, 11:94a
doctrine of, 12:13a f
Essenism and, 12:658a
modern, 11:279a f
as O.T. theme, 6:148a f
presumption of, 11:95b
weakness of, 7:12b
Pharisee and publican, parable of; see Parables of Christ
Pharisees: attitude of toward Rome, 7:106a
Christ and, 6:654a f; 7:134b; 8:105 f
Christ's condemnation of, 7:527 f, 527b f; 8:214 f, 214b f, 248 f
derivation of name, 8:105; 11:278b
description of, 7:293a f; 8:112a f
early church and, 8:214
heartlessness of, 7:529
identification of, 7:119a, 264, 638b; 8:105 f
judgment of, 7:293b
opposition of to Christ, 7:134b
opposition of to Christians, 11:278a f
as party, 12:13a f
Paul and, 7:206b f, 208a f
pride of, 7:265a f, 397b; 11:278b f
righteousness of, 7:293, 293a f
Sadducees and, 9:299b f
sins of, 8:214b f
virtues of, 11:278a f
Pharaoh: dream of, 1:773b f
the Exodus and, 1:836b
Ezekiel lamentations over, 6:238 f
Ezekiel oracle against, 6:223
fury of, 1:932a f
hardening of heart of, 11:330
hymn to, 4:14a
Phelps, William Lyon: on Bible, 1:460b
on happiness, 1:523a
on interesting people, 11:112a
Philadelphia: identification of, 12:393, 393a
letter to (Revelation), 12:393 f, 393a f, 559a f
loyalty of church in, 12:560b f
Philanthropy, self-sacrifice and, 10:170b f

Philemon (book of): authenticity of, 11:133a f, 555a
authorship of, 11:133a f, 555a
as church letter, 11:562 f
Colossians and, 11:133a
Ignatius' use of, 11:558a f
influence of on slavery, 11:561a
occasion of, 11:555a f
as personal letter, 11:560b f
place of origin of, 11:555b f
preservation of, 11:557b f
purpose of, 11:556a f
significance of, 11:560a f
text of, 11:560b
uniqueness of, 11:555a
Philetus, identification of, 11:489, 489b f
Philip: as disciple, 8:553a f; 9:107 f
Ethiopian eunuch and, 9:113 f, 113a f
Samaritan ministry of, 9:107 f, 108a f
Philippi: founding of church at, 9:217 f
history of, 11:3a f
identification of, 7:195b; 11:3a f
Luke and, 9:6b f; 11:4a
Pauline imprisonment at, 11:4a f
Pauline suffering at, 11:267
Pauline visit to, 11:3a f
Roman colonization at, 11:3b
Philippian church: Epaphroditus' mission to, 11:10a f, 67 f, 67b f
gift to Paul from, 11:9b f
Jewish hostility toward, 11:11b
officers in, 11:16
Paul sends Timothy to, 11:67 f, 67b f
Pauline affection for, 11:12a
Pauline relations with, 11:4b, 8a, 23 f, 54b
personal animosities in, 11:11a, 42a
Polycarp's communication with, 11:4b
quarrels in, 11:107 f
sufferings of, 11:10b f
titles of leaders in, 11:8b
women in, 11:11a
Philippians (book of): admonitions of, 11:105 f, 105a f
appeal of, 11:28a f
authenticity of, 11:8b f
benediction of, 11:129
chapter emphases of, 11:43a f
character of, 11:12a f, 14a f
Colossians and, 11:134a, 136a
composite form of, 11:8b f
contents of, 11:12a f
date of, 11:8a
destination of, 11:3a f
doxology of, 11:127
as expression of Christian way, 11:14a
as genuine letter, 11:13b
harmony of, 11:12b
as letter of thanksgiving, 11:9b f
integrity of, 11:8b f

occasion of, 11:3a f
Pauline authorship of, 11:8b
personal nature of, 11:17b f
place of writing of, 11:5a f, 136a
purpose of, 11:9b f, 67b f
salutation of, 11:15 f, 15a, 127 f
style of, 11:46 f
Timothy as co-author of, 11:15a
Philistia: conquest of, 1:279b
Ezekiel oracle against, 6:200 f
Hebrew conflicts with, 6:204
identification of, 4:449
punishment of (Joel), 6:755 f
Zephaniah oracle against, 6:1023 f
Philistines: Amos oracle against, 6:780 f
David's defeat of, 2:1074 f, 1074a f
identification of, 1:670; 2:897
Jeremiah oracle against, 5:1110 f
Shamgar and, 2:711
"Philistinism," meaning of, 2:907a
Phillips, J. B., on false teachers, 12:259
Phillips, Stephen, on involvement in wickedness, 5:689b
Philo of Alexandria, 1:107a; 7:97b; 8:452a f; 12:12b, 13b f
on God as light, 12:222
on oaths of God, 11:669b f
Philo Judaeus, law and, 1:37a f
Philological study, of O.T. world, 1:234b f
Philosopher: Hebrew as, 5:35b f
prophet and, 6:660a
Philosophical speculation, of Paul, 11:165a f
Philosophy: categories of, 4:370b
Christian attitude toward, 11:190 f
classical meaning of, 11:190 f
Colossian, 11:138a f
criterion of, 8:565b
function of, 7:88a; 11:224 f
in Greco-Roman world, 7:84b f
Greek (Aristotle), 7:85b f
Greek (Epicureanism), 7:86a f
Greek (Plato), 7:85a f
Greek (Stoicism), 7:86b f
in Hellenic culture, 7:84b f
Pauline attitude toward, 11:190a f, 191
poetry and, 4:228a f
"Pollyanna," 11:113a
religion and, 6:422b; 7:84b; 8:548b
Phinehas, identification of, 2:264a
Phoebe, Pauline introduction of, 9:653 f, 655a f
Phoenicia: coinage of, 3:764
rise of, 1:262a f

Phrygia, Jewish settlement in, 11:139b f
"Phrygian frenzy," 7:222a
Phygelus, identification of, 11:474 f
Physical, spiritual and, 11:673b f; 12:610b
Physical body: Christ's teachings on, 7:298a
Greek concept of, 7:321
Platonic concept of, 7:85b
Physical defect, contending with, 4:541a f
Physical energy, transforming of, 10:323a f
Physical resurrection; see Resurrection
Physical senses, age of, 12:240a
Physician: Asclepius as, 7:92a f
Christ as, 7:342a f
Ecclesiasticus attitude toward, 3:487b f
God as, 4:751a
Isaiah as, 5:378
lie to patient by, 3:305a
Luke as, 9:7b f; 11:515a
truthfulness of, 3:305a
Pi-Beseth, identification of, 6:231
Picture, 7:876b
Piety: Christian meaning of, 10:725a f
Ecclesiastes teaching on, 5:56 f
genuine, 4:77b f
patriotism and, 2:656a f
presumption and, 2:909b f
prosperity and, 3:910a f
"stabilized," 11:407a f
test of, 3:956b f
true, 3:1108b; 5:56
Pilate, 7:107b, 588a, 590 f, 590b f, 895a; 8:768a f
Christ before, 3:41b f; 7:590 f, 893 f, 893b f; 8:397 f, 397a f, 767 f, 768a f; 11:453 f; 12:433a
defense of, 8:775a
hand washing of, 7:598, 598a f
motivation of, 3:41b f
Pilgrim: attitude toward, 4:646b
Christian as, 12:88b f
Pilgrim Fathers: faith and courage of, 3:638a f
hardships of, 5:572a; 6:708a
national character of, 4:705b
Pilgrimage: I Peter as epistle of, 12:77a
Israelite, 4:647a
life as, 4:638b f; 6:394b; 11:451
song of, 4:646b f
Pilgrim's Progress (Bunyan), appeal of, 4:640a f
Pillar of cloud and fire, 1:930, 931a f
Pillars, identification of, 2:410; 6:598
"Pillars of earth," meaning of, 2:885
Pindar, on word and deed, 12:48b
"Pinnacle," derivation of, 5:639
Pioneer: Christ as, 7:292a f, 810b; 10:236b; 11:614, 614b f
Christian as, 11:381a f

Prophetic prediction, implications of, 1:207a f
Prophetic utterance, forms of, 1:206a f
Prophetic writings, canonization of, 1:43a
"Propitiation," etymology of, 1:230a
Proportion, sense of, 8:767b f
"Proselyte," meaning of, 7:533b
Proselyting, characterisics of, 7:533b f
Prosperity: danger of, 6:707b f
  divine favor of, 3:47b f
  effect of, 5:308a f
  as God's favor, 11:95b
  honesty and, 4:32a f
  morality and, 11:81a
  perils of, 8:119b f
  piety and, 3:910a f
  religion and, 3:289b f
  righteousness and, 3:234a f, 264a f; 11:450a f
  of sinner, 5:918a
  of wicked, 4:387, 807; 5:853b f; 913 f; 6:981a
Prosperity and reward, biblical promises of, 3:31a f
Prostitute, temple, 3:130 f, 322
Prostitution: Canaanite practice of, 1:760
  in Greco-Roman world, 7:82a
  Pauline teaching on, 10:74 f, 75a f
  psychological effects of, 10:75a f
  religious aspects of, 7:82a
Protestantism: adaptable spirit of, 11:466a
  divided, 11:292a f
  sense of duty of, 2:919b
"Protestant principle," 11:75b f
Protestant Reformation, 6:718a, 1137b f; 11:312b f
Proto-Luke, 7:66b; 8:16a f, 23a f
Protomartyr, Christ as, 12:369 f
Proud, abasement of, 4:403a
Proverb: lore of, 5:63a f
  meaning of, 4:256; 5:9a
  prudential, 3:1003b
  of Solomon, 4:838 f
Proverbs (book of): authorship of, 4:774b f, 779 f, 780a f
  Babylonian sources of, 4:767b f
  date of, 4:774b f
  divisions of, 4:477b f
  early care of, 1:214b f
  Egyptian parallels of, 4:768b f
  Egyptian sources of, 4:768b f
  eschatology of, 4:777a f
  ethical standard of, 4:777b
  motto of, 4:784 f
  N.T. and, 4:777b f
  parallelism types in, 4:776b
  poetic style of, 4:776a f
  practical character of, 4:776b f
  purpose of, 4:780 f
  Septuagint text of, 4:776a
  Solomonic origin of, 4:775a f
  sources of, 4:767a f

structure of, 1:214b f
style of, 4:775b f
teaching of, 4:776b f
text of, 4:775b f
themes of, 4:774b f, 780b f
wisdom of, 1:215b f, 381b
Proverbs of Ahikar, 4:767b f
Providence: meaning of, 9:214b f
  special, 3:76a f
  universalism and, 4:430b f
Prudery, example of, 11:93b
Psalmody, origins of, 1:182b
Psalm: meaning of, 4:9b
  nature of, 4:92a f
Psalmist: anguish of, 4:116 f
  character of, 4:88b f, 323b f, 625a f
  confidence of, 4:311a f, 492a f, 711a
  deliverance of from enemy, 4:657 f
  deliverance of from illness, 4:610 f, 610b f
  enemy of, 4:31 f, 32a f, 38 f, 89 f, 119 f, 166 f, 217 f, 217b f, 283a f, 307 f, 394b f, 718 f, 731
  faith of, 4:329 f, 709a
  fear of, 4:287a f
  foes of, 4:308 f, 323 f, 331 f
  friend of, 4:284b
  impatience of, 4:369a f
  imprecation of, 4:676 f, 676a
  integrity of, 4:142 f
  objectivity of, 4:535a f
  petition of to God, 4:214
  physical suffering of, 4:201 f, 201b f
  plight of, 4:27 f, 283, 362 f, 643, 727 f
  praise of, 4:144a f, 311
  prayer of, 4:143b f, 723a f
  self-pity of, 4:294a f
  silence of, 4:206 f
  sufferings of, 4:540 f, 540a, 726b f
  testimony of, 4:178, 178a f
  trust of in God, 5:22a f
  vindictiveness of, 4:332, 332a, 366, 366a f, 450 f, 450a f, 582 f, 582b f, 718b
  vow of, 4:271 f, 737 f
Psalms (book of): acrostic structure of, 4:11b f
  ancient Near East literature and, 4:14a f
  ancient versions of, 4:4a f
  antiphonal character of, 4:698
  appeal of, 4:507b
  Asaph authorship of, 4:393a f
  Asaphite, 4:260b f
  ascriptions of, 4:8a
  authorship of, 4:10a f, 691a
  bitterness in, 4:583a f
  canonization of, 4:11a
  character of, 4:661b f
  choirmaster superscription in, 4:8b
  Christianity and, 4:18a f
  as compilation, 4:7b f
  of confidence, 4:7a
  contents of, 4:512b f
  as covenant book, 1:336b
  date of, 4:10a f
  Davidic authorship of, 4:10a f, 22 f, 26 f, 266b f, 286a f, 292a f

Davidic superscription of, 4:8a f
  "Dedication of Temple" as superscription of, 4:8b
  devotional reading of, 4:159b, 327b f
  distinctiveness of, 4:3b f
  divisions of, 4:5a
  duplications within, 4:7b
  editing of, 4:639a
  as enthronement songs, 4:7a
  figures of speech in, 4:660
  general character of, 4:3a f
  Gunkel's classification of, 4:6b f
  hallelujah, 4:745 f
  Hebrew text of, 4:4a
  historical allusions in, 4:10a
  in human life, 3:403a f
  as "Hymnbook of Second Temple," 3:369a; 4:512b f
  hymns in, 4:6b, 694a f
  imprecatory, 4:582b f, 584 f, 703 f
  as individual laments, 4:7a
  as individual songs of thanksgiving, 4:7a
  instrumental music and, 4:762a f
  interpreting of, 4:17a f, 584a f
  in Jewish worship, 4:15a f
  as laments of community, 4:6b
  Latin version of, 4:4b f
  Leviticus and, 2:6b f
  as liturgical literature, 4:6a f
  liturgies in, 4:7a
  for marriage, 4:234 f
  memorizing of, 4:624a
  messianic interpretation of, 4:23
  messianism in, 4:236a f, 588
  in Mishnaic period, 4:15a f
  Mowinckel's study of, 4:7a f
  music and, 4:5a f, 762a f
  music of, 4:349a f
  musical instruments mentioned in, 4:5b f
  names for God in, 4:7b
  of nation, 4:227 f
  N.T. quotations from, 4:16a
  parallelism in, 4:11b
  "Pauline," 4:678a
  penitential, 4:168 f, 266 f, 539 f, 678a, 729 f
  pilgrim, 4:639a f
  place of in church, 4:16a f
  poetic structure of, 4:11a f
  poetry of, 4:343b f
  as private prayers, 4:6b
  process of compilation of, 4:8a
  prophetic influence in, 4:260 f
  as prophetic liturgies, 4:7a
  purpose of, 4:392b f, 437b
  purpose of composition of, 4:6a f
  reading of, 4:493b
  religion of, 1:336a f; 4:12a f
  rhythm of, 4:11a f
  royal, 4:6b f, 234 f, 379, 536 f, 587 f, 587b f

sacrificial concept in, 4:261 f
  Septuagint version of, 4:4a f
  significance of, 4:16b f, 545a
  as songs, 4:338b f
  of sons of Korah and Asaph, 4:8a
  spirit of, 4:534b, 582b f
  stanzas in, 4:11b
  superscriptions of, 4:8a
  Syriac version of, 4:4b
  text of, 4:4a
  title of, 4:3a, 8a
  types of, 4:6b f
  Ugaritic texts and, 4:15a
  universality of, 4:350a f
  use of in worship, 4:745a f
  variety of, 4:734b f
  as wisdom poetry, 4:7a, 254 f
  wisdom writing in, 4:667 f
Psalms of Solomon, 1:426b f
Psalteries, use of, 3:793
Psalterium Gallicanum, 4:4b
Psalterium iuxta Hebraeos, 4:4b f
Psalterium Romanum, 4:4b
Pseudonymity, in apocalypticism, 12:350a f
Pseudepigrapha: Alexandrian, 1:432a f
  apocalypses of, 1:427a f, 435b f
  hymns and psalms of, 1:425a f
  legendary history of, 1:433b f
  literature of, 1:421 f
  popular philosophy of, 1:434b f
  religion of, 1:421 f
  "Pseudepigrapha," meaning of, 1:421a
Pseudonymity, nature and practice of, 7:36a, 38b; 11:372a f; 12:166b
Psychoanalysis: method of, 6:163b
  task of, 8:567a f
Psychological mind, 11:52b f
Psychological warfare, 5:363b
Psychologist, achievements of, 4:741b
Psychology: aim of, 11:28b
  contribution of, 11:94b
  limitation of, 11:52b f
  Maginot-Line type of, 2:1069b f
  Pauline concept of, 9:369a f
Ptolemies: in Palestine, 6:342b
  Seleucids and, 6:513 f
Ptolemy I Soter, 6:514
Ptolemy II Philadelphus, 6:514 f
Ptolemy III Euergetes, 6:516
Ptolemy IV Philopator, 6:518, 527 f
Public, criticism of, 8:734a
Public affairs, religion and, 4:322a f
Public school, religious teaching in, 11:269b
Public worship: duty of, 11:396a f
  Israelite laws of (Numbers), 2:274 f
  pattern of, 11:419b
  privilege of, 11:396a f

for, 7:402 f, 445; 8: 210b f, 300b, 499a f
of Jonah, 8:210 f
Signs and wonders, as revelation of God, 1:366a; 10: 411b f
Silas: as author of Thessalonians, 11:250a f
identification of, 7:195a; 11:246b; 12:78b
imprisonment of, 11:4a f
Silence: breaking of, 6: 1022a f
caressing of, 4:103a f
of Christ; see Christ Jesus
cowardice of, 3:180a
deep, 7:443b
of God; see God
in heaven, 12:425, 574b
importance of, 12:574b
meaning of, 4:103a f; 8: 176b; 12:425a f
of nature, 4:103a f
non-golden, 8:339a
oppressiveness of, 5:891b
persuasiveness of, 12:121
power of, 7:890b
religious necessity of, 3: 207
significance of, 4:642b, 888b
speech and, 4:642b f, 888a f
strategy of, 5:227b f
"treasury" of, 7:306b
waiting in, 4:324, 324a f
way of, 4:762a
in worship, 4:513b f
Silesius, Angelus, on rose, 12:241b
Sill, Edward Rowland: on fellowship, 5:503b f
on hope, 5:607a
on love, 5:739a
on Sunday, 5:656a
on unintentional wrong, 11:389a
on words, 5:584a
Siloam, pool of, 8:516
Silvanus: identification of, 11:254
identified with Silas, 11: 246b, 254; 12:78b, 157 f
as joint-author of I Peter, 12:78b
Thessalonian ministry of, 11:246a f
Silver, Abba Hillel, on heritage of religion, 6:710b
Simeon: blessing of, 8:62
conquest of, 2:688 f
on silence, 4:642b
Simeonites, 3:360 f
Simile, 7: 166b
Simon, as name, 12:167
Simon, John, on preparation for war, 5:680a
Simon, Richard, biblical criticism of, 1:130a f
Simon the Charlatan, 9:109 f, 109b f; 11:194a
Simon of Cyrene, 7:142a, 600a f, 901, 901b; 8:403 f, 403b f, 452a
Simon the magician; see Simon the Charlatan
Simon the Pharisee, 8:143, 144a f
Simple things, enjoyment of, 4:556b f
Simplicity: contentment with, 7:280b
of God, 8:54b
Simpson, Hubert L.: on Enoch, 1:530b f

on pleasure, 2:1139b
Simpson, J. Y., on suffering of child, 3:1158a f
Simpson, P. Carnegie, on grace, 5:716b
Sin: abstract and specific, 5: 677b
acknowledgment of, 4: 170 f, 170b f, 897
of Adam (Pauline), 1: 501b f
anti-social character of, 4: 202b f
aspects of, 3:80b f
assimilation of, 3:130a f
atonement for, 1:380b; 2: 16a f
besetting, 11:498b f
biblical concept of, 6: 741b f; 11:676a f
blood and forgiveness of, 11:695 f, 695b
breeder of, 4:656a
causing others to, 7:469b f; 8:293 f
character of, 4:680a f, 790b
Christ as defender against, 12:300a f
Christ's expiation of (I John), 12:225
Christ's teachings on, 8: 334a
of civilization, 6:822b f
classes of, 11:653a
clinging to, 8:707b
of common people (Malachi), 6:1139 f
conceptions of, 3:85
concrete, 12:223a
condition of, 5:817a f
confession and, 2:166a f, 588b f; 4:170b f, 565a f, 679a f, 939a f; 8:275a f; 10:471a
confession of, 5:741a f, 931; 6:718b f; 12:223a f
conquest of, 1:509a f
consciousness of, 1:502a; 4: 570a, 679a; 6:624b, 632a f; 11:699a f
consequences of, 1:503b; 2: 1027a, 1104 f; 3:16a, 415b f; 4:681a, 791a f; 5: 692b f; 6:100a f; 8:341a; 9:396b f, 400b f
contempt as, 7:470b f
conviction of, 10:341b
cost of, 1:913b f
"covering" of, 12:140a
covetousness as, 5:674a f; 11:213b
creativeness and, 6:608b
crime and, 7:418a
Cross and, 8:407b
dead to (Pauline), 9: 472b f
death and, 10:638a f; 11: 617a
death and (Pauline), 9: 462 f, 464b, 510
death of, 11:702b
death of Christ and, 7:10a; 8:684, 771a, 779b
deceitfulness of, 11:625a f, 637b f
deception of, 6:582a f
definition of, 2:291b; 4: 680a f, 787; 9:428a; 11: 55b
degrees of, 12:299b f
deliberate, 11:653a
despair and, 4:340a
destructive nature of, 6: 585b f

as disease, 5:887b
disguise of, 3:910b f
distinctions of, 4:679b f
doubt as, 12:24a
drabness of, 6:584b f
dualism and, 10:738b
Ecclesiastes concept of, 5: 23b f
effect of, 8:275a; 11:695b f
Egyptian concept of, 1: 384b f
enslavement to (Pauline), 9:477b f
envy as, 2:981b f
etymology of, 1:226b f; 3: 85
evidences of, 11:272b
expiation for, 11:618
of fathers, 3:1069 f, 1069a f; 4:428b f; 6: 160a f, 575b f; 8:219b
forgetfulness as, 1:772a f; 4:565b f
forgiveness of, 4:680b f; 5: 219b; 6:720b; 7:670a f; 8: 145b f; 10:228a f, 341b f, 617b, 646b; 11:682b f
forgiveness of (Christ's teachings on), 7:253a, 349 f
forgiveness of (Hebrews), 11:706 f
forgiveness of (Iraelite concept of), 1:384a f
forgiveness of (modern attitude toward), 3:79b f
forgiveness of (Pauline), 9:181
forgiveness of (Psalms), 4:170 f
frustration of, 6:579a f
futility of, 6:580a f
against God, 2:1104b f; 4: 268b f, 680b
God's order and, 11:676a f
God's relation to, 5:737a f
gossip as, 11:438b f
great and little, 4:680a
greed as, 12:240a
habit of, 3:80b f
hatred of, 5:691b
Hebrew concept of, 3:24 f
against Holy Spirit, 5: 202a; 11:654a
idolatry as, 4:523b f; 6: 943a f
ignorance and, 6:581b f
impatience as, 4:372a f
importance to, 11:695b f
impurity as, 11:213b, 294b f
incompatibility of, 12:256 f
influence of, 3:81a
ingratitude as, 6:141b f
insatiability of, 6:608a f
irreverence as, 12:328 f
irrevocable, 11:745a f
of Israel; see Israel
Israelite concept of, 1: 384b f
jealousy as, 10:175a f
Jeremiah concept of, 5: 785b f
Jewish concept of, 7:109b
judgment of, 1:554a f
kinds of, 2:217a f; 3:105a f
long-range, 5:71a f
love and, 12:140a
Malachi concept of, 6: 1138 f
meaning of, 1:14b; 2:101; 5:1050a; 7:649b f; 11: 757a f

Mesopotamian concept of, 1:385a
of minister, 5:660a f
modern concept of, 1: 502a f; 9:369a, 428a f; 10:341a
as modern concern, 4:678a
monotony of, 5:499b
mortal, 12:299 f, 299b f
of Moses, 2:238a f
of nation, 3:1166b f
nature of, 1:369a; 2:291a f; 3:967b f, 1063a; 4:269b f; 9:396a f
nemesis of, 9:399b
O.T. concept of, 3:105
of omission, 1:772a f; 12: 61 f, 61b f
origin of, 1:492a; 8:611a
origin of (Pauline), 9: 464a
original: see Original sin
of orthodoxy, 11:109b
of other people, 4:399b f
overcoming of, 9:612a f
paradox of, 6:712b
of parent, 8:612
Pauline teaching on, 9: 369a, 396a f, 469 f, 569; 10:343 f, 343b f
penalty of, 4:153a, 501b f; 8:612a
penitence for, 4:203a f
perversion of, 6:865b f
of Pharisees, 8:214b f
pleasure of, 6:585a f; 11: 731b f
poverty and, 6:583a f
practice of, 3:937a
presumption as, 1:551b f; 3:1147a f; 5:261b
presumptuous, 4:107a f
preventive of, 11:744b
pride as; see Pride
proof of, 8:732b
prophetic concept of, 3:86
Psalms teaching on, 1: 338a
punishment and, 11:55b
punishment of, 6:488a f
punishment of (Hebrew), 3:80 f
purification for, 11:602a f
Puritan consciousness of, 4:388b
quality of, 4:200b
reality of, 4:566b f; 6:49b; 10:229a; 12:222b f
a rebellion, 3:86
record of, 3:80b
regret of, 7:282a
remorse for, 5:763b
repentance and, 2:699b
repudiation of, 6:310b f
responsibility for, 6:921a f
result of, 4:188a f, 501b f; 5:737b; 6:582b
retribution for, 3:92a f; 11: 319b f
salvation and, 12:229b
of sanctuaries (Amos), 6: 804 f
schism as, 3:282a f
scope and power of, 12: 257b f
scorn as, 4:654a f
Second Isaiah teaching on, 5:622, 686 f
self-assurance of, 1:556a; 8: 125b f
selfishness as, 12:311a f
sense of, 4:340a f, 570a, 678b f; 6:625a: 10:341a; 11:89b

Israelite itinerary through, 2:341 f

Trans-Jordan tribes, genealogy of, 3:362 f

Translation, problems of, 7:62a

Transmigration, doctrine of, 8:611a f

Transubstantiation: doctrine of, 8:573a

origin of, 7:86a

Travel, by river, 12:429b f

Treachery: description of, 4:288a

sin as, 6:642a f

Treasure, looted, 3:409a f

Treasury of merits, doctrine of, 11:177

Treasury of silence, 7:306b

Treaty: sanctity of (Ezekiel), 6:151b f

"smote" a, 3:53

Tree: beauty of, 5:711b f

duration of, 5:756

of Eden, 6:237

Ephraim as, 6:667a

forbidden (Eden), 1:496 f

fruitless (Jude metaphor), 12:333

of knowledge, 1:504a f

olive, 6:722

planting of, 1:641a f

as symbol, 2:437a f

twig and, 6:155b f

world, 6:233, 410

Tree of life: as religious figure, 12:542

Revelation vision of, 12:541 f, 542a

Tregelles, Samuel, on textual criticism, 12:624a, 625b

Trembling, causes of, 4:529a

Trench, Herbert, on failure of Christ, 11:755b

Trench, Richard, on love, 5:102b

"Trespass," meaning of, 7:316b

Trespass offering: Leviticus law of, 2:29b f, 30 f

ritual instructions, 2:35 f

Trespasses: forgiveness of (Pauline), 11:198

meaning of, 7:316b f

Trevelyan, George M.: on English Corn Laws, 6:604b

on motives, 5:691a

Trial: as cause of joy (James), 12:21 f

meeting of, 12:142a f

purpose of, 8:719a f

satisfaction and, 12:382a f

Tribes of Israel: position of on march and in camp, 2:148 f

Revelation reference to, 12:419

Tribulation: acceptance of, 8:725b

way of, 5:863b

Tribute, 1:546a

Trifles, 4:782a; 7:535 f

Trigon, as instrument, 6:397

Trinity, doctrine of, 7:622 f, 624a; 9:194a f

Trinitarianism, in I Peter, 12:89b

Trip, equipment for, 4:782b

Triumph: early Christian sense of, 12:93b f

pain and, 12:421b

Troas, Pauline visit to, 9:267a f; 10:297 f, 297b f

Troeltsch, Ernst, on Calvinism, 2:919a

Trollope, Anthony: on Caesar, 10:612b f

on preaching, 11:14b

on vengeance, 1:887b

Trophimus, identification of, 11:521

Trouble: anticipation of, 7:287b

assurance in, 4:72b f

cry of soul in, 4:148b f

getting into, 9:156a f

harvest of, 3:935 f

inevitability of, 4:641a

maker of, 2:965b f

meeting, 3:971b; 4:463a f

overcoming, 4:301a f

passing of, 3:995b f

personal, 4:540a f

prayer in, 4:463b f, 575a f

problem of, 4:462b f

purpose of, 3:336a f; 8:669a, 719a; 9:192a f; 11:277b, 321a

time of, 4:539a f; 6:540b f

Troy, fall of, 5:603b

Trudeau, Edward L., on courage, 1:768a

True light, I John teaching on, 12:232 f

True riches, Pastoral teaching on, 11:456 f, 456b f

Trueblood, Elton D.: on achievement of early church, 11:430b

on Christian heritage, 6:667a f

Truett, George W., on clerical vestments, 10:532b f

Trumpet: eschatological significance of, 12:426

of God, 11:306

identification of, 4:5b, 438

Israel's use of, 1:975a f; 4:438

kinds of (O.T.), 2:189; 3:594

Revelation reference to, 12:374

as symbol, 6:643a f

Trumpets, feast of; see Feast

Trust: betrayal of, 6:916a f

Christ's teaching on, 7:320 f, 320b f

doubt and, 4:232a f

fear and, 4:293b

in force, 7:713b

in God; see God

life as, 5:53b f

in man, 8:797a

psalms of, 4:322

securing of, 11:314b f

youth as, 5:82b f

Trusteeship, Christian, 10:52b f

Trustworthiness, need of, 4:896a

Truth: approach to (philosophy), 7:84b

approach to (religion), 7:84b

avoidance of, 5:869b

beauty and, 12:469b

belief in, 7:590a

biblical concept of, 5:798b

catholicity of, 11:153

Christ as, 1:232a; 7:253a; 8:595b, 701; 10:544b f

church as custodian of, 12:303b f

concealing of, 2:1154a f; 6:906a f

consequences and, 6:1059b f

conveying of, 8:40a

deathlessness of, 12:469a f

defense of, 6:1065a f

definition of, 8:151b

desire for, 11:26b

discovery of, 6:661a f; 11:25a f

doing of (I John), 12:224

durability of, 10:398b

etymology of, 1:231b f

exclusiveness of, 2:411b f

as expressed in persons, 11:119a f

faith in, 5:855b; 6:436b; 11:509b

falsehood and, 10:545a f; 11:209a f, 509b; 12:242 f

forces of, 6:1064a

freedom and, 10:544b f; 11:530a f

of God, 4:226a f; 6:1066a

God as source of, 11:25a f

half, 3:1039a f; 6:613b

idol of, 5:897a

immunity to, 5:212b f

incomplete, 11:92b

in inward being, 4:269b f

Johannine concept of, 8:474, 769 f; 12:231

light and, 4:226a f

love of, 8:590b

might and, 4:284b

mission of, 8:263a

nature of, 1:463a f; 8:768a f; 10:741a f

new attitude toward, 9:254a

objectivity of, 11:531a f

opposition to, 6:660b f

Pauline teaching on, 10:421, 421b; 11:119

of physician to patient, 3:305a

power of, 6:648b

prophetic, 6:661b

pursuit of, 5:862b f

rejection of, 6:127b

religion and, 7:84b; 9:66b

resisting of, 8:140a f

responsibility to, 2:450a f

revealed, 8:190a f

revelation of, 11:25a f

righteousness and, 11:524a

II John teaching on, 12:303, 303b f

in speech, 6:412a f; 10:348a

Spirit as (I John), 12:293 f

spirit of, 8:707, 708b f

suppression of, 4:676b

telling of, 1:988b

test of, 2:418b f

timelessness of, 6:671a f

witness of, 8:141a, 223b

word of, 11:488

worth of, 8:220a f

Truthfulness: practice of, 9:540b

in speech (Christ's teaching on), 7:299b f

Trying, limits of, 11:84a

Tubal, identification of, 6:213

Tullock, John, on F. D. Maurice, 12:220a

Turning back, 9:174a f

Turtle dove: identification of, 5:116

offering of, 2:18

Tusser, Thomas, on friendship, 2:1048b

Twells, Henry, on consciousness of sin, 11:701a

Twelve blessings, of Deuteronomy, 2:490 f

Twelve curses, of Deuteronomy, 2:490 f

Twelve tribes of Dispersion: identification of, 12:10a

James and, 12:9b f, 12a f, 20 f

Twenty-four elders, of Revelation, 12:402

"Twice dead," Clement of Alexander's interpretation of, 12:333

Twig, tree and, 6:155b f

"Twilight," meaning of, 2:185a

Two debtors, parable of; see Parables of Christ

"Two-document theory," 7:62b

Two-edged sword, of Revelation, 12:376, 385

Two impulses, Jewish doctrine of, 10:561

Two olive trees, Zechariah vision of, 6:1071 f, 1071b f

Two sons, parable of; see Parables of Christ

Two sticks, Ezekiel oracle of, 6:270 f

Two witnesses, of Revelation, 12:443 f, 582a f

Tychicus, identification of, 11:234 f, 515b f

Tyndale, William: English Bible and, 1:86b f

imprisonment of, 11:516b

Tyranny: disintegration of, 12:600b

downfall of, 6:472a f

Habakkuk teaching on, 6:990 f

Isaiah oracle on, 5:258 f, 258b f, 294 f, 294b f

majesty and, 6:690a

modern, 4:659a f

opposition to, 4:302b

rebellion against, 1:929b

religion and, 6:435a f

Second Zechariah teaching on, 6:1097 f, 1101 f

self-destructiveness of, 6:990 f

Tyrant, weakness of, 11:19a f

Tyre: Alexander's siege of, 6:1093 f

Amos oracle against, 6:781 f

Ezekiel lamentation over, 6:210

Ezekiel oracle against, 6:61b, 205 f, 217 f

identification of, 3:51; 4:449; 6:781

punishment of (Joel), 6:755 f

siege of, 6:205

Tyrrell, George: on Christianity, 6:821a

on clergy, 1:1046b

U

Ugaritic inscriptions, 1:305a

Ugaritic language, 1:220a f

Ugaritic texts, Psalms and, 4:15a

Ulai, identification of, 6:469

Unamuno y Jugo, Miguel de: on belief in God, 4:606a

Joppa

Bethlehem
2550'

Jerusalem
2593'

Jericho
820 FEET BELOW SEA LEVEL

DEAD
SEA
1292 FEET BELOW SEA LEVEL

Jord

PALESTINE
in New Testament Times

© PIERCE & SMITH